SOCIOLOGY

YOUR COMPASS FOR A NEW WORLD

FIFTH CANADIAN EDITION

ROBERT BRYM
UNIVERSITY OF TORONTO

LANCE W. ROBERTS
UNIVERSITY OF MANITOBA

LISA STROHSCHEIN
UNIVERSITY OF ALBERTA

JOHN LIE
UNIVERSITY OF CALIFORNIA, BERKELEY

NELSON EDUCATION

NELSON EDUCATION

Sociology: Your Compass for a New World, Fifth Canadian Edition
by Robert Brym, Lance W. Roberts, Lisa Strohschein, and John Lie

Vice President, Editorial Higher Education:
Anne Williams

Publisher:
Maya Castle and Leanna MacLean

Marketing Manager:
Terry Fedorkiw

Developmental Editor:
Toni Chahley

Photo Researcher and Permissions Coordinator:
Christine Elliott

Production Project Manager:
Jennifer Hare

Copy Editor:
Mariko Obokata

Proofreader:
Linda Szostak

Indexer:
Belle Wong

Design Director:
Ken Phipps

Managing Designer:
Franca Amore

Interior Design Revisions:
Jennifer Leung

Cover Design:
Trinh Truong

Cover Image:
Jennifer Leung; leolintang/ iStockphoto.com (hand with pen)

Compositor:
MPS Limited

Printed and bound in the United States
1 2 3 4 18 17 16 15

For more information contact Nelson Education Ltd., 1120 Birchmount Road, Toronto, Ontario, M1K 5G4. Or you can visit our Internet site at http://www.nelson.com

Additional credits for recurring images: oksana2010/Shutterstock.com (popcorn); Lightspring/ Shutterstock.com (tickets); Pincasso /Shutterstock (two one-way signs); Azure Dragon /Shutterstock (hand holding remote control); grzym/ Shutterstock (TV screen); Vitezslav Valka /Shutterstock (fork in road sign); K. Miri Photography/ Shutterstock (HD television)

Library and Archives Canada Cataloguing in Publication Data

Brym, Robert J., 1951-, author
Sociology : your compass for a new world / Robert Brym (University of Toronto), Lance W. Roberts (University of Manitoba), Lisa Strohschein (University of Alberta), John Lie (University of California, Berkeley).

Revision of: Sociology : your compass for a new world / Robert J. Brym ... [et al.]. — 4th Canadian ed. — Toronto : Nelson Education, [2012], ©2013.
Includes bibliographical references and index.
ISBN 978-0-17-653203-1 (pbk.)

1. Sociology—Textbooks. I. Lie, John, author II. Roberts, Lance W., 1950- author III. Strohschein, Lisa, 1966-, author IV. Title.

HM586.B7958 2015 301
C2014-906604-X

ISBN-13: 978-0-17-653203-1
ISBN-10: 0-17-653203-X

DEDICATION

Many authors seem to be afflicted with stoic family members who gladly allow them to spend endless hours buried in their work. I suffer no such misfortune. The members of my family have demanded that I focus on what really matters in life. I think that focus has made this a better book. I am deeply grateful to Rhonda Lenton, Shira Brym, Talia Lenton-Brym, and Ariella Lenton-Brym. I dedicate this book to them with thanks and love.

Robert Brym

To Charlie, our spirited little man: May your navigation through the social maze be revealing and fun.

Lance W. Roberts

To students past and present whose passion and enthusiasm continue to inspire me. And most of all, thanks to my husband, Frank, whose love and support sustains me through it all.

Lisa Strohschein

For Charis Thompson, Thomas Cussins, Jessica Cussins, and Charlotte Lie, with thanks and love.

John Lie

ROBERT BRYM (pronounced "brim") was born in Saint John, New Brunswick, studied sociology in Canada and Israel, and received his Ph.D. from the University of Toronto, where he is now the S. D. Clark Professor of Sociology and Associate Chair (Undergraduate) of the Department of Sociology. Bob's research focuses on the social bases of politics and social movements in Canada, Russia, and the Middle East. His most recent book is *Sociology as a Life or Death Issue*, Third Canadian Edition (Toronto: Nelson Education, 2014). He is now conducting research on violence and intolerance in the Middle East and North Africa. Bob is a Fellow of the Royal Society of Canada and has won several awards for his research and teaching, including the Northrop Frye Award and the University of Toronto's highest teaching honour, the President's Teaching Award. *Sociology: Your Compass for a New World* has been published in Canadian, Québécois, American, Brazilian, and Australian editions.

LANCE W. ROBERTS was born in Calgary, grew up in Edmonton, and received his Ph.D. from the University of Alberta. He is a Fellow of St. John's College and Professor of Sociology at the University of Manitoba, where he teaches Introductory Sociology as well as research methods and statistics courses. In the last decade, he has received several teaching awards, including his university's Dr. and Mrs. H. H. Saunderson Award for Excellence in Teaching. His current research interests cover the comparative charting of social change, educational concerns, and mental health issues. In addition to publishing in research journals, Lance recently coauthored *The Methods Coach*, *The Statistics Coach*, and *Understanding Social Statistics: A Student's Guide through the Maze* (Oxford University Press), all aimed at helping students master fundamental research techniques. He enjoys teaching Introductory Sociology and is currently developing a variety of tools to enlarge his students' sociological imaginations.

LISA STROHSCHEIN (rhymes with sunshine) was born in Ontario, Canada, and received her Ph.D. at McMaster University in 2002. She is currently Associate Professor and Associate Chair (Undergraduate) in the Department of Sociology at the University of Alberta. In her research, she investigates how family dynamics are related to health and well-being, with a specific focus on the impact of divorce on adults and children. Her current projects include a federally funded grant to describe and evaluate the social implications of new family forms in Canada and an international collaboration that will compare how Canadian and American youth navigated the transition to adulthood during the Great Recession.

JOHN LIE (pronounced "lee") was born in South Korea, grew up in Japan and Hawaii, and received his A.B., A.M., and Ph.D. degrees from Harvard University. His main interests are in social theory and political economy. Currently, he is the C. K. Cho Professor of Sociology at the University of California, Berkeley, where he previously served as the Dean of International and Area Studies. His recent publications include *Zainichi (Koreans in Japan)* (Berkeley: University of California Press, 2008) and *Modern Peoplehood: On Race, Racism, Nationalism, Ethnicity, and Identity*, paperback ed. (Berkeley: University of California Press, 2011).

BRIEF CONTENTS

CONTENTS

NEW IN THE FIFTH CANADIAN EDITION

Welcome to the fifth Canadian edition of *Sociology: Your Compass for a New World.* We have been gratified and moved by the positive response to earlier editions of this book. At the same time, we benefited from the constructive criticisms generously offered by numerous readers and reviewers. *Sociology: Your Compass for a New World*, Fifth Canadian Edition, is a response to many of their suggestions. Before we share the unique features that have characterized this text and have led to its success edition after edition, allow us to list the main innovations in this edition:

- Throughout, we added new research findings and incorporated data from the most recent Canadian census to keep the book as up-to-date as possible. The new edition contains more than 60 new figures.
- We have increased coverage of such timely issues as:
    - the "cultural turn" in sociology – Gramsci, Foucault, Bourdieu, and poststructuralism
    - the Occupy Movement, the Arab Spring, and Idle No More
    - qualitative research methods
    - ethics and social research
    - socialization across the life course
    - Canadian inequality in historical and comparative perspective
    - cyber-bullying
    - online networks
    - social media
    - critical race theory
    - First Nations
    - multiculturalism
    - third-wave feminism and postfeminism
    - the social construction of sexuality and sexual scripts
    - gender inequality from a global perspective
    - mate selection, including hooking up, friends with benefits, and same-sex relationships
    - cohabitation
    - divorce and step-parent families
    - the market model of religion
    - obesity
    - the social history of the tattoo
    - health policy and health inequality
    - intersectionality and health
- **Sociology at the Movies** was one of the most popular features of earlier editions among both faculty members and students. Building on this popularity, we wrote 16 new sociological reviews of movies including *12 Years a Slave, Zero Dark Thirty, The Dictator, The Secret Life of Walter Mitty, We Live in Public, Easy A, The Queen of Versailles, Searching for Sugar Man, RoboCop, Triangle: Remembering the Fire, The Ides of March, Friends with Benefits, The Lottery, Silver Linings Playbook, World War Z,* and *V for Vendetta.*
- Because of the success of our **Sociology at the Movies** feature, we decided to expand our coverage of popular culture by writing 20 **Sociology On The Tube** boxes. These boxes identify and explain the sociological significance of such popular TV shows *as Breaking Bad, Homeland, Game of Thrones, Sons of Anarchy, Toddlers*

and Tiaras, Here Comes Honey Boo-Boo, The Millers, Mr. D, The Newsroom, and *Duck Dynasty*.
- Our selection of other feature boxes has also been revitalized. We have written:
  - eight new **It's Your Choice boxes** on such timely topics as work conditions in overseas clothing factories, seasonal migrant workers, rape culture on college and university campuses, and euthanasia
  - five new **Social Policy boxes** on hot topics ranging from cyber-bullying to the legalization of recreational drugs to the Canadian oil pipeline debate

A COMPASS FOR A NEW WORLD

> It was the best of times, it was the worst of times, it was the age of wisdom, it was the age of foolishness, it was the epoch of belief, it was the epoch of incredulity, it was the season of Light, it was the season of Darkness, it was the spring of hope, it was the winter of despair, we had everything before us, we had nothing before us, we were all going direct to Heaven, we were all going direct the other way—in short, the period was so far like the present period, that some of its noisiest authorities insisted on its being received, for good or for evil, in the superlative degree of comparison only.
>
> —Charles Dickens, *A Tale of Two Cities* (2002 [1859])

Dickens refers to the end of the eighteenth century, yet he offers a prophetic description of the times in which we live. We, too, set sail at the dawn of an age of superlatives, an age of uncertainty.

Over the past couple of decades, we have torn old countries apart and created new ones. We proclaimed a new era of medical breakthroughs with the sequencing of the human genome, yet learned that the plague is still with us in the form of AIDS, expected to kill 85 million people by 2020. After some economists proclaimed that recessions were a thing of the past, we experienced two devastating economic crises that bankrupted many high-flying companies and individuals; we are still living through the aftermath of the second one. We saw the world's mood and its political and economic outlook buoyant one day, anxious the next, as terrorist attacks and wars led us further into an era of uncertainty.

The world is an unpredictable place. It is especially disorienting for students entering adulthood. We wrote this book to show undergraduates that sociology can help them make sense of their lives, however uncertain they may appear to be. We hope it will serve as their sociological compass in the new world they are entering as young adults. Moreover, we show that sociology can be a liberating practical activity, not just an abstract intellectual exercise. By revealing the opportunities and constraints we face, sociology can help us navigate our lives, teaching us who we are and what we can become in this particular social and historical context. We cannot know what the future will bring, but we can at least know the choices we confront and the likely consequences of our actions. From this point of view, sociology can help us create the best possible future. That has always been sociology's principal justification, and so it should be today.

UNIQUE FEATURES

We have tried to keep sociology's main purpose and relevance front and centre in this book. As a result, *Sociology: Your Compass for a New World*, Fifth Canadian Edition, differs from other major introductory sociology textbooks in four ways:

1. ***Drawing connections between one's self and the social world.*** To varying degrees, all introductory sociology textbooks try to show students how their personal experiences connect to the larger social world. However, we employ two devices to make

these connections clearer than in other textbooks. First, we illustrate key sociological ideas by using examples from popular culture that resonate deeply with student interests and experiences. For example, in Chapter 1 we illustrate the main sociological perspectives (functionalism, conflict theory, symbolic interactionism, and feminism) by analyzing changing fashions from Britney Spears to Lady Gaga. We analyze Canadian hockey to highlight central features of Durkheim's theory of religion in Chapter 3. In Chapter 21, we discuss the role of Facebook and Twitter in helping to mobilize the democratic movement in North Africa and the Middle East. We think these and many other examples speak directly to today's students about important sociological ideas in terms they understand, thus making the connection between self and society clear.

Second, we developed several unique pedagogical features to draw the connection between students' experiences and the larger social world. "Sociology at the Movies" and "Sociology on the Tube" take universal and popular elements of contemporary culture and render them sociologically relevant. We provide brief reviews of movies and television shows and highlight the sociological issues they raise and the sociological insights they embody. In each chapter, we repeatedly challenge students to consider how and why their own lives conform to, or deviate from, various patterns of social relations and actions. Many chapters feature an "It's Your Choice" box that sets out alternative approaches to a range of social problems and asks students to use logic and evidence to devise a course of action. Here we teach students that sociology can be a matter of the most urgent practical importance. Students also learn they can have a say in solving social problems.

2. ***What to think versus how to think.*** All textbooks teach students both *what* to think about a subject and *how* to think about it from a particular disciplinary perspective. In our judgment, however, introductory sociology textbooks usually place too much stress on the "what" and not enough on the "how." The result is that they sometimes read more like encyclopedias than enticements to look at the world in a new way. We have tipped the balance in the other direction. Of course, *Sociology: Your Compass for a New World* contains definitions and literature reviews. It features standard pedagogical aids, such as a list of **Chapter Aims** at the beginning of each chapter, a new **Time for Review** feature at the end of each major section in each chapter, a detailed **Summary** at the end of each chapter, and definitions of key terms in the margins of the text. However, we devote more space than other authors do to showing how sociologists think. The **Social Policy: What Do You Think** feature asks students to think critically and form an opinion about social policy issues by bringing logic and evidence to bear on them. We often relate an anecdote to highlight an issue's importance, present contending interpretations of the issue, and then adduce data to judge the merits of the various interpretations. We do not just refer to tables and graphs, we analyze them. When evidence warrants, we reject theories and endorse others. Thus, many sections of the book read more like a simplified journal article than an encyclopedia. If all this sounds just like what sociologists do professionally, then we have achieved our aim: to present a less antiseptic, more realistic, and therefore intrinsically exciting account of how sociologists practise their craft. Said differently, one of the strengths of this book is that it does not present sociology as a set of immutable truths carved in stone tablets. Instead, it shows how sociologists actually go about the business of solving sociological puzzles.

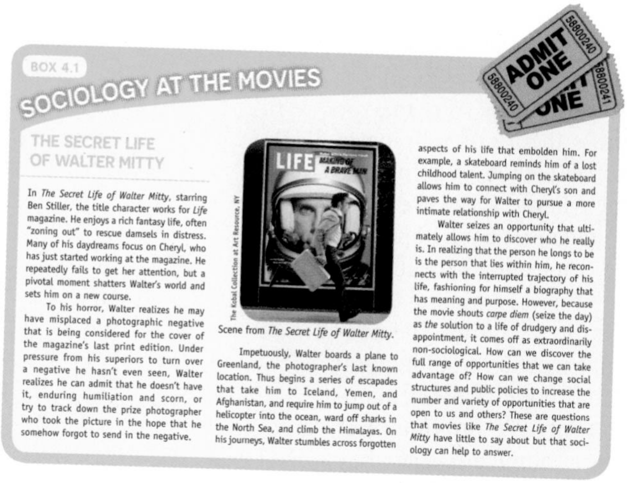

BOX 4.1

SOCIOLOGY AT THE MOVIES

THE SECRET LIFE OF WALTER MITTY

In *The Secret Life of Walter Mitty*, starring Ben Stiller, the title character works for *Life* magazine. He enjoys a rich fantasy life, often "zoning out" to rescue damsels in distress. Many of his daydreams focus on Cheryl, who has just started working at the magazine. He repeatedly fails to get her attention, but a pivotal moment shatters Walter's world and sets him on a new course.

To his horror, Walter realizes he may have misplaced a photographic negative that is being considered for the cover of the magazine's last print edition. Under pressure from his superiors to turn over a negative he hasn't even seen, Walter realizes he can admit that he doesn't have it, enduring humiliation and scorn, or try to track down the prize photographer who took the picture in the hope that he somehow forgot to send in the negative.

Scene from *The Secret Life of Walter Mitty*.

Impetuously, Walter boards a plane to Greenland, the photographer's last known location. Thus begins a series of escapades that take him to Iceland, Yemen, and Afghanistan, and require him to jump out of a helicopter into the ocean, ward off sharks in the North Sea, and climb the Himalayas. On his journeys, Walter stumbles across forgotten aspects of his life that embolden him. For example, a skateboard reminds him of a lost childhood talent. Jumping on the skateboard allows him to connect with Cheryl's son and paves the way for Walter to pursue a more intimate relationship with Cheryl.

Walter seizes an opportunity that ultimately allows him to discover who he really is. In realizing that the person he longs to be is the person that lies within him, he reconnects with the interrupted trajectory of his life, fashioning for himself a biography that has meaning and purpose. However, because the movie shouts *carpe diem* (seize the day) as *the* solution to a life of drudgery and disappointment, it comes off as extraordinarily non-sociological. How can we discover the full range of opportunities that we can take advantage of? How can we change social structures and public policies to increase the number and variety of opportunities that are open to us and others? These are questions that movies like *The Secret Life of Walter Mitty* have little to say about but that sociology can help to answer.

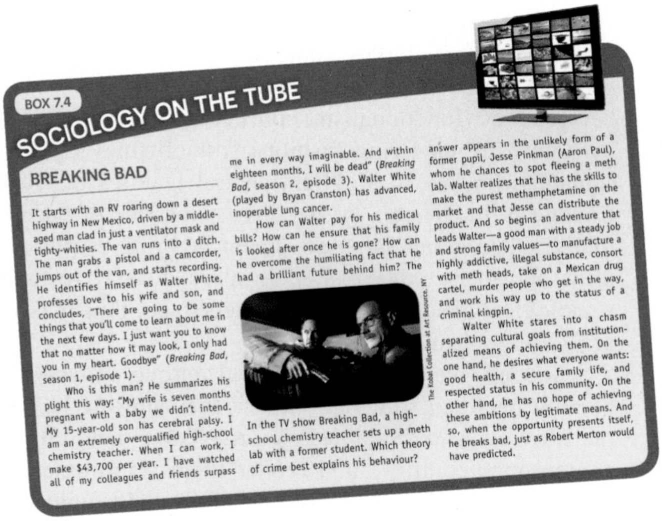

BOX 7.4

SOCIOLOGY ON THE TUBE

BREAKING BAD

It starts with an RV roaring down a desert highway in New Mexico, driven by a middle-aged man clad in just a ventilator mask and tighty-whities. The van runs into a ditch. The man grabs a pistol and a camcorder, jumps out of the van, and starts recording. He identifies himself as Walter White, professes love to his wife and son, and concludes, "There are going to be some things that you'll come to learn about me in the next few days. I just want you to know that no matter how it may look, I only had you in my heart. Goodbye" (*Breaking Bad*, season 1, episode 1).

Who is this man? He summarizes his plight this way: "My wife is seven months pregnant with a baby we didn't intend. My 15-year-old son has cerebral palsy. I am an extremely overqualified high-school chemistry teacher. When I can work, I make $43,700 per year. I have watched all of my colleagues and friends surpass me in every way imaginable. And within eighteen months, I will be dead" (*Breaking Bad*, season 2, episode 3). Walter White (played by Bryan Cranston) has advanced, inoperable lung cancer.

How can Walter pay for his medical bills? How can he ensure that his family is looked after once he is gone? How can he overcome the humiliating fact that he had a brilliant future behind him? The answer appears in the unlikely form of a former pupil, Jesse Pinkman (Aaron Paul), whom he chances to spot fleeing a meth lab. Walter realizes that he has the skills to make the purest methamphetamine on the market and that Jesse can distribute the product. And so begins an adventure that leads Walter—a good man with a steady job and strong family values—to manufacture a highly addictive, illegal substance, consort with meth heads, take on a Mexican drug cartel, murder people who get in the way, and work his way up to the status of a criminal kingpin.

Walter White stares into a chasm separating cultural goals from institutionalized means of achieving them. On the one hand, he desires what everyone wants: good health, a secure family life, and respected status in his community. On the other hand, he has no hope of achieving these ambitions by legitimate means. And so, when the opportunity presents itself, he breaks bad, just as Robert Merton would have predicted.

In the TV show Breaking Bad, a high-school chemistry teacher sets up a meth lab with a former student. Which theory of crime best explains his behaviour?

- **Sociology at the Movies** and **Sociology on the Tube** offer sociological insights gleaned from current films and popular television shows, and demonstrates sociology's vitality and relevance to students' lives. These features also encourage students to think critically about the films they watch.

BOX 11.3

IT'S YOUR CHOICE

DOES A RAPE CULTURE EXIST ON UNIVERSITY AND COLLEGE CAMPUSES?

Every Labour Day weekend, first-year university and college students flock to campus to take part in Frosh week. It's a way to welcome and orient first-year students to university and college life with live music, organized social gatherings, tours, and rallies—all intended to instill a sense of school spirit in the newcomers.

In 2013, the yearly event came under public scrutiny at the University of British Columbia in Vancouver and Saint Mary's University in Halifax. Videos posted to social media sites showed first-year male and female students yelling out an almost identical chant: "We like them YOUNG: Y is for your sister; O is for oh-so-tight; U is for underage; N is for no consent; G is for grab that ass."

Apparently, the chants were nothing new. They had been recited for years on both campuses and indeed at universities and colleges across Canada. This time, though, public outrage led university officials across the country to vow to take action.

For some people, the chants proved that Canadian universities were home to a "rape culture." A rape culture is said to exist in any environment where sexual violence is normalized, excused, and even condoned. For example, people who believe that men are naturally aggressive and that women are "just asking for it" foster an environment that is conducive to rape.

Others are uncertain that a rape culture exists on college and university campuses. They say that the problem lies with a small number of men who are sexual predators. Treating all men as potential sexual offenders is blatantly unfair.

Still others suggest that the problem is not just cultural but institutional (Armstrong, Hamilton, and Sweeney, 2006). Because college and university life can be stressful and alienating for first-year students, partying is an important opportunity for them to unwind and get to know others. Colleges and universities that fail to provide students with enough opportunities for socializing or those that adopt heavy-handed alcohol policies may unwittingly encourage students to attend private parties where men control nearly all aspects of the party experience, including choosing the venue, arranging transportation, and overseeing the flow of alcohol. From this point of view, if colleges and universities adopt policies that minimize the amount of private partying, the rate of sexual violence against women will fall.

What do you think? Is the problem of rape restricted to a small minority of men? Do student rallies that incite non-consensual sex provide evidence that a rape culture permeates campus life? Do you think that institutional factors contribute to the rate of sexual assault on university campuses? Could all three factors (individual, cultural, and institutional) play a role? How might one best begin to address the issue of sexual assault on Canadian college and university campuses?

How effective do you think this poster would be at deterring sexual assault on university and college campuses?

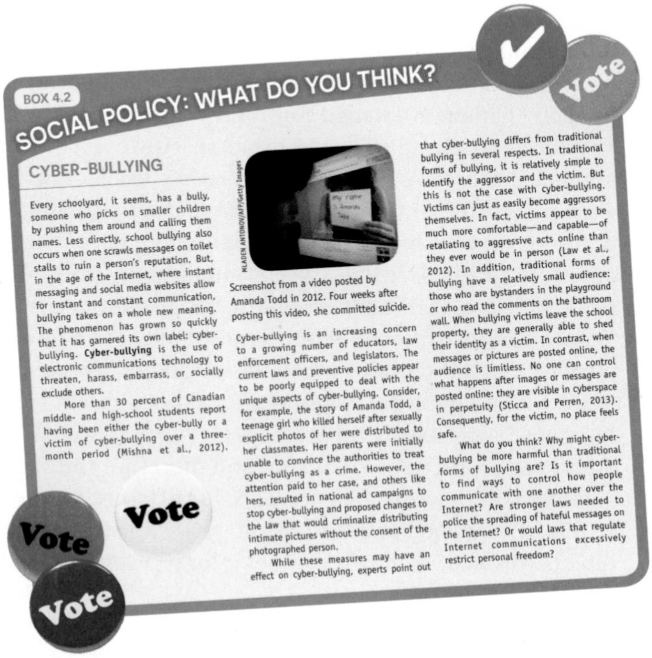

BOX 4.2

SOCIAL POLICY: WHAT DO YOU THINK?

CYBER-BULLYING

Every schoolyard, it seems, has a bully, someone who picks on smaller children by pushing them around and calling them names. Less directly, school bullying also occurs when one scrawls messages on toilet stalls to ruin a person's reputation. But, in the age of the Internet, where instant messaging and social media websites allow for instant and constant communication, bullying takes on a whole new meaning. The phenomenon has grown so quickly that it has garnered its own label: cyber-bullying. **Cyber-bullying** is the use of electronic communications technology to threaten, harass, embarrass, or socially exclude others.

More than 30 percent of Canadian middle- and high-school students report having been either the cyber-bully or a victim of cyber-bullying over a three-month period (Mishna et al., 2012).

Screenshot from a video posted by Amanda Todd in 2012. Four weeks after posting this video, she committed suicide.

Cyber-bullying is an increasing concern to a growing number of educators, law enforcement officers, and legislators. The current laws and preventive policies appear to be poorly equipped to deal with the unique aspects of cyber-bullying. Consider, for example, the story of Amanda Todd, a teenage girl who killed herself after sexually explicit photos of her were distributed to her classmates. Her parents were initially unable to convince the authorities to treat cyber-bullying as a crime. However, the attention paid to her case, and others like hers, resulted in national ad campaigns to stop cyber-bullying and proposed changes to the law that would criminalize distributing intimate pictures without the consent of the photographed person.

While these measures may have an effect on cyber-bullying, experts point out that cyber-bullying differs from traditional bullying in several respects. In traditional forms of bullying, it is relatively simple to identify the aggressor and the victim. But this is not the case with cyber-bullying. Victims can just as easily become aggressors themselves. In fact, victims appear to be much more comfortable—and capable—of retaliating to aggressive acts online than they ever would be in person (Law et al., 2012). In addition, traditional forms of bullying have a relatively small audience: those who are bystanders in the playground or who read the comments on the bathroom wall. When bullying victims leave the school property, they are generally able to shed their identity as a victim. In contrast, when messages or pictures are posted online, the audience is limitless. No one can control what happens after images or messages are posted online: they are visible in cyberspace in perpetuity (Sticca and Perren, 2013). Consequently, for the victim, no place feels safe.

What do you think? Why might cyber-bullying be more harmful than traditional forms of bullying are? Is it important to find ways to control how people communicate with one another over the Internet? Are stronger laws needed to police the spreading of hateful messages on the Internet? Or would laws that regulate Internet communications excessively restrict personal freedom?

- **It's Your Choice** teaches students that sociology can have urgent, practical importance—and that they can have a say in the development of public policy.
- **Social Policy: What Do You Think?** invites students to engage critically with issues related to social policy.

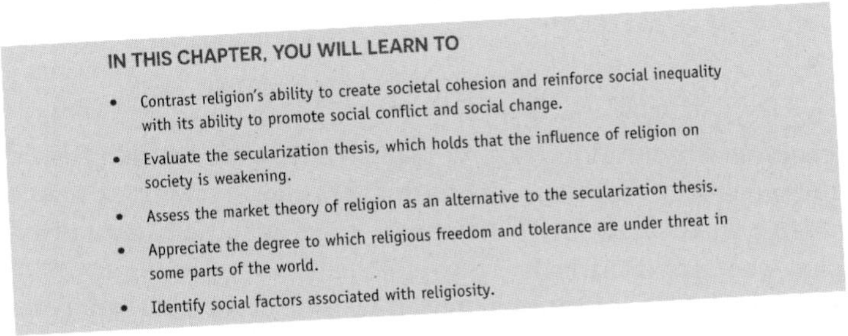

IN THIS CHAPTER, YOU WILL LEARN TO

- Contrast religion's ability to create societal cohesion and reinforce social inequality with its ability to promote social conflict and social change.
- Evaluate the secularization thesis, which holds that the influence of religion on society is weakening.
- Assess the market theory of religion as an alternative to the secularization thesis.
- Appreciate the degree to which religious freedom and tolerance are under threat in some parts of the world.
- Identify social factors associated with religiosity.

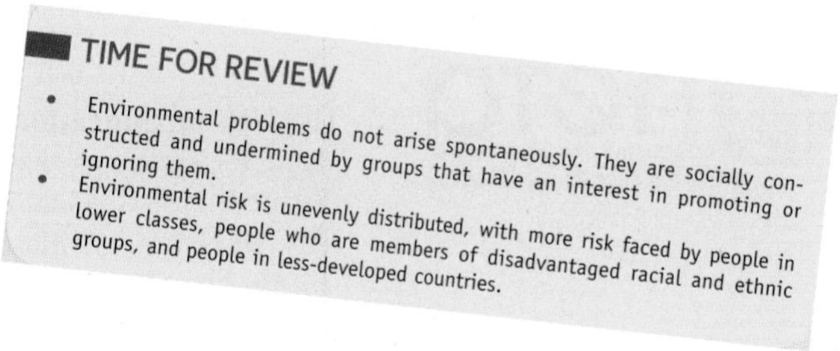

TIME FOR REVIEW

- Environmental problems do not arise spontaneously. They are socially constructed and undermined by groups that have an interest in promoting or ignoring them.
- Environmental risk is unevenly distributed, with more risk faced by people in lower classes, people who are members of disadvantaged racial and ethnic groups, and people in less-developed countries.

- The text features **student-tested pedagogical aids** and it shows how sociologists actually go about the business of solving sociological puzzles.

3. ***Objectivity versus subjectivity.*** Sociologists since Max Weber have understood that sociologists—indeed, all scientists—are members of society whose thinking and research are influenced by the social and historical context in which they work. Yet most introductory sociology textbooks present a stylized and unsociological view of the research process. Textbooks tend to emphasize sociology's objectivity and the hypothetico-deductive method of reasoning, for the most part ignoring the more subjective factors that go into the research mix. We think this emphasis is a pedagogical error. In our teaching, we have found that drawing the connection between objectivity and subjectivity in sociological research makes the discipline more appealing to students. It shows how research issues are connected to the lives of real flesh-and-blood women and men, and how sociology is related to students' existential concerns. Therefore, in most chapters of *Sociology: Your Compass for a New World* we include a personal anecdote that explains how certain sociological issues first arose in our own minds. We often adopt a narrative style because stories let students understand ideas on an emotional as well as an intellectual level, and when we form an emotional attachment to ideas, they stay with us more effectively than if our attachment is solely intellectual. We place the ideas of important sociological figures in social and historical context. We show how sociological methodologies serve as a reality check, but we also make it clear that socially grounded personal concerns often lead sociologists to decide which aspects of reality are worth checking on in the first place. We believe *Sociology: Your Compass for a New World* is unique in presenting a realistic and balanced account of the role of objectivity and subjectivity in the research process.
4. ***Diversity and a global perspective.*** It is gratifying to see how much less parochial introductory sociology textbooks are today than they were just a few decades ago. Contemporary textbooks highlight gender and race issues. They broaden the student's understanding of the world by comparing Canada with other societies. They show how global processes affect local issues and how local issues affect global processes. *Sociology: Your Compass for a New World* makes diversity and globalization prominent themes, too. We employ cross-national comparisons between Canada and countries as diverse as India and Sweden. We incorporate maps that illustrate the distribution of sociological variables globally and regionally, and the relationship among variables across time and space. We remain sensitive to gender and race issues throughout. This has been easy for us because we are members of racial and ethnic minority groups. We are multilingual. We have lived in other countries for extended periods. And we have published widely on countries other than Canada, including the United States, Russia, Israel, Palestine, South Korea, and Japan. As you will see in the following pages, our backgrounds have enabled us to bring greater depth to issues of diversity and globalization than other textbooks bring.

ANCILLARIES

A full range of high-quality ancillaries has been prepared to help instructors and students get the most out of *Sociology: Your Compass for a New World*, Fifth Canadian Edition.

SUPPLEMENTS FOR INSTRUCTORS

About the Nelson Education Teaching Advantage (NETA)

The **Nelson Education Teaching Advantage (NETA)** program delivers research-based instructor resources that promote student engagement and higher-order thinking to enable the success of Canadian students and educators. To ensure the high quality of these materials, all Nelson ancillaries have been professionally copy edited.

Be sure to visit Nelson Education's **Inspired Instruction** website at **www.nelson.com/inspired/** to find out more about NETA. Don't miss the testimonials of instructors who have used NETA supplements and seen student engagement increase!

Instructor Resources

All NETA and other key instructor ancillaries are provided in the Instructor Resources at **www.nelson.com/compass5ce**, giving instructors the ultimate tool for customizing lectures and presentations. Instructor materials can also be accessed through **www.nelson.com/login** and **login.cengage.com**.

NETA Test Bank: This resource was written by Ivanka Knezevic at the University of Toronto Mississauga. It includes over 2200 multiple-choice questions written according to NETA guidelines for effective construction and development of higher-order questions. The Test Bank was copy edited by a NETA-trained editor. Also included are true/false, short answer, and essay questions. Test Bank files are provided in Word format for easy editing and in PDF format for convenient printing, whatever your system.

The NETA Test Bank is available in a new, cloud-based platform. **Testing Powered by Cognero®** is a secure online testing system that allows you to author, edit, and manage test bank content from any place you have Internet access. No special installations or downloads are needed, and the desktop-inspired interface, with its drop-down menus and familiar, intuitive tools, allows you to create and manage tests with ease. You can create multiple test versions in an instant and import or export content into other systems. Tests can be delivered from your learning management system, your classroom, or wherever you want.

NETA PowerPoint: Microsoft® PowerPoint® lecture slides for every chapter have been created by Tamy Superle of Carleton University. There is an average of 30 slides per chapter, many featuring key figures, tables, and photographs from *Sociology: Your Compass for a New World*. NETA principles of clear design and engaging content have been incorporated throughout, making it simple for instructors to customize the deck for their courses.

Image Library: This resource consists of digital copies of figures, short tables, and photographs used in the book. Instructors may use these jpegs to customize the NETA PowerPoint or create their own PowerPoint presentations.

NETA Instructor's Manual: This resource was written by Peter Laurie at Fleming College. It is organized according to the textbook chapters and addresses key educational concerns, such as typical stumbling blocks student face and how to address them.

DayOne: Day One—Prof InClass is a PowerPoint presentation that instructors can customize to orient students to the class and their text at the beginning of the course.

MindTap: MindTap for *Sociology: Your Compass for a New World* is a personalized teaching experience with relevant assignments that guide students to analyze, apply, and elevate thinking, allowing you to measure skills and promote better outcomes with ease. A fully online learning solution, MindTap combines all student learning tools—readings, multimedia, activities, and assessments—into a single Learning Path that guides the student through your curriculum. You may personalize the experience by customizing the presentation of these learning tools to your students, even seamlessly introducing your own content directly into the Learning Path.

DVD Resources

Enhance your classroom experience with the exciting and relevant videos of ***Think Outside the Book: The Nelson Sociology DVD Collection,*** prepared to accompany *Sociology: Your*

Compass for a New World, Fifth Canadian Edition. Designed to enrich and support chapter concepts, this set of seven 30-minute video segments was created by Robert Brym to stimulate discussion of topics raised in sociology. Produced in conjunction with Face to Face Media (Vancouver), the Jesuit Communication Project (Toronto), and the National Film Board of Canada, the selections have been edited to optimize their impact in the classroom. Many of the selections are taken from films that have won national and international awards.

Student Ancillaries

Stay organized and efficient with **MindTap**—a single destination with all the course material and study aids you need to succeed. Built-in apps leverage social media and the latest learning technology. For example:

- ReadSpeaker will read the text to you.
- Flashcards are pre-populated to provide you with a jump start for review—or you can create your own.
- You can highlight text and make notes in your MindTap Reader. Your notes will flow into Evernote, the electronic notebook app that you can access anywhere when it's time to study for the exam.
- Self-quizzing allows you to assess your understanding.

Visit **www.NelsonBrain.com** to start using **MindTap**. Enter the Online Access Code from the card included with your text. If a code card is *not* provided, you can purchase instant access at NelsonBrain.com.

The following readers can be purchased at **www.NelsonBrain.com** in ebook or print-copy format:

- ***Sociology as a Life or Death Issue***, Second Canadian Edition, is a series of beautifully written essays in which Robert Brym introduces sociology by analyzing the social causes of death. It focuses on hip-hop culture, the social bases of cancer, suicide bombers, gender risk, and the plight of hurricane victims in the Caribbean region and on the coast of the Gulf of Mexico. In doing so, it reveals the powerful social forces that help to determine who lives and who dies and demonstrates the promise of a well-informed sociological understanding of the world. This brief and inexpensive volume is an eye-opener, an inspiration, and a guide for students of sociology and for anyone with an inquiring mind and hopes for a better world for future generations.
- ***Controversies in Canadian Sociology***, First Edition, by Reza Nakhaie, includes a range of classic and contemporary readings, employing the point-counterpoint method to challenge students to evaluate arguments on their merits and to develop their critical imaginations.
- ***Society in Question***, Sixth Edition, by Robert J. Brym, provides balanced coverage of the approaches and methods in current sociology, as well as unique and surprising perspectives on many major sociological topics. All readings have been chosen for their ability to speak directly to contemporary Canadian students about how sociology can enable them to make sense of their lives in a rapidly changing world.
- ***Images of Society: Readings that Inspire and Inform Society***, Second Edition, by Jerry P. White and Michael Carroll, is an exciting collection of readings designed for use in introductory sociology classes. The contents range from classic works in sociology to pieces illustrating recent sociological principles. Academic and journalistic readings have been selected by the authors to convey the distinctive way sociologists think. All readings are excerpts from longer pieces and are introduced with short prologues written by the editors.

ACKNOWLEDGMENTS

Anyone who has gone sailing knows that when you embark on a long voyage, you need more than a compass. Among other things, you need a helm operator blessed with a strong sense of direction and an intimate knowledge of likely dangers. You need crew members who know all the ropes and can use them to keep things intact and in their proper place. And you need sturdy hands to raise and lower the sails. On the voyage to complete the fifth Canadian edition of this book, the crew demonstrated all these skills. We are especially grateful to our publisher, **Maya Castle**, who saw this book's promise from the outset, understood clearly the direction we had to take to develop its potential, and on several occasions steered us clear of threatening shoals. We are also deeply indebted to the following crew members:

Toni Chahley, developmental editor
Jennifer Hare, production project manager
Terry Fedorkiw, marketing manager
Mariko Obokata, copy editor
Linda Szostak, proofreader
Christine Elliott, permissions coordinator and photo researcher
Tim Melnyk, research assistant

We thank the following reviewers for their critical comments on chapter drafts:

Laurie Forbes, Lakehead University
Helga Hallgrimsdottir, University of Victoria
Karen Kampen, University of Manitoba
Benjamin Kelly, Nipissing University
Ivanka Knezevic, University of Toronto
Barry McClinchey, University of Waterloo
Timothy MacNeill, University of Ontario Institute of Technology

We would also like to acknowledge the assistance of reviewers whose feedback helped shape the third and fourth Canadian editions:

Darlene Balandin, University of Western Ontario
Sonia Bookman, University of Manitoba
Christian Caron, Carleton University
Erling Christensen, Kwantlen Polytechnic University
Jim Cosgrave, Trent University
Slobodan Drakulic, Ryerson University
Kimberley A. Ducey, University of Winnipeg
Tara Fidler, University of Western Ontario and University of Toronto
Jean Golden, Ryerson University
Tom Groulx, St. Clair College
Jake Muller, Northwest Community College
Tamy Superle, Carleton University
Ron McGivern, Thompson Rivers University
Laurie Forbes, Lakehead University
Daniel Popowich, Mohawk College
Juergen Dankwort, Kwantlen Polytechnic University

Robert Brym

Lance Roberts

Lisa Strohschein

John Lie

PART 1

FOUNDATIONS

CHAPTER 1

A SOCIOLOGICAL COMPASS

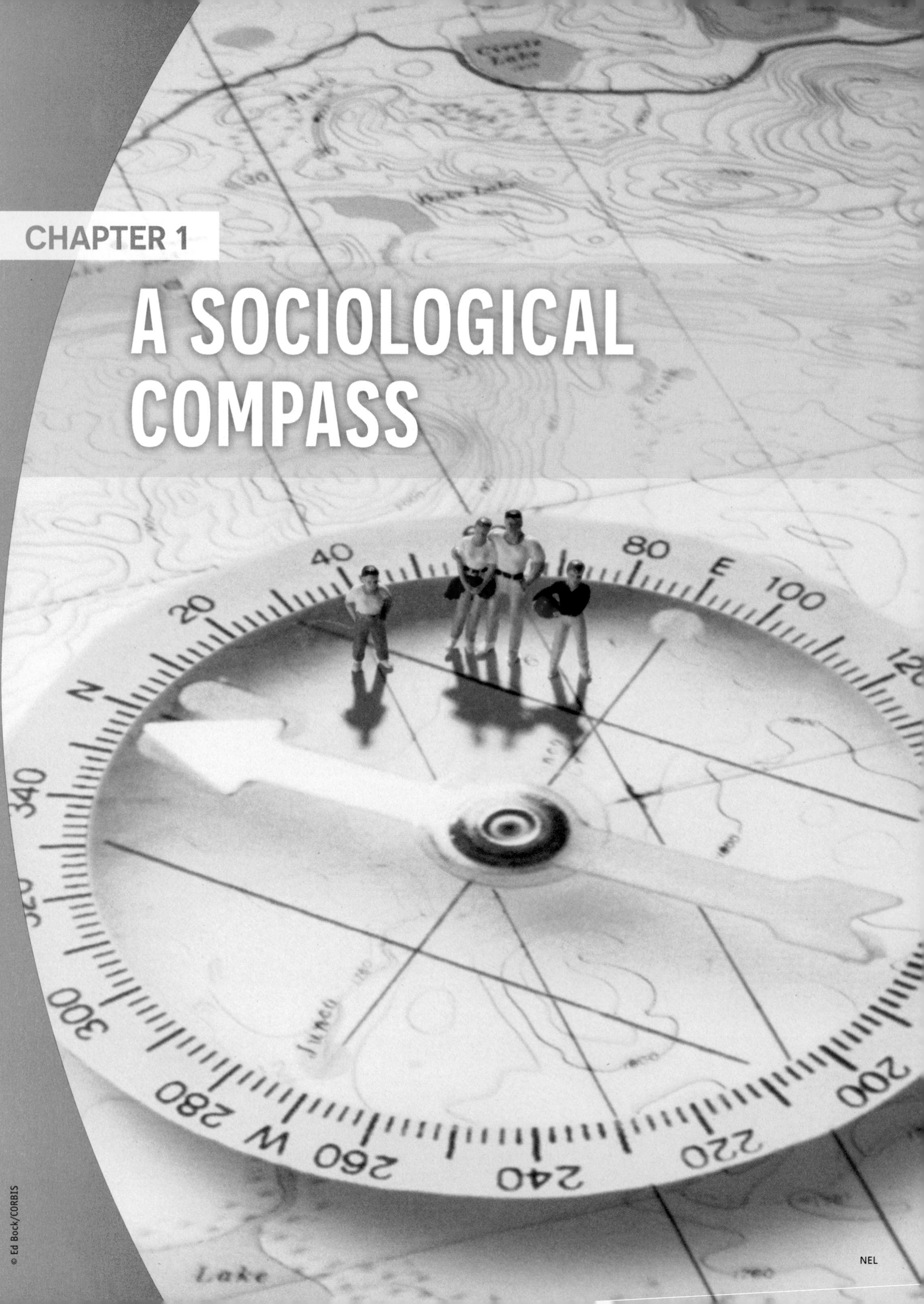

© Ed Bock/CORBIS

IN THIS CHAPTER, YOU WILL LEARN TO

- Define sociology.
- Identify the social relations that surround you, permeate you, and influence your behaviour.
- Describe how sociological research seeks to improve people's lives and test ideas using scientific methods.
- Summarize the main schools of sociological theory.
- Appreciate how sociology emerged out of the scientific, democratic, and industrial revolutions.
- Understand the main challenges facing society today.

INTRODUCTION

Why You Need a Compass for a New World

"When I was a small child growing up in New Brunswick in the 1950s, an Aboriginal woman would come to our home from time to time, and my mother would serve us lunch," recalls Robert Brym.

"The woman's name was Lena White. I was fond of Lena because she told good stories. During dessert, as we sipped tea with milk, Lena would spin tales about Gluskap, the Creator of the world.

"I liked Gluskap because he was mischievous and enormously powerful. He fought giants, drove away monsters, taught people how to hunt and farm, and named the stars. But he also got into trouble and learned from his mistakes. For example, one day the wind was blowing so hard Gluskap couldn't paddle his canoe into the bay to hunt ducks. So he found the source of the wind: the flapping wings of the Wind Eagle. He then tricked the Wind Eagle into getting stuck in a crevice where he could flap no more. Now Gluskap could go hunting. However, the air soon grew so hot he found it difficult to breathe. The water became dirty and began to smell bad, and there was so much foam on it he found it hard to paddle. When he complained to his grandmother, she explained that the wind was needed to cool the air, wash the earth, and move the waters to keep them clean. And so Gluskap freed the Wind Eagle and the winds returned to the earth. Gluskap decided it was better to wait for good weather and then go duck hunting, rather than to conquer the winds.

"Like the tale of the Wind Eagle, many of the Gluskap stories Lena told me were about the need for harmony among humans and between humans and nature. You can imagine my surprise, therefore, when I got to school and learned about the European exploration of what was called the New World. My teachers taught me all about the glories of the *conquest* of nature—and of other people. I learned that in the New World, a Native population perhaps a hundredth as large as Europe's occupied a territory more than four times larger. I was taught that the New World was unimaginably rich in resources. European rulers saw that by controlling it they could increase their power and importance. Christians recognized

Gluskap

new possibilities for spreading their religion. Explorers discerned fresh opportunities for rewarding adventures. A wave of excitement swelled as word spread of the New World's vast potential and challenges. I, too, became excited as I heard stories of conquest quite unlike the tales of Gluskap. Of course, I learned little about the violence required to conquer the New World."

In the 1950s, I was caught between thrilling stories of conquest and reflective stories that questioned the wisdom of conquest. Today, I think many people are in a similar position. On the one hand, we feel like the European explorers because we, too, have reached the frontiers of a New World. Like them, we are full of anticipation. Our New World is one of instant long-distance communication, global economies and cultures, weakening nation-states, and technological advances that often make the daily news seem like reports from a distant planet. In a fundamental way, the world is not the same place it was just 50 or 60 years ago. On the other hand, we understand that not all is hope and bright horizons. Our anticipation is mixed with dread. Gluskap stories make more sense than ever. Scientific breakthroughs are announced almost daily, but the global environment has never been in worse shape, and AIDS is now the leading cause of death for adults in Africa. Marriages and nations unexpectedly break up and then reconstitute themselves in new and unanticipated forms. We celebrate the advances made by women and minority groups only to find that some people oppose their progress, sometimes violently. Waves of people migrate between continents, establishing cooperation but also conflict between previously separated groups. New technologies make work more interesting and creative for some, offering unprecedented opportunities to become rich and famous. But they also make jobs more onerous and routine for others. The standard of living goes up for many people but stagnates or deteriorates for many more.

Amid all this contradictory news, good and bad, uncertainty about the future prevails. That is why my colleagues and I wrote this book. We set out to show undergraduates that sociology can help them make sense of their lives, however uncertain they may appear to be. Five hundred years ago, the early European explorers of North and South America set themselves the task of mapping the contours of the New World. We set ourselves a similar task here. Their frontiers were physical; ours are social. Their maps were geographical; ours are sociological. But in terms of functionality, our maps are much like theirs. All maps allow us to find our place in the world and see ourselves in the context of larger forces. Sociological maps, as the famous American sociologist C. Wright Mills wrote, allow us to "grasp the interplay of [people] and society, of biography and history" (Mills, 1959: 4). This book, then, shows you how to draw sociological maps so you can see your place in the world, figure out how to navigate through it, and perhaps discover how to improve it. It is your sociological compass.

We emphasize that sociology can be a liberating practical activity, not just an abstract intellectual exercise. By revealing the opportunities and constraints you face, sociology can help teach you who you are and what you can become in today's social and historical context. We cannot know what the future will bring, but we can at least know the choices we confront and the likely consequences of our actions. From this point of view, sociology can help us create the best possible future. That has always been sociology's principal justification, and so it must be today.

The Goals of This Chapter

This chapter has three goals:

1. The first goal is to illustrate the power of sociology to dispel foggy assumptions and help us see the operation of the social world more clearly. To that end, we examine a phenomenon that at first glance appears to be solely the outcome of breakdowns in *individual* functioning: suicide. We show that, in fact, *social* relations powerfully influence suicide rates. This exercise introduces you to the unique qualities of the sociological perspective.

2. The chapter's second goal is to show that, from its origins, sociological research has been motivated by a desire to improve the social world. Thus, sociology is not a dry, academic exercise but a means of charting a better course for society. At the same time, sociologists use scientific methods to test their ideas, thus increasing the validity of the results. We illustrate these points by briefly analyzing the work of the founders of the discipline.
3. The chapter's third goal is to suggest that sociology can help you come to grips with your century, just as it helped the founders of sociology deal with theirs. Today we are witnessing massive and disorienting social changes. As was the case 100 or 150 years ago, sociologists now try to understand social phenomena and suggest credible ways of improving society. By promising to make sociology relevant to you, this chapter is an invitation to participate in sociology's challenge.

Before showing how sociology can help you understand and improve your world, we briefly examine the problem of suicide. This examination will help illustrate how the sociological perspective can clarify and sometimes overturn commonsense beliefs.

THE SOCIOLOGICAL PERSPECTIVE

Analyzing suicide sociologically tests the claim that sociology takes a unique, surprising, and enlightening perspective on social events. After all, suicide appears to be a supremely antisocial and non-social act. First, it is condemned by nearly everyone in society. Second, it is typically committed in private, far from the public's intrusive glare. Third, it is comparatively rare: In 2011, there were 10.8 suicides for every 100 000 people in Canada (compared with the world average of about 16 suicides per 100 000 people; see Figure 1.1). And, finally, when you think about why people commit such acts, you are likely to focus on their individual states of mind rather than on the state of society—we are usually interested in the events that caused individuals to become depressed or angry enough to do something as awful as killing themselves. We do not usually think about the patterns of social relations that might encourage or inhibit such actions. If sociology can reveal the hidden social causes of such an apparently non-social and antisocial phenomenon, there must be something to it!

The Sociological Explanation of Suicide

At the end of the nineteenth century, Émile Durkheim (1951 [1897]) demonstrated that suicide is more than just an individual act of desperation that results from a psychological disorder, as was commonly believed at the time. Social forces, he showed, strongly influence suicide rates.

Durkheim made his case by examining the association between rates of suicide and rates of psychological disorder for different groups. The idea that psychological disorder causes suicide is supported, he reasoned, only if suicide rates tend to be high where rates of psychological disorder are high, and low where rates of psychological disorder are low. However, his analysis of European government statistics, hospital records, and other sources revealed nothing of the kind. For example, he discovered that insane asylums housed slightly more women than men, but there were four male suicides for every female suicide. Among the major religious groups in France, Jews had the highest rate of psychological disorder, but also the lowest suicide rate. Durkheim also found that psychological disorders occurred most frequently when a person reached adulthood, but suicide rates increased steadily with age.

Courtesy of A.C. Fine Art, Nova Scotia. Photographer: James Chambers

Alex Colville's *Pacific* (1967)

FIGURE 1.1

Map of Suicide Rates (per 100 000; most recent year available as of 2011)

Source: World Health Organization. 2013. "Suicide Prevention (SUPRE)." SUPRE Information leaflet pdf, 79kb. http://www.who.int/mental_health/management/en/SUPRE_flyer1.pdf?ua=1.

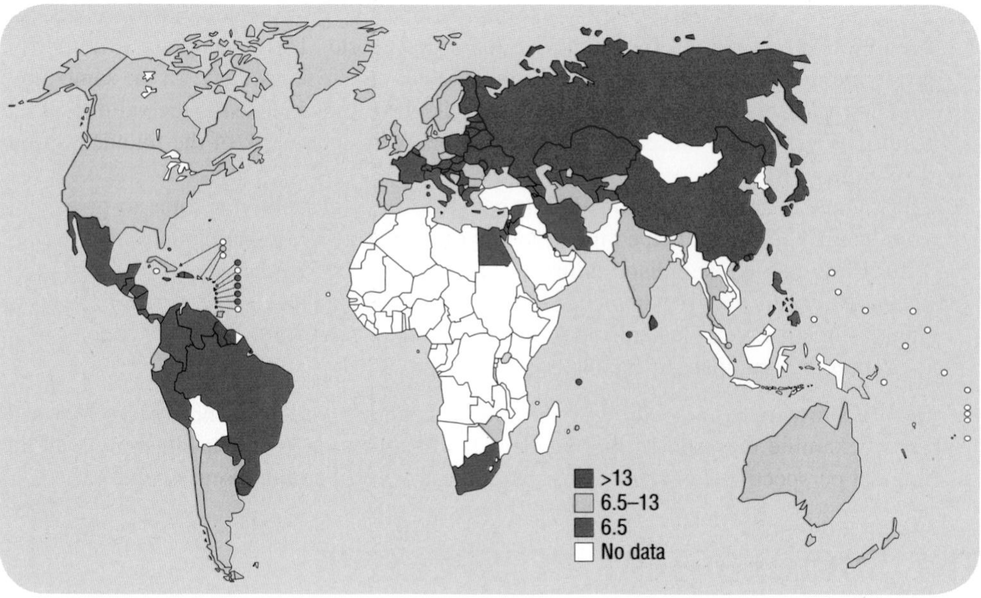

Social solidarity refers to (1) the degree to which group members share beliefs and values, and (2) the intensity and frequency of their interaction.

Clearly, suicide rates and rates of psychological disorder did not vary directly. In fact, they often appeared to vary inversely. Why? Durkheim held that suicide rates varied because of differences in the degree of **social solidarity** in various categories of the population. According to Durkheim, the greater the degree to which group members share beliefs and values, and the more frequently and intensely they interact, the more social solidarity the group exhibits. In turn, the more social solidarity a group exhibits, the more firmly anchored individuals are to the social world, and the less likely they are to take their own life when adversity strikes. In other words, Durkheim expected high-solidarity groups to have lower suicide rates than low-solidarity groups did—at least up to a point (see Figure 1.2).

To support his argument, Durkheim showed that married adults are half as likely as unmarried adults are to commit suicide because marriage creates social ties and a kind of moral cement that bind the individual to society. Similarly, he argued that women are less likely to commit suicide than men are because women are more involved in the intimate social relations of family life. Jews, Durkheim wrote, are less likely to commit suicide than Christians are because, after centuries of persecution, they have become a group that is more defensive and tightly knit. Older adults are more prone than the young and the middle-aged

FIGURE 1.2

Durkheim argued that the suicide rate declines and then rises as social solidarity increases.

Durkheim called suicide in high-solidarity settings *altruistic*. Soldiers who knowingly give up their lives to protect comrades commit altruistic suicide. Suicide in low-solidarity settings is *egoistic* or *anomic*. *Egoistic suicide* results from the poor integration of people into society because of weak social ties to others. For instance, someone who is unemployed has weaker social ties, and is thus more likely to commit suicide than someone who is employed. *Anomic suicide* occurs when vague norms govern behaviour. Thus, the rate of anomic suicide is likely to be high among people living in a society lacking a widely shared code of morality.

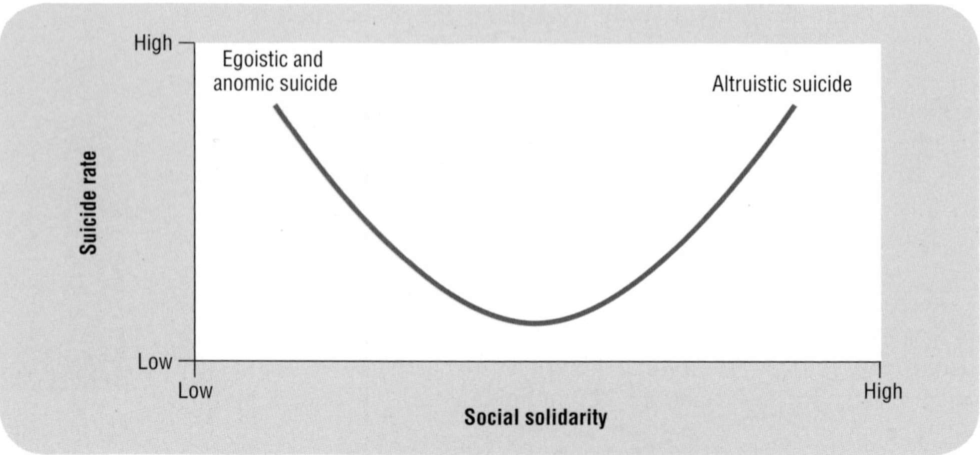

are to take their own lives in the face of misfortune because they are most likely to live alone, to have lost a spouse or partner, and to lack a job and a wide network of friends. In general, Durkheim wrote, "suicide varies with the degree of integration of the social groups of which the individual forms a part" (Durkheim, 1951 [1897]: 209). Note that his generalization tells us nothing about why a particular *individual* may take his or her life. That explanation is the province of psychology. But it does tell us that a person's likelihood of committing suicide decreases with the degree to which he or she is anchored in society. And it says something surprising and uniquely sociological about how and why the suicide rate varies across groups.

oliveromg/Shutterstock.com

Strong social bonds decrease the probability that a person will commit suicide when adversity strikes.

Suicide in Canada Today

Durkheim's theory is not just a historical curiosity; it sheds light on the factors that account for variations in suicide rates today. Consider Figure 1.3, which shows suicide rates by age and sex in Canada. Comparing rates for men and women, we immediately see that, as in Durkheim's France, men are three times more likely than women are to commit suicide. However, in other respects, Canada today differs from France more than a century ago. For example, in Durkheim's time, suicide was rare among youth. In Canada today, suicide is more common, having increased substantially since the 1960s.

Although the rate of youth suicide was low in Durkheim's France, his theory of social solidarity helps us understand why the youth suicide rate has risen in Canada. In brief, shared moral principles and strong social ties have eroded since the early 1960s, especially for Canadian youth. Consider the following facts:

- Church, synagogue, mosque, and temple attendance is down, particularly among young people. Well over half of Canadians attended religious services weekly in the 1960s. Today the figure is below one-third and is only 15 percent for people born after 1960.

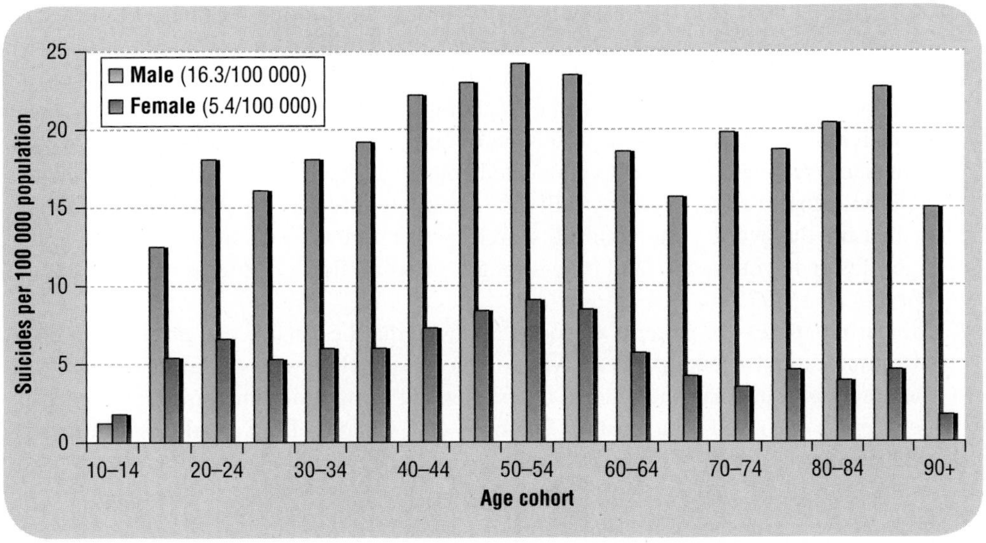

FIGURE 1.3

Suicide by Age and Sex, Canada, 2011

Source: Adapted from Statistics Canada. 2014b. "Suicides and suicide rate, by sex and by age group." http://www.statcan.gc.ca/tables-tableaux/sum-som/l01/cst01/hlth66d-eng.htm (retrieved 8 August 2014).

- Unemployment is up, especially for youth. The unemployment rate was around 3 percent for most of the 1960s, rose steadily to about 10 percent for most of the 1990s, and reached 13.4 percent in 1994. Since then, the unemployment rate has declined, but it is nearly twice as high for Canadians under the age of 25 as it is for Canadians above the age of 24 (in July 2014, 13.2 percent).
- The rate of divorce has increased sixfold since the early 1960s. Births outside of marriage are also much more common than they once were. As a result, more children are now being raised in single-parent families than was the case in the past, which suggests that, on average, they experience less adult supervision and less frequent and less intimate social interaction with their parents.

In sum, the figures cited above suggest that the level of social solidarity is now lower than it was just a few decades ago, especially for young people. Less firmly rooted in society, and less likely to share moral standards, young people in Canada today are more likely than they were half a century ago to take their own lives if they happen to find themselves in a deep personal crisis (see Box 1.1).

From Personal Troubles to Social Structures

You have known for a long time that you live in a society. Until now, you may not have fully appreciated that society also lives in you. That is, patterns of social relations affect your innermost thoughts and feelings, influence your actions, and thus help shape who you are. As we have seen, one such pattern of social relations is the level of social solidarity characteristic of the various groups to which you belong.

Social structures are relatively stable patterns of social relations.

Sociologists call relatively stable patterns of social relations **social structures**. One of the sociologist's main tasks is to identify and explain the connection between people's personal troubles and the social structures in which people are embedded. This task is harder work than it may seem at first. In everyday life, we usually see things mainly from our own point of view. Our experiences seem unique to each of us. If we think about them at all, social structures may appear remote and impersonal. To see how social structures influence us, we require sociological training.

Microstructures are the patterns of relatively intimate social relations formed during face-to-face interaction. Families, friendship circles, and work associations are examples of microstructures.

An important step in broadening our sociological awareness involves recognizing that three levels of social structure surround and permeate us. Think of these structures as concentric circles radiating out from you:

Macrostructures are overarching patterns of social relations that lie outside and above a person's circle of intimates and acquaintances. Macrostructures include classes, bureaucracies, and power systems, such as patriarchy.

Patriarchy is the traditional system of economic and political inequality between women and men.

1. **Microstructures** are patterns of intimate social relations. They are formed during face-to-face interaction. Families, friendship circles, and work associations are all examples of microstructures.

   Understanding the operation of microstructures can be useful. Let's say you are looking for a job. You might think you would do best to ask as many close friends and relatives as possible for leads and contacts. However, sociological research shows that people you know well are likely to know many of the same people. After asking a couple of close connections for help landing a job, you would do better by asking more remote acquaintances for leads and contacts. People to whom you are *weakly* connected (and who are weakly connected among themselves) are more likely to know *different* people. Therefore, they will give you more information about job possibilities and ensure that word about your job search spreads farther. You are more likely to find a job faster if you understand "the strength of weak ties" in microstructural settings (Granovetter, 1973).
2. **Macrostructures** are patterns of social relations that lie outside and above your circle of intimates and acquaintances.[1] Macrostructures include class relations, bureaucracies, and **patriarchy**, the traditional system of economic and political inequality between women and men in most societies (see Chapter 11, Sexualities and Gender Stratification).

BOX 1.1

IT'S YOUR CHOICE

SUICIDE AND THE INNU OF LABRADOR

The Canadians with the highest suicide rate are Aboriginal peoples. Among them, the Innu of Labrador have the highest suicide rate. They are probably the most suicide-prone people in the world. Among the Innu, the suicide rate is nearly 13 times the rate for all Canadians (Rogan, 2001; Samson, Wilson, and Mazower, 1999).

Durkheim's theory of suicide helps explain the Innu people's tragic propensity to commit suicide. Over the past six decades, the Innu's traditional norms and values have been destroyed. Moreover, the Innu were prevented from participating in stable and meaningful patterns of social interaction. In other words, social solidarity among the Innu has been cut to an abysmally low level.

How did this change happen? Historically, the Innu were a nomadic people who relied on hunting and trapping for their livelihood but in the mid-1950s, shortly after Newfoundland and Labrador became part of Canada, the provincial and federal governments were eager to gain more control of traditional Innu land to encourage economic development. Government officials reasoned that to accommodate new roads, mines, lumbering operations, hydroelectric projects, and low-level flight-training facilities for NATO air forces, the Innu would need to be concentrated in settlements. Furthermore, government officials believed that, to function in these new settlements, the Innu would need to learn practical and cultural skills associated with a modern industrial society. Consequently, governments put tremendous pressure on the Innu to give up their traditional way of life and settle in Davis Inlet and Sheshatshui.

CP Pictures Archive/Ryan Remiorz

Sniffing gasoline in Davis Inlet

In the new communities, Canadian laws, schools, and churches strongly discouraged the Innu from hunting, practising their religion, and raising their children in the traditional way. For example, Canadian hunting regulations limited Innu access to their age-old livelihood. Priests are known to have beaten children who missed church or school to go hunting, thus introducing interpersonal violence in a culture that formerly knew none. Teachers transmitted North American and European skills and culture, often denigrating Innu practices. At the same time, few alternative jobs existed in the new communities. Most Innu wound up living in despair and on welfare. In the absence of work, and lacking the stabilizing influence of their traditional culture, a people long known for their nonviolence and cooperative spirit became victims of widespread family breakdown, sexual abuse, drunkenness, and alcohol-related illness. In Sheshatshui in 2001, at least 20 percent of the children regularly got high by sniffing gasoline. In Davis Inlet, the figure was nearly 60 percent.

In 2002, the federal and provincial governments decided to move the people of Davis Inlet and create a safer community for them in Natuashish, 15 km away. The new community voted to abolish alcohol in 2008, but it is still smuggled into town, where a 40-ounce (1.2 litre) bottle of rye sells for $350. Some local mothers openly denounce people who supply alcohol and drugs, but substance abuse is still widespread and anti-abolitionists may still be found in the local government (Moore, 2010).

What can be done about the tragedy of the Innu? A 1984 study showed that a movement among the Innu to return to the land and to traditional hunting practices for up to seven months a year led to a dramatic improvement in health. They lived a vigorous outdoor life. Alcohol abuse stopped. Diet improved. Their emotional and social environments stabilized and became meaningful. Suicide was unknown (Samson, Wilson, and Mazower, 1999: 25).

Unfortunately, a big political obstacle stands in the way of a wide scale return of the Innu to their traditional lifestyle. The governments of Canada and Newfoundland and Labrador will not allow it. A widespread Innu return to the land would conflict with government and private economic development plans. For instance, the Lower Churchill Falls hydroelectric project (the second-biggest hydroelectric project in the world) and the Voisey's Bay nickel mine (the world's biggest deposit of nickel) are located in the middle of traditional Innu hunting and burial grounds. The Innu are vigorously attempting to regain control of their land. They also want to be able to decide on their own when and how to use Canadian health services, training facilities, and the like. Whether some compromise can be worked out between government and private plans for economic development and the continuity of the Innu people is unclear. What is clear is that, as a Canadian citizen, the outcome is partly your choice.

Understanding the operation of macrostructures is useful. Consider, for example, that when a marriage dissolves, partners commonly blame themselves and each other for their troubles. They tend to ignore the fact that, in our society, most married women who work full-time in the paid labour force are responsible for more housework, child care, and care for seniors than their husbands are. In most of Canada and in many other countries, governments and businesses support this arrangement insofar as they provide little assistance to families in the form of affordable and accessible daycare facilities, after-school programs for children, and the like. When spouses share domestic responsibilities equally, their marriages are happier and divorce is less likely, but the unequal division of work in the household—an aspect of patriarchy—is a major source of dissatisfaction in marriages, especially in families that cannot afford to buy services privately (Hochschild with Machung, 1989). Rather than explaining marriage breakups solely as the result of conflicting personalities, it is useful to understand how the macrostructure of patriarchy contributes to marital dissatisfaction. Changing that structure can help people to lead happier lives.

Global structures are patterns of social relations that lie outside and above the national level. They include international organizations, patterns of worldwide travel and communication, and the economic relations between countries.

3. The third level of society that surrounds and permeates us comprises **global structures**. International organizations, patterns of worldwide travel and communication, and economic relations between countries are examples of global structures. Global structures are increasingly important as inexpensive travel and communication allow all parts of the world to become interconnected culturally, economically, and politically.

   Understanding the operation of global structures can be useful, too. For instance, many people are concerned about the world's poor. They donate money to charities to help with famine and disaster relief. They support their government giving aid to poor countries. However, many of these people don't understand that charity and foreign aid alone will not end world poverty. Charity and foreign aid are unable to overcome the structure of social relations among countries that have created and sustain global inequality.

   As we will see in Chapter 9 (Globalization, Inequality, and Development), Britain, France, and other imperial powers locked some countries into poverty when they colonized them between the seventeenth and nineteenth centuries. In the twentieth century, the poor (or "developing") countries borrowed money from these same rich countries and Western banks to pay for airports, roads, harbours, sanitation systems, basic health care, and so on. Today, poor countries pay about seven times as much in interest on those loans as they receive in aid (United Nations, 2004: 201). Thus, it seems that relying exclusively on foreign aid and charity can do little to help solve the problem of world poverty. Understanding how the global structure of international relations created and helps maintain global inequality suggests new policy priorities for helping the world's poor. One such priority might involve campaigning for the cancellation of foreign debt in compensation for past injustices.

As these examples illustrate, personal problems are connected to social structures at the micro-, macro-, and global levels. Whether a personal problem involves finding a job, keeping a marriage intact, or figuring out a way to end world poverty, social-structural considerations broaden our understanding of the problem and suggest appropriate courses of action.

The Sociological Imagination

The **sociological imagination** is the quality of mind that enables a person to see the connection between personal troubles and social structures.

More than half a century ago, C. Wright Mills (1959) called the ability to see the connection between personal troubles and social structures the **sociological imagination**. He emphasized the difficulty of developing this quality of mind (see Box 1.2 and Box 1.3). His language is sexist by today's standards but his argument is as true and inspiring today as it was in the 1950s:

> When a society becomes industrialized, a peasant becomes a worker; a feudal lord is liquidated or becomes a businessman. When classes rise or fall, a man is employed or unemployed; when the rate of investment goes up or down, a man takes new heart or goes broke. When war happens, an insurance salesman becomes a rocket launcher; a store clerk, a radar man; a wife lives alone; a child grows up without a father. Neither the life of an individual nor the history of a society can be understood without understanding both.

BOX 1.2

SOCIOLOGY ON THE TUBE

HERE COMES HONEY BOO BOO: THE SOCIOLOGICAL IMAGINATION AND REALITY TV

The Thompsons are a loving family. They live beside the train tracks in a small town in rural Georgia. June and Mike, the parents, are high-school dropouts. Alana, age 7, goes by the nickname Honey Boo Boo. She has been competing in beauty pageants for two years with only modest success. Just before Honey Boo Boo goes on stage, Mama mixes up a special concoction to get her properly wired: a large glass of Red Bull and Mountain Dew that contains a couple of hundred calories of high-fructose corn syrup and as much caffeine as two cups of coffee. Mama calls it "Go Go Juice." In fact, the entire family runs on a high-sugar, high-fat diet, making all of them overweight and Mama obese (at age 32, she tips the scales at more than 136 kg).

The Thompsons have a special affinity for swine. They own a pet baby pig that lives in their house,

Noel Vasquez/Getty Images

Honey Boo Boo

and they apparently enjoy nothing so much as emulating its behaviour, squealing with unrestrained joy as they launch their bodies into big mud puddles on a hot summer's day after a good rain. At the annual Redneck Games, one of the older Thompson girls bobs not for apples but for uncooked pig's feet.

Mama helps to support the family by clipping coupons, receiving child support from the several men who sired her four daughters, and collecting payments from TLC, the TV channel that runs the show. The money must be good. *Here Comes Honey Boo Boo* was one of the station's most popular series until it was cancelled in October 2014, when reports surfaced that June was dating a convicted child molester.

In the mid-1990s, TLC was "The Learning Channel," but its educational programming earned poor ratings, so it began focusing on reality TV shows, which are inexpensive to produce and enormously popular. TLC turned around financially thanks to such hits as *Jon & Kate Plus 8, Extreme Couponing, My Big Fat Gypsy Wedding*, and *Here Comes Honey Boo Boo*.

The people in many reality TV shows represent small minorities—and, in the case of the southern white "rednecks" portrayed in *Here Comes Honey Boo Boo*, shrinking slices of the North American population. The reality they reflect is not the reality that most of us know, which is why viewers find these shows so fascinating. And not just fascinating: Viewers often feel better about themselves when they point and snicker at the statistical oddities that populate many reality TV shows. As such, *Here Comes Honey Boo Boo* and other similar programs perform an important social function. How much more upset might viewers be with their own lot in life if they did not have ready access to people they can ridicule? This sociological reality is rarely considered by the viewers of shows like *Here Comes Honey Boo Boo*. Arguably, *Here Comes Honey Boo Boo* deflects viewers' attention from important social issues and helps to minimize their political discontent.

TV programs, including reality TV shows, tell us important things about our society if we view them with a sociological eye. For that reason, in every chapter, we reflect on the fact that TV shows, while entertaining us, also have the potential to enlarge our sociological imagination.

Critical Thinking

1. Arguably, reality shows like *Here Comes Honey Boo Boo* help audience members feel better about themselves by giving them an opportunity to ridicule others. What similar social mechanisms operate in the schoolyard and in the workplace?
2. Under what conditions might such social mechanisms not operate?

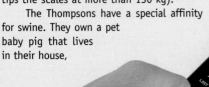

Yet men do not usually define the troubles they endure in terms of historical change. . . . The well-being they enjoy, they do not usually impute to the big ups and downs of the society in which they live. Seldom aware of the intricate connection between the patterns of their own lives and the course of world history, ordinary men do not usually know what this connection means for the kind of men they are becoming and for the kind of history-making in which they might take part. They do not possess the quality of mind essential to grasp the interplay of men and society, of biography and history, of self and world. They cannot cope with their personal troubles in such a way as to control the structural transformations that usually lie behind them.

BOX 1.3

SOCIOLOGY AT THE MOVIES

12 YEARS A SLAVE

At the Clerkenwell House of Correction in London in the late 1600s, it was not uncommon for a ship's captain to visit the girls awaiting trial for disorderly conduct, ply them with liquor and sweetmeats, and convince them that a better life awaited them in Jamaica. Presumably by monetary arrangement with the warden, many such girls were released, only to enter a life of servitude. Kidnappings helped to relieve labour scarcity in the New World.

Aboriginal people were the first slaves in the Americas, but neither they nor the white criminals brought over from England could satisfy the labour needs of sugar, tobacco, and cotton plantations. As a result, some 24 million West African blacks were rounded up like cattle and shipped across the Atlantic.

Still, kidnapping persisted into the nineteenth century. One case involved Solomon Northup, an educated, economically successful, free black man with a wife and two children. Abducted from Washington, D.C., in 1841, he was taken to Louisiana and enslaved there until an itinerant Canadian carpenter helped to free him in 1853.

Northup's 1855 memoir, *Twelve Years a Slave,* became the basis for a movie of the same name. Hailed as the first realistic cinematic portrayal of slavery in the New World, it won the Academy Award for best picture in 2013.

The movie is unspeakably upsetting, forcing audience members to wonder time and again how normal people could have engaged in such unrelenting cruelty toward other human beings. To the degree it provides an answer, it is this: the remorselessly brutal slave masters were anything but normal. The master of Solomon Northup (played by Chiwetel Ejiofor) is Edwin Epps (played by Michael Fassbender). He is portrayed as a madman who rapes, beats, whips, demeans, and psychologically tortures his slaves with gusto. And of course he is a racist, too, regarding blacks as more animal than human. When challenged by his Canadian carpenter to explain, "in the sight of God, what is the difference between a white man and a black man?" he replies, "You might as well ask what the difference is between a white man and a baboon. Now, I've seen one of them critters in Orleans that knowed just as much as any nigger I've got" (quoted in Northup, 1855: 266–67).

Notwithstanding the merits of *12 Years a Slave* as a movie, its explanations for slavery and the cruelties that derive from it are weak, sociologically speaking. Slavery did not rely on sadistic madmen like Epps to enslave and brutalize human beings. In the mid-nineteenth

> What they need … is a quality of mind that will help them to [see] … what is going on in the world and … what may be happening within themselves. It is this quality … that … may be called the sociological imagination.
> *(Mills, 1959: 3–4)*

The sociological imagination is a recent addition to the human repertoire. True, in ancient and medieval times, some philosophers wrote about society. However, their thinking was not sociological. They believed God and nature controlled society. They spent much of their time sketching blueprints for the ideal society and urging people to follow those blueprints. They relied on speculation rather than on evidence to reach conclusions about how society works (see Figure 1.4).

The **Scientific Revolution** began about 1550. It encouraged the view that sound conclusions about the workings of society must be based on solid evidence, not just on speculation.

Origins of the Sociological Imagination

The sociological imagination was born when three revolutions pushed people to think about society in an entirely new way:

1. The **Scientific Revolution** began about 1550. It encouraged the view that we should base conclusions about the workings of society on evidence, not speculation. People

The Kobal Collection at Art Resource, NY

Scene from *12 Years a Slave*

century, enslavement and brutalization were normal in the southern United States, the Caribbean, and South America. Nor was racism the cause of slavery, as is evident from the fact that white European prisoners served perfectly well as slaves. Rather, as Eric Williams (an historian and the first president of Trinidad and Tobago) wrote, "slavery was not born of racism; racism was the consequence of slavery" (Williams, 1944: 8). What Williams meant is that slavery derived from the profit motive in a context of labour scarcity; it was the basis for prosperity in America and Europe. Racism was a justification for it. Here, we have a sociological explanation for slavery and cruelty. This explanation focuses on the way social relations influence what people think and how they act.

Similarly for Epps's claim that blacks are no different from baboons. Mr. Bass, the Canadian carpenter (played by Brad Pitt) had the appropriate sociological response:

These niggers are human beings. If they don't know as much as their masters, whose fault is it? They are not allowed to know anything. You have books and papers, and can go where you please, and gather intelligence in a thousand ways. But your slaves have no privileges. You'd whip one of them if caught reading a book. They are held in bondage, generation after generation, deprived of mental improvement, and who can expect them to possess much knowledge!... If they are baboons ... you and men like you will have to answer for it. (Northup, 1855: 267–68)

Understanding the social constraints and possibilities for freedom that envelop us requires an active sociological imagination. The sociological imagination urges us to connect biography with history and social structure—to make sense of our lives and the lives of others against a larger historical and social background and to act in light of our understanding. Have you ever tried to put events in your own life in the context of history and social structure? Did the exercise help you make sense of your life? Did it in any way lead to a life more worth living? Is the sociological imagination a worthy goal?

Although for many people, movies are just entertainment, they often achieve by different means what the sociological imagination aims to accomplish. Therefore, in each chapter of this book, we review a movie to shed light on topics of sociological importance.

often link the Scientific Revolution to specific ideas, such as Newton's laws of motion and Copernicus's theory that Earth revolves around the Sun. However, science is less a collection of ideas than a method of inquiry. For instance, in 1609, Galileo pointed his newly invented telescope at the heavens, made some careful observations, and showed that his observations fit Copernicus's theory. This is the core of the scientific method: using evidence to make a case for a particular point of view. By the mid-seventeenth century, some philosophers, such as Descartes in France and Hobbes in England, were calling for a science of society. When sociology emerged as a distinct discipline in the nineteenth century, commitment to the scientific method was one firm pillar of the sociological imagination.

2. The **Democratic Revolution** began about 1750. It suggested that people are responsible for organizing society and that human intervention can therefore solve social problems. Four hundred years ago, most Europeans thought otherwise. For them, God ordained the social order. The American Revolution (1775–83) and the French Revolution (1789–99) helped to undermine that idea. These democratic upheavals showed that society could experience massive change in a short period and that *people* control society. The implications for social thought were profound. For if people could change society, then a science of society could help them improve it. Much of the

The **Democratic Revolution** began about 1750. It suggested that people are responsible for organizing society and that human intervention can therefore solve social problems.

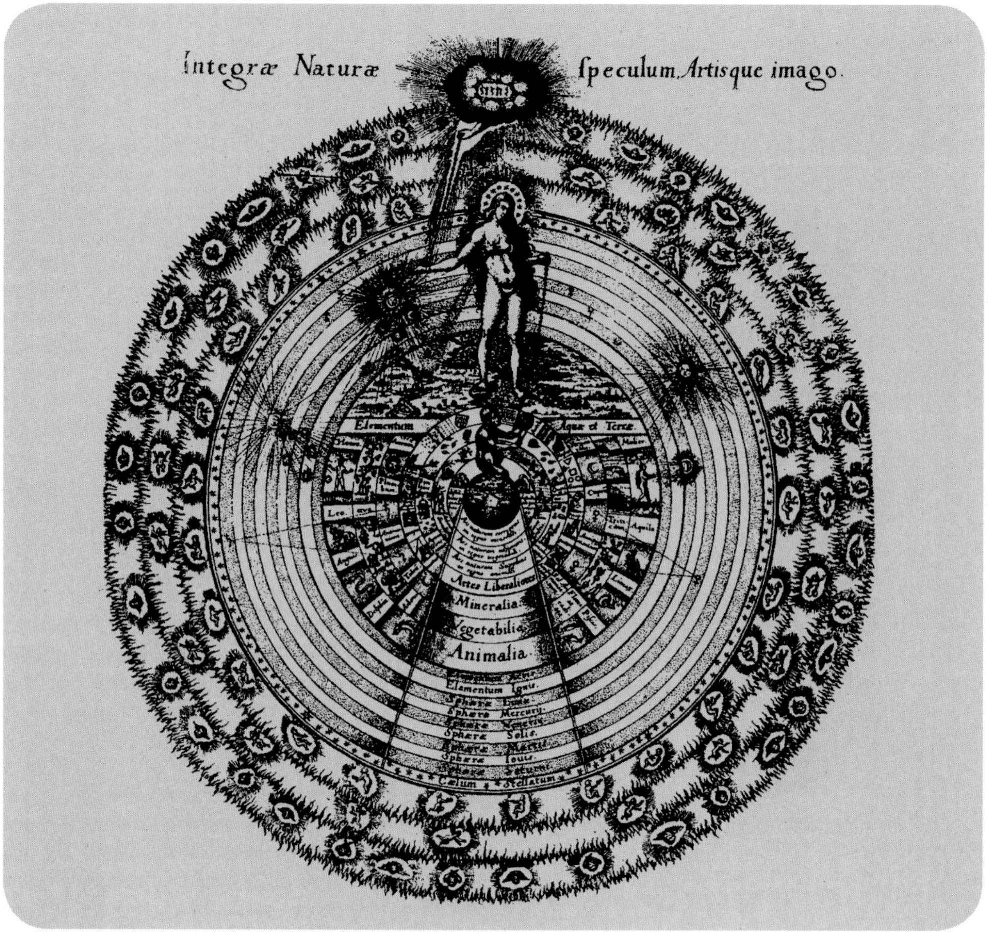

FIGURE 1.4

The European View of the World, about 1600

In Shakespeare's time, most educated Europeans pictured a universe in which God ultimately determines everything. Thus, in this early seventeenth-century engraving, a chain extends from God's hand to the hand of a woman representing Nature; she in turn holds a chain extending to the "ape of Nature," representing humankind. The engraving thus suggests that God and his intermediary, Nature, shape all human actions. Notice also that the engraving arranges all the elements of the universe—angels, heavenly objects, humans, animals, vegetables, minerals—in a hierarchy. It suggests that higher elements, such as the stars and the planets, influence lower elements, such as the fate of humans.

Source: Robert Fludd, *Ultriusque Cosmi Maioris Scilicet et Minoris Metaphysica, Physica Atqve Technica Historia*. 1617–19. (Oppenheim, Germany. Johan-Thedoride Bry.) By permission of Houghton Library, Harvard University.

justification for sociology as a science arose from the democratic revolutions that shook Europe and North America.

3. The **Industrial Revolution** began about 1780. It created a host of new social problems that attracted the attention of social thinkers. As a result of the growth of industry, masses of people moved from countryside to city, worked agonizingly long hours in crowded and dangerous mines and factories, lost faith in their religions, confronted faceless bureaucracies, and reacted to the filth and poverty of their existence with strikes, crime, revolutions, and wars. Scholars had never seen a sociological laboratory like this. The Scientific Revolution suggested that a science of society was possible. The Democratic Revolution suggested that people could intervene to improve society. The Industrial Revolution presented social thinkers with a host of pressing social problems crying out for a solution. They responded by giving birth to the sociological imagination.

The **Industrial Revolution**, often regarded as the most important event in world history since the development of agriculture and cities, refers to the rapid economic transformation that began in Britain in the 1780s. It involved the large-scale application of science and technology to industrial processes, the creation of factories, and the formation of a working class.

THEORY, RESEARCH, AND VALUES

French social thinker Auguste Comte (1798–1857) coined the term *sociology* in 1838 (Thompson, 1975). Comte tried to place the study of society on scientific foundations. He said he wanted to understand the social world as it was, not as he or anyone else imagined it should be. Yet there was a tension in his work. Although Comte was eager to adopt the scientific method in studying society, he was a conservative thinker, motivated by strong opposition to rapid change in French society. This inclination was evident in his writings. When he moved from his small, conservative hometown to Paris, Comte witnessed the democratic forces unleashed by the French Revolution, the early industrialization of society, and the rapid growth of cities. What he saw shocked and saddened him. Rapid social change was destroying much of what he valued, especially respect for traditional authority. He therefore urged slow change and the preservation of all that was traditional in social life. Thus, scientific methods of research *and* a vision of the ideal society were evident in sociology at its origins.

Although he praised the value of scientific methods, Comte never conducted any research. Neither did the second founder of sociology, British social theorist Herbert Spencer (1820–1903). However, Spencer believed that he had discovered scientific laws governing the operation of society. Strongly influenced by Charles Darwin's theory of evolution, he thought that societies evolve in the same way biological species do. Individuals struggle to survive, the unfit die before they can bear offspring, and the fittest survive. According to Spencer, this process allows "barbaric" societies to become "civilized." Deep social inequalities exist in society, but that is just as it should be if societies are to evolve, Spencer argued (1975 [1897–1906]).

Spencer's ideas, which came to be known as "social Darwinism," were popular for a time in North America and Great Britain. Wealthy industrialists, such as the oil baron John D. Rockefeller, found much to admire in a doctrine that justified social inequality and trumpeted the superiority of the wealthy and the powerful. Today, few sociologists think that societies are like biological systems. We have a better understanding of the complex economic, political, military, religious, and other forces that cause social change. We know that people can take things into their own hands and change their social environment in ways that no other species can. Spencer remains of interest because he was among the first social thinkers to assert that society operates according to scientific laws—and because his vision of the ideal society nonetheless showed through his writings.

To varying degrees, we see the same tension between belief in the importance of science and a vision of the ideal society in the work of the three giants in the early

traveler1116/Istockphoto.com

The Scientific Revolution began in Europe around 1550. Scientists proposed new theories about the structure of the universe and developed new methods to collect evidence so they could test those theories. Shown here is an astrolabe used by Copernicus to solve problems relating to the position of the Sun, the planets, and the stars.

Musée du Louvre, Paris/Giraudon, Paris/SuperStock

Eugene Delacroix's *Liberty Leading the People, July 28, 1830*. The democratic forces unleashed by the French Revolution suggested that people are responsible for organizing society and that human intervention can therefore solve social problems. As such, democracy was a foundation stone of sociology.

Diego Rivera's *Detroit Industry, North Wall* (1932–33). Fresco (detail). Copyright 1997. The Detroit Institute of Arts. The first Industrial Revolution began in the late eighteenth century. The so-called Second Industrial Revolution began in the early twentieth century. Wealthy entrepreneurs formed large companies. Steel became a basic industrial material. Oil and electricity fuelled much industrial production. At the same time, Henry Ford's assembly lines and other mass-production technologies transformed the workplace.

The Detroit Institute of Arts, USA/Gift of Edsel B. Ford/The Bridgeman Art Library

history of sociology: Karl Marx (1818–83), Émile Durkheim (1858–1917), and Max Weber (pronounced VAY-ber; 1864–1920). The lives of these three men spanned just over a century. They witnessed Europe's wrenching transition to industrial capitalism. They wanted to explain the great transformation of Europe and suggest ways of improving people's lives. They adopted scientific research methods in their work but they also wanted to chart a better course for their societies. The ideas they developed are not just diagnostic tools from which we can still learn but, like many sociological ideas, also prescriptions for combating social ills.

The tension between analysis and ideal, diagnosis and prescription, is evident throughout sociology. This tension becomes clear when we distinguish three important terms: theories, research, and values.

Theory

Theories are tentative explanations of some aspect of social life that state how and why certain facts are related.

Sociological ideas are usually expressed in the form of theories. **Theories** are tentative explanations of some aspect of social life. They state how and why certain facts are related. For example, in his theory of suicide, Durkheim related facts about suicide rates to facts about social solidarity, which enabled him to explain suicide as a function of social solidarity. In our broad definition, even a hunch qualifies as a theory if it suggests how and why certain facts are related (Einstein, 1954: 270).

Research

Research is the process of systematically observing reality to assess the validity of a theory.

After sociologists formulate theories, they can conduct research. **Research** is the process of systematically observing social reality, often to test a theory or assess its validity. For example, Durkheim collected suicide statistics from various government agencies to see whether the data supported or contradicted his theory. Because research can call a theory's validity into question, theories are only *tentative* explanations. We discuss the research process in detail in Chapter 2, How Sociologists Do Research.

Values

Before sociologists can formulate a theory, they must make certain judgments. For example, they must decide which problems are worth studying. They must make certain assumptions about how the parts of society fit together. If they are going to recommend ways of improving the operation of some aspect of society, they must even have an opinion about what the ideal society should look like. Sociologists' values shape these issues. **Values** are ideas about what is good and bad, right and wrong. Inevitably, values help sociologists formulate and favour certain theories over others (Edel, 1965; Kuhn, 1970 [1962]). As such, sociological theories may be modified and even rejected because of research, but they are often motivated by sociologists' values.

Values are ideas about what is good and bad, right and wrong.

Durkheim, Marx, and Weber stood close to the origins of the major theoretical traditions in sociology: functionalism, conflict theory, and symbolic interactionism. A fourth theoretical tradition, feminism, has arisen in recent decades to correct some deficiencies in the three long-established traditions. It will become clear as you read this book that many more theories exist in addition to these four. However, because these four traditions have been especially influential in the development of sociology, we present a thumbnail sketch of each one.

TIME FOR REVIEW

- How does the sociological study of suicide show that a distinctively *social* realm influences all human behaviour, even if the behaviour seems non-social or antisocial?
- What are microstructures, macrostructures, and global structures?
- How did the Scientific Revolution, the Industrial Revolution, and the Democratic Revolution influence the emergence of sociology?
- What is the relationship among values, theories, and research?

SOCIOLOGICAL THEORY AND THEORISTS

Functionalism

Durkheim

Durkheim's theory of suicide is an early example of what sociologists now call **functionalism**. Functionalist theories incorporate the following features:

Functionalism stresses that human behaviour is governed by relatively stable social structures. It underlines how social structures maintain or undermine social stability, emphasizes that social structures are based mainly on shared values or preferences, and suggests that re-establishing equilibrium can best solve most social problems.

1. They stress that relatively stable patterns of social relations, or social structures, govern human relations. For example, Durkheim emphasized how patterns of social solidarity influence suicide rates. Macrostructures are typically the social structures analyzed by functionalists.
2. Functionalist theories show how social structures maintain or undermine social stability. For example, Durkheim analyzed how the growth of industries and cities in nineteenth-century Europe lowered the level of social solidarity and contributed to social instability, which led, among other results, to a higher suicide rate.
3. Functionalist theories emphasize that social structures are based mainly on shared values or preferences. Thus, when Durkheim wrote about social solidarity, he sometimes meant the frequency and intensity of social interaction, but more often he thought of social solidarity as a sort of moral cement that binds people together.

Photo courtesy of Ed Clark

S. D. Clark (1910–2003) received his Ph.D. from the University of Toronto and later became that institution's first chair of the Department of Sociology. Born in Lloydminster, Alberta, he became known for his studies of Canadian social development as a process of disorganization and reorganization on a series of economic frontiers (Clark, 1968). The influence of functionalism on his work is apparent in his emphasis on the way society re-establishes equilibrium after experiencing disruptions caused by economic change.

4. Functionalism suggests that re-establishing equilibrium can best solve most social problems. Thus, Durkheim said that social stability could be restored in late–nineteenth-century Europe by creating new associations of employers and workers that would lower workers' expectations about what they could get out of life. If, said Durkheim, more people could agree on wanting less, then social solidarity would rise, resulting in fewer strikes, fewer suicides, and so on. Functionalism, then, was a conservative response to widespread social unrest in late–nineteenth-century France. A more liberal or radical response might have argued that if people are expressing discontent because they are getting less out of life than they expect, then discontent can be lowered by figuring out how they can get more out of life.

Functionalism in North America

Although functionalist thinking influenced North American sociology at the end of the nineteenth century, it was only during the continent's greatest economic crisis ever, the Great Depression of 1929–39, that functionalism took deep root here (Russett, 1966). With a quarter of the paid labour force unemployed and labour unrest rising, sociologists with a conservative frame of mind were, unsurprisingly, attracted to a theory focused on the restoration of social equilibrium. Functionalist theory remained popular for about 30 years. It experienced a minor revival in the early 1990s but never regained the dominance it enjoyed from the 1930s to the early 1960s.

Harvard sociologist Talcott Parsons was the foremost North American proponent of functionalism. Parsons is best known for identifying how various institutions must work to ensure the smooth operation of society as a whole. He argued that society is well integrated and in equilibrium when the family successfully raises new generations, the military successfully defends society against external threats, schools are able to teach students the skills and values they need to function as productive adults, and religions create a shared moral code among the people (Parsons, 1951).

Parsons was criticized for exaggerating the degree to which members of society share common values and social institutions contribute to social harmony. This criticism led North America's other leading functionalist, Robert Merton, to propose that social structures may have different consequences for different groups of people. Merton noted that some consequences may be disruptive or **dysfunctional** (Merton, 1968 [1949]). Moreover, said Merton, although **manifest** functions are obvious and intended, **latent** functions are unintended and less obvious. For instance, a manifest function of schools is to transmit skills from one generation to the next. A latent function of schools is to encourage the development of a separate youth culture that often conflicts with parents' values (Coleman, 1961; Hersch, 1998).

Dysfunctional consequences are effects of social structures that create social instability.

Manifest functions are obvious and intended effects of social structures.

Latent functions are non-obvious and unintended effects of social structures.

Conflict Theory

The second major theoretical tradition in sociology emphasizes the centrality of conflict in social life. **Conflict theory** incorporates the following features:

- Conflict theory generally focuses on large macrolevel structures, such as "class relations" or patterns of domination, submission, and struggle between people of high and low economic standing.
- Conflict theory shows how major patterns of inequality in society produce social stability in some circumstances and social change in others.
- Conflict theory stresses how members of privileged groups try to maintain their advantages while subordinate groups struggle to increase theirs. From this point of view, social conditions at a given time are the expression of an ongoing power struggle between privileged and subordinate groups.
- Conflict theory typically leads to the suggestion that eliminating privilege will lower the level of conflict and increase human welfare.

Conflict theory generally focuses on large macrolevel structures and shows how major patterns of inequality in society produce social stability in some circumstances and social change in others.

Marx

Conflict theory originated in the work of German social thinker Karl Marx. A generation before Durkheim, Marx observed the destitution and discontent produced by the Industrial Revolution and proposed a sweeping argument about the way societies develop (Marx, 1904 [1859]; Marx and Engels, 1972 [1848]). Marx's theory was radically different from Durkheim's. At the centre of Marx's ideas is the notion of **class conflict**, the struggle between classes to resist and overcome the opposition of other classes.

Class conflict is the struggle between classes to resist and overcome the opposition of other classes.

Marx argued that owners of industry are eager both to improve the way work is organized and to adopt new tools, machines, and production methods. These innovations allow them to produce more efficiently, earn higher profits, and drive inefficient competitors out of business. However, the drive for profits also causes capitalists to concentrate workers in larger and larger establishments, keep wages as low as possible, and invest as little as possible in improving working conditions. Thus, said Marx, a large and growing class of poor workers opposes a small and shrinking class of wealthy owners.

Marx believed that workers would ultimately become aware of belonging to the same exploited class. He called this awareness "class consciousness." He believed working-class consciousness would encourage the growth of trade unions and labour parties. According to Marx, these organizations would eventually seek to end private ownership of property, replacing it with a "communist" society where no private property exists and everyone shares wealth according to their needs.

Weber

Although some of Marx's ideas have been usefully adapted to the study of contemporary society, scholars have questioned his predictions about the inevitable collapse of capitalism. Max Weber, a German sociologist who wrote his major works a generation after Marx, was among the first to find flaws in Marx's argument (Weber, 1946). Weber noted the rapid growth of the service sector of the economy, with its many non-manual workers and professionals. He argued that many members of these occupational groups stabilize society because they enjoy higher status and income than do manual workers employed in manufacturing. In addition, Weber showed that class conflict is not the only driving force of history. In his view, politics and religion are also important sources of historical change (see below). Other writers pointed out that Marx did not understand how investing in technology would make it possible for workers to toil fewer hours under less oppressive conditions. Nor did he foresee that higher wages, better working conditions, and welfare state benefits would help to pacify manual workers.

John Porter (1921–79) was Canada's premier sociologist in the 1960s and 1970s. Born in Vancouver, he received his Ph.D. from the London School of Economics and spent his academic career at Carleton University in Ottawa. His major work, *The Vertical Mosaic* (1965), is a study of class and power in Canada. Firmly rooted in conflict theory, the book influenced a generation of Canadian sociologists in their studies on social inequality, elite groups, French–English relations, and Canadian–American relations.

Conflict Theory in North America

Conflict theory had some advocates in North America before the 1960s. Most noteworthy is C. Wright Mills, who laid the foundations for modern conflict theory in the 1950s. Mills conducted pioneering research on American politics and class structure. One of his most important books is *The Power Elite*, a study of the several hundred men who occupied the "command posts" of the American economy, military, and government. He argued that power is highly concentrated in American society, which is therefore less of a democracy than we are often led to believe (Mills, 1956).

Exceptions like Mills notwithstanding, conflict theory did not really take hold in North America until the 1960s, a decade rocked by growing labour unrest, Quebec separatism, anti-Vietnam War protests, the rise of the black power movement, and the revival of feminism, which had fallen dormant after its first stirrings in the late nineteenth and early twentieth centuries. Strikes, demonstrations, and riots were almost daily occurrences in the 1960s and early 1970s, and therefore many sociologists of that era considered conflict among classes, nations, races, and generations to be the very essence of society.

The Cultural Turn and Poststructuralism: Gramsci and Foucault

In the 1960s and 1970s, conflict theory took what has been called a "cultural turn." Increasingly, conflict theorists directed their attention to the ways in which language, music, literature, fashion, movies, advertising, and other elements of culture express domination by the powerful and resistance by others.

The origins of a cultural approach to the study of social conflict are found in essays written in the early twentieth century by Italian Marxist, Antonio Gramsci (pronounced GRAM-shee). In Gramsci's view, ruling classes establish their dominance partly by controlling jobs, using force, and the like. However, they also exercise power in softer ways. In particular, they fund the development, transmission, and learning of ideas that seem to embody the values of everyone but are actually biased in favour of upper-class dominance. Gramsci wrote that **cultural hegemony** exists when these values become so deeply entrenched that the great majority of people accept them as common sense (Gramsci, 1957, 1971). Subordinate classes can resist cultural hegemony, Gramsci wrote, but only if they develop ideas and institutions that express and support their own cultural preferences. Later writers extended Gramsci's argument to include dominant, taken-for-granted ideas about race, ethnicity, sexuality, and so on. (For an example of the way cultural hegemony works, refer to Box 1.2. See also Chapter 14, "Politics").

Cultural hegemony involves the control of a culture by dominant classes and other groups to the point where their values are universally accepted as common sense.

In France, from the 1950s to the 1980s, Michel Foucault (pronounced Foo-CŌ) further developed the notion that culture is the site of ongoing conflict between dominant and subordinate classes and other groups. Foucault made his case by studying new forms of regulation that accompany capitalist industrialization. He showed that, as the goal of maximizing economic productivity grows in importance, criminals, people with physically infirmities, people with mental illness, and ordinary students and workers are subjected to new structures of control in prisons, hospitals, institutions for the mentally ill, workplaces, schools, and universities. According to Foucault (1973, 1977, 1988), modern institutions sometimes use violence to regulate behaviour but they more often rely on new technologies and the *internalization* of control mechanisms. For example, modern institutions are physically, technologically, and socially designed so that authorities can easily observe the behaviour of inmates, patients, workers, and students. Authorities may not always watch their "clientele," but when inmates and others know that they *may* be under the watchful eye of authorities, they usually act as if they *are* being observed. Before capitalist industrialization, control took place almost exclusively through force, but now more subtle and effective mechanisms of regulation are employed.

According to Foucault, power is exercised in every social interaction, but every social interaction is also subject to resistance by subordinates. Thus, the exercise of power is unstable. Dominant groups and individuals must continuously renew their power relations to maintain control but sometimes they fail, providing subordinates the opportunity to assert their interests.

Foucault was part of a movement in French social thought known as **poststructuralism**. Earlier social thinkers had argued that social relations and cultures form structures, or stable determinants of the way people think and act. These "structuralists" typically categorized elements of social relations and of culture as binary opposites: male versus female, civilized versus uncivilized people, black versus white races, and so on (Derrida, 2004: 41). In contrast, poststructuralists, Foucault among them, denied the stability of social relations and of cultures, their capacity always to shape how people think and act, and their neat categorization of social and cultural elements as binary opposites. According to the poststructuralists, the social world is a more fluid and complex place, and people are more often the agents of their own destiny, than structuralists imagined.

Poststructuralism, a school of thought that originated in mid-twentieth-century France, denied the stability of social relations and of cultures, their capacity to always shape how people think and act, and their neat categorization of social and cultural elements as binary opposites.

To better understand these ideas, consider that many of us casually use the term "the opposite sex" in everyday speech without giving it much thought. Yet embedded in this term is a faulty set of assumptions based on a distribution of power that favours some categories of people at the expense of others. As you will learn in Chapter 11, Sexualities and Gender Stratification, it is factually incorrect to assume that men and women are opposites in their sexual identities, preferences, and behaviours. It is more accurate to say that men and women are arrayed along one scale with respect to their sexual identities, a second scale with respect to their sexual preferences, and a third scale with respect to their sexual behaviours; and their positions on these scales can change in different circumstances. When we perceive men as remaining clustered on one extreme of a single scale and women on the other extreme—when we view women and men as fixed "opposites"—we oversimplify the complexity of real flesh-and-blood people. We also ignore that many women and men are not so neatly pigeonholed. People who are not included in the conventional categorization are simply defined out of existence by our casual use of language and the underlying fact that some people have more power than others to name things.

Foucault's influence, and that of other poststructuralists, spans many areas of contemporary sociology. Foucault's ideas will be taken up again in Chapter 7, Deviance and Crime, Chapter 11, Sexualities and Gender Stratification, and Chapter 19, Health and Medicine. We will also come across Foucault's influence when we discuss the work of French sociologist Pierre Bourdieu in Chapter 8, Social Stratification, and Chapter 17, Education. Finally, we will encounter the legacy of poststructuralism when we review postcolonial theory in Chapter 9, Globalization, Inequality, and Development, and critical race theory in Chapter 10, Race and Ethnicity.

The **Protestant ethic** is the belief that religious doubts can be reduced, and a state of grace ensured, if people work diligently and live ascetically. According to Weber, the Protestant work ethic had the unintended effect of increasing savings and investment, and thus stimulating capitalist growth.

Symbolic Interactionism

Weber, Mead, and Goffman

We noted above that Weber criticized Marx's interpretation of the development of capitalism. Among other things, Weber argued that early capitalist development was caused not just by favourable economic circumstances but that certain *religious* beliefs also facilitated robust capitalist growth (Weber, 1958 [1904–5]). In particular, sixteenth- and seventeenth-century Protestants believed their religious doubts could be reduced and a state of grace ensured if they worked diligently and lived modestly. Weber called this belief the **Protestant ethic**. He believed it had an unintended effect: People who adhered to the Protestant ethic saved and invested more money than others did. Thus, capitalism developed most vigorously where the Protestant ethic took hold. Similarly, in much of his research, Weber emphasized the importance of empathically understanding people's motives and the meanings they attach to things to gain a clear sense of the significance of their actions. He called this aspect of his approach to sociological research the method of *Verstehen* ("understanding" in German).

American Sociological Association

Erving Goffman (1922–82) was born in Mannville, Alberta. He studied sociology and anthropology at the University of Toronto. He completed his Ph.D. at the University of Chicago and pursued his academic career at the University of California, Berkeley, and the University of Pennsylvania. Goffman developed an international reputation for his "dramaturgical" approach to symbolic interactionism.

The idea that any complete sociological analysis requires the analysis of subjective meanings and motives was only one of Weber's contributions to early sociological theory. Weber was also an important conflict theorist, as you will learn in later chapters. However, it is enough to note here that his emphasis on subjective meanings found rich soil in the United States in the late nineteenth and early twentieth centuries. His ideas resonated deeply with the individualism of American culture and the widely held belief that talent and initiative could enable anyone to achieve just about anything. Small wonder, then, that much of early American sociology focused on the individual or, more precisely, on the connection between the individual and the larger society.

This connection was the focus of sociologists at the University of Chicago, the most influential Department of Sociology in North America before World War II. For example, the University of Chicago's George Herbert Mead (1863–1931) was the driving force behind the study of how the individual's sense of self is formed in the course of interaction with other people. According to Mead, we learn who we are by taking the role of other people as we interact with them and by seeing ourselves as they see us. We discuss Mead's contribution in Chapter 4, Socialization. Here, we note only that the work of Mead and his colleagues gave birth to symbolic interactionism, a distinctively American theoretical tradition that continues to be a major force in sociology today.

Functionalist and conflict theories assume that people's group memberships—whether people are rich or poor, male or female, black or white—influence their behaviour. This approach can sometimes make people seem like balls on a pool table: They get knocked around and cannot choose their own destinies. However, we know from our everyday experience that people are not like that. We often make choices, sometimes difficult ones. We sometimes change our minds. Moreover, two people with similar group memberships may react differently to similar social circumstances because they interpret those circumstances differently.

Symbolic interactionism focuses on interaction in microlevel social settings and emphasizes that an adequate explanation of social behaviour requires understanding the subjective meanings people attach to their social circumstances.

Recognizing these issues, some sociologists focus on the subjective side of social life. They work in the symbolic interactionist tradition. **Symbolic interactionism** incorporates these features:

- Symbolic interactionism's focus on interpersonal communication in microlevel social settings distinguishes it from both functionalist and conflict theories.
- Symbolic interactionism emphasizes that social life is possible only because people attach meanings to things. It follows that an adequate explanation of social behaviour requires understanding the subjective meanings people associate with their social circumstances.
- Symbolic interactionism stresses that people help to create their social circumstances and do not merely react to them. For example, Canadian-born sociologist Erving Goffman (1922–82), one of the most influential symbolic interactionists, analyzed the many ways people present themselves to others in everyday life so as to appear in the best possible light. Goffman compared social interaction to a carefully staged play, complete with front stage, back stage, defined roles, and a wide range of props. In this play, a person's age, gender, race, and other characteristics may help to shape his or her actions, but there is much room for individual creativity as well (Goffman, 1959).
- By focusing on the subjective meanings people create in small social settings, symbolic interactionists sometimes validate unpopular and unofficial viewpoints. Their validation of other viewpoints increases our understanding and tolerance of people who may be different from us.

To understand symbolic interactionism better, let us briefly return to the problem of suicide. If a police officer discovers a dead person at the wheel of a car that has run into a tree, it may be difficult to establish whether the death was an accident or suicide. Interviewing friends and relatives to discover the driver's state of mind just before the crash may help rule out the possibility of suicide. As this example illustrates, understanding the intention or motive of the actor is critical to understanding the meaning of a social action and explaining it. A state of mind must be interpreted, usually by a coroner, before a dead body becomes a suicide statistic (Douglas, 1967).

For surviving family and friends, suicide is always painful and sometimes embarrassing. Insurance policies often deny payments to beneficiaries in the case of suicide. As a result, coroners are inclined to classify deaths as accidental whenever such an interpretation is plausible. Being human, they want to minimize a family's suffering after such a horrible event. Sociologists therefore believe that official suicide rates are about one-third lower than actual suicide rates.

Social Constructionism and Queer Theory

Social constructionism argues that apparently natural or innate features of life are often sustained by social processes that vary historically and culturally.

Social constructionism is a variant of symbolic interactionism that has become popular in recent years. Social constructionists argue that when people interact, they typically assume things are naturally or innately what they seem to be. But in reality, apparently natural or innate features of life are sustained by *social* processes that vary historically and culturally (Hannigan, 1995b).

For example, many people assume that differences in the way women and men behave are the result of their different biological makeup. In contrast, social constructionists show that many of the presumably natural differences between women and men depend on the way power is distributed between them and the degree to which certain ideas about women and men are shared (see Chapter 11, Sexualities and Gender

Stratification; Berger and Luckmann, 1966; West and Zimmerman, 1987). Since power distributions and ideas about gender vary over time and place, social constructionists are able to show how changing social conditions produce changes in the way people act out their gender identity. They conclude that gender is more a performance shaped by social conditions than part of a person's essence. People usually do such a good job of building natural-seeming identities in their everyday interactions—not just gender but also ethnicity, race, nationality, religion, and so on—that they do not notice the materials used in the construction process. Social constructionists identify those materials and analyze how people piece them together.

Queer theory takes the social constructionist argument a step further by denying the very existence of stable identities (Green, 2007). From the queer theorist's point of view, when we apply such labels as "male," "female," "gay," and "lesbian" to ourselves or others, we are adopting socially accepted labels that fail to capture the fluidity and variability of people's actual identities and performances. Such labels impose social conventions on people, thus acting as forms of control and domination and drawing attention away from the uniqueness of each individual (for more on queer theory, see Chapter 11, Sexualities and Gender Stratification).

Queer theory argues that people's sexual identities and performances are so variable that such conventional labels as "male," female," "gay," and "lesbian" fail to capture the sexual instability that characterizes the lives of many people.

In sum, the study of the subjective side of social life helps to take us beyond the official picture by deepening our understanding of how society works and supplementing the insights gained from macrolevel analysis.

Feminist Theory

Few women figured prominently in the early history of sociology. The strict demands placed on them by the nineteenth-century family and the lack of opportunity in the larger society prevented most women from earning a higher education and making major contributions to the discipline. Women who made their mark on sociology in its early years tended to have unusual biographies. Some of these exceptional people introduced gender issues that were largely ignored by Marx, Durkheim, Weber, Mead, and other early sociologists. Appreciation for the sociological contribution of these pioneering women has grown in recent years because concern with gender issues has come to form a substantial part of the modern sociological enterprise.

Margrit Eichler

Margrit Eichler (1942–) was born in Berlin, Germany. She took her Ph.D. at Duke University in the United States before beginning her academic career at the Ontario Institute for Studies in Education and the University of Toronto. She is internationally known for her work on feminist methodology (Eichler, 1987). Her work on family policy in Canada has strongly influenced students, professional sociologists, and policymakers (Eichler, 1988a).

Martineau and Addams

Harriet Martineau (1802–76) is often called the first female sociologist. Born in England to a prosperous family, she never married but was able to support herself comfortably from her journalistic writings. Martineau translated Comte into English, and she wrote one of the first books on research methods. She undertook critical studies of slavery, factory laws, and gender inequality. She was a leading advocate of voting rights for women, higher education for women, and gender equality in the family. As such, Martineau was one of the first feminists (Yates, 1985).

In the United States in the early twentieth century, a few women from wealthy families attended university, received training as sociologists, and wanted to become professors of sociology, but they were denied faculty appointments. Typically, they turned to social activism and social work instead. A case in point is Jane Addams (1860–1935). Addams was co-founder of Hull House, a shelter for destitute people in Chicago's slums, and she spent a lifetime fighting for social reform. She also provided a research platform for sociologists from the University of Chicago, who often visited Hull House to interview its clients. In recognition of her efforts, Addams received the 1931 Nobel Peace Prize.

Modern Feminism

Despite its early stirrings, feminist thinking had little impact on sociology until the mid-1960s, when the rise of the modern women's movement drew attention to the many remaining inequalities between women and men. Because of feminist theory's major influence on sociology, we regard it as sociology's fourth major theoretical tradition. Modern feminism has several variants (see Chapter 11, Sexualities and Gender Stratification). However, the various strands of **feminist theory** share the following features:

For the most part, **feminist theory** claims that patriarchy is at least as important as class inequality in determining a person's opportunities in life. It holds that male domination and female subordination are determined not by biological necessity but by structures of power and social convention. It examines the operation of patriarchy in both micro and macro settings. And it contends that existing patterns of gender inequality can and should be changed for the benefit of all members of society.

- Feminist theory focuses on various aspects of patriarchy, the system of male domination in society. Most feminists contend that patriarchy is as important as class inequality, if not more so, in determining a person's opportunities in life.
- Feminist theory holds that male domination and female subordination are determined not by biological necessity but by structures of power and social convention. From their point of view, women are subordinate to men only because men enjoy more legal, economic, political, and cultural rights.
- Feminist theory examines the operation of patriarchy in both microlevel and macrolevel settings.
- Feminist theory contends that existing patterns of gender inequality can and should be changed for the benefit of all members of society. The main sources of gender inequality include differences in the way boys and girls are reared; barriers to equal opportunity in education, paid work, and politics; the unequal division of domestic responsibilities between women and men; and (for Marxist feminists) the existing class structure.

As you will see in the following pages, sociologists have applied the four main theoretical traditions to all of the discipline's branches. They have elaborated and refined each of them. Some sociologists work exclusively within one tradition. Others conduct research that borrows from more than one tradition. However, all sociologists are deeply indebted to the founders of the discipline.

TIME FOR REVIEW

- What are the key features of the four main theoretical traditions? (Table 1.1 and Figure 1.5 will help you answer this question.)
- What was the "cultural turn" in the conflict tradition?

TABLE 1.1
The Main Theoretical Traditions in Sociology

Theoretical Tradition	Main Level of Analysis	Main Focus	Main Question	Image of Ideal Society
Functionalism	Macro	Values	How do the institutions of society contribute to social stability?	A state of equilibrium
Conflict theory	Macro	Class inequality	How do privileged groups seek to maintain their advantages and subordinate groups seek to increase theirs, often causing social change in the process?	The elimination of privilege, especially class privilege
Symbolic interactionism	Micro	Meaning	How do individuals communicate so as to make their social settings meaningful?	Respect for the validity of minority views
Feminist theory	Micro and macro	Patriarchy	Which social structures and interaction processes maintain male dominance and female subordination?	The elimination of gender inequality

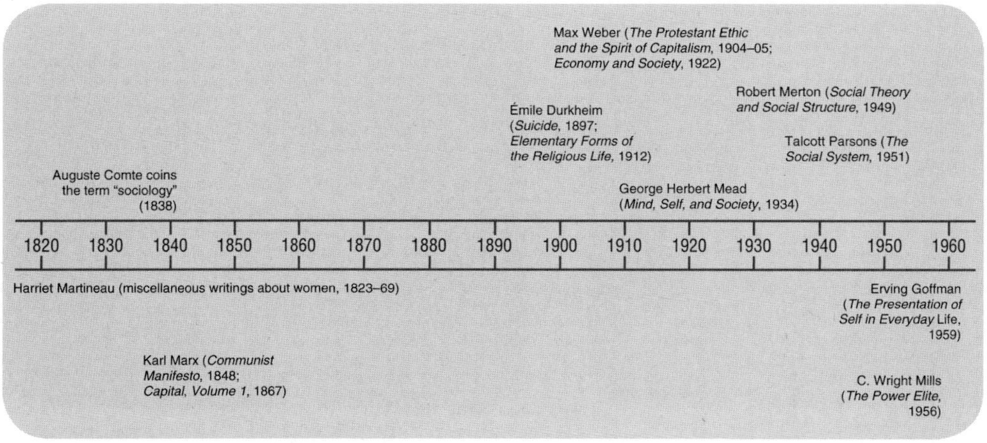

FIGURE 1.5
A Sociological Timeline of Some Major Figures in the Development of Sociological Theory, 1820–1960

To illustrate how much farther we are able to see by using theory as our guide, we now consider how the four traditions outlined above improve our understanding of an aspect of social life familiar to everyone: the world of fashion.

FASHION CYCLES AND THE FOUR THEORETICAL PERSPECTIVES

> "Oh. Two weeks ago I saw Cameron Diaz at Fred Siegel and I talked her out of buying this truly heinous angora sweater. Whoever said orange is the new pink is seriously disturbed."
> —*Elle Woods (Reese Witherspoon) in Legally Blond (2001)*

In 1998, one of the main fashion trends among white, middle-class girls between the ages of 11 and 14 was the Britney Spears look: bare midriff, highlighted hair, wide belt, glitter purse, big wedge shoes, and Skechers Energy sneakers. However, in 2002, a new pop star, Avril Lavigne, was rising in the pop charts. Nominated for a 2003 Grammy Award in the "Best New Artist" category, the 17-year-old skater punk from the small town of Napanee in eastern Ontario affected a shaggy, unkempt look. She sported worn-out T-shirts, 1970s-style plaid Western shirts with snaps, baggy pants, undershirts, ties, backpacks, chain wallets, and, for shoes, Converse Chuck Taylors. As Avril Lavigne's popularity soared, some young girls switched their style from glam to neo-grunge (Tkacik, 2002).

That switch is just one example of the fashion shifts that occur periodically and with increasing frequency in popular culture. A rock idol or movie star helped by a carefully planned marketing campaign captures the imagination of some people who soon start dressing in the style of the star—until another star catches their fancy and influences yet another style change.

Why do fashion shifts take place? How and why do they affect you? Sociologists explain fashion cycles in four ways. Each explanation derives from a major theoretical tradition in sociology.

Functionalism

From the functionalist viewpoint, fashion trends come and go because they enable social inequality to persist. If they didn't have this purpose, we wouldn't have fashion cycles. Specifically, exclusive fashion houses in Paris, Milan, New York, and London show new styles every season. Some of the new styles catch on among the rich clientele of big-name designers. The main appeal of wearing expensive, new fashions is that wealthy clients can distinguish themselves from people who are less well off. Thus, fashion performs an important social function. By allowing people of different rank to distinguish themselves from one another, it helps to preserve the ordered layering of society into classes.

Britney Spears versus Avril Lavigne

© Reuters NewMedia Inc./Corbis

Frederic Legrand/Shutterstock.com

According to functionalists, the ebb and flow of fashion sped up in the twentieth century thanks to technological advances in clothes manufacturing. Inexpensive knock-offs could now quickly reach lower-class markets. Consequently, new styles needed to be introduced more often so fashion could continue to perform its function of helping to maintain an orderly class system. Fashion cycles sped up.

Functionalism offers a pretty accurate account of the way fashion trends worked until the 1960s, but after that, fashion became more democratic. Paris, Milan, New York, and London are still important fashion centres. However, new fashion trends are increasingly being initiated by lower classes, minority racial and ethnic groups, and people who spurn "high" fashion altogether. Napanee is, after all, pretty far from Paris. Today, big-name designers are more likely to be influenced by the inner-city styles of hip-hop rather than vice versa. New fashions no longer trickle down from the upper classes and a few high-fashion centres. People in the upper classes are nearly as likely to adopt lower-class fashion trends that can originate just about anywhere. Functionalism no longer provides a satisfying explanation of fashion cycles.

Conflict Theory

Some sociologists turned to conflict theory for an alternative view of the fashion world. Conflict theory highlights the tensions underlying existing social arrangements and the capacity of those tensions to burst into the open and cause social change. From this point of view, fashion cycles are a means by which owners and other big players in the clothing, advertising, and entertainment industries make big profits. They introduce new styles frequently because they make more money when they encourage people to buy new clothes often. Doing so has the added advantage of keeping consumers distracted from the many social, economic, and political problems that might otherwise cause them to express dissatisfaction with the existing social order and even rebel against it. Conflict theorists therefore believe that fashion helps to maintain a *precarious* social equilibrium that could be disrupted by the underlying tensions between consumers and big players in fashion-related industries.

Conflict theorists have a point. Fashion *is* a big and profitable business. Owners *do* introduce new styles frequently to make more money. They have, for example, created the Color Marketing Group (known to insiders as the "Color Mafia"), a committee that meets regularly to help change the palette of colour preferences for consumer products. According to one committee member, the Color Mafia makes sure that "the mass media ... fashion magazines and catalogs, home shopping shows, and big clothing chains all present the same options" each season (Mundell, 1993).

Yet the Color Mafia and other influential elements of the fashion industry are not all-powerful. Remember what Elle Woods said after she convinced Cameron Diaz not to buy that heinous angora sweater: "Whoever said orange is the new pink is seriously disturbed." Like many consumers, Elle Woods *rejected* the advice of the fashion industry. And in fact, some of the fashion trends initiated by industry owners flop.

Fashion flops hint at one of the main problems with the conflict interpretation of fashion cycles: They make it seem as if fashion decisions are dictated entirely from above. Reality is more complicated. Fashion decisions are made partly by consumers.

Symbolic Interactionism

Symbolic interactionism is best understood by thinking of clothes as symbols or objects that represent ideas. Clothing allows us to communicate with others by telling them who we are and allowing us to learn who they are. This insight derives from symbolic interactionism, which, you will recall, examines how various aspects of social life convey meaning and thereby assist or impede communication (Davis, 1992).

A person's identity or sense of self is always a work in progress. True, we develop a self-conception as we mature. We come to think of ourselves as members of one or more families, occupations, communities, classes, ethnic and racial groups, and countries. We develop patterns of behaviour and belief associated with each of these social categories. Nonetheless, social categories change over time, and so do we, as we move through those categories and as we age. Consequently, our identities are always in flux. When our identities change, we become insecure or anxious about who we are. Clothes help us express our shifting identities. They convey whether you are "straight," sexually available, athletic, conservative, and much else, thus telling others how you want them to see you and the kinds of people with whom you want to associate. At some point, you may become less conservative, less sexually available, and so on. Your clothing style is likely to change accordingly. (Of course, the messages you try to send are subject to misinterpretation.) For its part, the fashion industry feeds on the ambiguities in us, investing much effort in trying to discern which new styles might capture current needs for self-expression.

Feminism

Gender—the personal sense of being masculine or feminine as conventionally defined—is a central part of everyone's identity. It is also the main focus of sociological feminism. Because clothes are one of the most important means of expressing gender, feminist sociologists have done a lot of interesting work on fashion.

Traditional feminists view fashion as an aspect of patriarchy, the system of male domination of women. They note that fashion is mainly a female preoccupation; that it takes a lot of time and money to choose, buy, and clean clothes; and that fashionable clothing is often impractical and uncomfortable, sometimes even unhealthy. They conclude that fashion imprisons women. In addition, fashion's focus on youth, slenderness, and eroticism diminishes women by turning them into sexual objects. When Lady Gaga gets strip-searched in the "Prison for Bitches" at the start of her 2010 "Telephone" video, and then enters the prison exercise yard clad in little more than chains, some feminists think she is glorifying rape and female domination. By fastening vanity plates on her car that identify it as a "Pussy Wagon," she is arguably reducing women to sexual objects for the pleasure of men.

However, some feminists offer a different interpretation. They see Lady Gaga as a continuation of the girl power movement that first emerged in 1996, with the release of the Spice Girls' hit single, "Wannabe." From their point of view, Lady Gaga is all about asserting women's power. They note that, in "Telephone," Lady Gaga and Beyoncé go so far as to poison the men who treat them as sexual objects, and that at the 2009 MuchMusic Video Awards show, Lady Gaga's bra shot flames, suggesting that she is not just hot but also powerful and independent. As Lady Gaga once said, "Some women choose to follow men, and some women choose to follow their dreams. If you're wondering which way to go, remember that your career will never wake up and tell you it doesn't love you anymore" (Spines, 2010: 54; see also Bauer, 2010; Powers, 2009).

Arthur Mola/WireImage/Getty Images

Lady Gaga

In sum, functionalism helps us understand how fashion cycles operated until the 1960s. Conflict theory helps us see the class tensions underlying the apparently stable social arrangements of the fashion industry. Symbolic interactionism explains how fashion assists communication and the drawing of boundaries between different population categories. Feminism explores the ambiguities of gender identity that underlie the rise of new fashion trends. Although each type of sociological explanation clarifies a different aspect of fashion, all four allow us to probe beneath a taken-for-granted part of our world and learn something new and surprising about it. That is the promise of the four main types of sociological explanation.

A SOCIOLOGICAL COMPASS

Our summary of the major theoretical perspectives in sociology suggests that the founders of the discipline developed their ideas in an attempt to solve the great sociological puzzle of their time—the causes and consequences of the Industrial Revolution. This fact raises two interesting questions. What are the great sociological puzzles of *our* time? How are today's sociologists responding to the challenges presented by the social settings in which *we* live? We devote the rest of this book to answering these questions in depth. In the remainder of this chapter, we outline what you can expect to learn from this book.

It would be wrong to suggest that just a few key issues animate the research of tens of thousands of sociologists around the world. Viewed up close, sociology today is a heterogeneous enterprise enlivened by hundreds of theoretical debates, some focused on small issues relevant to particular fields and geographical areas, others focused on big issues that seek to characterize the entire historical era for humanity as a whole.

The **Postindustrial Revolution** refers to the technology-driven shift from manufacturing to service industries and the consequences of that shift for virtually all human activities.

Among the big issues, two stand out. Perhaps the greatest sociological puzzles of our time are the causes and consequences of the **Postindustrial Revolution** and globalization. The Postindustrial Revolution is the technology-driven shift from manufacturing to service industries—the shift from employment in factories to employment in offices—and the consequences of that shift for nearly all human activities (Bell, 1973; Toffler, 1990). For example, because of the Postindustrial Revolution, non-manual occupations now outnumber manual occupations, and women have been drawn into the system of higher education and the paid labour force in large numbers. The shift to service industries has transformed the way we work and study, our standard of living, the way we form families, and much else.

Globalization is the process by which formerly separate economies, states, and cultures become tied together and people become increasingly aware of their growing interdependence.

Globalization is the process by which formerly separate economies, states, and cultures become tied together and people become increasingly aware of their growing interdependence (Giddens, 1990: 64; Guillén, 2001). Especially in recent decades, rapid increases in the volume of international trade, travel, and communication have broken down the isolation and independence of most countries and people. Also contributing to globalization is the growth of many institutions that bind corporations, companies, and cultures together. These processes have led us to depend more than ever on people in other countries for products, services, ideas, and even a sense of identity.

Sociologists agree that globalization and postindustrialism promise many exciting opportunities to enhance the quality of life and increase human freedom. However, they also see many social-structural barriers to the realization of that promise. We can summarize both the promise and the barriers by drawing a compass—a sociological compass (see Figure 1.6). Each axis of the compass contrasts a promise with the barriers to its realization. The vertical axis contrasts the promise of equality of opportunity with the barrier of inequality of opportunity. The horizontal axis contrasts the promise of individual freedom with the barrier of constraint on that freedom. Let us consider these axes in detail because much of our discussion in the following chapters turns on them.

Equality versus Inequality of Opportunity

Optimists forecast that postindustrialism will provide more opportunities for people to find creative, interesting, challenging, and rewarding work. In addition, they say, the postindustrial era will generate more "equality of opportunity"—that is, better chances for *all* people to get an education, influence government policy, and find good jobs.

You will find evidence to support these claims in this book. For example, we show that the average standard of living and the number of good jobs have increased in the postindustrial era. Women have made rapid strides in the economy, the education system, and other institutions. Postindustrial societies like Canada are characterized by a decline in discrimination against

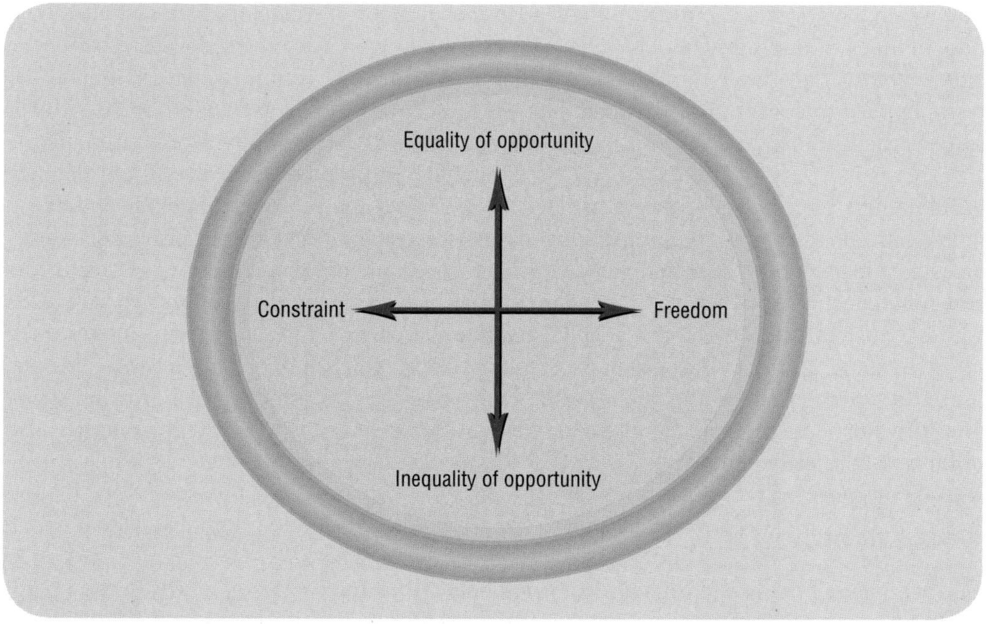

FIGURE 1.6
A Sociological Compass

members of minority groups, while democracy is spreading throughout the world. People living in desperate poverty form a declining percentage of the world's population.

Yet, as you read this book, it will also become clear that all these seemingly happy stories have a dark underside. For example, the number of routine jobs with low pay and few benefits is growing faster than the number of creative, high-paying jobs. An enormous opportunity gulf still separates women from men. Racism and discrimination are still a big part of our world. Our health care system is in crisis, just as our population is aging rapidly and most in need of health care. Many of the world's new democracies are only superficially democratic, while Canadians and citizens of other postindustrial societies are increasingly cynical about the ability of their political systems to respond to their needs. Many people are looking for alternative forms of political expression. The *absolute* number of the world's population that is living in desperate poverty continues to grow, as does the gap between rich and poor nations. Some people attribute the world's most serious problems to globalization and have formed organizations and movements—some of them violent—to oppose it. In short, equality of opportunity is an undeniably attractive ideal, but it is unclear whether it is the inevitable outcome of a globalized, postindustrial society.

Freedom versus Constraint

Growing freedom is also evident—but within limits. In an earlier era, most people retained their religious, ethnic, racial, and sexual identities for a lifetime, even if they were not particularly comfortable with them. They often remained in social relationships, even if they made them unhappy. One of the major themes of this book is that many people are now freer to construct their identities and form social relationships in ways that suit them. More than ever, you can *choose* who you want to be, with whom you want to associate, and how you want to associate with them. The postindustrial and global era frees people from traditional constraints by encouraging virtually instant global communication, international migration, greater acceptance of sexual diversity and a variety of family forms, the growth of ethnically and racially diverse cities, and so on. For instance, in the past, people often stayed in marriages even if they were dissatisfied with them. Families often involved a father working in the paid labour force and a mother keeping house and raising children without pay. Today, people are freer to end unhappy marriages and create family structures that are more suited to their individual needs.

Again, however, we must face the less rosy aspects of postindustrialism and globalization. In many of the following chapters, we point out how increased freedom is experienced only within certain limits and how, in some spheres of life, social diversity is limited by a strong push to conformity. For example, we can choose from a far wider variety of consumer products than ever before, but consumerism itself increasingly seems compulsory, although it is a way of life that threatens the natural environment. Meanwhile, some new technologies, such as surveillance cameras, cause us to modify our behaviour and act in more conformist ways. Large, impersonal bureaucracies and standardized products and services dehumanize both staff and customers. The tastes and the profit motives of vast media conglomerates, most of them American-owned, govern most of our cultural consumption and arguably threaten the survival of distinctive national cultures. Powerful interests are trying to shore up the traditional nuclear family even though it does not suit some people. As these examples show, the push to uniformity counters the trend toward growing social diversity. Postindustrialism and globalization may make us freer in some ways, but they also place new constraints on us.

Why Sociology?

Our overview of themes in *Sociology: Your Compass for a New World* drives home a point made by Anthony Giddens, renowned British sociologist and adviser to former British prime minister Tony Blair. According to Giddens, we live in an era "suspended between extraordinary opportunity ... and global catastrophe" (Giddens, 1990: 166). The quality of our everyday lives continues to be profoundly affected by a whole range of environmental issues; profound inequalities in the wealth of nations and of classes; religious, racial, and ethnic violence; and unsolved problems in the relations between women and men. Despair and apathy are possible responses to these complex issues, but they are not responses that humans favour. If it were our nature to give up hope, we would still be sitting around half-naked in the mud outside a cave. People are more inclined to look for ways of improving their lives, and this period of human history is full of opportunities to do so. For example, we have advanced to the point where, for the first time, we have the means to feed and educate everyone in the world. Similarly, it now seems possible to erode some of the inequalities that have always been the major source of human conflict.

Careers in Sociology

Sociology offers useful advice on how to achieve the goals of equality and freedom because it is more than just an intellectual exercise. Sociology is an applied science with practical, everyday uses in the realms of teaching and public policy, and in the creation of laws and regulations by organizations and governments (see Box 1.4). That is because sociologists are trained not just to see what is but also to see what is possible.

Students often ask: "Can I get a good job with a sociology degree?" "Exactly what kind of work could I do with a major in sociology?" "Aren't all the good jobs these days in technical areas and the natural sciences?" To answer these questions, consider the following:

A sociology B.A. improves your understanding of the diverse social conditions affecting men and women, people with different sexual orientations, and people from different countries, regions, classes, races, and ethnic groups. Therefore, people with a B.A. in sociology tend to be attracted to jobs requiring good "people skills," and jobs involved with managing and promoting social change (see Table 1.2).

Often, people with a B.A. in sociology go on to graduate school and obtain professional degrees in related fields, including law, urban planning, industrial relations, social work, and public policy. You will therefore find many people with bachelor's degrees in sociology working as lawyers, urban planners, city managers, statisticians, and healthcare and education administrators.

Most people with a graduate degree in sociology teach and conduct research in universities, with research being a more important component of the job in larger and more

BOX 1.4

SOCIAL POLICY: WHAT DO YOU THINK?

ARE CORPORATE SCANDALS A PROBLEM OF INDIVIDUAL ETHICS OR SOCIAL POLICY?

The Sloan School of Management at MIT conducted a survey of 600 graduates as part of its 50th anniversary observance. Sixty percent of respondents said that honesty, integrity, and ethics are the main characteristics of a good corporate leader. Most alumni felt that living a moral professional life is more important than pulling in large paycheques and generous perquisites.

Unfortunately, the behaviour of North American executives often fails to reflect high ethical standards. For example, thousands of ordinary Canadians lost billions of dollars, including substantial pension savings, when senior executives of telecommunications giant Nortel grossly overstated the company's profitability and prospects, earned huge bonuses based on false accounting, and then watched the stock price slide from a high of $124.50 per share in July 2000 to 64 cents per share in October 2002. Several senior executives lost their jobs, but they were not prosecuted and they all kept their ill-gotten gains. In 2004, a group of Canadian investors launched a class-action lawsuit against newspaper baron Conrad Black and other executives of Hollinger International for $4 billion in damages. The suit claimed market losses may have been caused by controversies involving Black's management and allegations that he and associates quietly pocketed $400 million to which they were not entitled. (Black was eventually found guilty in an American court of fraud and obstruction of justice, and was sentenced to a 42-month jail term and a $125,000 fine.)

Can we rely on individual morality or ethics to show senior executives how to behave responsibly—that is, in the long-term interest of their companies and society as a whole? Ethics courses have been taught at all business schools for years but, as the dean of one business school noted, these courses can't "turn sinners into saints.... If a company does a lot of crazy stuff but its share price continues to rise, a lot of people will look the other way and not really care whether senior management is behaving ethically or not" (quoted in Goll, 2002).

Because individual ethics often seem weak in the face of greed, some observers have suggested that new public policies—laws and regulations passed by organizations and governments—are required to regulate executive compensation. For example, some people think stiff jail terms should be imposed on anyone who engages in accounting fraud, and strong legal protection should be offered to anyone who "blows the whistle" on executive wrongdoing.

Sociology helps us focus on what may appear to be personal issues and see them in the larger context of public policy. Even our tendency to act ethically or unethically is shaped in part by public policy—or the lack of it. Therefore, we review a public policy debate in each chapter of this book. It is good exercise for the sociological imagination, and it will help you gain more control over the forces that shape your life.

prestigious institutions. However, many sociologists do not teach. Instead, they conduct research and give policy advice in a wide range of settings outside the system of higher education. For example, in many federal government agencies, sociologists are employed as researchers and policy consultants. Sociologists also conduct research and policy analysis in trade unions, nongovernmental organizations, and professional and public interest associations. In the private sector, you can find sociologists practising their craft in firms specializing in public opinion polling, management consulting, market research, standardized testing, and "evaluation research," which assesses the impact of particular policies and programs before or after they go into effect.

One way of seeing the benefits of a sociological education is to compile a list of some of the famous practical idealists who studied sociology in university. That list includes several former heads of state, among them President Fernando Cardoso of Brazil, President Tomas Masaryk of Czechoslovakia, Prime Minister Edward Seaga of Jamaica, and President Ronald Reagan of the United States. The current first lady of the United States, Michelle Obama, has a sociology degree. Before she became first lady, she worked as commissioner of planning and development in Chicago City Hall, and as the founding executive director of a program that prepares youth for public service. In her current role, she continues to shape public policy regarding nutrition and childhood obesity. The former vice-president of the Liberal Party of Canada and former president and vice-chancellor of York University in Toronto, Lorna Marsden, is a sociologist. Anthony Giddens, former director of the London School of Economics and adviser to former British Prime Minister Tony Blair, earned a graduate degree in sociology. So did the heads of two of Canada's leading public opinion firms: Martin Goldfarb, chairman, president, and CEO of The Goldfarb Corporation; and Michael Adams and Donna Dasko, president and former

TABLE 1.2

Jobs Commonly Held by Canadians with Degrees in Sociology

Source: Neil Guppy & R. Alan Hedley. 1993. *Opportunities in Sociology* (Montreal: Canadian Sociology and Anthropology Association). Reprinted with permission of the Canadian Sociological Association.

Government
Community affairs officer
Urban/regional planner
Legislative aide
Affirmative action/employment equity worker
Foreign service officer
Human rights officer
Personnel coordinator

Research
Social research specialist
Consumer researcher
Data analyst
Market researcher
Survey researcher
Census officer/analyst
Demographer/population analyst
Systems analyst

Community Affairs
Occupational/career counsellor
Homeless/housing worker
Public health/hospital administrator
Child development technician
Public administration assistant
Social assistance advocate
Resident planning aide
Group home worker
Rehabilitation program worker
Rural health outreach worker
Housing coordinator
Fundraising director/assistant
Caseworker/aide
Community organizer
Youth outreach worker

Corrections
Corrections officer
Criminology assistant
Police officer
Rehabilitation counsellor
Criminal investigator
Juvenile court worker
Parole officer

Teaching
College/university placement worker
Public health educator
Teacher
Admissions counsellor

Business
Market analyst
Project manager
Sales representative
Real estate agent
Journalist
Public relations officer
Actuary
Insurance agent
Human resources manager
Production manager
Labour relations officer
Administrative assistant
Quality control manager
Merchandiser/purchaser
Computer analyst
Data entry manager
Publishing officer
Advertising officer
Sales manager

Note: While more recent data have not been compiled, we have little reason to believe that the job picture has changed significantly since this table was first created.

senior vice-president, respectively, of Environics. Alex Himelfarb, former clerk of the Privy Council (Canada's highest ranking civil servant), holds a sociology Ph.D., too, as did Daniel Hill, the first full-time director of the Ontario Human Rights Commission and former Ontario Ombudsman. All of these people enjoyed careers that nicely answer the question, "What can you do with a sociology degree?" You can change the world.

In sum, although sociology does not offer easy solutions to the question of how the goal of improving society may be accomplished, it does provide a useful way of understanding our current predicament and seeing possible ways of dealing with it, of leading us a little farther away from the mud outside the cave. You sampled sociology's ability to tie personal troubles to social-structural issues when we discussed suicide. You reviewed the major theoretical perspectives that enable sociologists to connect the personal with the social-structural. When we outlined the half-fulfilled promises of postindustrialism and globalization, you saw sociology's ability to provide an understanding of where we are and where we can go.

We frankly admit that the questions we raise in this book are tough to answer. Sharp controversy surrounds them all. However, we are sure that if you try to grapple with these issues, you will enhance your understanding of your society's, and your own, possibilities. In brief, sociology can help you figure out where you fit into society and how you can make society fit you.

TIME FOR REVIEW

- What are some of the greatest social tensions in our time?
- These tensions have emerged in a particular social context. What are the chief features of that context?

SUMMARY

1. What is sociology?
   Sociology is the systematic study of human behaviour in social context. The sociological perspective analyzes the connection between personal troubles and social structures.

2. Where are the social relations that surround you, permeate you, and influence your behaviour?
   Social relations exist in micro- (small-scale, face-to-face), macro- (large-scale, more impersonal), and global (very large scale, cross-cultural and cross-country) social structures. To varying degrees, people are aware of these structures, which therefore also exist in people's minds. Insofar as these social structures open up some opportunities and close off others, they influence human behaviour.

3. How does sociological research seek to test ideas using scientific methods and thereby improve people's lives?
   Sociological research begins with values—ideas about what is good and bad, right and wrong. Values often motivate sociologists to define which problems are worth studying and to make initial assumptions about how to explain sociological phenomena. These explanations are theories—tentative explanations of some aspect of social life. Theories state how and why specific facts are connected. Research is the process of systematically observing social reality to test the validity of a theory. Sociological theories may be modified and even rejected through research. Thus, sociological research uses scientific methods to evaluate ideas but the desire to improve people's lives often motivates the research.

4. What are the main theoretical traditions in sociology?
   Sociology has four major theoretical traditions. Functionalism analyzes how social order is supported by macrostructures. The conflict approach analyzes how social inequality is maintained and challenged. Symbolic interactionism analyzes how meaning is created when people communicate in microlevel settings. Feminist theories focus on the social sources of patriarchy in both macrolevel and microlevel settings.

5. How did sociology emerge out of the Scientific Revolution, the Democratic Revolution, and the Industrial Revolutions?
   The Scientific Revolution encouraged the view that sound conclusions about the workings of society must be based on evidence, not just on speculation. The Democratic Revolution suggested that people are responsible for organizing society and that human intervention can therefore solve social problems. The Industrial Revolution created a host of new and serious social problems that attracted the attention of many social thinkers.

6. What are the main challenges facing society today?
   The Postindustrial Revolution is the technology-driven shift from manufacturing to service industries. Globalization is the process by which formerly separate economies, states, and cultures become tied together and people become increasingly aware of their growing interdependence. The causes and consequences of postindustrialism and globalization form the great sociological puzzles of our time. The tensions between equality and inequality of opportunity, and between freedom and constraint, are among the chief interests of sociology today.

NOTE

1. Sociologists also distinguish *mesostructures*, which are social relations that link microstructures and macrostructures. See Chapter 6, Networks, Groups, Bureaucracies, and Societies.

CHAPTER 2

HOW SOCIOLOGISTS DO RESEARCH

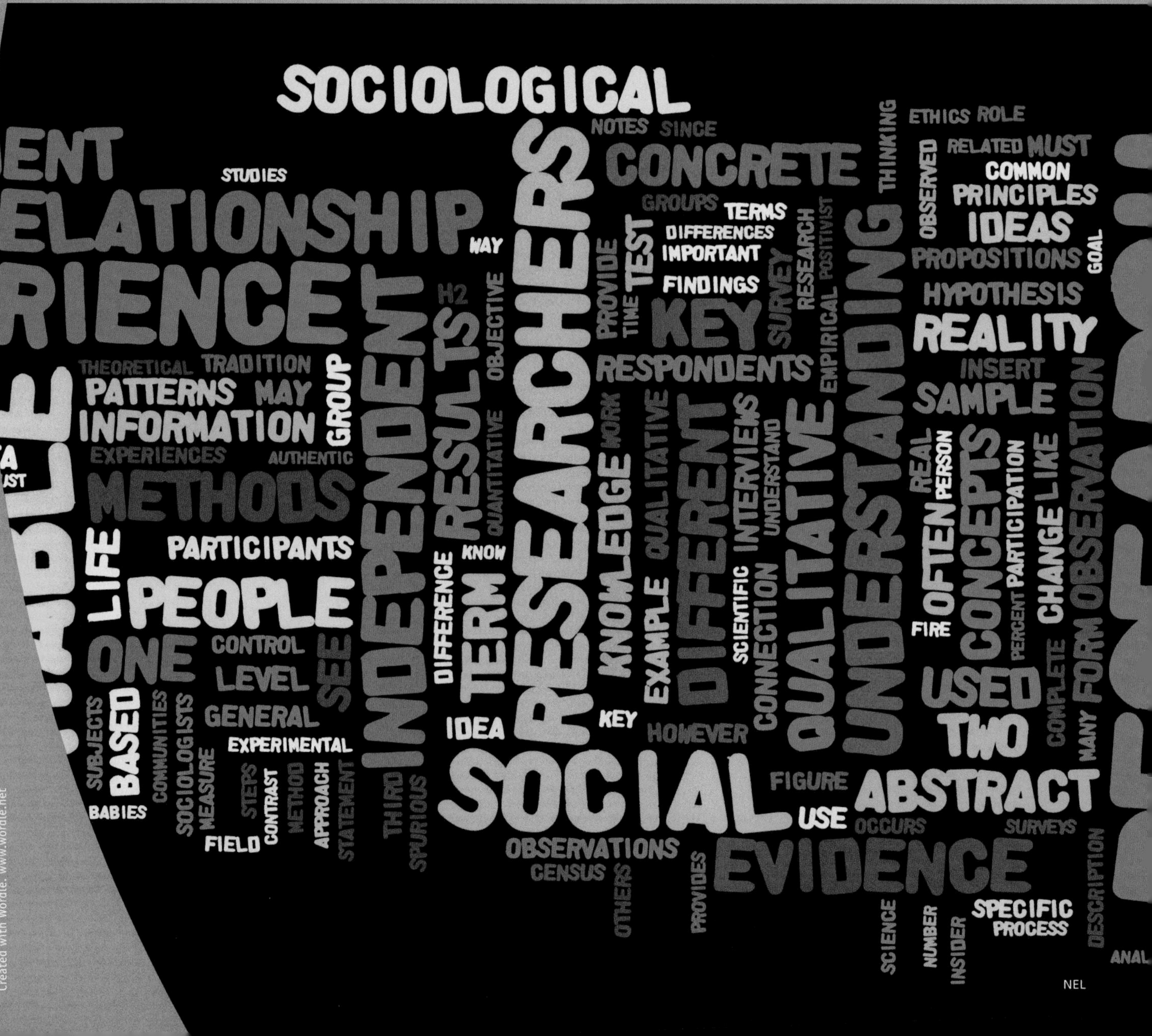

Created with Wordle. www.wordle.net

IN THIS CHAPTER YOU WILL LEARN TO

- Identify the meaning and components of different levels of experience.
- Appreciate common mistakes in unscientific thinking.
- Understand how viewpoint affects understanding.
- List the major steps in qualitative and quantitative research.
- Outline the ethical norms guiding sociological research.
- Contrast the experimental and survey methods used by quantitative researchers with the participant observation and interviewing methods used by qualitative researchers.

SCIENCE AND EXPERIENCE

OTTFFSSENT

"Okay, Mr. Smarty Pants, see if you can figure this one out." That's how Robert Brym's 11-year-old daughter, Talia, greeted him one day when she came home from school. "I wrote some letters of the alphabet on this sheet of paper. They form a pattern. Take a look at the letters and tell me the pattern."

Robert took the sheet of paper from Talia and smiled confidently. "Like most North Americans, I'd had a lot of experience with this sort of puzzle," says Robert. "For example, most IQ and SAT tests ask you to find patterns in sequences of letters, and you learn certain ways of solving these problems. One of the most common methods is to see if the 'distance' between adjoining letters stays the same or varies predictably. For example, in the sequence ADGJ, there are two missing letters between each adjoining pair. Insert the missing letters and you get the first 10 letters of the alphabet: A(BC)D(EF)G(HI)J.

"This time, however, I was stumped. On the sheet of paper Talia had written the letters OTTFFSSENT. I tried to use the distance method to solve the problem. Nothing worked. After 10 minutes of head scratching, I gave up."

"The answer's easy," Talia said, clearly pleased at her father's failure. "Spell out the numbers 1 to 10. The first letter of each word—one, two, three, and so on—spells OTTFFSSENT. Looks like you're not as smart as you thought. See ya." And with that she bounced off to her room.

"Later that day, it dawned on me that Talia had taught me more than just a puzzle. She had shown me that experience sometimes prevents people from seeing things. My experience with solving letter puzzles by using certain set methods kept me from solving the unusual problem of OTTFFSSENT."

Said differently, reality (in this case, a pattern of letters) is not just a thing "out there" we can learn to perceive "objectively." As social scientists have

Experience helps determine how we see "reality."

appreciated for more than a century, *experience* helps determine how we perceive reality, including what patterns we see and whether we can see patterns at all (Hughes, 1967: 16). To understand how sociologists use science to conduct research, it is helpful to distinguish two levels of experience.

Levels of Experience

To understand our experience, it is useful to distinguish concrete levels from abstract levels. Each level has unique characteristics.

Concrete experience is obtained by seeing, touching, tasting, smelling, or hearing.

Percepts are the smallest bits of concrete experience.

Patterns are collections of related percepts.

Let's begin with the concrete level. You obtain **concrete experience** by seeing, touching, tasting, smelling, and hearing. The parts of concrete experience are **percepts**, which form **patterns** when aggregated. For example, a single dot on a page is a percept, while a collection of dots constitutes a pattern. Likewise, when you hear the loud initial "beep" of a garbage truck reversing, you experience a percept; when you hear "beep, beep, beep," you distinguish a pattern (see Figure 2.1).

Two characteristics of concrete experience are worth noting. First, we share the concrete level of experience with all other living creatures. Your pet parakeet experiences life at the concrete level, as does a dog walking down the street. Second, the concrete level of experience is meaningless by itself. If life were experienced exclusively at the concrete level, it would be full of sensations but devoid of meaning. The experience of a newborn infant approximates this condition. What must it be like to leave the warm, muffled world of the womb and be thrust into a barrage of electric light, strange smells, and odd sensations? William James described this uncontaminated concrete experience as "one great blooming, buzzing confusion" (James, 1890: 462).

Abstract experience is the imaginary world of the mind.

Fortunately, you do not live exclusively at the concrete level; your experience is not confined to meaninglessness. The abstract level of experience saves you from a state of confusion. **Abstract experience** occurs in your mind. It is the world of imagination, of fantasy.

Concepts are abstract terms used to organize concrete experience.

The abstract level is composed of **concepts**. Concepts are abstract terms for organizing sensory experience. Place six pens in front of you. Examine the pens. You will likely experience each one differently—as objects of different length, diameter, and colour. Some may contain teeth marks, while others are unflawed. Notice, however, that you refer to each of these concretely different objects by the same abstract concept. Each of them, to your mind, is a "pen." Through this naming process, called *conceptualization*, you organize your concrete experience by placing the different objects into a single, meaningful category.

FIGURE 2.1
Levels of Experience

Level of Experience	Components	Aggregates
Abstract (meaningful experience; occurs in the mind)	Concepts ("bits" of ideas)	Propositions (related concepts)
		⇕ Research methods link the concrete to the abstract
Concrete (meaningless experience; occurs through the senses)	Percepts ("bits" of perception)	Patterns (related percepts)

Your mind is full of concepts that enable you to organize and give meaning to your concrete experience. Your mind also relates concepts to one another and, in doing so, forms **propositions**. Propositions are abstract statements that express the relationship between two or more concepts. Imagine someone says, "Watch, table, education, income." After hearing this list of concepts, you are unlikely to say, "Now that's a good idea!" Concept lists are not propositions. Propositions emerge when your mind connects concepts in a meaningful way. Two examples of propositions are "The watch is on the table" and "More educated people tend to earn more income."

Propositions are ideas that result from finding the relationship between concepts.

Almost everyone expresses propositions. If someone approaches you in the bar next Saturday evening and says, "I think I love you," you are being "propositioned." Similarly, a proposition is evident when a political commentator says, "This provincial government is the most corrupt in Canada."

Social issues, such as poverty, deviance, and educational attainment (and all the others that fill this textbook), are often on people's minds, as is evident by browsing through newspapers or blogs. Citizens use concepts to characterize these issues and express propositions about how concepts are related. In the marketplace of ideas, propositions about almost any topic span the whole range of possibilities. Sociologists add their voices to the chorus.

Ideas about social life are like all propositions: they reside in the abstract world of people's minds; they are fantasies. The distinguishing feature of *sociological* ideas is that sociologists connect their abstract concepts and propositions to concrete percepts and patterns. In other words, sociology is interested in sorting out which ideas on a topic best describe experience. In doing so, sociologists try to distinguish groundless speculation from reality.

The methods of social science research are the principles, protocols, and tools sociologists use to link the abstract and concrete levels of experience. This chapter introduces common methodological procedures used by sociological practitioners to formulate propositions that are sustained by evidence. We begin our review by contrasting scientific and unscientific thinking.

Scientific versus Unscientific Thinking

In science, seeing is believing. But in everyday life, believing is seeing. In other words, in everyday life, our biases easily influence our observations. This circumstance often leads us to draw incorrect conclusions about what we see. In contrast, scientists, including sociologists, develop ways of collecting, observing, and thinking about evidence that minimize their chance of drawing biased conclusions.

On what basis do you decide statements are true in everyday life? Below we describe 10 types of unscientific thinking (Babbie, 2000). As you read about each one, ask yourself how frequently you think unscientifically. If you often think unscientifically, this chapter will help you develop more objective ways of thinking.

1. "Chicken soup helps get rid of a cold. *It worked for my grandparents, and it works for me*." This statement represents knowledge based on *tradition*. Although some traditional knowledge is valid (sugar will rot your teeth), some is not (masturbation will not blind you). Science is required to separate valid from invalid knowledge.
2. "Weak magnets can be used to heal many illnesses. *I read all about it in the newspaper*." This statement represents knowledge based on *authority*. We often think something is true because we read it in an authoritative source or hear it from an expert. However, authoritative sources and experts can be wrong. Scientists question authority to arrive at more valid knowledge.
3. "The car that hit the cyclist was dark brown. I was going for a walk last night when *I saw* the accident." This statement represents knowledge based on *casual observation*. Unfortunately, we are usually pretty careless observers. In general, uncertainty can be reduced by observing in a conscious and deliberate manner and by recording observations. That is just what scientists do.

4. "If you work hard, you can get ahead. *I know because several of my parents' friends started off poor but are now comfortably middle class.*" This statement represents knowledge based on *overgeneralization*. For instance, if you know a few people who started off living in poverty, worked hard, and became rich, you may think any person living in poverty can become rich if he or she works hard enough. You may not know about the more numerous people living in poverty who work hard and remain poor or about the rich people who never worked hard. A scientist, however, can study a **sample** that is representative of an entire **population**. Sampling enables them to avoid overgeneralization. They also avoid overgeneralization by repeating research, which ensures that they do not draw conclusions from an unusual set of research findings.

A **sample** is the part of the population of research interest that is selected for analysis.

A **population** is the entire group about which the researcher wants to generalize.

5. "I'm right because *I can't think of any contrary cases*." This statement represents knowledge based on *selective observation*. Sometimes we unconsciously ignore evidence that challenges our firmly held beliefs. Thus, you may actually know some people who work hard but remain poor. However, to maintain your belief that hard work results in wealth, you may keep them out of mind. The scientific requirement that evidence be drawn from representative samples of the population minimizes bias arising from selective observation.
6. "Mr. Smith lives in poverty even though he works hard, but that's because he has a disability. People with disabilities are the only *exception to the rule* that if you work hard you can get ahead." This statement represents knowledge based on *qualification*. Qualifications or "exceptions to the rule" are often made in everyday life, as they are in science. The difference is that in everyday life, qualifications are easily accepted as valid, whereas in scientific inquiry, they are treated as statements that must be carefully examined in the light of evidence.
7. "The Toronto Blue Jays won 50 percent of their baseball games over the last three months but 65 percent of the games they played on Thursdays. *Because it happened so often before*, I bet they'll win next Thursday." This statement represents knowledge based on *illogical reasoning*. In everyday life, we may expect the recurrence of events without reasonable cause, ignoring the fact that rare sequences of events sometimes occur just by chance. For example, it is possible to flip a coin 10 times and have it come up heads each time. On average, 10 heads in a row will happen once every 1024 times you flip a coin 10 times. In the absence of any apparent reason for this happening, it is merely coincidental. It is illogical to believe otherwise. Scientists refrain from illogical reasoning. They also use statistical techniques to distinguish between events that are probably due to chance and those that are not.

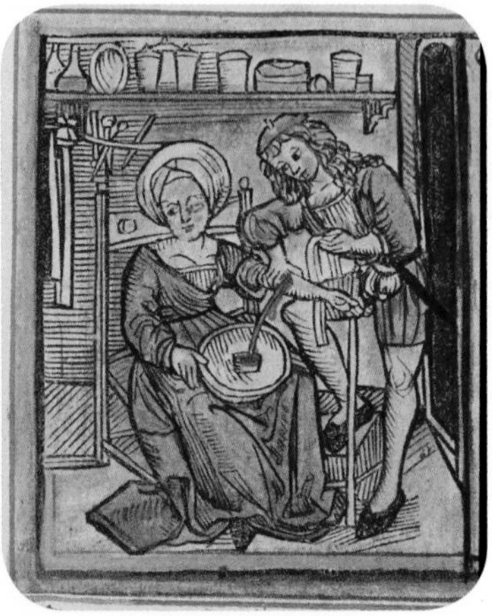

Blood letting, from 'Tractatus de Pestilencia' (vellum), Albik, M. (15th century) / Private Collection, Archives Charmet / The Bridgeman Art Library

The first major advance in modern medicine took place when doctors stopped using unproven interventions in their treatment of patients and started relying on research to assess the value of their interventions. One such unproven intervention involved bleeding patients, shown here in a medieval drawing.

8. "*I just can't be wrong*." This statement represents knowledge based on *ego-defence*. Even scientists may be passionately committed to the conclusions they reach in their research because they have invested much time, energy, and money in them. It is other scientists—more accurately, the whole institution of science, including its commitment to publishing research results and critically scrutinizing findings—that put strict limits on ego-defence in scientific understanding.
9. "*The matter is settled once and for all*." This statement represents knowledge based on the *premature closure of inquiry*. This way of thinking involves deciding that all the relevant evidence has been gathered on a particular subject. Science, however, is committed to the idea that all theories are only temporarily true. Matters are never settled.
10. "*There must be supernatural forces at work here*." This statement represents knowledge based on *mystification*. When we can find no rational explanation for a phenomenon, we may attribute it to forces that cannot be observed or fully understood. Although such forces may exist, scientists remain skeptical. They are committed to discovering observable causes of observable effects.

TIME FOR REVIEW

- How does the abstract level of experience differ from the concrete level?
- A child asks her mother: "Why do I have to go to bed so early?" She responds: "Because I said so!" In what sense is the mother's response unscientific?
- The term "research" literally means "look again." What thinking error is most closely associated with someone uninterested in research?

RESEARCH PRELIMINARIES

Research Approaches

Reality Construction and Confirmation

Imaginary, abstract experience differs from concrete, empirical experience. Everyone uses some method for linking these two kinds of experience. The resulting connections determine a person's understanding of what is "real."

Through the process of linking abstract understanding to concrete sensations, we construct social realities. For example, the actor Jennifer Lawrence believes ghosts are real. She reports, "I'm scared of ghosts. Just yesterday when I moved into a new room at the hotel, I was deeply convinced that I shouldn't wash my face, because if I would look into the mirror, I would actually see a ghost" (perezhilton, 2013). J. Law is not alone among celebrities in believing ghosts are real. Sharing this belief are Michelle Williams, Halle Berry, Lily Collins, Ryan Gosling, Demi Lovato, Matthew McConaughey, Dylan McDermott, and Paul McCartney. Each of them acquired this understanding by matching the concept of ghost with some empirical experience. Do you think ghosts are real? If so, you probably went through a similar reality-construction process.

Statements about reality, both scientific and unscientific, are assertions backed by empirical evidence. Assertions are abstract thoughts: Canada's Prime Minister is unpopular; Your professor is a fool; Most Canadians favour public schooling. Evidence is concrete: public opinion surveys, personal observations, historical documents, and the like. Supporting assertions with empirical evidence constitutes a demonstration that a claim is real. Without evidence, assertions are fantasy (for example, "Hobbits are real."). Research methods link abstract claims to concrete patterns to sort fact from fantasy. In the sciences, including sociology, the use of demanding research methods constitutes adequate demonstrations of reality.

One goal of scientific research is to produce "objective" results. It is worth clarifying what objectivity means, since the concept is subject to confusing stereotypes. Objectivity is not the result of researchers suspending their values, freeing themselves of bias, and producing uncontaminated statements about reality. Scientists are not special types of humans. Just like everyone else, scientists have values and biases. Their ideas and observations, like everyone's, are necessarily subjective. The impressive record of science is not based on its practitioners enjoying an unusual gift for being dispassionate. Science gets its power from its methods, its procedures, from how it goes about generating results.

In this context, when scientists speak of **objectivity** they mean "inter-subjective reliability." All initial observations in science are subjective, since they are generated by real people who cannot escape themselves or society. Objectivity emerges as independent researchers examining the same object produce consistent (that is, reliable) observations. More independent observations and more consistency yield stronger evidence of objectivity.

Objectivity is assessed by the degree of consistency between the observations of independent observers.

Producing objective findings is difficult and demanding work that results from the scientific method, not the special character of scientists.

The Importance of Viewpoint

Abstract experience is composed of concepts and principles existing in our minds. The abstract terms we have in mind play a central role in the reality we can construct. If such terms as "black hole," "Oedipus complex," and "structural strain" are not meaningful terms in your vocabulary, then they do not form part of your reality. Reality is limited by the concepts and principles at our command—which, by the way, underscores the benefit of a liberal arts education. People exposed to a wider range of ideas have the potential to construct richer realities. A reporter asked Shaquille O'Neal if he'd visited the Parthenon during his trip to Greece: "I can't really remember the names of the clubs that we went to." "No, no, I didn't go to England," Paris Hilton is reported as saying. "I went to London." What do O'Neill's and Hilton's responses imply about the realities they have constructed (Davis, 2013)?

Concepts and principles do more than limit reality; they shape it. Looking at the world from a particular viewpoint shapes what you experience. Capitalists see the world in terms of markets, communists in terms of central planning, Christians in terms of Jesus, many atheists in humanistic terms. This principle applies to every form of endeavour. Viewpoint matters to the realities experienced.

As discussed in Chapter 1, sociological viewpoints are expressed in terms of sociological concepts and theories. Theories are narratives composed of propositions that help us understand, explain, and potentially predict social realities. Structural functionalists have one version of social reality, conflict theorists another. The same holds true of feminists and symbolic interactionists. Different sociological theories offer contrasting versions of social reality. The versions are dissimilar because the theories use different concepts and principles, and marshal various types of evidence to support their claims.

Insiders and Outsiders

A useful way to classify viewpoints relies on the distinction between "insiders" and "outsiders." You will appreciate this difference if you have ever navigated a maze. A maze is a walking puzzle filled with many paths. Some paths lead to dead ends, while others advance you toward the exit. When you enter a maze, the goal is to find the route that leads to the exit.

You traverse the maze as an "insider," which, like all viewpoints, has both limitations and benefits. In this case, one limitation is the sense of confusion and frustration that occurs because the tall sides of every path restrict your vision. At every turn, your view and understanding are restricted by what surrounds you. At the same time, however, you have an intimate appreciation of the surrounding details.

Owners of mazes often provide help for people in the maze. Help typically comes from either a map or a sentinel who stands on a platform overseeing the maze's operation. Both the map and the sentinel provide an "outsider's" view, which is helpful because it provides a global, bird's-eye perspective. By not becoming overwhelmed by the extensive details of an insider's perspective, the outsider's perspective provides a view of the forest rather than the trees.

The maze is analogous to social life. People find themselves in groups and organizations of all sorts. As members of these communities, people are bound to have detailed experiences and insights. This knowledge constitutes an insider's appreciation of how the community operates. For example, Aboriginal people have a rich and detailed appreciation of reservation life that urban dwellers lack. The inner workings of Hells Angels are well understood by full-patch members but are foreign to outsiders. The same holds true for all manner of ethnic, racial, gender, and class communities (Ryan, Kofman, and Aaron, 2011; Kulik et al., 2012). In sociological terms, an insider's position and unique experiences provide intimate sensitivities and understandings that are inaccessible to outsiders.

Outsiders offer a different perspective. It may be that only members of particular communities are able to understand certain features of those communities. However, an insider's perspective restricts them from understanding what non-members can see. For example, foreigners visiting Canada for the first time can offer insights about our country that are not obvious to us. RCMP task force members see things about the Hells Angels organization that its members don't appreciate. You have a different awareness of your partner's virtues and vices than he or she does (and vice versa). We conclude that our social position shapes our perspective and what we know. No person or group has a monopoly on knowledge.

Positivist and Interpretive Traditions

In sociology, outsider viewpoints emphasize the "objective" nature of social realities, while insider perspectives emphasize the importance of "subjective" understanding. Unpacking these perspectives helps us understand the positivist and interpretive traditions in the discipline.

The positivist tradition in sociology began with one of the originators of the discipline, Auguste Comte. His goal, like the goal of **positivists** who continue in this tradition, was to model sociology after the natural sciences, which is evident in his preferred name for the discipline—social physics.

Positivists assume that social realities are objective and are best studied through quantitative research methods.

Positivists assume that social realities exist independent of observers and are "out there" waiting to be discovered. In this tradition, social realities are objective, in the sense that they are the same for you as they are for me. From the positivist viewpoint, the task of sociological methods is to develop tools to observe and measure objective social reality in a *quantitative* manner, which often entails using surveys and statistics. Positivists believe that continuing sociological research will result in the steady accumulation of reliable, valid knowledge of the social world that, in turn, can be used to guide constructive social change.

Sociologists working in the interpretive tradition are skeptical of the positivists' worldview. **Interpretivists** emphasize the importance of subjectivity and insiders' understanding. The interpretive tradition does not believe in a universal, independent social reality. Its practitioners believe that all understanding is contingent and meaningfully constructed based on historical, cultural, and social experience. Interpretivists emphasize that the key drivers of human conduct (meanings and motives) cannot be observed directly. Therefore, they reason, trying to apply the methods of the physical sciences to social realities will result, at best, in trivial results. In contrast, the interpretivist tradition favours using *qualitative* methods to gain insight into how differing definitions of reality shape social outcomes. This methodology usually entails systematically observing social settings and describing one's observations by using words, not numbers.

Interpretivists assume that social realities are subjectively constructed and are best studied through qualitative research methods.

The sociological theories introduced in Chapter 1 are organized in the positivist and interpretive traditions. Functionalists, such as Durkheim, are generally guided by the positivist tradition. They argue that social systems have objective structural characteristics that can be understood through quantitative research, and that these structural characteristics are external to, and affect, individuals. By contrast, symbolic interactionists argue that understanding individuals' unique definitions of experience provide key insights into their conduct and that such understanding must be obtained through research methods tailored for this purpose. Conflict theorists and feminist theorists draw on a mixture of both traditions.

Quantitative and Qualitative Research Traditions

Viewpoints shape perspective. Outsiders see things differently from how insiders do. Sociology's theoretical traditions give different emphases to insider and outsider perspectives. These differences have consequences for how researchers working in these theoretical traditions gather evidence to test their ideas. Researchers employing a positivist approach emphasize *deductive* reasoning and quantitative methods. Researchers working in the interpretive tradition utilize *inductive* reasoning and qualitative methods. Appreciating these differences can assist in understanding the strengths of the evidence provided in support of the ideas proposed.

Look again at Figure 2.1. Notice that research methods are the approaches and techniques that investigators use for linking the abstract and concrete levels of experience. Research methods are, in other words, techniques for drawing conclusions about what is real. The reality construction process used in the positivist and interpretive traditions start in different positions and take different forms.

Researchers working in the positivist tradition begin at the abstract level and employ deduction to make connections to empirical experience. By contrast, researchers in the interpretive tradition begin at the concrete level and employ induction to make connections to the abstract level.

Deductive reasoning begins with general ideas and proceeds to test their validity on specific cases.

The deductive approach used by positivists is a "top-down" process. It begins with the general case and moves to specific instances. **Deductive reasoning** begins with some general idea and then tests whether the idea is credible. The original propositions used in deduction come from theoretical reasoning that occurs at the abstract level. For example, before making any empirical observations, there may be good theoretical reasons for thinking that contemporary students are less empathetic than those of previous generations, or that the European Union will collapse by 2025. By themselves, these abstract assertions are speculations—but they are propositions that can be tested empirically. If empirical tests confirm these abstract propositions, then the result is new knowledge. In this way, deduction moves from the abstract to the concrete levels of experience.

Inductive reasoning begins with concrete cases and proceeds to identify general patterns and themes.

Inductive reasoning is the process of going from the specific case to the general one. It is "bottom-up" in its method. Inductive reasoning begins when observations are made of specific, empirical instances. If you go on a blind date and enjoy the company of your brown-eyed partner, you have made one observation. If your next 50 blind dates all reveal that brown-eyed people are more fun than others, a pattern emerges. From your experiences, you might generalize about the connection between eye colour and fun: Brown-eyed dates are more fun. Such knowledge might become your rule for understanding the reality of the dating world. You may generalize that it is prudent to pass over the green-eyed and the blue-eyed if you want to have fun.

Stated more formally, inductive reasoning looks for commonalities among different cases and then generalizes from these shared characteristics. Induction begins at the concrete level of experience, and after observing a certain number of cases, formulates a general insight at the abstract level. The goal is not quantitative measurement but interpretive understanding. By concentrating on fewer cases in a more intensive manner, qualitative researchers using inductive methods seek to understand the richness of reality as experienced by participants in social life.

The Research Act: Connecting Ideas to Evidence

Unscientific thinking often results in a distorted understanding of the social world. Sociological research seeks to provide a more complete, accurate understanding of social realities. Whether quantitative or qualitative techniques are employed, the goal of research is to connect ideas to empirical evidence. Because quantitative and qualitative researchers begin their search in different places, they follow different steps in making the connection.

Qualitative research takes the following steps:

1. Identify a research interest based on concrete experience(s).
2. Collect evidence from one or more cases of the same type.
3. Analyze the cases to identify common patterns and themes.
4. Using sociological concepts and principles, provide an interpretation of the patterns and themes that stresses the context in which the concrete experiences took place.

Notice that this process represents an inductive approach. You begin with a concrete experience that sparks an interest. From there, the steps lead you to progressively deeper understanding, first by examining additional cases of the same type, and then coming to a generalized interpretation. The qualitative model assumes contextualized understanding is critical, so immersion in well-chosen cases is central to subjective understanding.

Courtesy of Carol Wainio

Carol Wainio's *We Can Be Certain* (1982). Research involves taking the plunge from speculation to testing ideas against evidence, or emerging from concrete experiences to make sense of what was experienced.

Quantitative research follows a different path, based on deduction. This model includes the following steps:

1. Identify a theoretical idea of interest.
2. Translate the abstract idea into a testable hypothesis.
3. Collect and analyze data.
4. Accept or reject the hypothesis.

This approach is deductive since it begins with a general idea and then proceeds to test the idea on specific cases. The approach is quantitative insofar as the hypothesis test is conducted on precisely measured variables.

Quantitative and qualitative research projects are rooted in contrasting viewpoints and result in different sorts of understanding. Quantitative understanding is based in numbers and statistics; qualitative understanding, in narratives and stories. Quantitative studies provide a broad understanding that focuses on a relatively small number of variables; qualitative studies provide a narrower understanding that is rich in detail. For example, a quantitative study that carefully examines how two features of schools (school facilities and teacher commitment) affect student performance in 1000 Canadian schools provides a different kind of understanding from an investigation that observes and interviews students and teachers in a single school over a year-long period. One approach is not better than the other. Their appropriateness for solving a particular problem depends on the research goals. Each of these research approaches provides unique, valuable insights that are beyond the reach of the other.

The quantitative and qualitative research traditions provide *complementary* understandings that can enrich each other. Each generates a specific type of knowledge of social reality by linking ideas and evidence. Taken together, they form a continuous loop that connects abstract ideas to concrete experience, as illustrated in Figure 2.2.

Ethical Considerations

Qualitative and quantitative research both require the merger of evidence with ideas. Empirical evidence in sociology is generally collected from individuals. We interview people, observe them, ask them to complete questionnaires, and examine their personal records in official sources. Collecting such evidence has the potential to disrupt the lives of participants. Imagine how upsetting it might be to ask people about traumatic memories they have long suppressed, or to observe them acting in ways that are shameful, or to uncover biographical information that is at odds with their present identity. No matter how fascinating or important sociologists believe their studies to be, they have no right to proceed in ways that override the rights of others.

To protect the rights of others, sociological research is guided by a code of ethics. Research ethics are principles that determine whether research procedures are admissible or inadmissible. The standards specified by research ethics do not focus on specific acts; rather, they are norms

FIGURE 2.2
The Research Cycle

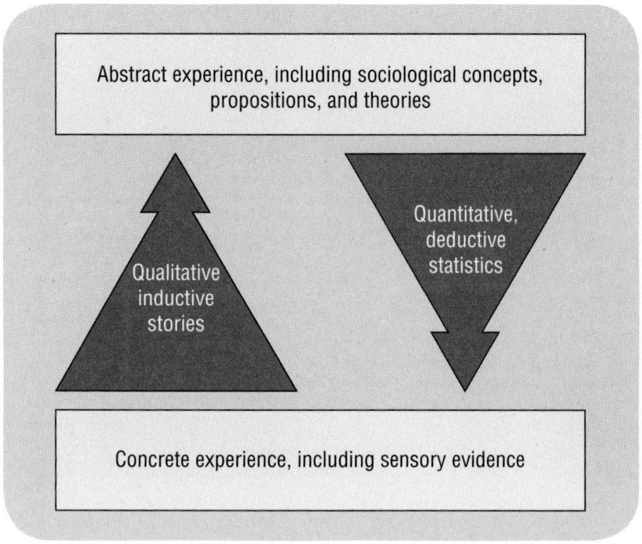

that researchers are required to aspire to. Like most ethical issues, the gap between ethical ideals and their application in real world circumstances varies. In Canada, the Canadian Sociological Association has codified the relevant professional ethics (www.csa-scs.ca/code-of-ethics). The basic principles include voluntary participation, harm minimization, privacy, and authenticity (Babbie and Benaquisto, 2010: 62–72). Let us review each of these principles in turn.

The principle of *voluntary participation* requires that subjects participate because they have chosen to do so. Participants should not be forced to participate. In extreme instances, the application of this principle is clear. But, like all ethical issues, ambiguity enters as we move from the extreme. For example, if a professor asks students to participate in a half-hour survey as a component of their course grade or to research and write a 5000-word term paper, is participation completely voluntary?

A second ethical principle centres on *harm minimization*, sometimes called the right to safety. Even if participants participate voluntarily, they have the right not to be injured. Here, injury is broadly defined to include not just bodily harm but also psychological and social harm. Again, while the application of this principle at the extremes is clear, it becomes problematic in many situations. Given the wide variation in human character traits and temperament, how can a researcher know in advance which data collection techniques will upset which respondents?

Informed consent is participants' acknowledgment that they are aware of the risks of participation and are participating voluntarily.

These first two ethical principles are merged in the concept of **informed consent**. Informed consent requires that voluntary participation be based on a full understanding of the risks of participation (Babbie and Benaquisto, 2010: 66). For that reason, participants are commonly asked to sign an informed consent form that outlines the attendant risks and acknowledges their voluntary participation.

Anonymity occurs when the researcher cannot make a connection between respondents and evidence.

Confidentiality occurs when the researcher can make a connection between respondents and evidence but agrees not to do so.

Third, research participants should enjoy the right to privacy. In other words, participants' identities must be protected. The right to privacy takes two forms, one stronger than the other. The stronger form guarantees respondents' anonymity. **Anonymity** requires that both the researcher and the consumers of the research do not know how particular respondents answered questions. With anonymity, the evidence is not linked to any information on the identity of the people from whom the evidence was collected. Without any link, privacy is guaranteed. However, in many cases, anonymity is impossible to guarantee. For example, if respondents are contacted by telephone, their phone number serves as an identity marker. In these cases, privacy is established through confidentiality. **Confidentiality** occurs when the researcher possesses the link between respondents and evidence but agrees not to share this information. Confidentiality represents a weaker form of privacy since respondents must trust the researcher not to disclose their identities.

The fourth principle of research ethics concerns authenticity. Authenticity occurs when appearances match reality. When they are mismatched, deception occurs. Protecting the dignity of research subjects requires that they not be deceived. Deception can take many forms but commonly includes not informing subjects that they are being studied and lying to them about the goals of the study. Deception does occur in some research studies, often because the research could not proceed otherwise. In instances where respondents are duped, researchers need to be particularly careful. This care typically takes two forms. First, researchers must have a compelling argument stating why the importance of the study's results override authenticity concerns. Second, researchers must debrief subjects. **Debriefing** involves interviewing participants at the close of the investigation to inform them of what actually took place and manage any evident concerns.

Debriefing involves interviewing participants after a study to clarify what occurred and deal with any fallout related to deception.

In general, research ethics focuses on the rights of participants (see Box 2.1). However, these ethical principles also extend to consumers of research. On this account, researchers are required to conduct their data analyses honestly and report their findings fully and fairly. Otherwise, those who consume the research findings will be deceived.

You now have a general understanding of how sociological research proceeds and what ethical issues it encounters. Now let's turn our attention to learning more about the details of the quantitative and qualitative research traditions.

BOX 2.1

SOCIOLOGY AT THE MOVIES

ZERO DARK THIRTY

The terrorist attacks on the World Trade Center in September 2001 (9/11) killed about 3000 people, wounded untold numbers physically and psychologically, shattered infrastructure, and disrupted commerce. The devastation was bound to provoke serious retaliation. Even before al-Qaeda leader Osama bin Laden took responsibility, the hunt for him and his associates was on. *Zero Dark Thirty* traces the 10-year search for bin Laden and his assassination by a U.S. Navy SEAL team in 2011.

Torture plays a central role in the film. The movie is filled with scenes of detainees being waterboarded, held in crates, suffering sleep deprivation, being beaten, and the like—all in service of getting information about the whereabouts of bin Laden. The brutal interrogations portrayed in the film are really a form of data collection, specifically a type of interview. Like all interviews, the objective is to obtain valid information from the respondent. And the interrogators, like all interviewers, face the issue of motivation. Why should the respondent reveal what he knows? The answers offered by interviewers and interrogators frame the ethics of their data collection.

The ethics of scientific research restricts interviewers to motivating respondents in ways that respect their dignity. The norms of voluntary consent, harm minimization, privacy, and authenticity ensure that subjects are treated respectfully. Torture dismisses these normative constraints and finds support in the belief that the ends (obtaining information) are justified by any motivational means. Torture is morally repugnant, and its portrayal in *Zero Dark Thirty* typically elicits disgust.

Snap Stills/Rex Features/CP Picture Archive

A U.S. Navy SEAL team invades bin Laden's hideout in Zero Dark Thirty.

Whether evidence is collected ethically, once obtained, it requires interpretation. On this issue, *Zero Dark Thirty* illustrates a quandary faced by all researchers—how to handle uncertainty. The interrogators want evidence about bin Laden's whereabouts so they can send a team to kill him. U.S. politicians, from the President on down, know they are treading on risky political ground. The costs of mistakes are high. Assassinating the wrong target or killing innocent bystanders would lead to unwanted national and international political fallout. In the film, we repeatedly see CIA operatives bringing evidence to their political masters, only to have it dismissed as insufficient. The politicians want certainty.

Finally, after repeated efforts to find more evidence of bin Laden's position, a meeting is called. Most of the CIA analysts around the table believe that the evidence suggests a 60 percent probability that bin Laden is in an identified Pakistani location. The heroine, Maya, played by Jessica Chastain, asserts the probability is 100 percent. She feels certain, the way many qualitative researchers do after they have been immersed in their study for an extended period. But of course there are no guarantees. As with both quantitative and qualitative researchers, the CIA analysts must make decisions without having complete information. The data are never all in; there is always risk that conclusions are in error. Sociological research comprises a set of strategies and techniques for reliably reducing decision risks and it does so in an ethical manner. But there are other ways to gather reliable data, not all of them ethical and not all of them as reliable.

TIME FOR REVIEW

- What components must come together for something to be considered real?
- Someone claims, "You are a fool." Is this statement subjective or objective? What is required to turn it from one kind of statement into the other?
- Give an example of how an outsider's view of a hockey team differs from an insider's view.
- How would a positivist's view of your classroom differ from an interpretivist's view?
- Explain how induction and deduction connect abstract and concrete experience.
- Where do theoretical ideas fit in both quantitative and qualitative approaches to research?
- If your professor takes your class's final grades, analyzes sex differences in performance, and publishes the results, are any ethical codes being violated? If so, which ones?

QUANTITATIVE APPROACHES

Operationalization is the process of translating concepts into variables and propositions into hypotheses.

Quantitative methods are used by sociologists who seek an objective understanding of social phenomena using the deductive approaches modelled after natural science. Quantitative researchers proceed by translating theoretical ideas into hypotheses, which are then tested through careful measurement and statistical analysis. Experiments and surveys are quantitative methods in sociology. Before describing them, we need to be clear about the place of variables and hypotheses in quantitative methods.

Measuring Variables

A **variable** is a measure of a concept that has more than one value or score.

All sociological methods are concerned with connecting abstract ideas to empirical evidence. Quantitative methods begin at the abstract level and proceed to test theoretical ideas against empirical experience (see Figure 2.3).

Quantitative methods begin with a theoretical idea. Figure 2.3 illustrates this as a proposition (arrow 1), which expresses an idea about the relationship between concepts. For example, a researcher may have good theoretical reasons for proposing that people with more education earn higher incomes. This abstract proposition states the relationship between the concepts "education" and "income."

FIGURE 2.3
Translating Propositions into Hypotheses

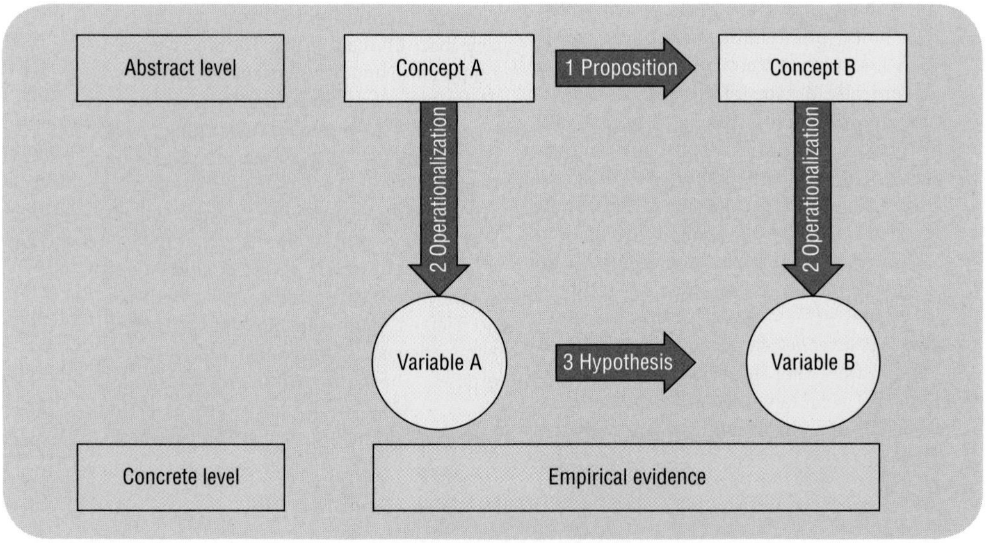

Quantitative researchers immediately encounter a problem in testing abstract ideas. The problem exists because abstract concepts and propositions are imaginary. Has anyone ever seen, touched, heard, tasted, or smelled "education"? How about "income"? The reason we haven't experienced these concepts in a sensory way is that concepts are mental images. They lack concrete properties.

To overcome this problem, quantitative researchers translate abstract propositions into testable forms through operationalization. **Operationalization** is the process by which a concept is translated into a variable (see Figure 2.3, arrows 2). A **variable** is a measure of a concept that has more than one value or score. For example, consider the abstract concept "education." Operationalization asks us to consider what variables would indicate whether one person is more or less educated than another. One operationalization might be "years of schooling." What variables might be used to measure "income?" One possibility is "annual before-tax income from employment and other sources."

After operationalization, the original proposition, which expressed a relationship between concepts, is translated into a relationship between variables. The result of this translation is a hypothesis, the testable form of a proposition (see Figure 2.3, arrow 3). In our example, the hypothesis is "People with more years of schooling have higher gross taxable annual income." A **hypothesis** is the testable form of a proposition because you can imagine being able to experience (measure) different levels of the variables in concrete form.

Most students understand that a hypothesis is an educated guess. Figure 2.3 shows what this statement actually means. The "educated" part of an "educated guess" refers to the fact that a hypothesis is informed by an idea. It is a thoughtful guess, not a wild one. A hypothesis remains a guess insofar as we don't know how well it fits observable evidence. Evidence collected through research is used to test hypotheses. In quantitative research, experiments and surveys are methods for conducting such tests.

Experiments

Experiments are not widely used in sociological research, although some key insights have resulted from this approach (Milgram, 1974; Zimbardo, 2008). However, understanding experiments is important because it lays bare some fundamental principles of quantitative thinking.

Experiments begin with a hypothesis about how one variable affects another. The variable considered the cause is called an **independent variable**, while the outcome or effect is identified as the **dependent variable**. An **experiment** is a carefully controlled artificial situation that allows researchers to isolate presumed causes and measure their effects precisely (Campbell and Stanley, 1963).

To identify the independent variable's effects on the dependent variable, experimenters first create two groups of subjects. They accomplish this task by means of **randomization**, which assigns individuals to the groups by chance processes. Randomization ensures that the two groups are equivalent. Next, experimenters measure both groups on the dependent variable. Since the groups are initially equivalent, the group scores on the dependent variable are the same. Experimenters then proceed to introduce the independent variable to only one of the groups. The independent variable is the hypothesized agent of change. The group experiencing the independent variable is called the **experimental group**. The group left alone is called the **control group**. The final step in the experimental method is to remeasure the dependent variable on the experimental and control groups after the independent variable has been administered. Because the groups were initially equivalent, any observed final differences in the dependent variable are considered effects of the independent variable (see Box 2.2).

Although the results of experimental procedures can be impressive, their application in sociology is limited. A key limitation centres on considerations of **validity**. Valid results are results that accurately reflect reality. **Reliability,** which refers to consistency of results, is a necessary condition for validity. A watch that is two minutes slow provides a reliable but invalid measure of time. If you glance at the watch again in several seconds, you get a similar, inaccurate report. Researchers who use hat size as a measure of intelligence also achieve consistent but invalid measures (Rushton and Ankney, 2009). Sociological researchers continually work at improving the reliability and validity of their measures of

A **hypothesis** is the testable form of a proposition.

An **independent variable** is the presumed cause in a cause-and-effect relationship.

A **dependent variable** is the presumed effect in a cause-and-effect relationship.

An **experiment** is a carefully controlled artificial situation that allows researchers to isolate hypothesized causes and measure their effects precisely.

Randomization in an experiment involves assigning each individual by chance processes.

The **experimental group** is the group that is exposed to the independent variable.

The **control group** is the group that is not exposed to the independent variable.

Validity is the degree to which results reflect reality.

Reliability is the degree to which procedures yield consistent results.

In a **survey**, sociologists ask respondents questions about their knowledge, attitudes, or behaviour, either in a face-to-face or telephone interview or in a paper-and-pencil format.

key concepts. Their aim, like that of the target shooter, is to hit the bull's eye (validity) consistently (reliability).

The strictly controlled, artificial conditions in experiments often compromise validity. For example, a common experimental measure of aggression is willingness to press a button that supposedly administers a shock to an unseen person in another room (Subra et al., 2010). But is pressing that button really equivalent to beating someone on the street with a baseball bat? Is sharing jelly beans with someone in a laboratory test the same as being cooperative with others outside the lab? Does placing your finger on an iPhone camera connected to some software fully capture your level of stress (Azumio Inc., 2014)? In addition, the fact that experimental participants are not a cross-section of the population makes it difficult to know how experimental findings apply to non-laboratory conditions.

BOX 2.2

SOCIAL POLICY: WHAT DO YOU THINK?

GOVERNMENT NUTRITIONAL EXPERIMENTS IN RESIDENTIAL SCHOOLS

In 1942, federal government researchers visiting remote reserve communities in northern Manitoba found the Aboriginal people to be in bad shape. They were malnourished and demoralized. One researcher characterized them as marked by "shiftlessness, indolence, improvidence and inertia" (Mosby, 2013: 147).

Although the obvious response to a malnourished population under government care is to provide increased support, government researchers saw this situation as an opportunity for a field experiment. The researchers had encountered a ready-made laboratory. By defining Aboriginal malnourishment and demoralization as dependent variables and vitamin supplements as independent variables, the design

F. Royal/National Film Board of Canada/ Library and Archives Canada/

A doctor attends to an Aboriginal boy as part of an experiment testing the effect of vitamins—and vitamin deprivation—on the Norway House Cree in Northern Manitoba, 1942.

was set to learn how different nutritional supplements affected health outcomes. The first experiments were conducted in 1942 on a population of 300 Norway House Cree in northern Manitoba. The experimental group of 125 received vitamin supplements. These supplements were withheld from the control group.

Recognizing that Aboriginal children in government-controlled residential schools provided ideal experimental subjects, the research program spread. By 1947, experiments involving 1,300 Aboriginal students in six residential schools were in place in British Columbia, Alberta, Manitoba, Ontario, and Nova Scotia. In some experiments, milk rations were reduced to half the recommended levels for two years to observe the effects. In other research, different combinations of vitamin and mineral supplements were provided to one group and not another. Since an important indicator of the dependent variable (health) was measured by observing the health of students' gums, dental services were withdrawn from participating students since fixing the children's teeth and gums would contaminate the results.

When these experiments were conducted in the 1940s, codified ethics for the treatment of human subjects in scientific research were just beginning. Still, one has to wonder how researchers could purposely deprive children in government care from adequate nutrition and health care. Did the researchers see these children only as experimental subjects and not as human beings? Did the fact that they were Aboriginal contribute to their mistreatment? Or was the higher purpose of scientific advancement used to justify the means? Even today, the lead researcher's son defends his father's actions by rationalizing, "He was just trying to do good work" (Livingstone, 2013).

Surveys

Surveys are the most widely used sociological research method. In a **survey**, sociologists ask people about their knowledge, attitudes, or behaviour. All survey researchers aim to study part of a group—a sample—to learn about the whole group of interest—the population. To generalize reliably about the population based on findings from a sample, researchers must be sure that the characteristics of the people in the sample match those of the population (see Box 2.3). To draw a sample from which they can safely generalize, researchers choose respondents (people who answer the survey questions) at random.

BOX 2.3

IT'S YOUR CHOICE

PRIVACY, POLITICS, AND THE CANADIAN CENSUS

Beginning in 1871, the Canadian census was conducted every 10 years. In 1956, the frequency changed to every five years. Academics, businesses, government agencies, and non-governmental organizations came to rely on the breadth, depth, and accuracy of the census to develop their strategic plans. Because of the importance of census information in economic and social planning, the law required all adults to complete the census questionnaire. Penalties for refusing include fines and imprisonment.

In recent decades, Statistics Canada issued two types of census questionnaires, a "short" and a "long" form. The short form consisted of about eight basic questions about age, sex, and the like. The long form consisted of about 60 questions on topics such as home life, work, and ethnicity. Statistics Canada distributed the short form to all households. It distributed the long form to 20 percent of households chosen at random.

In 2010, the federal Conservative government announced that, beginning in 2011, it would replace the mandatory long-form census with a voluntary National Household Survey (NHS) distributed to 33 percent of households. The Conservatives justified their decision largely on ethical grounds, declaring the long-form census to be a coercive violation of privacy rights. In the words of Tony Clement, the minister responsible for the decision: "The government does not believe it is appropriate to force Canadians to divulge personal information under threat of prosecution" (Meahan, 2010).

Scrapping the long-form census incited a groundswell of opposition from a wide range of interest groups, including provincial and municipal governments, ethnic and religious bodies, community organizations, unions, and academic and professional organizations. Public opinion, by contrast, was ambivalent. About half of the general population agreed that the mandatory long-form census was an invasion of privacy, but two-thirds considered it to be a reasonable intrusion.

This proposal for abolishing the census was not the first such suggestion by a Conservative government. The idea was previously put forward in 1986. However, the first effort to abolish the census was quickly shelved because, in addition to the opposition groups in 2010, the business community had expressed outrage in 1986. But the business community's voice was largely absent in 2010 because information sources had changed dramatically over the last quarter century. Business can now access alternative, current, market-specific data from computers, smartphones, and other personal technologies. Census data are increasingly irrelevant to business (Brym, 2014c).

Without the business lobby pressuring the government to change its plans, the Conservatives proceeded with the voluntary survey in 2011. As the experts predicted, the survey resulted in a dramatic decline in the quality of data. Fewer people participate in voluntary surveys than in mandatory ones, so the margins of error are wider. The 2006 census saw 94 percent of eligible adults respond. The 2011 NHS achieved a response rate of 68 percent. This difference in participation has important consequences for estimating the social profiles of Canadian communities. In particular, since disadvantaged communities have lower survey participation rates, their number and characteristic situations are underestimated, while the opposite is true for privileged communities.

Are changes observed between 2006 (and earlier) findings and 2011 results real social trends, or do they result from low-quality 2011 data? Does less reliable evidence about disadvantaged Canadian communities provide governments with more freedom to make policies based on ideology rather than on evidence? Such questions underscore the importance of high-quality empirical evidence for shaping public policy in this country.

Do you agree with the government's decision to institute the NHS? Is it too intrusive to require citizens to share information about their personal, home, and work lives? Is the long-form census a case where the collective good should prevail over individual interests? As a citizen who is influenced by policy decisions that are based in part on the accuracy of census data, it's your choice.

When researchers use surveys to collect information, they identify people in a representative sample and then ask them a set of identical questions. People interviewed on a downtown street corner do *not* constitute a representative sample of Canadian adults: such a sample does not include people who live outside the urban core, it underestimates the number of seniors and people with disabilities, it does not take into account regional diversity, and so on.

Sparky/Getty Images

Sociologists often conduct surveys through telephone interviews. Within organizational settings, either face-to-face interviews or self-administered questionnaires are common. In face-to-face interviews, a trained interviewer asks and records the answers to a set of predetermined questions. In a self-administered survey, respondents read the questions and provide their answers to the predetermined questions on a paper questionnaire. Increasingly, questionnaires are available for on-line completion.

Surveys typically contain two types of questions. Closed-ended questions provide the respondent with a list of permitted answers. Each answer is assigned a numerical code for purposes of statistical analysis. By contrast, open-ended questions allow respondents to answer in their own words. Open-ended questions are particularly useful when researchers don't have enough knowledge to create a meaningful and complete list of possible answers.

In a **probability sample**, the units have a known and nonzero chance of being selected.

Sampling

Survey methods benefit from high reliability. Done properly, different surveys yield consistent results. This outcome is illustrated by the close clustering of opinion poll results near election times. Selecting representative samples is central to survey reliability.

To acquire a representative sample, researchers can't just recruit volunteers or select people who are easy to reach. Instead, they must choose respondents who constitute a **probability sample**. Probability samples are samples in which every member of a population has a known, nonzero chance of being selected.

Creating a probability sample begins with a *sampling frame*, a list of all the people in the population of interest. A random selection method is then used to select individual cases. This process ensures that every person in the population has a known and nonzero chance of being selected. Creating sampling frames are a continuing challenge to survey researchers, since most organizational membership lists are incomplete or outdated. For general population surveys, researchers typically rely on computer-generated random-digit dialling, which captures telephone numbers of all types (including unlisted numbers and cellphones). Still, this method is imperfect because it excludes persons without phones (about 3 percent of the population). For these reasons, disadvantaged groups such as homeless persons, Aboriginal peoples, and illegal immigrants are generally underrepresented in survey research studies.

Mikael Damkier/Shutterstock.com

Homelessness is increasingly a focus of public policy. But public support may not be adequate if homeless people are not counted properly. Statistics Canada first included a count of homeless people in the 2001 census. However, these numbers are only estimates because the count is based on information about the use of shelters and soup kitchens, combined with an attempt at street counts.

Sample Size and Statistical Significance

Survey researchers carefully select respondents so that the sample results reflect the population. When researchers are confident that sample results reflect the population, they refer to the findings as being *statistically significant*. Statistical significance should not be confused with *substantive significance*, which refers to the importance of the results. The importance of research findings is a separate issue from whether the sample results can be confidently generalized to the population.

An important determinant of statistical significance is sample size. As sample size grows, so does the likelihood of finding statistically significant results. However, collecting evidence from sample members is a costly undertaking, leading to a trade-off between data collection costs and sample accuracy. In general, a random sample of 1500 people provides acceptably accurate results, no matter how large the population.

TABLE 2.1
Sex and Frequency of Traffic Accidents

Frequency of Traffic Accidents	Sex: Male	Female	Total
Few	70%	40%	104
Many	30%	60%	96
Total	80	120	200

Reading Tables

Survey researchers work in the quantitative tradition. They test theories by converting ideas into hypotheses, which express an expected pattern of relationship between independent and dependent variables. The variables are measured on members of a sample, whose responses are expected to reflect the views of the population because of the design of the sample. Survey findings are quantitative because counts are made of the frequency of responses to different variables. So, for example, in a survey in which the independent variable is the respondent's "sex" and the dependent variable is "frequency of traffic accidents," the results may show:

Sex

(1) Males = 80
(2) Females = 120

Frequency of Traffic Accidents

(1) Low = 104
(2) High = 96

These quantitative results show how many people in the sample were of each sex and how many had different numbers of traffic accidents. But let's say that a research hypothesis stated that "Women have more traffic accidents than men do." How could these results be used to test the hypothesis?

The answer involves reading a contingency table. This skill is very handy since many survey findings are expressed in this form.

A **contingency table** is a cross-classification of cases by at least two variables that allows you to determine how the variables are related. Table 2.1 shows the contingency table for the relationship between sex and frequency of traffic accidents. Notice that, by convention, the independent variable (sex) and its values (male, female) are listed across the top of the table, while the dependent variable (frequency of traffic accidents) and its values (few, many) are listed on the left side of table.

A **contingency table** is a cross-classification of cases by at least two variables that allows you to see how, if at all, the variables are associated.

The information *inside* the table shows how (if at all) the variables are related. Notice that the information in the table is expressed in terms of column percentages. This use of percentages is important because percentages allow you to compare the column information. If the evidence in a contingency table is not expressed as column percentages, you need to convert it to this form to proceed.

A **relationship** exists between two variables if the values of one variable change systematically with the values of the other.

A **relationship** exists between two variables if the values of one variable change systematically with the values of the other. The **strength** of a relationship is determined by the degree to which change in the independent variable is associated with change in the dependent variable. Tables 2.2 and 2.3 show two extremes of strength. Table 2.2 shows the

The **strength** of a relationship is determined by the degree to which change in the independent variable is associated with change in the dependent variable.

TABLE 2.2
No Relationship between Sex and Frequency of Traffic Accidents

Frequency of Traffic Accidents	Sex: Male	Female	Total
Few	70%	70%	104
Many	30%	30%	96
Total	80	120	200

TABLE 2.3
Maximum Relationship between Sex and Frequency of Traffic Accidents

Frequency of Traffic Accidents	Sex		
	Male	**Female**	**Total**
Few	100%	0%	104
Many	0%	100%	96
Total	80	120	200

situation where no connection (strength of association) exists between the two variables. Table 2.3 presents the situation where the independent variable makes all the difference to the dependent variable.

Here's how you determine the strength of a relationship in a contingency table. Step 1: Compute the differences between the adjacent cells in each row inside the table. Step 2: Average these differences. Applied to Table 2.2, Step 1 yields 70 minus 70 = 0 percent difference, and 30 − 30 = 0 percent difference. Step 2 yields an average difference of (0 + 0) / 2 = 0 percent. In short, in Table 2.2, sex makes no difference to the frequency of traffic accidents. Now apply the same steps to Table 2.3. Step 1: 100 − 0 = 100, and 0 − 100 = 100. (Note: Don't worry about negative numbers. Just look for differences). Step 2, the average difference is 100 percent (100 + 100) / 2. Therefore, in Table 2.3, sex makes all the difference to the frequency of traffic accidents.

Tables 2.2 and 2.3 represent the extremes of a relationship. Most actual evidence shows differences somewhere between these extremes. Larger differences indicate that the independent variable is having a stronger effect (making more of a difference) on the dependent variable. You can now apply these two steps to determine the strength of the relationship between sex and frequency of traffic accidents in Table 2.1. Do the findings support or disconfirm the research hypothesis?

Determining Causes

The meaning of "relationship" in research is the same as in everyday life. Relationships exist when the changes in two things are systematically connected. If a change in your life systematically changes someone else's life, the two of you are related in some way. If the relationship weakens, what you do in your life makes less of a difference to the other person. If the relationship disintegrates, a change in your life makes no difference to that of the other person. Life goes on, but the connection is lost. In research, the same holds true, except that the components are not people but variables.

Ultimately, quantitative researchers are interested in establishing *causal* relationships. Does change in education cause change in income? Does more foreign aid improve the standard of living in receiving nations? Does increasing age at marriage reduce the divorce rate? To establish whether an independent variable causes change in a dependent variable, researchers must satisfy three criteria. We will review these criteria and illustrate them by examining the question, "Do storks cause babies to appear?"

The first causal criterion requires the researcher to demonstrate that the variables systematically change together. This demonstration is the *relationship* test, which establishes that the variables are in fact associated. In our example, the researcher needs to demonstrate that regions with higher numbers of storks also have higher birth rates. In fact, this relationship is the case in Scandinavia, where regions with fewer storks have lower fertility rates, and areas with more storks have higher fertility rates.

As a second causal criterion, researchers must establish *sequencing*, showing that the independent variable changes before changes in the dependent variable occur. If the hypothesis is that storks cause babies to appear, the researcher must demonstrate that the storks arrived prior to the babies (and not vice versa). The first two causal criteria are straightforward. The third one, *non-spuriousness*, requires more elaboration.

Relationships between people do not exist in isolation, and neither do relationships between independent and dependent variables. Instead, connections between variables and people always exist in a context. In research, a **control variable** (or several control variables) specifies the context of a relationship. For example, a young man may declare his undying love for his date on a Saturday night, but the wise date will understand that this declaration may be influenced by the context and ask, "What will he say when he's sober on Sunday morning?" Similarly, the relationship between family income and the years of schooling a person attains in various countries may depend on whether the national postsecondary system is funded privately or by the state. High-quality state-funded schools will mute the effect of family income on years of education attained. Contexts affect relationships. In our example, the contextual issue is whether variables other than stork sightings are influencing the observed relationship between stork sightings and babies appearing.

A **control variable** identifies the context for the relationship between an independent variable and a dependent variable.

The existence of control variables has an important implication for the interpretation of relationships: The appearance of a relationship between two variables does not always signify that the relationship is real. Appearance and reality do not always coincide. Just ask any broken-hearted former sweetheart.

In quantitative research, an important reason for the imperfect alignment between the appearance and the reality of relationships is the operation of control variables. Control variables may affect the nature of any apparent relationship between two variables. Since researchers are interested in identifying real relationships, before they are willing to declare that a relationship between two variables is authentic, they must investigate the influences of potentially contaminating control variables. They do this to avoid being fooled by appearances.

A relationship between an independent variable and a dependent variable may be authentic (real) or phony. Authenticity is the third criterion researchers use to determine causality. Researchers call phony relationships **spurious**. *Spuriousness occurs when change in a control variable causes change in both the independent and dependent variables.* To understand why an inauthentic relationship between two variables may appear real, you need to recall that variables exert effects when they change. This outcome is true of all variables, including the control variables that form the context for an independent–dependent variable relationship.

The relationship between an independent variable and a dependent variable is said to be **spurious** when a control variable causes change in both the independent and dependent variables.

Figure 2.4 illustrates a spurious relationship. Note that no line connects the independent and dependent variables, suggesting that the two variables are not really connected. Follow the arrows and you will see how spuriousness operates. Variation in the third variable, the control variable, causes change in both the independent and dependent variables. Consequently, if you examined only the independent and dependent variables—that is, if you ignored the context—you would see the independent and dependent variables changing together systematically. Under spurious circumstances,

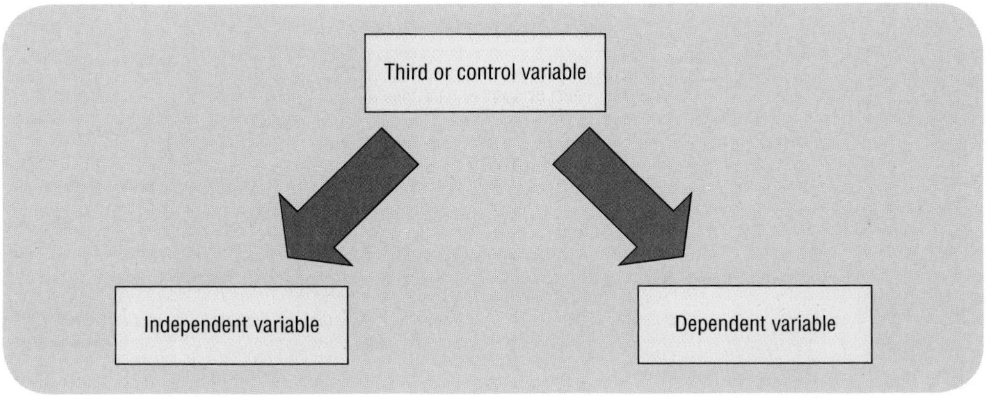

FIGURE 2.4
How Spurious Relationships Occur

you would see that independent and dependent variables are related when, in fact, they are not. You would be fooled by phony appearances.

Consider the following illustrations of spurious relationships. Earlier we introduced the relationship between the number of storks in a region (the independent variable) and the number of births in the region (the dependent variable). This apparent relationship is, in fact, spurious. In this case, the relevant third variable is whether the region is rural or urban. Rural regions have more stork sightings and higher birth rates than urban regions do. In other words, the apparent connection between stork sightings and babies appearing is not authentic; changes in both are due to regional differences.

Nobody likes to be fooled, least of all researchers. Therefore, researchers test for potential spuriousness in independent–dependent variable relationships. The easiest way to understand the test for spuriousness is to contrast Figure 2.4 with Figure 2.5, which illustrates a genuine relationship. In Figure 2.5, the independent and dependent variables are *actually* related, as evidenced by the double-headed arrow connecting them. Moreover, in this diagram, the third variable is *unconnected* to either the independent or dependent variable.

Comparing the two diagrams, we see that the operation of the control variable has either nothing to do with the independent–dependent variable connection (the authentic case, Figure 2.5) or everything to do with the appearance of such a connection (the spurious case, Figure 2.4). Based on this crucial difference between the authentic and inauthentic models, researchers have devised a test for determining the existence of spuriousness. The key idea of the test involves examining the independent–dependent variable relationship under two conditions—first, when the third variable is allowed to *change* and, second, when the third variable is *held constant*. Where a variable is held constant, it is fixed and does not change. Using these comparisons, the test for spuriousness works as follows. If the independent–dependent variable relationship is authentic, then the original independent–dependent variable relationship is evident under both conditions; that is, both when the third variable is allowed to vary and when it is held constant. By contrast, if the original relationship is spurious, the independent–dependent variable connection is evident only when the third variable is changing (the first condition) and disappears when the third variable is held constant (the second condition).

You can better appreciate this logic by returning to our examples. If the connection between storks and babies were authentic (real), then it would be unaffected by the third variable, region. Here is how the test would occur. Under the first condition, the researcher would examine the connection between stork sightings and babies appearing for both rural and urban regions. In this condition, the third variable (region) is being allowed to change. As reported previously, the relationship between stork sightings and babies appearing is evident under this condition. Next, under the second condition, the researcher would examine the storks–babies connection *only for rural regions* and then *only for urban*

FIGURE 2.5
How Authentic Relationships Occur

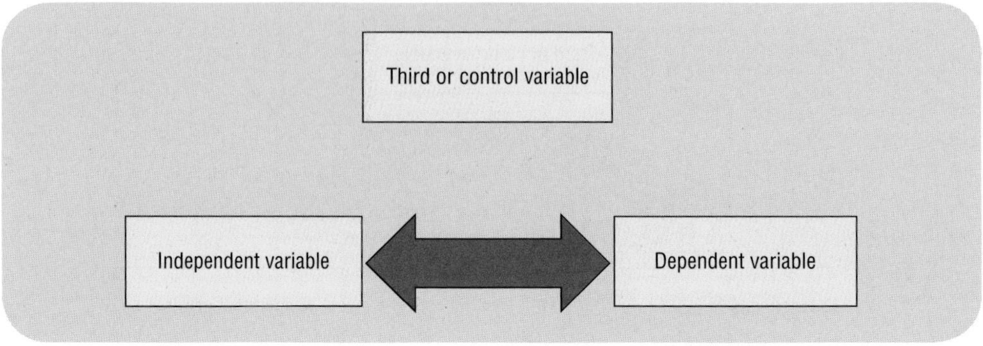

regions. In doing so, the researcher would be examining the independent–dependent variable connection with the third variable being held constant. This second test would reveal no connection between stork sightings and babies appearing. The researcher would then conclude the storks–babies relationship is spurious because the relationship is evident in the first condition but disappeared in the second condition.

This understanding of the test for spuriousness parallels the situation in everyday life. Imagine you meet someone in a bar this weekend and, after a night of partying, you declare love for each other. Three variables are operating in this situation: your feelings, the other person's feelings, and alcohol. How can you test whether your declaration is authentic or spurious? If the declaration is authentic, it will remain the same when the third variable is removed (when you sober up). If the declaration is spurious, it will disappear when the third variable is no longer operating.

To summarize, researchers conclude a causal connection exists between two variables when they successfully demonstrate that

1. the variables systematically change together (the relationship criterion);
2. the independent variable changed before observed changes in the dependent variable (the sequencing criterion); and
3. the observed relationship is authentic (the non-spuriousness criterion).

Survey research, including the analysis of the quantitative data that surveys generate to test hypotheses, illustrates the deductive, objective approach to sociological research based on natural science models. Sociologists also conduct qualitative research that relies on induction and subjective understanding to generate knowledge of social reality. The following section introduces the qualitative tradition.

TIME FOR REVIEW

- What variables could be used to operationalize the concept of "happiness?"
- Construct a plausible hypothesis between the variables "dropping out of high school" and "drug abuse," using "drug abuse" as the independent variable. Now construct a plausible hypothesis between these same variables, using "dropping out of high school" as the independent variable.
- Explain how a bathroom scale could produce reliable but invalid results.
- A local television news channel invites viewers to participate in their Web poll question of the day. Do the results constitute a probability sample? Why or why not?
- What control variable might reveal that the relationship between sex and traffic accidents in Table 2.1 is spurious?

QUALITATIVE APPROACHES

Qualitative methods are used by sociologists who seek a subjective understanding of social phenomena using the inductive approach. You have seen that quantitative research is organized around the measurement of variables, which are properties of social objects. In this way, quantitative research concentrates on specific parts of social life. The goal is to test hypotheses about the relationships between the components of social life, such as social class, gender, and inequality. Qualitative research is designed for different purposes.

Qualitative research focuses on wholes, not parts. It emphasizes that meaning and motives are central to understanding human experience—and that these features cannot be measured quantitatively or understood in isolation. Rather than trying to measure objective features of social life, qualitative research centres on understanding how people interpret social experience. The uniqueness of human experience requires methods tailored for that purpose, not methods modelled on the natural sciences.

Around 1900, when sociology was emerging as an academic discipline, German sociologists debated the appropriateness of applying natural science methods to interpret social life. In contrast to searching for general laws of social life, Max Weber and others participating in this debate emphasized that sociology should seek **Verstehen** (understanding). According to Weber, the search for understanding social experience must centre on how people subjectively define and interpret their own and others' actions. This task, in turn, requires the study of wholes, not parts (Truzzi, 1974).

Verstehen is a methodological approach the goal of which is to understand the meaning of social experience to participants in social life.

The qualitative research methodologies evolved within the tradition of *Verstehen*. Their basic emphasis is that sociological methods should centre on **empathy**. Understanding human social experience requires using our imagination to become aware of the internal life of others. Qualitative research is a broad category that includes several research methods. We now introduce you to two of these research methods: participant observation and qualitative interviewing.

Empathy is the process of using imagination to become aware of how others define and interpret their experience.

Participant Observation

In participant observation, researchers take part in the social group being studied and, while part of the action, systematically observe what occurs and why. The goal of participant observation is to experience and understand what it is like to be a member of a specific community. For example, in one classic participant observation study, researchers, under false pretenses, had themselves admitted as patients into 12 different psychiatric hospitals (Rosenhan, 1973). They arrived at the hospitals complaining that they heard voices saying "empty," hollow," and "thud." None of the psychiatric, nursing, or custodial staff knew they were anything but newly admitted patients. During the course of the researchers' stay, their participation in the organization's routines and observation of their own and others' experiences taught them much about how the label "mentally ill" shapes the way others interpret and react to the actions of people labelled mentally ill.

Like all qualitative research, participant observation emphasizes careful description, attention to social process and context, and flexibility. Because this research method requires sensitivity to social surroundings, it lacks a codified set of procedures. However, participant observation studies typically confront the following issues (see Box 2.4).

Determining the Researcher's Role

How involved will the researcher be with the group being studied? At one end of the continuum, researchers can be complete participants; whereas, at the other end, they are complete observers. More frequently, they fall somewhere in between (Gold, 1958). When acting as complete participants, researchers seek to become full members of the community and conceal their identity as researchers from community members. Selecting this role has advantages and disadvantages. The biggest advantage is that it minimizes problems of **reactivity**. Reactivity refers to observed people concealing certain things or exaggerating their authentic actions in an effort to impress the researcher. One reason the Rosenhan study of mental institutions is so compelling is that the mental institution staff did not know the participants were researchers. If they did, you can easily imagine how the staff would have adjusted their actions. On the other hand, the role of complete participant involves serious ethical concerns. For instance, how would you feel if you learned that one of your sexual

Reactivity occurs when the presence of a researcher causes the observed people to conceal certain things or act artificially to impress the researcher.

BOX 2.4

SOCIOLOGY ON THE TUBE

UNDERCOVER BOSS

Episodes of *Undercover Boss* follow a general formula. Chief Executive Officers (CEOs) decide to find out what is happening outside the executive office. To accomplish this goal, the CEOs, wearing a disguise and presenting themselves as employees in training, are paired with experienced staff members in various positions within the organization. After some training from the senior staff member, the CEOs try their hand at the tasks associated with their new role. During each assignment, the CEO bonds with the staff member, asking questions about the company, the division, the position, and the employee's personal life.

In each episode, the undercover CEO undertakes a set of steps that parallel those in a qualitative research project employing participant observation. Participant observation involves observing people's activities by participating in their lives. It creates a sympathetic understanding of the subjects' motivations and actions. It is just this type of understanding that is sought by the CEO in each episode. Having looked at their company's profit and loss statements and spreadsheets of their company's performance, these undercover CEOs are looking for the information that does not show up on these reports.

To achieve their goal, undercover bosses, like participant observers, face challenges in gaining access, identifying key informants, assembling field notes, and constructing a narrative. When regular employees talk with a boss, they restrict the information they share. To encourage employees to speak freely, bosses must gain access in some way that doesn't identify their real status. In *Undercover Boss*, access is gained through disguises and introductions that present the boss as an ordinary person. Here, reality TV and qualitative research diverge significantly. In the field, locating an informant who provides trustworthy information to the researcher is a huge challenge. In *Undercover Boss*, it is a non-issue. Reality TV shows are carefully produced, and the employee who works with the boss is pre-selected to fit the show's style and narrative. Still, surprises occur, such as the time in a British episode when a frustrated employee punched his boss, knocked him to the ground, and dislocated 14 of his teeth (Dailymash, 2014).

David M. Russell/© CBS/Courtesy: Everett Collection/CP Picture Archive

A CEO serves hot dogs and soft drinks in *Undercover Boss*.

Once accepted, the undercover boss is well positioned to observe what occurs at ground level and to learn through discussion how employees experience the workplace. The challenge is to keep note of the key features of the experience. The undercover bosses are often seen sneaking into a private location to record their observations. On other occasions, what is observed (such as sexual harassment or health code violations) is so disturbing that the CEO immediately reports it to an authority for correction.

The final step in the research process involves making sense of one's experiences. This task is always a challenge for the undercover bosses. Often, they call home after their shift to discuss events with their spouses. The bosses are commonly filmed displaying emotions ranging from anger to sadness as they come to terms with what they have learned. In the show, the bosses' understanding of their experiences is revealed to the employees in private debriefing interviews and in a gathering of the company's executives and staff.

In the final analysis, what we witness on *Undercover Boss* is not scientific research, but entertainment. We enjoy witnessing high-status bosses struggling with tasks routinely completed with competence by people well below their pay grade. Tension emerges from seeing the collision between higher and lower views of the same organization. And there is drama in peeling back the layers of role performance and learning how real people cope with their jobs. Although the results are not scientific, the form followed in episodes of *Undercover Boss* parallels the steps in participant observation.

encounters had been observed by an unidentified researcher? You can imagine how people felt when one sociologist conducted an infamous participant observation study in just this way (Humphrey, 1970; Babbie, 2004).

Less immersed in the social setting is the *participant-as-observer*. In this form, participants know the researcher's status and goals. Until the researcher gains the trust of participants, the role is accompanied by reactivity concerns but reduces ethical breaches. With time and sensitivity, reactivity is reduced, and the role can yield useful insights about communities of interest. Canadian illustrations of this approach include Wilson's (2002) investigation of Toronto raves, Totten's (2001) study of youth gangs, and Clancey's (2001) inquiry into the work of scientists in the Arctic. The complete observer role is rarely employed since non-participation denies the researcher the kind of insider experience that is key to qualitative investigations.

Gaining Access

A second issue confronting participant observation research involves answering the question, "How will the researcher gain access to the group or community under study?" The level of challenge this presents varies with how open or closed the group is. Gaining access to fast-food courts, hospital waiting areas, and rock concerts is relatively easy. Entering corporate boardrooms, religious cult ceremonies, and Supreme Court deliberations is difficult—but in some cases not impossible, as illustrated by Barker's study of the Unification Church (Barker, 1984).

The Unification Church is a worldwide religious community that, in the 1990s, had a high public profile. Until his death in 2012, Reverend Sun Myung Moon led the church, whose followers were named Moonies. The church was accused of being a cult that brainwashed practitioners (Saner, 2012). The exotic perception of this community was enhanced by its public weddings, in which thousands of couples were married in a single ceremony (Boorstein, 2010).

It took sociologist Eileen Barker an extended period to negotiate access for her study of the Moonies. For both ethical and practical reasons, she was unwilling to pretend to become a member, so she put out feelers to the community. Unexpectedly, she was approached by a member of the community who asked her to write a response to the negative publicity the group was receiving. Barker argued she could not write anything without conducting a proper research study that included independent funding and a complete membership roster so she could interview a random sample of members. It took two years from the time of initial contact for Barker's research conditions to be satisfied. Only then did her field research start.

There are no foolproof keys for gaining access to closed communities. Strategic plans and perseverance are usually necessary conditions, but good luck often plays an important role. Most groups have "gatekeepers" whose role is to control access to the community. Gaining the trust of the person(s) in this role is helpful. So is finding a sponsor. Sponsors are organizational insiders who are willing to use their influence to overcome barriers to access. To perform this function, successful sponsors are typically high-status community members.

Identifying Key Informants

Key informants are community members who are willing and able to provide credible information about an organization's culture, issues, and activities.

Third, after gaining entry to a community, how do researchers become oriented in their unfamiliar surroundings? A helpful tool is a social map that provides an overview of the community's culture, social structure, and major issues. **Key informants** can provide such a map, thereby smoothing the researcher's integration into the community. William Whyte's famous study of a youth gang in Boston was aided by "Doc," a leader who gave him valuable information about members and events (Whyte, 1943). Elliott Liebow's investigation of African American men who spent their days hanging out on a street corner relied on Tally, a member of the group, to help his understanding (Liebow, 1967). Likewise, Eileen

Barker's six-year investigation of the Moonies relied on vital information provided her by "moles" (Barker, 1984).

However, researchers need to be careful whom they select as informants. A common problem is that those who want to be key informants are poorly positioned to provide credible information. The best informants are often those who are least willing to play this role, since they play key roles in the organization. It is often optimal if sponsors can double as a key informant.

Assembling Field Notes

Fourth, how can researchers record their observations of the community? The goal of participant observation is to understand and interpret the experience of a community and its members. In doing so, researchers gather a rich trove of observations. Since these observations are collected over time and are subject to memory distortion, researchers need methods for assembling accurate "field notes." The following principles are generally applicable. First, mental notes are fragile and should be recorded as soon as possible. However, writing notes increases the likelihood of reactivity, so researchers can often only jot their field notes. These jottings should be transformed into full field notes not later than the end of each day. Field notes should be as complete as possible. Err on the side of recording too much rather than too little, since the value of specific points is often not evident until later in the analysis. Be sure to distinguish what was observed from how the researcher reacted to various experiences. Both are valid sources of information but they are analytically different. Finally, keep separate track of **analytic memos**. Analytic memos are field notes that record a researcher's initial interpretations of experiences in the field. Such memos are first approximations of the meaning of the observations and are important for the next step in participation observation research.

Analytic memos are field notes that record a researcher's initial understanding of witnessed events.

Constructing a Narrative

Finally, how do researchers interpret their field notes? The task is more art than craft. However, some useful guidelines can be gleaned from the best participant observation work.

Given the rich observations contained in field notes, it is easy to get lost in the details. It is important not to let that happen. Remember the purpose of the project: to identify and interpret empirical patterns. Pattern recognition requires looking for similarities and differences. Identifying the types of thoughts, feelings, and behaviours that are common to specific contexts is the key to identifying cultural and structural patterns. Looking at deviant cases helps the researcher identify the limits of the patterns.

Once patterns are identified, they require interpretation. Participant observation is not journalism. It does not end with description. In the final analysis, a participant observer's goal is to embed the findings in a framework of more general sociological concepts. This task is usually accomplished through a series of successive approximations, which begins with the identification of **sensitizing concepts**. Sensitizing concepts are not necessarily sociological concepts. They are concepts that a researcher invents to make initial sense of the field notes (Bowen, 2006) and, in doing so, highlights key features of social interaction.

Sensitizing concepts are used to capture the first impressions about meaningful patterns in field notes.

By using sensitizing concepts, the researcher becomes clearer on what the identified patterns mean. As the patterns become clearer, opportunities emerge for casting the patterns in terms of sociological concepts and principles. In this task, familiarity with prior research is helpful. However, "grounded theory" efforts often lead to the construction of novel sociological concepts based on careful observation and induction.

As our overview of participant observation indicates, the inductive techniques used in this qualitative method are less codified than the steps used in quantitative investigations. While less codification can enhance uncertainty, anxiety, and frustration, it also opens up opportunities for creative insight and expression.

Qualitative Interviewing

Structured interviews follow carefully crafted protocols to acquire the respondent's view on pre-determined subjects.

Unstructured and semi-structured interviews employ loose, open-ended formats, allowing respondents to speak their minds.

Our earlier discussion of quantitative survey research noted that surveys often rely on interviews. Qualitative research employs a different kind of interview from those used in surveys. In general, survey research utilizes **structured interviews**. In structured interviews, all the questions (typically closed-ended) are crafted in advance to measure specific variables. The variables are components of hypotheses that, in turn, reflect the theoretical ideas being tested. Qualitative research, by contrast, uses **unstructured** or **semi-structured interviews**. These interviews have minimal formatting and employ open-ended questions. Where structured interviews seek specific information from the respondent, their unstructured counterparts use interview questions and probes to encourage respondents to share their thoughts, feelings, actions, and events.

Qualitative methods seek to have respondents open up and share the character and meaning of their experience *from the insider's point of view.* In contrast, structured interviews used in quantitative methods inquire about what the researcher thinks is important. Unstructured and semi-structured interviews used in qualitative methods focus on what the respondents define as important. Accordingly, qualitative interviews are fluid and flexible.

The content of qualitative interviews provides the content that researchers use to constructive the narrative from their investigation. Therefore, these interviews are shaped by guidelines to organize the content so results are comparable and themes are detectable (Bryman and Teevan, 2005).

Cases are used in qualitative research to exemplify how insiders experience social realities.

Case studies focus on the rich description of a single case.

Authenticity is the extent to which qualitative investigation captures social realities as experienced by insiders.

Member validation asks respondents who were observed and/or interviewed to judge the authenticity of the research narrative.

Qualitative interviews are a method of collecting evidence. To obtain a full, accurate record of their experience, it is not unusual for respondents to be interviewed more than once. Interviews are conducted on one or more cases. **Cases** are illustrative instances of some individual or organization. **Case studies** provide rich descriptions of a single case. Qualitative studies often include a small number of cases. The intensive study of social processes, interactions, and meanings between cases allows researchers to identify patterns and themes that become the centre of their narrative.

Qualitative researchers use authenticity, rather than validity and reliability, as the criterion for judging their work. **Authenticity** refers to whether the narrative provides a genuine description of social realities as experienced by the participants. One common technique for checking on the authenticity of the narrative product is to have the report reviewed by participants who were observed and/or interviewed. This technique is called **member validation**.

In qualitative research, authenticity has the same meaning as it does when analyzing quantitative data tables or in relation to research ethics. Across these different topics, when something is inauthentic, appearances do not match reality. In research ethics, where inauthenticity occurs, deception is present. In analyzing quantitative data tables, inauthenticity indicates spuriousness. In qualitative research, inauthenticity indicates superficiality. Qualitative studies are attractive because they provide readers with a full sense of the lives of others.

Similar to different sociological theories offering a variety of perspectives, different research methods offer a variety of views of social reality. And, similar to different theories, different research methods are complementary. No single theory or research method can fully capture the rich complexity of social reality. The mission of sociology is to systematically build on our understanding of complex social realities one study at a time. Over time, these investigations provide successively more complete understandings of the social contexts and processes that surround social action.

The roster of research methods noted in this chapter is far from a complete list of the strategies used by sociologists to enlarge our understanding of social reality. For example, sociological research also uses the analysis of official statistics, focus groups, and the content analysis of personal documents and media outputs ranging from photographs to worldwide tweets. Whatever specific techniques are employed, they generally fit within either the positivist or interpretive traditions. In doing so, any study carries the strengths and weaknesses of its viewpoint and associated tactics of inquiry. Table 2.4 contrasts the basic considerations underlying the quantitative and qualitative approaches.

TABLE 2.4
Comparison of Quantitative and Qualitative Methods

Source: Brym, Robert. 2014. *2011 Census Update: A Critical Interpretation*. Toronto: Nelson Education; Meahan, Lynn. 2010. "Statement on 2011 Census." Office of the Honourable Tony Clement, Minister of Industry.

	Quantitative Methods	**Qualitative Methods**
Methodological Tradition	Positivist	Interpretive
Viewpoint	Outsider	Insider
General Approach	Structured	Flexible
Logical Approach	Deduction	Induction
Connection to Theory	Theory testing	Theory generating
Sample Sizes	Large	Small
Sample Selection	Representative	Illustrative
Scope	Few variables	Many variables
Breadth	Multi-context generalization	Context-specific analysis
Goal	Explanation	Understanding
Methodological Emphasis	Reliability and validity	Authenticity
Nature of Evidence	Numbers and statistics	Narratives and stories

TIME FOR REVIEW

- How can reactivity affect a photograph you take of your mother?
- If you wanted to complete a participant observation study of a biker gang, how might you gain access?
- What strategy could a groom use for taking field notes at his wedding ceremony?
- How do interviews used in quantitative studies differ from qualitative interviews?

THE IMPORTANCE OF BEING SUBJECTIVE

You now have a pretty good idea of the basic methodological issues that confront any sociological research project. You also understand the strengths and weaknesses of the different research traditions.

Our synopsis of sociology's tools for checking the reality status of ideas should not obscure the fact that sociological research questions often spring from real-life experiences and the pressing concerns of the day. However, before any sociological analysis occurs, we rarely see things as they are. We see them as *we* are. Then, a sort of waltz begins. Subjectivity leads; objectivity follows. When the dance is finished, we see things more accurately.

Feminism provides a prime example of this process. Feminism represents a *political* movement of people and ideas that, since the 1960s, has helped shape the sociological *research* agenda. For example, before the rise of the modern feminist movement, many concerns were considered sociological non-issues, such as the division of labour in the household, violence against women, the effects of child-rearing responsibilities on women's careers, and the social barriers to women's participation in politics and the armed forces. Sociologists did not study these issues. Effectively, the issues did not exist for the sociological community (although they did, of course, exist for women). However, subjectivity led. Feminism, as a political movement, brought these concerns and many others to the attention of the Canadian public. Objectivity followed. Large parts of the sociological community began doing rigorous research on feminist-inspired issues and greatly refined our knowledge of them.

The entire sociological perspective began to shift as a growing number of scholars abandoned gender-biased research (Eichler, 1988b; Tavris, 1992). Thus, approaching sociological problems from an exclusively male perspective is now less common than it once was. For instance, it is less likely in 2016 than it was in 1966 that a sociologist would study work but ignore unpaid housework as one type of labour. Similarly, sociologists now frown on using data on one gender to draw conclusions about all people. As these advances in sociological thinking show, and as has often been the case in the history of the discipline, objective sociological knowledge has been enhanced as a result of subjective experiences. And so the waltz continues. As in *Alice in Wonderland*, the question now is, "Will you, won't you, will you, won't you, will you join the dance?"

TIME FOR REVIEW

- What place do subjectivity and objectivity have in conducting sociological research?

SUMMARY

1. **What are the meaning and components of different levels of experience?**
Concrete experiences are empirical and relate to your five senses. Such sensations are composed of percepts that are aggregated into patterns. Abstract experiences are imaginary and occur in your mind. These meaningful ideas are composed of concepts that are connected to form propositions. Making connections between abstract and concrete levels of experience forms realities that are described and interpreted by sociological methods.

2. **What are the common mistakes in unscientific thinking?**
Unscientific thinking includes a wide range of errors, including uncritically accepting statements passed on through tradition or by authority; relying on casual, unrepresentative, or selective observations; using qualifications without examining them in the light of evidence; reasoning illogically; ego-defence; premature closure; and mystification. In different ways, these errors produce results that are invalid expressions of reality.

3. **How does viewpoint shape understanding?**
Viewpoints radically shape experience. A principal distinction exists between insider and outsider viewpoints. Insiders are people who are members of a particular group or community. They have a detailed, specific understanding of their social setting. Outsiders are persons who do not belong to a group or community. They are often able to see broader, more general patterns of organization.

4. **What are the major steps in the qualitative and quantitative research models?**
Qualitative research uses induction and takes the following steps: 1. Identify a research interest based on concrete experience. 2. Collect evidence from one or more cases of the same type. 3. Analyze the case(s) to identify common patterns and themes. 4. Provide a contextualized interpretation of the patterns and themes using sociological concepts and principles. Quantitative research follows a different path, based on deduction. The steps in this model include: 1. Identify a theoretical idea of interest. 2. Translate the idea into a testable hypothesis. 3. Collect and analyze data. 4. Accept or reject the hypothesis.

5. What ethical norms guide sociological research?
Sociological research is guided by ethical principles, including voluntary participation, harm minimization, privacy, and authenticity. Voluntary participation and harm minimization are included in informed consent, which means that subjects must be aware of possible negative consequences and freely decide to participate. Privacy requires that the participant identifiers be anonymous, or at least confidential. Authenticity requires that both participants and consumers of research be honestly informed about research procedures and results.

6. How are experimental and survey methods used by quantitative researchers?
Experimental and survey methods are data collection techniques often used by quantitative researchers. Both procedures test hypotheses about how variables are related among carefully selected participants. The results are subject to statistical analyses that lead to either confirmation or rejection of hypotheses.

7. How do qualitative researchers use participant observation and interviewing methods?
Both participant observation and interviewing procedures gather insider information about the meaning and motives of participants' experience. Researchers use inductive procedures to analyze the results. In doing so, they look for common themes that indicate context-specific understanding.

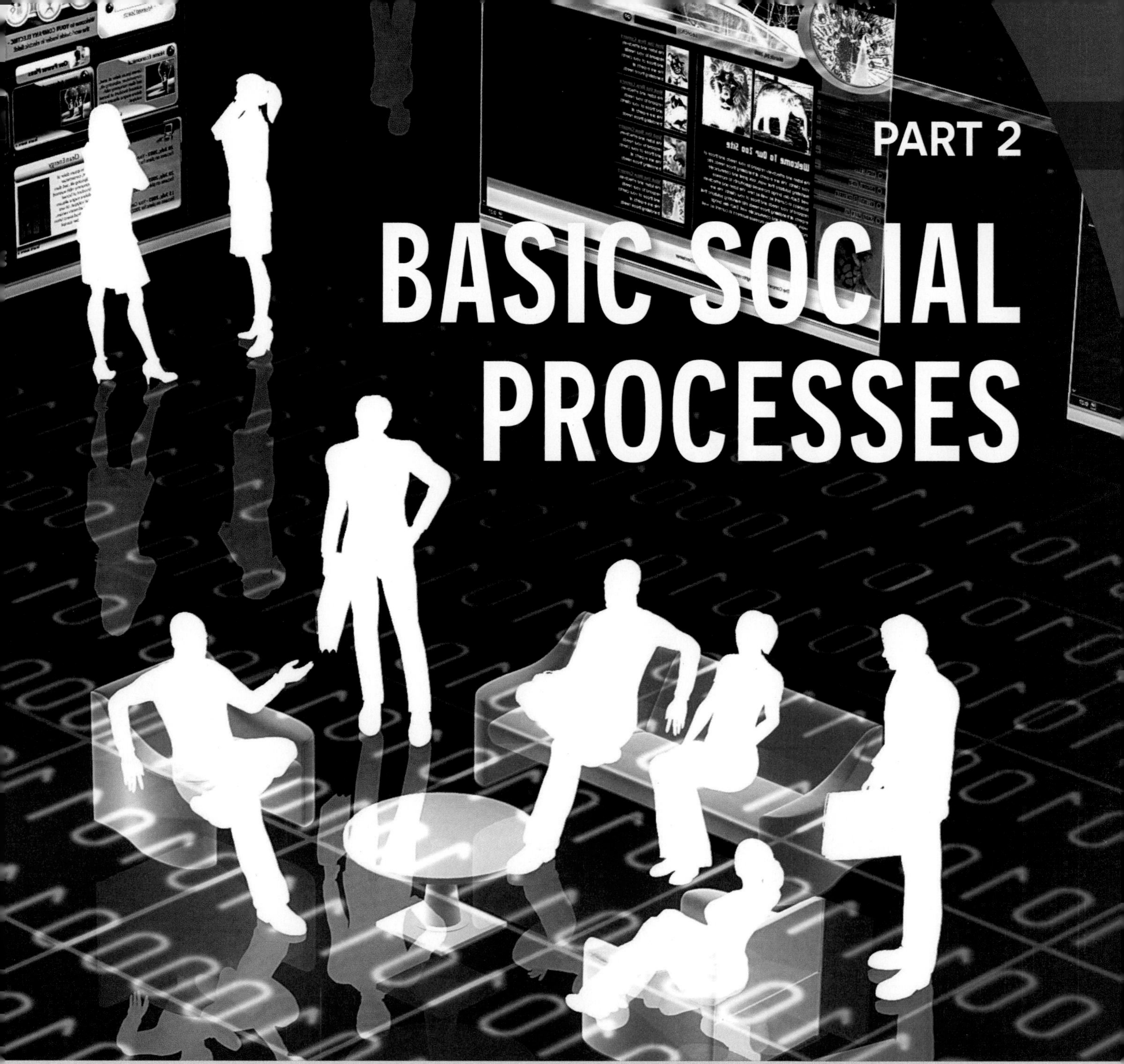

PART 2
BASIC SOCIAL PROCESSES

Nmedia/Can Stock Photo Inc.

CHAPTER 3

CULTURE

© Picture Hooked/LOOP IMAGES/Loop Images/Corbis

IN THIS CHAPTER YOU WILL LEARN TO

- Explain the role of culture in generating meaning and solving problems.
- Contrast biological and cultural explanations.
- Appreciate differences among functionalist, symbolic interactionist, and conflict approaches to understanding culture.
- See how culture operates as a force that both increases human freedom and constrains social action by shaping social organization.

CULTURE AS PROBLEM SOLVING

If you follow sports, you probably know that many athletes perform little rituals before each game. Canadian hockey legend Sidney Crosby is a prime example. On game day, he enters the home arena through a circuitous route to ensure he doesn't pass the visitors' locker room, tapes his sticks in a specific way, eats a peanut butter and jam sandwich at precisely 5 p.m., performs a sequenced series of stretches, suits up in a programmed manner, and performs a unique pre-game handshake before stepping on the ice.

Bruce Bennett/Thinkstock

Sidney Crosby

The superstitious practices of athletes make some people chuckle. However, such rituals put athletes at ease. Many students have rituals that serve the same function when they are under exam stress. Some wear a lucky piece of jewellery or item of clothing. Others say special words or a quick prayer. Still others cross themselves. Others engage in more elaborate rituals. One study reports on a student who felt she would do well only if she ate a sausage and two eggs sunny-side up on the morning of each exam. She always placed the sausage vertically on the left side of her plate and the eggs to the right of the sausage—so they formed the "100" percent she was aiming for (Albas and Albas, 1989). Of course, the ritual likely had a more direct influence on her cholesterol level than on her grades. Yet, it may have indirectly had the desired effect. To the degree the ritual helped relieve her anxiety and help her relax, she may have done better on her exams.

Like all elements of culture, superstitions help people to solve the challenges of life. Whether the challenge involves winning a hockey game, performing well on exams, building a house, or facing death, humans turn to their culture for solutions. At the root of culture is solving the problem of meaning.

CULTURE AS MEANING GENERATOR

Chapter 2 introduced a distinction between concrete and abstract levels of experience. The concrete level is composed of your empirical sensations of touch, taste, smell, sound, and sight. Viewing the squiggles in Figure 3.1 will give you several examples of concrete experience. Examine them carefully. What do the squiggles on each line mean to you?

For most readers of this book, the squiggles will be meaningless. This result does not occur because your eyesight is poor. It occurs because concrete, physical sensations, by themselves, are meaningless.

Now read the following sentence: *Were it otherwise, you would understand the marks on this page without learning to read English.* The squiggles in the preceding sentence are meaningful, English words. Culture gives concrete experience meaning.

By the way, the first line in Figure 3.1 is gobbledygook. The remaining three lines are not. They are translations of the italicized sentence in the previous paragraph, expressed in

FIGURE 3.1
Four Texts

🕈♋❒♏ ♏⬧ ♋■♎♏❒⬧📪 🙰□■■⧫♏■ ⬧♓♏ ♎♓♏ ☠□⧫♏■
♋◆♐ ♎♓♏⬧♏❒ ⬧♏♓⧫♏ ❖♏❒⬧⧫♏♒♏■ □♒■♏ ♎♋⬧
⬧♓♏ ♋◆♐ 👍♏◆⧫⬧♍♒ ●♏⬧♏■ ●♏❒■⧫♏■📫

在相反的情况下，你可以不必学习汉语就能明白此页中的标记。

În caz contrar, ar trebui să înțeleagă notele de pe această pagină, fără a învăța să citească în limba română.

Wäre es anders, könnten Sie die Noten auf dieser Seite verstehen ohne das Sie auf Deutsch lesen lernten.

High culture is culture consumed mainly by upper classes (opera, ballet, etc.).

Popular culture (or mass culture) is culture consumed by all classes.

Culture consists of the shared symbols and their definitions that people create to solve real-life problems.

Symbols are concrete objects or abstract terms that represent something else.

Abstraction is the ability to create general concepts that meaningfully organize sensory experience.

Beliefs are cultural statements that define what community members consider real.

Cooperation is the capacity to create a complex social life by establishing generally accepted ways of doing things and ideas about what is right and wrong.

Chinese, Romanian, and German. If you are appropriately connected to Chinese, Romanian, or German culture, the respective lines in Figure 3.1 would be just as meaningful to you as their English counterpart.

The power of culture is that it makes our sensory experiences meaningful. Once your cultural experience conditions you to interpret concrete experiences in a certain way, this perspective becomes your reality. As evidence, notice that you cannot interpret the squiggles on this page as anything but English words. In a similar way, readers of Chinese cannot see the second line in Figure 3.1 as anything but Chinese, and readers of Germans cannot see the final line as anything but German.

Culture Defined

In everyday speech, "culture" often refers to **high culture** (opera, ballet, etc.) or **popular culture** (movies, pop music, etc.). For sociologists, however, the definition of culture is much broader. Sociologically speaking, **culture** consists of the shared symbols and their definitions that people create to solve real-life problems. To understand this definition, we need to elaborate on its components. Let's start with the term "symbol."

Symbols are concrete objects or abstract terms that represent something else. A gold ring on the third finger is an object that represents marital status. The term "Big Mac" is an abstract term that represents a particular type of hamburger supplied by a fast-food establishment. Symbols fill human experience.

The meaning of a symbol is not in the symbol; the meaning resides in what the symbol refers to. For this reason, symbols always have an abstract dimension. This abstract feature of symbols is what is referred to by the words "and their definitions" in the key term definition of culture. A symbol's "definition" informs us what a symbol represents.

Our definition of culture notes that symbols are *shared*. Idiosyncratic symbols are not part of culture. A psychotic person who believes that rain clouds represent happiness is using a symbol that is not part of culture. So too are the special terms and signs of endearment that lovers create for themselves. Culture is composed of symbols whose meanings are shared among a substantial number of people. The definition of a pencil as an instrument for writing is part of your culture. So is the idea that obtaining a university degree will improve your life. Members of a community who acquire a set of shared, meaningful symbols participate in a common culture.

Culture is the primary driver of what people do because individuals respond to the meaning of events, and the meaning of events is defined by our culture. Culture intervenes between concrete experience and our responses by assigning significance. As a child, you looked at the night sky and saw only a pattern of twinkling lights. Over time, your culture provided you with such concepts as "star" and "Big Dipper." Now, when you look up at night, you can distinguish stars, planets, comets, and constellations. The same holds for all your experiences. First you "look" (the concrete behaviour part), then you "name" (the cultural part), and then you "see" (the abstract understanding part).

The Origins of Culture

Culture is the primary means by which humans adapt to their environments; that is why our definition of culture emphasizes that we create culture to solve real-life problems. You can appreciate the importance of culture for human survival by considering the predicament of early humans about 100 000 years ago. They lived in harsh natural environments and had poor physical endowments, making them slower runners and weaker fighters than many other animals. Yet, despite these disadvantages, they survived. They prospered largely because they were the smartest creatures around. Their sophisticated brains enabled them to create cultural "survival kits" of enormous complexity and flexibility. These cultural survival kits contained three main tools. Each tool was a uniquely human talent that gave rise to a different element of culture.

The first tool in the cultural survival kit is **abstraction**, the ability to create general concepts that organize sensory experience in meaningful ways. You learned about this process in Chapter 2, which discussed the conceptualization process. The concepts that result from abstraction are the most pervasive type of symbols in human cultures. This is why language is so important to the preservation of any culture.

Concepts allow humans to organize, classify, interpret, and generalize their experiences. For instance, we recognize that we can sit on many objects but that only some of them have four legs, a back, and space for one person. We distinguish the latter from other objects by giving them a name: chairs. By the time most babies reach the end of their first year, they have heard the word "chair" often and understand that it refers to a certain class of objects.

Cultural concepts provide the foundation for beliefs. **Beliefs** are statements about what members of a community define as real. Remember that culture is composed of a set of *shared* symbols. When beliefs are widely shared in a community, members accept such beliefs as truth. Cultural constructions of reality and truth do not necessarily coincide with scientifically established fact. Consider the following three statements: "The Sun orbits around Earth." "Opposites attract." "God is love." The first of these statements is demonstrably false, the second is only conditionally true (that is, true under some circumstances), while the third is scientifically untestable. Nonetheless, all these beliefs have been considered true in one culture or another, and community members have acted on the basis of such understandings.

Cooperation is the second tool in the human cultural survival kit. It is the capacity to create a complex social life by establishing **norms** (generally accepted ways of doing things) and **values** (statements that identify desirable or preferable conditions). For example, family members cooperate to raise children, and in the process, they develop and apply norms and values about which child-rearing practices are appropriate and desirable. Note, however, that different times and places give rise to different norms and values. Contemporary parents might ground children for swearing, but in pioneer times, parents would typically "beat the devil out of them." As this example suggests, by analyzing how people cooperate and produce norms and values, we can learn much about what distinguishes one culture from another.

Production is the third main tool in the human cultural survival kit. Cultural production takes two main forms. First, it involves making and using tools and technology. Tools and technology improve our ability to take what we want from nature. We call such tools and techniques **material culture** because they are tangible, whereas symbols, norms, values, and other elements of **non-material culture** are intangible. All animals take from nature to subsist, and apes may sometimes use rocks to break other objects, or walking sticks to steady themselves as they cross fast-flowing streams. However, only humans are intelligent and agile enough to

Norms are generally accepted ways of doing things.

Values are ideas that identify desirable states (conditions that are true, good, or beautiful).

Production is the human capacity to make and use the tools and technology that improve our ability to take what we want from nature.

Material culture comprises the tools and techniques that enable people to accomplish tasks.

Non-material culture is composed of symbols, norms, and other intangible elements.

By cooperating, people are able to accomplish more than the same number of people working individually could accomplish.

TABLE 3.1
The Building Blocks of Culture

Source: Adapted from Bierstedt (1963).

The human capacity for...	Abstraction	Cooperation	Production
Gives rise to these elements of culture	Beliefs	Norms and values	Material culture and social organization
In medicine, for example...	*Theories* are developed about how a certain drug might cure a disease.	*Experiments* are conducted to test whether the drug works as expected.	*Treatments* are developed on the basis of the experimental results.

Social organization is the orderly arrangement of social interaction.

Folkways are norms that specify social preferences. Because they are the least important norms, violating them evokes the least severe punishment.

Mores (pronounced MOR-ays) are core norms that most people believe are essential for the survival of their group or their society.

Taboos are among the strongest norms. When someone violates a taboo, it causes revulsion in the community and punishment is severe.

Laws are norms that are codified and enforced by the state.

manufacture tools and use them to produce everything from food to satellites. In this sense, production is a uniquely human activity.

A second result of cultural production is social organization. Culture is often characterized as a blueprint or design for living with others. **Social organization** is the orderly arrangement of social interaction. Within many species, ordered activities are a result of genetic programming. For example, ants are born to build colonies and bees are born to build hives. Not so with humans. Our organized social conduct is rooted in a cultural blueprint. Understanding, interpreting, and putting this blueprint into coordinated action is the key to community survival.

Table 3.1 lists each of the human capacities we have discussed and illustrates their cultural offshoots in the field of medicine. As in medicine, so in all fields of human activity: abstraction, cooperation, and production give rise to specific kinds of beliefs, norms, values, social organization, tools, and technologies that help us deal with real-life problems.

Four Types of Norms: Folkways, Mores, Taboos, and Laws

If a man walks down a busy street wearing nothing on the top half of his body, he is violating a folkway. If he walks down the street wearing nothing on the bottom half of his body, he is violating a more (the Latin word for "custom," pronounced MOR-ay). **Folkways** are norms that specify social *preferences*. **Mores** are norms that specify social *requirements*. People are usually punished when they violate norms, but the punishment is usually minor when the norm is a folkway. Some onlookers will raise their eyebrows at the shirtless man. Others will shake their head in disapproval. In contrast, the punishment for walking down the street without pants is bound to be moderately harsh. Someone is bound to call the police, probably sooner than later (Sumner, 1940 [1907]). The strongest and most central norms, however, are **taboos**. When someone violates a taboo, it causes revulsion in the community, and punishment is severe. Incest is one of the most widespread taboos.

Folkways, mores, and taboos form a continuum that displays a community's understanding of the importance of each type of norm for community life. Because of the importance of mores and taboos, these norms are often transformed into laws. **Laws** are norms that have codified and enforced punishments by the state. Robbery, for example, is against the law. According to the law, it is unacceptable to take someone's property by using violence or the threat of violence. Further, the law specifies the forms of punishment (fines, imprisonment, etc.) to be experienced by people convicted of robbery.

TIME FOR REVIEW

- What are the similarities and differences among high culture, popular culture, and the sociological definition of culture?
- Is the concept "banana" a symbol? Why or why not?
- How is it possible for cultural beliefs to be scientifically false?
- What are similarities and differences among folkways, mores, and taboos?

CULTURE AND BIOLOGY

The Evolution of Human Behaviour

We have seen how the human capacity for abstraction, cooperation, and production enables us to create culture and makes us distinctively human. This capacity is built on a solid biological foundation. Biology, as every sociologist recognizes, sets broad human limits and potentials, including the potential to create culture.

Some biologically trained students of human behaviour go a step further. For example, evolutionary psychologists claim that genes—chemical units that carry traits from parents to children—account not just for physical characteristics but also for specific behaviours and social practices (Mealey, 2010; Neuberg, Kenrick, and Schaller, 2010; Pinker, 2002). They deny the significance of culture. Such thinking is growing in popularity, and it undermines the sociological perspective. As the following example illustrates, it is also misguided.

Male Promiscuity, Female Fidelity, and Other Myths

Evolutionary psychologists employ a three-step argument for their biological explanation of human behaviour and social arrangements. First, they identify a supposedly universal human behavioural trait. Next, they offer an explanation for why this behaviour increases survival chances through reproduction. Finally, they conclude that the behaviour in question cannot easily be changed. For example, they explain alleged male promiscuity and female fidelity as follows:

1. *Universal claim*: Men are more likely than women are to want many sexual partners.
2. *Survival-value argument*: Every time a man ejaculates, he produces hundreds of millions of sperm, while fertile women typically release only one egg per month. Based on these sex differences, men and women develop different strategies to increase the chances of reproducing their genes. Because a woman produces few eggs, she improves her chance of reproducing her genes if she has a mate who stays around to help and protect her while she is pregnant, giving birth, and nursing a small infant. By contrast, because a man's sperm is plentiful, he improves his chance of reproducing his genes if he tries to impregnate as many women as possible.
3. *Conclusion*: These biologically based reproductive strategies are encoded or "hard-wired" in our genes. Therefore, male promiscuity and female fidelity are necessary.

Let's apply the table-reading and causal analysis skills you learned in Chapter 2 to illustrate the problems with this argument.

Table 3.2 contains data from a survey of a representative sample of the American population. It shows that a minority of adult American men (21 percent) claimed having more than one sex partner in the previous year. The figure for adult American women was significantly lower (10 percent). However, if we control for marital status, as in Table 3.3, the figures fall to 5 percent for men and 1 percent for women, a much smaller difference. These differences indicate that certain *social arrangements*, such as the institution of marriage, account in substantial measure for variation in male promiscuity. There is no *universal* propensity to male promiscuity.

TABLE 3.2
Number of Sex Partners by Respondent's Sex, United States (in percent)

	Respondent's Sex	
Number of Sex Partners	**Male**	**Female**
0 or 1	79	90
More than 1	21	10
Total	100	100
n (number of respondents)	1004	1233

Source: From National Opinion Research Center, 2004, *General Social Survey, 1972–2002* (Chicago: University of Chicago), machine-readable file. Reprinted with permission.

TABLE 3.3
Number of Sex Partners by Respondent's Sex, United States, Married Respondents Only (in percent)

Source: From National Opinion Research Center, 2004, *General Social Survey, 1972–2002* (Chicago: University of Chicago), machine-readable file. Reprinted with permission.

	Respondent's Sex	
Number of Sex Partners	**Male**	**Female**
0 or 1	95	99
More than 1	5	1
Total	100	100
n (number of respondents)	499	534

Still, the data in Table 3.2 indicate that 11 percent more men than women said they had more than one sex partner in the preceding year. Among unmarried people, the male–female difference was 14 percent. Sociologists attribute these gender differences to two main factors (McConaghy, 1999: 311–14). First, on average, men are more likely than women are to have same-sex sexual relations, and gay men are more likely than lesbians are to have many sex partners. This finding contradicts the evolutionary psychologists' argument that male promiscuity reflects an adaptive reproductive strategy because, clearly, gay men do not have sex with other men to make babies. Moreover, in-depth interviews suggest that men tend to exaggerate how many sexual partners they have because our *culture* puts a premium on male sexual performance. Genes and reproductive strategies play no role in this regard. We conclude that the evolutionary psychologists' claims about male promiscuity and female fidelity are false. So are many of their other claims about so-called behavioural universals.

An additional problem with the evolutionary psychologists' argument is that little evidence links specific behaviours and social arrangements to specific genes. Finally, even if researchers discover an association between particular genes and particular behaviours, it would be wrong to conclude that variations among people are due only to their genes. Genes *never* develop without environmental influence (see Figure 3.2).

In sum, your genes do not hardwire your behaviour patterns. Changes in social environment produce physical and, to an even greater degree, behavioural change. To determine the effects of the social environment on human behaviour, we need to abandon the premises of evolutionary psychology and use sociological skills to analyze the effects of social structure and culture.

FIGURE 3.2
A Genetic Misconception

When scientists announced they had finished sequencing the human genome on June 26, 2000, some people thought all human characteristics could be read from the human genetic "map." They cannot. The functions of most genes are still unknown. Moreover, because genes mutate randomly and interact with environmental (including social) conditions, the correspondence between genetic function and behavioural outcome is highly uncertain.

Source: *The National Post*, Toronto, Canada, 2000. Gary Clement.

Language and the Sapir-Whorf Thesis

Language is one of the most important parts of any culture. A language is a system of symbols strung together to communicate thought. Equipped with language, we can share understandings, pass experience and knowledge from one generation to the next, and make plans for the future. In short, language allows culture to develop. Consequently, sociologists commonly think of language as a cultural invention that distinguishes humans from other animals.

In the 1930s, Edward Sapir and Benjamin Lee Whorf proposed an influential argument about the connection between experience, thought, and language. It is now known as the **Sapir-Whorf thesis** (Skerrett, 2010; Whorf, 1956). The thesis holds that we experience important things in our environment and form concepts about those things (path 1 to 2 in Figure 3.3). Then, we develop language to express our concepts (path 2 to 3). Finally, language itself influences how we see the world (path 3 to 1).

The **Sapir-Whorf thesis** holds that we experience certain things in our environment and form concepts about those things. We then develop language to express our concepts. Finally, language itself influences how we see the world.

For example, different types of camels are important in the environment of nomadic Arabs, and different types of snow are important in the lives of Inuit in Canada's Far North (path 1 to 2). Consequently, nomadic Arabs have developed many words for different types of camels and Inuit have developed many words for different types of snow (path 2 to 3). Distinctions that these people see elude us because types of camels and snow are less important in our environment.

In turn, language obliges people to think in certain ways (path 3 to 1). If you're walking in a park, you will know whether a certain tree is in front of you, behind you, to the left, or to the right. When asked where the tree is, you will use such directions to describe its position. We think "egocentrically," locating objects relative to ourselves. However, egocentric directions have no meaning for speakers of Tzeltal in southern Mexico or of Guugu Yimithirr in Queensland, Australia. These speakers lack concepts and words for "left," "right," and so on. They think geographically, and will say that the tree is to the "north," "south, "east," or "west." Trained from infancy to attend to geographic direction, Tzeltal speakers are obliged to think in those terms. If a tree to the north is located behind them and they are asked where the tree is, they will point to themselves, as if they don't exist. Reportedly, a Tzeltal speaker can be blindfolded, put in a dark room, and spun around 20 times until he's dizzy yet still point without hesitation to the north, south, east, and west (Boroditsky, 2010; Deutscher, 2010).

For an example closer to home, consider that income and power inequality between women and men encourages some men to refer to women by using such terms as *fox, babe, bitch, ho,* and *doll*. However, the use of such words in itself influences men to think of women simply as sexual objects. If such men are ever to think of women as their equals, gender inequality will need to be reduced, but the language such men use to refer to women will also need to change.

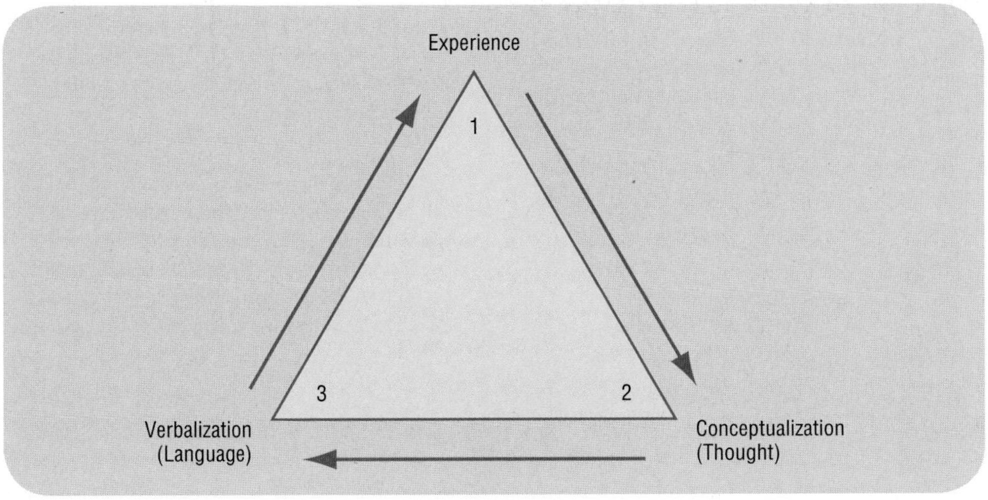

FIGURE 3.3
The Sapir-Whorf Thesis

CULTURE AS FREEDOM AND CONSTRAINT

A Functionalist Analysis of Culture: Culture and Ethnocentrism

Despite culture's central importance in human life, it is often invisible. People tend to take their culture for granted. Its expression seems so sensible and natural, they rarely think about it. In contrast, people are often startled when confronted by cultures other than their own. The beliefs, norms, techniques, and practices of other cultures frequently seem odd, irrational, and even inferior.

Ethnocentrism is the tendency for people to judge other cultures exclusively by the standards of their own culture.

Judging another culture exclusively by the standards of our own culture is known as **ethnocentrism** (see Box 3.1). Ethnocentrism impairs sociological analysis. We can illustrate this point by discussing a practice that seems bizarre to many Westerners: cow worship among Hindu peasants in India.

Hindu peasants refuse to slaughter cattle and eat beef because, for them, the cow is a religious symbol of life. Pinup calendars throughout rural India portray beautiful women with the bodies of fat, white cows, milk jetting out of each teat. Cows are permitted to wander the streets, defecate on the sidewalks, and stop to chew their cud in busy intersections and on railroad tracks, causing traffic to come to a complete halt. In Madras, police

BOX 3.1

SOCIOLOGY AT THE MOVIES

BORAT AND THE DICTATOR

In *Borat* and *The Dictator*, Borat Sagdiyev, a journalist from Kazakhstan, and Haffaz Aladeen, supreme leader of the mythical Middle Eastern country of Wadiya, visit the United States to learn about American culture and democracy. Both plan to return home with useful lessons. The humour of both movies turns on the apparent differences between, on the one hand, the culture of Borat and Aladeen, and, on the other hand, their audience and the people they meet. Their values, beliefs, and norms offend the people they encounter. Since Borat and Aladeen are capable of seeing the world only from their own cultural viewpoint, the movies are, at one level, stories of ethnocentrism gone mad.

Then the lens switches to the audience. During a scene in *Borat*, Borat persuades a rodeo organizer in Salem, Virginia, to let him sing the national anthem before the show begins. Borat first makes a little speech: "My name Borat, I come from Kazakhstan. Can I say first, we support your war of terror. [applause and cheers] May U.S. and A. kill every single terrorist! [*applause and cheers*] May George Bush drink the blood of every single man, woman, and child of Iraq! [*applause and cheers*] May you destroy their country so that for the next 1000 years not even a single lizard will survive in their desert! [*applause and cheers*]" After thus highlighting the inhumanity of his audience, Borat sings the Kazakh national anthem in English to the tune of the United States national anthem:

Kazakhstan is the greatest country in the world.
All other countries are run by little girls.
Kazakhstan is number one exporter of potassium.
Other Central Asian countries have inferior potassium.
Kazakhstan is the greatest country in the world.
All other countries is the home of the gays.

To the suggestion that another country exceeds the United States in glory, the audience responds with jeers and boos that grow so loud, one fears for Borat's life.

Similarly, although jokes about Middle Eastern culture pepper *The Dictator*, the lens often turns on the United States. This is how Aladeen addresses the United Nations Security Council:

Why are you guys so anti-dictators? Imagine if America was a dictatorship. You can let one percent of the people have all the nation's wealth. You can help your rich friends get richer by capping their taxes and bailing them out when they gamble and lose. You could ignore the needs of the poor

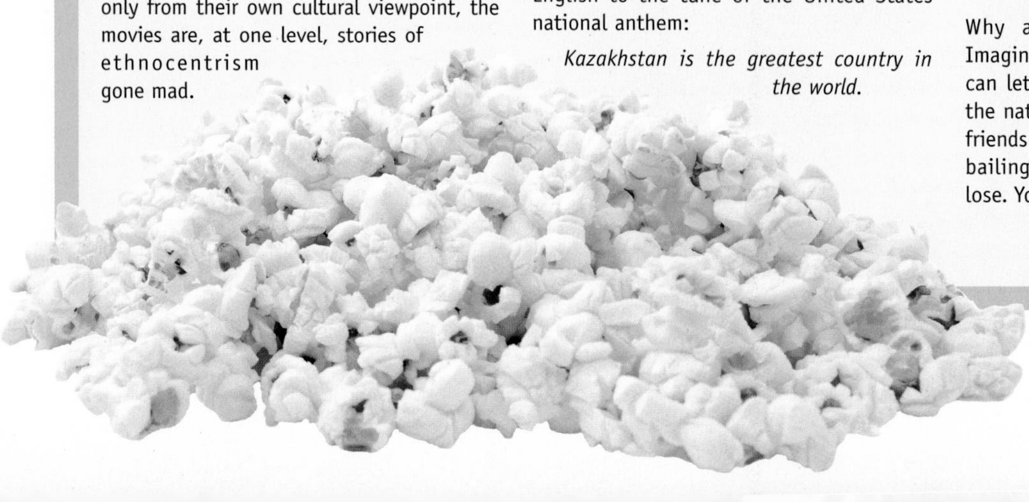

stations maintain fields where stray cows that have fallen ill can graze and be nursed back to health. The government even runs old-age homes for cows where dry and decrepit cattle are kept free of charge. All this fuss seems utterly inscrutable to most Westerners, for it takes place amid poverty and hunger that could presumably be alleviated if only the peasants would slaughter their "useless" cattle for food instead of squandering scarce resources to feed and protect these animals.

According to anthropologist Marvin Harris, however, ethnocentrism misleads many Western observers (Harris, 1974: 3–32). Cow worship, it turns out, is an economically rational practice in rural India. For one thing, Indian peasants cannot afford tractors, so cows are needed to give birth to oxen, which are in high demand for plowing. For another, the cows produce hundreds of millions of kilograms of recoverable manure, about half of which is used as fertilizer and half as a cooking fuel. With oil, coal, and wood in short supply, and with the peasants unable to afford chemical fertilizers, cow dung is, well, a godsend. What is more, cows in India don't cost much to maintain since they eat mostly food that is not fit for human consumption. And they represent an important source of protein and a livelihood for members of low-ranking castes, who have the right to dispose of the bodies of dead cattle. These "untouchables" eat beef and form the workforce of India's large leather-craft industry. The protection of cows by means of cow worship is thus a perfectly sensible and highly efficient economic practice. It only seems irrational when judged by the standards of Western agribusiness.

for healthcare and education. ... You could lie about why you go to war. You could fill your prisons with one particular racial group and no one would complain!

Aladeen thus questions how democratic and just the United States is.

Some people consider *Borat* and *The Dictator* to be long, prejudiced rants against Americans, Jews, Kazakhs, blacks, gays, women, and so on. However, the real objects of its satire are the world's racists, sexists, anti-Semites, and homophobes, regardless of their race, creed, or national origin. The deeper message of *Borat* is anything but ethnocentric: respect for human dignity is a value that rises above all cultures, and people who think otherwise deserve to be laughed at.

The Kobal Collection at Art Resource, NY

Aladeen wins a race after shooting his competitors in *The Dictator*.

Critical Thinking Questions

- Do *Borat* and *The Dictator* help you see the prejudices of other people more clearly?
- Do *Borat* and *The Dictator* help you see your own prejudices more clearly?
- Borat and Aladeen talk and act like bigots from the opening title to the closing credits. Do you think that the expression of bigotry is inherently offensive and should always be avoided? Or do you believe that the satirical expression of bigotry can usefully reveal hidden prejudices?

Source: McClintock, Pamela. 2012. "Box Office Preview: Sacha Baron Cohen's 'Dictator' Takes a Shot at 'Avengers'." *The Hollywood Reporter* 15 May. http://www.hollywoodreporter.com/news/box-office-dictator-sacha-baron-cohen-324560 (retrieved 24 October 2012).

Many Westerners find the Indian practice of cow worship bizarre. However, cow worship performs a number of useful economic functions and is in that sense entirely rational. By viewing cow worship exclusively as an outsider (or, for that matter, exclusively as an insider), we fail to see its rational core.

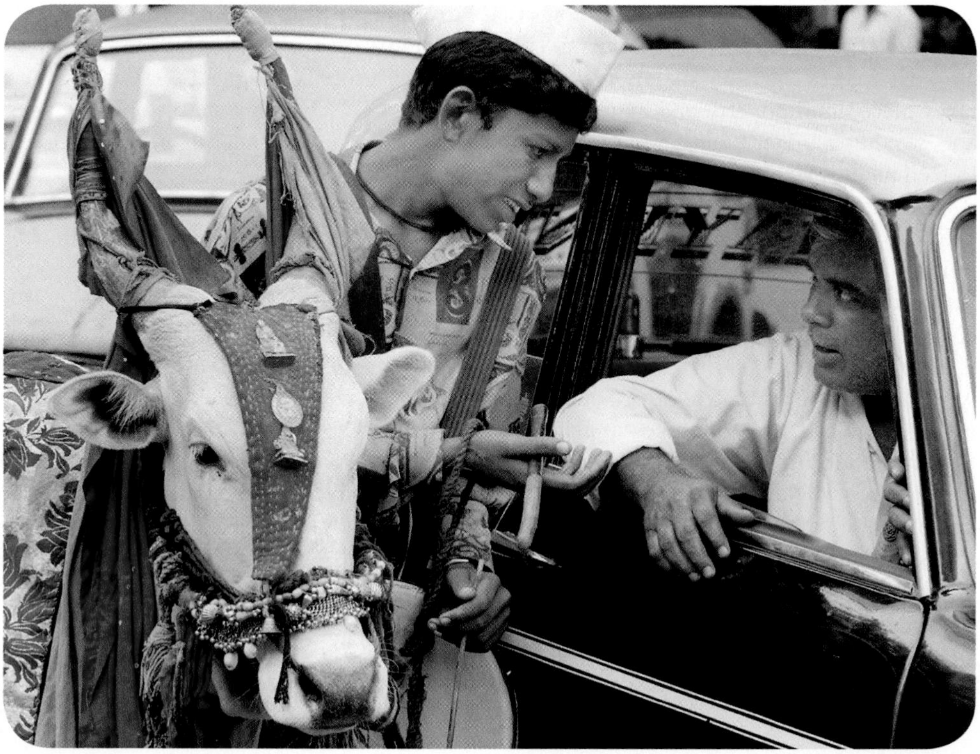

Rob Elliott/AFP/Getty Images

Harris's analysis of cow worship in rural India is interesting for two reasons. First, it illustrates how functionalist theory can illuminate otherwise mysterious social practices. Harris uncovers a range of latent functions performed by cow worship, thus showing how a particular social practice has unintended and unobvious consequences that make social order possible. Second, we can draw an important lesson about ethnocentrism from Harris's analysis. If you refrain from taking your own culture for granted and judging other cultures by the standards of your own, you take an important first step toward developing a sociological understanding of culture.

TIME FOR REVIEW

- What is the Sapir-Whorf hypothesis? Provide an example of how it operates from your personal experience.
- The works of Bach, Beethoven, Mozart, and their peers are typically labelled "classical" music. How might such labelling be interpreted as ethnocentrism?

CULTURE AS FREEDOM

Culture has two faces. First, culture provides us with an opportunity to exercise our *freedom*. We use and elaborate elements of culture in our everyday life to solve practical problems and express our needs, hopes, joys, and fears.

However, creatively utilizing culture is just like any other act of construction; we need raw materials to get the job done. The raw materials for the culture we create consist of cultural elements that either existed before we were born or are created by other people after our birth. We may put these elements together in ways that produce something genuinely new. However, there is no other well to drink from, so our existing culture limits what we can think and do. In that sense, culture *constrains* us. This constraint is culture's second face. In the rest of this chapter, we take a close look at both faces of culture.

Symbolic Interactionism and Cultural Production

Until the 1960s, most sociologists argued that culture is a "reflection" of society. Using a term introduced in Chapter 2, we can say that they regarded culture as a dependent variable. Harris's analysis of rural Indians certainly fits that mould. In Harris's view, the social necessity of protecting cows led to the cultural belief that cows are holy.

In recent decades, the symbolic interactionist tradition we discussed in Chapter 1 has influenced many sociologists of culture. Symbolic interactionists are inclined to regard culture as an *independent* variable. In their view, people do not accept culture passively. We are not empty vessels into which society pours a defined assortment of beliefs, symbols, and values. Instead, we actively produce and interpret culture, creatively fashioning it and attaching meaning to it in accordance with our diverse needs.

The idea that people actively produce and interpret culture implies that, to a degree, we are at liberty to choose how culture influences us.

Cultural Diversity

Part of the reason we are increasingly able to choose how culture influences us is that Canadian society has diversified. Like many societies in the world, Canada is undergoing rapid cultural diversification because of a rising number of immigrants and the wide range in their countries of origin (Roberts et al., 2013). In fact, among the high-income, developed nations of the Organisation for Economic Co-operation and Development (OECD), Canada scores the highest level of ethnic diversity (see Figure 3.4).

FIGURE 3.4
Ethnic Fractionalization in 30 OECD Countries
Source: Patsiurko, et al. 2012. p. 206

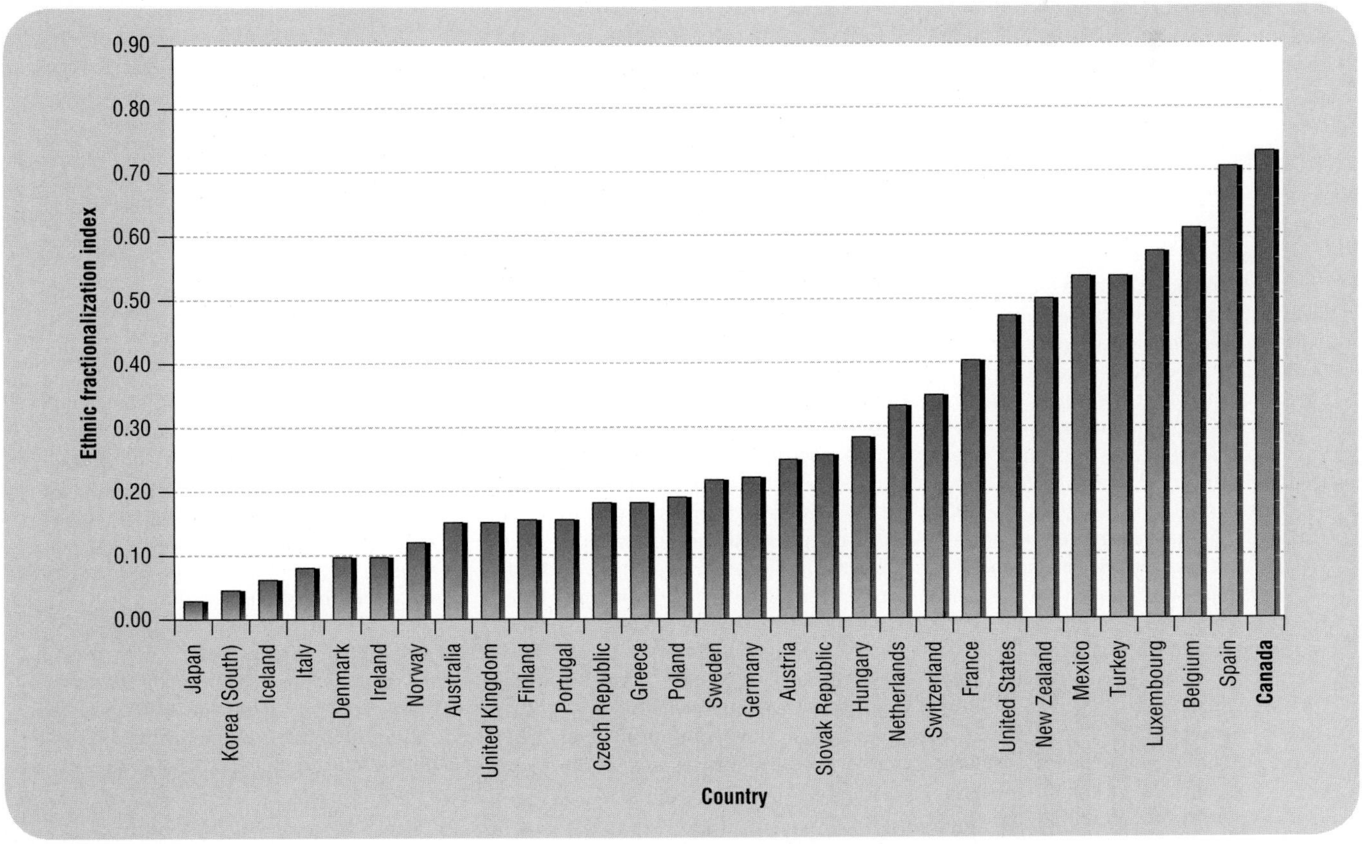

The ethnic fractionalization index reported in Figure 3.4 measures the probability that two randomly selected people from the same country are *not* of the ethnic, linguistic, or cultural group. The index ranges between 0 and 1.0, with higher scores indicating greater cultural diversity. Canada's fractionalization score (over 0.70) is more than 10 times higher than the scores for relatively homogeneous countries such as Japan and Italy, almost three times as high as the scores for Germany and Sweden, and almost 50 percent higher than the score for the United States.

Multiculturalism

At the political level, cultural diversity has become a source of conflict (see Box 3.2). The conflict is most evident in the debates that have surfaced in recent years concerning curricula in the Canadian educational system.

Although each provincial and territorial government in Canada has jurisdiction over education, until recent decades, schools across Canada stressed the common elements of our culture, history, and society. Students learned the historical importance of the "charter groups"—the English and the French. School curricula typically neglected the contributions to Canada's development by non-whites, non-French, and non-English. Moreover, students learned little about the less savoury aspects of Canadian history, including immigration policies that sought to preserve Canada's "English stock" by restricting or denying entry to

BOX 3.2

SOCIAL POLICY: WHAT DO YOU THINK?

Vote

SHOULD RELIGIOUS SYMBOLS BE BANNED IN PUBLIC SPACES?

In Canada, Québec is identified as a "distinct society." This designation is rooted in the founding of Canada—the union of Lower Canada (now Québec) with Upper Canada (now Ontario), New Brunswick, and Nova Scotia merged the country's English and French "charter groups." From the outset, Québec had special linguistic and constitutional rights, including special representation in the House of Commons and distinctive civil law. Until the 1950s, Québec's central social institutions—the family, the education system, and the health care system—were shaped by the Roman Catholic Church. Its control was especially strong in rural areas (Gauvreau, 2008).

Rural, conservative, French, Catholic distinctiveness weakened in the 1960s as Québec began its "Quiet Revolution." The Quiet Revolution was a period of dramatic political and cultural change that transformed Québec into a province characterized by secularism, cosmopolitanism, and a strong welfare state (Dickinson and Young, 2008). Today, Québec's distinct society is evident in its generous support of public institutions (for example, tuition accounts for 17 percent of university costs in Québec compared with 35 percent in Ontario), its nationalism (for example, the Parti Québécois wants Québec to become an independent country), and the liberal values of its population (for example, Québeckers are more likely to support euthanasia and public funding of abortion than are Canadians in the rest of the country).

Québec uses public policy tools to retain its distinctiveness. A recent example was the proposed Québec Charter of Values, which, if passed, would have forbidden public employees from wearing religious symbols while at work. Under the proposal, turbans, burkas, hijabs, kipot, and "large" crosses would not have been allowed. In addition, people receiving government services would not have been permitted to cover their face (Dougherty, 2013).

Cultural values are central to the construction of meaning in both individual and community life. Values express what is considered desirable or preferable. Québec's proposed Charter of Values was directed at maintaining the cultural distinctiveness of the province and reinforcing the secular character of public institutions and services. These are collective values. Québec's population is diverse and multicultural. Broad groups of citizens are deeply committed to their Christian, Jewish, Islamic, or other religious values and wish to symbolize their commitments in the way they dress. So the stage was set for a clash between minority and majority values. The result was a heated public policy debate in Québec about the balance between cultural freedom of expression and cultural constraints.

Where do you stand on this issue? Are you offended when public servants display their private religious commitments while on the job? Or are such expressions a tribute to Canada's commitment to multiculturalism and religious tolerance?

Canada continues to diversify culturally.

certain groups (Chapter 10, Race and Ethnicity). In general, history books were written from the perspective of the victors, not the vanquished.

For the past few decades, multiculturalists have argued that school, college, and university curricula should present a more balanced view of Canadian history, society, and culture. Curricula that reflect the country's ethnic and racial diversity will presumably allow minority groups to gain respect, dignity, and power and, in doing so, bring the educational system into line with Canada's status as the first officially multicultural society (Joshee and Sinfield, 2012). In 1971, the Canadian government declared that Canada, while officially bilingual, had no "official" culture—that is, none of the distinguishable cultures in Canada takes precedence over the others. With the passage of the Canadian Multiculturalism Act in 1988, the federal government confirmed its commitment to the recognition of all Canadians as full and equal participants in Canadian society. Multiculturalists conclude that to the extent that existing curricula are biased, they fail to provide students with the type of education demanded by a country truly devoted to multiculturalism.

Most critics of multiculturalism in education do not argue against teaching cultural diversity. What they fear is that multicultural education is being taken too far (Bliss, 2006; Gregg, 2006). Specifically, they say multiculturalism has three negative consequences:

1. Critics believe that multicultural education hurts students who are members of minority groups by forcing them to spend too much time on non-core subjects. To get ahead in the world, they say, students need to be skilled in English, French, math, and science. By taking time away from these subjects, multicultural education impedes the success of minority group members in the work world. Multiculturalists counter that minority group students develop self-esteem from a curriculum that stresses cultural diversity, which helps them get ahead in the work world.
2. Critics also believe that multicultural education leads to political disunity and results in more inter-ethnic and interracial conflict. Therefore, they want curricula to stress the common elements of the national experience and highlight Europe's contribution to Canadian culture. Multiculturalists reply that political unity and inter-ethnic and interracial harmony maintain inequality in Canadian society. Conflict, they say, while unfortunate, is often necessary to achieve equality between majority and minority groups.
3. Finally, critics complain that multiculturalism encourages the growth of **cultural relativism**. Cultural relativism is the opposite of ethnocentrism. It is the belief that all

Cultural relativism is the belief that all cultures have equal value.

cultures and all cultural practices have equal value. The trouble with this view is that some cultures oppose the most deeply held values of most Canadians. Critics argue that, to the degree that it promotes cultural relativism, a truly multicultural system of education might encourage respect for practices that are abhorrent to most Canadians (Box 3.3). Multiculturalists reply that we don't have to take cultural relativism to such an extreme. *Moderate* cultural relativism encourages tolerance, and we should promote it.

Clearly, multiculturalism in education is a complex and emotional issue. Globally, cultures are becoming more heterogeneous. This trend has important social and political consequences that are best faced through informed debate (Kymlicka, 2010; Reitz et al., 2009).

A Conflict Analysis of Culture: The Rights Revolution

What are the social roots of cultural diversity and multiculturalism? Conflict theory suggests where to look for an answer. Recall from Chapter 1 the central argument of conflict theory:

BOX 3.3

IT'S YOUR CHOICE

FEMALE GENITAL MUTILATION: CULTURAL RELATIVISM OR ETHNOCENTRISM?

The World Health Organization (WHO) defines female genital mutilation (FGM) as "procedures that intentionally alter or injure female genital organs for non-medical reasons" (World Health Organization, 2013a). FGM has no medical benefits. It usually involves partial or total removal of the clitoris and sometimes includes partial or total removal of the "lips" that surround the vagina and the surgical narrowing of the vaginal opening. It can result in severe bleeding, problems urinating, cysts, infection, infertility, and complications in childbirth, including increased risk of newborn death. Other effects include humiliation, trauma, and loss of sexual pleasure. Only about 18 percent of FGM procedures are carried out by trained medical personnel, although in Egypt the figure is 77 percent (UNICEF, 2013: 2).

More than 125 million girls and women worldwide have undergone FGM, the great majority of them in Africa. However, increased international migration has brought FGM to Canada and other countries. Egypt, Ethiopia, Nigeria, and Sudan account for 83 percent of FGM cases worldwide; more than 150 000 Canadians claim to be at least partly of Egyptian, Ethiopian, Nigerian, and Sudanese ethnic origin (Statistics Canada, 2014; UNICEF, 2013:2).

Proponents of FGM often claim that women who have not experienced genital mutilation are inclined to "masculine" levels of sexual interest and activity. In contrast, women who have undergone FGM are considered more likely to remain virgins before marriage and faithful within marriage. Moreover, proponents often assert that FGM enhances fertility.

One reaction to FGM takes a "human rights perspective." In this view, the practice is an aspect of gender-based oppression that women experience to varying degrees in societies worldwide. Adopting this perspective, the United Nations defines FGM as a form of violence against women. Many international, regional, and national agreements commit governments to preventing FGM, assisting women at risk of undergoing it, and punishing people who commit it. In Canada, FGM is against the law.

Cultural relativists regard the human rights perspective as ethnocentric. They view interference with the practice as little more than neo-imperialist attacks on African cultures. From their point of view, talk of "universal human rights" denies cultural rights to less powerful peoples. Moreover, opposition to FGM undermines tolerance and multiculturalism while reinforcing racist attitudes. Cultural relativists therefore argue that we should affirm the right of other cultures to practise FGM even if we regard it as destructive, senseless, oppressive, and abhorrent. We should respect the fact that other cultures regard FGM as meaningful and as serving useful functions.

Which of these perspectives do you find more compelling? Do you believe that certain principles of human decency transcend the particulars of any culture? If so, what are those principles? If you do not believe in the existence of any universal principles of human decency, then does anything go? Would you agree that, say, genocide is acceptable if most people in a society favour it? Or are there limits to your cultural relativism? In a world where supposedly universal principles often clash with the principles of particular cultures, where do you draw the line?

Social life is an ongoing struggle between more and less advantaged groups. Privileged groups try to maintain their advantages while subordinate groups struggle to increase theirs. And sure enough, if we probe beneath cultural diversification and multiculturalism, we find what has been called the **rights revolution**, the process by which socially excluded groups have struggled to win equal rights under the law and in practice.

The **rights revolution** is the process by which socially excluded groups struggled to win equal rights under the law and in practice beginning in the second half of the twentieth century.

After the outburst of nationalism, racism, and genocidal behaviour among the combatants in World War II, the United Nations proclaimed the Universal Declaration of Human Rights in 1948. It recognized the "inherent dignity" and "equal and inalienable rights of all members of the human family" and held that "every organ of society" should "strive by teaching and education to promote respect for these rights and freedoms and by progressive measures, national and international, to secure their universal and effective recognition and observance" (United Nations, 1998). Fanned by such sentiment, the rights revolution was in full swing by the 1960s. Today, women's rights, minority rights, gay and lesbian rights, the rights of people with special needs, constitutional rights, and language rights are key parts of our political discourse. Because of the rights revolution, democracy has been widened and deepened (Chapter 14, Politics). The rights revolution is by no means finished. Many categories of people are still discriminated against socially, politically, and economically. However, in much of the world, all categories of people now participate more fully than ever in the life of their societies (United Nations Development Programme, 2013).

The rights revolution raises some difficult issues. For example, some members of groups that have suffered extraordinarily high levels of discrimination historically, such as Aboriginal Canadians, Chinese Canadians, and others, have demanded reparations in the form of money, symbolic gestures, land, and political autonomy (Chapter 10, Race and Ethnicity). Much controversy surrounds the extent of the obligation of current citizens to compensate for past injustices.

Such problems notwithstanding, the rights revolution is here to stay and it profoundly affects our culture. Specifically, the rights revolution fragments Canadian culture by legitimizing the grievances of groups that were formerly excluded from full social participation and renewing their pride in their identity and heritage. Our history books, our literature, our music, our use of languages, our very sense of what it means to be Canadian have diversified culturally. White, male, heterosexual property owners of north European origin are still disproportionately influential in Canada, but our culture is no longer dominated by them in the way that it was just a half century ago.

From Diversity to Globalization

The cultural diversification we witness today is not evident in preliterate or tribal societies. In such societies, cultural beliefs and practices are virtually the same for all group members. For example, many tribal societies organize **rites of passage**. These cultural ceremonies mark the transition from one stage of life to another (for example, from childhood to adulthood) or from life to death (for example, funerals and memorial services). They can involve elaborate procedures, such as body painting and carefully orchestrated chants and movements. They are often conducted in public, and no variation from prescribed practice is allowed. In simple societies, culture is homogeneous (Durkheim, 1976 [1915]).

Rites of passage are cultural ceremonies that mark the transition from one stage of life to another (for example, baptisms, confirmations, weddings) or from life to death (for example, funerals and memorial services).

In contrast, preindustrial Western Europe and North America were rocked by artistic, religious, scientific, and political forces that fragmented culture. The Renaissance, the Protestant Reformation, the Scientific Revolution, the French and American revolutions—between the fourteenth and eighteenth centuries, all these movements involved people questioning old ways of seeing and doing things. Science placed skepticism about established authority at the very heart of its method. Political revolution proved there was nothing ordained about who should rule and how they should do so. Religious dissent ensured that the Catholic Church would no longer be the supreme interpreter of God's will in the eyes of all Christians. Authority and truth became divided as never before.

Cultural fragmentation picked up steam during industrialization as the variety of occupational roles grew and new political and intellectual movements crystallized. Its pace is

Sean Pavone/Shutterstock.com

The idea of globalization first gained prominence in marketing strategies in the 1970s. In the 1980s, such companies as Coca-Cola and McDonald's expanded into non-Western countries to find new markets.

Globalization is the process by which formerly separate economies, states, and cultures are tied together and people become aware of their growing interdependence.

quickening again today in the postindustrial era as a result of globalization. **Globalization** is the process by which formerly separate economies, states, and cultures are tied together and people become aware of their growing interdependence.

The international influences characterizing globalization take many forms and are evident in politics, religion, the mass media, and styles of clothing and music. One of the most important roots of globalization is the expansion of international trade and investment. Even the most patriotic of Canadians has probably dined at least once at McDonald's—and even a business as "American" as McDonald's has 58 percent of its stores in 117 countries outside of the United States, generating 61 percent of its profits (McDonald's Corporation, 2012). At the same time, members of different ethnic and racial groups are migrating and coming into sustained contact with one another. Influential transnational organizations, such as the International Monetary Fund, the World Bank, the European Union, Greenpeace, and Amnesty International, are multiplying. Relatively inexpensive international travel and communication make contacts among people from diverse cultures routine. The mass media make Ryan Gosling and the latest Spiderman movie nearly as well known in Warsaw as in Winnipeg. MTV brings rock music to the world via stations in Canada, Brazil, Japan, India, China, Australia, Korea, Russia, and so on. Globalization, in short, destroys political, economic, and cultural isolation, bringing people together in what Canadian media analyst Marshall McLuhan (1964) called a "global village." Because of globalization, people are less obliged to accept the culture into which they are born and freer to combine elements of culture from a wide variety of historical periods and geographical settings. Globalization is a schoolboy in New Delhi, India, listening to Rihanna on his iPhone as he rushes to slip into his Levis, wolf down a bowl of Kellogg's Basmati Flakes, and say goodbye to his parents in Hindi because he's late for his English-language school.

The Globalization of English

A good indicator of the influence and extent of globalization is the spread of English. In 1600, English was the mother tongue of between four million and seven million people. Not even all people in England spoke it. Today, more than a billion people speak English worldwide, more than half as a second language. With the exception of the many varieties of Chinese, English is the most widespread language on Earth. English is dominant because, for more than 200 years, Britain and the United States were the world's most powerful and influential countries—economically, militarily, and culturally. In recent decades, the reach of the English language has increased because of the global spread of capitalism, the popularity of Hollywood movies and American TV shows, and the widespread access to instant communication via telephone and the Internet. English is becoming the common language of scientific and educational communication. The Politecnico di Milano, one of Italy's most respected universities, announced that, beginning in 2014, all its courses would be taught in English. Other universities in Europe and Asia are following suit (Dyer, 2012).

Because of the rise of English (as well as the influence of French, Spanish, and the languages of a few other colonizing nations), several thousand languages around the world are being eliminated. These endangered languages are spoken by the tribes of Papua New Guinea; the native peoples of the Americas; the national and tribal minorities of Asia, Africa, and Oceania; and marginalized European peoples, such as the Irish and the Basques (see Figure 3.5). Experts estimate that the 5000 to 6000 languages spoken in the world today will be reduced to between 1000 and 3000 in a century. Since much of culture is encoded in language, the loss of languages amounts to the displacement of local traditions and identity by the traditions and identity of the colonial power. Television and the Internet play an important role in the trend toward homogeneity, even though social media can provide a record of endangered languages before extinction (Gray, 2012).

The corrosive effect of English on non-English cultures is evident in Canada, too. Of the 60 Aboriginal languages listed in the 2011 census, only a few (Cree, Ojibway, Oji-Cree, and Dene) are "strong and viable" (Canadian Press, 2012). But even those languages experienced decline in the preceding five years. On the other hand, Québec is surrounded by English-speaking provinces and the United States, yet 94 percent of Québec's population speak French. This fact is a tribute to the development and enforcement of language laws and other policies aimed at language retention. The contrasting experiences of Québec and Canada's First Nations illustrate that the globalization of English will continue eroding traditional languages and cultures unless vigorous, sustained efforts are mounted to resist the trend.

Aspects of Postmodernism

Some sociologists think that so much cultural fragmentation and reconfiguration has taken place in the last few decades that a new term is needed to characterize the culture of our

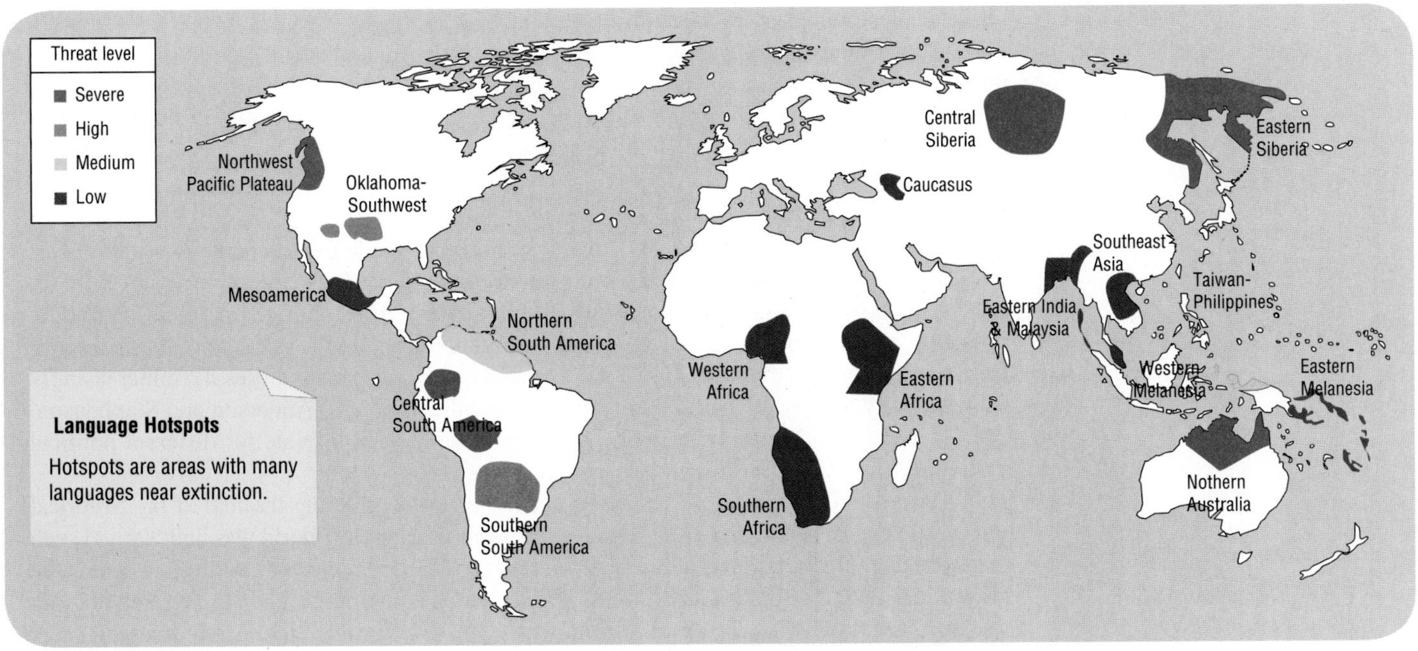

FIGURE 3.5
Language Regions at Risk

Source: Ngs Staff/National Geographic Creative

Postmodernism is characterized by an eclectic mix of cultural elements, the erosion of authority, and the decline of consensus around core values.

times: **postmodernism**. Scholars often characterize the last half of the nineteenth century and the first half of the twentieth century as the era of modernity. During this hundred-year period, much of Western culture was characterized by belief in the inevitability of progress, respect for authority, and consensus around core values. In contrast, postmodern culture involves an eclectic mix of elements from different times and places, the erosion of authority, and the decline of consensus around core values. Let us consider, in turn, each of these aspects of postmodernism.

An Eclectic Mix of Elements from Different Times and Places

In the postmodern era, it is easier to create personalized belief systems and practices by blending facets of different cultures and historical periods. Consider religion. Between 1991 and 2011, census figures report that people with "no religious affiliation" increased from 12.6 to 23.9 percent of the population. During the same two decades, those identifying themselves as Christian declined from 83 to 67.3 percent (Statistics Canada, 2013i). Canadians are increasingly willing to feast from a religious buffet that combines a conventional menu with a wide assortment of less conventional beliefs and practices, including astrology, tarot, New Age mysticism, psychic phenomena, and communication with the dead (Bibby, 2011, 2013). Many people now draw on religions in much the same way consumers shop in a mall. Meanwhile, churches, mosques, temples, synagogues, and other religious institutions have diversified their services to appeal to the spiritual, leisure, and social needs of religious consumers and retain their loyalties in the competitive market for congregants and parishioners (Finke and Stark, 2005).

The mix-and-match approach we see when it comes to religion is evident in virtually all spheres of culture. Although purists may scoff at such cultural blending, it has an important social consequence. People who engage in cultural blending are likely to be more tolerant and appreciative of ethnic, racial, and religious groups other than their own.

The Erosion of Authority

Half a century ago, Canadians were more likely than they are today to defer to authority in the family, schools, politics, medicine, and so forth. As the social bases of authority and truth have multiplied, however, we are more likely to challenge authority. Authorities once widely respected, including parents, physicians, and politicians, have come to be held in lower regard by many people. In the 1950s, Robert Young played the firm, wise, and always-present father in the TV hit series *Father Knows Best*. Six decades later, the typical TV father is more like Homer Simpson: a fool. Compared with their counterparts in the twenty-first century, Canadian teenagers in the 1980s were more likely to express confidence in our police, politicians, court system, and religious organizations (Bibby, 2009). Today, both young and old Canadians are likely to be critical of social institutions, including those, such as religious organizations, that previously enjoyed special respect. The rise of Homer Simpson and the decline of confidence in government both reflect the erosion of traditional authority (Nevitte, 1996; Roberts et al., 2005).

The Decline of Consensus around Core Values

Half a century ago, people's values remained relatively stable over the course of their adult lives, and many values were widely accepted. Today, value shifts are more rapid, and consensus has broken down on many issues (Roberts et al., 2005). For example, in the middle of the twentieth century, the great majority of adults remained loyal to one political party from one election to the next. However, specific issues and personalities have increasingly eclipsed party loyalty as the driving forces of Canadian politics (Anderson and Stephenson, 2011). Today, people are more likely than they were in 1950 to vote for different political parties in successive elections.

We may also illustrate the decline of consensus by considering the fate of big historical projects. For most of the past 200 years, consensus throughout the world was built around such monumental projects. Various political and social movements convinced people they could take history into their own hands and create a glorious future just by signing up. German Nazism was one such big historical project. Its followers expected the Reich to enjoy a thousand years of power. Communism was an even bigger historical project, mobilizing hundreds of millions of people for a future that promised to end inequality and injustice for all time. However, the biggest and most successful historical project was not so much a social movement as a powerful idea—the belief that progress is inevitable, that life will always improve, mainly because of the spread of democracy and scientific innovation.

The twentieth century was unkind to big historical projects. Russian communism lasted 74 years. German Nazism endured a mere 12. The idea of progress fell on hard times as 100 million soldiers and civilians died in wars; the forward march of democracy took wrong turns into fascism, communism, and regimes based on religious fanaticism; and pollution from urbanization and industrialization threatened the planet. In the postmodern era, more and more people recognize that apparent progress, including scientific advances, often has negative consequences (Easton, 2011). As the poet E.E. Cummings once wrote, "nothing recedes like progress."

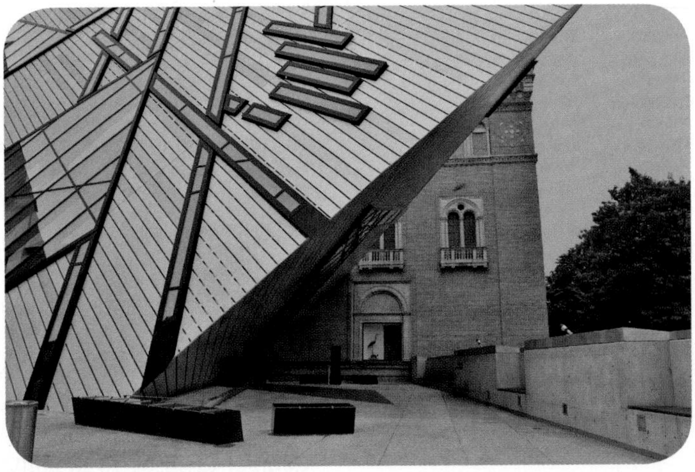

Lissandra Melo/Shutterstock.com

A hallmark of postmodernism is the combining of cultural elements from different times and places. For example, the Michael Lee-Chin Crystal that was added to the Royal Ontario Museum created a postmodern nightmare in the eyes of some critics.

Postmodernism worries many parents, teachers, politicians, religious leaders, and professors. Given the eclectic mixing of cultural elements from different times and places, the erosion of authority, and the decline of consensus around core values, how can we make binding decisions? How can we govern? How can we teach children and adolescents the difference between right and wrong? How can we transmit accepted literary tastes and artistic standards from one generation to the next? These are the kinds of issues that plague people in positions of authority today.

Although their concerns are legitimate, many authorities seem not to have considered the other side of the coin. The postmodern condition empowers ordinary people and makes them more responsible for their own fate. It frees people to adopt religious, ethnic, and other identities they are comfortable with, rather than accepting identities imposed on them by others. It makes people more tolerant of difference—which is no small matter in a world torn by group conflict. The postmodern attitude also encourages healthy skepticism about rosy and naive scientific and political promises.

Canada: The First Postmodern Culture?

Until the mid-1960s, most sociologists' image of Canadians was that of a stodgy people: peaceful, conservative, respectful of authority, and therefore quite unlike our American cousins.

According to conventional wisdom, the United States was born in open rebellion against the British motherland. Its Western frontier was lawless. Vast opportunities for striking it rich bred a spirit of individualism. Thus, American culture became an anti-authoritarian culture.

Canada developed differently according to the conventional view. It became an independent country not through a revolutionary upheaval but in a gradual, evolutionary manner. The North-West Mounted Police and two hierarchical churches (Roman Catholic and Anglican) established themselves on the Western frontier *before* the era of mass settlement, allowing for the creation of an orderly society rather than an American-style Wild West. Beginning with the Hudson's Bay Company, large corporations quickly came to dominate the Canadian economy, hampering individualism and the entrepreneurial spirit. Thus, Canadian culture became a culture of deference to authority. That, at least, was the common view until the 1960s (Lipset, 1963).

Although the contrast between deferential Canadian culture and anti-authoritarian American culture may have had some validity half a century ago, it is an inaccurate characterization today (Adams, 2004). As we have seen, the questioning of authority spread throughout the Western world beginning in the 1960s. Nowhere did it spread as quickly and thoroughly as in Canada. Canadians previously expressed more confidence in big business than Americans did, but surveys now show the opposite. Canadians were once more religious than Americans were, but that is no longer the case. Fewer Canadians (in percentage terms) say they believe in

God and fewer attend weekly religious services. Confidence in government has eroded more quickly in Canada than in the United States. Americans are more patriotic than Canadians are, according more respect to the state. Finally, Americans are more likely than Canadians are to regard the traditional nuclear family as the ideal family form and to think of deviations from tradition—same-sex couples, single-parent families, cohabitation without marriage—as the source of a whole range of social problems. Thus, whether sociologists examine attitudes toward the family, the state, the government, religion, or big business, they now find that Americans are more deferential to traditional institutional authority than Canadians are.

Because Canadians are less deferential to traditional institutional authority than Americans are, some commentators say that Canadians lack a distinct culture. For example, American patriotism sparks awareness of great national accomplishments in art, war, sports, and science. Anthems, rituals, myths, and celebrations commemorate these accomplishments and give Americans a keen sense of who they are and how they differ from non-Americans. Not surprisingly, therefore, a larger percentage of Americans than Canadians think of themselves in unhyphenated terms—as "Americans" plain and simple rather than, say, Italian-Americans. In Canada, a larger percentage of the population thinks of itself in hyphenated terms; compared with the Americans, our identity is qualified, even tentative.

Does this mean that Canadians lack a distinct national culture? Hardly. However, demonstrating the distinctiveness of Canadian culture is not simple. Sociological research into this question uses both the qualitative and quantitative methods introduced in Chapter 2. One recent quantitative investigation compared Canada and the United States on the World Values Survey, which uses representative national samples to compare nations on standardized indicators (Boucher, 2013). The trends in Canadian and U.S. differences are summarized in Figure 3.6.

The trends in Figure 3.6 are clear. In the economic domain, which includes values related to such issues as support for free markets, the importance of self-actualizing work, and the importance of meritocracy, Canada was similar to the United States but is becoming more distinct over time. The same trend is apparent in the social domain, which includes civil permissiveness, trust, tolerance of cultural differences, and egalitarianism. Regarding the moral dimension, which includes such values as moral permissiveness, church attendance, and subjective religiosity, Canada's distinctiveness is growing over time. The gap between

FIGURE 3.6

Trends in Canadian and U.S. Value Differences

Source: Boucher, Christian. "Canada-US Values Distinct, Inevitably Carbon Copy, or Narcissism of Small Differences?" Featured article from *Horizons, Volume 7, Number 1—North American Linkages Navigating Between Scylla and Charybdis*, Policy Research Initiative, Government of Canada, 2004.

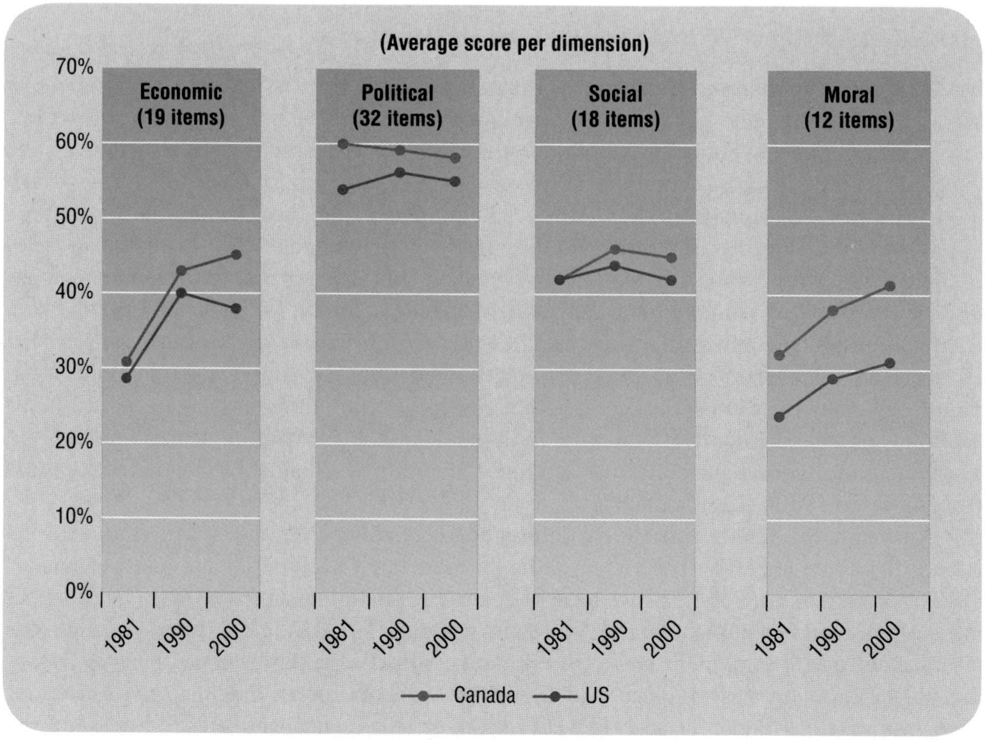

Canada and the United States is narrowing only in the political dimension, which includes values related to national pride, cosmopolitanism, and confidence in public institutions. Still, a significant difference remains between the values orientations of the two nations.

Canada continues its trend toward postmodernism as its values become more progressive and secular. As public opinion pollster Michael Adams writes:

> Canadians feel *strongly* about their *weak* attachments to Canada, its political institutions and their fellow citizens. In other words, they feel strongly about the right to live in a society that allows its citizens to be detached from ideology and critical of organizations, and not to feel obliged to be jingoistic or sentimentally patriotic. Canadians' *lack* of nationalism is, in many ways, a distinguishing feature of the country.
> *(Adams, 1997: 171)*

In short, Canadian culture *is* distinctive, and its chief distinction may be that it qualifies us as the first thoroughly postmodern society. This distinctiveness is recognized around the globe as Canada continues to rank as the nation with the best reputation in the world (Reputation Institute, 2013).

TIME FOR REVIEW

- How has the rights revolution contributed to cultural diversity in Canada?
- How does multiculturalism as a fact of Canadian society differ from multiculturalism as a Canadian value?
- What are the cultural advantages and disadvantages of the globalization of English?
- What societal features characterize a postmodern nation?
- In what ways does Canadian culture differ from the culture of the United States? In what ways is it similar?

Rationalization is the application of the most efficient means to achieve given goals and the unintended, negative consequences of doing so.

CULTURE AS CONSTRAINT

We noted previously that culture has two faces. One we labelled freedom, the other constraint. On the one hand, diversity, globalization, the rights revolution, and postmodernism are aspects of the new freedoms that culture encourages today. On the other hand, as you will now learn, rationalization, consumerism, and cultural capital act as constraining forces on our lives. Culture also operates as a force for social control and the replication of privilege.

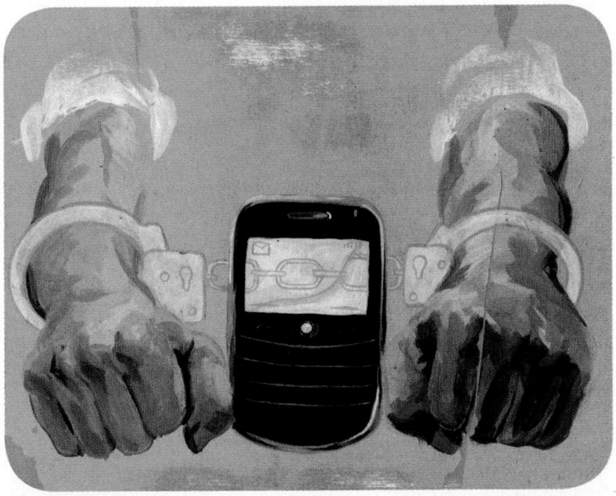

© David Murray

BlackBerry devices and iPhones allow people to stay in touch with friends and work every waking moment. Many people have mixed feelings about these devices. Sometimes they seem pleasurable and efficient. At other times, they prevent relaxation and intimacy. As such, they typify the two faces of culture.

Rationalization and Time Use

Max Weber coined the term **rationalization** to describe the application of the most efficient means to achieve given goals and the unintended, negative consequences of doing so. He claimed that rationalization has crept into all spheres of life. In Weber's view, rationalization is one of the most constraining aspects of contemporary culture, making life akin to living inside an "iron cage."

The constraining effects of rationalization are evident, for example, in the way we measure and use time. People did not always let the clock determine the pace of daily life. The first mechanical clocks were installed in public squares in Germany 700 years ago to signal the beginning of the workday, the timing of meals, and quitting time. Workers were accustomed to enjoying a flexible and vague work schedule regulated only approximately by the seasons and the rising and setting of the Sun. The strict regime imposed by the work clocks made their lives harder. They staged uprisings to silence the clocks, but to no

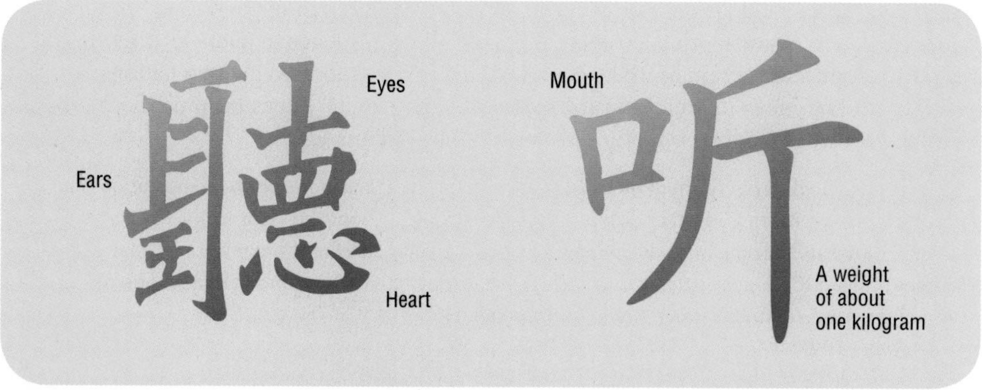

Reprinted here are the Chinese characters for "listening" *(t'ing)* in traditional Chinese script (left) and simplified, modern script (right). Each character comprises several word-symbols. In classical script, listening is depicted as a process involving the eyes, the ears, and the heart. It implies that listening demands the utmost empathy and involves the whole person. In contrast, modern script depicts listening as something that involves merely one person speaking and the other "weighing" speech. Modern Chinese script has been rationalized. Has empathy been lost in the process?

avail. City officials sided with employers and imposed fines for ignoring the work clocks (Thompson, 1967).

Today, few people rebel against the work clock. This is especially true of urban North American couples who are employed full-time in the paid labour force and have young children. For them, life often seems an endless round of waking up at 6:30 a.m.; getting everyone washed and dressed; preparing the kids' lunches; getting them out the door in time for the school bus or the car pool; driving to work through rush-hour traffic; facing the speedup at work resulting from the recent downsizing; driving back home through rush-hour traffic; preparing dinner; taking the kids to their soccer game; returning home to clean up the dishes and help with homework; getting the kids washed, their teeth brushed, and then into bed; and (if they have not brought some office work home) grabbing an hour of TV before collapsing, exhausted, for six hours' sleep before the story repeats itself. Life is less hectic for residents of small towns, unmarried people, couples without young children, retirees, and people who are unemployed. But the lives of others are typically so packed with activities that almost a third of Canadians report having no time for fun (Statistics Canada, 2011d). After 700 years of conditioning, allowing clocks to precisely regulate our activities seems the most natural thing in the world, although there is, of course, nothing natural about it.

Consumerism is the tendency to define ourselves in terms of the goods we purchase.

The regulation of time ensures efficiency. It maximizes how much work you accomplish in a day. It enables trains to run on schedule, university classes to begin punctually, and business meetings to start on time. However, many people complain that life has become too hectic to enjoy. In recent decades, the percentage of Canadians working non-standard hours (other than 9 to 5) has increased from 23 percent to 29 percent. The percentage of Canadians who say they routinely experience a serious "time crunch" has gone up from 16 percent to 20 percent. The percentage of Canadian teenagers regularly eating meals with adults has plummeted from 64 percent to 38 percent (Brooker and Hyman, 2010).

Have we come to depend too heavily on the work clock? Harold Lloyd in *Safety Last!* (1923).

Consumerism

The second constraining aspect of culture that we examine is **consumerism**, the tendency to define ourselves in terms of the goods and services we purchase. As artist Barbara Kruger put it, "I shop, therefore I am" (see Box 3.4).

Recent innovations in advertising take full advantage of our tendency to define ourselves in terms of the goods we purchase. For example, when personal video recorders (PVRs) enabled TV viewers to skip ads that cost millions of dollars to produce, advertisers had to think up new ways of drawing products to the attention of consumers. One idea they hit on was paying to place their products in TV shows and movies. Product-placement advertising helps consumers associate the product with characters they identify with. The product becomes part of who we are or who we want to be, and, as a result, sales often soar.

BOX 3.4

SOCIOLOGY ON THE TUBE

MY SHOPPING ADDICTION AND HOARDERS: IS CONSUMERISM A SOCIAL DISEASE?

The Diagnostic and Statistical Manual of Mental Disorders (DSM) is the psychiatrist's "bible." It lists defining criteria for hundreds of ailments. One is "compulsion." According to the DSM, people suffer from a compulsion if they feel they need to perform repetitive behaviour to reduce stress, even though the behaviour cannot realistically neutralize stress.

For example, the October 2012 premier of *My Shopping Addiction* introduced viewers to Heather, who, when her grandmother died, became the sole heir of millions of dollars. The jealousy and resentment of her parents and siblings led Heather to an isolated existence on the outskirts of Las Vegas, where she rents a mansion for $9000 a month. To compensate for her loneliness, she shops for clothes, shoes, and beauty products. Her monthly shopping bill averages $30 000. At that rate, she will be broke and alone in four years.

Not that you need to be rich to be a compulsive shopper. The premier also featured Roshanda, a part-time DJ who spends $300 a month buying juice, socks, dishwasher liquid, chewing gum—just about anything she can get her hands on—at a 99¢ store. She can't pay her rent or her utility bills. To feed her shopping addiction, she has borrowed thousands of dollars from her family and friends, whom she has thoroughly alienated. "What do you like better," asks the intervening psychologist, "your best friend or the 99¢ store?" "I like the store," Roshanda answers.

The Kobal Collection at Art Resource, NY

Scene from *Hoarders*.

Hoarding is listed as a compulsive disorder in the latest edition of the DSM, released in 2013. Nonetheless, some psychiatrists may not appreciate the sociological fact that different social settings create opportunities for expressing compulsions in different forms. In intensely spiritual sixteenth-century Spain, the compulsive behaviour of Ignatius of Loyola, a devout priest and the founder of the Jesuits, took a religious form. He was never satisfied that he had confessed his sins sufficiently and could not stop himself from compulsively going to confession many times a day, although doing so tormented him (Ganss, 1991: 77–78). The United States and, to a somewhat lesser degree, Canada are consumer societies. We don't earn enough to buy all that we want, so we borrow money to feed our compulsion; on average, Canadians owed 163 percent more than they earned in 2014, down just 1 percent from the record high in 2013 (Babad, 2014). Do we all, to varying degrees, suffer from a compulsive disorder?

The effectiveness of advertising encourages businesses to produce even more advertising. As advertising becomes more pervasive, it becomes accepted as a normal part of daily life. In fact, people often *become* ads. They proudly display consumer labels as marks of their status and identity. Advertisers teach us to associate the words "Gucci" and "Nike" with different kinds of people, and when people display these labels on their clothes, they are telling us something about the kind of people they are. Advertising becomes us.

The rationalization process, when applied to the production of goods and services, enables us to produce more efficiently, to have more of just about everything than previous generations did. However, it is consumerism that ensures we will buy most of the goods that are produced. Of course, we have lots of choice. We can select from dozens of styles of running shoes, cars, toothpaste, and all the rest. We can also choose to buy items that help define us as members of a particular **subculture**, adherents of a set of distinctive values, norms, and practices within a larger culture. But individual tastes aside, we all have one thing in common. We tend to be good consumers. We are motivated by advertising, which is based on the accurate insight that people will tend to be considered cultural outcasts if they fail to conform to stylish trends. By creating those trends, advertisers push us to buy, even if doing so requires that we work more and incur large debts (Phelps, 2010). That is

A **subculture** is a set of distinctive values, norms, and practices within a larger culture.

"Untitled" (I shop therefore I am) 1987. Copyright © Barbara Kruger. Courtesy Mary Boone Gallery, New York.

Consumerism ties identities to purchases.

why the "shop-till-you-drop" lifestyle of many North Americans prompted French sociologist Jean Baudrillard to remark pointedly that even what is best in North America is compulsory (Baudrillard, 1988). And it is why many sociologists say that consumerism, like rationalization, acts as a powerful constraint on our lives.

From Counterculture to Subculture

In concluding our discussion of culture as a constraining force, we note that consumerism is remarkably effective at taming countercultures. **Countercultures** are subversive subcultures. They oppose dominant values and seek to replace them. The hippies of the 1960s formed a counterculture and so do environmentalists today. Countercultures rarely pose a serious threat to social stability. Most often, the system of social control, of rewards and punishments, keeps countercultures at bay. In our society, consumerism acts as a social control mechanism that normally prevents countercultures from disrupting the social order. It does that by transforming deviations from mainstream culture into means of making money and by enticing rebels to become entrepreneurs (Frank, 2009).

Countercultures are subversive subcultures.

Consider hip hop. It originated in the 1970s, when manufacturing industries were leaving the American inner city, unemployment among black American youth rose to more than 40 percent, and conservative governments were cutting school and welfare budgets, thus deepening the destitution of ghetto life (Piven and Cloward, 1977: 264–361, 1993; Wilson, 1987). With few legitimate prospects for advancement, many poor black American youth in the inner city turned to crime and, in particular, the trade in crack cocaine. Turf wars spread as gangs tried to outgun each other for control of the local traffic (Davis, 1990).

These shocking conditions gave rise to a shocking musical form: hip hop. Stridently at odds with the values and tastes of both whites and middle-class black Americans, hip hop described and glorified the mean streets of the inner city while holding the police, the mass media, and other pillars of society in utter contempt. In their 1988 album, *It Takes a Nation to Hold Us Back*, Chuck D and Public Enemy accused the mass media of maliciously distributing lies about blacks, charged the FBI and the CIA with assassinating Martin Luther King, Jr. and Malcolm X, the two great leaders of the African American community in the 1960s, and blamed the federal government for organizing the fall of the Black Panthers, the radical black nationalist party of the 1960s. Here, it seemed, was an angry expression of subcultural revolt that could not be tamed.

However, the seduction of big money did much to mute the political force of hip hop. As early as 1982, hip hop began to win acclaim from mainstream rock music critics. With the success of Run–D.M.C. and Public Enemy in the late 1980s, it became clear there was a big audience for hip hop. Significantly, much of that audience was composed of white youths, who "relished ... the subversive 'otherness' that the music and its purveyors represented" (Neal, 1999: 144). Sensing the opportunity for profit, major media corporations signed distribution deals with the small independent recording labels that had formerly been the exclusive distributors of hip hop CDs. In 1988, *Yo! MTV Raps* debuted on MTV, bringing hip hop to middle America.

Most hip hop recording artists proved they were eager to forgo political relevancy for commerce. Some started their own clothing lines, while Tommy Hilfiger, Versace, and others began marketing clothing influenced by ghetto styles. Puff Daddy reminded his audience in a 1999 CD that "get money, that's simply the plan." Bling—not to mention Bentley automobiles and Cîroc vodka—became the emblems of hip hop. Hip hop was no longer just a musical form but a commodity with spinoffs.

Helga Esteb/Shutterstock.com

Hip hop counterculture is commodified.

Radical political currents still exist in hip hop, but mainly outside North America. "*Rais Lebled* [Mr. President]," a song by a Tunisian rapper, became the anthem of young people participating in the democratic uprisings in Tunisia, Egypt, and Bahrain in 2011: "Mr. President, your people are dying / People are eating rubbish / Look at what is happening / Miseries everywhere, Mr. President / I talk with no fear / Although I know I will get only trouble / I see injustice everywhere" (Ghosh, 2011). However, in North America, hip hop has become, for the most part, an apolitical commodity that increasingly appeals to a racially heterogeneous, middle-class audience. Rebellion has been turned into mass consumption. Hip hop's radicalism has given way to the lure of commerce. Under the impact of consumerism, a counterculture has become a subculture.

Cultural Capital

Yet another way that culture constrains us is through the use of cultural capital. Capital comes in many forms. Financial capital (money) is the most common. The French sociologist Pierre Bourdieu (1986) identified cultural capital as another important resource used for accomplishing goals. **Cultural capital** refers to the beliefs, tastes, norms, and values that people draw upon in their everyday life. People with different socialization histories occupy different social positions and have different amounts and types of cultural capital. The Aboriginal female who has spent most of her life living on an isolated reserve in northern Saskatchewan likely has very different beliefs, tastes, norms, and values from the man from a privileged family of English origin who heads a large corporation in Montreal.

Cultural capital refers to the beliefs, tastes, norms, and values that people draw upon in everyday life.

Cultural capital is not just about differences. It is about differences with important social consequences. Communities and organizations are bounded by different types of cultural capital, which form an important component of what makes them distinct. In a stratified society, the distinctive cultural capital of privileged groups and organizations is used as a means of protecting privilege and keeping outsiders out. This gatekeeping function occurs when dominant groups define their specific kinds of cultural capital as prerequisites for recruitment and selection.

As Bourdieu emphasizes, differences in cultural capital are connected to social classes. For instance, public schools are mostly governed by middle-class cultural capital. Success does not depend solely on intelligence and hard work. Succeeding in the school system requires being comfortable with a wide range of expectations rooted in cultural capital. Students need to be punctual. They need to be clean. They need to sit still. They need to be courteous. And so on. When students from lower-class or immigrant backgrounds attend such schools, the cultural capital at their command is often misaligned with existing school culture. Such misalignment makes adaptation more challenging. It commonly results in the subordination and marginalization of the non–middle-class students.

The same process of social sorting takes place in the employment market. How comfortable would you be if a prospective employer took you to a sophisticated restaurant where your manners were deficient, the conversation involved references to books and ballets you knew nothing about, and you were asked for opinions about political policies that you didn't understand? You would likely end the dinner with a clear sense that you would not be a good fit with this place of employment. And the potential employer would likely draw the same conclusion. Although cultural capital is symbolic, not material, it plays an important role shaping your fate in society.

In an era when individualism and autonomy are valued, it is not surprising to see the emergence of pockets of resistance to cultural constraints. Culture jamming is a good example. **Culture jamming** involves individuals and groups challenging dominant cultural beliefs, tastes, norms, and values. Cultural jammers resist mainstream culture in creative ways, including altering billboards, conducting street protests, and cloning websites (Gramigna, 2012). The point of this activity is to draw attention to the cultural assumptions and consequences of capitalist, consumerist culture. It is a form of cultural consciousness-raising. The Canadian magazine, *Adbusters*, is well known internationally for promoting cultural jamming aimed at transforming corporate advertisements into

Cultural jamming refers to the creative methods used by individuals and groups to challenge dominant cultural beliefs, tastes, norms, and values.

anti-consumption, anti-capitalist campaigns. In fact, the idea for the Occupy Movement came from *Adbusters*.

The Occupy Movement began in New York City as Occupy Wall Street (OWS). OWS mobilized protesters against the growing social and economic inequality rooted in corporate greed and corruption. Beginning in 2011 with protesters occupying a park near Wall Street, the protest gained worldwide publicity. Soon Occupy protests were replicated in dozens of cities. The slogan for the Occupy protest movement was "We are the 99%," referring to the recent, dramatic wealth accumulation among the richest one percent of the population. The entire OWS movement originated from a senior *Adbusters* editor distributing an email to magazine subscribers proposing a peaceful protest by occupying a location near Wall Street. When the perceived injustice of existing cultural arrangements is sparked by individual protest and fanned by a social organization supported by social media, the result is considerable pressure on the status quo.

Cultural jamming illustrates the paradoxical nature of culture. People create culture to aid problem solving and adaptation but, once created, culture becomes an entity to which humans must adapt to varying degrees. Culture generates possibilities for autonomy and independence at the same time as it constrains individual conduct. Languages that direct our thinking are the same vehicles by which we express our unique thoughts and feelings. Culture creates mass media from iPhones to Twitter accounts and, in turn, these material media create content that transforms symbolic culture. Cultural production is not a static phenomenon but a complicated interactive flow that is both the product and producer of human action.

TIME FOR REVIEW

- How does rationalization account for the differences between a game of street hockey and games in a hockey tournament?
- How has consumerism constrained your life? Has it made you freer in any way?
- Is cultural jamming a counterculture or a subculture?
- Explain how cultural capital is similar to, and different from, financial capital.

SUMMARY

1. What role does culture play in generating meaning and solving problems?
   By itself, concrete experience is meaningless. Experience must be interpreted to be meaningful. Interpretations require bringing cultural concepts and ideas to concrete experiences. The meaning of all individual and collective experience is rooted in culture. Whatever challenges environments pose to individuals and communities, the solutions to such problems are found in the possibilities and constraints afforded by culture.

2. How do biological explanations differ from cultural explanations?
   Biologists argue that surviving in harsh environments requires adaptations that, over time, are selected into the gene pool. They argue that conduct is hardwired into our DNA. If this were really the case, either there would be substantial variation in the genetic profile of humans (which there is not), or human actions would display limited variation (which they do not). Cultural differences provide a more appropriate accounting of the remarkable differences in human activity over time and place.

3. What do functionalism, symbolic interactionism, and conflict theory teach us about the operation of culture?
Functionalism, symbolic interactionism, and conflict theory teach us that the character and operation of culture in everyday life are multi-faceted. Functionalism emphasizes the constraining character of culture by highlighting how culture guides individual conduct toward collective goals. Conflict theory emphasizes that cultural blueprints for action are usually biased toward the interests and goals of privileged groups. Symbolic interaction reminds us that culture is a human creation. Consequently, people can resist and change cultural blueprints that they find unacceptable.

4. How does culture operate as a liberating force?
Cultural beliefs, norms, tastes, and values are selective in their emphasis. They give higher priority to some ideas, preferences, and rules than others. In modern and post-modern societies, the emphasis on rights, multiculturalism, and the expression of unique identities all provide opportunities for individuals to determine their own courses of action. Symbolic interactionists stress the importance of individual interpretation and choice. For them, culture is a system created by means of human action. Since culture is fluid, it can be reshaped if individuals decide to support alternate beliefs, norms, and values. Conflict theorists argue the privileged groups exercise more power in shaping the dominant culture. Consequently, if members of subordinate groups are to avoid exploitation, their rights must be guaranteed.

5. How does culture operate as a constraining force?
Culture is composed of a shared set of meaningful symbols that help to organize people socially, and pattern or constrain their behaviour. Rationalization is the belief that efficiency should drive actions to achieve goals. Consumerism is a value that encourages us to define ourselves in terms of the goods and services we purchase. Cultural capital is knowledge that supports success in particular environments. Each of these cultural elements constrains individuals. Rationalization leads to a hurried, stressful life governed by the clock. Consumerism locks individuals into judging their worth by fashionable acquisitions. Cultural capital bars those without certain kinds of knowledge from entering valuable social spheres.

CHAPTER 4

SOCIALIZATION

I must not copy what I see on the Simpsons
I must not copy what I see on the Simpsons
I must not copy what I see on the Simpsons
I must not copy what I see on the Simpsons
I must not copy what I see on the Simpsons
I must not copy what I see on the Sim
I must not copy what I see on the

IN THIS CHAPTER, YOU WILL LEARN TO

- Appreciate the degree to which social interaction unleashes human abilities, including the ability to see oneself as different from others.
- Evaluate how stages in life are influenced by the historical period in which people live.
- Contrast the declining socializing influence of the family with the rising socializing influence of schools, peer groups, and the mass media over the past century.
- Compare the greater speed, frequency, and comprehensiveness of identity change today with the lower speed, frequency, and comprehensiveness of identity change just a few decades ago.

THE CONSEQUENCES OF SOCIAL ISOLATION IN CHILDHOOD

One day in 1800, a 10- or 11-year-old boy was captured in the woods in southern France. He was filthy, naked, unable to speak, and had not been toilet trained. The boy was taken to Paris to be scrutinized by medical experts. How had he come to be living in the forest? A scar on his neck suggested a horrific past. Was the boy an unwanted child, left to die in the woods after an unknown person slit his throat? No one knew.

Equally challenging was determining what was wrong with the boy, who became known as "the savage of Aveyron." Some experts said the boy was mentally retarded, others that he was a deaf-mute. One ambitious young doctor, Jean Marc Itard, expressed a different view. He hypothesized that the boy's strangeness might be due to the effects of having been raised in extreme isolation. Intrigued by the mysterious boy, Itard took over his care, called him Victor, and conducted an initial assessment of his capabilities. Next, Itard tried to teach Victor a few basic skills. The task was daunting. As he began his work, Itard recorded in his journal that Victor was a "disgustingly dirty child affected with spasmodic movements, and often convulsions, who swayed back and forth ceaselessly like certain animals in a zoo, who bit and scratched those who opposed him, who showed no affection for those who took care of him, and who was, in short, indifferent to everything and attentive to nothing" (Itard, cited in Lane, 1976: 4).

Itard's efforts to train Victor led to great fame for the doctor but little success with Victor. After a few years of trying to teach Victor how to read and communicate with others, Itard gave up. He wrote up his findings in a formal report, concluding that the project to educate and civilize Victor had been a total failure. Despite intensive training, Victor never mastered speech, displayed limited intellectual engagement, and failed to develop emotional attachments to people (Benzaquen, 2006).

Sadly, over the years, other cases have emerged of children lacking human contact at a critical stage in their development. An especially shocking case, because of its mass scale, became known in 1989, shortly after the rule of a corrupt Romanian dictator came to an abrupt end when he and his wife were executed by their own people on Christmas Day. In the following months, the world learned the shocking details of how children had been treated by the regime. Because of harsh economic conditions, nearly 100 000 children had been abandoned by their families. Left in the hands of the state, these children were warehoused in orphanages that provided little food and even less love. The toll appeared greatest for those who had been abandoned at birth. Starving and listless, many babies were also strangely cross-eyed. Had they developed a strange illness? No. Because they had spent their short lives lying on their backs and staring at the blank ceiling overhead, these infants

Mary Evans Picture Library

Known as the savage of Aveyron, Victor never mastered speech, nor did he develop emotional bonds with others beyond those who took care of him.

had no opportunity to focus on objects, an activity that would have allowed them to develop their vision properly.

Stunned by the deplorable conditions of the orphanages, families around the world descended on Romania to adopt the children. Approximately 600 of these children were adopted by Canadian parents. Seizing the opportunity to learn more about the long-term effects of early life deprivation, researchers in Canada and elsewhere began to study some of these children. They wondered whether these children could overcome their early neglect and grow up to become functioning adults.

The results were mixed. A decade later, Romanian orphans who had been adopted by Canadian parents had caught up to Canadian children in weight and height (Le Mare and Audet, 2006). However, as in Victor's case, researchers discovered that the emotional scars of neglect run deep. The brains of the adopted Romanian children were smaller and less developed than they should have been, resulting in a wide array of emotional and intellectual deficits. As young adults, many of the children reported struggling to fit in, and some were convicted of crimes.

The lesson seems clear. During the first few months of life, children must be exposed to other humans who will care for and love them. Otherwise, the neural structures that are responsible for emotional and intellectual development wither and die (Nelson, Fox, and Zeanah, 2014).

The examples of Victor and the Romanian orphans suggest that the ability to become human is only a potential. To be actualized, **socialization** must unleash the potential. Socialization is the process by which people learn to function in social life. They do so by (1) entering and disengaging from a succession of roles and (2) becoming aware of themselves as they interact with others. A **role** is the behaviour expected of a person occupying a particular position in society.

To paint a picture of the socialization process, we first review the main theories of how a sense of self develops during childhood, during which the contours of the self are first formed.

Socialization is the process by which people learn to function in social life and become aware of themselves as they interact with others.

TIME FOR REVIEW

- What evidence suggests that children require contact with others to realize their human potential?
- How and why might prolonged social isolation affect adults differently from the way it affects young children?

A **role** is the behaviour expected of a person occupying a particular position in society.

FORMATION OF THE SELF

Driven by elemental needs, infants cry out. Those who hear their cries, usually their parents, respond by providing the infant with food, comfort, and affection. At first, infants do not seem able to distinguish themselves from their main caregivers. However, continued social interaction enables infants to begin developing a self-image or sense of **self**—a set of ideas and attitudes about who they are as independent beings.

The **self** consists of your ideas and attitudes about who you are.

Freud

Austrian psychoanalyst Sigmund Freud proposed the first social-scientific interpretation of the process by which the self emerges (Freud, 1962 [1930], 1973 [1915–17]). He noted that infants demand immediate gratification but begin to form a self-image when their demands are denied—when, for example, parents decide not to feed and comfort them every time they wake up in the middle of the night. The parents' refusal at first incites howls of protest. However, infants soon learn to eat more before going to bed, sleep for longer periods, and go back to sleep when they wake up. Equally important, the infant begins to sense that its needs differ from those of its parents, it has an existence independent of others, and it must balance its needs with the realities of life. Because of many such lessons in self-control, the child eventually develops a sense of what constitutes appropriate behaviour and a moral sense of right and wrong. Soon a personal conscience crystallizes. It is a storehouse of cultural standards. In addition, a psychological mechanism develops that normally balances the pleasure-seeking and restraining components of the self. Earlier thinkers believed that the self emerges naturally, the way a seed germinates. In a revolutionary departure from previous thinking on the subject, Freud argued that only social interaction allows the self to emerge.

Cooley's Symbolic Interactionism

American scholars took ideas about the emergence of the self in a still more sociological direction. Notably, Charles Horton Cooley introduced the idea of the "looking-glass self," making him a founder of the symbolic interactionist tradition and an early contributor to the sociological study of socialization.

Cooley observed that when we interact with others, they gesture and react to us. This response allows us to imagine how we appear to others. We then judge how others evaluate us. Finally, from these judgments we develop a self-concept or a set of feelings and ideas about who we are. In other words, our feelings about who we are depend largely on how we see ourselves evaluated by others. Just as we see our physical body reflected in a mirror, so we see our social selves reflected in people's gestures and reactions to us (Cooley, 1902).

For instance, when teachers evaluate students negatively, students may develop a negative self-concept that causes them to do poorly in school. Poor performance may have as much to do with teachers' negative evaluations as with students' innate abilities (Sanchez and Roda, 2003). Here, succinctly put, we have the hallmarks of what came to be known as symbolic interactionism—the idea that in the course of face-to-face communication, people engage in a creative process of attaching meaning to things.

Mead

George Herbert Mead (1934) further developed the idea of the looking-glass self. Like Freud, Mead noted that a subjective and impulsive aspect of the self is present from birth. Mead called it simply the **I**. Again like Freud, Mead argued that a repository of culturally approved standards emerges as part of the self during social interaction. Mead called this objective, social component of the self the **me**. However, while Freud focused on the denial of the impulsive side of the self as the mechanism that generates the self's objective side, Mead drew attention to the unique human capacity to "take the role of the other" as the source of the me.

The **I**, according to Mead, is the subjective and impulsive aspect of the self that is present from birth.

The **me**, according to Mead, is the objective component of the self that emerges as people communicate symbolically and learn to take the role of the other.

Mead's Four Stages of Development: Role Taking

Mead saw the self as developing in four stages of role taking:

1. At first, children learn to use language and other symbols by imitating important people in their lives, such as their mother and father. Mead called such people **significant others**.
2. Next, children pretend to be other people. That is, they use their imaginations to role-play in games such as "house," "school," and "doctor."
3. Then, about the time they reach the age of seven, children learn to play complex games that require them to simultaneously take the role of several other people. In baseball, for example, the infielders need to be aware of the expectations of everyone in the infield. A shortstop may catch a line drive. If she wants to make a double play, she must almost instantly be aware that a runner is trying to reach second base and that the person playing second base expects her to throw there. If she hesitates, she probably cannot execute the double play.

Significant others are people who play important roles in the early socialization experiences of children.

4. Once a child can think in this complex way, she can begin the fourth stage in the development of the self, which involves taking the role of what Mead called the **generalized other**. Years of experience may teach an individual that other people, employing the cultural standards of their society, usually regard her as funny, temperamental, or intelligent. A person's image of these cultural standards and how they are applied to her is what Mead meant by the generalized other.

The **generalized other**, according to Mead, is a person's image of cultural standards and how they apply to him or her.

Since Mead, psychologists interested in the problem of childhood socialization have analyzed how the style, complexity, and abstractness of thinking (or "cognitive skills") develop in distinct stages from infancy to the late teenage years (Piaget and Inhelder, 1969). Other psychologists have analyzed how the ability to think in abstract moral terms develops in stages (Kohlberg, 1981). However, from a sociological point of view, it is important to recognize that the development of cognitive and moral skills is more than just the unfolding of a person's innate characteristics. As you will now see, the structure of a person's society and his or her place in it also influences socialization.

TIME FOR REVIEW

- What makes Cooley's depiction of the "looking-glass self" a *sociological* insight?
- According to Mead, what is the distinction between me and I?

AT THE INTERSECTION OF BIOGRAPHY AND HISTORY

It is true that a newborn baby's interaction with caring adults sets socialization in motion, but socialization does not happen only at the beginning of life. Socialization is a lifelong process. From birth to death, the expectations and behaviour of the people around us change, and in response we change, too.

Earlier we discussed how the self emerges in stages. Yet the crystallization of the self is more than a developmental process. A person's potential is also shaped by the unique slice of history through which he or she lives. Said differently, success and failure occur in part because of circumstances beyond our control. We tend to think that we are masters of our destiny but we are equally a product of our society: what we can become is made possible (or not) because of the historical circumstances in which we live.

Lisa Strohschein, one of this book's co-authors, knows this from her own family history. "My grandfather, James, was born on a farm in Holland in 1915. He married his childhood sweetheart and, in the hope of giving their growing family a better future, they immigrated to Ontario in the 1950s, raising six sons and two daughters. They worked hard on their farm, but to make ends meet, James worked as a carpenter on the side. Four of his sons followed James into carpentry. Two of them capitalized on James's skill as a human calculator. James had the uncanny ability to quickly add, subtract, multiple, and divide numbers in his head—a useful skill on the farm and in carpentry. When the computer age arrived, however, two of his sons put their inherited skill with numbers to a new use. They studied computer science and became very successful in a rapidly growing industry. My grandfather was proud of all of his sons, but I remember him wondering aloud just before he died in 2005 what his own life would have looked like if he had been born in 1955 instead of 1915. It's an interesting sociological question that highlights the importance of history and society in the development of the self. The shifting structures and institutions that compose our society are the scaffolding that enables us to construct our biography and the canvas upon which we create our lives."

BOX 4.1

SOCIOLOGY AT THE MOVIES

THE SECRET LIFE OF WALTER MITTY

In *The Secret Life of Walter Mitty*, starring Ben Stiller, the title character works for *Life* magazine. He enjoys a rich fantasy life, often "zoning out" to rescue damsels in distress. Many of his daydreams focus on Cheryl, who has just started working at the magazine. He repeatedly fails to get her attention, but a pivotal moment shatters Walter's world and sets him on a new course.

To his horror, Walter realizes he may have misplaced a photographic negative that is being considered for the cover of the magazine's last print edition. Under pressure from his superiors to turn over a negative he hasn't even seen, Walter realizes he can admit that he doesn't have it, enduring humiliation and scorn, or try to track down the prize photographer who took the picture in the hope that he somehow forgot to send in the negative.

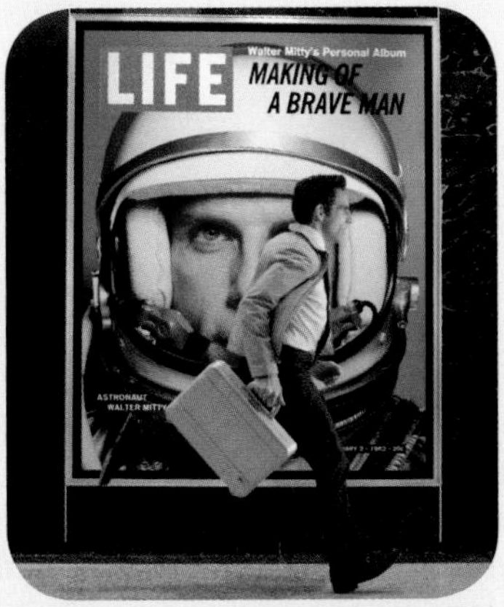

The Kobal Collection at Art Resource, NY

Scene from *The Secret Life of Walter Mitty*.

Impetuously, Walter boards a plane to Greenland, the photographer's last known location. Thus begins a series of escapades that take him to Iceland, Yemen, and Afghanistan, and require him to jump out of a helicopter into the ocean, ward off sharks in the North Sea, and climb the Himalayas. On his journeys, Walter stumbles across forgotten aspects of his life that embolden him. For example, a skateboard reminds him of a lost childhood talent. Jumping on the skateboard allows him to connect with Cheryl's son and paves the way for Walter to pursue a more intimate relationship with Cheryl.

Walter seizes an opportunity that ultimately allows him to discover who he really is. In realizing that the person he longs to be is the person that lies within him, he reconnects with the interrupted trajectory of his life, fashioning for himself a biography that has meaning and purpose. However, because the movie shouts *carpe diem* (seize the day) as *the* solution to a life of drudgery and disappointment, it comes off as extraordinarily non-sociological. How can we discover the full range of opportunities that we can take advantage of? How can we change social structures and public policies to increase the number and variety of opportunities that are open to us and others? These are questions that movies like *The Secret Life of Walter Mitty* have little to say about but that sociology can help to answer.

What is true in this regard for individuals is true for the characteristic way that entire civilizations develop. Contrast ancient China with ancient Greece. In large part because of complex irrigation needs, the rice agriculture of ancient southern China required substantial cooperation among neighbours. It needed to be centrally organized in an elaborate hierarchy within a large state. Harmony and social order were therefore central to ancient Chinese life. Ancient Chinese thinking, in turn, tended to stress the importance of mutual social obligation and consensus rather than debate. Ancient Chinese philosophy focused on the way whole systems, not discrete analytical categories, cause processes and events.

In contrast, the hills and seashores of ancient Greece were suited to small-scale herding and fishing, so ancient Greece was less socially complex than ancient China was, and it was more politically decentralized. Ancient Greek citizens had more personal freedom than the ancient Chinese did. Consequently, the ancient Greek philosophies tended to be analytical, which meant, among other things, that processes and events were viewed as the result of discrete categories rather than whole systems. Markedly different cultures—patterns of behaviour and styles of thinking—grew up on these contrasting cognitive foundations. Civilizational differences depended less on the innate characteristics of the ancient Chinese and Greek peoples than on the structure of their societies (Nisbett et al., 2001; see Box 4.1).

Sociologists who study socialization focus on the following questions: As individuals move through life, how does society shape their identities, attitudes, and behaviour? How do societies differ in the ways they organize life transitions, life stages, and life trajectories? What are the relationships among changing societies, changing biographical patterns, and the subjective experiences of the individual? In the next sections of this chapter, we touch on each of these questions (Shanahan and MacMillan, 2008).

A Sociology of the Life Course

The **life course** refers to the distinct phases of life through which people pass. These stages vary from one society and historical period to another.

Rites of passage are cultural ceremonies that mark the transition from one stage of life to another (e.g., baptisms, confirmations, weddings) or from life to death (funerals).

All individuals pass through distinct stages of life, which, taken together, sociologists call the **life course**. These stages are often marked by **rites of passage**, or rituals signifying the transition from one life stage to another (Fried and Fried, 1980). Among the best-known rites of passage in Canada are baptism, confirmation, the bar mitzvah and bat mitzvah, high-school graduation, college or university convocation, the wedding ceremony, and the funeral. Rituals do not mark all transitions in the life course, however. For example, in Canada people often complain about the "terrible twos," when toddlers defy parental demands in their attempt to gain autonomy. Similarly, when some Canadian men reach the age of about 40, they experience a "mid-life crisis," in which they attempt to defy the passage of time and regain their youth. (It never works.)

Some stages of the life course are established not just by norms but also by law. For example, most societies have laws that stipulate the minimum age for buying tobacco, drinking alcohol, driving a vehicle, and voting. Most societies also have a legal retirement age. Moreover, the duration of each stage of life differs from one society and historical period to the next. For example, there are no universal rules for when a person becomes an adult. In preindustrial societies, adulthood arrived soon after puberty. In Japan, a person becomes an adult at 20. In Canada, adulthood arrives at 18 (the legal voting age and the legal drinking age in some provinces) or 19 (the legal drinking age in other provinces). Until the 1970s, the legal voting age was 21, and the legal drinking age ranged between 18 and 21.

Finally, although some life-course events are universal—birth, puberty, marriage, and death—not all cultures attach the same significance to them. Thus, ritual practices marking these events vary. For example, formal puberty rituals in many preindustrial societies are extremely important because they mark the transition to adult responsibilities. However, adult responsibilities do not immediately follow puberty in industrial and postindustrial societies because of our prolonged period of childhood and adolescence. Therefore, formal puberty rituals are less important in such societies.

Childhood and Adolescence

Even the number of life stages varies historically and across societies. For instance, childhood was a brief stage of development in medieval Europe (Ariès, 1962 [1960]). In contrast, childhood is a prolonged stage of development in rich societies today, and adolescence is a new phase of development that was virtually unknown just a few hundred years ago (Gillis, 1981).

How did childhood and adolescence come to be recognized as distinct stages of life? In preindustrial societies, children were considered small adults. From a young age, they were expected to conform as much as possible to the norms of the adult world. They were put to work as soon as they could contribute to the welfare of their families. This often meant doing chores by the age of 5 and working full-time by the age of 10 or 12. Marriage, and thus the achievement of full adulthood, was common by the age of 15 or 16.

Children in Europe and North America fit this pattern until the late seventeenth century, when the idea emerged of childhood as a distinct stage of life. At that time, the feeling grew among well-to-do Europeans and North Americans that boys should be permitted to play games and receive an education that would allow them to develop the emotional, physical, and intellectual skills they would need as adults. Girls continued to be treated as "little women" (the title of Louisa May Alcott's 1869 novel) until the nineteenth century. Most working-class boys did not enjoy much of a childhood until the twentieth century. Thus, it was only in the last century or so that the idea of childhood as a distinct and prolonged period of life became universal in the West.

The idea of childhood emerged when and where it did because of social necessity and social possibility. Prolonged childhood was necessary in societies that required better-educated adults to do increasingly complex work because childhood gave young people a chance to prepare for adult life. Prolonged childhood was possible in societies where improved hygiene and nutrition allowed most people to live more than 35 years, the average lifespan in Europe in the early seventeenth century. In other words, before the late seventeenth century, most people did not live long enough to permit the luxury of childhood. Moreover, young people faced no social need for a period of extended training and development before the comparatively simple demands of adulthood were thrust upon them.

In general, wealthier and more complex societies whose populations enjoy a long average life expectancy stretch out the pre-adult period of life. For example, we saw that in seventeenth-century Europe, most people reached mature adulthood by the age of about 16. In contrast, in Canada and other postmodern countries, most people are considered to reach mature adulthood only in their early 30s, by which time they have usually completed their formal education, married, and "settled down." Once teenagers were relieved of adult responsibilities, a new term was coined to describe the teenage years: *adolescence*. Subsequently, the term *young adulthood* entered popular usage as an increasingly large number of people in their late teens, 20s, and early 30s delayed marriage to attend university.

Age Cohort

As you pass through the life course, you learn new patterns of behaviour that are common to people about the same age as you. Sociologically speaking, a category of people born in the same range of years is called an **age cohort**. For example, all Canadians born between 1980 and 1989 form an age cohort. **Age roles** are patterns of behaviour that we expect of people in different age cohorts. Age roles also form an important part of our sense of self and others (Riley, Foner, and Waring, 1988). As we pass through the stages of the life course, we assume different age roles. To put it simply, a child is supposed to act like a child, an older person like an older person. We may see a 5-year-old dressed in a suit and think it cute but look askance at a lone 50-year-old on a merry-go-round. "Act your age" is a demand that we make when people of any age do not conform to their age roles. Many age roles are informally known by character types, such as "the rebellious teenager" and "the wise old woman." We formalize some age roles by law. For instance, establishing a minimum age for smoking, drinking, driving, and voting formalizes certain aspects of the adolescent and adult roles.

An **age cohort** is a category of people born in the same range of years.

Age roles are norms and expectations about the behaviour of people in different age cohorts.

We find it natural that children in the same age cohort, such as preschoolers in a park, should play together or that people of similar age cluster together at parties. Conversely, many people view romance and marriage between people who are widely separated by age to be problematic and even repulsive.

At the same time, no two cohorts have the same experience as they pass through the age structure. As the members of a cohort move through a given range of years, they both change and are changed by their experiences.

Generation

A **generation** is a special type of age cohort. Many people think of a generation as people born within a 15- to 30-year span. Sociologists, however, usually define generation more narrowly. From a sociological point of view, a generation comprises members of an age cohort who have unique and formative experiences during their youth. Age cohorts are statistically convenient categories, but members of a generation form a group with a collective identity and shared values.

A **generation** is an age cohort that shares unique formative experiences during the first few decades of life, which help to shape a collective identity and set of values.

Not all cohorts can become a generation. Generations are most likely to form during times of rapid social change. When society is in upheaval, young people seeking to find their way in the world can no longer rely on the predictable patterns of the past but must carve out new trails. Revolutionary movements, whether in politics or the arts, are often led by members of a young generation who aggressively displace the ideas of an older generation (Eisenstadt, 1956; Mannheim, 1952).

Canada has five identifiable generations today. In describing them, we recognize that generations tend to be clearest at their centre and fuzzier at their boundaries. The generation that is currently passing away and whose experiences are increasingly known only through history books is often called "the greatest generation." Born between the early 1900s and 1928, members of this generation were at least 88 years old in 2016. They are called the greatest generation because they came of age during the Great Depression (1929–39) and then went on to endure World War II (1939–45). By rising to the formidable challenges of these two events, the greatest generation laid the groundwork for economic prosperity and stability in Canada in the decades ahead.

The greatest generation was followed by "the silent generation," whose members became the parents of Canada's most well-known generation, the "baby boomers." Members of the silent generation were born between 1929 and 1945; in 2016, they were between the ages of 71 and 87. The silent generation is sometimes called the traditionalist generation because of their shared values of hard work, thriftiness, and conformity. Occasionally, they are referred to as the lucky generation because they were old enough to be shaped by the events of World War II, but too young to have experienced combat. Craving security, the silent generation is risk-averse, patriotic, and community-minded. As a generation, its chief shortcoming is that it was not especially innovative. Its members often felt threatened by change.

As soldiers returned home after World War II and wanted to settle down to family life, Canada experienced a baby boom that lasted until the mid-1960s. During this period, approximately 400 000 children were born each year. In 2016, baby boomers between the ages of 51 and 70 made up 29 percent of Canada's population (Statistics Canada, 2012j). When this cohort came of age in the 1960s and 1970s, they turned the stolid, comfortable world of their parents upside down. Baby boomers were the leading edge of a cultural revolution. They were bound together by the war in Vietnam, Trudeaumania, Canada's centenary, and popular music (the songs of the Beatles, the Rolling Stones, and the Guess Who). Baby boomers have been characterized as idealistic, tolerant, and creative. In the workplace, they are highly competitive, independent, and innovative. Their main weakness is the need for instant gratification. Because of their relative greed and self-absorption, baby boomers are often vilified for leaving massive debt for future generations (Higgs and Gilleard, 2010).

"Generation X" followed the baby boomers. Born between 1966 and 1981, they were between 35 and 50 years old in 2016. Members of Generation X faced a period of relatively slow economic growth and a job market glutted by the baby boomers. Consequently, many of them resented having to take so-called McJobs when they entered the labour force. Vancouver's Douglas Coupland, the novelist who invented the term Generation X, cuttingly defined a McJob as a "low pay, low-prestige, low-dignity, low-benefit, no-future job in the service sector. Frequently considered a satisfying career choice by people who have never held one" (Coupland, 1991: 5). Fortunately, as Gen Xers settled into their careers, their lives eventually improved.

As a group, Gen Xers tend to be skeptical, individualistic, adept with technology, and conservative with money (Gordinier, 2008; Watson, 2013). They are entrepreneurial but desire work–life balance. Moreover, they have little loyalty to their employer: if they see a better job, they will switch. Their lack of loyalty is sometimes seen as a liability, as is their difficulty in working collaboratively.

Finally, the Millennials, born after 1982, are so named because they came of age at the beginning of the twenty-first century (Howe and Strauss, 2009). They are also sometimes referred to as Generation Y, Generation Next, or Generation Me. Because of the growing number of immigrants to Canada who come from around the world, Millennials are more ethnically diverse than are previous generations of Canadians. They are also on track to be the most educated generation in history. But don't be misled into thinking that being well educated has helped them get ahead. The Great Recession (2008–09) put a damper on many of their career aspirations. Today, Millennials are likely to be struggling to fit into the labour market, living with their parents, and uncertain when they will finally make it on their own.

Although their parents were sometimes overly involved in their lives, Millennials are emotionally close to their parents (Winograd and Hais, 2011). Millennials are environmentally conscious, have an unshakable faith that they can make a positive

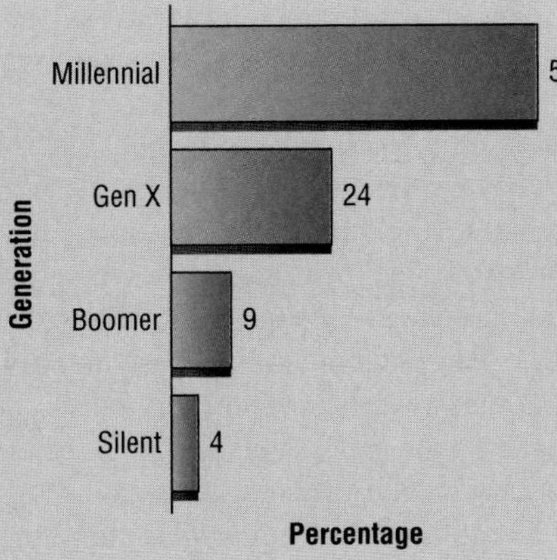

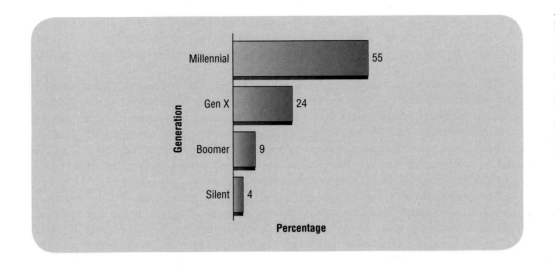

FIGURE 4.1
Percentage of Americans who have shared a selfie on a social media site

Source: Pew Research Center. 2014. "Millennials in Adulthood: Detached from Institutions, Networked with Friends." Washington, DC: Author. (page 6).

difference in their world, and are always on the search for new experiences (Pew Research Center, 2014). They are passionate and open with their opinions. They value teamwork, and they take technological advances such as the Internet for granted. As Figure 4.1 illustrates, Millennials in the United States are far more comfortable posting pictures of themselves on social media than are members of older generations. (There is no Canadian data on the subject but we may safely assume that Canadian trends probably are similar.) Moreover, many Millennials have never sent a letter by Canada Post—the 15-year-old daughter of one of this textbook's authors thought that "snail mail" meant email!

Do you consider yourself a Millennial? You may find that you share some of the values that define Millennials, but it is equally likely that a new generation is on the verge of forming. If so, what values and experiences do you think this new generation will share?

TIME FOR REVIEW

- In what ways do the number and duration of life stages vary across societies and historical periods?
- What transforms a cohort into a generation?

HOW SOCIALIZATION WORKS

Some people are passive, others aggressive. Some are serious, others humorous. Some are selfish, others altruistic. It is instructive to ask how socialization contributes to such wide variation in character type.

A detailed answer to this question is complex, but the basic principles are not: People are surrounded and influenced by real or imagined others, who constitute a person's **social environment**. To satisfy individual needs and interests, every person needs to adapt to his or her environment. **Adaptation** involves arranging one's actions to maximize the degree to which an environment satisfies one's needs and interests.

The **social environment** is composed of the real or imagined others to whom individuals must adapt to satisfy their own needs and interests.

Adaptation is the process of changing one's actions to maximize the degree to which an environment satisfies one's needs and interests.

The challenge of learning to ride a bicycle illustrates these concepts. If a girl wants to ride a bicycle, she cannot act any way she likes. To be successful, she must adjust her behaviour to satisfy the characteristics of the physical environment. In this case, the dominant environmental characteristic is gravity. On her first attempt, the novice cyclist will do her best, but her adaptive behaviour will likely be imperfect. As a result, the environment provides feedback in the form of skinned knees, scraped hands, and bruised legs. These are all signals that the environment is not cooperating. To gain cooperation and satisfy her bike-riding interests, the girl must learn how to balance herself on the bicycle. She does, and eventually learns the role of cyclist.

The same process occurs in social environments, each of which has distinctive requirements. Different types of families make different kinds of demands on their children. Different kinds of schools have distinctive expectations of students. Neighbourhood environments differ, and so do friendship groups and every other social setting. Each of these environments shapes its participants through socialization. In an abusive family, the adaptive strategies that children learn, and the kind of persons they become, differ from what other children learn and become in a warm, supportive family.

As these examples make clear, socialization is fundamentally an evolutionary process. Simply stated, the steps in the process are as follows: (1) In any environment, a person acts on the basis of his or her existing personal characteristics and interests. (2) The environment responds to the person's actions more or less cooperatively. (3) The environmental response shapes the individual's conduct by either reinforcing existing patterns (cooperation) or encouraging change (resistance). In short, individual character leads to actions to which environments respond selectively. When environments respond cooperatively—when they satisfy individual needs—the rewards reinforce existing individual characteristics. When environments frustrate individual needs, change (learning) is encouraged.

When this socialization process occurs in infants and children, the results are profound because the immediate social environment (the family) is so demanding and powerful relative to the child's resources. As children grow older and become more fully socialized, they have a wider range of adaptive options at their disposal. This means their characters are more stable, since they are more skilled at getting environments to cooperate. Still, at all stages of life, dramatic resocialization is possible if the social environment is sufficiently imposing. For example, cults can transform recruits into people who are unrecognizable to their former friends and family members by employing the same socialization principles that transform participants in *The Biggest Loser*.

Theories and Agents of Socialization

Functionalists emphasize how socialization helps to maintain orderly social relations. They also play down the freedom of choice that individuals enjoy in the socialization process. Conflict and feminist theorists typically stress the discord based on class, gender, and other divisions that is inherent in socialization and that sometimes leads to social change. Symbolic interactionists highlight the creativity of individuals in attaching meaning to their social surroundings. They focus on the many ways in which we often step outside of, and modify, the values and roles that authorities try to teach us. Socialization—whether it maintains order or engenders conflict, shapes us or allow us to shape it—operates through a variety of social institutions, including families, schools, peer groups, and, in modern times, the mass media. We now consider how these various "agents of socialization" work. As we do so, please take careful note of the functionalist, conflict, symbolic interactionist, and feminist interpretations embedded in our discussion.

Families

Primary socialization is the process of acquiring the basic skills needed to function in society during childhood. Primary socialization usually takes place in a family.

The family is the most important agent of **primary socialization**, the process of mastering the basic skills required to function in society during childhood. The family is well suited to providing the kind of careful, intimate attention required for primary socialization. It is a small group, its members are in frequent face-to-face contact, and most parents love their children and are highly motivated to care for them. These characteristics make most families ideal for teaching small children everything from language to their place in the world.

The family into which you are born also exerts an *enduring* influence over the course of your life. Consider the long-term effect of the family's religious atmosphere. Research shows that the main way religious groups grow is by recruiting and retaining children whose parents already belong to the group (Bibby, 2001: 115). Parents are the key source of their children's religious identification throughout life. Even Canadians who say they have abandoned the religious faith of their parents—or claim to have no religious identification—typically readopt the religious identities of their parents when they participate in rites of passage, such as marriage and baptism (Bibby, 2001: 200).

ONOKY - Fabrice LEROUGE/Getty Images

As the first major agent of socialization, families help children to learn basic skills and internalize the values of their society.

Note, however, that the socialization function of the family was more pronounced a century ago, partly because adult family members were more readily available for child care than they are today. As industry grew, families left farming for city work in factories and offices. Especially after the 1950s, many women needed to work outside the home for a wage to maintain an adequate standard of living for their families. Fathers partially compensated by spending more time with their children. However, because divorce rates are higher now than in the 1950s and many fathers have less contact with their children after divorce, children see less of their fathers on average now than they did half a century ago. Because of these developments, child care—and therefore child socialization—became a big social problem.

Schools: Functions and Conflicts

For children over the age of 5, the child-care problem was partly resolved by the growth of the public school system, which was increasingly responsible for **secondary socialization**, or socialization outside the family after childhood. Industry needed better-trained and educated employees. In response, by the early twentieth century, Canadian provinces passed laws prescribing school attendance. In 2011, 87 percent of adult Canadians had completed high school, and 64 percent had postsecondary qualifications (Statistics Canada, 2013c). Canadians are among the most highly educated people in the world.

Secondary socialization is socialization outside the family after childhood.

Instructing students in academic and vocational subjects is just one part of the school's job. In addition, a **hidden curriculum** teaches students what will be expected of them in the larger society once they graduate; more generally, it teaches them how to be "good citizens."

The **hidden curriculum** in school involves teaching obedience to authority and conformity to cultural norms.

What is the content of the hidden curriculum? In the family, children tend to be evaluated on the basis of personal and emotional criteria. As students, however, they are led to believe that they are evaluated solely on the basis of their performance on impersonal tests. They are told that similar criteria will be used to evaluate them in the work world. The lesson is only partly true. As you will see in Chapters 8 (Social Stratification), 10 (Race and Ethnicity), 11 (Sexualities and Gender Stratification), and 17 (Education), it is not just performance but also class, gender, sexual orientation, and racial criteria that help determine success in school and in the work world. But the accuracy of the lesson is not the issue here. The important point is that the hidden curriculum has done its job if it convinces students that they are judged on the basis of performance alone. Similarly, a successful hidden curriculum teaches students punctuality, respect for authority, the importance of competition in leading to excellent performance, and other conformist behaviours and beliefs that are expected of good citizens, conventionally defined.

The idea of the hidden curriculum was first proposed by conflict theorists, who see an ongoing struggle between privileged and disadvantaged groups whenever they probe beneath the surface of social life (Willis, 1984 [1977]). Their research highlights that many students from disadvantaged backgrounds struggle with the hidden curriculum. Disproportionate numbers reject the hidden curriculum because it is poorly aligned with lessons they have already internalized—that the privileged always end up on top and that conventionally good behaviour will get them nowhere. Consequently, students from disadvantaged backgrounds often do poorly in school and eventually enter the work world near the bottom of the socioeconomic hierarchy. Paradoxically, the resistance of underprivileged students to the hidden curriculum helps to sustain the overall structure of society, with its privileges and disadvantages.

Learning disciplined work habits is an important part of the socialization that takes place in schools.

Monkey Business Images/Shutterstock.com

Symbolic Interactionism and the Self-Fulfilling Prophecy

The **Thomas theorem** states, "Situations we define as real become real in their consequences."

A **self-fulfilling prophecy** is an expectation that helps bring about what it predicts.

Early in the twentieth century, symbolic interactionists proposed the **Thomas theorem**, which holds that "situations we define as real become real in their consequences" (Thomas, 1966 [1931]: 301). They also developed the closely related idea of the **self-fulfilling prophecy**, an expectation that helps to cause what it predicts. Our analysis of the hidden curriculum suggests that the expectations of working-class and racial-minority students often act as self-fulfilling prophecies. Expecting to achieve little if they play by the rules, they reject the rules and so achieve little.

Self-fulfilling prophecies can also affect teachers. In one famous study, two researchers informed teachers in a primary school that they would administer a special test to the pupils to predict intellectual "blooming." In fact, the test was just a standard IQ test. After the test, the researchers told the teachers which students they could expect to become high achievers and which they could expect to become low achievers. In fact, the researchers randomly assigned pupils to the two groups. At the end of the year, the researchers repeated the IQ test. They found that the students singled out as high achievers scored significantly higher than those singled out as low achievers. Since the only difference between the two groups of students was that teachers expected one group to do well and the other to do poorly, the researchers concluded that teachers' expectations alone influenced students' performance (Rosenthal and Jacobson, 1968). The clear implication of this research is that if a teacher believes that children living in poverty or children who are members of minority groups are likely to do poorly in school, chances are they will. This relationship has been borne out in subsequent research. Teachers' lowered expectations for children living in poverty and children who are members of minority groups predict educational outcomes fairly well (Becker, 2013; Rubie-Davis, Hattie, and Hamilton, 2006).

A person's **peer group** comprises people who are about the same age and of similar status as the individual. The peer group acts as an agent of socialization.

Peer Groups

Status refers to a recognized social position an individual can occupy.

Like schools, peer groups are agents of socialization whose importance grew in the twentieth century. A **peer group** consists of individuals who are not necessarily friends but who are about the same age and of similar status. (**Status** refers to a recognized social position an individual can occupy.) Peer groups help children and adolescents separate from their families and develop independent sources of identity. They are especially influential over such lifestyle issues as appearance, social activities, and dating. In fact, from middle childhood through adolescence, the peer group is often a dominant socializing agent.

As you have probably learned from experience, conflict often erupts between the values promoted by the family and those promoted by the adolescent peer group. Adolescent peer groups are controlled by youth, and through them young people begin to develop their own identities. They do this by rejecting some parental values, experimenting with new elements of culture, and engaging in various forms of rebellious behaviour. In contrast, families are controlled by parents and represent the values of childhood. Under these circumstances, some issues are likely to become points of conflict between the generations, among them, hair and dress styles; music; curfews; tobacco, drug, and alcohol use; and political views.

We should not, however, overstate the significance of adolescent–parent conflict. For one thing, the conflict is usually temporary. Once adolescents mature, the family exerts a more enduring influence on many important issues. Research shows that families have more influence than peer groups do on the educational aspirations and the political, social, and religious preferences of adolescents and university students (Crosnoe and Johnson, 2011; Simons-Morton and Chen, 2009).

A second reason not to exaggerate the extent of adolescent–parent discord is that peer groups are not just sources of conflict. They also help *integrate* young people into the larger society. A study of preadolescent children in a small North American city illustrates the point. Over eight years, sociologists Patricia and Peter Adler conducted in-depth interviews with school children between the ages of 8 and 11. The children lived in a well-to-do community comprising about 80 000 whites and 10 000 racial minority-group members (Adler and Adler, 1998). In each school the Adlers visited, they found a system of cliques arranged in a strict hierarchy, much like the arrangement of classes and racial groups in adult society. In schools with a substantial number of students who were members of a visible minority, cliques were divided by race. The cliques comprising members of a visible minority were usually less popular than the white cliques were. In all schools, the most popular boys were highly successful in competitive and aggressive, achievement-oriented activities, especially athletics. The most popular girls came from well-to-do and permissive families. One of the main bases of their popularity was that they had the means and the opportunity to participate in the most interesting social activities, ranging from skiing to late-night parties. Physical attractiveness was also an important basis of girls' popularity. Thus, elementary-school peer groups prepared these youngsters for the class and racial inequalities of the adult world and the gender-specific criteria that would often be used to evaluate them as adults, such as competitiveness in the case of boys and physical attractiveness in the case of girls. (For more on gender socialization, see the discussion of the mass media below and Chapter 11, Sexualities and Gender Stratification.) What we learn from this research is that peer groups function not only to help adolescents form an independent identity by separating them from their families but also to teach them how to adapt to the ways of the larger society.

The Mass Media

Like the school and the peer group, the mass media have become increasingly important socializing agents in the twenty-first century. The mass media include television, radio, movies, videos, music downloads, the Internet, newspapers, magazines, and books.

The fastest-growing mass medium is the Internet. Worldwide, the number of Internet users jumped from just 36 million in 1996 to more than 2.4 billion in 2012 (Internet World Statistics, 2013b). The Internet has begun to replace television as the medium that Canadians spend the most amount of time using on a daily basis. However, this fact overlooks a profound change in user behaviour. Canadians multi-task: increasingly, they surf the Internet and chat online while they watch TV. Young people, in particular, use social media sites such as Facebook and Twitter to exchange comments as they watch TV shows. These changing habits force advertisers to find new ways of engaging their increasingly distracted audience.

BOX 4.2

SOCIAL POLICY: WHAT DO YOU THINK?

CYBER-BULLYING

Every schoolyard, it seems, has a bully, someone who picks on smaller children by pushing them around and calling them names. Less directly, school bullying also occurs when one scrawls messages on toilet stalls to ruin a person's reputation. But, in the age of the Internet, where instant messaging and social media websites allow for instant and constant communication, bullying takes on a whole new meaning. The phenomenon has grown so quickly that it has garnered its own label: cyber-bullying. **Cyber-bullying** is the use of electronic communications technology to threaten, harass, embarrass, or socially exclude others.

More than 30 percent of Canadian middle- and high-school students report having been either the cyber-bully or a victim of cyber-bullying over a three-month period (Mishna et al., 2012).

MLADEN ANTONOV/AFP/Getty Images

Screenshot from a video posted by Amanda Todd in 2012. Four weeks after posting this video, she committed suicide.

Cyber-bullying is an increasing concern to a growing number of educators, law enforcement officers, and legislators. The current laws and preventive policies appear to be poorly equipped to deal with the unique aspects of cyber-bullying. Consider, for example, the story of Amanda Todd, a teenage girl who killed herself after sexually explicit photos of her were distributed to her classmates. Her parents were initially unable to convince the authorities to treat cyber-bullying as a crime. However, the attention paid to her case, and others like hers, resulted in national ad campaigns to stop cyber-bullying and proposed changes to the law that would criminalize distributing intimate pictures without the consent of the photographed person.

While these measures may have an effect on cyber-bullying, experts point out that cyber-bullying differs from traditional bullying in several respects. In traditional forms of bullying, it is relatively simple to identify the aggressor and the victim. But this is not the case with cyber-bullying. Victims can just as easily become aggressors themselves. In fact, victims appear to be much more comfortable—and capable—of retaliating to aggressive acts online than they ever would be in person (Law et al., 2012). In addition, traditional forms of bullying have a relatively small audience: those who are bystanders in the playground or who read the comments on the bathroom wall. When bullying victims leave the school property, they are generally able to shed their identity as a victim. In contrast, when messages or pictures are posted online, the audience is limitless. No one can control what happens after images or messages are posted online: they are visible in cyberspace in perpetuity (Sticca and Perren, 2013). Consequently, for the victim, no place feels safe.

What do you think? Why might cyber-bullying be more harmful than traditional forms of bullying are? Is it important to find ways to control how people communicate with one another over the Internet? Are stronger laws needed to police the spreading of hateful messages on the Internet? Or would laws that regulate Internet communications excessively restrict personal freedom?

One strategy is to invite television viewers to access additional content online, blurring the boundaries between these two mass media.

Irrespective of whether they are simultaneously online, Canadians watch about four hours of television daily on average (Television Bureau of Canada, 2014). Low-income Canadians watch more TV than high-income earners do, men watch more than women do, people over age 54 watch more than younger Canadians do, and those living in the North watch more than those in other regions do.

Cyber-bullying is the use of electronic communications technology to threaten, harass, embarrass or socially exclude others.

Canadians increasingly live in a world of continuous connectivity (Turkle, 2011). There are benefits to be sure. Parents can better track their children's whereabouts. We can share pictures of our vacation while still on vacation. And if you've ever wondered what song was playing on the mall audio system, an app will identify it after just a few phrases and link you to a website where you can buy it. However, researchers wonder whether continuous connectivity comes at a cost. What does it mean that there is almost no possibility of being truly alone or unavailable? How does one take back a comment or a picture that was posted in haste but that can be seen immediately by others and re-posted many times over? As Box 4.2 illustrates, these issues are particularly relevant in the case of cyber-bullying.

The Mass Media and the Feminist Approach to Socialization

The mass media expose individuals to influences that shape their ideas, attitudes, expectations, values, and behaviour. This is especially true for children and adolescents. Although people are to some extent free to choose socialization influences from the mass media, they choose some influences more often than others. Specifically, they tend to choose influences that are more pervasive, fit existing cultural standards, and are made especially appealing by those who control the mass media. We can illustrate this fact by considering how feminist sociologists analyze gender roles. **Gender roles** are widely shared expectations about how males and females are supposed to act. These expectations are of special interest to feminist sociologists, who claim that people are not born knowing how to express masculinity and femininity in conventional ways. Instead, say feminist sociologists, people *learn* gender roles, partly through the mass media.

Gender roles are the set of behaviours associated with widely shared expectations about how males and females are supposed to act.

The learning of gender roles through the mass media begins when small children see that only a kiss from Prince Charming will save Snow White from eternal sleep. Here is an early lesson about who can expect to be passive and who potent. The lesson continues in magazines, romance novels, television, advertisements, music, and the Internet. For example, a central theme in Harlequin romance novels (the world's top sellers in this genre, based in Toronto) is the transformation of women's bodies into objects for men's pleasure. In the typical Harlequin romance, men are the sexual aggressors. They are typically more experienced and promiscuous than the women are. Similarly, *Fifty Shades of Grey* features a young college graduate who enters into a sexual relationship with a wealthy young man who is dominant, while she is submissive. The bestselling *Twilight* trilogy starts with a teenage girl who meets and falls under the spell of a mysterious boy who is actually a 104-year-old vampire. The common theme in all of these novels is that females are sexually inexperienced and need strong, skillful men to fulfill them sexually.

People do not passively accept messages about appropriate gender roles. They often interpret them in unique ways and sometimes resist them. For the most part, however, people try to develop skills that will help them perform conventional gender roles (Eagly and Wood, 1999: 412–13). Of course, conventions change. It is important to note in this regard that what children learn about femininity and masculinity today is less sexist than what they learned just a few generations ago. For example, comparing *Snow White and the Seven Dwarfs* (1937) and *Cinderella* (1950) with *Tangled* (2010) and *Tangled Ever After* (2012), we see immediately that children going to Disney movies today are sometimes presented with more assertive and heroic female role models than the passive heroines of

Richard Levine / Alamy

Harlequin romance books

previous generations. However, the amount of change in gender socialization should not be exaggerated. *Cinderella* and *Snow White* are still popular movies. Moreover, for every *Tangled* there is a *Little Mermaid* (1989), a movie that simply modernizes old themes about female passivity and male conquest.

As the learning of gender roles through the mass media suggests, not all media influences are created equal. We may be free to choose which media messages influence us, but most people are inclined to choose the messages that are most widespread, most closely aligned with existing cultural standards, and made most enticing by the mass media. In the case of gender roles, these messages usually support conventional expectations about how males and females are supposed to act.

Resocialization and Total Institutions

Resocialization occurs when powerful socializing agents deliberately cause rapid change in a person's values, roles, and self-conception, sometimes against a person's will.

An **initiation rite** is a ritual that signifies a person's transition from one group to another and ensures his or her loyalty to the new group.

Total institutions are settings in which people are isolated from the larger society and under the strict control and constant supervision of a specialized staff.

In concluding our discussion of socialization agents, we must highlight the importance of **resocialization** in contributing to the lifelong process of social learning. Resocialization takes place when powerful socializing agents deliberately cause rapid change in people's values, roles, and self-conception, sometimes against their will.

You can see resocialization at work in the ceremonies that are staged when someone joins a fraternity, a sorority, a sports team, or a religious order. Such a ceremony, or **initiation rite**, signifies the transition of the individual from one group to another and ensures his or her loyalty to the new group. Initiation rites require new recruits to abandon old self-perceptions and assume new identities. Typically, these rites comprise a three-stage ceremony involving (1) separation from the old status and identity (ritual rejection); (2) degradation, disorientation, and stress (ritual death); and (3) acceptance of the new group culture and status (ritual rebirth).

Much resocialization takes place in what Erving Goffman (1961) called **total institutions**. Total institutions are settings in which people are isolated from the larger society and under the strict control and constant supervision of a specialized staff. Asylums and prisons are examples of total institutions. Because of the "pressure cooker" atmosphere in such institutions, resocialization in total institutions is often rapid and thorough, even in the absence of initiation rites.

A famous failed experiment illustrates the immense resocializing capacity of total institutions (Haney, Banks, and Zimbardo, 1973; Zimbardo, 1972). In the early 1970s, a group of researchers created their own mock prison in what was known as the Stanford prison experiment (Zimbardo, 2008). They paid about two dozen male volunteers to act as guards and inmates. The volunteers were mature, emotionally stable, intelligent university students from middle-class homes in the United States and Canada. None had a criminal record. By the flip of a coin, half the volunteers were designated prisoners, the other half guards. The guards made up their own rules for maintaining order in the mock prison. The prisoners were picked up by city police officers in a squad car, searched, handcuffed, fingerprinted, booked at the police station, and taken blindfolded to the mock prison. At the mock prison, each prisoner was stripped, deloused, put into a uniform, given a number, and placed in a cell with two other inmates.

To better understand what it means to be a prisoner or a prison guard, the researchers intended to observe and record social interaction in the mock prison for two weeks. However, they were forced to end the experiment abruptly after only six days because they were frightened by what they witnessed. In less than a week, the prisoners and prison guards could no longer tell the difference between the roles they were playing and their "real" selves. Much of the socialization these young men had undergone over a period of about 20 years had been quickly suspended.

About a third of the guards began to treat the prisoners like despicable animals, taking pleasure in cruelty. Even the guards who were regarded by the prisoners as tough but fair stopped short of interfering in the tyrannical and arbitrary use of power by the most sadistic guards.

All the prisoners became servile and dehumanized, thinking only about survival, escape, and their growing hatred of the guards. Had they been thinking as university students, they could have walked out of the experiment at any time. Some of the prisoners did, in fact, beg for parole. However, by the fifth day of the experiment, they were so programmed to think of themselves as prisoners that they returned docilely to their cells when their request for parole was denied.

The Stanford prison experiment suggests that your sense of self and the roles you play are not as fixed as you may think. Radically alter your social setting and, like the university students in the experiment, your self-conception and patterned behaviour are also likely to change. Such change is most evident among people undergoing resocialization in total institutions. However, the sociological eye is able to observe the flexibility of the self in all social settings, including those that greet the individual in adult life.

TIME FOR REVIEW

- How does a conflict theorist view socialization?
- How does the hidden curriculum influence successful school performance?
- What is a self-fulfilling prophecy?
- What messages do the mass media send about appropriate roles for men and women?
- Why are total institutions ideal for resocialization?

SOCIALIZATION AND THE FLEXIBLE SELF

The development of the self is a lifelong process. When young adults enter a profession or get married, they must learn new occupational or family roles. Retirement and old age present an entirely new set of challenges. Giving up a job, seeing children leave home and start their own families, and losing a spouse and close friends—all these changes later in life require that people think of themselves in new ways and redefine who they are. Many new roles are predictable. To help us learn them we often engage in **anticipatory socialization**, which involves beginning to take on the norms and behaviours of the roles to which we aspire. (Think of 15-year-old fans of *Girls* learning from the TV show what it might mean to be a young adult.) Other new roles are unpredictable. You might unexpectedly fall in love and marry someone from a different ethnic, racial, or religious group. You might experience a sudden and difficult transition from peace to war. If so, you will need to learn new roles and adopt new cultural values, or at least modify your old ones. Even in adulthood, then, the self remains flexible.

Anticipatory socialization involves taking on the norms and behaviours of the role to which we aspire.

Today, people's identities change faster, more often, and more completely than they did just a few decades ago. One factor contributing to the growing flexibility of the self is globalization. As we saw in Chapter 3 (Culture), people are now less obliged to accept the culture into which they are born. Because of globalization, they are freer to combine elements of culture from a wide variety of historical periods and geographical settings.

A second factor that increases our freedom to design our selves is our growing ability to fashion new bodies from old. People have always defined themselves partly in terms of their bodies; your self-conception is influenced by whether you're a man or a woman, tall or short, healthy or ill, conventionally attractive or plain. However, our bodies were once fixed by nature. People could do nothing to change the fact that they were born with certain features and grew older at a certain rate.

Now, however, you can change your body, and therefore your self-conception, radically and virtually at will—if, that is, you can afford it. Bodybuilding, aerobic exercise, and weight-reduction regimens are more popular than ever. Plastic surgery allows people to buy new breasts, noses, lips, eyelids, and hair—and to remove unwanted fat, skin, and hair from various parts of their bodies. Although we lack Canadian data on the subject, American trends are probably similar: in 2013, nearly 1.7 million Americans underwent cosmetic surgery, 5.7 times as many as in 1992. Another 13.4 million Americans underwent collagen, Botox, and other "minimally invasive" procedures, 195 times as many as in 1992 (American Society of Plastic Surgeons, 2013). Other body-altering procedures include sex-change operations and organ transplants. At any given time, more than 50 000 North Americans are waiting for a replacement organ. Brisk, illegal international trade in human hearts, lungs, kidneys, livers, and eyes enables well-to-do people to enhance and extend their lives (Cohen, 2013; Rothman, 1998). Modern bionics makes it possible to wire realistic prosthetic limbs into brain circuitry that, with practice, can function almost like the original limbs. Technologies are also being developed to restore vision and hearing using cameras, microphones, and microscopic electrodes. As these examples illustrate, in recent decades, science and technology have introduced many exciting opportunities for changing our bodies, and therefore our self-conceptions (see Box 4.3).

BOX 4.3

SOCIOLOGY ON THE TUBE

SELF-TRANSFORMATION: EXTREME MAKEOVER AND ITS SPINOFFS

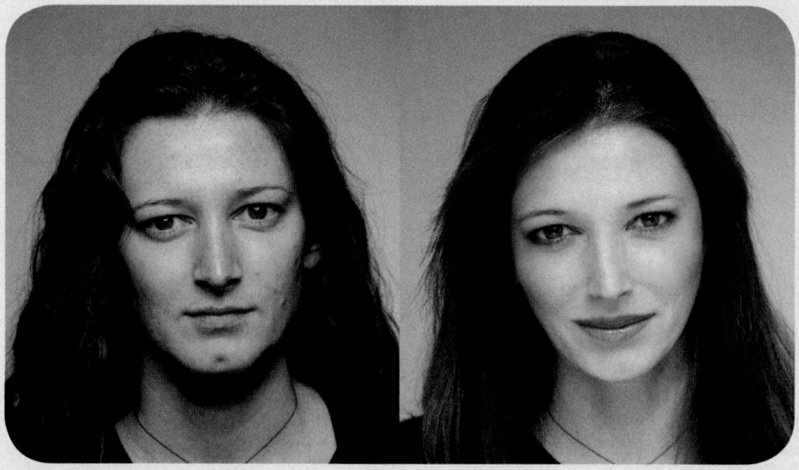

Rubberball/Mark Andersen/Getty Images

Before and after photos, *Extreme Makeover*

In a typical episode of *Extreme Makeover*, a team comprising a plastic surgeon, a personal trainer, a hairdresser, and a wardrobe consultant refashion a woman's exterior. The cameras record the woman's doubts and suffering but also her resilience and determination. In the end, when she sees the finished product, her self-esteem skyrockets, and her family and friends wax ecstatic over her Cinderella transformation.

Extreme Makeover first aired in 2002. Since then, it has bred a host of copycats proposing quick fixes to other life problems. Each adheres to strict conventions about what is good, beautiful, and valuable. Each seeks to convince people that the key to a happy interior life involves quickly and radically transforming exterior aspects of one's self, according to set patterns. Such shows as *Extreme Makeover: Home Edition*, *The Apprentice*, *The Bachelor*, and *Say Yes to the Dress* offer fast solutions to problems of housing, career, intimate relations, and wardrobe, respectively. Canadian variants of many of these shows are available for the patriotic viewer.

Of course, almost every adult wants to be attractive and have a good job, a long-lasting intimate relationship with another adult, and material comforts. However, shows such as those listed earlier teach viewers that all we need to be happy is to achieve commercially manufactured ideas of what constitutes the perfect body, face, career, partner, house, and wardrobe. Said differently, their common message is that the surest path to self-awareness and self-fulfillment involves accepting images that others have generated as ideals.

Mead would say these shows make it seem as if all worthwhile self-development comes from the "me"—the objectifications supplied, in this case, largely by marketing experts—not from thoughtful exploration of the creative "I." The tough questions posed by ancient Greek philosophy—Who am I? What do I need to make me happy?—have no relevance in this context. Arguably, *Extreme Makeover* and its spinoffs turn answers to these difficult questions into instant and, for most people, unrealistic solutions focusing on the commercial images others provide. They teach us nothing about how to know ourselves and, by doing so, how to find our own way to living happily.

Source: Weber, Brenda R. and Karen W. Tice. 2009. "Are You Finally Comfortable in Your Own Skin?" *Genders* 49. http://www.genders.org/g49/g49_webertice.html (retrieved 2 May 2014).

Self-Identity and the Internet

Further complicating the process of identity formation today is the growth of the Internet. In the 1980s and early 1990s, most observers believed that social interaction by means of computer would involve only the exchange of information between individuals. They were wrong. Computer-assisted social interaction can profoundly affect how people think of themselves (Brym and Lenton, 2001; Haythornthwaite and Wellman, 2002).

Internet users interact socially by exchanging text, images, and sound via email, instant messaging, Internet phone, Facebook, Twitter, videoconferencing, computer-assisted work groups, online dating services, and so on. In the process, they often form **virtual communities**. Virtual communities are associations of people scattered across the country or the planet, who communicate via computer about subjects of common interest.

Virtual communities are associations of people scattered across the country, continent, or planet who communicate via computer about a subject of common interest.

Because virtual communities allow interaction using concealed identities, people are free to assume new identities and are encouraged to discover aspects of themselves they were formerly unaware of. In virtual communities, shy people can become bold; normally assertive people can become voyeurs; older people can become young; straight people can become gay; women can become men, and vice-versa (Turkle, 1995). Experience on the Internet thus reinforces our main point: in recent decades, the self has become increasingly flexible, and people are now freer than ever to shape their selves as they choose.

TIME FOR REVIEW

- In what ways have globalization, various medical advances, and the pervasiveness of the Internet led to new, more flexible selves?

SUMMARY

1. Why is social interaction necessary to unleash human potential?
   Studies show that children raised in extreme isolation do not develop normally. They often lack the intellectual and emotional capacity of children raised in conventional environments. Various theories suggest that socialization leads to the formation of self. Freud argued that a self-image begins to emerge when a baby's impulsive demands are denied. Because of many lessons in self-control, a child eventually develops a sense of what constitutes appropriate behaviour, a moral sense of right and wrong, and a personal conscience. Ongoing social interaction is thus necessary for the self to emerge. Like Freud, Mead noted that an impulsive aspect of the self (the "I") is present from birth. Developing Cooley's idea of the "looking-glass self," Mead also argued that a repository of culturally approved standards emerges as part of the self during social interaction. Mead drew attention to the unique human capacity to take the role of the other as the source of the "me." People develop, he wrote, by first imitating and pretending to be their significant others, then learning to play complex games that require understanding several roles simultaneously, and finally developing a sense of cultural standards and how they apply.

2. How are stages in the life course influenced by the historical period in which people live?
   The stages of the life course have been structured differently across history. For example, in the past, childhood and adolescence were not recognized as distinct stages, with the consequence that children were expected to live in much the same way that adults did. Accordingly, children entered the labour market as soon as they were able to perform

work tasks. A new view of childhood, which emerged a little over a century ago, began to treat children as unsocialized people who needed instruction and training to develop properly. In response, school attendance became mandatory, and labour laws prohibited children from working in the paid labour market. In each historical period then, we can see that socialization prepares individuals to become the people society needs them to be.

3. In what ways has the socializing influence of the family decreased in the twentieth century, while the influence of schools, peer groups, and the mass media increased?
Families remain an important and enduring agent of socialization. However, their influence has dwindled as the reach of other institutions and social forces has grown. The transfer of knowledge and skills that, in the past, would have been the primary if not sole responsibility of families increasingly occurs outside of the family system. Thus, what parents teach their children may be offset by what they learn in other settings. For example, sex education in the curriculum of Canadian schools may reflect values that conflict with what children learn in the home. Similarly, peers and the mass media may introduce children to perspectives that differ from what they are typically exposed to through their families.

4. In what sense is the self more flexible than it once was?
People's self-conceptions are subject to more flux now than they were even a few decades ago. Cultural globalization, medical advances, and computer-assisted communication are among the factors that have made the self more flexible.

CHAPTER 5

SOCIAL INTERACTION

Multi-bits/Getty Images

IN THIS CHAPTER YOU WILL LEARN TO

- Identify the sociological "building blocks" of social interaction.
- Describe how feminist theory highlights the role of emotions in social interaction.
- Explain the importance of power in social interaction according to conflict theory.
- Appreciate how symbolic interactionism improves our understanding of verbal and nonverbal communication.

THE BUILDING BLOCKS OF INTERACTION

At nearly half a million square metres, the West Edmonton Mall is among the world's largest shopping complexes. It includes more than 800 stores and kiosks, a huge indoor water park, an ice hockey rink, 14 movie theatres (including an IMAX), and so on. "When I first entered the enormous structure, I was disoriented," Lance Roberts reports. "The volume of sights, sounds, people, noise, and shopping alternatives was overwhelming."

"My experience was typical, which is why every mall entry includes a 'You are here' map. These maps help orient newcomers to an initially overwhelming environment. The locator arrow specifies where you are in three-dimensional space. Knowing your location better equips your navigation to where you want to go.

"The three dimensions of space (height, width, and depth) do not provide a complete picture of your surroundings. A fourth dimension—time—matters too. After all, if you ask a friend to meet you for coffee but don't set a time, it is unlikely that you will connect.

"My first year of employment as a professor at the University of Manitoba demonstrated the importance of yet a fifth dimension. I found the university was overwhelming. I had to organize and teach several new courses but lacked understanding of effective pedagogy. I had started a program of research but being introduced to the 'publish or perish' environment was draining. And then there was committee work, demands for supervision by graduate students, colleagues' solicitations for advice and support, professional gossip—all of which demanded time and talents that I lacked. Clearly, Woody Allen's quip that "80 percent of success is just showing up" was a gross overestimate. I had the space and time coordinates down pat but felt far from successful.

"What I lacked was an adequate understanding of the fifth dimension in which my newly minted professorship was located (Brym, 2014b). The fifth dimension is *social*; it is the dimension that sociologists study. In my case, I lacked a full appreciation of what I was in for when I took my first university appointment. New entrants into any social scene experience similar disorientation. Do first-year students; newlyweds; retirees; first-time marathoners, heroin users, or political candidates really know what they are getting into? For the same reasons that a road map is useful, a map of the *social* space surrounding us is helpful for figuring out where we want to go."

Walter Bibikow/AGE Fotostock

The West Edmonton Mall

Sociology seeks to understand the social space in which actions unfold. In some respects, this effort parallels the way physicists seek to understand the physical space that surrounds us. Physicists use special terms to characterize the features of physical space and have ideas about how those features are related. Similarly, sociological concepts and principles highlight important characteristics and relationships in social space. This section introduces some of the fundamental sociological building blocks for understanding social space.

The sociological imagination thrives by exploring the linkages between personal experience and the surrounding society. So let's begin with the person. A **person** is an individual whose uniqueness is captured in his or her personality, which comprises the constellation of traits that reliably define an individual's singularity. In sociology, **character** is a synonym for person. Just as you are a person, so is every other individual in your Introductory Sociology class because each of you has a unique character.

A **person** is a unique individual, whose distinctiveness is captured in his or her "personality."

In sociology, **character** is a synonym for "person."

We spend most of our lives connected to other people. They constitute our **social environment**. Social environments are typically organized, which means that the persons in the environment act in an orderly, patterned way. Observe any university classroom, sports arena, place of worship, or shopping centre, and you will see the social order. The order is not perfect but shows patterns of behaviour. On occasion, students may yell at a professor, one fan might throw another off a balcony, gunshots might ring out in a mosque, or a riot may occur in a mall—but such outbursts are not what you typically expect or generally experience. The fact that people are surprised by such events is evidence that an orderly pattern usually prevails.

A person's **social environment** is composed of real or imagined others to whom the person is connected.

Consider a university classroom. Every student in the class is a unique person. Each one is physically capable at any moment of yelling at a classmate, bursting into song, dancing in the aisles, smoking pot, or performing in myriad other ways not typically seen in class. Your professor is similarly capable. So why isn't the classroom chaotic?

The basic answer is that classrooms are organizations. **Organizations** are collectivities characterized by *social structure*. The structure is evident in the fact that individuals in organizations act in patterned ways. Professors are typically at the front of the classroom and follow the routine of lecturing, illustrating, asking questions, and the like. Students usually sit facing the professor, listening and taking notes.

Organizations are collectivities characterized by structure that encourages patterns in individual action.

Organizations are the social space where persons find themselves connected to others. Describing this fifth dimension requires identifying the components of an organization and their relationships. Information about organizational components and connections constitutes a social map in which you can locate yourself.

The locations on a social map of an organization are called statuses. A **status** is a culturally defined position in an organization. Statuses are connected in systematic ways, which gives any organization its structure. The connections between statuses are **norms**, which you learned in Chapter 2 are generally accepted ways of doing things. The reason your classroom is not chaotic, then, is that the individuals enter positions (statuses such as professor or student) that have expectations for the type of conduct that is appropriate and inappropriate (norms). In short, people know their location on a social map and typically follow specified routes (actions; see Box 5.1).

A **status** is a culturally defined position or social location.

Norms are generally accepted ways of doing things.

Note that statuses and norms are defined by culture. Different cultures invent different kinds of statuses and associated expectations for action. Some cultures encourage democratic governments, others demand authoritarian ones. Some underwrite nuclear families, others embrace extended ones. In this sense, culture is a blueprint for social organization. Note also that people *occupy* statuses but a person is not a status. You are not reducible to the status of a student, a lover, a son, or a daughter. You are a unique, precious human being. Finally, note that organizations exist independently of individuals. If you withdraw from Introductory Sociology, the university class endures. If your professor leaves, a replacement will be found; the organizational pattern persists.

People bring statuses to life. Associated with any status are norms about how a person should think, feel, and act when they occupy the social position. These status-related

BOX 5.1

SOCIOLOGY ON THE TUBE

SONS OF ANARCHY

Sons of Anarchy is an award-winning television series about a fictional motorcycle club in a California town. The Sons are a gang of outlaws, so beatings, gun running, narcotics consumption, influence peddling, pornography production, and killing are routine. Customized Harley-Davidsons symbolize that the Sons are rebels. So does their "Men of Mayhem" patch. But although these mavericks operate outside the law, they do not exist outside the laws of sociology.

In a world centred on violence, imprisonment and death are inevitable, so club membership changes between episodes. However, membership hovers around 10 and includes a cast of interesting personalities, including Jax, the son of the club's founder, who is torn by ambivalence about his career; his manipulative mother, Gemma, with her distorted views of family; Opie, a gentle, mountainous killer; and Tig, the loyal sidekick with low impulse control.

These characters display widely varying personalities. If they were assessed using standard psychiatric criteria, few would escape serious clinical diagnosis. Yet, when viewed with a sociological eye, their conduct seems remarkably orderly because they adhere to clearly articulated statuses, roles, and norms.

Thus, the club has a president, vice-president, secretary, and sergeant-at-arms. There are also hang-arounds, whose identifying patches mark them as probationary club members. Each of these statuses has specific, role-related responsibilities. The secretary is responsible for keeping the club's records and accounts in order. The sergeant-at-arms is responsible for discipline. Regular meetings are held in the club's boardroom and major decisions are decided by majority vote.

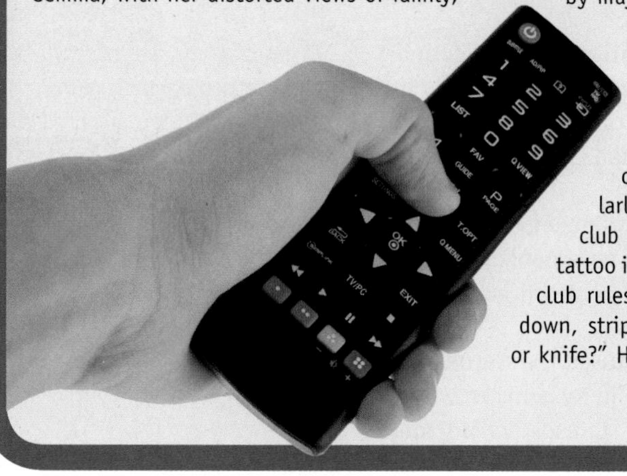

Once statuses are assigned and group decisions are made, norm compliance is mandatory. Harsh sanctions follow noncompliance. In one particularly gruesome episode, a former club member returns with his club tattoo intact, which is strictly against club rules. The club members pin him down, strip off his shirt, and ask, "Fire or knife?" His choice of the former leads to a painful encounter between his tattoo and a blowtorch.

The Kobal Collection at Art Resource, NY

Even anarchistic criminals are organized by social statuses and governed by social norms.

Sons of Anarchy is a highly glamourized version of biker gangs. For example, the club members are well groomed and enjoy sparkling white teeth. Still, the series illustrates an important point about social life. For ongoing interaction to be successful, it must be guided by a social structure of statuses, roles, and norms. This social reality cannot normally be violated by law-abiding citizens—or by anarchistic criminals.

Roles are clusters of expectations about thoughts, feelings, and actions appropriate for occupants of a particular status.

Role-playing involves conforming to existing performance expectations.

clusters of norms form **roles**, which occupants are expected to perform. The liveliness of a classroom, sports team, religious ceremony, or any other organized event is the result of people occupying statuses and engaging in role performance, the execution of role expectations.

In role performance, we see both the freedom and the constraint that is always present in social life. Constraint occurs in the form of role-playing. If someone performs a role in exactly the way social convention prescribes, it is an act of conformity. Sociologists call such performance **role-playing**. When military officers issue orders, they expect their orders to be obeyed precisely. However, in many circumstances, role

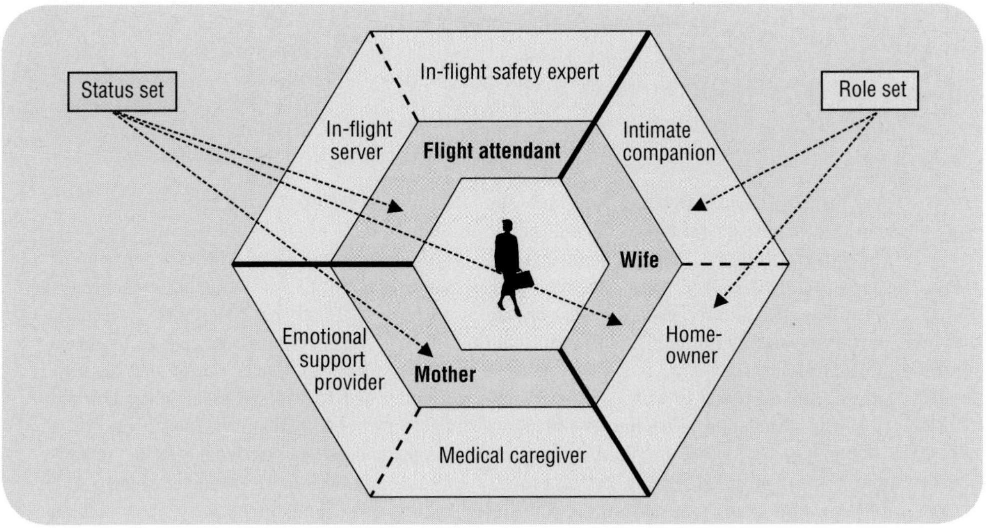

FIGURE 5.1
Role Set and Status Set

A person occupies several recognized positions or statuses at the same time—for example, mother, wife, and flight attendant. All of these statuses together form a status set. Each status is composed of several sets of expected behaviours or roles—for example, a wife is expected to act as an intimate companion to her husband and to assume certain legal responsibilities as co-owner of a house. In Figure 5.1, dashed lines separate roles and solid lines separate statuses.

expectations are unclear, incomplete, or contradictory (see Figures 5.1 and 5.2). How should you act on a first date? Or when you come across a serious traffic accident? Or when your best friend asks you to lie? In other circumstances, a person's character may prohibit him or her from conforming to clear role expectations. Vegans refuse to eat Thanksgiving turkey at grandmother's house. Teenagers refuse to rat on their friends when the principal asks who vandalized the gym. In these situations, persons engage in role-making. **Role-making** is the creative process by which individuals generate and perform roles. Through role-making, people display their individuality and autonomy.

Role-making is the creative process by which individuals generate role expectations and performances.

Social interaction, the process by which role performers act in relation to others, is an ongoing mixture of role-making and role-taking. In all social contexts, people are, to varying degrees, governed by the dictates of the surrounding social structures and agents who shape their own actions (see Box 5.2). Social interaction gives both shape and fluidity to patterned interactions with others. Studies of emotional life illustrate this point well.

Social interaction is the process by which role performers act in relation to others.

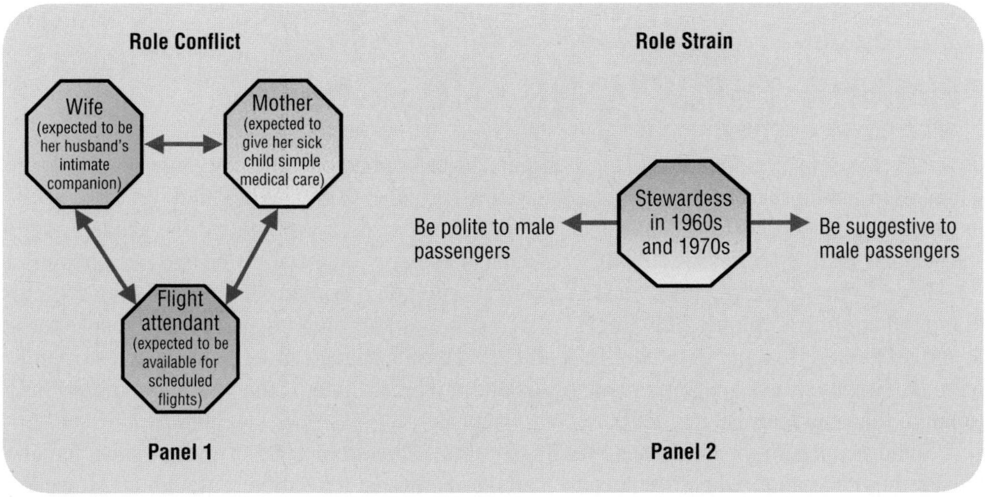

FIGURE 5.2
Role Conflict and Role Strain

(Panel 1): Role conflict takes place when different role demands are placed on a person who holds two or more statuses at the same time. How might a flight attendant experience role conflict because of the contradictory demands of the statuses diagrammed in the figure?

(Panel 2): Role strain occurs when incompatible role demands are placed on a person in a single status. Why was the status of stewardess in the 1960s and 1970s high in role strain?

BOX 5.2

SOCIOLOGY AT THE MOVIES

WE LIVE IN PUBLIC

We Live in Public tells the story of Josh Harris, an Internet pioneer. After making a small fortune, Harris used some of his money to conduct an "experiment" to see how the Internet might shape social interaction in the future. The project, which Harris called "Quiet: We Live in Public," invited more than 100 people to live in specially constructed, closed living quarters for free. The catch was that the entire complex was outfitted with cameras and microphones that captured every action.

The Kobal Collection at Art Resource, NY

Quiet: We Live in Public raises the question of what happens to our behaviour when others can see us at all times—similar to the situation in an era of social media, surveillance cameras, and consumer tracking on the Web.

Any resident could watch the feed from any of the cameras, as could the general public through the Internet. With cameras in every recreation and dining area, sleeping pod, washroom, and shower, even the most private moments were captured. The residents paid no money for their stay but gave up their privacy and all rights to what was recorded.

The mood and behaviour of residents changed as the project unfolded. As one resident later reflected, "It was sort of aggressively weird. Energy was turning." Another resident claimed that the environment was "turning people into beasts." Residents took guns from the firing range and threatened others. In the dining hall, some slammed the table demanding food, while others paraded on the table dressed as clowns. To a degree, the social environment that Harris's project created paralleled the virtual environment the Internet creates through social media. Twitter feeds and Facebook pages contain much benign interaction, but they also give licence to outrageous behaviour, some of it highly aggressive. One example is the 2014 "neknomination" drinking challenge on Facebook, which began in Australia and reportedly led to the death of several young men in the United Kingdom. Apparently, if people know they always have an audience, they perform for it, but not always in a way that is thoughtful or safe.

Social interaction requires that we play roles, but given the conflicts and strains associated with role performance, from time to time we need to retreat from the action and relax. Harris's experiment illustrates that, with an audience always present and with no possibility of retreat, people's capacity for productive social interaction decreases. Thus, Harris and his girlfriend lived for an extended period under full Internet surveillance. They began as a happy couple, moved from routine, meaningful interaction to extended silence and indifference, and ended with Josh forcing his girlfriend to have sex with him. Harris's personal experience confirmed his prediction that the cost of spending more time interacting with virtual audiences is a decline in the quality of face-to-face interaction.

Harris claimed his experiment predicted how the Internet would affect people. In today's wired world, how are our constant status updates and tweets, and the Google analytics that track all of our clicks, similar to the environment of *Quiet: We Live in Public*? If an audience is always present, where can we retreat to?

Josh Harris apparently learned a lesson from his experiment. After *Quiet: We Live in Public*, he and some friends took a cruise. Later, he retreated to an apple farm that he tended himself. After an unsuccessful attempt to found a social media company, he moved to Africa, where he now shuns all digital technology and teaches basketball to young people.

FEMINIST THEORY AND EMOTIONS

Several years ago, a researcher and his assistants eavesdropped on 1200 conversations of people laughing in public places, such as shopping malls (Provine, 2000). When they heard someone laughing, they recorded who laughed (the speaker, the listener, or both) and the genders of the speaker and the listener. To simplify their research, they eavesdropped only on two-person groups.

They found a clear status-related pattern to laughter: women laugh more than men do in everyday conversations. The biggest discrepancy in laughing occurs when the speaker is a woman and the listener is a man. In such cases, women laugh more than twice as often as men do. However, even when a man speaks and a woman listens, the woman is more likely to laugh than the man is.

Some people might think these findings confirm the stereotype of the giggling female. Others might say that, when it comes to men, women have a lot more to laugh at. However, sociological research suggests that, in general, differences in role performance are often related to gender status. For example, men are more likely than women are to engage in long monologues and interrupt when others are talking (Speer and Stokoe, 2011). Men are less likely to ask for help or directions because doing so would imply a reduction in their authority. Much male–female conflict results from these differences. A stereotypical case is the lost male driver and the helpful female passenger. The female passenger, seeing that the male driver is lost, suggests that they stop and ask for directions. The male driver does not want to ask for directions because he thinks that would make him look incompetent. If both parties remain firm in their positions, an argument is bound to result.

Blaj Gabriel/Shutterstock.com

If, in general, statuses shape patterns of social interaction, feminist sociologists are especially sensitive to gender differences in social interaction like those just described. They see that gender often structures interaction patterns. The case of laughter follows a predictable pattern. It is generally true that people with higher status (in this case, men) get more laughs, while people with lower status (in this case, women) laugh more. Perhaps that is why class clowns are nearly always boys. Laughter in everyday life, it turns out, is not as spontaneous as you may think. It is often a signal of who has higher or lower status. Social structure influences who laughs more.

Emotion Management

Some scholars think that laughter and other emotions are like the common cold. In both cases, an external disturbance causes a reaction that people presumably experience involuntarily. The external disturbance could be a grizzly bear attack that causes us to experience fear, or exposure to a virus that causes us to catch a cold. In either case, according to some researchers, we can't control our body's response. Emotions, like colds, just happen to us (Thoits, 1989: 319).

It is not surprising that feminists were among the first sociologists to note the flaw in the view that emotional responses are typically involuntary (Hochschild, 1979, 1983). Seeing how often women, as status subordinates, must *control* their emotions, they generalized the idea. Emotions don't just happen to us, they argued. We manage them. If a grizzly bear attacks you in the woods, you can run as fast as possible or calm yourself, lie down, play dead, and silently pray for the best. You are more likely to survive the grizzly bear attack if you control your emotions and follow the second strategy. You will also temper your fear with a new emotion: hope (see Figure 5.3).

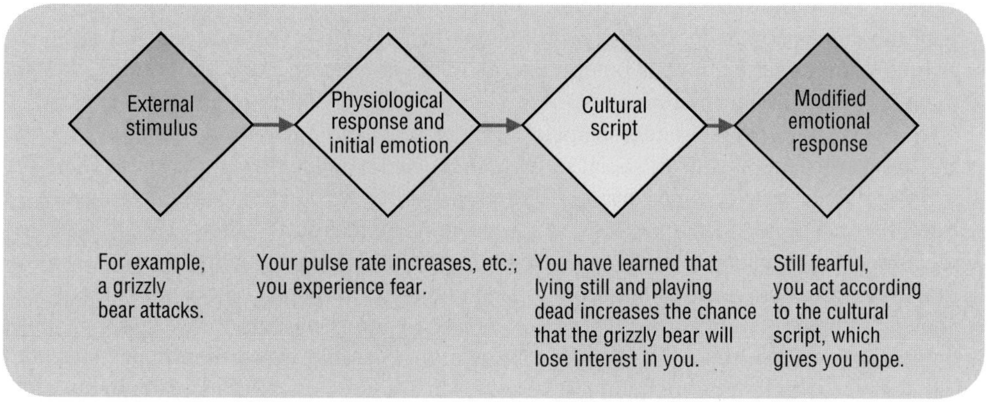
External stimulus
Physiological response and initial emotion
Cultural script
Modified emotional response
For example, a grizzly bear attacks.
Your pulse rate increases, etc.; you experience fear.
You have learned that lying still and playing dead increases the chance that the grizzly bear will lose interest in you.
Still fearful, you act according to the cultural script, which gives you hope.

FIGURE 5.3
How We Get Emotional

In general, when people manage their emotions, they usually follow certain cultural "scripts," such as the culturally transmitted knowledge that lying down and playing dead gives you a better chance of surviving a grizzly bear attack. That is, individuals usually know the culturally designated emotional response to a particular external stimulus and try to respond appropriately. If they don't succeed in achieving the culturally appropriate emotional response, they are likely to feel guilt, disappointment, or (as in the case of the grizzly bear attack) something much worse.

Emotion management involves people obeying "feeling rules" and responding appropriately to the situations in which they find themselves.

Sociologist Arlie Russell Hochschild is a leading figure in the study of **emotion management**. In fact, she coined the term. She argues that emotion management involves people obeying "feeling rules" and responding appropriately to the situations in which they find themselves (Hochschild, 1983, 2012). For example, people may talk about the "right" to feel angry, or they may acknowledge that they "should" have mourned a relative's death more deeply. People have conventional expectations not only about what they should feel but also about how much they should feel, how long they should feel it, and with whom they should share those feelings. For example, we are expected to mourn the end of a love relationship. Canadians today regard shedding tears in response as completely natural, though if you shot yourself—a fad among some European Romantics in the early nineteenth century—then the average Canadian would consider you deranged. If you date someone new just minutes after your long-time love unexpectedly broke up with you, most people will regard you as weird. Norms and rules govern our emotional life.

Emotion Labour

Emotion labour is emotion management that many people do as part of their job and for which they are paid.

Hochschild distinguishes emotion management (which everyone does in their everyday life) from **emotion labour** (which many people do as part of their job and for which they are paid). We've all seen teachers discipline students who routinely hand in assignments late, pass notes, chatter during class, talk back, and act as class clowns. Those teachers do emotion labour. Similarly, sales clerks, nurses, and flight attendants must be experts in emotion labour. They spend a considerable part of their workday dealing with other people's misbehaviour, anger, rudeness, and unreasonable demands. They spend another part of their workday in what is essentially promotional and public relations work on behalf of the organizations that employ them. ("We hope you enjoyed your flight on Air Canada and that we can serve you again the next time you travel.") In all these tasks, they carefully manage their own emotions while trying to render their clientele happy and orderly. Hochschild estimates that in the United States, nearly half the jobs women do and one-fifth of the jobs men do involve substantial amounts of emotion labour. More women than men do emotion labour because they are typically better socialized to undertake caring and nurturing roles.

Note, too, that as the focus of the economy shifts from the production of goods to the production of services, the market for emotion labour grows. More and more people are selected, trained, and paid for their skills in emotion labour. That is why, since the mid-1990s, job applicants have been increasingly assessed for their "emotional intelligence" in addition to their other skills (Dann, 2008). Consequently, business organizations increasingly govern the expression of feelings at work, which becomes less spontaneous and authentic over time. This process affects women more than it does men because, on average, women do more emotion labour than men do.

As always, however, conduct in social settings is not fully governed by social expectations. To a degree, occupants of social statuses shape and manage their experience. Consider the way supermarket clerks perform customer service. Research shows that clerks give two reasons for managing their emotions at the customer checkout (Tolich, 1993). The first involves constraint: because store management insists on politeness and helpfulness, it monitors and regulates emotion labour, taking disciplinary action when clerks consistently and seriously violate emotion norms. The second reason centres on autonomy: clerks manage their emotions to have fun and make the routine more bearable. According to one checkout clerk, "I am constantly talking, telling jokes, and stuff. I get a little circus going in my unit"

(Tolich, 1993: 375). Regulated emotion management fosters alienation because others shape it, but autonomous emotion management is liberating to the degree it allows actors to control their displays of emotion.

Emotions in Historical Perspective

Social structure impinges on emotional experiences in many ways. As we have seen, status hierarchies influence patterns of laughter. Cultural scripts and the expectations of others influence the way we manage our emotions in our personal lives. The growth of the economy's service sector requires more emotion labour, turns it into a commodity, and decreases the ability of people to experience emotions spontaneously and authentically. In these and other ways, the commonsense view of emotions as unique, spontaneous, uncontrollable, authentic, natural, and perhaps even rooted exclusively in our biological makeup proves to be misguided.

We can glean additional evidence of the impact of society on our emotional life from socio-historical studies. It turns out that feeling rules take a range of forms under different social conditions, which vary historically. Three examples from the social history of emotions help illustrate the point:

- *Grief.* Among other factors, the crude death rate (the annual number of deaths per 1000 people in a population) helps determine our experience of grief (Lofland, 1985). In Europe, as late as 1600, life expectancy was only 35 years. Many infants died at birth or in their first year of life. Infectious diseases decimated populations. The medical profession was in its infancy. The risk of losing family members, especially babies, was thus much greater than it is today. One result of this situation was that people invested less emotionally in their children than we typically do. Their grief response to the death of children was shorter and less intense than ours is; the mourning period was briefer and people became less distraught. Over the years, as health conditions improved and the infant mortality rate fell, people's emotional investment in children increased. It intensified especially in the nineteenth century when women starting having fewer babies on average as a result of industrialization (Chapter 20, Population and Urbanization). As emotional investment in children increased, the grief response to children's deaths intensified and lasted longer.
- *Anger.* Industrialization and the growth of competitive markets in nineteenth-century North America and Europe turned the family into an emotional haven from a world increasingly perceived as heartless (Chapter 15, Families). In keeping with the enhanced emotional function of the family, anger control, particularly by women, became increasingly important for the establishment of a harmonious household. The early twentieth century witnessed mounting labour unrest and the growth of the service sector. Avoiding anger thus became an important labour relations goal, too. This trend also influenced family life. Child-rearing advice manuals increasingly stressed the importance of teaching children how to control their anger (Stearns and Stearns, 1985, 1986).
- *Disgust.* Manners in Europe in the Middle Ages were disgusting by our standards. Even the most refined aristocrats spat in public and belched shamelessly during banquets. Members of high society did not think twice about scratching themselves in places we regard as private and passing gas at the dinner table, where they ate with their hands and speared food with knives. What was acceptable then causes revulsion now because feeling rules have changed. Specifically, manners began to change with the emergence of the modern political state, especially after 1700. The modern political state raised armies and collected taxes, imposed languages, and required loyalty. All this coordination of effort necessitated more self-control on the part of the citizenry. Changes in standards of public conduct—signalled by the introduction of the fork, the nightdress, the handkerchief, the spittoon, and the chamber pot—accompanied the rise of the modern state.

Christie's Images Ltd./SuperStock

Manners in Europe during the Middle Ages were disgusting by today's standards.

Good manners also served to define who had power and who lacked it. For example, there is nothing inherently well mannered about a father sitting at the head of the table carving the turkey and children waiting to speak until they are spoken to. These rules about the difference between good manners and improper behaviour were created to signify the distribution of power in the family by age and gender (Elias, 1994 [1939]; Scott, 1998).

We thus see that although emotions form an important part of all social interactions, they are neither universal nor constant. They have histories and deep sociological underpinnings in statuses, roles, and norms. This observation flies in the face of common sense. We typically think of our interactions as outcomes of our emotional states. We commonly believe that we interact differently with people depending on whether they love us, make us angry, or make us laugh. We usually think our emotions are evoked involuntarily and result in uncontrollable action. However, emotions are not as unique, involuntary, and uncontrollable as people often believe. Underlying the turbulence of emotional life is a measure of order and predictability governed by sociological principles that vary historically.

Just as building blocks need cement to hold them together, norms, roles, and statuses require a sort of "social cement" to turn them into a durable social structure and to prevent them from falling apart. What is the nature of the cement that holds the building blocks of social life together? Asked differently, exactly how is social interaction maintained? That is the most fundamental sociological question one can ask, for it is really a question about how social structures, and society as a whole, are possible. It is the subject of the next two sections of this chapter.

TIME FOR REVIEW

- How does a status differ from a person?
- How does role-playing differ from role-making? How are these concepts connected to the ideas of freedom and constraint?
- What is the difference between emotional management and emotional labour?
- What do historical differences in emotional expression tell us about norms of conduct?

CONFLICT THEORIES OF SOCIAL INTERACTION

Competing for Attention

Have you ever been in a conversation where you couldn't get a word in edgewise? If you are like most people, this situation is bound to happen occasionally. The longer this kind of one-sided conversation persists, the more neglected you feel. You may make increasingly forceful attempts to turn the conversation your way. However, if you fail, you may decide to end the interaction altogether. If this experience repeats itself—if the person you are talking to persistently monopolizes conversations—you are likely to want to avoid getting into conversations with him or her in the future. Maintaining interaction (and maintaining a relationship) requires that both parties' need for attention is met.

Most people do not consistently try to monopolize conversations. If they did, there wouldn't be much talk in the world. In fact, turn-taking is one of the basic norms that govern conversations; people take turns talking to make conversation possible. Nonetheless, a remarkably large part of all conversations involves a subtle competition for attention. Consider the following snippet of dinner conversation:

John: "I'm feeling really starved."
Mary: "Oh, I just ate."
John: "Well, I'm feeling really starved."
Mary: "When was the last time you ate?"

Charles Derber recorded this conversation (Derber, 1979: 24). John starts by saying how hungry he is. The attention is on him. Mary replies that she is not hungry; the attention shifts to her. John insists he is hungry, shifting attention back to him. Mary finally allows the conversation to focus on John by asking him when he last ate. John thus "wins" the competition for attention.

Derber recorded 1500 conversations in family homes, workplaces, restaurants, classrooms, dormitories, and therapy groups. He concluded that North Americans usually try to turn conversations toward themselves. They usually do so in ways that go unnoticed. Nonetheless, claims Derber, the typical conversation is a covert competition for attention. In Derber's words, there exists

> a set of extremely common conversational practices which show an unresponsiveness to others' topics and involve turning them into one's own. Because of norms prohibiting blatantly egocentric behaviour, these practices are often exquisitely subtle.... Although conversationalists are free to introduce topics about themselves, they are expected to maintain an appearance of genuine interest in [topics] about others in a conversation. A delicate face-saving system requires that people refrain from openly disregarding others' concerns and keep expressions of disinterest from becoming visible. (1979: 23)

You can observe the competition for attention yourself. Record a couple of minutes of conversation in your dorm, home, or workplace. Then play back the recording. Evaluate each statement in the conversation. Does the statement try to change which person is the subject of the conversation? Or does the statement say something about the *other* conversationalists or ask them about what they said? How does not responding or responding by merely saying "uh-huh" shift attention? What other conversational techniques are especially effective in shifting attention? Who "wins" the conversation? What is the winner's gender, race, and class position? Is the winner popular or unpopular? Is there a connection between the person's status in the group and his or her ability to win? You might even want to record yourself to see how you participate in conversational competition.

Derber's analysis is influenced by conflict theory, which holds that social interaction involves competition over valued resources. Such resources include attention, approval, prestige, information, money, and so on (Coleman, 1990; Cook and Whitmeyer, 1992). According to conflict theorists, competitive interaction involves people seeking to gain the most—socially, emotionally, and economically—while paying the least.

Power and Social Interaction

Many conflict theorists of social interaction emphasize that when people interact, their statuses are often arranged in a hierarchy. People on top enjoy more **power** than those on the bottom—that is, they are "in a position to carry out [their] own will despite resistance" (Weber, 1947: 152). In face-to-face communication, the degree of inequality strongly affects the character of social interaction between interacting parties (Bourdieu, 1977 [1972]; Collins, 1982; Wilkinson and Pickett, 2010). For example, research shows that rich people tend to care less about others than do people who are not rich. Unless rich people are interacting with other rich people, they often turn a blind eye, give others the cold shoulder, look down on others, or look right through them. People who are not rich tend to treat others with greater care, respect, and empathy (see Box 5.3) (Kraus and Keltner, 2009).

Power is the capacity to carry out one's own will despite resistance.

BOX 5.3

SOCIAL POLICY: WHAT DO YOU THINK?

HAVE SOCIAL MEDIA RUINED INTERPERSONAL COMMUNICATION?

"While my wife and I were dining at a favourite Italian restaurant, a couple in their early 20s entered," Lance Roberts recalls. "My wife commented on their fashionable clothes and said something like, 'What an impressive looking couple.' The couple was seated where we could easily observe them. They each ordered a glass of wine, and what do you think they did next? You're right if you guessed they got out their cellphones and began to read and text. When their wine arrived, they each took a sip and returned to their respective virtual experiences. My wife asked, 'What are they doing? How can they ignore one another like that?' She declined my offer to go over and interview the couple in search of answers to her questions. Instead, we satisfied ourselves by paying attention to our fine meal and each other."

"The couple in the restaurant represents a new normal; you can observe the same interaction style by individuals and couples in social settings ranging from family dinners to hockey games. Cheap, reliable interconnectivity makes it possible to engage in constant updating and communicating with others. I share my wife's critical commentary on this state of affairs. But we are now grandparents, so what can you expect? Still, it's worth asking what is lost when making virtual social connections takes precedence over face-to-face interaction.

"One plausible loss is the capacity for empathy. Empathy is the ability to understand and be sensitive to the internal life and needs of others. Empathy is learned, and some people have more empathy than others do because they have been socialized differently. Likewise, generational differences may affect one's level of empathy. Evidence suggests that today's university and college students may be less empathic than previous generations were."

Seventy-two studies of university undergraduates conducted over the past three decades measured empathic concern about the misfortunes of others, the ability to imagine other people's viewpoints, and the level of anguish over others' misfortunes. Here is how recent undergraduates compare with earlier generations (Konrath, 2010):

- A significant decline has occurred in empathic concern (48 percent) and perspective-taking (34 percent).
- Post-2000 undergraduates are far less likely than pre-2000 undergraduates to agree with statements like "I often have tender, concerned feelings for people less fortunate than me" and "I sometimes try to understand my friends better by imagining how things look from their perspective."
- The largest decline in empathy scores occurred after 2000, when social networking sites and smartphones began to flourish.
- Decline in empathy is related to a rise in narcissism—self-absorption that sees other people as means to an end (Twenge and Campbell, 2009).

Self-centredness and decreased levels of kindness and helpfulness have led the generation of university-aged students to be labelled "Generation Me." Slogans such as "Believe in yourself," "Be yourself," and "You must love yourself before you can love someone else" define the generational style (Twenge, 2006).

Since empathy is a learned capacity, it is not surprising that reduced empathy is rooted in early social experiences. Many members of the current generation of university-aged students come from single-child families where they have been the centre of attention. Many come from dual-income families where parents have had less time to model and reinforce empathy. Many went to schools with "no fail" and other policies that provided little corrective feedback. Many are surrounded by digital technologies that make it possible to be connected to others without caring much about them. Many find themselves in educational and employment situations where the only paths to success are individualism and competition.

Whatever the causes, this characteristic generational shift will have important social consequences. Perhaps a couple ignoring each other over dinner in favour of their smartphones is nobody's business but theirs. But low empathy is no isolated phenomenon. It is correlated with many forms of antisocial behaviour. Considering this larger connection leads to wondering about many things. How will workplaces organized around role conformity need to change to accommodate Generation Me? What consequences will reduced empathy have on the future stability of marriage partnerships and childrearing? How will this generation treat their parents as they become progressively disabled?

How well do the characteristics of Generation Me describe you and your friends? What signs do you see in your everyday experiences that indicate a lack of empathy? Do you think your generation is more self-centred than your parent's generation? If so, what strategies could be used to increase empathy in the next generation?

To get a better grasp on the role of power in social interaction, consider two extreme cases and the case that lies at the midpoint between the extremes (Table 5.1). **Domination** represents one extreme type of interaction. In social interaction based on domination, nearly all power is concentrated in the hands of people of high status, whereas people of low status enjoy almost no power. Two examples of social interaction based on domination are guards versus inmates in a concentration camp, and landowners versus slaves on plantations in the American South before the Civil War. In extreme cases of domination, subordinates live in a state of near-constant fear.

Domination is a mode of interaction in which nearly all power is concentrated in the hands of people of high status. Fear is the dominant emotion in systems of interaction based on domination.

The other extreme involves interaction based on **cooperation**. Here, power is more or less equally distributed between people of different status. Cooperative interaction is based on feelings of trust. For instance, marriages are happier when spouses equitably share housework and child care. Perceived inequity breeds resentment and dissatisfaction. It harms intimacy. It increases the chance that people will have extramarital affairs and divorce. In contrast, a high level of trust between spouses is associated with marital stability and enduring love (Shallcross and Simpson, 2012).

Cooperation is a basis for social interaction in which power is more or less equally distributed between people of different status. The dominant emotion in cooperative interaction is trust.

Between the two extremes of interaction based on domination, and interaction based on cooperation, is interaction based on **competition**. In this mode of interaction, power is unequally distributed but the degree of inequality is less than in systems of domination. If trust is the prototypical emotion of relationships based on cooperation, and fear is the characteristic emotion of subordinates involved in relationships based on domination, envy is an important emotion in competitive interaction.

Competition is a mode of interaction in which power is unequally distributed but the degree of inequality is less than in systems of domination. Envy is an important emotion in competitive interactions.

Significantly, an organization's mode of interaction strongly influences its efficiency or productivity—that is, its ability to achieve its goals at the least possible cost. Thus, black slaves on plantations in the pre–Civil War South and Jews in Nazi concentration camps were usually regarded by their masters as slow and inept workers (Collins, 1982: 66–69). This characterization was not just a matter of prejudice. Slavery *is* inefficient because, in the final analysis, fear of coercion is the only motivation for slaves to work. Yet as psychologists have known for many decades, punishment is a far less effective motivator than reward is (Skinner, 1953). Slaves hate the tedious and often back-breaking labour; they get little in exchange for it, and therefore they typically work with less than maximum effort.

In a competitive mode of interaction, subordinates receive more benefits, including prestige and money. Prestige and money are stronger motivators than the threat of coercion is. Thus, if bosses pay workers reasonably well and treat them with respect, they will work more efficiently than slaves will, even if the workers do not particularly enjoy their work or fail to identify with the goals of the company. Knowing they can make more money by working harder and that their efforts are appreciated, workers will often put in extra effort (Collins, 1982: 63–65).

As sociologist Randall Collins and others have shown, however, the most efficient workers are those who enjoy their work and identify with their employer (Collins, 1982: 60–85; Lowe, 2000). Employers can help to create high worker morale and foster a more cooperative work environment by giving workers a bigger say in decision making, encouraging worker creativity, and ensuring that salaries and perks are not too highly skewed in favour of those on top. Activities that help workers feel they are in harmony with their employer and are playing on the same team include company picnics, baseball games, and, in Japan, the singing of company songs before the workday begins. Similarly, although sales meetings and other conferences have an instrumental purpose (the discussion of sales strategies, new products, and so on), they also offer opportunities for friendly social interaction

TABLE 5.1
Main Modes of Interaction

	Mode of Cooperation		
Mode of Interaction	**Domination**	**Competition**	**Cooperation**
Level of inequality	High	Medium	Low
Characteristic emotion	Fear	Envy	Trust
Efficiency	Low	Medium	High

that increases workers' identification with their employer. When workers identify strongly with their employers, they will be willing to undergo self-sacrifice, take initiative, and give their best creative effort, even without the prospect of increased material gain.

Power and Position

As noted earlier, power is the ability to achieve desired outcomes. It is exercised in all modes of interaction. It is not simply a reflection of personality but is mostly a product of social circumstances. Power is embedded in the statuses that people occupy and in the relationships they derive from those positions. We can understand this point better by exploring the connection between power and social status.

Social statuses are typically ranked in terms of access to valuable financial, physical, social, or cultural resources. Occupants of preferred statuses have access to many valuable resources and use them to perpetuate privilege. For instance, rich people have the means to hire accountants, tax lawyers, and investment counsellors who can advise them on how to minimize their tax bills and maximize the amount of money they can pass on to their children. Similarly, people in positions of great power can make and enforce norms that benefit them. That is why lower-status perpetrators of "street crimes" typically receive more severe punishments than do higher-status agents of "suite crime." Such differences are built into the architecture of society.

Power, then, is a principal determinant of successful action. Unequal power is part of the way people (mainly powerful people) design organizations. Taken together, these considerations highlight that some people are more successful than others are, not because of their intelligence, hard work, thriftiness, and so on, but by virtue of the statuses they occupy, which, to a considerable degree, they may have inherited. You might ask why this state of affairs is tolerated. Why don't the powerless routinely protest? One important reason relates to our "cultural scaffolding."

Cultural scaffolding is the set of cultural values and beliefs that legitimate existing power arrangements, making them seem reasonable and giving them a natural, taken-for-granted quality (Roscigno, 2012). Take language use, for example. No students arrive at university without having had their written and spoken language constantly corrected over an extended period. You spent considerable time and energy memorizing standard spellings and distinguishing which words are correct in specific circumstances (can/may; effect/affect).

You didn't refuse to learn these things because of the cultural scaffolding surrounding you. The pressure to learn Standard English is a like a conspiracy; the pressure is on wherever you turn—from parents, teachers in every grade, extended family members, and outsiders. Almost everyone takes it for granted that Standard English is the correct way to express oneself. But where do these rules and regulations come from? Here's a clue. In elementary school, we are taught what is sometimes called "the Queen's English." As this expression suggests, culturally prescribed language rules legitimate and institutionalize the conduct of the rich and the powerful. The rich and the powerful are privileged in all social institutions. Micro-social conduct is played out in a context where the rules of the game are often biased.

TIME FOR REVIEW

- Conflict theorists view interaction as a competition for valued resources. Explain how this principle applies to ordinary conversations.
- What are the main characteristics of domination? How do they differ from the main characteristics of cooperation?
- What signs tell you that a person is powerful?
- What role does cultural scaffolding play in the perpetuation of privilege?

SYMBOLIC INTERACTION

Is social interaction *always* a competitive and conflict-prone struggle over valued resources, as conflict theorists suggest? A moment's reflection suggests otherwise. People frequently act in ways they consider fair or just, even when doing so fails to maximize their personal gain (Batson, 2011). Some people even engage in altruistic or heroic acts from which they gain nothing and risk much. The plain fact is that social life is richer than conflict theorists would have us believe. Selfishness and conflict are not the only bases of social interaction.

When people behave fairly or altruistically, they are interacting with others based on norms they have learned. These norms say they should act justly and help people in need, even when doing so costs a lot. How then do people learn norms (as well as roles and statuses)? The first step involves what George Herbert Mead called "taking the role of the other," that is, seeing yourself from the point of view of the people with whom you interact (Chapter 4, Socialization). According to Mead, we interpret other people's words and nonverbal signals to understand how they see us, and we adjust our behaviour to fit their expectations about how we ought to behave. During such symbolic interaction, we learn norms and adopt roles and statuses.

Such social learning differs from studying a user manual or a textbook. As we interact with others, our social learning involves constantly negotiating and modifying the norms, roles, and statuses that we meet, shaping them to suit our preferences. People learn norms, roles, and statuses actively and creatively, not passively and mechanically (Berger and Luckmann, 1966; Blumer, 1969; Strauss, 1993). Let us explore this theme by considering the ingenious ways in which people manage the impressions they give to others during social interaction.

Goffman's Dramaturgical Analysis

One of the most popular variants of symbolic interactionism is **dramaturgical analysis**. As first developed by Erving Goffman (1959), and briefly discussed in Chapter 1, A Sociological Compass, dramaturgical analysis takes literally Shakespeare's line from *As You Like It:* "All the world's a stage, and all the men and women merely players."

Dramaturgical analysis views social interaction as a sort of play in which people present themselves so that they appear in the best possible light.

From Goffman's point of view, people constantly engage in role-playing. This fact is most evident when we are "front stage" in public settings (see Box 5.4). Just as being front stage in a play requires the use of props, set gestures, and memorized lines, so does acting in public space. A server in a restaurant, for example, must dress in a uniform, smile, and recite fixed lines ("How are you? My name is Sam and I'm your server today. May I get you a drink before you order your meal?"). When the server goes "back stage," he or she can relax from the front-stage performance and discuss it with fellow actors ("Those kids at table six are driving me nuts!"). Thus, we often distinguish between our public roles and our "true" selves. Note, however, that even while back stage, we engage in role-playing and impression management; it's just that we are less likely to be aware of it. For instance, in the kitchen, a server may try to present herself in the best possible light to impress another server so that she can eventually ask him out for a date. Thus, the implication of dramaturgical analysis is that there is no single self, just the ensemble of roles we play in various social contexts. Servers in restaurants play many roles when off the job. They play on basketball teams, sing in church choirs, and hang out with friends at shopping malls. Each role is governed by norms about what kinds of clothes to wear, what kind of conversation to engage in, and so on. Everyone plays on many front stages in everyday life.

We do not always play our roles enthusiastically. If a role is stressful, people may engage in role distancing. **Role distancing** involves giving the impression of just "going through the motions" but lacking serious commitment to a role. Thus, when people think a role they are playing is embarrassing or beneath them, they typically want to give their peers the impression that the role is not their "true" self. My parents force me to sing in the church choir; I'm working at McDonald's just to earn a few extra dollars, but I'm going back to college next semester; this old car I'm driving is just a loaner. These are the kinds of rationalizations individuals offer when distancing themselves from a role.

Role distancing involves giving the impression that we are just "going through the motions" but actually lack serious commitment to a role.

Onstage, people typically try to place themselves in the best possible light; they engage in "impression management." For example, when students enter medical school, they quickly adopt a new medical vocabulary and wear a white lab coat to set themselves apart from patients. They try to model their behaviour after the doctors who have authority over them. When dealing with patients, they may hide their ignorance under medical jargon to maintain their authority. They may ask questions they know the answer to so that they can impress their teachers. According to one third-year student, "The best way of impressing [advisers] with your competence is asking questions you know the answer to. Because if they ever put it back on you, 'Well what do you think?' then you can tell them what you think and you'd give a very intelligent answer because you knew it. You didn't ask it to find out information. You asked it to impress people" (Haas and Shaffir, 1987). Medical students don't take a course in how to act like a doctor, but they learn their new role in the course of impression management (Lewin and Reeves, 2011).

Let us now inquire briefly into the way people use words and nonverbal signals to communicate in face-to-face interaction. As we shall see, something as apparently straightforward as having a conversation is actually a wonder of intricate complexity.

Ethnomethodology

Goffman's view of social interaction seems cynical. He portrays people as being inauthentic or constantly playing roles but never really being themselves.

However discomforting Goffman's cynicism may be, we should not overlook his valuable sociological point: The stability of social life depends on our adherence to norms, roles, and statuses. If that adherence broke down, social life would become chaotic. Take something as simple as walking down a busy street. Hordes of pedestrians rush toward you yet rarely collide with you. Collision is avoided because of a norm that nobody actually teaches and few people are aware of but almost everyone follows. If someone blocks your way, you move to the right. When you move to the right and the person walking toward you moves to the right (your left), you avoid bumping into each other. Similarly, consider the norm of "civil inattention." When we pass people in public, we may establish momentary eye contact out of friendliness but we usually look away quickly. According to Goffman, such a gesture is a "ritual" of respect, a patterned and expected action that affirms our respect for strangers. Imagine what would happen if you fixed your stare at a stranger for a few seconds longer than the norm. Rather than being seen as respectful, your intention might be viewed as rude, intrusive, or hostile. Thus, we would not even be able to walk down a street in peace were it not for the existence of certain unstated norms. These and many other norms, some explicit and some not, make an orderly social life possible (Goffman, 1963, 1971).

By emphasizing how we construct social reality in the course of interaction, symbolic interactionists downplay the importance of norms and understandings that *precede* any given interaction. **Ethnomethodology** tries to correct this shortcoming. Ethnomethodology is the study of the methods ordinary people use, often unconsciously, to make sense of what others do and say. Ethnomethodologists stress that everyday interactions could not take place without preexisting shared norms and understandings. The norm of moving to the right to avoid bumping into an oncoming pedestrian and the norm of civil inattention are both examples of preexisting shared norms and understandings.

Ethnomethodology is the study of how people make sense of what others do and say by adhering to preexisting norms.

To illustrate the importance of preexisting shared norms and understandings, Harold Garfinkel conducted a series of breaching experiments. **Breaching experiments** illustrate the importance of everyday, ritualistic interactions by disrupting interaction patterns. In one such experiment, he asked one of his students to interpret a casual greeting in an unexpected way (Garfinkel, 1967: 44):

Breaching experiments illustrate the importance of everyday, ritualistic interactions by disrupting interaction patterns.

> Acquaintance: [waving cheerily] How are you?
>
> Student: How am I in regard to what? My health, my finances, my schoolwork, my peace of mind, my ...?
>
> Acquaintance: [red in the face and suddenly out of control] Look! I was just trying to be polite. Frankly, I don't give a damn how you are.

As this example shows, social interaction requires tacit agreement between the actors about what is normal and expected. Without shared norms and understandings, no sustained interaction can occur. When someone violates the assumptions underlying the stability and meaning of daily life, people are likely to become upset and end the interaction. The reaction of shock and outrage generated by breaching experiments, coupled with the rush to restore orderly interaction, illustrates the place and importance of daily interaction rituals (Collins, 2013).

Assuming the existence of shared norms and understandings, let us now inquire briefly into the way people communicate in face-to-face interaction. This issue may seem trivial. However, as you will soon see, having a conversation is actually a wonder of intricate complexity.

Verbal and Nonverbal Communication

In the 1950s, an article appeared in the British newspaper *News Chronicle*, trumpeting the invention of an electronic translating device at the University of London. According to the article, "[a]s fast as [a user] could type the words in, say, French, the equivalent in Hungarian or Russian would issue forth on the tape" (quoted in Silberman, 2000: 225). The report was an exaggeration, to put it mildly. It soon became a standing joke that if you ask a computer to translate into Russian the New Testament proverb, "The spirit is willing, but the flesh is weak," the output would read, "The vodka is good, but the steak is lousy." Today, we are closer to high-quality machine translation than we were in the 1950s. However, a practical Universal Translator exists only on *Star Trek*.

The Social Context of Language

Why can people translate better than computers can? Because computer programs find it difficult to make sense of the social and cultural context in which language is used. The same words can mean different things in different settings, so computers, lacking contextual cues, routinely botch translations. That is why machine translation works best when applications are restricted to a single social context—say, weather forecasting or oil exploration. In such cases, specialized vocabularies and meanings specific to the context of interest are built into the program. Ambiguity is reduced and computers can "understand" the meaning of words well enough to translate them with reasonable accuracy. Humans must also be able to reduce ambiguity and make sense of words to become good translators but they do so by learning the nuances of meaning in different cultural and social contexts over an extended time. Nonverbal cues assist them in this task.

Status Cues

As noted earlier, social life involves relationships between individuals occupying social positions. Participants need information to define the status of others and announce their own status to others. As Goffman (1959) observed, when individuals come into contact, they try to acquire information that will help them define the situation and thus make interaction easier. Status identification is assisted by attending to **status cues**, which are visual indicators of a person's social position.

Status cues are visual indicators of a person's social position.

Status cues come in many forms, ranging from the way people dress and speak to where they live and how they furnish their homes. Although status cues can be useful in helping people define the situation and thus greasing the wheels of social interaction, they also pose a social danger; status cues can quickly degenerate into stereotypes, or rigid views of how members of various groups act, regardless of whether individual group members really behave that way. **Stereotypes** create social barriers that impair interaction or prevent it altogether. For instance, in some places, police officers routinely stop young black male drivers without cause to check for proper licensing, possession of illegal goods, and other similar violations. In this case, a social cue has become a stereotype that guides police policy. Young black males, the great majority of whom never commit an illegal act, view this police practice as harassment. Racial stereotyping therefore helps perpetuate the sometimes poor relations between young black men and law enforcement officials.

Stereotypes are rigid views of how members of various groups act, regardless of whether individual group members really behave that way.

In addition to status cues, verbal communication and interaction are assisted by interpretations of body language and facial expression.

Body Language and Facial Expressions

Earlier you learned that female status is usually associated with less power than male status is. Evidence of gender inequality at the micro-sociological level is evident in the conversation analysis studies reported earlier in the chapter. Such verbal communication inequalities are reinforced through non-verbal communication (see Figure 5.4).

Consider, for example, characteristics of body language that are widely considered to be "feminine." A feminine person "keeps her body small and contained," makes sure she "doesn't take up too much space or impose herself," and "walks and sits in tightly packaged ways" (Wade, 2013:1). In contrast, expansive body postures indicate power and entitlement. Recent studies thus show that expansive body postures lead people to feel more powerful and that such feelings encourage deviant conduct (Yap et al., 2013). Whether these postures are assumed consciously or not makes little difference. Under experimental conditions, people who assume expansive postures are more likely to cheat on a test, steal money, and commit traffic violations. These facts about body language show how structural inequality between women and men shows up in everyday, micro-level interaction.

Despite the wide variety of facial expressions in the human repertoire, research suggests that the facial expression of emotion is quite similar across cultures (Ekman, 1999). Cultural similarities are found in the facial expression of not only happiness, sadness, anger, disgust, fear, and surprise, but also the more complex emotions of amusement, contempt, contentment, embarrassment, excitement, guilt, pride, relief, satisfaction, sensory pleasure, and shame. But, like all symbols, facial expressions require interpretation, which are prone to misreading (Fernandez-Dols et al., 1997). Typically, untrained observers cannot distinguish fake from genuine smiles more often than one could expect based on chance (Wade, 2010). Facial expressions made when lying are also prone to misinterpretation. With training, however, the accuracy of reading facial expressions can be markedly improved.

FIGURE 5.4
Body Language

Among other things, body language can communicate both the degree to which people conform to gender roles and widely shared expectations about how males or females are supposed to act. In these photos, which postures suggest power and aggressiveness? Which suggest pleasant compliance? Which are "appropriate" to the gender of the person?

Source: Courtesy of Robert Brym.

Theory	Focus
Feminist	Status differences between women and men structure social interaction.
Conflict	The competitive exchange of valued resources structures social interaction.
Symbolic Interactionist	Social interaction involves the interpretation, negotiation, and modification of norms, roles, and statuses.

TABLE 5.2
Theories of Social Interaction

Symbolic interpretation is always embedded in a cultural context, and different cultural expectations can lead to colossal misunderstandings. For instance, until recently, it was considered rude among educated Japanese to say no. Disagreement was instead conveyed by discreetly changing the subject and smiling politely. Consequently, it was common for visiting North Americans to think that their Japanese hosts were saying yes because of the politeness, the smile, and the absence of a no, when in fact they were saying no.

Similarly, no gestures or body postures mean the same thing in all societies and all cultures. In our society, people point by using an outstretched hand and an extended finger. However, people raised in other cultures tip their head or use their chin or eyes to point out something. We nod our heads yes and shake no, but others nod no and shake yes.

Finally, we must note that in all societies, people communicate by manipulating the space that separates them from others (Hall, 1959, 1966). Sociologists commonly distinguish four zones that surround us. The size of these zones varies from one society to the next. In North America, an intimate zone extends about 0.5 metres from the body. It is restricted to people with whom we want sustained, intimate physical contact. A personal zone extends from about 0.5 metres to 1.5 metres away. It is reserved for friends and acquaintances. We tolerate only a little physical intimacy from such people. The social zone is situated in the area roughly 1.5 metres to 3.5 metres away from us. Apart from a handshake, no physical contact is permitted from people we restrict to that zone. The public zone starts around 3.5 metres from our bodies. It is used to distinguish a performer or a speaker from an audience.

As these examples show, face-to-face interaction may at first glance appear to be straightforward and unproblematic—and most of the time, it is. However, underlying the surface of human communication is a wide range of cultural assumptions, unconscious understandings, and nonverbal cues that make interaction possible (see Table 5.2).

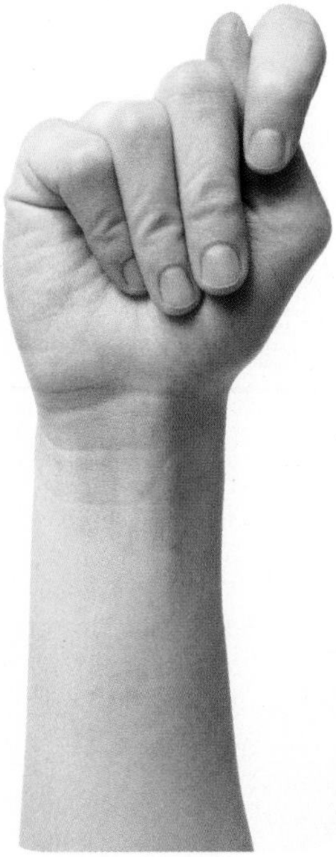
Dreamstime

Like many hand gestures, the "fig" means different things in different times and places. We probably know it as a sign that adults make when they play with children and pretend "I've got your nose." But in ancient Rome, the fig was meant to convey good luck; in India it represents a threat; and in Russia, Turkey, and South Korea, it means "screw you." It means "T" in the American Sign Language alphabet, but was modified in the International Sign Language alphabet to avoid giving offence.

TIME FOR REVIEW

- What is role distancing? How might it be evident in a 12-year-old assigned the chore of cleaning the toilet?
- What are breaching experiments? What do they tell us about social life?
- What is the difference between front-stage and back-stage role performances?
- Give an example from your everyday experience where using status cues successfully supported interaction. Give an example where using status cues failed to support interaction.
- Interlock your fingers and place your connected hands behind your head. Your arms will now form "elephant ears." How does this posture affect your feeling of dominance or submissiveness? Why?

DmitryOnishchik/Thinkstock.com

Society fits together like a set of nested Russian dolls, with face-to-face interaction constituting the smallest doll in the set.

FROM SMALL PROCESSES TO BIG STRUCTURES

In this chapter, we referred to norms, roles, and statuses as the "building blocks" of social life. These building blocks form the microstructures within which face-to-face interaction takes place. In concluding, we add that sustained microlevel interaction often gives rise to higher-level structures—"mesostructures," such as networks, groups, and organizations. In the next chapter, we examine these intermediate-level structures. Then, in Part 4 of this book, we show how these intermediate-level structures can form macrolevel structures known as *institutions*.

Society, it will emerge, fits together like a set of nested Russian dolls, with face-to-face interaction constituting the smallest doll in the set. Big structures set limits to the operation of small structures (see Box 5.4). However, it is within small structures that people interpret, negotiate, and modify their immediate social settings, thus giving big structures their dynamism and their life.

BOX 5.4

IT'S YOUR CHOICE

DOES NEGOTIATING SOCIAL ORDER TAKE TOO MUCH TIME AND ENERGY?

Lance Roberts reports the following recent experiences: "I am seated on a crowded bus, stand up, and offer my seat to an older woman. She replies in a brisk tone, 'I am fully capable of standing.' A student (who received a D on a recent test) and his mother appear during office hours to argue that I should 'cut him some slack' because he is a 'hockey star.' I am walking down the right side of a busy mall and must stay alert to avoid bumping into people who are walking on the same side in the opposite direction. Students whom I do not know send me emails that begin by addressing me by my first name. Despite public announcements, a stranger beside me at the movies continues to text during the film.

"For me, each of these events was annoying. In each social encounter, I thought the norms were clear: When someone offers you a seat, you gratefully accept it; you do not bring your mother to office hours; you walk on the right side of a corridor; strangers do not use first names; you follow public reminders to turn off your phone. I was annoyed by these interactions because social order was not taken for granted. In each case, I was required to negotiate a solution."

Interaction occurs in a social context. Micro interactions between you and others may seem like isolated experiences, but they are not. They are embedded in a larger social network, which conditions what you think is normal and take for granted.

One important feature of the social settings in which everyday experience occurs is their degree of social rigidity. Using this dimension, social contexts can be ranked from "tight" to "loose" (Gelfand et al., 2011). Tight social contexts are characterized by strong norms that are imposed on the situation and accepted by participants. Loose social contexts are characterized by weak norms that are proposed to and interpreted by participants (von Below et al., 2013). In relatively tight societies, social expectations for most situations are clearly defined and deviance is not tolerated. In relatively loose societies, social arrangements are negotiated and flexible.

The annoyance I experienced in the examples cited earlier resulted from low situational constraint. The situations were governed by vague norms that had to be negotiated, rather than clear ones that could be taken for granted. I was annoyed because I have more interesting things to do with my time and energy than negotiate ordinary courses of action. What do you think? Are you regularly surprised or annoyed by how others act in public? Would your life be more enjoyable if situational norms were clearer and conformity more reliable? Would you change your mind if you learned that societies with stronger situational constraints had fewer civil liberties, higher religiosity, more police presence, stronger criminal justice penalties, and more inequality?

SUMMARY

1. What are the key building blocks for the study of social interaction?
Social life is generally organized; it is underwritten by patterns. The patterns are mapped by identifying social statuses and the norms attached to them. Persons are unique individuals who bring organizations to life when they occupy statuses governed by norms. Organized social life is expressed by roles. When norms are simple, direct, and clear, roles are played. However, the norms guiding social action are often incomplete, inappropriate, ambiguous, or contradictory. These conditions encourage the use of individual autonomy through role-making.

2. How does feminist theory help us understand the role of emotions in social interaction?
Gender differences exist in interaction patterns and emotional expression. Feminists relate these differences to power inequalities between women and men. On average, women inhabit lower statuses. They are required to perform more emotional management and emotion labour than men are.

3. How does conflict theory help us understand the role of power in social interaction?
Power differences between people influence the form and emotional character of social interaction. In terms of achieving their desired outcomes, people with more power are generally more successful than are people with less power. They achieve their desired outcomes partly by influencing the construction of cultural scaffolding that defines some outcomes as preferable to others.

4. How does symbolic interactionism help us understand social interaction?
People rely on culture to understand themselves and their surroundings. Culture is composed of shared symbols that require interpretation to be meaningful. Symbolic interactionists focus on how people create meaning in the course of social interaction and on how they negotiate and modify roles, statuses, and norms. Symbolic interactionism has several variants. Dramaturgical analysis is based on the idea that people play roles in their daily lives in much the same way actors on stage play roles. Ethnomethodology analyzes the methods people use to make sense of what others do and say. It insists on the importance of preexisting shared norms and understandings in making everyday interaction possible. While language plays a central role in interaction, nonverbal symbols are also important. Status cues, body language, and facial expression operate to direct lines of communication and coordinate action.

CHAPTER 6

NETWORKS, GROUPS, BUREAUCRACIES, AND SOCIETIES

Nmedia/Can Stock Photo Inc.

IN THIS CHAPTER, YOU WILL LEARN TO

- Appreciate that although people usually act to satisfy their interests and emotions, social collectivities often influence people to suppress their emotion and act against their interests.
- Recognize that we live in a surprisingly small world in which only a few social ties separate us from complete strangers.
- Distinguish social networks, groups, bureaucracies, and societies.
- Identify ways in which social groups impose conformity on members and draw boundaries between those who belong and those who do not.
- Describe the ways in which bureaucracies can be made more efficient.
- Explain how humans' changing relationship to nature has affected population size, the permanence of settlements, the specialization of work tasks, labour productivity, and social inequality.

BEYOND INDIVIDUAL MOTIVES

The Holocaust

In 1941, the large stone and glass train station was one of the proudest structures in Smolensk, a provincial capital of about 100 000 people on Russia's western border. Always bustling, it was especially busy on the morning of June 28. Besides the usual passengers and well-wishers, hundreds of Soviet Red Army soldiers were nervously talking, smoking, writing hurried letters to their loved ones, and sleeping fitfully on the station floor waiting for their train. Nazi troops had invaded the nearby city of Minsk in Belarus a couple of days before. The Soviet soldiers were being positioned to defend Russia against the inevitable German onslaught.

Robert Brym's father, then in his 20s, had been standing in line for nearly two hours to buy food when he noticed flares arching over the station. Within seconds, Stuka bombers, the pride of the German air force, swept down, releasing their bombs just before pulling out of their dive. Inside the station, shards of glass, blocks of stone, and mounds of earth fell indiscriminately on sleeping soldiers and nursing mothers alike. Everyone panicked. People trampled on one another to get out. In minutes, the train station was rubble.

Nearly two years earlier, Robert's father had managed to escape Poland when the Nazis invaded his hometown near Warsaw. Now, he was on the run again. By the time the Nazis occupied Smolensk a few weeks after their dive-bombers had destroyed its train station, Robert's father was deep in the Russian interior serving in a workers' battalion attached to the Soviet Red Army.

"My father was one of 300 000 Polish Jews who fled eastward into Russia before the Nazi genocide machine could reach them," says Robert. "The remaining three million Polish Jews were killed in various ways. Some died in battle. Many more, like my father's mother and younger siblings, were rounded up like diseased cattle and shot. However, most of Poland's Jews wound up in the concentration camps. Those deemed unfit were shipped to the gas

AFP/Getty Images

Majdanek concentration camp near Lublin, Poland, 1944

chambers. Those declared able to work were turned into slaves until they could work no more. Then they, too, met their fate. A mere 9 percent of Poland's 3.3 million Jews survived World War II. The Nazi regime was responsible for the death of six million Jews in Europe (Burleigh, 2000).

"One question that always perplexed my father about the war was this: How was it possible for many thousands of ordinary Germans—products of what he regarded as the most advanced civilization on earth—to systematically murder millions of defenceless and innocent Jews, Roma ('Gypsies'), homosexuals, communists, and people with mental disabilities in the death camps? To answer this question adequately, we must borrow ideas from the sociological study of networks, groups, and bureaucracies."

How Social Groups Shape Our Actions

How could ordinary German citizens commit the crime of the twentieth century? The conventional, non-sociological answer is that many Nazis were evil, sadistic, or deluded enough to think that Jews and other "undesirables" threatened the existence of the German people. Therefore, in the Nazi mind, the innocents had to be killed. This answer is given in the 1993 movie *Schindler's List* and in many other accounts.

Yet it is far from the whole story. Sociologists emphasize three other factors:

1. *Norms of solidarity demand conformity.* When we form relationships with friends, lovers, spouses, teammates, and comrades-in-arms, we develop shared ideas or "norms of solidarity" about how we should behave toward them to sustain the relationships. Because these relationships are emotionally important to us, we sometimes pay more attention to norms of solidarity than to the morality of our actions. For example, a study of Nazis who roamed the Polish countryside to shoot and kill Jews and other "enemies" of Nazi Germany found that the soldiers often did not hate the people they systematically slaughtered, nor did they have many qualms about their actions (Browning, 1992). They simply developed deep loyalty to one another. They felt they had to get their assigned job done or face letting down their comrades. Thus, they committed atrocities partly because they just wanted to maintain group morale, solidarity, and loyalty. They committed evil deeds not because they were extraordinarily bad but because they were quite ordinary in the sense that they acted to sustain their friendship ties and to serve their group, just like most people do.

   The case of the Nazi regime may seem extreme, but other instances of going along with criminal behaviour uncover a similar dynamic at work. Why do people rarely

The Everett Collection/CP Picture Archive

German industrialist Oskar Schindler (Liam Neeson, centre) searches for his plant manager, Itzhak Stern, among a trainload of Polish Jews about to be deported to Auschwitz-Birkenau in *Schindler's List*. The movie turns the history of Nazism into a morality play, a struggle between good and evil forces. It does not probe into the sociological roots of good and evil.

report crimes committed by corporations? Employees may worry about being reprimanded or fired if they become whistleblowers, but they also worry about letting down their co-workers. Why do gang members engage in criminal acts? They may seek financial gain, but they also regard participating in criminal activity as a way of maintaining a close social bond with their fellow gang members (see Box 6.1).

A study of the small number of Polish Christians who helped save Jews during World War II helps clarify why some people violate group norms (Tec, 1986). The

BOX 6.1

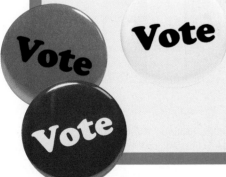

SOCIAL POLICY: WHAT DO YOU THINK?

GROUP LOYALTY OR BETRAYAL?

Glen Ridge, New Jersey, is an affluent suburb of about 8000 people. It was the site of a terrible rape case in 1989. A group of 13 teenage boys lured a sweet-natured young woman with an IQ of 49 into a basement. There, four of them raped her while three others looked on; six left when they realized what was going to happen. The rapists used a baseball bat and a broomstick. The boys were the most popular students in the local high school. The young woman was not a stranger to them. Some of them had known her since she was five years old, when they had convinced her to lick the point of a ballpoint pen that had been coated in dog feces.

Weeks passed before anyone reported the rape to the police. Years later, at trial, many members of the community rallied behind the boys, blaming and ostracizing the victim. The courts eventually found three of the four young men guilty of first-degree rape, but they were allowed to go free for eight years while their cases were appealed. In the end, they received only light sentences in 1997. One was released from jail in 1998, two others in 1999. Why did members of the community refuse to believe the clear-cut evidence? What made them defend the rapists? Why were the boys let off so easily?

Bernard Lefkowitz interviewed 250 key players and observers in what became known as the Glen Ridge rape case. Ultimately, he indicted the *community* for the rape. He concluded that "[the rapists] adhered to a code of behaviour that mimicked, distorted, and exaggerated the values of the adult world around them," while "the citizens supported the boys because they didn't want to taint the town they treasured" (Lefkowitz, 1997a: 493). What were some of the community values the elders upheld and the boys aped?

- *The subordination of women.* All the boys grew up in families where men were the dominant personalities. Only one of them had a sister. Not a single woman occupied a position of authority in Glen Ridge High School. The boys classified their female classmates either as "little mothers" who fawned over them or as "bad girls" who were simply sexual objects.
- *Lack of compassion for the weak.* According to the minister of Glen Ridge Congregational Church, "[a]chievement was honored and respected almost to the point of pathology, whether it was the achievements of high school athletes or the achievements of corporate world conquerors." Adds Lefkowitz: "Compassion for the weak wasn't part of the curriculum" (Lefkowitz, 1997a: 130).
- *Tolerance of male misconduct.* The boys routinely engaged in delinquent acts, including one spectacular trashing of a house. However, their parents always paid damages, covered up the misdeeds, and rationalized them with phrases like "boys will be boys." Especially because they were town football heroes, many people felt they could do no wrong.
- *Intense group loyalty.* "The guys prized their intimacy with each other far above what could be achieved with a girl," writes Lefkowitz (1997a: 146). The boys formed a tight clique, and team sports reinforced group solidarity. Under such circumstances, the probability of someone "ratting" on his friends was very low.

In the end, there was a "rat." His name was Charles Figueroa. He did not participate in the rape but he was an athlete, part of the jock clique, and therefore aware of what had happened. Significantly, he was one of the few black boys in the school, tolerated because of his athletic ability but never trusted because of his race. Behind his back, his teammates often called him a nigger. This young man's family was highly intelligent and morally sensitive. He was the only one to have the courage to betray the group (Lefkowitz, 1997a, 1997b).

The Glen Ridge rape case raises the important question of where we ought to draw the line between group loyalty and group betrayal. Considering your own group loyalties, have you ever regretted not having spoken up? Have you ever regretted not having been more loyal? What is the difference between these two types of situations? Can you specify criteria for deciding when loyalty is required and when betrayal is the right thing to do? You may have to choose between group loyalty and betrayal on more than one occasion, so thinking about these criteria—and clearly understanding the values for which your group stands—will help you make a more informed choice.

heroism of these Polish Christians was not correlated with their educational attainment, political orientation, religious background, or even attitudes toward Jews. In fact, some Polish Christians who helped save Jews were anti-Semitic. Instead, these Christian heroes were, for one reason or another, estranged or cut off from mainstream norms. Because they were poorly socialized into the norms of their society, they were freer not to conform and instead to act in ways they believed were right. We could tell a roughly similar story about corporate whistleblowers or people who turn in their fellow gang members. They are disloyal from an insider's point of view but heroic from an outsider's viewpoint, often because they have been poorly socialized into the group's norms.

2. *Structures of authority tend to render people obedient.* Most people find it difficult to disobey authorities because they fear ridicule, ostracism, and punishment. This fact was strikingly demonstrated in an experiment conducted by social psychologist Stanley Milgram (1974). Milgram informed his experimental subjects they were taking part in a study on punishment and learning. He brought each subject to a room where a man was strapped to a chair. An electrode was attached to the man's wrist. The experimental subject sat in front of a console. It contained 30 switches with labels ranging from "15 volts" to "450 volts" in 15-volt increments. Labels ranging from "slight shock" to "danger: severe shock" were pasted below the switches. The experimental subjects were told to administer a 15-volt shock for the man's first wrong answer and then increase the voltage each time he made an error. The man strapped in the chair was, in fact, an actor. He did not actually receive a shock. As the experimental subject increased the current, however, the actor began to writhe, shouting for mercy and begging to be released. If the experimental subjects grew reluctant to administer more current, Milgram assured them the man strapped in the chair would be fine and insisted that the success of the experiment depended on the subject's obedience. The subjects were, however, free to abort the experiment at any time. Remarkably, 71 percent of experimental subjects were prepared to administer shocks of 285 volts or more even though the switches starting at that level were labelled "intense shock," "extreme intensity shock," and "danger: severe shock" and despite the fact that the actor appeared to be in great distress at this level of current (see Figure 6.1).

Milgram's experiment teaches us that as soon as we are introduced to a structure of authority, we are inclined to obey those in power. This is the case even if the authority structure is new and highly artificial, even if we are free to walk away from it with no penalty, and even if we think that by remaining in its grip we are inflicting terrible pain on another human being. In this context, the actions and inactions of German citizens in World War II become more understandable if no more forgivable.

FIGURE 6.1

Social Distance Increases Obedience to Authority

Milgram's experiment supports the view that separating people from the negative effects of their actions increases the likelihood of compliance. When the subject and actor were in the same room and the subject was told to force the actor's hand onto the electrode, 30 percent of subjects administered the maximum 450-volt shock. When the subject and actor were merely in the same room, 40 percent of subjects administered the maximum shock. When the subject and actor were in different rooms but the subject could see and hear the actor, 62.5 percent of subjects administered the maximum shock. When subject and actor were in different rooms and the actor could be seen but not heard, 65 percent of subjects administered the maximum shock.

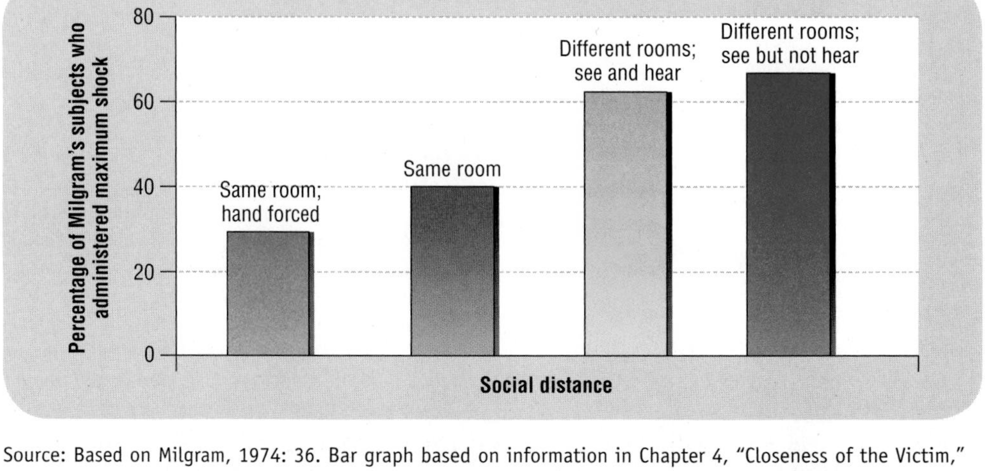

Source: Based on Milgram, 1974: 36. Bar graph based on information in Chapter 4, "Closeness of the Victim," from Obedience to Authority by Stanley Milgram. Copyright © 1974 by Stanley Milgram. Reprinted by permission of HarperCollins Publishers, Inc.

3. *Bureaucracies are highly effective structures of authority.* The Nazi genocide machine was effective because it was bureaucratically organized. As Max Weber (1978) defined the term, a **bureaucracy** is a large, impersonal organization comprising many clearly defined positions arranged in a hierarchy. A bureaucracy has a permanent, salaried staff of qualified experts and written goals, rules, and procedures. Staff members usually try to find ways of running their organization more efficiently. *Efficiency* means achieving the bureaucracy's goals at the least cost. The goal of the Nazi genocide machine was to kill Jews and other so-called undesirables. To achieve that goal with maximum efficiency, the job was broken into many small tasks. Most officials performed only one function, such as checking train schedules, organizing entertainment for camp guards, maintaining supplies of Zyklon B gas, or removing ashes from the crematoria. The full horror of what was happening eluded many officials or at least could be conveniently ignored as they concentrated on their jobs, most of them far removed from the gas chambers and death camps in occupied Poland. Many factors account for variations in Jewish victimization rates across Europe during World War II. One factor was bureaucratic organization. Not coincidentally, the proportion of Jews killed was highest not in the Nazi-controlled countries, such as Romania, where the hatred of Jews was most intense, but in countries such as Holland, where the Nazi bureaucracy was best organized (Bauman, 1991; Sofsky, 1997 [1993]).

Getty Images

Dr. Jeffrey Wigand was one of the most famous whistleblowers of the 1990s. Vice-president of research and development at Brown and Williams Tobacco Corp., Wigand was fired after he discovered that the company was adding ammonia and other chemicals to cigarettes to enhance nicotine absorption and speed up addiction. Despite threats and harassment, Wigand told all on the CBS public affairs program *60 Minutes*, ultimately leading to a US$368 billion suit against big tobacco for health-related damages. The story is the subject of the 1999 movie *The Insider*, starring Russell Crowe.

In short, the sociological reply to the question posed by Robert's father is that it was not just blind hatred but the nature of groups and bureaucracies that made it possible for the Nazis to kill innocent people so ruthlessly.

People commonly think *individual* motives prompt our actions, and for good reason. As we saw in Chapter 5, Social Interaction, we often make rational calculations to maximize gains and minimize losses. In addition, deeply held emotions partly govern our behaviour. However, this chapter asks you to make a conceptual leap beyond the individual motives that prompt us to act in certain ways. We ask you to consider the way four kinds of social *collectivities* shape our actions: networks, groups, bureaucratic organizations, and whole societies. The limitations of an analysis based exclusively on individual motives should be clear from our discussion of the social roots of evil. The advantages of considering how social collectivities affect us should become clear below. We begin by considering the nature and effects of social networks.

A **bureaucracy** is a large, impersonal organization comprising many clearly defined positions arranged in a hierarchy. A bureaucracy has a permanent, salaried staff of qualified experts and written goals, rules, and procedures. Ideally, staff members always try to find ways of running the bureaucracy more efficiently.

TIME FOR REVIEW

- What are norms of solidarity and how do they work to render people obedient?
- How do authority structures help to ensure conformity?
- Why are bureaucracies especially efficient means of ensuring conformity?

SOCIAL NETWORKS

It's a Small World

Suppose someone asked you to deliver a letter to a complete stranger on the other side of the country by using only acquaintances as intermediaries. You give the letter to an acquaintance, who can give the letter to one of his or her acquaintances, and so on. Research shows that, on average, it would take no more than six acquaintances to get the letter to the stranger. This fact suggests that we live in a small world; just a few social ties separate us from everyone else (Travers and Milgram, 1969).

Our world is small because we are enmeshed in overlapping sets of social relations, or social networks. Although any particular individual may know a small number of people, his or her family members, friends, co-workers, and others know many more people who extend far beyond that individual's personal network. So, for example, the authors of this textbook are likely to be complete strangers to you. Yet your professor may know one of us or at least know someone who knows one of us. Probably no more than three links separate us from you. Put differently, although our personal networks are small, they lead quickly to much larger networks. We live in a small world because our social networks connect us to the larger world (see Box 6.2).

BOX 6.2

SOCIOLOGY AT THE MOVIES

THE SOCIAL NETWORK

Facebook is one of the world's most popular websites, with more than half a billion users. Its main source of revenue is selling information about its users to advertisers. Mark Zuckerberg, its 30-year-old founder and principal shareholder, is the world's youngest self-made billionaire, with a net worth of $33 billion in 2014. *The Social Network* is the remarkable story of how Zuckerberg hatched Facebook in a Harvard dorm room in 2004 and cooked up a corporate omelette valued at $150 billion just ten years later—necessarily breaking a few eggs in the process.

Sociologists have mined Facebook for data to test theories about relationships, identity, self-esteem, popularity, collective action, race, and political engagement (Rosenbloom, 2007). However, the movie pays no attention to this research. Instead, it asks whether Zuckerberg's success was due more to his genius, cunning, or greed. Aaron Sorkin, who wrote the crisp, witty, exhilarating screenplay, seems to think it was a little of all three. If Sorkin had read more sociology, he might have concluded that social networks were also partly responsible for Facebook's stunning ascent.

Merrick Morton/© Columbia Pictures/Courtesy Everett Collection/CP Picture Archive

Mark Zuckerberg invents Facebook in *The Social Network.*

Think of the way Zuckerberg's personal network made the resources needed to create Facebook available to him. Zuckerberg was an undergraduate at Harvard, which regularly published a hard-copy *Facebook* containing photos and brief bios of Harvard students. Moreover, anyone even fleetingly familiar with the Internet in 2004—let alone a programming nerd like Zuckerberg—knew of the existence of popular dating and social networking sites operating on principles similar to those that Facebook would later adopt (Brym and Lenton, 2001).

Strong and weak ties led Zuckerberg to more specifically useful resources. Harvard upperclassmen Cameron and Tyler Winklevoss hired Zuckerberg to write code for a Harvard-based social-networking site. Zuckerberg liked their idea so much that, while he was ostensibly working for them, he developed Facebook on his own. (The Winklevosses later sued Zuckerberg, settling for $65 million.) For Facebook's start-up costs, Zuckerberg borrowed $15 000 from his roommate, Eduardo Saverin, whom he later defrauded for his share in Facebook. (Saverin also successfully sued.) According to Zuckerberg, he even got the idea of extending Facebook beyond Harvard from Dustin Moskovitz, another roommate. It may have taken a genius to see the enormous potential of a general Web-based social networking site and a combination of cunning and greed to "borrow" useful ideas and money from people in his personal network, but the raw materials for Facebook were in the air for anyone in Zuckerberg's position, and Zuckerberg's personal ties led him to them ("Bloomberg Game Changers," 2010; Wright, 2010).

The irony at the centre of *The Social Network* is that Zuckerberg, who invents the world's most powerful friendship machine, can't keep a friend. In the opening scene, his girlfriend dumps him, and myriad other failed relationships litter the movie. The irony of the irony is that Zuckerberg had just enough of the right kind of friends—or at least access to useful nodes in his personal network—to help make him what he is.

Sociologists define a **social network** as a bounded set of individuals linked by the exchange of material or emotional resources, everything from money to friendship. The patterns of exchange determine the boundaries of the network. Members exchange resources more frequently with one another than with non-members. They also think of themselves as network members. Social networks may be formal (defined in writing) or informal (defined only in practice). The people you know personally form the boundaries of your personal network. However, each of your network members is linked to other people. In this way, you can be connected to people you have never met, creating a small world that extends far beyond your personal network.

A **social network** is a bounded set of individuals who are linked by the exchange of material or emotional resources. The patterns of exchange determine the boundaries of the network. Members exchange resources more frequently with one another than with non-members. They also think of themselves as network members. Social networks may be formal (defined in writing), but they are more often informal (defined only in practice).

The Value of Network Analysis

The study of social networks is not restricted to ties among individuals (Berkowitz, 1982; Wasserman and Faust, 1994; Wellman and Berkowitz, 1997). The units of analysis or *nodes* in a network can be individuals, groups, organizations, and even countries. Thus, social network analysts have examined everything from intimate relationships between lovers to diplomatic relations among nations.

Unlike organizations, most networks lack names and offices. For example, there is a Scouts Canada but no North American Trading Bloc. In a sense, networks lie beneath the more visible collectivities of social life, but that makes them no less real or less important. Some analysts claim that by focusing on highly visible collectivities, we can gain only a partial sense of why certain things happen in the social world. From their point of view, getting the whole story requires probing below the surface and examining the network level. The study of social networks clarifies a wide range of social phenomena, including how people find jobs and how they form communities.

Finding a Job

Many people learn about important events, ideas, and opportunities from their social networks. Friends and acquaintances often introduce you to everything from an interesting college or university course or a great restaurant to a satisfying occupation or a future spouse. Of course, social networks are not the only source of information, but they are highly significant.

Consider how people find jobs. Do you look in the "Help Wanted" section of your local newspaper, scan the Internet, or walk around town looking for "Employee Wanted" signs? Although these strategies are common, people often learn about employment opportunities

The Everett Collection/CP Picture Archives

Parents can help their graduating children find jobs by getting them plugged into the right social networks. Here, in the 1967 movie *The Graduate*, a friend of the family advises Dustin Hoffman that the future lies in the plastics industry.

from other people. But what kind of people? According to Mark Granovetter (1973), you may have strong or weak ties to another person. You have strong ties to people who are close to you, such as family members and friends. You have weak ties to acquaintances, such as people you meet at parties and friends of friends. In his research, Granovetter found that weak ties are more important than strong ties are in finding a job, which is contrary to common sense. You might reasonably assume that an acquaintance would not do much to help you find a job whereas a close friend or relative would make a lot more effort in that regard. However, by focusing on the flow of information in personal networks, Granovetter found something different. Acquaintances are more likely to provide useful information about employment opportunities than friends or family members are because people who are close to you typically share overlapping networks. Therefore, the information they can provide about job opportunities is often redundant. In contrast, acquaintances are likely to be connected to *diverse* networks. They can therefore provide information about many different job openings and introduce you to many different potential employers. Moreover, because people typically have more weak ties than strong ties, the sum of weak ties holds more information about job opportunities than the sum of strong ties. These features of personal networks allow Granovetter to conclude that the "strength of weak ties" lies in their diversity and abundance.

Urban Networks

We rely on social networks for a lot more than job information. Consider everyday life in the big city. We often think of big cities as cold and alienating places where few people know one another. In this view, urban acquaintanceships tend to be few and functionally specific; we know someone fleetingly as a bank teller or a server in a restaurant but not as a whole person. Even dating often involves a long series of brief encounters. In contrast, people often think of small towns as friendly, comfortable places where everyone knows everyone else (and everyone else's business). Some of the founders of sociology emphasized just this distinction. Notably, German sociologist Ferdinand Tönnies (1988 [1887]) contrasted "community" with "society." According to Tönnies, a community is marked by intimate and emotionally intense social ties, whereas a society is marked by impersonal relationships held together largely by self-interest. A big city is a prime example of a society in Tönnies's judgment.

Tönnies's view prevailed until network analysts started studying big-city life in the 1970s. Where Tönnies saw only sparse, functionally specific ties, network analysts found elaborate social networks, some functionally specific and some not. For example, Barry Wellman and his colleagues studied personal networks in Toronto (Wellman, Carrington, and Hall, 1997). They found that each Torontonian has an average 400 social ties, including immediate and extended kin, neighbours, friends, and co-workers. These ties provide everything from emotional aid (e.g., visits after a personal tragedy) and financial support (e.g., small loans) to minor services (e.g., fixing a car) and information of the kind studied by Granovetter. Strong ties that last a long time are typically restricted to immediate family members, a few close relatives and friends, and a close co-worker or two. Beyond that, however, people rely on a wide array of ties for different purposes at different times. Compared with 50 years ago, it may be less common now to see downtown residents sitting on their front porch on a summer evening, sipping soft drinks and chatting with neighbours as the kids play road hockey. However, the automobile, public transportation, the telephone, and the Internet help people stay in close touch with a wide range of contacts for a variety of purposes (Haythornthwaite and Wellman, 2002). Far from living in an impersonal and alienating world, Torontonians' lives are network-rich. Research conducted elsewhere in North America reveals much the same pattern of urban life.

Online Networks

Some people believe that cellphones and the Internet impair social interaction, isolate individuals, and ruin community life. They note that friends meeting for coffee in 1990 would pay close attention to each other, whereas friends meeting for coffee today routinely interrupt their interaction to check and respond to messages on their smartphone. Similarly, widespread Internet access allows people to spend an enormous amount of time staring at a computer screen instead of interacting face-to-face with family members and neighbours. From this point of view, the Internet disrupts and destroys social life.

When sociologists examine Internet-based social interaction, they find a different reality. One study shows that the top three audiences for undergraduate Facebook users are "my old high school friends," "people in my classes," and "other friends." "Total strangers" are the fourth-ranked audience, followed by "someone I met at a party" and "family." Even when students meet total strangers online, they tend to be strangers within a known and trusted institution, notably their college or university. Facebook does not usually break down existing social ties. As undergraduates use Facebook, they tend to gain information and emotional support, solidifying existing offline relationships and strengthening community ties (Ellison, Steinfeld, and Lampe, 2007).

The Building Blocks of Social Networks

Researchers often use mathematical models and computer programs to analyze social networks. However, no matter how sophisticated the mathematics or the software, network analysts begin from an understanding of the basic building blocks of social networks.

The most elementary network form is the **dyad**, a social relationship between two nodes or social units (e.g., people, firms, organizations, countries). A **triad** is a social relationship among three nodes. The difference between a dyad and a triad may seem small. However, the social dynamics of these two elementary network forms are fundamentally different, as sociologist Georg Simmel showed early in the twentieth century (Simmel, 1950; see Figure 6.2).

A **dyad** is a social relationship between two nodes or social units (e.g., people, firms, organizations, countries).

A **triad** is a social relationship among three nodes or social units (e.g., people, firms, organizations, countries).

In a dyadic relationship, such as a marriage, both partners tend to be intensely and intimately involved. Moreover, for the dyad to exist, it needs both partners—but to "die" it needs only one to opt out. A marriage, for example, can endure only if both partners are intensely involved; if one partner ceases active participation, the marriage is over in practice if not in law. The need for intense involvement on the part of both partners is also why a dyad can have no "free riders," or partners who benefit from the relationship without contributing to it. Finally, in a dyadic relationship, the partners must assume full responsibility for all that transpires. Neither partner can shift responsibility to some larger collectivity because no larger collectivity exists beyond the relationship between the two partners.

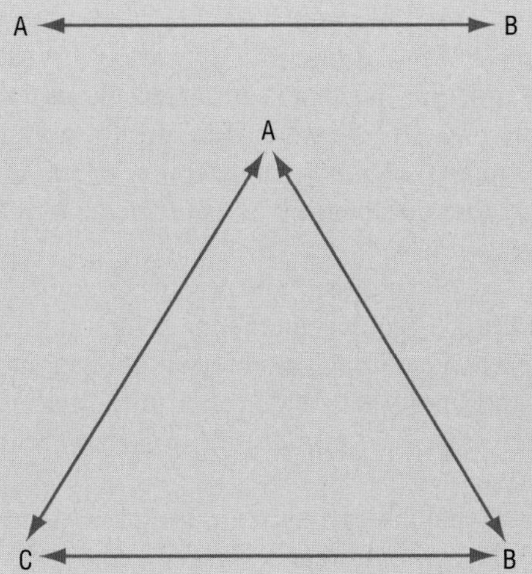

Characteristics of the dyad:
1. Both partners are intensely absorbed in the relationship.
2. The dyad needs both partners to live but only one to die.
3. No "free riders" are possible.
4. Neither partner can deny responsibility by shifting it to a larger collectivity.

Characteristics of the triad:
1. Intensity and intimacy are reduced.
2. The triad restricts individuality by allowing a partner to be constrained for the collective good. A partner may be outvoted by a majority, for example.
3. Coalitions are possible.
4. Third-party mediation of conflict between two partners is possible.
5. Third-party exploitation of rivalry between two partners is possible.
6. A third-party divide-and-conquer strategy is possible.
7. "Free riders" are possible.
8. It is possible to shift responsibility to the larger collectivity.

FIGURE 6.2
Dyad and Triad

In contrast, when a third person enters the picture, thereby creating a triad, relationships tend to be less intimate and intense. Equally significantly, the triad restricts individuality by allowing one partner to be constrained for the collective good. This situation occurs when a majority outvotes one partner. The existence of a triad also allows the formation of coalitions or factions. Furthermore, a triad allows one partner to mediate conflict between the other two, exploit rivalry between the other two, or encourage rivalry between the other two to achieve dominance. Thus, the introduction of a third partner makes possible a completely new set of social dynamics that are structurally impossible in a dyadic relationship.

TIME FOR REVIEW

- Why are any two strangers connected by just a few social links?
- How can weak ties yield strong results when searching for a job?
- When the scale of a network increases from two to three nodes, what new possibilities for social interaction emerge?

A **social group** comprises one or more networks of people who identify with one another and adhere to defined norms, roles, and statuses.

A **social category** comprises people who share a similar status but do not identify with one another.

In **primary groups**, norms, roles, and statuses are agreed on but are not put in writing. Social interaction leads to strong emotional ties. It extends over a long period, and involves a wide range of activities. It results in group members knowing one another well.

Secondary groups are larger and more impersonal than primary groups are. Compared with primary groups, social interaction in secondary groups creates weaker emotional ties. It extends over a shorter period, and it involves a narrow range of activities. It results in most group members having at most a passing acquaintance with one another.

IS GROUP LOYALTY ALWAYS FUNCTIONAL?

Love and Group Loyalty

Intensity and intimacy characterize many dyadic relationships. However, outside forces can destroy these relationships. For instance, the star-crossed lovers in *Romeo and Juliet* are torn between their love for each other and their loyalty to the feuding Montague and Capulet families. In the end, Romeo and Juliet die, victims of the feud.

Love thwarted by conflicting group loyalty is the stuff of many tragic plays, novels, and movies. Most audiences have no problem grasping that group loyalty is often more powerful than romantic love is. However, it is unclear why group loyalty holds such power over us. Also unclear is whether the power of group loyalty is always beneficial, as functionalists are inclined to argue. Before delving into the insights that the sociological study of groups offers on these issues, it will prove useful to define a few terms.

Primary and Secondary Groups

Social groups are composed of one or more networks of people who identify with one another, routinely interact, and adhere to defined norms, roles, and statuses. We usually distinguish social groups from **social categories**, people who share similar status but do not identify with one another. Coffee drinkers form a social category. They do not normally share norms and identify with one another. In contrast, members of a family, sports team, or college are aware of shared membership. They think of themselves as members of a collectivity and routinely interact. They form groups.

Many kinds of social groups exist. However, sociologists make a basic distinction between primary and secondary groups. In **primary groups**, members agree on norms, roles, and statuses but do not define them in writing. Social interaction creates strong emotional ties. It extends over a long period and involves a wide range of activities. It results in group members knowing one another well. The family is the most important primary group.

Secondary groups are larger and more impersonal than primary groups are. Compared with primary groups, social interaction in secondary groups creates weaker emotional ties. It extends over a shorter period and involves a narrow range of activities. It results in most group members having at most a passing acquaintance with one another. Your sociology class is an example of a secondary group.

Bearing these distinctions in mind, we can begin to explore the power of groups to ensure conformity.

The main primary group is the family, which is an enduring, multifunctional social unit characterized by unwritten consensus concerning norms, roles and statuses, emotional intensity, and intimacy.

Benefits of Group Conformity

Television's first reality TV show was *Candid Camera*. On an early episode, an unsuspecting man waited for an elevator. When the elevator door opened, he found four people, all confederates of the show, facing the elevator's back wall. Seeing the four people with their backs to him, the man at first hesitated. He then tentatively entered the elevator. However, rather than turning around so he would face the door, he remained facing the back wall, just like the others. The scene was repeated several times. Men and women, black and white, all behaved the same way. Confronting unanimously bizarre behaviour, they chose conformity over common sense.

Conformity is an integral part of group life, and primary groups generate more pressure to conform than do secondary groups. Strong social ties create emotional intimacy. They also ensure that primary group members share similar attitudes, beliefs, and information. Beyond the family, friendship groups (or cliques) and gangs demonstrate these features. Conformity ensures group cohesion.

A classic study of soldiers in World War II demonstrates the power of conformity to get people to face extreme danger. Samuel Stouffer and his colleagues (1949) showed that primary group cohesion was the main factor motivating soldiers to engage in combat. Rather than belief in a cause, such as upholding liberty or fighting the evils of Nazism, the feeling of camaraderie, loyalty, and solidarity with fellow soldiers supplied the principal motivation to face danger. Brigadier General S.L.A. Marshall (1947: 160–61) famously wrote: "A man fights to help the man next to him. … Men do not fight for a cause but because they do not want to let their comrades down." Or as one soldier says in the 2001 movie *Black Hawk Down*: "When I go home people will ask me, 'Hey, Hoot, why do you do it, man? Why? Are you some kinda war junkie?' I won't say a goddamn word. Why? They won't understand. They won't understand why we do it. They won't understand it's about the men next to you. And that's it. That's all it is." As such, if you want to create a great military force, you need to promote group solidarity and identity—which explains the importance of wearing uniforms, singing anthems, displaying insignia, hoisting flags, conducting drills, training under duress, and instilling hatred of the enemy.

The same processes operate in everyday life, as the 2004 movie, *Mean Girls*, shows. *Mean Girls* is the story of 17-year-old Cady Heron (played by Lindsay Lohan), who was home-schooled in Africa by her archaeologist parents and is then plunked into a suburban American high school when the family moves back to the United States. The ways of the school bewilder her, so a friend prepares "Cady's Map to North Shore High School." It shows the layout of the cafeteria, with tables neatly labeled "Varsity Jocks," "J.V. Jocks," "Plastics," "Preps," "Fat Girls," "Thin Girls," "Black Hotties," "Asian Nerds," "Cool Asians," "Cheerleaders," "Burnouts," and so on. If you drew a map of your high school cafeteria—for that matter, even your college or university cafeteria—the labels might be different, but chances are they would represent cliques that are just as segregated as North Shore High was.

Cady Heron (Lindsay Lohan) receives instruction about the cliques of North Shore High School in *Mean Girls*.

Everywhere, group members tend to dress and act alike, use the same slang, like and dislike the same kind of music, and demand loyalty, especially in the face of external threat. All groups demand conformity and, to varying degrees, they get it, although, of course, group loyalties may change with changing social circumstances (see Box 6.3).

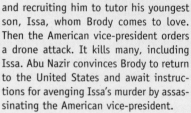

BOX 6.3

SOCIOLOGY ON THE TUBE

HOMELAND AND THE AMBIGUITIES OF GROUP MEMBERSHIP

From the 1950s to the 1980s, a few big TV networks dominated the airwaves. They developed middle-of-the-road programs that appealed to a mass audience and shunned controversy.

TV series were just collections of stand-alone episodes. You didn't need to see early installments to fully appreciate what was going on in later ones because characters and plot lines remained pretty much the same for the duration.

Little changed when cable TV took off in the 1970s. The new technology merely brought previously inaccessible network programs within reach. For example, Canadians could now tune into American stations even if they happened to live far from the international border.

In contrast, the 1980s and especially the 1990s saw independent cable TV stations starting to appeal to specific audience segments by developing their own programs. They fragmented the mass audience. TV stations were devoted to one type of program—news, sports, children's shows, food, popular music, pornography, old movies, and so on.

Didier Baveral/© Showtime Network/ Courtesy: Everett Collection/CP Picture Archive

CIA agent Carrie Mathison (played by Claire Danes) in *Homeland*.

One previously ignored market segment—sophisticated viewers—was attracted by new dramatic series boasting multifaceted characters and intricate story lines stretching over many episodes. For the first time in the history of the medium, dramatic series that avoided stereotypes and mirrored the complexities of real life appeared. The first of the new breed was *The Sopranos*. It debuted in January 1999 and captivated its audience for 86 hour-long episodes until June 2007. *The Sopranos* paved the way for such critical and popular hits as *The Wire, Battlestar Galactica, Deadwood, Breaking Bad, Friday Night Lights, Mad Men,* and *Homeland* (Sepinwall, 2012).

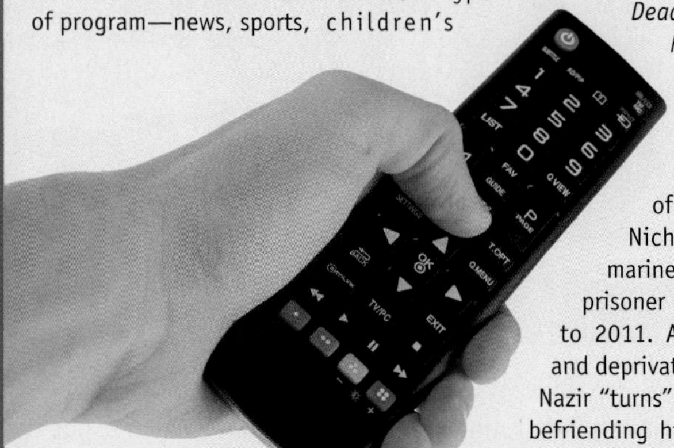

Ambiguities of group membership generate much of *Homeland*'s dramatic tension. Nicholas Brody is an American marine sergeant, captured and held prisoner by al-Qaeda in Iraq from 2003 to 2011. After Brody's years of torture and deprivation, al-Qaeda mastermind Abu Nazir "turns" Brody by treating him kindly, befriending him, converting him to Islam, and recruiting him to tutor his youngest son, Issa, whom Brody comes to love. Then the American vice-president orders a drone attack. It kills many, including Issa. Abu Nazir convinces Brody to return to the United States and await instructions for avenging Issa's murder by assassinating the American vice-president.

On Brody's return to the United States, he is welcomed as a war hero and soon wins a seat in the U.S. Congress. However, CIA agent Carrie Mathison has intelligence that leads her to suspect that Brody is an al-Qaeda agent. To gain more information, she engineers an affair with Brody, who is married and has two children. They seem to fall in love.

Mathison eventually discovers evidence confirming Brody's affiliation with Abu Nazir. Confronted with the evidence, Brody is forced to become a CIA double agent charged with helping to bring down Abu Nazir. The operation is headed by Peter Quinn, whose boss, we discover, is not in the CIA. Quinn seems to have instructions to kill Brody after Brody disposes of Abu Nazir.

Is Brody loyal to the CIA or to Abu Nazir? Is he loyal to his wife or to Mathison? Is Mathison loyal to Brody or to the CIA? Is Quinn loyal to the CIA or to some other body? In the old days of TV, the good guys and the bad guys looked and talked differently and remained dedicated to their respective groups. Good drama on TV today is more realistic sociologically, recognizing that group loyalties can shift as circumstances change. In *Homeland*, we are even left wondering who are the good guys and who are the bad guys—the Americans, who suffer lethal terrorist attacks, or Abu Nazir, whose land was invaded by the Americans and whose innocent young son was killed by them. We are even asked to question our own group loyalties.

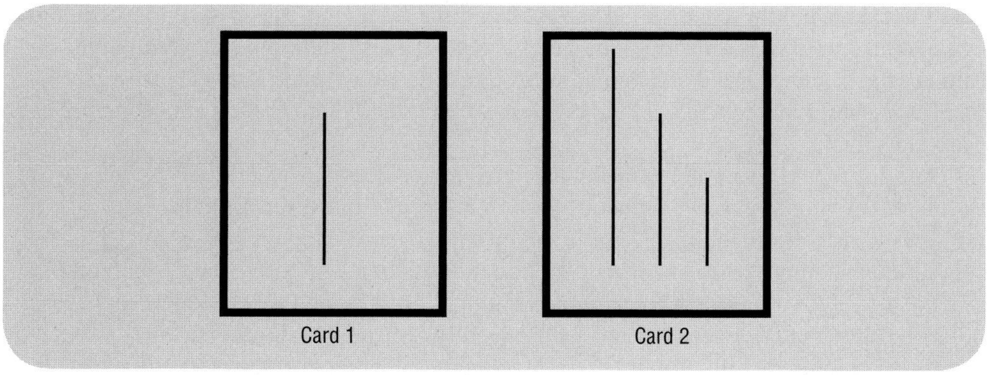

FIGURE 6.3
The Asch Experiment

The Asch Experiment

A famous experiment conducted by social psychologist Solomon Asch also demonstrates how group pressure creates conformity (Asch, 1955). Asch assembled a group of seven men. One of them was the experimental subject; the other six were Asch's confederates. Asch showed the seven men a card with a line drawn on it. He then showed them a second card with three lines of varying length drawn on it (see Figure 6.3). One by one, he asked the confederates to judge which line on card 2 was the same length as the line on card 1. The answer was obvious. One line on card 2 was much shorter than the line on card 1. One line was much longer. One was exactly the same length. Yet, as instructed by Asch, all six confederates said that either the shorter or the longer line was the same length as the line on card 1. When it came time for the experimental subject to make his judgment, he typically overruled his own perception and agreed with the majority. Only 25 percent of Asch's experimental subjects consistently gave the right answer. Asch thus demonstrated how easily group pressure can overturn individual conviction and result in conformity.

Asch's work and subsequent research show that several factors affect the likelihood of conformity (Sternberg, 1998: 499–500). First, the likelihood of conformity increases as *group size* increases to three or four members. For groups larger than four, the likelihood of conformity generally does not increase. Second, as *group cohesiveness* increases, so does the likelihood of conformity. Where greater intimacy and sharing of values occur, group members are less likely to express dissent. Third, *social status* affects the likelihood of conformity. People with low status in a group (e.g., because of their gender or race) are less likely to dissent than are people with high status. Fourth, *culture* matters. People in individualistic societies, like Canada, tend to conform less than do people in collectivist societies, like China. Fifth, the *appearance of unanimity* affects the likelihood of conformity. Even one dissenting voice greatly increases the chance that others will dissent.

Disadvantages of Group Conformity

Groupthink and Bystander Apathy

As functionalists note, the power of groups to ensure conformity is often a valuable asset. Armies could not operate without willingness to undergo personal sacrifice for the good of the group, nor could sports teams excel. However, being a good team player can have a downside because the consensus of a group can sometimes be misguided or dangerous. Dissent might save the group from making mistakes, but the pressure to conform despite individual misgivings—sometimes called **groupthink**—can lead to disaster (Janis, 1972).

Groupthink is group pressure to conform despite individual misgivings.

The dangers of groupthink are greatest in high-stress situations. For example, groupthink was at work in high-level meetings preceding the space shuttle *Columbia* disaster in 2003. Transcripts of those meetings show that the NASA official who ran the shuttle management meetings, a non-engineer, believed from the outset that foam insulation debris could not damage the spacecraft. She dismissed the issue and cut off discussion when an engineer expressed his concerns. The others present quickly fell into line with the manager running the meeting (Wald and Schwartz, 2003). A few days later, damage caused by foam insulation debris caused *Columbia* to break apart on re-entry into Earth's atmosphere. Seven astronauts died.

Bystander apathy occurs when people observe someone in an emergency but offer no help.

The concept of **bystander apathy** is related to the idea of groupthink. Bystander apathy occurs when people observe someone in an emergency but offer no help. One case that attracted worldwide attention in 2011 involved a two-year-old toddler in Foshan, China, who was seriously injured when she wandered into the path of a van. Surveillance footage shows that the driver did not stop. A truck then drove over her a second time. Again, the driver did not stop. More than a dozen of people subsequently turned a blind eye when they walked by the critically injured child. Finally, a trash collector pulled her off the road and managed to track down her mother. The child later died in hospital (see the YouTube video of this incident at www.youtube.com/verify_age?next_url=/watch%3Fv%3D05P0mjtnoD8). Studies of bystander apathy suggest that, in general, as the number of bystanders increases, the likelihood of any one bystander helping another decreases because the greater the number of bystanders, the less responsibility any one individual feels. This behaviour shows that people usually take their cues for action from others and again demonstrates the power of groups over individuals.

Group Conformity, Group Conflict, and Group Inequality

Functionalists often emphasize the benefits of group conformity. They are inclined to overlook the ways in which conflict within groups can avert disaster. By emphasizing the benefits of group conformity, functionalists are also inclined to ignore the ways in which group conformity encourages conflict and reinforces inequality.

In-group members are people who belong to a group.

Out-group members are people who are excluded from an in-group.

If a group exists, it follows that some people must not belong to it. Accordingly, sociologists distinguish **in-group** members (those who belong) from **out-group** members (those who do not). Members of an in-group typically draw a boundary separating themselves from members of the out-group and they try to keep out-group members from crossing the line. Anyone who has gone to high school knows all about in-groups and out-groups. They have seen first-hand how race, class, athletic ability, academic talent, and physical attractiveness act as boundaries separating groups.

Group Boundaries: Competition and Self-Esteem

Why do group boundaries crystallize? One theory is that group boundaries emerge when people compete for scarce resources. For example, old immigrants may greet new immigrants with hostility if the latter are seen as competitors for scarce jobs (Levine and Campbell, 1972). Another theory is that group boundaries emerge when people are motivated to protect their self-esteem. From this point of view, drawing group boundaries allows people to increase their self-esteem by believing that out-groups have low status (Tajfel, 1981).

The classic experiment on prejudice, *The Robber's Cave Study* (Sherif et al., 1988 [1961]), supports both theories. Researchers brought two groups of 11-year-old boys to a summer camp at Robber's Cave State Park in Oklahoma in 1954. The boys were strangers to one another and for about a week the two groups were kept apart. They swam, camped, and hiked. Each group chose a name for itself, and the boys printed their group's name on their caps and T-shirts. Then the two groups met. A series of athletic competitions was set up between them. Soon, each group became highly antagonistic toward the other. Each group came to hold the other in low esteem. The boys ransacked cabins, started food fights, and stole various items from members of the other group. Thus, under competitive conditions, the boys drew group boundaries starkly and quickly.

Natural or artificial boundaries—rivers, mountains, highways, railway tracks—typically separate groups or communities.

The investigators next stopped the athletic competitions and created several apparent emergencies whose solution required cooperation between the two groups. One such emergency involved a leak in the pipe supplying water to the camp. The researchers assigned the boys to teams of members from *both* groups. Their job was to inspect the pipe and fix the leak. After engaging in several such cooperative ventures, the boys started playing together without fighting. Once cooperation replaced competition and the groups ceased to hold each other in low esteem, group boundaries melted away as quickly as they had formed.

Significantly, the two groups were of equal status—the boys were all white, middle class, and 11 years old—and their contact involved face-to-face interaction in a setting where norms established by the investigators promoted a reduction of group prejudice. Social scientists today recognize that all these conditions must be in place before the boundaries between an in-group and an out-group fade (Sternberg, 1998: 512).

Dominant Groups

The boundaries separating groups often seem unchangeable and even "natural." In general, however, dominant groups construct group boundaries in particular circumstances to further their goals (Barth, 1969; Tajfel, 1981). Consider Germans and Jews. By the early twentieth century, Jews were well integrated into German society. They were economically successful, culturally innovative, and politically influential, and many of them considered themselves more German than Jewish. In 1933, the year Hitler seized power, 44 percent of marriages involving at least one German Jew were marriages to a non-Jew. In addition, some German Jews converted before marrying non-Jewish Germans (Gordon, 1984). Yet, although the boundary separating Germans from Jews was quite weak, the Nazis chose to redraw and reinforce it. Defining a Jew as anyone who had at least one Jewish grandparent, the Nazis passed a series of anti-Jewish laws and, in the end, systematically slaughtered the Jews of Europe. The division between Germans and Jews was not "natural." It came into existence because of its perceived usefulness to a dominant group.

We conclude that both the functionalist and conflict perspectives contribute much to our appreciation of how social groups operate. By emphasizing the benefits of group conformity, functionalists increase our understanding of the means by which individuals are mobilized to achieve group goals. In contrast, conflict theorists caution us to recognize that too much conformity can be dangerous: failure to dissent can have disastrous consequences and high levels of group conformity often reinforce group inequality.

Groups and Social Imagination

In concluding this section, we note that group interaction is not always face to face. Often, people interact with other group members in their imagination.

Consider reference groups, which are composed of people against whom an individual evaluates his or her situation or conduct. Members of a **reference group** function as role models. Reference groups may influence us even though they represent a largely imaginary ideal. For instance, the advertising industry promotes certain body ideals that many people try to emulate, although we know that hardly anyone can look like a runway model.

A **reference group** comprises people against whom an individual evaluates his or her situation or conduct.

JPL/NASA

Is it possible to imagine everyone in the world as a community? Why or why not? Under what conditions might it be possible?

We need to exercise our imaginations vigorously to participate in the group life of a society like ours because much social life in a complex society involves belonging to secondary groups without knowing or interacting with most group members. It is impossible for an individual to interact with any more than a small fraction of the more than 35 million people living in this country. Nonetheless, most Canadians feel a strong emotional bond to other Canadians. Similarly, think about the employees and students at your college or university. They know they belong to the same secondary group and many of them are probably loyal to it. Yet how many people at your school have you met? Probably no more than a small fraction of the total. One way to make sense of the paradox of intimacy despite distance is to think of your postsecondary institution or Canada as "imagined communities." They are imagined because you cannot possibly meet most members of the group and can only speculate about what they must be like. They are, nonetheless, communities because people believe strongly in their existence and importance (Anderson, 1991).

Many secondary groups are **formal organizations**, secondary groups designed to achieve explicit objectives. In complex societies like ours, the most common and influential formal organizations are bureaucracies. We now turn to an examination of these often frustrating but necessary organizational forms.

Formal organizations are secondary groups designed to achieve explicit objectives.

TIME FOR REVIEW

- How is conformity to group norms useful?
- How is conformity to group norms dangerous?
- How can conformity to group norms increase or reinforce social inequality?

BUREAUCRACIES

Bureaucratic Inefficiency

Earlier, we noted that Weber regarded bureaucracies as the most efficient type of secondary group. This sentiment runs against the grain of common knowledge. In everyday speech, when someone says *bureaucracy*, people commonly think of bored clerks sitting in small cubicles spinning out endless trails of "red tape" that create needless waste and frustrate the goals of clients. So it may seem odd to think of bureaucracies as being efficient.

How can we square the reality of bureaucratic inefficiencies with Weber's view that bureaucracies are the most efficient type of secondary group? The answer is twofold. First, we must recognize that when Weber wrote about the efficiency of bureaucracy, he was comparing it with older organizational forms that operated on the basis of either traditional practice ("We do it this way because we've always done it this way") or the charisma of their leaders ("We do it this way because our chief inspires us to do it this way"). Compared with such "traditional" and "charismatic" organizations, bureaucracies *are* generally more efficient. Second, we must recognize that Weber thought bureaucracies could operate efficiently only in the ideal case. He wrote extensively about some of bureaucracy's less admirable aspects in the real world. In other words, he understood that reality is often messier than the ideal case. So should we. In reality, bureaucracies vary in efficiency. Therefore, rather than proclaiming bureaucracy as being efficient or inefficient, we should find out what makes bureaucracies work well or poorly.

Traditionally, sociologists have lodged four main criticisms against bureaucracies. First is the problem of **dehumanization**. Rather than treating clients and personnel as people with unique needs, bureaucracies sometimes treat clients as standard cases and personnel as cogs in a giant machine. This treatment frustrates clients and lowers worker morale. Second is the problem of **bureaucratic ritualism** (Merton, 1968 [1949]). Bureaucrats sometimes become so preoccupied with rules and regulations that they make it difficult for the organization to fulfill its goals. Third is the problem of **oligarchy**, or "rule of the few" (Michels, 1949 [1911]). Some sociologists have argued that in all bureaucracies, power tends to become increasingly concentrated in the hands of a few people at the top of the organizational pyramid. This tendency is particularly problematic in political organizations because it hinders democracy and renders leaders unaccountable to the public. Fourth is the problem of **bureaucratic inertia**. Bureaucracies are sometimes so large and rigid that they lose touch with reality and continue their policies even when their clients' needs change.

Two main factors underlie bureaucratic inefficiency: size and social structure. Consider size first. The larger the bureaucracy, the more difficult it is for functionaries to communicate. Moreover, bigger bureaucracies make it easier for rivalries and coalitions to form. As Figure 6.4 shows, only one dyadic relationship can exist between two people, whereas three dyadic relationships can exist among three people and six dyadic relationships among four people. The number of potential dyadic relationships increases exponentially with the number of people. Hence, 300 dyadic relationships are possible among 25 people and 1225 dyadic relationships are possible among 50 people. The possibility of clique formation, rivalries, conflict, and miscommunication rises as quickly as the number of possible dyadic social relationships in an organization.

The second factor underlying bureaucratic inefficiency is social structure. Figure 6.5 shows a typical bureaucratic structure: a hierarchy. The bureaucracy has a head. Below the head are three divisions. Below the divisions are six departments. As you move up the hierarchy, the power of the staff increases. Note also the lines of communication that join the various bureaucratic units. Departments report only to their divisions. Divisions report only to the head.

Usually, the more levels in a bureaucratic structure, the more difficult communication becomes because people must communicate indirectly, through department and division heads, rather than directly with each other. Information may be lost, blocked, reinterpreted, or distorted as it moves up the hierarchy, or an excess of information may cause top levels to become engulfed in a paperwork blizzard that prevents them from clearly seeing the needs of the organization and its clients. Bureaucratic heads may have only a vague and imprecise idea of what is happening "on the ground" (Wilensky, 1967).

Dehumanization occurs when bureaucracies treat clients as standard cases and personnel as cogs in a giant machine. This treatment frustrates clients and lowers worker morale.

Bureaucratic ritualism involves bureaucrats becoming so preoccupied with rules and regulations that they make it difficult for the organization to fulfill its goals.

Oligarchy means "rule of the few." All bureaucracies have a supposed tendency for power to become increasingly concentrated in the hands of a few people at the top of the organizational pyramid.

Bureaucratic inertia refers to the tendency of large, rigid bureaucracies to continue their policies even when their clients' needs change.

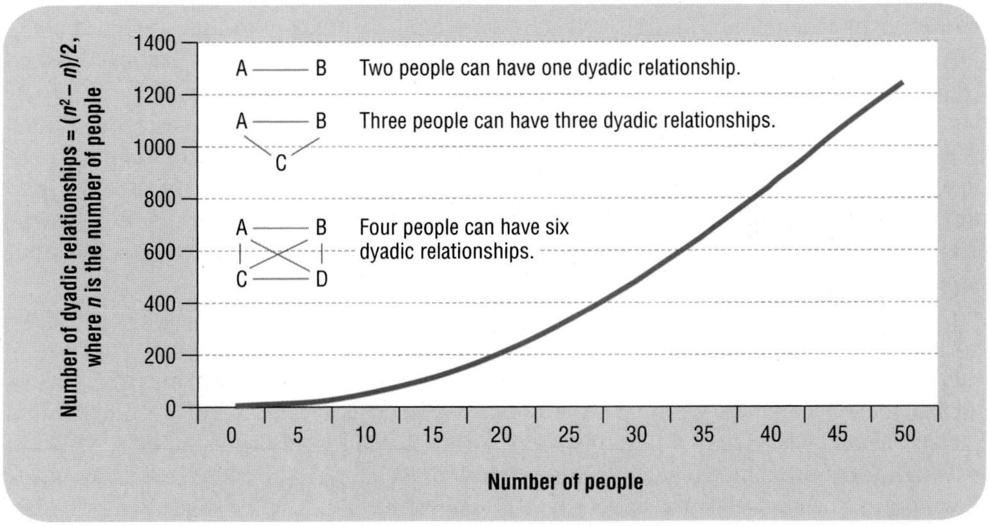

FIGURE 6.4
Number of Possible Dyadic Relationships by Number of People in Group

FIGURE 6.5
Bureaucratic Structure

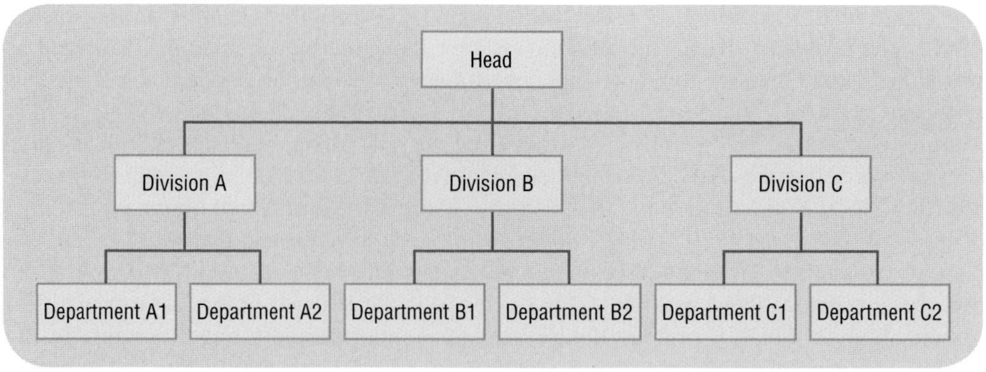

Consider also what happens when the lines of communication directly joining departments or divisions are weak or nonexistent. As the lines joining units in Figure 6.5 suggest, department A1 may have information that could help department B1 do its job better but may have to communicate that information indirectly through the division level. At the division level, the information may be lost, blocked, reinterpreted, or distorted. Thus, just as people who have authority may lack information, people who have information may lack the authority to act on it directly (Crozier, 1964 [1963]).

Below we consider some ways of overcoming bureaucratic inefficiency. As you will see, these solutions typically involve establishing patterns of social relations that flatten the bureaucratic hierarchy and cut across the sort of bureaucratic rigidities illustrated in Figure 6.5. As a useful prelude to this discussion, we first note some shortcomings of Weber's analysis of bureaucracy. Weber tended to ignore both bureaucracy's informal side and the role of leadership in influencing bureaucratic performance. Yet, as you will learn, it is precisely by paying attention to such issues that we can make bureaucracies more efficient.

Bureaucracy's Informal Side

Weber was concerned mainly with the formal structure or chain of command in a bureaucracy. He paid little attention to the social networks that underlie the chain of command.

Evidence for the existence of social networks and their importance in the operation of bureaucracies date back to the 1930s. Officials at the Hawthorne plant of the Western Electric Company near Chicago wanted to see how various aspects of the work environment affected productivity. They sent social scientists in to investigate. Among other things, researchers found that workers in one section of the plant had established a norm for daily output. Workers who failed to meet the norm were helped by co-workers until their output increased. Workers who exceeded the norm were chided by co-workers until their productivity fell. Company officials and researchers previously had regarded employees merely as individuals who worked as hard or as little as they could in response to wage levels and work conditions. However, the Hawthorne study showed that employees are members of social networks that regulate output (Roethlisberger and Dickson, 1939).

In the 1970s, Rosabeth Moss Kanter conducted another landmark study of informal social relations in bureaucracies (Kanter, 1977). Kanter studied a corporation in which most women were sales agents. They were locked out of managerial positions. However, she did not find that the corporation discriminated against women as a matter of policy. She did find a male-only social network whose members shared gossip, went drinking, and told sexist jokes. The cost of being excluded from the network was high: To achieve good raises and promotions, a person needed to be accepted as "one of the boys" and be sponsored by a male executive, which was impossible for women. Thus, despite a company policy that did not discriminate against women, an informal network of social relations ensured that the company discriminated against women in practice.

Despite their overt commitment to impersonality and written rules, bureaucracies rely profoundly on informal interaction to get the job done (Barnard, 1938; Blau, 1963). This fact is true even at the highest levels. For example, executives usually decide important matters in face-to-face meetings, not in writing or via the phone. That is because people feel more comfortable in intimate settings, where they can get to know "the whole person." Meeting face to face, people can use their verbal and nonverbal interaction skills to gauge other people's trustworthiness. Socializing—talking over dinner, for example—is an important part of any business because the establishment of trust lies at the heart of all social interactions that require cooperation (Gambetta, 1988).

Jupiterimages/Thinkstock.com

Informal interaction is common even in highly bureaucratic organizations. A water cooler, for example, can be a place for exchanging information and gossip, and even a place for decision making.

The informal side of bureaucracy operates at lower levels, too. For instance, while on the job, some office workers take time to text-message or email their colleagues and friends. Some analysts believe this kind of behaviour is dysfunctional, as it lowers office productivity. Others think it is functional. It gives workers a chance to communicate quickly and easily with colleagues about matters of importance to the workplace. It also allows them to step out of their routine by, say, sharing a joke and then return to their work tasks refreshed. Over time, such behaviour can strengthen friendship ties. The line between functional and dysfunctional informal communication seems to depend on how much and what kind of chatter takes place. Too much chatter unrelated to work may indeed hamper productivity but, within limits, communication via the informal side of bureaucracy seems to be beneficial.

Laissez-faire leadership allows subordinates to work things out largely on their own, with almost no direction from above. It is the least effective type of leadership.

Leadership

Apart from overlooking the role of informal relations in the operation of bureaucracies, Weber also paid insufficient attention to the issue of leadership. Weber thought the formal structure of a bureaucracy largely determines how it operates. However, sociologists now realize that leadership style also has a big bearing on bureaucratic performance (Barnard, 1938; Ridgeway, 1983).

Authoritarian leadership demands strict compliance from subordinates. Authoritarian leaders are most effective in a crisis, such as a war or the emergency room of a hospital.

Research shows that the least effective leader is the one who allows subordinates to work things out largely on their own, with almost no direction from above. This leadership style is known as **laissez-faire leadership**, from the French expression "let them do." Note, however, that laissez-faire leadership can be effective under some circumstances. It works best when group members are highly experienced, trained, motivated, and educated, and when trust and confidence in group members are high. In such conditions, a strong leader is not really needed for the group to accomplish its goals. At the other extreme is **authoritarian leadership**. Authoritarian leaders demand strict compliance from subordinates. They are most effective in a crisis, such as a war or the emergency room of a hospital. They may earn grudging respect from subordinates for achieving the group's goals in the face of difficult circumstances, but they rarely win popularity contests. **Democratic leadership** offers more guidance than the laissez-faire variety but less control than the authoritarian type. Democratic leaders try to include all group members in the decision-making process, taking the best ideas from the group and moulding them into a strategy that all can identify with. Except during crisis situations, democratic leadership is usually the most effective leadership style.

Democratic leadership offers more guidance than the laissez-faire variety but less control than the authoritarian type. Democratic leaders try to include all group members in the decision-making process, taking the best ideas from the group and moulding them into a strategy with which all can identify. Except during crisis situations, democratic leadership is usually the most effective leadership style.

In sum, contemporary researchers have modified Weber's characterization of bureaucracy in two main ways. First, they have stressed the importance of informal social networks in shaping bureaucratic operations. Second, they have shown that democratic leaders are most effective in non-crisis situations because they tend to widely distribute decision-making authority and rewards. As you will now see, these lessons are important when it comes to thinking about how to make bureaucracies more efficient.

Overcoming Bureaucratic Inefficiency

In the business world, large bureaucratic organizations sometimes find themselves unable to compete against smaller, innovative firms, particularly in industries that are changing quickly (Burns and Stalker, 1961). This situation occurs partly because innovative firms tend to have flatter and more democratic organizational structures, such as the network illustrated in Figure 6.6. Compare the flat network structure in Figure 6.6 with the traditional bureaucratic structure in Figure 6.5. Note that the network structure has fewer levels than the traditional bureaucratic structure does. Moreover, in the network structure, lines of communication link all units. In the traditional bureaucratic structure, information flows only upward.

Much evidence suggests that flatter bureaucracies with decentralized decision making and multiple lines of communication produce more satisfied workers, happier clients, and bigger profits (Kanter, 1989). Some of this evidence comes from Sweden and Japan. Beginning in the early 1970s, such corporations as Volvo and Toyota were at the forefront of bureaucratic innovation in those countries. They began eliminating middle-management positions. They allowed worker participation in a variety of tasks related to their main functions. They delegated authority to autonomous teams of a dozen or so workers who were allowed to make many decisions themselves. They formed "quality circles" of workers to monitor and correct defects in products and services. As a result, product quality, worker morale, and profitability improved. Today, these ideas have spread well beyond the Swedish and Japanese automobile industry and are evident in such companies as General Motors, Ford, Boeing, and Caterpillar. In the 1980s and 1990s, companies outside the manufacturing sector introduced similar bureaucratic reforms, again with positive results.

Organizational Environments

An **organizational environment** comprises a host of economic, political, and cultural forces that lie outside an organization and affect the way it works.

If flatter organizations are more efficient, why aren't all bureaucracies flatter? Mainly, say sociologists, because of the environment in which they operate. An **organizational environment** comprises a host of economic, political, and cultural factors that lie outside an organization and affect the way it works (Aldrich, 1979; Meyer and Scott, 1983). Some organizational environments are conducive to the formation of flatter, network-like bureaucracies. Others are not. We can illustrate the effects of organizational environments by discussing two cases that have attracted much attention in recent years: the United States and Japan.

In the 1970s, American business bureaucracies tended to be more hierarchical than their Japanese counterparts were. This was one reason that worker dissatisfaction was high and

FIGURE 6.6
Network Structure

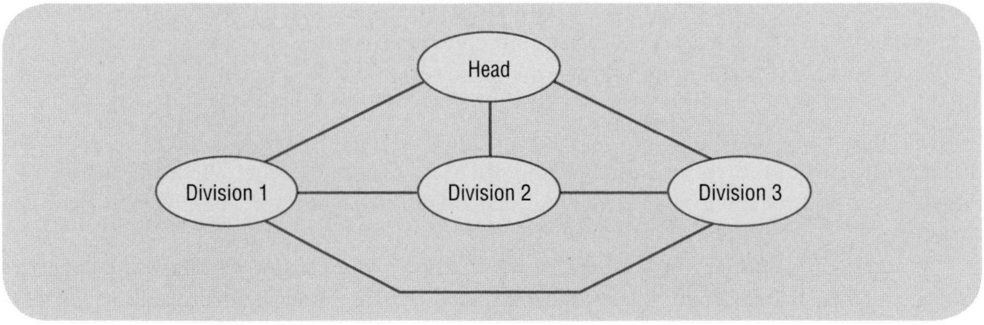

labour productivity was low in the United States. In Japan, where corporate decision making was more decentralized, worker morale and productivity were high (Dore, 1983). Several aspects of the organizational environment help to explain Japanese–American differences in the 1970s:

- *Japanese workers were in a position to demand and achieve more decision-making authority than American workers were.* After World War II, the proportion of Japanese workers in unions increased, whereas the proportion of American workers in unions declined. Unions gave Japanese workers more clout than their American counterparts enjoyed.
- *International competition encouraged bureaucratic efficiency in Japan.* Many big Japanese corporations matured in the highly competitive post–World War II international environment. Many big American corporations originated earlier, in an international environment with few competitors. Thus, Japanese corporations had a bigger incentive to develop more efficient organizational structures (Harrison, 1994).
- *The availability of external suppliers allowed Japanese firms to remain lean.* Many large American companies matured when external sources of supply were scarce. For example, when IBM entered the computer market in the 1950s, it needed to produce all components internally because nobody else was making them. This situation led IBM to develop a large, hierarchical bureaucracy. In contrast, Japanese computer manufacturers could rely on many external suppliers in the 1970s. Therefore, they could develop flatter organizational structures (Podolny and Page, 1998).

Today, Japanese–American differences have substantially decreased because most big businesses in the United States have introduced Japanese-style bureaucratic reforms (Tsutsui, 1998). For instance, Silicon Valley, the centre of the American computer industry today, is full of companies that fit the "Japanese" organizational pattern. These companies originated in the 1980s and 1990s, when external suppliers were abundant and international competitiveness was intense. In addition, American companies started to copy Japanese business structures because they saw them as successful (DiMaggio and Powell, 1983). We thus see how changes in the organizational environment help to account for convergence between Japanese and American bureaucratic forms.

The experience of the United States over the past few decades suggests hope for increasing bureaucratic efficiency and continuing the growth of employee autonomy and creativity at work. It does not mean that bureaucracies in Japan and the United States will be alike in all respects in 20 or 50 or 100 years. The organizational environment is unpredictable, and sociologists are just beginning to understand its operation. It is therefore anyone's guess how far convergence will continue.

TIME FOR REVIEW

- What does it mean when we talk about the efficiency of an organization?
- Compared with what kinds of organizations are bureaucracies considered to be efficient?
- What kinds of bureaucracies are relatively inefficient?

SOCIETIES

Societies are collectivities of interacting people who share a culture and, usually, a territory.

Networks, groups, and bureaucracies are embedded in **societies**, collectivities of interacting people who share a culture and, usually, a territory. (Note, however, that for "virtual societies" on the Internet, a shared territory is unnecessary.) Like smaller collectivities, societies help shape human action. They influence the kind of work we do and how productively we work. They mould patterns of class, gender, racial, and ethnic inequality. They impinge on the way religious, family, and other institutions operate. They affect the way we govern and the way we think of ourselves.

Despite the pervasiveness of these influences, most people are blind to them. We tend to believe that we are free to do what we want. Yet the plain fact is that societies affect even our most personal and intimate choices. For example, deciding how many children to have is one of the most intensely private and emotional issues a woman or a couple must face. So why is it that tens of millions of women and couples have decided in the space of just a few decades to have an average of two babies instead of six, or eight babies instead of four? Why do so many individuals make almost exactly the same private decision at almost precisely the same historical moment? The answer is that certain identifiable social conditions prompt them to reach the same conclusion, in this case to have fewer or more babies. And so it is with most decisions. Identifiable social conditions increase the chance that we will choose one course of action over another.

The relationship between people and nature is the most basic determinant of how societies are structured and therefore how people's choices are constrained. Accordingly, researchers have identified six stages of human evolution, each characterized by a shift in the relationship between people and nature. As we review each of these stages, note what happens to the human–nature relationship: With each successive stage, people are less at the mercy of nature and thus transform it more radically. The changing relationship between people and nature has huge implications for all aspects of social life. Let us identify these implications as we sketch the evolution of human society in bold strokes.

Foraging Societies

Foraging societies are societies in which people live by searching for wild plants and hunting wild animals. Such societies predominated until about 10 000 years ago. Inequality, the division of labour, productivity, and settlement size are very low in such societies.

Until about 10 000 years ago, all people lived in **foraging societies**. They sustained themselves by searching for wild plants and hunting wild animals (Lenski, Nolan, and Lenski, 1995; O'Neil, 2004; Sahlins, 1972). They depended on nature passively, taking whatever it made available and transforming it only slightly to meet their needs. They built simple tools, such as baskets, bows and arrows, spears, and digging sticks. They sometimes burned grasslands to encourage the growth of new vegetation and attract game, but they neither planted crops nor domesticated many animals.

Most foragers lived in temporary encampments, and when food was scarce they migrated to more bountiful regions. Harsh environments could support one person per 25 to 130 square kilometres (10 to 50 square miles). Rich environments could support 25 to 80 people per square kilometre (10 to 30 people per square mile). Foraging communities or bands averaged about 25 to 30 people but could be as large as 100 people. *Aquatic foragers*, such as those on the western coast of North America, concentrated on fishing and hunting marine mammals. *Equestrian foragers*, such as the Great Plains Aboriginal peoples of North America, hunted large mammals from horseback. *Pedestrian foragers* engaged in diversified hunting and gathering on foot and could be found on all continents.

Until the middle of the twentieth century, most social scientists thought that foragers lived brief, grim lives. In their view, foragers were engaged in a desperate struggle for existence that was typically cut short by disease, starvation, pestilence, or some other force of nature. We now know that this characterization says more about the biases of early anthropologists than about the lives foragers actually lived. Consider the !Kung of the Kalahari Desert in southern Africa, who maintained their traditional way of life until the 1960s (Lee, 1979). Young !Kung did not fully join the workforce until they reached the age of 20. Adults worked only about 15 hours a week. Mainly because of disease, children faced a much smaller chance of surviving childhood than is the case in contemporary society, but about 10 percent of the !Kung were older than 60, the same percentage as Canadians in the early 1970s. It thus seems that the !Kung who survived childhood lived relatively long, secure, leisurely, healthy, and happy lives. They were not unique. The tall totem poles, ornate wood carvings, colourful masks, and elaborate clothing of the Kwakiutl on Vancouver Island serve as beautiful reminders that many foragers had the leisure time to invest considerable energy in ornamentation.

Equestrian foragers were hierarchical, male-dominated, and warlike, especially after they acquired rifles in the nineteenth century. However, the social structure of pedestrian foragers—the great majority of all foragers—was remarkably non-hierarchical. They shared what little wealth they had, and women and men enjoyed approximately equal status.

Aquatic foragers had much leisure time to invest in ornamentation, suggesting that their lives were by no means a constant struggle for survival.

Pastoral and Horticultural Societies

Substantial social inequality became widespread about 10 000 years ago, when some bands began to domesticate various wild plants and animals, especially cattle, camels, pigs, goats, sheep, horses, and reindeer (Lenski, Nolan, and Lenski, 1995; O'Neil, 2004). By using hand tools to garden in highly fertile areas (**horticultural societies**) and herding animals in more arid areas (**pastoral societies**), people increased the food supply and made it more dependable. Nature could now support more people. Moreover, pastoral and horticultural societies enabled fewer people to specialize in producing food and more people to specialize in constructing tools and weapons, making clothing and jewellery, and trading valuable objects with other bands. Some families and bands accumulated more domesticated animals, cropland, and valued objects than others did. As a result, pastoral and horticultural societies developed a higher level of social inequality than was evident in most foraging societies.

As wealth accumulated, feuding and warfare grew, particularly among pastoralists. Men who controlled large herds of animals and conducted successful predatory raids acquired much prestige and power and came to be recognized as chiefs. Some chiefs formed large, fierce, mobile armies. The Mongols and the Zulus were horse pastoralists who conquered large parts of Asia and Africa, respectively.

Most pastoralists were nomadic, with migration patterns dictated by their animals' needs for food and water. Some pastoralists migrated regularly from the same cool highlands in the summer to the same warm lowland valleys in the winter and were able to establish villages in both locations. Horticulturalists often established permanent settlements beside their croplands. These settlements might include several hundred people. However, the development of large permanent settlements, including the first cities, took place only with the development of intensive agriculture.

Horticultural societies are societies in which people domesticate plants and use simple hand tools to garden. Such societies first emerged about 10 000 years ago.

Pastoral societies are societies in which people domesticate cattle, camels, pigs, goats, sheep, horses, and reindeer. Such societies first emerged about 10 000 years ago.

Agricultural Societies

Especially in the fertile river valleys of the Middle East, India, China, and South America, human populations flourished—so much so that, about 5000 years ago, they could no longer be sustained by pastoral and horticulture techniques. It was then that **agricultural societies** originated. The plow was invented to harness animal power for more intensive and efficient agricultural production. The plow allowed farmers to plant crops over much larger areas and dig below the topsoil, bringing nutrients to the surface and thus increasing yield (Lenski, Nolan, and Lenski, 1995; O'Neil, 2004).

Agricultural societies are societies in which plows and animal power are used to substantially increase food supply and dependability as compared with horticultural and pastoral societies. Agricultural societies first emerged about 5000 years ago.

A medieval painting shows peasants harvesting outside the walls of their lord and master's castle. Why is it significant that the church is situated inside the walls?

Because the source of food was immobile, many people built permanent settlements, and because people were able to produce considerably more food than was necessary for their own subsistence, surpluses were sold in village markets. Some of these centres became towns and then cities, home to rulers, religious figures, soldiers, craft workers, and government officials. The population of some agricultural societies numbered in the millions.

The crystallization of the idea of private property was one of the most significant developments of the era. Among pedestrian foragers, there was no private ownership of land or water. Among horticulturalists, particular families might be recognized as having rights to some property, but only while they were using it. If the property was not in use, they were obliged to share it or give it to a family that needed it. In contrast, in societies that practised intensive agriculture, powerful individuals succeeded in having the idea of individual property rights legally recognized. It was possible for people to buy land and water, to call them their own, and to transmit ownership to their offspring. People could now become rich and, through inheritance, make their children rich.

Ancient civilizations thus became rigidly divided into classes. Royalty surrounded itself with loyal landowners, protected itself with professional soldiers, and justified its rule with the help of priests, whose job, in part, was to convince ordinary peasants that the existing social order was God's will. Government officials collected taxes and religious officials collected tithes, thus enriching the upper classes with the peasantry's surplus production. In this era, inequality between women and men also reached its historical high point (Boulding, 1976).

Industrial Societies

Stimulated by international exploration, trade, and commerce, the Industrial Revolution began in Britain in the 1780s. A century later, it had spread to all of Western Europe, North America, Japan, and Russia. Industry required the use of fuel—at first, waterpower and steam—to drive machines and thereby greatly increase productivity, as measured by the quantity of goods that could be produced with a given amount of effort.

Industrial societies are societies that use machines and fuel to greatly increase the supply and dependability of food and finished goods. The first such society emerged in Great Britain in the last decades of the eighteenth century.

If you have ever read a Charles Dickens novel, such as *Oliver Twist*, you know that hellish working conditions and deep social inequalities characterized early **industrial societies**. Work in factories and mines became so productive that owners amassed previously unimaginable fortunes, but ordinary labourers worked 16-hour days in dangerous conditions and earned barely enough to survive. They struggled for the right to form and join unions and expand the vote to all adult citizens, hoping to use union power and political influence to improve their working and living conditions. At the same time, new technologies and ways of organizing work made it possible to produce ever more goods at a lower cost per unit. The increase in productivity made it possible to meet many of the workers' demands and raise living standards for the entire population.

Increasingly, businesses required a literate, numerate, and highly trained workforce. To raise profits, they were eager to identify and hire the most talented people. They encouraged everyone to develop their talents and rewarded them for doing so by paying higher salaries. Inequality between women and men began to decrease because of the demand for talent and women's struggles to enter the paid workforce on an equal footing with men. Why hire an incompetent man over a competent woman when you can profit more from the services of a capable employee? Put in this way, women's demands for equality made good business sense. For all these reasons, class and gender inequality declined as industrial societies matured.

Postindustrial Societies

In the early 1970s, sociologist Daniel Bell (1973) argued that industrial society was rapidly becoming a thing of the past. According to Bell, just as agriculture gave way to manufacturing as the driving force of the economy in the nineteenth century, so did manufacturing give way to service industries by the mid-twentieth century, resulting in the birth of **postindustrial societies**.

Postindustrial societies are societies in which most workers are employed in the service sector and computers spur substantial increases in the division of labour and productivity. Shortly after World War II, the United States became the first postindustrial society.

Even in pre-agricultural societies, a few individuals specialized in providing services rather than in producing goods. For example, a person considered adept at tending to the ill, forecasting the weather, or predicting the movement of animals might be relieved of hunting responsibilities to focus on these services. However, such jobs were rare because productivity was low. Nearly everyone needed to contribute physical work for the tribe to survive. Even in early agricultural societies, 80 to 100 farmers were needed to support one non-farmer (Hodson and Sullivan, 1995: 10). Only at the beginning of the nineteenth century in industrialized countries did productivity increase to the point where a quarter of the labour force could be employed in services. Today, about three-quarters of Canadian workers are in the service sector.

In postindustrial societies, women have been recruited to the service sector in disproportionately large numbers, which has helped to ensure a gradual increase in equality between women and men in terms of education, income, and other indicators of rank (Chapter 11, Sexualities and Gender Stratification). But the picture with respect to inequality between classes is more complex. Most postindustrial societies, and especially the United States, have experienced large increases in class inequality. Other postindustrial societies, such as Canada, have experienced smaller increases. A few postindustrial societies, such as France, had less inequality in 2000 than in 1977, bucking the broader trend (Smeeding, 2004). We discuss the reasons for these different patterns in Chapter 8, Social Stratification.

During the final decades of the twentieth century, rapid change in the composition of the labour force was made possible by the computer. The computer automated many manufacturing and office procedures. It created jobs in the service sector as quickly as it eliminated them in manufacturing. The computer is to the service sector what the steam engine was to manufacturing, the plow was to intensive agriculture, domestication was to horticulture and pastoralism, and simple hand tools were to foraging.

Postnatural Societies

On February 28, 1953, two men walked into a pub in Cambridge, England, and offered drinks all around. "We have discovered the secret of life!" proclaimed one of the men. He was James Watson. With his colleague, Francis Crick, he had found the structure of deoxyribonucleic acid, or DNA, the chemical that makes up genes. During cell division, a single DNA molecule uncoils into two strands. New, identical molecules are formed from each strand. In this way, growth takes place and traits are passed from one generation to the next. It was one of the most important scientific discoveries ever (Watson, 1968).

By the early 1970s, scientists were beginning to develop techniques for manipulating DNA (so-called **recombinant DNA**). Soon they could cut a segment out of a DNA strand and join the remaining sections together, or they could take a DNA strand and connect it to segments of DNA from another living thing. This ability meant that scientists could create new life forms, a capability that had until then been restricted in the popular imagination to God. Enthusiasts proclaimed a "second genesis" as they began to speculate about the potential of the new technology to rid the world of hereditary disease; feed the hungry with higher-yield, disease-resistant farm products; and even create more intelligent, beautiful,

Recombinant DNA involves removing a segment of DNA from a gene or splicing together segments of DNA from different living things, thus effectively creating a new life form.

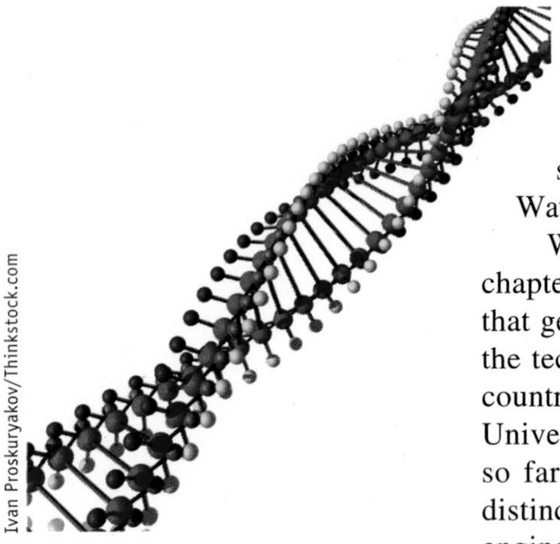
Ivan Proskuryakov/Thinkstock.com

The DNA molecule

and athletic children. For many millions of years, nature had selected the "fittest" living things for survival. Now it seemed possible for humans to speed up natural selection, thus escaping the whims of nature and creating a more perfect society under their control. The invention of recombinant DNA marked the onset of a new social era—what we prefer to call the era of **postnatural society** (Dyson, 1999; Watson, 2000).

We consider some of the perils of postnatural society in detail in this book's online chapter, Chapter 22, Technology and the Global Environment. Here we emphasize only that genetic engineering could easily result in increased social inequality. For example, the technology for creating more perfect babies will undoubtedly be expensive, so rich countries and rich people are more likely than others are to benefit from it. Princeton University biologist Lee Silver and Nobel Prize–winning physicist Freeman Dyson go so far as to speculate that the ultimate result of genetic engineering will be several distinct human species. People who are in a position to take full advantage of genetic engineering will be better looking, more intelligent, less likely to suffer from disease, and more athletic. People who are not so fortunate will face nature's caprice in handing out talents and disadvantages, just as our foraging ancestors did (Brave, 2003). The main, and perhaps only, safeguard against such an outcome is true democracy, which would allow ordinary people to decide which risks are worth taking and how the benefits of genetic engineering should be distributed within and across populations (Häyry and Lehto, 1998).

Postnatural societies are societies in which genetic engineering enables people to create new life forms.

TIME FOR REVIEW

- As societies evolve, what happens to human dependence on nature?
- How do levels of class and gender inequality change as societies evolve?

FREEDOM AND CONSTRAINT IN SOCIAL LIFE

Throughout this chapter, we emphasized the capacity of networks, groups, bureaucracies, and societies to constrain human behaviour. As we have seen, such social collectivities can even encourage dangerously high levels of conformity, compel people to act against their better judgment, dominate people in a vice of organizational rigidities, and affect the level of social inequality in society.

We stressed the constraining aspect of social collectivities because we wanted to counter the commonsense view that motives alone determine the way people act. In conclusion, however, we should remember that people are often free to exercise two options other than bowing to the will of their social collectivities (Hirschman, 1970). In some circumstances, they can leave the social collectivities to which they belong. In other circumstances, they can struggle against the constraints their social collectivities seek to impose on them. After all, it is always possible to say no, even to the worst tyrant. Less dramatically but no less importantly, knowledge, including sociological knowledge, can increase the ability of people to resist the constraints imposed on them. Recall the Milgram experiment we discussed at the beginning of this chapter, in which subjects administered what they thought were painful shocks to people just because the experimenters told them to. When the experiment was repeated years later, many of the subjects refused to go along with the demands of the experimenters. Some invoked the example of the Nazis to justify their refusal to comply. Others mentioned Milgram's original experiment. Their knowledge, some of it perhaps gained in sociology courses, enabled them to resist unreasonable demands (Gamson, Fireman, and Rytina, 1982).

Paradoxically, to succeed in challenging social collectivities, people must sometimes form a new social collectivity—a lobby, a union, a political party, a social movement (Lipset, Trow, and Coleman, 1956). People are always free to form new social collectivities that can counteract old ones. Embedded in social relations, we can use them for good or evil.

SUMMARY

1. Do people act the way they do only because of their interests and emotions?
   People's motives are important determinants of their actions, but social collectivities also influence the way they behave. Because of the power of social collectivities, people sometimes act against their interests, values, and emotions.
2. Is it a small world?
   Yes. Most people interact repeatedly with a small circle of family members, friends, and co-workers. However, our personal networks overlap with other social networks, which is why only a few links separate us from complete strangers.
3. What are social networks, groups, bureaucracies, and societies?
   Networks are bounded set of individuals linked by the exchange of material or emotional resources. Groups are clusters of people who identity with one another. Bureaucracies are large, impersonal organization comprising many clearly defined positions arranged in a hierarchy, a permanent, salaried staff of qualified experts and written goals, rules, and procedures. Societies are collectivities of interacting people who share a culture and, usually, a territory.
4. How do social groups impose conformity on members and draw boundaries between those who belong and those who do not?
   Social groups impose conformity on members by establishing norms of solidarity and structures of authority. They draw boundaries between those who belong and those who do not by creating cultural and legal differences between them.
5. Is it possible to overcome bureaucratic inefficiency?
   Bureaucratic inefficiency increases with size and degree of hierarchy. However, efficiency can often be improved by flattening bureaucratic structures, decentralizing decision-making authority, and opening lines of communication between bureaucratic units.
6. How does the relationship of humans to nature change as societies evolve?
   Over the past 100 000 years, the growing human domination of nature has increased the supply and dependability of food and finished goods, productivity, the division of labour, and the size and permanence of human settlements. Class and gender inequality increased until the nineteenth century and then began to decline. Class inequality began to increase in some societies in the last decades of the twentieth century and may continue to increase in the future.

PART 3

INEQUALITY

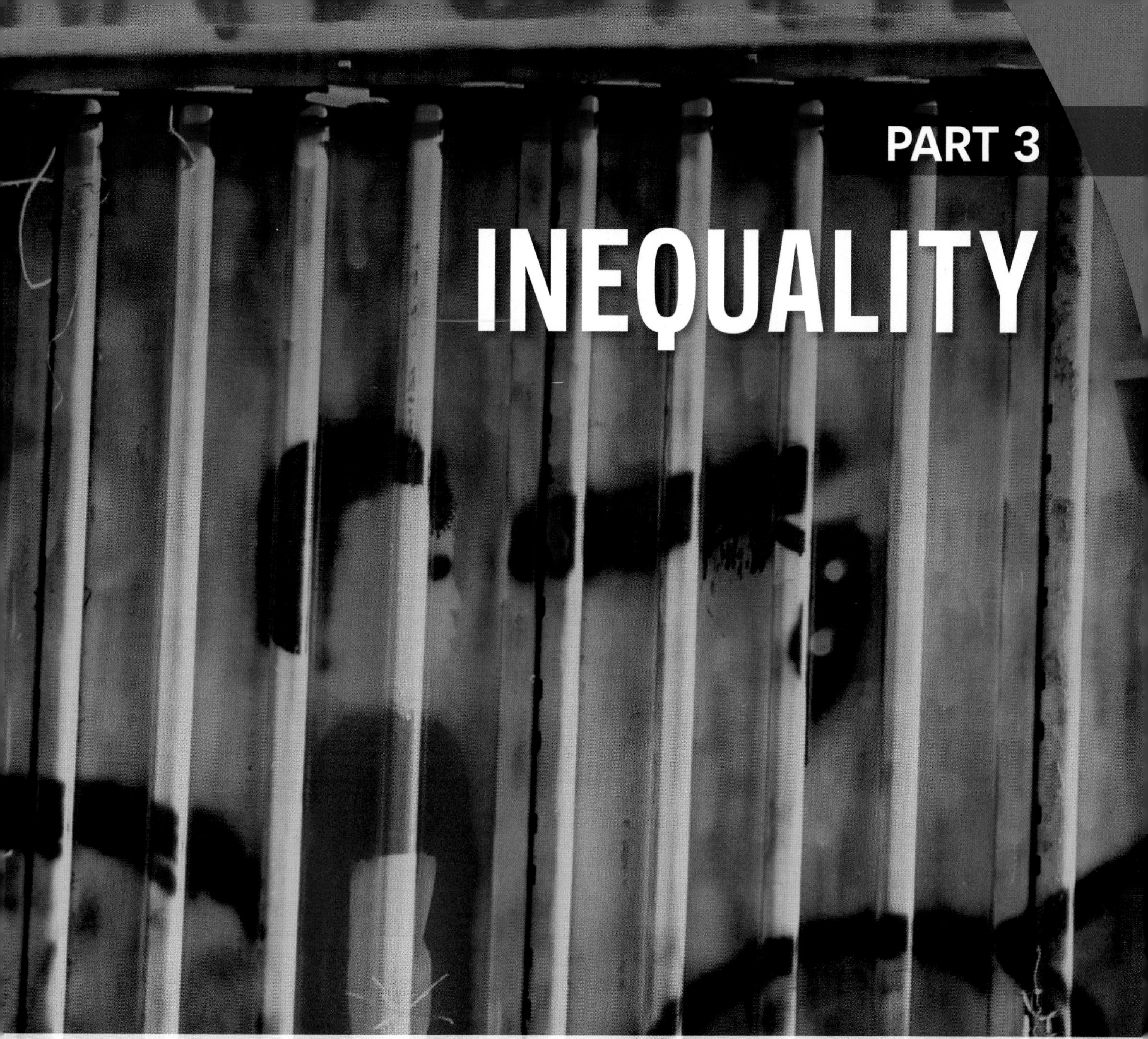

CHAPTER 7

DEVIANCE AND CRIME

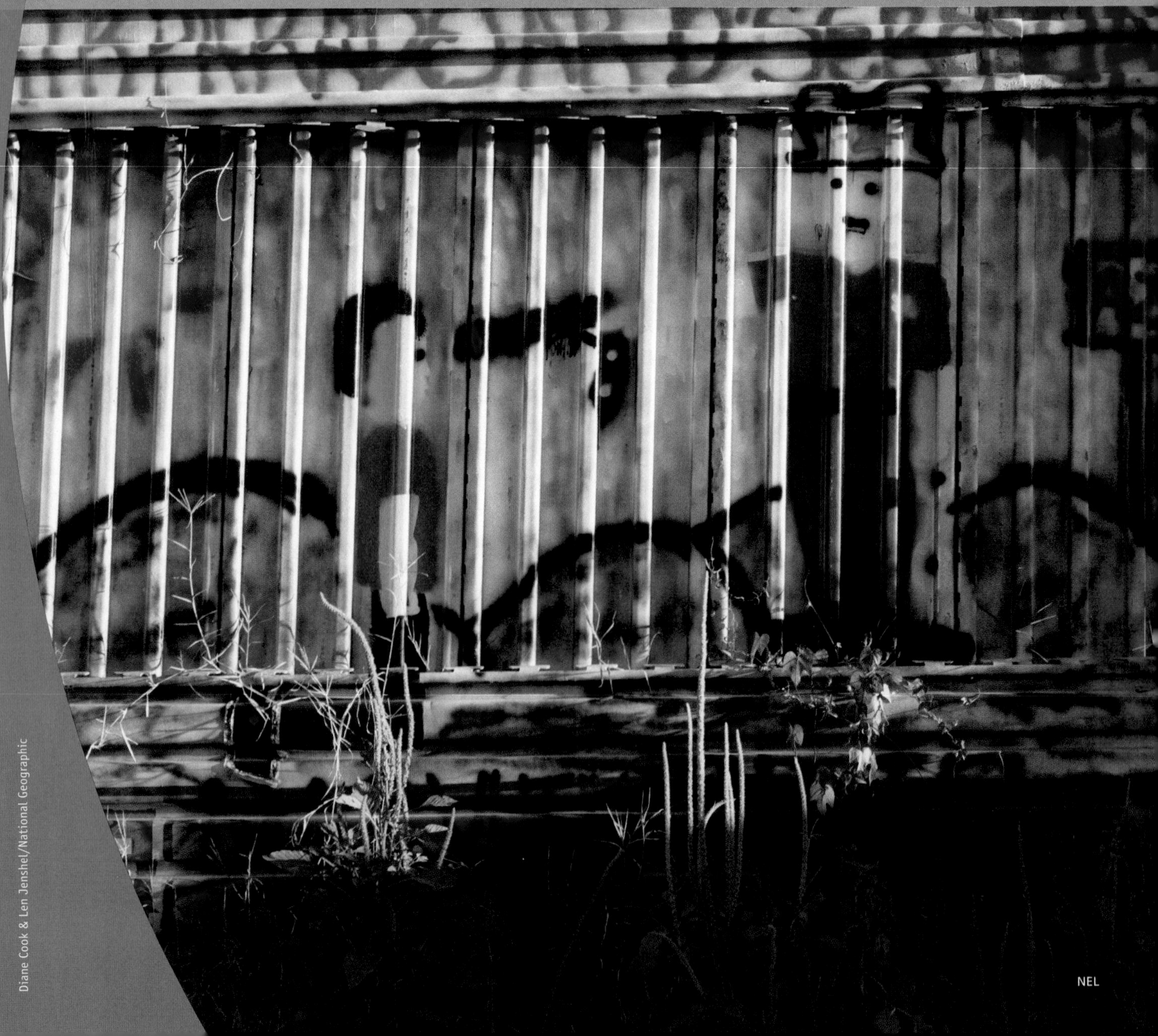

Diane Cook & Len Jenshel/National Geographic

IN THIS CHAPTER YOU WILL LEARN TO

- Define and measure crime.
- Distinguish crime from deviance.
- Compare and contrast the major sociological explanations of deviance and crime.
- Recognize the principal trends in social control and regulation.

THE SOCIAL DEFINITION OF DEVIANCE AND CRIME

Deviance occurs when someone departs from a norm and evokes a negative reaction from others.

Crime is deviance that is against the law.

A **law** is a norm stipulated and enforced by government bodies.

If you happen to come across members of the Tukano tribe in northern Brazil, don't be surprised if they greet you with a cheery "Have you bathed today?" You might find the question insulting, but think how you would feel if you were greeted by the Yanomamö people in Brazil's central highlands. An anthropologist reports that when he first encountered the Yanomamö, they rubbed mucus and tobacco juice into their palms, then inspected him by running their filthy hands over his body (Chagnon, 1992). He must have been relieved to return to urban Brazil and be greeted with a simple kiss on the cheek.

Rules for greeting people vary widely from one country to the next and among different cultural groups within one country (Swanson et al., 2014). Violating local norms can cause offence, a fact that one businessman discovered too late when visiting South Korea. Noticing his host in the restaurant where they were scheduled to meet, he beckoned him with an index finger. The host spoke little during the meal, and the deal they had been working on fell through. Later the visitor found out why. Koreans use their index finger to beckon only cats and dogs. If you want to politely beckon another person in South Korea, you should do so with all four fingers facing down, much like Canadians wave goodbye.

This anecdote illustrates that norms vary widely, so deviance is relative. What some people consider normal, others consider deviant, and vice versa. No act is deviant in itself. People commit deviant acts only when they break a norm and cause others to react negatively. From a sociological point of view, *everyone* is deviant in one social context or another.

CP Picture Archive/Frank Gunn

Nelson Mandela spent decades imprisoned in South Africa for his activities that were designed to end apartheid. Today Mandela is hailed as a hero. He was awarded the Nobel Peace Prize in 1993 and served as the first democratically elected president of South Africa from 1994 to 1999.

The Difference between Deviance and Crime

Deviance involves breaking a norm and evoking a negative reaction from others. Societies establish some norms as laws. **Crime** is deviance that breaks a **law**, which is a norm stipulated and enforced by government bodies.

Just as deviance is relative, so too is crime. Consider a list of famous people who have been labelled criminals: Socrates; Jesus; Martin Luther; Louis Riel; Mahatma Gandhi; Martin Luther King, Jr.; and Nelson Mandela. For many people today, these figures are heroes. In contrast, people who planned and participated in the extermination of Jews, Roma (Gypsies), and homosexuals in Nazi Germany were acting in a way that had been defined in Germany as law-abiding. You would probably consider the actions taken by the Nazis in Germany to be deviant or criminal, but not the actions of Jesus or Martin Luther. That is because norms and laws have changed dramatically. Today, under Canadian law, it is a crime to advocate or promote genocide. We conclude that what is considered a crime at one time and place may be considered perfectly normal in another time and place.

Sanctions

Informal punishment involves a mild sanction that is imposed during face-to-face interaction, not by the judicial system.

People who are **stigmatized** are negatively evaluated because of a marker that distinguishes them from others and that is labelled as socially unacceptable.

Formal punishment takes place when the judicial system penalizes someone for breaking a law.

Most people don't notice many deviant acts, and, if they do, many consider them too trivial to warrant punishment. More serious acts of deviance, if noticed, are typically punished, either informally or formally. **Informal punishment** is mild. It may involve raised eyebrows, gossip, ostracism, shaming, or stigmatization (Braithwaite, 1989). When people are **stigmatized**, they are negatively evaluated because of a marker that distinguishes them from others (Goffman, 1963). One of this book's authors, John Lie, was stigmatized as a young child and often bullied by elementary-school classmates because he was a Korean student in a Japanese school. "I was normal in other ways," says John. "I played the same sports and games; watched the same television shows; and looked, dressed, and acted like other Japanese students. However, my one deviation was enough to stigmatize me. It gave licence to some of my classmates to beat me up from time to time. I wondered at the time why no rules banned bullying and why no law existed against what I now call racial discrimination. If such a law did exist, my classmates would have been subject to formal punishment, which is more severe than informal punishment."

Formal punishment results from people breaking laws. For example, criminals may be formally punished by being sentenced to serve time in prison or perform community service.

Types of deviance and crime vary in terms of the *severity of the social response*, which varies from mild disapproval to capital punishment (Hagan, 1994). Types of deviance and crime also vary in terms of *perceived harmfulness*. Note that *actual* harmfulness is not the only issue here—*perceived* harmfulness also plays a role. Coca-Cola got its name because, in the early part of the twentieth century, it contained a derivative of cocaine. Today, cocaine is an illegal drug because people's perceptions of its harmfulness have changed. Finally, deviance and crime vary in terms of the *degree of public agreement* about whether an act should be considered deviant or criminal. Even the social definition of murder varies over time and across cultures and societies. Thus, in the nineteenth century, Inuit communities sometimes allowed newborns to freeze to death. Life in the Far North was precarious. Killing newborns was not considered a punishable offence if community members agreed that investing scarce resources in keeping the newborn

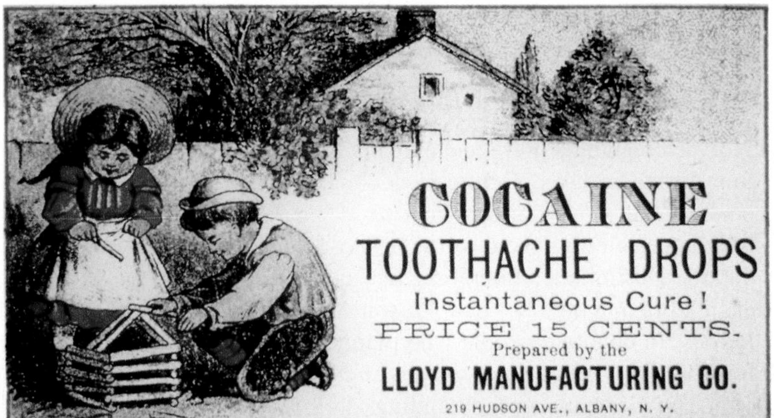

National Library of Medicine, Washington, DC

One of the determinants of the seriousness of a deviant act is its perceived harmfulness. Perceptions vary historically. For instance, until the early part of the twentieth century, cocaine was considered a medicine. It was an ingredient in Coca-Cola and toothache drops; in these two forms, cocaine was commonly consumed by children.

BOX 7.1

IT'S YOUR CHOICE

VIOLENCE AND HOCKEY: DEVIANT, CRIMINAL, OR NORMATIVE?

For more than a century, violence has been part of NHL hockey. The violence takes many forms—nasty stick work, kicking, hitting from behind, brawls, and abuse of officials. In one memorable incident in 2004, Todd Bertuzzi of the Vancouver Canucks stalked and assaulted Steve Moore of the Colorado Avalanche. Late in the game, without provocation, Bertuzzi pursued Moore from one end of the rink to the other. When Moore tried to avoid Bertuzzi by turning his back and skating away, Bertuzzi grabbed the back of Moore's jersey, delivered a sucker punch, and used his body to drive Moore face first into the ice. Moore's NHL career was done, while Bertuzzi paid a fine of $500, completed 80 hours of community service, and was suspended for 17 months. He then returned to the NHL.

Hockey violence continues. The 2013 season opened with a fight that required Montreal Canadien George Parros to be removed from the game on a stretcher, and in December of that year, Boston Bruin Shawn Thornton beat Pittsburgh Penguin Brooks Orpik unconscious after grabbing him from behind. Thornton was suspended 15 games. Any review of recent games will provide you with examples of on-ice conduct that, if it occurred on the street, would result in criminal charges. Still, many fans consider violence an enjoyable part of the game. At www.hockeyfights.com/, fans of hockey violence can even scan statistics on fights by player and year, enjoy videos of fights, and vote on who won them.

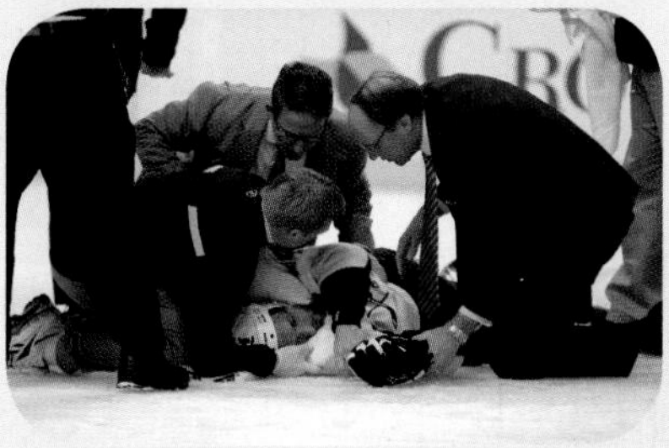

© Fred Kfoury/Icon SMI/Corbis

The Boston Bruin's Shawn Thornton beat Pittsburgh Penguin Brooks Orpik unconscious on December 7, 2013.

Social pressure is growing for change in a current norms regarding hockey violence. The Canadian Medical Association recently condemned the complacency of NHL team owners regarding this issue (Picard, 2013). Fear of brain injury is making concerned parents reluctant to register their children in the sport and is encouraging record numbers to drop out (Hume, 2013). Ex-players have launched a class action suit against the NHL over the cumulative impact of the game's violence on their lives (O'Connor, 2013). It remains to be seen how the NHL will respond to pressures for normative change.

Do you think hockey has too much violence? Should athletes who commit assaults while playing contact sports be treated differently under the law from people who engage in assaults outside of contact sports? If so, should the perpetrators be treated differently when their cases involve severe injury or death? Do you think severe injury and death are just risks that are part of playing such sports? Or is a crackdown needed on sports violence? Should more athletes be charged? Should coaches be charged if they have encouraged violent activity?

alive could endanger everyone's well-being. Similarly, whether we classify the death of a miner as accidental or a case of manslaughter depends on the kind of worker safety legislation in place. Some societies have more stringent worker safety rules than others do, and deaths considered accidental in some societies are classified as criminal offences in others (Takala et al., 2013). So we see that, even when it comes to serious crimes, social definitions vary (see Box 7.1).

Figure 7.1 allows us to classify four types of deviance and crime:

1. **Social diversions** are minor acts of deviance. One example is participating in fads and fashions such as dyeing your hair purple. People usually perceive such acts as harmless. They evoke, at most, a mild societal reaction, such as amusement or disdain, because many people are apathetic or unclear about whether social diversions are, in fact, deviant.
2. **Social deviations** are more serious acts. Because large numbers of people agree that these acts are deviant and in some ways harmful, social deviations are usually subject to institutional sanction. For example, at John Lie's high school in Hawaii, a rule made long hair on boys a fairly serious deviation punishable by a humiliating public haircut.

Social diversions are minor acts of deviance that are generally perceived as relatively harmless. They evoke, at most, a mild societal reaction, such as amusement or disdain.

Social deviations are non-criminal departures from norms that are nonetheless subject to official control. Some members of the public regard them as being in some ways harmful, while other members of the public do not.

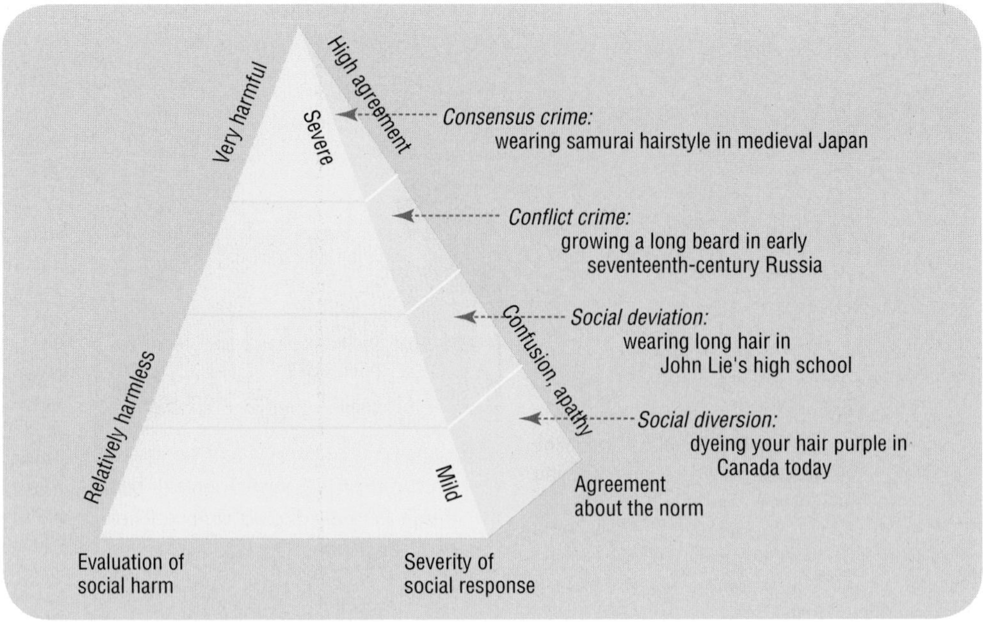

FIGURE 7.1
Types of Deviance and Crime

Source: From *Crime and Disrepute* by John Hagan. Copyright © 1994 Pine Forge Press. Reprinted by permission of Sage Publications.

Conflict crimes are illegal acts that many people consider harmful to society. However, other people believe the acts to be not so harmful. People who commit conflict crimes are punishable by the state.

Consensus crimes are illegal acts that nearly all people agree are bad in themselves and harm society greatly. The state inflicts severe punishment for consensus crimes.

3. **Conflict crimes** are deviant acts that the state defines as illegal but whose definition is controversial in the wider society (see Box 7.2). For instance, Tsar Peter the Great of Russia, who wanted to Westernize and modernize his empire, viewed long beards as a sign of backwardness. On September 1, 1698, he imposed a tax on beards to discourage men from growing them. Many Russians disagreed with his policy. Others agreed that growing long beards harmed Russia because it symbolized Russia's past rather than its future. Because of disagreement about the harmfulness of the practice, wearing a long beard in late–seventeenth-century Russia can be classified as a conflict crime.
4. Finally, **consensus crimes** are widely recognized to be bad in themselves. Little controversy surrounds their seriousness. The great majority of people agree that such crimes should be met with severe punishment. For instance, in medieval Japan, hairstyle was an important expression of people's status. If you were a peasant and sported the hairstyle of the samurai (warrior caste), you could be arrested and even killed because you were seen to be calling the entire social order into question.

As these examples show, people's conceptions of deviance and crime vary substantially over time and between societies. Under some circumstances, an issue that seems quite trivial to us, such as hairstyle, can be a matter of life and death.

Measuring Crime

Some crimes are more common than others are, and rates of crime vary by place and time and among different social groups. We now describe some of these variations. Then we review the main sociological explanations of crime and deviance.

First, a word about crime statistics. The main source of crime statistics is the information on crimes that is collected by the police. Since 1962, Canada has used the Uniform Crime Reporting (UCR) Survey to collect data from more than 1200 police detachments across Canada on 91 detailed categories of crime. Annually, the government publishes data on types of offences and characteristics of offenders.

Victimless crimes involve violations of the law in which no victim steps forward and is identified.

These statistics have two main shortcomings. First, much crime is not reported to the police. For example, so-called **victimless crimes** are violations of the law in which no victim steps forward and is identified. Victimless crimes include communicating for the purposes of prostitution, illegal gambling, and the use of illegal drugs. In addition, many common assaults go unreported because the assailant is a friend or relative of the victim;

BOX 7.2

SOCIAL POLICY: WHAT DO YOU THINK?

SHOULD RECREATIONAL DRUGS BE LEGALIZED?

In the mid-1960s, Lance Roberts was young, rebellious, and, like many of his generation, attracted to the counterculture of the day, which emphasized sex, drugs, and rock and roll. Lance recalls, "My friends and I enjoyed our share of comforting chemicals. Alcohol was always present at parties, but our favourite was marijuana. We called it Mary Jane. Suppliers were few but, fortunately, my girlfriend's older brother was "connected" so we were usually able to fill our needs. In telephone conversations where our parents might be listening, we used the code phrase 'dating Mary Jane (MJ).'

"My dates with MJ began in high school and carried on into university. One day I was walking across campus and my friend ran up and said, 'Did you hear the news about Larry? He got busted dating MJ last night!' Larry was not one of our inner circle, but we knew him well. Larry went to trial, was found guilty, and was sentenced to jail time! I can no longer remember how long his sentence was but it certainly shocked us. Some members of our group quit dating MJ immediately, and the rest of us were a lot more careful after Larry's encounter with the courts.

"In the decades since my early dates with MJ, Canadians' experience with marijuana drug has broadened (University of Ottawa, 2014). There are now about 2.3 million Canadian users. Their average age is 15. About a quarter of a million teenagers report using weed daily, making Canadian youth the world leaders among developed countries in cannabis use (Hui, 2013). Strains of the drug have increased in potency, and their effects are more targeted."

Canada spends about $500 million annually enforcing marijuana laws. Since 2006, enforcing these laws has left about half a million Canadians (mostly youth) with criminal records. More than two-thirds (69 percent) of adults support either decriminalization for casual users (34 percent) or outright legalization and taxation (36 percent) (Forum Research, 2013). Opinion polls indicate support for the decriminalization/legalization is trending upward.

Arguments for decriminalization and legalization take several forms. Supporters claim that majority public opinion should be followed, that the limited effective enforcement of the law degrades legal authority, that saddling youth with criminal records is stigmatizing and unproductive, that current practices support criminal organizations, and that potential tax revenues are being overlooked. By contrast, those opposing legal change argue that using drugs is immoral, that consumption causes psychological and social damage, and that using soft drugs is the gateway to harder drug use.

The issue is becoming more prominent. Political parties are taking public policy stands, as are medical and police associations. Where do you stand? Do you think the current laws should be changed? What justifies your position? Do you favour decriminalization? Decriminalization can take several forms; arrests can be replaced with tickets, fines, or police turning a blind eye. Which do you support? What about legalization? Should the state take over supply and/or distribution, or should all kinds of suppliers and distributors be legalized? How do you justify your opinion?

many victims of sexual assault are reluctant to report the crime because they are afraid they will be humiliated, not believed, or stigmatized.

The second main shortcoming of official statistics is that authorities and the wider public decide which criminal acts to report and which to ignore. If, for instance, the authorities decide to crack down on illegal drug use, then more drug-related crimes will be counted, not necessarily because more drug-related crimes have occurred but because more drug criminals are apprehended. Changes in legislation, which either create new offences or amend existing offences, also influence the number of recorded offences. Recognizing these difficulties, students of crime often supplement official crime statistics with other sources of information.

In **self-report surveys**, respondents are asked to report their involvement in criminal activities, either as perpetrators or as victims.

Self-report surveys are especially useful. In such surveys, respondents are asked to report their involvement in criminal activities, either as perpetrators or as victims. Self-report surveys compensate for many of the problems associated with official statistics. In general, self-report surveys report approximately the same rate of serious crime as official statistics do but find two or three times the rate of less serious crimes. Consequently, *indirect measures* of crime are sometimes also used. For instance, sales of syringes are a good index of the use of illegal intravenous drugs. However, indirect measures are unavailable for many types of crime.

Self-report surveys are also useful because they tell us that most Canadians have engaged in some type of criminal activity and that, in any given year, about a quarter of the population believe they have been the victim of a crime. These large proportions remind us that committing an act in violation of the law does not automatically result in being officially labelled a criminal. To be so identified, an individual's law-violating behaviour must first be observed and be deemed to justify action. The behaviour must be reported to the police who, in turn, must respond to the incident, decide whether it warrants further investigation, file a report, and make an arrest. Next, the accused person must appear at a preliminary hearing, an arraignment, and a trial. If the person does not plead guilty, the possibility always exists that he or she will not be convicted because guilt has not been proven beyond a reasonable doubt.

Victimization surveys are surveys in which people are asked whether they have been victims of crime.

In **victimization surveys**, people are asked whether they have been victims of crime. Although these types of surveys date back to the mid-1960s in the United States, no national victimization survey was done in Canada until 1988 (Fattah, 1991).

The most reliable victimization data in Canada comes from the General Social Survey (GSS) on Victimization. This survey is conducted every five years on a representative sample of Canadians. It asks respondents for their accounts of eight types of crime: sexual assault, robbery, physical assault, break and enter, motor vehicle/parts theft, theft of household property, vandalism, and theft of personal property.

Highlights of the most recent evidence (Perreault and Brennan, 2010) include the following. Victimization rates in Canada have remained stable since 2004, with about a quarter of the population reporting themselves as victims of crime in the past year. The majority of reported incidents were nonviolent, the highest proportion being theft of personal property (34%). Among violent incidents, the most common was physical assault (19%). Generally, the victimization rate is higher in western provinces than eastern provinces; higher among single people than married people; and higher among younger Canadians than older Canadians.

A large proportion of the criminal events reported through victimization surveys are not reported to police, and therefore never become part of the official record. The best estimates are that such non-reporting occurs for about 70 percent of violent and personal property theft victimization. For this reason, the GSS Victimization survey results differ from the official UCR Survey results.

The UCR data are used to generate two official estimates of crime in Canada that track the volume of crime: the traditional, police-reported crime rate and the crime severity index. Traditional crime rate accounts can be strongly affected by changes in commonly occurring events that are of low severity. For example, a sharp decline in small thefts can result in a reduced crime rate even when such serious crimes as homicide are on the rise. To compensate for such distortions, the crime severity index gives greater weight to serious crimes such as homicide before including them in the measure.

Figures 7.2 and 7.3 show Canadian crime trends in recent decades. Figure 7.2 illustrates that crime followed a 30-year uptrend after 1962 but has been on a steady decline in recent decades. Figure 7.3 uses the crime severity index to show the pattern of decline in violent activity over the last decade. These trends run counter to many Canadians' views

FIGURE 7.2
Police-Reported Crime Rates, 1962–2012

Source: Perreault, 2013.

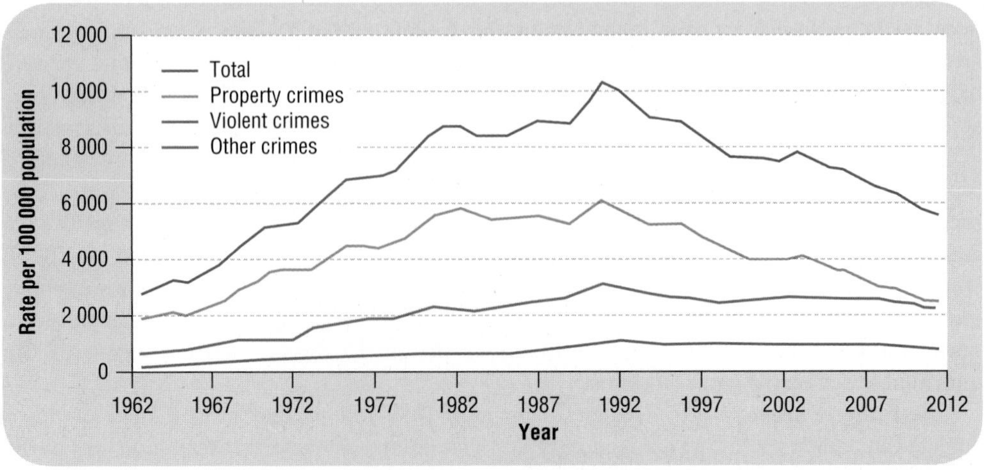

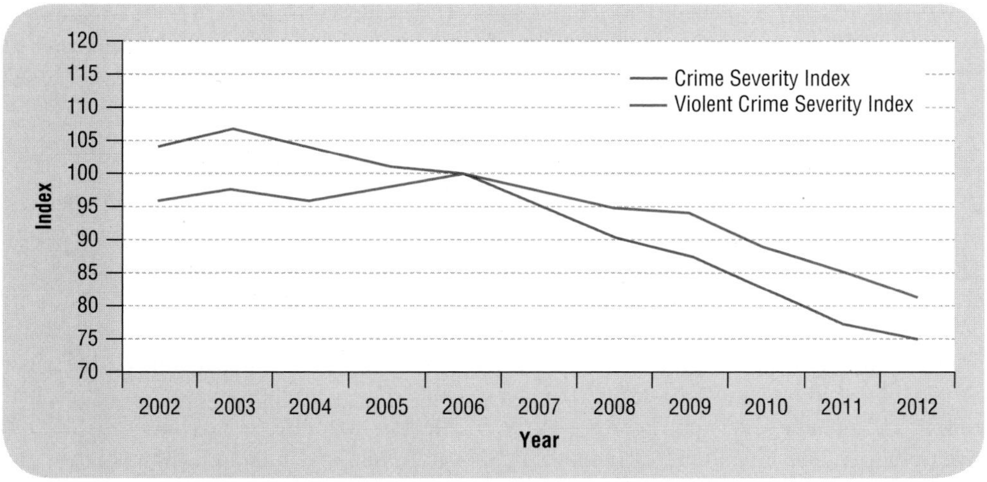

FIGURE 7.3
Police-Reported Crime Severity Indexes, 2002–2012

Source: Perreault, 2013.

of increasing crime, which have been shaped by the dramatic crimes reported each day in newspaper headlines and on the nightly news.

Explanations for Declining Crime Rates

Four explanations exist for the decline in Canadian crime rates. First, the "war against crime" is increasingly being fought by a substantially enlarged corps of better trained and better equipped law enforcement and correctional officers (Wilson and Petersilia, 2011). Recent declines in Canada's crime rate may reflect the introduction of new community policing initiatives, enforcement efforts that target specific types of crime and attempt to reduce their incidence, the refinement of case-management methods, improvements in the field of forensics, and efforts directed toward crime prevention (Royal Canadian Mounted Police, 2012).

Second, young men are most prone to crime, but Canada is aging and the number of young people in the population has declined. Specifically, the 15- to 24–year-old age cohort decreased in size by 6 percent between 1980 and 2010 (Statistics Canada, 2010b). Unlike the 1980s, when the baby boomers born between 1947 and 1966 entered their years of highest risk for crime, the 1990s saw a "baby bust." Because birth rates plummeted between 1967 and 1979, since the 1990s the pool of people at high risk of criminal behaviour has shrunk.

Third, the unemployment rate is strongly correlated with the crime rate (Cook, Watson, and Parker, 2014). Poor economic conditions in the 1980s made it hard to find a job and contributed to the high crime rate in that decade (Ouimet, 2002). Conversely, following a steep recession in 1990–91, the economy grew in 208 of the 226 months between January 1992 and October 2010 (Trading Economics, 2010). The modest growth continues, creating economic conditions that favour a decrease in crime.

Finally, and more controversially, some researchers argue that declining crime rates may be linked to the legalization of abortion (Donahue and Levitt, 2001). They observe that the crime rate started to decline about two decades after abortion was legalized in Canada and the United States. These researchers believe the drop occurred because, with the legalization of abortion, proportionately fewer unwanted children were brought into the population. They argue that, compared with wanted children, unwanted children are more prone to criminal behaviour because they tend to receive less parental supervision and guidance.

Criminal Profiles

Several social statuses are correlated with criminal behaviour, including sex, age, and race.

Of the 2011–12 Canadian criminal court cases in which the sex of the accused was reported, 81 percent involved a male accused and 19 percent, a female accused (Boyce, 2013). This pattern reappears for cases processed in youth courts. In 2010–11 youth cases in which the sex of the accused was reported, males accounted for 77 percent of cases and women for 23 percent (Brennan, 2012).

People who have not reached middle age commit most crime. The 15- to 24-year-old age cohort is the most prone to criminal behaviour. Although 15- to 24-year-olds represented just 12 percent of the Canadian population in 2012, they accounted for 76 percent of cases in youth court and 30 percent of cases in adult court (Boyce, 2013).

Race and Incarceration

Official statistics show that race is also a factor in crime. Aboriginal people composed 4 percent of the Canadian population according to the 2011 National Household Survey. However, they accounted for 27 percent of people in custody in provincial/territorial prisons and 23 percent of those in federal prisons (Dauvergne, 2012; Office of Correctional Investigator, 2013). In both types of institutions, the overrepresentation of Aboriginal people in prisons is trending upward (Perreault, 2009). Between 2001 and 2011, the number of incarcerated Aboriginal people increased by almost 40 per cent (Sapers, 2012). The overrepresentation of Aboriginal people in Canada's prisons is particularly marked in the Prairie provinces. Although Aboriginal people constitute 12 percent of Saskatchewan's population, they account for 78 percent of adults sentenced to custody in that province. In Alberta, where Aboriginal people make up 5 percent of the population, they account for 41 percent of custodial sentences. Aboriginal people were also a majority among those sentenced to custody in Nunavut, the Northwest Territories, Yukon, Saskatchewan, and Manitoba (see Figure 7.4).

The literature offers four explanations for the overrepresentation of Aboriginal people in Canada's prisons (Hartnagel, 2000). First, a disproportionately large number of Aboriginal people live in poverty. Although the great majority of people living in poverty are law-abiding, poverty and its handicaps are associated with elevated crime rates. Second, Aboriginal people tend to commit so-called **street crimes**—breaking and entering, robbery, assault, and the like—that are more detectable than **white-collar crimes** such as embezzlement, fraud, copyright infringement, false advertising, and so on. Third, the police, the courts, and other institutions may discriminate against Aboriginal people. Consequently, Aboriginal people may be more likely to be apprehended, prosecuted, and convicted. Fourth, contact with Western culture has disrupted social life in many Aboriginal communities (Chapter 10, Race and Ethnicity). Disruption has led to a weakening of social control over community members. Some people think that certain "races" are *inherently* more law abiding than others, but they are able to hold such an opinion only by ignoring the powerful *social* forces that cause so many Aboriginal people to be incarcerated in Canada (Roberts and Gabor, 1990).

Street crimes include arson, break and enter, assault, and other illegal acts disproportionately committed by people from lower classes.

White-collar crimes refer to illegal acts committed by respectable, high-status persons in the course of their work.

FIGURE 7.4
Aboriginal Canadians Sentenced to Custody, by Jurisdiction, 2010–11

Source: Dauvergne, 2013.

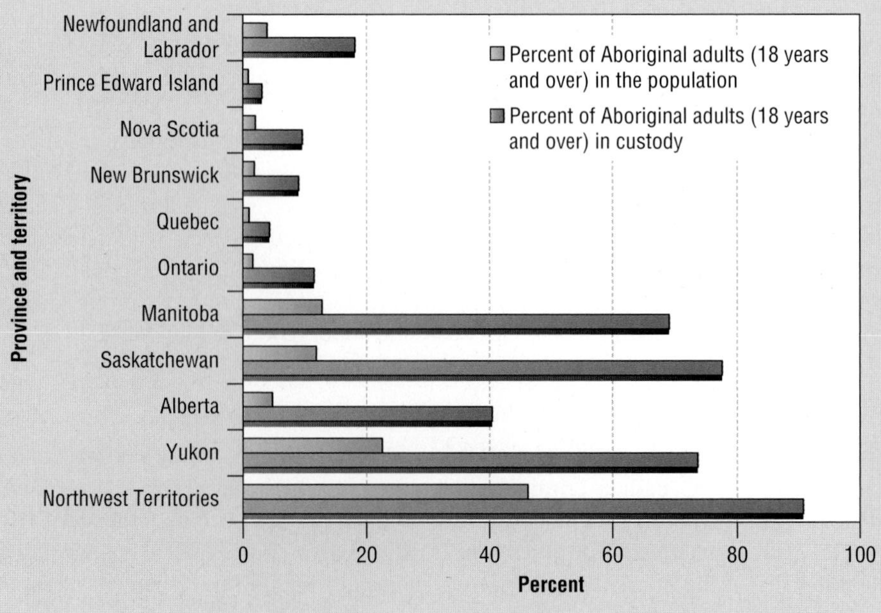

Most of the factors listed above also account for the above-average incarceration rate among black Canadians. Black people are more likely than are whites to occupy a lower-class position, to engage mainly in street crime as opposed to white-collar crime, and to face a discriminatory criminal justice system. They are also more likely than white people are to be motivated to commit criminal acts; to be detected and apprehended engaging in criminal acts; and to be prosecuted, convicted, and jailed.

The claim that the criminal justice system engages in discriminatory practices based on race may be difficult for some Canadians to accept, but research suggests that the claim is credible. For example, a Toronto survey showed that older and better-educated whites and Asians with no criminal record are significantly less likely to be stopped for police searches than are younger and less well-educated whites and Asians who have a criminal record. In contrast, age, education, and lack of a criminal record do not insulate blacks from searches. In fact, better-educated and well-to-do blacks are *more* likely to be stopped and searched by police than are less well-educated and poorer blacks. These findings suggest that Toronto police keep a closer eye on blacks than they do on whites and Asians, and are particularly suspicious of blacks who have education and money (Wortley and Tanner, 2011).

AF archive / Alamy

Oscar Grant III was a 22-year-old black man and father from Oakland, California. On New Year's Eve, 2009, he and his friends hopped aboard a rapid transit train. During the ride, someone provoked a fight with him. Police officers responded, removing Grant and several other black men from the train and detaining them. While Grant was restrained and lying face down, officer Johannes Mehserle shot him in the back, killing him. Mehserle spent just 11 months in jail. These events illustrate the persistence of racial bias in the criminal justice system and are depicted in the 2013 movie, *Fruitvale Station.* Actual video of the shooting is on YouTube at www.youtube.com/watch?v=SOP8TSP2YJU.

TIME FOR REVIEW

- How does crime differ from deviance? Give examples of each.
- Explain why official crime statistics are conservative estimates.
- What factors help explain the recent trend in declining crime rates?
- Some Aboriginal leaders deplore Canada as a racist society. What criminal statistics can be used to support their claim?

EXPLAINING DEVIANCE AND CRIME

> Lep: "I remember your li'l ass used to ride dirt bikes and skateboards, actin' crazy an' shit. Now you want to be a gangster, huh? You wanna hang with real muthaf—and tear shit up, huh? Stand up, get your li'l ass up. How old is you now anyway?"
>
> Kody: "Eleven, but I'll be twelve in November."
> —*Sanyika Shakur*
> *(Monster: The Autobiography of an L.A. Gang Member. New York: Penguin, 1993)*

"Monster" Kody Scott eagerly joined the notorious gang the Crips in South Central Los Angeles in 1975 when he was in grade 6. He was released from Folsom Prison on parole in 1988, at the age of 24. Until about three years before his release, he was one of the most ruthless gang leaders in Los Angeles and the California prison system. In 1985, however, he decided to reform. He adopted the name Sanyika Shakur, became a black nationalist, and began a crusade against gangs. Few people in his position have chosen that path. In Scott's heyday, about 30 000 gang members roamed Los Angeles County. Today there are more than 150 000.

What makes engaging in crime an attractive prospect to so many people? In general, why do deviance and crime occur at all? For explanations, sociologists rely on symbolic interactionism, functionalism, conflict theories, and feminist theories.

Symbolic Interactionist Approaches to Deviance and Crime

People may learn deviant and criminal behaviour when they interact with others. Identifying the social circumstances that promote the learning of deviant and criminal roles is a traditional focus of symbolic interactionists.

Learning Deviance

The idea that becoming a habitual deviant or criminal is a learning process that occurs in a social context was firmly established by Howard S. Becker's classic study of marijuana users (Becker, 1963: 41–58). In the 1940s, Becker financed his Ph.D. studies by playing piano in Chicago jazz bands. He used the opportunity to carefully observe 50 fellow musicians, informally interview them in depth, and write up detailed field notes after performances.

Becker found that his fellow musicians passed through a three-stage learning process before becoming regular marijuana users. Failure to pass a stage meant failure to learn the deviant role and become a regular user. These are the three stages:

1. *Learning to smoke the drug in a way that produces real effects.* First-time marijuana smokers do not generally get high. To do so, they must learn how to smoke the drug in a way that ensures a sufficient dosage to produce intoxicating effects (taking deep drags and holding their breath). This process takes practice, and some first-time users give up, typically claiming that marijuana has no effect on them or that people who claim otherwise are just fooling themselves. Others are more strongly encouraged by their peers to keep trying. If they persist, they are ready to move on to stage two.
2. *Learning to recognize the effects and connect them with drug use.* Those who learn the proper smoking technique may not recognize that they are high or they may not connect the symptoms of being high with smoking the drug. They may get hungry, laugh uncontrollably, play the same song for hours on end, and yet still fail to realize that these are symptoms of intoxication. If so, they will stop using the drug. Becker found, however, that his fellow musicians typically asked experienced users how they knew whether they were high. Experienced users identified the symptoms of marijuana use and helped novices make the connection between what they were experiencing and their smoking of the drug. Once they made that connection, novices were ready to advance to stage three.
3. *Learning to enjoy the perceived sensations.* Smoking marijuana is not inherently pleasurable. Some users experience a frightening loss of self-control (paranoia). Others feel dizzy, uncomfortably thirsty, itchy, forgetful, or dangerously impaired in their ability to judge time and distance. If these negative sensations persist, marijuana use will cease. However, Becker found that experienced users typically helped novices redefine negative sensations as pleasurable. They taught novices to laugh at their impaired judgment, take special pleasure in quenching their deep thirst, and find deeper meaning in familiar music. If and only if novices learned to define the effects of smoking as pleasurable did they become habitual marijuana smokers.

Learning *any* deviant or criminal role requires a social context in which experienced deviants or criminals teach novices the "tricks of the trade." It follows that more exposure to experienced deviants and criminals increases the chance that an individual will come to value a deviant or criminal lifestyle and consider it normal (Sutherland, 1939, 1949). Moreover, the type of deviant or criminal that predominates in one's social environment has a bearing on the type of deviant or criminal that a novice will become. For example, depending on the availability of different types of deviants and criminals in their neighbourhoods, delinquent youths will turn to different types of crime. In some areas, delinquent youths are recruited by organized crime, such as the Mafia. In areas that lack organized crime networks, delinquent youths are more likely to create violent gangs. Thus, the relative availability of different types of deviants and criminals influences the type of deviant or criminal role a delinquent youth learns (Cloward and Ohlin, 1960).

Labelling

One night in downtown Regina, Saskatchewan, after a night of heavy drinking, two 20-year-old university students, Alex Ternowetsky and Steven Kummerfield, both white and middle class, picked up Pamela George, an Aboriginal single mother who occasionally worked as a prostitute. They drove the 28-year-old woman outside the city limits, had her perform oral sex without pay, and then savagely beat her to death. Although the two young men were originally charged with first-degree murder, a jury later found them guilty of the lesser charge of manslaughter. Justice Ted Malone of the Saskatchewan Court of Queen's Bench instructed the jurors to consider that the two men had been drinking and that George was "indeed a prostitute." Members of the victim's family were appalled, Native leaders outraged. Tone Cote of the Yorkton Tribal Council said the sentence would send the message that "it's all right for little white boys to go out on the streets, get drunk and use that for an excuse to start hunting down our people."

BananaStock/Thinkstock.com

A variant of symbolic interactionism known as **labelling theory** holds that deviance results not just from the actions of the deviant but also from the responses of others, who define some actions as deviant and other actions as normal. As the above example suggests, such terms as *deviant* and *criminal* are not applied automatically when a person engages in rule-violating behaviour. Some individuals escape being labelled as deviants despite having engaged in deviant behaviour. Others, like Ternowetsky and Kummerfield, are labelled deviant but found to be guilty of a lesser charge than would typically be the case. Still others, such as Pamela George, who are the victims of such acts, may find themselves labelled as deviant (Matsueda, 1988, 1992).

Labelling theory holds that deviance results not so much from the actions of the deviant as from the response of others, who label the rule breaker a deviant.

Aaron Cicourel (1968) demonstrated labelling's important role in who is caught and charged with crime. Cicourel examined the tendency to label rule-breaking adolescents as juvenile delinquents if they came from families in which the parents were divorced. He found that police officers tended to use their discretionary powers to arrest adolescents from divorced families more often than adolescents from intact families who committed similar delinquent acts. Judges, in turn, tended to give more severe sentences to adolescents from divorced families than to adolescents from intact families who were charged with similar delinquent acts. Sociologists and criminologists then collected data on the social characteristics of adolescents who were charged as juvenile delinquents, "proving" that children from divorced families were more likely to become juvenile delinquents. Their finding reinforced the beliefs of police officers and judges. Thus, the labelling process acted as a self-fulfilling prophecy.

Functionalist Explanations

While symbolic interactionists focus on the learning and labelling of deviant and criminal roles, functionalists direct their attention to the social dysfunctions that lead to deviant and criminal behaviour.

Durkheim

Functionalist thinking on deviance and crime originated with Durkheim (1938), who made the controversial claim that deviance and crime are beneficial for society. For one thing, he wrote, when someone breaks a rule, it provides others with a chance to condemn and punish the transgression, remind them of their common values, clarify the moral boundaries of the group to which they belong, and thus reinforce social solidarity (see Box 7.3). For another, deviance and crime help societies adapt to social change. Martin Luther King, Jr. was arrested in Alabama in February 1965 for taking part in a demonstration supporting the idea that blacks should be allowed to vote, but later that year, the passage of the Voting Rights Acts made it a crime to *prevent* blacks from voting in the United States. King's crime

BOX 7.3

SOCIOLOGY AT THE MOVIES

EASY A

Olive Penderghast (Emma Stone) is embarrassed to admit she spent the weekend at home alone, so she tells her pushy high-school friend, Rhi (Aly Michalka), she had a date with a college guy. On Monday, the following dialogue ensues:

Rhi: "The whole weekend?"
Olive: "Yup."
Rhi: "Whoa, whoa. Wait a minute. You didn't have. . . ."
Olive: "No, no. Of course not."
Rhi: "You liar. . . ."
Olive: "Rhi, I'm not that kind of girl."
Rhi: "Oh really? The kind that does it or the kind that does it and doesn't have the lady balls to tell her best friend?"

Rhi then drags Olive into a school restroom and insists on knowing the "truth." To shut her up, Olive finally "admits" she had sex with the mythical college guy. Big mistake. Marianne (Amanda Bynes) overhears the conversation. She is a self-righteous Christian enthusiast who promptly lets everyone in the school know that Olive is a fallen woman.

The school's norms are sexist and homophobic. They prohibit premarital sex for females but encourage it for males. They view only heterosexual sex as acceptable. So although Olive is seen as a slut, the male students—outsiders and misfits in particular—see her as an opportunity. One male student who is gay, another who is obese, and a third who is a nerd get Olive to help them out by pretending she had sex with them. They become socially acceptable as Olive's reputation plummets.

The Kobal Collection at Art Resource, NY

Becoming labelled as a sexual deviant allows Olive Penderghast (Emma Stone) to help other deviants become normalized. In what sense does *Easy A* out-Durkheim Durkheim?

Easy A is a well-written and funny movie, but what makes it sociologically interesting is the story it tells about the functions of norms and norm-breaking. Durkheim observed that norm-breakers like Olive reinforce group solidarity insofar as they encourage group members to publicly display outraged opposition to norm-breaking (Durkheim, 1964 [1895]). If Durkheim saw *Easy A*, he would immediately notice that everyone's gossiping and finger-pointing in reaction to Olive's alleged sexual transgression acted to strengthened the norm that premarital sex for females is unacceptable. But *Easy A* also teaches us a sociological principle that Durkheim did not remark upon: Norm-breakers can provide outsiders with the opportunity to become insiders. In *Easy A*, the gay, obese, and nerdy males become socially acceptable once they say they had sex with Olive. Olive the transgressor transforms them from outcasts to integral group members. In their functionalist interpretation of norms and norm-breaking, the writers of *Easy A* out-Durkheim Durkheim.

Critical Thinking

1. Can you think of a situation in your own experience—at school, in your neighbourhood, during summer camp, in church, mosque, or synagogue—where norm-breaking reinforced group solidarity? Write a paragraph describing this situation.
2. Can you think of a situation where a norm-breaker gave outsiders an opportunity to become integrated into a group? Write a paragraph describing this situation.

(and similar crimes by other civil rights activists) brought about positive social change, demonstrating the validity of Durkheim's point about the positive functions of deviance and crime.

Merton

Strain theory holds that people may turn to deviance when they experience strain. Strain results when a culture teaches people the value of material success and society fails to provide enough legitimate opportunities for everyone to succeed.

Robert Merton (1938) further developed Durkheim's theory by emphasizing the *dysfunctions* of deviance and crime. Merton argued that cultures often teach people to value material success. Just as often, however, societies do not provide enough legitimate opportunities for everyone to succeed. In Merton's view, **strain theory** suggests that such a discrepancy between cultural ideals and structural realities is dysfunctional and leads to strain, which increases a person's likelihood of turning to deviance.

Most people who experience strain will nonetheless force themselves to adhere to social norms, Merton wrote. He called this option "conformity." The rest adapt by engaging in one of four types of action. Rejecting the society's goals and its institutionalized means of achieving them, they may drop out of conventional society ("retreatism"). Rejecting the goals of conventional society but continuing to follow them, they may engage in "ritualism." Accepting cultural goals and creating novel means of achieving them results in "innovation." Although some innovators are business geniuses like Henry Ford and Steve Jobs, others are criminals (see Box 7.4). Finally, rejecting cultural goals and finding new means of achieving new goals involves "rebellion"—the Hippies of the 1960s represent this last form of adaptation to strain (see Figure 7.5).

Criminal Subcultures

It is not only individuals who adapt to the strain caused by social dysfunction. Social groups also adapt—by forming criminal gangs. Gang members feel the legitimate world has rejected them. They return the favour by rejecting the legitimate world. In the process, they develop distinct norms and values—a criminal **subculture** (Cohen, 1955).

A **subculture** is a set of distinctive values, norms, and practices within a larger culture.

An important part of any gang subculture consists of the justifications its members spin for their criminal activities. These justifications make illegal activities appear morally acceptable and normal, at least to the gang members. Typically, criminals deny personal responsibility for their actions ("It wasn't my fault!") or deny the wrongfulness of the act ("I was just borrowing it."). They condemn those who pass judgment on them ("The cops are bigger crooks than anyone!"). They claim their victims get what they deserve ("She had it coming to her."). And they appeal to higher loyalties, particularly to friends and family ("I had to do it because he dissed my gang."). Such

BOX 7.4

SOCIOLOGY ON THE TUBE

BREAKING BAD

It starts with an RV roaring down a desert highway in New Mexico, driven by a middle-aged man clad in just a ventilator mask and tighty-whities. The van runs into a ditch. The man grabs a pistol and a camcorder, jumps out of the van, and starts recording. He identifies himself as Walter White, professes love to his wife and son, and concludes, "There are going to be some things that you'll come to learn about me in the next few days. I just want you to know that no matter how it may look, I only had you in my heart. Goodbye" (*Breaking Bad*, season 1, episode 1).

Who is this man? He summarizes his plight this way: "My wife is seven months pregnant with a baby we didn't intend. My 15-year-old son has cerebral palsy. I am an extremely overqualified high-school chemistry teacher. When I can work, I make $43,700 per year. I have watched all of my colleagues and friends surpass me in every way imaginable. And within eighteen months, I will be dead" (*Breaking Bad*, season 2, episode 3). Walter White (played by Bryan Cranston) has advanced, inoperable lung cancer.

How can Walter pay for his medical bills? How can he ensure that his family is looked after once he is gone? How can he overcome the humiliating fact that he had a brilliant future behind him? The answer appears in the unlikely form of a former pupil, Jesse Pinkman (Aaron Paul), whom he chances to spot fleeing a meth lab. Walter realizes that he has the skills to make the purest methamphetamine on the market and that Jesse can distribute the product. And so begins an adventure that leads Walter—a good man with a steady job and strong family values—to manufacture a highly addictive, illegal substance, consort with meth heads, take on a Mexican drug cartel, murder people who get in the way, and work his way up to the status of a criminal kingpin.

The Kobal Collection at Art Resource, NY

In the TV show Breaking Bad, a high-school chemistry teacher sets up a meth lab with a former student. Which theory of crime best explains his behaviour?

Walter White stares into a chasm separating cultural goals from institutionalized means of achieving them. On the one hand, he desires what everyone wants: good health, a secure family life, and respected status in his community. On the other hand, he has no hope of achieving these ambitions by legitimate means. And so, when the opportunity presents itself, he breaks bad, just as Robert Merton would have predicted.

FIGURE 7.5
Merton's Strain Theory of Deviance

Source: Adapted from Merton, 1938

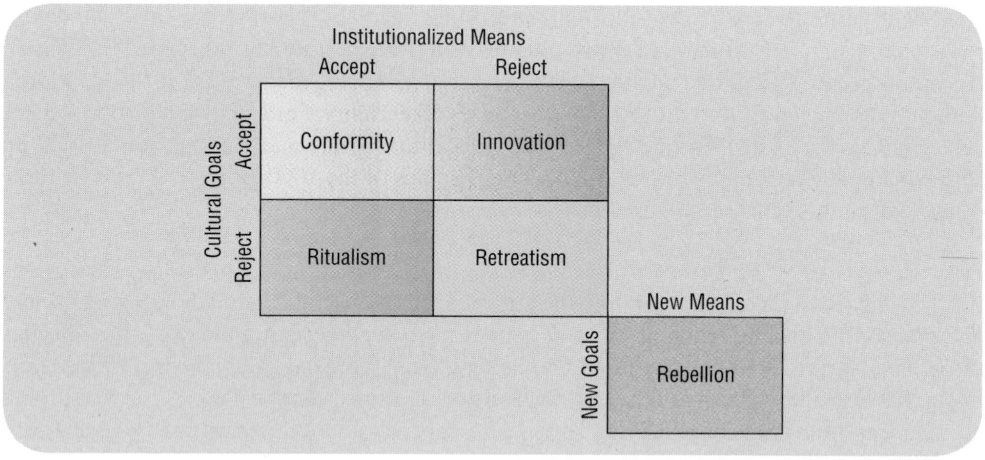

© Viviane Moos/CORBIS

rationalizations enable criminals to clear their consciences and get on with the job (Sykes and Matza, 1957).

Although deviants may depart from mainstream culture in many ways, they are strict conformists when it comes to the norms of their own subculture. They tend to share the same beliefs, dress alike, eat similar food, and adopt the same mannerisms and speech patterns. Although most members of the larger society consider gang subcultures to be deviant, gang members strongly discourage deviance *within* the subculture.

Functionalism and the Relationship Between Crime and Class

One of the main problems with functionalist accounts is that they exaggerate the connection between crime and class. Many self-report surveys find, at most, a weak tendency for criminals to come disproportionately from lower classes. Some self-report surveys report no such tendency at all, especially among young people and for less serious types of crime (Weis, 1987). A stronger correlation exists between *serious street crimes* and class. Armed robbery and assault, for instance, are more common among people from lower classes. A stronger correlation also exists between *white-collar* crime and class. Middle- and upper-class people are most likely to commit fraud and embezzlement, for example. Thus, generalizations about the relationship between class and crime must be qualified by taking into account the severity and type of crime (Braithwaite, 1981). Note also that official statistics usually exaggerate class differences because they are more accurate barometers of street crime than suite crime; more police surveillance occurs in lower-class neighbourhoods than in upper-class boardrooms, and widely cited police statistics do not record some white-collar crimes because they are handled by agencies other than the police. As we will now see, conflict theories help to overcome functionalism's inadequate explanation of the relationship between crime and class.

Conflict Theories

Conflict theorists maintain that rich and powerful members of society impose deviant and criminal labels on others, particularly those who challenge the existing social order.

Meanwhile, the rich and powerful are usually able to use their money and influence to escape punishment for their own misdeeds.

Steven Spitzer (1980) summarizes this school of thought. He notes that capitalist societies are based on private ownership of property. Moreover, their smooth functioning depends on the availability of productive labour and respect for authority. When thieves steal, they challenge private property. Theft is therefore a crime. When so-called bag ladies and drug addicts drop out of conventional society, they are defined as deviant because their refusal to engage in productive labour undermines a pillar of capitalism. When young, politically volatile students demonstrate and militant trade unionists strike, they, too, represent a threat to the social order. Authorities may therefore define them as deviant or criminal.

Of course, Spitzer notes, the rich and the powerful also engage in deviant and criminal acts. However, they are less likely than other people are to be reported, convicted, and prosecuted for criminal acts (Blumberg, 1989; Clinard and Yeager, 1980; Hagan, 1989; Sherrill, 1997; Snider, 1999; Sutherland, 1949). *Reporting* is less frequent because much white-collar crime takes place in private and is therefore difficult to detect. For instance, supposedly competing corporations may decide to fix prices and divide markets—both crimes—but executives may make such decisions in boardrooms, private clubs, and homes that are not generally subject to police surveillance. *Conviction* and *prosecution* are less frequent partly because wealthy white-collar criminals can afford legal experts, public relations firms, and advertising agencies that advise their clients on how to bend laws, build up their corporate image in the public mind, and influence lawmakers to pass laws "without teeth." In addition, the law is more lenient in meting out punishment for white-collar crime than for street crime. Compare the crime of break and enter with that of fraud. Fraud almost certainly costs society more than break and enter does, but breaking and entering is a street crime committed mainly by lower-class people, while fraud is a white-collar crime committed mainly by middle- and upper-class people. Not surprisingly, prison sentences are nearly twice as likely in break-and-enter convictions than in fraud convictions (Thomas, 2002: 9).

In sum, conflict theorists emphasize the connection between power and crime. Differential access to economic resources results in differences, both in power and in the ability to achieve the desired outcomes (Chapter 5, Social Interaction). Power, in turn, is commonly used to perpetuate privilege. Since the sanctions applied to criminal and deviant conduct are unpleasant and constraining, members of privileged classes use their power to avoid being defined as criminal and, if so defined, from suffering serious consequences.

The earlier distinction between street crime and suite (white-collar) crime is relevant here. Street crime is associated with the threat or application of force or violence. In contrast, white-collar crime relies on deceit, concealment, and the violation of trust. The connection between class and type of crime is clear. Economic need motivates crime among occupants of lower-class positions, while economic greed motivates crime among occupants of privileged classes. Public attention is focused mainly on street crime, whereas the suffering associated with white-collar crime, although widespread, is largely underappreciated. For example, the Canadian Securities Commission estimates that more than a million Canadian adults are victims of investment fraud, with a third of them experiencing "extreme or significant impacts on their personal finances" (Canadian Business Journal, 2013). Substantial financial loss also influences psychological, physical, and emotional health. While the federal government is taking steps to increase punishment for suite crime, Canada ranks poorly compared to other countries in terms of its laws, policies, and practices that sanction it (Brown, 2012; Federal Accountability Initiative for Reform, 2013).

Social Control

Conflict theorists argue that the rich and the powerful exercise disproportionate control over the criminal justice system and are therefore able to engage in deviance and crime with

Control theory holds that the rewards of deviance and crime are ample. Therefore, nearly everyone would engage in deviance and crime if they could get away with it. The degree to which people are prevented from violating norms and laws accounts for variations in the level of deviance and crime.

relative impunity. This argument is generalized by one variant of conflict theory, known as **control theory**. According to control theorists, nearly everyone would like to have the fun, pleasure, excitement, and profit that deviance and crime promise. Moreover, they say, if we could get away with it, most of us would commit deviant and criminal acts to acquire more of these rewards. For control theorists, the reason most of us do not engage in deviance and crime is that we are prevented from doing so. In contrast, deviants and criminals break norms and laws because social controls imposed by various authorities are too weak to ensure conformity.

Travis Hirschi developed the control theory of crime (Hirschi, 1969; Gottfredson and Hirschi, 1990). He argued that, compared with adults, adolescents are more prone to deviance and crime because they are incompletely socialized and therefore lack self-control. Adults and adolescents may both experience the impulse to break norms and laws, but adolescents are less likely to control that impulse. Hirschi went on to show that the adolescents who are most prone to delinquency are likely to lack four types of social control. They tend to have few social *attachments* to parents, teachers, and other respectable role models; few legitimate *opportunities* for education and a good job; few *involvements* in conventional institutions; and weak *beliefs* in traditional values and morality. Because of the lack of control stemming from these sources, these adolescents are relatively free to act on their deviant impulses. For similar reasons, boys are more likely to engage in juvenile delinquency than girls are, and people who experience job and marital instability are more likely than others are to engage in crime (Giordano, 2014; Hagan et al., 1987; Peters, 1994; Sampson and Laub, 1993). Tighter social control by authorities in all spheres of life decreases the frequency of deviant and criminal acts.

Feminist Contributions

Although conflict theory shows how the distribution of power in society influences the definition, detection, and prosecution of deviance and criminality, it neglects the consequences of what you will learn about in detail in Chapter 11, Sexualities and Gender Stratification: on average, women are less powerful than men are in all social institutions. Feminist sociologists hold that gender-based power differences influence the framing of laws and therefore the definition and detection of crime and the prosecution of criminals. They point out that historically, because of their less privileged status, to be female is to be deviant.

To support their claim, feminists note that, until recently, many types of crime against women were largely ignored in Canada and most other parts of the world. This was true even when the crime involved non-consensual sexual intercourse, an act that prior to 1983 was defined under Canadian criminal law as *rape* and is now considered a form of *sexual assault*. Admittedly, the authorities sometimes severely punished rape involving strangers. However, date rape and acquaintance rape were rarely prosecuted, while Canadian law viewed marital rape as a contradiction in terms, as if it were logically impossible for a woman to be raped by her husband. Law professors, judges, police officers, rapists, and even victims did not think date rape was "real rape" (Estrich, 1987). Similarly, until the 1970s, judges, lawyers, and social scientists rarely discussed sexual harassment and physical violence against women. Governments did not collect data on the topic, and few social scientists showed any interest in the subject. Relative powerlessness allowed many women to be victimized while the violence against them went unnoticed by the larger society and their assailants went free.

It follows from the feminist argument that a shift in the distribution of power between women and men would alter this state of affairs. And in fact, that is precisely what happened after about 1970. A series of changes to Canadian criminal law since 1970 have emphasized that non-consensual sexual acts are sexual assaults. The new laws

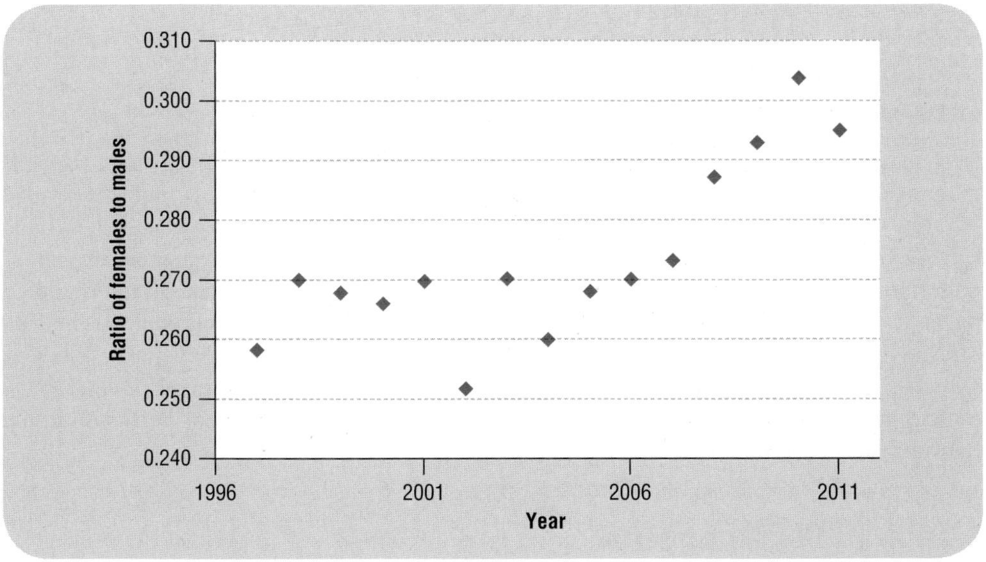

FIGURE 7.6
The Ratio of Female to Male Youth Admitted to Correctional Services, Canada, 1997–2011

Source: Statistics Canada. 2014. Adapted from Statistics Canada CANSIM Database, Table 251-0011. Retrieved June 12, 2014. http://www5.statcan.gc.ca/cansim/home-accueil?lang=eng&p2=49&MM

have helped raise people's awareness of date rape, acquaintance rape, and marital rape. Sexual assault is more often prosecuted now than it once was. The same is true for other types of violence against women and for sexual harassment. These changes occurred because, since 1970, women's position has improved in the economy, the family, and other social institutions. Women now have more autonomy in the family, earn more, and enjoy more political influence. Women also created a movement for women's rights that heightened concern about crimes disproportionately affecting them (MacKinnon, 1979). Social definitions of crimes against women changed as women became more powerful in Canadian society.

In the 1970s, some feminists expected that growing gender equality would also change the historical tendency for women to be far less crime-prone than men are. They reasoned that control over the activities of girls and women would weaken, thus allowing women to behave more like men. Widely publicized cases of violent crime by teenage girls add weight to such claims, and official data support them. For instance, the ratio of women to men convicted of youth crime rose by 14.3 percent from 1997 to 2011 (see Figure 7.6).

Our overview shows that many theories contribute to understanding the social causes of deviance and crime. Each focuses on a different aspect of the phenomenon, so familiarity with all of them allows us to develop a fully rounded appreciation of the complex processes surrounding the sociology of deviance and crime.

TIME FOR REVIEW

- What role do self-fulfilling prophecies play in labelling theory?
- How would a conflict theorist explain why street crimes receive more attention from the criminal justice system than does suite crime?
- A parent of a juvenile delinquent seeks your advice on how to get her daughter to conform. Based on control theory, what advice would you give?
- What have feminist researchers added to our understanding of criminal conduct?

SOCIAL CONTROL AND REGULATION

Internal and External Social Control

Social control refers to the ways in which a social system attempts to regulate people's thoughts, feelings, appearance, and behaviour.

Internal social control regulates people through socialization and shapes people's minds so they come to regard deviant actions as undesirable.

External social control regulates people by imposing punishments and offering rewards.

Responses to deviance are matters of **social control**, the ways that a social system attempts to regulate people's thoughts, feelings, appearance, and behaviour. Social control is divided into two main types: internal and external. **Internal social control** regulates people through socialization. It is directed at shaping people's minds so they view deviant actions as undesirable. The socialization process generates internal social control by internalizing norms. In contrast, **external social control** regulates people by imposing punishments and offering rewards. This method of control is enacted by police officers, lawmakers, judges, parents, teachers, and other authority figures. As we will now see, different proposals and policies for social control place more or less emphasis on reshaping minds versus imposing punishments and offering rewards.

Trends in Social Control

No discussion of crime and deviance would be complete without considering social control and punishment because all societies impose sanctions on rule breakers. However, the *degree* of social control varies over time and from one society to the next. *Forms* of punishment also vary. Below we focus on how social control and punishment have changed historically.

Consider first the difference between preindustrial and industrial societies. Beginning in the late nineteenth century, many sociologists argued that preindustrial societies are characterized by strict social control and high conformity, while industrial societies are characterized by less stringent social control and low conformity (Tönnies, 1988 [1887]). Similar differences were said to characterize small communities versus cities. As an old German proverb says, "City air makes you free."

There is much truth in this point of view. Whether they are fans of opera or reggae, connoisseurs of fine wine or marijuana, city dwellers in industrialized societies find it easier than do people in preindustrial societies to belong to a group or subculture of their choice. In general, the more complex a society, the less likely many norms will be widely shared. In fact, in a highly complex society, such as Canada today, it is difficult to find an area of social life in which everyone is alike or in which one group can impose its norms on the rest of society without resistance.

Nonetheless, some sociologists believe that in some respects social control has intensified over time. They recognize that individuality and deviance have increased but insist this increase has happened only within strict limits, beyond which it is now *more* difficult to move. In their view, many crucial aspects of life have become more regimented, not less.

Much of the regimentation of modern life is tied to the growth of capitalism and the state. Factories require strict labour regimes, with workers arriving and leaving at a fixed time and, in the interim, performing routine tasks at a set pace. Workers initially rebelled against this regimentation since they had been accustomed to enjoying many holidays and a flexible and vague work schedule regulated only approximately by the seasons and the rising and setting of the sun. But they had little alternative as wage labour in industry overtook feudal arrangements in agriculture (Thompson, 1967). Meanwhile, as French social theorist Michel Foucault demonstrated in detail, institutions linked to the growth of the modern state—armies, police forces, public schools, health care systems, and other bureaucracies—also demanded strict work regimes, curricula, and procedures. These institutions existed on a much smaller scale in preindustrial times or did not exist at all. Today, such institutions penetrate our lives and sustain strong norms of belief and conduct (Foucault, 1977).

A **panopticon** is a prison design that allows inmates to be constantly observed without their knowledge. This term derives from the word *panoptic*, meaning "all seeing."

The growth of modern surveillance, social control, and associated discipline is metaphorically captured in an idea introduced by English philosopher Jeremy Bentham. A **panopticon** is an architectural design for prisons consisting of an inner ring and an outer

XINHUA/ActionPress/CP Picture Archive

When the Vancouver Canucks lost Game 7 of the Stanley Cup playoffs to the Boston Bruins in 2011, rioting broke out in Vancouver. Surveillance cameras caught much of the action, and police reviewed more than 5000 hours of digital imagery, leading to hundreds of arrests. Some experts believe that once the public better appreciates the capacity of surveillance cameras to help identify rioters and demonstrators, many people will be inhibited from participating not just in hockey riots but also in political demonstrations.

ring. The outer ring comprises prisoners' cells that are open to light on both sides. The inner ring is a tower with large windows that houses the guards. The key to the design is that guards can observe prisoners at all times but the inmates do not know when they are being watched. The effect is "to induce in the inmate a state of conscious and permanent visibility" (Foucault, 1977: 201).

Although only a few prisons approximate the panopticon design, the model is a metaphor for the level of surveillance and its effects in a wide range of institutional settings. In postindustrial societies, digital surveillance technology is almost everywhere—exemplified by cookies, spyware, clickstream, fingerprinting, in-store video-surveillance, closed-circuit television, credit cards, metal detectors, drug and DNA testing, health records, highway toll passes, and searchable databases. Anonymity is quickly becoming impossible, so authorities can exercise more effective monitoring and social control than ever before. We live in a **surveillance society** that uses all-encompassing surveillance technology to optimize social control (Gilliom and Monahan 2012; Bauman and Lyon, 2013).

A **surveillance society** uses all-encompassing surveillance technology to optimize social control.

As always, where social forces work to constrain and control individual autonomy, other efforts are made to counter the trend. One example is the emergence of organizations aimed at protecting personal privacy. For instance, the Institute of Applied Autonomy (www.appliedautonomy.com/) charts the location of urban surveillance cameras so activists and interested others can move through "paths of least surveillance." Privacy International (www.privacyinternational.org/) has launched a series of research and intervention projects to make citizens aware of how their privacy is compromised and what can be done to resist. However, given the powerful interests that control information technologies—Google, for example, controls two-thirds of the search engine market and captures every click—it seems likely that resisting the trend toward enhanced surveillance and reduced privacy will, at best, reduce the pace of movement toward an entirely transparent society.

The Prison

In October 2001, a 63-year-old man who had Parkinson's disease and was addicted to cocaine was arrested in Ottawa. A passerby had noticed that he had a 32-gauge shotgun in his gym bag and notified the police. The man, who was charged with possession of a weapon, did not resist arrest, perhaps because he knew well what awaited him. Roger Caron, dubbed Mad Dog Caron by the press, had first been sentenced to prison at the age

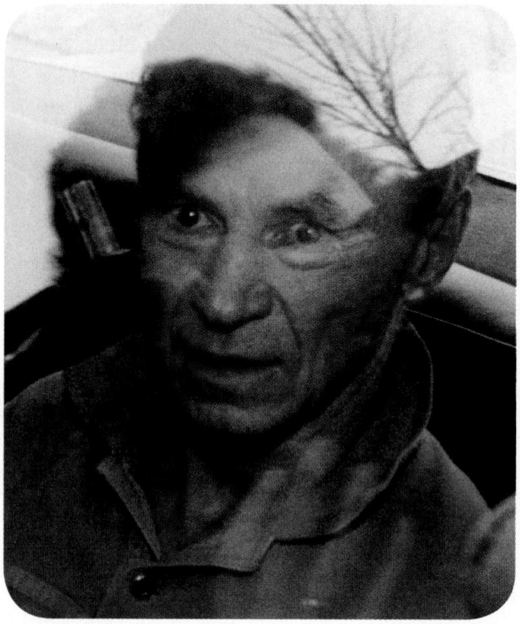

CP Picture Archive/Fred Chartrand

Roger Caron, who was 16 years old when he was first sentenced to prison for breaking and entering, spent much of his life behind bars. His prison experiences turned him into a career criminal.

of 16 for breaking and entering. He had spent most of his adult life as an inept robber, using the gates of Canada's major prisons like revolving doors: Guelph, Kingston, Collins Bay, Millhaven, Stony Mountain, St. Vincent de Paul, Dorchester, and Penetanguishene.

While incarcerated in the 1970s and after having already spent almost 20 years in prison, Caron wrote a chilling account of his life behind bars. He was still in prison when *Go-Boy!* was published in 1978. The book describes in harrowing detail the harshness of the prison experience—the violence; the festering hatreds; the hard labour; the horrors of solitary confinement; the twisted, manipulative friendships; and the brutal use of corporal punishment. He describes the use of the "paddle"—"three leather straps with wooden handles so thick and coarse as to barely sag. Each one was perforated with hundreds of tiny holes designed to trap and rip the flesh from the buttocks." When he was first paddled in 1955, "[w]hite searing pain exploded throughout my being and blood gushed from my lips as I struggled to stifle a scream. It was brutal and it was horrible" (Caron, 1979: 59; see also Farrell, n.d.).

Go-Boy! was honoured in 1978 with the Governor General's Award for literature and, in the years that followed, Caron wrote other books. However, he was unable to leave his past life totally. Following imprisonment for another botched robbery attempt, Caron was released from prison in 1998 and was still on parole at the time of his 2001 arrest. Regardless of the initial factors that caused Caron to turn to crime, it was his experience in prison that turned him into a career criminal (CyberPress, 2001).

Caron's experience follows a pattern long known to sociologists. Prisons are agents of socialization, and new inmates often become more serious offenders as they adapt to the culture of the most hardened, long-term prisoners (Wheeler, 1961). Because prison often turns criminals into worse criminals, it is worth pondering the institution's origins, development, and current dilemmas.

As societies industrialized, imprisonment became one of the most important forms of punishment for criminal behaviour (Garland, 1990; Morris and Rothman, 1995). In preindustrial societies, criminals were publicly humiliated, tortured, or put to death, depending on the severity of their transgressions. In the industrial era, depriving criminals of their freedom by putting them in prison seemed less harsh, more "civilized" (Durkheim, 1973 [1899–1900]).

Rationales for Incarceration

Some people still take a benign view of prisons, seeing them as opportunities for *rehabilitation*. They believe that prisoners, while serving time, can be taught how to be productive citizens on release. In Canada, the rehabilitative ethos predominated from the 1950s to the early 1970s, when many prisons sought to reform criminals by offering them psychological counselling, drug therapy, skills training, education, and other programs that would help at least the less violent offenders reintegrate into society (McMahon, 1992; Smith and Schweitzer, 2013).

Today, however, many Canadians scoff at the idea that prisons can rehabilitate criminals. We have adopted a tougher line. Politicians routinely campaign on promises of a get-tough approach to crime and to criminals. Some people see prison as a means of *deterrence*. In this view, people will be less inclined to commit crimes if they know they are likely to get caught and serve long and unpleasant prison terms. Others think of prisons as institutions of *revenge*. They believe that depriving criminals of their freedom and forcing them to live in poor conditions is fair retribution for their illegal acts. Still others see prisons as institutions of *incapacitation*. From this viewpoint, the chief function of the prison is to keep criminals out of society as long as possible to ensure they can do no more harm (Feeley and Simon, 1992; Simon, 1993; Zimring and Hawkins, 1995).

No matter which of these views predominates, one thing is clear. Since the 1960s, the Canadian public has demanded that more criminals be arrested and imprisoned, and it has got what it wanted. On any given day, about 14 800 youth (aged 14 to 17) and 38 200 adults are in custody in Canada (Dauvergne, 2012; Munch, 2012). Although Canada's incarceration rate is higher than that of most West European countries, it is much lower than that of the United States (Figure 7.7). The United States has the world's highest incarceration rate at 743 prisoners per 100 000 population, followed by Russia (568 per 100 000 population).

New York Public Library

In preindustrial societies, criminals who committed serious crimes were put to death, often in ways that seem cruel by today's standards. One method involved hanging the criminal with starving dogs.

Moral Panic

What accounts for our increased enthusiasm for get-tough policies? One answer is that the mass media tends to report crime in a way that frightens us. Mass media crime reporting is distorted in several ways (Canadian Resource Centre for Victims of Crime, 2013). A first distortion concerns level of coverage. After sports, general interest, and business, crime is the fourth most commonly reported issue in the media. This level of coverage grossly exaggerates the amount of criminal activity in Canada. A second distortion involves the type of coverage. More than half of crime stories in the media relate to violent offences, which is several times the actual prevalence. A third distortion concerns the nature of coverage. For their own purposes, the media have a bias for highlighting extreme or unusual events. Homicides in Canada, for example, are relatively rare events (Perreault, 2013). About 600 murders are committed in this country every year—a tiny percentage of the roughly 2.2 million Criminal Code incidents reported to the police annually. However, when a homicide occurs, it receives enormous media coverage. The same holds true for coverage of crimes committed by strangers. Children are much more likely to be abducted by a parent than by a stranger, and adults are much more likely to experience violence at the hands of an intimate partner than someone unknown, but media coverage gives the opposite impression.

Given media biases, it is not surprising that many members of the public fear strangers, exaggerate levels of violence, and overestimate the risk of becoming a victim. To the extent we believe that the crimes in the headlines are typical of crime in Canada, we may believe that the battle to win the "war against crime" requires the most punitive measures.

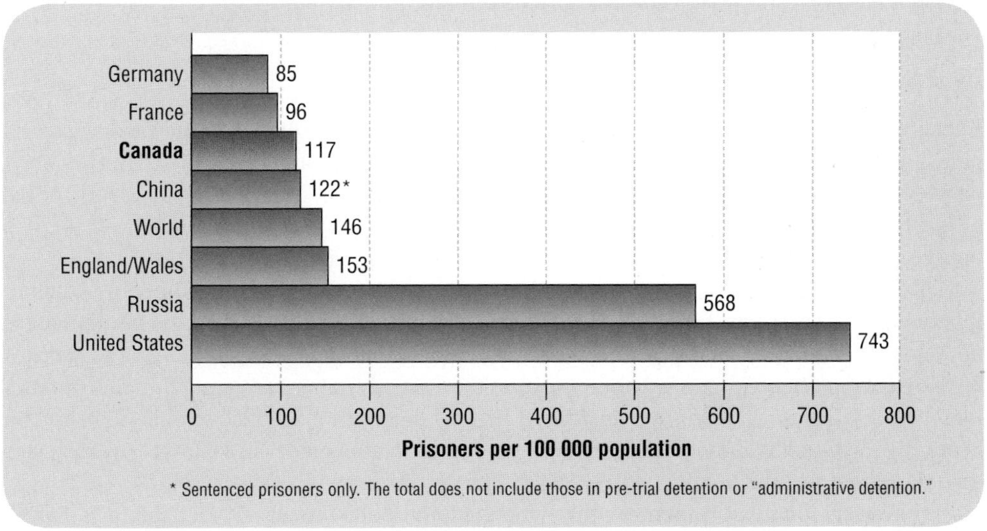

FIGURE 7.7
World Prison Population, 2011

Source: Roy Walsley, Director World Prison Population List. Publisher International Centre for Prison Studies.

A **moral panic** is an extreme over-response that occurs when many people fervently believe that some form of deviance or crime poses a profound threat to society's well-being.

In short, media presentations of the crime problem may serve to promote a **moral panic**. That is, in response to lurid headlines that direct attention to the most notorious—and atypical—crimes and criminals, the public may conclude that most crime is violent and predatory, that all criminals are dangerous, and that our crime rate signals a grave threat to our society's well-being (Hier, 2011). Are you part of the moral panic? Have you and your family taken special precautions to protect yourself from the "growing wave" of criminality? Even if you're not part of the moral panic, chances are you know someone who is. Therefore, to put things in perspective, you need to recall an important fact from our discussion of recent trends in crime rates: According to official statistics, the moral panic is taking place during a period when major crime indexes have been *falling* for two decades.

Why, then, the moral panic? Does anyone benefit from it? There may be several interested parties. First, the mass media benefit from moral panic because it allows them to rake in hefty profits. They publicize every major crime because crime draws big audiences, and big audiences mean more revenue from advertisers. After all, a front-page photograph of Karla Homolka or Paul Bernardo still generates newspaper sales two decades after their convictions—even if the story that accompanies it is abbreviated or banal (Jeffords, 2013). Fictional crime programs also draw millions of viewers to their TVs.

Second, the criminal justice system is a huge bureaucracy with thousands of employees. They benefit from moral panic because increased spending on crime prevention, control, and punishment secures their jobs and expands their turf.

Third, and probably most importantly, the moral panic is useful politically. Since the early 1970s, many politicians have based entire careers on get-tough policies. At election time, they make combating crime a focal point of their campaign promises. Over the objections of most Canadian criminologists, sociologists, and lawyers, and despite pleas from law enforcement officials as far away as Texas, where "get-tough" measures failed to curb crime, the Conservative government passed a crime bill in 2012 that ratcheted up the moral panic in this country despite falling crime rates. Bill C-10 introduced new criminal offences, new and increased mandatory minimum sentences, longer waiting times before criminals can apply for pardons, harsher sentencing for young offenders, and other tough measures. The Conservatives plan to expand the prison system to accommodate the expected increase in the incarcerated population. This approach to punishment will cost a lot of taxpayers' money and serve only to create a larger class of hardened criminals.

CP PHOTO/Frank Gunn

Intensive media coverage of the most notorious and violent crimes and criminals may lead to a heightened fear of crime and demands for tougher penalties. Karla Homolka, who with her husband, Paul Bernardo, was responsible for the sexual assault and brutal murder of Tammy Homolka, Leslie Mahaffy, and Kristen French in the early 1990s, is still the subject of media attention.

Alternative Forms of Punishment

Two of the most contentious issues concerning the punishment of criminals are these: (1) Should we reintroduce the death penalty to punish the most violent criminals? (2) Should we explore alternatives to prison for less serious crimes? In concluding this chapter, we briefly consider each of these questions.

Capital Punishment

Execution has a long history and is still widely used today (see Figure 7.8). In Canada, capital punishment has not been used since 1962, and it was formally abolished in 1976. However, polls show that many Canadians favour its reintroduction. According to recent polls, 63 percent of Canadian adults favour the reintroduction of the death penalty, 30 percent oppose it, and 7 percent are undecided (AngusReidGlobal, 2013).

Although the death penalty ranks high as a form of revenge, it is questionable whether it is much of a deterrent. First, murder is often committed in a rage, when the perpetrator is not thinking rationally. Many murderers are unlikely to consider the costs and consequences of their actions. Second, critics point out that the United States has a much higher murder rate than do Canada and Western European nations that do not practise capital punishment. Moreover, within the United States, states without the death penalty have lower murder rates than those that use the death penalty (Death Penalty Information Center, 2012).

Moreover, we must remember that where capital punishment *is* practised, it is hardly a matter of blind justice. Figure 7.9 summarizes the U.S. experience and shows how much

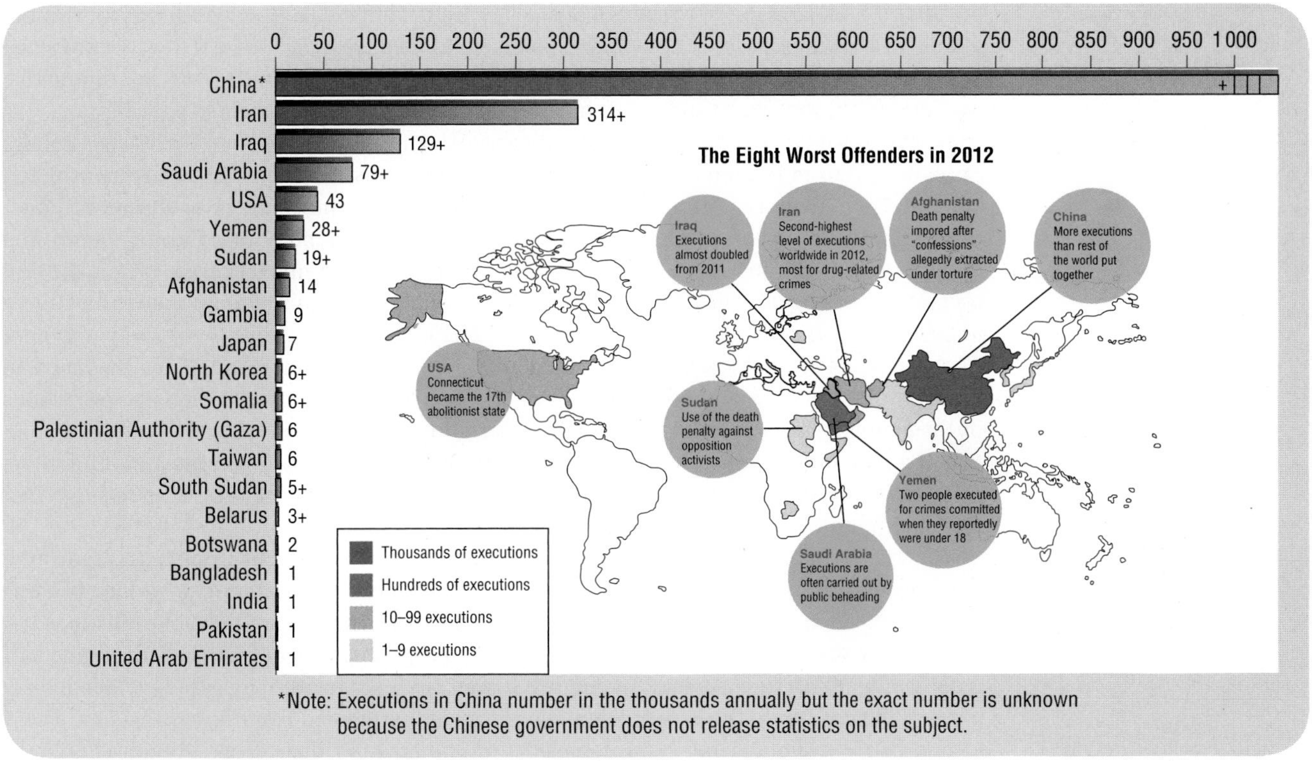

FIGURE 7.8
International Executions, 2012. Capital punishment continues in wide use around the globe.

Source: © 2013 Amnesty International USA. Used with permission.

race matters. Murderers who kill white victims are typically executed. Murderers who kill people of colour rarely receive the death penalty. Given this patent racial bias, we cannot view the death penalty as a justly administered punishment.

Finally, in assessing capital punishment, we must remember that mistakes are common. Nearly 40 percent of death sentences in the United States are overturned because of new evidence or a mistrial (Haines, 1996). In Canada, the wrongful convictions of Donald Marshall, Guy Paul Morin, David Milgaard—and many others in recent times—for murders they did not commit should be sufficient to remind us that the wheels of justice do not always turn smoothly.

Alternative Strategies

In recent years, analysts have suggested two main reforms to our current prison regime. First, some analysts have argued that we should reconsider our stance on rehabilitation. Advocates of rehabilitation suggest that the **recidivism rate**, the rate at which convicted offenders commit another crime, can be reduced through such programs as educational and job training, individual and group therapy, substance abuse counselling, and behaviour modification (Demleitner, 2010). Second, they have argued that, whenever possible, we should attempt to reduce rather than increase the number of incarcerated offenders. Drawing on labelling theory, they suggest we pursue a policy of "radical non-intervention," diverting offenders from formal processing in the criminal justice system. Proponents of this idea say that at least part of the increase in crime we have witnessed since the 1960s is attributable to the introduction of new and

The **recidivism rate** is the rate at which convicted offenders commit another crime.

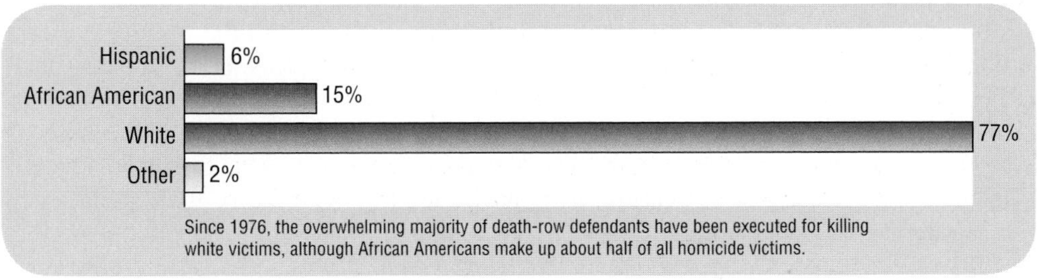

FIGURE 7.9
Race of U.S. Homicide Victims in Cases Resulting in an Execution since 1976

Source: © 2013 Amnesty International USA. Used with permission.

broadened definitions of criminal conduct. They believe that charging and imprisoning more and more Canadians, especially youth, is unlikely to help these individuals develop prosocial behaviour (Department of Justice, 2013). Accordingly, they advise us to seek alternative methods that divert adults and youth from formal criminal justice system processing.

Although alternative procedures vary across provinces and territories, their use generally arises after the police or Crown prosecutor recommends that an offender be considered suitable for "diversion." One example of an alternative measure is a victim–offender reconciliation program (VORP), in which victim and offender meet under controlled circumstances. The victim has an opportunity to describe the impact of the criminal event on himself or herself. The offender might, for example, be required to apologize and agree to compensate the victim financially (Wood, 2012). Cases dealt with in this way are more likely to involve male than female offenders. Young offenders selected for inclusion in these programs are usually over 15 years of age, and they generally complete the provisions of the agreements they make. Most cases referred for diversion involve theft under $5000, which is not surprising: to be recommended for diversion, the offence must be minor. As well, to be considered as candidates for diversion, offenders must first acknowledge that they are guilty of the act they have been accused of committing.

In like fashion, proponents of *decarceration* recommend that such options as fines (the most commonly used penal sanction in Canada), probation, and community service become more widely used as alternatives to imprisonment. However, not everyone favours this strategy. Some argue that the increased use of community programs does not reduce the numbers of individuals subject to formal social control. Rather, such strategies may simply widen the net through the creation of more intensive, intrusive, and prolonged control mechanisms. These efforts might more accurately be labelled *transcarceration* than decarceration (Lowman, Menzies, and Palys, 1987). Noting such objections, some analysts suggest that we go further still and lobby for legislative reform that would decriminalize certain categories of conduct currently prohibited under Canadian criminal law, such as marijuana possession.

Finally, we must mention the recent changes to the Criminal Code that have attempted to address the overrepresentation of Aboriginal people in Canada's inmate population. For example, section 718.2 specifies that "all available sanctions other than imprisonment that are reasonable in the circumstances should be considered for all offenders, with particular attention to the circumstances of Aboriginal offenders." Although being an Aboriginal person does not automatically result in a lesser sentence, the Supreme Court of Canada has urged judges sentencing an Aboriginal offender to recognize the "broad systemic and background factors affecting Aboriginal people" (Lonmo, 2001: 8). The Court recognizes that sociological factors contribute to the incarceration rate of Aboriginal people being ten times higher than the rate for non-Aboriginal people. These factors include "the history of colonialism, displacement, and residential schools and how that history continues to translate into lower educational attainment, lower incomes, higher unemployment, higher rates of substance abuse and suicide, and of course higher levels of incarceration for Aboriginal peoples" (Office of Correctional Investigator, 2013).

TIME FOR REVIEW

- Explain the difference between internal and external controls. How can these concepts be applied to the way university tests are conducted?
- Imagine that a newspaper report of three deaths resulting from binge drinking on university campuses this year inspired a moral panic. What form might it take?
- Explain the differences between punishments aimed at rehabilitation, deterrence, and revenge. How does a death penalty sentence fit in this classification?
- How could recidivism rates be used to test the credibility of alternative sentencing programmes?

SUMMARY

1. How does crime differ from deviance? How is crime measured?
Deviance occurs when a norm is violated. Crime results from violating a particular type of norm called a law. Crime is measured through official statistics and self-reports. Official crime rates are generated from police reports and published in Uniform Crime Reporting (UCR) Surveys. Self-reported measures use representative samples to gather evidence of the types and frequencies of victimization the public experiences.

2. What are the major sociological explanations of crime and their contributions?
Symbolic interactionists draw attention to the role that labels play in the formation of deviant and criminal identities. Once labelled, a deviant or criminal identity becomes self-generating. Functionalists emphasize how misalignments between culturally defined goals and social opportunities create the motivation for crime and deviance. Conflict theorists stress that upper classes use their power to perpetuate privilege by downplaying their own misconduct and classifying others as deviant and criminal. Feminists show that, historically, because of their less privileged status, crimes against women have often been ignored.

3. What are the main trends in social control and regulation?
The sophistication and prevalence of digital technologies supports the rise of a surveillance society in which individual conduct can be continuously monitored and regulated. Moral panics have invigorated a trend toward increasing the incarceration rate.

4. What are the main forms of punishment for criminal behaviour, and how have they changed over time?
As societies industrialized, the use of prisons as a form of punishment became widespread. The rationales for imprisonment include incapacitation, rehabilitation, deterrence, and revenge. The death penalty is the most extreme form of punishment. Although banned in many Western countries, the death penalty is still widely applied around the globe. The high expense and questionable effectiveness of imprisonment encourage the development of alternative types of sentencing. These alternatives include community service, fines, and victim–offender reconciliation.

CHAPTER 8

SOCIAL STRATIFICATION

IN THIS CHAPTER YOU WILL LEARN TO

- Identify and measure trends in economic inequality in Canada.
- Compare the contribution of different types of capital to economic achievement.
- Analyze the key characteristics of poverty in Canada.
- Contrast Marxist, Weberian, and functionalist explanations of stratification.
- Distinguish how different classes view the class system.

PATTERNS OF SOCIAL INEQUALITY

Shipwrecks and Inequality

Writers and filmmakers sometimes tell stories about shipwrecks and their survivors to make a point about **social stratification**, the organization of society in layers or strata. They use the shipwreck as a literary device. It allows them to sweep away all traces of privilege and social convention. What remains are human beings stripped to their essentials, guinea pigs in an imaginary laboratory for the study of wealth and poverty, power and powerlessness, esteem and disrespect.

Social stratification refers to the way in which society is organized in layers or strata.

The tradition began with Daniel Defoe's *Robinson Crusoe*, first published in 1719. Defoe tells the story of an Englishman marooned on a desert island. His strong will, hard work, and inventiveness turn the poor island into a thriving colony. Defoe was one of the first writers to portray capitalism favourably. He believed that people get rich if they possess the virtues of good businesspeople—and stay poor if they don't.

The 1975 Italian movie *Swept Away* tells almost exactly the opposite story. In the movie, a beautiful woman, one of the idle rich, boards her yacht for a cruise in the Mediterranean. She treats the hardworking deckhands in a condescending and abrupt way. The deckhands do their jobs but seethe with resentment. Then comes the storm. The yacht is shipwrecked. Only the beautiful woman and one handsome deckhand remain alive, marooned on a desert island. Now equals, the two survivors soon have passionate sex and fall in love. All is well until the day of their rescue. As soon as they return to the mainland, the woman resumes her haughty ways. She turns her back on the deckhand, who is reduced again to the role of a common labourer. Thus, the movie sends the audience three harsh messages. First, it is possible to be rich without working hard, because a person can inherit wealth. Second, people can work hard without becoming rich. Third, something about the structure of society causes inequality, for inequality disappears only on the desert island, in the absence of society as we know it.

Titanic is a more recent movie on the shipwreck-and-inequality theme. At one level, the movie shows that class differences are important. For example, in first class, living conditions are luxurious, whereas in third class, they are cramped. Indeed, on the *Titanic*, class differences spell the difference between life and death. After the *Titanic* strikes the iceberg off the coast of Newfoundland and Labrador, the ship's crew prevents second- and third-class passengers from entering the few available lifeboats. They give priority to rescuing first-class passengers. Consequently, 75 percent of third-class passengers perished, compared with 39 percent of first-class passengers. As the tragedy of the *Titanic* unfolds, however, another, contradictory theme emerges. Under some circumstances, we learn, class differences can be insignificant. In the movie, the sinking of the *Titanic* is the backdrop to a fictional love story about a wealthy young woman in first class and a working-class youth in the decks below. The sinking of the *Titanic* and the collapse of its elaborate class structure give the young lovers an opportunity to cross class lines and profess their devotion

A 1912 ad for the Titanic's maiden voyage

to each other. At one level, then, *Titanic* is an optimistic tale that holds out hope for a society in which class differences matter little.

Robinson Crusoe, Swept Away, and *Titanic* raise many of the issues we address in this chapter. What are the sources of social inequality? Do determination, industry, and ingenuity shape the distribution of advantages and disadvantages in society, as *Robinson Crusoe* suggests? Or is *Swept Away* more accurate? Do certain patterns of social relations underlie and shape that distribution? Is *Titanic's* first message of social class differences still valid? Does social inequality still have big consequences for the way we live? What about *Titanic's* second message? Can people overcome or reduce inequality in society? If so, how?

To answer these questions, we first sketch patterns of social inequality in Canada, paying special attention to change over time. We then assess major theories of social inequality in the light of logic and evidence.

Economic Inequality in Canada

Canada has grown richer over time and ranks as one of the world's most prosperous countries. Today, the average Canadian family earns about 20 times more than it did in 1951. This gain is less impressive than it seems, however, because of inflation. A soft drink that cost a dime a few decades ago now costs more than a dollar. Moreover, the average number of earners per family has increased as more women have entered the paid labour force. Consequently, more people now contribute to the income of the average family than was the case in 1951. Even so, Canadian families earn considerably more now than they did 60 years ago, partly because they are more productive. Today, the average worker earns more because he or she is more skilled and uses more sophisticated technology to produce more goods and services per hour of work.

Averages simplify reality. Because income is not equally shared, many families are not average. Some are rich, some are poor, and many are in between. One measure sociologists use to observe income inequality and its change over time is the **income quintile share**. Here are the steps for computing income quintile shares:

The **income quintile share** measures the share of total income earned by each income-ranked fifth of the population.

1. *Rank* families in the population from those with lowest incomes to those with highest incomes.
2. Compute the total income generated by *all families.*
3. Divide the rank-ordered families (Step 1) into five *equal-sized* categories (quintiles). These categories represent the fifth with the lowest incomes through the fifth with the highest incomes.
4. Compute the total income for *each quintile.*
5. Divide the total income for each quintile (Step 4) by the total family income (Step 2) to create the income quintile share.

Figure 8.1 reports the quintile shares among Canadian families for 1976 and 2010. Note that this figure reports family incomes *after* taxes and government transfers. In other words, these numbers represent the situation after income taxes, Employment Insurance, goods and services tax (GST) credits, and so on have redistributed family incomes to reduce inequality. Through these redistributions, the richest Canadians lose about a fifth of their income, while the poorest fifth see their incomes increase by nearly two-thirds. If Canadians relied only on the market to distribute income, inequality would be much greater than the situation reported in Figure 8.1.

In 2010, the bottom quintile of families and unattached individuals earned just 4.8 percent of all income, while the top quintile earned 44.3 percent. On average, the richest fifth of families in Canada retained about 9.2 times as much income as the poorest fifth of families. Almost half of all family income goes to the top 20 percent. This description provides an indicator of the level of income inequality in Canada.

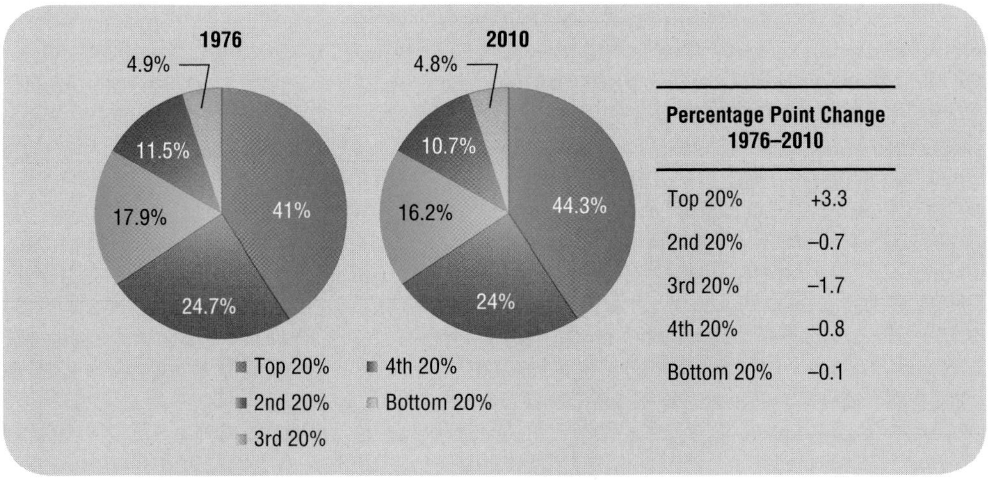

FIGURE 8.1

The Distribution of After-Tax Income Among Families and Unattached Individuals, Canada, 1976 and 2010

Source: From BRYM/LIE. *SOC+* 2CE. © 2015 Nelson Education Ltd. Reproduced by permission. ww.cengage.com/permissions

Comparing the 2010 results with the 1976 results provides a sense of how income inequality has changed over time. All quintiles earned a smaller share of total national income in 2010 than in 1976—except for the top quintile, which earned 3.3 percent more. This pattern mirrors the trend in most rich countries: income gaps have been widening for nearly three decades (Fortin et al., 2012). The rich are getting richer, as Figure 8.2 illustrates for Canada.

Another measure commonly used to track income inequality is the **Gini coefficient**, which compares the actual income distribution in a population to perfect equality. The result tells us what proportion of a society's income would have to be redistributed for perfect equality to occur. Gini coefficients vary between 0 (every family earns exactly the same amount) and 1.0 (one family earns everything). Figure 8.3 shows changes in the Canadian Gini index since 1976. Clearly, income inequality has increased substantially in recent decades.

The **Gini coefficient** reports the proportion of total income that would have to be redistributed for perfect equality to exist.

No society enjoys perfect income equality. To appreciate the Canadian situation it is helpful to compare it to that of other nations. Figure 8.4 compares Canada with the United States over the past several decades. It shows that Canada enjoys more income equality than the United States does and that inequality has grown much more quickly in the United States than in Canada.

Because the United States has the highest level of income inequality of any wealthy country, it is useful to place Canada in the broader context of Figure 8.5, which shows the Gini index for all major wealthy countries. We immediately see that Canada ranks in the top third. The northern European countries do a much better job than Canada does of redistributing income by means of government policies.

Reg Innell/GetStock.com

The Canadian Press/Bill Becker

The Canadian Press/Darren Calabrese

The Thomsons, Canada's wealthiest family, ranked 24th on the *Forbes Magazine* list of the world's richest people in 2013. Their assets totalled $26.1 billion. Sir Kenneth Thomson, who died in June 2006, handed over the reins of the Thomson electronic media, publishing, and information services empire to his son, David. The Thomsons are an example of success through both hard work and family connections.

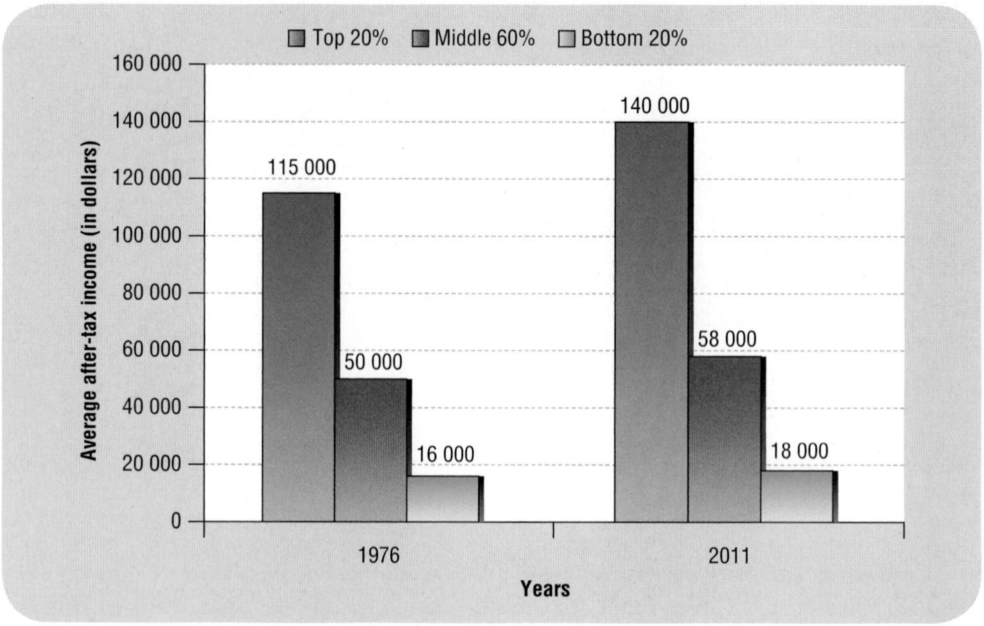

FIGURE 8.2
Average After-Tax Inflation-Adjusted Income by Income Group, Canada, 1976–2011

Source: Employment and Social Development Canada. "Financial Security—Income Distribution." http://www4.hrsdc.gc.ca/.3ndic.1t.4r@-eng.jsp?iid=22. Retrieved December 16, 2013.

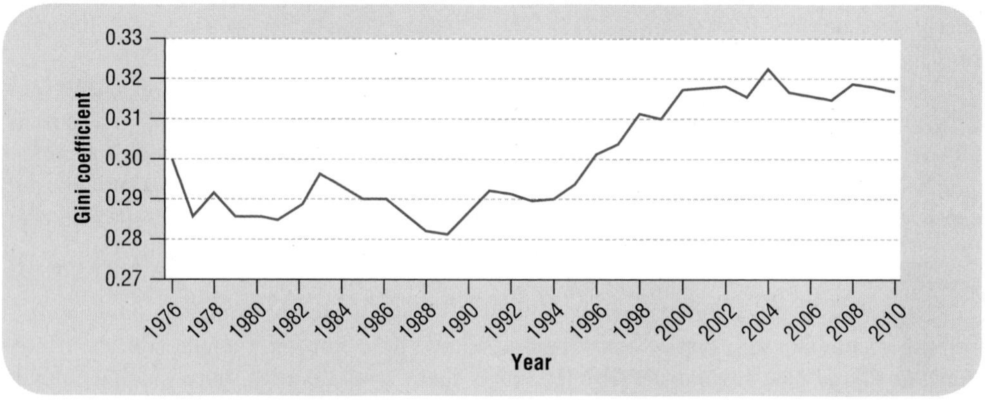

FIGURE 8.3
Canadian Gini Coefficients, 1976–2010

Source: Conference Board of Canada, 2013. "Income Inequality." www.conferenceboard.ca/hcp/details/society/income-inequality.aspx. Retrieved December 16, 2013. Used with permission.

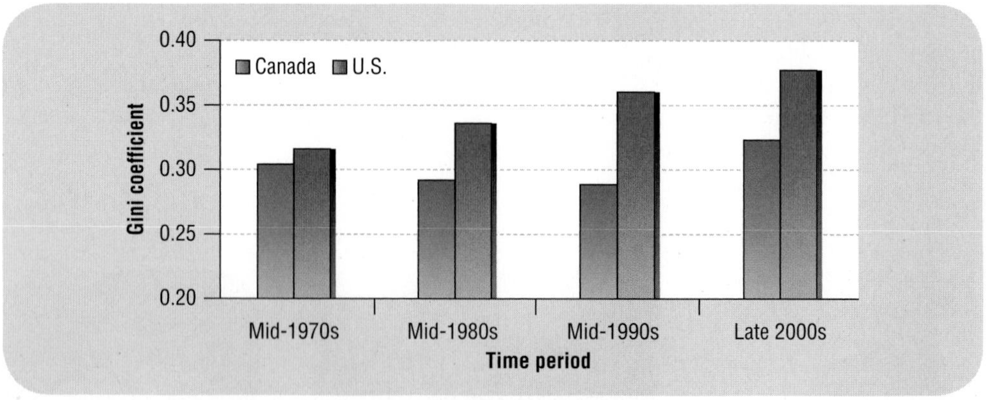

FIGURE 8.4
Growing Inequality in Canada and the United States

Source: Conference Board of Canada, 2013 "Income Inequality." www.conferenceboard.ca/hcp/details/society/income-inequality.aspx. Retrieved December 16, 2013. Used with permission.

Explanations of Income Inequality

Why do some people fall into the highest quintile and others into the lowest? What explains income distribution? The job a person holds plays a large role. Bank presidents earn more than branch managers do, who in turn earn more than bank tellers do. Other jobs not only pay less well but also involve restricted hours of work or periods of unemployment. Thus,

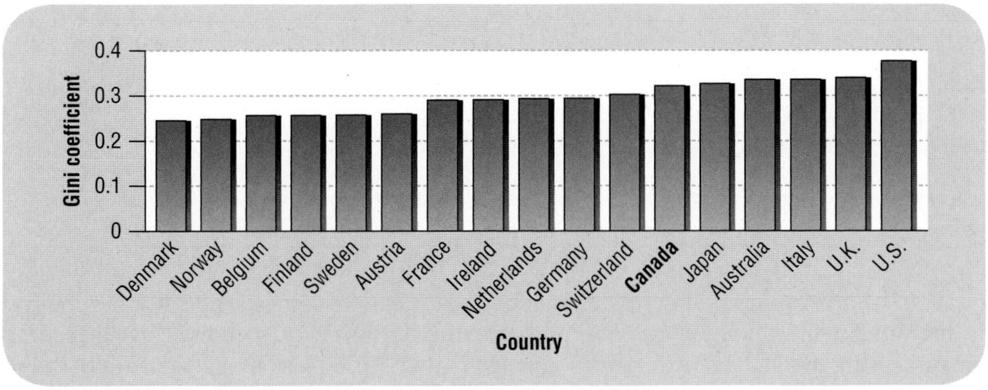

FIGURE 8.5
Inequality in Wealthy Countries

Source: Conference Board of Canada, 2013. "Income Inequality." www.conferenceboard.ca/hcp/details/society/income-inequality.aspx. Retrieved December 16, 2013. Used with permission.

much about income inequality traces back to what kinds of work a person is able to obtain (see Table 8.1).

We know that some individuals earn high salaries because their natural talent allows them to take jobs that pay a lot. Sidney Crosby (hockey player), Steve Nash (basketball player), Drake (rap musician), Ryan Gosling (actor), and James Cameron (film producer) are Canadians whose success on the world stage has provided them with substantial earnings. The principal reason for their excellence is a natural endowment in music, athletics, and so on. A genetic gift sets them apart. At the other end of the economic spectrum, some people have the genetic misfortune of Down syndrome or autism, conditions that prevent them from earning big salaries. Such people, at both ends of the spectrum, are exceptional. For the great majority of people, genes play only a minor role in determining income.

Even for people with a natural talent in the performing arts or athletics, effort is essential. Practice and years of dedication to the basics of a profession are common to all who enjoy success. Effort is also significant for many Canadians who spend long hours at work—whether amassing billable hours in a law practice, doing the endless chores required by a small business, or working overtime on a construction site. However, although diligence and perseverance might be necessary conditions for rewards, they are not sufficient. Effort alone does not result in high income (see Figure 8.6).

Raw talent needs to be sharpened. Training, coaching, schooling—these are crucial ways in which skills are developed and nurtured. Natural talents and our efforts are important ingredients in this process, to be sure, but education matters. Indeed, the importance of education as a determinant of occupation and income continues to increase (Baer, 1999; Statistics Canada, 2003: 9). As the Canadian occupational structure moves further away from its traditional resource-based foundation to a more mature knowledge-driven economy, the importance of education will continue to grow.

TABLE 8.1
Average Annual Earnings by Selected Occupational Groups, 2010

Occupational Group	Average Annual Earnings ($)
Managerial	76 300
Natural and applied sciences	64 600
Health	56 900
Social science, education, government service, and religion	48 900
Trades, transport, and equipment operators	42 500
Processing, manufacturing, and utilities	37 500
Art, culture, recreation, and sport	31 900
Primary industry	31 600
Sales and service	25 000

Source: Statistics Canada. 2012h. "Earnings of individuals, by selected characteristics and National Occupational Classification (NOC-S), 2010 constant dollars, annually." CANSIM Table 2020106. http://dc2.chass.utoronto.ca.myaccess.library.utoronto.ca/cgi-bin/cansimdim/c2_getArrayDim.pl. Retrieved December 25, 2012.

Natural talent → **Rewards**

Natural talent + Effort → **Rewards**

Natural talent + Effort + Skill-rich environments + Developed skills → **Rewards**

Natural talent + Effort + Skill-rich environments + Developed skills + Social and cultural capital → **Rewards**

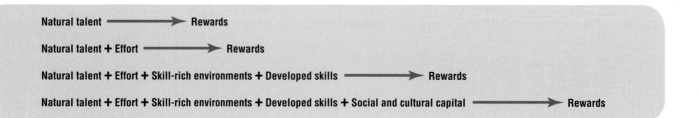

FIGURE 8.6
Explanations for Income Inequality

If physical capital is investment in industrial plants and equipment, **human capital** is investment in education and training. Just as productivity increases by upgrading manufacturing plants and introducing new technology, productivity gains can also result from investment in the skills and abilities of people. Jobs requiring advanced skills are increasingly numerous in Canada. Better-educated workers are more skilled and productive in these jobs because they have invested in acquiring the skills and knowledge essential to our economy (Betcherman and Lowe, 1997).

Human capital is the sum of useful skills and knowledge that an individual possesses.

Much evidence supports a human capital interpretation of the link between schooling and income (Gu and Wong, 2010). However, this interpretation does not provide a complete explanation for why people earn what they earn. For example, in the legal profession, almost everyone makes the same human capital investment. Every lawyer acquires a law degree. Yet economic rewards vary, even for people with the same educational experience and the same type of legal practice. In particular, female lawyers with the same credentials and work experience as male lawyers tend to earn less than male lawyers do (Kay and Hagan, 1998).

Part of the reason that people with the same amount of human capital may receive different economic rewards is that they possess different amounts of social capital. **Social capital** refers to people's networks or connections. Individuals are more likely to succeed when they have strong bonds of trust, cooperation, mutual respect, and obligation with well-positioned individuals or families. Knowing the right people, and having strong links to them, helps in finding opportunities and taking advantage of them (Coleman, 1988).

Social capital refers to the networks or connections that individuals possess.

A related version of this argument is captured in the notion of **cultural capital** (Bourdieu and Passeron, 1990). Cultural capital comprises people's social skills: their ability to impress others, to use tasteful language and images effectively, and thus to influence and persuade people. Although the notion of social capital stresses your networks and connections with others, the idea of cultural capital emphasizes your impression management skills, your ability to influence others. In different ways, both concepts emphasize being part of the right "social club."

Cultural capital is the stock of knowledge, tastes, and habits that legitimate the maintenance of status and power.

The concepts of social and cultural capital also share the idea that families higher in the social hierarchy enjoy more capital of all types. Connections and culture help you find a good job. The hiring of new recruits, then, depends not only on the talent, effort, and skills that people bring to the interview but also on their connections and culture. Indeed, culture and connections often influence who gets an interview.

In sum, natural talent and effort are important, and for a few occupations, very significant. For most Canadians, level of education (or developed skill) is a critical factor in finding continuous, well-paying employment. In addition, social and cultural capital are consequential for many people in finding economic success. Explaining an individual's position in the income hierarchy depends on several factors, but the four themes outlined in Figure 8.6 are crucial (see Box 8.1).

Income versus Wealth

How long would it take you to spend a million dollars? If you spent $1000 a day, it would take you nearly three years. How long would it take you to spend a *billion* dollars? If you spent $2500 a day, you couldn't spend the entire sum in a lifetime—at that rate of spending, a billion dollars would last for more than 1000 years. (This scenario assumes you don't invest the money; if you invested it sensibly, you could never exhaust a billion dollars by spending $10 000 a day.) Thus, a billion dollars is an almost unimaginably large sum

BOX 8.1

SOCIAL POLICY: WHAT DO YOU THINK?

Vote

CAN GOVERNMENT INFLUENCE INEQUALITY?

Among rich nations, Canada ranks slightly above the middle in terms of its level of income inequality. Considerable evidence indicates that inequality is systematically associated with a wide-range of undesirable individual and social outcomes. For example, Wilkinson and Pickett (2010) show the connection between increased inequality and several undesirable outcomes: lower life expectancy, higher infant mortality, lower numeracy and literacy, more homicides and imprisonment, more teenage births and obesity, lower trust and social mobility, and higher mental illness.

Is it realistic to think that governments can do anything to reduce inequality and its correlated ills? Exploring this question requires appreciating that income inequality results from a combination of economic and political factors. First, some economic systems generate more inequality than others do. This baseline is then affected by government intervention in the form of taxes and transfers. Some political systems redistribute more income to reduce inequality than others do.

Figure 8.7 shows the effect of economic and political institutions on the Gini index of inequality for Canada and several other nations. The red diamonds indicate the level of inequality resulting from the operation of economic forces. The blue bars indicate the results after governments have intervened to reduce market inequality.

Three points are worth highlighting. First, economic forces operate to produce important differences in the amount of inequality. The Italian economic system produces the most inequality and the Swiss the least. Second, government policies vary considerably in the amount they reduce inequality—signified by the distance between each country's red diamond and black bar. The countries in Figure 8.7 are ranked from left to right in terms of decreasing government impact on inequality. Belgium produces the largest impact (45 percent decrease); the United States the least (22 percent decrease). Canada's reduction through taxes and transfers is 27 percent. Finally, as a result of the interaction between economic and political forces, societies end up with a range of levels of inequality—indicated by the height of the blue bars.

What do you think of Canada's tolerance for inequality relative to other modern nations? Should Canada be doing more to redistribute income through taxes and transfers? Would you be willing to have more of your income redistributed? If not yours, then whose incomes should be redistributed? What consequences would you expect if your proposal became law?

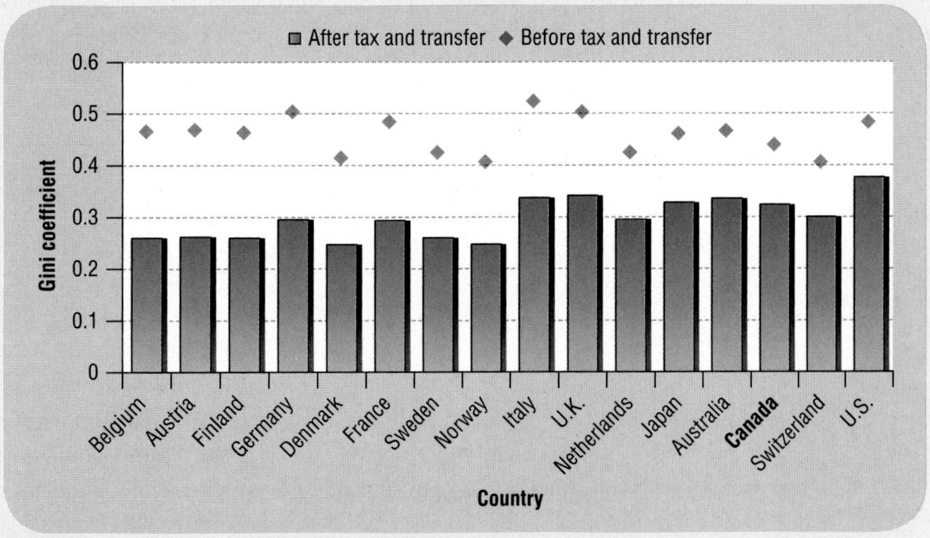

FIGURE 8.7

Gini Coefficient Before and After Taxes and Transfers, Late 2000s

Source: Conference Board of Canada. 2013. "Income Inequality." Retrieved April 8, 2014. http://www.conferenceboard.ca/hcp/details/society/income-inequality.aspx. Used with permission.

of money. Yet between 2004 and 2013, the estimated fortune of Canada's richest person, David Thomson, increased 20.4 percent, from $21.67 billion to $26.1 billion. In contrast, a full-time worker earning the average Canadian minimum wage earns about $21 000. Just the *increase* in Thomson's wealth between 2004 and 2013 was equal to the total annual income of 210 952 minimum-wage earners. The top 100 CEOs in Canada earn close to $8 million a year on average. At that rate, each CEO earned an amount equal to the *annual* income of the average Canadian worker between 12:01 a.m. on January 1 and 1:11 p.m. on January 2, 2014 ("Top Canadian CEOs," 2014). We list the 10 richest Canadians in Table 8.2.

What are the sources of the fortunes listed in Table 8.2? For some names on the list (Thomson, Irving, Weston), inheritance is a critical factor. These are family dynasties. Other people on the top-10 list had merely well-to-do or solid middle-class parents. None rose from rags to riches. On the whole, Table 8.2 suggests the key determinants of wealth are a mix of inheritance and business acumen.

Only a very few families acquire the great wealth of major business enterprises. However, most families own some assets, which add up to greater or lesser family wealth. For most adults, assets include a car (minus the car loan) and some appliances, furniture, and savings (minus the credit-card balance). Wealthier families also have equity in a house (the market value minus the mortgage). More fortunate families are able to accumulate other assets, such as stocks and bonds, retirement savings, and vacation homes.

Figure 8.8a shows the distribution of wealth among Canadian families in 1999, 2005, and 2012. The families are divided into quintiles. Notice that the bottom 40 percent of families own almost no assets (as represented by net worth). In fact, people in the bottom 20 percent owe more than they own. Notice also that the assets owned by the bottom 40 percent of families actually decreased over the 13 years covered by the graph, whereas the assets owned by the top 60 percent of families grew.

Wealth inequality in Canada is even more severe than income inequality, as illustrated for 2012 in Figure 8.8b. While the *incomes* of the richest quintile are about three times that of the middle quintile, their *wealth* (as represented by net worth) is about seven times greater. For both income and wealth, the gains since 1999 have disproportionately flowed to the

TABLE 8.2
Ten Wealthiest Canadians, 2013

Individual or Family	Estimated Wealth	Assets
1. Thomson family	$26.1 billion	Media, information distribution; Thomson Reuters; Woodbridge Co. Ltd.
2. Galen Weston	$10.4 billion	Food, groceries, retail, real estate; George Weston Ltd.; Loblaw Cos. Ltd.; Holt Renfrew
3. Irving family	$7.85 billion	Oil, forestry products, gas stations, media, transportation, real estate; Irving Oil Ltd.; J.D. Irving Ltd.
4. Rogers family	$7.6 billion	Cable TV, communications, media, pro sports; Rogers Communication Inc.
5. James Pattison	$7.39 billion	Auto sales, food, media, forestry products, entertainment, export services; Jim Pattison Group
6. Saputo family	$5.24 billion	Food, real estate, transportation; Saputo Inc.
7. Estate of Paul Desmarais Sr.	$4.93 billion	Financial services, media; Power Corp. of Canada
8. Jeff Skoll	$4.92 billion	Internet, media; eBay Inc., Participant Media
9. Richardson Family	$4.45 billion	agri-food, energy, real estate, financial services; James Richardson & Sons
10. Carlo Fidani	$4.08 billion	real estate, construction; Orlando Corp.

Source: Adapted from http://www.huffingtonpost.ca/2013/11/21/wealthiest-people-canadian-business_n_4316065.html. Retrieved December 16, 2013. © Canadian Business. PROFIT & MoneySense. Rogers Publishing Ltd. Used with permission.

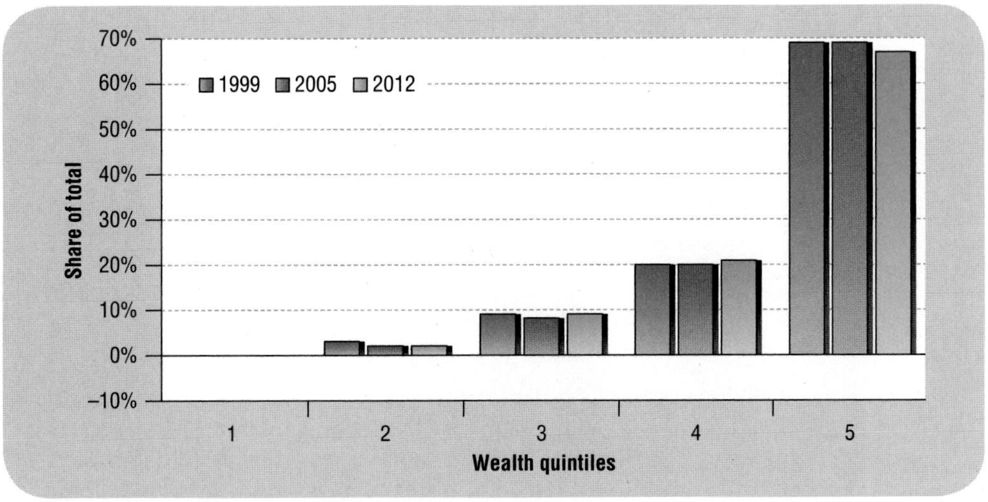

(a) Quintiles of Net Worth 1999, 2005, 2012.

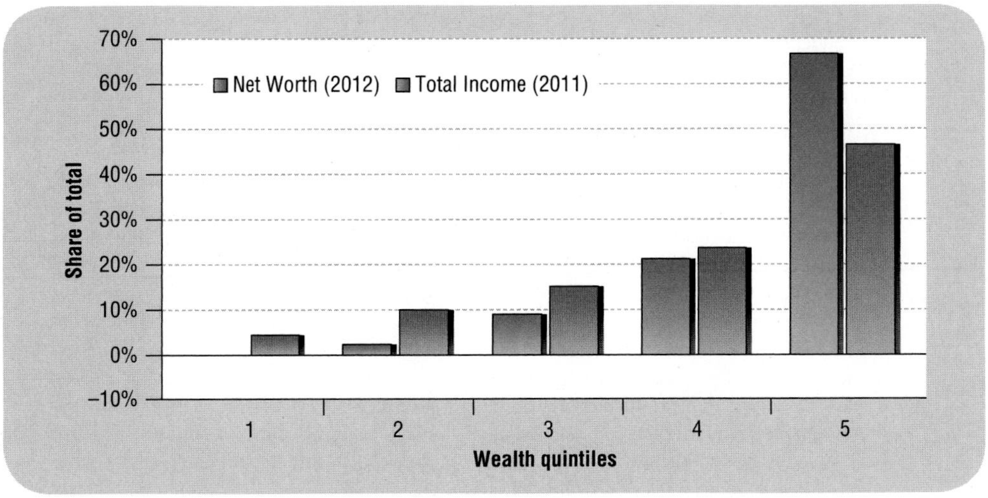

(b) Inequality of Income and Wealth, 2012.

FIGURE 8.8

Income and wealth inequalities in Canada are large, with most increases going to the richest Canadians.

Source: Macdonald, David 2014. "Outrageous Fortune: Documenting Canada's Wealth Gap." Canadian Centre for Policy Alternatives. Retrieved April 5, 2014. https://www.policyalternatives.ca/outrageous-fortune

richest Canadians. The level of wealth among the richest is difficult for average Canadians to comprehend (see Box 8.2). For example, the wealth of the 86 richest Canadians is enough to buy *all* the private assets (houses, cottages, vehicles, land, stocks, bonds, jewellery, furniture, savings, pensions, and so on) of all 755 000 residents of New Brunswick with the exception of New Brunswick's Irving and McCain families who are in the list of 86 (Macdonald, 2014: 10).

Finally, note that only a modest correlation exists between income and wealth. Some wealthy people have low annual incomes and some people with high annual incomes have little accumulated wealth. As such, annual income may not be the best measure of a person's wealth. Policies that seek to redistribute income from the wealthy to the poor, such as income-tax laws, may not get to the root of economic inequality because income redistribution does not have a strong effect on the distribution of wealth (Conley, 1999; Oliver and Shapiro, 1995).

Income and Poverty

At the bottom of the income distribution are people who are homeless. In recent decades, the number of people with no fixed address has shot up. But we do not know exactly how

BOX 8.2

SOCIOLOGY AT THE MOVIES

THE QUEEN OF VERSAILLES

The Queen of Versailles is an award-winning film that documents the experience of David and Jackie Siegel, owners of the world's largest time-share company. It begins by introducing the family and their plans to build the largest single-family house in the United States in Orlando, Florida. The house is modelled after the palace of Versailles in Paris. With its grand staircases, stained-glass domed roof, 30 bathrooms, 11 kitchens, 30-car garage, and indoor skating rink, the building is a monument to wealth and conspicuous consumption.

The construction of the 90 000-square-foot house halts as the business falters due to the 2008 economic crisis. The film then documents the struggles involved in trying to keep the business afloat, the stress in the household, and the lifestyle and character changes among family members.

Various sociological concepts are illustrated by *The Queen of Versailles*. The first centres on mobility. Jackie Siegel comes from a modest, working-class background. She overcame a bad first marriage, became an engineer, and landed a job with IBM. After winning a beauty pageant, it becomes clear to her that it is easier to achieve intragenerational mobility through marriage than employment. She does so by marrying David, a billionaire 30 years her senior.

Preserving wealth in challenging economic times turns out to be a lot harder than earning it in good times (as David did) or marrying it (as Jackie did). The documentary shows David's mounting frustration, irritability, and disconnection as he fights downward mobility and retreats into isolation. It turns out that the way rich people cope with downward mobility is not so different from the way less privileged people do.

The Kobal Collection at Art Resource, NY

Jackie Siegel in front of her mansion in *The Queen of Versailles*.

The documentary provides a glimpse of the lifestyles of the rich during good times. As their new home is under construction, the family has to make do in a 26 000-square-foot house, including a staff of 19, and an annual clothing budget of more than a million dollars. The parents and their seven children are pampered at every turn. Whenever her children don't amuse her, Jackie passes them along to a nanny. When dogs poop on the floor, maids are summoned to clean up. Exotic pets die because the children don't feed them. Unused goods are piled everywhere.

Change comes with the economic collapse and the arrival of hard times. Of course, "hard times" are relative. The Siegels are distraught at the thought of having to move their children from private school to public school. With the private plane and yacht gone, the family faces the exotic experience of flying commercial. In one revealing scene, Jackie is at the Hertz rental car kiosk in an airport and asks the attendant: "Where's my driver?"

While the documentary provides some entertaining insights into the extravagances of the elite, the most jarring scenes arise from the juxtaposition between the Siegels and those they employ. As the Siegels struggle to maintain their billionaire lifestyle, we see the challenges faced every day by their nanny and limo driver. Virginia, the nanny, displays unwavering commitment to the overly privileged children. Even though she has not seen her own son in more than 20 years, she relentlessly cleans, cooks, and cares—all so she can send money home to her family in the Philippines. At the end of his full day of service, the limo driver borrows the Rolls Royce to try to make a little bit of extra money to feed his family.

Like many successful businessmen, David sees himself as self-made; he attributes his success to himself and his ability to use power. As the documentary makes clear, however, his attribution of success to personal initiative is a delusion. Social conditions always play an important role; in David's case, his success rests on a public policy that made cheap money easily available. When this policy changed, his fortunes collapsed. He "blames the system" for his "addiction" to cheap money. Suddenly, his fate is not his fault.

The Queen of Versailles is a revealing demonstration of how excessive wealth can insulate the privileged from the realities of ordinary people. Along the way, it clarifies how income inequality can corrode people's character.

many Canadians are homeless. In cities across the country, people sleep under bridges, in back alleys, behind dumpsters, and in thickets in public parks. They do so night after night, month after month. Recent estimates suggest that every year, at least 200 000 Canadians use homeless shelters or sleep outside (Gaetz et al., 2013). These numbers represent only the visibly homeless people. Including the "hidden homeless" (people who stay with family or friends temporarily), the number rises to as high as 900 000 (Wellesley Institute, 2010).

Homelessness is one manifestation of poverty. Exactly how many Canadians live in poverty is a matter of intense debate. Poverty lacks an agreed-on definition. A first disagreement occurs around whether poverty should be defined in absolute or relative terms.

An absolute definition of poverty focuses on bare essentials, suggesting that poor families have resources inadequate for acquiring the basic necessities of life (food, shelter, clothing). Agreement on "bare essentials" depends on values and judgments (Sarlo, 2001). What is essential varies from time to time, place to place, and group to group. Many of our ancestors lived without indoor plumbing, and some Canadians still do, but most people would define indoor plumbing as essential. A family could survive on a steady diet of cod and potatoes, but most would define such a family as poor.

A relative poverty line also has drawbacks. Two questions are central: Relative to what? How relative? This second area of disagreement relates to whether poverty ought to be defined narrowly, in terms of economic measures (e.g., income), or more broadly, with respect to community standards (e.g., safety of working conditions, environmental quality, housing stock). Most definitions tend to be narrow, focusing primarily on income. But even if a relative poverty line is defined narrowly, how relative ought it to be? One-third of average income? one-half? some other fraction?

Yet another disagreement plagues any definition. Should poverty be defined on the basis of income or consumption? Since "bare essentials" is a core idea in any definition of poverty, it makes good sense to ask about, and measure, poverty as the cost of purchasing bare essentials. Deprivation occurs when a family cannot acquire the essentials, not necessarily when income is too low. Income and consumption are correlated, of course, but people with high net wealth can live off their savings even when earning a low income.

In one sense, the definition of poverty means little to a homeless woman sleeping on top of a hot-air vent. The immediate experience of poverty by families in remote coastal communities, by single parents in the urban core, and by farmers on the Prairies is unaffected by whether poverty is defined absolutely or relatively, narrowly or broadly, by income or by consumption. However, the definition of poverty is consequential for these people, insofar as social policies are enacted, or not enacted, based on levels and trends in poverty. Definitions matter.

Social policy has a profound impact on the distribution of opportunities and rewards in Canada. Politics can reshape the distribution of income and the system of inequality by changing the laws governing people's right to own property, entitling people to various welfare benefits, and redistributing income through tax policies. When politicians de-emphasize poverty, legislative efforts to maintain or expand welfare benefits and redistribute income are less likely. A definition of poverty that shows fewer Canadians living in poverty implies little need for government action. Conversely, for politicians and political parties advocating for the poor, their cause benefits from a definition of poverty that shows a growing proportion of people living in poverty.

Unlike some countries, such as the United States, Canada does not have an official definition of poverty. Statistics Canada argues that there is no internationally accepted definition of poverty and that any definition is arbitrary. Therefore, it does not attempt to estimate the number of Canadians who are living in poverty. Instead, Statistics Canada reports what it calls a **low-income cutoff**. This cutoff conveys "the income level at which a family may be in straitened circumstances because it has to spend a greater proportion of its income [at least 20 percent] on necessities than the average family of similar size" (Statistics Canada, 2000b: 122). The threshold is reported for seven different family sizes and for five sizes of community because "straitened circumstances" depend on the number of people in your family and where you live. Most advocates for the poor interpret these thresholds, shown for 2011 in Table 8.3, as poverty lines. For example, in Canada's largest cities, a family of four with after-tax income of less than $36 504 would be considered to be living in poverty.

Low-income cutoff is Statistic Canada's term for the income threshold below which a family devotes at least 20 percent more of its income to the necessities of food, shelter, and clothing than does an average family.

In recent decades, the prevalence of low income among Canadians peaked at 15.7 percent in 1996, declined to around 12 percent by 2007, and then rose to about 13 percent during the financial crisis of 2008–09 (Figure 8.9). Note, however, that the trajectory of low-income patterns varies by socio-economic group (Murphy, Zhang, and Dionne, 2012). For example, in recent decades, the prevalence of low income among single parents declined steeply, from

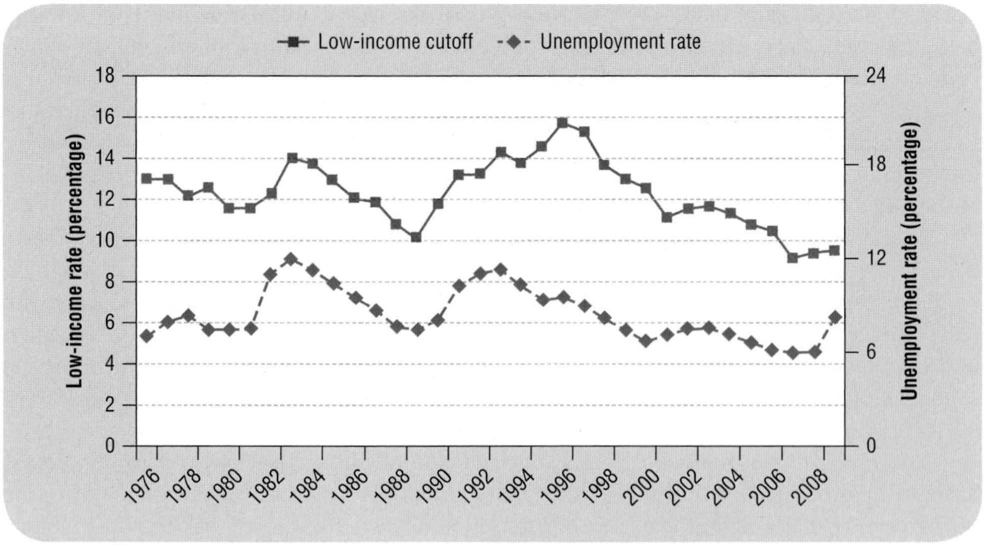

FIGURE 8.9
Canadian Low-Income Rates and Unemployment Rates, 1976–2009

Source: Survey of Consumer Finances (1976 to 1995), Survey of Labour and Income Dynamics (1996 to 2009) and Labour Force Survey (CANSIM Table 282-0002), Statistics Canada. Captured from Murphy, Zhang, and Dionne, 2012: 14.

40 to 20 percent. The low-income rate for seniors declined significantly between the 1970s and mid-1990s but has since risen. The low-income rate for children in low-income families declined steadily over this period.

Myths about the Poor

The language we use to speak about people living in poverty is often revealing. For example, referring to someone as "poor but honest" implies that we view such a combination as so unlikely that people who have both characteristics are exceptions to the rule. Popular mythology also depicts people living in poverty—especially those who receive public assistance ("welfare")—as lazy, irresponsible, and lacking in motivation, abilities, and moral values. These images are potent and contribute to stereotypes of the "deserving" and the "undeserving" poor (for example, war veterans and children versus "welfare bums" and people "looking for a handout"). However, research conducted in the past few decades shows that many of the stereotypes about people living in poverty are myths:

- Myth 1: People are poor because they don't want to work. This myth ignores that many people cannot work because of a disability or because they must care for their young children because of inadequate or inaccessible child-care facilities. This myth also ignores that many people who live in poverty work full-time, and many more work part-time. However, having a job is no guarantee of escaping poverty because of the low minimum wage set by provincial and territorial governments. In September 2014, the hourly minimum wage varied from $10.20 (in Alberta) to $11.00 (in Ontario and Nunavut), with an unweighted provincial and territorial average of $10.33 (Retail Council of Canada, 2014). A person living in a large Canadian city working 50 weeks at 40 hours a week for $10.33 an hour would earn only $20 660 a year—just $1353 above the low-income cutoff (see Table 8.3). But it gets worse. In terms of purchasing power

TABLE 8.3
Selected After-Tax Low-Income Cutoffs, 2011 ($)

Source: Statistics Canada. 2012l. "Low Income Lines, 2010–2011." www.statcan.gc.ca/pub/75f0002m/75f0002m2012002-eng.htm. Retrieved December 25, 2012.

	Population of Community	
Family Size	**Rural**	**Urban over 500 000**
1	12 629	19 307
4	23 879	36 504
7+	33 121	50 631

(that is, taking inflation into account), the minimum wage fell by about 25 percent across Canada from the mid-1970s to the mid-2000s. The low minimum wage helps to ensure widespread poverty.

- Myth 2: Most people living in poverty are immigrants. Actually, only recent immigrants experience poverty rates that are significantly higher than the poverty rates of the Canadian-born, and recent immigrants are only a small fraction of all Canadian immigrants. Moreover, once immigrants are established, they typically have lower poverty rates than do people born in Canada (National Council of Welfare, 2004).
- Myth 3: Most poor people are trapped in poverty. In fact, more than 92 percent of people with low income in a given year escape poverty in less than two years; 80 percent escape in less than a year. Fewer than 8 percent are mired in poverty for more than two years (Statistics Canada, 2010d). We conclude that most people try to move out of difficult financial circumstances—and most succeed, at least for a time.

Explaining Poverty

Why do some people live in poverty and others do not? Answers to this question vary from individual-level to structural explanations.

Individual-Level Explanations

Individual-level explanations focus on the attributes of poor people, asking how they differ from people who are not poor. This type of explanation focuses on causes that lie "within the person." Using this logic, someone is poor because of a personal characteristic, such as low intelligence or a behaviour abnormality.

Some evidence suggests that *individual attributes* explain a small amount of poverty. For example, we know that people with a disability have a higher risk of living in poverty than others do. However, not all people with a disability live in poverty, and the vast majority of people living in poverty have no disability. On balance, this type of evidence teaches us that poverty is, for the most part, not a consequence of individual attributes, even though these attributes are important in some cases.

A related explanation focuses on the acquired *attitudes* of individuals, such as low self-esteem, lack of achievement motivation, and an inability to delay gratification. Using this logic, poverty persists because families who are poor employ child-rearing practices that enhance bad attitudes. A related version of this argument stresses a "culture of poverty," a way of thinking and acting that is supposedly shared by families who live in poverty. This culture presumably reinforces and perpetuates itself through inadequate upbringing and ill-formed personalities.

Two objections undermine this type of explanation. First, descriptions of poverty that stress a culture of depression, lack of hope, and fatalism may be accurate, but these states of mind are typically *effects* of poverty, not causes. Second, many people who are poor work, are religious, don't smoke or drink, and so on. Therefore, evidence that supports explanations founded on these personal deficits is often lacking.

Economic Organization

Another type of explanation has greater currency in sociology. It stresses the *organization of the economy* as the principal cause of poverty. Capitalist economies feature cyclical booms and busts, periods of low unemployment and high profits, followed by high unemployment and low profits. During recessions, many people lose their jobs and fall into poverty. Moreover, as we have seen, people with minimum-wage jobs don't earn enough to escape poverty. The lack of good jobs is thus a major cause of poverty (see Figure 8.9).

Social Policy

Other analysts stress *social policy* as a factor affecting poverty levels. For example, as noted above, if you received the minimum hourly wage while working full-time, year-round, you would barely escape poverty, especially if you had children to support. In this sense, minimum-wage legislation is a social policy that creates a group of working poor.

The social world is not quite so simple, of course. If minimum wages were to rise too much or too quickly, so too might the level of unemployment because some employers might not be able to afford a sudden big jump in wages. Debate over these issues continues, but the point is that our social policies affect people's well-being, and understanding the consequences of such policies is important.

The system of tax collection and tax allocation illustrates another way that social policies affect poverty (see Box 8.3). In a progressive tax system, as incomes rise, a greater *proportion* of income is paid in tax. For example, those who earn \$100 000 would pay a larger percentage of their income as tax than do those who earn \$50 000. In Canada, although our income tax system is progressive, the overall tax system is relatively neutral. Most Canadian families pay about the same percentage of their total income in tax. This situation occurs because two interrelated factors undermine the "Robin Hood" effect of progressive income taxes. First, taxes other than income tax, such as the GST and fuel taxes, are regressive, which means they are not based on the income of the taxpayer. You pay the same tax on a \$100 chair as does David Thomson, Canada's richest man. Second, those who earn more are able to shelter much of their income from taxation in registered education saving plans and registered retirement savings plans, through capital gains tax exemptions, and so on. As a result, the tax system does less to erode poverty than you might imagine.

BOX 8.3

IT'S YOUR CHOICE

INCOME REDISTRIBUTION AND TAXATION

The idea of "rugged individualism" implies that our personal fortunes ought to rest on our own shoulders. People who work hard, persevere, and make wise decisions supposedly deserve big rewards. By implication, those who are lazy and unwise deserve less.

In contrast, the idea of "collective responsibility" implies that as members of a community, we ought to look out for one another. Those who have should share. The interests of the many should come before the riches of a few.

Few Canadians support either of these extremes, but examples of each principle are easy to find. The notion of rugged individualism is consistent with the unequal distribution of income in Canada and the high salaries of the presidents of large corporations. The concept of collective responsibility is embodied in government support for post-secondary education and health care.

How much tax revenue should governments collect, and should they redistribute that revenue in ways that benefit lower-income groups? Should governments exercise more collective responsibility by giving more tax dollars to support hospitals and schools, or should people act more as rugged individualists and pay for medical care and education themselves? These questions relate to social policy.

Here are some of the arguments for and against income redistribution, arguments that are fundamental to some of the major political debates in many countries in recent years. What choices would you make if you could run the government for a few years?

AGAINST REDISTRIBUTION

1. Taking from the rich and giving to the poor decreases the motivation for people in both groups to work hard.
2. The cost of redistribution is high. Taking from one group and giving to another requires a government agency to collect money and then to reallocate it.
3. Some individuals and families cheat. They hide or misrepresent their earnings, either to pay less in tax or to receive more government money through welfare. Redistribution promotes tax cheats and welfare frauds.

FOR REDISTRIBUTION

1. A society with a low level of inequality is a better place to live than is a society with a high level of inequality.
2. An extra dollar to a family living in poverty is more helpful than an extra dollar to a family that is wealthy.
3. Improving the material well-being of a poor family enhances the well-being of a rich family because it encourages less crime and less political discord.

Ideology

Finally, some sociologists stress ways of thinking, or ideology, as an explanation for poverty. Negative images of various groups lead to an undervaluing of the ways of life of some people, such as First Nations people, recent immigrants, and members of visible minority groups. Discrimination follows from such undervaluation. Discrimination causes poverty because it leads to less success in finding good jobs.

Is poverty an inevitable feature of society? It may be, at least to the extent that inequality is known to exist in all societies. However, the extent of poverty in Canada could be reduced if we chose to follow the example of Western European nations. Many countries in Western Europe have poverty rates well below Canada's because their governments have established job-training and child-care programs that allow people who are living in poverty to take jobs with livable wages and benefits. This option is, however, clearly a political choice. Many Canadians argue that providing welfare benefits dampens the work ethic and perpetuates poverty. Although the Western European evidence does not support that view, Canadians do not currently seem to have the political will to change our social policies and thereby alleviate poverty.

These basic patterns and trends characterize social stratification in Canada. Bearing them in mind, we now examine how major sociologists have explained social stratification. We begin with Karl Marx, who formulated the first major sociological theory of stratification in the middle of the nineteenth century (Marx and Engels, 1972 [1848]; Marx, 1904 [1859]).

TIME FOR REVIEW

- What would be the income quintile shares for a society with a Gini index score of 0? What would the income quintile shares be for a society with a Gini score of 1?
- How does social capital differ from individual capital? What social capital differences would you expect to find when comparing a public school with an exclusive private school?
- Imagine the Canadian government instituted a 100 percent inheritance tax. How would this tax affect the list of the richest people in Canada?
- The Bible claims that "the poor will always be with us." Does the credibility of this claim change when using a relative definition of poverty rather than an absolute definition of poverty?
- How do individual-level and structural explanations differ in terms of where they locate the primary causes of poverty?

THEORIES OF STRATIFICATION

Conflict Perspectives

Marx

In medieval Western Europe, peasants worked small plots of land owned by landlords. Peasants were legally obliged to give their landlords a set part of the harvest and to continue working for them under any circumstance. In turn, landlords were required to protect peasants from marauders. They were also obliged to open their storehouses and feed the peasants if crops failed. This arrangement was known as **feudalism**.

Feudalism was a legal arrangement in preindustrial Europe that bound peasants to the land and obliged them to give their landlords a set part of the harvest. In exchange, landlords were required to protect peasants from marauders and open their storehouses to feed the peasants if crops failed.

According to Marx, by the late fifteenth century, several forces were beginning to undermine feudalism. Most important was the growth of exploration and trade, which increased the demand for many goods and services in commerce, navigation, and industry. By the seventeenth and eighteenth centuries, some urban craftsmen and merchants had opened small manufacturing enterprises and had saved enough capital to expand production. However, they faced a big problem: To increase profits they needed more workers. Yet the biggest potential source of workers—the peasantry—was legally bound to the land. Thus, feudalism needed to wither if agricultural peasants were to become industrial workers. In Scotland, for example, this happened when enterprising landowners recognized they could make more money raising sheep and selling wool than by having their peasants till the soil. Consequently, they turned their cropland into pastures, forcing peasants off the land and into the cities. The former peasants had no choice but to take jobs as urban workers.

In Marx's view, relations between workers and industrialists first encouraged rapid technological change and economic growth. After all, industrial owners wanted to adopt new tools, machines, and production methods so they could produce more efficiently and earn higher profits. But such innovation had unforeseen consequences. In the first place, some owners, driven out of business by more efficient competitors, were forced to become members of the working class. Together with former peasants pouring into the cities from the countryside, this influx caused the working class to grow. Second, the drive for profits motivated owners to concentrate workers in larger and larger factories, keep wages as low as possible, and invest as little as possible in improving working conditions. Thus, as the ownership class grew richer and smaller, the working class grew larger and more impoverished.

Class consciousness refers to being aware of membership in a class.

Class, in Marx's sense of the term, is determined by a person's relationship to the means of production. In Weber's usage, class is determined by a person's "market situation."

Marx felt that workers would ultimately become aware of their exploitation. Their sense of **class consciousness** would, he wrote, encourage the growth of unions and workers' political parties. These organizations would eventually try to create a communist system in which there would be no private wealth. Instead, under communism, everyone would share wealth, said Marx.

According to Marx, the **bourgeoisie** are owners of the means of production, including factories, tools, and land. They do not do any physical labour. Their income derives from profits.

Marx's theory includes several noteworthy points. First, according to Marx, a person's **class** is determined by the source of his or her income, or, to use Marx's term, by a person's "relationship to the means of production." For example, members of the capitalist class (or **bourgeoisie**) own the means of production, including factories, tools, and land. They do not do any physical labour. They are thus in a position to earn profits. In contrast, members of the working class (or **proletariat**) do physical labour. They do not own the means of production. They are thus in a position to earn wages. In Marx's view, classes are distinguished by their source of income, not by the amount of income they earn.

The **proletariat**, in Marx's usage, is the working class. Members of the proletariat do physical labour but do not own means of production. They are thus in a position to earn wages.

A second noteworthy point about Marx's theory is that it recognizes more than two classes in any society. In particular, the **petite bourgeoisie** is a class of small-scale capitalists who own means of production but employ only a few workers or none at all. Their situation forces them to do physical work themselves. In Marx's view, as capitalism develops, members of the petite bourgeoisie are bound to disappear because they are economically inefficient. According to Marx, every economic era is characterized by just two great classes: landlords and serfs during feudalism, the bourgeoisie and proletariat during capitalism.

Critique of Marx

The **petite bourgeoisie**, in Marx's usage, is the class of small-scale capitalists who own means of production but employ only a few workers or none at all, forcing them to do physical work themselves.

Marx's ideas strongly influenced the development of conflict theory (Chapter 1, A Sociological Compass). Today, however, sociologists generally agree that Marx did not accurately foresee some aspects of capitalist development:

- Industrial societies did not polarize into two opposed classes engaged in bitter conflict. Instead, a large and heterogeneous middle class of "white-collar" workers emerged. Some of them are non-manual employees; others are professionals. Many of these workers enjoy higher income and higher status than manual workers do. With a bigger stake in capitalism than that of manual workers with no property, non-manual employees and professionals generally act as a stabilizing force in society. To take account of these changes, some neo-Marxists recognize *two* main divisions in the social relations of work—between owners and non-owners, and between supervisors/managers and non-supervisors/managers. The class of supervisors and managers is sometimes called the "new middle class." Members of the new middle class take direction from owners and are responsible for coordinating the work of other employees (Clement and Myles, 1994).

- Marx correctly argued that investment in technology makes it possible for capitalists to earn high profits. However, he did not expect investment in technology to make it possible for workers to earn higher wages and toil fewer hours under less oppressive conditions. Yet that is just what happened. Improved living standard tended to pacify workers, as did the availability of various welfare state benefits, such as employment insurance.
- Communism took root not where industry was most highly developed, as Marx predicted, but in semi-industrialized countries, such as Russia in 1917 and China in 1949. Moreover, instead of evolving into classless societies, new forms of privilege emerged under communism, where elite communist party members could enjoy scarce Western goods at nominal prices, luxurious country homes, free trips abroad, and so on. According to a Russian quip from the 1970s, "Under capitalism, one class exploits the other, but under communism it's the other way around."
- Businesspeople developed new ways to avert economic crises and prolong the life of capitalism by stimulating demand. To encourage people to buy more things, they began advertising, which created new "needs." To give people the means to buy new things they could not otherwise afford, businesspeople created easy credit. And to ensure that people frequently replaced the new things they bought, they started designing things to break down. Among the abundant fruits of such "planned obsolescence" are light bulbs with short, 1000-hour life spans, hosiery that develops runs after being worn just a few times, and inkjet printers containing a chip that makes them die after printing a set number of pages.

Weber

Writing in the early twentieth century, Max Weber foretold most of the developments outlined above. He did not think communism would create classlessness. He understood the significance of the growth of the middle class. Consequently, Weber developed a much different approach to social stratification from Marx's approach.

Weber, like Marx, saw classes as economic categories (Weber, 1946: 180–95). However, he did not think that class position was determined by a single criterion—ownership versus non-ownership of property. Class position, wrote Weber, is determined by a person's "market situation," including the individual's possession of goods, opportunities for income, level of education, and degree of technical skill. For Marx, class is a *relational* concept; different classes reflect oppositional relationships to the means of production. For Weber, class is a *distributional* concept; gradations in class are associated with an individual's value in the marketplace.

According to Weber, society is divided into four main classes: large-property owners, small-property owners, employees who are relatively highly educated but do not own property, and manual workers who lack higher education and do not own property. Thus, in Weber's scheme, white-collar employees and professionals emerge as a large class.

If Weber broadened Marx's idea of class, he also recognized that two types of groups other than class have a bearing on the way a society is stratified: status groups and parties.

Status groups differ from one another in the prestige or social honour they enjoy and in their style of life. Consider members of a particular minority ethnic community who

Status groups differ from one another in terms of the prestige or social honour they enjoy and also in terms of their style of life.

have recently immigrated. They may earn relatively high income but endure relatively low prestige. The longer-established members of the majority ethnic community may look down on the newcomers as vulgar "new rich." If their cultural practices differ from those of the majority ethnic group, their style of life may also become a subject of scorn. Thus, the position of the minority ethnic group in the social hierarchy does not derive only from its economic position but also from the esteem in which it is held.

Parties, in Weber's usage, are organizations that seek to impose their will on others.

In Weber's usage, **parties** are not just political groups but, more generally, organizations that seek to impose their will on others. Control over parties, especially large bureaucratic organizations, does not depend solely on wealth or some other class criterion. One can head a military, scientific, or other bureaucracy without being rich, just as one can be rich yet still endure low prestige.

Weber argued that to draw an accurate picture of a society's stratification system, we must analyze classes, status groups, and parties as independent bases of social inequality. But to what degree are they independent of one another? Weber said that the importance of status groups as a basis of stratification is greatest in pre-capitalist societies. Under capitalism, classes and parties (especially bureaucracies) become the main bases of stratification.

Functionalism

Marx and Weber were Germans who wrote their major works between the 1840s and the 1910s. Inevitably, their theories bear the stamp of the age in which they wrote. The next major developments in the field occurred in the United States in the mid-twentieth century. Just as inevitably, these innovations were coloured by the optimism, dynamism, and prejudices of that time and place.

Functionalism, you will recall, views society as an integrated system of parts. The operation of the parts shares a common purpose, which makes the contribution of each part "functional." For functionalists, a useful purpose is served by even those components of society that appear problematic, such as poverty. Some functionalists thus point out that people who live in poverty are willing to undertake menial jobs, thus ensuring that low-wage, "dirty work" gets done. Middle-class social workers, police officers, and owners of thrift stores depend on the people who live in poverty for jobs insofar as the poor are often their clients. People living in poverty created jazz and the blues, and they have made other magnificent cultural contributions. Their reliable record of not voting helps shape stable election outcomes (Gans, 1972). For functionalists, then, social systems are always organized to advance collective interests.

The **functional theory of stratification** argues that (1) some jobs are more important than others are, (2) people must make sacrifices to train for important jobs, and (3) inequality is required to motivate people to undergo these sacrifices.

A general **functional theory of stratification** was proposed by Kingsley Davis and Wilbert Moore at the end of World War II (Davis and Moore, 1944). Davis and Moore observed that jobs differ in importance. A judge's work, for example, contributes more to society than does the work of a janitor. This discrepancy presents a problem: How can people be motivated to undergo the long training they need to serve as judges, physicians, engineers, and so on? Higher education is expensive. You earn little money while training. Long and hard study rather than pleasure seeking is essential. Clearly, an incentive is needed to motivate the most talented people to train for the most important jobs. The incentives, said Davis and Moore, are money and prestige. Thus, social stratification is necessary (or "functional") because the prospect of high rewards motivates people to undergo the sacrifices needed to achieve a higher education. Without substantial inequality, they conclude, the most talented people would have no incentive to become judges, physicians, and so on.

Although the functional theory of stratification may at first seem plausible, we can conduct what Weber called a "thought experiment" to uncover one of its chief flaws. Imagine a society with just two classes of people—physicians and farmers. The farmers grow food. The physicians tend the ill. Then, one day, a rare and deadly virus strikes. The virus has the odd property of attacking only physicians. Within weeks, our imaginary society has no more doctors. As a result, the farmers are much worse off. Cures and treatments for their ailments are no longer available. Soon the average farmer lives fewer years than his or her predecessors did. The society is less well off, though it survives.

Now imagine the reverse. Again we have a society comprising only physicians and farmers. Again a rare and lethal virus strikes. This time, however, the virus has the odd property of attacking only farmers. Within weeks, the physicians' stores of food are depleted. After a few more weeks, the physicians start dying of starvation. The physicians who try to become farmers catch the new virus and expire. Within months, there is no more society. Who, then, does the more important work, physicians or farmers? Our thought experiment suggests that farmers do, for without them society cannot exist.

From a historical point of view, we can say that *none* of the jobs regarded by Davis and Moore as "important" would exist without the physical labour done by people in "unimportant" jobs. To sustain the witch doctor in a tribal society, hunters and gatherers needed to produce enough for their own subsistence plus a surplus to feed, clothe, and house the witch doctor. To sustain the royal court in an agrarian society, serfs needed to produce enough for their own subsistence plus a surplus to support the royal family. By using taxes, tithes, and force, government and religious authorities have taken surpluses from ordinary working people for thousands of years. These surpluses were used, among other things, to establish the first institutions of higher learning in the thirteenth century. Out of these early institutions, modern universities developed.

The question of which occupations are most important is thus unclear. To be sure, most physicians earn a lot more money than most family farmers do today and they also enjoy much more prestige. But that is not because their work is more important in any objective sense of the word. (On the question of why physicians and other professionals earn more than non-professionals do, see Chapter 17, Education).

A second problem with the functional theory of stratification is that it stresses how inequality helps society discover talent but ignores the pool of talent lying undiscovered because of inequality (Tumin, 1953). Bright and energetic adolescents may be forced to drop out of high school to help support themselves and their families. Capable and industrious high-school graduates may be forced to forgo a postsecondary education because they can't afford it. Inequality may encourage the discovery of talent but only among those who can afford to take advantage of the opportunities available to them. For the rest, inequality prevents talent from being discovered.

Third, the functional theory of stratification fails to examine how advantages are passed from generation to generation. Like Robinson Crusoe, the functional theory correctly emphasizes that talent and hard work often result in high material rewards. However, it is also true that inheritance allows parents to transfer wealth to children regardless of their talent. For example, glancing back at Table 8.3, we see that many of the largest personal fortunes in Canada were inherited. Even rich people who do not inherit large

Agriculture and Agri-Food Canada

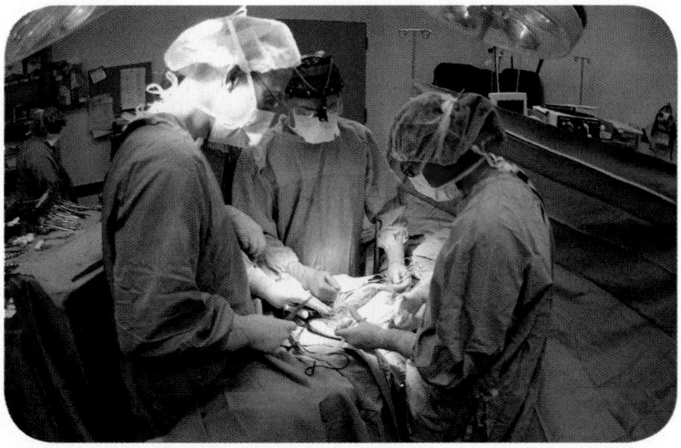

Photos.com

According to the functional theory of stratification, "important" jobs require more training than "less important" jobs. The promise of big salaries motivates people to undergo that training. Therefore, the functionalists conclude, social stratification is necessary. As the text makes clear, however, one of the problems with the functional theory of stratification is that it is difficult to establish which jobs are important, especially when we take a historical perspective.

fortunes often start near the top of the stratification system. Bill Gates, for example, is one of the richest people in the world. He did not inherit his fortune. However, his father was a partner in one of the most successful law firms in Seattle. Gates himself went to the most exclusive and expensive private schools in the city, followed by a stint at Harvard. In the late 1960s, his high school was one of the first in the world to boast a computer terminal connected to a nearby university's mainframe. Gates's early fascination with computers dates from this period. Gates is without doubt a highly talented man, but surely the social advantages he was born with, and not just his talents, helped to elevate him to his present lofty status (Wallace and Erickson, 1992). An adequate theory of stratification must take inheritance into account, while recognizing how inequality prevents the discovery of talent.

Many of the ideas reviewed above emphasize the economic sources of inequality. However, as Weber correctly pointed out, inequality is not based on money alone. It is also based on prestige and power.

Power

In 2010, Tom and Sharon Brown moved from Calgary to tiny Parrsboro, Nova Scotia, with their teenage daughter, Courtney. In the local high school and on Facebook, Courtney was mercilessly bullied. She started skipping classes and opened a second Facebook account, but to no avail. Things got so bad that on March 30, 2011, Courtney committed suicide. It was the second teen suicide in Nova Scotia caused by bullying in just over two months (Paperny, 2011). When 14-year-old Dawn-Marie Lesley of Mission, B.C., hanged herself in her bedroom with a dog leash almost 11 years earlier, she left a suicide note that spoke for the predicament of many such young people: "If I try to get help it will get worse. They are always looking for a new person to beat up and they are the toughest girls. If I ratted they would get suspended and there would be no stopping them. I love you all so much" (quoted in O'Malley and Ali, 2001).

Bullying was probably part of your upbringing, too. Recall your years in the schoolyard. Remember how some people had the power to "name," while others were forced to "wear" those names? "Four eyes," "fatty," and "spaz" were common names in many schools. If you had the misfortune of needing glasses, having a visible birthmark, or even having an unusual name, you might have been the victim of verbal abuse.

Why are so many children publicly shamed and humiliated? Because doing so makes those with the power to name feel superior and proud. The peer group is a place to "earn points" and win friends. To become one of the in-crowd, a child must disparage outsiders. If a person is part of the out-crowd, he or she must disparage members of the in-crowd as a defence aimed at maintaining self-esteem. Often it is cliques who do the mocking. Cliques are often defined by their social class, ethnicity, grade level, or neighbourhood.

Power is ability to impose one's will on others despite resistance.

Bullying is one form of power in action. Max Weber defined **power** as the ability of individuals or groups to get their own way, even in the face of resistance from others (Weber, 1947: 152). However, it is a mistake to think that power is an attribute that you either have or don't have. That is because less powerful groups may organize and resist; and organization and resistance are themselves bases of power. Accordingly, less powerful groups may become more powerful when the power holders seek to impose their will. Sometimes, less powerful groups may even prevent power holders from achieving their aims. Power is therefore not an all-or-nothing attribute but a *social relationship*, and the exercise of power may cause less powerful people to become more powerful. In Nova Scotia, a movement has grown quickly to combat bullying in schools. In April 2011, the movement's leaders convinced the provincial government to agree to set up a task force to deal with the problem; and in 2013, the province passed legislation giving victims of cyberbullying the right to sue cyberbullies.

Authority is legitimate, institutionalized power.

Sociologists distinguish power from authority. **Authority** rests on moral consent—I comply with your demands not because you force me to but because I believe your demands are legitimate. We agree that bringing a gun to school is inappropriate and that halting at stop

BOX 8.4

SOCIOLOGY ON THE TUBE

TREME: HOW INEQUALITY SHAPES DISASTER

New Orleans, situated on the Gulf Coast of Louisiana, is famous for its jazz, its bourbon, and its carnivals. In that region, hurricane season is an annual autumn event. New Orleans is particularly vulnerable. Most of the city is below sea level, some parts as much as 2.5 meters (8 feet) below. New Orleans sits like a saucer in a pool, surrounded by bodies of salt water. Hurricane winds of more than 200 km per hour create devastating storm surges. On August 25, 2005, Hurricane Katrina struck with brutal force, leaving 2300 dead, $100 billion in damage, and more than three-quarters of the population evacuated from their homes.

Among American cities, New Orleans is exceptionally poor, black, segregated, violent, and unequal (Fussell, 2006). After World War II, many whites moved to the suburbs. When Katrina hit, more than two-thirds of New Orleans' residents were black. One-third of them were poor. Poor blacks were concentrated in the low-lying, least desirable areas of the city. In New Orleans, race and class inequalities met to create widespread social risk.

Treme is a poor neighbourhood in New Orleans that is the setting for David Simon's television series focusing on Katrina's aftermath. It is organized around fascinating characters who struggle to cope with the dislocation Katrina wrought. They include Creighton Bernette (John Goodman), a college professor tortured by writer's block and the devastation of his beloved city; Creighton's wife, Toni (Melissa Leo), a civil rights lawyer frantically working to help the oppressed; Davis McAlary (Steve Zahn), a part-time radio disc jockey and band member who alternates between alienation and enthusiasm; Albert Lambreaux (Clarke Peters), who struggles to reunite his Mardi Gras Indian tribe in his old neighbourhood; and underemployed trombonist Antoine Batiste (Wendell Pierce), whose love of jazz overrides his commitment to marriage and family.

Treme is wonderful, dramatic television. The characters are compelling, each engaged in his or her heroic struggles. And if you are a fan of jazz, you'll find special satisfaction in the unusually long musical interludes. What *Treme* lacks, though, is the sociological context in which the post-Katrina nightmare is embedded. The Hurricane Katrina disaster and its aftermath were not unpredictable acts of God for which no one is responsible (Brym, 2014). Individuals need not have been left to struggle and cope as best they could. Social policies had created New Orleans' inequality, segregation, violence, and poverty. Repeated legislative decisions were taken not to invest in flood mitigation engineering. Behind the slow, weak emergency response was a conservative federal government's ideology emphasizing individualism. As the sociological imagination emphasizes, individual experience is always embedded in historically shaped social arrangements. *Treme* illustrates the extent of individual dislocation and suffering that results when governments permit inequalities to flourish. It falls short, though, of identifying the social underpinnings of the disaster.

REUTERS/Rick Wilking/Landov

New Orleans immediately after Hurricane Katrina (2005)

signs is essential for safety. Most people obey these rules not out of fear of sanctions, but because they agree that they are sensible, legitimate practices.

The use of power is often invisible (see Box 8.4). Powerful people often don't have to do anything to get their way because others understand it would be futile to resist. Extremely powerful individuals or groups are even able to set agendas, frame issues, and shape ideas—that is, to decide the topics that will be debated and how they will be debated. Their power enables them to exclude potentially contentious issues from debate. They may then win battles without having to fight them because others often haven't even conceived of the need to raise certain issues or at least the need to raise them in certain ways. For those who hold power, the invisible use of power is less risky than allowing contentious issues to be put on an agenda, which might lead less powerful individuals and groups to organize and resist, and perhaps even require the use of force to win an issue. Patradioxically, the use of force is a sign of relative weakness.

TIME FOR REVIEW

- What are the main arguments and criticisms of the Marxist view of stratification?
- According to Weber, what are the main social classes? How do social classes differ from status groups and parties?
- What are the main arguments and limitations of the functionalist view of stratification?
- What is the key difference between a relationship based on power and one based on authority?

SOCIAL MOBILITY

Mordecai Richler's *The Apprenticeship of Duddy Kravitz* is one of the classics of modern Canadian literature (Richler, 1959). Made into a 1974 film starring Richard Dreyfuss as Duddy, it is the story of a poor 18-year-old Jewish Montrealer in the mid-1940s desperately seeking to establish himself in the world. To that end, he waits on tables, smuggles drugs, drives a taxi, produces wedding and bar mitzvah films, and rents out pinball machines. He is an obnoxious charmer with relentless drive, a young man so fixed on making it that he is even willing to sacrifice his girlfriend and his only co-worker to achieve his goals. We cannot help but admire Duddy for his ambition and his artfulness even while being shocked by his guile and his single-mindedness.

Part of what makes *The Apprenticeship of Duddy Kravitz* universally appealing is that it could be a story about anyone on the make. It is not just some immigrants and their children who may start out as pushy little guys engaged in shady practices and unethical behaviour. As Richler reminds us repeatedly, some of the wealthiest establishment families in Canada and elsewhere started out in just this way. Duddy, then, is a universal symbol of "upward mobility"—and the compromises a person must sometimes make to achieve it.

Much of our discussion to this point has focused on how we describe inequality and how we explain its persistence. Now we take up a different, although related, set of questions. Is our position in the system of inequality fixed? To what extent, if at all, are we trapped in a disadvantaged social position or assured of maintaining an advantaged position? At birth, do all people have the same freedom to gain wealth and fame? Are opportunities equally accessible to everyone?

Sociologists use the term *social mobility* to refer to the dynamics of the system of inequality and, in particular, to movement up and down the stratification system. If we think about inequality as either a hierarchy of more or less privileged positions or a set of higher and lower social classes, an important question emerges: how much opportunity do people have to change their positions? Typically, change has been measured using one of two benchmarks: your first position in the hierarchy (your first full-time job) or your parents' position in the hierarchy. Comparing your first job with your current job is an examination of occupational or **intragenerational mobility**. Comparing parents' occupations with their children's occupations is an examination of the inheritance of social position or **intergenerational mobility**.

Intragenerational mobility is social mobility that occurs within a single generation.

Intergenerational mobility is social mobility that occurs between generations.

Whichever benchmark is used, social mobility analysts are interested in the openness, or fluidity, of society. Open, or fluid, societies are characterized by greater equality of access to all positions in the hierarchy of inequality. Thus, in more open societies, regardless of your social origins, you are more likely to rise or fall to a position that reflects your capabilities. In contrast, in closed or rigid societies, your social origins determine where you are located in the hierarchy of inequality. In such societies, poverty begets poverty, wealth begets wealth; being born into a particular position is a life sentence. For example, in medieval Europe, laws ensured that peasants remained peasants and lords remained lords. In the

Indian caste system, religion ensured that Brahmins remained Brahmins and untouchables remained untouchables.

More recently, societies have become more open in the sense that social origin does not completely determine one's fate. Think about the changes in Canadian society over the last century. A mainly agrarian, resource-based economy has transformed into an advanced, postindustrial country. We have experienced substantial growth in well-paying occupations in finance, marketing, management, and the professions. To what extent have people from all walks of life, from all economic backgrounds, been able to benefit from this transformation? This question introduces a second, related theme to discussions of mobility—equality of opportunity.

In the 1950s and 1960s, proponents of the functional theory of stratification and human capital theory thought that equality of opportunity would become the rule. They argued that as more and more skilled jobs are created in the new economy, the best and the brightest must rise to the top to take those jobs and perform them diligently. We would then move from a society based on *ascription* to one based on *achievement*. In a system of inequality based on ascription, your family's station in life determines your own fortunes. In a system based on achievement, your own talents and hard work determine your lot in life. If you achieve good grades in school, you increase your chance of acquiring a professional or managerial job.

Other sociologists cautioned that this scenario of high individual social mobility might not follow from the transformation of the economy. They focused on the reproduction of inequality, emphasizing how advantaged families have long attempted to ensure that their offspring inherit their advantages (Collins, 1979). On the world stage, Blossfeld and Shavit (1993) demonstrated that in 11 of 13 advanced industrial countries, little evidence supports the view that greater equality of opportunity is associated with expanding education systems (Sweden and the Netherlands are the two exceptions). In short, the openness or fluidity of the system of inequality did not increase over the last half of the twentieth century.

Richard Wanner (1999) tested these ideas using Canadian data. He set himself the task of examining whether the growth of education—more high schools, colleges, and universities—benefited people from all social backgrounds equally. He reasoned that if ascription is weaker now than in previous decades, then parents' **socioeconomic status (SES)**—an index combining data on income, education, and occupational prestige—should now have less effect on a child's education than it once had. If in earlier decades the chances of children from disadvantaged families going to university were small, then, in more recent decades, as ascription weakened, these chances should have increased. As measures of socioeconomic background, Wanner used mother's and father's education and father's occupation. He tested his central question by using detailed information from a representative sample of 31 500 Canadians.

Socioeconomic status (SES) combines data on income, education, and occupational prestige in a single index of a person's position in the socioeconomic hierarchy.

Wanner found that class-based ascription still operates strongly. Despite the fact that more Canadians are acquiring more years of schooling and more degrees than ever before, the long arm of family socioeconomic background continues to exert a strong hold on educational attainment. The link has not weakened between family advantage and children's educational achievement.

Explanations for how and why this link remains strong remain a matter of controversy (Davies, 1999). The school system has become increasingly differentiated. Students from lower socioeconomic backgrounds tend to predominate in high-school vocational programs and college diploma programs. Students from higher socioeconomic backgrounds typically attend university. Also, new high-school programs have proliferated, including storefront schools for "at-risk" students in disadvantaged neighbourhoods, language-immersion streams, private schools, and enriched learning tracks. These types of schools tend to enrol students from diverse socioeconomic backgrounds. In other words, educational opportunities are now more numerous for everyone, but they are highly stratified and therefore tend to perpetuate inequalities rather than erase them.

To emphasize this last point, sociologists distinguish "equality of opportunity" from "equality of condition." Equality of opportunity focuses on the chances of participation, while equality of condition focuses on the chances of succeeding. Both forms of equality are connected to social class. Not only do students from lower economic classes experience restricted access to certain types of schooling, but they have weaker supports for taking advantage of available opportunities (Reardon, 2011). By way of analogy, we may all be able to enter the race, but if you come with track shoes and good coaching and I come with boots and no coaching, your chances of winning are higher, assuming we have equal athletic skills.

Finally, we must note that young people are especially likely to experience limited upward mobility if they enter the job market during a recession, a period of declining economic activity (Harvey and Kalwa, 1983). During a recession, unemployment increases, making it more difficult to find a job. Young people who do find a job must often take work below the level for which they are trained. When the economic downturn ends, and employment picks up, employers are inclined to hire not the young people who have been unemployed or underemployed for a few years but a still more junior cohort of young people, who tend to be better trained and more willing to work for lower wages. Thus, young people who enter the job market during a recession are likely to experience relatively low upward mobility over their entire careers. For example, the global recession of 2008–09 created a cohort of job market entrants, many of them with university and college degrees, who now realize that they may never achieve the economic successes of their parents' generation (Smith, 2012).

TIME FOR REVIEW

- What does social mobility research tell us about the extent of upward mobility in Canada?
- What are the implications of social mobility research for functionalist theory?
- How does equality of opportunity differ from equality of condition?

PERCEPTIONS OF CLASS INEQUALITY

We expect you have had some strong reactions to our review of sociological theories and research on social stratification. You may therefore find it worthwhile to reflect more systematically on your own attitudes to social inequality. To start with, do you consider the family in which you grew up to have been lower class, working class, middle class, or upper class? Do you think the gaps between classes in Canadian society are big, moderate, or small? How strongly do you agree or disagree with the view that big gaps between classes are needed to motivate people to work hard and maintain national prosperity? How strongly do you agree or disagree with the view that inequality persists because it benefits the rich and the powerful? How strongly do you agree or disagree with the view that inequality persists because ordinary people don't join together to get rid of it? Answering these questions will help you clarify the way you perceive and evaluate the Canadian class structure and your place in it. If you take note of your answers, you can compare them with the responses of representative samples of Canadians, which we review below.

Surveys show that few Canadians have trouble placing themselves in the class structure when asked to do so. Most Canadians consider themselves to be middle class or working class. They also think that the gaps between classes are relatively large. But do Canadians think that these big gaps are needed to motivate people to work hard, thus increasing their own wealth and the wealth of the nation? Some Canadians think so, but most do not. A survey conducted in 18 countries, including Canada, asked more than 22 000 respondents whether large differences in income are necessary for national prosperity. Canadians were among the most likely to disagree with that view (Pammett, 1997: 77).

So, Canadians know that they live in a class-divided society. They also tend to think that deep class divisions are not necessary for national prosperity. Why then do Canadians think inequality persists? The 18-nation survey cited above sheds light on this issue. One of the survey questions asked respondents how strongly they agree or disagree with the view that "inequality continues because it benefits the rich and powerful." Most Canadians agreed with that statement. Only about a quarter of them disagreed with it in any way. Another question asked respondents how strongly they agree or disagree with the view that "inequality continues because ordinary people don't join together to get rid of it." Again, most Canadians agreed, with less than one-third disagreeing in any way (Pammett, 1997: 77–78).

Despite widespread awareness of inequality and considerable dissatisfaction with it, most Canadians are opposed to the government playing an active role in reducing inequality. Most do not want government to provide citizens with a basic income. They tend to oppose government job-creation programs. They even resist the idea that government should reduce income differences through taxation (Pammett, 1997: 81). Most Canadians remain individualistic and self-reliant. On the whole, they persist in the belief that opportunities for mobility are abundant and that it is up to the individual to make something of those opportunities by means of talent and effort.

Significantly, however, all the attitudes summarized above vary by class position. For example, discontent with the level of inequality in Canadian society is stronger at the bottom of the stratification system than at the top. The belief that Canadian society is full of opportunities for upward mobility is stronger at the top of the class hierarchy than at the bottom. The idea that government should reduce inequality has considerably less opposition as we move down the stratification system. We conclude that, if Canadians allow inequality to persist, it is because the balance of attitudes—and of power—favours continuity over change. We take up this important theme again in Chapter 14 (Politics), where we discuss the social roots of politics.

TIME FOR REVIEW

- How do Canadians view the level of social inequality in Canada and the possible means for reducing it?
- How do Canadians' perceptions of the class system vary by social class?

SUMMARY

1. **How is economic inequality measured?**
   Standard measures of economic inequality are based on income quintile shares. One measure compares the income quintile share of the top 20 percent of families to that of the bottom 20 percent. A second measure is the Gini index, which ranges from 0 (perfect equality, where each household earns the same amount) to 1 (perfect inequality, where one household earns everything).

2. **How has the level of income inequality changed over time?**
   Since the early 1990s, the level of economic inequality in Canada has increased substantially. Income inequality is lower in Canada than in the United States but considerably higher than in many Western European countries.

3. **What types of capital contribute to economic success?**
   Capital refers to useful assets. Everyone is endowed with some measure of natural talent, which is cultivated through education and training to form *human capital*. The transformation of human capital is enhanced through the social networks that comprise *social capital* and the social skills (including manners and tastes) that comprise *cultural capital*.

4. What are some of the key characteristics of poverty in Canada?
Canada does not have an official measure of poverty. However, the low-income cutoff suggests that about 13 percent of Canadians are poor. Poverty is surrounded by several myths, including the idea that those living in poverty lack motivation, are mostly immigrants, and stay poor for extended periods. Structural explanations provide better accounts of poverty than do individualistic explanations.

5. What are the main differences between Marxist, Weberian, and functionalist theories of stratification?
Marx's theory of stratification distinguishes classes on the basis of their role in the productive process. It predicts inevitable conflict between the bourgeoisie and the proletariat and the birth of a communist system. Weber distinguished between classes based on their "market relations." His model of stratification included four main classes. He argued that class consciousness may develop under some circumstances but is by no means inevitable. Weber also emphasized prestige and power as important non-economic sources of inequality. Functionalists argue that all components of society—including poverty and the existing level of stratification—contribute to the collective good. Davis and Moore's functional theory of stratification argues that (1) some jobs are more important than others, (2) people need to make sacrifices to train for important jobs, and (3) inequality is required to motivate people to undergo these sacrifices. In this sense, stratification is functional.

6. How do Canadians view the class system?
Most Canadians are aware of the existence of the class system and their place in it. They believe that large inequalities are not necessary to achieve national prosperity. Most Canadians also believe that inequality persists because it serves the interests of the most advantaged members of society and because those who are disadvantaged do not join together to change things. However, most Canadians disapprove of government intervention to lower the level of inequality.

CHAPTER 9

GLOBALIZATION, INEQUALITY, AND DEVELOPMENT

emarto/Thinkstock.com

IN THIS CHAPTER, YOU WILL LEARN TO

- Describe how globalization occurs as people and institutions across the planet become increasingly aware of, and dependent on, one another.
- Appreciate that globalization creates a world that is more homogeneous in some ways and more localized in others.
- Analyze change in the magnitude of inequality on a world scale.
- Assess competing explanations for the persistence of global inequality.
- Identify differences between countries that have recently emerged from poverty and those that have not.
- Understand how the disadvantages of globalization can be minimized.

THE CREATION OF A GLOBAL VILLAGE

© diego_cervo/Istockphoto.com

We are all connected.

Suppose you want to travel to Europe. You might check the Internet to buy an inexpensive plane ticket. You would then get your passport and perhaps download a guidebook. Depending on the kind of person you are, you might spend a lot of time planning and preparing for the trip or you might just pack the basics—your passport, your ticket, a backpack full of clothes, your credit card—and embark on an adventure.

How different things were just 30 years ago. Then, you probably would have gone to see a travel agent first, as most people did when they wanted airline tickets. Next, you would have had to make sure you had not only a valid passport but also visas for quite a few countries. Obtaining a visa was a tedious process. You had to travel to an embassy or a consulate or mail in your passport. Then you had to wait days or weeks to receive the visa. Today, fewer countries require visas.

The next step in organizing the European trip would have involved withdrawing money from your bank account. Automated teller machines (ATMs) were rare, so you likely had to stand in line at the bank to speak to a teller. Next, you had to take the money to the office of a company that sold traveller's cheques because banks did not sell them. When you arrived in Europe, you needed to have local currency, which you could buy only from large banks and moneychangers. Few students had credit cards 30 years ago. Even if you were one of the lucky few, you could use it only in large stores and restaurants in big cities. If you ran out of cash and traveller's cheques, you were in big trouble. You could look for another Canadian tourist and try to convince him or her to take your personal cheque. Alternatively, you could go to a special telephone for international calls, phone home, and have money wired to a major

Jason Dewey/Getty Images

Jason Dewey/Getty Images

Currency conversion, then and now

bank for you. That was time consuming and expensive. Today, most people have credit cards and ATM cards. Even in small European towns, you can charge most of your shopping and restaurant bills on your credit card without using local currency. If you need local currency, you go to an ATM and withdraw money from your home bank account or charge it to your credit card; the ATM automatically converts your dollars to local currency.

Most European cities and towns today have many North American–style supermarkets. Speakers of English are numerous, so social interaction with Europeans is easier. You would have to try hard to get very far from a McDonald's. It is also easy to receive news and entertainment from back home though the Internet. In contrast, each country you visited 30 years ago would have featured a distinct shopping experience. English speakers were rarer. North American fast-food outlets were practically non-existent. Apart from the *International Herald-Tribune*, which was available only in larger towns and cities, North American news was hard to come by. TV featured mostly local programming. You might see an American show now and then, but it would not be in English.

Clearly, the world seems a much smaller place today than it did 30 years ago. Some people go so far as to say that we have created a "global village." But what exactly does that mean? Is the creation of a global village uniformly beneficial? Or does it also have a downside?

The Triumphs and Tragedies of Globalization

As suggested by our two imaginary trips to Europe, separated by a mere 30 years, people throughout the world are now linked together as never before. **Globalization** is occurring as people and institutions across the planet become increasingly aware of, and dependent on, one another. Consider these facts (and see Table 9.1 and Figure 9.1):

Globalization occurs as people and institutions across the planet become increasingly aware of, and dependent on, one another.

- International telecommunication has become easy and inexpensive. In 1930, a three-minute New York–London phone call cost more than $300[1] in today's dollars and only

TABLE 9.1
Indicators of Globalization, 1981/82–2012

	1981/82	2012
International tourist arrivals (millions of people)	277	1,035
Foreign direct investment (billions of dollars)	59	1,400
Internet hosts	213	909 million
International organizations	14 273	66 000+

Source: OECD. 2013. "FDI in Figures." http://www.oecd.org/daf/inv/FDI%20in%20figures.pdf (accessed August 10, 2013); Internet Systems Consortium. 2013. "ISC Domain Survey." http://www.isc.org/services/survey/ (accessed August 10, 2013); Union of International Associations. 013. "The Yearbook of International Organizations." http://www.uia.org/yearbook?qt-yb_intl_orgs=2#qt-yb_intl_orgs (accessed August 10, 2013); World Tourism Organization. 2013. http://www2.unwto.org/ (accessed August 10, 2013).

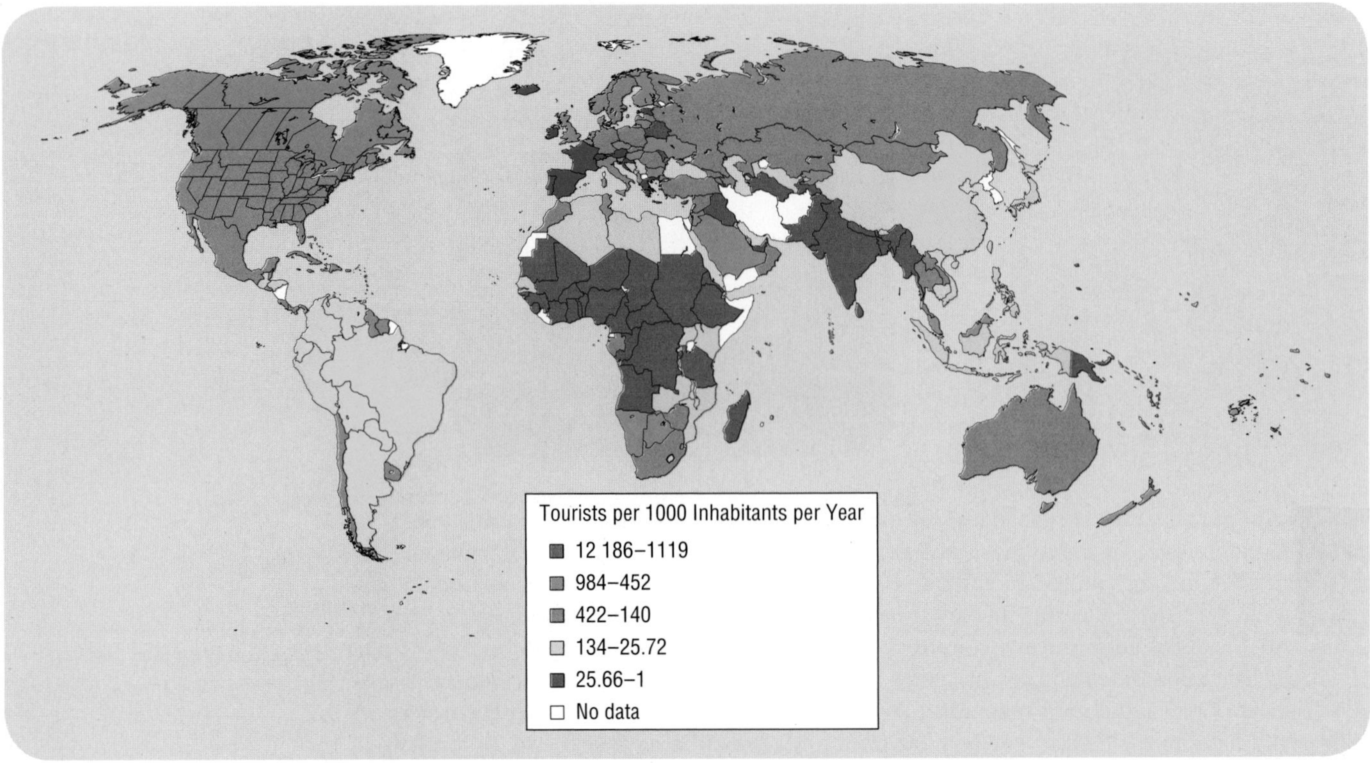

FIGURE 9.1
Foreign Visitors

International tourism leads to the sense that the world forms one society. However, exposure to international tourism is higher in some countries than in others. This map shows the number of foreign visitors who travelled to each country per 1000 country residents in 2008. Which countries are most exposed to international tourism? Which countries are least exposed? What consequences might differential exposure have for people's self-identity?

NationMaster.com. 2013. "Tourist arrivals (per capita) (most recent) by country." www.nationmaster.com/graph/eco_tou_arr4_perap-economy-tourist-arrivals-per-capita. Accessed August 10, 2013.

Imperialism is the economic domination of one country by another.

a minority of North Americans had telephones in their homes. In 2016, you can talk for free on Skype for as long as you want to anyone who has an Internet connection.

- Between 1982 and 2012, the world's population increased by 52 percent but the number of international tourists increased by 274 percent.
- International trade and investment have increased rapidly. For example, from 1982 to 2008, worldwide investment across national borders ("foreign direct investment") increased by a remarkable 2273 percent.
- Many more international organizations and agreements now span the globe. In 1981, about 14 000 international organizations existed. By 2012, there were more than four-and-a-half times as many. Individual nation-states give up some of their independence when they join international organizations or sign international agreements. For example, when Canada, the United States, and Mexico entered the North American Free Trade Agreement (NAFTA) in 1994, they agreed that trade disputes would be settled by a three-country tribunal. The autonomy of nation-states has, to some degree eroded with the creation of many such "transnational" bodies and treaties.
- In 1981, there were just 213 Internet hosts. In 2012, there were 909 million hosts. They connect 2.4 billion people from around the world through instant messaging, email, file transfers, websites, and videoconferencing.

The benefits of the rapid movement of capital, commodities, culture, and people across national boundaries should be clear from comparing our imaginary trips to Europe today and 30 years ago. What was a struggle for a North American traveller three decades ago is easy today. In this and many other ways, globalization has transformed and improved the way we live.

Yet not everyone is happy with globalization. Inequality between rich and poor countries remains staggering. In some respects, it is increasing. Arguably, rather than spreading the wealth, globalized industries and technologies may be turning the world into a more unequal place. Many people also oppose globalization because it may be hurting local cultures and the natural environment. Some anti-globalization activists even suggest that globalization is a form of **imperialism**, the economic domination of one country by another.

From their point of view, globalization puts the entire world under the control of powerful commercial interests. Moreover, it contributes to the homogenization of the world, the cultural domination of less powerful countries by more powerful countries. It is one thing, they say, for Indonesians and Italians to have closer ties to North Americans, but do Indonesians and Italians really want to become *like* North Americans?

In the next section, we first explore what globalization is and how it affects our everyday lives. To make the impact of globalization concrete, we trace the global movement of a commodity familiar to everyone: athletic shoes. This exercise illuminates the many ways in which far-flung individuals are bound together. Next, we consider the causes of globalization, emphasizing the importance of political, economic, and technological factors. We then analyze whether globalization is forcing different parts of the world to become alike. We also explore how globalization generates its own opposition. Finally, we take a longer view and examine the roots of globalization historically.

The second task we set ourselves is to examine the nature and causes of global inequality. We note that the gap between rich and poor countries is wide and, according to some measures, is getting wider. We then discuss the major theories that seek to explain global inequality and conclude that poor countries are not doomed to remain poor. We close by considering what people can do to alleviate global inequality and poverty.

TIME TO REVIEW

- What is globalization?
- What contrasting effects has globalization had on different categories of people?

THE SOURCES AND CONTOURS OF GLOBALIZATION

Globalization in Everyday Life

When we buy a commodity, we often tap into a **global commodity chain**, a worldwide "network of labour and production processes, whose end result is a finished commodity" (Hopkins and Wallerstein, 1986: 159).

A **global commodity chain** is a worldwide network of labour and production processes whose end result is a finished commodity.

We can better understand the web of global social relations by tracing the way one commodity—athletic shoes—binds consumers and producers in a global commodity chain. Until the 1970s, most sports shoes were manufactured in the United States. Today, such corporations as Nike produce all their shoes abroad. Manufacturing plants moved because governments eliminated many of the laws, regulations, and taxes that acted as barriers to foreign investment and trade. Consequently, Nike and other manufacturers started setting up overseas plants, where they could take advantage of low labour costs. The result was a new international division of labour. High-wage management, finance, design, and marketing services were concentrated in the United States and other advanced industrial countries, low-wage manufacturing in the less developed, industrializing countries (Fröbel, Heinrichs, and Kreye, 1980; Chapter 13, Work and the Economy). Not just Nike but General Motors, General Electric, and many other large corporations closed some or all their plants in the United States and Canada (high-wage countries) and established factories in Mexico, Indonesia, and other developing economies.

In Vietnam, Nike workers make 20 cents an hour. At that rate, the labour cost for a $100 pair of Nikes is 37 cents ("Campaign for Labour Rights," 2004). Many Indonesian workers must work as much as six hours overtime each day. Reports of beatings and sexual harassment by managers are common. When the Indonesian workers tried to form a union, organizers were fired and the military was brought in to restore order (LaFeber, 1999: 142). When Michael Jordan became Nike's poster boy in 1976, his $20 million endorsement fee was bigger than the combined yearly wages of all 25 000 Indonesian workers who made the shoes (LaFeber, 1999: 107). Kobe Bryant's endorsement fee, negotiated in 2005, was $45 million ("Kobe Bryant," 2005).

When people buy a pair of Nike athletic shoes, they insert themselves in a global commodity chain. Of course, the buyers do not create the social relations that exploit Indonesian labour and enrich Kobe Bryant. Still, it would be difficult to deny the buyers' part, however small, in helping those social relations persist (see Box 9.1).

Sociology makes us aware of the complex web of social relations and interactions in which we are embedded. The sociological imagination allows us to link our biography with history and social structure. Globalization extends the range of that linkage, connecting our biography with global history and global social structure.

BOX 9.1

SOCIAL POLICY: WHAT DO YOU THINK?

Vote

CAN WORK CONDITIONS BE IMPROVED IN CLOTHING FACTORIES IN DEVELOPING COUNTRIES?

Chances are, most of the clothes you wear come from China, Bangladesh, India, Sri Lanka, and Vietnam. In these countries, labour is relatively inexpensive, environmental and safety standards are comparatively lax, and out of economic necessity, poorly paid workers (mainly women, some of them children) routinely work much longer hours than they do in Canada. We want inexpensive clothing, so most of us prefer not to think much about who makes our clothes and how the workers are treated.

Yet at around 9 a.m. on 24 April 2013, when a clothing factory collapsed near Dhaka, the Bangladeshi capital, Canadians did notice. So did the rest of the world. Some 1132 people died, and more than 2500 were injured because of shoddy building construction, ineffective safety inspections, overcrowding, the desires of the factory owner and Western companies to maximize profits, and Western demand for inexpensive clothing.

After the tragedy, some Western companies, the Bangladeshi government, and the Bangladesh Garment Manufacturers and Exporters Association vowed to compensate the families of the victims and improve working conditions in the country's garment factories (Hossain, 2013). A European-led safety accord was signed by H&M, Zara, and Fast Retailing (Asia's biggest retailer). Other companies, including Walmart, Target, Gap, and Canada's Loblaws (which sells Joe Fresh clothing, made in the collapsed factory) adopted their own initiatives to tighten safety regulations and improve working conditions.

It remains to be seen how much improvement these promises will yield. However, it is worth remembering that in the two years after 146 Jewish and Italian immigrant women died in the 1911 Triangle Shirtwaist Factory fire in New York City, the public outcry and union pressure resulted in 60 new laws being passed, improving safety conditions in the city's factories. It is a sad reflection on the human condition that we must often witness mass death before we are motivated to make the world a better place.

© K. M. Asad/Demotix/Corbis

The Rana Plaza factory collapse, Bangladesh, 24 April 2013.

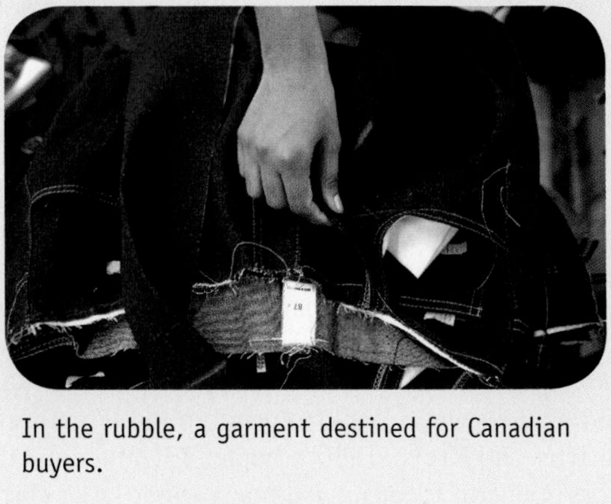

© ANDREW BIRAJ/Reuters/Corbis

In the rubble, a garment destined for Canadian buyers.

Critical Thinking

1. Do you think working conditions in Asian garment factories will improve as a result of the 2013 fire? Why or why not?
2. What would be the most effective means of pressuring Canadian retailers to help improve working conditions in Asian garment factories. Why?

The Sources of Globalization

Few people doubt the significance of globalization. Although social scientists disagree on its exact causes, most of them stress the importance of technology, politics, and economics.

Technology

Technological progress has made it possible to move goods and information over long distances quickly and inexpensively. The introduction of commercial jets radically shortened the time necessary for international travel, and its cost dropped dramatically after the 1950s. Similarly, various means of communication, such as telephone, fax, and email, allow us to reach people around the globe inexpensively and almost instantly. Whether we think of international trade or international travel, technological progress is an important part of the globalization story. Without modern technology, it is hard to imagine how globalization would be possible.

Politics

Globalization could not occur without advanced technology, but advanced technology on its own could never bring about globalization. Think of the contrast between North Korea and South Korea. Both countries are about the same distance from North America. You have probably heard of major South Korean companies, like Hyundai and Samsung, and may have met people from South Korea or Korean Canadians. Yet unless you are an expert on North Korea, you probably will have had no contact with North Korea and its people. We have the same technological means to reach the two Koreas. Yet although we enjoy strong relations and intense interaction with South Korea, Canada did not extend diplomatic recognition to North Korea until 2001. As of 2011, Canada had not yet opened an embassy there. There is no trade between the two countries. The reason is political. The South Korean government has been an ally of Canada since the Korean War in the early 1950s and has sought greater political, economic, and cultural integration with the outside world. North Korea, in an effort to preserve its authoritarian political system and communist economic system, has remained isolated from the rest of the world. As this example shows, politics is important in determining the level of globalization.

Economics

Finally, economics is an important source of globalization. As we saw in our discussion of global commodity chains and the new international division of labour, industrial capitalism is always seeking new markets, higher profits, and lower labour costs. Put differently, capitalist competition has been a major spur to international integration (Gilpin, 2001; Stopford and Strange, 1991).

Transnational corporations—also called multinational or international corporations—are the most important agents of globalization in the world today. They differ from traditional corporations in five ways (Gilpin, 2001; LaFeber, 1999):

Transnational corporations are large businesses with head offices in rich countries. They that rely increasingly on foreign labour and foreign production; skills and advances in design, technology, and management; world markets; and massive advertising campaigns. They are increasingly autonomous from national governments.

1. Traditional corporations rely on domestic labour and domestic production. Transnational corporations depend increasingly on foreign labour and foreign production.
2. Traditional corporations extract natural resources or manufacture industrial goods. Transnational corporations increasingly emphasize skills and advances in design, technology, and management.
3. Traditional corporations sell to domestic markets. Transnational corporations depend increasingly on world markets.
4. Traditional corporations rely on established marketing and sales outlets. Transnational corporations depend increasingly on massive advertising campaigns.
5. Traditional corporations work with or under national governments. Transnational corporations are increasingly autonomous from national governments.

Technological, political, and economic factors do not work independently in leading to globalization. For example, governments often promote economic competition to help transnational corporations win global markets. Consider Philip Morris, the company that makes Marlboro cigarettes (Barnet and Cavanagh, 1994). Philip Morris introduced the Marlboro brand in 1954. It soon became the best-selling cigarette in the United States, partly because of the success of an advertising campaign featuring the Marlboro Man. The Marlboro Man

© John Van Hasselt/Corbis Sygma

symbolized the rugged individualism of the American frontier, and he became one of the most widely recognized icons in American advertising. Philip Morris was the smallest of the country's six largest tobacco companies in 1954, but it rode on the popularity of the Marlboro Man to become the country's biggest tobacco company by the 1970s.

In the 1970s, the anti-smoking campaign began to have an impact, leading to slumping domestic sales. Philip Morris and other tobacco companies decided to pursue globalization as a way out of the doldrums. Economic competition and slick advertising alone did not win global markets for American cigarette makers, however. The tobacco companies needed political influence to make cigarettes one of the country's biggest and most profitable exports. To that end, the U.S. trade representative in the Reagan administration, Clayton Yeutter, worked energetically to dismantle trade barriers in Japan, Taiwan, South Korea, and other countries. He threatened legal action for breaking international trade law and said the United States would restrict Asian exports unless these countries allowed the sale of American cigarettes. Such actions were critically important in globalizing world trade in cigarettes. In 1986, the commercial counsellor of the U.S. Embassy in Seoul, South Korea, wrote to the public affairs manager of Philip Morris Asia as follows: "I want to emphasize that the embassy and the various U.S. government agencies in Washington will keep the interests of Philip Morris and the other American cigarette manufacturers in the forefront of our daily concerns" (quoted in Frankel, 1996). As the case of Philip Morris illustrates, economics and politics typically work hand in hand to globalize the world.

"I want to emphasize that the embassy and the various U.S. government agencies in Washington will keep the interests of Philip Morris and the other American cigarette manufacturers in the forefront of our daily concerns."

A World Like the United States?

We have seen that globalization links people around the world, often in ways that are not obvious. We have also seen that the sources of globalization lie in closely connected technological, economic, and political forces. Now let us consider one of the consequences of globalization, the degree to which globalization is homogenizing the world and, in particular, making the whole world look like the United States (see Figure 9.2).

Much impressionistic evidence supports the view that globalization homogenizes societies. Many economic and financial institutions around the world now operate in roughly the same way. For instance, transnational organizations, such as the World Bank and the

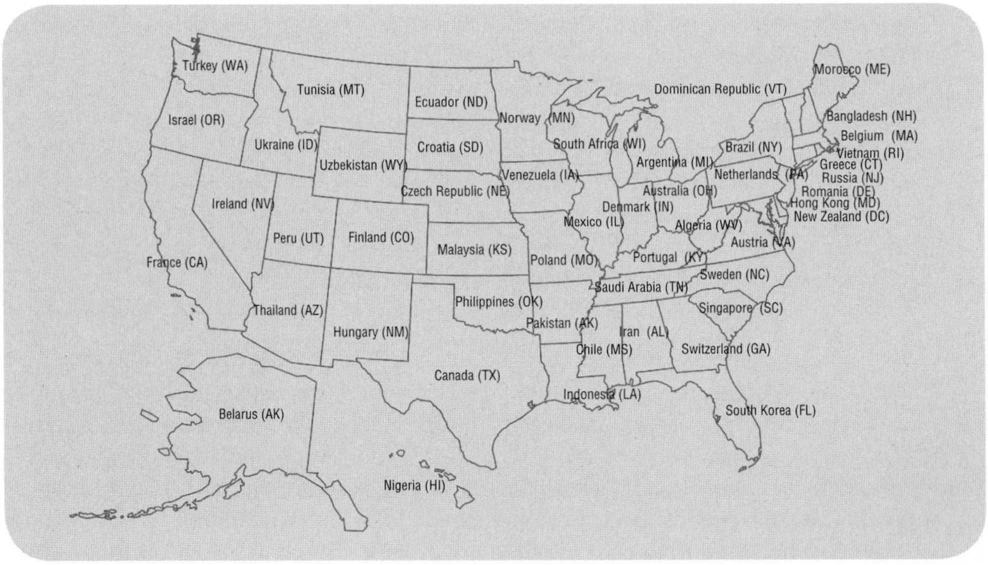

FIGURE 9.2

The Size and Influence of the American Economy

This map will help you gauge the enormous importance of the United States in globalization because it emphasizes just how large the American economy is. The economy of each American state is as big as that of a whole country. Specifically, this map shows how the gross domestic product (GDP) of various countries compares with that of each state. For example, the GDP of California is equal to that of France, the GDP of New Jersey is equal to that of Russia, and the GDP of Texas is equal to that of Canada.

Source: From *The Globe and Mail*, March 8, 2003, p. F1. Reprinted with permission from The Globe and Mail.

International Monetary Fund, have imposed economic guidelines for developing countries that are similar to those governing advanced industrial countries. In the realm of politics, the United Nations (UN) engages in global governance, whereas Western ideas of democracy, representative government, and human rights have become international ideals. In the domain of culture, American icons circle the planet: supermarkets, basketball, Hollywood movies, Disney characters, Coca-Cola, MTV, CNN, McDonald's, and so on.

Indeed, one common shorthand expression for the homogenizing effects of globalization is **McDonaldization**. George Ritzer (1996: 1) defines McDonaldization as "the process by which the principles of the fast-food restaurant are coming to dominate more and more sectors of American society as well as of the rest of the world." The idea of McDonaldization extends Weber's concept of rationalization, the application of the most efficient means to achieve given ends (Chapter 3, Culture). Because of McDonaldization, says Ritzer, the values of efficiency, calculability, and predictability have spread from North America to the entire planet and from fast-food restaurants to virtually all spheres of life. As Ritzer shows, McDonald's leaves nothing to chance. McDonald's is even field-testing self-service kiosks in which an automated machine cooks and bags French fries while a vertical grill takes patties from the freezer and grills them to your liking (Carpenter, 2003). Significantly, McDonald's now does most of its business outside the United States. You can find McDonald's restaurants in nearly every country in the world. McDonaldization has come to stand for the global spread of values associated with the United States and its business culture.

McDonaldization is a form of rationalization. It refers to the spread of the principles of fast-food restaurants—efficiency, predictability, and calculability—to all spheres of life.

However, anyone familiar with symbolic interactionism should be immediately suspicious of sweeping claims about the homogenizing effects of globalization. After all, it is a central principle of symbolic interactionism that people create their social circumstances and do not merely react to them, that they negotiate their identities and do not easily settle for identities imposed on them by others. Accordingly, some analysts find fault with the view that globalization is making the world a more homogeneous place based on North American values. They argue that people always interpret globalizing forces in terms of local conditions and traditions. Globalization, they say, may in fact sharpen some local differences. They have invented the term **glocalization** to describe the simultaneous homogenization of some aspects of life and the strengthening of some local differences under the impact of globalization (Shaw, 2000).

Glocalization is the simultaneous homogenization of some aspects of life and the strengthening of some local differences under the impact of globalization.

They note, for example, that McDonald's serves different foods in different countries (Watson, 1997). A burger at a Taiwanese McDonald's may be eaten with betel nuts. Vegetarian burgers are available at Indian McDonald's, and kosher burgers are the norm at Israeli McDonald's. Dutch McDonald's serves the popular McKrocket, made of 100 percent beef ragout fried in batter. In Hawaii, McDonald's routinely serve Japanese ramen noodles with their burgers. McDonald's began serving poutine in Québec, and the practice has spread across Canada to consumers undeterred by McDonald's nutrition guide, which lists a large serving as providing 130 percent of the recommended daily allowance for saturated fat (McDonald's Corporation, 2005). Although the Golden Arches may suggest that the world is becoming the same everywhere, once we go through them and sample the fare, we find much that is unique.

Those who see globalization merely as homogenization also ignore the **regionalization** of the world, the division of the world into different and often competing economic, political, and cultural areas. The argument here is that the institutional and cultural integration of countries often falls far short of covering the whole world. Figure 9.3 illustrates one aspect of regionalization. World trade is unevenly distributed across the planet and it is not dominated by just one country. Three main trade blocs exist—an Asian bloc dominated by Japan and China, a North American bloc dominated by the United States, and a European bloc dominated by Germany. These three trade blocs contain just over a fifth of the world's countries but account for more than three-quarters of world economic activity as measured by gross domestic product.[2] Most world trade takes place *within* each of these blocs. Each bloc competes against the others for a larger share of world trade. Politically, we can see regionalization in the growth of the European Union. Most Western European–bloc countries now share the same currency, the euro, and they coordinate economic, political, military, social, and cultural policies.

Regionalization is the division of the world into different and often competing economic, political, and cultural areas.

FIGURE 9.3
The Regionalization of World Trade

Source: Geoffrey York. "Asian Trade Bloc Would Rival NAFTA, EU." *Globe and Mail*. August 24, 2006. Pg. B1.

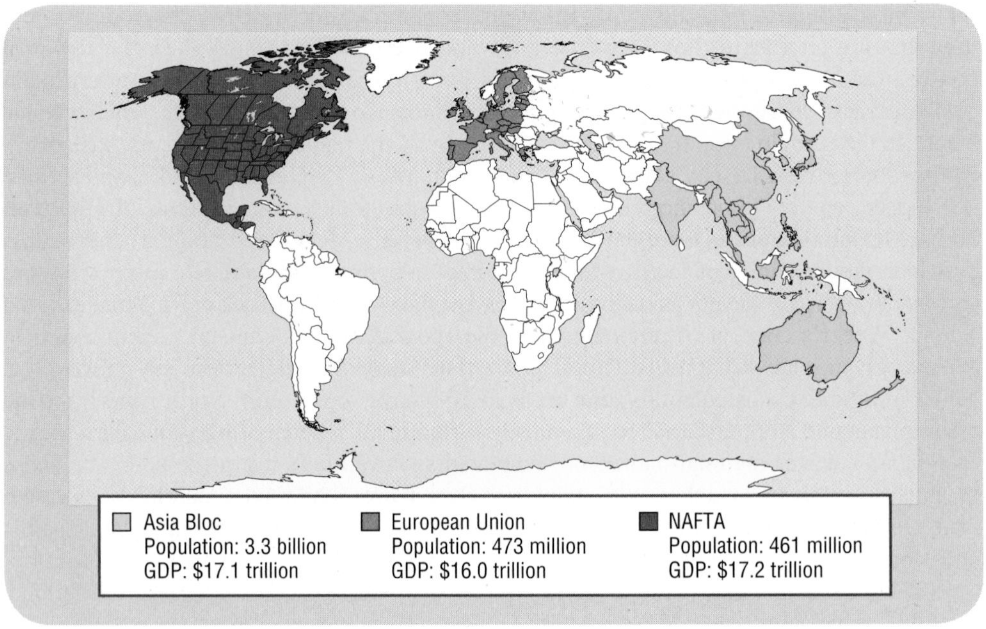

We conclude that globalization does not have a simple, one-way, and inevitable consequence. In fact, as you will now learn, its impact is often messy. Globalization has generated much criticism and opposition, unleashing a growing anti-globalization movement.

Globalization and Its Discontents: Anti-globalization and Anti-Americanism

In 1996, political scientist Benjamin Barber published an important book titled *Jihad vs. McWorld*. Barber argued that globalization (the making of what he called "McWorld") was generating an anti-globalization reaction, which he called *jihad*. *Jihad* means "striving" or "struggle" in Arabic. Traditionally, Muslims use the term to refer to perseverance in achieving a high moral standard. The term can also suggest the idea of a holy war against those who harm Muslims. In the latter sense, it represents an Islamic fundamentalist reaction to globalization. The most spectacular and devastating manifestations of fundamentalist Islamic *jihad* were the September 11, 2001, jet hijackings that led to the crash of an airliner in Pennsylvania and the destruction of the World Trade Center and part of the Pentagon. About 3000 people, 24 of them Canadians, lost their lives as a result of these attacks. The operatives of the al-Qaeda network sought to roll back the forces of globalization by attacking what they considered to symbolize the global reach of godless American capitalism.

Islamic fundamentalism is the most far-reaching and violent of many reactions against globalization throughout the world. A much less violent reaction is the anti-globalization movement in the advanced industrial countries (Klein, 2000). In 1994, the governments of 134 countries set up the World Trade Organization (WTO) to encourage and referee global commerce. When the WTO met in Seattle in December 1999, some 40 000 union activists, environmentalists, supporters of worker and peasant movements in developing countries, and other opponents of transnational corporations staged protests that caused property damage and threatened to disrupt the proceedings. The police and the National Guard responded with concussion grenades, tear gas, rubber bullets, and mass arrests.

In 2010–11, the Arab Spring and the Occupy Movement were widely identified as rebellions caused partly by globalization. The Occupy Movement sought to publicize and protest growing inequality—not just between the richest and the poorest countries but also between the richest and poorest people in rich countries. Since the 1970s, multinational corporations had been shutting down North American factories and relocating their operations in low-wage countries, resulting in bigger profits for shareholders and salaries for executives, but fewer good jobs for North American workers. Following the 2008–09 financial crisis, which resulted in even more layoffs, government cutbacks, and mortgage foreclosures, members of the Occupy Movement took to the streets.

Some Occupy Movement protesters were inspired by the rebellion against authoritarian regimes that originated in Tunisia, spread throughout the Middle East and North Africa, and came to be known as the Arab Spring. Authoritarian regimes in Egypt and elsewhere in the region have been supported for decades by American military and civilian aid, yet little economic progress took place outside the oil-producing countries. Democracy remained a pipe dream. The Arab Spring sought to rectify this state of affairs.

The Occupy Movement and the Arab Spring will be discussed in greater detail in Chapter 21, Collective Action and Social Movements. Mentioning them here highlights two facts. First, globalization is far from universally welcome. Second, the anti-globalization movement has many currents. Some are extremely violent, others nonviolent. Some reject only what they regard as the excesses of globalization, others reject globalization in its entirety. This complexity supports our view that globalization is not a simple process with predictable consequences. It is a multifaceted phenomenon, the outcome of which is unclear.

The History of Globalization

The extent of globalization since about 1980 is unprecedented in world history. Sociologist Martin Albrow therefore argues that the "global age" is only a few decades old (Albrow, 1997). He dates it from the spread of global awareness and skepticism about the benefits of modernization. However, Albrow and others are inclined to exaggerate the extent of globalization (Gilpin, 2001; Hirst and Thompson, 1999). The nation-state is still a major centre of power in the world. National borders remain important. Most companies concentrate their business in a single country. Most foreign trade occurs between advanced industrial countries and, as we have seen, within distinct regional groups of advanced industrial countries. Many developing countries are poorly integrated in the global economy. Most people in the world have little or no access to the advanced technologies that exemplify globalization, such as email. Cultural differences remain substantial across the planet.

Furthermore, globalization is not as recent as Albrow would have us believe. Anthony Giddens (1990) argues that globalization is the result of industrialization and modernization, which picked up pace in the late nineteenth century. And, in fact, a strong case can be made that the world was highly globalized 100 or more years ago. In the late nineteenth century, people could move across national borders without passports. The extent of international trade and capital flow in the late twentieth century only restored the level achieved before World War I (1914–18; Hirst and Thompson, 1999).

World War I and the Great Depression (1929–39) undermined the globalization of the late nineteenth and early twentieth centuries. They incited racism, protectionism, and military build-up and led to Nazi and communist dictatorships that culminated in World War II (1939–45; Hobsbawm, 1994; James, 2001). International trade and investment plummeted between 1914 and 1945, and governments erected many new barriers to the free movement of people and ideas. A longer view of globalization suggests that globalization is not an inevitable and linear process. Periods of accelerated globalization—including our own—can end.

An even longer historical view leads to additional insight. Some sociologists, such as Roland Robertson (1992), note that globalization is as old as civilization itself and is in fact the *cause* of modernization rather than the other way around. Archaeological remains show that long-distance trade began 5000 years ago. People have been migrating across continents and even oceans for thousands of years. Alexander the Great conquered vast stretches of Europe, western Asia, and northern Africa, while Christianity and Islam spread far beyond their birthplace in the Middle East. All these forces contributed to globalization in Robertson's view.

So is globalization 30, 125, or 5000 years old, as suggested by, respectively, Albrow, Giddens, and Robertson? The question has no correct answer. The answer depends on what we want globalization to mean. A short historical view—whether 125 or 30 years—misses the long-term developments that have brought the world's people closer to one another.

Yet if we think of globalization as a 5000-year-old phenomenon, the definition and value of the term are diluted.

Colonialism is the direct political control of one country by another.

We prefer to take an intermediate position, by thinking of globalization as a roughly 500-year-old phenomenon. We regard the establishment of colonies and the growth of capitalism as the main forces underlying globalization, and both **colonialism** and capitalism began about 500 years ago, symbolized by Columbus's voyage to the Americas. (Colonialism is the direct political control of one country by another.) As you will now see, the main advantage of thinking of globalization in this way is that it tells us much about the causes of development or industrialization and the growing gap between rich and poor countries and people. These topics will now be the focus of our attention.

TIME TO REVIEW

- What are the main causes of globalization?
- What tendencies suggest that globalization does not always "homogenize" people?
- When did globalization begin on a wide scale?

DEVELOPMENT AND UNDERDEVELOPMENT

John Lie decided to study sociology because he was concerned about the poverty and dictatorships he had read about in books and observed during his travels in Asia and Latin America. "Initially," says John, "I thought I would major in economics. In my economics classes, I learned about the importance of birth-control programs to cap population growth, efforts to prevent the runaway growth of cities, and measures to spread Western knowledge, technology, and markets to people in less economically developed countries. My textbooks and professors assumed that if only the less-developed countries would become more like the West, their populations, cities, economies, and societies would experience stable growth. Otherwise, the developing countries were doomed to suffer the triple catastrophe of overpopulation, rapid urbanization, and economic underdevelopment.

"Equipped with this knowledge, I spent a summer in the Philippines working for an organization that offered farmers advice on how to promote economic growth. I assumed that, as in North America, farmers who owned large plots of land and used high technology would be more efficient and better off. Yet I found the most productive villages were those in which most farmers owned *small* plots of land. In such villages, there was little economic inequality. The women in these villages enjoyed low birth rates and the inhabitants were usually happier than were the inhabitants of villages in which there was more inequality.

"As I talked with the villagers, I came to realize that farmers who owned at least some of their own land had an incentive to work hard. The harder they worked, the more they earned. With a higher standard of living, they didn't need as many children to help them on the farm. In contrast, in villages with greater inequality, many farmers owned no land but leased it or worked as farm hands for wealthy landowners. They didn't earn more for working harder, so their productivity and their standard of living were low. They wanted to have more children to increase household income.

"Few Filipino farms could match the productivity of high-tech North American farms, because even large plots were small by North American standards. Much high-tech agricultural equipment would have been useless there. Imagine trying to use a harvesting machine in a plot not much larger than some suburban backyards.

"Thus, my Western assumptions turned out to be wrong. The Filipino farmers I met were knowledgeable and thoughtful about their needs and desires. When I started listening to them, I started understanding the real world of economic development. It was one of the most important sociological lessons I ever learned."

Let us begin our sociological discussion of economic development by examining trends in levels of global inequality. We then discuss two theories of development and underdevelopment, both of which seek to uncover the sources of inequality among nations. Next, we analyze some cases of successful development. Finally, we consider what we can do to alleviate global inequality in light of what we learn from these successful cases.

Levels and Trends in Global Inequality

We learned in Chapter 8 (Social Stratification) that Canada is a highly stratified society. When we shift our attention from the national to the global level, we find an even more dramatic gap between rich and poor. In a Manhattan restaurant, pet owners can treat their cats to $100-a-plate birthday parties. In Cairo (Egypt) and Manila (the Philippines), garbage dumps are home to entire families who sustain themselves by picking through the refuse. People who travel outside the two dozen or so highly industrialized countries of North America, Western Europe, Japan, and Australia often encounter scenes of unforgettable poverty and misery. The UN calls the level of inequality worldwide "grotesque" (United Nations, 2002: 19). The term is justified when you consider that that the citizens of the two dozen richest countries spend more on cosmetics or alcohol or ice cream or pet food than it would take to provide basic education, or water and sanitation, or basic health and nutrition for everyone in the world (Table 9.2).

Has global inequality increased or decreased over time? That depends on how you measure it. If you define inequality as the difference between the average incomes of rich and poor countries, you find that income inequality was very high in 1950 and is even higher now (see the bottom line in Figure 9.4). However, this comparison gives equal weight to each country, whether it is a behemoth like China or a tiny city-state like Monaco.

It makes sense to count populous countries more heavily in our calculations. Doing so reveals that income inequality between countries was extremely high in 1950 but declined thereafter, mainly because China started to prosper in the early 1980s and India and Brazil followed suit a little later (see the middle line in Figure 9.4). The emergence of large, new middle classes in these populous countries caused the level of income inequality among countries weighted for population size to fall. Nevertheless, economic conditions in some parts of the world deteriorated. In the four decades between 1972 and 2012, per capita income in sub-Saharan Africa fell by nearly 10 percent taking inflation into account (United Nations, 2010b, 2013).

Photo by Miro Cernetig, Globe & Mail, Toronto, Canada

A half-hour's drive from the centre of Manila, the capital of the Philippines, an estimated 70 000 Filipinos live on a 22-hectare (55-acre) mountain of rotting garbage, 45 metres (150 feet) high. It is infested with flies, rats, dogs, and disease. On a lucky day, residents can earn up to $5 retrieving scraps of metal and other valuables. On a rainy day, the mountain of garbage is especially treacherous. In July 2000, an avalanche buried 300 people alive. People who live on the mountain of garbage call it "The Promised Land."

TABLE 9.2

Global Priorities: Annual Cost of Various Goods and Services (in US$ billion)

Note: Items in italics represent estimates of what they would cost to achieve. Other items represent estimated actual cost.

Good or Service	Cost (in US$ billions)
Additional annual cost, basic education for everyone in the world	6.3
Additional annual cost, water and sanitation for everyone in the world	12.4
Annual dog and cat food sales, USA	18.6
Additional annual cost, reproductive health care for all women in the world	18.6
Additional annual cost, basic health and nutrition for everyone in the world	20.1
Annual global perfume sales	27.5
Annual TV advertising, USA	60.0
Annual global revenue, strip clubs	75.0
Annual global revenue, cocaine sales (2008)	88.0
Annual beer sales, USA	96.0
Annual global arms sales	1700.0

Sources: Bureau of Labor Statistics. "CPI Inflation Calculator." http://data.bls.gov/cgi-bin/cpicalc.pl?cost1=1&year1=1998&year2=2011 (accessed December 28, 2012); Negative Population Growth. "Total Midyear World Population, 1950-2050." www.npg.org/facts/world_pop_year.htm (accessed December 28, 2012); United Nations. World Development Report 1998 (New York: Oxford University Press): 37. United Nations data for 1998 are adjusted for world population increase, 1998–2011, and the US consumer price index, 1998–2011; Pet Food Institute. 2012. "U.S. Pet Food Sales." www.petfoodinstitute.org/Index.cfm?Page=USPetFoodSales (accessed December 28, 2012); Statistic Brain. 2012. www.statisticbrain.com/ (retrieved 28 December 2012); United Nations. 2012. "The Global Cocaine Market." www.unodc.org/documents/wdr/WDR_2010/1.3_The_globa_cocaine_market.pdf (accessed December 28, 2012); Global Issues. "World Military Expenditures." 2012. www.globalissues.org/article/75/world-military-spending#WorldMilitarySpending (accessed December 28, 2012).

FIGURE 9.4

Three Concepts of World Inequality

A Gini index of 0 indicates that every income recipient receives exactly the same amount of income. A Gini index of 1.0 indicates that a single income recipient receives all of the income. To put things in perspective, note that the Gini index of inequality for individuals worldwide is about 0.70, while the Gini index for individuals in Brazil, which has one of the highest levels of inequality of any country, is about 0.52.

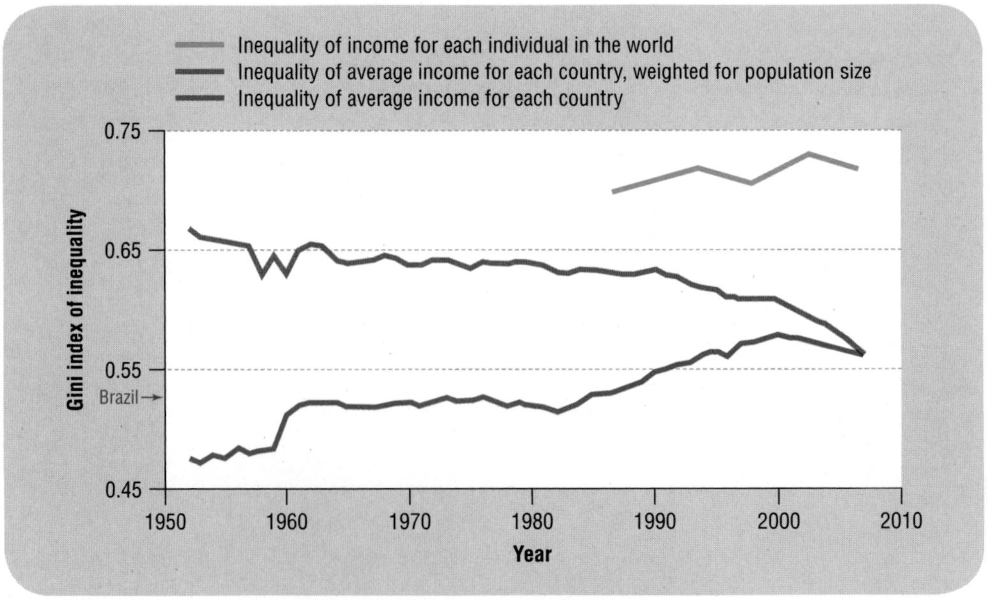

Source: Milanovic, Branko. 2010. "The Consequences of Inequality and Wealth Distribution." Accessed February 16, 2010 (http://ineteconomics.org/people/participants/branko-milanovic).

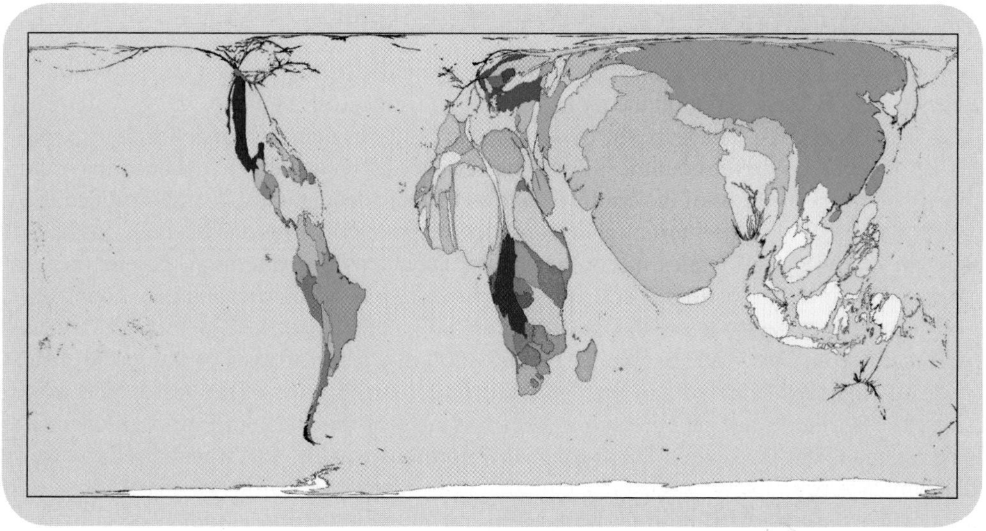

FIGURE 9.5
World Poverty.

Note: The size of each country is proportional to the percentage of people in that country living on US$2 a day or less in purchasing power.

Source: University of Sheffield. 2006. "Absolute Poverty."

A problem remains. Comparing country averages ignores the fact that poor people live in rich countries and rich people live in poor countries. Country averages fail to capture the extent of inequality between the richest of the rich and the poorest of the poor. That is why it makes most sense to examine income inequality among *individuals* rather than among countries. Doing so, we discover that income inequality was astoundingly steep in 1985 and has risen even higher since then (see the top line in Figure 9.4). Today, the richest 1 percent of the world's population (about 70 million people) earn as much as the bottom 66 percent (about 4.6 billion people) (Milovic, 2010). About 14 percent of the world's people live on less than $1 a day, and 37 percent on less than $2 a day (see Figure 9.5). Most people living in desperate poverty are women. On the slightly brighter side, the absolute number of people in the world living on less than $1 a day peaked in 1950 and then started declining. In percentage terms, the proportion of people living on less than $1 a day fell from about 84 percent in 1820 to less than 20 percent today (United Nations, 2007: 24).

Statistics never speak for themselves. We need theories to explain them. Let us now outline and critically assess the two main theories that seek to explain the origins and persistence of global inequality.

Modernization Theory: A Functionalist Approach

Two main sociological theories claim to explain global inequality. The first, **modernization theory**, is a variant of functionalism. According to modernization theory, global inequality results from various dysfunctional characteristics of poor societies themselves. Specifically, modernization theorists say the citizens of poor societies lack sufficient *capital* to invest in Western-style agriculture and industry. They lack rational, Western-style *business techniques* of marketing, accounting, sales, and finance. As a result, their productivity and profitability remain low. They lack stable, Western-style *governments* that could provide a secure framework for investment. Finally, they lack a Western *mentality*: values that stress the need for savings, investment, innovation, education, high achievement, and self-control in having children (Inkeles and Smith, 1976; Rostow, 1960). Societies characterized by these dysfunctions are considered to be poor. It follows that people living in rich countries can best help their poor cousins by transferring Western culture and capital to them and eliminating the dysfunctions. Only then will the poor countries be able to cap population growth, stimulate democracy, and invigorate agricultural and industrial production. Government-to-government foreign aid can accomplish some of this change. However, much work also needs to be done to encourage Western businesses to invest directly in poor countries and to increase trade between rich and poor countries.

Modernization theory holds that economic underdevelopment results from poor countries lacking Western attributes. These attributes include Western values, business practices, levels of investment capital, and stable governments.

Dependency Theory: A Conflict Approach

Dependency theory views economic underdevelopment as the result of exploitative relations between rich and poor countries.

Proponents of **dependency theory**, a variant of conflict theory, have been quick to point out the chief flaw in modernization theory (Baran, 1957; Cardoso and Faletto, 1979; Wallerstein, 1974–89). For the past 500 years, the most powerful countries in the world deliberately impoverished the less powerful countries. Focusing on internal characteristics blames the victim rather than the perpetrator of the crime. It follows that an adequate theory of global inequality should not focus on the internal characteristics of poor countries themselves. Instead, it ought to follow the principles of conflict theory and focus on patterns of domination and submission—specifically, in this case, on the *relationship* between rich and poor countries.

According to dependency theorists, less global inequality existed in 1500 and even in 1750 than today. However, beginning around 1500, the armed forces of the world's most powerful countries subdued and then annexed or colonized most of the rest of the world. Around 1780, the Industrial Revolution began. It enabled the Western European countries, Russia, Japan, and the United States to amass enormous wealth, which they used to extend their global reach. They forced their colonies to become sources of raw materials, cheap labour, investment opportunities, and markets for the conquering nations. The colonizers thereby prevented industrialization and locked the colonies into poverty.

In the decades following World War II, nearly all the colonies in the world became politically independent. However, the dependency theorists say that exploitation by direct political control was soon replaced by new means of achieving the same end: substantial foreign investment, support for authoritarian governments, and mounting debt.

- *Substantial foreign investment.* Many people assume that investment is always a good thing. According to dependency theorists, however, investment by multinational corporations has positive consequences for rich countries and negative consequences for poor countries. According to these theorists, investment in poor countries is typically used only to extract raw materials, create low-wage jobs, and siphon off wealth in the form of profits. The raw materials are used to create high-wage jobs in design, research, manufacturing, and administration back in the rich countries, where multinational corporations situate their head offices. Some of the manufactured goods are then sold back to the poor, unindustrialized countries for additional profit. Dependency theorists conclude that, for poor countries, the disadvantages of foreign investment far outweigh the advantages.
- *Support for authoritarian governments.* According to dependency theorists, multinational corporations and rich countries continued their exploitation of the poor countries in the postcolonial period by extending economic and military support to local authoritarian governments. These governments managed to keep their populations subdued most of the time. When that was not possible, Western governments sent in troops and military advisers, engaging in what became known as "gunboat diplomacy." The term was coined in colonial times. In 1839, the Chinese rebelled against the British importation of opium into China, and the British responded by sending a gunboat up the Yangtze River, which started the Opium War. This war resulted in Britain winning control of Hong Kong and access to five Chinese ports; what started as gunboat diplomacy ended as a rich feast for British traders. In the postcolonial period, the United States has been particularly active in using gunboat diplomacy in Central America. A classic case is Guatemala in the 1950s (LaFeber, 1993). In 1952, the democratic government of Guatemala began to redistribute land to impoverished peasants. Some of the land was owned by the United Fruit Company, a United States multinational corporation and the biggest landowner in Guatemala. Two years later, the CIA backed a right-wing coup in Guatemala, preventing land reform and allowing the United Fruit Company to continue its highly profitable business as usual.
- *Mounting debt.* The governments of the poor countries struggled to create transportation infrastructure, including airports, roads, and harbours; build their education systems; and deliver safe water and the most basic health care to their people. To accomplish these tasks, they needed to borrow money from Western banks and governments. Some

rulers also squandered money on luxuries. So it came about that debt—and the interest payments that inevitably accompany debt—grew every year. By 2008, the total debt of poor countries amounted to \$3.7 trillion. Interest payments were \$1.6 billion a day. Government foreign aid helps, but not much. It amounts to less than 10 percent of interest payments (Jubilee Debt Campaign, 2010: 6; OECD, 2008: 6).

Weidenfeld and Nicolson Archives

In 1893, leaders of the British mission pose before taking over what became Rhodesia and is now Zimbabwe. To raise a volunteer army, every British trooper was offered about 23 square kilometres (9 square miles) of native land and 20 gold claims. The Matabele and Mashona peoples were subdued in a three-month war. Nine hundred farms and 10 000 gold claims were granted to the troopers and about 100 000 cattle were looted, leaving the native survivors without a livelihood. Forced labour was subsequently introduced by the British so that the natives could pay a £2 a year tax.

Core, Periphery, and Semiperiphery

Although dependency theory provides a more realistic account of the sources of global inequality than modernization theory does, it leaves a big question unanswered: how have some countries managed to escape poverty and start rapid economic development? After all, the world does not consist just of **core capitalist countries** that are major sources of capital and technology (the United States, Japan, and Germany) and **peripheral capitalist countries** that are major sources of raw materials and cheap labour (the former colonies). In addition, a middle tier of **semiperipheral capitalist countries** consists of former colonies that are making considerable headway in their attempts to become prosperous (South Korea, Taiwan, and Israel, for example; Wallerstein, 1974–89). Comparing the poor peripheral countries with the more successful semiperipheral countries presents us with a useful natural experiment. The comparison suggests the circumstances that help some poor countries overcome the worst effects of colonialism.

The semiperipheral countries differ from the peripheral countries in four main ways (Kennedy, 1993: 193–227; Lie, 1998), which we outline below.

Type of Colonialism

Around the turn of the twentieth century, Taiwan and Korea became colonies of Japan. They remained so until 1945. However, in contrast to the European colonizers of Africa, Latin America, and other parts of Asia, the Japanese built up the economies of their colonies. They established transportation networks and communication systems. They built steel, chemical, and hydroelectric power plants. After Japanese colonialism ended, Taiwan and South Korea were thus at an advantage compared with Ghana, for example, at the time Britain gave up control of that country. South Korea and Taiwan could use the Japanese-built infrastructure and Japanese-trained personnel as springboards to development.

Geopolitical Position

Although the United States was the leading economic and military power in the world by the end of World War II, it began to feel its supremacy threatened in the late 1940s by the Soviet Union and China. Fearing that South Korea and Taiwan might fall to the communists, the United States poured unprecedented aid into both countries in the 1960s. It also extended large, low-interest loans and opened its domestic market to Taiwanese and South Korean products. Because the United States saw Israel as a crucially important ally in the Middle East, it also received special economic assistance. Other countries with less strategic importance to the United States received less help in their drive to industrialize.

State Policy

A third factor that accounts for the relative success of some countries in their efforts to industrialize and become prosperous concerns state policies. As a legacy of colonialism, the Taiwanese and South Korean states were developed on the Japanese model. They kept workers' wages low, restricted trade union growth, and maintained quasi-military discipline in factories. Moreover, by placing high taxes on consumer goods, limiting the import of foreign goods, and preventing their citizens from investing abroad, they encouraged their citizens to put much of their money in the bank. These policies created a large pool of capital for industrial expansion. The South Korean and Taiwanese states also gave subsidies, training grants, and tariff protection to export-based industries from the 1960s onward. (Tariffs are

Core capitalist countries are rich countries that are the world's major sources of capital and technology (the United States, Japan, and Germany).

The **peripheral capitalist countries** are former colonies that are poor and are major sources of raw materials and cheap labour.

The **semiperipheral capitalist countries** consist of former colonies that are making considerable headway in their attempts to industrialize (South Korea, Taiwan, and Israel are examples).

taxes on foreign goods.) These policies did much to stimulate industrial growth. Finally, the Taiwanese and South Korean states invested heavily in basic education, health care, roads, and other public goods. A healthy and well-educated labour force combined with good transportation and communication systems laid solid foundations for economic growth.

Social Structure

Taiwan and South Korea are socially cohesive countries, which makes it easy for them to generate consensus around development policies. It also allows them to get their citizens to work hard, save a lot of money, and devote their energies to scientific education.

Social solidarity in Taiwan and South Korea is based partly on the sweeping land reform they conducted in the late 1940s and early 1950s. By redistributing land to small farmers, both countries eliminated the class of large landowners, who usually oppose industrialization. Land redistribution eliminated a major potential source of social conflict. In contrast, many countries in Latin America and Africa did not undergo land reform. The United States often intervened militarily in Latin America to prevent land reform because U.S. commercial interests profited handsomely from the existence of large plantations (LaFeber, 1993).

Another factor underlying social solidarity in Taiwan and South Korea is that neither country suffered from internal conflicts like those that wracked sub-Saharan Africa. British, French, and other Western European colonizers often drew the borders of African countries to keep antagonistic tribes living side by side in the same jurisdiction and sought to foment tribal conflict. Keeping tribal tensions alive made it possible to play one tribe off against another, making it easier for imperial powers to rule. This policy led to much social and political conflict in postcolonial Africa. Today, the region suffers from frequent civil wars, coups, and uprisings. It is the most conflict-ridden area of the world. For example, the civil war in the Democratic Republic of Congo from 1998 to 2003 resulted in millions of deaths, and renewed conflict beginning in 2008 killed many more Congolese. This high level of internal conflict acts as a barrier to economic development in sub-Saharan Africa.

In sum, postcolonial countries that enjoy a solid industrial infrastructure, strategic geopolitical importance, strong states with strong development policies, and socially cohesive populations are in the best position to join the ranks of the rich countries in the coming

Seoul is the capital of South Korea, one of the semiperipheral countries making rapid strides toward prosperity.

Brand X Pictures/Jupiter Images

decades. We may expect countries that have *some* of these characteristics to experience some economic growth and increase in the well-being of their populations in the near future. Such countries include China, India, Chile, Thailand, Indonesia, Mexico, and Brazil (see Figure 9.6). In contrast, African countries south of the Sahara are in the worst position of all. They have inherited the most damaging consequences of colonialism, and they enjoy few of the conditions that could help them escape the history that has been imposed on them.

Canada as a Semiperipheral Country

Many analysts regard Canada as a semiperipheral country that has managed to achieve prosperity despite its colonial past (Brym with Fox, 1989: 34–56; Laxer, 1989):

- The *type of colonialism* that Canada experienced is sometimes called "white settler colonialism." Like Australia, New Zealand, and the United States, Canada was settled by large numbers of Europeans who soon overwhelmed the Aboriginal population. They were determined to reproduce or improve the standard of living they enjoyed in the old country. Much of the wealth they produced was therefore reinvested locally. In contrast, when the European powers colonized Africa, they set up only small enclaves of white settlers. Their main aim was to exploit local resources and populations, sending nearly all of the wealth back to Europe.[3]
- Canada's *geopolitical position* has always been highly favourable to economic development. That is because Canada has served as a major supplier of raw materials and other goods to France, Great Britain, and the United States, and has fallen under the protective wing of each of these countries, all of which have viewed Canada as a staunch ally. For example, Canada played a disproportionately large role in World War II as a training ground, source of raw materials, and supplier of arms and soldiers to the Allies.
- Canada's *state policy* has sometimes acted to protect and stimulate the growth of Canadian industry, although not as consistently as the state policy of, say, South Korea. For example, Canada's 1879 National Policy established a duty on imported manufactured goods. It sheltered the growth of Canadian industry, then in its infancy, by making foreign-made manufactured goods more expensive. Similarly, the 1965 Auto Pact required that foreign automobile companies wanting to sell cars in Canada duty-free manufacture cars in Canada and use a certain proportion of

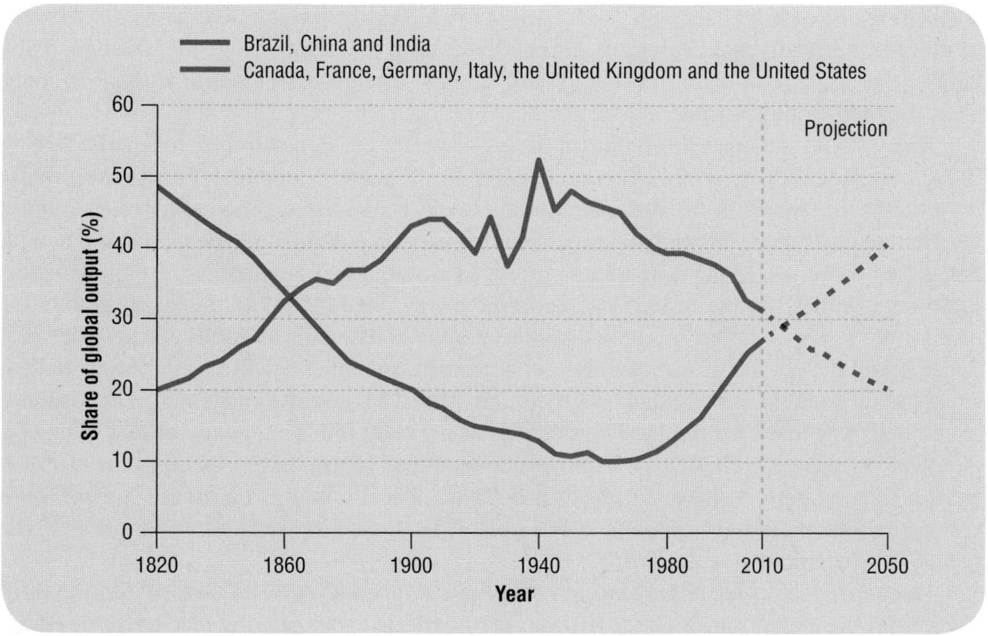

FIGURE 9.6
Share of World Gross Domestic Product by Selected Countries, 1820–2050 (projected, in percent)

Source: United Nations Development Programme. 2013. Human Development Report 2013: Human Progress in a Diverse World. New York: p. 13. www.undp.org/content/dam/undp/library/corporate/HDR/2013GlobalHDR/English/HDR2013%20Report%20English.pdf (retrieved 10 August 2013).

Canadian-made components. The Auto Pact thus stimulated the growth of an industry that, directly or indirectly, was responsible for the employment of one-sixth of Ontario's labour force.

- Canada's *social structure* has arguably had fewer positive effects on economic development than is the case in such countries as South Korea and Taiwan. In Canada, the French–English conflict has drawn attention away from development policy. And although strong farmers' and workers' movements have pushed governments in other countries to attend closely to development issues, these movements have been relatively weak in Canada (Brym, 1992; Laxer, 1989). Canada is not a world centre of capital. Our manufacturing sector is proportionately smaller than that of Germany, the United States, and Japan. An unusually large percentage of our industry is foreign-owned. Still, Canada is one of the wealthiest countries in the world. Our semiperipheral status is clear.

TIME TO REVIEW

- What are the main trends in patterns of global inequality in recent decades?
- What are the main principles of modernization theory?
- What are the main principles of dependency theory?
- Why have some previously poor countries developed rapidly in recent decades?

NEOLIBERAL VERSUS DEMOCRATIC GLOBALIZATION

Globalization and Neoliberalism

Neoliberal globalization is a policy that promotes private control of industry; minimal government interference in the running of the economy; the removal of taxes, tariffs, and restrictive regulations that discourage the international buying and selling of goods and services; and the encouragement of foreign investment.

For some political and economic leaders, the road sign that marks the path to prosperity reads "**neoliberal globalization**." Neoliberal globalization is a policy that promotes private control of industry; minimal government interference in the running of the economy; the removal of taxes, tariffs, and restrictive regulations that discourage the international buying and selling of goods and services; and the encouragement of foreign investment. Advocates of neoliberal globalization resemble the modernization theorists of a generation ago. They believe that if the poor countries would only emulate the successful habits of the rich countries, they too would prosper.

Many social scientists are skeptical of this prescription. For example, Joseph E. Stiglitz (2002), the Nobel Prize–winning economist and former chief economist of the World Bank, argues that the World Bank and other international economic organizations often impose outdated policies on developing countries, putting them at a disadvantage in comparison with developed countries. In the African country of Mozambique, for example, foreign debt was 4.5 times the GNP in the mid-1990s. In other words, the amount of money Mozambique owed to foreigners was four-and-a-half times more than the value of goods and services produced by all the people of Mozambique in a year. Facing an economic crisis, Mozambique sought relief from the World Bank and the International Monetary Fund (IMF). The response of the IMF was that Mozambique's government-imposed minimum wage of less than $1 a day was "excessive." The IMF also recommended that Mozambique spend twice as much as its education budget and four times as much as its health budget on interest payments to service its foreign debt (Mittelman, 2000: 104). How such crippling policies might help the people of Mozambique is unclear.

Does historical precedent lead us to believe that neoliberalism works? To the contrary, with the exception of Great Britain, neoliberalism was *never* a successful development strategy in the early stages of industrialization. Germany, the United States, Japan, Sweden, and other rich countries became highly developed economically between the first decades of the nineteenth century and the early twentieth century. South Korea, Taiwan, Singapore, and other semiperipheral countries became highly developed economically in the second half of the twentieth century. Today, China and India are industrializing quickly. These countries did not pursue privatization, minimal government intervention in the economy, free trade, and foreign investment in the early stages of industrialization. Rather, the governments of these countries typically intervened to encourage industrialization. They protected infant industries behind tariff walls, invested public money heavily to promote national industries, and so on. Today, China and India maintain among the highest barriers to international trade in the world (Chang, 2002; Gerschenkron, 1962; Laxer, 1989). Typically, it is only after industrial development is well under way and national industries can compete on the global market that countries begin to advocate neoliberal globalization to varying degrees. As one political economist writes, "The sensible ones liberalise in line with the growth of domestic capacities—they try to expose domestic producers to enough competition to make them more efficient, but not enough to kill them" (Wade in Wade and Wolf, 2002: 19). The exception that proves the rule is Great Britain, which needed less government involvement to industrialize because it was the first industrializer and had no international competitors. Even the United States, one of the most vocal advocates of neoliberal globalization today, invested a great deal of public money subsidizing industries and building infrastructure, including roads, schools, ports, airports, and electricity grids, in the late nineteenth and early twentieth centuries. It was an extremely protectionist country until the end of World War II. As late as 1930, the Smoot–Hawley Tariff Act raised tariffs on foreign goods 60 percent. Today, the United States still subsidizes large corporations in a variety of ways and maintains substantial tariffs on a range of foreign products, including agricultural goods, softwood lumber, and textiles. In this respect, the United States differs very little from Japan, France, and other rich countries.

In sum, there is good reason to be skeptical about the benefits of neoliberal globalization for poor countries (Bourdieu, 1998a; Brennan, 2003; see Box 9.2). Yet, as you will now see, globalization can be reformed so that its economic and technological benefits are distributed more uniformly throughout the world.

Foreign Aid, Debt Cancellation, and Tariff Reduction

In the film *About Schmidt* (2002), Jack Nicholson plays Warren Schmidt, a former insurance executive. Retirement leaves Schmidt with little purpose in life. His wife dies. His adult daughter has little time or respect for him. He feels his existence lacks meaning. Then, while watching TV one night, Schmidt is moved to support a poor child in a developing country. He decides to send a monthly $27 cheque to sponsor a Tanzanian boy named Ndugu. He writes Ndugu long letters about his life. While Schmidt's world falls apart before our eyes, his sole meaningful human bond is with Ndugu. At the end of the movie, Schmidt cries as he looks at a picture Ndugu drew for him: an adult holding a child's hand.

It does not take a Warren Schmidt to find meaning in helping the desperately poor. Many people contribute to charities that help developing countries in a variety of ways. Many more people contribute development aid indirectly through the taxes they pay to the federal government. Many Canadians think our contributions are generous. Do you? A 2002 survey found that while 71 percent of Canadians thought foreign aid important, only 51 percent favoured the government's announced plan of gradually increasing the total (Asia Pacific Foundation of Canada, 2002).

Was foreign aid by Canada already at a high level? The UN urges the world's 22 richest countries to contribute 0.7 percent of their GDP to development aid. (This goal was set at the urging of then Canadian prime minister Lester Pearson in 1969.) In 2012, only five countries reached that goal: Luxembourg, Sweden, Norway, Denmark, and the

BOX 9.2

SOCIOLOGY AT THE MOVIES

CAPTAIN PHILLIPS

On April 8, 2009, four pirates boarded the *Maersk Alabama* 440 km off the coast of Somalia. They held Captain Richard Phillips and two crew members on the bridge. The 17 remaining crew members hid in the engine room, allowing them to disable the freighter, capture one of the pirates, and free one of the hostages. Frustrated, the pirates abandoned the *Maersk Alabama* in a lifeboat, taking Captain Phillips hostage. They hoped that they would be able to ransom him for millions.

Within 24 hours, U.S. Navy war ships reached the *Maersk Alabama*, and on April 12, marksmen from SEAL Team 6 shot and killed the three pirates in the lifeboat. Captain Phillips was freed, and the sole surviving pirate was eventually sentenced to more than 33 years in a U.S. prison.

Captain Phillips incorporates classic Hollywood themes to tell the story of the *Maersk Alabama*. There is the everyman-hero, Captain Phillips, played by Tom Hanks. There are the dark-skinned bad guys, played by Barkhad Abdi, Barkhad Abdirahman, Faysal Ahmed, and Mahat M. Ali. And there is the might, precision, and long reach of the U.S. military. Captain Phillips, his crew, and the American sailors remain calm and exercise great cunning, discipline, and bravery. The Somali pirates are quarrelsome and disorganized, and they chew khat, a plant containing an amphetamine-like stimulant that makes them high. In the end, good triumphs over evil.

The movie is 127 minutes long. Just before the 110-minute mark, Abdumali Muse, the pirate leader, utters the only two sentences that provide some sociological context for truly understanding the story of the *Maersk Alabama*: "Big ships come to our water, take all the fish out. What's left for us to fish?"

The Indian Ocean off the coast of Somalia is rich in tuna, shrimp, lobster, and other valuable species. The Somalis developed a viable commercial fishery to take advantage of this bounty. However, at the end of the twentieth century, giant foreign trawlers started scooping up hundreds of millions of dollars worth of fish every year, destroying the livelihood of local fishermen. Around the same time, European hospitals and factories hired firms to dispose of toxic waste, including mercury, cadmium, lead, and spent nuclear fuel. These firms, apparently controlled by the Italian Mafia, dumped leaking barrels of the waste off the coast of Somalia. Particularly after the 2005 Indian Ocean tsunami, the barrels started washing ashore. Somalis reported rashes, nausea, malformed babies, radiation sickness, and hundreds of deaths (Hari, 2009; Stuhldreher, 2008). That is when piracy started on a large scale.

The Somali government had collapsed back in 1991, so it was impossible for local authorities to police the waters and prevent illegal fishing and dumping by foreigners. As regional warlords took control of most of Somalia, they used local grievances to mobilize support for piracy operations.

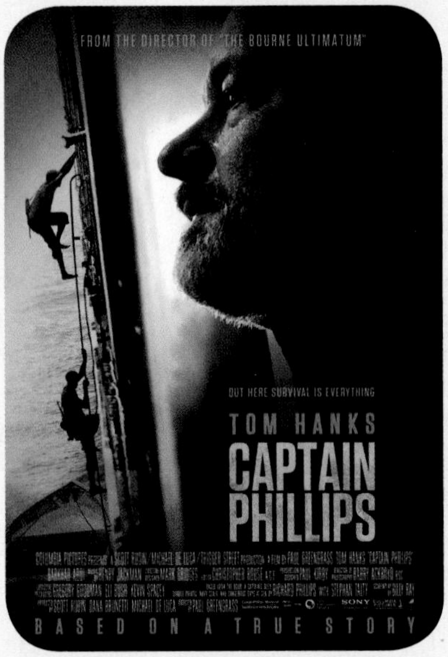

The Kobal Collection at Art Resource, NY

Movie poster from *Captain Phillips*.

Capturing foreign vessels and extracting ransom for their release became an important source of income for the warlords and a livelihood for displaced fishermen and their families (Sone, 2010).

The larger, sociological context of the story of the *Maersk Alabama* is that of globalization—or at least a particular form of globalization that prevents many poor nations from enjoying economic development, encourages some of them to turn to illegal alternatives, and allows Westerners to stereotype their populations as the dark-skinned bad guys. *Captain Phillips* aids in that effort.

Netherlands (see Figure 9.7). Canada ranked fourteenth among the 24 rich nations with its contribution of 0.32 percent of its GDP. The United States ranked nineteenth at 0.19 percent. A World Bank official compared (1) the subsidies rich countries gave to farms and businesses within their borders with (2) the amount of development aid they gave developing countries. He concluded that "[t]he average cow [in a rich country] is supported by three times the level of income of a poor person in Africa" (quoted in Schuettler, 2002).

Since the United States is by far the world's richest country, it is the American contribution to foreign aid that potentially makes the greatest difference. But even if the United States quadrupled its foreign aid budget to meet UN guidelines, some foreign aid as presently delivered is not an effective way of helping the developing world. Foreign aid is often accompanied by high administrative and overhead costs. It is often given on condition that it is used to buy goods from donor countries that are not necessarily high-priority items for recipient countries. Food aid often has detrimental effects on poor countries. One expert writes: "As

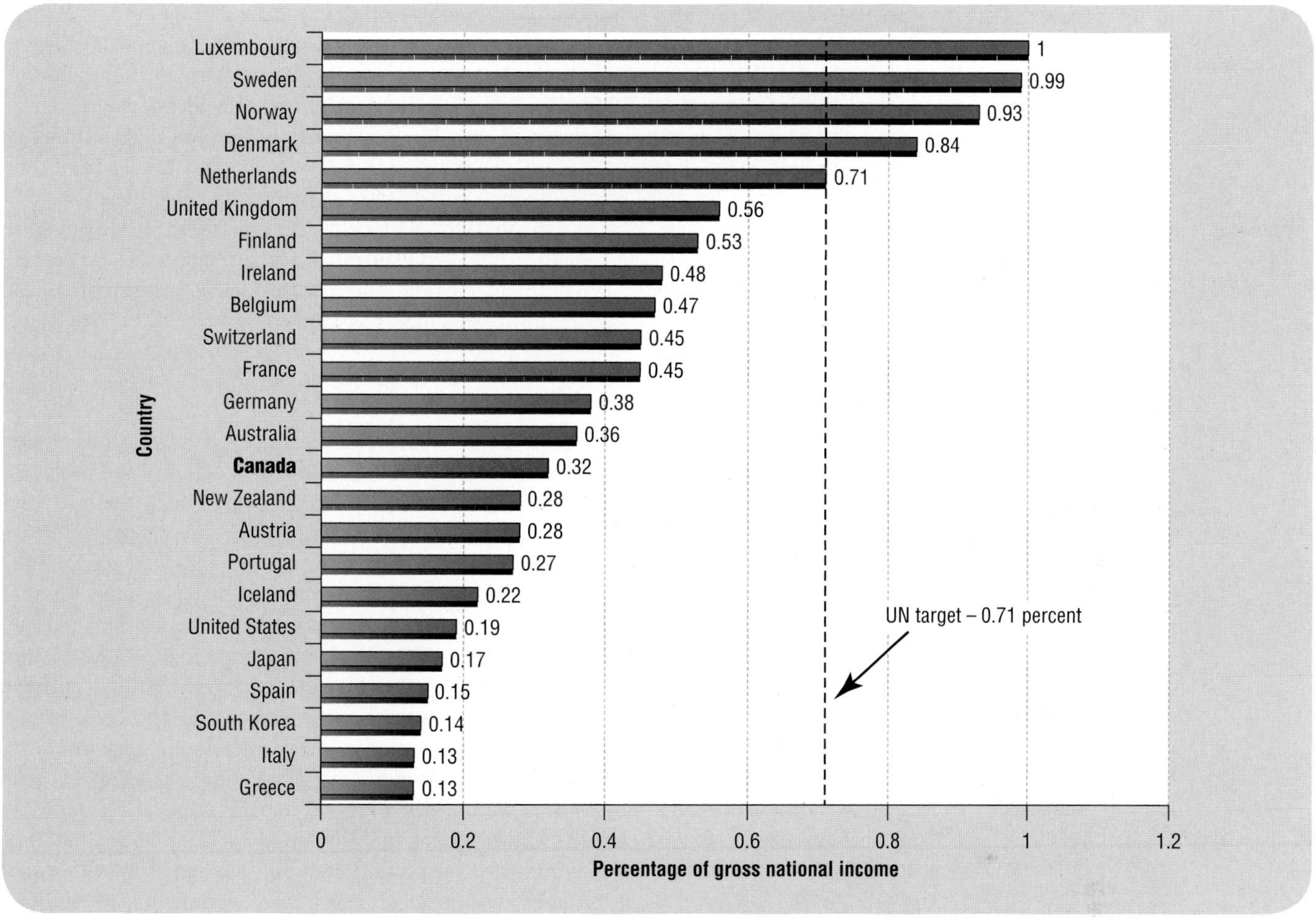

FIGURE 9.7
Official Foreign Aid as Percentage of Gross National Income, 2012

Source: OECD. 2013a. "Official Development Assistance–April 2013 Update." www.oecd.org/dac/stats/oda2012-interactive.htm. Accessed August 10, 2013.

well as creating expensive [dependence on] nonindigenous cereals, and discouraging export-production of items like corn and rice in which the U.S.A. is expanding its own trade, [U.S. food aid] has frequently served as a major disincentive to the efforts of local farmers to grow food even for domestic consumption" (Hancock, 1989: 169). Some foreign aid organizations, such as Oxfam and Caritas Internationalis, waste little money on administration and overhead expenses because they are driven by high principles, pay their staffs low salaries, build partnerships with reputable local organizations, work with their partners to identify the most pressing needs of poor countries, and focus their efforts on meeting those needs (Ron, 2007). The efforts of such organizations remind us that foreign aid can be beneficial and that strict oversight is required to ensure that foreign aid is not wasted but is directed to truly helpful projects, such as improving irrigation and sanitation systems and helping people acquire better farming techniques. Increasing the amount of foreign aid and redesigning its delivery can thus help mitigate some of the excesses of neoliberal globalization.

So can debt cancellation. Many analysts argue that the world's rich countries and banks should simply write off the debt owed to them by the developing countries in recognition of historical injustices. They reason that the debt burden of the developing countries is so onerous that it prevents them from focusing on building up economic infrastructure, improving the health and education of their populations, and developing economic policies that can help them emerge from poverty. This proposal for blunting the worst effects of neoliberal globalization may be growing in popularity among politicians in the developed countries. For example, former Canadian prime minister Paul Martin, former British prime minister Tony Blair, and former U.S. president Bill Clinton, among others, support the idea. Former U.S. president George W. Bush and Prime Minister Stephen Harper support limited versions of this proposal.

A third reform proposed in recent years involves rich countries eliminating or at least lowering agricultural tariffs and subsidies. Such tariffs and subsidies prevent developing countries from exporting goods that could earn them money for investment in agriculture, industry, and infrastructure. Eliminating or lowering tariffs and subsidies would require training some farmers in rich countries for new kinds of work, but it would also stimulate economic growth in the developing world. The overall trend in recent decades has been slow but in the right direction. For instance, in the United States, government subsidies to agriculture fell from 11 percent of farm income in 1995–97 to 9 percent in 2009–11. However, in Norway, Switzerland, Japan, and South Korea, farm subsidies still amount to 50–60 percent of farm income. And in Canada, government subsidies have been stuck at 15 percent of farm income since the mid-1990s ("Agricultural Subsidies," 2012).

Democratic Globalization

The final reform we consider involves efforts to help spread democracy throughout the developing world. A large body of research shows that democracy lowers inequality and promotes economic growth (Pettersson, 2003; Sylwester, 2002; United Nations, 2002). Democracies have these effects for several reasons. They make it more difficult for elite groups to misuse their power and enhance their wealth and income at the expense of the less well-to-do. They increase political stability, thereby providing a better investment climate. Finally, because they encourage broad political participation, democracies tend to enact policies that are more responsive to people's needs and benefit a wide range of people from all social classes. For example, democratic governments are more inclined to take steps to avoid famines, protect the environment, build infrastructure, and ensure such basic needs as education and health. These measures help to create a population better suited to pursue economic growth.

Although democracy has spread in recent decades, by 2012, only 90 countries with 46 percent of the world's population were fully democratic (Freedom House, 2013; Chapter 14, Politics). For its part, the United States has supported as many anti-democratic as democratic regimes in the developing world. Especially between the end of World War II in 1945 and the collapse of the Soviet Union in 1991, the U.S. government gave military and financial aid to many anti-democratic regimes, often in the name of halting the spread of Soviet influence. These actions often generated unexpected and undesirable consequences, or what the Central Intelligence Agency (CIA) came to call "blowback" (Johnson, 2000). For example, in the 1980s, the U.S. government supported Saddam Hussein when it considered Iraq's enemy, Iran, the greater threat to U.S. security interests. The United States also funded Osama bin Laden when he was fighting the Soviet Union in Afghanistan. Only a decade later, these so-called allies turned into the United States' worst enemies (Chomsky, 1991; Johnson, 2000; Kolko, 2002).

In sum, we have outlined four reforms that could change the nature of neoliberal globalization and turn it into what we would like to call democratic globalization. These reforms include offering stronger support for democracy in the developing world, contributing more and better foreign aid, forgiving the debt owed by developing countries to the rich countries, and eliminating many of the tariffs that restrict exports from developing countries. These kinds of policies could plausibly help the developing world overcome the legacy of colonialism and join the ranks of the well-to-do. They would do much to ensure that the complex process we call globalization would benefit humanity as a whole.

TIME TO REVIEW

- What is neoliberal globalization?
- How could the level of global inequality be lowered?

SUMMARY

1. What is globalization and why is it taking place?
Globalization is the growing interdependence and mutual awareness of individuals and economic, political, and social institutions around the world. It is a response to many forces, some technological (e.g., the development of inexpensive means of rapid international communication), others economic (e.g., burgeoning international trade and investment), and still others political (e.g., the creation of transnational organizations that limit the sovereign powers of nation states).

2. In what sense does globalization create a world that is both more homogeneous and more localized?
Globalization homogenizes us insofar as it creates a common world culture of movies, commodities, political ideals, economic policies, and so on. However, these cultural elements are adapted to local conditions, creating unique hybrids. Moreover, globalization has evoked an anti-globalization reaction in many places.

3. What are the main trends in global inequality and poverty?
Global inequality and poverty are staggering and in some respects are worsening. The income gap between rich and poor countries weighted for population size has declined since 1950, but the gap between rich and poor individuals has grown worldwide.

4. What are the main sociological theories of economic development?
Modernization theory argues that global inequality occurs as a result of some countries lacking sufficient capital, Western values, rational business practices, and stable governments. Dependency theory counters with the claim that global inequality results from the exploitative relationship between rich and poor countries.

5. What are the differences between countries that have recently emerged from poverty and those that have not?
The poor countries best able to emerge from poverty have a colonial past that left them with industrial infrastructures. They also enjoy a favourable geopolitical position. They implement strong, growth-oriented economic policies, and they have socially cohesive populations. Countries that have not emerged from poverty tend to lack these characteristics.

6. How can the disadvantages of globalization be minimized?
Neoliberal globalization can be reformed so that the benefits of globalization are more evenly distributed throughout the world. Possible reforms include offering stronger support for democracy in the developing world, contributing more and better foreign aid, forgiving the debt owed by developing countries to the rich countries, and eliminating tariffs that restrict exports from developing countries.

NOTES

1. All dollar references are to U.S. currency unless otherwise indicated.

2. Gross national product (GNP) is the total dollar value of goods and services produced in a country in a year. It allocates goods and services based on the nationality of the owners. Gross domestic product (GDP) is a similar measure, but instead allocates goods and services based on the location of the owners. So, for example, goods and services produced overseas by foreign subsidiaries would be included in GNP but not in GDP.

3. From this point of view, South Africa and, to a lesser degree, Zimbabwe (formerly Rhodesia) represent intermediate cases between the rest of Africa on the one hand, and Canada, the United States, Australia, and New Zealand on the other.

CHAPTER 10

RACE AND ETHNICITY

© Bob Brym

IN THIS CHAPTER, YOU WILL LEARN TO

- Distinguish race from ethnicity, identify how both are socially constructed, and analyze how social structure supports them.
- Identify ways in which social interaction influences ethnic and racial identity.
- Evaluate the role of power and privilege in preserving ethnic and racial inequality.
- Forecast the likely future place of race and ethnicity in Canada.

DEFINING RACE AND ETHNICITY

The Great Brain Robbery

About 150 years ago, Dr. Samuel George Morton of Philadelphia was the most distinguished scientist in North America. Among other things, Morton collected and measured human skulls. The skulls came from various times and places. Their original occupants were members of different races. Morton believed he could show that the bigger your brain, the smarter you were. To prove his point he packed BB-sized shot into a skull until it was full. Next he poured the shot from the skull into a graduated cylinder. He then recorded the volume of shot in the cylinder. Finally, he noted the race of the person from whom each skull came. Using this procedure, he thought, would allow him to draw conclusions about the average brain size of different races.

As he expected, Morton found that the races ranking highest in the social hierarchy had the biggest brains, while those ranking lowest had the smallest brains. He claimed that the people with the biggest brains were whites of European origin. Next were Asians. Then came Native North Americans. The people at the bottom of the social hierarchy—and those with the smallest brains—were blacks.

Morton's research had profound sociological implications, for he claimed to show that the system of social inequality in North America and throughout the world had natural, biological roots. If, on average, members of some racial groups are rich and others poor, some highly educated and others illiterate, some powerful and others powerless, that was, said Morton, due to differences in brain size and mental capacity. Moreover, because he used science to show that Native North Americans and blacks *naturally* rested at the bottom of the social hierarchy, his ideas were used to justify two of the most oppressive forms of domination and injustice: colonization and slavery.

© CEFutcher /Istockphoto.com

Ethnic and racial diversity is especially pronounced among young Canadians in urban areas.

Despite claims of scientific objectivity, not a shred of evidence supported Morton's ideas. For example, in one of his three main studies, Morton measured the capacity of skulls robbed from Egyptian tombs. He found that the average volume of black people's skulls was 65.5 millilitres (4 cubic inches) smaller than the average volume of white people's skulls. This fact seemed to prove his case. Today, however, we know that three main issues compromise his findings:

1. Morton claimed to be able to distinguish the skulls of white and black people by the shapes of the skulls. Since it is not possible to do so, Morton's sorting of skulls is invalid.

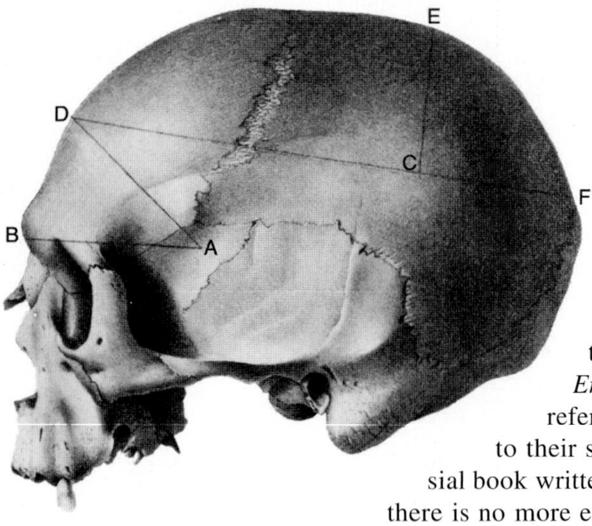

Samuel Morton's Crania Americana (1839)

In the nineteenth century, brain size was falsely held to be one of the main indicators of intellectual capacity. Average brain size was incorrectly said to vary by race. Researchers who were eager to prove the existence of such correlations are now widely regarded as practitioners of a racist quasi-science.

2. Morton's skulls formed a small, unrepresentative sample of 72 skulls.
3. Morton's racial samples were incomparable with respect to gender. Females comprised 71 percent of the "Negroid" group and only 48 percent of the "Caucasian." Given that women's bodies are, on average, smaller than men's, these group comparisons are unfair. Morton's findings are biased in favour of larger, white, male skulls.

Scientifically speaking, Morton's findings are meaningless. Yet they were influential for a long time, and some people still believe them. For example, in 1963, the author of an article about race in the *Encyclopedia Britannica*, then the world's most authoritative general reference source, wrote that blacks have "a rather small brain in relation to their size" (Buxton, 1963: 864A). That claim was repeated in a controversial book written by a Canadian psychologist in the mid-1990s (Rushton, 1995). Yet there is no more evidence today than there was in 1850 that whites have bigger brains than blacks do.[1]

Race, Biology, and Society

Biological arguments about racial differences have grown more sophisticated over time. However, the scientific basis of these arguments is just as shaky now as it always has been.

In medieval Europe, some aristocrats saw blue veins under their pale skin but could not see blue veins under the peasants' suntanned skin. They concluded that the two groups must be racially distinct. The aristocrats called themselves "blue bloods." They ignored the fact that the colour of blood from an aristocrat's wound was just as red as the blood from a peasant's wound.

About 80 years ago, some scholars expressed the belief that racial differences in average IQ scores were genetically based. Thus, in 1927, Canadian professor Peter Sandiford argued that Canada must institute selective immigration to ensure that only the best and the brightest arrived on our shores and that we keep out "misfits" and "defectives." He encouraged the recruitment of people of British, German, and Danish stock, and discouraged the recruitment of Poles, Italians, and Greeks. Sandiford provided IQ test results supporting his selective immigration policy. He argued that his data showed the mental superiority of Northern Europeans compared with Eastern and Southern Europeans. However, his testing results also provided what he regarded as "profoundly disturbing" evidence. People of Japanese and Chinese ancestry had the highest intelligence scores—results he had not predicted. He dismissed this finding by asserting that a few clever Asians had apparently entered Canada. They were exceptions, he wrote, and should not detract from the "need" to also keep Asians out of Canada (McLaren, 1990).

Similarly, in the United States, Jews scored below non-Jews on IQ tests in the 1920s. Their lower scores were used as an argument against Jewish immigration. More recently, African Americans have on average scored below European Americans on IQ tests. Some people say their lower scores justify slashing budgets for schools in the inner city, where many African Americans live. Why invest good money in inner-city schooling, such people ask, if low IQ scores are rooted in biology and therefore fixed (Herrnstein and Murray, 1994)? However, the people who argued against both Jewish immigration and better education for inner-city African Americans ignored two facts. First, Jewish IQ scores rose as Jews moved up the class hierarchy and could afford better education. Second, enriched educational facilities have routinely boosted the IQ scores of inner-city African American children (Frank Porter Graham Child Development Center, 1999; Heckman, 2011; Nisbett, 2011). Much evidence shows that the social setting in which a person is raised and educated has a big impact on IQ. The claim that racial differences in IQ scores are biologically based is about as strong as evidence that aristocrats have blue blood (Cancio, Evans, and Maume, 1996; Fischer et al., 1996; Chapter 17, Education).[2]

If we cannot reasonably maintain that racial differences in average IQ scores are based in biology, what about differences in athletic prowess or other abilities? For example, some people insist that, for genetic reasons, black people are better than whites at singing and sports, but are more prone to crime. Is there any evidence to support these beliefs?

At first glance, the supporting evidence might seem strong. Consider sports. Aren't 73 percent of NBA players and 67 percent of NFL players black? Don't blacks of West African descent hold the 200 fastest 100-metre-dash times, all under 10 seconds? Don't North and East Africans regularly win 40 percent of the top international distance-running honours yet represent only a fraction of 1 percent of the world's population (Entine, 2000; Lapchick, 2011)? Although these facts are undeniable, the argument for the genetic basis of black athletic superiority begins to falter once we consider two additional points. First, no gene linked to general athletic superiority has been identified. Second, athletes of African descent do not perform unusually well in many sports, such as swimming, hockey, cycling, tennis, gymnastics, and soccer. The idea that people of African descent are in general superior athletes is simply untrue.

AP Photo/Petr David Josek

Athletic heroes, such as P.K. Subban, are often held up as role models for black youth, even though the chance of making it as an athlete is much less than the chance of attaining a postsecondary education and succeeding in professional work. Racial stereotypes about black athletic prowess and intellectual inferiority are often reinforced through the idolization of sports heroes.

Sociologists have identified certain *social* conditions that lead to high levels of participation in sports (and in entertainment and crime). These social conditions operate on all groups of people, whatever their race. Specifically, people who face widespread prejudice and discrimination often enter sports, entertainment, and crime in disproportionately large numbers for lack of other ways to improve their social and economic position. For these people, other avenues of upward mobility are often blocked because of prejudice and discrimination.

Prejudice is an attitude that judges a person on his or her group's real or imagined characteristics. **Discrimination** is unfair treatment of people because of their group membership. For example, it was not until the 1950s that prejudice and discrimination against North American Jews began to decline appreciably. Until then, Jews had played a prominent role in some professional sports. Thus, when the New York Knicks played their first game on November 1, 1946, beating the Toronto Huskies 68–66, the starting lineup for New York consisted of Ossie Schechtman, Stan Stutz, Jake Weber, Ralph Kaplowitz, and Leo "Ace" Gottlieb—an all-Jewish squad (National Basketball Association, 2000). Similarly, Koreans in Japan today are subject to much prejudice and discrimination, and they often choose to pursue careers in sports and entertainment. In contrast, Koreans in Canada face less prejudice and discrimination, and few of them become athletes and entertainers. Instead, they are often said to excel in engineering and science. As these examples suggest, then, social circumstances have a big impact on athletic and other forms of behaviour.

Prejudice is an attitude that judges a person on his or her group's real or imagined characteristics.

Discrimination is unfair treatment of people because of their group membership.

The idea that people of African descent are genetically superior to whites in athletic ability is the complement of the idea that they are genetically inferior to whites in intellectual ability. Both ideas reinforce black–white inequality.[3] For although there are just a few thousand professional athletes in North America, there are millions of pharmacists, graphic designers, lawyers, systems analysts, police officers, nurses, and people in other interesting occupations that offer steady employment and good pay. By promoting only the P.K. Subbans and Kevin Durants of the world as suitable role models for youth, the idea of "natural" black athletic superiority and intellectual inferiority in effect asks blacks to bet on a high-risk proposition—that they will make it in professional sports. At the same time, it deflects attention from a much safer bet—that they can achieve upward mobility through academic excellence (Guppy and Davies, 1998; Duncan and Murnane, 2011).

An additional problem undermines the argument that genes determine the behaviour of racial groups. It is impossible to neatly distinguish races based on genetic differences. Relatively consistent differences are observed only when comparing people from distant locales, such as Norway versus Eastern Asia. Within continental landmasses, genetic contrasts are negligible for adjacent populations because migration and conquest bring about genetic mixing. Such mixing prevails whenever supposedly distinct groups have been in contact for more than a few generations. In North America, for instance, it was not uncommon for white male slave owners to rape black female slaves, who then gave birth to children of mixed race. Many Europeans had children with Aboriginal people in the eighteenth and nineteenth centuries. This fact undermines attempts to sort populations into distinct racial types. Many of today's supposed racial schemas, including the well-known "colour-code" contrasting red, yellow, brown, and white, are contrasts that derive from European seafarers' early encounters with groups then unfamiliar to them.

We know from the census that ethnic and racial intermarriage has been increasing in Canada at least since 1871. The increase in intermarriage is one factor explaining why, in the 2011 National Household Survey, 42 percent of respondents reported multiple ethnic or racial identities (Statistics Canada, 2013c). Usually, people who report multiple ethnic or racial identities have parents of two different ethnic or racial origins (Kalbach and Kalbach, 1998). A growing number of North Americans are similar to Tiger Woods. Woods claims he is of "Cablinasian" ancestry—part Caucasian, part black, part Native American Indian, and part Asian. As these examples illustrate, the differences among black, white, Asian, and so forth, are often anything but clear-cut. In fact, some respected scholars believe we all belong to one human race, which originated in Africa (Cavalli-Sforza, Menozzi, and Piazza, 1994).

In modern times, humanity has experienced so much intermixing that race as a biological category has lost nearly all meaning. Some biologists and social scientists therefore suggest we drop the term "race" from the vocabulary of science. Most sociologists, however, continue to use the term "race." They do so because *perceptions* of race continue to affect the lives of most people profoundly. Everything from your wealth to your health is influenced by whether others see you as black, white, brown, or something else. Race as a *sociological* concept is thus an invaluable analytical tool. It refers to the existence of classification schemes that are widely understood and widely taken to be relevant. It is invaluable, however, only to the degree that people who use the term remember that it refers to *social significance* that is widely attached to physical differences (e.g., skin colour) rather than to biological differences that shape behaviour patterns.

Said differently, perceptions of racial difference are socially constructed and often arbitrary. The Irish and the Jews were regarded as "blacks" by some people a hundred years ago, and today some northern Italians still think of southern Italians from Sicily and Calabria as "blacks" (Gilman, 1991; Ignatiev, 1995; Roediger, 1991). During World War II, some people made arbitrary physical distinctions between Chinese allies and Japanese enemies that helped justify the Canadian policy of placing Japanese Canadians in internment camps. These examples show that racial distinctions are social constructs, not biological givens.

Race is a social construct used to distinguish people in terms of one or more physical markers, usually with profound effects on their lives.

Finally, then, we can define **race** as a social construct used to distinguish people in terms of one or more physical markers. However, this definition raises an interesting question. If race is merely a social construct and not a useful biological term, why are perceptions of physical difference used to distinguish groups of people in the first place? Why, in other words, does race matter? Most sociologists believe that race matters because it allows social inequality to be created and perpetuated. The English who colonized Ireland, the Americans who went to Africa looking for slaves, and the Germans who used the Jews as a scapegoat to explain their deep economic and political troubles after World War I all created systems of racial domination. (A **scapegoat** is a disadvantaged person or category of people whom others blame for their own problems.) Once colonialism, slavery, and concentration camps were established, behavioural differences developed between subordinates and superordinates. For example, North American slaves and Jewish concentration camp inmates, with little motivating them to work hard except the ultimate threat of the master's whip, tended to do only the minimum work necessary to survive. Their masters noticed this tendency and characterized their subordinates as inherently slow and unreliable workers (Collins, 1982: 66–69). In this way, racial stereotypes are born. The stereotypes then embed themselves in literature, popular lore, journalism, and political debate, which reinforces racial inequalities (see Figure 10.1). We thus see that race matters to the degree that it helps to create and maintain systems of social inequality.

A **scapegoat** is a disadvantaged person or category of people whom others blame for their own problems.

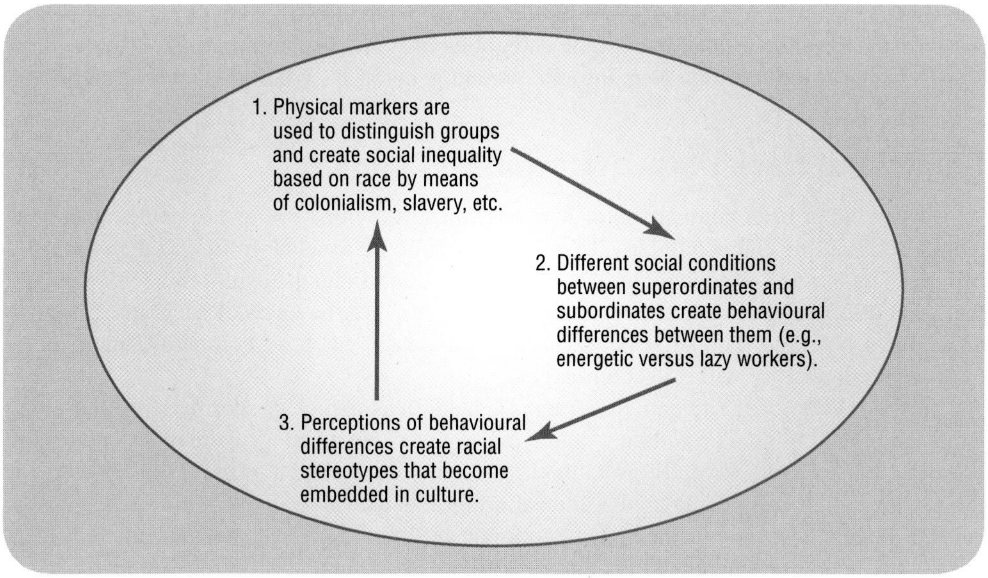

FIGURE 10.1
The Vicious Circle of Racism

Ethnicity, Culture, and Social Structure

Race is to biology as ethnicity is to culture. A race is a socially defined category of people whose perceived *physical* markers are deemed significant. An **ethnic group** comprises people whose perceived *cultural* markers are deemed significant. Ethnic groups differ from one another in terms of language, religion, customs, values, ancestors, and the like. However, just as physical distinctions don't *cause* differences in the behaviour of various races, so cultural distinctions are often not by themselves the major source of differences in the behaviour of various ethnic groups. In other words, ethnic values and other elements of ethnic culture have less of an effect on the way people behave than we commonly believe. That is because *social structural* differences frequently underlie cultural differences.

An **ethnic group** comprises people whose perceived cultural markers are deemed socially significant. Ethnic groups differ from one another in terms of language, religion, customs, values, ancestors, and the like.

An example will help drive home the point. People often praise Jews, Koreans, and other economically successful groups for their cultural values, including an emphasis on education, family, and hard work. People less commonly notice, however, that Canadian immigration policy has been highly selective. For the most part, the Jews and Koreans who arrived in Canada were literate, urbanized, and skilled. Some even came with financial assets (Brym, Shaffir, and Weinfeld, 1993; Li, 1995; Wong and Ng, 1998). They certainly confronted prejudice and discrimination, but far less than did blacks and Aboriginal people in Canada. These *social-structural* conditions facilitated Jewish and Korean success. They gave members of these groups a firm basis on which to build and maintain a culture emphasizing education, family, and other middle-class virtues. In contrast, in the first decades of the twentieth century, Aboriginal people and the black descendants of slaves were typically illiterate and unskilled, and they experienced more prejudice and discrimination than did other ethnic or racial groups in Canada. These social-structural disadvantages—not their culture—led to them being, on average, less economically successful than Jews and Koreans.

In general, much Canadian research supports the argument that culture, in and of itself, is unimportant in determining the economic success of racial or ethnic groups. Substantial differences *do* exist in the average annual incomes of some racial groups. For example, the average annual income of Aboriginal people is substantially below that of white Canadians. So is the average annual income of non-white immigrants. The point, however, is that these differences are due largely to such factors as the years of education attained by the average Aboriginal person in Canada and the number of years the non-white immigrant has been living in Canada. Little income difference separates white Canadians from the Canadian-born children of non-white immigrants. A professor of law who happens to be of Aboriginal origin earns about as much as a professor of law who happens to be white. The problem is that Canada has so few Aboriginal professors of law. Note, however, that because of persistent racism, the annual income of some categories of non-white immigrants, notably black men, remains below average even into the second generation. We discuss this issue below.

Ethnic and Racial Stratification in Canada

As we saw in our brief comparison of Koreans and Jews with Aboriginal people, what matters in determining the economic success of an ethnic or a racial group are the *resources* people possess, such as education, literacy, urbanity, and financial assets. We may now add that what also matters in determining economic success are the kinds of economic *opportunities* open to people. The latter point can be seen clearly when we compare Canada in the mid-twentieth century with Canada today.

In the middle of the twentieth century, Canada was a society sharply stratified along ethnic and racial lines. The people with the most power and privilege were of British origin. WASPs (white Anglo-Saxon Protestants) in particular controlled almost all the big corporations in the country and dominated politics. Immigrants who arrived later enjoyed less power and privilege. Even among them, big economic differences were evident, with European immigrants enjoying higher status than immigrants of Asian ancestry, for example.

John Porter, one of the founders of modern Canadian sociology, referred to mid–twentieth-century Canada as an ethnically and racially stratified "vertical mosaic." He thought the retention of ethnic and racial culture was a big problem in Canada because it hampered the upward mobility of immigrants. In his view, the "Canadian value system" encouraged the retention of ethnic culture, making Canada a low-mobility society (Porter, 1965, 1979: 91).

By the 1970s, however, many Canadian sociologists, including Porter himself, needed to qualify their view that ethnic and racial culture determine economic success or failure. Certain events upset their earlier assumptions. The Canadian economy grew quickly in the decades after World War II. Many members of ethnic and racial minority groups were economically successful despite ethnic and racial prejudice and discrimination. Economic differences diminished among ethnic groups and, to a lesser degree, among racial groups. Ethnic and racial diversity increased among the wealthy, politicians at all levels of government, and professional groups. Visible minority status, whether Asian, Caribbean, or Hispanic, had little bearing on educational, occupational, and income attainment in Canada, at least among those who were Canadian-born (Boyd, Goyder, Jones, McRoberts, Pineo, and Porter, 1985; Brym with Fox, 1989: 103–13; Guppy and Davies, 1998; Lian and Matthews, 1998; Nakhaie, 1997; Ogmundson and McLaughlin, 1992; Pendakur and Pendakur, 1998; Pineo and Porter, 1985; Reitz and Breton, 1994). On the whole, the children of immigrants who were members of visible minority groups actually achieved above-average success in obtaining education (Boyd, 2002; see Table 10.1). Apparently, then, for the great majority of Canadians after World War II, ethnic and racial culture mattered less than the structure of mobility opportunities in determining economic success.

Beginning in the 1990s, recent immigrants who were members of visible minority groups were less successful economically than one would expect, given their educational and other resources (Kazemipur and Halli, 2001; Li, 2000). However, cultural values had little to do with this tendency. Canada experienced an unusually high rate of unemployment in the 1990s, hovering near 10 percent until late in the decade. That situation made it more difficult than in previous decades for recently arrived members of visible minority groups to succeed economically. In addition, although such immigrants were selected to come to Canada because they were highly educated, their credentials were often not recognized by Canadian employers. The accreditation mechanisms for foreign credentials are poorly developed in this country and need to be improved (Reitz, 2011). The relative lack of success of recent immigrants who are members of visible minorities thus reinforces our point. In addition to the resources a person possesses, the structure of opportunities for economic advancement determines income and occupational and educational attainment. Ethnic or racial culture by itself plays at most a minor role.

TABLE 10.1
Percentage with Below-Average Income by Ethnic Identity and Place of Birth, Canada, 2001

Source: Adapted from Statistics Canada (2005b).

	Born Abroad (%)	Born in Canada (%)
British	53	51
French	51	52
Other European	59	45
African	65	20
Arab	67	35
Other Asian	64	27
Caribbean	67	20
Other Latin, Central, and South American	55	34
Aboriginal	77	54
Canadian	62	50

Note: Data are for a random sample of 31 100 Canadian residents who gave a single ethnic origin in the 2001 census. Average individual annual income was $27 141. The income data were truncated at $200 000.

Canadian Multiculturalism

Canada's **multiculturalism** policy emphasizes tolerance of ethnic and racial differences.

The structural opportunities that shape immigration operate in the context of Canada's **multiculturalism** policy, which emphasizes tolerance of ethnic and racial differences. Although Canadian multiculturalism is promoted worldwide as a successful model of immigrant incorporation, considerable confusion surrounds its meaning (Berry and Sam, 2013; Roberts et al., 2013). Before proceeding, ask yourself: What activities or organizations do you associate with multiculturalism?

The multiculturalism policy that Canada initiated in 1971 promoted cultural diversity (the maintenance and development of immigrant cultures) and equity and inclusion (the reduction of barriers to equitable participation in Canadian society) (Government of Canada, 1971). In practice, Canadian policy first emphasized cultural diversity, so multiculturalism became associated with the promotion of ethnic cultures through annual festivals, such as Winnipeg's Folklorama and Toronto's Caribana.

The emphasis on cultural diversity generated considerable criticism (Ryan, 2010). For example, the former premier of British Columbia, Ujjal Dosanjh, said the policy supports "anything anyone believes—no matter how ridiculous and outrageous it might be, [it] is ... acceptable in the name of diversity" (quote in Reitz, 2010: 3). Parallel criticisms are expressed elsewhere. Leaders in Germany, the Netherlands, and the United Kingdom hold that multiculturalism encourages the development of distinct ethnic enclaves with cultures that support strange and sometimes unacceptable values and practices. In this view, multiculturalism is a failure insofar as it marginalizes cultural minorities (Economist, 2007).

In contrast, multicultural policy in Canada currently focuses less on cultural pluralism than on incorporating immigrants into the larger society (Fleras, 2009). The policy's purpose is to enable members of cultural minorities to continue identifying with their heritage while eliminating barriers to their full participation in Canadian society—for insistence, by preventing discrimination and encouraging public education, voting, and other forms of civic integration (Berry, 2013).

Identifying the effects of multicultural policy is difficult because many variables beyond policy influence the immigrant experience. Research suggests that differences between Canadian and U.S. policies account for only small differences in the economic and social incorporation of immigrants (Reitz, 2010, 2011). However, Canada is distinct from the United States in terms of its treatment of members of cultural minority groups, as evidenced by even seemingly small differences, such as Canada's higher rate of citizenship acquisition and stronger support for maintaining a high level of immigration (Bloemraad, 2006; Citrin, Johnson, and Wright, 2012).

Over the last several decades, pollsters have asked Canadians what made them most proud of Canada. "Multiculturalism" has steadily risen in the rankings and currently occupies

BOX 10.1

SOCIOLOGY ON THE TUBE

LITTLE MOSQUE ON THE PRAIRIE

Little Mosque on the Prairie, a Canadian comedy series that ran from 2007 to 2012, follows the everyday lives of people in the fictional town of Mercy, Saskatchewan. It challenges common misperceptions about Muslims and depicts them as essentially no different from anyone else.

Converts to any religion are sometimes more orthodox than those born into it. Because they are highly motivated to convert in the first place, and sometimes feel the need to prove their faith to their co-religionists through overt displays of zeal, converts can become, as the saying goes, "more papist than the Pope." In season one of *Little Mosque on the Prairie*, we meet such a convert, a young man by the name of Marlon. After converting, Marlon dons the *taqiya* (short, round cap) and the *kurta* (long, loose shirt). He questions and denounces any Muslim who is not 100 percent committed to the most traditional and antiquated precepts of the faith. Before long, he has established himself as a nuisance to the lifelong Muslims in Mercy. Fed up, they plot ways to show Marlon how illiberal and annoying he has become. Through humour, the episode serves to undermine the stereotype that most Muslims are extreme in their beliefs.

Throughout the series, relations are harmonious between Mercy's Muslims and non-Muslims. For instance, Mercy's non-Muslim community had practically no response when Marlon decided to convert. In the final season of *Little Mosque on the Prairie*, the mosque's *imam*, Amaar, becomes the best friend of Duncan, the town's Anglican minister.

Some critics say that *Little Mosque on the Prairie* papers over serious problems in the lives of Canadian Muslims. They have a point. According to one survey, 37 percent of Canadians say they have a negative impression of Islam and 10 percent say they have neither a positive nor a negative impression (Trudeau Foundation, 2006). Canadian Muslims are mainly immigrants from Pakistan and the Middle East. They often experience lower rates of upward mobility than immigrants did between the end of World War II and the 1980s. But such issues are not raised in *Little Mosque on the Prairie*.

On the other hand, the situation is decidedly better in Canada than in other Western countries. Canadian Muslims form the most highly educated community of Muslims in the world. In France and in England, Muslim immigrants are on the whole much worse off economically and in terms of mobility prospects than they are

second place (Adams, 2007; Reitz, 2010). The Canadian record in welcoming and supporting the integration of immigrants is something that deserves to be celebrated (see Box 10.1) (Berry, 2013). Still, racial and ethnic inequalities remain.

Such inequalities are more deeply rooted in social structure than in biology and culture. Said differently, the biological and cultural aspects of race and ethnicity are secondary to their sociological character when it comes to explaining inequality. Moreover, the distinction between race and ethnicity is not as simple as the difference between biology and culture. As noted above for the Irish and the Jews, groups once socially defined as races may be later redefined as ethnicities, even though they do not change biologically. Social definitions, not biology and not culture, determine whether a group is viewed as a race or an ethnic group. The interesting question from a sociological point of view is why social definitions of race and ethnicity change. We now consider that issue.

TIME FOR REVIEW

- How can social differences account for racial differences in athletic performance?
- What role does culture play in determining the success of ethnic and racial minorities in Canada?
- What are the central features of Canada's multiculturalism policy?

in Canada. Especially in France, they are prevented from certain public displays of their religious heritage. In both European countries, Muslims have occasionally rioted to protest the conditions of their existence, something that Canada has never seen. Not surprisingly in this context, Muslims in France and England more frequently adopt extremist attitudes than they do in Canada.

Similarly, in the United States, antipathy to Muslims is more widespread than it is in Canada. Some Americans have sought to prevent the construction of mosques, in at least one case even going so far as to set fire to a construction site. In 2011, the American television station TLC launched a reality show called *All-American Muslim* documenting the lives of Muslims outside Detroit. However, after a member of the Christian Florida Family Association objected that the show was pro-Muslim propaganda, the show lost sponsors (including Lowes, the home improvement chain). It was cancelled in its first season (Freedman, 2011).

Canadians' reception of *Little Mosque on the Prairie* was much warmer. It became one of the most popular Canadian comedy series ever aired. In 2007, it won Gemini's Canada Award for media representation of multiculturalism and was nominated for a host of other prizes by the Directors Guild of Canada, the Gemini Awards, and the Canadian Comedy Awards. Thus, despite ignoring unpleasant realities that require the attention of all Canadians, *Little Mosque on the Prairie* accurately reflects the fact that Muslims in Canada are on the whole better off and more respected than are their co-religionists in other Western countries.

The cast of *Little Mosque on the Prairie*

Courtesy of WestWind Pictures

RACE AND ETHNIC RELATIONS: THE SYMBOLIC INTERACTIONIST APPROACH

Labels and Identity

John Lie moved with his family from South Korea to Japan when he was a baby. He moved from Japan to Hawaii when he was 10 years old, and again from Hawaii to the American mainland when he started university. The move to Hawaii and the move to the U.S. mainland changed the way John thought of himself in ethnic terms.

In Japan, Koreans form a minority group. Before 1945, when Korea was a colony of Japan, some Koreans were brought to Japan to work as miners and unskilled labourers. The Japanese thought the Koreans who lived there were beneath and outside Japanese society (Lie, 2001). Not surprisingly, then, Korean children in Japan, including John, were often teased and occasionally beaten by their Japanese schoolmates. "The beatings hurt," says John, "but the psychological trauma resulting from being socially excluded by my classmates hurt more. In fact, although I initially thought I was Japanese like my classmates, my Korean identity was literally beaten into me.

"When my family immigrated to Hawaii, I was sure things would get worse. I expected Americans to be even meaner than the Japanese were. (By Americans, I thought only of white European Americans.) Was I surprised when I discovered that most of my schoolmates were not white European Americans, but people of Asian and mixed ancestry! Suddenly I was a member of a numerical majority. I was no longer teased or bullied. In fact, I found that students of Asian and non-European origin often singled out white European Americans (called *haole* in Hawaiian) for abuse. We even had a 'beat up *haole* day' in school. Given my own experiences in Japan, I empathized somewhat with the white Americans. But I have to admit that I also felt a great sense of relief and an easing of the psychological trauma associated with being Korean in Japan.

"As the years passed, I finished public school in Hawaii. I then went to college in Massachusetts and got a job as a professor in Illinois. I associated with, and befriended, people from various racial and ethnic groups. My Korean origin became a less and less important factor in the way people treated me. There was simply less prejudice and discrimination against Koreans during my adulthood in the United States than in my early years in Japan. I now think of myself less as Japanese or Korean than as American. When I lived in Illinois, I sometimes thought of myself as a Midwesterner. Now that I have changed jobs and moved to California, my self-conception may shift again; my identity as an Asian American may strengthen given the large number of Asians who live in California. Clearly, my ethnic identity has changed over time in response to the significance others have attached to my Korean origin. I now understand what the French philosopher Jean-Paul Sartre meant when he wrote that 'the anti-Semite creates the Jew'" (Sartre, 1965 [1948]: 43).

The Formation of Racial and Ethnic Identities

The details of John Lie's life are unique. But experiencing a shift in racial or ethnic identity is common. Social contexts and, in particular, the nature of the relations with members of other racial and ethnic groups, shape and continuously reshape a person's racial and ethnic identity. Change your social context and your racial and ethnic self-conception eventually changes too (Miles, 1989; Omi and Winant, 1986).

Consider Italian Canadians. Around 1900, Italian immigrants thought of themselves as people who came from a particular town or perhaps a particular province, such as Sicily or Calabria. They did not usually think of themselves as Italians. Italy had become a unified country only in 1861. A mere 40 years later, many Italian citizens still did not identify with their new Italian nationality. In both Canada and the United States, however, government officials and other residents identified the newcomers as Italians. The designation at first seemed odd to many of the new immigrants. Over time, however, it stuck. Immigrants from Italy started thinking of themselves as Italian Canadians because others defined them that way. A new ethnic identity was born (Yancey, Ericksen, and Leon, 1979).

As symbolic interactionists emphasize, the development of racial and ethnic labels, and ethnic and racial identities, is typically a process of negotiation. For example, members of a group may have a racial or an ethnic identity, but outsiders may impose a new label on them. Group members then reject, accept, or modify the label. The negotiation between outsiders and insiders eventually results in the crystallization of a new, more or less stable ethnic identity. If the social context changes again, the negotiation process begins a new.

One such case involves the labelling of the Indigenous peoples of North America by European settlers. When Christopher Columbus landed in North America in 1492, he assumed he had reached India. He called the Indigenous peoples *Indians* and the misnomer stuck—not only among European settlers but also among many Indigenous peoples themselves. Indigenous peoples still identified themselves in tribal terms—as Mi'kmaq or Mohawk or Haida—but they typically thought of themselves collectively and *in opposition to European settlers* as Indians. A new identity was thus grafted onto tribal identities because Indigenous peoples confronted a group that had the power to impose a name on them.

In time, however, an increasingly large number of Indigenous people began to reject the term *Indian*. White settlers and their governments took land from the Indigenous peoples and forced them onto reserves, which led to growing resentment, anger, and solidarity.

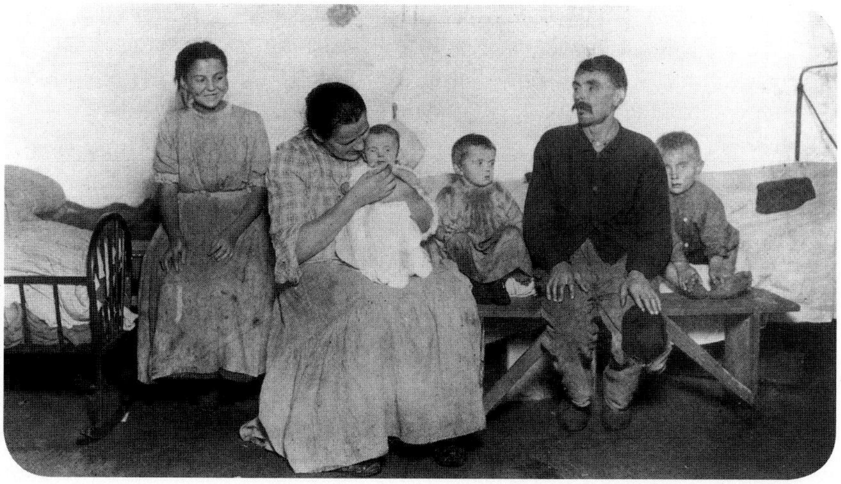
National Archives of Canada/C-030939

Many white Canadians lived in poor urban ghettos in the nineteenth and early twentieth centuries. However, a larger proportion of them experienced upward mobility than was the case for African Canadians in the late twentieth century. This photo shows a family in a Manitoba tenement in 1912.

Especially since the 1960s, Indigenous North Americans have begun to fight back culturally and politically, asserting pride in their languages, art, and customs, and making legal claims to the land that had been taken from them. One aspect of their resistance involved questioning the use of the term *Indian*. In Canada, many prefer instead to be referred to as Native Canadians, Indigenous people, Aboriginal people, or First Nations. These new terms, especially the last one, are assertions of new-found pride. Today, many North Americans of European origin accept these new terms out of respect for Indigenous North Americans and in recognition of their neglected rights. New, more or less stable ethnic identities have thus been negotiated as the power struggle continues between Indigenous people and more recent settlers. As the social context changed, the negotiation of ethnic identities proceeded apace.

Ethnic and Racial Labels: Imposition versus Choice

The idea that race and ethnicity are socially constructed does not mean that everyone can always freely choose their racial or ethnic identity. The degree to which people can exercise such freedom of choice varies widely over time and from one society to the next. Moreover, in a given society at a given time, different categories of people are more or less free to choose their racial or ethnic identity.

In Canada, the people with the most freedom to choose are white European Canadians whose ancestors arrived more than two generations ago. For example, identifying yourself as an Irish Canadian no longer has negative implications, as it did in, say, 1900. Then, in a city like Toronto, with a substantial concentration of Irish immigrants, the English Protestant majority typically regarded working-class Irish Catholics as often drunk, inherently lazy, and born superstitious. This strong anti-Irish sentiment, which sometimes erupted into conflict, meant the Irish found it difficult to escape their ethnic identity even if they wanted to. Since then, however, Irish Canadians have followed the path taken by many other white European groups. They have achieved upward mobility and blended with the majority.

As a result, Irish Canadians no longer find their identity imposed on them. Instead, they may *choose* whether to march in a St. Patrick's Day parade, enjoy the remarkable contributions of Irish authors to English-language literature and drama, and take pride in the athleticism and precision of Riverdance. For them, ethnicity is largely a *symbolic* matter, as it is for the other white European groups that have undergone similar social processes. Herbert Gans defines **symbolic ethnicity** as "a nostalgic allegiance to the culture of the immigrant generation, or that of the old country; a love for and a pride in a tradition that can be felt without having to be incorporated in everyday behavior" (Gans, 1991: 436).

Symbolic ethnicity is a nostalgic allegiance to the culture of the immigrant generation, or that of the old country, that is not usually incorporated in everyday behaviour.

In contrast, most African Canadians lack the freedom to enjoy symbolic ethnicity. They may well take pride in their cultural heritage and participate in such cultural festivals as Caribana. However, their identity as people of African descent is not an option

Racism is the belief that a visible characteristic of a group, such as skin colour, indicates group inferiority and justifies discrimination.

because a considerable number of non-blacks are racists and impose the identity on them. **Racism** is the belief that a visible characteristic of a group, such as skin colour, indicates group inferiority and justifies discrimination (see Box 10.2). Surveys show that between 30 percent and 55 percent of Canadians (depending on the wording of the question) hold racist views of varying intensity (Henry

BOX 10.2

SOCIOLOGY AT THE MOVIES

SEARCHING FOR SUGARMAN

Apartheid was the brutal system of racial segregation that governed South Africa from 1948 to 1994. Nelson Mandela is known around the world as the black leader who heroically protested that racist system. He was imprisoned for 27 years for resisting apartheid but emerged to become the country's president.

Although apartheid privileged South African whites, many were disgusted by its social injustices. Those whites joined with blacks and, over the decades, protested and resisted the governing regime. During the same period, more than 15 000 km away, blacks and whites in the United States were protesting the system of segregation that denied people of colour their civil rights.

Protesting oppressive institutional arrangements is a grind and it is often dangerous. It requires focus, organization, persistence, and bravery. Those in power do not give up their privileges easily. Protest movements continually look for tools to inspire their members and keep them on task. Around the world, one important tool for rallying demonstrators is the protest song (Cullum, 2011).

Many protest singers participated in the American civil rights protests of the 1960s and 1970s. One of the most famous was Bob Dylan. But while Dylan was gaining international fame, record producers discovered a Latino singer–songwriter working in Detroit. They were confident he would be as big as Dylan. Sixto Rodriguez released two critically successful albums. However, they were commercial flops, and Rodriguez's recording contract was promptly cancelled. He returned to a life of obscurity as a construction worker.

Rex Features via AP Images

Sixto Rodriguez

Rodriguez thought his musical career was done. But he was wrong. A bootlegged copy of his *Cold Play* album made its way to South Africa, where it reached an enthusiastic audience among apartheid protesters. Its songs became rallying cries for the opposition. Rodriguez obtained a cult-like following, reinforced by the false rumour of his on-stage suicide (Titlestad, 2013).

Searching for Sugar Man is a documentary of two South African protesters' journey in the late 1990s to determine the circumstances of Rodriguez's death. Much to their surprise, they find him living an anonymous life in Detroit. The documentary mixes archival footage and interviews to provide insights into how racial discrimination operates in South Africa and the United States. It reveals that although Rodriguez's albums have worldwide sales of between 500,000 and 1 million copies, he has never received a penny in royalties (Frere-Jones, 2012).

Searching for Sugar Man won the best-documentary Academy Award in 2013. It is of sociological interest on several accounts. First, it reminds us how racist and oppressive Western political institutions were only a few decades ago. Second, it provides a sense of the sustained effort required to overturn racially unjust institutional arrangements. Regime change is not for weak-willed romantics. Finally, we see an illustration of how interconnected the global village is. A neglected, protest singer of colour in the United States inspires white apartheid demonstrators half way around the world. Their actions, in turn, reignite Rodriguez's late-in-life musical career.

et al., 2001: 147–51). Racism is not confined to individuals. Racism is often embedded in the policies and practices of organizations. Where this occurs it is called **institutional racism**.

As the contrast between Irish Canadians and African Canadians suggests, then, relations among racial and ethnic groups can take different forms. We now turn to conflict theories, which seek to explain why racial and ethnic relations take different forms in different times and places.

Institutional racism occurs where organizational policies and practices systematically discriminate against people of colour.

CONFLICT THEORIES OF RACE AND ETHNICITY

Many whites of European origin have assimilated into Canadian society. Their families have been here for generations, and they have stopped thinking of themselves as Italian Canadian or Irish Canadian or German Canadian. Today, they think of themselves just as Canadians because, over time, they have achieved rough equality with members of the majority group (Boyd, 1999; Boyd and Norris, 2001). In the process, they began to blend in with them.

In contrast, assimilation is less widespread among Aboriginal people, Québécois, African Canadians, and Asian Canadians. Conflict theories explain why.

Internal Colonialism

One conflict theory is the theory of **internal colonialism** (Blauner, 1972; Hechter, 1974). *Colonialism* involves people from one country invading another country. In the process, the invaders change or destroy the native culture. They gain virtually complete control over the native population. They develop the racist belief that the native inhabitants are inherently inferior. And they confine the native people to work considered demeaning. *Internal colonialism* involves much the same processes but within the boundaries of a single country. Internal colonialism prevents assimilation by segregating the colonized people in terms of jobs, housing, and social contacts ranging from friendship to marriage. To varying degrees, Canada, the United States, Great Britain, Australia, France, Italy, Spain, Russia, and China have engaged in internal colonialism. In Canada, the main victims of internal colonialism are Aboriginal people, the Québécois, and people of African descent.

Internal colonialism involves one race or ethnic group subjugating another in the same country. It prevents assimilation by segregating the subordinate group in terms of jobs, housing, and social contacts.

Aboriginal People in Canada

The single word that best describes the treatment of Aboriginal people in Canada by European immigrants in the nineteenth century is *expulsion*. **Expulsion** is the forcible removal of a population from a territory claimed by another population.

Expulsion is the forcible removal of a population from a territory claimed by another population.

Expulsion is dramatically illustrated by the plight of the Beothuk (pronounced bee-**aw**-thik), an Aboriginal people who lived in what is today Newfoundland and Labrador. The Beothuk were Algonkian-speaking people who probably numbered fewer than a thousand at the time of European contact. In the sixteenth century, Europeans used Newfoundland and Labrador as a fishing port, returning to Europe each year after the fishing season. In the seventeenth century, year-round European settlement began. This caused a revolution in the life of the Beothuk because the Europeans viewed them as a nuisance. They even offered incentives to the Mi'kmaq of Nova Scotia to kill off the Beothuk. The Beothuk population declined and gradually withdrew from European contact.

As European settlement grew in the eighteenth century, the Beothuk were squeezed into the interior. There they competed with fur traders for scarce resources. Eventually the Beothuk were reduced to a small refugee population along the Exploits River system, living off the meagre resources of the Newfoundland and Labrador interior. The expulsion of the Beothuk from their traditional territories because of European colonization led to the tribe's eventual extinction. Today, about all that remains of the Beothuk, aside from their tragic history and a few artefacts, is a statue outside the Newfoundland and Labrador provincial legislature.

The story of the Beothuk is an extreme case. However, *all* Aboriginal tribes had broadly similar experiences. In the eighteenth and nineteenth centuries, as the European settlers' fur trade gave way to the harvesting of timber, minerals, oil, and gas, Aboriginal peoples were shunted aside so the Canadian economy could grow. At the time, Europeans thought they were

The Canadian policy of assimilation: In its annual report of 1904, the Department of Indian Affairs published the photographs of Thomas Moore of the Regina Industrial School "before and after tuition." These images are "a cogent expression of what federal policy had been since Confederation and what it would remain for many decades. It was a policy of assimilation, a policy designed to move Aboriginal communities from their 'savage' state to that of 'civilization' and thus to make in Canada but one community—a non-Aboriginal one" (Milloy, 1999).

Saskatchewan Archives Board, R-82239[1] and R-82239[2]

Saskatchewan Archives Board, R-82239[1] and R-82239[2]

"assimilating" the Aboriginal peoples. The Indian Act spoke of the need to transform a hunting-gathering people into an agricultural labour force (Menzies, 1999). Sir John A. Macdonald, Canada's first prime minister, spoke of the need "to do away with the tribal system and assimilate the Indian people in all respects with the inhabitants of the Dominion, as speedily as they are fit to change" (quoted in Montgomery, 1965: 13). In contrast, many Aboriginal peoples understood the settlers' actions—the passage of the Indian Act, the establishment of the reserve system, the creation of residential schools, and so forth—less as an attempt to assimilate them than as an attempt to obliterate their heritage. It is in this sense that the government of Canada has been accused by some Aboriginal peoples of perpetuating cultural genocide (Cardinal, 1977). **Genocide** is the intentional extermination of an entire population defined as a "race" or a "people."

Genocide is the intentional extermination of an entire population defined as a "race" or a "people."

Adding insult to injury, early historical writing about Canada depicted Aboriginal peoples as either irrelevant or evil. Typically, in *The History of the Dominion of Canada*, a book widely used in Canadian schools at the turn of the twentieth century, only five pages were devoted to Aboriginal peoples (Clement, 1897). They are described as "cruel," "rude," "false," "crafty," "savages," and "ferocious villains" who plotted against the Europeans with "fiendish ingenuity" (Francis, 1992; Richardson, 1832; Roberts, 1915). Canadian schoolbooks continued to portray Aboriginal peoples in pretty much this way until the mid-twentieth century.

So we see that, throughout North America, the confrontation with European culture undermined the way of life of the Aboriginal peoples. Because of internal colonialism and, in particular, expulsion from their traditional lands, Aboriginal peoples in Canada were prevented from practising their traditional ways and assimilating into the larger society. Most of them languished on reservations and, in more recent times, in urban slums. There they experienced high rates of unemployment, poverty, ill health, and violence (see Table 10.2).

Especially since the 1960s, Canada's First Nations have periodically demonstrated in protest against the conditions of their existence. The most recent of these protests, the "Idle No More" movement, erupted in late 2012, after the federal government, eager to see new oil and gas pipelines built from Alberta to the British Columbia coast, weakened the consultation and approval process for construction along Canada's waterways. Such pipeline construction increases the risk of serious environmental damage, and some of the affected territory is on Native reserves. First Nations demonstrations against the new legislation began in Saskatchewan, and protesters later began blocking rail lines in British Columbia, Ontario, and Québec. The chief of a reserve in northern Ontario went on a hunger strike to

TABLE 10.2
Social Conditions among Aboriginal Peoples in Canada, circa 2006

	Aboriginal Peoples	Non-Aboriginal Peoples
Adult population with university degree (%)	7.0	25.0
Population residing in dwellings requiring major repair (%)	45.0[1]	7.5
Median income (index: non-Aboriginal = 100.0)	66.7	100.0
Population in low-income families (%)	31.2	12.4
Unemployment rate (%)	12.3	6.3
Projected life expectancy, 2017 (years)	68.5	81.5
Suffered major depressive attitude in past year (%)	13.2	7.3
Population with diabetes (%)	19.7[1]	5.2
Ethnic status of adult population in federal and provincial prisons (%)	18.0	3.1

[1]On-reserve only.

Sources: Perreault, Samuel. 2009. "The Incarceration of Aboriginal People in Adult Correctional Services." Juristat July. Accessed January 5, 2013 (www.statcan.gc.ca/pub/85-002-x/2009003/article/10903-eng.htm#a1); Reading, Charlotte Loppie, and Fred Wien. 2009. "Health Inequalities and Social Determinants of Aboriginal Peoples' Health." National Collaborating Centre for Aboriginal Health. Accessed January 4, 2013 (http://ahrnets.ca/files/2011/02/NCCAH-Loppie-Wien_Report.pdf); Statistics Canada. 2010a. "Aboriginal Statistics at a Glance." Accessed January 4, 2013 (www.statcan.gc.ca/pub/89-645-x/89-645-x2010001-eng.htm).

force a meeting with the prime minister and publicize the plight of her people. As of this writing, the effect of this latest wave of Aboriginal protest is unclear. What is certain is that it raised once again the question of whether and in what form non-Aboriginal Canadians should take responsibility for past and current injustices, a subject to which we return later.

The Québécois

A second form of internal colonialism involves not expulsion but **conquest**, the forcible capture of land and the economic and political domination of its inhabitants. For example, as part of their centuries-long struggle to control North America, the English conquered New France and its 60 000 settlers in 1759. The English thereby created a system of ethnic stratification that remained in place for more than 200 years and turned out to be a major source of political conflict (McRoberts, 1988).

Conquest is the forcible capture of land and the economic and political domination of its inhabitants.

The British recognized that any attempt to impose their language, religion, laws, and institutions in the former French colony could result in unacceptably high levels of resistance and conflict. Therefore, they tried to accommodate farmers and the Catholic clergy by reinforcing their rights and privileges. The British believed this approach would win the allegiance of these two groups, who would in turn help build loyalty to Britain among the population as a whole. In contrast, the British undermined the rights and privileges of merchants engaged mainly in the fur trade. So while agriculture, religion, and politics remained the province of the French, the British took over virtually all large-scale commerce.

As noted, this pattern of ethnic stratification remained intact for two centuries. True, by 1950, most farmers had been transformed into urban, industrial workers. A contingent of Québécois had become physicians, lawyers, and members of the "new middle class" of administrators, technicians, scientists, and intellectuals. However, the upper reaches of the stratification system remained overwhelmingly populated by people of British origin. Social separation reinforced economic segregation. The French and the British tended to speak different languages, live in different towns and neighbourhoods, interact occasionally, befriend one another infrequently, and intermarry rarely. Characteristically, the novel that became emblematic of the social relations between French and English in Québec is entitled *Two Solitudes* (MacLennan, 1945).

Apart from its rigid system of ethnic stratification, Québec in the middle of the twentieth century was remarkable because of its undeveloped government services. Health, education, and welfare were largely controlled by the Catholic Church. Government intervention in economic matters was almost unknown. Because of this political backwardness, in the late 1940s, members of Québec's new middle class, together with blue-collar workers, began campaigning to modernize the provincial political system. They pressed for more liberal labour laws that would recognize the right of all workers to form unions and strike. They wanted state control over education and a new curriculum that stressed the natural and social sciences rather than classical languages and catechism. They desired a government that would supply a wide range of social services to the population. They demanded that the state provide better infrastructure for economic development and help francophone entrepreneurs expand their businesses. The partial realization of these aims in the 1960s came to be known as the Quiet Revolution.

However, the modernization of the Québec state failed to resolve four issues:

1. *The potential demographic decline of the Québécois.* By 1981, Québécois women were giving birth to fewer children on average than were women in any other province. In fact, they were having fewer than the 2.1 children that women must bear on average to ensure that the size of the population does not decline (Romaniuc, 1984: 14–18). Noticing this trend in the 1970s, many Québécois felt they were becoming an endangered species.
2. *The assimilation of immigrants into English culture.* Fears of demographic decline were reinforced by the preference of most new immigrants to have their children educated in English-language schools. Together with the falling birth rate, this development threatened to diminish the size—and therefore, potentially, the power—of Québec's francophone population.
3. *Persistent ethnic stratification.* The Quiet Revolution helped to create many thousands of jobs for highly educated francophones—but almost exclusively in the government bureaucracy, the educational system, and in new Crown corporations, such as Hydro-Québec. It became apparent in the 1970s that management positions in the private sector remained the preserve of English-origin Canadians.
4. *The continued use of English as the language of private industry.* English remained the language of choice in the private sector because the largest and technologically most advanced businesses were controlled by English Canadians and Americans. This situation was felt particularly keenly when the expansion of the state sector, and therefore the upward mobility of the francophone new middle class, slowed in the 1970s.

Because of the above-listed issues, many Québécois felt that the survival and prosperity of their community required vigorous state intervention in non-francophone institutions. For example, many Québécois came to believe that most shares of banks, trust companies, and insurance firms should be held in Québec and that these financial institutions should be obliged to reinvest their profits in the province. They argued that the state should increase its role as economic planner and initiator of development and should forbid foreign ownership of cultural enterprises. Finally, the Québécois increasingly demanded compulsory French-language education for the children of most immigrants, obligatory use of French among private-sector managers, and French-only signs in public places. Most Québécois regarded these proposals as the only means by which their community could survive and attain equality with the English. Moreover, since the Québec state did not have the legal authority to enact some of the proposed changes, many Québécois felt that the province ought to negotiate broader constitutional powers with the federal government. A large minority of Québécois went a step further. They became convinced that Québec ought to become a politically sovereign nation, albeit a nation economically associated with Canada.

The pro-independence Parti Québécois won the provincial election in 1976. In 1980, it held a referendum to see whether Québeckers favoured "sovereignty-association." Nearly 60 percent voted no. A second referendum was held in 1995. This time, the forces opposed to sovereignty-association won by the narrowest of margins—about 1 percent. The sovereignty question then subsided, and the Parti Québécois lost provincial elections in 2003, 2007, and 2008. The Parti Québécois declined to hold another referendum when it formed the province's governing party from 2012 to 2014. Nonetheless, Canada's future is still uncertain because of the economic, social, and cultural segregation of the Québécois from English Canada that is a legacy of the conquest.

Black Canadians

We have seen that internal colonialism, whether it is accomplished by means of expulsion or conquest, creates big barriers to assimilation that can endure for centuries. A third form of internal colonialism—slavery—creates similar barriers. **Slavery** is the ownership and control of people.

By 1800, 24 million Africans had been captured and placed on slave ships headed to North America, Central America, and South America. Because of violence, disease, and shipwreck, fewer than half survived the passage. Black slaves were bought and sold in Canada at least until the 1820s. Only in 1833, when the British government banned slavery throughout the British Empire, did the practice become illegal in Canada. Slavery was abolished in the United States 30 years later.

It is true that the extent of slavery in Canada paled in comparison with its widespread use in the United States, where tobacco and cotton production depended entirely on the work of dirt-cheap black labour. It is also true that for decades Canada served as the terminus of the "underground railway," a network of assistance that smuggled escaped slaves out of the United States to freedom in Canada. However, after the American Civil War (1861–65) the practice of encouraging black settlement in Canada was reversed. Government policy required the rejection of most immigration applications by black people. This policy reflected a deeply felt prejudice on the part of the Canadian population that persisted throughout the twentieth century (Sissing, 1996). Moreover, social relations between black Canadians and the white European majority were anything but intimate and based on equality. Until the middle of the twentieth century, African Canadians tended to do unskilled labour and be residentially and socially segregated—for example, in the Halifax community of Africville, established around 1850 by runaway American slaves (Clairmont and Magill, 1999).

Canadian immigration policy was liberalized in the 1960s. Racial and ethnic restrictions were removed. Immigrants were now admitted on the basis of their potential economic contribution to Canada, their close family ties with Canadians, or their refugee status (see Table 10.3). As a result, Canada became a much more racially and ethnically diverse society (see Figure 10.2). Today, about three-quarters of Canadian immigrants are members of visible minority groups, most of them from Africa, Asia, South America, and Central America. Among them, according to the 2011 census, are 945 000 blacks. They form Canada's third

TO BE SOLD,

A BLACK WOMAN, named PEGGY, aged about forty years ; and a Black boy her ſon, named JUPITER, aged about fifteen years, both of them the property of the Subſcriber.

The Woman is a tolerable Cook and waſher woman and perfectly underſtands making Soap and Candles.

The Boy is tall and ſtrong of his age, and has been employed in Country buſineſs, but brought up principally as a Houſe Servant—They are each of them Servants for life. The Price for the Wowan is one hundred and fifty Dollars—for the Boy two hundred Dollars, payable in three years with Intereſt from the day of Sale and to be properly ſecured by Bond &c.—But one fourth leſs will be taken in ready Money.

PETER RUSSELL.

York, Feb. 10th 1806.

Upper Canada Gazette, February 10, 1806

Black Slave for Sale: Many distinguished persons were slave owners, including Peter Russell, who held positions in the executive and legislative councils and became administrator of Upper Canada.

Slavery is the ownership and control of people.

Category	Number	Percentage
Family class	56 446	22.7
Economic immigrants	156 121	62.8
Refugees	27 872	11.2
Other	8 306	3.3
Not stated	4	0
Total	248 748	100.0

Source: Citizenship and Immigration Canada. 2012. "Facts and Figures: Immigration Overview Permanent and Temporary Residents 2011" p. 5. www.cic.gc.ca/english/pdf/research-stats/facts2011.pdf (accessed January 5, 2013). Adapted and reproduced with the permission of the Minister of Public Works and Government Services Canada, 2010.

TABLE 10.3
Canadian Immigrants by Category, 2011

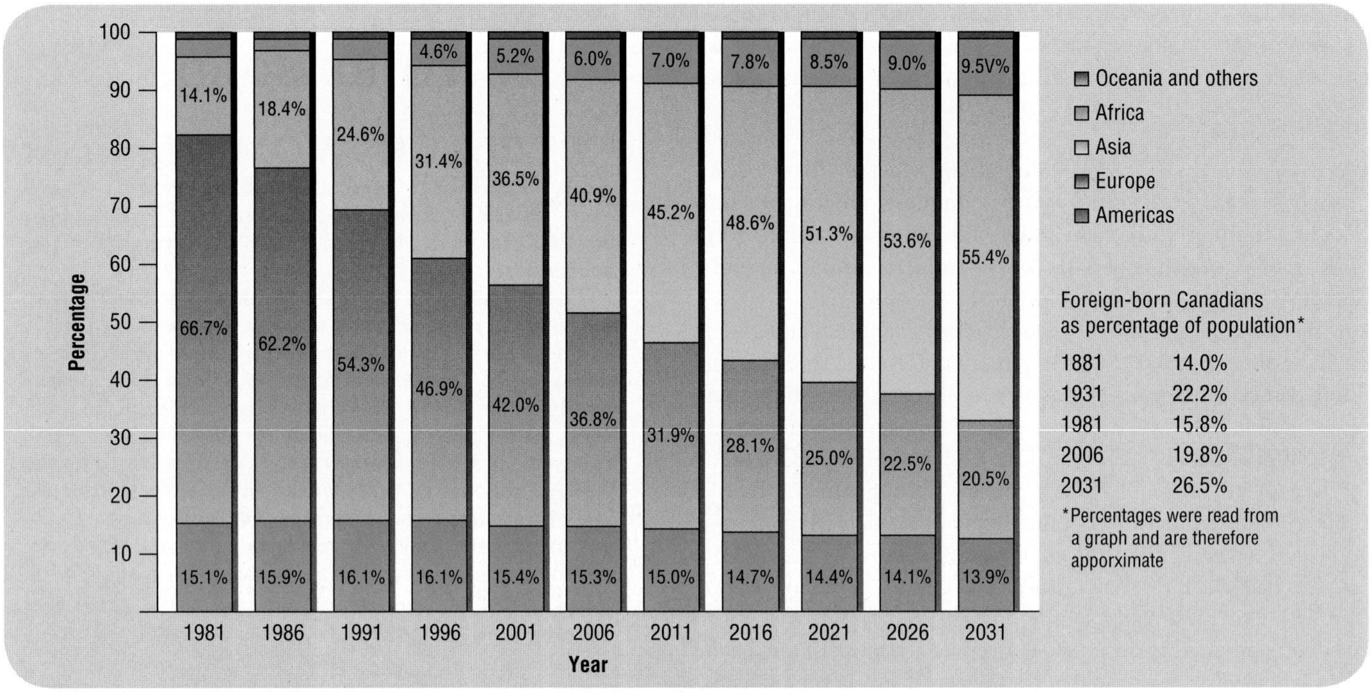

FIGURE 10.2

Canada's Foreign-Born Population by Continent of Birth, 1981 to 2031 (projected)

Source: Statistics Canada. 2006. Projections of the Diversity of the Canadian Population, 2006 to 2031, 91-551-XIE 2010001 2006 to 2031. Released March 9, 2010.

largest visible minority (after Chinese and East Indians), representing 2.8 percent of the total population and 15.1 percent of the population of visible minority people (see Table 10.4.). With the influx of new immigrants in recent decades, the social standing of Canada's black community has improved significantly. Many new immigrants had completed postsecondary education before their arrival. Others attended colleges and universities in Canada. Nonetheless, black Canadians still tend to interact little with white Canadians of European descent, especially in their intimate relations, and they still tend to live in different neighbourhoods. Like the aftermath of expulsion and conquest, the aftermath of slavery—prejudice, discrimination, disadvantage, and segregation—continues to act as a barrier to assimilation.

TABLE 10.4

Canadian Population by Visible Minority Group, 2006 and 2031 (projected)

Source: Statistics Canada. 2006. Projections of the Diversity of the Canadian Population, 2006 to 2031, 91-551-XIE 2010001 2006 to 2031. Released March 9, 2010.

	2006		2031	
Group	**Thousands**	**Percentage**	**Thousands**	**Percentage**
South Asian	1320	4.1	3640	8.7
Chinese	1269	3.9	2714	6.4
Black	815	2.5	1809	4.3
Filipino	427	1.3	1020	2.4
Latin American	317	1.0	733	1.7
Arab	276	0.8	930	2.2
Southeast Asian	250	0.8	449	1.1
West Asian	164	0.5	523	1.2
Korean	148	0.5	407	1.0
Japanese	85	0.3	142	0.3
Other	213	0.7	489	1.2
Subtotal	5285	16.3	12855	30.6
Rest of population	27237	83.7	29222	69.4
Total	32522	100.0	42078	100.0

You can easily judge for yourself the strength of social barriers between Canadians of different ethnic and racial backgrounds. You can also determine how this barrier has changed over time. Draw up a list of your five closest friends and note the ethnic or racial background of each one. Now ask one of your parents to do the same for *their* five closest friends. Finally, ask one of your grandparents to draw up a similar list. How racially and ethnically diverse is your friendship network? How do you explain its racial and ethnic diversity or lack of diversity? How racially and ethnically diverse is your friendship network compared with the friendship network of your parent and grandparent? How do you explain differences between generations?

The Theory of the Split Labour Market and the Case of Asian Canadians

We have seen how the theory of internal colonialism explains the persistence of inequality and segregation between racial and ethnic groups. A second theory that focuses on the social-structural barriers to assimilation is the theory of the **split labour market**, first proposed by sociologist Edna Bonacich (1972). Bonacich's theory explains why racial identities are reinforced by certain labour market conditions. In brief, she argues that where low-wage workers of one race and high-wage workers of another race compete for the same jobs, high-wage workers are likely to resent the presence of low-wage competitors and conflict is bound to result (see Box 10.3). Consequently, racist attitudes develop or are reinforced.

The theory of the **split labour market** holds that where low-wage workers of one race and high-wage workers of another race compete for the same jobs, high-wage workers are likely to resent the presence of low-wage competitors and conflict is bound to result. Consequently, racist attitudes develop or are reinforced.

This situation is certainly what happened during the early years of Asian immigration in Canada. Chinese, then Japanese, and later Sikhs were allowed into Canada from about the 1850s to the early 1920s for one reason: to provide scarce services and cheap labour in the booming West. By the early twentieth century, Chinese-owned restaurants, grocery stores, laundries, and import businesses dotted the West and especially British Columbia (Li, 1998; Whitaker, 1987). Numerically more important, however, were the Asian labourers who worked in lumbering, mining, and railway construction. For example, 15 000 Chinese men were allowed into Canada to complete construction of the final and most difficult section of

BOX 10.3

IT'S YOUR CHOICE

MORE SEASONAL AND MIGRANT WORKERS?

In 2013, the Royal Bank of Canada dismissed 50 high-tech information technology employees and replaced them with temporary foreign workers from India (Tomlinson, 2013). In 2014, several McDonald's franchises in British Columbia were found recruiting temporary foreign workers from the Philippines, while passing over fully qualified Canadian applicants (Gollom, 2014). These incidents caused much controversy because temporary foreign workers are not allowed to be hired if Canadian citizens or permanent residents are available to take the jobs in question. However, the number of temporary foreign workers is rising rapidly in Canada. Hiring now stands at 340 000 per year (Beltrame, 2014).

Temporary foreign workers arrive on temporary visas to take specific jobs. Their rights are ambiguous. Farm labourers and nannies make up about 2 percent of temporary foreign workers (Ramos, 2012). Some 25 percent of them are professionals.

Arguments exist for and against the current policy. Supporters argue that temporary foreign workers only want to earn some money and then return home (Ramos, 2012). Critics argue that the policy is racist and sexist insofar as it recruits a disproportionate number of women and persons of colour to low-level jobs, where exploitation and harassment are common. They also argue that temporary foreign workers take jobs away from unemployed Canadians and drive wages down (National Union of Public and General Employees, 2013).

The Canadian public is split on the issue (Trudeau Foundation, 2011). One-third oppose recruiting more temporary foreign workers, one-third support more recruitment, and one-third have no opinion. Into which category do you fall? What are the likely long-term consequences of your position?

the Canadian Pacific Railway (CPR), which involved blasting tunnels and laying rail along dangerous Rocky Mountain passes. The Chinese were paid half the wages of white workers. It is said that they "worked like horses." It is also said that they "dropped like flies" due to exposure, disease, malnutrition, and explosions. Three Chinese workers died for every kilometre of track laid.

Asian immigration in general was widely viewed as a threat to cherished British values and institutions, an evil to be endured only as long as absolutely necessary. Therefore, once the CPR was completed in 1885, the Chinese were no longer welcomed in British Columbia. A prohibitively expensive "head tax" equal to two months' wages was placed on each Chinese immigrant. The tax was increased tenfold in 1903. In 1923, Chinese immigration was banned altogether. During the Great Depression, more than 28 000 Chinese were deported because of high unemployment, and Asian immigration did not resume on a large scale until the 1960s, when racial criteria were finally removed from Canadian immigration regulations.

Underlying European Canadian animosity against Asian immigration was a split labour market. The fact that Asian immigrants were willing to work for much lower wages than were European Canadians fuelled deep resentment among European Canadians, especially when the labour market was flooded with too many job seekers. European Canadians formed "exclusion leagues" to pressure the government to restrict Asian immigration, and on occasion they even staged anti-Asian riots. Such actions solidified racial identities among both the throwers and the victims of the bricks and made assimilation impossible (on the 1907 anti-Asian riots in Vancouver, see Chapter 21, Collective Action and Social Movements).

In sum, the theory of split labour markets, like the theory of internal colonialism, emphasizes the social-structural roots of race and ethnicity. The groups that have had the most trouble assimilating into the British values and institutions that dominate Canadian society are those that were subjected to expulsion from their native lands, conquest, slavery, and split labour markets. These circumstances left a legacy of racism that created social-structural impediments to assimilation—impediments such as forced segregation in low-status jobs and low-income neighbourhoods.

Some Advantages of Ethnicity

The theories of internal colonialism and split labour markets emphasize how social forces outside a racial or an ethnic group can force its members together, preventing their assimilation into a society's dominant values and institutions. These theories focus on the

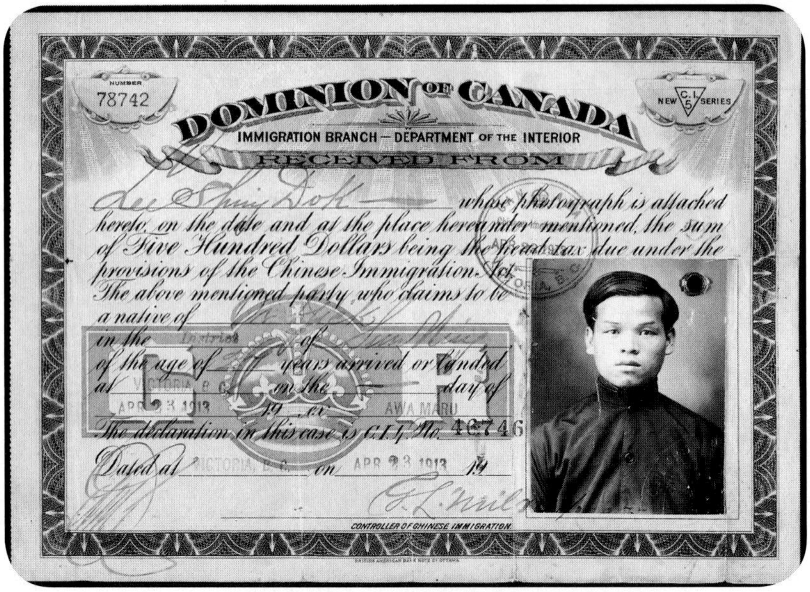

Head tax certificate: Immigrants from China were required by law to pay a "head tax" to enter Canada between 1885 and 1923. The tax began as a fee of $50 and rose as high as $500.

National Archives of Canada/C149236

Courtesy of the Pier 21 Society

Pier 21 is located at 1055 Marginal Road, Halifax. Many immigrants entered Canada at Pier 21, which opened its doors in 1928. As the era of ocean travel was coming to an end in March 1971, the Immigration Service left Pier 21. It is now the site of the Canadian Museum of Immigration at Pier 21.

disadvantages of race and ethnicity. Moreover, they address only the most disadvantaged minority groups. The theories have less to say about the internal conditions that promote group cohesion and, in particular, the *value* of group membership. And they don't help us to understand why some European Canadians, such as those of Greek or Polish or German origin, continue to participate in the life of their ethnic communities, even when their families have been in the country more than two or three generations.

The sociological literature suggests that three main factors enhance the value of ethnic group membership for some white European Canadians who have lived in the country for many generations:

1. *Ethnic group membership can have economic advantages.* The economic advantages of ethnicity are most apparent for immigrants, who often lack extensive social contacts and fluency in English or French. They commonly rely on members of their ethnic group to help them find jobs and housing. In this way, immigrant communities become tightly knit. However, some economic advantages extend into the second generation and beyond. For example, community solidarity is an important resource for "ethnic entrepreneurs," businesspeople who operate largely within their ethnic community. They draw on their community for customers, suppliers, employees, and credit, and they may be linked economically to the homeland as importers and exporters. They often pass on their businesses to their children, who in turn can pass the businesses on to the next generation. In this way, strong economic incentives encourage some people to remain ethnic group members, even beyond the immigrant generation (Light, 1991; Portes and Manning, 1991).
2. *Ethnic group membership can be politically useful.* Consider, for instance, the way some Canadians reacted to the rise of separatism in Québec in the 1960s. To bridge the growing divide between francophone Québec and the rest of the country, the federal government under Pierre Trudeau's Liberals promoted a policy of bilingualism. French and English were made official languages, which meant that federal government services would be made available in both languages, and instruction in French, including total immersion instruction, would be encouraged in English schools. Members of some ethnic groups, such as people of Ukrainian origin in Western Canada, felt neglected and alienated by this turn of events. They saw no reason for the French to be accorded special status and wanted a share of the resources available for promoting ethnic languages and cultures. As a result, the Trudeau government proclaimed a new policy

of multiculturalism in 1971. Federal funds became available for the promotion of Ukrainian and all other ethnic cultures in Canada. This entire episode of Canadian ethnic history bolstered Western support for the Liberal Party for nearly a decade and softened Western opposition to bilingualism. Moreover, it helped to stimulate ethnic culture and ethnic identification throughout the country. We thus see that ethnicity can be a political tool for achieving increased access to resources. This is part of the reason for the persistence of ethnic identification for some white European Canadians whose families have lived in the country for many generations.

Canadian Pacific Airline/National Archives of Canada/C-45080

With the introduction of the point system in 1967, nationality and race were removed as selection criteria from the Immigration Act.

3. *Ethnic group membership tends to persist because of the emotional support it provides.* Like economic benefits, the emotional advantages of ethnicity are most apparent in immigrant communities. Speaking the ethnic language and sharing other elements of native culture are valuable sources of comfort in an alien environment. Even beyond the second generation, however, ethnic group membership can perform significant emotional functions. For example, some ethnic groups have experienced unusually high levels of prejudice and discrimination involving expulsion or attempted genocide. For people who belong to such groups, the resulting trauma is so severe it can be transmitted for several generations. In such cases, ethnic group membership offers security in a world still seen as hostile long after the threat of territorial loss or annihilation has disappeared (Bar-On, 1999). Ethnic group membership also offers emotional support beyond the second generation by providing a sense of rootedness. Especially in a highly mobile, urbanized, technological, and bureaucratic society such as ours, ties to an ethnic community can be an important source of stability and security (Isajiw, 1978).

The three factors listed above make ethnic group membership useful to some Canadians whose families have been in the country for many generations. In fact, retaining ethnic ties beyond the second generation has never been easier. Inexpensive international communication and travel allow ethnic group members to maintain strong ties to their ancestral homeland in a way that was never possible in earlier times. Immigration once involved cutting all or most ties to a person's country of origin. Travel by sea and air was expensive, long-distance telephone rates were prohibitive, and the occasional letter was about the only communication most immigrants had with relatives in the old country. Lack of communication encouraged assimilation into the newly adopted countries. Today, however, ties to the ancestral communities are often maintained in ways that sustain ethnic culture. For example, roughly 25 000 Jews have emigrated from the former Soviet Union to Canada since the early 1970s, settling mainly in Toronto. They frequently visit relatives in the former Soviet Union and Israel, speak with them on the phone, and use the Internet to exchange email. They also receive Russian-language radio and TV broadcasts, act as conduits for foreign investment, and send money to relatives abroad (Brym, 2001; Brym with Ryvkina, 1994; Markowitz, 1993). This sort of intimate and ongoing connection with the motherland is typical of most recent immigrant communities in North America. Thanks to inexpensive international travel and communication, some ethnic groups have become **transnational communities** whose boundaries extend between countries.

Transnational communities are communities whose boundaries extend between or among countries.

In sum, ethnicity remains a vibrant force in Canadian society for a variety of reasons. Even some white Canadians whose families settled in this country more than two generations ago have reason to identify with their ethnic group. Bearing this in mind, what is the likely future of race and ethnic relations in Canada? We conclude by offering some tentative answers to that question.

TIME FOR REVIEW

- How does the theory of internal colonialism explain the historical processes through which Aboriginal peoples have been decimated, the Québécois threatened, and African Canadians exploited?
- How does split labour market theory help explain how powerful groups exploit ethnic differences to perpetuate dominance?
- What economic, political and socio-emotional advantages accompany the maintenance of connections to an ethnic community?

THE FUTURE OF RACE AND ETHNICITY IN CANADA

The world comprises nearly 200 countries and more than 5000 ethnic and racial groups. As a result, no country is ethnically and racially homogeneous and, in many countries, including Canada, the largest ethnic group forms less than half the population (see Table 10.5 and Figure 10.3). Canada's British roots remain important. Our parliamentary democracy is based on the British model. The Queen's representative, the governor general, is our titular head of state. We still celebrate May 24, Queen Victoria's birthday. And English is the country's predominant language, with more than 56 percent of Canadians claiming it as their mother tongue. Our French patrimony is also strong, especially of course in Québec. Nationwide, 22 percent of Canadians claim French as their mother tongue (Statistics Canada, 2010e). Nonetheless, Canada is one of the most racially and ethnically heterogeneous societies, and it will become still more diverse in coming decades (Pendakur, 2000).

As racial and ethnic diversity has increased, Canadian ethnic and race relations have changed radically. Two hundred years ago, Canada was a society based on expulsion, conquest, slavery, and segregation. Today, we are a society based on segregation, pluralism, and

TABLE 10.5
Canada's 25 Largest Ethnic Groups

1	Canadian	10 563 805	14	Filipino	662 600
2	English	6 509 500	15	British Isles	576 030
3	French	5 065 690	16	Russian	550 520
4	Scottish	4 714 970	17	Welsh	458 705
5	Irish	4 544 870	18	Norwegian	452 705
6	German	3 203 330	19	Métis	447 655
7	Italian	1 488 425	20	Portuguese	429 850
8	Chinese	1 487 580	21	American	372 575
9	First Nations (North American Indian)	1 369 115	22	Spanish	368 305
10	Ukrainian	1 251 170	23	Swedish	341 845
11	East Indian	1 165 145	24	Hungarian	316 765
12	Dutch	1 067 245	25	Jewish	309 650
13	Polish	1 010 705			

Source: Brym, 2014c: 18.
Note: Respondents could select more than one ethnicity.

FIGURE 10.3

Percentage of Population Accounted for by the Country's Largest Ethnic Group

No country is ethnically homogeneous, and in many countries the largest ethnic group forms less than half the population. This map illustrates the world's ethnic diversity by showing the percentage of each country's population that is accounted for by the country's largest ethnic group. How ethnically diverse is Canada compared with other countries?

Sources: "Ethnic Groups," 2001; Central Intelligence Agency, 2001.

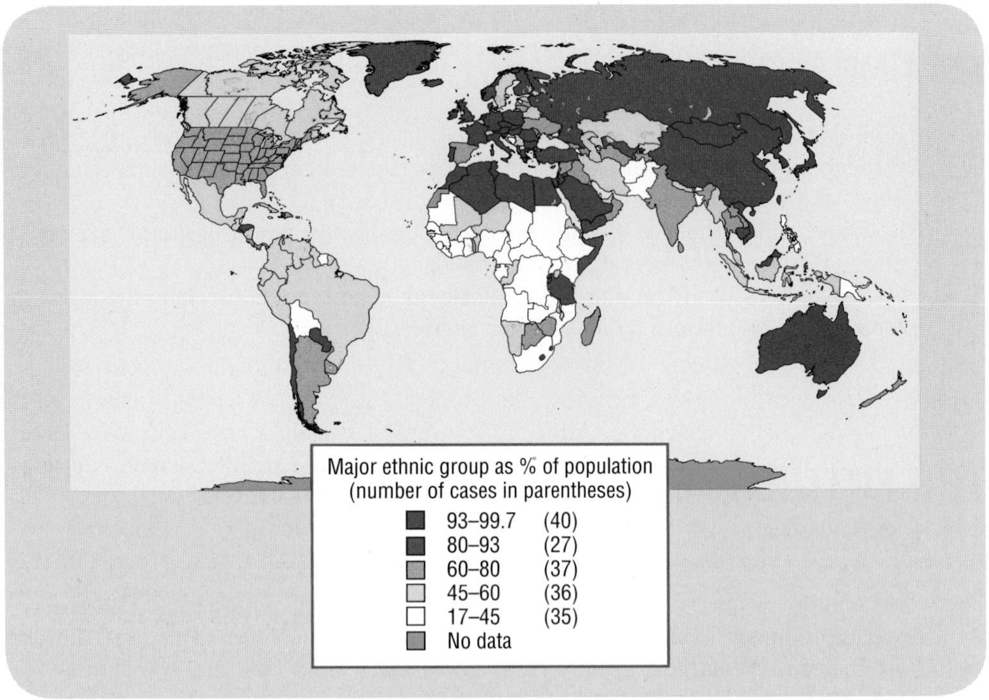
Major ethnic group as % of population
(number of cases in parentheses)
93–99.7 (40)
80–93 (27)
60–80 (37)
45–60 (36)
17–45 (35)
No data

Pluralism is the retention of racial and ethnic culture combined with equal access to basic social resources.

assimilation, with **pluralism** being understood as the retention of racial and ethnic culture combined with equal access to basic social resources. Thus, on a scale of tolerance, Canada has come a long way in the past 200 years (see Figure 10.4).

Canada is also a tolerant land compared with other countries. In the late twentieth and early twenty-first centuries, racial and ethnic tensions in some parts of the world erupted into wars of secession and attempted genocide. In the 1990s, conflict among Croats, Serbs, and other ethnic groups tore Yugoslavia apart. Russia fought two bloody wars against its Chechen ethnic minority. In Rwanda, Hutu militia and soldiers massacred many thousands of Tutsi civilians. A few years later, Tutsi soldiers massacred many thousands of Hutu civilians. Comparing Canada with countries that are not rich, stable, and postindustrial may seem to stack the deck in favour of concluding that Canada is a relatively tolerant society. However, even when we compare Canada with other rich, stable, postindustrial countries, it seems relatively tolerant by most measures. For example, a survey of 44 countries found that "only in Canada does a strong majority

FIGURE 10.4

Six Degrees of Separation: Types of Ethnic and Racial Group Relations

Source: From *KORNBLUM. *ACP SOCIOLOGY IN A CHANGING WORLD, 4E. © 1997 Wadsworth, a part of Cengage Learning, Inc. Reproduced by permission. www.cengage.com/permissions.

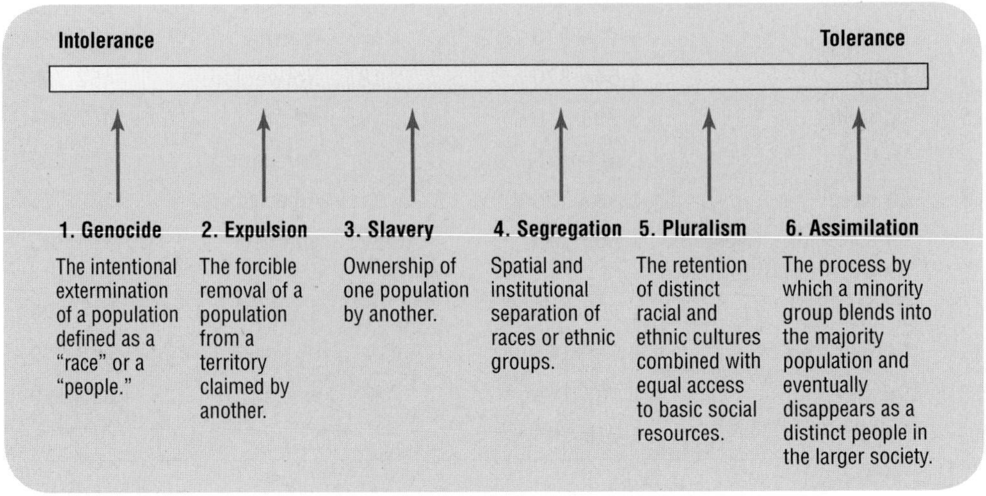
Intolerance
Tolerance
1. Genocide
The intentional extermination of a population defined as a "race" or a "people."
2. Expulsion
The forcible removal of a population from a territory claimed by another.
3. Slavery
Ownership of one population by another.
4. Segregation
Spatial and institutional separation of races or ethnic groups.
5. Pluralism
The retention of distinct racial and ethnic cultures combined with equal access to basic social resources.
6. Assimilation
The process by which a minority group blends into the majority population and eventually disappears as a distinct people in the larger society.

of the population (77 percent) have a positive view of immigrants." Far behind in second place came the United States, at 49 percent (Pew Research Center, 2002: 43; see also Figure 10.5).

Growing tolerance does not imply the absence of ethnic and racial discrimination and stratification (see Box 10.1). Although Canada is becoming less ethnically and racially stratified from one census to the next, serious problems remain (Lautard and Guppy, 2014). For one thing, the upward mobility of immigrants has slowed since the early 1990s, partly because many highly educated immigrants are finding it difficult to gain academic and professional recognition for credentials earned abroad (Reitz, 2011). For another, Aboriginal people are making slow progress in their efforts to raise their educational and economic standings. They remain clustered at the bottom of Canada's socioeconomic hierarchy. Finally, while the Canadian-born children of most immigrants are not disadvantaged because of their ethnicity or race, the same is not true for black men. Even black men who are Canadian-born face persistent discrimination and below-average earnings. It follows that, if present trends continue, Canada's mosaic will continue to be stratified, mainly along racial lines. Unless dramatic changes occur, a few groups will continue to enjoy less wealth, income, education, good housing, health care, and other social rewards than other Canadians do.

Political initiatives could decrease racial stratification, speeding up the movement from segregation to pluralism and assimilation for the country's most disadvantaged groups. Such political initiatives include more compensation for historical injustices committed against Aboriginal peoples. The historic 2008 apology by Prime Minister Harper for the havoc wrought on Aboriginal communities by Canada's residential schools, the $1.9 billion compensation package for victims of those schools, and the recent settlement of some Native land disputes gives hope in that regard (see Box 10.4). In addition, ethnic and racial equality would be increased, and disadvantaged Canadians would benefit from the following policies: instituting affirmative action or **employment equity** programs that encourage the hiring of qualified members of disadvantaged minority groups; government-subsidized job training and child care; and the creation of a system for efficiently upgrading credentials earned abroad to meet Canadian standards.

Employment equity is a policy giving preference to minority group members if equally qualified people are available for a position.

Institutional reforms can also play an important role. **Critical race theory** argues that racism is not necessarily the product of conscious decisions made by individuals. Rather, it is often the outcome of common practices that are embedded in Canada's political, legal, and other institutions but that many people are not aware of (Aylward, 1999). For example, the education system promotes students based on merit. However, many students from disadvantaged racial backgrounds cannot compete with other students on an equal footing because, in their families, they could not gain the language and other skills required for demonstrating merit in school. The principle of merit thus sounds fair but, in practice, it

Critical race theory holds that racism is often the outcome of common practices that are embedded in Canada's political, legal, and other institutions but that many people, especially those in dominant positions, are not aware of.

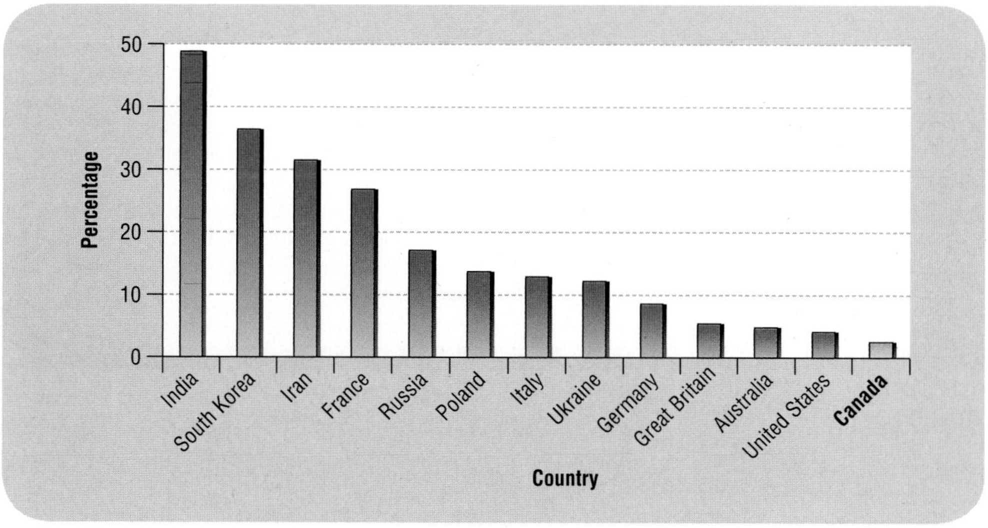

FIGURE 10.5
Percentage Not Wanting a Neighbour of a Different Race, Selected Countries

Source: World Values Survey. 2005. Machine readable data set. Ann Arbor MI: Inter-University Consortium for Political and Social Research. Reprinted with permission.

BOX 10.4

SOCIAL POLICY: WHAT DO YOU THINK?

SHOULD WE PAY THE PRICE OF PAST WRONGS?

July 28, 2001, was a hot, muggy day in Toronto, and Randall Robinson added to the heat with his fiery oration to the African Canadian Legal Clinic (ACLC). "We're owed at least $11 trillion," he exhorted. "America must pay for slavery." The Harvard-educated Robinson was championing the cause of reparations for the descendants of American slaves—monetary compensation for past injustices. Americans of African descent, he argued, have been "bottom-stuck" since they were slaves. Their disadvantaged position today, he argued, is the legacy of slavery.

Although slavery was abolished in Canada in 1833, Robinson's arguments were endorsed by the ACLC and by other Canadian groups that are not of African descent. Japanese, Chinese, Aboriginal, and Jewish Canadians all had representatives and gave advice at the meeting of the ACLC in July 2001.

- *Japanese Canadians.* In 1942, three months after Japan attacked Pearl Harbor, the Canadian government invoked the War Measures Act. All people of Japanese origin residing within 160 kilometres (100 miles) of the Pacific Coast were removed from their homes. With about 24 hours' notice, almost 21 000 Japanese Canadians, 75 percent of them Canadian citizens, were moved to prisoner of war camps, work camps, and internment camps. Japanese Canadians sought and eventually received reparations for this historical injustice.
- *Chinese Canadians.* As noted earlier, the descendants of many Chinese Canadians were forced to pay a highly discriminatory head tax between 1885 and 1903. Chinese Canadians received compensation for this mistreatment only in 2006.
- *Aboriginal peoples.* In the twentieth century, many Aboriginal children were taken from their parents and placed in residential schools. Many of them were physically and sexually abused in these schools. Aboriginal peoples also claim that much land was illegally taken from them. They, too, have sought and received a redress of grievances.
- *Jewish Canadians.* The Nazis enslaved and slaughtered European Jews by the millions during World War II. Jews were the first group to seek reparations (from the German government) for the historical injustices they suffered. Jewish Canadians have sought compensation from the Canadian government for refusing to allow a boatload of Jews fleeing Nazi Germany to land in Canada in 1939.

Other aggrieved groups who were apparently not represented at the meeting include Ukrainian and Croatian Canadians (some of whom were placed in internment camps during World War I), Italian and German Canadians (some of whom were placed in internment camps during World War II), and Sikh Canadians (a boatload of whom were refused entry in Vancouver in 1914).

In the past, what was past was past. The vanquished were vanquished and the powerful wrote the history books, taking no responsibility for what their ancestors had done. Today, things are different. Aggrieved groups in Canada and around the world are demanding reparations (Orsorio, 2014). Fertile terrain for this historical turn has been provided by the recognition of fundamental human rights, signified first by the Human Rights Declaration of the United Nations in 1948, and the widespread delegitimization of racial and ethnic discrimination. The mobilization of shame has triggered a revolutionary change in how some people and governments view past injustices.

What do you think about the reparations issue? Should *you* compensate African Canadians for slavery, Chinese Canadians for the head tax, Japanese Canadians for the internment camps, and Aboriginal peoples for residential schools and land? How responsible should *you* be for events that took place 50 or 200 years ago? In 1988, the Canadian government condemned the internment of Japanese Canadians during World War II, offered individual and community compensation to Japanese Canadians, and provided a $24 million endowment for the Canadian Race Relations Foundation. In 2005, $50 million in compensation was promised to Canadians of Chinese, Italian, Ukrainian, Croatian, German, Jewish, and Sikh origin. Also in 2005, a settlement was reached to compensate each former student of Aboriginal residential schools with $10 000 for the first year they spent in residence and $3000 for each additional year. So far the adjudication process has paid out about 80 000 claims. Does this seem fair to you? What about the far larger demands of Aboriginal peoples for self-government and land rights, given that they were pushed onto reserves to make way for exploration and resource development? Should Canada recognize its guilt and compensate those who have suffered? If not, why not? If so, what limits, if any, should be placed on reparations?

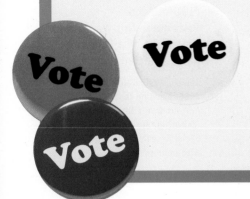

establishes a subtle form of racism and inhibits serious reform (Aylward, 1999). To deal with this problem, critical race theorists propose new programs to improve the preparation of students from disadvantaged racial backgrounds for the general school curriculum and to do a better job of recognizing the value of instructing students in their native languages about their own cultures and histories.

Critical race theorists argue that the privileged position of even well-intentioned members of dominant groups constrains their ability to understand, document, propose, and enact policies to address latent discrimination. In this view, the interests attached to privilege and power always predominate. It follows that a serious effort to address ongoing minority inequities must begin by listening to what minority group members have to say about their experience of injustice and inequality. This approach can begin to uncover the many ways in which apparently neutral policies framed in terms of "merit," "colour blindness," "equity," "opportunity," and the like actually reproduce privilege (Warner, 2006).

TIME FOR REVIEW

- What is the likely future of race and ethnicity in Canada?
- How does Canada compare with other countries in terms of its level of tolerance of immigrants and ethnic and racial minorities?
- What programs and policies are likely to reduce racial and ethnic inequality? What challenges are these programs and policies likely to face?

SUMMARY

1. How are race and ethnicity socially constructed? What roles do culture and social structure play in their perpetuation?
Biologists suggest that race is not a meaningful or useful term because the biological differences that distinguish races do not predict differences in social behaviour. However, sociologists note that *perceptions* of racial difference have important consequences for people's lives. Whether a person is seen as belonging to one race or another can affect that person's health, wealth, and many others aspects of life.

A race is a category of people whose perceived *physical* markers are deemed socially significant. An ethnic group is a category of people whose perceived *cultural* markers are deemed socially significant. Just as physical distinctions do not cause differences in the behaviour of races, cultural distinctions are often not in themselves the major source of differences in the behaviour of various ethnic groups. *Social-structural* differences are typically the most important sources of differences in social behaviour.

2. How are ethnic and racial identities shaped through social interaction?
Symbolic interactionists argue that race and ethnicity are not fixed and they are not inherent in people's biological makeup or cultural heritage. Rather, the way race and ethnicity are perceived and expressed depends on the history and character of race and ethnic relations in particular social contexts. These social contexts shape the way people formulate (or "construct") their perceptions and expressions of race and ethnicity. Thus, racial and ethnic labels and identities are variables. They change over time and place. For example, cordial group relations hasten the blending of labels and identities, whereas ethnic and racial animosity hardens them.

3. What role do power and privilege play in preserving ethnic and racial inequalities?
The theory of internal colonialism highlights the way powerful and privileged groups change or destroy Indigenous cultures, gaining virtually complete control over Indigenous populations, developing the racist belief that Indigenous people are inherently inferior, and confining them to work they consider to be demeaning. Internal colonialism prevents assimilation by segregating the colonized in terms of jobs, housing, and social contacts ranging from friendship to marriage. The theory of the split labour market highlights the way low-wage workers of one race and high-wage workers of another race may compete for the same jobs. In such circumstances, high-wage workers are likely to resent the presence of low-wage competitors. Conflict is bound to result and racist attitudes are likely to develop or get reinforced.

4. What is the future of race and ethnicity in Canada?
Racial and ethnic identities and inequalities are likely to persist into the foreseeable future. Affirmative action programs, more job training, improvements in public education, the creation of training courses designed to upgrade the credentials of foreign-trained professionals, and state-subsidized health care and child care would promote racial and ethnic equality. However, institutional racism is subtly embedded in Canadian institutions, making progressive policies and programmes challenging to implement.

NOTES

1. Controversy surrounds the terminology used throughout this chapter. In defining ethnicity and race, some scholars prefer to emphasize common descent and culture by using terms like *African Canadian* and *European Canadian* rather than *black* and *white*. However, terms that emphasize descent and culture can be ethnocentric. For example, there are millions of black immigrants from former British and French colonies in Europe. Therefore, *European Canadian* does not accurately signify the white majority in Canada. Because there is no perfect set of terms to denote racial or ethnic communities, we use *white* and *European Canadian*, as well as *black*, *African Canadian*, and *African American*.

2. Although sociologists commonly dispute a genetic basis of mean intelligence for races, evidence suggests that *individual* differences in intelligence are partly genetically transmitted (Bouchard et al., 1990; Lewontin, 1991: 19–37; Scarr and Weinberg, 1978; Schiff and Lewontin, 1986).

3. The genetic argument also belittles the athletic activity itself by denying the role of training in developing athletic skills.

CHAPTER 11

SEXUALITIES AND GENDER STRATIFICATION

Don Bayley/Getty Images

IN THIS CHAPTER, YOU WILL LEARN TO

- Distinguish sex (which is biologically determined) from gender (which is largely shaped by social structure and culture).
- Identify the main social forces that influence people to develop conventional gender roles and attitudes toward heterosexuality.
- Analyze how the conventional social distinction between men and women serves to create gender inequality in the workplace.
- Appreciate that gender inequality contributes to male aggression against women.

SEX VERSUS GENDER

Is It a Boy or a Girl?

On April 27, 1966, eight-month-old identical twin boys were taken to a hospital in Winnipeg to be circumcised. For the procedure, doctors used an electrical cauterizing needle—a device that seals blood vessels as it cuts. However, because of equipment malfunction or doctor error, the needle entirely burned off one baby's penis. The parents desperately sought medical advice. No matter whom they consulted, they received the same prognosis. As one psychiatrist summed up the baby's future, "He will be unable to consummate marriage or have normal heterosexual relations; he will have to recognize that he is incomplete, physically defective, and that he must live apart" (quoted in Colapinto, 1997: 58).

One evening, more than half a year after the accident, the parents, now deeply depressed, were watching TV. They heard Dr. John Money, a psychologist from Johns Hopkins Hospital in Baltimore, say that he could *assign* babies a male or female identity. Money had been the driving force behind the creation of the world's first sex-change clinic at Johns Hopkins. He was well known for his research on **intersexed** infants, babies born with ambiguous genitals because of a hormone imbalance in the womb or some other cause. It was Money's opinion that infants with ambiguous genitals should be assigned a sex by surgery and hormone treatments, and reared in accordance with their newly assigned sex. According to Money, these strategies would lead to the child developing a self-identity consistent with its assigned sex.

Intersexed infants are babies born with ambiguous genitals because of a hormone imbalance in the womb or some other cause.

The Winnipeg couple wrote to Dr. Money, who urged them to bring their child to Baltimore immediately. After consulting various physicians, including Money, the parents agreed to have their son's sex reassigned. In anticipation of what would follow, the boy's parents stopped cutting his hair, dressed him in feminine clothes, and changed his name from Bruce to Brenda. Doctors performed surgical castration when the child was 22 months old.

Early reports of the child's progress indicated success. In contrast to her biologically identical brother, Brenda was said to disdain cars, gas pumps, and tools. She was supposedly fascinated by dolls, a dollhouse, and a doll carriage. Brenda's mother reported that, at the age of four and a half, Brenda took pleasure in her feminine clothing: "[S]he is so feminine. I've never seen a little girl so neat and tidy . . . and yet my son is quite different. I can't wash his face for anything. . . . She is very proud of herself, when she puts on a new dress, or I set her hair" (quoted in Money and Ehrhardt, 1972: 11).

The case generated worldwide attention. Textbooks in medicine and the social sciences were rewritten to incorporate Money's reports of the child's progress (Robertson, 1987: 316). But then, in March 1997, two researchers dropped a bombshell. A biologist from the University of Hawaii and a psychiatrist from the Canadian Ministry of Health unleashed a scientific scandal when they published an article showing that Bruce/Brenda had, in fact, struggled against his/her imposed girlhood from the start (Diamond and Sigmundson, 1999). Brenda insisted on urinating standing up, refused to undergo additional "feminizing" surgeries that had been planned, and, from age seven, daydreamed of her ideal future self "as a twenty-one-year-old male with a moustache, a sports car, and surrounded by admiring friends" (Colapinto, 2001: 93). She experienced academic failure and rejection and ridicule from her classmates, who dubbed her "Cavewoman." At age nine, Brenda had a nervous breakdown. At age 14, in a state of acute despair, she attempted suicide (Colapinto, 2001: 96, 262).

In 1980, when she was 14, Brenda learned the details of her sex reassignment from her father. At age 16, she decided to have her sex reassigned once more and to live as a man rather than as a woman. Advances in medical technology made it possible for Brenda, who now adopted the name David, to have an artificial penis constructed. At age 25, David married a woman and adopted her three children, but that did not end his ordeal (Gorman, 1997). In May 2004, at the age of 38, David Reimer committed suicide.

CP PHOTO/Winnipeg Free Press

David Reimer at about 30 years of age.

Gender Identity and Gender Role

The story of Bruce/Brenda/David introduces the first big question of this chapter. What makes us male or female? Of course, part of the answer is biological. Your **sex** depends on whether you were born with distinct male or female genitals and a genetic program that released male or female hormones to stimulate the development of your reproductive system.

Your **sex** depends on whether you were born with distinct male or female genitals and a genetic program that released either male or female hormones to stimulate the development of your reproductive system.

However, the case of Bruce/Brenda/David also shows that more is involved in becoming male or female than biological sex differences. Recalling his life as Brenda, David said, "[E]veryone is telling you that you're a girl. But you say to yourself, 'I don't *feel* like a girl.' You think girls are supposed to be delicate and *like* girl things—tea parties, things like that. But I like to *do* guy stuff. It doesn't match" (quoted in Colapinto, 1997: 66; our emphasis). As this quotation suggests, being male or female involves not just biology but also certain "masculine" and "feminine" feelings, attitudes, desires, and behaviours. These characteristics—sociologists refer to them as features of a person's **gender**—may or may not align with a person's biological sex.

Gender refers to the feelings, attitudes, desires, and behaviours that are associated with a particular sexual category.

Gender has three components:

1. **Sexuality** refers to a person's capacity for erotic experiences and expressions.
2. **Gender identity** refers to a person's sense of belonging to a particular sexual category ("male," "female," "homosexual," "lesbian," "bisexual," and so on).
3. **Gender role** refers to behaviour that conforms to widely shared expectations about how members of a particular sexual category are supposed to act.

Sexuality refers to a person's capacity for erotic experiences and expressions.

Gender identity refers to a person's sense of belonging to a particular sexual category.

Contrary to first impressions, the case of Bruce/Brenda/David suggests that, unlike sex, gender is not determined solely by biology. Research shows that babies first develop a vague sense of being a boy or a girl at about the age of one. They develop a full-blown sense of gender identity between the ages of two and three (Fausto-Sterling, Coll, and Lamarre, 2012). We can therefore be confident that Bruce/Brenda/David already knew he was a boy when he was assigned a female gender identity at the age of 22 months. He had, after all, been raised as a boy by his parents and treated as a boy by his brother for almost two years. He had seen boys behaving differently from girls on TV and in storybooks. He had played with stereotypical boys' toys. After his gender reassignment, the constant presence of his twin brother reinforced those early lessons on how boys ought to behave. In short, baby Bruce's *social* learning of his gender identity was already far advanced by the time he had his sex-change operation. Many researchers believe that if gender reassignment occurs before the age of 18 months, it will usually be successful (Creighton et al., 2014; Hughes et al., 2006). However, once the social learning of gender has taken hold, as with baby

Gender role refers to behaviour that conforms to widely shared expectations about how members of a particular sexual category are supposed to act.

Bruce, it is apparently very difficult to undo, even by means of reconstructive surgery, hormones, and parental and professional pressure. The main lesson we draw from this story is not that biology is destiny but that the social learning of gender begins very early in life.

The first half of this chapter helps you understand what makes people conventionally male or female. We first outline two competing perspectives on gender differences. The first argues that gender is inherent in our biological makeup and that society must reinforce those tendencies if it is to operate smoothly. Functionalist theory is compatible with this argument. The second perspective argues that gender is constructed mainly by social influences and may be altered to benefit society's members. Conflict, feminist, and symbolic interactionist theories are compatible with the second perspective.

Heteronormativity is the belief that sex is binary (one must be either male or female as conventionally understood) and that sex ought to be perfectly aligned with gender (one's sexuality, gender identity, and gender role ought to be either male or female as conventionally understood).

Heterosexuality is the preference for members of the "opposite" sex as sexual partners.

In our discussion, we examine how people learn conventional gender roles in the course of everyday interaction, during socialization in the family and at school, and through advertising. We show that most of this learning is "heteronormative." **Heteronormativity** is the belief that sex is binary (one ought to be either male or female as conventionally understood) and that sex ought to be perfectly aligned with gender (one's sexuality, gender identity, and gender role ought to be either male or female as conventionally understood). Thus, most people regard **heterosexuality**—the preference for members of the "opposite" sex as sexual partners—as being normal, and they seek to enforce this preference. Yet, for reasons that are still poorly understood, some people resist and even reject the gender that is assigned to them based on their biological sex. When such resistance occurs, negative sanctions are often applied to get them to conform or to punish them for their deviance. People often use emotional and physical violence to enforce conventional gender roles.

The second half of the chapter examines one of the chief consequences of people learning conventional gender roles. Gender, as currently constructed, creates and maintains social inequality. We illustrate this point in two ways. We investigate why gender is associated with an earnings gap between women and men in the paid labour force. We also show how gender inequality encourages sexual harassment, sexual assault, and spouse abuse. In concluding our discussion of sexuality and gender, we discuss social policies that sociologists have recommended to decrease gender inequality and thereby improve women's safety.

TIME FOR REVIEW

- How do sex and gender differ?
- What are the consequences for people who have non-heteronormative appearance and behaviour?

THEORIES OF GENDER

Essentialism is a school of thought that views gender differences as a reflection of biological differences between women and men.

Most arguments about the origins of gender differences in human behaviour adopt one of two perspectives. Some analysts see gender differences as a reflection of naturally evolved dispositions. Sociologists call this perspective **essentialism** because it views gender as part of the nature or "essence" of a person's biological makeup (Gelman, 2003). Other analysts see gender differences as a reflection of the different social positions occupied by women and men. Sociologists call this perspective *social constructionism* because it views gender as being "constructed" by people living in historically specific social structures and cultures. Conflict, feminist, and symbolic interactionist theories focus on various aspects of the social construction of gender. We now summarize and criticize essentialism. We then turn to social constructionism.

Modern Essentialism: Sociobiology and Evolutionary Psychology

Sigmund Freud (1977 [1905]) offered an early essentialist explanation of male–female differences. However, in recent decades, sociobiologists and evolutionary psychologists have offered the most influential variant of the theory. According to sociobiologists and evolutionary psychologists, all humans instinctively try to ensure that their genes are passed on to future generations. However, men and women develop different strategies to achieve this goal. A woman has a bigger investment than a man does in ensuring the survival of offspring because she produces only a small number of eggs during her reproductive life and, at most, can give birth to about 20 children. It is therefore in a woman's best interest to maintain primary responsibility for her genetic children and to find the best mate with whom to fertilize her eggs. He is the man who can best help support the children after birth. In contrast, most men can produce hundreds of millions of sperm in a single ejaculation, and this feat can be repeated often. Thus, a man increases the chance that his and only his genes will be passed on to future generations when he is promiscuous yet jealously possessive of his partners. Moreover, since men compete with other men for sexual access to women, men evolve competitive and aggressive dispositions that include physical violence (Ainsworth and Maner, 2012). Women, says one evolutionary psychologist, are greedy for money, whereas men want casual sex with women, treat women's bodies as their property, and react violently to women who incite male sexual jealousy. These are "universal features of our evolved selves" that presumably contribute to the survival of the human species (Buss, 2000, 2013). From the point of view of sociobiology and evolutionary psychology, then, gender differences in behaviour are based in biological differences between women and men.

Functionalism and Essentialism

Functionalists reinforce the essentialist viewpoint when they claim that traditional gender roles help to integrate society (Parsons, 1942). In the family, wrote Talcott Parsons, women traditionally specialize in raising children and managing the household. Men traditionally work in the paid labour force. Each generation learns to perform these complementary roles by means of gender role socialization.

For boys, noted Parsons, the essence of masculinity is a series of "instrumental" traits, such as rationality, self-assuredness, and competitiveness. For girls, the essence of femininity is a series of "expressive" traits, such as nurturance and sensitivity to others. Boys and girls first learn their respective gender traits in the family as they see their parents going about their daily routines. The larger society also promotes gender role conformity. It instills in men the fear that they won't be attractive to women if they are too feminine, and it instills in women the fear that they won't be attractive to men if they are too masculine. In the functionalist view, then, learning the essential features of femininity and masculinity integrates society and allows it to function properly.

A Critique of Essentialism from the Conflict and Feminist Perspectives

Conflict and feminist theorists disagree sharply with the essentialist view. They lodge four main criticisms against it.

First, *essentialists ignore the historical and cultural variability of gender and sexuality*. Wide variations exist in what constitutes masculinity and femininity. Wide variations are also evident in the level of gender inequality, the rate of male violence against women, the criteria used for mate selection, and other gender differences that appear to be universal to the essentialists. These variations deflate the idea that women and men are separated by essential and universal behavioural differences. Three examples help illustrate the point:

1. Since the 1960s, as a result of the rapid entry of women into the paid labour force, a shift has occurred in the qualities that men and women seek in their mates. Compared

Definitions of *male* and *female* traits vary across societies. For example, the ceremonial dress of male Wodaabe nomads in Niger may appear "feminine" by conventional North American standards.

M. ou Me. Desjeux, Bernard/CORBIS

with half a century ago, women today are less motivated to seek men who will be good providers, instead preferring men with good looks. Men increasingly prefer women with good financial prospects and are less swayed by women's domestic skills (Eagly and Wood, 1999, 2013; Smiler, 2011).

2. Most researchers reject the long-standing assumption that males are *naturally* superior to females in math and science because evidence shows that males tend to perform better than females only in countries where gender inequality is high. Where males and females are treated equally, gender differences in math and science scores disappear (Ayalon and Livneh, 2013; Hyde and Mertz, 2009).
3. The assumption that all men want to have sex with as many women as possible may be true of some men—note the infidelities of Tiger Woods and Sandra Bullock's ex-husband, Jesse James—but the "Casanova complex" turns out to be an exception not the rule (Smiler, 2013). Moreover, it appears that "hooking up" is practised to the same extent by male and female college and university students, although males are more likely than are women to exaggerate the frequency of their sexual encounters (Currier, 2013).

As these examples show, gender differences are not constants and are not inherent in men and women. They vary with social conditions.

The second problem with essentialism is that *it tends to generalize from the average, ignoring variations within gender groups.* On average, women and men do differ in some respects. For example, one of the best-documented gender differences is that men are, on average, more verbally and physically aggressive than women are. However, when essentialists say men are inherently more aggressive than women are, they make it seem as if that is true of all men and all women. As Figure 11.1 illustrates, it is not. When trained researchers measure verbal or physical aggressiveness, scores vary widely within gender groups. Men and women show considerable overlap in their aggressiveness. Many women are more aggressive than the average man and many men are less aggressive than the average woman.

Third, *little or no evidence directly supports the essentialists' major claims.* Sociobiologists and evolutionary psychologists have not identified any of the genes that, they claim, cause male jealousy, female nurturance, the unequal division of labour between men and women, and so forth.

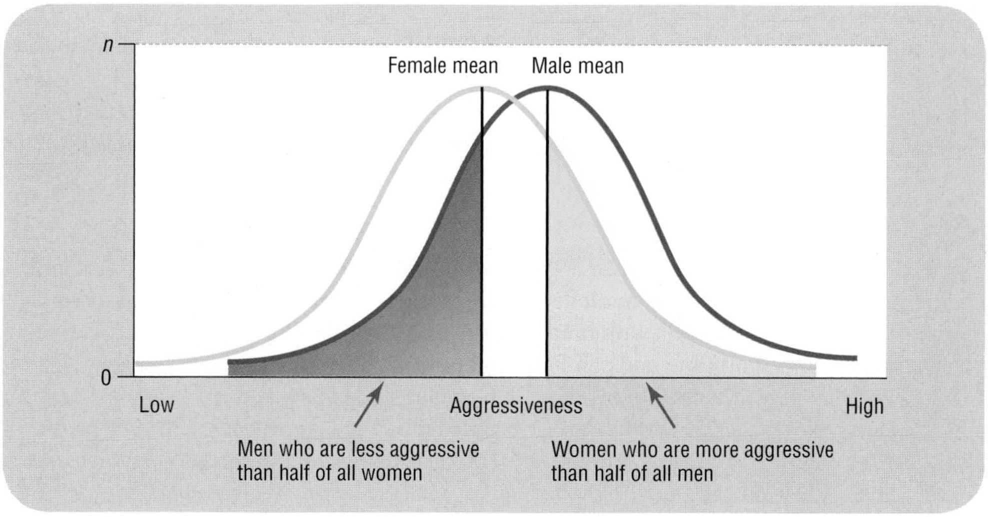

FIGURE 11.1
The Distribution of Aggressiveness among Men and Women

Finally, *essentialists' explanations for gender differences ignore the role of power.* Essentialists assume that existing behaviour patterns help to ensure the survival of the species and the smooth functioning of society. However, as conflict and feminist theorists argue, essentialists generally ignore the fact that, compared with women, men are more likely to be in positions of greater power and authority.

Conflict theorists dating back to Marx's collaborator, Friedrich Engels, have located the root of male domination in class inequality (Engels, 1970 [1884]). According to Engels, men gained substantial power over women when preliterate societies were first able to produce more than the amount needed for their own subsistence. At that point, some men gained control over the economic surplus. They soon devised two means of ensuring that their offspring would inherit the surplus. First, they imposed the rule that only men could own property. Second, by means of socialization and force, they ensured that women remained sexually faithful to their husbands. As industrial capitalism developed, Engels wrote, male domination increased because industrial capitalism made men still wealthier and more powerful while it relegated women to subordinate, domestic roles.

Many feminist theorists doubt that male domination is so closely linked to the development of industrial capitalism. For one thing, they note that gender inequality is greater in pre-capitalist, agrarian societies than in industrial capitalist societies. For another, male domination is evident in societies that call themselves socialist or communist. These observations lead many feminists to conclude that male domination is rooted less in industrial capitalism than in the patriarchal authority relations, family structures, and patterns of socialization and culture that exist in most societies (Lapidus, 1978: 7).

Despite this disagreement, conflict and feminist theorists concur that behavioural differences between women and men result less from any essential differences between them than from men being in a position to impose their interests on women. From the conflict and feminist viewpoints, functionalism, sociobiology, and evolutionary psychology can themselves be seen as examples of the exercise of male power, that is, as rationalizations for male domination and sexual aggression.

Social Constructionism and Symbolic Interactionism

Essentialism is the view that masculinity and femininity are inherent and universal traits of men and women, whether because of biological or social necessity or some combination of the two. In contrast, social constructionism is the view that *apparently* natural or innate features of life, such as gender, are actually sustained by *social* processes that vary historically and culturally. As such, conflict and feminist theories may be regarded as types of social constructionism. So may symbolic interactionism. Symbolic interactionists, you will

© skodonnell/Istockphoto.com

"She is the perfect person when you are little that everyone wants to be like."

recall, focus on the way people attach meaning to things in the course of their everyday communication. One of the things to which people attach meaning is what it means to be a man or a woman. We illustrate the symbolic interactionist approach by first considering how boys and girls learn masculine and feminine roles in the family and at school. We then show how gender roles are maintained in the course of everyday social interaction and through advertising in the mass media.

Gender Socialization

Barbie dolls have been around since 1959. Based on the creation of a German cartoonist, Barbie is the first modern doll modelled after an adult. Some industry experts predicted mothers would never buy dolls with breasts for their little girls. Were *they* wrong! Barbie is the bestselling doll of all time and can be found in more than 150 countries.

What do girls learn when they play with Barbie? One study that asked young adolescent girls about their experiences and views of Barbie recorded the following response: "I think Barbie is one of those things that never goes out of style. Barbie is a great doll for girls to play with when they are little. And even older women collect them. She is the perfect person when you are little that everyone wants to be like. And girls want to dress her up and she is something that can be brought places and not worried about being broke" (Kuther and McDonald, 2004: 48).

One dream that Barbie stimulates among many girls concerns body image. After all, Barbie is a scale model of a woman with a 40-18-32 figure (Hamilton, 1996: 197). Researchers who compared Barbie's gravity-defying proportions with the actual proportions of several representative groups of adult women concluded that the probability of this body shape is less than 1 in 100 000 (Norton et al., 1996). (Ken's body shape is far more realistic, having a probability of 1 in 50.)

Nevertheless, since the 1960s, Barbie has served as an identifiable symbol of stereotypical female beauty (Magro, 1997). Playing with Barbie socializes young girls to want to be slim, blonde, shapely, and, implicitly, pleasing to men. Moreover, Barbie exerts a powerful influence on what young girls think bodies should look like. In experimental studies, young girls who played with Barbie were more likely than girls who played with an average-proportioned doll to identify ultra-thin bodies as the ideal body size. In addition, they viewed their own bodies more negatively (Anschutz and Engels, 2010; Dittmar, Halliwall, and Ive, 2006).

Toys are only part of the story of gender socialization and hardly its first or final chapter. As managers of their children's lives, parents often shape resources and opportunities for their children (McHale, Crouter, and Whiteman, 2003). A girl is more likely than a boy to have her bedroom painted in yellows, pinks, and purples. Few parents enroll their boys in pottery or sewing classes, choosing instead to sign them up for sports activities. Parents, and especially fathers, are more likely to encourage their sons to engage in boisterous and competitive play and discourage their daughters from doing likewise. In general, parents tend to encourage girls to engage in cooperative, role-playing games (Fagot, Rodgers, and Leinbach, 2000; Gauvain et al., 2002; Parke, 2001, 2002). Boys are more likely than girls are to receive praise for assertiveness, and girls are more likely than boys are to receive rewards for compliance (Kerig, Cowan, and Cowan, 1993). Given this early socialization, it seems perfectly "natural" that boys' toys stress aggression, competition, spatial manipulation, and outdoor activities, while girls' toys stress nurturing, physical attractiveness, and indoor activities (Hughes, 1995). Still, what seems natural must be continuously socially reinforced. Presented with a choice between playing with a tool set and a dish set, preschool boys are about as likely to choose one as the other—unless the dish set is presented as a girl's toy and they think their fathers would view playing with it as "bad." Then, they tend to go for the tool set (Raag and Rackliff, 1998).

It would take someone who has spent very little time in the company of children to think they are passive objects of socialization. They are not. Parents, teachers, and other authority figures typically try to impose their ideas of appropriate gender behaviour on children, but children creatively interpret, negotiate, resist, and self-impose these ideas all the time. Gender is something that is done, not just given (Messner, 2000; West and Zimmerman, 2009). Said differently, gender is more than a characteristic of the individual. It is produced through social processes. This fact is nowhere more evident than in the way children play.

Gender Segregation and Interaction

Consider the grade 4 and 5 classroom that sociologist Barrie Thorne (1993) observed. The teacher periodically asked the children to choose their own desks. With the exception of one girl, the children always segregated *themselves* by gender. The teacher then drew on self-segregation by pitting boys against girls in spelling and math contests. The contests were characterized by cross-gender antagonism and expression of within-gender solidarity. Similarly, when children played chasing games in the schoolyard, groups often *spontaneously* crystallized along gender lines. These games had special names, some of which had clear sexual meanings, such as "chase and kiss." Provocation, physical contact, and avoidance were all sexually charged parts of the game.

Although Thorne found that contests, chasing games, and other activities often involved self-segregation by gender, she observed many cases of boys and girls playing together. She also noticed much boundary crossing, involving boys playing stereotypically girls' games and girls playing stereotypically boys' games. The most common form of boundary crossing involved girls playing sports that were central to the boys' world: soccer, baseball, and basketball. When girls demonstrated skill at these activities, boys often accepted them as participants.

Thorne also observed occasions when boys and girls interacted without strain and without strong gender identities. For instance, activities requiring cooperation, such as taking part in a group radio show or art project, lessened the attention to gender. Another situation that lessened strain between boys and girls, causing gender to recede in importance, occurred when adults organized mixed-gender encounters in the classroom and during physical education periods. On such occasions, adults legitimized cross-gender contact. Mixed-gender interaction was also more common in less public and less crowded settings. Thus, boys and girls were more likely to play together in a relaxed way in the relative privacy of their neighbourhoods. In contrast, in the schoolyard, where their peers could scrutinize them, gender segregation and antagonism were more evident.

A **gender ideology** is a set of interrelated ideas about what constitutes appropriate masculine and feminine roles and behaviour.

In sum, Thorne's research makes two important contributions to our understanding of gender socialization. First, children are actively engaged in the process of constructing gender roles. They are not merely passive recipients of adult demands. Second, although schoolchildren tend to segregate themselves by gender, boundaries between boys and girls are sometimes fluid and sometimes rigid, depending on social circumstances. The content of children's gendered activities is by no means fixed.

We do not mean to suggest that adults lack gender demands and expectations. They do have such demands and expectations, which contribute importantly to gender socialization. For instance, many schoolteachers think that boys succeed in math because of their natural ability, whereas girls who succeed in math do so because of effort (Espinoza, da Luz Fontes, and Arms-Chavez, 2014). Parents often reinforce gender expectations in their evaluation of their children's school and sports activities (Fredericks and Eccles, 2005; Gunderson et al., 2012).

Adolescents usually start choosing courses in school by the age of 14 or 15. By then, they have a well-formed **gender ideology**, a set of interrelated ideas about what constitutes appropriate masculine and feminine roles and behaviour. One aspect of gender ideology becomes especially important around grades 9 and 10: adolescents' ideas about whether, as adults, they will focus mainly on the home, paid work, or a combination of the two. Adolescents usually make course choices with gender ideologies in mind. Boys are strongly inclined to consider only their careers when making course choices. Most girls are inclined to consider both home responsibilities and careers, although a minority considers only home responsibilities and another minority considers only careers. Consequently, boys tend to choose career-oriented courses, particularly in math and science, more often than girls do. College and university accentuate the pattern (Chapter 17, Education).

Myrleen Cate/Index Stock

In her research on schoolchildren, sociologist Barrie Thorne noticed much "boundary crossing" between boys and girls. Most commonly, boys accepted girls as participants in soccer, baseball, and basketball games when the girls demonstrated skill at these sports.

Lisa Strohschein, one of this book's authors, still has vivid memories of her high-school experiences during the early 1980s. As a straight "A" student in elementary school, she was shocked when she entered high school. "I still got As in English and the social sciences but my math marks dropped like a rock. To my horror, I failed my first math test. I was devastated. Today, I recognize that there were large deficits in the math curriculum of my elementary school that didn't adequately prepare me for high-school math. But back then, I thought the problem was with me. So I went to the math teacher to find out what I needed to do to get better marks. He said, 'Lisa, it's not all that important for you to do well in math. After all, where are you going to use it anyway? Housewives don't really need algebra or geometry.'

"As it turns out, I became a sociologist specializing in statistical analysis. Without advanced math skills, I wouldn't be able to do my research. I still wonder what my life would look like if I had taken my high-school teacher's comments to heart and hadn't ventured to enroll in a statistics class once I entered university."

The Mass Media and Body Image

The social construction of gender does not stop at the school steps. Outside school, children, adolescents, and adults continue to negotiate gender roles as they interact with the mass media.

If you systematically observe the roles played by women and men in television, movies, magazines, music videos, TV commercials, and print media advertisements, you will discover a long-established pattern. Although females comprise half the population, they are generally underrepresented as characters on television and on the big screen. One study analyzed the gender of all characters in the 90 top-grossing general audience–rated films between 1990 and 2005. The authors found that for every 2.6 male characters, there was only one female character (Smith et al., 2010). To the extent that males are shown more frequently in movies than are females, researchers suggest that girls may view their stories as less important than the stories of boys.

When female characters are featured, they tend to be portrayed in stereotypical ways. Women are often seen cleaning house, taking care of children, making meals, and modelling clothes. Men are not (Michelle, 2012; Paek, Nelson, and Vilela, 2010). Women are generally more concerned than men are about their physical attractiveness, signalling to the audience that women are supposed to serve as objects of male desire. Men, on the other hand, tend to be cast as playboys who spend their waking moments in search of sexual conquests (Zayer et al., 2012). Among couples in romantic movies, the men are often considerably older than the women are (see Figure 11.2). Moreover, men are more likely than women are to be

FIGURE 11.2

George Clooney's Movie Romances, 1996–2011

Source: Compiled from Internet Movie Database (www.imdb.com/name/nm0000123/?ref_=fn_al_nm_1)

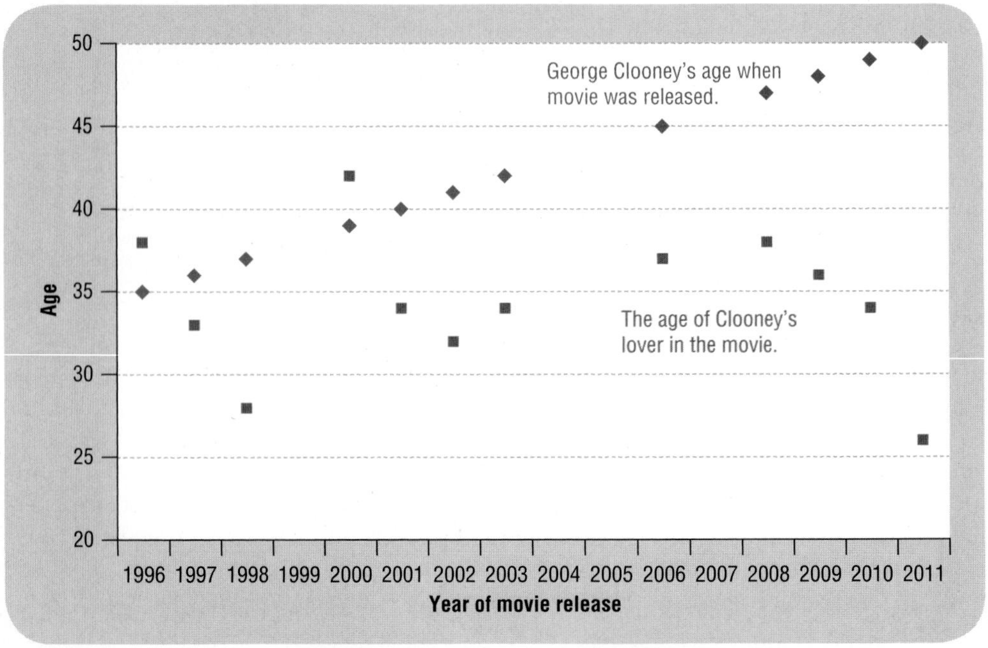

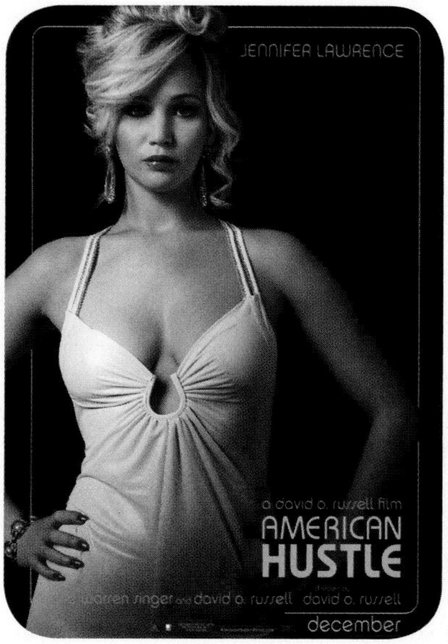

Marilyn Monroe was widely considered the most attractive woman in the world in the 1950s. Today, Jennifer Lawrence is considered one of America's sexiest women. What attributes do you think made these women so attractive in their respective periods? Are these attributes the same or different?

portrayed in work roles and to be seen as being financially successful. In popular sitcoms such as *Modern Family*, *Big Bang Theory*, *2 Broke Girls*, and *Surviving Jack*, it is the women who lack stable, well-paying jobs or are stay-at-home moms even as the men are invariably accomplished professionals.

Media images present a view of the world that is promoted as normal, expected, and desirable. By framing our reality, they powerfully influence our behaviour. Some people even try to shape their own bodies and physical appearance after the images they see on TV (Wegenstein and Ruck, 2011). The ideal female form in contemporary North American culture is sexualized and thin, so most women strive for those ideals in their own bodies.

Women are increasingly expected to present themselves as sex objects. True, women have always been expected to base their worth on whether men find them physically attractive. But more than ever, images of women in the media are now hypersexualized. Advertisements routinely show women in scantily clad and sexually provocative poses. Often, the camera is frozen on a sexually charged moment, capturing the vulnerability of a woman on the verge of being overpowered by a man or group of men. Such poses are sometimes adopted straight out of violent pornography. Researchers found that nearly 10 percent of ads in the top-selling magazines of 2002 showed lifeless or unconscious women posing sexually, or men sexually dominating women, lying to or tricking them, or watching them without their knowledge in inappropriate settings (Stankiewicz and Roselli, 2008).

Some researchers say that our culture has become "pornified," meaning that we have erased the previously well-established boundary between mainstream media and pornography (Paasonen, Nikunen, and Saarenmaa, 2007). Sexually explicit materials in the mass media are more common and increasingly socially acceptable. Typically, Burger King promotes its "super seven incher burger" with a wide-eyed, open-mouth blonde, blood-red lipstick adorning her lips, apparently ready to fellate her meal (see a photo of the ad at http://gawker.com/5301856/eating-a-burger-king-super-seven-incher-is-just-like-giving-a-blow-job).

Approximately 10 percent of print advertisements depict women as sexual victims.

Think, too, of the ways stripper poles, G-strings, pasties, and other paraphernalia associated with exotic dancers and strip clubs have become common accessories for today's female pop stars. In their respective top-selling music videos in 2013, Rihanna gyrates on a stripper pole, and Nicki Manaj appears topless except for nipple pasties. During a live performance in Vancouver in 2014, Miley Cyrus flaunted her sequin-studded thong as she simulated oral sex on a Bill Clinton impersonator in front of a mostly teenaged audience. Then there's twerking.

Men and women are sexual creatures but what is promoted in pornified mass media today is a restrictive and demeaning version of female sexuality. Rather than women being characterized as individuals with unique sexual needs and desires, they are usually treated as standardized sex objects to be bought and sold for the sexual gratification and pleasure of men.

Even young girls are not immune to such pressures (Goodin et al., 2011). Increasingly, they are persuaded that sexualized clothing, identity, and behaviour can make them popular and accepted by their peers (Graff, Murnen, and Smolak, 2012). One popular American chain sells thong underwear to children with the words "eye candy" emblazoned on the front. Thongs and padded bras are big selling items in pre-teen clothing stores. As Box 11.1 illustrates, the sexualization of young girls begins when they are toddlers.

In the same way that women are persuaded that they must be sexy, thinness is held out as the ideal body shape—and it seems to be getting thinner every year. Thus, between 1922 and 1999, Miss America beauty pageant winners became only a little taller but much thinner (Curran, 2000). As one eating disorders expert observed, "Beauty pageants, like the rest of our media-driven culture, give young women in particular a message, over and over again, that it's exceedingly important to be thin to be considered successful and attractive" (quoted in Curran, 2000).

The rake-thin models who populate modern ads are not promoting good health. They are promoting an extreme body shape that is unattainable for most people (Tovee et al., 1997).

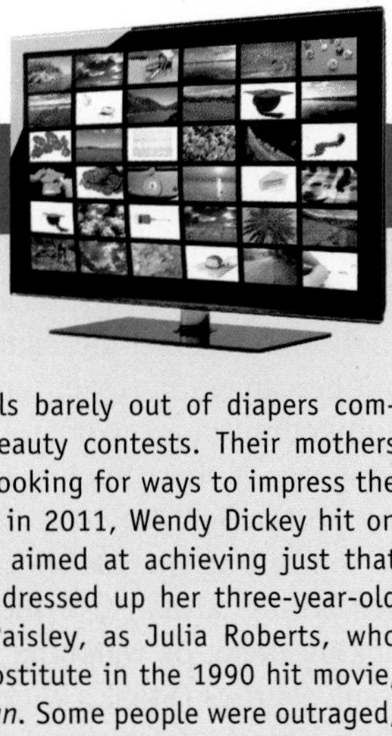

BOX 11.1

SOCIOLOGY ON THE TUBE

TODDLERS & TIARAS

© Corbis

Paisley Dickey, age 3

"Unleash your passion!" screams the banner on the Bratz home page (www.bratz.com/). Passion may seem beyond the emotional maturity of the average Bratz customer, a five- to eight-year-old girl. However, Bratz is willing to push boundaries. The company sells skinny, breasted dolls named Yasmin, Cloe, Jade, and Sasha. They wear tight miniskirts, tight tops that expose their midriffs, fishnet stockings, high-heeled shoes, and boas. Their flaming red or bubble-gum pink lips, always pouting, seem to have been injected with massive doses of collagen. The dolls are moulded to strike provocative poses. Passion may be a stretch for the little girls who play with these dolls, but Bratz is undeniably preparing them to become sex objects.

Some girls are sexualized even before they reach the age of five. Consider the reality TV series, *Toddlers & Tiaras,* which features girls barely out of diapers competing in beauty contests. Their mothers are always looking for ways to impress the judges, and in 2011, Wendy Dickey hit on a cute idea aimed at achieving just that effect. She dressed up her three-year-old daughter, Paisley, as Julia Roberts, who played a prostitute in the 1990 hit movie, *Pretty Woman*. Some people were outraged, but Paisley's mom chalked up their reaction to jealousy and other base emotions. Psychologists tell us that the sexualization of young girls contributes to poor cognitive functioning, low self-esteem, depression, eating disorders, and diminished sexual health (Zurbriggen et al., 2010). However, Wendy Dickey and other pageant moms think they know better. After all, Paisley won the beauty pageant. For her mom, that's all that really counts.

They do so because it is good business. The industries devoted to fitness, weight-loss diets, low-calorie food, and cosmetic surgery do billions of dollars of business every year in North America (Hesse-Biber, 1996). Bankrolled by these industries, advertising in the mass media blankets us with images of slim bodies and makes these body types appealing. Once people become convinced that they need to develop bodies like the ones they see in ads, many of them are really in trouble because, for most people, these body images are impossible to attain.

Research shows just how widespread dissatisfaction with our bodies is. One survey of American, Brazilian, and Argentinian female university students showed that more than 80 percent of women in each country were dissatisfied with their overall appearance (Forbes et al., 2012). Among adults in the United States, nearly half of women and one in three men expressed dissatisfaction with their weight (Fallon, Harris, and Johnson, 2014). Studies have consistently shown that when men and women are presented with slim images in the media, they more negatively evaluate their own appearance (Aubrey, 2010; Fernandez and Pritchard, 2012).

One 26-country study analyzed women's body dissatisfaction worldwide (Swami et al., 2010). Researchers presented samples of men and women with a chart showing a series of female figures. They then asked respondents to indicate which figure they preferred and which figure most closely resembled their own (see Figure 11.3). The average age of respondents was 24.7 years. Even though the sample was young (and therefore relatively slim), the overwhelming majority of women wanted to be slimmer than they were. Their body ideal varied from one region to the next, but their actual self-reported body image was heavier than their body ideal in every world region. North American and South American women were more dissatisfied with their bodies than were women from other regions, and North American and South American men viewed heavier women more unfavourably than did men from other regions. Still, men everywhere actually preferred heavier women than women thought men preferred. Significantly, women's level of body dissatisfaction did not vary greatly from one region to the next, probably because more exposure to Western and Western-style mass media was associated with greater preference for thin women, and respondents tended to be highly exposed to such mass media and its strong emphasis on female thinness.

Body dissatisfaction motivates many people—girls and boys, women and men—to follow weight-loss diets (Mendes et al., 2014; Mooney, Farley, and Strugnell, 2010). Some are willing to live dangerously. About a quarter of women and a sixth of men in North America say they would willingly trade more than three years of their life to achieve their weight goals. Half of female smokers and 30 percent of male smokers say they smoke to control their weight. Surveys suggest that between 1 percent and 5 percent

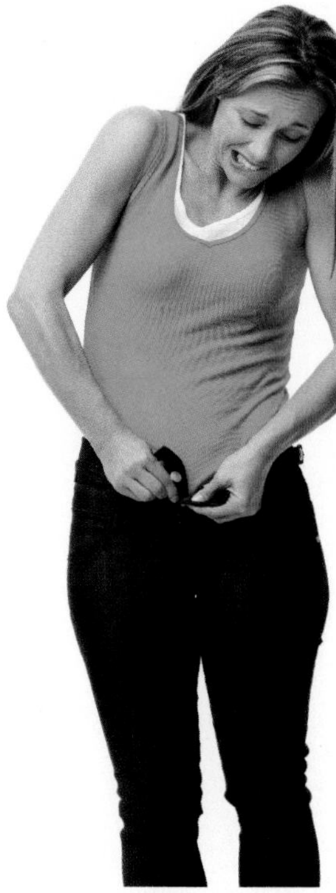

The low-calorie and diet-food industry promotes an ideal of slimness that is often impossible to attain and that generates widespread body dissatisfaction.

FIGURE 11.3
Female Figure Rating across World Regions

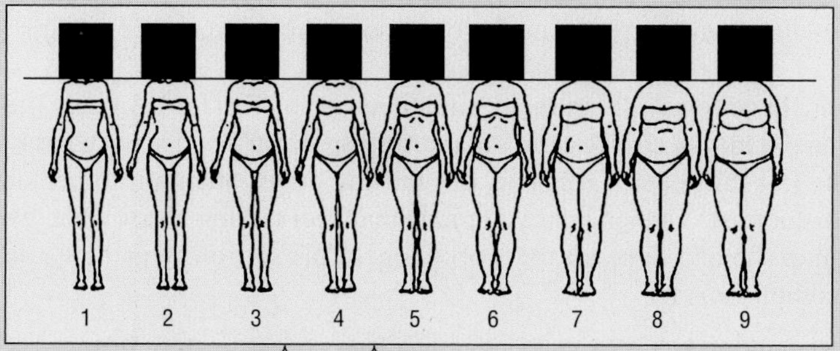

Women's Dissatisfaction Score*	
North America	1.4
South America	1.4
Africa	1.3
Scandinavia	1.1
East Asia	1.1
Western Europe	1.0
Southeast Asia	0.9
Eastern Europe	0.8
Oceania	0.8
South & West Asia	0.5

*Actual self-reported regional average minus ideal regional average

Source: Swami, Viren et al. 2010. "The Attractive Female Body Weight and Female Body Dissatisfaction in 26 Countries across 10 World Regions: Results of the International Body Project I." *Personality and Social Psychology Bulletin 36*, 3: 309–25.

of North American women suffer from anorexia nervosa (characterized by weight loss, excessive exercise, food aversion, distorted body image, and an intense and irrational fear of body fat and weight gain). About the same percentage of North American female college and university students suffer from bulimia, characterized by cycles of binge eating and purging (through self-induced vomiting or the use of laxatives, purgatives, or diuretics).

Male–Female Interaction

The gender roles children learn in their families, at school, and through the mass media form the basis of their social interaction as adults. For instance, by playing team sports, boys tend to learn that social interaction is most often about competition, conflict, self-sufficiency, and hierarchical relationships (leaders versus the led). They understand the importance of taking centre stage and boasting about their talents (Messner, 1995). Because many of the most popular video games for boys exclude female characters (it wasn't named *Game Boy* for nothing!), depict women as sex objects, or involve violence against women, they reinforce some of the most unsavoury lessons of traditional gender socialization (Collins, 2011). For example, in the 20 top-selling video games, 43 percent of female characters versus 4 percent of male characters are shown partially or totally nude (Downs and Smith, 2010). In contrast, by playing with dolls and baking sets, girls tend to learn that social interaction is most often about maintaining cordial relationships, avoiding conflict, and resolving differences of opinion through negotiation (Subrahmanyam and Greenfield, 1998). They learn the importance of giving advice and not promoting themselves or being bossy.

Because of these early socialization patterns, misunderstandings between men and women are common. A stereotypical example: Harold is driving around lost. However, he refuses to ask for directions because doing so would amount to an admission of inadequacy and therefore a loss of status. Meanwhile, it seems perfectly natural to Sybil to want to share information, so she urges Harold to ask for directions. The result: conflict between Harold and Sybil (Tannen, 1990: 62).

Gender-specific interaction styles also have serious implications for who is heard and who gets credit at work. Here are two cases uncovered by Deborah Tannen's research (1994: 132–59):

- A female office manager doesn't want to seem bossy or arrogant. She is eager to preserve consensus among her co-workers. Therefore, she spends a good deal of time soliciting their opinions before making an important decision. She asks questions, listens attentively, and offers suggestions. She then decides. However, her male boss sees her approach as indecisive and incompetent. When recruiting a leader for an upper-management position, he overlooks the woman and selects an assertive man.
- Male managers are inclined to say "I" in many situations, as in "I'm hiring a new manager and I'm going to put him in charge of my marketing division" or "This is what I've come up with on the Lakehill deal." This sort of phrasing draws attention to personal accomplishments. In contrast, Tannen heard a female manager talking about what "we" had done, when in fact she had done all the work alone. This sort of phrasing camouflages women's accomplishments.

The contrasting interaction styles illustrated above can result in female managers not gaining credit for competent performance. That may be part of the reason why women sometimes complain about a **glass ceiling**, a social barrier that makes it difficult for them to rise to the top level of management. As we will soon see, the glass ceiling is also supported by factors other than interaction styles, such as outright discrimination and women's generally greater commitment to family responsibilities. Yet gender differences in interaction styles seem to play an independent role in constraining women's career progress.

The **glass ceiling** is a social barrier that makes it difficult for women to rise to the top level of management.

TIME FOR REVIEW

- How does essentialism support the functionalist depiction of traditional gender roles?
- According to conflict theorists and feminists, what are the weaknesses of essentialism?
- What evidence suggests that gender is largely learned through socialization processes?
- What are the consequences for girls and women when the mass media promote sexualized bodies and thin as a cultural ideal?

SEXUALITY

Sexuality and Resistance

The preceding discussion outlines some powerful social forces that push us to define ourselves as conventionally masculine or feminine in behaviour and appearance. For most people, gender socialization by the family, the school, and the mass media is compelling and sustained by daily interactions. However, a minority of people resists conventional gender roles, suggesting that there are varying degrees of "maleness" and "femaleness." Other people reject the idea that men should only be sexually attracted to women and that women should only be sexually attracted to men.

In the same way that feminists have questioned the links between sex and gender, queer theorists challenge the idea that sexuality is an essential and unchanging aspect of sexual identity. According to queer theory, one's capacity for erotic expression may extend beyond the sexual category in which one has been placed. Labels force people into categories that may or may not capture their reality. Borrowing from feminism, queer theorists say that sexuality is something that one does, not something that one is. When sexuality is viewed as a performance rather than a characteristic of the individual, it is possible to see that sexuality is socially constructed. Said differently, both heterosexuality and homosexuality are culturally and historically determined phenomena whose meanings continue to change over time and in different contexts (Fischer, 2013). Consequently, it cannot be said that heterosexuality is natural or normal and that homosexuality is unnatural and deviant, only that they have been defined in this way.

Foucault argued that homosexuality is a relatively recent invention. It emerged in the 1870s when medical practitioners began to frame same-sex acts as a characteristic of a certain kind of individual rather than a temptation to which anyone might succumb (Foucault, 1981). Although same-sex relations between men have existed throughout history, Foucault claimed it was only when homosexuality emerged as a distinct social category that a culture and an identity began to form around homosexuality. The notion of "coming out of the closet" is a modern invention: declaring oneself to be gay became possible only when homosexuality was socially recognized as a sexual identity.

Queer theorists and feminists do not always see eye to eye. That is because feminists view *gender* as the fundamental category that organizes social relations. For them, the basic conflict in society is between women and men. Queer theorists counter that *sexuality* is the fundamental category that organizes social relations. For them, the basic conflict in society is between those who regard sexual identity as fixed and those who regard it as fluid. And not all gay or lesbian activists identify with queer theory, partly because some do not agree with the view that sexual identities are fundamentally fluid. With these differences in mind, we now turn to a brief description of sexual identities in Canada today.

Transgendered people break society's gender norms by defying the rigid distinction between male and female.

People who identify as **transgendered** defy society's gender norms and blur widely accepted gender roles (Cole et al., 2000: 151). For example, some people who identify as transgendered are cross-dressers. They gender-identify with one sex and sometimes dress in clothing generally considered appropriate to the "opposite" sex. In North America, about 1 in 5000 to 10 000 people is transgendered. Some people who identify as transgendered also see themselves as **transsexuals**. They identify with a gender that is culturally inconsistent with their biological sex. People who identify as transsexuals believe they were born with the "wrong" body. They identify with, and want to live fully as, members of the "opposite" sex. They often take the lengthy and painful path to a sex-change operation. About 1 in 30 000 people in North America is a transsexual (Nolen, 1999). Transsexuals may or may not be sexually attracted to members of another sex. People who identify as **homosexuals** prefer sexual partners of the same sex, and those who identify as **bisexuals** enjoy sexual partners of either sex. People usually call homosexual men *gay* and homosexual women *lesbians*. **Asexuals** identify themselves as people who are not sexually attracted to anyone at all.

Transsexuals believe they were born with the "wrong" body. They identify with, and want to live fully as, members of the "opposite" sex.

Homosexuals are people who prefer sexual partners of the same sex. People usually call homosexual men gay and homosexual women *lesbians*.

Bisexuals are people who enjoy sexual partners of both sexes.

Asexuals are people who lack interest in sexual activity of any kind.

Fewer than 2 percent of Canadians describe themselves as homosexual or bisexual (Tjepkema, 2008). However, sexual identities are more varied on university campuses. A recent study at the University of Alberta found that 7.5 percent of students identified as asexual, whereas 3 and 1 percent respectively identified their sexual identity as gay and lesbian (Kinkartz, Wells, and Hillyard, 2013). Another 2 percent said they questioned their sexual identity.

At the same time, many people who have had same-sex sexual experiences or desires consider themselves to be heterosexual. They may resist other labels because they experience homosexual urges only intermittently or rarely, and also because they want to avoid facing the widespread animosity directed toward non-heterosexuals (Flowers and Buston, 2001; Herdt, 2001; Laumann et al., 1994: 299).

A 2004 survey of North American university students showed that homosexual experiences and desires are far more frequent than homosexual identification. Men were 3.5 times as likely to say they had homosexual experiences and desires as they were to identify as gay. Women were 5.6 times as likely to say they had same-sex sexual experiences or desires as to identify as lesbians (see Figure 11.4).

In 2010, one of this book's authors (Brym) surveyed students of his large introductory sociology class at the University of Toronto on their sexual orientation. Interestingly, he found a considerably higher percentage of homosexual identifiers than found in the 2004 North American university survey. Probable reasons for the difference include the following: (1) Toronto is a large urban centre where liberal attitudes, including attitudes toward sexuality, are more widespread than they are in North America as a whole; (2) six years had passed between the two surveys, during which attitudes became more liberal; and (3) Toronto comprises one of the three biggest homosexual communities in North America (the others are New York and San Francisco) and is therefore especially attractive to homosexuals.

More remarkably, fully 35 percent of women in the U of T survey said they had some same-sex experience or desire, twice as many as the corresponding percentage for men. What might account for this difference? One plausible explanation is that many heterosexual men find

FIGURE 11.4
Homosexuality Indicators, North American University Students, 2004, and University of Toronto SOC101 Students, 2010 (in percent)

Sources: Brym (2010b); Ellis, Robb, and Burke (2005: 572–73).

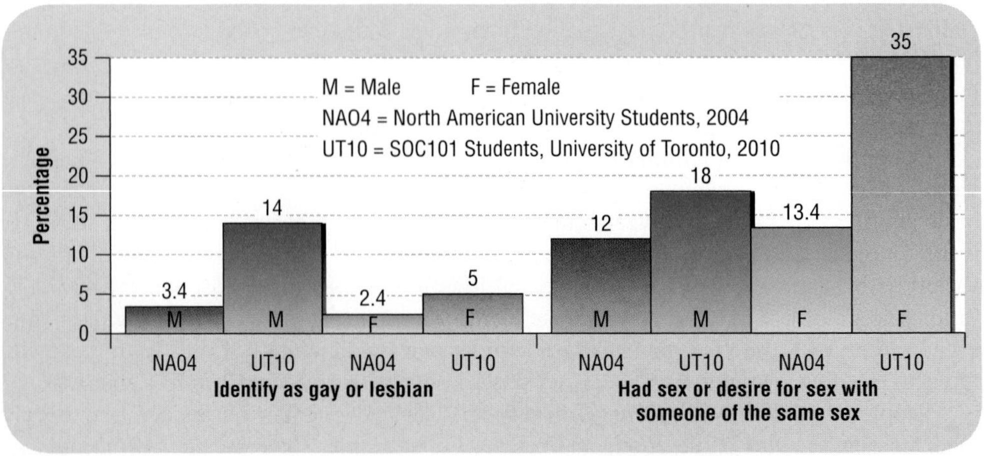

sex between women titillating, so a considerable number of young women engage in sexual acts with other women for the benefit of men—a growing phenomenon according to analysts who, in recent years, have observed the party, bar, and club scenes (Rupp and Taylor, 2010).

Enforcing Heteronormativity

Transgendered people, transsexuals, bisexuals, homosexuals, and asexuals have lived in every society. Some societies have held such people in high regard. Ancient Greece encouraged homosexuality. Many Aboriginal North American nations celebrate what the Ojibwa call "two-spirited" people, who are said to incorporate both masculine and feminine attributes. Traditionally, two-spirited people were given high-prestige roles, such as healer or fortune-teller. Some tribes recognized as many as six genders (Cameron, 2005; Lang, 1998).

More frequently, societies have forbidden non-heteronormative behaviour. For example, nearly 80 countries have laws against homosexuality (see Figure 11.5). In Saudi Arabia, Yemen, and Mauritania, those convicted of homosexuality may face the death penalty (Itaborahy and Zhu, 2013). At the same time, gains have been made in legalizing same-sex marriage. Sixteen countries allow same-sex marriage and recognize it countrywide. Several countries permit same-sex marriage in some but not all jurisdictions.

We do not yet well understand why some individuals develop homosexual orientations. Some scientists believe that the cause of homosexuality is mainly genetic, others think it is chiefly hormonal, while still others point to life experiences during early childhood as the most important factor (Jannini et al., 2010). The scientific consensus is that homosexuality "emerges for most people in early adolescence without any prior sexual experience. … [It] is not changeable" (American Psychological Association, 1998). A study of homosexual men in the United States found that 90 percent believed they had been born with their homosexual orientation and only 4 percent felt that environmental factors were the sole cause (Lever, 1994). Polls suggest that the general public increasingly believes that homosexuality is not so much a preference as an innate orientation. People who believe that homosexuality is a preference tend to be less tolerant of gays and lesbians than are those who think homosexuality is innate (Rosin and Morin, 1999: 8).

In general, sociologists are less interested in the origins of homosexuality than in the way it is socially constructed, that is, in the wide variety of ways homosexuality is expressed and repressed (Plummer, 1995). It is important to note in this connection that homosexuality has become less of a stigma over the past century. Two factors are chiefly responsible for homosexuality gaining greater acceptance, one scientific, the other political. In the

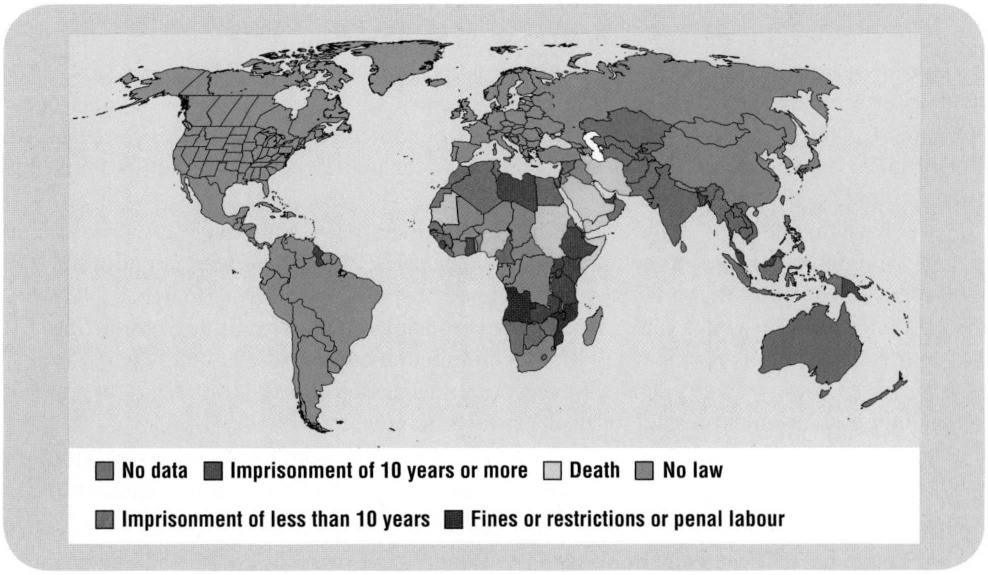

FIGURE 11.5
Punishment for Male–Male Sexual Relations, 2010

Source: International Gay, Lesbian, Bisexual, Trans and Intersex Association, 2010.

Especially since the 1970s, gays and lesbians have gone public with their lifestyles, thus helping to legitimize homosexuality and sexual diversity in general.

© tirc83/Istockphoto.com

twentieth century, sexologists—psychologists and physicians who study sexual practices scientifically—first recognized and stressed the wide diversity of existing sexual practices. Alfred Kinsey was among the pioneers in this field. He and his colleagues interviewed thousands of men and women. In the 1940s, they concluded that homosexual practices were so widespread that homosexuality could hardly be considered an illness affecting a tiny minority (Kinsey, Pomeroy, and Martin, 1948; Kinsey et al., 1953).

If sexologists provided a scientific rationale for belief in the normality of sexual diversity, sexual minorities themselves provided the social and political energy needed to legitimize sexual diversity among an increasingly large section of the public. Especially since the 1970s, gays and lesbians have built large communities and subcultures, particularly in major urban areas and have gone public with their lifestyles (Greenhill, 2001; Ingram, 2001; Owen, 2001). They have organized demonstrations, parades, and political pressure groups to express their self-confidence and demand equal rights with the heterosexual majority (Goldie, 2001). These activities have done much to legitimize homosexuality and sexual diversity in general.

The evidence for greater acceptance of homosexuals in society is clear. In 1975, 63 percent of Canadians thought that homosexuality is always wrong (*Maclean's*, 2002: 12). Today, 80 percent of Canadians think that society should accept homosexuals (Pew Research Center, 2013b). Elsewhere, acceptance of same-sex relations is less widespread. For instance, in Pakistan, Nigeria and Uganda, fewer than 5 percent of adults think that society should accept homosexuals.

Everywhere and at all stages of the life cycle, there exists some level of opposition to people who don't conform to conventional gender roles. When you were a child, did you ever poke fun at a sturdily built girl who was good at sports by referring to her as a "dyke"? As an adolescent or a young adult, have you ever insulted a man by calling him a "fag?" If so, your behaviour was not unusual. Many children and adults believe that heterosexuality is superior to homosexuality, and they are not embarrassed to say so. "That's so gay!" is commonly used as an expression of disapproval among teenagers.

Moreover, many homosexuals fear the antipathy and hostility of others. A study of about 500 young adults in the San Francisco Bay Area, perhaps the most sexually tolerant area in the world, found that 1 in 10 admitted having physically attacked or threatened people he or she believed were homosexuals. Twenty-four percent reported having engaged in anti-gay name-calling. Among male respondents, 18 percent reported having acted in a violent or threatening way and 32 percent reported having engaged in name-calling. In addition, a third of those who had *not* engaged in anti-gay aggression said they would do so if a homosexual flirted with, or propositioned, them (Franklin, 1998; see also Bush and Sainz, 2001; Faulkner and Cranston, 1998).

The consequences of such attitudes can be devastating. For example, 14-year-old Christian Hernandez of Niagara Falls, Ontario, told his best friend that he was gay. "He told me he couldn't accept it," recalls Hernandez. "And he began to spread it around." For two years, Hernandez was teased and harassed almost daily. After school one day, a group of boys waited for him. Their leader told Hernandez that "he didn't accept faggots, that we brought AIDS into the world" and stabbed him in the neck with a knife. Hernandez required a week's hospitalization. When he told his parents what had happened, his father replied that he'd "rather have a dead son than a queer son" (Fisher, 1999).

Research suggests that some anti-gay crimes may result from repressed homosexual urges on the part of the aggressor (Adams, Wright, and Lohr, 1998). From this point of view, aggressors are **homophobic**, or afraid of homosexuals, because they cannot cope with their own, possibly subconscious, homosexual impulses. Their aggression is a way of acting out a denial of these impulses. Although this psychological explanation may account for some anti-gay violence, it seems inadequate when set alongside the finding that fully half of all young male adults admitted to some form of anti-gay aggression in the San Francisco study cited above. An analysis of the motivations of these San Franciscans showed that some of them did commit assaults to prove their toughness and heterosexuality. Others committed assaults just to alleviate boredom and have fun. Still others believed they were defending themselves from aggressive sexual propositions. A fourth group acted violently because they wanted to punish homosexuals for what they perceived as moral transgressions (Franklin, 1998). It seems clear, then, that anti-gay violence is not just a question of abnormal psychology but a broad cultural problem with several sources (see Box 11.2).

Homophobic people are afraid of homosexuals.

BOX 11.2

SOCIOLOGY AT THE MOVIES

MILK (2008)

Until he was 40, Harvey Milk worked in a large investment firm in New York and supported the Republican Party. However, he was a closet homosexual and was bored with his life, so he decided to do something that one would least expect from a member of the pinstripe crowd. He joined a hippie theatre troupe, fell in love with another man, came out of the closet, and opened a camera store in the Castro district, the centre of San Francisco's gay community. There, Milk felt at home.

It was the mid-1970s, however, and even in San Francisco, the gay community was harassed and persecuted, not least by the San Francisco police. Anti-gay discrimination radicalized and politicized Milk. In 1977, he became the first openly gay man to hold public office in the United States when he brought together a gay-liberal-union-black-Latino alliance and was elected to the San Francisco Board of Supervisors.

Milk, starring the extraordinary Sean Penn in the title role, tells the inspiring story of Harvey Milk's political and romantic life from the time of his fateful decision at the age of 40 until he was murdered (along with San Francisco's mayor, George Moscone) in 1978 at the age of 48. The murderer was Dan White, another member of the Board of Supervisors, a married and deeply religious anti-gay activist who fought his own homosexual impulses and eventually became psychologically unstable under the strain.

The Kobal Collection at Art Resource, NY

Harvey Milk (played by Sean Penn)

TIME FOR REVIEW

- How do queer theory and feminist theory differ?
- Why are homosexual experiences and desires more frequent than homosexual identification?
- In what ways are individuals pressured to conform to conventional heterosexual gender roles?

GENDER INEQUALITY

How does gender influence the life experiences and life chances of boys and girls, women and men worldwide? One way of comparing countries according to how well women and men are treated is the Global Gender Gap Index. The index takes into account the inequality between men and women in terms of health, participation in the paid labour force, educational attainment, and political influence. A score of 1 indicates perfect equality of women and men on these four dimensions, while a score of 0 indicates maximum inequality.

As Figure 11.6 shows, seven of the ten most gender-egalitarian countries in the world are in Europe. Canada ranks 20th. In general, gender inequality is less pronounced in rich countries than in poor countries. Gender equality is partly a function of economic development. However, gender equality is also a function of government policy. Thus, in some former communist countries in Eastern European and Central Asia, gender inequality is lower than we would expect, given their level of economic development. Meanwhile, in some Islamic countries, gender inequality is higher than we would expect, given their level of economic development. These anomalies exist because the former communist countries made gender equality a matter of public policy, whereas many Islamic-majority countries have done the opposite (Brym, 2014b).

FIGURE 11.6
Global Gender Gap Index, Top Ten and Bottom Ten Countries Plus Canada

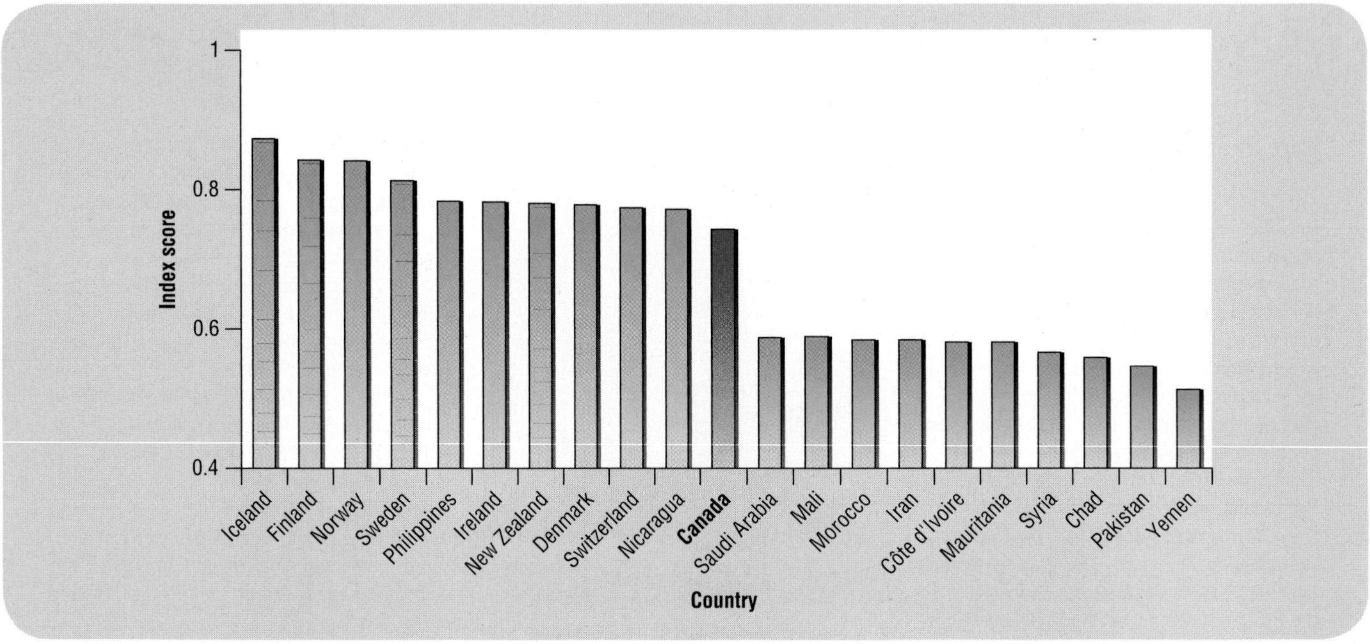

Source: Adapted from World Economic Forum, 2013. "Global Gender Gap Index 2013 Rankings," Table 3a, The Global Gender Gap Report, 2013. Geneva, Switzerland.

The Origins of Gender Inequality

Let us now turn to the question of how gender inequality originated. Contrary to what essentialists say, men have not always enjoyed much more power and authority than women have. Substantial inequality between women and men was socially constructed and has existed for only about 6000 years. Three major socio-historical processes account for the growth of gender inequality: long-distance warfare and conquest, plow agriculture, and the separation of public and private spheres.

Long-Distance Warfare and Conquest

The anthropological record suggests that women and men were about equal in status in nomadic, foraging societies, the dominant form of society for 90 percent of human history. Rough gender equality was based on women producing a substantial amount of the band's food, up to 80 percent in some cases (Chapter 15, Families).

The archaeological record from "Old Europe" tells a similar story. Old Europe is a region stretching roughly from Poland in the north to the Mediterranean island of Crete in the south, and from Switzerland in the west to Bulgaria in the east. Between 7000 and 3500 BCE, men and women enjoyed approximately equal status throughout the region. In fact, the regions' religions gave primacy to fertility and creator goddesses. Kinship was traced through the mother's side of the family. Then, sometime between 4300 and 4200 BCE, all this began to change. Old Europe was invaded by successive waves of warring peoples from the Asiatic and European northeast (the Kurgans) and the deserts to the south (the Semites). Both the Kurgan and Semitic civilizations were based on a steeply hierarchical social structure in which men were dominant. Their religions gave primacy to male warrior gods. They acquired property and slaves by conquering other peoples and imposed their religions on the vanquished. They eliminated, or at least downgraded, goddesses as divine powers. God became a male who willed that men should rule women. Laws reinforced women's sexual, economic, and political subjugation to men. Traditional Judaism, Christianity, and Islam all embody ideas of male dominance, and they all derive from the tribes that conquered Old Europe in the fifth millennium BCE (Eisler, 1987; Lerner, 1986).

Plow Agriculture

Long-distance warfare and conquest catered to men's strengths, greatly enhancing male power and authority. A similar effect resulted from large-scale farming that used plows harnessed to animals. Plow agriculture originated in the Middle East approximately 5000 years ago. It required that strong adults remain in the fields all day for much of the year. It also reinforced the principle of private ownership of land. Since men were on average stronger than women were, and since women were restricted in their activities by pregnancy, childbirth, and nursing, plow agriculture made men more powerful socially. Thus, men owned land, and ownership was passed from the father to the eldest son (Coontz and Henderson, 1986).

The Separation of Public and Private Spheres

In the agricultural era, economic production was organized around the household. Men may have worked apart from women in the fields but the fields were still part of the *family* farm. In contrast, during the early phase of industrialization, men's work moved out of the household and into the factory and the office. Most men became wage or salary workers. Some men assumed decision-making roles in economic and political institutions. Yet while men went public, women who could afford to do so remained in the domestic or private sphere. The idea soon developed that this situation represented a natural division of labour. This idea persisted until the second half of the twentieth century, when a variety of social circumstances, ranging from the introduction of the birth control pill to women's demands for entry into higher education, finally allowed women to enter the public sphere in large numbers.

We thus see that, according to social constructionists, gender inequality derives not from any inherent biological features of men and women but from three main socio-historical circumstances: the arrival of long-distance warfare and conquest, the development of plow agriculture, and the assignment of women to the domestic sphere and men to the public sphere during the early industrial era.

The Twentieth Century

The twentieth century witnessed growing equality between women and men in many countries. In Canada, the decline of the family farm made children less economically useful and more costly to raise. As a result, women started having fewer children. The industrialization of Canada, and then the growth of the economy's service sector, also increased demand for women in the paid labour force. Such changes blurred the lines between the public and private spheres and made it possible for women to work in the paid labour market. In addition, the women's movement fought and won key battles, extending to women the basic rights that had previously been enjoyed only by men. As we will see, the women's movement developed in three waves over the course of the twentieth century.

The Women's Movement

The first wave of the women's movement emerged during the late nineteenth century and endured until the early 1920s. Its most important public achievements in Canada were the right to vote and the right to be considered persons, and not personal property, under Canadian law. In 1916, women in Alberta, Manitoba, and Saskatchewan were granted the right to vote in provincial elections. All the other provinces followed suit by 1925 except Québec, which granted women the right to vote only in 1940. These rights were first granted to white women. Women from certain ethnic and racial groups did not receive the franchise until later (Nelson and Robinson, 2002).

CP Picture Archive/Jonathan Hayward

The second wave of the women's movement started in the mid-1960s. Members of the movement advocated equal rights with men in education and employment, the elimination of sexual violence, and control over their own reproduction.

In the mid-1960s, the second wave of the women's movement emerged. Second-wave feminists were inspired in part by the successes of the civil rights movement in the United States. They argued that women's concerns were largely ignored despite persistent and pervasive gender inequality. Like their counterparts more than half a century earlier, they held demonstrations, lobbied politicians, and formed women's organizations to further their cause. They demanded equal rights with men in education and employment, the elimination of sexual violence, and control over their own reproduction.

The third wave of the feminist movement began to build in the 1990s, when it was recognized that women were oppressed in different ways and to varying degrees. In particular, working class, non-white women began to resent middle- and upper-class white women for portraying themselves as champions of gender equality while hiring women of colour as low-paid nannies and maids and dismissing the experiences of women of different races, abilities, and classes as relevant to the feminist enterprise (Cassidy, Lord, and Mandell, 1998: 26). The feminist movement thus started to splinter. Black feminist scholars began to develop theories that explored how women's lives are rooted in particular historical and racial experiences (hooks, 1984). Analysts influenced by queer theory argued for paying attention to women with non-heteronormative sexual orientations.

Today, considerable diversity exists in the feminist movement concerning ultimate goals. Three main streams can be distinguished:

1. *Liberal feminism* is the most popular perspective. Its advocates believe that the main sources of women's subordination are learned gender roles and the denial of opportunities to women. Liberal feminists advocate nonsexist methods of socialization and

education, more sharing of domestic tasks between women and men, and the extension to women of all the educational, employment, and political rights and privileges men enjoy.
2. *Socialist feminists* regard women's relationship to the economy as the main source of women's disadvantages. They believe that the traditional nuclear family emerged along with inequalities of wealth and that the economic and sexual oppression of women has its roots in capitalism. Socialist feminists assert that the reforms proposed by liberal feminists are inadequate because they can do little to help working-class women, who are too poor to take advantage of equal educational and work opportunities. Socialist feminists conclude that only the elimination of private property and the creation of economic equality can bring about an end to the oppression of all women.
3. *Radical feminists* find the reforms proposed by liberals and the revolution proposed by socialists to be inadequate. Patriarchy—male domination and norms justifying that domination—is more deeply rooted than capitalism, say the radical feminists. After all, patriarchy predates capitalism. Moreover, it is just as evident in self-proclaimed communist societies as it is in capitalist societies. Radical feminists conclude that the very idea of gender must be changed to bring an end to male domination. Some radical feminists argue that new reproductive technologies, such as in vitro fertilization, are bound to be helpful in this regard because they can break the link between women's bodies and child bearing (Chapter 15, Families). However, the revolution envisaged by radical feminists reaches beyond the realm of reproduction to include all aspects of male sexual dominance. From their point of view, pornography, sexual harassment, restrictive contraception, sexual assault, incest, sterilization, and physical assault must be eliminated for women to reconstruct their sexuality on their own terms.

The newest strand in the women's movement consists of "postfeminists," young women who take their equality with men for granted (Everingham, Stevenson, and Warner-Smith, 2007). They think they can have it all—careers and families—if they want, and that if some women choose not to have a career or a family, then that decision is solely their choice. These young women do not see how traditional feminism can help them. Although they are eager to express their empowerment as women, they tend to do so by buying clothes that make them look and feel sexy and allow them to express and taking control of their sexuality. Sometimes they call this approach "girl power."

In sum, the women's movement fought for, and won, increased economic, political, and legal rights for women. For many Canadians, the women's movement brought about a fundamental reorientation of thinking in terms of what women could and should do. Thus, despite varying perspectives on how to resolve the issue of gender inequality, the women's movement has achieved much over the past century.

Gender Inequality in the Labour Market

After reading this brief historical overview of the feminist movement, you might be inclined to dismiss gender inequality as ancient history. If so, your decision would be hasty. True, women are almost as likely as men to be employed in the paid labour market, a far cry from the situation half a century ago. However, men and women still differ in their labour market experiences. We can see this distinction clearly by focusing on the earnings gap between men and women, one of the most important expressions of gender inequality (Figure 11.7).

Canadian data on the earnings of women and men were first reported in 1967. At that time, the ratio of female to male earnings stood at around 58 percent. In 1992, the ratio passed 70 percent and, since then, has fluctuated near that level (Baker and Drolet, 2010). Although the ratio of female to male earnings is relatively high in a couple of occupational categories, women earn less than men do in every category (Table 11.1).

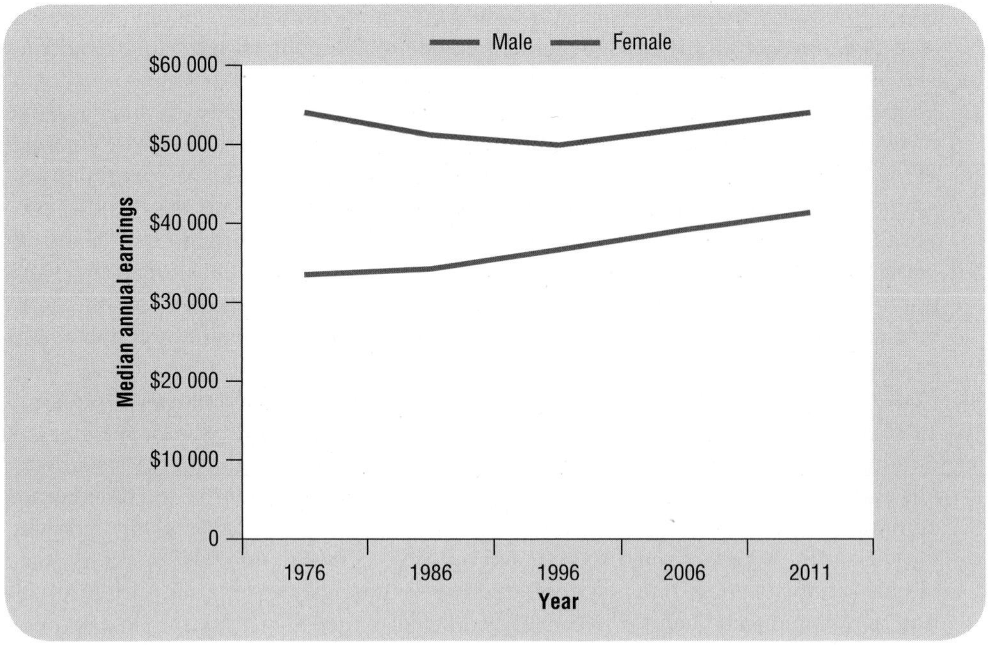

FIGURE 11.7
Median Annual Earnings of Full-time Workers (2011 Dollars), by Sex, Canada 1976–2011

Source: Adapted from Statistics Canada. 2014a. Distribution of earnings, by sex, 2011 constant dollars, annual, 1976–2011 CANSIM (database), Table 202-0101 (retrieved April 27, 2014).

Reasons for the Gender Gap in Earnings

Four main factors contribute to the gender gap in earnings (Bianchi and Spain, 1996; England, 1992):

1. *Gender discrimination.* In February 1985, when Microsoft already employed about 1000 people, it hired its first two female executives. According to a well-placed source involved in the hirings, both women got their jobs because Microsoft was trying to win a U.S. Air Force contract. According to the government's guidelines, Microsoft didn't

TABLE 11.1
Women in Broad Occupational Categories, Canada, 1989, 1999, and 2009

Source: Adapted from Statistics Canada, 2008b, 2008c, CANSIM Table 282-0010 and Table 202-0106. http://dc1.chass.utoronto.ca.myaccess.library.utoronto.ca/cgi-bin/cansimdim/c2_getArrayDim.pl (retrieved November 20, 2010).

	Percentage Females in Occupation			Women's Earnings as a Percentage of Men's Earnings, 2008
	1989	1999	2009	
Management	32.0	35.1	37.0	66.3
Business, finance, and administrative	71.5	71.2	71.0	61.5
Natural and applied science	19.5	20.7	22.3	82.5
Health	78.2	78.5	80.5	52.1
Social science, education, government service, and religion	59.2	64.8	69.6	63.4
Art, culture, recreation, and sport	50.1	54.1	54.4	84.4
Sales and service	55.4	5673	56.9	54.1
Trade, transport, equipment operators	5.4	6.0	6.4	61.0
Primary industry	20.2	21.6	19.5	45.4
Processing, manufacturing, utilities	31.4	32.2	30.1	54.9

have enough women in top management positions to qualify. The source quotes then 29-year-old Bill Gates, president of Microsoft, as saying, "Well, let's hire two women because we can pay them half as much as we will have to pay a man, and we can give them all this other 'crap' work to do because they are women" (quoted in Wallace and Erickson, 1992: 291). This incident is a clear illustration of **gender discrimination**, rewarding women and men differently for the same work. Discrimination on the basis of sex is against the law in Canada. Yet progress is slow; as noted earlier, the female–male earnings ratio has not improved much since 1992.

Gender discrimination involves rewarding men and women differently for the same work.

2. *Women tend to be concentrated in low-wage occupations and industries.* The second factor leading to lower earnings for women is that the programs they select in high school and afterward tend to limit them to jobs in low-wage occupations and industries. The concentration of women in certain occupations and men in others is referred to as *occupational sex segregation*. Although women have made big strides since the 1970s, they are still concentrated in lower-paying clerical and service occupations and underrepresented in higher-paying occupations (see Table 11.1). This situation is particularly true for women of colour, Aboriginal women, and women with disabilities (Chard, 2000: 229).
3. *Heavy domestic responsibilities reduce women's earnings.* Raising children can be one of the most emotionally satisfying experiences. However, we should not be blind to the fact unpaid domestic work decreases the time women have available for education, training, and paid work. Because women are disproportionately involved in child rearing, they experience the brunt of this economic reality. They devote fewer hours to paid work than men do, experience more labour-force interruptions, and are more likely than men are to take part-time jobs, which pay less per hour and offer fewer benefits than full-time work does (Waldfogel, 1997). Globally, women do between two-thirds and three-quarters of all unpaid child care, housework, and care for aging parents (Boyd, 1997: 55). Even when they work full-time in the paid labour force, women continue to shoulder a disproportionate share of domestic responsibilities (Chapter 15, Families).
4. Finally, people commonly consider work done by women to be less valuable than work done by men because they view it as involving fewer skills. Women tend to earn less than men do because the skills involved in their work are often undervalued (Figart and Lapidus, 1996; Sorenson, 1994). For example, kindergarten teachers (nearly all of whom are women) earn significantly less than office machine repair technicians (nearly all of whom are men). It is, however, questionable whether it takes less training and skill to teach a young child the basics of counting and cooperation than it takes to get a photocopier to collate paper. As this example suggests, we sometimes apply arbitrary standards to reward different occupational roles. In our society, these standards systematically undervalue the kind of skills needed for jobs where women are concentrated.

We thus see that the gender gap in earnings is based on several *social* circumstances, not on any inherent differences between women and men. This fact means that we can reduce the gender gap if we want to. Below, we discuss social policies that could create more equality between women and men.

Eliminating the Gender Gap in Earnings

Two main policy initiatives will probably be required in the coming decades to bridge the gender gap in earnings. One is the development of a better child-care system. The other is the development of a policy of "equal pay for work of equal value." Let us consider each of these issues in turn.

Child Care

High-quality, government-subsidized, affordable child care is widely available in most Western European countries but not yet in Canada outside Québec (Chapter 15, Families). Sixty percent of children in the United Kingdom are in regulated child care, as are

69 percent of children in France and 78 percent in Denmark. In contrast, Canada's child-care efforts are a patchwork that has been chronically underfunded. Currently, there are only enough regulated daycare spaces for one in every five children under the age of six in Canada (Canadian Child Care Federation, 2013). As a result, many Canadian women with young children are either unable to work outside the home or able to work outside the home only on a part-time basis.

A universal system of daycare was proposed in Canada as early as 1970, but little was done at the federal level or in most provinces and territories. Québec is an exception. In 1997, that province introduced a comprehensive family policy that attempts to integrate family benefits, paid parental leave, child care, and kindergarten. Its child-care component heralded universally available, affordable child care. Once women had access to child care, rates of labour market participation among Québec women began to climb steadily (Stalker and Ornstein, 2013).

In 2004, affordable, high-quality, regulated daycare was a central electoral promise of the victorious Liberal Party. By mid-2005, the beginnings of a national system began to take shape when the federal government reached child-care agreements with Saskatchewan, Manitoba, Ontario, and Newfoundland and Labrador. Had it taken root across the country, the system might have paid for itself. One study estimated that a high-quality, affordable, universal system of child care and early child-care education would cost $7.9 billion, while the increased employment of mothers would be worth $6.2 billion and the improvement in child development would be worth $4.3 billion (Cleveland and Krashinsky, 1998). However, after Stephen Harper became prime minister in 2006, he scrapped the agreements in favour of annual tax benefits of $1200 paid to parents for each child under age six. The amount and the targeting were widely criticized as failing to address what women who work for pay needed to support their families. Given that the average monthly cost to place a child in daycare in the city of Vancouver is approximately $1250 per month, the amount provided by the federal government falls far short of the actual cost ("By the Numbers," 2013). By comparison, the average monthly cost to place a child in daycare in Montreal is a mere $140.

Equal Pay for Work of Equal Value

On paper, Canadian women have had the right to equal pay for the same jobs done by men since the 1950s. Unfortunately, although early laws proclaimed lofty goals, they failed to result in fair wages.

In the 1980s, researchers found that women earn less than men do, partly because jobs in which women are concentrated are valued less than jobs in which men are concentrated. The researchers therefore tried to establish gender-neutral standards by which they could judge the dollar value of work. These standards included such factors as the education and experience required to do a particular job and the level of responsibility, amount of stress, and working conditions associated with it. Researchers thought that, by using these criteria to compare jobs in which women and men are concentrated, they could identify pay inequities. The underpaid could then be compensated accordingly. In other words, women and men would receive **equal pay for work of equal value**, even if they did different jobs.

Equal pay for work of equal value refers to the equal dollar value of different jobs. It is established in gender-neutral terms by comparing jobs in terms of the education and experience needed to do them and the stress, responsibility, and working conditions associated with them.

In 1985, Manitoba became the first Canadian province to implement equal pay for work of equal value (or "pay equity") in the public service. Pay equity is now official policy in 10 of 13 Canadian jurisdictions; Alberta, Saskatchewan, and the Northwest Territories are the exceptions. However, the provisions vary widely. Enforcement mechanisms are weak, and employers have found ways to argue that unequal wages do not signify discrimination based on sex.

In light of the meagre advances in Canadian public policy that we have outlined, it is easy to understand why the earnings gap persists between women and men. It is probably less evident that continued gender inequality encourages male violence against women, an issue to which we now turn.

Male Aggression against Women

One evening in December 2012, Jyoti Singh Pandey, a 23-year-old physiotherapy student, went out with her boyfriend to see *The Life of Pi* at a movie theatre in a suburb of Delhi, India. After the movie, the couple hopped on a minibus for the trip home. Six men were aboard, including the driver. After taunting the woman for going out in the evening, and therefore failing to behave with appropriate modesty, they beat the boyfriend unconscious with an iron rod and gagged and bound him. The men proceeded to drag Jyoti to the back of the bus, where they raped her repeatedly and penetrated her with the iron rod. They then threw Jyoti and her boyfriend from the moving bus onto the road. The driver backed up, attempting to kill her, but her boyfriend somehow managed to get her out of the way. Jyoti nonetheless died of her injuries a few weeks later. Soon after she died, *The Times of India* reported the words of Hindu spiritual leader Asaram Bapu: "The victim is as guilty as her rapists" ("Delhi Gang-Rape Victim," 2013; Kaul, 2012).

Sexual violence, the neglect or murder of infant girls, disputes over dowries, domestic violence, and poor care of elderly women are responsible for the deaths of hundreds of thousands of girls and women in India every year (Anderson and Ray, 2012; Harris, 2013). Much of the population is outraged by this state of affairs, so it is not surprising that mass protests against the treatment of women in India broke out in the days and weeks following Jyoti Singh Pandey's rape.

However, the words of a religious authority like Asaram Bapu prevent us from dismissing her rape as just the work of half a dozen sick individuals. For when one man's belief is multiplied a million or a hundred million times over, it forms part of a culture; and for any element of a culture to endure, it must be supported by social arrangements that render it useful to some people. Asaram Bapu gave voice to a belief that is widespread, although far from universal, in India: women deserve what they get when they fail to subordinate themselves to men and behave with abject modesty. To the degree people like Asaram Bapu believe Jyoti was in any way responsible for the tragedy that befell her, we must regard the crime against her as a phenomenon with deep social and cultural roots.

We do not mean to suggest that all men endorse the principle of male dominance, much less that all men are inclined to engage in sexual assault or other acts of aggression against women. Many men favour gender equality, and most men never abuse a woman (Messerschmidt, 1993). Yet the fact remains that many cultures legitimize male dominance, making it seem valid or proper. For example, pornography, jokes about "dumb blondes," and leering might seem harmless. However, at a subtler, sociological level, such activities are assertions of the appropriateness of women's submission to men. Such frequent and routine reinforcements of male superiority increase the likelihood that some men will consider it their right to assault women physically or sexually if the opportunity to do so exists or can be created. "Just kidding" has a cost.

In the following sections, we examine various forms of male aggression against women, including sexual harassment, sexual assault and spouse abuse.

Sexual Harassment

Sexual harassment can be divided in two types. **Quid pro quo sexual harassment** takes place when sexual threats or bribery are made a condition of employment decisions—the exchange of a promotion for sexual favours, for example. (The Latin phrase *quid pro quo* means "something for something.") **Hostile environment sexual harassment** involves sexual jokes, comments, and touching that interferes with work or creates a hostile work environment. Research suggests that relatively powerless women are the most likely to be sexually harassed. Specifically, women who are young, unmarried, and employed in non-professional jobs are most likely to become objects of sexual harassment, particularly when they are temporary workers, when the ratio of women to men in the workplace is low (as is the case in the military), and when the organizational culture of the workplace tolerates sexual harassment (Gill and Febbraro, 2013; Rogers and Henson, 1997; Welsh, 1999).

Quid pro quo sexual harassment takes place when sexual threats or bribery are made a condition of employment decisions.

Hostile environment sexual harassment involves sexual jokes, comments, and touching that interferes with work or creates an unfriendly work environment.

Sexual Assault

Serious acts of aggression between men and women are common. Most such acts are committed by men against women. Worldwide, 7.2 per cent of women 15 years of age and older reported that they have been sexually assaulted by someone other than an intimate partner at least once in their lives (Abrahams et al., 2014). In Canada, more than 6 percent women under the age of 25 report having been sexually assaulted and 9 percent report having been stalked (Johnson, 2006: 36).

In one study, more than 20 percent of female Canadian postsecondary students reported having given in to unwanted sexual intercourse because they were overwhelmed by a man's continued arguments and pressure. Nearly 7 percent reported they had unwanted sexual intercourse because a man threatened or used some degree of physical force. Nearly 14 percent claimed that, while they were either intoxicated or under the influence of drugs, a man had attempted unwanted sexual intercourse (DeKeseredy and Kelly, 1993).

Another study found that half of first- and second-year university women reported unwanted attempts at intercourse by males of their acquaintance, one-third of them involving "strong" physical force. The women seemed constrained by traditional roles in their negative responses: 37 percent did nothing, 26 percent responded verbally, and 14 percent responded physically. The stronger the victim's response, the less likely it was that the attempted rape was completed. Half of the attacks succeeded. None of the women reported the attack to the authorities, and half talked to no one about it. The rest told friends. Eleven percent ended the relationship, whereas almost three-quarters either accepted the situation or ignored the attack. Half continued to have sex with, date, or maintain a friendship with the assailant. Most blamed themselves at least partially for the incident (Murnen, Perot, and Byrne, 1989; see Box 11.3). A more recent study revealed that university women remain hesitant in labelling unwanted sexual experiences as rape or sexual assault (Deming et al., 2013).

Some people think rapists are men who suffer a psychological disorder that compels them to achieve immediate sexual gratification even if violence is required. Others think rape occurs because of flawed communication. They believe some victims give mixed signals to their assailants by, for example, drinking too much and flirting with them.

Such explanations are not completely invalid. Interviews with victims and perpetrators show that some offenders do suffer from psychological disorders. Others misinterpret signals in what they regard as sexually ambiguous situations (Hannon et al., 1995). But such cases account for only a small proportion of the total. Men who commit sexual assaults are rarely mentally disturbed and it is abundantly clear to most assailants that they are doing something their victims strongly oppose (Senn et al., 2000).

What then accounts for sexual assault being as common as it is? The fact that sexual assault is not about sexual gratification at all—some offenders cannot ejaculate or even achieve an erection—suggests a sociological answer. All forms of sexual assault involve domination and humiliation as principal motives. It is not surprising, therefore, that some offenders were physically or sexually abused in their youth. They develop a deep need to feel powerful as psychological compensation for their early powerlessness. Others are men who, as children, saw their fathers treat their mothers as potentially hostile figures who needed to be controlled or as mere objects available for male gratification. They saw their fathers as emotionally cold and distant. Raised in such an atmosphere, rapists learn not to empathize with women. Instead, they learn to want to dominate them (Lisak, 1992).

Certain social situations increase the rate of sexual aggression. One such situation is war. In wartime, conquering male soldiers often feel justified in wanting to humiliate the vanquished, who are powerless to stop them. Rape is often used for this purpose, as was especially well documented in the ethnic wars that accompanied the breakup of Yugoslavia in the 1990s and in the civil war in the Democratic Republic of Congo from 1998 until the present.

BOX 11.3

IT'S YOUR CHOICE

DOES A RAPE CULTURE EXIST ON UNIVERSITY AND COLLEGE CAMPUSES?

Every Labour Day weekend, first-year university and college students flock to campus to take part in Frosh week. It's a way to welcome and orient first-year students to university and college life with live music, organized social gatherings, tours, and rallies—all intended to instill a sense of school spirit in the newcomers.

In 2013, the yearly event came under public scrutiny at the University of British Columbia in Vancouver and Saint Mary's University in Halifax. Videos posted to social media sites showed first-year male and female students yelling out an almost identical chant: "We like them YOUNG: Y is for your sister; O is for oh-so-tight; U is for underage; N is for no consent; G is for grab that ass."

Apparently, the chants were nothing new. They had been recited for years on both campuses and indeed at universities and colleges across Canada. This time, though, public outrage led university officials across the country to vow to take action.

For some people, the chants proved that Canadian universities were home to a "rape culture." A rape culture is said to exist in any environment where sexual violence is normalized, excused, and even condoned. For example, people who believe that men are naturally aggressive and that women are "just asking for it" foster an environment that is conducive to rape.

Others are uncertain that a rape culture exists on college and university campuses. They say that the problem lies with a small number of men who are sexual predators. Treating all men as potential sexual offenders is blatantly unfair.

Still others suggest that the problem is not just cultural but institutional (Armstrong, Hamilton, and Sweeney, 2006). Because college and university life can be stressful and alienating for first-year students, partying is an important opportunity for them to unwind and get to know others. Colleges and universities that fail to provide students with enough opportunities for socializing or those that adopt heavy-handed alcohol policies may unwittingly encourage students to attend private parties where men control nearly all aspects of the party experience, including choosing the venue, arranging transportation, and overseeing the flow of alcohol. From this point of view, if colleges and universities adopt policies that minimize the amount of private partying, the rate of sexual violence against women will fall.

What do you think? Is the problem of rape restricted to a small minority of men? Do student rallies that incite non-consensual sex provide evidence that a rape culture permeates campus life? Do you think that institutional factors contribute to the rate of sexual assault on university campuses? Could all three factors (individual, cultural, and institutional) play a role? How might one best begin to address the issue of sexual assault on Canadian college and university campuses?

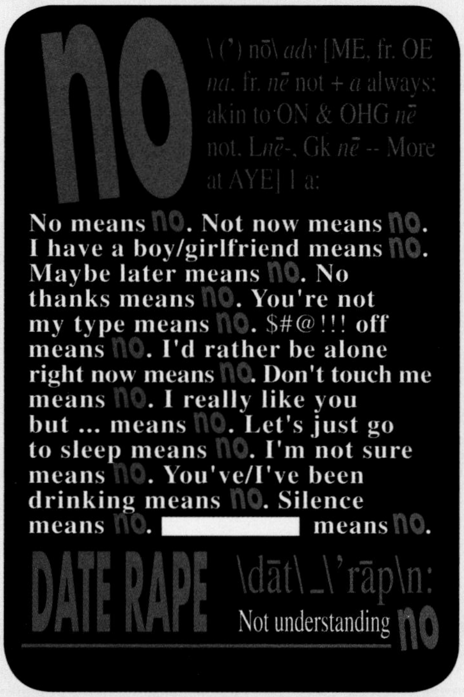

Courtesy of the Canadian Federation of Students

How effective do you think this poster would be at deterring sexual assault on university and college campuses?

Spouse Abuse

About 26 percent of police-reported violent crime in Canada involves spousal violence, and 80 percent of victims of spousal violence are women (Sinha, 2013). Women are far more likely than are men to experience severe physical aggression, such as being beaten, choked, strangled, sexually assaulted, and killed (Stewart, MacMillan, and Wathen, 2013).

There are three main types of spousal violence: (Johnson, 1995; Johnson and Ferraro, 2000):

- *Common couple violence* occurs when partners have an argument, and one partner lashes out physically at the other. For a couple that engages in this type of violence, violent acts are unlikely to occur often, escalate over time, or be severe. Both partners are about equally likely to engage in common couple violence, regardless of their gender.

- *Intimate terrorism* is part of a general desire of one partner to control the other. Where one partner engages in intimate terrorism, violent acts are likely to occur often, escalate over time, and be severe. Among heterosexual couples, the aggressor is usually the man.
- *Violent resistance* is the third main type of domestic violence. Among heterosexual couples, violent resistance typically involves a woman violently defending herself against a man who has engaged in intimate terrorism.

For heterosexual couples, spousal violence is positively associated with the level of gender inequality in the family It is also more common in families where men believe that male domination is justified, and among couples who had witnessed their mothers being abused and who had themselves been abused when they were children (Cui et al., 2011; Franklin and Kercher, 2012; Murrell, Christoff, and Henning, 2007; Stewart MacMillan, and Wathen, 2013). In short, the incidence of domestic violence is highest where a big power imbalance exists between men and women, where norms justify the male domination of women, and where early socialization experiences predispose men to behave aggressively toward women.

We conclude that male aggression against women and gender inequality are not separate issues. Gender inequality is the foundation of aggression against women. Gender equality is not just a matter of justice. It is also a question of safety.

TIME FOR REVIEW

- What three socio-historical forces led to the widening of gender inequality?
- What were the main achievements of each of the three waves of feminism?
- How might the establishment of a universally accessible system of high-quality child care and the implementation of a universal system of equal pay for work of equal value lower the level of gender inequality?
- How is gender inequality linked to male violence against women?

SUMMARY

1. Are sex and gender rooted in nature?
   Sex refers to certain anatomical and hormonal features of a person, while gender refers to the culturally appropriate expression of masculinity and femininity. Sex is largely rooted in nature, although people can change their sex by undergoing a sex-change operation and hormone therapy. In contrast, social and biological forces strongly influence gender. Sociologists study the way social conditions affect the expression of masculinity and femininity.

2. What major social forces channel people into performing culturally appropriate gender roles?
   Various agents of socialization channel people into performing culturally approved gender roles. The family, the school, and the mass media are among the most important of these agents of socialization. Once the sex of children is known (or assumed), parents and teachers tend to treat boys and girls differently in terms of the kind of play, dress, and learning they encourage. The mass media reinforce the learning of masculine and feminine roles by making different characteristics seem desirable in boys and girls, men and women.

3. What is homosexuality? Why does it exist?
Homosexuals are people who prefer sexual partners of the same sex. We do not yet understand well the causes of homosexuality—whether it is genetic, hormonal, psychological, or some combination of the three. We do know that homosexuality does not appear to be a choice and that it emerges for most people in early adolescence and without prior sexual experience. Sociologists are, in any case, more interested in the way homosexuality is expressed and repressed. For example, they have studied how, in the twentieth century, scientific research and political movements made the open expression of homosexuality more acceptable. Sociologists have also studied the ways in which various aspects of society reinforce heterosexuality and treat homosexuality as a form of deviance subject to tight social control.

4. How does the existence of sharply defined gender roles influence men's and women's experiences in the labour market?
The gender gap in earnings derives from outright discrimination against women, women's disproportionate domestic responsibilities, women's concentration in low-wage occupations and industries, and the undervaluation of work typically done by women. Among the major reforms that could help eliminate the gender gap in earnings and reduce the level and expression of gender inequality are the development of an affordable, accessible system of high-quality daycare, and the remuneration of men and women on the basis of their work's actual worth.

5. What explains male aggression against women?
Male aggression against women is rooted in gender inequality. Thus, where women and men are more equal socially, and norms justify gender equality, the rate of male aggression against women is lower. Male aggression against women, including sexual harassment, sexual assault, and spouse abuse, is encouraged by a lesson most of us still learn at home, in school, at work, through much of organized religion, and in the mass media—that it is natural and right for men to dominate women. Daily patterns of gender domination, viewed as legitimate by most people, are built into our courtship, sexual, family, and work norms.

CHAPTER 12

SOCIOLOGY OF THE BODY: DISABILITY, AGING, AND DEATH

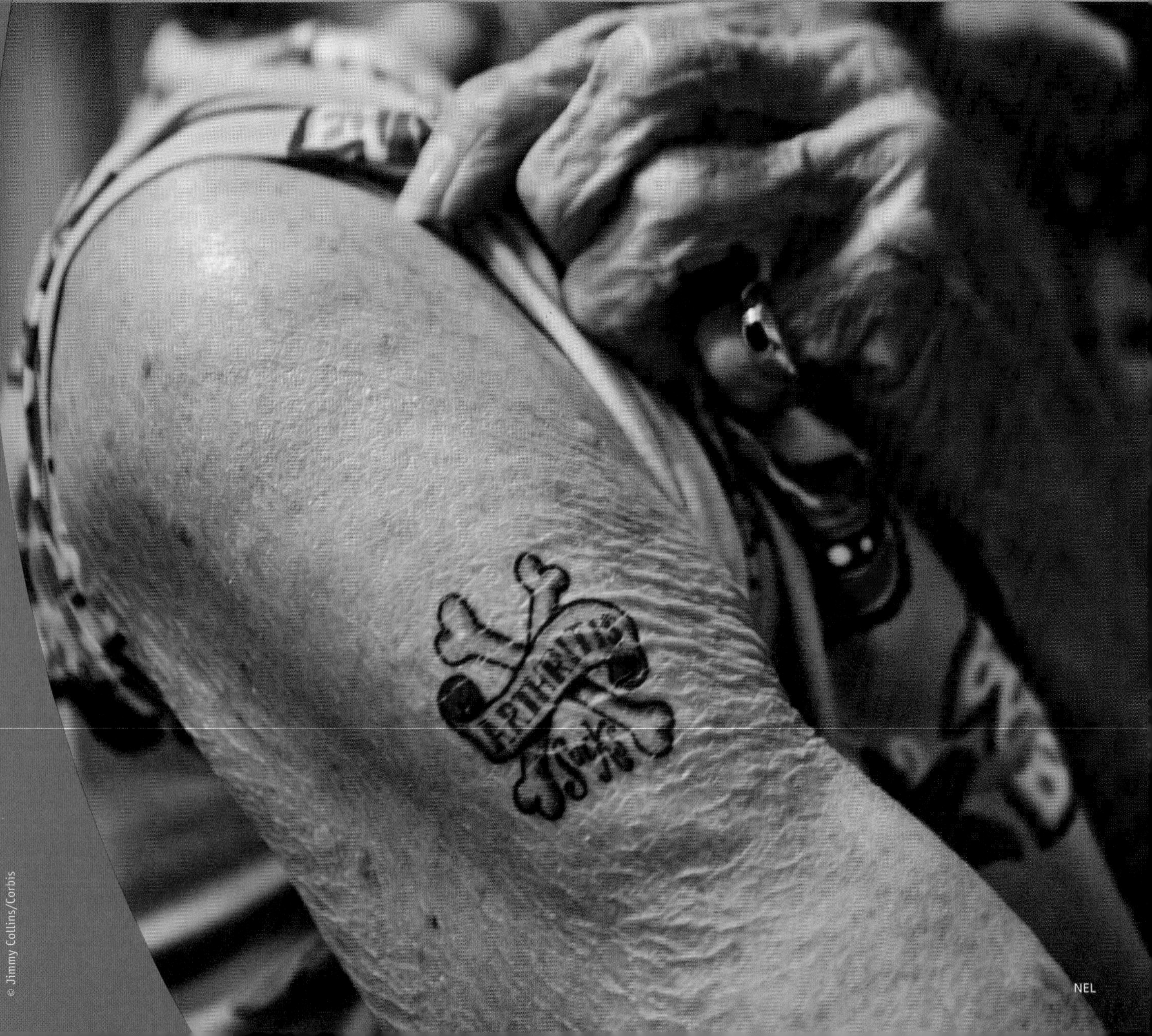

© Jimmy Collins/Corbis

IN THIS CHAPTER, YOU WILL LEARN TO

- Recognize that the way people make their bodies appear has social causes and social consequences.
- Understand that individuals modify their bodily appearance to express identity and difference, yet typically do so in ways that reflect conformity to cultural norms.
- Compare definitions of disability and responses to disability over time and place.
- Evaluate the potential for population aging to reduce discriminatory attitudes and affect power imbalances between young and old.
- Appreciate that death and dying are influenced by sociological processes.

THINKING ABOUT THE HUMAN BODY SOCIOLOGICALLY

Have you ever thought about the ways in which people are increasingly able to do things in this world without a physical presence? Take online courses. You don't need to get dressed, wait for a bus, or look for a seat in the classroom. Instead, by logging on to a computer, you can listen to the instructor, participate in class discussion, and write an exam, all from the comfort of your home.

Or think about modern warfare. Instead of a traditional battlefield where combatants gather to fight face to face, war in the twenty-first century does not necessarily require that enemies be physically present in the same place. Unmanned aerial vehicles (UAVs), or drones, are at the forefront of a new and emerging age of robotic warfare (Bhatt, 2012). Praised for their precision and their ability to insulate pilots from harm, the use of drones has escalated dramatically under U.S. President Barack Obama.

Every day, hundreds of American men and women, dressed in military uniform, arrive to work at a set of bunkers at bases in New Mexico, Nevada, and South Dakota. Seated in ergonomic chairs and surrounded by computer screens in dimly lit, heavily air-conditioned rooms, these soldiers operate drones in Pakistan, Afghanistan, and Yemen. Their mission is to conduct surveillance on "high-value" targets, provide protection and reconnaissance to American soldiers on the ground, and rain missiles on enemies.

You might think that sociologists of the body would have little interest in studying virtual activities such as drone warfare. After all, it is the technological wizardry that gets all the attention in the mass media. Yet in three ways, drone warfare piques the interest of sociologists who think about the human body.

MASSOUD HOSSAINI/AFP/Getty Images

In service since the 1990s, the Predator is a common type of unmanned aerial vehicle (UAV) used by the United States military.

First, sociologists are interested in how the human body is marked so it can be socially regulated. To make this point, a sociologist might ask why, if bodies are truly irrelevant in drone warfare, why do the soldiers who operate the drones wear uniforms? Outsiders cannot see them in their military garb. For all it matters, the soldiers operating the drones could be sitting in their underwear or in a party dress.

A sociological response to this question is that social institutions always make demands on bodily appearance as a means of exerting social control. An army uniform indicates membership in an organization and allegiance to a state. It makes the wearer's status visible to oneself and others, serving as a constant reminder that one belongs to certain collectivities and identifies with their goals. Uniforms also give legitimacy to certain activities, sanctioning behaviour that otherwise would be problematic—such as killing people. In short, to wear a military uniform is to confirm one's identity as a highly trained and fully compliant soldier who behaves in expected ways.

Drone operators must be skilled in reading and interpreting the bodies they observe. Emotional expression, gesture, stance, and dress provide clues to a person's status and purpose. By correctly interpreting the bodily appearance and behaviour of potential targets, drone operators can distinguish enemy combatants from civilians, glean information on foes, and take action against them. Sociologists also study human bodies—not to destroy them, of course, but to analyze them as social products, entities that bear the imprint of society. For instance, although height and weight are often taken for granted as natural or biological features, they are qualities influenced by social conditions and norms.

Bodies are also vehicles for expressing individuality. Although some people have altered their bodies in various ways throughout history, increasingly in many societies a tendency exists for the body to be seen as a "project" that people shape to achieve a unique identity (Shilling, 2013). Some people spend time in the gym, cultivating a muscular appearance. Others dye their hair to hide signs of aging. Still others use piercings, tattoos, and other forms of body modification to create bodies intended to be admired as pieces of art. The body can also be marked unintentionally, as occurs when illness and disability disfigure one's appearance or impose bodily restrictions. Regardless of circumstance, embedded in the idea that our bodies reflect both our selves and our society is a sociological principle that is the main lesson of this chapter. The human body is more than a wonder of biology. It is also a sociological wonder insofar as it is central to constructing culture, personhood, and identity (Fox, 2012; Turner, 1996).

Embodiment refers to the physical and mental experience of existence.

A second reason why sociologists of the human body are drawn to studying drone warfare relates to the issue of embodiment. **Embodiment** refers to the physical and mental experience of existence. Said differently, a body is not just something that one has; it is also something that one is. We can better understand the nature of embodiment by looking at a common misconception about the effects of drone warfare on soldiers. Many people assume that because the soldiers operating drones are fighting a virtual war, their experiences lack the same intensity as those of soldiers who are physically present in battle. Therefore, it is common for drone operators to be mocked by other soldiers and to be derided as "cubicle warriors" or worse (Gregory, 2011).

Do drone operators merit such a dismissive label? Their bodies suggest otherwise. Even though they are not physically present in the battlefield, drone operators experience the same adrenaline rush as do soldiers engaged physically in battle. When drone operators launch a missile from the safety of their bunkers, their bodies sweat, their hearts race, and their breathing becomes shallow and rapid. These bodily signs, characteristic of the fight-or-flight response, cannot be suppressed despite the absence of any physical threat to the soldier and the distance that separates the soldier from the target. This physical response tells us that the experience of killing, whether in person or not, is always "embodied." The body and the mind are not easily separated. Even virtual war has a material reality (Holmqvist, 2013).

Not only does drone warfare elicit a physical response, it may also have mental health consequences. A common mental health diagnosis among soldiers is post-traumatic stress disorder (PTSD), which involves the unwanted and repeated reliving of traumatic events through nightmares and flashbacks. Research shows that drone operators experience PTSD as frequently, or perhaps even more frequently, than do soldiers in the battlefield. One reason for their PTSD is that drone operators can see high-resolution images of death and destruction that are often not visible to soldiers in the battlefield (Holmqvist, 2013).

Paying attention to embodiment also alerts sociologists to the ways in which we often ignore what it means for people to inhabit bodies that are ill, aged, or disabled. Hospital personnel often reduce people to their medical problem, referring to "the lymphoma in room 203" or "the geriatric case down the hall." Such administrative categories can make it difficult to see beyond the label. In contrast, sociologists seek to understand the lived experience of being ill, elderly, or disabled. As we will see, taking embodiment into account can move us past the tyranny of stereotypes and into the realm of subjective experience.

There is a third way in which drone warfare captures the interest of those who think about the body sociologically. Today, possibilities exist for shaping bodies that would have been seen as science fiction just a few decades ago. For example, people with spinal cord injuries are beginning to benefit from brain technology interface devices. When implanted in the brain, these devices wirelessly transmit information to micro-electric stimulators in the body, bypassing the spinal cord to produce the desired movement. Breakthroughs have also been made in the treatment of diabetes. Beeper-sized computer devices track blood sugar level and deliver insulin continuously via a small pump under the skin, eliminating the routine of painful finger pricks and better mimicking normal pancreatic processes. Moreover, these devices can be controlled by smartphones, and the gathered information can be relayed to health care practitioners.

A **cyborg** (short for cybernetic organism) is an entity that embodies elements both living and dead, human and machine, natural and unnatural (Haraway, 1991). We have entered the age of cyborgs, and their existence raises the question of exactly what human bodies are and what they might become (Sandel, 2007; Shilling, 2013). For example, should there be limits on which technologies are employed to change the human body? Should we use technology merely to improve the lives of people with disabilities so their experiences are comparable to those who are considered normal? Or should we strive to enhance all human performance, enabling us to acquire senses and capacities far beyond our present capabilities? From *Frankenstein* to the latest version of *RoboCop*, movies that feature cyborgs represent our collective effort to grapple with such sociological questions (see Box 12.1).

Cyborgs are entities that embody elements both living and dead, human and machine, natural and unnatural.

BOX 12.1

SOCIOLOGY AT THE MOVIES

ROBOCOP (2014)

RoboCop is the latest iteration in a long line of movies that reflect society's preoccupation with the increasingly blurred line between human and machine. Set in 2028, the film opens with a dilemma confronting OmniCorp, a multinational company that has made billions by developing and selling drones and androids deployed overseas. The company wants to sell in the North American market but is stymied by a wary public and government officials who question whether robots can act acceptably when they cannot really know what it means to take a human life.

OmniCorp sees a golden opportunity when Detroit police officer Alex Murphy is critically injured by a car bomb in the line of duty. OmniCorp scientists encase Murphy in a robotic body that gives him superhuman capabilities. Although Murphy is led to believe that his mind remains intact, his brain is manipulated with software and drugs. The intent is to sharpen his skills so he can perform beyond normal human capabilities without emotions and conscience getting in the way. OmniCorp believes that if it can turn Murphy into an efficient, weaponized human being, it can sway public opinion in favour of putting a RoboCop on every street corner. OmniCorp cares little for Murphy as a person and is willing to overwrite his humanity in the name of profit.

© Orion Pictures/courtesy Everett Collection/CP Photos

Joel Kinnaman plays Alex Murphy in *RoboCop*

Initially, the public responds enthusiastically to RoboCop. Nonetheless, questions linger. Is RoboCop a machine? A man? A machine that thinks it's a man? A man who is afraid he is just a machine? The movie provides an answer. In the climax, Murphy's wife and son are held hostage by OmniCorp employees. Murphy overrides his programming, rescues his family, and kills his corrupt handlers. In doing so, he makes it clear that humanity cannot be suppressed, regardless of how technology is merged with human bodies by companies eager to control humans for profit. Time will tell whether the movie is right.

In this chapter, we discover the ways in which having and being a body lie at the core of all social engagement. As we have shown, bodies are socially regulated and marked; they are the surface on which one conveys social status and identity; they are the basis for our social existence in the world; and they are the source of considerable debate as technology erases the boundaries between human and machine. These themes are woven throughout this chapter as we consider the ways in which bodily appearance, disability, aging, death, and dying are more than just physical occurrences, but also have social significance.

TIME FOR REVIEW

- Why do uniforms help to produce desired behaviour?
- What are the three ways in which drone warfare piques the interest of sociologists interested in the human body?
- Why is it important to understand the implications of embodiment?
- How do cyborgs blur the boundaries between human and machine?

SOCIETY AND THE HUMAN BODY

The Body and Social Status: A Feminist Interpretation

The human body means different things and has a variety of consequences in different cultures and historical periods and for various categories of people. For example, a person's height, weight, and attractiveness may seem to be facts of nature. However, the standards by which we define a "normal" or "desirable" body vary historically. Moreover, because of the social value that is placed on a person's height, weight, and perceived attractiveness, these bodily features influence income, health, likelihood of getting married, and much else. Let us explore in detail the relationship between body characteristics and social status.

Height

In an experiment, four people of the same height and roughly similar appearance were introduced to a group of students. The first person was introduced as another undergraduate, the second as a graduate student, the third as an assistant professor, and the fourth as a full professor. Members of the group were asked to rank the four people in terms of their height. Despite the fact that all four were of equal stature, the students estimated that the full professor was the tallest, the assistant professor next tallest, then the graduate student, and finally the undergraduate. Apparently believing that physical stature reflects social stature, the students correlated social status with height ("Short Guys Finish Last," 1995–96).

Is this perception accurate? Do tall people really tend to enjoy high social status? And why are some people tall in the first place? We can begin to answer these questions by first acknowledging that genes are an important determinant of any particular individual's height. However, the great majority of human *populations* are almost exactly the same genetically. A complex set of *social* factors determines the average height of most populations, whether the population consists of members of a country, a class, a racial or an ethnic group, and so on. Moreover, a complex set of social consequences flow from differences in height.

Figure 12.1 shows some of the main social causes and consequences of stature. For purposes of illustration, consider just the impact of income on height. When incomes rise in a population, parents can better afford to feed their children a higher-quality diet (especially one rich in protein), helping their offspring to grow taller in adulthood. Replicated over successive generations, average height in the population gradually increases. Thus, Danish men were on average nearly thirteen centimetres (five inches) taller in 1980 than in 1860 (Hatton and

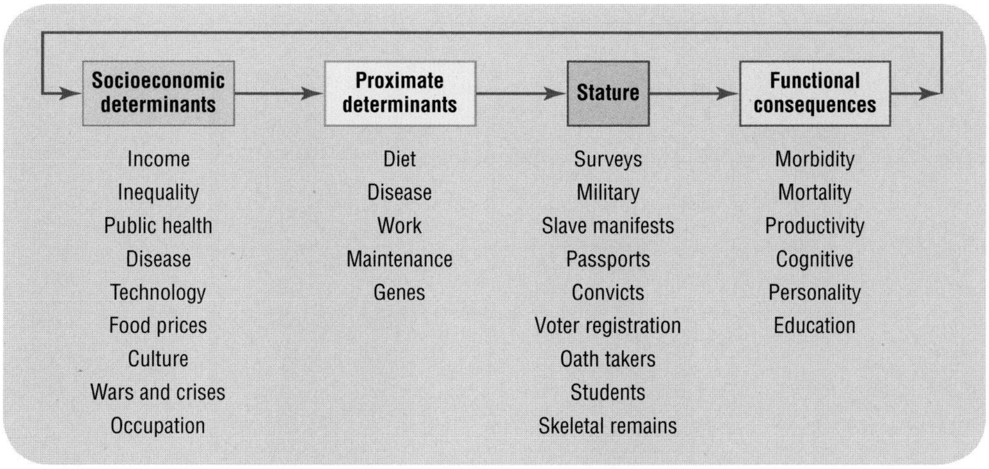

FIGURE 12.1

A flow diagram of determinants and consequences of stature in human populations

Source: Steckel, Richard H. 2013. "Biological Measures of Economic History." *Annual Reviews of Economics 5:* 401–423.

Bray, 2010). Japanese men were on average five centimetres (two inches) taller at the end of the twentieth century than they were at mid-century, and are projected to be the same height as men in North America within a generation (Health Service Bureau, 2009). In each case, the main cause of growing stature is the same: A higher standard of living led to an improved diet that allowed the human body to come closer to realizing its full growth potential.

As we might expect, within countries, we also find a correlation between stature and class position. Class differences in height are smaller than they were centuries ago (Silventoinen, 2003). Even today, however, members of upper classes are on average taller than are members of middle classes, who are in turn taller than members of working classes are.

The consequences of stature are also notable. Scrutiny of many sources, ranging from U.S. Army records since the Civil War to all Norwegian X-ray records from the 1950s, reveals that, on average, tall people live longer than others do (Steckel, 2013). Tall people also perform better on intelligence tests, earn more money, and tend to reach the top of their profession more quickly than do shorter people (Case and Paxson, 2008; Lindqvist, 2012). In Canada, researchers have found that men who are taller are more likely than are shorter men to be in positions of authority in their workplace (Gawley, Perks, and Curtis, 2009). For Canadian men and women, height is positively associated with income (Perks, 2005). Thus, in one year, a Canadian man who is ten centimetres (4 inches) taller than another man but like him in all other relevant respects will earn, on average, $222 more.

At least part of the reason that short people tend to be less successful in some ways than are tall people is that they experience subtle discrimination based on height. In other words, the belief that shorter people are inferior to taller people will produce its expected reality. Consider where you sit in the status hierarchy based on height. Have you ever felt advantaged or disadvantaged because of how tall you are?

Weight

Just as better access to high-quality food has made it possible for us to grow taller, it has also allowed us to increase our weight. In some cases, the wide availability of food has led to overeating. Overweight is the result of consuming more food than the body needs. In Canada and other industrialized nations, the percentage of overweight people is relatively high (see Figure 12.2).

The modern environment encourages people to overeat (Mitchell et al., 2011). In highly industrialized and postindustrial societies, food tends to be inexpensive and abundant. Moreover, few Canadians need to expend much energy to secure food, find shelter, and travel. As more Canadians become accustomed to eating more food and settling into sedentary lifestyles, even more of us are predicted to become overweight.

Ironically, just as overweight is on the rise, it is the slender body that is perceived to be the ideal body shape in most societies. Let us assume that *Playboy* "Playmates of the Month"

FIGURE 12.2

Percentage of Adults Who Are Overweight, Selected Countries, 2013

Note: Overweight adults have a BMI of 25 or higher (BMI is weight in kilograms divided by the square of height in metres).

Source: OECD (2013b). "Overweight and obesity," in OECD Factbook 2013: Economic, Environmental and Social Statistics, OECD Publishing. Retrieved July 8, 2014 (http://dx.doi.org/10.1787/factbook-2013-100-en).

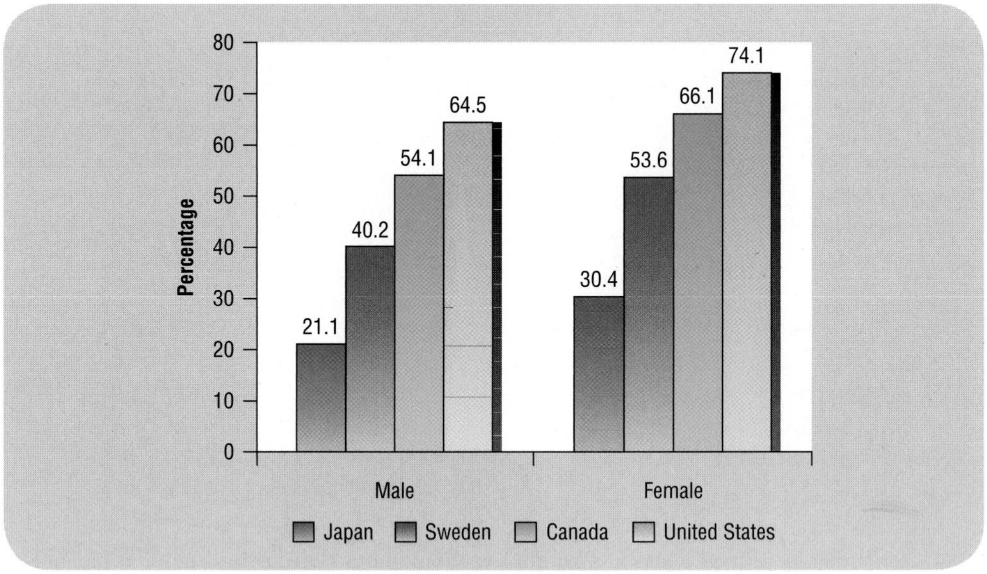

(or "centrefolds") represent the North American ideal body type for women. From information in the magazine, it is possible to calculate the body mass index (BMI) of 609 centrefolds from December 1953 to January 2009 (see Figure 12.3). (The body mass index is equal to one's body mass in kilograms divided by the square of one's body height in metres.) The BMI of *Playboy* centrefolds fell 7 percent from 1953 to 2009. According to the accepted standard, a BMI of less than 18.5 indicates an underweight woman. By this benchmark, the average *Playboy* centerfold has been underweight since about 1960. A BMI greater than 25.0 is the accepted standard for an overweight woman. From 1978–79 to 2004, the average BMI for Canadian women rose 6 percent, from 25.2 to 26.7. Here, then, is a recipe for rising anxiety about one's body: a body ideal that is growing slimmer and an average body type that is becoming bulkier.

Media images consistently display bodies that have been airbrushed to thin "perfection," projecting an unattainable vision of beauty and redefining what is seen as desirable. Perhaps in a society where food has become plentiful, those who restrict food intake and sculpt their bodies to be as thin as possible should be celebrated for their achievement. If true, do well-rounded bodies evoke the opposite reaction? It appears so. North Americans consistently rate

FIGURE 12.3

Body Mass Index (BMI) of 609 *Playboy* Centrefolds, December 1953–January 2009

Source: Tjepkema, Michael. 2006. "Measured Obesity: Adult obesity in Canada: Measured height and weight." Ottawa, ON: Statistics Canada; Gammon, Katherine. 2009. "Infoporn: Today's Playmates Are More Like Anime Figures Than Real Humans." *Wired* 17, 2.

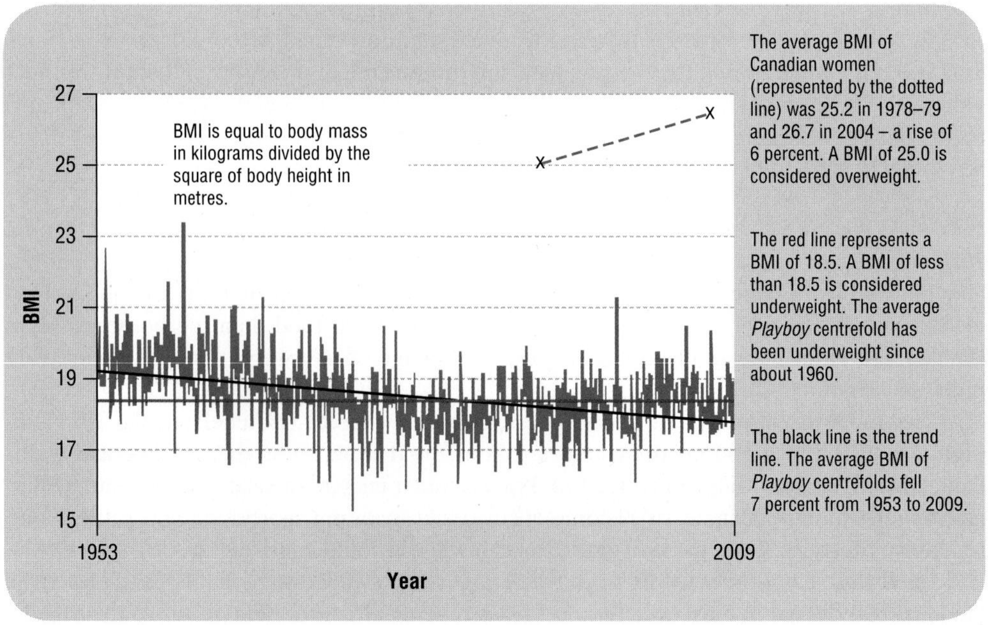

overweight people as less attractive, less industrious, and less disciplined than thin people (Puhl and Heuer, 2009). In our culture, fat has become repugnant.

Because of North America's cultural preference for thinness and its corresponding distaste for round bodies, body weight influences status. Women, however, pay a higher penalty than do men for being overweight. Thus, while both men and women who are overweight are less likely to be married than are men and women of average weight, marriage rates are lowest for overweight women (Kark and Karnehed, 2012; Sobal and Hanson, 2011). Similarly, overweight women earn less than women of average weight. The income of men is less influenced by weight (Bozoyan and Wolbring, 2011; Judge and Cable, 2011).

Allan Bregg/Shutterstock.com

Miley Cyrus was #1 on *Maxim* magazine's "Hot 100" list for 2013. What made her "hot"?

The thin body is not the ideal everywhere. In Mauritania and other countries in West Africa, plump women are highly prized. In these regions, food is in short supply, so having a fat wife signifies high social status. For this reason, thin girls are seen as unmarriageable and unwanted. To ensure that their daughters will one day attract prospective suitors, many parents encourage and sometimes force young girls to eat far more than they want, producing fat bodies (Ouldzeidoune et al., 2013). Whereas camel's milk, rich in fat, would have been the substance of choice in the past, today, appetite-inducing pills achieve the same result.

The cult of thinness was not cherished in the past either. In preindustrial societies, people generally favoured well-rounded physiques because they signified wealth and prestige. At a time when food was not readily available, those who were wealthy cultivated round bodies as a sign to others that they had more than enough to eat. Not surprisingly, beautiful women as depicted by the great artists of the past tend to be on the heavy side by today's standards.

Our discussion suggests that fat *is* a feminist issue (Fikkan and Rothblum, 2012). Women's bodies tend to be subject to greater scrutiny and social control than are the bodies of men (Smith, 2012). In particular, most women and girls are socialized to believe that their bodies are always subject to the judgment of the male gaze. Hence, they come to believe that their value derives from presenting themselves in ways that are pleasing to men (McKinley, 2011). Men tend to be criticized more on their performance rather than on their weight. This double standard may explain why women who violate weight expectations are more negatively sanctioned than men are.

We can extend this observation to consider other ways in which patriarchal ideas about the body have historically influenced how women have lacked control over their bodies. In Canada and other developed countries, people tend to think they have rights over their own bodies. For instance, the feminist movement asserts the right of every woman to control her own reproductive functions (Neyer and Bernardi, 2011). Yet people have not always endorsed this view, and some Canadians still contest it. Slaves' bodies are the property of their owners. (There are still about 30 million slaves in the world; Fisher, 2013.) Masters can generally use their slaves' bodies for anything they want, including hard labour and sex. Similarly, in deeply patriarchal societies, a husband effectively owns his wife's body. He can rape his wife with impunity (Brym, 2014a).

Bridgeman Art Library/SuperStock

Rubens's *The Toilette of Venus* (1613). Venus, the Roman goddess of beauty, as depicted by Peter Paul Rubens four centuries ago. Would Venus need a tummy tuck to be considered beautiful today?

Body Projects

Despite the widespread view that people have rights over their own bodies, most people do not treat their bodies in wildly idiosyncratic ways. Instead, we tend to be influenced by norms of body practice. In part, these norms are determined by the social groups to which we belong. For example, Catholic priests are defined partly by sexual abstinence. Male Jews and Muslims are defined partly by circumcision. Many of the most important social distinctions—gender, race, age, tribe, and so on—are "written" on the body by different styles of dress, jewellery, tattoos, cosmetics, and so forth. People have always attempted to affect their body shape and appearance, but they do so according to principles laid out by society.

Not only do people alter their bodily appearance to conform to social norms and expectations, but subjectivity also comes into play. How individuals experience their self is based on whether and how they are able to produce a body that meets cultural ideals (Dworkin and Wachs, 2009). That is, the body becomes personally meaningful through attempts to modify its shape and appearance.

When individuals take on the responsibility of designing their own bodies, they do so because of a transformative shift in how society views the body. While we once might have thought of the body as a fixed biological entity, individuals today are increasingly compelled to see the body as an unfinished object that needs to be shaped and stylized. As noted by Cher, whose relatively youthful appearance is the culmination of countless cosmetic surgeries: "Nature isn't always the best. I have the money to improve on nature and I don't see why I shouldn't" (Hancock et al., 2000: 3). Thus, our bodies have become projects. A **body project** is an enterprise that involves shaping one's body to express one's identity and meet cultural expectations of beauty and health (Rose, 2007; Shilling, 2013).

A **body project** is an enterprise that involves shaping one's body to express one's identity and meet cultural expectations of beauty and health.

Perhaps you think that body projects are just for celebrities. Not at all. Body projects are for everyone, as we can see once we understand that they involve four different types of activities: camouflaging, extending, adapting, and redesigning (Atkinson, 2003). *Camouflaging* involves temporary and non-invasive attempts to hide or mask aspects of the body that are seen as undesirable. It includes putting on makeup and applying deodorant and perfume. *Extending* involves overcoming a natural limitation of the body through a technological device. It includes wearing glasses and prosthetic limbs. *Adapting* is the effort to maintain the physical appearance of the body by reducing or eliminating parts of the body that elicit unfavourable responses from others. Examples include mole removal, using dye to hide greying hair, and losing weight. Finally, *redesigning* involves permanently reconstructing the body, usually for purposes of self-expression and aesthetics. It includes breast augmentation surgery, hair implants, and tattooing and piercing.

A brief review of the social history of the tattoo illustrates how body projects produce identities that vary from one social setting to the next (Atkinson, 2003). Europeans first encountered tattoos during their conquest of other civilizations, where tattoos were used for tribal rituals, to convey status, or to ward off evil spirits. Europeans viewed tattoos as exotic and primitive. They sometimes brought North American Aboriginal people to Europe to display them as curious exhibits of the New World and to highlight the contrast between the painted savage and the civilized European body as a means of justifying colonization.

Over time, sailors began to use tattoos as souvenirs of their travel to far-flung places. Still seen as curiosities, tattooed bodies were also displayed in carnival freak shows. Carnival workers eventually turned to tattooing their own bodies. By the 1900s, tattooing was less likely to be seen as exotic and more likely to be associated with disrepute. This association developed because tattooed women gained notoriety for their risqué carnival performances in which clothing was removed one piece at a time to reveal their tattoos.

During World Wars I and II, men tattooed military insignia, national flags, and the names of loved ones on their bodies. In this context, tattoos signified masculinity, national pride, and citizenship. When World War II ended, tattooing once again became unsavoury, as criminal elements took up tattooing to display gang affiliation and convey antisocial sentiment, as illustrated by the initials "FTW," short for "fuck the world." Rebelliousness also appealed to the dissident youth cultures that emerged in the 1960s, which used tattoos to express empowerment and freedom from cultural constraints. Increasingly, women had themselves tattooed. For instance, a woman who had a small, delicate tattoo on her breast could be seen as expressing sexual independence and control of her body.

As tattooing diffused throughout the population, it shed its marginal status and became a widely accepted practice, particularly when the tattoo was in a discrete location. During the late 1990s, tattooing went mainstream, with studios vigorously competing with each other to create personalized works of art on the bodies of their clients. Television shows such as *Miami Ink* and *Inked* soared in popularity.

Today, tattoos adorn the bodies of many celebrities such as Vin Diesel, Dennis Rodman, Johnny Depp, Rhianna, Pink, Tommy Lee, and Adam Levine, to name a few. Angelina

Jolie's highly personalized tattoos produce a media frenzy every time she acquires another (she has 18 as of this writing). Deciphering the meaning of each of her tattoos has become a pastime of the tabloid press. Contrast this eager social response with the frosty reception that Angelina's tattoos would have garnered a century ago. Think, too, about the ways in which her tattoos are embodied: her body is being used to make an intentional statement about the type of person she is and how she wants others to see her.

Do you have a tattoo? If so, for what reason did you decide to get one? What do you think your tattoo says about you? Is your tattoo visible so that everyone can see it? Why or why not? When, or if, others have seen your tattoo, how did they respond? Given that social meanings of tattoos are continually changing, what do you think tattoos represent in today's culture? How do you think the meaning of your tattoo might change in, say, 20 years?

Francois Durand/Getty Images

Angelina Jolie displays two of her tattoos, Buddhist sayings.

TIME FOR REVIEW

- What are the social causes and consequences of height and weight?
- What is a feminist interpretation of the social pressures that are exerted to achieve the ideal body type?
- Which of the four types of body projects are most intrusive and permanent?
- How does the social history of the tattoo help us to understand that body projects are expressions of self that conform to cultural norms?

DISABILITY

For those who think that the body can be endlessly shaped to express one's identity, disability and disease are stark reminders that the body has biological limits. Bodies that do not look or perform in the same way that other bodies do are commonly interpreted as different and sometimes as disabled. But what is disability? By one definition, a disability is a physical or mental characteristic that keeps some people from performing within the range of normal human activity. In this view, disability is a characteristic of *individuals*. Proponents of this definition are likely to believe that people with disabilities need to be cured or rehabilitated before they can participate in the broader society. They may also see people with disabilities as objects of charity, medical treatment, and social protection.

A second definition regards disability as a *social relationship*. From this point of view, a physical or social barrier may restrict the opportunity of some people to participate in the normal life of a community on a level equal with others. Parents, teachers, religious leaders, athletic coaches, and doctors, among others, act to enforce the norms that guide their respective institutions. Consequently, those in authority have the power to define what is normal and to decide what disabled people can do and what they can become. For example, Helen, a schoolteacher who is partially sighted, described her own childhood experiences in elementary school this way:

> One insecure young [teacher] made life rather difficult for me. When he took over my group, he told everyone where to sit, sending tall people to the back. I tried to explain that I needed to sit at the front, but he just would not listen. He told me to keep quiet. He then put some work on the board and told us to get on with it. I put up my hand to tell him that I couldn't read what was on the board, but he told me to put my hand down and get on with my work. When I started to say that I couldn't read what was on the board, he sent me out of the room and afterwards gave me detention for arguing. [The teacher] said that I was a lazy, idle good-for-nothing who had never done a stroke of work ... (Thomas, 1999: 21)

As this example suggests, the teacher's attempts to impose order in the classroom by seating children according to their height is what produced Helen's disability (Thomas, 1999). Her disability became more apparent when the rules of the institution were prioritized over her own needs.

Defining disability as a social relationship makes it easier to recognize that the distinction between an able body and a disabled body is socially constructed and that it varies over time and place, as do strategies for dealing with disabilities. We will illustrate such variation shortly, but before doing so we briefly discuss disability in the Canadian context.

Disability in Canada

In Canada, approximately 3.8 million adults (nearly 13 percent of the adult population) identify themselves as having a disability (Statistics Canada, 2013b). Disability, for Statistic Canada's purposes, is assessed by asking respondents whether they are limited in their daily activities because of a long-term problem or health condition. Measured in this way, disability tends to be more common among older people than among younger people and among women than among men (see Figure 12.4).

The Canadian constitution prohibits discrimination against people with disabilities. However, it protects people who have disabilities only from the actions of the federal government, not from private organizations and individuals (Barnett, Nicol, and Walker, 2012). Unlike the United States, Canada lacks national legislation to mandate accommodation in the workplace for people with disabilities. Consequently, Canada has a patchwork of different provincial and territorial laws that vary in their ability to assure equal treatment for Canadians with disabilities in the workplace.

Evidence suggests that Canadians with disabilities do encounter barriers in their places of employment. Compared with the average Canadian, Canadians with disabilities are less likely to be employed when they are of working age. When they are employed, they are less likely to advance to a position of authority (Battams, 2013; Jones, 2008; Williams, 2006). They are more likely to experience involuntary retirement (Denton, Plenderleith, and Chowhan, 2013). In addition, people with disabilities are more likely to be poor than are other Canadians (Galarneau and Radalescu, 2009). While some scholars debate whether the employment experiences of people with disabilities reflect discrimination or other factors, many researchers believe that as much as half of the wage gap can be attributed to discrimination against people with disabilities (Jones, 2008).

FIGURE 12.4
Age and Gender Differences in the Prevalence of Disability in Canada, 2012

Source: Statistics Canada. 2013b. Disability in Canada: Initial findings from the Canadian Survey on Disability. Catalogue No. 89-654-X — No. 002. Ottawa, ON: Author. Page 4.

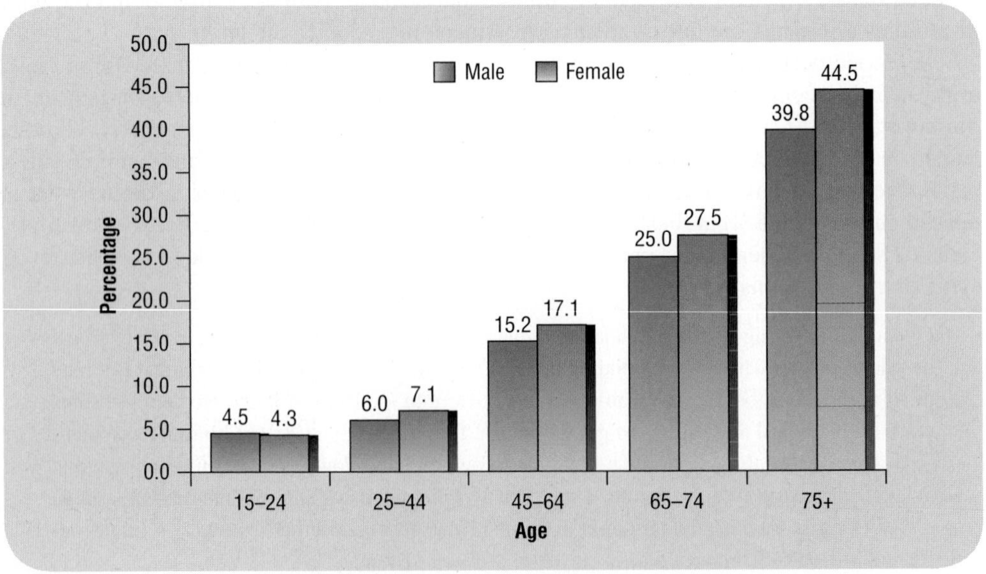

Some types of disability are associated with more disadvantages than other types of disability are. For instance, people who are blind are often quickly identified as unemployable. Consequently, they are more than twice as likely as are other Canadians with disabilities to be unemployed (Benoit et al., 2013). People with disabilities other than blindness often find it easier to pass as being able-bodied, thereby enduring less discrimination than those with such an obvious impairment.

The incidence of disability has declined because of improvements in prenatal care and nutrition and widespread inoculation against infectious diseases. At the same time, by making it possible to save the lives of those who are horrifically injured or dangerously ill, medical advances swell the ranks of the population with disabilities. Some scholars suggest that our rapid pace of life also increases the risk of disability because (1) moving fast can be dangerous and (2) those who cannot keep up with the fast pace become conspicuous and are thus marked as abnormal (Wendell, 1996). In sum, social conditions influence the incidence of disability in society and, as we will now see, the very definition of what constitutes a disability.

The Social Construction of Disability

Pity the poor lefty, for centuries considered inferior. About 400 years ago, the Catholic Church declared left-handed people servants of the Devil and burned some of them at the stake. Then it forced lefties to become right-handed in school. In Japan, as recently as the early twentieth century, left-handedness in a wife was grounds for divorce. Maori women in New Zealand weave ceremonial cloth with the right hand because they believe that using the left desecrates the cloth. Some African tribes along the Niger River do not allow women to prepare food with the left hand for fear of being poisoned. Almost universally, people have considered left-handedness to be a disability, so much so that the sentiment has been embedded in many languages. In Russian, to do something *na levo* means to do it under the table or illegally, but literally it means "on the left." In English, the word *left* derives from an Old English word that means "weak" or "worthless." Also in English, *gauche* means "ill-mannered"—but the French from which it is derived means "left." (In contrast, *adroit* means "proper" in English—but the French from which it is derived means "to the right.") In Latin, "right" is *dexter* (as in the English *dextrous*, a desirable attribute) while "left" is *sinister*, which of course means "evil" in English. *Linkisch* is German for "leftish"—and "awkward."

Today, negative attitudes toward left-handedness seem nonsensical. We don't think of left-handed people—roughly 10 percent of the population—as being disabled or deficient in physical or mental capacity. The fact that so many people once thought otherwise suggests that definitions of disability are not based on self-evident biological realities. Instead, they vary socially and historically. Note also that some people, but not others, consider a 1.5-metre-tall (4-foot-tall) person to have a disability, and that most people must be convinced by advertising that erectile dysfunction in a 75-year-old man is a disability. These examples suggest that definitions of disability differ across societies and historical periods, and that in any one time and place, people may disagree over these definitions.

Rehabilitation and Elimination

Modern western approaches to disability emerged in the nineteenth century. All scientists and reformers of the time viewed disability as a self-evident biological reality. Some scientists and reformers sought the **rehabilitation** of people with disabilities. Rehabilitation involves curing disabilities to the extent possible through medical and technological intervention. It also entails trying to improve the lives of people with disabilities by means of care, training, and education. Finally, it seeks to integrate people with disabilities into society (Longmore, 2003).

Rehabilitation involves curing disabilities to the extent possible through medical and technological intervention; trying to improve the lives of people with disabilities by means of care, training, and education; and integrating people with disabilities into society.

The desire for rehabilitation motivated the establishment of schools for children who are blind, the widespread use of prosthetics, the construction of wheelchair-accessible buildings, and so forth. It also prompted the passage of laws that benefit those with disabilities by mandating accessibility to buildings, public transportation, and jobs. These laws have done much to help integrate people with disabilities into society.

At the same time, rehabilitation has had its problems. Many rehabilitation strategies were implemented without consulting people with disabilities. Instead, medical doctors and social service agencies were presumed to be experts and imposed their preconceptions about disability on their clients. People with disabilities have often been critical of the paternalistic attitudes inherent in rehabilitation, insisting that their own experience and their knowledge of their own bodies make them authorities on how people with disabilities should be accommodated.

Other scientists and reformers took a more sinister tack. They sought to eliminate disability altogether by killing people who had a disability or by sterilizing them and preventing them from having children. The Nazis adopted this approach in Germany beginning in 1933. They engineered the sterilization and killing of the mentally "deficient" and the physically "deviant," including people who were blind and those who were deaf (Proctor, 1988).

One of the ugliest chapters in Canadian history involves the government-funded, forced sterilization of those deemed to be mentally defective. The practice was systematically carried out by medical authorities. In Alberta, for example, sexual sterilization was performed on nearly 3000 people between 1928 and 1972 (Grekul, Krahn, and Odynak, 2004). As with the Nazis, those who were advocates of sexual sterilization in Canada were swayed by their faith in eugenics. **Eugenics** is the belief that the human race can be improved by controlling which people can become parents. Science has provided compelling evidence that disability is rarely a heritable characteristic but some people nonetheless continue to endorse eugenics.

Eugenics is the belief that the human race can be improved by controlling which people can become parents.

Ableism

Because the human environment is structured largely around the norms of those without disabilities, people with disabilities suffer many disadvantages. Specifically, people routinely stigmatize people with disabilities, negatively evaluating them because of a characteristic that supposedly sets them apart from others. People also employ stereotypes when dealing with people with disabilities, expecting them to behave according to a rigid and often inaccurate view of how everyone with that disability acts. The resulting prejudice and discrimination against people with disabilities is called **ableism**. A historical example of ableism is the widespread belief among nineteenth-century Western educators that people who are blind are incapable of high-level or abstract thought. Because of this prejudice, people who were blind were systematically discouraged from pursuing intellectually challenging tasks and occupations. Similarly, an 1858 article in the *American Annals of the Deaf and Dumb* held that "the deaf and dumb are guided almost wholly by instinct and their animal passions. They have no more opportunity of cultivating the intellect and reasoning facilities than the savages of Patagonia or the North American Indians" (quoted in Groce, 1985: 102). Racists think of members of racial minorities as naturally and incurably inferior. Ableists think of people with disabilities in the same way. As the preceding quotation suggests, racists and ableists were often the same people.

Ableism is prejudice and discrimination against people who have disabilities.

Ableism involves more than active prejudice and discrimination. It also involves the largely unintended *neglect* of the conditions of people with disabilities. This point should be clear to anyone who needs a wheelchair to get around. Many buildings were constructed without the intention of discriminating against people in wheelchairs, yet they are extremely inhospitable to them. Thus, physical impairments become disabilities when the human environment is constructed largely on the basis of ableism. Ableism exists through both intention and neglect.

Challenging Ableism: The Normality of Disability

© Lightscapes Photography, Inc./CORBIS

Architecture and urban planning that neglect some modes of mobility make life difficult for people who depend on wheelchairs.

In 1927, science fiction writer H. G. Wells published a short story called "The Country of the Blind" (Wells, 1927). It provocatively reversed the old saying that "in the country of the blind, the one-eyed man is king." In the story, the protagonist, Nuñez, survives an avalanche high in the Andes. When he revives in a mountain valley, he discovers he is on the outskirts of an isolated village whose members are all blind because of a disease that struck 14 generations earlier. For them, words like *see*, *look*, and *blind* have no meaning.

Because he can see, Nuñez feels vastly superior to the villagers; he thinks he is their "Heaven-sent King and master." Over time, however, he realizes that his sight places him at a disadvantage vis-à-vis the villagers. Their senses of hearing and touch are more highly developed than his are, and they have designed their entire community for the benefit of people who cannot see. Nuñez stumbles where his hosts move gracefully and he constantly rants about seeing—which only proves to his hosts that he is out of touch with reality. The head of the village concludes that Nuñez is "an idiot. He has delusions; he can't do anything right." In this way, Nuñez's vision becomes a disability. He visits a doctor who concludes there is only one thing to do. Nuñez must be cured of his ailment, namely, he must be blinded. Thus, Wells suggests that in the land of the blind, the man who sees must lose his vision or be regarded as a raving idiot.

Wells's tale is noteworthy because it makes blindness seem normal. Its depiction of the normality of blindness comes close to the way many people with disabilities today think of their disabilities—not as a form of deviance but as a different form of normality. As one blind woman wrote, "If I were to list adjectives to describe myself, blind would be only one of many, and not necessarily the first in significance. My blindness is as intrinsically a part of me as the shape of my hands or my predilection for salty snacks.... The most valuable insight I can offer is this: blindness is normal to me" (Kleege, 1999: 4).

The idea of the normality of disability has partly supplanted the rehabilitation ideal. Although reformers without disabilities originally led the rehabilitation movement, the situation began to change in the 1960s. Inspired by other social movements of the era, people with disabilities began to organize themselves (Campbell and Oliver, 1996). The founding of the Disabled Peoples International in 1981 and inclusion of the rights of those with disabilities in the United Nations Universal Declaration of Human Rights in 1985 signified the growth—and growing legitimacy—of the new movement globally. Since the 1980s, people with disabilities have begun to assert their autonomy and the "dignity of difference" (Barnes and Mercer, 2003). Rather than requesting help from others, they insist on self-help. Rather than seeing disability as a personal tragedy, they see it as a social problem. Rather than regarding themselves as deviant, they think of themselves as inhabiting a different but quite normal world.

The deaf community typifies the new challenge to ableism. Increasingly, people who are deaf share a collective identity with others who are deaf (Dolnick, 1993). Rather than feeling humiliated by the seeming disadvantage of deafness, they take pride in their condition. Indeed, many people in the deaf community see themselves as members of a minority cultural group, defined by their use of sign language, not as people defined by their disability. For this reason, many people who are deaf are eager to remain deaf even though cochlear implants now make it possible for them to hear (Sparrow, 2010). As one deaf activist put it, "I'm happy with who I am... I don't want to be 'fixed.'... In our society everyone agrees that whites have an easier time than blacks. But do you think a black person would undergo operations to become white?" (quoted in Dolnick, 1993: 38).

Although ableism is deeply entrenched in our society, attempts to overcome stereotypes and misperceptions are gaining momentum. One example is Michael J. Fox's attempt to subvert ableism on his television show (see Box 12.2).

BOX 12.2

SOCIOLOGY ON THE TUBE

THE MICHAEL J. FOX SHOW

Michael J. Fox is a famous Canadian who, since the mid-1980s, has starred in numerous blockbuster movies (*Back to the Future*, *Teen Wolf*, *Doc Hollywood*) and award-winning television shows (*Family Ties* and *Spin City*). But just when he seemed to have it all, his life fell apart. Diagnosed at the age of 30 with Parkinson's disease, Fox knew that hard decisions were ahead. He continued in his role on *Spin City*, developing numerous tricks to help him appear healthy in front of the camera. As the disease progressed, however, his tremors and rocking made it impossible for him to disguise his illness. At the peak of *Spin City*'s popularity, Fox resigned from the show and then withdrew from show business altogether. It appeared that the public had seen the last of Michael J. Fox.

But he didn't stay out of the limelight for long. Within months, Fox became an advocate for research on Parkinson's disease, establishing a fundraising charity in his name and becoming the public face of the disease. More than a decade later, he returned to acting. It started with bit parts on several shows, but in 2013, Fox landed his own show.

Debby Wong/Shutterstock.com

Michael J. Fox

The Michael J. Fox Show focuses on the life of Mike Henry, a well-liked former news anchor in New York City who gave up his job four years ago because he was diagnosed with Parkinson's disease. In the series premiere, Henry is encouraged by his family to return to work—they say he is driving them all crazy. Henry agrees but emphasizes to his producer, "I don't want a pity job." Thrust back into the world of work, the show follows Henry's efforts to achieve work–life balance in the context of his disability.

Make no mistake. The show is not intended as a poignant drama that encourages the audience to feel sorry for Henry because he has a degenerative condition. Members of the audience are fully aware that they are watching a humorous yet frank depiction of what it is like to live with a disability. The show dispels some common stereotypes of disability. Henry is neither tragic and pitiable nor heroic and inspirational. Indeed, his family appears to love and be frustrated by Henry in equal measure. In short, *The Michael J. Fox Show* presents viewers with a typical family—with the sole difference that one of its members, who has the same needs, wants, and struggles as anyone else, happens to have a disability. In this way, it is a radical departure from the way disability was handled in many older TV shows and movies.

TIME FOR REVIEW

- What evidence suggests that disability is socially constructed?
- How did historical forms of treatment perpetuate disability stereotypes and harm disabled people?
- In what ways does ableism negatively affect the lives of Canadians?

AGING

The Sociology of Aging

Disability affects some people. Aging affects us all. Many people think of aging as a natural process that inevitably thwarts our best attempts to delay death. Sociologists, however, see aging in a more complex light. For them, the sociological nature of aging is also evident in the fact that its significance varies from one society to the next. That is, different societies attach different meanings to aging bodies.

Menopause, for example, occurs in all mature women. In Canada, we often see it as a major life event. Thus, the old euphemism for menopause was the rather dramatic expression "change of life." In contrast, menopause is a relatively minor matter in Japan. Moreover, while menopausal Canadian women may experience hot flashes, menopausal Japanese women tend to complain mainly about stiff shoulders (Melby, Lock, and Kaufert, 2005). As this example shows, aging is not just a biological process but is also deeply rooted in society and culture.

Age can also be a basis for social division. Some observers believe that in Canada and other aging societies, older people are gaining power at the expense of younger people. Others note that our cultural preoccupation with youthfulness continues to fuel distaste for aging bodies and to promote negative perceptions of older people (Calasanti, 2007). On the following pages, we describe the phenomenon of population aging, and then we assess whether demographic change is influencing the power and treatment of older people.

Population Aging in Canada and around the World

Canada's population is greying. In 1901, only 5 percent of Canadians were 65 or older but in 2011 the corresponding figure was nearly 15 percent (Statistics Canada, 2012d). One way to visualize population aging in Canada is by examining **population pyramids**, graphs that show the percentage of the population in various age/sex "cohorts," where the length of each coloured bar represents the number of men or women in each five-year age range (Figure 12.5 and Figure 12.6). In 1901, Canada's population pyramid looked like a true pyramid. The base was wide, indicating that most people were young, and the

Population pyramids are graphs that show the percentage of the population in various age and sex cohorts.

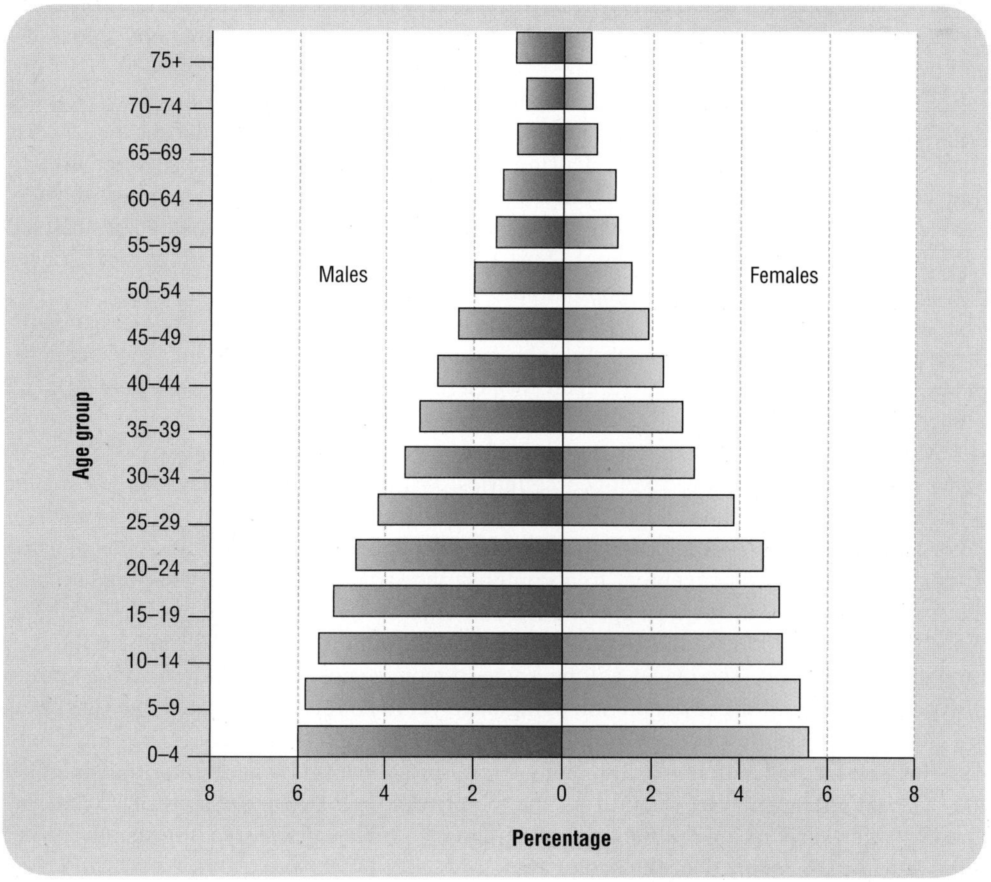

FIGURE 12.5
Population Pyramid, Canada, 1901

Source: McVey and Kalbach, 1995.

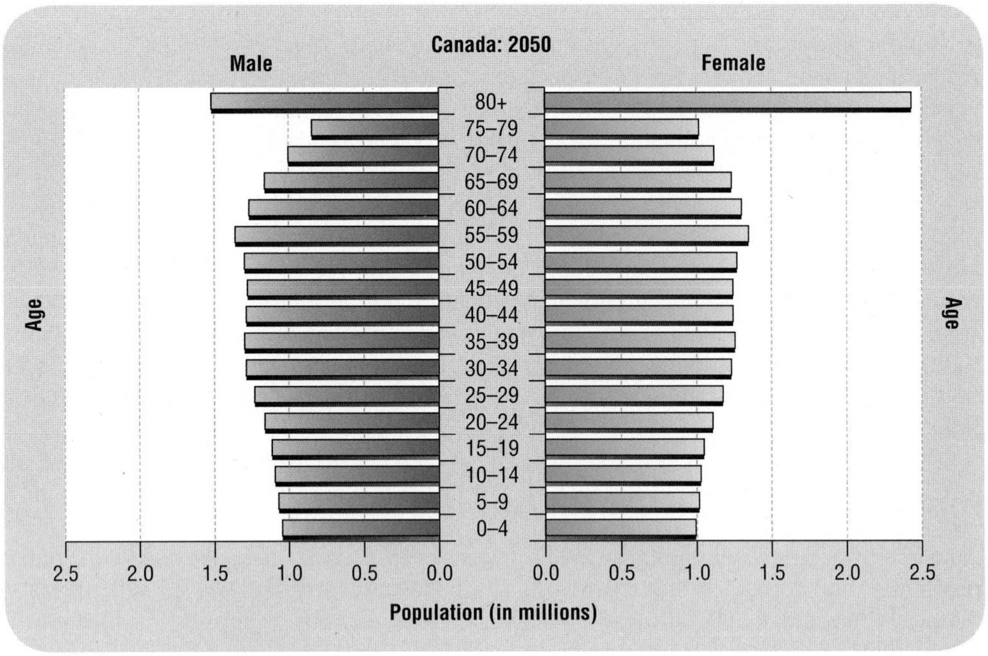

FIGURE 12.6
Population Pyramid, Canada, 2050 (projected)

Source: U.S. Census Bureau, International Database.

top was narrow, suggesting a small senior population. By 2050, however, Canada's population pyramid will look more like a T, indicating roughly the same percentage of people in all age cohorts except the oldest, which will be considerably more numerous. Because older and younger people have different needs, this change in population composition has wide-ranging implications for housing, education, employment, pensions, and health care.

The number of seniors in Canada has increased for three main reasons. First, nearly a third of Canada's citizens (approximately 10 million people) were born during the 20-year "baby boom" after World War II. During that period, Canadian women gave birth to four children on average (Wister, 2005). Second, **life expectancy** (the number of years people are expected to live on average) has increased because of improvements in medical care, sanitation, nutrition, and housing. Third, Canada's low birth rate contributes to a higher percentage of older people in the population.

Life expectancy is the number of years people are expected to live on average.

Canada is not the only country with an aging population. In many other middle- and high-income countries, population aging is also a pressing issue. Canada has a smaller percentage of seniors than are found in Japan (23 percent), Germany (21 percent), Italy (20 percent), and France (17 percent) (Statistics Canada, 2012d).

Moreover, population aging is a global phenomenon because developing countries are aging more rapidly than are developed countries. Within the next two decades, the senior population in Brazil, China, South Korea, and Thailand will double from 7 to 14 percent (World Health Organization, 2011). To put these increases into perspective, consider that it took France more than a century to accomplish the same feat! Overall, the population of the world's seniors will see a staggering rise, from just over half a billion in 2010 to more than 1.5 billion in 2050. Said differently, at some point in the next decade and for the first time in human history, the planet will be home to more seniors than children under the age of five. The implications of population aging have yet to be fully appreciated, but its effects will surely be felt almost everywhere.

Because the population is aging, many sociologists now find it necessary to distinguish the "old old" (people 85 or older) from the merely "old" (between the ages of 75 and 84) and the "young old" (between the ages of 65 and 74). Increasingly, sociologists are paying more attention to people over the age of 99.

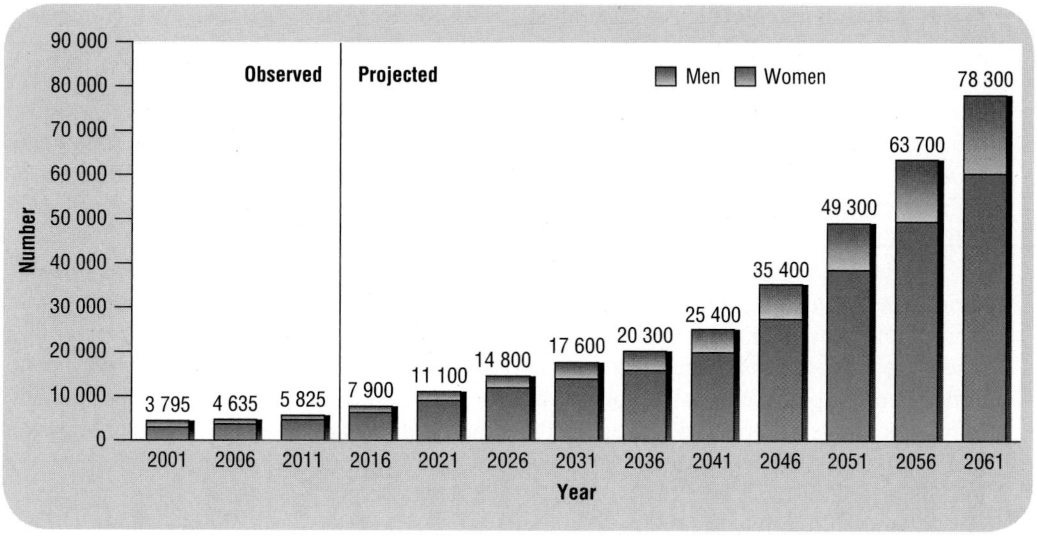

FIGURE 12.7
Number of Centenarians by Sex, Canada, 2001–2061

Source: Statistics Canada. 2012d. The Canadian Population in 2011: Age and Sex. Ottawa, ON: Minister of Industry. Page 2.

Centenarians

Centenarians are people who are 100 or more years old. The 2011 census counted 5825 centenarians in Canada. By 2061, they are projected to number 78,300 (see Figure 12.7). Centenarians are thus among the fastest growing segments of the population. Over the next 50 years, the number of centenarians worldwide will increase ten-fold, whereas the number of seniors aged 65 to 74 will merely double (World Health Organization, 2011).

Centenarians are people who have reached 100 years of age or more.

Researchers have much to learn about the lives of centenarians, which will be a growing area of research in the future. Here is some of what researchers now know about centenarians living in Canada today. Given that men live shorter lives on average than do women (Chapter 19), Canadian women are nearly five times more likely than men are to reach the age of 100 (Statistics Canada, 2012f). Although more than 90 per cent of seniors over the age of 65 live independently, among those who are 100 or older, only one in three maintains his or her own residence (Statistics Canada, 2012k). The most common health conditions for centenarians in the province of Ontario are dementia (58 percent) and arthritis (54 percent); and while 95 percent of centenarians visited a doctor in the past year, fewer than 20 percent are hospitalized (Rochon et al., 2014). Thus, while an overall pattern of poorer health has been observed after the age of 100, many centenarians continue to enjoy good health.

Intergenerational Tensions: A Conflict Interpretation

According to conflict theorists, the struggle for power may sometimes pit older people against younger people. For example, some people believe that ancient China and other preindustrial societies were **gerontocracies**, or societies in which the oldest citizens enjoyed the most prestige and power. Although some societies may approximate a gerontocracy, its extent has been exaggerated. Today's powerful, wealthy, and prestigious leaders are often mature, but rarely the oldest, people in a society.

A **gerontocracy** is a society ruled by older people.

In general, true gerontocracy is rare. Like King Lear, seniors often give up power and become marginalized. Even in traditional societies that held seniors in high esteem, aging was not usually seen as an unambiguous good. Ambivalence about aging—especially as people reach the oldest age cohorts—is a cultural universal. As one historian writes, "Youth has always and everywhere been preferred to old age. Since the dawn of history, old people have regretted [the loss of] their youth and young people have feared the onset of old age" (Minois, 1989 [1987]).

Just as true gerontocracy is uncommon, so is rule by youth. True, relatively young age cohorts sometimes supply most of a country's political leadership. This situation happened in revolutionary France in the late eighteenth century, revolutionary Russia in the early twentieth century, and revolutionary China in the mid-twentieth century. However, youthful ruling cadres may become gerontocracies in their own right, especially in non-democratic societies, as was the case with the Russian communist leadership in the 1980s and the Chinese communist leadership in the 1990s; the young generation that had grabbed power half a century earlier still clung on as old age approached.

While neither young nor old wield absolute control in Canada today, tensions can simmer between young and old. Young adults, who struggle to gain a foothold in the labour market and must make do with jobs that offer low wages and little security, sometimes resent the success of older generations who benefited from a period of steady employment, strong pension plans, and rising housing prices. In a similar way, members of older generations look with consternation on young adults' delayed transition to independence. They fail to recognize that the world that today's young adults are struggling to enter has fewer good job opportunities than does the world they inhabited only a generation or two ago. Such misperceptions can fuel intergenerational conflict, particularly during hard economic times (Furstenberg, 2010; Walker, 2012). However, no evidence suggests that intergenerational conflict is a serious political problem or that it is nudging Western societies toward gerontocracy (Krieger and Ruhose, 2013).

Ageism

Ageism is prejudice and discrimination against older people.

Especially in a society that puts a premium on vitality and youth, being older is a social stigma. **Ageism** is prejudice about, and discrimination against, older people. Ageism is evident, for example, when older men are stereotyped as "grumpy" or "feeble" and treated accordingly.

Stereotypes of aging convey the message that the lives of older people are filled with decline, loss, and dependency. Because disease and death are more likely to occur when one is old, some people assume that all aging bodies must be sickly and decrepit. Loss is also assumed to pervade all aspects of the lives of older people. Typically, the loss of one's role as a worker signals entry into old age. As one ages, the deaths of one's contemporaries thin out social relationships, leading to isolation. The death of a spouse is perceived as the most devastating loss, and it too occurs more frequently in later life. Finally, because seniors no longer engage in paid work and sometimes require assistance from others, particularly when they fall ill, seniors are often seen as dependent—as care recipients rather than those who give care.

In reality, although health certainly declines with age, seniors are in better health today than ever before. Their good health is due to their healthier lifestyles and the medical advances of recent decades. Similarly, although seniors do experience a thinning out of their social networks, they can and often do develop new roles that enrich their lives. Volunteering allows seniors to remain engaged in their communities and to forge new social ties. Grandparenthood is a deeply rewarding and highly anticipated role in later life (Clarke and Roberts, 2004). Few seniors miss full-time work, particularly when they are able to plan for and control the circumstances of their retirement, but many continue to work part-time. Finally, the overwhelming majority of seniors live independently. Fewer than 8 percent of seniors live in senior citizens' residences or health care facilities (Statistics Canada, 2012k). Thus, evidence shows that seniors are generally healthy, socially active, and contributing members of society.

The active life of many seniors today is a far cry from traditional stereotypes.

Some analysts suggest that precisely because our population includes more seniors than ever, the stereotypes of aging are slowly dissipating. Do we have a newfound appreciation for older people? A supporting example is Betty White, a beloved television actress whose career has spanned more than 60 years. Now in her 90s, she has recently starred in *Betty White's Off Their Rockers* and *Hot in Cleveland* and appeared as the host of *Saturday Night Live*—but her pedigree extends all the way back to *Golden Girls* in the 1980s and *The Mary Tyler Moore Show* in the 1960s. Does Betty White's case suggest that stereotypes of aging are receding? Or is she an exception?

Mary Clavering/Young Hollywood/Getty Images

Does the star power of Betty White suggest that ageism is declining?

The Wealth and Power of Seniors in Canada

Conflict theorists argue that age influences power insofar as, compared with younger people, older people may have more money and political authority and thus may be held in higher regard. From this point of view, one way of assessing the power of seniors is to examine their poverty rate. The lower their poverty rate, the greater their power.

Starting in the 1970s, poverty rates among Canadian seniors fell dramatically, from about 25 percent to approximately 7 per cent by the turn of the century (Milligan, 2008). Their improved economic status was the outcome of new income security programs, such as the Guaranteed Income Supplement (GIS) and the Old Age Security (OAS) pension (Schirle, 2013). These policies have been so successful that, among high-income countries, Canada boasts one of the lowest rates of poverty for seniors, behind only the Netherlands and France.

This success is tempered by recent changes. The poverty rate among seniors has started to creep up in Canada, even as poverty rates for seniors are declining in other countries (OECD, 2013c). Pension reform, enacted partly to offset the projected economic burden of aging populations, will reduce benefits for Canadian seniors in the future. For example, effective in 2023, the eligibility age for OAS will rise from 65 to 67. Smaller payouts in the future will force Canadians to save more during their working years so they will have enough to support themselves later in life. Growing economic disparity among seniors is likely to result; people with private pensions will be better able to meet their needs in retirement than will people who lack such pensions. Thus, while the current generation of seniors can use their economic resources to prolong their health and live independently, future generations of seniors may not have the resources they need to age in the same way.

TIME FOR REVIEW

- In what ways is population aging a global phenomenon?
- What makes centenarians distinct from other seniors?
- What evidence disproves the stereotypes of aging?
- Why might Canadian seniors be poorer in the future than they are today?

DEATH AND DYING

It may seem odd to say so, but the ultimate social problem everyone must face is his or her own demise. Why are death and dying *social* problems and not just religious, philosophical, and medical issues?

For one thing, attitudes toward death vary widely across time and place. So do the settings within which death typically takes place. Thus, although people have always dreaded death, most people accepted it (Ariès, 1982). Their acceptance came partly because most people believed in life after death, whether in the form of a continuation of life in Heaven or in cyclical rebirth. What also made death easier to accept is that the dying were not isolated from other people. They continued to interact with household members and neighbours, who offered them continuous emotional support. Finally, because those who were dying had previous experience giving emotional support to dying people, they had learned to accept death more easily as a part of everyday life.

In contrast, today in North America, we tend to separate dying and death from everyday life. Most terminally ill patients want to die peacefully and with dignity at home, surrounded by their loved ones. Yet most Canadians die in hospitals or long-term institutions. In such settings, they are likely to be surrounded by medical professionals and life-prolonging technologies. Moreover, death has been separated from everyday life; we are unlikely to encounter death outside of a funeral home or hospital. Dying used to be public. It is now hidden. Consequently, we are less prepared for death than our ancestors were.

Our reluctance to accept death is evident from the many euphemisms we use as a means of symbolically separating ourselves from the horror of death. We say that the dead have "passed away" or "gone to meet their maker" or are "in a better place." Sometimes we use humorous expressions as a distancing mechanism. We comment that people have "croaked" or "kicked the bucket" or "cashed in their chips" or that they are "pushing up daisies."

Psychiatrist Elisabeth Kübler-Ross's analysis of the stages of dying also suggests the extent to which we are reluctant to accept death (Kübler-Ross, 1969). She based her analysis on interviews with patients who were told they had an incurable disease. At first, the patients went into *denial*, refusing to believe their death was imminent. Then they expressed *anger*, seeing their demise as unjust. *Bargaining* followed; they pled with God or with fate to delay their death. Then came *depression*, when they resigned themselves to their fate but became deeply despondent. Only then did the patients reach the stage of *acceptance*, when they put their affairs in order, expressed regret over not having done certain things when they had the chance, and perhaps spoke about going to Heaven.

Subsequent research has not provided strong evidence that those five stages are experienced by all dying people or that they are experienced in the sequence Kübler-Ross originally described. However, Kübler-Ross herself cautioned against a formulaic approach to death, suggesting that attempts to categorize death could dehumanize the experience. Rather, she instructed others to "use the stages as an 'algorithm' to remind you to listen, and to respect the depths of the patient's experience" (Dugan, 2004: W26).

Biological Death and Social Death

Death is usually perceived as a binary category—one is either alive or one is dead. In reality, the boundary between life and death is fuzzy. It becomes even more clouded when we distinguish between biological death and social death. Biological death involves the end of the living body; social death is the termination of its social presence.

Social and biological deaths do not necessarily occur together (Seale, 1998). Social death may take place after biological death—sometimes long after. Dead people may retain a social presence when loved ones visit their gravesite and talk aloud to them. In China, a connection with the dead is institutionalized in the practice of ancestor worship. On the other hand, social death may precede biological death. For example, Alzheimer's disease can erase memories and one's identity to the point that loved ones feel that a person has already departed, despite the continuation of vital signs. As Box 12.3 illustrates, negotiating the ambiguity between social and biological death in these situations can pose wrenching ethical dilemmas.

Final Disposition of the Body

Once biological death has been certified, the formal process can begin to mark the transition of the deceased person from the land of the living. Funeral rites are a way to release the deceased person from their earthly obligations and to allow the living to repair the rift in the social fabric that is created when death occurs. As such, funerals are symbolic and full of meaning. Nonetheless, sociologists may interpret what happens at funerals in different ways. Whereas functionalists would suggest that the emotional outpouring that occurs bonds community members to one another, conflict theorists would point out that funerals are also

BOX 12.3

IT'S YOUR CHOICE

NEGOTIATING THE AMBIGUITY BETWEEN SOCIAL AND BIOLOGICAL DEATH

Today, physicians preside over death. They are considered experts in determining whether to engage in interventions that prolong or save life and in deciding when death occurs. Technological advances have complicated a doctor's decision, but the precise moment of death has always been elusive. In the past, the determination of death would have rested on simple indicators such as breath and heartbeat. On occasion, mistakes were made, with unwitting victims prematurely buried, only to gain consciousness in a coffin. Indeed, fear of being buried alive prompted numerous inventions and contraptions throughout history to avoid such a fate (King, 2008).

Once cardiopulmonary resuscitation (CPR) technologies made it possible to resuscitate people whose hearts had stopped, new criteria for death were needed. Attention switched from the heart and lungs to the brain. In 1968, the American Medical Association established lack of brain function as the new standard for death. Brain death entailed loss of awareness, lack of reflexes, and the absence of response to stimuli. However, even these criteria are not clear-cut, thrusting into the spotlight complex issues around decision making at the end of life. One of these debates centres on what to do when people are not brain dead but remain in an intermediate condition known as "persistent vegetative state" (PVS). In PVS, the body remains capable of growth and development, but is largely devoid of sensation and thought (Laureys, Owen, and Schiff, 2004).

Such complexities play out in disconcerting ways. In some situations, families that want everything done to save their loved one are pitted against doctors who are reluctant to perform interventions that, in their opinion, are futile. An example is Hassan Rasouli, who suffered brain damage in 2010 as a result of infection following surgery. Doctors at Toronto's Sunnybrook Health Sciences Centre informed the family that Hassan was in PVS and they planned to withdraw life support. The family contested the decision, believing that Hassan was recovering and would soon gain consciousness. This right-to-life case made it all the way to the Supreme Court of Canada, which ruled in 2013 that doctors do not have a unilateral right to overrule the wishes of the family. Unexpectedly, several months after his ordeal began, Hassan showed signs of responding inconsistently to stimuli, which led doctors to upgrade him to an even more nebulous condition known as a minimally conscious state. His long-term prognosis remains uncertain.

In other situations, families struggle to have their loved ones who are in PVS removed from life support. In 2014, national attention was drawn to an end-of-life care conflict between a nursing home and the family of Margot Bentley, age 82. Diagnosed more than a decade earlier with Alzheimer's disease, Margot had prepared for the inevitable by issuing an end-of-life directive that instructed health care providers to allow her to die when she had reached an advanced stage of the disease. Once Margot deteriorated to the level of PVS and could no longer communicate her own wishes, the family acted on her behalf to insist that Margot should no longer be fed. In response, the nursing home insisted that food is not treatment and that patients who accept food confirm by their actions that they want to eat. In the eyes of the family, Margot's response to being spoon-fed was merely a reflex, and they reiterated that her wish to die should be respected. For its part, the nursing home appeared to be motivated by concern that health care workers who fail to provide a patient with the necessities of life could be charged with criminal negligence. Regardless of what happens to Margot, her family has vowed to take their right-to-die battle to the Supreme Court of Canada.

Right-to-life and right-to-die struggles pivot around the same issue: when a person is neither fully alive nor fully dead, who decides what happens? What do you think? Are doctors always in the best position to decide? Should the wishes of the patient and the family always take precedence over the advice of doctors? Are individual cases so unique that general rules cannot be designed? Or can you suggest some rules that might be helpful in reaching painful decisions about when to prolong life or bring it to an end?

moments when family members may feud with one another, compete for the dead person's possessions, and let their emotions get the best of them. As a lawyer once said, "where there's a will, there's a relative."

Funerals were once steeped in tradition and therefore were pretty much standardized. For example, it was customary among Christians in North America to hold funerals with black hearses, wooden coffins, sombre garb for mourners, and the singing of hymns at a church service followed by a graveside ceremony (King, 2008). This unvarying routine has since given way to new and diverse practices. Increasingly, the focus is on the person rather than the body (McManus, 2013). Although this trend has many manifestations, we briefly discuss new trends in the disposition of the body to demonstrate the ways in death has become personalized.

In the not-so-distant past, decisions about the final resting place of the body were focused on finding a suitable plot in an appropriate cemetery. Today, most Canadians are cremated when they die. Moreover, an ever-expanding range of options are available for the final resting place of the dead. Ashes may be kept in an urn by family members, scattered on private property or in open public space such as the sea, buried in a cemetery, or placed in a memorial facility for the storage of the remains. In keeping with the desire to imbue the body with unique meaning, one may transform the remains into a diamond (by compressing the ashes—largely carbon—under extremely high pressure) or produce art objects out of them (by incorporating the ashes in paint or glass). Family members may then wear the diamonds or display the artwork at home as a reminder of their loved one. Even more exotic choices exist. Celestis Inc. places ashes in a capsule that is shot into Earth's orbit until it vaporizes when re-entering the atmosphere. As these examples illustrate, we no longer need to seclude the dead in cemeteries. We can allow the dead to participate in the activities of the living.

Some sociologists suggest that the modern preoccupation with finding unique ways to dispose of human bodies and an accompanying desire for individuals to design their own funerals signal a new openness to death and a corresponding shift away from the denial of death (Seale, 1998; McManus, 2013). Whether we have actually become more accepting of death will undoubtedly become a subject of continuing sociological research and debate.

TIME FOR REVIEW

- In what ways has death become less public and more hidden?
- What are the implications of distinguishing between biological and social death?

SUMMARY

1. **What are the social causes and consequences associated with bodily appearance and presentation?**
   The human body cannot be fully understood without appreciating its social dimension. Consider body weight. Economic development and agricultural advances have made it possible for more people to meet their nutritional requirements. Average body weight rose as societies became more affluent. Eventually, an abundant food supply and sedentary lifestyle enticed people to eat more than they needed, turning overweight into a social problem. These changes were matched by a shift in preference for the ideal body type. Once people had enough to eat, round bodies ceased to be symbolic of wealth and privilege. Particularly in Western society, fat bodies have become undesirable and stigmatized, so social sanctions are imposed on people who exceed what is deemed to be an acceptable body weight.

2. **In what sense are body projects both social and personal?**
   People have always adorned and modified their bodies. In the past, bodies were usually altered using traditional signs, and the practice of altering the body served purely social functions. Today, however, people are preoccupied with the appearance of the body as an expression of *individual* identity. Even so, these expressions generally conform to

existing norms about how bodies ought to look. Tattoos exemplify the dual nature of body projects. Over time, the meaning of the tattoo has changed, affecting the content of tattoos, their placement on the body, and the probability that certain categories of people will acquire one. In this sense, a tattoo reveals membership in a group and the group's relationship to the rest of society. Within these social parameters, people are free to shape, decorate, and train their bodies to express who they are.

3. How have definitions and responses to disability varied over time and place?
In the nineteenth century, disability was described as a physical or mental problem that kept a person from performing within the range of normal human activity. Defined in this way, disability became a problem in need of a cure. Moreover, this definition justified a rehabilitation approach that forced people with disabilities to depend on health care professionals to cure and reintegrate them into normal society. In response, sociologists and disability activists have defined disability as the loss of opportunity to take part in the normal life of a community on an equal level due to a physical or social barrier. This definition suggests that society needs to change more than does the individual who has the disability. It also conveys that disability is socially constructed, occurring when some people have the power to apply the label of disability to others. To the extent that this definition acknowledges the personhood of people with disabilities and accepts the normality of difference, it has the potential to alleviate the prejudice and discrimination that people with disabilities often encounter.

4. How might population aging reduce ageist attitudes and affect power imbalances between young and old?
Because of the global trend toward rising life expectancy and reduced fertility, the planet will soon be home to more seniors than children under the age of five. The implications of population aging are profound, affecting countries' policies around housing, employment, pensions, health care, and much more. It is unclear, however, whether, as a result of population aging, ageist attitudes will decline or whether the current balance of power between young and old will shift. Contemporary Western culture places high social value on youth, health, and independence. Ageist stereotypes continue to paint older people as sickly, in decline, and dependent on others, despite evidence to the contrary. While neither the young nor the old hold absolute power in any modern society, both young and old may perceive that their generation is being unfairly treated. These sentiments may fuel intergenerational conflict, particularly in difficult economic times, but, so far, do not appear to be appreciably altering the balance of power toward any age group.

5. What is sociological about death and dying?
Death is more than the end of one's material existence. It is a socially recognized and managed phenomenon. For example, funerals undertake the practical task of disposing of human remains but also symbolically represent the movement of the dead person out of the world of the living. The different ways in which societies negotiate the dying process and engage in death practices reveal fundamental features of social life in a given time and place. In short, our approach to death informs how we live.

PART 4
INSTITUTIONS

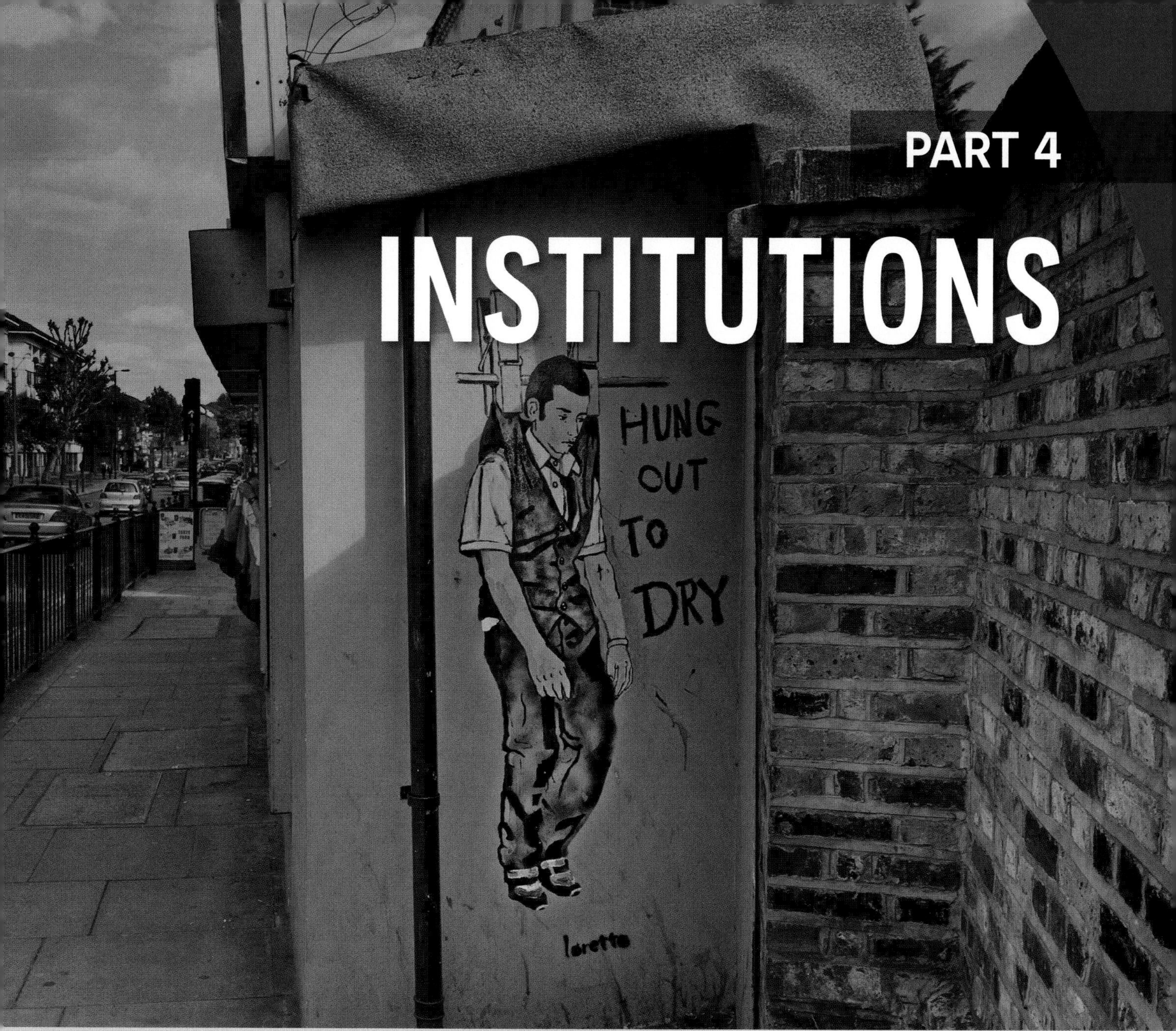

CHAPTER 13

WORK AND THE ECONOMY

IN THIS CHAPTER, YOU WILL LEARN TO

- Outline the characteristics of three work-related revolutions—in agriculture, in manufacturing, and in the provision of services—and understand how they have altered the way people earn a living and organize their social life.
- Identify the most important trends in the changing nature of work in the last century.
- Describe how people seek to control work through unions, professional organizations, corporations, and markets.
- Recognize how large corporations and global markets have transformed work and will increasingly influence your choices as a member of the labour force and a citizen.

THE PROMISE AND HISTORY OF WORK

Salvation or Curse?

The computerization of the office began in earnest in the early 1980s. Soon, the image of the new office emerged. It was a checkerboard of three-metre-by-three-metre cubicles. Three padded walls, two metres high, framed each cubicle. Inside, a computer terminal sat on a desk. A worker quietly tapped away at a keyboard, seemingly entranced by the glow of a video screen.

Sociologist Shoshana Zuboff visited many such offices soon after they were computerized. She sometimes asked the office workers to draw pictures capturing their job experience before and after computerization. The pictures were strikingly similar. Smiles changed to frowns, mobility became immobility, sociability was transformed into isolation, freedom turned to regimentation. Two of the workers' pictures are shown in Figure 13.1. In these drawings, work automation and standardization emerge as profoundly degrading and inhuman processes (Zuboff, 1988).

The image conveyed by these drawings is just one view of the transformation of work in the Information Age. But there is another view, and it is vastly different. Leading thinkers say we are entering a "second machine age" in which digital technology is radically transforming human possibilities (Brynjolfsson and McAfee, 2014). Google cars that drive themselves and computers that beat the best human Jeopardy competitors are early indicators of what the future holds for medicine, commerce, industry, entertainment, education, and so on. These revolutionary changes will certainly produce serious dislocations for some people. The hope, however, is that they will free many more from drudgery. This vision is well captured by an arresting cover of *Wired* magazine reprinted as Figure 13.2. According to *Wired*, digital technologies free us. They allow us to become more mobile and more creative. Computerized work allows our imaginations to leap and our spirits to soar.

These strikingly different images form the core questions of the sociology of work, our focus in this chapter. Is work a salvation or a curse? Or is it perhaps both at once? Is it more accurate to say that work has become more of a salvation or a curse over time? Or is work a salvation for some and a curse for others?

To answer these questions, we first sketch the three work-related revolutions of the past 10 000 years. Each revolution has profoundly altered the way we sustain ourselves and the way we live. Next, we examine how job skills have changed over the past century. We also trace changes in the number and distribution of "good" and "bad" jobs over time

FIGURE 13.1

One View of the Effects of Computers on Work

Shoshana Zuboff asked office workers to draw pictures representing how they felt about their jobs before and after a new computer system was introduced. Here are before and after pictures drawn by two office workers.

Source: Shosanna Zuboff. *In the Age of the Smart Machine: The Future of Work and Power* (Basic Books: New York), 1988. Pg. 146–7. © 1988 Basic Books, Inc. Reprinted by permission of Basic Books, a member of Perseus Books, L.L.C.

"Before I was able to get up and hand things to people without having someone say, what are you doing? Now, I feel like I am with my head down, doing my work."

"My supervisor is frowning because we shouldn't be talking. I have on the stripes of a convict. It's all true. It feels like a prison in here."

and project these changes into the near future. We then analyze how people have sought to control work through unions, professional organizations, corporations, and markets. Finally, we place our discussion in a broader context. The growth of large corporations and markets on a global scale has shaped the transformation of work over the past quarter century.

FIGURE 13.2

Another View of the Effect of Computers on Work

Wired magazine is always on high about the benefits of computer technology.

Porto/Wired/Condé Nast Archive. Copyright © Condé Nast

Analyzing these transformations will help you appreciate the work-related choices you face both as a member of the labour force and as a citizen.

Economic Sectors and Revolutions

The **economy** is the social institution that organizes the production, distribution, and exchange of goods and services. Conventionally, analysts divide the economy into three sectors. The *primary* sector includes farming, fishing, logging, and mining. In the *secondary* sector, raw materials are turned into finished goods through manufacturing. Finally, in the *tertiary* sector, services are bought and sold. These services include the work of nurses, teachers, lawyers, hairdressers, computer programmers, and so on. These three sectors of the economy are often called the agricultural, manufacturing, and service sectors.

The **economy** is the institution that organizes the production, distribution, and exchange of goods and services.

Each economic sector rose to dominance through a revolution in the way people work, and each revolution sharply restructured social inequality (Gellner, 1988; Nolan and Lenski, 2005):

- *The Agricultural Revolution.* Ten thousand years ago, nearly all humans lived in nomadic tribes. Then, people in the fertile valleys of the Middle East, Southeast Asia, and South America began to herd cattle and grow plants by using simple hand tools. Stable human settlements spread. About 5000 years ago, farmers invented the plow. By attaching plows to large animals, they substantially increased the land under cultivation. **Productivity**—the amount produced for every hour worked—soared.
- *The Industrial Revolution.* International exploration, trade, and commerce helped stimulate the growth of markets from the fifteenth century on. **Markets** are social relations that regulate the exchange of goods and services. In a market, prices are established by how plentiful goods and services are (supply) and how much they are wanted (demand). In the late 1700s, the steam engine, railroads, and other technological innovations greatly increased the ability of producers to supply markets. This was the era of the Industrial Revolution. Beginning in England, the Industrial Revolution spread to Western Europe, North America, Russia, and Japan within a century, making manufacturing the dominant economic sector.
- *The Postindustrial Revolution.* Service jobs were rare in pre-agricultural societies because nearly everyone needed to do physical work for the tribe to survive. As productivity increased, however, service-sector jobs became numerous. By automating much factory and office work, the computer accelerated this shift in the last third of the twentieth century. In Canada today, more than three-quarters of the labour force is employed in the service sector (see Figure 13.3).

Productivity refers to the amount of goods or services produced for every hour worked.

Markets are social relations that regulate the exchange of goods and services. In a market, the prices of goods and services are established by how plentiful they are (supply) and how much they are wanted (demand).

The Division and Hierarchy of Labour

Besides increasing productivity and causing shifts between employment sectors, the Agricultural Revolution, the Industrial Revolution, and the Postindustrial Revolution altered the way work was socially organized. For one thing, the **division of labour** increased. That is, work tasks became more specialized with each successive revolution. People living in pre-agrarian societies had four main jobs: hunting wild animals, gathering edible wild plants, raising children, and tending to the tribe's spiritual needs. In contrast, a postindustrial society, such as Canada's, boasts tens of thousands of different kinds of jobs.

The **division of labour** refers to the specialization of work tasks. The more specialized the work tasks in a society, the greater the division of labour.

In some cases, increasing the division of labour involves creating new skills, such as website design and laser eye surgery. Some new types of jobs require long periods of study that result in creative, well-paying work. Foremost among these are the professions, such as medicine, law, and engineering. In other cases, increasing the division of labour involves breaking a complex skill into a series of simple routines that involve little or no creativity and yield relatively low pay.

FIGURE 13.3
Estimated Distribution of Canadian Labour Force in Goods Production and Services, 1946–2013

Source: Adapted from Crompton and Vickers, 2000; Statistics Canada, 2005a; Statistics Canada 2014b.

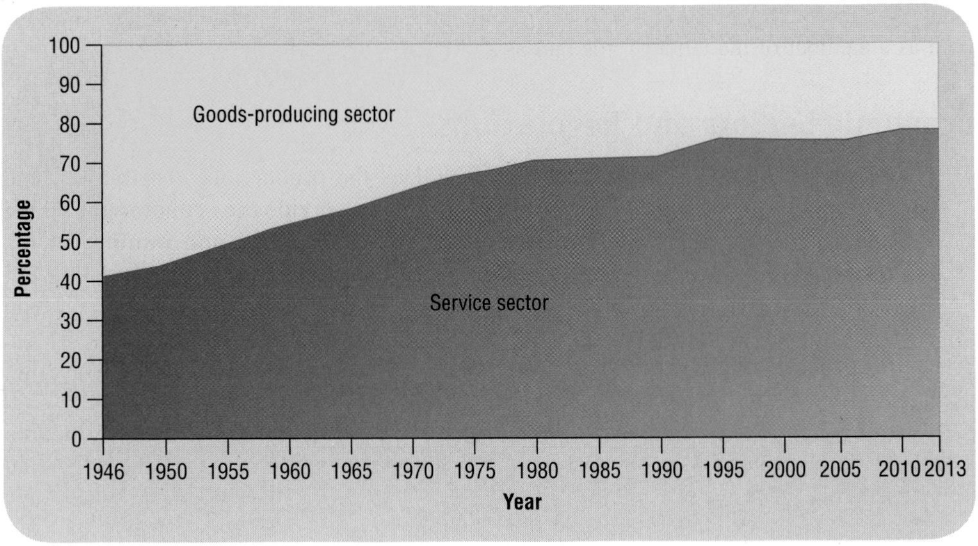

One way of summarizing these changes is to say that the division of labour has become increasingly complex. As social complexity grew, work relations became more hierarchical, with superordinates exercising authority and subordinates following commands. At the same time, the work of superordinates becomes more creative and lucrative, while the work of subordinates becomes less creative and comparatively unrewarding financially.

TIME FOR REVIEW

- What are the pessimistic and optimistic forecasts associated with the ongoing digital revolution?
- How do economic institutions change as societies move from agricultural, through industrial, to postindustrial revolutions?
- What is the division of labour? What is its historical trend?

"GOOD" VERSUS "BAD" JOBS

John Lie once landed a job as a factory worker in Honolulu, where he grew up. "The summer after my second year in high school," John recalls, "I decided it was time to earn some money. I had expenses, after all, but only an occasionally successful means of earning money: begging my parents. Scouring the help wanted ads in the local newspaper, I soon realized I wasn't really qualified to do anything in particular. Some friends at school suggested I apply for work at a pineapple-canning factory. So I did.

"At the factory, an elderly man asked me a few questions and hired me. I was elated—but only for a moment. A tour of the factory floor ruined my mood. Row upon row of conveyor belts carried pineapples in various states of disintegration. Supervisors urged the employees to work faster yet make fewer mistakes. The smell, the noise, and the heat were unbearable. After the tour, the interviewer announced I would get the graveyard shift (11 p.m. to 7 a.m.) at minimum wage.

"The tour and the prospect of working all night finished me off. Now dreading the idea of working in the factory, I wandered over to a mall. I bumped into a friend there. He told me a bookstore was looking for an employee (9 to 5, no pineapple smell, and air-conditioned, although still minimum wage). I jumped at the chance. Thus, my career as a factory worker ended before it began.

"A dozen years later, just after I got my Ph.D., I landed one of my best jobs ever. I taught for a year in South Korea. However, my salary hardly covered my rent. I needed more work desperately. Through a friend of a friend, I found a second job as a business consultant in a major corporation. I was given a big office with a panoramic view of Seoul and a personal secretary who was both charming and efficient. I wrote a handful of sociological reports that year on how bureaucracies work, how state policies affect workers, how the world economy had changed in the past two decades, and so on. I accompanied the president of the company on trips to the United States. I spent most of my days reading books. I also went for long lunches with colleagues and took off several afternoons a week to teach."

What is the difference between a "good" and a "bad" job, as these terms are usually understood? As John Lie's anecdote illustrates, bad jobs don't pay much and require the performance of routine tasks under close supervision. Working conditions are unpleasant, sometimes dangerous. Bad jobs require little formal education. In contrast, good jobs often require higher education. They pay well. They are not closely supervised and they encourage workers to be creative in pleasant surroundings. Other distinguishing features of good and bad jobs are not apparent from the anecdote. Good jobs offer secure employment, opportunities for promotion, and other significant benefits. In a bad job, you can easily be fired, you receive few if any fringe benefits, and the prospects for promotion are few (Adams, Betcherman, and Bilson, 1995; Lowe, 2000). Bad jobs are often called "dead-end" jobs and growth in the number of such jobs has alarmed many observers (Standing, 2011).

Most social scientists who discuss today's service revolution tend to have both good and bad jobs in mind. Yet most jobs fall between the two extremes sketched above. They have some mix of good and bad features. What can we say about the overall mix of jobs in Canada? Are there more good jobs than bad jobs? And what does the future hold? Are good jobs or bad jobs likely to become more plentiful? What are your job prospects? These are tough questions, not least because some conditions that influence the mix of good and bad jobs are unpredictable. Nonetheless, social research sheds some light on these issues (Krahn and Lowe, 1998; Kalleberg, 2013).

The Deskilling Thesis

Harry Braverman (1974) proposed one view of the future of work. He argued that owners (capitalists) organize work to maximize profits. One way to increase profits is to break complex tasks into simple routines. This increased division of labour in the workforce has three important consequences. First, employers can replace workers with machinery. Second, given the simplification of work, employers can replace skilled workers with less expensive, unskilled workers. Third, employers can control workers more directly since less worker discretion and skill is needed to complete each task. As a result, the future of work, as Braverman saw it, involves a **deskilling** trend.

We can best understand deskilling as the separation of conceptualization from execution in work. For example, in the 1910s, Henry Ford introduced the assembly line. It enabled him to produce affordable cars for a mass market. Workers executed highly specialized, repetitive tasks requiring little skill at a pace set by their supervisors. Automotive designers and managers conceived of the end product and the machinery necessary to build it. The workers merely executed the instructions of their superiors. The term **Fordism** is now often used to refer to mass-production, assembly-line work.

Around the same time, Frederick W. Taylor developed the principles of **scientific management**. After analyzing the movements of workers as they did their jobs, Taylor trained them to eliminate unnecessary actions and greatly improve their efficiency. Workers became cogs in a giant machine known as the modern factory.

Sociologists lodged several criticisms against Braverman's deskilling thesis, perhaps the most serious of which was that he was not so much wrong as irrelevant. That is, even if his characterization of factory work was accurate, factory workers represent only a small

Deskilling refers to the process by which work tasks are broken into simple routines requiring little training to perform. Deskilling is usually accompanied by the use of machinery to replace labour wherever possible and increased management control over workers.

Fordism is a method of industrial management based on assembly-line methods of producing inexpensive, uniform commodities in high volume.

Scientific management, developed in the 1910s by Frederick W. Taylor, is a system for improving productivity. After analyzing the movements of workers as they did their jobs, Taylor trained them to eliminate unnecessary actions. This technique is also known as Taylorism.

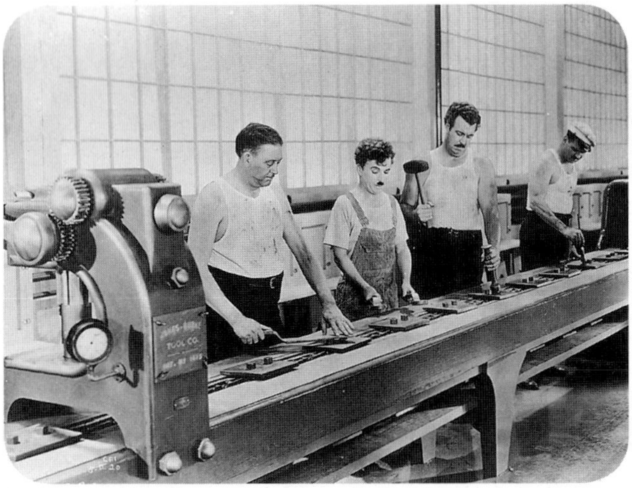

The Everett Collection/CP Picture Archive

Charlie Chaplin's 1929 movie *Modern Times* was a humorous critique of the factory of his day. In the movie, Chaplin gets a tic and moves like a machine on the assembly line. He then gets stuck on a conveyor belt and run through a machine. Finally, he is used as a test dummy for a feeding machine. The film thus suggests that workers were being used for the benefit of the machines rather than the machines being used for the benefit of the workers.

proportion of the labour force—and a smaller proportion every year, as the manufacturing sector shrinks and the service sector expands. According to some of Braverman's critics, the vital question is not whether jobs are becoming worse in manufacturing but whether good jobs or bad jobs are growing in services, the sector that accounts for about three-quarters of Canadian jobs today. Put another way, does the deskilling thesis apply to both industrial labour and service work?

Shoshana Zuboff's analysis of office workers, mentioned at the beginning of this chapter, suggested that Braverman's insights apply beyond the factory walls (Zuboff, 1988; Lowe, 1987). Zuboff argues that the computerization of the office in the 1980s involved increased supervision of deskilled work. And she is right, at least in part. The computer did eliminate many jobs and routinize others. It allowed supervisors to monitor every keystroke, thus intensifying worker control. Today, employees who consistently fall behind a prescribed work pace or use their computers for personal purposes can easily be identified and then retrained, disciplined, or fired.

Part-Time Work

The growth of part-time work in Canada has added to concern about the erosion of meaningful, dignified employment. The proportion of part-time workers in the Canadian labour force more than doubled between 1976 and 2013. In 2013, 18.9 percent of people in the Canadian labour force were part-timers, working fewer than 30 hours a week. Among men, the figure was 12.2 percent, among women, 26.5 percent (Statistics Canada, 2014b).

For two reasons, the expansion of part-time work is not a serious problem in itself. First, some part-time jobs are good jobs in the sense we defined above. Second, some people want to work part time and can afford to do so (Marshall, 2001). For example, some people who want a job also want to devote a large part of their time to family responsibilities. Part-time work affords them that flexibility. Similarly, many high-school and university students who work part-time are happy to do so.

Although the growth of part-time jobs is not problematic for voluntary part-time workers or people who have good part-time jobs, an increasingly large number of people depend on part-time work for the necessities of full-time living (Kalleberg, 2013; Standing 2011). And the plain fact is that most part-time jobs are bad jobs. Thus, part-time workers make up about two-thirds of the people working at or below minimum wage. Moreover, the fastest-growing category of part-time workers comprises *involuntary* part-timers. Involuntary part-time workers work part-time but would prefer full-time work. About 840 000 Canadians were in the involuntary category in 2010 (Gilmore and LaRochelle-Côté, 2011).

The downside of part-time work is not only economic, however. Nor is it just a matter of coping with dull routine. If you've ever had a bad part-time job, you know that one of its most difficult aspects involves maintaining your self-respect in the face of low pay, no benefits, lack of job security, low status, and no outlet for creativity. In the words of Dennis, a McDonald's employee interviewed by one sociologist, "This isn't really a job.... It's about as low as you can get. Everybody knows it" (quoted in Leidner, 1993: 182).

And, Dennis might have added, nearly everybody lets you know he or she knows it. Ester Reiter (1991) studied fast-food workers in Toronto, many of whom were teenagers working part-time. These workers are trained, Reiter noted, to keep smiling no matter how demanding or rude their customers may be. The trouble is you can only count backward from 100 so many times before feeling utterly humiliated. Anger often boils over.

The difficulty of maintaining your dignity as a fast-food worker is compounded by the high premium most young people place on independence, autonomy, and respect. The problem this creates for teenagers who take jobs in fast-food restaurants is that their constant deference to customers violates the norms of youth culture. Therefore, fast-food workers are typically stigmatized by their peers and are frequently the brunt of insults and ridicule (Newman, 1999: 97).

Fast-food workers undoubtedly represent an extreme case of the indignity endured by part-timers. However, the problem exists in various guises in many part-time jobs. For instance, if you work as a "temp" in an office, you are more likely than are other office workers to be the victim of sexual harassment (Welsh, 1999). You are especially vulnerable to unwanted advances because you lack power in the office and are considered "fair game." Similar challenges to status legitimacy and personal integrity are found among "substitute teachers" (Clifton and Roberts, 1993). Thus, the form and depth of degradation may vary from one part-time job to another but, as your own work experience may show, degradation seems to be a universal feature of this type of deskilled work.

A Critique of the Deskilling Thesis

The deskilling thesis captures the trend toward the simplification of previously complex jobs, but it paints an incomplete picture insofar as it focuses on the bottom of the occupational hierarchy. Taking a broader perspective and examining the entire occupational structure, we find that not all jobs are being deskilled. Deskilling seems to be occurring mainly in jobs that are characteristic of the "old" economy, such as assembly-line manufacturing, rather than the "new" economy, such as biotechnology and informatics. In fact, even on Ford's assembly line, not all jobs were deskilled. A new group of workers was required to design the assembly line and the new production machinery. New jobs higher up the skill hierarchy were therefore necessary.

In general, if deskilling has occurred for some jobs, has this trend been offset by the "reskilling" or "upskilling" of other jobs? Evidence suggests that although much of the growing service sector is associated with the growth of "dead-end" jobs, more of it is associated with an enlargement of skilled employment. Table 13.1 uses national survey evidence from five countries to examine the skill levels of workers in the goods-producing and the service sectors. Skilled jobs were identified as those requiring high levels of conceptual autonomy and complexity. The results show that, in all countries, jobs in the service sector require higher levels of skill than do jobs in the goods-producing sector. They undermine the notion that the overall workforce is becoming deskilled because higher skill requirements are reported in the service economy, which is the fastest-growing sector.

Braverman and Zuboff underestimated the continuing importance of skilled labour in the economy. Assembly lines and computers may deskill many factory and office jobs, but if deskilling is to take place, then some members of the labour force must invent, design, advertise, market, install, repair, and maintain complex machines, including computerized and robotic systems. Most of these people have better jobs than the factory and office workers analyzed by Braverman and Zuboff. Moreover, although technological innovations kill off entire job categories, they also create entire new industries with many good jobs. This trend is illustrated by the rapid growth of digital research and development communities in Silicon Valley, Waterloo, and Kanata (outside Ottawa).

Our analysis of good and bad jobs raises another question: How has the introduction of information technology affected workers' skills and income? Research suggests that computers magnify pay differences among skill levels. They augment high-skill levels but replace low-skill levels. People in high-skill occupations, like architecture or machine design, earn higher wages when they use computers to do their work. In contrast, people

	Country				
Economic Sector	**Canada**	**United States**	**Norway**	**Sweden**	**Finland**
Goods-producing sector	26	25	31	23	25
Service sector	42	38	47	43	46
Difference between sectors	16	13	16	20	21

TABLE 13.1
Percentage of Employees in Skilled Jobs by Sector and Country

Source: Clement and Myles, 1994: 7.

Lanny Ziering/Jupiter Images

LWA-JDC/CORBIS

The growing service sector includes routine jobs requiring little training and creative jobs requiring a higher education.

who use, say, a computerized cash register require little new training. Their hourly wage is unaffected by the introduction of the new technology—but their work hours are often reduced. These findings suggest that the introduction of computers tends to enlarge the number and quality of good jobs and reduce the number of bad jobs. However, it does not improve the quality of bad jobs (Pabilonia and Zoghi, 2005a, 2005b; Kalleberg, 2013).

In sum, the information technology revolution has transformed work, but little evidence suggests that it has degraded work overall. On the other hand, it is causing the income gap to grow, both between skilled workers who use information technology and those who do not, and between skilled and less skilled workers.

The Social Relations of Work

The rise of a more knowledge-intensive economy has had a big impact on the *social relations* of work. The Industrial Revolution began an era of work that required brute force and obedience to authority. With the spinning jenny, the assembly line, and the increasing use of machinery in production, more and more work became industrialized. Workers were closely supervised in factory settings, and an increasing division of labour meant that the skill content of certain jobs eroded.

It is misleading, however, to think that it takes less skill now than it did in previous centuries to produce the goods and services we use today. We may be misled to reach this conclusion when we focus on the skills associated with specific jobs or job tasks, but not when we focus on the skills associated with the entire process of providing goods and services. If anything, this overall process requires more skill because of the complexity of goods and services we now produce.

As Clement and Myles (1994) argue, the skill content of the entire labour process has risen, although much of that skill content now resides in managerial and administrative spheres. After the Industrial Revolution, a managerial revolution took place. It involved the separation of conceptualization from execution. More of the job of conceptualization shifted to the managerial and administrative realm. Before the mass-produced sweater, individual artisans determined the patterns and colours they would use. Now, workers in most textile sweatshops have no discretion over what they produce. Managers choose patterns and colours and they pass along orders to supervisors who direct shop floor production.

The rise of a managerial class that began with the advent of the manufacturing era has intensified in the postindustrial service revolution. Many service-sector jobs are knowledge-intensive, and "postindustrial services employ more skilled managers than firms in goods and distribution" (Clement and Myles, 1994: 80). As well, these managers tend less often to have surveillance and supervision roles, and more often to have real decision-making power.

The net result is the rise of a new middle class with greater power to make decisions about what is to be done and how to do it.

The newer social relations of work are starkly illustrated in Silicon Valley. Some top executives there earn many millions of dollars annually. Even at less lofty levels, there are many thousands of high-paying, creative jobs in the Valley (Bjorhus, 2000; Tam, 2012). Amid all this wealth, however, the electronics-assembly factories in Silicon Valley are little better than high-tech sweatshops. Most workers in the electronics factories earn less than 60 percent of the Valley's average wage, work long hours, are frequently exposed to toxic substances, and suffer industrial illnesses at three times the average rate for other manufacturing jobs. Although the opulent lifestyles of Silicon Valley's millionaires are often featured in the mass media, a more accurate picture of the Valley also incorporates those who execute the demands of the knowledge workers and executives.

Figure 13.4 illustrates the changing nature of the Canadian occupational structure. Based on projections by Human Resources Development Canada, the chart shows, across a set of skill dimensions, the high-growth areas of the economy. This pattern is consistent with the pattern of growing income inequality discussed in Chapter 8, Social Stratification. There, you will recall, we noted growing inequality between the top 40 percent of income earners and the remaining 60 percent.

Labour Market Segmentation

Labour market segmentation is the division of the market for labour into distinct settings. In these settings, work is found in different ways and workers have different characteristics. There is only a slim chance of moving from one setting to another.

The processes described above are taking place in the last of the three stages of labour market development identified by David Gordon and his colleagues (Gordon, Edwards, and Reich, 1982). The period from about 1820 to 1890 was one of *initial proletarianization* in North America. During this period, a large industrial working class replaced craft workers in small workshops. Then, from the end of the nineteenth century until the start of World War II, the labour market entered the phase of *labour homogenization*. Extensive mechanization and deskilling took place during this stage. Finally, the third phase of labour market development is that of **labour market segmentation**. During this stage, which began after World War II

Emerging (Growth) Sector	University	College/Technical	High School or Less Than High School
Environment	Biophysicist, agrologist, professional forester, environmental engineer	Air quality specialist, environmental technologist, pollution prevention officer, regulations officer	Landfill equipment operator, sylviculture and forestry worker, aquaculture and marine harvest labourer
Biotechnology	Biologist, biophysicist, food science engineer, food scientist, food biochemist, pharmacist, bioethicist, clinical ethicist	Chemical technician, biological technician, water supply manager, inspector in public and environmental health	Information clerk; reporting, scheduling, and distribution occupations; labourer
Multimedia	Lawyer specializing in protecting intellectual property rights, translator, network architect, information librarian	Animation designer, Web designer, production designer, ideas manager, videographer	Product tester, information clerk
Aerospace	Aeronautics specialist, aerospace engineer, software engineer, astrophysicist, sales and marketing specialist	Mechanic, aircraft inspector, machinist, tool and die maker, industrial design technologist	Assembler, machinist, aircraft electronic assembler

FIGURE 13.4
Sample Occupations in Emerging Sectors

Source: Adapted from Human Resources Development Canada, 2000.

and continues to the present, large business organizations emerged. Thousands of small businesses continue to operate at this stage. However, different kinds of jobs are associated with small businesses than with large business organizations. Good jobs with security and relatively high wages tend to be concentrated in large firms, while smaller businesses cannot afford to offer the same wages and job security provisions. The result is a *segmented* labour market. In these two different settings, workers, and the work they do, have different characteristics:

The **primary labour market** comprises mainly highly skilled, well-educated workers. They are employed in large corporations that enjoy high levels of capital investment. In the primary labour market, employment is secure, earnings are high, and fringe benefits are generous.

- The **primary labour market** is made up disproportionately of highly skilled, well-educated workers. They are employed in large corporations that enjoy high levels of capital investment. In the primary labour market, employment is relatively secure, earnings are high, fringe benefits are generous, and opportunities for advancement within the firm are good. Often the work is unionized because workers have the collective ability to exert pressure on their large employer.
- The **secondary labour market** contains a disproportionately large number of women and members of ethnic minority groups, especially recent immigrants. Employees in the secondary labour market tend to be unskilled and lack higher education. They work in small firms with low levels of capital investment. Employment is insecure, earnings are low, fringe benefits are meagre, and mobility prospects are limited. These firms are often subcontracted by large corporations that minimize their risk by off-loading seasonal work (for example, in logging and oil exploration) and work for which demand is volatile (for example, in auto parts supply and house construction).

The **secondary labour market** contains a disproportionately large number of women and members of ethnic minorities, particularly recent immigrants. Employees in the secondary labour market tend to be unskilled and lack higher education. They work in small firms that have low levels of capital investment. Employment is insecure, earnings are low, and fringe benefits are meagre.

This characterization may seem to advance us only a little beyond our earlier distinction between good jobs and bad jobs. However, proponents of labour market segmentation theory offer fresh insights into two important issues. First, they argue that people find work in different ways in the two labour markets. Second, they point out that social barriers make it difficult for individuals to move from one labour market to the other. To appreciate these points, it is vital to note that workers do more than just work. They also seek to control their work and prevent outsiders from gaining access to it. In this regard, some workers are more successful than others. Understanding the social roots of their success or failure permits us to see why the primary and secondary labour markets remain distinct. Therefore, we now turn to a discussion of forms of worker control.

Worker Resistance and Management Response

One of the criticisms lodged against Braverman's analysis of factory work is that he inaccurately portrays workers as passive victims of management control. In reality, workers often resist the imposition of task specialization and mechanization by managers. They go on strike, change jobs, fail to show up for work, sabotage production lines, and so on (Dunk, 1991; Agboola and Salawu, 2011). In these ways, worker resistance causes management to modify its organizational plans.

The **human relations school of management** emerged in the 1930s as a challenge to Taylor's scientific management approach. It advocated less authoritarian leadership on the shop floor, careful selection and training of personnel, and greater attention to human needs and employee job satisfaction.

In the 1930s, the **human relations school of management** emerged as a challenge to Frederick W. Taylor's scientific management approach. It advocated less authoritarian leadership on the shop floor and encouraged careful selection and training of personnel and greater attention to human needs and employee job satisfaction.

In the following decades, owners and managers of big companies in all the rich industrialized countries realized they needed to make still more concessions to labour if they wanted a loyal and productive workforce. These concessions included not just higher wages but also more decision-making authority about product quality, promotion policies, job design, product innovation, company investments, and so on. The biggest concessions to labour were made in countries with the most powerful trade union movements, such as Sweden, which has a unionization rate of about 70 percent. In these countries, unions are organized in nationwide umbrella organizations that negotiate directly with centralized business organizations and governments over wages and labour policy. At the other extreme is the United States, where less than 12 percent of the non-agricultural work force is unionized (OECD, 2014b).

Canada is located between these two extremes, although closer to the American than the Swedish model. In Canada, about 30 percent of Canadian employees belong to a union (Statistics Canada, 2013j). Here, however, there is no centralized, nationwide bargaining among unions, businesses, and governments. Two indicators of the relative inability of Canadian workers to wrest concessions from their employers are given in Figure 13.5 and Figure 13.6. Canadians work more hours per week than people do in many other rich industrialized countries. Canadians also have fewer paid vacation days per year (see Box 13.1). However, Canadian workers are better off than their American counterparts are on these two measures.

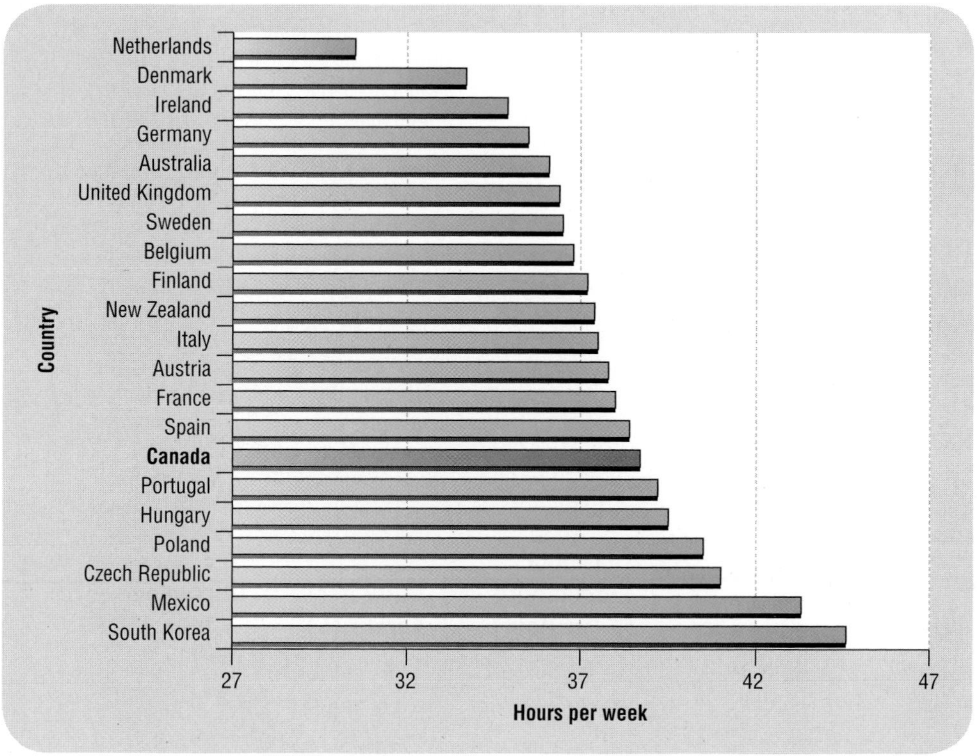

FIGURE 13.5

Average Hours Worked per Week, Selected Countries, 2011

Source: OECD. 2014a. "Average Usual Weekly Hours Worked on the Main Job." *OECD StatExtracts*. Retrieved February 15, 2014 (http://stats.oecd.org/Index.spx?DataSetCode=ANHRS).

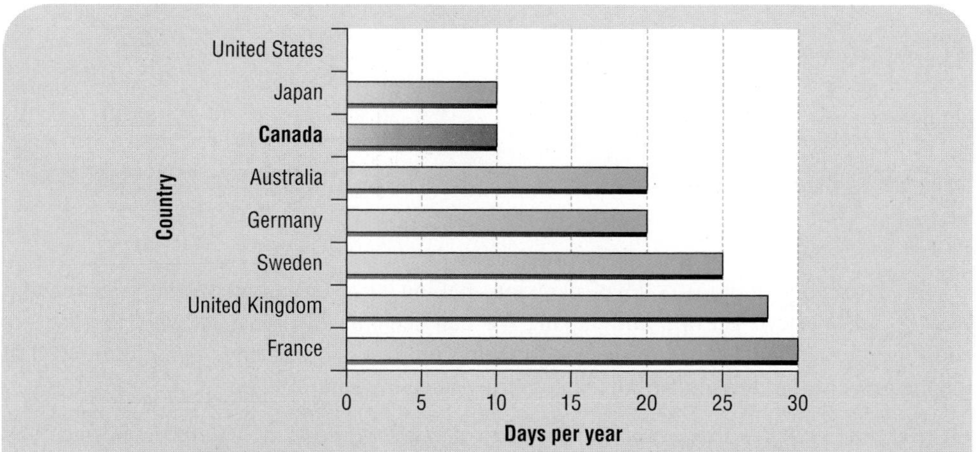

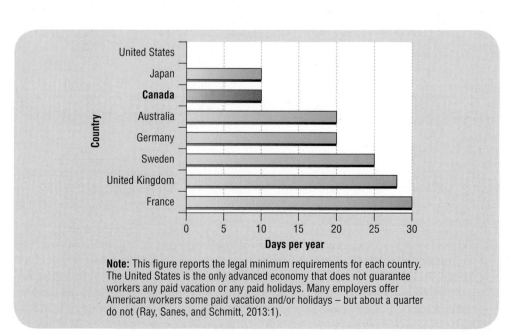

Note: This figure reports the legal minimum requirements for each country. The United States is the only advanced economy that does not guarantee workers any paid vacation or any paid holidays. Many employers offer American workers some paid vacation and/or holidays – but about a quarter do not (Ray, Sanes, and Schmitt, 2013:1).

FIGURE 13.6

Annual Paid Vacation Days per Year, Selected Countries, 2013

Source: Ray, Rebecca, Milla Sanes, and John Schmitt. 2013. *No-Vacation Nation Revisited*. Washington, DC: Center for Economic and Policy Research. www.cepr.net

BOX 13.1

IT'S YOUR CHOICE

THE IMPORTANCE OF VACATIONS

Work is often stressful. Employees are pressed to work more efficiently while the pervasiveness of smartphones and wireless connections makes disconnecting from work difficult. The under- and unemployed are stressed because they don't have access to employment stress. Achieving work–life balance is challenging for everyone.

Vacations are intended to provide a break from employment stress. They are times for rest and recovery. However, national standards for paid vacations and holidays vary widely. The United States has no legal guarantees for paid vacation or holidays. Canada guarantees 10 days a year. Some countries offer up to 35 days each year (see Table 13.2).

Time off is time not spent on productive work, so perhaps guaranteed vacations are a detriment to national productivity. On the other hand, it may be that rested, refreshed workers are more productive, which implies that mandating vacations is a sound economic plan. The following table reports the situation for the eight countries providing the most vacation and holidays. Included in the table are the annual number of mandated days off, as well as standardized measures of labour productivity, gross domestic product (GDP) per capita, and the unemployment rate.

If vacations are systematically related to economic outcomes, we should expect little variation in economic performance among these nations with generous vacation benefits. But that is not what the data show. The generous paid days off among these countries is related to both high labour productivity (Belgium) and low labour productivity (Portugal), high GDP (Austria) and low GDP (Portugal), and high unemployment rates (Spain) and low unemployment rates (Austria). Nationally mandated paid vacations and holidays do not meaningfully influence the macro economy.

Taking holidays and vacations does, however, have micro effects. Your experience in paid employment is like your experience in university. If you put in more time, you generally do better. On the other hand, taking time off is definitely related to your physical and mental wellness (Joudrey and Wallace, 2009). What kind of balance between productive work and time off do you think is optimal for yourself and others? After graduating, if an excellent paying job offer came along, how much vacation time would it need to provide? What if the offer paid well but offered little or no time off? Do underemployed and unemployed people deserve some kind of vacation support? If so, how much?

TABLE 13.2
Are Vacations Economically Beneficial?

Country	Days Off per Year	Labour Productivity ($ Per Hour)	GDP per Capita ($)	Unemployment Rate (%)
Austria	35	51.60	42 409	4.4
Portugal	35	32.40	23 385	15.9
Germany	34	55.80	30 028	5.5
Spain	34	47.50	30 557	25.1
France	31	57.70	35 548	10.3
Belgium	30	59.50	37 883	7.6
Italy	30	46.60	30 136	10.7
New Zealand	30	34.10	29 730	6.9

Source: Hess, Alexander. 2013. "On holiday: Countries with the most vacation days." *The Wall Street Journal*. June 8. Retrieved April 15, 2014.

The **quality of work life** movement originated in Sweden and Japan. It involves small groups of a dozen or so workers and managers collaborating to improve both the quality of goods produced and communication between workers and managers.

In the realm of industry-level decision making, too, Canadian workers lag behind workers in Western Europe and Japan. We can see this discrepancy when we briefly consider the two main types of decision-making innovations that have been introduced in the factories of the rich industrialized countries since the early 1970s:

1. *Reforms that give workers more authority on the shop floor* include those advanced by the **quality of work life** movement. *Quality circles* originated in Sweden and Japan. They involve small groups of a dozen or so workers and managers collaborating to improve both the quality of goods produced and the communication between workers and managers. In some cases, this approach has evolved into a system that results in high productivity gains and worker satisfaction. Quality circles have been introduced in

some Canadian industries, including automotive and aerospace. However, they are less widespread here than in Western Europe and Japan.

2. *Reforms that allow workers to help formulate overall business strategy* give workers more authority than do quality circles. For example, in much of Western Europe, workers are consulted not just on the shop floor but also in the boardroom. In Germany, this system is known as **codetermination**. German workers' councils review and influence management policies on a wide range of issues, including when and where new plants should be built and how capital should be invested in technological innovation. North America has a few examples of this sort of worker involvement in high-level decision making, mostly in the auto industry. Worker-participation programs were widely credited with improving the quality of North American cars and increasing the auto sector's productivity in the 1980s and 1990s, making it competitive again with Japanese carmakers.

Codetermination is a German system of worker participation that allows workers to help formulate overall business strategy. German workers' councils review and influence management policies on a wide range of issues, including when and where new plants should be built and how capital should be invested in technological innovation.

Unions have clearly played a key role in increasing worker participation in industrial decision making since the 1920s and especially since the 1970s. To varying degrees, owners and managers of big corporations have conceded authority to workers to create a more stable, loyal, and productive workforce. In Canada, governments too have ceded some workplace authority to unionized workers. Public sector employees who work for government, Crown corporations, public schools, and the health care system are much more likely than their private sector counterparts are to be unionized. Seventy-one percent of the public sector is unionized compared with about 16 percent of the private sector. Understandably, workers who enjoy more authority in the workplace, whether unionized or not, have tried to protect the gains they have won. As we will now see, they have thereby contributed to the separation of primary and secondary labour markets.

Unions and Professional Organizations

Unions are organizations of workers that seek to defend and promote their members' interests. By bargaining with employers, unions have succeeded in winning improved working conditions, higher wages, and more worker participation in industrial decision making for their members. One indicator of the power of unions is that the hourly wage gap between unionized and nonunionized full-time workers is about \$4, and the hourly wage gap between unionized and nonunionized part-time workers is about \$8 (Uppal, 2011).

Unions are organizations of workers that seek to defend and promote their members' interests.

In conjunction with employers, unions have also helped develop systems of labour recruitment, training, and promotion. These systems are sometimes called **internal labour markets** because they control pay rates, hiring, and promotions within corporations (Tate and Yang, 2012). At the same time, they reduce competition between a firm's workers and external labour supplies.

Internal labour markets are social mechanisms for controlling pay rates, hiring, and promotions within corporations while reducing competition between a firm's workers and external labour supplies.

In an internal labour market, training programs that specify the credentials required for promotion govern advancement through the ranks. Seniority rules specify the length of time a person must serve in a given position before being allowed to move up. These rules also protect senior personnel from layoffs according to the principle of "last hired, first fired." Finally, in internal labour markets, recruitment of new workers is usually limited to entry-level positions. In this way, the intake of new workers is controlled. Senior personnel are assured of promotion and protection from outside competition. For this reason, internal labour markets are sometimes called "labour market shelters."

Labour market shelters operate not only among unionized factory workers but also among professionals, such as doctors, lawyers, and engineers. **Professionals** are people with specialized knowledge acquired through extensive higher education. They enjoy a high degree of work autonomy and usually regulate themselves and enforce standards through professional associations. The Canadian Medical Association is probably the best known and one of the most powerful professional associations in the country. Professionals exercise authority over clients and subordinates. They operate according to a code of ethics that emphasizes the altruistic nature of their work. Finally, they specify the credentials needed to enter their professions and thus maintain a cap on the supply of new professionals.

Professionals are people with specialized knowledge acquired through extensive higher education.

This practice reduces competition, ensures high demand for their services, and keeps their earnings high. In this way, the professions act as labour market shelters, much like unions do. (For further discussion of professionalization, see Chapter 17, Education.)

Barriers between the Primary and Secondary Labour Markets

We saw above that many workers in the secondary labour market do not enjoy the high pay, job security, and benefit packages shared by workers in the primary labour market, many of whom are members of unions and professional associations. We can now add that these workers find it difficult to exit the "job ghettos" of the secondary labour market because three social barriers make the primary labour market difficult to penetrate:

1. *The primary labour market often has few entry-level positions.* One set of circumstances that contributes to the lack of entry-level positions in the primary labour market is corporate "downsizing" and plant shutdowns. Both took place on a wide scale in Canada and the United States throughout the 1980s and early 1990s, as well as during the "Great Recession" of 2008–09. The lack of entry-level positions is especially acute during periods of economic recession. Big economic forces, such as plant shutdowns and recessions, prevent upward mobility and often result in downward mobility.
2. *Workers often lack informal networks linking them to good job openings.* People frequently find out about job availability through informal networks of friends and acquaintances (Granovetter, 1995; Zhao and Zhang, 2013). These networks often consist of people with the same ethnic and racial backgrounds. Recent immigrants, and especially refugees, who compose a disproportionately large share of workers in the secondary labour market and tend not to be white, are less likely than others are to find out about job openings in the primary labour market, where the labour force is disproportionately white. Even within ethnic groups, the difference between getting good work and having none is sometimes a question of having the right connections.
3. *Workers often lack the required training or certification for jobs in the primary labour market.* What is more, because of their low wages and scarce leisure time, workers in the secondary labour market often cannot afford to upgrade either their skills or their credentials. Impersonal economic forces, a lack of network ties, and insufficient education often lead to people being stuck in the secondary labour market.

The Time Crunch and Its Effects

Although the quality of working life is higher in the primary labour market than in the secondary labour market, we must be careful not to exaggerate the differences. Overwork and lack of leisure have become central features of our culture, and are experienced by workers in both labour markets. We are experiencing a growing time crunch. In most Canadian households, all the adults work full-time in the paid labour force, and many adolescents work part-time. Some people work two jobs to make ends meet. Many managers, truck drivers, and professionals work 10 or more hours a day because of tight deadlines, demands for high productivity, and a trimmed-down workforce.

Over the past 50 years, the average number of hours that people spend working at their primary job has remained stable at between 35 and 40 hours per week. However, given the growth of part-time labour discussed earlier, the average workweek has remained stable over the last half century only because a growing number of Canadians are working longer hours (Shields, 1999). The result is that Canadians are spending more time working to sustain our society, as evidenced by the following calculation.

The total amount of time available to all Canadians in a year is 365 days × 24 hours × the number of people living in Canada. Of the total available time, how much is spent performing paid work? In 1976, 8.7 percent of our time was devoted to work. By 2012, that figure increased to 10 percent (Statistics Canada, 2012a). The increase occurred while the percentage of Canadians in the paid labour force fell. We conclude that Canadians in the paid labour force are working more hours, raising their stress levels.

Stress is the feeling of being unable to cope with life's demands given one's resources. Work is the leading source of stress throughout the world. Over a quarter of working adults in Canada report that their lives are "highly stressful" (Crompton, 2011). Sixty percent of this group identify work as the primary cause. High stress levels are particularly prevalent among people who are well educated and have "good jobs." Because women tend to undertake more family responsibilities than do men, women tend to experience more stress.

In turn, high stress levels reduce productivity—the quantity and quality of work tasks that can be completed in an hour. Working under high stress also increases both absenteeism and disability claims (Arsenault and Sharpe, 2009). Stress-related consequences are not confined to work. Mental health suffers from stress through increased anxiety, depression, fatigue, insomnia, and substance abuse. Physical health also deteriorates from chronic stress as evidenced by elevated rates of heart disease, ulcers, and stroke (Heart and Stroke Foundation, 2011).

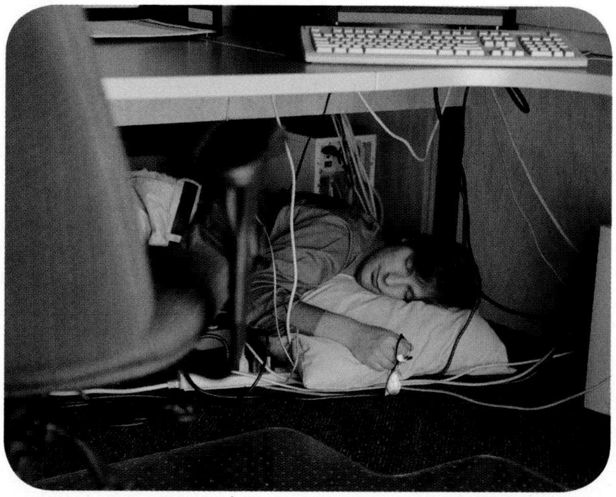

Are Canadians working too many hours per week?

There are three main reasons that leisure is on the decline and the pace of work is becoming more frantic for many people in the paid labour force (Schor, 1992). First, effective corporate advertising is pushing Canadians to consume goods and services at higher and higher levels all the time. To satisfy these advertising-induced "needs," people must work longer. Second, most corporate executives apparently think it is more profitable to push employees to work more hours than to hire new employees and pay expensive benefits for them. Third, most Canadian workers in the private sector are not in a position to demand reduced working hours and more vacation time because few of them are unionized. They lack clout and suffer the consequences in terms of stress, depression, and other work-related ailments.

TIME FOR REVIEW

- How has the drive for profits affected job deskilling and part-time work?
- What major work differences contribute to large income gaps?
- What means do workers use to control their work and create better employment outcomes?

THE PROBLEM OF MARKETS

One conclusion we can draw from the preceding discussion is that the secondary labour market is a relatively **free market**. That is, the supply and demand for labour regulate wage levels and other benefits. If supply is high and demand is low, wages fall. If demand is high and supply is low, wages rise. Workers in the secondary labour market lack much power to interfere in the operation of the forces of supply and demand.

In a **free market**, prices are determined only by supply and demand.

In contrast, the primary labour market is a more **regulated market**. Wage levels and other benefits are not established by the forces of supply and demand alone; workers and professionals are in a position to influence the operation of the primary labour market to their advantage.

In a **regulated market**, various social forces limit the capacity of supply and demand to determine prices.

Our analysis suggests that the freer the market, the higher the resulting level of social inequality. In the freest markets, many of the least powerful people are unable to earn enough to subsist, while a few of the most powerful people can amass huge fortunes. Because of this propensity to growing inequality, the secondary labour market cannot be entirely free. Canadian governments have had to establish a legal minimum wage to prevent the price of unskilled labour from dropping below the point at which people are literally unable to make a living (see Box 13.2).

The question of whether free or regulated markets are better for society lies at the centre of much debate in economics and politics, but the dichotomy is too simplistic. First, no markets are completely unregulated. Regulation is always a matter of degree, as demonstrated by the varied structure of markets across cultures and historical periods (Lie 1992). Second, the degree and type of market regulation depends on how power, norms, and values are distributed among various social groups. Consequently, the costs and benefits of regulation may be socially distributed in many different ways.

The "neoclassical" school of contemporary economics challenges this understanding of the social dimension of markets (Becker, 1976; Mankiw, 1998). Instead of focusing on how power, norms, and values shape markets, neoclassical economists argue that free markets maximize economic growth. We can use the minimum wage to illustrate their point. According to neoclassical economists, if the minimum wage is eliminated, everyone will be better off. For example, in a situation where labour is in low demand and high supply, wages will fall, increasing profits. Higher profits will in turn allow employers to invest more in expanding their businesses. The new investment will create new jobs, and rising demand for labour will drive wages up. Social inequality may increase but eventually *everyone* will be better off thanks to the operation of the free market.

One real-world difficulty with neoclassical theory is that resistance to the operation of free markets increases as you move down the social hierarchy. People at the low end of the social hierarchy usually fight falling wages. A social environment full of strikes, riots, and industrial sabotage is unfavourable to high productivity and new capital investment. That is why the economic system of a society at a given time is a more or less stable set of

BOX 13.2

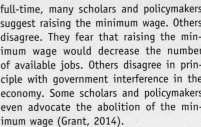

SOCIAL POLICY: WHAT DO YOU THINK?

SHOULD WE ABOLISH THE MINIMUM WAGE?

In Canada, the provinces and territories set the hourly minimum wage. In 2014, it ranged from $9.95 in Alberta to $11.00 in Ontario, with most provinces and territories around the $10 range. At about $10 an hour, a minimum-wage job may be fine for teenagers, many of whom are supported by their parents. However, it is difficult to live on your own, much less to support a family, on a minimum-wage job, even if you work full-time. This is the problem with the minimum wage: It does not amount to a living wage for many people.

In Ontario in 2011, about 40 percent of minimum-wage workers were over the age of 24. The minimum wage was $10.25 an hour. The annual income of someone working 52 weeks a year at 40 hours a week was $21320. If that person lived in Brampton, Hamilton, Mississauga, Ottawa, or Toronto, he or she earned 8.4 percent less than the low-income cutoff (Block, 2013: 5; Statistics Canada, 2013). Welcome to the world of the "working poor." Could you live on $21320 a year in one of Ontario's big cities, especially if you are over the age of 24 and thinking about starting a family?

Given the thousands of Canadians who cannot lift themselves and their children out of poverty even while they work full-time, many scholars and policymakers suggest raising the minimum wage. Others disagree. They fear that raising the minimum wage would decrease the number of available jobs. Others disagree in principle with government interference in the economy. Some scholars and policymakers even advocate the abolition of the minimum wage (Grant, 2014).

What do you think? Should the minimum wage be raised? Should someone working full-time be entitled to live above the low-income cutoff? Or should businesses be entitled to hire workers at whatever price the market will bear?

compromises between advocates and opponents of free markets. Markets are only as free as people are prepared to tolerate, and their degree of tolerance varies historically and among cultures (Berger and Dore, 1996; Doremus et al., 1998).

In the rest of this chapter, we offer several illustrations of how sociologists analyze markets. First, we compare capitalism, communism, and democratic socialism, the main types of economic system in the world today. Second, we examine the ability of big corporations to shape Canadian markets. Finally, we extend our analysis of corporate and free market growth to the global level. We identify advocates and opponents of these developments and sketch the main work-related decisions that face us in the twenty-first century.

ACCOUNT OF THE

SALE of a WIFE, by J. NASH,

IN THOMAS-STREET MARKET,

On the 29th of May, 1823.

This day another of those disgraceful scenes which of late have so frequently annoyed the public markets in this country took place in St. Thomas's Market, in this city; a man (if he deserves the name) of the name of John Nash, a drover, residing in Rose-mary-street, appeared there leading his wife in a halter, followed by a great concourse of spectators; when arrived opposite the Bell-yard, he publicly announced his intention of disposing of his better half by Public Auction, and stated that the biddings were then open; it was a long while before any one ventured to speak, at length a young man who thought it a pity to let her remain in the hands of her present owner, generously bid 6d.! In vain did the anxious seller look around for another bidding, no one could be found to advance one penny, and after extolling her qualities, and warranting her sound, and free from vice, he was obliged, rather than keep her, to let her go at that price. The lady appeared quite satisfied, but not so the purchaser, he soon repented of his bargain, and again offered her to sale, when being bid nine-pence, he readily accepted it, and handed the lady to her new purchaser, who, not liking the transfer, made off with her mother, but was soon taken by her purchaser, and claimed as his property, to this she would not consent but by order of a magistrate, who dismissed the case. Nash, the husband, was obliged to make a precipitate retreat from the enraged populace.

Copy of Verses written on the Occasion:

COME all you kind husbands who have scolding wives,
Who tho' living together are tired of your lives,
If you cannot persuade her nor good natur'd make her
Place a rope round her neck & to market pray take her

Should any one bid, when she's offer'd for sale,
Let her go for a trifle lest she should get stale,
If six-pence be offer'd, & that's all can be had,
Let her go for the same rather than keep a lot bad.

Come all jolly neighbours, come dance sing & play,
Away to the wedding where we intend to drink tea;
All the world assembles, the young and the old,
For to see this fair beauty, as we have been told.

Here's success to this couple to keep up the fun,
May bumpers go round at the birth of a son;
Long life to them both, and in peace & content
May their days and their nights for ever be spent.

Shepherd, Printer, No. 6, on the Broad Weir, *Bristol*.

An unregulated market creates gross inequalities. Here is an account of a wife sold by her husband for nine pence in Britain in 1823. Similar events inspired Thomas Hardy's classic novel, *The Mayor of Casterbridge* (1886).

Capitalism is the dominant economic system in the world. Private ownership of property and competition in the pursuit of profit characterize capitalist economies.

Corporations are legal entities that can enter into contracts and own property. They are taxed at a lower rate than individuals are and their owners are normally not liable for the corporation's debt or any harm it may cause the public.

CAPITALISM, COMMUNISM, AND DEMOCRATIC SOCIALISM

Capitalism

The world's dominant economic system today is **capitalism**. Capitalist economies have two distinctive features (see Box 13.3).

1. *Private ownership of property*. In capitalist economies, individuals and corporations own almost all the means of producing goods and services. Individuals and corporations are therefore free to buy and sell just about anything. Like individuals, **corporations** are legal entities. They can enter contracts and own property. However, corporations are taxed at a lower rate than individuals are. Moreover, the corporation's owners typically are not liable if the corporation harms consumers or goes bankrupt. Instead, the corporation is legally responsible for damage and debt.

BOX 13.3

SOCIOLOGY ON THE TUBE

DRAGONS' DEN

"Welcome to *Dragons' Den*, where hopeful entrepreneurs tempt wealthy dragons with the best business ideas money can buy. And remember, they must get all the money they came for or they leave with nothing." That is how the host begins each Canadian-produced episode of the second highest-rated television show. (*Hockey Night in Canada* is first.) The premise of the show is simple: people with a business proposition seek financial support from a panel of venture capitalists (the "dragons"). Like many talent-search reality television shows, the episodes include the good, the bad, and the ugly. Compared with other talent shows, what determines the success of a pitch is clear. First, the dragons assess the size of the market for the business and, if large enough, they are interested. Second, dragons consider whether the requested investment is reasonable, given the share of the company and the level of control being offered.

While entertainment is provided by the drama of negotiations, bickering among the dragons, and the comedy of poor pitches, the *Dragons' Den* illustrates the basic tenets of a capitalistic marketplace. Capitalistic economies have two distinctive features: private ownership of property and competition in the pursuit of profit. The budding entrepreneurs on *Dragons' Den* pitch their business idea and its sales history. They are always asked if they have full ownership of their company and its assets. Their pitch is dead if they report anything other than full private ownership. If the first condition is satisfied, then the competition begins. On the show, it takes two forms. First, there is competition between the interested dragons and the entrepreneur about the required share of the company and the type of control each wants. This negotiation is key to each side's future profits, so the bargaining can be intense. Second, the dragons often compete for a stake in the business. When dragons bid against each other for access to the business, demand exceeds supply, which means a potential increase in the entrepreneur's profit.

Canadian Broadcasting Corporation

The dragons

Canada's *Dragons' Den* is a franchise owned by the international, capitalist conglomerate, Sony. Versions of this television program are found in more than 20 countries, from Afghanistan to the United States. Wherever it is broadcast, the essentials of the program are the same—and so is its popularity. People are apparently fascinated to see this microcosm of capitalism in action. What viewers don't see in the *Dragons' Den* is how the ruthless pursuit of profit leads to decisions that can deskill a workforce, outsource jobs, lay off employees, and generate appalling social inequalities.

2. *Competition in the pursuit of profit.* The second hallmark of capitalism is that producers compete to offer consumers desired goods and services at the lowest possible price. In a purely capitalist economy, the government does not interfere in the operation of the economy. Presumably, everyone benefits; the most efficient producers make profits, consumers can buy at low prices, and many jobs are created.

In reality, no economy is perfectly free. The state needed to intervene heavily to create markets in the first place. For example, 500 years ago, the idea that land was a commodity that could be bought, sold, and rented on the free market was an utterly foreign concept to Aboriginal people in North America. To turn North American land into a marketable commodity, European armies had to force Aboriginal people off the land and eventually onto reserves. Governments had to pass laws regulating the ownership, sale, and rent of land. Without the military and legal intervention of government, no market for land would exist.

Today, governments must also intervene in the economy to keep the market working effectively. For instance, governments create and maintain roads and ports to make commerce possible. And to protect workers and consumers from the excesses of corporations, governments pass laws governing the minimum wage, occupational health and safety, child labour, and industrial pollution (see Box 13.4). If very large corporations get into

BOX 13.4

SOCIOLOGY AT THE MOVIES

TRIANGLE: REMEMBERING THE FIRE

Since the early days of capitalism, factory work has often been the site of bad jobs. Workers sell their labour to factories, and the profit motive encourages business owners to minimize inputs such as the cost of labour and maximize output (the number of goods or services produced). Poor working conditions often accompany exploitation.

On March 15, 1911, a workforce of mostly young, immigrant women was working at the Triangle Shirtwaist factory in Manhattan. They made women's blouses. Only when a fire broke out did the panicking workers learn that the owners kept all the doors locked to prevent employee theft. In this inferno, workers attempted to escape however they could. Many jumped from the 10-storey building. Thirty died with the flesh worn off their hands from sliding down the steel elevator cable. The building was a gruesome scene of 146 broken, charred, dead bodies. Most of the workers were recent Jewish and Italian immigrant women between the ages of 16 and 23. *Triangle: Remembering the Fire* tells the story and commemorates the tragedy (Connell, 2011).

A century ago, the Triangle fire triggered important social consequences. Garment workers' unions were energized and successfully fought for better working conditions,

Kheel Center, Cornell University

The aftermath of the Triangle fire

higher wages, and improved job safety and health. Governments passed higher minimum standards for factory working conditions. Attention was drawn to the level of exploitation of young, immigrant, low-skilled workers in the secondary labour market.

Although working conditions improved following the Triangle fire, workers in the secondary labour market still struggle with many of the same concerns. In Canada, immigrant workers are prone to abuse, exploitation, and lax government oversight (Kauri, 2012). Unions continue to struggle and resist the excesses of capitalistic enterprises (Cheadle, 2012). Obtaining minimum-wage policies that generate a decent standard of living is an ongoing challenge (Battle, 2011). Over the last century, most garment and other factory work has been relocated offshore. While this shift changes the location of the abuses, the same issues remain: worker safety, pay, and rights. The 1100 workers killed in a Bangladesh garment factory collapse in 2013 exemplify the ongoing risks (CBC News, 2013).

Capitalism is an impressive form of social organization for producing goods and services. However, amid the abundance that capitalistic enterprises produce, it is easy to forget the central sociological insight that all institutions, economic and otherwise, are social constructions created for the betterment of humans. Institutions are means, not ends. As such, they should be judged by how well they serve human purposes; human purposes should not be judged by how well they serve institutions. When we lose sight of this insight, misery and tragedy are not far away. The story of *Triangle: Remembering the Fire* is a vivid reminder of this important sociological lesson.

FIGURE 13.7
The World Competitiveness Scoreboard, 2013

Source: IMD International, 2010, "The World Competitiveness Scoreboard 2013." Retrieved February 16, 2014. (www.imd.org/wcc/news-wcy-ranking/pdf).

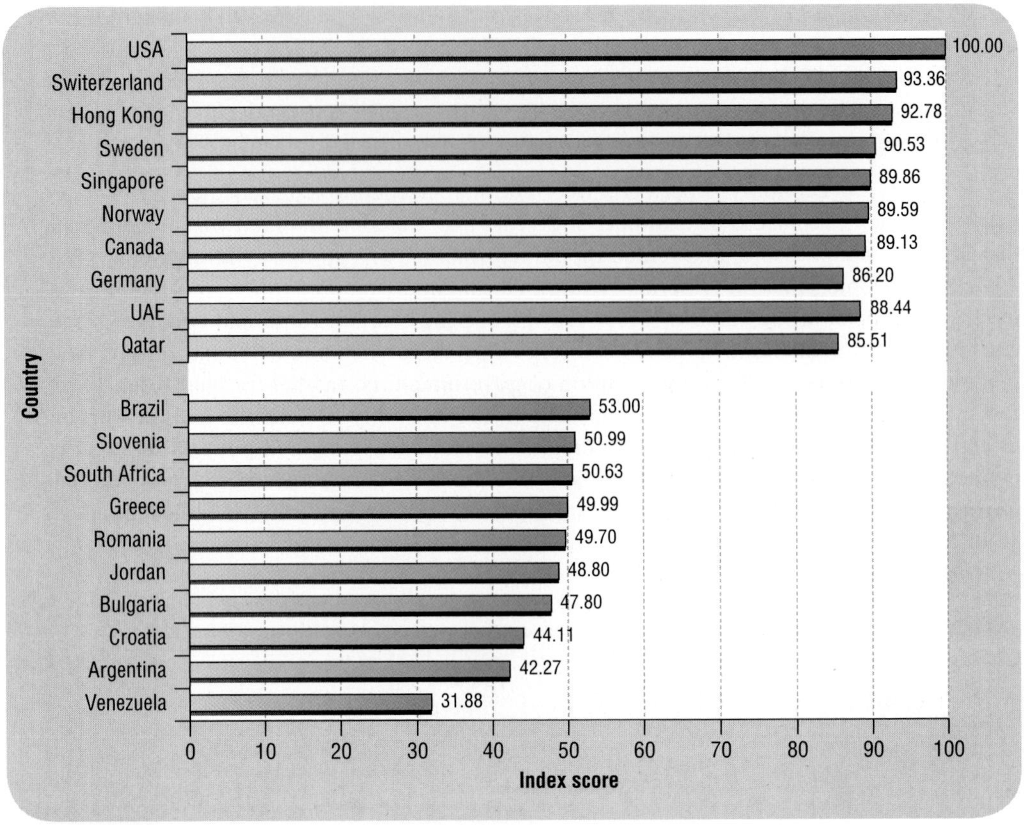

financial trouble, they can expect the government to bail them out, rationalizing their need by claiming that their bankruptcy would be devastating to the economy. This situation happened most recently during the Great Recession of 2008–09, when the government gave GM Canada and Chrysler Canada low-interest loans to prevent bankruptcy. The government also plays an influential role in supporting some leading companies, such as Bombardier Inc. in Montreal, manufacturer of aerospace and rail equipment.

Which capitalist economies are the most free and which are the least free? The International Institute for Management Development (IMD International) in Switzerland publishes a widely respected annual index of competitiveness. The index is based on the amount of state ownership of industry and other indicators of market freedom. Figure 13.7 gives the scores for the 10 most competitive and 10 least competitive countries in 2013. The most competitive countries are the United States (scoring 100), Switzerland (93.36), and Hong Kong (92.78). Venezuela ranks as the least competitive of the 60 nations, with a score of 31.88. Canada ranks seventh, with a score of 89.13.

Communism

Communism is a social and an economic system in which property is owned by public bodies; government planning, not the market, determines production and distribution.

Communism is the name Karl Marx gave to the classless society that, he said, is bound to develop out of capitalism. Socialism is the name usually given to the transitional phase between capitalism and communism. No country in the world is or ever has been communist in the pure sense of the term. About two dozen countries in Asia, South America, and Africa consider themselves to be socialist countries, including China, North Korea, Vietnam, and Cuba. As an ideal, however, communism is an economic system with two distinct features:

1. *Public ownership of property.* Under communism, the state owns almost all the means of producing goods and services. Private corporations do not exist. Individuals are not free to buy and sell goods and services. The stated aim of public ownership is to ensure that all individuals have equal wealth and equal access to goods and services.

2. *Government planning.* Five-year state plans establish production quotas, prices, and most other aspects of economic activity. The political officials who design the state plans, not the forces of supply and demand, determine what is produced, in what quantities, and at what prices. A high level of control is required to implement these rigid state plans. As a result, democratic politics is not allowed to interfere with state activities. Only one political party exists—the Communist party. Elections are held regularly, but only members of the Communist party are allowed to run for office (Zaslavsky and Brym, 1978).

Until recently, the countries of Central and Eastern Europe and Central Asia were single-party, socialist societies. The most powerful of these countries was the Soviet Union, which was composed of Russia and 14 other socialist republics. In perhaps the most surprising and sudden change in modern history, the countries of the region began introducing capitalism and holding multi-party elections in the late 1980s and early 1990s.

The collapse of socialism in Central and Eastern Europe and Central Asia is attributable to several factors. For one thing, the citizens of the region enjoyed few civil rights. For another, their standard of living was only about half as high as that of people in the rich industrialized countries of the West. The gap between East and West grew as the arms race between the Soviet Union and the United States intensified in the 1980s. The standard of living fell as the Soviet Union mobilized its economic resources to try to match the quantity and quality of military goods produced by the United States. Dissatisfaction was widespread and expressed itself in many ways, including strikes and political demonstrations. It grew as television and radio signals beamed from the West made the gap between socialism and capitalism more apparent to the citizenry. Eventually, the Communist parties of the region felt they could no longer govern effectively and so began to introduce reforms.

Democratic Socialism

Several prosperous and highly industrialized countries in northwestern Europe, such as Sweden, Denmark, and Norway, are democratic socialist societies. So are France and Germany, albeit to a lesser degree. Such societies have two distinctive features (Olsen, 2002):

1. *Public ownership of certain basic industries.* In democratic socialist countries, the government owns certain basic industries entirely or in part. Still, as a proportion of the entire economy, the level of public ownership is not high—far lower than the level of public ownership in socialist societies. The great bulk of property is privately owned, and competition in the pursuit of profit is the main motive for business activity, just as in capitalist societies.
2. *Substantial government intervention in the market.* Democratic socialist countries enjoy regular, free, multi-party elections. However, unlike in Canada, political parties backed by a strong trade union movement have formed governments in democratic socialist countries for much of the post–World War II period. The governments that these unions back intervene strongly in the operation of markets for the benefit of ordinary workers. Taxes are considerably higher than they are in capitalist countries. Consequently, social services are more generous, and workers earn more, work fewer hours, and enjoy more paid vacation days. Since the 1980s, the democratic socialist countries have moved in a more capitalistic direction. In particular, they have privatized some previously government-owned industries and services. Still, these countries retain their distinct approach to governments and markets, which is why democratic socialism is sometimes called a "third way" between capitalism and socialism.

THE CORPORATION

Oligopolies are giant corporations that control part of an economy. When just a few corporations dominate an economic sector, they can influence prices, thus forcing consumers to pay more for goods and services. They can also exercise excessive influence on governments

Oligopolies are giant corporations that control part of an economy. They are few in number and tend not to compete against one another. Instead, they can set prices at levels that are most profitable for them.

to deregulate their operations or help them in other ways. However, in Canada and other Western countries, so-called antitrust laws limit their growth. In 1889, Canada first introduced legislation restricting businesses from combining or colluding to control markets. Replaced in 1923 by the Combines Investigation Act, the law allows government to review corporate mergers and acquisitions.

However, the law has been only partly effective in stabilizing the growth of oligopolies. You need look no further than your local gas station to find an example that continues to suggest price competition is not as vigorous as the idea of "antitrust" implies. Canadian banking provides another illustration of corporate concentration. Canada has only 29 domestic banks. Several of them are so small you have likely never heard of them. The top five banks, as ranked by the value of their assets, control about 90 percent of all banking assets in the country. Such concentration is a world apart from the early nineteenth century, when most businesses, including banks, were family owned and served only local markets (National Council of Welfare, 1998; Whittington, 1999).

Conglomerates are large corporations that operate in several industries at the same time.

An important effect of Canadian competition law is to encourage big companies to diversify. That is, rather than corporations increasing their share of control in their own industry, they often move into new industries in an effort to avoid antitrust laws. Big companies that operate in several industries at the same time are called **conglomerates**. One example of a rapidly expanding Canadian conglomerate is Bell Canada Enterprises (BCE), which has telephone, television, newspaper, Internet, and other interests. In wave after wave of corporate mergers, big companies are swallowed up by still bigger ones (Mizruchi, 1982, 1992). Google represents a startling example. Since 2001, it has acquired more than 150 companies and is currently acquiring new companies at a rate of one a week.

Interlocking directorates are formed when an individual sits on the board of directors of two or more non-competing companies.

Outright ownership of one company by a second company in another industry is only one way corporations may be linked. **Interlocking directorates** are another. Interlocking directorates are formed when an individual sits on the board of directors of two or more non-competing companies. (Antitrust laws prevent an individual from sitting on the board of directors of a competitor.) For instance, the board of directors of BCE includes, among others, members connected to Petro-Canada, WestJet, the Bank of Montreal, Telus, and Bombardier. Such interlocks enable corporations to exchange valuable information and form alliances for mutual benefit. They also create useful channels of communication to, and influence over, government since some board members of major corporations are likely to be former senior politicians (Marchak, 1991; Nawfal, 2011).

Of course, small businesses, defined as those with fewer than 100 employees, continue to exist. In Canada, about 70 percent of workers in the private sector work for small businesses (see Figure 13.8). Small firms, which are a critical feature of the Canadian economy, are particularly important in the service sector. However, compared with large firms, profits in small firms

FIGURE 13.8

Share of Total Private Employment by Size of Business, 2012

Source: Statistics Canada, Labour Force Survey, 2012, and calculations by Industry Canada. Retrieved February 18, 2014 (www.ic.gc.ca/eic/site/061.nsf/eng/02805.html).

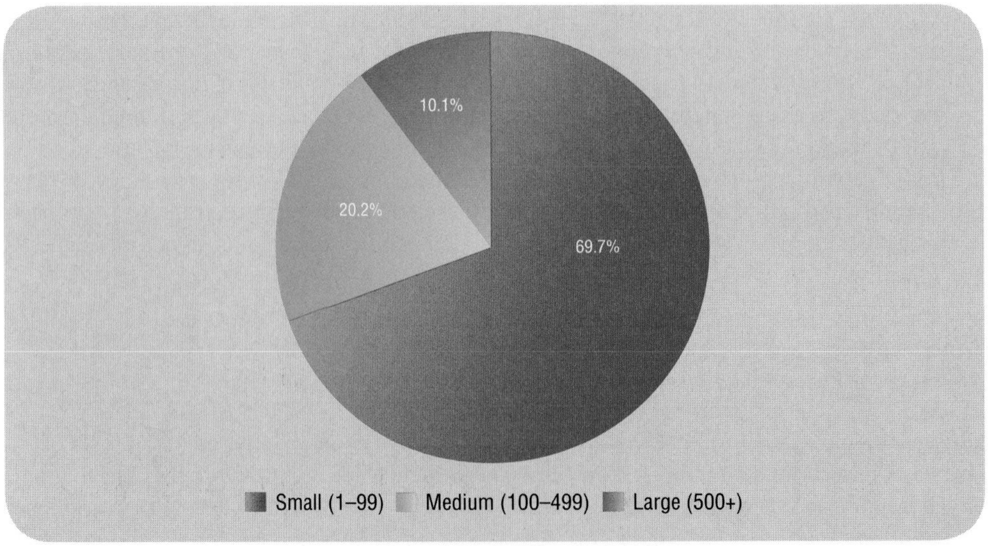

are typically low and bankruptcies are common. Small firms often use outdated production and marketing techniques. Jobs in small firms frequently have low wages and meagre benefits.

Some 10 percent of the Canadian labour force works in large corporations, defined as businesses with more than 500 employees. Among Canada's largest private sector employers is the Loblaw food chain, owned by George Weston Ltd., with more than 155 000 employees. Onex Corporation, a conglomerate, employs more than 238 000 Canadians in diverse firms that include interests in health care, hotels, gas stations, and insurance.

GLOBALIZATION

As noted earlier, since the early 1980s, Canada has been hit by wave after wave of corporate downsizing. Especially in older manufacturing industries, thousands of blue-collar workers and middle managers have lost their jobs. Periodically, unemployment has soared, and social problems, such as alcoholism and domestic violence, have become acute. Some people blame government for the plant shutdowns. They say taxes are so high, big corporations can no longer make decent profits. Others blame the unemployed people themselves. They say powerful unions drive up the hourly wage to the point where companies lose money.

Beginning in the 1980s, workers, governments, and corporations became involved as unequal players in the globalization of the world economy. Japan and Germany had fully recovered from the devastation of World War II. With these large and robust industrial economies now firing on all cylinders, American and Canadian-based multinationals were forced to cut costs and become more efficient to remain competitive. On a scale far larger than ever before, they began to build branch plants in low-wage countries, such as Mexico and China, to take advantage of cheap labour and low taxes. Multinational corporations based in Japan and other highly industrialized countries followed suit.

Although multinational corporations could easily move investment capital from one country to the next, workers were rooted in their communities, and governments were rooted in their nation-states. Multinationals thus had a big advantage over the other players in the globalization game. They could threaten to move their plants unless governments and workers made concessions. They could play one government off against another in the bidding war for new plants. And they could pick up and leave when it became clear that relocation would do wonders for their bottom line.

Today, nearly four decades after the globalization game began in earnest, the clear winners are the stockholders of multinational corporations whose profits have soared. The losers are blue-collar workers. To cite just one example, in the past two decades, General Motors has cut its workforce in Canada and the United States by about one-half in the face of stiff competition from automotive giants in Japan and Germany in particular.

Even while these cuts were being made, however, some large manufacturers were hiring. For instance, employment at Bombardier grew dramatically, and this Canadian-owned rail and aerospace firm is now a world leader. In the service sector, employment soared, as we have seen.

Globalization in the Less Developed Countries

It is still too soon to tell whether the governments and citizens of the less developed countries will be losers or winners in the globalization game. On the one hand, it is hard to argue with the assessment of the rural Indonesian woman interviewed by Diane Wolf. She prefers the regime of the factory to the tedium of village life. In the village, the woman worked from dawn till dusk doing household chores, taking care of siblings, and feeding the family goat. In the factory, she earns less than $1 a day sewing pockets on men's shirts in a hot factory. Yet because work in the factory is less arduous, pays something, and holds out the hope of even better work for future generations, the woman views it as nothing less than liberating (Wolf, 1992). Feeling much the same way are many workers in other regions of the world where branch plants of multinationals have sprung up in recent decades. A wage of $4 an hour is excellent pay in Mexico, and workers rush to fill jobs along Mexico's northern border with the United States.

Yet the picture is not all bright. The governments of developing countries attract branch plants by imposing few if any pollution controls on their operations, with dangerous consequences for the environment. Typically, fewer jobs are available than the number of workers who are drawn from the countryside to find work in the branch plants. The overabundance of people for the available jobs results in the growth of urban slums that suffer from high unemployment and unsanitary conditions. High-value components are often imported. Therefore, the branch plants create few good jobs involving design and technical expertise. Finally, some branch plants—particularly clothing and shoe factories in Asia—exploit children and women, requiring them to work long workdays at paltry wages and in unsafe conditions.

Companies such as Nike and the Gap have been widely criticized for conditions in their overseas sweatshops. Nike is the market leader in sports footwear. It has been at the forefront of moving production jobs overseas to such places as Indonesia. There, Nike factory workers make about 10 cents an hour, which is why labour costs account for only about 4 percent of the price of a pair of Nike shoes. Workdays in the factories stretch as long as 16 hours. Substandard air quality and excessive exposure to toxic chemicals are normal. An international campaign aimed at curbing Nike's labour practices has had only a modest impact (Nisen, 2013).

THE FUTURE OF WORK AND THE ECONOMY

Although work and the economy have changed enormously over the years, one thing has remained constant for centuries. Businesses have always looked for ways to cut costs and boost profits. Two of the most effective means they have adopted for accomplishing these goals involve introducing new technologies and organizing the workplace in more efficient ways. Much is uncertain about the future of work and the economy. However, it is a pretty safe bet that businesses will continue to follow these established practices.

Just how these practices will be implemented is less predictable. For example, it is possible to use technology and improved work organization to increase productivity by complementing the abilities of skilled workers. Worldwide, the automotive, aerospace, and computer industries have tended to adopt this approach. They have introduced automation and robots on a wide scale, while constantly upgrading the skills of their workers. And they have proven the benefits of small autonomous work groups for product quality, worker satisfaction, and therefore the bottom line. Conversely, new technology and more efficient work organization can be used to replace workers, deskill jobs, and employ low-cost labour—mainly women and minority group members—on a large scale. Women are entering the labour force at a faster rate than men are. Competition from low-wage industries abroad remains intense. Therefore, the second option is especially tempting in some industries.

Our analysis suggests that each of the scenarios described above will tend to predominate in different industries and labour markets. The pressure of competition will continue to prompt innovation and restructuring. However, we have also suggested that workplace struggles have no small bearing on how technologies are implemented and work is organized. To a degree, therefore, the future of work and the economy is up for grabs.

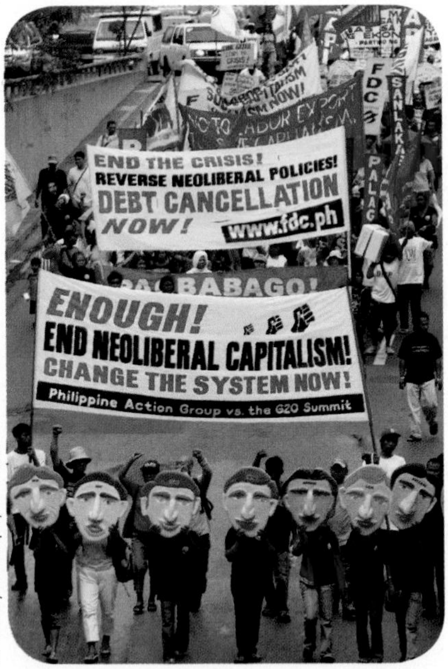

AP Photo/Pat Roque/CP Photo

Some people in the rich, industrialized countries oppose the globalization of commerce. Shown here are demonstrators marching in the streets of Toronto in 2010 as part of a protest against the G20 economic summit.

TIME FOR REVIEW

- What characteristics distinguish free markets from regulated markets?
- What features characterize each of the three main economic systems in the world?
- How do corporations disproportionately influence the economy and politics?
- How do multinational corporations maximize shareholder profits?

SUMMARY

1. How did the three work-related revolutions alter the organization of work and society as a whole?

The first work-related revolution began about 10 000 years ago when people established permanent settlements and started herding and farming. The second work-related revolution began about 240 years ago when various mechanical devices, such as the steam engine, greatly increased the ability of producers to supply markets. The third revolution in work is marked by growth in the provision of various services. It accelerated in the final decades of the twentieth century with the widespread use of the computer.

Each revolution in work increased productivity and the division of labour, caused a sectoral shift in employment, and made work relations more hierarchical. However, for the past three decades the degree of hierarchy has been lowered in some industries, resulting in productivity gains and more worker satisfaction.

2. What trends changed the nature of work in the last century?

Deskilling and the growth of part-time jobs were two of the main trends in the workplace in the last century. However, skilled labour has remained important in the economy. Good jobs have become more plentiful but the number of bad jobs is also growing rapidly. The result is a segmentation of the labour force into primary and secondary labour markets. Various social barriers limit mobility from the secondary to the primary labour market.

3. How do workers try to increase their control over their jobs?

Workers have resisted attempts by their bosses to deskill and control jobs. As a result, business has had to make concessions by giving workers more authority, both on the shop floor and in formulating overall business strategy. Such concessions have been biggest in countries where workers are more organized and powerful. Workers have also responded by forming unions and professional organization, which establish internal labour markets to control pay rates, hiring, and promotions and reduce competition with external labour supplies.

4. What are some of the consequences of the growth of large corporations and global markets?

Corporations are the dominant economic players in the world today. They exercise disproportionate economic and political influence by forming oligopolies, conglomerates, and interlocking directorates. Growing competition has led big corporations to cut costs by building branch plants in low-wage, low-tax countries. Stockholders have profited from this strategy. However, the benefits for workers in both the industrialized and the less developed countries have been mixed at best.

CHAPTER 14

POLITICS

IN THIS CHAPTER, YOU WILL LEARN TO

- Analyze the distribution of power in society and its consequences for political behaviour and public policy.
- Trace the influence of social structures and state institutions on politics.
- Describe the three waves of democratization that have swept the world in the past two centuries.
- Explain why some societies become highly democratic.
- Recognize that social inequality limits democracy even in the richest countries.
- See the association between changing state structures and changing patterns of warfare.

INTRODUCTION

Free Trade and Democracy

Just four days before what some people call the most important Canadian election of the twentieth century—the "free trade election" of 1988—the outcome seemed clear. A Gallup poll published on November 17 showed the Liberals with a commanding 43 percent of the popular vote. The Progressive Conservatives (PCs) trailed far behind at 31 percent. The New Democratic Party (NDP) stood at 22 percent.

However, just 100 hours before the first votes were cast, a little-known organization, the Canadian Alliance for Trade and Job Opportunities (CATJO), swung into high gear. With a campaign budget larger than that of the two opposition parties combined, CATJO funded a media blitz promoting the PCs and their free trade policies. A barrage of brochures, newspaper ads, and radio and television commercials supported the idea that Canadian prosperity depended on the removal of all taxes and impediments to trade between Canada and the United States. CATJO argued that if goods and services could be bought and sold across the border without hindrance, and capital invested without restraint, good jobs would proliferate and Canada's prosperity would be assured.

Before the media blitz, an Angus Reid poll disclosed that most Canadians disagreed with CATJO's rosy assessment: 54 percent opposed free trade and 35 percent supported it. A majority of Canadians sensed that free trade might open Canada to harmful competition with giant American companies, leading to job losses and deteriorating living standards. Yet the CATJO onslaught succeeded in overcoming some of these fears. Its media campaign hammered the pro-free-trade message into the minds of the Canadian public and drew attention away from the opposition. Then, on election day, the unexpected happened. The PCs won with 43 percent of the popular vote. A mere six weeks later, on January 1, 1989, the Canada–U.S. Free Trade Agreement was implemented. In October 1992, as shown in the photo on this page, officials initialled the North American Free Trade Agreement, bringing Mexico into the free trade zone established in 1989 by Canada and the United States. The agreement went into effect January 1, 1994.

Who backed CATJO? Its sole sponsor was the Business Council on National Issues (BCNI), an organization comprising the chief executive officers of 150 of Canada's leading corporations. These were people with a clear stake in free trade. Their companies stood to benefit from increased business activity between Canada and the United States and unrestricted freedom to invest wherever profits promised to be higher (Richardson, 1996).

George Bush Presidential Library

Mexican, American, and Canadian ministers initial NAFTA in October 1992.

The degree to which the Canadian people as a whole have benefited from free trade is a matter of ongoing debate.

The 1988 free trade election raises important political questions. Does the victory of the PCs illustrate the operation of government "of the people, by the people, for the people," as Abraham Lincoln defined democracy in his famous speech at Gettysburg in 1863? The election certainly allowed a diverse range of Canadians to express conflicting views. In the end, the people got the government they elected. This fact suggests that Lincoln's characterization of politics applied as well to Canada in 1988 as it did to the United States in 1863.

However, big business's access to a bulging war chest might lead us to doubt that Lincoln's definition applies. Few groups can act like CATJO and put together $18 million for a media campaign aimed at swaying the opinions of Canadians. Should we therefore conclude that (in the words of one wit) Canada is a case of government "of the people, by the lawyers, for the businessmen"?[1]

The free trade election of 1988 raises questions that lie at the heart of political sociology. What accounts for the degree to which a political system responds to the demands of all its citizens? As you will see, political sociologists have often answered this question by examining the effects of social structures, especially class structures, on politics. Although this approach contributes much to our understanding of political life, it is insufficient by itself. A fully adequate theory of democracy requires that we also examine how state institutions and laws affect political processes. We elaborate these points in the second section of this chapter.

From the mid-1970s until the early 1990s, a wave of competitive elections swept across many formerly non-democratic countries. Most dramatically, elections were held in the former Soviet Union at the end of this period. Western analysts were ecstatic. By the mid-1990s, however, it became clear that their optimism was naive. Often, the new regimes turned out to be feeble and limited democracies. As a result, political sociologists began to reconsider the social preconditions of democracy. We review of some of their work in this chapter's third section. We conclude that genuine democracy is not based solely on elections. In addition, for democracy to take root and grow, large classes of people must win legal protection of their rights and freedoms. This protection has not been secured in most of the world. Finally, in this chapter's fourth section, we discuss some of the ways in which people step outside the rules of normal electoral politics to change society. We focus on two types of "politics by other means": war and terrorism.

Some analysts believe that politics in the rich industrialized countries is less likely to be shaped by class inequality in the future. Our reading of the evidence is different. In concluding this chapter, we argue that persistent class inequality is the major barrier to the progress of democracy in countries such as Canada.

Before developing these themes, we define some key terms.

What Is Politics? Key Terms

Power is the ability to impose one's will on others.

Politics is a machine that helps to determine "who gets what, when, and how" (Lasswell, 1936). Power fuels the machine. **Power** is the ability to control others, even against their will (Weber, 1947: 152). Having more power than others do gives you the ability to get more valued things sooner. Having less power than others do means you get fewer valued things later. Political sociology's chief task is figuring out how power drives different types of political machines.

The use of power sometimes involves force. For example, one way of operating a system for distributing jobs, money, education, and other valued things is by throwing people who do not agree with the system in jail. In this case, people obey political rules because they are afraid to disobey. More often, people agree with the distribution system or at least accept it grudgingly. For instance, most people pay their taxes without much pressure from the Canada Revenue Agency. They pay their parking tickets without serving jail time. They recognize the right of their rulers to control the political machine. When most people basically agree with how the political machine is run, raw power becomes **authority**. Authority is legitimate, institutionalized power. Power is *legitimate* when people regard its use as morally correct or justified. Power is *institutionalized* when the norms and statuses of social organizations govern its use. These norms and statuses define how authority should be used, how individuals can achieve authority, and how much authority is attached to each status in the organization (see Box 14.1).

Authority is legitimate, institutionalized power.

BOX 14.1

SOCIOLOGY ON THE TUBE

GAME OF THRONES

"Someday you will sit on the throne and the truth will be what you make it... The world will be exactly as you want it to be." With these words, Queen Cersei Lannister informs her eldest son, Crown Prince Joffrey Baratheon, of a fundamental truth in the world of the Seven Kingdoms: might makes right (*Game of Thrones*, season 1, episode 3).

This idea pervades *Game of Thrones*. It often seems that no principle or higher authority guides political action. Instead, people, divided into clans, are driven only by murderous self-interest in their quest to control the Iron Throne. Every success is followed by the spinning of a story covering up or glorifying the actions of the winners and ignoring or speaking ill of the losers. When a boy discovers the Queen and her brother are involved in an incestuous relationship, the boy must be killed immediately to protect legitimate authority, and his fate must be called an accident. On a larger scale is the Red Wedding (*Game of Thrones*, season 3, episode 9).

The Starks secure the cooperation of the Freys in their bid to capture the Iron Throne. In exchange, the Freys demand that Robb Stark marry one of Lord Walder Frey's daughters so that both clans will be linked to the Throne by marriage. Robb Stark agrees but then breaks his promise.

Under the guise of forgiveness, Lord Walder Frey invites the Starks and their army to another wedding celebration in his castle. After much drinking and gaiety, Frey's soldiers, disguised as musicians, massacre key members of the Stark family. Tents hosting Stark soldiers are collapsed and set on fire.

Game of Thrones is based on a book that describe how, for their role in ending the rebellion, the Freys are granted many benefits and important positions. The authority of the Baratheons and the Lannisters is secured. Jared Frey invents a story blaming the Red Wedding massacre on the Starks. Truth becomes what the winners make it.

Significantly, however, something changes. The people of the Seven Kingdoms are angered and disgusted by the actions of the Freys, who have violated a sacred tradition guaranteeing the safety and security of all guests. And so we learn that the Seven Kingdoms are not in fact devoid of higher political principles.

The Kobal Collection at Art Resource, NY

Does might make right?

What is more, in the simmering negative reaction of the people of the Seven Kingdoms to the Frey massacre, we see that repression and violence have lasting effects that may sow the seeds of future rebellion against oppressive authority. We even begin to suspect that Abraham Lincoln may have had a point when he implored his audience to "have faith that right makes might, and in that faith, let us, to the end, dare to do our duty as we understand it."

Max Weber (1947) described three ideal bases on which authority can rest (while stressing that real-world cases often rest on varying mixes of the pure types):

1. **Traditional authority.** Particularly in tribal and feudal societies, rulers inherit authority through family or clan ties. The right of a family or a clan to monopolize leadership is widely believed to derive from the will of a god.
2. **Legal-rational authority.** In modern societies, authority derives from respect for the law. Laws specify how a person can achieve office. People generally believe these laws are rational. If someone achieves office by following these laws, his or her authority is respected.
3. **Charismatic authority.** Sometimes, extraordinary, charismatic individuals challenge traditional or legal-rational authority. They claim to be inspired by a god or some higher principle that transcends other forms of authority. One such principle is the idea that all people are created equal. Charismatic figures sometimes emerge during a **political revolution**, an attempt by many people to overthrow existing political institutions and establish new ones. Political revolutions take place when widespread and successful movements of opposition clash with crumbling traditional or legal-rational authority.

Traditional authority, the norm in tribal and feudal societies, involves rulers inheriting authority through family or clan ties. The right of a family or clan to monopolize leadership is widely believed to derive from the will of a god.

Legal-rational authority is typical of modern societies. It derives from respect for the law. Laws specify how a person can achieve office. People generally believe these laws are rational. If someone achieves office by following these laws, people respect his or her authority.

Charismatic authority is based on a belief in the claims of extraordinary individuals that they are inspired by a god or some higher principle.

A **political revolution** is the overthrow of political institutions by an opposition movement and its replacement by new institutions.

Politics takes place in all social settings—intimate face-to-face relationships, families, universities, and so on. However, political sociology is concerned with institutions that specialize in the exercise of power and authority. Taken together, these institutions form the **state**. The state comprises institutions that formulate and carry out a country's laws and public policies. In performing these functions, the state regulates citizens in **civil society**. Civil society is "made up of areas of social life—the domestic world, the economic sphere, cultural activities and political interaction—which are organized by private or voluntary arrangements between individuals and groups outside the direct control of the state" (Held, 1987: 281; see Figure 14.1).

In turn, citizens in civil society control the state to varying degrees. In an **authoritarian** state, citizen control is sharply restricted. In a **totalitarian** state, it is virtually nonexistent. In a **democracy**, citizens exert a relatively high degree of control over the state. They do this partly by choosing representatives in regular, competitive elections.

The **state** consists of the institutions responsible for formulating and carrying out a country's laws and public policies.

Civil society is the private sphere of social life.

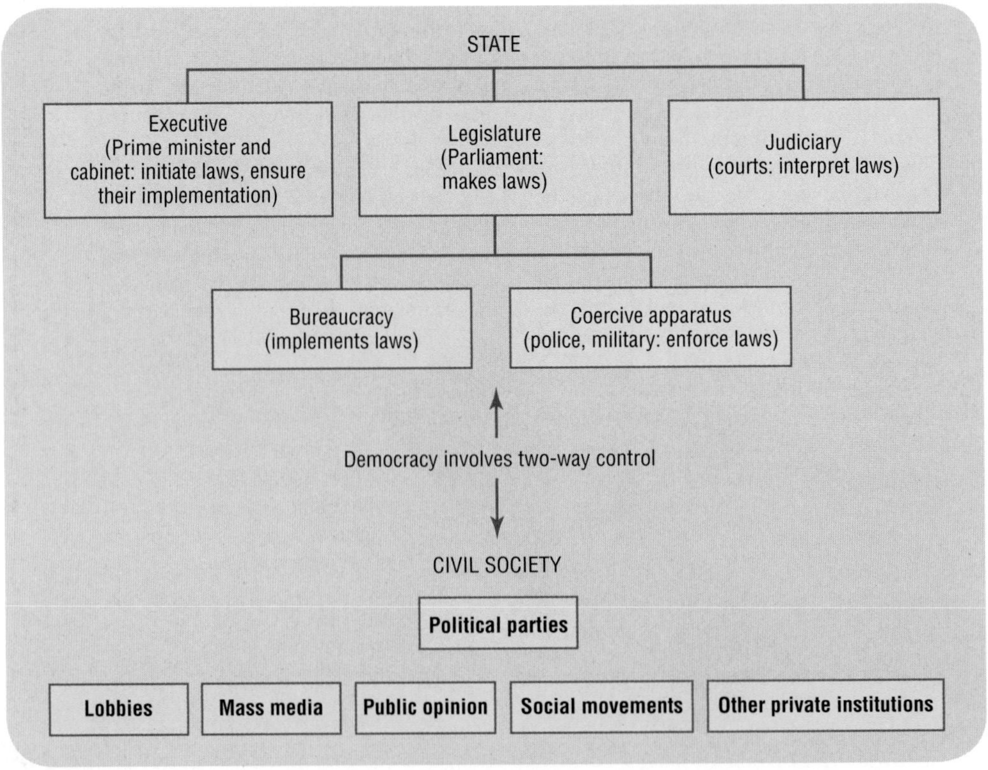

FIGURE 14.1
The Institutions of State and Civil Society

© hrstklnkr/istockphoto.com

SuperStock

© EdStock/istockphoto.com

The three faces of authority according to Weber: traditional authority (King Louis XIV of France, circa 1670), charismatic authority (Vladimir Lenin, Bolshevik leader of the Russian Revolution of 1917), and legal-rational authority (Stephen Harper in the 2008 Canadian federal election campaign).

In modern democracies, citizens do not control the state directly. They do so through a variety of organizations. **Political parties** compete for control of government in regular elections. They put forward policy alternatives and rally adult citizens to vote. **Lobbies** are formed by special interest groups, such as trade unions and business associations, which advise politicians about their members' desires. They also remind politicians of the value of their members' votes, organizing skills, and campaign contributions. The **mass media** keep a watchful and critical eye on the state. They keep the public informed about the quality of government. **Public opinion** refers to the values and attitudes of the adult population as a whole. It is expressed mainly in polls, emails, and letters to lawmakers, and it gives politicians an overview of citizen preferences. Finally, when dissatisfaction with normal politics is widespread, protest sometimes takes the form of **social movements**. A social movement is a collective attempt to change all or part of the political or social order. Social movements help to keep governments responsive to the wishes of the citizenry (Chapter 21, Collective Action and Social Movements).

Bearing these definitions in mind, we now consider the merits and limitations of various sociological theories of democracy.

Authoritarian states sharply restrict citizen control of the state.

In a **totalitarian** state, citizens lack almost any control of the state.

In a **democracy**, citizens exercise a high degree of control over the state. They do this mainly by choosing representatives in regular, competitive elections.

Political parties are organizations that compete for control of government. In the process, they give voice to policy alternatives and rally adult citizens to vote.

TIME FOR REVIEW

- What forms can the exercise of power take?
- How do political systems vary depending on the relationship between state and civil society?

THEORIES OF DEMOCRACY

Lobbies are organizations formed by special interest groups to advise and influence politicians.

The **mass media** are print, radio, television, and other communication technologies. In a democracy, the mass media help keep the public informed about the quality of government.

Public opinion refers to the values and attitudes of the adult population as a whole.

Social movements are collective attempts to change all or part of the political or social order by means of rioting, petitioning, striking, demonstrating, and establishing lobbies, unions, and political parties.

Pluralist theory holds that power is widely dispersed. As a result, no group enjoys disproportionate influence, and decisions are usually reached through negotiation and compromise.

Elite theory holds that small groups occupying the command posts of the most influential institutions make important decisions that profoundly affect all members of society. Moreover, they do so without much regard for elections or public opinion.

Elites are small groups that control the command posts of institutions.

A Functionalist Account: Pluralist Theory

In the early 1950s, New Haven, Connecticut, was a city of about 150 000 people. It had seen better times. As in many other American cities, post–World War II prosperity and new roads had allowed much of the white middle class to resettle in the suburbs, eroding the city's tax base. It also left much of the downtown to residents living in poverty and members of minority groups. Some parts of New Haven became slums.

Beginning in 1954, Mayor Richard Lee decided to do something about the city's decline. He planned to attract new investment, eliminate downtown slums, and stem the outflow of the white middle class. Urban renewal was a potentially divisive issue. However, according to research conducted at the time, key decisions were made in a highly democratic manner. The city government listened closely to all major groups. It adopted policies that reflected the diverse wants and interests of city residents.

The social scientists who studied New Haven politics in the 1950s followed **pluralist theory** (Dahl, 1961; Polsby, 1959). They argued that the city was highly democratic because power was widely dispersed. They showed that few of the most prestigious families in New Haven were economic leaders in the community. Moreover, neither economic leaders nor the social elite monopolized political decision making. Different groups of people decided various political issues. Some of these people had low status in the community. Moreover, power was more widely distributed than in earlier decades. The pluralists concluded that no single group exercised disproportionate power in New Haven.

The pluralists believed that politics worked much the same way in the United States as a whole and in other democracies, such as Canada. Democracies, they said, are heterogeneous societies with many competing interests and centres of power. No single power centre can dominate consistently. Sometimes one category of voters or one set of interest groups wins a political battle, sometimes another. Most often, however, politics involves negotiation and compromise between competing groups. Because no one group is always able to control the political agenda or the outcome of political conflicts, democracy is guaranteed, argued the pluralists.

Pluralists closely followed the functionalist script. They viewed the political system as an institution that helps society achieve its collective goals and interests, in the process integrating its members and keeping it in equilibrium (Parsons, 1963). Foreign to the pluralist mindset were the notions that different segments of society might have fundamentally opposing goals and interests, that some groups are consistently more powerful than others are, and that politics could be a disruptive endeavour that sometimes promotes disequilibrium and on occasion even tears a society apart.

Conflict Approaches I: Elite Theory

Followers of **elite theory** sharply disagreed with the pluralist perspective. They argued that groups with opposing goals and interests confront each other in the political arena, and that while conflict is not always overt, it is never far below the surface of political affairs. Moreover, powerful groups exercise far more control over political life than less powerful groups do.

Foremost among early elite theorists was C. Wright Mills (1956). Mills defined **elites** as small groups that occupy the command posts of a society's most influential institutions. In the United States, the country Mills analyzed, these institutions include the 200 to 300 biggest corporations, the executive branch of government, and the military. Mills wrote that the people (nearly all men) who control these institutions make important decisions that profoundly affect all members of society. Moreover, they do so without much regard for elections or public opinion.

Mills showed the connections among the corporate, state, and military elites. People move from one elite group to another during their careers. Their children intermarry. They maintain close social contacts. They tend to be recruited from upper-middle and upper classes.

Yet Mills denied that these connections turn the three elites into what Marx called a **ruling class**, a self-conscious and cohesive group of people, led by big corporate shareholders, who act to shore up capitalism. Mills insisted that the three elites are relatively independent of one another. They may see eye to eye on many issues, but each has its own sphere of influence; conflict among elite groups is frequent (Alford and Friedland, 1985: 199; Mills, 1956: 277).

A **ruling class** is a self-conscious, cohesive group of people in elite positions. They act to advance their common interests, and are typically led by corporate executives.

The Elitist Critique of Pluralism

Most political sociologists today question the pluralist account of democratic politics. They dispute pluralism's viewpoint because research has established the existence of large, persistent, wealth-based inequalities in political influence and political participation.

John Porter's *The Vertical Mosaic* (1965) was the first in a series of Canadian studies that demonstrate the weaknesses of pluralism and corroborate aspects of elite theory (Brym, 1989; Clement, 1975; Olsen, 1980). These studies show that a disproportionately large number of people in Canada's political and other elites come from upper-class and upper-middle-class families. For example, about 40 percent of Canadian prime ministers, premiers, and cabinet ministers were born into the richest 10 percent of families in the country (Olsen, 1980: 129). In their youth, members of Canada's elite are likely to have attended expensive private schools. As adults, they tend to marry the offspring of other elite members and belong to exclusive private clubs. In the course of their careers, they often move from one elite group to another. Arguably, people with this sort of background cannot act dispassionately on behalf of all Canadians, rich and poor. Controversy persists over whether Canada's elites form a ruling class. Porter (1965), noting frequent conflict among elites, argued against the view that a ruling class controls Canada. Some of his students disagreed. They argued that the interests of large corporations dominate Canadian political life (Clement, 1975; Olsen, 1980). However, both Porter and his students did agree on one point: Contrary to pluralist claims, well-to-do Canadians consistently exercise disproportionate influence over political life in this country.

Studies of political participation in Canada add weight to the elitist view. Many surveys show that political involvement and social class are positively correlated (see Figure 14.2;

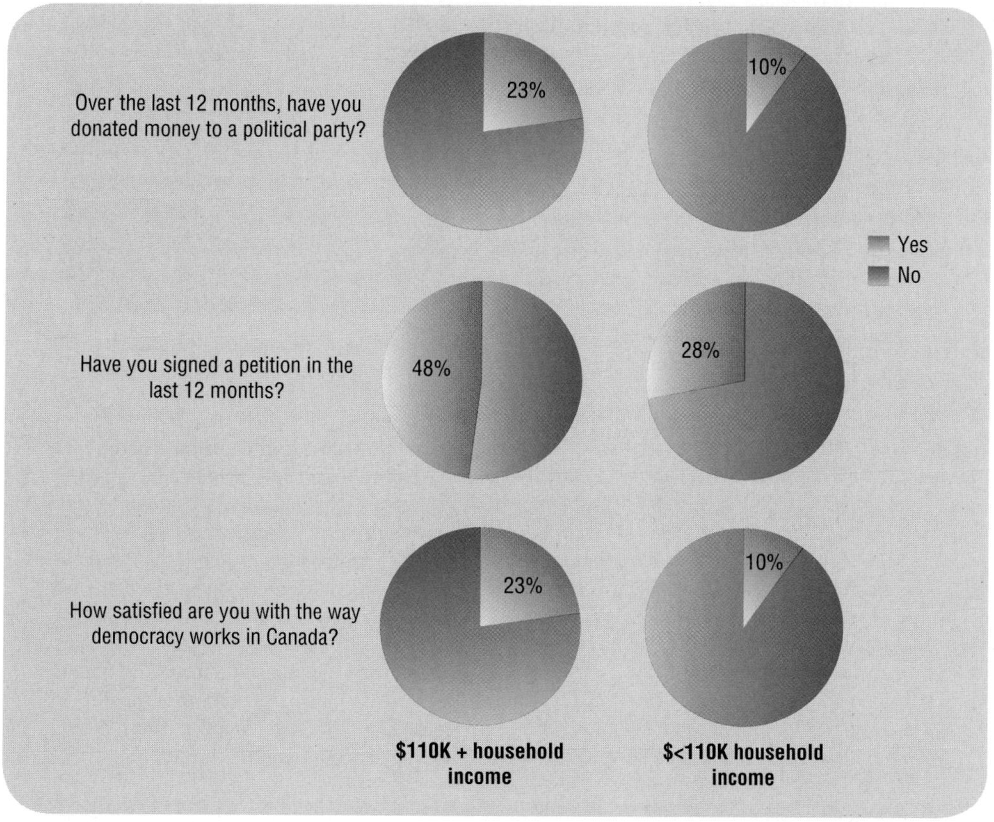

FIGURE 14.2
Class Differences in Political Participation and Satisfaction, Canada, 2011

Source: Compiled from Fournier, Patrick, Fred Cutler, Stuart Soroka, and Dietlind Stolle. 2011. The 2011 Canadian Election Study. [dataset] http://ces-eec.org/pagesE/surveys.html (retrieved August 14, 2013).

also Box 14.2). For example, the likelihood of voting depends on a person's class position. As we move down the class hierarchy, we see a steep decline in the likelihood of phoning—or writing—a member of Parliament, helping a candidate in an election campaign, contributing money to a political party, or running for office. As the intensity of political participation declines, so does political influence (Eagles, 1993). Consequently, although political apathy and cynicism are high among Canadians, the poorest Canadians are the most politically apathetic and cynical (see Box 14.3). They have less interest in politics than do well-to-do

BOX 14.2

IT'S YOUR CHOICE

INCREASING THE PARTICIPATION OF WOMEN IN CANADIAN POLITICS

Just as political participation decreases with social class, so it varies by gender. On the whole, women are less politically active than men are. The gender gap in political participation is due to sociological and historical factors. In recent years, the gender gap has been reduced by political pressure and resulting public policy innovations. It can be further reduced by the same means.

By demonstrating, petitioning, and gaining the support of influential liberal-minded men, Canadian women won the right to vote federally in 1917 and in Yukon and all provinces except Québec by 1925. Québec fell into line in 1940 and the Northwest Territories in 1951. Some women have since been elected to Parliament and to provincial and territorial legislatures. As of 2011, women represented 24.6 percent of federal members of Parliament and provincial or territorial members of legislative assemblies. However, critics emphasize that this level was reached in the late 1990s and then more or less stabilized. Over that same period, fewer women than men were put forward as candidates by their parties. Many fewer women were appointed to cabinet positions. And only once, between June and October 1993 did Canada have a female prime minister (Kim Campbell). As these facts suggest, the more influential the type of political activity, the fewer women we find (Bashevkin, 1993; Equal Voice, 2005).

Active involvement in political life, especially running for office, requires time and money. Women are disadvantaged in this regard. As you saw in Chapter 11, Sexualities and Gender Stratification, women have, on average, lower socioeconomic status than men do. Women are also saddled with more domestic responsibilities than men are. These factors prevent many women from running for office. In addition, political parties influence the nomination of candidates for elected office and thus help determine where women run. Most parties tend to assign female candidates to ridings where their chances of winning are low (Brodie, 1991).

CP Picture Archive/Tom Hanson

Kim Campbell, Canada's only female prime minister, June to October 1993

Public policy analysts note that female political participation would likely increase if these barriers were removed (Boyd, 2001; Brodie, 1991). For example, laws could be passed that would allow candidates to take unpaid leave from their jobs to contest nominations and elections, set spending limits for nomination and election campaigns, make contributions for nomination campaigns tax-deductible, treat child-care and housekeeping costs as reimbursable campaign expenses, and so on. Additionally, laws could be enacted that make government subsidies to political party campaigns dependent on the proportion of their elected candidates that are women. In such a system, party subsidies would increase with the proportion of women elected, thus creating a powerful disincentive for parties to place most female candidates in ridings where they are likely to lose. The means to increase the participation of women in politics are available. Whether these means are implemented is your choice.

BOX 14.3

SOCIOLOGY AT THE MOVIES

THE IDES OF MARCH

Mike Morris (George Clooney) is campaigning for the presidency of the United States. He is a secularist and an environmentalist. He opposes war and favours job creation by government. He is charming and handsome. His decades-long marriage is apparently rock-solid. He is backstopped by a talented and devoted staff.

All is idealism, brains, and beauty until Morris's campaign staffer, Stephen Meyers (Ryan Gosling) takes two fateful steps. First, he sleeps with intern Molly Stearn (Evan Rachel Wood) and discovers that Stearn is pregnant after having had an affair with Morris. Second, Meyers meets with the campaign manager of Morris's opponent in the presidential race, who tries to convince Meyers to switch sides. When Morris's campaign manager, Paul Zara (Philip Seymour Hoffman) finds out about the meeting, he fires Meyers. But in the end, Meyers blackmails Morris with his knowledge of the affair. He forces Morris to give him Zara's job.

The movie's clear message is that many cynical, self-serving, and corrupt politicians and advisers slither underneath the apparent idealism, brains, and beauty of political life. This will be news only to viewers living on remote desert islands lacking print and electronic media. In recent years, sex scandals involving presidents, prime ministers, and other high public officials have come to light in the United States, the United Kingdom, Italy, France, Israel, Canada, and elsewhere. Indeed, what was initially surprising about the 2013 spectacle of Canadian senators padding their expense accounts with hundreds of thousands of dollars in false travel and housing claims was less the evidence of corruption than the Canadian public's muted reaction to the revelations. Yet, on reflection, given the way many politicians behave, is it any wonder that many citizens of Canada and other Western democracies are apathetic and cynical about mainstream politics?

The Kobal Collection at Art Resource, NY

Political corruption breeds public cynicism.

citizens, and they are more likely to think that government does not care what they think. As one of the twentieth century's leading political sociologists wrote, "The combination of a low vote and a relative lack of organization among the lower-status groups means that they will suffer from neglect by the politicians who will be receptive to the wishes of the more privileged, participating, and organized strata" (Lipset, 1981: 226–27).

Conflict Approaches II: Marxist Rejoinders to Elite Theory

Although elite theory is compelling in some respects, it has its critics, Marxists foremost among them. One group of Marxists, known as "instrumentalists," denies that elites enjoy more or less equal power. Actually, they say, elites form a ruling class dominated by big business. From their point of view, the state is an arm (or "instrument") of the business elite. Big business gains control of the state in three main ways. First, members of wealthy families occupy important state positions in highly disproportionate numbers. Second, government officials rely mainly on the representatives of big business for advice. Third, political parties rely mainly on big business for financial support. According to some Marxists, members of different elites may disagree about specific issues. However, because of the three control mechanisms just listed, they always agree about one issue: the need to maintain the health of the capitalist system (Miliband, 1973 [1969]).

A second group of Marxists, known as "structuralists," offers an alternative interpretation of why the state in capitalist society is necessarily biased in favour of big business. For structuralists, it is not so much the *social origins* of high government officials or the *social ties* linking them with big business that encourages the state to act with a pro-capitalist bias. Rather, the capitalist state acts as an arm of big business because it is constrained to do so by *the nature of the capitalist system itself.* For example, if Canadian government officials take actions that deeply damage capitalist interests, investment would be redirected to countries with regimes that are kinder to company profits. Such a move would cost Canada jobs and prosperity. It would be highly unpopular. The government could easily fall. Fearing this outcome, governments in capitalist societies find their field of action restricted to policies that ensure the well-being of big business. According to structuralists, it is the very fact that the state is embedded in a capitalist system that forces it to act in this way (Poulantzas, 1975 [1968]).

It follows from both the instrumentalist and the structuralist positions that ordinary citizens, especially members of the working class, rarely have much influence over state policy. According to Marxists, true democracy can emerge only if members of the working class and their supporters overthrow capitalism and establish a socialist system (see Chapter 13, Work and the Economy).

Conflict Approaches III: Power Resource Theory

Both Marxist and elite theories leave big questions unanswered. For one thing, they pay little attention to how political parties lose office while other political parties get elected. Nor are they much concerned with the effect of one party or another on public policy. In fact, for Marxist and elite theorists, elections are little more than sideshows. They believe that elites or a ruling class always control society, regardless of election outcomes. Therefore, they contend, the victory of one party over another does not deserve much sociological attention because it does not substantially affect the lives of ordinary men and women.

In contrast, many political sociologists today think it matters a great deal which party is in office. After all, the lives of ordinary men and women are hugely affected by whether the governing party supports or opposes free trade, weaker environmental standards, less publicly funded medical care, bigger government subsidies for child care, abortion on demand, and so forth. Elite theorists are correct to claim that power is concentrated disproportionately in the hands of the well-to-do, but we still need a theory that accounts for the successes and failures of different parties and policies in different times and places. For these purposes, **power resource theory** is helpful. It focuses on how *variations* in the distribution of power affect the fortunes of parties and policies over the long term.

Power resource theory holds that the distribution of power among major classes partly accounts for the successes and failures of different political parties over the long term.

To understand power resource theory, first consider your own party preference. For many reasons, you may support one political party over another. Your family may have a long tradition of voting for one party. You may have never really questioned this support. Maybe you support a party because you admire the energy, integrity, or track record of its leader. Or you might support a party because you agree with its policies on a range of issues. What factors lead *you* to prefer one party over another?

If a party's policies influence your vote, you are like many Canadians. In fact, Canadian voters cluster in two main policy groups. Voters on the *left* promote extensive government involvement in the economy. Among other things, they favour a strong "social safety net" of health and welfare benefits to help the less fortunate members of society. As a result, left-wing policies often lead to less economic inequality. In contrast, voters on the *right* favour a reduced role for government in the economy. They want to see a smaller welfare state and emphasize the importance of individual initiative in promoting economic growth. Economic issues aside, leftists and rightists also tend to differ on social or moral issues. Leftists tend to support equal rights for women and racial and sexual minorities. Rightists tend to support more traditional social and moral values.

Figure 14.3 shows one indicator of how left and right sentiments translated into support for Canada's four main political parties in 2011. Using data from the most recent Canadian Election Survey, we first found, for supporters of each party, the percentage of people who favour corporate tax cuts. This viewpoint is one indicator of the percentage of people on the right. We then found the percentage of people who support more federal spending on welfare. This viewpoint is one indicator of the percentage of people on the left. Finally,

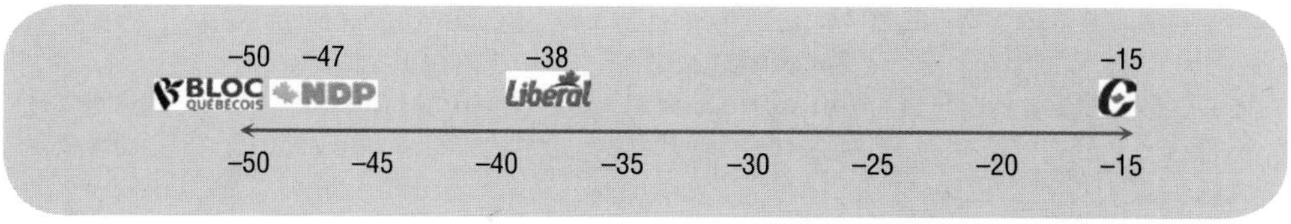

FIGURE 14.3
Left Versus Right, Canadian Federal Parties, 2011

Source: Fournier, Patrick, Fred Cutler, Stuart Soroka, and Dietlind Stolle. 2011. The 2011 Canadian Election Study. [dataset] http://ces-eec.org/pagesE/surveys.html (retrieved August 14, 2013).

we subtracted the percentage on the left from the percentage on the right. This difference is what we call the "left–right index." The higher the value of the left-right index, the more right-wing a party is. Clearly, big differences separate Canada's main political parties. Supporters of the Conservatives are farthest to the right. Supporters of the Liberals are closest to the middle of the Canadian political spectrum. The New Democrats and the Bloc Québécois are furthest to the left. Do you think of yourself as a supporter of one of these parties? Is your choice related to its policies?

The policies favoured by different parties have diverse effects on different categories of people. Therefore, different parties tend to be supported by different classes, regions, religious communities, races, and other groups. Do you think the policies of your preferred party favour the class, region, religious group, or race to which you belong? If so, how? If not, why not?

In most Western democracies, one of the main factors distinguishing political parties is differences in *class* support (Korpi, 1983: 35; Lipset and Rokkan, 1967; Manza, Hout, and Brooks, 1995). However, the tendency for people in different classes to vote for different parties varies from one country to the next. In Canada, the tendency is relatively weak.

The strength of the tendency for people in different classes to vote for different parties depends on many factors. One of the most important factors is the extent to which classes are socially organized or cohesive (Brym with Fox, 1989: 57–91; Brym, Gillespie, and Lenton, 1989). For example, an upper class that can create such organizations as the Business Council on National Issues and CATJO, which supported the PCs so effectively in the 1988 free trade election, is more powerful than an upper class that cannot take such action. If an upper class makes such efforts, while a working class fails to organize itself, right-wing candidates have a better chance of winning office. Conservative policies are more likely to become law. Similarly, a working class that can unionize many workers is more powerful than one with few unionized workers. That is because unions often collect money for the party that is more sympathetic to union interests. Unions also lobby on behalf of their members and try to convince their members to vote for the pro-union party. If workers become more unionized, while an upper class fails to organize itself, then left-wing candidates have an improved chance of winning office. In this situation, policies that favour lower classes are more likely to become law. This is the main insight of power resource theory. *Organization is a source of power. Change in the distribution of power between major classes partly accounts for the fortunes of different political parties and different laws and policies* (Esping-Andersen, 1990; Korpi, 1983; O'Connor and Olsen, 1998; Shalev, 1983).

You can see how power resource theory works by looking at Table 14.1, which divides 18 industrialized democracies in the three decades after World War II into three groups. In group one are countries like Sweden, where democratic socialist parties usually controlled government. (Democratic socialist parties are at least as left wing as the NDP in Canada.) In group two are countries like Australia, where democratic socialist parties sometimes controlled, or shared in control of, government. In group three are countries like Canada, where democratic socialist parties rarely or never shared in control of government. The group averages in column one show that democratic socialist parties are generally more successful in countries where more workers are unionized. The group averages in columns two and three show more economic inequality exists in countries that are weakly unionized and have no democratic socialist governments. In other words, by means of taxes and social policies, democratic socialist governments ensure that people

TABLE 14.1
Some Consequences of Working-Class Power in 18 Rich Industrialized Countries, 1946–1976

	Percentage of Non-agricultural Workforce Unionized	Percentage of Total Percentage Poor National Income to Top 10% of Earners	Percentage Poor
Mainly democratic socialist countries (Sweden, Norway)	68.5	21.8	4.3
Partly democratic socialist countries (Austria, Australia, Denmark, Belgium, UK, New Zealand, Finland)	46.6	23.6	7.8
Mainly non-democratic-socialist countries (Ireland, West Germany, Netherlands, USA, Japan, Canada, France, Italy, Switzerland)	28.0	28.3	10.8

Note: "Percentage Poor" is the average percentage of the population living in relative poverty according to OECD standards, with the poverty line standardized according to household size.

Source: Korpi, 1983: 40, 196.

CP Picture Archive/Michel Euler

In the 2002 election for the French presidency, right-wing candidate Jean-Marie Le Pen placed second. Le Pen's anti-immigrant campaign highlighted the degree to which political cleavages in France are based not just on class but also on race. (A 2014 poll showed that Le Pen's daughter, Marine, would win the French presidency if an election were held on the day of the poll.)

who are rich earn a smaller percentage of national income and people who are poor form a smaller percentage of the population. Studies of pensions, medical care, and other state benefits in the rich industrialized democracies reach similar conclusions. In general, where working classes are more organized and powerful, disadvantaged people are economically better off (Lindert, 2004; Myles 1989; O'Connor and Brym, 1988; Olsen and Brym, 1996).

Class is not the only factor that distinguishes political parties. Historically, *religion* has also been an important basis of party differences. For example, in Western European countries with large Catholic populations, such as Switzerland and Belgium, political parties differ partly on the basis of the religious affiliation of their supporters. In recent decades, *ethnicity and race* have become cleavage factors of major and growing importance in some countries. For example, in the United States, African Americans have overwhelmingly supported the Democratic Party since the 1960s (Brooks and Manza, 1997). Ethnicity has become an increasingly important division in French politics because of heavy Arab immigration from Algeria, Morocco, and Tunisia since the 1950s and growing anti-immigration sentiment among a substantial minority of whites (Veugelers, 1997). *Regional* groups distinguish parties in other countries, such as Canada, where some parties have been particularly attractive to Westerners, others to Québécois. Power resource theory focuses mainly on how the shifting distribution of power between working and upper classes affects electoral success. However, we can also use the theory to analyze the electoral fortunes of parties that attract different religious groups, races, regional groups, and so on.

Conflict Approaches IV: State-Centred Theory

Democratic politics is a contest among various class, racial, ethnic, religious, and regional groups to control the state for their own advantage. When power is substantially redistributed because of such factors as change in the cohesiveness of these social groups, old ruling parties usually fall and new ones take office.

Note, however, that a winner-take-all strategy would be nothing short of foolish. If winning parties passed laws that benefited only their supporters, they might cause mass outrage and even violent opposition. And it would be bad politics to allow opponents to become angry, organized, and resolute. After all, winners want more than just a moment of glory. They want to be able to enjoy the spoils of office over the long haul. To achieve stability, they must give people who lose elections a voice in government. That way, even determined opponents are likely to recognize the government's legitimacy. Pluralists thus make a good point when they say that democratic politics is about accommodation and compromise. They lose sight only of how accommodation and compromise typically give more advantages to some rather than others, as stressed by both elite theorists and power resource theorists.

There is, however, more to the story of politics than conflict between classes, religious groups, regions, and so forth. Theda Skocpol and others who follow **state-centred theory** show how the state itself can structure political life (Block, 1979; Evans, Rueschemeyer, and Skocpol, 1985; Skocpol, 1979). They regard senior elected officials and state bureaucrats not as agents of economic elites but as major political players in their own right. Moreover, they hold that major political struggles become embodied in the very structure of states. That is, historically important political battles typically end with the passage of new laws and the creation of new political institutions. These laws and institutions go on to influence political life until political conflict becomes serious enough to alter them once again. Until then, the state influences political life *to some degree independently of day-to-day political conflict and the distribution of power at a given time.* This argument is a valuable supplement to power resource theory (see Table 14.2).

State-centred theory holds that the state itself can structure political life, to some degree, independently of the way power is distributed between classes and other groups at a given time.

To illustrate state-centred theory, recall first that all societies are divided into classes, religious groups, regions, and so on. In principle, any one or a combination of these social divisions may be reflected in the policies of different political parties and the social characteristics of party supporters. For example, in some societies, politics is mostly about the attempts of different *classes* to control the state for their own advantage; in other societies, politics is more about the attempts of different *regions* to control the state for their own advantage; and so forth. What then determines which social division—class, region, or another factor—will predominate in political life? State-centred theory provides useful insights into this issue. According to state-centred theory, the state may be organized in such a way as to bias politics toward one social division or another.

Consider Canada. We saw above that different Canadian political parties tend to attract people from different social classes. However, that tendency is weak. Compared with most other democracies, class differences among parties are small in Canada. In contrast, regional differences are comparatively large (Butovsky, 2001; Gidengil, 1992). These large regional differences are evident, for example, in the results of the 2011 federal election (see Figure 14.4).

TABLE 14.2
Five Sociological Theories of Capitalist Democracy Compared

	Pluralist	**Elite**	**Marxist**	**Power-Resource**	**State-Centred**
How is power distributed?	Dispersed	Concentrated	Concentrated	Concentrated	Concentrated
Who are the main power holders?	Various groups	Elites	Ruling class	Upper class	State officials
On what is their power based?	Holding political office	Controlling major institutions	Owning substantial capital	Owning substantial capital	Holding political office
What is the main basis of public policy?	The will of all citizens	The interests of major elites	Capitalist interests	The balance of power among classes, etc.	The influence of state structures
Do lower classes have much influence on politics?	Yes	No	Rarely	Sometimes	Sometimes

FIGURE 14.4
Results of 2011 Canadian Federal Election

Source: Elections Canada. 2011. "Official Voting Results: Forty-First General Election 2011." www.elections.ca/scripts/ovr2011/default.html (retrieved September 6, 2011).

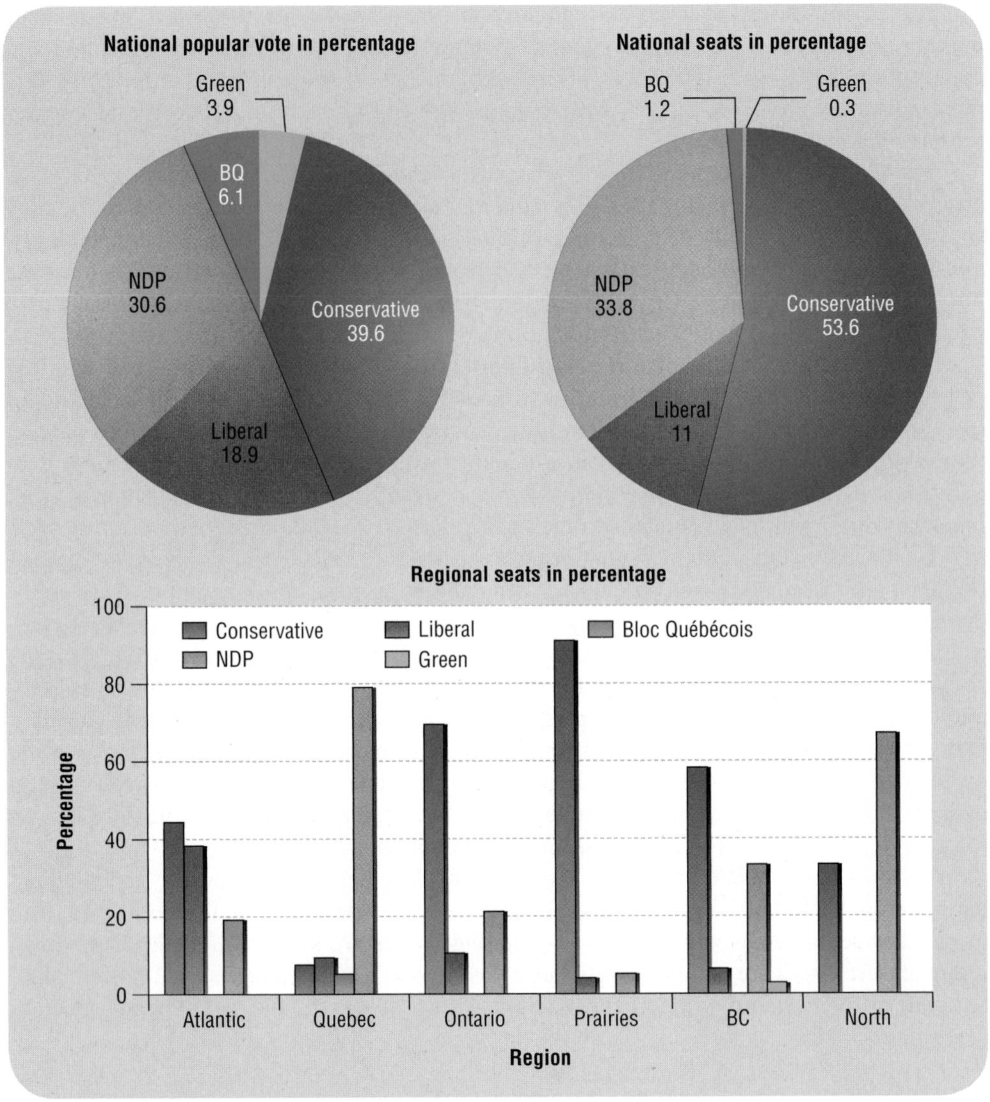

The Bloc Québécois was the most popular federal political party in Québec from the time it first ran federally (1993) until 2011. Although Québec voters have twice rejected referenda calling for sovereignty, most Bloc supporters favour holding a third referendum in the hope of achieving the separation Québec from Canada. In the 2011 federal election, the province swung wildly toward the NDP. Although the NDP is not in favour of sovereignty for Québec, the party supports more autonomy for Québec than the Conservatives and the Liberals do.

The Conservative Party grew from a merger between the Conservative Alliance, which was almost entirely limited to the West, and the remnants of the Progressive Conservatives, mainly from Ontario eastward. The former Conservative Alliance members retain a strong belief that the central government neglects Western interests; some MPs have even advocated separation from Canada as the ultimate remedy. In the 2011 election, the Conservatives made big gains in Ontario, but they still have their strongest support in the Prairies.

What produces such a strong regional bias (and a correspondingly weak class bias) in Canadian political life? The answer lies in the history of Canadian politics and, in particular, in the way that history has structured the laws and policies of the Canadian state. In other words, the explanation for the regional bias of Canadian politics is state-centred.

Before Confederation in 1867, the British North American colonies enjoyed few unifying ties. Vast geographical barriers separated them. No railway or telegraph line linked them all. Lower Canada (now Québec) had become part of British North America by military conquest just a century earlier. It was divided from the other colonies by religion (Catholic versus Protestant), ethnicity (French versus English), and lingering resentment.

Despite these divisions, British North American businessmen tried to forge a union among the colonies in the mid-1860s. They did so because they faced a big problem that only unification could solve: the loss of their export markets. The British were dismantling the protected market known as the British Empire. The Americans had turned against free trade. To make matters worse, the British North American colonies had accumulated a crippling debt load by borrowing to help finance railroad construction, while certain elements in the United States were threatening to expand the border of their country northward. In this context, the business and political leaders of British North America regarded Confederation as a means of creating a new market and an expanded tax base by encouraging mass immigration and promoting economic growth.

However, to unify the British North American colonies, the Fathers of Confederation needed to be careful. For one thing, they needed to avoid consulting ordinary citizens for fear of having their plan rejected. They knew the colonies had little in common and that most ordinary citizens had no interest in union (Ryerson, 1973: 355).

The Fathers of Confederation also found it necessary to draft a founding document, the British North America (BNA) Act, which played down the deep divisions between the British North American colonies. Most important, the BNA Act left ambiguous the question of how power would be distributed between federal and provincial governments. This vagueness enabled the Fathers of Confederation to form their union, but it also left the door open to the bickering and bargaining that has characterized federal–provincial/territorial relations ever since 1867. Especially after World War II, the BNA Act (and later the Canadian Constitution) allowed power to continue to drift from the federal to the provincial and territorial governments and thus entrenched regionalism in Canadian political life.

A landmark in the decentralization and regionalization of Canadian politics was reached in 1959. In that year, Québec and the federal government agreed that a provincial or territorial government not wanting to participate in a federal program could receive federal funds to set up its own parallel program. Thereafter, the provincial and territorial right to opt out of federal programs was widely used not just Québec but also by the other provinces and territories, which insisted on having the same rights as Québec (Bélanger, 2000). Power continued to decentralize and regionalize as the provinces gained more control over taxation, resource revenues, immigration policy, language use, and so on. Canada was a deeply regionally divided society from the start, and the state—through the country's basic laws and policies—entrenched regional divisions. The result was a country in which politics is defined less as a struggle between classes than as a struggle between regions (Brym, 1992). Said differently, from the perspective of state-centred theory, class conflict is given less voice than is regional conflict in Canada because of the way the state structures politics.

TIME FOR REVIEW

- What are the main claims of the pluralist theory of politics?
- What are the main claims of the elite theory of politics?
- What are the main claims of the Marxist theory of politics?
- What are the main claims of the power resource theory of politics?
- What are the main claims of the state-centred theory of politics?

THE FUTURE OF DEMOCRACY

Two Cheers for Russian Democracy

In the winter of 1989, the Institute of Sociology of the Russian Academy of Science invited Robert Brym and nine other Canadian sociologists to attend a series of seminars in Moscow. The seminars were designed to acquaint some leading sociologists in the Soviet Union with Western sociology. The weather was frigid, but the country was in the midst of a great thaw. Totalitarianism was melting, leaving democracy in its place. Soviet sociologists had never been free to read and research what they wanted, and they were eager to learn from North American and European scholars (Brym, 1990).

"Or at least so it seemed," says Robert. "One evening about a dozen of us were sitting around comparing the merits of Canadian whisky and Russian vodka. Soon, conversation turned from Crown Royal versus Moskovskaya to Russian politics. 'You must be so excited about what's happening here,' I said to my Russian hosts. 'How long do you think it will be before Russia will have multi-party elections? Do you think Russia will become a liberal democracy like Canada, or a socialist democracy like Sweden?'

"One white-haired Russian sociologist slowly rose to his feet. His colleagues privately called him 'the dinosaur.' It soon became clear why. '*Nikogda*,' he said calmly and deliberately—'never.' '*Nikogda*,' he repeated, his voice rising sharply in pitch, volume, and emphasis. Then, for a full minute he explained that capitalism and democracy were never part of Russia's history, nor could they be expected to take root in Russian soil. 'The Russian people,' he proclaimed, 'do not want a free capitalist society. We know *freedom* means the powerful are free to compete unfairly against the powerless, exploit them, and create social inequality.'

Although luxury businesses like Versace do brisk business in Moscow, the streets are filled with homeless people. That is because the richest 10 percent of Russians earn 15 times as much as the poorest 10 percent, making Russia one of the most inegalitarian countries in the world.

ALEXANDER MEMENOV/AFP/Getty Images

"Everyone else in the room disagreed with the dinosaur's speech, in whole or in part. However, not wanting to cause any more upset, we turned the conversation back to lighter topics. After 15 minutes, someone reminded the others that we had to rise early for the next day's seminars. The evening ended, its great questions unanswered."

Today, the great questions of Russian politics remain unanswered. And it now seems there was some truth in the dinosaur's speech after all. Russia first held multi-party elections in 1991. Surveys found that most Russians favoured democracy over other types of rule. However, support for democracy soon fell because the economy collapsed and the poverty rate jumped (Gerber and Hout, 1998; see Chapter 13, Work and the Economy).

Democratic sentiment weakened as economic conditions worsened (Whitefield and Evans, 1994). In elections held in the mid-1990s, support for democratic parties plunged as support for communist and extreme right-wing nationalist parties surged (Brym, 1995, 1996). National surveys find that as many as 97 percent of the citizens of some countries view democracy as the ideal form of government. In Russia, the figure was just 51 percent (Klingemann, 1999). Democracy allowed a few Russians to enrich themselves at the expense of most others. Therefore, many citizens equated democracy not with freedom but with economic distress.

Russia's political institutions reflect the weakness of Russian democracy. Power is concentrated in the presidency to a much greater degree than in the United States. The Russian Parliament and the judiciary do not act as checks on executive power. Only a small number of Russians belong to political parties. Voting levels are low. National television stations are tightly state-controlled. Minority ethnic groups (especially Muslims from the Caucasus) are sometimes treated arbitrarily and cruelly. Clearly, Russian democracy has a long way to go before it can be considered on par with democracy in the West.

The limited success of Russian democracy raises an important question. What social conditions must exist for a country to become fully democratic? We turn to this question next. To gain perspective, we first consider the three waves of democratization that have swept the world since 1828 (Huntington, 1991: 13–26; see Figure 14.5).

The Three Waves of Democracy

The first wave of democratization began when more than half the white adult males in the United States became eligible to vote in the 1828 presidential election. By 1926, 33 countries enjoyed at least minimally democratic institutions: the United States, most countries in Western Europe, the British dominions (Australia, Canada, and New Zealand), Japan, and four Latin American countries (Argentina, Colombia, Chile, and Uruguay). However, a democratic reversal occurred between 1922 and 1942. During that period, fascist,

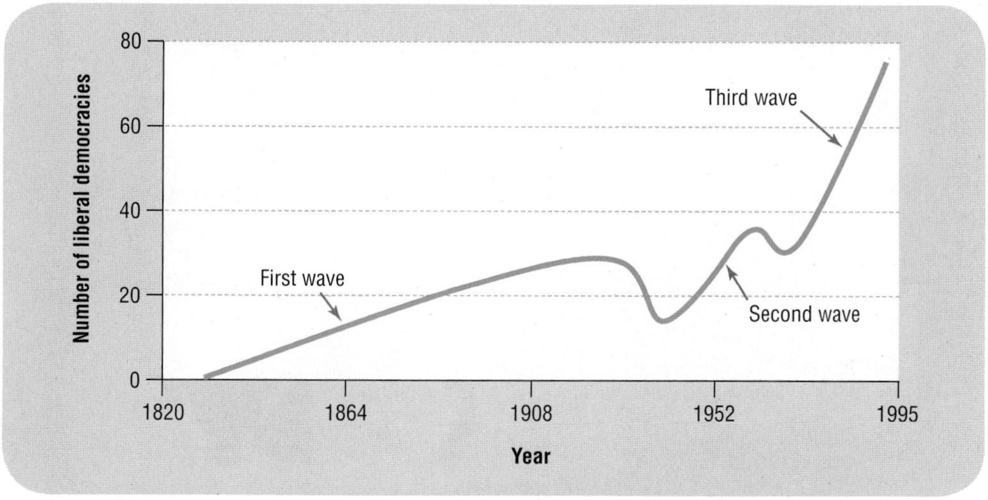

FIGURE 14.5
The Three Waves of Democratization, 1828–1995

Sources: Diamond, 1996: 28; Huntington, 1991: 26.

communist, and militaristic movements caused two-thirds of the world's democracies to fall under authoritarian or totalitarian rule.

The second wave of democratization swept across a large part of the world between 1943 and 1962. The Allied victory in World War II returned democracy to many of the defeated powers, including West Germany and Japan. The end of colonial rule brought democracy to some states in Africa and elsewhere. Some Latin American countries formed limited democracies. However, even by the late 1950s, the second wave was beginning to exhaust itself. Soon, the world was in the midst of a second democratic reversal. Military dictatorships replaced many democracies in Latin America, Asia, and Africa. One-third of the democracies that existed in 1958 were authoritarian regimes by the mid-1970s.

The third and biggest wave of democratization began in 1974 with the overthrow of military dictatorships in Portugal and Greece. It crested in the early 1990s. In Southern and Eastern Europe, Latin America, Asia, and Africa, a whole series of authoritarian regimes fell. In 1991, Soviet communism collapsed. By 1995, 117 of the world's 191 countries were democratic in the sense that their citizens could choose representatives in regular, competitive elections. That amounts to 61 percent of the world's countries containing nearly 55 percent of the world's population (Diamond, 1996: 26).

Formal democracy involves regular, competitive elections.

In **liberal democracies**, citizens enjoy regular, competitive elections *and* the freedoms and constitutional protections that make political participation and competition meaningful.

The third wave seems less dramatic, however, when we bear in mind that these figures refer to **formal democracies**—countries that hold regular, competitive elections. Many of these countries are not **liberal democracies**. That is, like Russia, they lack the freedoms and constitutional protections that make political participation and competition meaningful. In formal but non-liberal democracies, substantial political power may reside with a military that is largely unaffected by the party in office. Certain cultural, ethnic, religious, or regional groups may not be allowed to take part in elections. The legislative and judicial branches of government may not constrain the power of the executive branch. Citizens may not enjoy freedom of expression, assembly, and organization. Instead, they may suffer from unjustified detention, exile, terror, and torture. At the end of 1995, 40 percent of the world's countries were liberal democracies, 21 percent were non-liberal democracies, and 39 percent were non-democracies, but the percentage of liberal democracies was already falling (Diamond, 1996: 28; U.S. Information Agency, 1998–99). The third wave was subsiding.

Nigeria celebrates independence from Britain in 1960. In 1993, General Sani Abacha annulled the presidential election, became head of state, and began a reign of brutal civil rights violations. The world's third wave of democratization was drawing to a close.

William Vanderson/Hulton Archive/Getty Image

The Social Preconditions of Democracy

Liberal democracies emerge and endure when countries enjoy considerable economic growth, industrialization, urbanization, the spread of literacy, and a gradual decrease in economic inequality (Huntington, 1991: 39–108; Lipset, 1981: 27–63, 469–76, 1994; Moore, 1967; Rueschemeyer, Stephens, and Stephens, 1992; Zakaria, 1997). Economic development creates middle and working classes that are large, well organized, literate, and well off. When these classes become sufficiently powerful, the state must recognize their demands for civil liberties and the right to vote and run for office. If powerful middle and working classes are not guaranteed political rights, they may initiate revolutionary upsurges that sweep away kings, queens, landed aristocracies, generals, and authoritarian politicians. In contrast, democracies do not emerge where middle and working classes are too weak to wrest big political concessions from pre-democratic authorities. In intermediate cases—where, say, a country's military is about as powerful a political force as its middle and working classes—democracy is precarious and often merely formal. The history of unstable democracies is largely a history of internal military takeovers (Germani and Silvert, 1961).

Apart from the socioeconomic conditions noted above, favourable external political and military circumstances help liberal democracy endure. Liberal democracies, even strong ones such as France, can collapse when fascist, communist, and military regimes and empires defeat them. They revive when democratic alliances win world wars and authoritarian empires break up. Less coercive forms of outside political intervention are also sometimes effective. For example, in the 1970s and 1980s, the European Union helped liberal democracy in Spain, Portugal, and Greece by integrating these countries in the Western European economy and giving them massive economic aid.

In sum, powerful, pro-democratic foreign states and strong, prosperous middle and working classes are liberal democracy's best guarantees. It follows that liberal democracy will spread in the less economically developed countries only if they prosper and enjoy support from the United States and the European Union, the world centres of liberal democracy.

Recognizing the importance of the United States and the European Union in promoting democracy in many parts of the world should not obscure two important facts. First, the United States is not always a friend of democracy. For example, between the end of World War II and the collapse of the Soviet Union in 1991, democratic regimes that were sympathetic to the Soviet Union were often destabilized by the United States and replaced by anti-democratic governments. American leaders were willing to export arms and offer other forms of support to anti-democratic forces in Iran, Indonesia, Chile, Nicaragua, Guatemala, and other countries because they believed it was in the United States' political and economic interest to do so (Chapter 9, Globalization, Inequality, and Development). For similar reasons, the United States supports non-democratic regimes in Saudi Arabia, Kuwait, and elsewhere today. Desire for access to oil, copper, and even bananas (among other commodities), combined with fear of communist and radical Islamist influence, have often outweighed democratic ideals in the United States. Anti-American attitudes in many parts of the world are based on American *opposition* to popular rule.

Second, just because the United States promotes democracy in many parts of the world, we should not assume that liberal democracy has reached its full potential in that country or, for that matter, in any of the other rich postindustrial countries that promote democracy internationally, including Canada. We saw otherwise in our discussion of the limited participation and influence of disadvantaged groups in Canadian politics. It seems fitting, therefore, to briefly assess the future of liberal democracy in Canada.

Postmaterialism and the Dilemma of Canadian Politics

A recent school of thought, **postmaterialism**, holds that economic or material issues are becoming less important in Canadian politics. Postmaterialists argue as follows: Liberal democracies are less stratified than are non-liberal democracies and non-democracies.

Postmaterialism claims that growing equality and prosperity in the rich industrialized countries have resulted in a shift from class-based to value-based politics.

That is, in liberal democracies, the gap between rich and poor is less extreme and society as a whole is more prosperous. In fact, say the postmaterialists, prosperity and the moderation of stratification have reached a point where they have fundamentally changed political life in Canada. They claim that, as recently as half a century ago, most people were politically motivated mainly by their economic or material concerns. As a result, parties were distinguished from one another chiefly by the way they attracted voters from different classes. Now, however, according to the postmaterialists, many if not most Canadians have had their basic material wants satisfied. Young people in particular, who grew up in relatively prosperous times, are less concerned with material issues, such as whether their next paycheque can feed and house their family. They are more concerned with postmaterialist issues, such as women's rights, civil rights, and the environment. The postmaterialists conclude that the old left–right political division, based on class differences and material issues, is being replaced. The new left–right political division, they say, is based on age differences and postmaterialist issues (Clark and Lipset, 1991; Clark, Lipset, and Rempel, 1993; Inglehart, 1997).

Although Canada is certainly more prosperous and less stratified than are the less developed countries of the world, it seems to us that postmaterialists are wrong to think that affluence is universal in this country or that inequality is decreasing. Chapter 8, Social Stratification, documents these facts at length. Canada has a comparatively high poverty rate among rich industrialized countries, and income inequality has been increasing for decades. Unemployment and poverty are particularly widespread among youth—the people who, in the postmaterialist view, are the most affluent and least concerned with material issues. About two-thirds of single Canadians under the age of 25 live below the low-income cut-off. This high level of poverty suggests that, today, more new voters are poor than at any time since at least 1980, when data on youth poverty were first collected. Under these circumstances, we should not be surprised that Canadian public opinion polls repeatedly show Canadians' leading concerns to be unemployment and related economic issues.

We thus arrive at the key dilemma of Canadian politics. Material issues—essentially problems of class inequality—continue to loom large in the minds of most Canadians. Yet, as we have seen, Canadian politics focuses on regional, not class issues. There exists a disconnect between Canadian priorities and Canadian political life.

One reform that could help remedy this situation is the adoption of a new type of electoral system. Ours is based on the British, "first-past-the-post" model. The country is divided into constituencies or ridings. In an election, candidates from different parties run in each riding. The candidate receiving the most votes in each riding wins. The trouble with this system is twofold. First, if more than two candidates run in a riding, the winning candidate may receive a minority of votes cast. People who vote for losing candidates are thus unrepresented in Parliament. Second, a party winning x votes in a particular region sometimes wins more seats than does a party receiving x + y votes that happen to be widely dispersed across the country. Votes for a particular party that are geographically concentrated tend to count for more than votes that are widely geographically distributed.

A more democratic alternative is the "list" electoral system used in France, Germany, and other continental Western European countries. In this system, each party presents a list of candidates to voters in the country as a whole. People vote for parties, not candidates. A party's top candidate wins a seat in Parliament for the first, say, 75 000 votes the party receives from anywhere in the country. The party's second candidate on the list wins a seat for the next 75 000 votes cast for the party, and so on. By this method, nearly all votes are translated into parliamentary representation. The system is more democratic than the first-past-the-post system—far fewer votes are "wasted" on losing candidates—so ordinary people feel they have more say in political affairs. This model is not without flaws,[2] but it is more democratic than the first-past-the-post system is.

Canada's major political parties oppose the list system because it would weaken them. Meanwhile, Canadians' harbour a growing sense that they are not well represented in Parliament. Their unease probably accounts in part for the 18 percentage point drop in voter turnout between 1958 and 2011. It probably also accounts in part for Canadians'

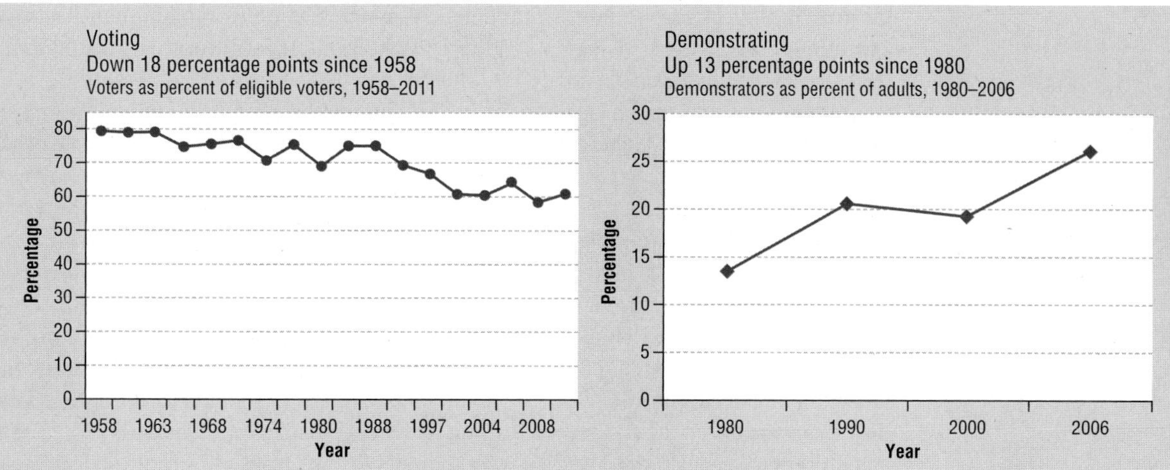

FIGURE 14.6
Canada: Voting Down, Demonstrating Up

Source: Elections Canada. 2013. "Voter Turnout at Federal Elections and Referendums." www.elections.ca/content.aspx?section=ele&dir=turn&document=index&lang=e (retrieved August 14, 2013); World Values Survey. 2013. "Online Data Analysis." www.wvsevsdb.com/wvs/WVSAnalize.jsp?Idioma=I (retrieved August 14, 2013).

increasing rate of participation in unconventional means of influencing public policy. For instance, the percentage of Canadian who said they participated or would be willing to participate in a demonstration increased 13 percentage points between 1980 and 2006 (see Figure 14.6). Recent examples of the way in which an increasing number of Canadians are expressing their political demands include the Occupy Movement demanding lower economic inequality (2011–12) and the Idle No More movement demanding environmental protection and justice for First Nations people (2012–13). We take up the idea that the future of Canadian politics may lie in part outside "normal" politics in Chapter 21, Collective Action and Social Movements.

Participating in social movements is not the only way people step outside the rules of normal electoral politics to change society. We conclude our discussion by considering two other types of "politics by other means": war and terrorism.

TIME FOR REVIEW

- When did the three waves of democracy sweep the world? What were their main characteristics? What changes followed each wave?
- What social conditions generally precede the crystallization of liberal democracy?

POLITICS BY OTHER MEANS

Much political conflict is constrained by rules that all sides accept. Yet people sometimes reject the rules. In extreme cases, each side in a conflict denies the legitimacy of the other side and uses force to disempower the others. The result is war.

War

A **war** is a violent armed conflict between politically distinct groups who fight to protect or increase their control of territory. Humanity has spent much of its history preparing for war, fighting it, and recovering from it. War has broken out some 14 000 times between 3600 BCE and the present. It has killed more than a billion soldiers and two billion civilians, approximately 3 percent of the people born in the last 5600 years. (This percentage is an underestimate because it necessarily ignores armed conflict among people without a recorded history.) Overall, however, and taking a long historical view, wars have become more

A **war** is a violent armed conflict between politically distinct groups who fight to protect or increase their control of territory.

destructive over time with "improvements" in the technology of human destruction. The twentieth century was history's deadliest, with about 100 million war deaths (Beer, 1974; Brzezinski, 1993; Haub, 2011).

War is an expensive business, and the United States spends far more than any other country financing it. The United States accounts for about a third of world military expenditures and nearly 30 percent of world arms export agreements (Grimmett, 2006).

Wars take place between countries (interstate wars) and within countries (civil or societal wars). A special type of interstate war is the colonial war, which involves a colony engaging in armed conflict with an imperial power for the purpose of gaining independence. Figure 14.7 shows the number of active armed conflicts in the world for each type of war from 1946 to 2009. You will immediately notice two striking features of the graph. First, after reaching a peak between the mid- to late 1980s, the number of armed conflicts dropped sharply. Second, since the mid-1950s, most armed conflict in the world has been societal rather than interstate. Today, countries infrequently go to war against each other. They often go to war with themselves as contending political groups fight for state control or seek to break away and form independent states. Don't let the mass media distort your perception of global war. Wars like the recent U.S.–Iraq war account for little of the total magnitude of armed conflict, although they loom large in the media. Wars like the recent conflict in the Democratic Republic of Congo account for most of the total magnitude of armed conflict yet are rarely mentioned in the mass media. From 2003 to 2007, the U.S.–Iraq war killed roughly 170 000 combatants and civilians. Between 1998 and 2003, deaths caused by the civil war in the Democratic Republic of Congo numbered in the millions (CBC News, 2007; Coghlan et al., 2006; "Iraq Body Count," 2008; "Iraq Coalition Casualty Count," 2008).

War risk varies from one country to the next (Figure 14.8), but what factors determine the risk of war on the territory of a given country? We can answer that question by classifying the countries of the world by government type and level of prosperity (Marshall and Gurr, 2003: 11). Government types include democracy, autocracy (absolute rule by a single person or party), and "intermediate" forms. Intermediate types of government include some elements of democracy (e.g., regular elections) and some elements of autocracy (e.g., no institutional checks on presidential power).

FIGURE 14.7

Global Trends in Violent Conflict, 1946–2012

Source: "Global Trends in Armed Conflict, 1946–2012", p. 19 in Backer, David A., Jonathan Wilkenfeld, and Paul K. Huth. 2014. *Peace and Conflict 2014*. Boulder: Paradigm Publishers.

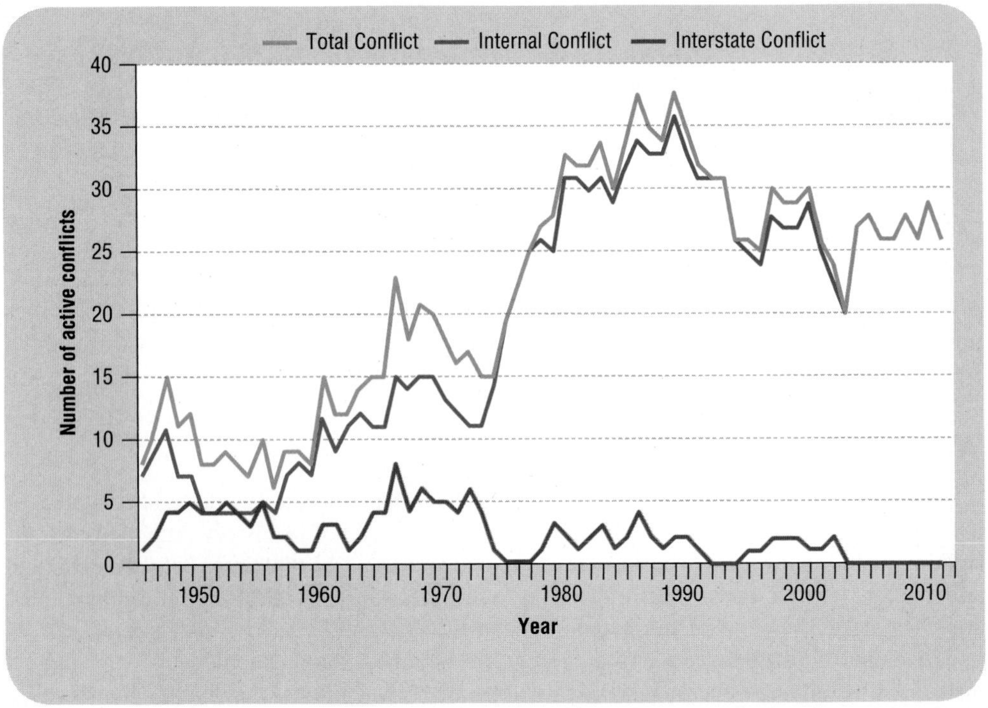

Jon Jones/Sygma/Corbis

The civil war in the Democratic Republic of Congo (1994–2003) caused millions of deaths.

Given our earlier discussion of the social preconditions of democracy, it should be no surprise that in prosperous countries, democracy is more common and autocracy less common. What is particularly interesting is the distribution of countries with *intermediate* types of government. Countries with intermediate types of government are at the highest risk of war, especially societal or civil war. Why? A democratic government tends to be stable because it enjoys legitimacy in the eyes of its citizens. An autocratic government tends to be stable because it rules with an iron fist. In contrast, an intermediate type of government is characterized neither by high legitimacy nor by iron rule. It is therefore most prone to collapsing into societal war, with armed political groups fighting each other for state control. We conclude that economic development and democratization are the two main factors leading to less war. (Of course, countries that avoid war on their own territory may nonetheless engage in war elsewhere, the United States being the prime example. Since 1850, the United States has intervened militarily in other countries more than once a year on average; see Kohn, 1988).

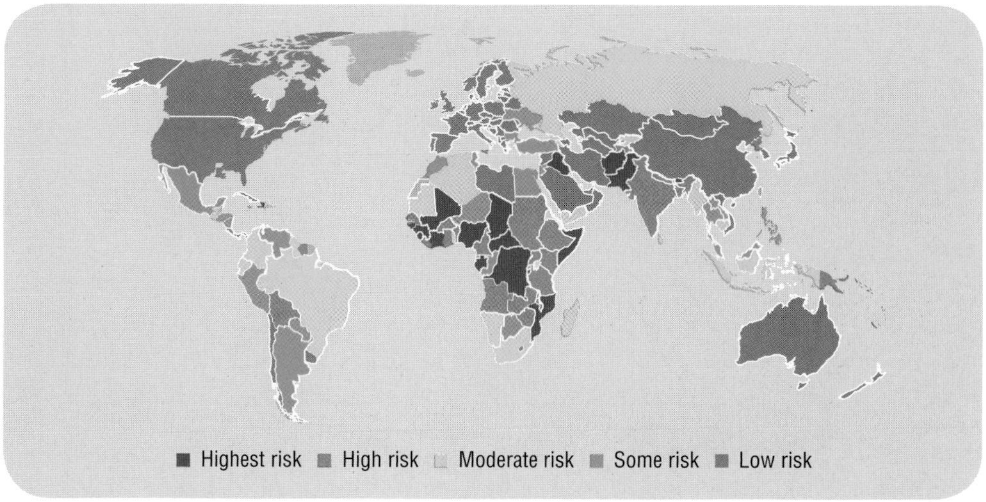

FIGURE 14.8
Risk of Future Instability, 2010–12

Source: Backer, David A., Jonathan Wilkenfeld, and Paul K. Huth. 2014. *Peace and Conflict 2014*. Boulder: Paradigm Publishers.

Terrorism and Related Forms of Political Violence

We can learn much about the predicament of the world today by lingering a moment on the question of why societal warfare has largely replaced interstate warfare since World War II. As usual, historical perspective is useful (Tilly, 2002).

From the rise of the modern state in the seventeenth century until World War II, states increasingly monopolized the means of coercion in society. This had three important consequences. First, as various regional, ethnic, and religious groups came under the control of powerful central states, the number of regional, ethnic, and religious wars declined, and interstate warfare became the norm. Second, because states were powerful and monopolized the means of coercion, conflict became more deadly. Third, civilian life was pacified because the job of killing for political reasons was largely restricted to state-controlled armed forces. Thus, even as the death toll from war rose, civilians were largely segregated from large-scale killing. As late as World War I (1914–18), civilians accounted for only 5 percent of war deaths.

All this changed after World War II (1939–45). Since then, there have been fewer interstate wars and more civil wars, guerrilla wars, massacres, terrorist attacks, and instances of attempted ethnic cleansing and genocide perpetrated by militias, mercenaries, paramilitaries, suicide bombers, and the like. Moreover, large-scale violence has increasingly been visited on civilian rather than on military populations. By the 1990s, civilians composed fully 90 percent of war deaths. The mounting toll of civilian casualties is evident from data on terrorist attacks (Figure 14.9).

Change in the form of collective violence came about for three main reasons (Tilly, 2002). First, decolonization and separatist movements roughly doubled the number of independent states in the world, and many of these new states, especially in Africa and Asia, were too weak to control their territories effectively. Second, especially during the Cold War (1946–91), the United States, the Soviet Union, Cuba, and China often subsidized and sent arms to domestic opponents of regimes that were aligned against them. Third, the expansion of international trade in contraband provided rebels with new means of support. They took advantage of inexpensive international communication and travel to establish support communities abroad for the export of heroin, cocaine, diamonds, dirty money, and so forth. In sum, the structure of opportunities for engaging in collective violence shifted radically after World War II. As a result, the dominant form of collective violence changed from interstate to societal warfare.

FIGURE 14.9
Total and Fatal Terrorist Attacks, 1970–2011

Source: LaFree, Gary and Laura Dugan, "Global Trends in Terrorism, 1970–2011," p. 30 in Backer, David A., Jonathan Wilkenfeld, and Paul K. Huth. 2014. *Peace and Conflict 2014*. Boulder: Paradigm Publishers.

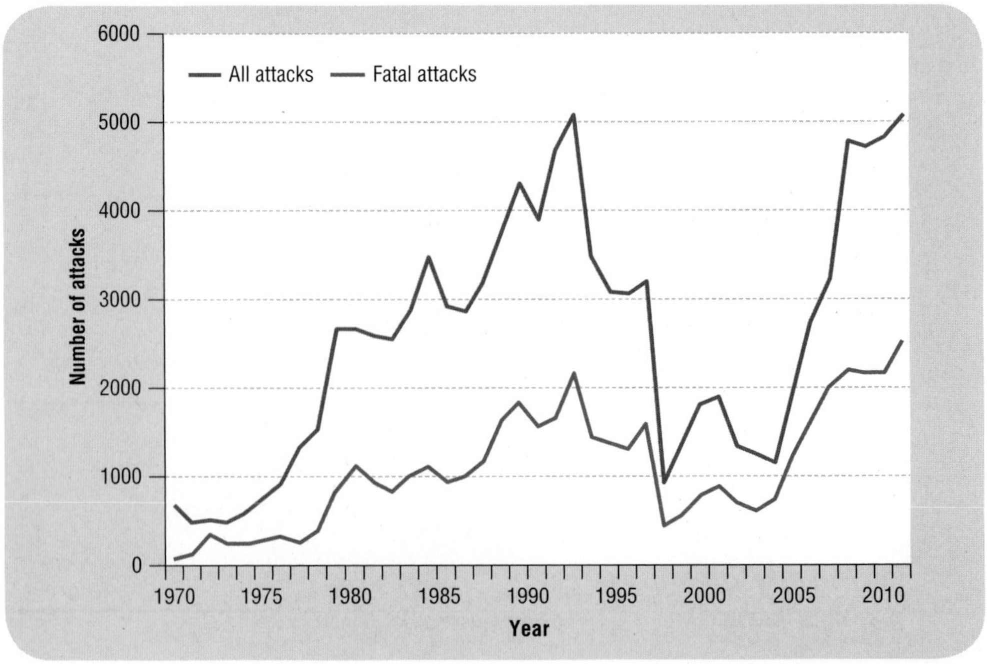

Al-Qaeda

From this perspective, and whatever its individual peculiarities, al-Qaeda is a typical creature of contemporary warfare. It originated in Afghanistan, a notoriously weak and dependent state. The United States supported al-Qaeda's founders militarily in their struggle against the Soviet occupation of Afghanistan in the 1980s. Al-Qaeda organized international heroin, diamond, and money-laundering operations. It established a network of operatives around the world. All of this was made possible by changes in the structure of opportunities for collective violence after World War II.

International terrorists often demand autonomy or independence for some country, population, or region (Pape, 2003). For example, among Al-Qaeda's chief demands are Palestinian statehood and the end of American support for the wealthy regimes in Saudi Arabia, Kuwait, and the Gulf states. Al-Qaeda has turned to terror as a means of achieving these goals because other ways of achieving them have largely been closed off. The United States considers support for the oil-rich Arab countries to be in its national interest. It has so far done little to further the cause of Palestinian statehood. Staunch opponents of American policy cannot engage in interstate warfare with the United States because they lack states of their own. At most, they are supported by states, such as Iran, that lack the resources to engage in sustained warfare with the United States. Because the existing structure of world power closes off other possibilities for achieving political goals, terror emerges as a viable alternative for some people.

TIME FOR REVIEW

- How did warfare change as the modern state started monopolizing the means of coercion in society?
- How did warfare change when many weak states emerged after World War II?
- Why did civil wars proliferate after World War II?

SUMMARY

1. How does the distribution of power in society influence politics?
   The level of democracy in a society depends on the distribution of power. When power is concentrated in the hands of few people, society is less democratic than it is when it is distributed among many people.

2. What do the main theories of democratic politics say about the relationship between political life, on the one hand, and social structures and state institutions, on the other?
   Pluralists correctly note that democratic politics is about negotiation and compromise. However, they fail to appreciate that economically advantaged groups have more power than disadvantaged groups do. *Elite theorists* correctly note that power is concentrated in the hands of advantaged groups. However, they fail to appreciate how variations in the distribution of power influence political behaviour and public policy. *Marxists* correctly argue that the interests of large business are generally off-limits to challenges. However, they understate the degree to which ordinary citizens, including members of the working class, sometimes influence state policy. *Power resource theorists* usefully focus on changes in the distribution of power in society and their effects. However, they fail to appreciate what *state-centred theorists* emphasize—that state institutions and laws also independently affect political behaviour and public policy.

3. What were the three waves of democracy?
During three periods, democracy spread rapidly in the world. Then the spurt of democratization slowed or reversed. The first wave began when more than half the white adult males in the United States became eligible to vote in the 1828 presidential election. By 1926, 33 countries enjoyed at least minimally democratic institutions. However, between 1922 and 1942, fascist, communist, and militaristic movements caused two-thirds of the world's democracies to fall under authoritarian or totalitarian rule. The second wave of democracy began after World War II, when Allied victory returned democracy to many fascist states, and wars of colonial independence led to the formation of a series of new democracies. Military dictatorships then replaced many of the new democracies; a third of the democracies in 1958 were authoritarian regimes by the mid-1970s. The third wave of democracy began in Portugal in 1974. It had slowed and in some cases reversed by the end of the twentieth century.

4. Under what conditions do some societies become highly democratic?
Citizens win legal protection of rights and freedoms when their middle and working classes become large, organized, and prosperous; and when powerful, friendly, pro-democratic foreign states support them.

5. Is Canada completely democratic?
No. Postmaterialists think Canada has reached a new and higher stage of democratic development but enduring social inequalities prevent even the most advanced democracies from being fully democratic.

6. How has the nature of the state affected patterns of warfare?
The rise of the modern state in the seventeenth century led to the monopolization of the means of coercion in society. Once centralized state armies became the major military force in society, interstate warfare became the norm, warfare became more deadly, and relatively few civilians died in war. However, the emergence of many weak states after World War II encouraged the outbreak of societal or civil wars, which are now the norm. Civilian deaths now account for most war deaths. Societal wars gain impetus when hostile outside powers get involved in them and rebels take advantage of increased opportunities to engage in illegal trade and establish support communities abroad. International terrorism has benefited greatly from the combination of weak states, outside support, and new ways of mobilizing resources.

NOTES

1. We say "businessmen" advisedly. Very few women are among Canada's richest people.
2. First, the list system can allow many parties to win parliamentary seats; as a result, unstable coalition governments may often form. This is the situation in Italy, which has had more than 60 governments since World War II. Second, small parties that are needed to form coalition governments may wield more power than their popularity justifies. This situation exists in Israel, where orthodox religious parties have been part of the government since the founding of the state in 1948. These outcomes can be avoided by establishing a high threshold for the total number of votes a party must receive before it can have any representation in Parliament. By keeping small parties out of parliament, stability is achieved, albeit at the cost of a measure of democracy.

CHAPTER 15

FAMILIES

© Per-Anders Pettersson/Corbis

IN THIS CHAPTER, YOU WILL LEARN TO

- Distinguish between the traditional "nuclear" family and the more structurally diverse, complex, and smaller families that are common today.
- Compare functionalist, conflict, and feminist accounts of family life.
- Describe courtship and couple formation in contemporary society.
- Assess the impact of divorce on adults and children.
- Outline the variety of family structures that children experience in Canadian society.
- Identify policies that can be implemented to accommodate different family forms.

IS "THE FAMILY" IN DECLINE?

Social-structural arrangements are "tight" to the degree they demand conformity to norms. Lance Roberts grew up in a structurally tight, middle-class, suburban family in Edmonton in the 1950s that bears little resemblance to most families today.

Ruslan Guzov/Shutterstock.com

The nuclear ideal

"By the standards of the time, everything in my neighbourhood appeared normal. The streets were filled with new, thousand-square-foot bungalows. All the houses were built by a single developer, following one of six standardized floor plans. When you entered a friend's house you could tell it was a replica of yours, or some other friend's. Every yard was fenced, almost all in one of three conventional styles. Building variation was evident only in the garages. Most were the single-car variety, built of second-hand materials by neighbourhood fathers. Their varying degrees of design knowledge and construction technique mostly accounted for differential results. The one major exception was 'the Doctor' (whose title was always expressed with deference, and who was actually a veterinarian). As my father pointed out, his double-car garage was built 'by professionals.'

"Many of the fathers in the neighbourhood, including mine, worked at the nearby Imperial Oil refinery. The only exceptions were 'the Doctor' and an immigrant from Holland—'the Dutchman.' He delivered bread in a van and always honked his horn three times when he finished his deliveries mid-afternoon. That was the full extent of deviance I can recall.

"Not surprisingly, I took the conformity pervading my childhood for granted. However, in my final year of elementary school, two cracks appeared in my social life. First, during a Christmas holiday a new kid who had moved into the neighbourhood disappeared with his family. When he returned in January, he told stories of his holiday in an exotic place called Hawaii. I repeated his stories about this tropical paradise at dinner and asked why our family didn't go there. I was told that our family couldn't afford such luxury and, then, with a dismissive tone, my father added that my friend's father 'let the mother work.' As I lay in bed that evening I remember thinking, 'Mothers can work? And this leads to Hawaii?'

"The second crack in the facade of normality opened up during a school civics project on the importance of voting. While having an after-school snack I asked my mother if she voted in the last election. She replied, 'Yes, of course; it's our civic responsibility.' I then inquired how she voted. She replied, 'The same as your father.' 'Why the same as dad?' I asked. The logic of my mother's reply astounded me: 'Because if I voted any differently, I would cancel out his vote.' Try as I might I could not rationalize that ballots should be cast to avoid 'cancelling out' a spouse's vote.

"These childhood revelations about the possibility of mothers working and spousal voting independence were the thin edge of a wedge that eventually shattered my structurally tight understanding of families. In the course of a generation, the world of Canadian families changed from structurally tight to structurally loose. Social expectations about family life shifted from impositions that required conformity to suggestions that required interpretation. Recent changes in Canadian families have been so extensive that my adult children find reports of my childhood family's rigid structure as remote from their experience as I found my friend's report on Hawaii."

For better or for worse, our most intense emotional experiences are bound up with our families. We love, hate, protect, hurt, express generosity toward, and envy nobody as much as our parents, siblings, children, and mates. Some families are islands of domestic bliss. A few are sites of the most violent acts imaginable. As many as one-third of solved homicides in Canada occur in family or intimate relationships (Statistics Canada, 2013e). Given the intensity of our emotional involvement with our families, should we be surprised that most people are passionately concerned with the rights and wrongs, the do's and don'ts, of family life? Should we be surprised that family issues lie close to the centre of political debate in this country?

Because families are emotional minefields, few subjects of sociological inquiry generate as much controversy. Much of the debate centres on whether the family is in decline and, if so, what should be done about it. This issue has been discussed since the mid-nineteenth century. Listen to John Laing, a Protestant minister in Ontario, in 1878: "We may expect to see further disintegration until the family shall disappear.... In all things civil and sacred the tendency of the age is towards individualism ... its plausible aphorisms and popular usages silently undermining the divine institution of the family" (quoted in Pence and Jacobs, 2001).

When people speak about "the decline of the family," they are often referring to the **nuclear family**. The nuclear family comprises two married, opposite-sex parents and their biological children who share the same residence. Others refer more narrowly to the **traditional nuclear family**. The traditional nuclear family is a nuclear family in which the wife works in the home without pay while the husband works outside the home for money.

A **nuclear family** comprises two married opposite-sex parents and their biological children who share the same residence.

A **traditional nuclear family** is a nuclear family in which the husband works outside the home for money and the wife works without pay in the home.

Although the nuclear family remains the cultural ideal, fewer Canadian families follow this model today than in the past. In contemporary society, families come in many different forms. Variations include single-parent families, families without children, same-sex couple households that may or may not have children, families in which partners are not legally married to one another, and step-parent families that include children from more than one union.

Moreover, because people are freer now than they were in the past to leave unhappy relationships and to find new partners, contemporary families are also more complex. That is, when people enter into unions, each person is likely to have a history of previous partners. Past unions have a way of intruding on current relationships, particularly when one partner has a child from a previous relationship. In addition, complex families must negotiate their roles in the absence of institutional cues about who is in or out of the family system (Brown and Manning, 2009; Seltzer and Bianchi, 2013). These **family boundary ambiguities** are confusing for everyone. For example, what does a girl call the woman who has married her noncustodial father? What obligations, if any, do adult step-children have to a step-parent when the step-parent is no longer married to their biological parent? If a child is spending equal time in two households following divorce, which place is "home"? (Lamanna and Riedmann, 2009).

Family boundary ambiguities refer to a state in which family members are uncertain about who is in or out of their family or who is performing tasks or roles within the family system.

Finally, families are much smaller than ever. Rising life expectancy and falling fertility are producing a **verticalization of family structure**: more surviving generations but fewer family members within each generation (Connidis, 2010). The contemporary family no longer resembles a wide, bushy tree, but instead looks more like a tall, skinny beanpole. Some sociologists even use the term "beanpole family" to describe its new character.

Verticalization of family structure refers to the increased number of living generations in a family, accompanied by fewer members within each generation.

What should we make of the growing diversity, increased complexity, and smaller size of families? Some sociologists, many of them functionalists, view the erosion of the nuclear family as an unmitigated disaster (Blankenhorn, 2007; Popenoe, 1998). In their view, a host of social ills—rising rates of crime, illegal drug use, poverty, and welfare dependency—result when children do not grow up in stable married-parent households. They call for various legal and cultural reforms to shore up marriage. For instance, they want to make it more difficult to get a divorce and they want people to place less emphasis on individual happiness at the expense of family responsibility.

Other sociologists, influenced by conflict and feminist theories, disagree with the functionalist assessment (Coontz, 2004; Ferree, 2010). They argue it is incorrect to believe that families have only one legitimate form. They emphasize that families can be structured in many ways and that the diversity of family forms increases as people adapt to new social pressures. They also contend that changing family forms do not necessarily represent deterioration in the quality of people's lives. Different family forms can *improve* the way people live, especially when accompanied by economic and political reforms, such as the creation of an affordable nationwide daycare system.

We have organized this chapter around the debate concerning the alleged decline of the Canadian family. We first outline the functional theory of the family because the issues raised by functionalism remain a focus of sociological controversy. We next present a critique of functionalism, borrowing from the work of conflict theorists and feminists. In particular, we show that the nuclear family became the dominant and ideal family form as a result of specific social and historical conditions. When these conditions changed, the nuclear family became less prevalent, and new family forms emerged. We describe the characteristics of these new family forms in Canada in the twenty-first century, highlighting their implications for families and the broader society. As we will see, although new family forms solve some problems, they are not an unqualified blessing. The chapter's concluding section therefore considers the kinds of policies that might help alleviate some of the most serious concerns faced by families today.

© John Springer Collection/CORBIS

Bob D'Amico/© ABC/Courtesy: Everett Collection

Father Knows Best was one of the most popular TV sitcoms of the 1950s. It portrayed a smoothly functioning, happy, white, middle-class, mother-homemaker, father-breadwinner family. *Modern Family* reached the TV screen in 2009. Jay, a white Anglo-Saxon man in his 60s, is divorced and married to Gloria, who is Colombian, divorced, in her 30s, and has a young son from her first marriage (Manny). Jay has two adult children—Claire (married with three children) and Mitchell (who, with his male partner, have adopted a Vietnamese baby). Comparing family sitcoms from the 1950s with today's sitcoms, we see that age, ethnicity, race, sexual orientation, and marital status have been transformed from constants into variables.

TIME FOR REVIEW

- What differentiates the nuclear family from the traditional nuclear family?
- In what ways do contemporary families differ from families of the past?

FUNCTIONALISM AND THE NUCLEAR IDEAL

Functional Theory

For any society to survive, its members must cooperate economically. They must have babies. The offspring must be raised in an emotionally supportive environment so they can learn the ways of the group and eventually operate as productive adults. Since the 1940s, functionalists have argued that the nuclear family is ideally suited to meet these challenges. In their view, the nuclear family performs five main functions: it provides a basis for regulated sexual activity, economic cooperation, reproduction, socialization, and emotional support (Murdock, 1949: 1–22; Parsons, 1955).

Functionalists cite the pervasiveness of the nuclear family as evidence of its ability to perform these functions. They acknowledge that other family forms exist. **Polygamy** expands the nuclear unit "horizontally" by adding one or more spouses (almost always wives) to the household. Polygamy is still legally permitted in many less industrialized countries of Africa and Asia. However, the overwhelming majority of families are monogamous because they cannot afford to support several wives and many children. The **extended family** expands the nuclear family "vertically" by adding another generation—one or more of the spouses' parents—to the household. Extended families were once common throughout the world. They still are in some places. However, according to the functionalists, the basic building block of the extended family (and of the polygamous family) is the nuclear unit.

Polygamy expands the nuclear family "horizontally" by adding one or more spouses (usually women) to the household.

The **extended family** expands the nuclear family "vertically" by adding another generation—one or more of the spouses' parents—to the household.

George Murdock was a functionalist who, in the 1940s, conducted a famous study of 250 mainly preliterate, foraging societies (sometimes called "hunting-and-gathering societies"). Murdock wrote, "Either as the sole prevailing form of the family or as the basic unit from which more complex familial forms are compounded, [the nuclear family] exists as a distinct and strongly functional group in every known society" (Murdock, 1949: 2). Moreover, Murdock continued, the nuclear family is always based on **marriage**. He defined marriage as a socially approved, presumably long-term, sexual and economic union between a man and a woman. It involves rights and obligations between spouses and between spouses and their children.

Marriage is a socially approved, presumably long-term sexual and economic union between a man and a woman. It involves reciprocal rights and obligations between spouses and between parents and children.

Does this functionalist account provide an accurate picture of family relations across history? To assess its adequacy, we discuss families in the two settings on which functionalists focused their attention: (1) foraging societies, and (2) middle-class North American families in the 1950s.

Foraging Societies

Foraging societies are nomadic groups of 100 or fewer people. They have a gendered division of labour. Most men hunt and most women gather wild, edible plants. Women also do most of the child care. However, research on foragers shows that men often tend to babies and children in such societies (Leacock, 1981; Lee, 1979). When men return from an unsuccessful hunt, they often gather food. In some foraging societies, women hunt. Thus, the gender division of labour is less strict than functionalists assume. Moreover, the gender division of labour is not associated with large differences in power and authority because women produce up to 80 percent of the food. Overall, men have few privileges that women don't also enjoy.

A rough gender equality is found among the !Kung-San, a foraging society in the Kalahari Desert in Botswana. Women play a key economic role by providing food.

© Peter Johnson/Corbis

Foragers travel in small camps or bands. The band decides by consensus when to send out groups of hunters. When they return from the hunt, they distribute game to all band members based on need. Hunters do not hunt based on their nuclear family's needs. Nor do hunters distribute game only to their nuclear family. Contrary to Murdock (1949), the band, not the nuclear family, is the most efficient social organization for providing everyone with valuable food sources.

Life in foraging societies is highly cooperative. Women and men often care for each other's children. In contrast to the functionalists' claim that socialization is the "basic and irreducible" function of the nuclear family, the band, not the nuclear family, assumes responsibility for child socialization in foraging societies. Socialization is more a public than a private matter. As a seventeenth-century Innu man from northern Québec said to a Jesuit priest who was trying to convince him to adopt European ways of raising children, "Thou hast no sense. You French people love only your own children; but we all love all the children of our tribe" (quoted in Leacock, 1981: 50).

In sum, research on foraging societies calls into question many of the functionalists' generalizations. In foraging societies, relations between the sexes are generally egalitarian. Each nuclear unit does not execute its important economic and socialization functions in isolation and in private. Instead, cooperative band members execute most economic and socialization functions in public.

Let us now assess the functionalist theory of the family in the light of evidence concerning Canadian families in the years just after World War II, the second focus of the functionalists' attention.

Courtesy of the artist and Bau-Xi Gallery, Toronto ON, Canada

Mimi Matte's *Family Outing* (1998): In the 1950s, married women often hid their frustrations with family life.

The Canadian Family in the 1950s

As a description of family patterns in the 15 years after World War II, functionalism has some merit. During the Great Depression (1929–39) and World War II (1939–45), Canadians were forced to postpone marriage (if they married at all) because of widespread poverty, government-imposed austerity, and physical separation. After this long and dreadful ordeal, many Canadians just wanted to settle down, have children, and enjoy the peace, pleasure, and security that family life seemed to offer. Conditions could not have been better for doing just that. The immediate postwar era was one of unparalleled

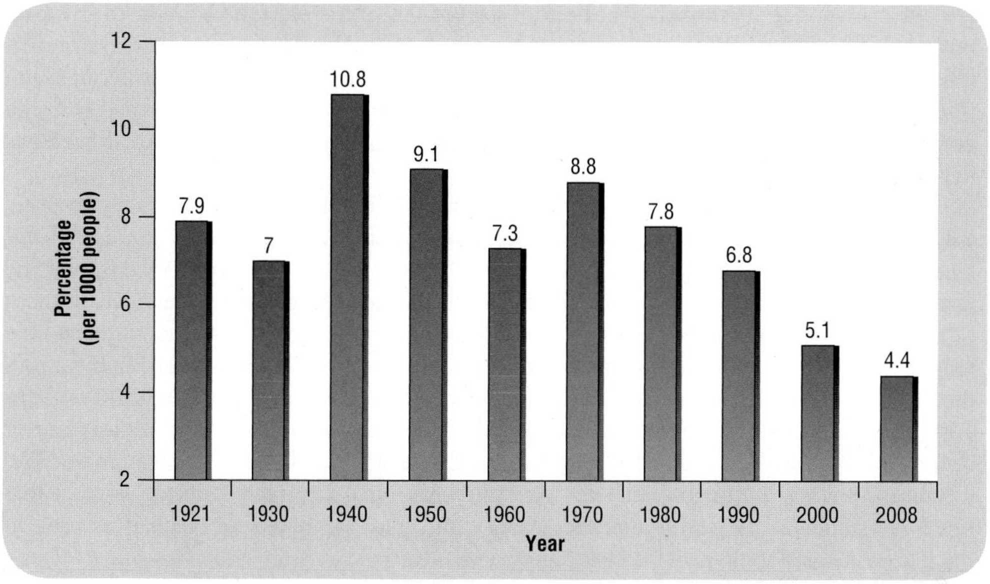

FIGURE 15.1
Marriage Rates, 1921–2008

Source: Employment and Social Development Canada. 2014. "Family Life–Marriage." Retrieved July 14, 2014 (www4.hrsdc.gc.ca/.3ndic.1t.4r@-eng.jsp?iid=78&bw=1).

optimism and prosperity. Real per capita income rose, as did the percentage of Canadians who owned their own homes. By the mid-1950s, employment and personal income reached all-time highs. Various services and legislative amendments that had been introduced during World War II to encourage wives and mothers to join the labour force were rescinded. The expectation was that a return to "normal" meant the resumption of the men's role as providers and women's role as housewives (Kingsbury and Scanzoni, 1993).

These conditions resulted in a "marriage boom" (see Figure 15.1). Increasingly, Canadians lived in married-couple families. The proportion of "never married" Canadians decreased and the average age at first marriage dropped between 1941 and 1956 from 24.4 to 23.4 years for brides and from 27.6 to 26.1 years for bridegrooms (McVey and Kalbach, 1995: 225; see Figure 15.2). A second result was a baby boom. During this period, there was a spike in the number of children born. And unlike the situation today, married men were much more likely than married women were to be working for pay. For example, in 1951, 90 percent of married men but only 11 percent of married women were in the paid labour force.

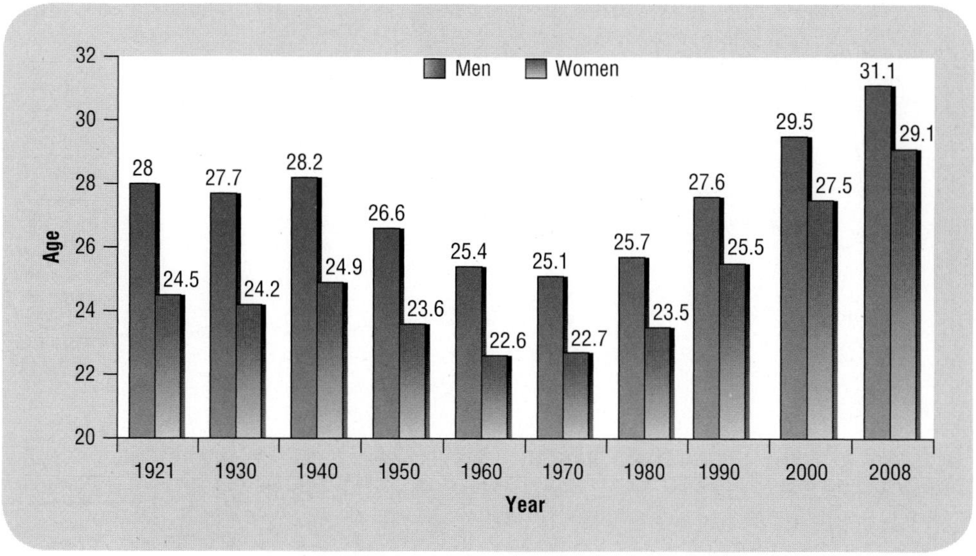

FIGURE 15.2
Average Age at First Marriage, by Gender, 1921–2008

Source: Employment and Social Development Canada. 2014. "Family Life—Marriage." Retrieved July 14, 2014 (www4.hrsdc.gc.ca/.3ndic.1t.4r@-eng.jsp?iid=78&bw=1).

Of course, not all women could afford to stay out of the workforce. Women living in poverty have often worked both inside and outside the home. However, middle-class women tended overwhelming to engage only in domestic activities, devoting increasing attention to child rearing and housework. Women and men became increasingly concerned with the emotional quality of family life, as love and companionship became firmly established as the main motivation for marriage (Cherlin, 2009).

The immediate postwar situation described by the functionalists was in many respects a historical aberration. Trends in marriage, divorce, and fertility show a gradual *weakening* of the nuclear family from the early 1900s until the end of World War II, and the resumption of a weakening trend beginning in the 1960s. The **marriage rate** (the number of marriages that occur in a year for every 1000 people in the population) never attained the heights reached in the immediate postwar period. Instead, marriage rates fell sharply from the 1970s onward. The **divorce rate** (the number of divorces that occur in a year for every 1000 people in the population) increased in the 1960s with the introduction of more liberal divorce laws. However, in the 1990s, the divorce rate stabilized and then began to decline. The decline was not due to a renewed commitment to marriage, but reflected the fact that fewer Canadians were getting married. Finally, the **total fertility rate** reached its peak in the late 1950s and then dropped (see Figure 15.3).

The marriage rate is the number of marriages that occur in a year for every 1000 people in the population.

The divorce rate is the number of divorces that occur in a year for every 1000 people in the population.

The total fertility rate is the average number of children that would be born to a woman if she were to live to the end of her childbearing years and experienced the same age-specific fertility rates observed in a given year.

The early functionalists, it seems, generalized too hastily from the families they knew best—their own. By the early 1960s, the earlier trends in Canada had reasserted themselves. Thus, as the retreat from marriage intensified and family forms began to diversify, the functionalist view of the family increasingly fell out of step with the experiences of Canadian families.

In fact, changes in family life have been so pervasive over the past 50 years that tracking how Canadians enter and exit unions poses greater challenges today than it once did. In 2011, the federal government announced that it would no longer calculate the marriage rate and divorce rate annually (which explains why Figures 15.1 and 15.2 report data only until 2008). This decision was partly due to government cutbacks but it also reflected a new reality: couples increasingly prefer cohabiting relationships over marriage. Because marriage requires a licence and divorce requires a court order, both can be accurately measured. In contrast, no government organization or legal authority must be consulted when a cohabiting relationship begins or ends. Thus, while government statistics could be reliably used in the past to track patterns of union formation and dissolution among Canadians, researchers must seek out other data sources to obtain an accurate portrait of these patterns in Canada today.

Functionalists missed the big picture largely because they ignored the degree to which (1) the traditional nuclear family is based on gender inequality and (2) changes in power

FIGURE 15.3
Total Fertility Rate, Canada, 1921–2011

Source: Adapted from Statistics Canada. 2013f. Fertility: Overview, 2009 to 2011. Catalogue no. 91-209-X. Ottawa, ON: Minister of Industry (page 10).

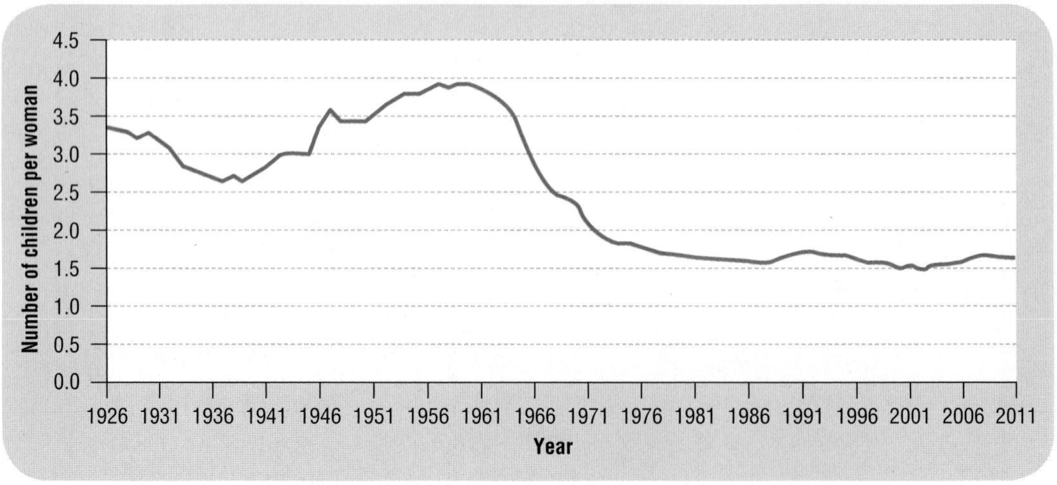

relations between women and men alter family structures. Sociologists working in the conflict and feminist traditions have developed these points, as we will now see.

CONFLICT AND FEMINIST THEORIES

The idea that power relations between women and men explain the prevalence of different family forms was first suggested by Marx's close friend and coauthor, Friedrich Engels. Engels argued that the traditional nuclear family emerged as a result of inequalities of wealth. Once wealth was concentrated in the hands of a man, wrote Engels, he became concerned about how to transmit it to his children, particularly his sons. Engels asked, How could a man safely pass on an inheritance? His answer: Only by controlling his wife sexually and economically. Economic control ensured that the man's property would not be squandered and would remain his and his alone. Sexual control, in the form of enforced female monogamy, ensured that his property would be transmitted only to *his* offspring. Engels concluded that only the elimination of private property and the creation of economic equality—in a word, communism—could bring an end to gender inequality and the traditional nuclear family (Engels, 1970 [1884]: 138–9).

Engels was right to note the long history of male economic and sexual domination in the traditional nuclear family. Early Canadian law was informed by a vision of the family in which the wife's labour belonged to her husband. Although a series of legal reforms have altered the situation, as recently as the mid-twentieth century, a wife could not rent a car, qualify for a loan, or sign a contract without her husband's permission.

However, Engels was wrong to think that communism would eliminate gender inequality in the family. Gender inequality has been as common in societies that call themselves communist as in societies that call themselves capitalist. For example, the Soviet Union left "intact the fundamental family structures, authority relations, and socialization patterns crucial to personality formation and sex-role differentiation. Only a genuine sexual revolution [or, as we prefer to call it, a *gender revolution*] could have shattered these patterns and made possible the real emancipation of women" (Lapidus, 1978: 7).

Because gender inequality exists in non-capitalist (including pre-capitalist) societies, most feminists believe something other than, or in addition to, capitalism accounts for gender inequality and the persistence of the traditional nuclear family. In the feminist view, *patriarchy*—male dominance and norms justifying that dominance—is more deeply rooted in the economic, military, and cultural history of humankind than suggested by the classical Marxist account. For feminists, only a genuine gender revolution can alter this state of affairs.

Just such a revolution gained force in Canada and other rich industrialized countries about 60 years ago. It produced broad social change. Women's employment in the paid labour market rose dramatically. Women caught up with and then overtook men in rates of college and university completion. Women demanded more rights over their own bodies. As their economic power increased and their leisure time dwindled, women began to insist that men shoulder more of the housework.

Despite these remarkable changes, most scholars today concede that the revolution produced uneven results (England, 2010). We can observe the mixed outcomes of the gender revolution by examining gender inequality in the context of the gender division of labour.

The Gender Division of Labour

In a traditional nuclear family, men are expected to go out and earn a family wage, whereas women are expected to perform domestic chores and care for family members. Today, more than 70 percent of Canadian women with children under the age of 16 are in paid employment (Ferraro, 2010). This statistic tells us the traditional nuclear family is no longer the norm. Has the twenty-first century ushered in a more equitable distribution in the amount of time Canadian men and women spend in paid work and housework? The answer is both yes and no.

The answer is yes because patterns of paid and unpaid work have changed over time. Participation in the paid labour force has increased sharply for women and fallen slightly for men (Lindsay, 2008a). Time spent doing household chores has increased for men and fallen for women.

But the answer is also no. Despite signs of convergence, gender differences persist. On average, men still spend more time than women do working for pay. Women still do more unpaid domestic work than men do (Bianchi et al., 2012; Evertsson, 2014; Lindsay, 2008a).

A traditional gender division of labour is most common in households with young children (Bianchi et al., 2012; Marshall, 2011). While young, dual-earner couples tend to participate equally in paid and unpaid work when there are no children in the household, the situation changes soon after childbirth. Mothers tend to reduce their hours of paid work while fathers boost their hours of paid employment.

Two main factors shrink the gender gap in domestic chores. First, the smaller the gap between the husband's and the wife's earnings, the more equal the division of household labour. Apparently, women are routinely able to translate earning power into domestic influence. Their increased status enables them to get their husbands to do more around the house. In addition, women who earn relatively high incomes are able to use some of their money to pay outsiders to do domestic work.

Attitude is the second factor that shrinks the gender gap in domestic labour. The more a husband and wife agree that there *should* be equality in the household division of labour, the more equality there is. Seeing eye to eye on this issue is often linked to both spouses having a postsecondary education (Greenstein, 1996). It follows that for greater equality between men and women doing household chores, two things need to happen. There must be greater equality between men and women in the paid labour force and broader cultural acceptance of the need for gender equality.

Summing up, we can say that conflict theorists and feminists have performed a valuable sociological service by emphasizing the importance of power relations in structuring family life. The gender revolution, however, is but one piece of the dramatic transformation of family life over the past 60 years. We next examine changes in attitudes toward mate selection and describe the variety of ways in which partnering occurs in Canada today.

TIME FOR REVIEW

- In what ways were families in foraging societies and Canadian families in the postwar period different from what structural-functionalists expected?
- How was Engels both right and wrong about the role of capitalism in reinforcing gender inequality in family life?
- How has the gender division of labour both changed and remained the same?

MATE SELECTION

Love and Mate Selection

We expect love to be an essential ingredient in marriage. Yet in most societies throughout human history, love had little to do with marriage (Abbott, 2011). Third parties, not brides and grooms, typically arranged marriages. The selection of marriage partners was based

The Everett Collection/CP Picture Archive

Clark Gable and Vivien Leigh in *Gone with the Wind* (1939): Hollywood glamorized heterosexual, romantic love and solidified the intimate linkage between love and marriage that we know today.

mainly on calculations intended to maximize their families' prestige, economic benefits, and political advantages.

The idea that love should guide the choice of a marriage partner first gained currency in the eighteenth century with the rise of liberalism and individualism, philosophies that stressed freedom of the individual over community welfare (Beck and Beck-Gernsheim, 1995; Cherlin, 2009). However, the intimate link between love and marriage that we know today emerged only in the early twentieth century, when Hollywood and the advertising industry began to promote self-gratification on a grand scale. For these new spinners of fantasy and desire, an important aspect of self-gratification was heterosexual romance leading to marriage.

In the past, when marriages were arranged by others, couples may have had the opportunity to know one another only *after* they were married. Today, marriage is rarely the first step couples take when forming a relationship. Instead, nearly all young people today engage in prolonged courtship rituals. Dating often starts in early adolescence, as youth attend parties, dances, or sporting events together. Romantic relationships in these contexts rarely last more than a few months but provide youth with opportunities for sexual discovery and experimentation. As adolescence progresses into young adulthood, dating shifts from attending events in groups to spending time as a couple. The purpose of dating also changes. In preparation for adult roles, romantic relationships become the basis for testing physical and emotional compatibility with another person.

In the past, couples followed a fairly direct path from dating to engagement to marriage. Today, young adults have a variety of options available to them. We discuss differences between marriage and cohabitation before describing other types of couple relationships that exist in Canada today.

Marriage and Cohabitation

The vast majority of Canadians will marry at least once in their lifetimes but, for a growing number of people, the transition from being single to being married is likely to involve cohabitation as an intermediate step (Clark and Crompton, 2006).

Marriage and cohabitation are similar in some ways. Both involve regular sexual relations and a common residence. Marriage, however, is a contract that is accomplished through ritual and legal authority. All marriages start with a wedding, which requires a licence and involves an exchange of vows before an authorized official and witnesses. Cohabitation typically starts without fanfare.

Another difference is that marriage has clearly defined roles and expectations. For example, marriage connects spouses to a larger kinship network that can be called upon for support. In contrast, couples who cohabit must create their own "scripts." They must agree on whether and how they will share money and other assets. They must also decide whether and how they want their employers, health care providers, and families to recognize their union. Because kinship ties can be nebulous in cohabiting relationships, social support from families is not guaranteed. Sometimes, families may not even know about a cohabiting relationship; one study found that 10 percent of young adults did not even tell their parents about their first cohabiting relationship (Thornton, Axinn, and Xie, 2007).

Finally, marriages are more enforceable than are cohabiting relationships (Cherlin, 2010). Said differently, the penalties for ending a marriage are greater than those for ending cohabiting relationships. For example, when couples choose to go their separate ways, rights to property are more clearly specified in marriages than in cohabiting relationships. These differences mean that marriage is a social institution (Nock, 2009). Cohabitation is not.

Since the Canadian census first started collecting information on cohabitation in 1981, the rate has more than tripled from 5.6 percent to 16.7 percent of all families in 2011 (Statistics Canada, 2012m). Growing rates of cohabitation in Canada mirror what is occurring in other high-income countries, albeit with some variation. Cohabitation is the norm in Sweden and Denmark, but remains rare (though it is on the rise) in Italy, Greece, and Poland (Perrelli-Harris et al., 2012; Sobotka and Toulemon, 2008).

Rates of cohabitation are not uniform across Canada either. In Québec, rates of cohabitation have soared above the national average for several decades (LeBourdais and Lapierre-Adamcyk, 2004; Pollard and Wu, 1998). In addition, cohabitors in Québec are significantly less likely to convert their relationships to marriages and are less likely to experience the breakdown of the relationship than are cohabitors in the rest of Canada (Wu and Pollard, 2000). Together, these trends suggest that cohabitation is quickly replacing marriage as the modal way of family life in Québec.

Why are rates of cohabitation so much higher in Québec than they are in the rest of Canada? Researchers point to the Quiet Revolution of the 1960s that severed Québec's longstanding links with the Roman Catholic Church and rapidly transformed the province into a secular society (Laplante, 2013). Once the church lost its grip on social life, a new generation of Québeckers were free to reject conservative religious teaching on marriage and to adopt a more liberal stance towards intimate relationships.

Today, most Canadians between the ages of 20 and 29 experience a common-law relationship as their first union (Kerr, Moyser, and Beaujot, 2006). Few Canadians, especially those who are younger, think there is anything wrong with cohabiting. Still, cohabitation tends to be short-lived. In Canada, the average length of a cohabiting relationship is a little over three years (Heuveline and Timberlake, 2004). Of the cohabiting relationships that end, about one-third are converted into marriages. The others involve a breakup.

Couples cohabit for many reasons (Sassler, 2010). Some couples fit into our earlier description of using cohabitation as an intermediate step on the path to marriage. For them, cohabitation is a trial marriage. Other couples view cohabitation as an alternative to living alone. They opt for the convenience, efficiency, and pleasure of living with someone but have few if any expectations for the future. Still others view cohabitation as an alternative to marriage. For these couples, cohabitation is a permanent living arrangement that best meets their needs.

The reasons people give for cohabiting tend to vary by age. Young adults are more likely to see cohabitation as a way of testing compatibility. They treat marriage as the end goal. In contrast, older adults, particularly those who are coming out of a previous marriage, tend to view cohabitation as an alternative to marriage. For many of them, marriage is the last thing on their minds.

Recently, new types of relationships have begun to spring up in the gap between singlehood and cohabitation. One such relationship is known as **friends with benefits** (FWB). FWB involves having occasional sexual relations with someone who is a friend, but without commitment or romantic purpose. **Hookups** represent another arrangement. Hookups typically involve a sexual encounter with a stranger or acquaintance that is unplanned and unlikely to be repeated.

Friends with benefits involves occasional sexual relations with a friend, without commitment or romantic feelings for one another.

Hookups and FWB are relatively common on university and college campuses. Are these relationships as self-serving and shallow as some people think? Some sociologists argue that it is exploitive to engage in sex simply to fulfill physical needs while waiting for a better prospect to come along (Williams and Adams, 2013). They also wonder whether an established pattern of uncommitted sexual encounters can permanently impair a young person's capacity or desire to achieve emotional intimacy with another person.

Hookups are spontaneous, one-time sexual encounters between strangers or acquaintances.

Other sociologists think that FWB relationships exist because they serve a larger social purpose. When interviewed about FWB relationships, young adults said they enjoy the relative security of having sex with someone they know and find such relationships less awkward than casual sex (Karlsen and Træen, 2013). More importantly, young people assert that one of the chief criteria by which contemporary relationships are judged to be successful is whether one is a good lover. Hookups and FWB relationships may be socially accepted means for young people to improve their love-making techniques and demonstrate their sexual competence to others.

Generally, FWB relationships last only a few months. Fewer than one in five FWB relationships turns into a romantic relationship (Owen, Fincham, and Manthos, 2013). This fact has not stopped Hollywood from idealizing FWB relationships as a means of finding true love (see Box 15.1).

Living Apart Together

Another new living arrangement that falls between singlehood and cohabitation is living apart together (LAT). **LAT** relationships are living arrangements in which intimate partners, who regard themselves as a couple and are recognized as such by others, share living quarters on an intermittent basis but maintain separate households and finances (Cherlin, 2010). For some scholars, LAT represents just a transitory new stage on the path to possible cohabitation and marriage. Other scholars view LAT relationships as a new family form that allows partners to maximize their desire for intimacy and personal freedom (Duncan and Phillips, 2011). One thing is clear. LAT relationships challenge the traditional notion that a committed intimate relationship can only occur within the confines of a single household (Karlsson and Borell, 2002).

LAT, which stands for living apart together, is a living arrangement in which each person maintains his or her own separate residence, but both people consider themselves to be in a committed intimate relationship.

Research suggests that 8 percent of the Canadian population aged 20 and over identified themselves as LAT in 2011, with older adults less likely to enter this type of relationship than are younger Canadians (Turcotte, 2013). Older adults, however, are much more likely than are younger Canadians to view this living arrangement as a deliberate lifestyle choice rather than a temporary or involuntary circumstance (Turcotte, 2013). Older adults give two reasons for preferring LAT relationships over cohabitation (de Jong Gierveld and Merz, 2013). First, many older adults in LAT relationships are reluctant to give up their own home and established routines. Second, maintaining their own residence allows older adults to preserve ties to adult children who may not accept their parent's new relationship.

Same-Sex Marriage and Civil Unions

In 2001, the Netherlands became the first country to legalize same-sex marriage. Following suit were Belgium, Spain, Canada, South Africa, Norway, Iceland, Portugal, Sweden, Argentina, Denmark, France, Brazil, Uruguay, New Zealand, and the United Kingdom. Many other Western European countries allow same-sex couples to register their partnerships under the law in so-called civil unions. Civil unions recognize the partnerships as having some or all of the legal rights of marriage.

BOX 15.1

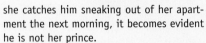

SOCIOLOGY AT THE MOVIES

FRIENDS WITH BENEFITS

In the well-established tradition of romantic comedies, *Friends with Benefits* conveys the message that, if you wait long enough and try hard enough, you will surely find your soulmate. In most romantic comedies, the path of true love starts with a hint of romance. Not so with this film. *Friends with Benefits* shows that the path to true love can begin with a booty call.

Jamie (Mila Kunis), a headhunter from New York, recruits Dylan (Justin Timberlake), an art director from Los Angeles, to take a new position at *GQ* magazine in New York. Unfamiliar with the city, Dylan begins to hang out with Jamie, and they find they have much in common. One thing they share is fear of emotional commitment. As they regale each other with stories of relationship letdowns and failures, they wonder what it would be like to be in a relationship with no strings attached and no possibility of disappointment. After talking it over, the two decide to enter into a "friends with benefits" relationship. They'll have sex with one another but won't let themselves fall in love with one another.

And so the couple embarks on mutually satisfying booty calls, all the while reminding one another about the terms of their relationship. After a while,

Kristina Nikishina/Epsilon/Getty Images

Mila Kunis and Justin Timberlake, the stars of *Friends with Benefits*.

however, Jamie wants a change. Taking a walk through Central Park, they encourage each other to try to pick someone up. Dylan starts talking to a woman who turns out to be married and uninterested. Jamie approaches a man and invites him on a date. Jamie falls hard for him. Feeling apprehensive and mindful of her past hurts, she tells him they won't have sex until after the fifth date. They enjoy five magical dates. As the night of the fifth date draws to a close, she asks him to spend the night. When she catches him sneaking out of her apartment the next morning, it becomes evident he is not her prince.

Jamie is heartbroken. She turns to Dylan for comfort. Dylan recommends that she accompany him back to Los Angeles for a weekend away at his family's place. There, Jamie meets Dylan's dad, sister, and nephew who take to her instantly. Over the course of the weekend, Jamie and Dylan appear to be rekindling their relationship. But the moment is short-lived—Jamie overhears Dylan telling his sister that Jamie doesn't mean anything to him. Feeling betrayed once again, Jamie abruptly leaves and flies home alone.

Dylan returns to New York City, pondering what Jamie really means to him. It takes a heart-to-heart moment with his father to get him to face the truth. Dylan's father urges his son not to let the love of his life get away. If he does, Dylan will regret it. Dylan springs into action, employing all of his romantic impulses to sweep Jamie off of her feet and convince her that he is the one for her.

Is the film formulaic? Absolutely! But it was also successful at the box office. In sharing their past romantic heartbreaks and growing discouragement over finding love, Dylan and Jamie help us to accept and even laugh at our own disappointments. But even as it decries the perils of modern love, the film manages to reinvigorate the main message that is the essence of all romantic comedies—that for each of us, our one true love awaits. We just need to keep the faith.

Still, there has been a sea change in the expression of romantic feelings. In a previous era, movie viewers accepted that the height of passion was achieved the moment lovers' lips met. Love in the twentieth century requires a much more thorough test.

The 2011 census recorded 64 575 same-sex couple households, which accounts for less than 1 percent of all couple households in Canada (Statistics Canada, 2012m). Figure 15.4 describes the characteristics of same-sex couple households in Canada. Same-sex couple households are slightly more likely to be male than female. Nine out of ten same-sex couple households have no children and just under a third involve legal marriage.

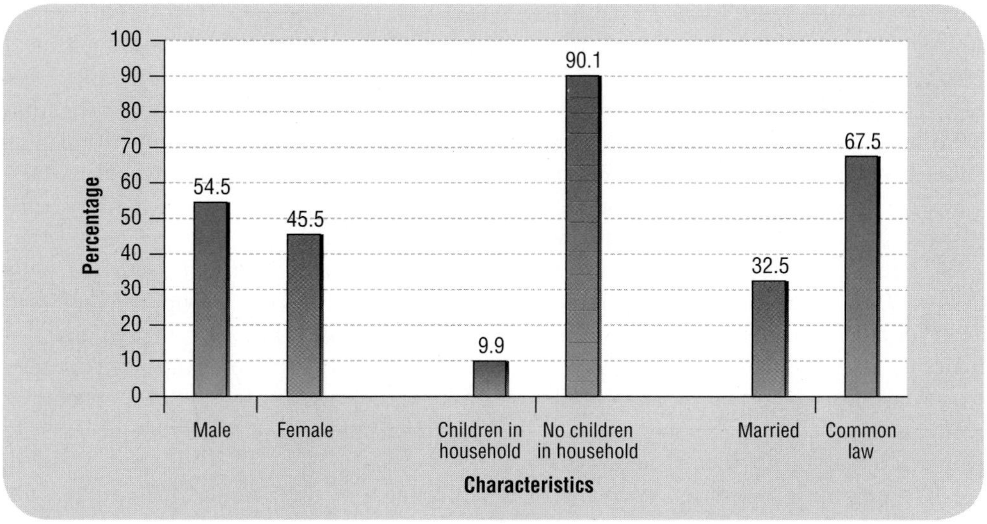

FIGURE 15.4
Characteristics of Same-Sex Couples in Canada, 2011

Source: Adapted from Statistics Canada. 2012g. "Conjugal Status, Opposite/Same-sex Status and Presence of Children for the Couple Census Families in Private Households of Canada, Provinces, Territories and Census Metropolitan Areas, 2011 Census." Retrieved July 14, 2014 (www12.statcan.gc.ca/census-recensement/2011/dp-pd/tbt-tt/Rp-eng.cfm?LANG=E&APATH=3&DETAIL=0&DIM=0&FL=A&FREE=0&GC=0&GID=0&GK=0&GRP=1&PID=102659&PRID=0&PTYPE=101955&S=0&SHOWALL=0&SUB=0&Temporal=2011&THEME=89&VID=0&VNAMEE=&VNAMEF=). Statistics Canada. 2011a. Census of Population, Statistics Canada Catalogue no. 98-312-XCB2011046. Statistics Canada. 2012m. Portrait of Families and Living Arrangements in Canada: Families, Households and Marital Status, 2011 Census of Population. Catalogue no. 98-312-X2011001. Ottawa: Minister of Industry.

Worldwide, and often amid sharp controversy, the legal and social definition of "family" is being broadened to include same-sex partners in long-term relationships. This change reflects the fact that most homosexuals, like most heterosexuals, want a long-term, intimate relationship with one other adult (Chauncey, 2005). Moreover, many same-sex partners want their relationships to be formally recognized by the state so that they can enjoy the same legal rights as do married heterosexual couples. For example, marriage allows same-sex partners to participate in medical decision making, jointly own property, and inherit property when one partner dies.

Even so, same-sex cohabiting relationships are much more likely to break up than either cohabiting or married different-sex relationships (Andersson et al., 2006; Kalmijn, Loeve, and Manting, 2007; Lau, 2012). Because the option of same-sex marriage is very recent, it will be many years before researchers will be able to assess whether same-sex marriages are as likely to end in divorce as different-sex marriages.

TIME FOR REVIEW

- What makes marriage a social institution?
- What new and emerging family forms exist in Canada?
- Why do same-sex relationships tend to be more fragile than opposite-sex relationships?

DIVORCE

Though few people enter marriage with the expectation that it will fail, the reality is that many marriages do not last. Before 1968, divorce was a complex legal process, and it was rare. Adultery was the only grounds for divorce in Canada, except in Nova Scotia, where cruelty was sufficient grounds even before Confederation (Morrison, 1987). The Divorce Act of 1968 expanded the grounds for granting a divorce to include mental or physical cruelty, rape, gross addiction to alcohol or other drugs, sodomy, bestiality, and homosexual acts. The dissolution of a marriage was also permitted on grounds of unspecified "marital breakdown" if couples lived apart for a number of years. The 1985 amendment of Canada's Divorce Act specified only one ground for divorce—marital breakdown, defined in three ways: (1) the spouses lived apart for one year, (2) one of the spouses committed adultery, or (3) one spouse treated the other with mental or physical cruelty.

Currently, 41 percent of all marriages end in divorce before the thirtieth year of marriage (Kelly, 2012). In nearly all cases, divorces are granted on the basis of a couple having lived apart for at least one year (Statistics Canada, 2011b). Remember, however, that divorce statistics no longer provide an accurate picture of the number of family breakups because they do not include the formation and dissolution of cohabiting relationships. Since cohabiting relationships are less stable than marriage is, the rate of union dissolution must necessarily be much higher than the divorce rate implies.

We now turn to a brief overview of the correlates of divorce and then address its consequences.

Predictors of Divorce

Unhappiness with one's spouse is an obvious correlate of divorce (Guven, Senik, and Stichnoth, 2012; Sayer et al., 2011). So are other interpersonal factors. Thus, relationships characterized by high levels of conflict, including violence, are likely to end in divorce. Equally fragile are relationships where one or both partners struggle with substance abuse or mental health problems (Kreager et al., 2013; Strohschein, 2012). Infidelity is also associated with divorce (Finch and Beacham, 2010).

Demographic and social factors also make a difference. Women are more likely than men are to initiate divorce. Divorce is more likely to occur in the earlier years of marriage (Clark and Compton, 2006). Couples who are religious are less likely to divorce, particularly when they belong to the same religion (Lyngstad and Jalovaara, 2010). Social factors associated with an increased risk of divorce include living in poverty, having less education, cohabiting with one's spouse before marriage, having a premarital birth or a previous marriage, and having grown up in a household without two continuously married parents (Amato, 2010; Bumpass and Wu, 2000; Clark and Compton, 2006; Lyngstad and Jalovaara, 2010; Woods and Emery, 2002; Wu and Pollard, 2000; Wolfinger, 2011).

Interestingly, premarital cohabitation may be weakening as a predictor of divorce (Hewitt and DeVaus, 2009; Liefbroer and Dourleijn, 2006; Manning and Cohen, 2012). Researchers suspect that as cohabitation becomes more common and accepted as an intermediate step on the path to marriage, those who cohabit before marriage will no longer be prone to divorce. Family researchers are following this trend closely.

Kevin Mazur/Getty Images for J/P Haitian Relief Organization

Gwyneth Paltrow and Chris Martin filed for divorce in 2014, assuring the public that their amicable divorce could shield their two children, Apple and Moses, from any emotional harm.

Consequences of Divorce

Although divorce enables spouses to leave unhappy marriages, serious questions have been raised about the consequences of divorce, particularly in the long term. When it comes to the consequences for children, some scholars claim that divorcing parents are trading their children's well-being for their own happiness. Celebrities like Gwyneth Paltrow, who announced her divorce to Coldplay musician Chris Martin in 2014, have a different opinion. In her blog, Paltrow stated that if divorcing parents engage in "conscious uncoupling," they can protect their children from the emotional harms of divorce. This viewpoint implies that there may be such a thing as a good divorce. What does research say about this issue?

Research perspectives have shifted dramatically regarding the effects of parental divorce on a child's well-being. In the past, researchers viewed divorce as a catastrophic event in the lives of children. They evaluated children's well-being in both intact and divorced-parent households and consistently found deficits in the well-being of children in divorced-parent households. Children of divorce were said to grow into adults who struggled with high levels of depression and anxiety, battled ongoing drug and alcohol abuse, and had difficulty forming intimate relationships (Wallerstein, Lewis, and Blakeslee, 2000).

These early studies were deeply flawed. For example, researchers identified three main issues with a landmark 25-year study of divorced children (Amato, 2003). First, the children in the study were all known to be struggling with divorce and received counselling in exchange for participating in the study. Second, the study did not include a control group of children in intact households, making it impossible to test whether any real differences existed between children from divorced and non-divorced families. Third, the study did not allow researchers to evaluate whether some of the problems detected in children after divorce had existed prior to divorce.

These criticisms ushered in more rigorous standards for how researchers ought to investigate the consequences of divorce on children's well-being. A research design that follows intact families over time makes it possible to compare outcomes between children whose parents remain married and those whose parents subsequently divorce. Such a research design also makes it possible to know whether and when in the divorce process children start developing adjustment issues.

As it turns out, researchers have learned that children experience adjustment issues even before their parents file for divorce (Cherlin, Chase-Lansdale and McRae, 1998; Strohschein, 2012). Part of the reason is because in the period leading up to divorce, the quality of the marital relationship deteriorates. Parents may withdraw from one another emotionally. They may argue more frequently and with greater intensity. Tension between parents is emotionally distressing for everyone in the family, including children. Thus, it is not uncommon for children and their parents to develop adjustment issues prior to divorce.

Today, most researchers study divorce from the perspective of stress theory. Stress theory suggests that experiences such as divorce require adjustment to new circumstances but do not necessarily threaten well-being. How well people are able to rebound and adjust following divorce depends on the resources they can draw on, the extent to which divorce is accompanied by other disruptions, and their attitudes about the divorce (Amato, 2000). For example, divorce is less stressful when parents continue to provide their children with reassurance and affirmation, when there are relatively few changes to children's daily routines, and when children are encouraged to talk about their feelings. Conversely, adjustment is more difficult when parents are too overwhelmed to be effective caregivers, when divorce forces children to move out of their neighbourhoods and away from peers and positive adult role models, and when children are encouraged to take the side of one parent over another.

To understand why some children are more adversely affected by parental divorce than others are, we must examine what happens to children throughout the divorce process. Researchers have identified three main factors associated with child adjustment to divorce: economic hardship, reduced contact with the non-residential parent, and changes in family structure.

Economic Hardship

Women's income usually falls after divorce, while men's income usually changes little (Gadalla, 2008; La Rochelle-Côté, Myles, and Picot, 2012). This result occurs because husbands tend to earn more than wives do, children typically live with their mothers after divorce, and child-support payments are often inadequate.

In the past, Canadian laws regarding the division of marital assets on divorce and the awarding of alimony contributed to women's declining living standards post-divorce. For example, in the early 1970s, Irene Murdock, a farm wife, claimed that her labours over the course of 15 years had earned her a share in the family farm. However, the Supreme Court of Canada ruled that her work was simply that of an "ordinary farm wife" and did not entitle her to share in the property that she and her husband had accumulated during their marriage (Steel, 1987: 159).

Although all Canadian provinces and territories now have laws requiring spouses to share assets in the event of marital breakdown, the precise definition of what constitutes a "family asset" varies and creates inconsistencies across jurisdictions (Dranoff, 2001: 257). In addition, although the monetary value of tangible "family assets," such as a house or money in the bank, can be calculated and shared, the valuable "new property" in today's society is the earning power of a professional degree, highly paid employment, work experience, a skilled trade, or other human capital. On divorce, the wife *may* receive an equal share of tangible property, but that does not usually result in her beginning post-divorce life on an equal footing with her former husband—especially if she retains physical custody of the couple's children and if she previously sacrificed her education and career so he could earn a college or university degree.

Child support involves money paid by the non-custodial parent to the custodial parent for the purpose of supporting the children of a separated marital, cohabiting, or sexual relationship.

Child support is money paid by the non-custodial parent to the custodial parent for the purpose of supporting the children of a separated marital, cohabiting, or sexual relationship. Under the Divorce Act, either parent may be ordered to pay child support. However, because mothers retain custody in most cases—and because women are more likely to be economically disadvantaged—the vast majority of those ordered to pay child support are fathers.

Every jurisdiction in Canada requires parents to support their children following separation or divorce. However, court orders do not guarantee that child support will be paid. In practice, default rates have been high, and orders for child and spousal support have often been difficult to enforce. All Canadian provinces and territories now have programs to prevent non-payment of child support. Nonetheless, the problem of "deadbeat parents" remains significant. In an effort to address the problem, Alberta and Ontario have recently taken to posting on their websites the names and photos of people who default on child support payments. Naming them and asking for the public's help in finding them is presumed to increase the pressure on defaulters. Whether this tactic works is unknown.

What is known is that economic hardship following parental divorce makes it difficult for children to cope. When divorced parents cannot achieve the same standard of living they had prior to divorce, feelings of loss may be amplified. If the family falls into poverty, the inability to meet basic needs is a potent threat to a child's well-being. Economic hardship can also disrupt previously established routines, leaving children feeling disconnected and adrift. If economic troubles force a family to move away from a familiar school and neighbourhood, disruption is greater still.

Reduced Contact with the Non-Residential Parent

Because after divorce, children more often live with their mothers than with their fathers, divorced children are more likely to lose touch with their fathers (Juby, LeBourdais, and Marcil-Gratton, 2005; Sinha, 2014). It was once thought that contact with the non-residential parent had few effects on child outcomes and that the economic contributions of the non-residential parent mattered most (Amato and Gilbreth, 1999). Today, sociologists understand that the relationship between children and their non-residential parent is important for children's well-being, particularly when contact is not superficial. However, the nature of contact with a non-residential parent and its benefits to children are often determined by the amount of conflict between ex-spouses. Non-residential fathers typically reduce contact with their children when they have ongoing conflict with their former spouse.

Children's well-being suffers most when parents persist in or escalate hostilities after divorce. Conversely, children benefit from contact with their non-residential parent when ex-spouses get along with each other. In short, it is not the amount of contact with a non-residential parent that makes a difference, but the degree of cooperation and commitment to shared parenting that determine whether such contact helps or hinders a child's adjustment to parental divorce (Sobolewski and King, 2005).

Additional Changes in Family Structure

After divorce, parents may seek new partners. Up to one-half of divorced parents subsequently remarry or cohabit. Scholars once thought that remarriage was a positive influence on children. But research now shows that a favourable outcome is often not the case. Many children living in step-parent households derive little benefit from the additional income and supervision that a step-parent brings to the household. This lack of benefit results for a few reasons. For example, because remarriages often occur between people who have had previous unions, a new spouse may be supporting non-resident children from previous relationships, which reduces the financial resources available to the current household. Similarly, after remarriage, children may find themselves competing with the step-parent for the attention of the biological parent. If new children are born into the union, the current children may come to resent their newborn half-siblings or feel relegated to the outskirts of the family.

In addition, the entry of another adult figure in the household introduces the possibility that the new relationship will also fail. If that relationship breaks down, children who experience this second marital disruption may be particularly vulnerable. Researchers in Canada and the United States have found that children who experience multiple changes in family structure fare more poorly than do children who experience a single divorce in childhood (Fomby and Cherlin, 2007; Fomby and Sennott, 2013; Strohschein, Roos and Brownell, 2009). One study followed all children born to married-parent households in 1984 in Manitoba. Tracking these children until they reached young adulthood, the researchers tested whether the number of changes in family structure they experienced from birth until age 18 predicted high-school graduation. The results are shown in Figure 15.5.

Children who remained in a married-parent household throughout their childhood had the highest rate of high-school graduation. Children who experienced one change in family structure, either through parental death or divorce, were significantly less likely to finish high school. Note that remarriage did not improve the graduation rate to the level of continuously married parents. The rate of high-school completion was by far the lowest among children who had experienced three or more family structure transitions between birth and age 18.

These results suggest that the effects of parental divorce may be wide-ranging and long-lasting. Parents do not want divorce to harm their children. They typically go to great lengths to protect them. However, it is difficult to foresee all of the ways in which parental divorce will alter children's living conditions and life trajectories (see Box 15.2).

That brings us back to our original question: Is there such a thing as a good divorce? When we examine the ways in which parental divorce can reduce the family's economic circumstances, downgrade the quality of the parent-child relationship, and open the door

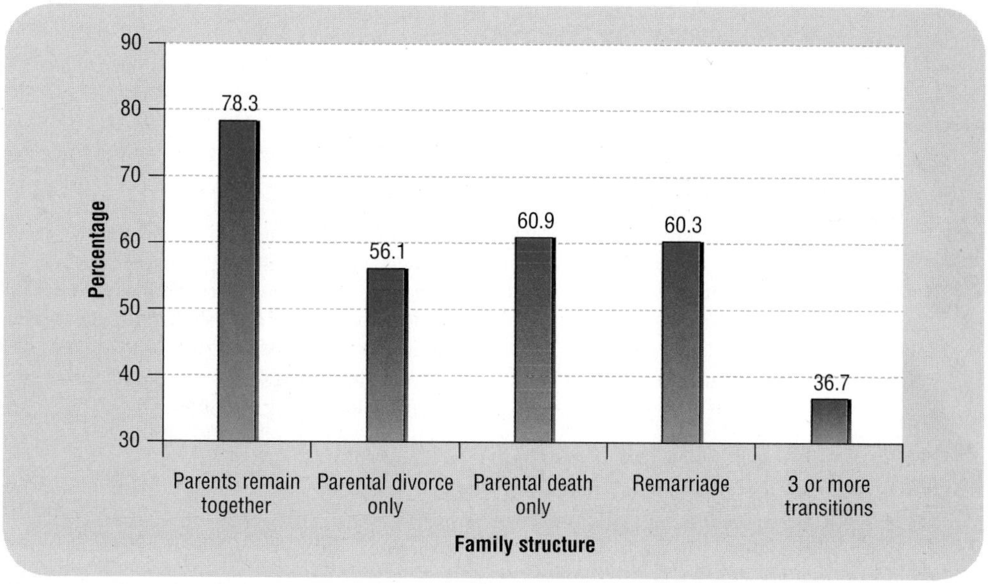

FIGURE 15.5

Percent Graduating from High School, by Number of Changes in Family Structure, 1984 Manitoba Birth Cohort, Born into a Married-Parent Household

Adapted from Strohschein, Lisa, Noralou Roos, and Marni Brownell. 2009. "Family structure histories and high school completion: Evidence from a population based registry." *Canadian Journal of Sociology 34*(1): 83–103.

BOX 15.2

SOCIOLOGY ON THE TUBE

THE MILLERS

Richard Foreman/CBS via Getty Images

Nate referees the arguments between his newly separated parents.

Does parental divorce touch only the lives of young children living under their parents' roof? If the story of the Millers, a hit TV show on CBS, is any indication, the answer is a resounding no. Divorce can alter family dynamics even when it occurs years after children have grown up and moved away.

After three years of marriage, Nate Miller, a local news reporter, has just split up with his wife. Nate is terrified of his parents' reaction and will go to any lengths to prevent them from finding out. One day, his parents, Tom and Carol (played by Beau Bridges and Margo Martindale) show up unannounced at his condo. Somehow, the secret spills out. It has the most surprising effect on his parents. Once they recover from the initial shock, Tom declares that he is following his son's lead. He wants a divorce from Carol, to whom he has been married for 43 years. Pandemonium ensues. When the dust settles, Carol has moved in with Nate and Tom is hunkering down with Nate's sister, Debbie, and her husband Adam. Hence, the show's tagline: The only thing more painful than having your parents split up is having them move in.

The show illustrates how Nate and Debbie, along with their divorcing parents, come to terms with the new family living arrangements. There are plenty of laughs along the way. To its credit, however, the show attempts to capture the deep emotional undercurrents that can accompany divorce. Indeed, the show delivers some sociological insights through its depiction of the adjustments that adult children and aging parents make in response to parental divorce.

First, both Nate and his sister are forced to examine their rose-tinted perception of their childhood experiences, eventually recognizing that their parents' constant bickering and marital unhappiness often had unsettling effects on their own well-being. This observation corresponds with sociological research finding that one reason why children are in poorer mental health long before parental divorce occurs is because of the conflict they were exposed to while their parents were still together. The insight that their family life was less than ideal also makes Nate and Debbie rethink their knee-jerk plan to reunite their parents. They acknowledge that their parents' marriage cannot be salvaged. The realization is bittersweet. They remain saddened over what their parents' relationship has become but are emotionally ready to move on.

Second, the show vividly demonstrates that uncoupling isn't the clean break some people might think or want it to be. A shared history is not so easily discarded, despite one's best intentions. Accustomed to dealing with their parents as a unit, Nate and Debbie must now treat their parents as separate people. Divorce appears to have transformed their parents into people whom their adult children are no longer sure they really know. Perhaps most challenging of all is the emotional minefield. Because Tom and Carol are focused on their own inner turmoil and are largely oblivious to the needs and personal space of their adult children, the task seems particularly difficult. The show makes clear that there is no easy roadmap for Nate and Debbie to follow: each step forward will be hard fought.

That's not to say that separation is any easier for Carol and Tom. They bicker every time they see one another. They seek to humiliate one another other, trying to show that life as a single person is far better than their past married life. Yet, they miss some aspects of their former life. In one naughty episode, they sneak off to have sex. It becomes just another piece of information to hide from their kids. They seem to know intuitively that muddying their status as divorcing parents will be too much for their kids to handle. Their kids now see them as separated; slowly, they must learn how to see themselves that way too.

Gladskikh Tatiana/Shutterstock.com

A high level of parental conflict creates long-term distress among children. If their parents divorce, children may escape a stressful environment, leading to a post-divorce reduction in their aggression.

to further changes in family structure, it is clear that divorce often acts as a trigger for further disruptions. Some parents avoid such disruptions. Good divorces certainly take place. However, when disruptions accumulate and pervade daily life, the likelihood that children will cope well decreases dramatically (Amato, Kane, and James, 2011).

There appears to be only one situation in which children *always* fare better following divorce. In highly dysfunctional households that have a high level of parental conflict, children tend to experience a reduction in their aggressive behaviour after their parents split up (Morrison and Coiro, 1999; Strohschein, 2005). In such cases, parental divorce represents a relief from the tensions of an openly hostile environment.

TIME FOR REVIEW

- What demographic and social factors predict divorce?
- What further disruptions are commonly experienced by children whose parents divorce?
- Under what circumstances is a good divorce possible?

REPRODUCTION

The transformation of marriage has been accompanied by an equally dramatic revolution in reproduction. Lifelong marriage, once the only socially sanctioned means for raising children, is today just one option available for those who desire to be parents. In the twenty-first century, parenthood often precedes marriage. Consequently, the average age at which women give birth to their first child is now younger than the average age at which women enter their first marriage. In addition, technological advances have weakened the link between sex and procreation. Oral contraceptives and safer abortion procedures allow women to dictate the circumstances under which childbearing occurs. In vitro fertilization makes it possible to have a baby without the physical act of sex. In the following sections, we discuss the ways in which Canadian women exercise reproductive choice before describing the different types of households that children now grow up in.

Reproductive Choice

Children are increasingly expensive to raise. They no longer give the family economic benefits, as they once did on the family farm. Most women want to work in the paid labour force, and many pursue a career. Consequently, most women decide to have fewer children, to have them further apart, and to have them starting at an older age. Some decide to have none at all (Ravanera and Beaujot, 2009).

A woman's decision not to have children may be carried out by means of contraception or abortion. Abortion was declared a criminal offence in Canada in 1892. In the 1960s, an abortion reform movement spearheaded by Dr. Henry Morgentaler urged the repeal of abortion laws that, in his words, "compelled the unwilling to bear the unwanted" (quoted in Dranoff, 2001: 16). In 1969, the law was changed to permit "therapeutic abortion" if performed by a physician in an accredited hospital and if a three-member committee certified that the continuation of the pregnancy would likely endanger the health of the mother. In 1988, the Supreme Court of Canada struck down the law on abortion on the grounds that it contravened a woman's right to control her own reproductive life and, as such, contravened her constitutionally protected guarantee to security of her person. In 1989, the Supreme Court unanimously determined that the civil law in Québec, the Québec Charter, and the common law do not protect fetal life or interests. In 1993, the Supreme Court of Canada struck down legislation that banned abortion clinics. Today, abortion clinics operate in most Canadian provinces; the exceptions are Nova Scotia, New Brunswick, Prince Edward Island, and Saskatchewan.

In 2010, the latest year for which data are available, 64 641 abortions took place in Canada (Canadian Institute for Health Information [CIHI], 2014). This count excludes Québec, which reported 27 139 abortions in 2009. Thus, the abortion rate in Canada is approximately 14 per 1000 women between the ages of 15 and 44. The abortion rate in Canada is about the same as it is in the United States (Pazol et al., 2013). Of those countries in the world where abortion data are collected, Russia has the highest abortion rates at approximately 37 per 1000 women.

Attitudes toward abortion in Canada are mixed. Surveys consistently show that one-third of Canadian women believe that the life of a fetus should be protected at conception, one-third believe it should be protected at some point during pregnancy, and one-third believe that legal protection should start at birth (CIHI, 2014). Abortion attitudes vary by age. Young adults are more likely than are older adults to approve of the availability of legal abortion for any reason (Bibby, 2001). Ninety percent of adults and 84 percent of teenagers support the availability of legal abortion when rape is involved.

Researchers argue that a repeal of abortion laws would likely return us to the situation that existed in the 1960s (Sedgh et al., 2012). Many abortions took place then, but because they were illegal, they were expensive, difficult to obtain, and posed dangers to women's health. If abortion laws were repealed, many researchers predict that women living in poverty and their unwanted children would suffer most. Taxpayers would wind up paying bigger bills for welfare and medical care.

Reproductive Technologies

For most women, exercising reproductive choice means being able to prevent pregnancy and birth by means of contraception and abortion. For some women, however, it means *facilitating* pregnancy and birth by means of reproductive technologies. Some couples are infertile. With a declining number of desirable children available for adoption, and a persistent and strong desire by most people to have children, demand exists for techniques to help infertile couples, some same-sex couples, and single women have babies.

Reproductive technologies are used in four main ways. In *artificial insemination*, a donor's sperm is inserted in a woman's vaginal canal or uterus during ovulation. In *surrogate motherhood*, a donor's sperm is used to artificially inseminate a woman who has signed a contract to surrender the child at birth in exchange for a fee. In *in vitro fertilization*, eggs are surgically removed from a woman and joined with sperm in a culture dish; a resulting embryo is then transferred back to the woman's uterus. Finally, various *screening techniques* are used on sperm and fetuses to increase the chance of giving birth to a baby of the desired sex and to end pregnancies deemed medically problematic.

Social, Ethical, and Legal Issues

Reproductive technologies raise several sociological and ethical issues (Gerrits et al., 2013). One is discrimination. Most reproductive technologies are expensive. Surrogate mothers can charge $20 000 or more to carry a child. In vitro fertilization can cost $100 000 or more. Poor and middle-income earners who happen to be infertile cannot afford these procedures. In addition, some members of the medical profession have a strong tendency to deny single women and same-sex couples access to reproductive technologies; the medical community discriminates not just against those of modest means but also against non-nuclear families.

A second problem introduced by reproductive technologies is that they render the terms *mother* and *father* obsolete, or at least vague. Is the mother the person who donates the egg, carries the child in her uterus, or raises the child? Is the father the person who donates the sperm or raises the child? As these questions suggest, a child conceived through a combination of reproductive technologies and raised by a heterosexual couple could have as many as three mothers and two fathers! But it is not just a problem of terminology. If it were, we could just introduce new distinctions to reflect the new reality, such as "egg mother," "uterine mother," and "social mother." The real problem is social and legal. It is unclear who has what rights and obligations to the child, and what rights and obligations the child has vis-à-vis each parent. This lack of clarity has already caused anguished court battles over child custody. In 2011, a British court may have set a precedent by permitting a surrogate mother to keep the baby she carried despite having signed a contract to hand it over to a couple for £4500 ($7400; Allen, Ellicott, and Eccles, 2011). Reproductive technologies, in short, have caused people to rethink the very nature of the family.

Public debate on a wide scale is needed to decide who will control reproductive technologies and to what ends. Reproductive technologies may bring the greatest joy to infertile people. They may also prevent the birth of children with diseases such as muscular dystrophy and multiple sclerosis. However, reproductive technologies may continue to benefit mainly the well-to-do, reinforce traditional family forms that are no longer appropriate for many people, and cause endless legal wrangling and heartache.

In the next few pages, we consider a variety of different family configurations in which Canadian children may grow up. We begin, however, by considering zero-child families.

Zero-Child Families

In Canada, what we prefer to call "zero-child families" are increasingly common. Our admittedly clumsy term seems necessary because the alternatives are so value laden: a "childless family" implies that a family without children lacks something it should have, while the more recent "child-free family" suggests that a family without a child is unencumbered and that a child is therefore a burden. To maintain neutrality, we resort to clumsiness.

Roughly a fifth of North American women between the ages of 40 and 44 have never given birth (Ravanera and Beaujot, 2009). To explain this fact we must first recognize that not having a child may be the result of circumstances beyond a couple's control. For example, one or both partners may be infertile, and some evidence suggests that infertility is a growing issue, perhaps because of chemical pollutants in the air and water. It seems

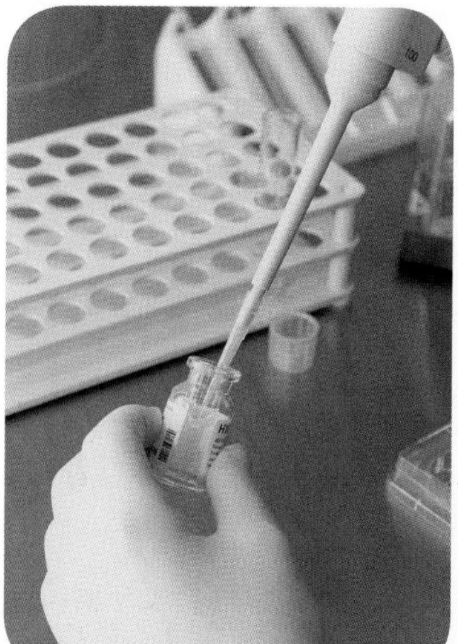

Fertilizing an egg in vitro

that not having a child is more often a matter of choice, however, and the main reasons for the increasing prevalence of zero-child families are the rising cost of raising a child and the growth of attractive alternatives.

Just how expensive are children? This is a matter for debate. In 2011, *Money Sense* magazine reported that it cost parents a whopping $243 660 to raise a child to the age of 19. Note that this estimate does not include the costs of postsecondary education. Couples also incur non-economic costs when they have a child, the most important of which is stress. The birth of a child requires that couples do more work in the home, give up free time and time together, develop an efficient daily routine, and divide responsibilities. All these requirements introduce sources of disagreement and tension in daily life, so it is little wonder that relationship satisfaction declines with a child in the house (Nomaguchi and Milkie, 2005).

Alternative attractions decrease the desire of some couples to have a child. People with high income, high education, and professional and managerial occupations are most likely to have zero-child families. Such people tend to place an especially high value on mobility, careers, and leisure-time pursuits. The desire to postpone having children to achieve other goals can turn a couple's "waiting game" into eventual acceptance of their permanent status as a zero-child family (Ravanera and Beaujot, 2014). Usually, such adults are neither frustrated nor unhappy that they do not have a child. Despite their tendency to feel negatively stereotyped as "selfish," they tend to be more satisfied with their marriage than are couples with a child (Lamanna and Riedmann, 2009).

Lone-Parent Families

During the first half of the twentieth century, lone-parent families generally resulted because of the death of one parent. Today, solo parenting is usually the product of separation or divorce. A third route to lone parenthood involves single, never-married mothers who give birth to children on their own. The biological father may be in the picture, but he does not live with the child. Changes in the distribution of these routes to lone-parenthood are illustrated in Figure 15.6.

In 2011, 16 percent of Canadian families were headed by a lone parent, with more than eight in ten lone-parent families headed by women (Statistics Canada, 2012m). Poverty is far more prevalent among female-headed single-parent families than among any other type

FIGURE 15.6

Distribution of the Legal Marital Status of Lone Parents, Canada, 1961–2011.

Statistics Canada. 2012i. Fifty Years of Families in Canada, 1961–2011: Families, Households and Marital Status, 2011 Census of Population. Catalogue no. 98-312-X2011003. Ottawa, ON: Minister of Industry. Page 3.

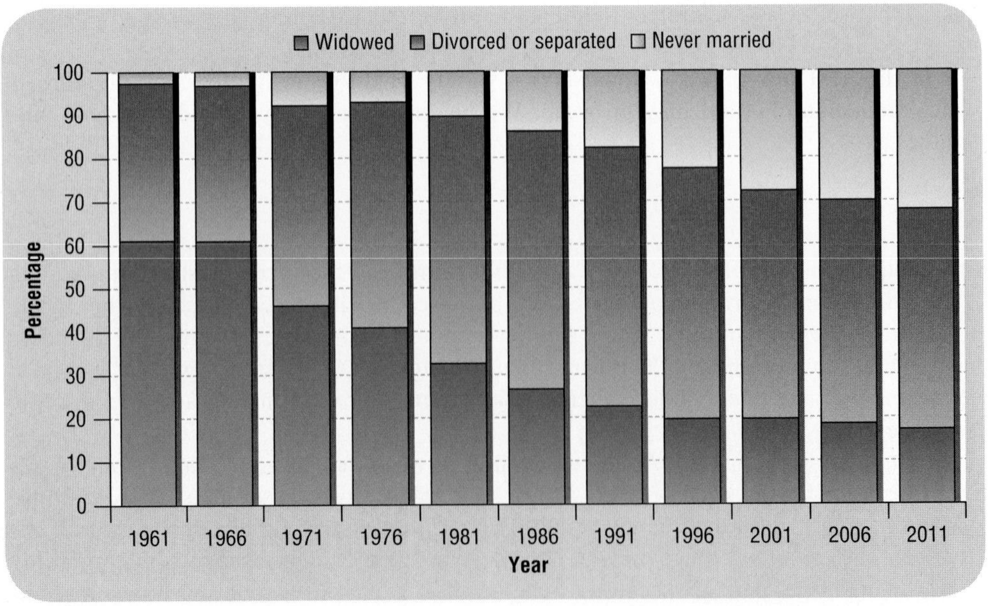

MoMo Productions/Getty Images

Divorce is responsible for the majority of lone-parent families in Canada today. Female-headed lone-parent families are far more common than male-headed lone-parent families.

of family. The poverty rate in female-headed single-parent families is more than double the rate in male-headed single-parent families.

Step-Parent Families

About one in ten children under the age of 14 lives in a step-parent family (Statistics Canada, 2012m). Simple step-parent families exist when only one adult has children from a prior union living in the household. A complex step-parent household exists when (1) both adults have one or more children from a previous relationship living in the household or (2) only one parent has one or more children from a prior relationship in the household but new children are born into the household from the current relationship. Over the past 15 years, the proportion of simple step-parent families has declined while the proportion of complex step-parent families has increased (Vezina, 2012).

Children in Same-Sex Couple Households

Some same-sex couples are raising children who (1) were the offspring of previous, heterosexual marriages, (2) were adopted, or (3) resulted from artificial insemination. Many people believe that children raised by same-sex parents will develop a confused sexual identity, exhibit a tendency to become homosexuals themselves, and suffer discrimination from children and adults in the "straight" community. Unfortunately, there is little research in this area and much of it is based on small, unrepresentative samples. Nevertheless, the research findings are consistent. They suggest that children who grow up in same-sex parent families are much like children who grow up in heterosexual families (Tasker and Golombok, 1997).

Families with same-sex parents differ from families with heterosexual parents in some respects. Same-sex couples tend to be more egalitarian than heterosexual couples are, sharing most decision making and household duties equally (Goldberg, Smith, and Perry-Jenkins, 2012; Rosenbluth, 1997). Their egalitarian approach may result because they are more likely to reject traditional marriage patterns. The fact that they tend to experience similar gender socialization and earn about the same income also encourages equality (Kurdek, 1998). In sum, available research suggests that raising children in same-sex parent families has no apparent negative consequences for the children.

In 2002, in a precedent-setting move hailed by gay-rights activists as the first of its kind in the world, full parental rights were extended to homosexual couples in Québec. Here, lesbians react as the Québec legislature passes the law.

TIME FOR REVIEW

- How has technology facilitated the weakening of the links between reproduction and sex?
- Why is non-marital childbearing a concern?
- In what ways have children's family structures become more diverse?

FAMILY POLICY

Having discussed several aspects of the decline of the traditional nuclear family and the proliferation of diverse family forms, we can now return to the big question posed at the beginning of this chapter: Is the decline of the nuclear family a bad thing for society? Do families with two biological parents—particularly those with stay-at-home moms—provide the kind of discipline, role models, help, and middle-class lifestyle that children need to stay out of trouble with the law and grow up to become well-adjusted, productive members of society? Conversely, are family forms other than the traditional nuclear family the main source of teenage crime, poverty, welfare dependency, and other social ills?

The answer suggested by research is clear: although the decline of the traditional nuclear family can be a source of many social problems, it doesn't have to be that way (Brown, 2010; McLanahan, Tach, and Schneider, 2013). The United States demonstrates how social problems can emerge from the decline of the nuclear family. Sweden illustrates how such problems can be averted. These two cases represent two models that Canadians should consider when thinking about our own family policies. The top panel of Table 15.1 shows that *on most indicators of nuclear family decline, Sweden leads the United States.* In Sweden, men and women get married at a later age than in the United States. Rates of

TABLE 15.1
The "Decline" of the Nuclear Family and the Well-Being of Children: The United States and Sweden Compared

Indicators of Nuclear Family "Decline"	United States	Sweden	#1 "Decline"
Median age at first marriage			
Men	28.3	35.5	Sweden
Women	25.6	32.9	Sweden
Non-marital birth rate	38.5	54.7	Sweden
One-parent households with children aged <18 as % of all households with children aged <18	17.6	15.2	U.S.A.
Percentage of mothers with children aged <3 in labour force	54.2	71.9	Sweden
Indicators of Child Well-Being	**United States**	**Sweden**	**#1 "Well Being"**
Mean reading performance score at age 14	507	504	U.S.A.
Percentage of children in poverty	21.6	7.0	Sweden
Public spending on families as a percent of GDP	1.2	3.1	Sweden
Infant mortality rate	6.7	2.5	Sweden
Suicide rate for children aged 15–19 (per 100 000)	8.0	4.3	Sweden

Source: Adapted from OECD 2011 and Copen et al., 2012.

non-marital childbearing are higher in Sweden than in the United States. Compared with American women, a much larger proportion of Swedish women with children under the age of three work in the paid labour force.

The bottom panel of Table 15.1 shows that *on most measures of children's well-being, Sweden also leads the United States*. Only on reading scores do American children score slightly higher than do children in Sweden. The child poverty rate is far lower in Sweden than it is in the United States. Public spending on families as a percent of gross domestic product (GDP) is much higher in Sweden than in the United States. Moreover, the infant mortality rate and the youth suicide rate are far lower in Sweden than in the United States. Overall, then, the decline of the traditional nuclear family has gone further in Sweden than in the United States, but children are better off on average. How is this possible?

One explanation is that Sweden has something the United States lacks: a substantial family-support policy. When a child is born in Sweden, parents are entitled to a total of 16 months of parental leave that can be shared between them. Government benefits pay 80 percent of the parent's salary for the first 14 months, then a reduced rate for the final two months. Parents are entitled to free consultations at "well-baby clinics." Like all citizens of Sweden, they receive free health care from the state-run system. Temporary parental benefits are available for parents with a sick child under the age of 12. One parent can take up to 60 days off work per sick child per year at 80 percent of his or her salary. All parents can send their children to heavily government-subsidized, high-quality daycare.

Among industrialized countries, the United States stands at the other extreme. Since 1993, a parent is entitled to 12 weeks of *unpaid* parental leave. Under the Affordable Care Act that will be fully operational in 2016, six million Americans will still lack health care coverage. There is no system of state daycare. The value of the dependant deduction on income tax has fallen by nearly 50 percent in current dollars since the 1940s. Thus, when an unwed Swedish woman has a baby, she knows she can rely on state institutions to maintain her standard of living and help give her child an enriching social and educational environment. When an unwed American woman has a baby, she is pretty much on her own. She stands a good chance of sinking into poverty, with all the negative consequences that will have for her and her child.

Canada stands midway between these two extremes. In a study of 33 countries, Canada tied for fifth place on the number of weeks it allows new parents to take off work, but it stood fifteenth in terms of generosity of maternity leave payments (Smyth, 2003). Canada has enough regulated daycare spaces for only a fifth of Canadian children up to age 12, and the average annual government allocation for child care is less than $500 per child. An international comparison of early childhood services placed Sweden at the top, but ranked the United States and Canada near the bottom (UNICEF, 2008). Policy debates often revolve around the direction should Canada pursue in the future, given these options. Should Canadians move closer to the American or Swedish model?

In Canada, people commonly raise three criticisms against generous family-support policies. First, some people say such policies encourage illegitimate births, long-term dependence on welfare, and the breakup of two-parent families. However, research shows that neither the divorce rate nor the rate of births to unmarried mothers is higher when welfare payments are more generous (Albelda and Tilly, 1997; Ruggles, 1997; Sweezy and Tiefenthaler, 1996).

A second criticism of generous family-support policies focuses on child care. Some critics say that non-family child care is bad for children under the age of three. In their view, only parents can provide the love, interaction, and intellectual stimulation infants and toddlers need for proper social, cognitive, and moral development. However, when studies compare family care and daycare involving a strong curriculum, a stimulating environment, plenty of caregiver warmth, low turnover of well-trained staff, and a low ratio of caregivers to children, they find that daycare has no negative consequences for children over the age of one (Clarke-Stewart, Gruber, and Fitzgerald, 1994; Harvey, 1999). Research also shows that daycare has some benefits, notably enhancing a child's ability to make friends. The benefits of high-quality daycare are even more evident in low-income families, which often cannot provide the kind of stimulating environment offered by high-quality daycare.

The third criticism lodged against generous family-support policies is that they are expensive and need to be paid for by high taxes. That is true. Swedes, for example, pay

Painting class in a state-subsidized daycare facility in Stockholm, Sweden

Jonathan Blair/Corbis

higher taxes than just about anyone else in the world. They have made the political decision to pay high taxes partly to avoid the social problems and associated costs that emerge when the traditional nuclear family is replaced with other family forms and no institutions are available to help family members in need.

While few people want to pay higher taxes, it is important to note that generous family-support policies provide offsetting economic benefits. For example, Québec alone among Canadian provinces has established an inexpensive, universally accessible, high-quality, provincially regulated daycare system not unlike Sweden's. Research shows that, since the inception of the program in 1997, it has enabled many women to enter the paid labour force, increased gender equality, helped to boost median household income by a third, and lowered the level of income inequality in the province (Gignac, 2014). We thus see that such a daycare system is beneficial not just for women and not just for families. It benefits society as a whole.

TIME FOR REVIEW

- What reasons do Canadians generally give for opposing generous family-support policies?
- What are the benefits of generous family-support policies?

SUMMARY

1. **How does the traditional nuclear family differ from the contemporary Canadian family?**
   The traditional nuclear family consists of a married-parent household with at least one child, where the father is the provider and the mother is the homemaker. Today, such families are in the minority. Contemporary families are more diverse, more complex, and smaller than they used to be.

2. **What is the functionalist theory of the family? According to conflict theorists and feminists, what are the problems with this theory?**
   The functionalist theory holds that the nuclear family is a distinct and universal family form because it performs five important functions in society: sexual regulation, economic cooperation, reproduction, socialization, and emotional support. The theory is most accurate in depicting families in North America in the two decades after World War II. Families today and in other historical periods depart from the functional model in important respects. Marxists stress how families are tied to the system of capitalist ownership. They argue that only the elimination of capitalism can end gender inequality in families. Feminists note that gender inequality existed before capitalism and in communist societies. They stress how the patriarchal division of power and patriarchal norms reproduce gender inequality.

3. **How do patterns of couple formation in contemporary society differ from couple formation in the past?**
   In the past, marriages were arranged by families as a way of forging alliances between different kinship groups. As such, family needs and obligations had priority over personal preferences. Today, couples are expected to marry for love, and they spend significant amounts of time and effort to vet potential mates for physical and emotional compatibility. As the path from singlehood to marriage has become less linear and more ambiguous, new and emerging family forms have sprung up in the gap between them.

4. Is there such a thing as a good divorce?
Yes, but a good divorce can be difficult to achieve because it assumes that parents can accurately foresee and protect their children from the damaging effects of divorce. In actuality, parents often underestimate the amount of change that divorce brings into their lives. Whether children can adjust positively to divorce depends on the resources that can be drawn on, the occurrence of subsequent disruptions to their lives, and attitudes about the divorce. Disruptions such as a decline in living standards, estrangement from their parents, and a revolving-door of new adults entering and exiting their household make it difficult for children to cope well with parental divorce.

5. What types of family structures do children experience in Canadian society?
The continuously married, two-biological-parent household has given way to a proliferation of new family forms. Both non-marital childbearing and divorce have increased the number of children who spend time in a lone-parent household. The desire to find intimacy with a new partner has resulted in a growing number of step-parent households. Similarly, growing acceptance of same-sex relationships has increased the number of children being raised in such settings.

6. What sorts of policies can countries adopt to accommodate different family forms?
People sometimes blame the decline of the traditional nuclear family for increasing poverty, welfare dependence, and crime. However, some countries have adopted policies that largely prevent these problems. Therefore, these social problems are in a sense a political choice.

CHAPTER 16

RELIGION

Paper Boat Creative/Getty Images

IN THIS CHAPTER, YOU WILL LEARN TO

- Contrast religion's ability to create societal cohesion and reinforce social inequality with its ability to promote social conflict and social change.
- Evaluate the secularization thesis, which holds that the influence of religion on society is weakening.
- Assess the market theory of religion as an alternative to the secularization thesis.
- Appreciate the degree to which religious freedom and tolerance are under threat in some parts of the world.
- Identify social factors associated with religiosity.

RELIGION AND SOCIETY

Robert Brym started writing the first draft of this chapter just after returning from a funeral. "Roy was a fitness nut," says Robert, "and cycling was his sport. One perfect summer day, he was out training with his team. I wouldn't be surprised if the sunshine and vigorous exercise turned his thoughts to his good fortune. At 41, he was a senior executive in a medium-sized mutual funds firm. His boss, who treated him like a son, was grooming him for the presidency of the company. Roy had three vivacious children, ranging in age from 1 to 10, and a beautiful, generous, and highly intelligent wife. He was active in community volunteer work and everyone who knew him admired him. But on this particular summer day, he suddenly didn't feel well. He dropped back from the pack and then suffered a massive heart attack. Within minutes, he was dead.

"During *shiva*, the ritual week of mourning following the death of a Jew, hundreds of people gathered in the family's home and on their front lawn. I had never felt such anguish before. When we heard the steady, slow, clear voice of Roy's 10-year-old son solemnly intoning the mourner's prayer, we all wept. And we asked ourselves and one another the inevitable question: Why?"

In 1902, the great psychologist William James observed that this question lies at the root of all religious belief. Religion is the common human response to the fact that we all stand at the edge of an abyss. It helps us cope with the terrifying fact that we must die (James, 1976 [1902]: 116). It offers us immortality, the promise of better times to come, and the security of benevolent spirits who look over us. It provides meaning and purpose in a world that might otherwise seem cruel and senseless.

The motivation for religion may be psychological, as James argued. However, the content and intensity of our religious beliefs, and the form and frequency of our religious practices, are influenced by the structure of society and our place in it. In other words, the religious impulse takes literally thousands of forms. It is the task of the sociologist of religion to account for this variation. Why does one religion predominate here, another there? Why is religious belief more fervent at one time than at another? Under what circumstances does religion act as a source of social stability and under what circumstances does it act as a force for social change? Are we becoming more or less religious? Are we becoming more or less tolerant toward religious diversity? These are all questions that have occupied the sociologist of religion, and we touch on all of them here. Note that we will not have anything to say about the truth of religion in general or the value of any particular religious belief or practice. These are questions of faith, not science. They lie outside the province of sociology.

The cover of *Time* magazine once asked, "Is God Dead?" As a sociological observation, there can be little doubt about the answer. In Canada, 80 percent of adults believe that God exists (Environics Institute, 2011). By this measure (and by other measures we will examine below), God is still very much alive. Nonetheless, as we will show, the scope of religious authority has declined in Canada and in other parts of the world. That is, religion governs fewer aspects of life than it once did. Some Canadians still look to religion to deal with all of life's problems. But, increasingly, Canadians expect that religion can help them deal with only a restricted range of spiritual issues. Other institutions—medicine, psychiatry, criminal justice, education, and so forth—have grown in importance as the scope of religious authority has declined.

Stockbyte/Getty

Religion gives meaning to life and helps us cope with the terrifying fact that we must die.

At the same time, religious issues continue to intrude on public life, sometimes in unexpected ways. Television programs are starting to portray religious dilemmas (see Box 16.1). Governments cannot avoid being drawn into debates about religion because they are often framed in the language of rights. When religious rights are pitted against other rights, the state has the difficult task of finding an acceptable solution. Decisions often have an impact on our lives. As we will see, religion is far from being only a private matter.

Although a growing number of Canadians say they are not religious, other evidence suggests a religious awakening in some quarters. For instance, new religious movements are springing up, attracting converts daily. Moreover, fundamentalist and conservative religious traditions are gaining strength as liberal traditions become less appealing. Some sociologists have argued that viewing the field of religion as a kind of market comprising "sellers" and "buyers" of religious services can help us to understand how and why an overall pattern of decline in religious observance can be observed alongside growing religious intensity.

Before we address the issues just noted, let us see how the founding fathers of sociology and some important contemporary innovators in the field have treated the issue of religion in society.

THEORETICAL APPROACHES TO THE SOCIOLOGY OF RELIGION

Durkheim's Functionalist Approach

More than one person has said that hockey is Canada's "national religion." Do you agree with that opinion? Before making up your mind, consider that 80 percent of Canadians tuned in to at least part of the gold medal men's hockey game between Canada and the United States at the 2010 Vancouver Winter Olympics, making them the largest TV audience in Canadian history. And when Canada's men's hockey team came from behind to defeat the Soviets in 1972, the nation virtually came to a standstill ("Gold Medal," 2010).

Apart from drawing a huge audience, the Stanley Cup playoffs generate a sense of what Durkheim would have called "collective effervescence." That is, the Stanley Cup excites us by making us feel part of something larger than we are: the Montreal Canadiens, the Edmonton Oilers, the Toronto Maple Leafs, the Vancouver Canucks, the Calgary Flames, the Ottawa Senators, the Winnipeg Jets, the institution of Canadian hockey, the spirit of Canada itself. As celebrated Canadian writer Roch Carrier (1979: 77) wrote in his famous short story, "The Hockey Sweater": "School was . . . a quiet place where we could prepare for the next hockey game, lay out our next strategies.

BOX 16.1

SOCIOLOGY ON THE TUBE

FROM DUCK DYNASTY TO THE GOOD WIFE

Afraid of offending audiences and advertisers, television shows have traditionally shied away from characters that are overtly religious. When featured, religious characters have tended to be depicted stereotypically. One such example is born-again Christian Ned Flanders on the *The Simpsons*. Ned's overly pious nature habitually annoys his neighbour, Homer Simpson, and even exasperates his pastor, Reverend Lovejoy.

More recently, reality TV shows have taken to broadcasting the extreme lifestyles of some religious groups. *Sister Wives* reveals the complicated lives of a polygamous family, who belong to an offshoot of the Church of Latter Day Saints. *Duck Dynasty* showcases the outrageous antics of the eccentric but religiously devout Robertson family. Affiliated with the Church of Christ, the family ends each episode with a prayer.

Jeffrey Neira/CBS via Getty Images

Alicia Florrick and her husband, Peter, in *The Good Wife*.

There are some recent exceptions to the stereotypical and sensationalist depictions of religious characters on television. For example, the Canadian sitcom *Little Mosque on the Prairie* employed both humour and sensitivity in showing Muslims and Christians sharing their church building in rural Saskatchewan. Another exception is the hugely successful American drama, *The Good Wife*. The main character, Alicia Florrick, played by Julianna Margulies, relaunches her career as a lawyer when her husband, Peter, who works for the state attorney's office, is sent to jail for misusing public funds to pay for prostitutes. As Alicia contemplates and then attempts to repair her marriage to Peter (played by Chris Noth), other characters also develop their own storylines. One of these subplots involves the absorption of Peter and Alicia's teenaged daughter, Grace, with Christianity. Their daughter's religiosity puzzles her parents, neither of whom can understand what prompted their daughter's spiritual turn.

A few episodes later, a reporter asks Alicia whether she believes in God. It's a loaded question because her husband is running for the governorship. In the United States, politicians and their families who don't profess belief in God are considered unelectable. Nonetheless, Alicia responds truthfully. She tells the reporter that she is an atheist. Peter's campaign team is aghast. Has she sabotaged her husband's aspirations to the governorship? Apparently not. Her response elicits no change in her husband's approval ratings. Perhaps, the show implies, society has become more accepting of religious diversity.

The dynamics of living in a family where its members hold discrepant religious views presents an interesting opportunity for the show's writers, who might explore how religious diversity can be successfully managed. So far, the show's writers have not gone down this path. If they do, will the writers provide a fresh perspective and move past the caricatures employed by other television shows? Viewers can only watch and wait.

As for church, . . . there we forgot school and dreamed about the next hockey game. Through our daydreams it might happen that we would recite a prayer: we would ask God to help us play as well as Maurice Richard." For many hours each year, hockey enthusiasts transcend their everyday lives and experience intense enjoyment by sharing the sentiments and values of a larger collective. In their fervour, they banish thoughts of their own mortality. They gain a glimpse of eternity as they immerse themselves in institutions that will outlast them and athletic feats that people will remember for generations to come.

So do you think the Stanley Cup playoffs are a religious event? There is no god of the Stanley Cup (although the nickname of Canadian hockey legend Wayne Gretzky—The Great One—suggests that, for at least some fans, he may have transcended the status of a mere mortal). Nonetheless, the Stanley Cup playoffs meet Durkheim's definition of a religious experience. Durkheim said that when people live together, they come to share common sentiments and values. These common sentiments and values form a **collective conscience** that is larger than any individual's. On occasion, we experience the collective conscience directly. This causes us to distinguish the secular, everyday world of the **profane** from the religious, transcendent world of the **sacred**. We designate certain objects as symbolizing the sacred. Durkheim called these objects **totems**. We invent certain public practices to connect us with the sacred. Durkheim referred to these practices as **rituals**. According to him, the effect (or function) of rituals and of religion as a whole is to reinforce social solidarity.

Sergei Bachlakov/Shutterstock.com

From a Durkheimian point of view, the Stanley Cup playoffs can be considered a religious ritual.

Durkheim would have found support for his theory in research showing that major sporting events are linked to suicide rates (Andriessen and Krysinska, 2009). In the United States, the suicide rate is lower on Super Bowl Sunday than it is on other Sundays (Joiner, Hollar, and Van Orden, 2006). Similarly, when France hosted the FIFA World Cup, suicide rates dipped for younger Frenchmen (Encrenaz et al., 2012). In Québec from 1951 to 1992, the early ousting of the Montreal Canadiens from the Stanley Cup playoffs was associated with an increased tendency for young men to commit suicide during the hockey series (Trovato, 1998). These patterns are consistent with Durkheim's theory of suicide, which predicts a lower suicide rate when social solidarity increases and a higher suicide rate when social solidarity decreases (Chapter 1, A Sociological Compass).

The **collective conscience** comprises the common sentiments and values that people share as a result of living together.

Durkheim would consider the Stanley Cup and the team insignia to be totems. The insignia represent groups we identify with. The trophy signifies the qualities that professional hockey stands for: competitiveness, sportsmanship, excellence, and the value of teamwork. The hockey games themselves are public rituals enacted according to strict rules and conventions. We suspend our everyday lives as we watch the ritual unfold. The ritual heightens our experience of belonging to certain groups, increases our respect for certain institutions, and strengthens our belief in certain ideas. These groups, institutions, and ideas all transcend us. Thus, the Stanley Cup playoffs may be regarded as a sacred event in Durkheim's terms. They cement society in the way Durkheim said all religions do (Durkheim, 1976 [1915]). Do you agree with this Durkheimian interpretation of the Stanley Cup playoffs? Do you see any parallels between the Durkheimian analysis of the Stanley Cup playoffs and sports in your community or university?

The **profane** refers to the secular, everyday world.

The **sacred** refers to the religious, transcendent world.

Religion, Feminist Theory, and Conflict Theory

Durkheim's theory of religion is a functionalist account. It offers useful insights into the role of religion in society. Yet conflict and feminist theorists lodge two main criticisms against it. First, Durkheim's theory overemphasizes religion's role in maintaining social cohesion. In reality, religion often incites social conflict. Second, it ignores the fact that when religion does increase social cohesion, it often reinforces social inequality.

Totems are objects that symbolize the sacred.

Rituals in Durkheim's usage are public practices designed to connect people to the sacred.

Religion and Social Inequality

Consider first the role of major world religions and social inequality (see Figure 16.1 and Table 16.1). Little historical evidence helps us understand the social conditions that gave rise to the first world religions, Judaism and Hinduism, 3800 to 4000 years ago. But we know enough about the rise of Buddhism, Christianity, and Islam between 2700 and 1500 years ago to say that the impulse to find a better world is often encouraged by adversity in this one. We also know that Moses, Jesus, Muhammad, and Buddha all promoted a message of equality and freedom. Finally, we know that over generations, the charismatic leadership of

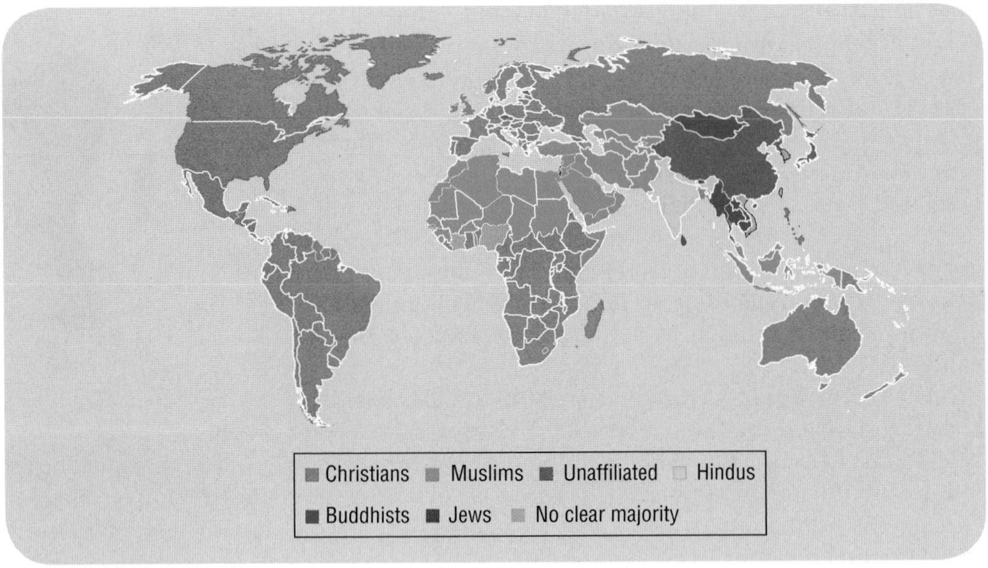

FIGURE 16.1
This map shows the dominant religion in each of the world's countries, defined as the religion to which more than 50 percent of a country's population adheres.

Source: Pew Research Center. "The Global Religious Landscape." © 2012. http://www.pewforum.org/2012/12/18/global-religious-landscape-exec/

The **routinization of charisma** is Weber's term for the transformation of divine enlightenment into a permanent feature of everyday life.

the world religions became "routinized." The **routinization of charisma** is Weber's term for the transformation of divine enlightenment into a permanent feature of everyday life. It involves turning religious inspiration into a stable social institution with defined roles, such as interpreters of the divine message, teachers, dues-paying laypeople, and so forth. The routinization of charisma typically makes religion less responsive to the needs of ordinary people, and it often supports social inequalities and injustices, as you will now see.

Religion and the Subordination of Women

It was Marx who first stressed how religion often tranquilizes the underprivileged into accepting their lot in life. He called religion "the opium of the people" (Marx, 1970 [1843]: 131).

We can draw evidence for Marx's interpretation from many times, places, and institutions. For example, as feminists note, the major world religions have traditionally placed women in a subordinate position, reinforcing patriarchy. Consider the following scriptural examples of the subordination of women:

- Corinthians in the *New Testament* emphasizes that "women should keep silence in the churches. For they are not permitted to speak, but should be subordinate, as even the law says. If there is anything they desire to know, let them ask their husbands at home. For it is shameful for a woman to speak in church."
- The *Sidur*, the Jewish prayer book, includes this morning prayer, which is recited by Orthodox and ultra-Orthodox men: "Blessed are you, Lord our God, King of the Universe, who did not make me a woman."
- The *Qur'an*, the holy book of Islam, contains a Book of Women in which it is written that "righteous women are devoutly obedient.... As to those women on whose part you fear disloyalty and ill-conduct, admonish them, refuse to share their beds, beat them."

It is also significant that Catholic priests and Muslim mullahs must be men, as must Jewish rabbis in the Conservative and Orthodox denominations. However, the major world religions are becoming less patriarchal in many parts of the world. Vibrant feminist movements exist among Muslims, Catholics, Orthodox Jews, and so on. Women have been allowed to serve as Protestant ministers since the mid-nineteenth century and as rabbis in the more liberal branches of Judaism since the 1970s. In the United Church of Canada, one-third of ordained ministers are female (United Church of Canada, 2013). In the meantime, there is a serious shortage of male candidates for the priesthood among Roman Catholics, perhaps portending change in that church as well.

TABLE 16.1
The Five World Religions: Origins, Beliefs, and Divisions

	Origins	Beliefs	Divisions
Judaism 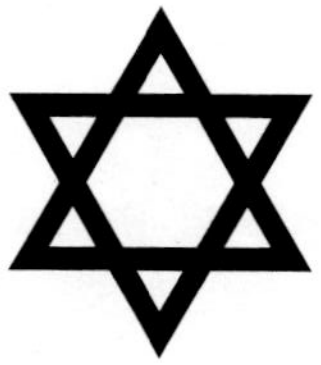	Judaism originated about 4000 years ago in what is now Iraq, when Abraham first asserted the existence of just one God. About 800 years later, Moses led the Jews out of Egyptian bondage. The emancipation of the Jews from slavery was a defining moment in the history of Judaism.	The central teachings rest on belief in one God (Yahweh) and on the idea that God sanctions freedom and equality. The 613 divine commandments (*mitzvot*) mentioned in the Five Books of Moses (Torah) form the core of orthodox Jewish practice The *mitzvot* include prescriptions for justice, righteousness, and observance: rest and pray on the Sabbath, honour the old and the wise, do not wrong a stranger in buying or selling, do not seek revenge or hold a grudge, etc. The Torah forms part of the Old Testament.	In seventeenth-century Eastern Europe, ecstatic Chasidic sects broke away from the bookish Judaism of the time. In nineteenth-century Germany, the Reform movement allowed prayer in German, the integration of women in worship, etc. Orthodox Judaism was a reaction against the liberalizing tendencies of Reform and involved a return to traditional observance. Conservative Judaism crystallized in Britain and the United States in the nineteenth century to reconcile what its practitioners regarded as the positive elements in Orthodoxy with the dynamism of Reform. Reconstructionism is a liberal twentieth-century movement known for its social activism and gender egalitarianism.
Christianity 	Christianity originated about 35 CE in what is now Israel. Jesus, a poor Jew, criticized the Judaism of his time for its external conformity to tradition and ritual at the expense of developing a true relationship to God as demanded by the prophets.	Believe in God and love him; love your neighbour—these are the two main lessons of Jesus. These teachings were novel because they demanded that people match outward performance with inner conviction. It was not enough not to murder. One could not even hate. Nor was it enough not to commit adultery. One could not even lust after a neighbour's wife (Matthew V, 21–30). These teachings made Jesus anti-authoritarian and even revolutionary. Admonishing people to love their neighbours impressed upon them the need to emancipate slaves and women. Christians retained the Jewish Bible as the Old Testament, adding the gospels and letters of the apostles as the New Testament.	In 312 CE, the Roman Emperor converted to Christianity and turned Christianity into a state religion, after which the Church became the dominant institution in Europe. In the sixteenth century, Martin Luther, a German priest, challenged the Christian establishment by seeking to establish a more personal relationship between the faithful and God. His ideas quickly captured the imagination of half of Europe and led to the split of Christianity into Catholicism and Protestantism. In the Middle Ages, Christianity had split into Western and Eastern halves, the former centred in Rome, the latter in Constantinople (now Istanbul, Turkey). Various Orthodox churches today derive from the Eastern tradition. Protestantism has been especially prone to splintering because it emphasizes the individual's relationship to God rather than a central authority. Today, there are hundreds of different Protestant churches.
Islam 	Islam originated about 600 CE in what is now Saudi Arabia. The powerful merchants of Mecca had become greedy and corrupt, impoverishing and enslaving many people. Also, fear grew that the Persian and Roman Empires might soon fall, bringing the end of the world. Into this crisis stepped Muhammad, who claimed to have visions from God.	People who profess Islam have five duties. At least once in their life they must recite the Muslim creed aloud, correctly, with full understanding, and with heartfelt belief. (The creed is "There is no god but Allah and Muhammad is his prophet.") Five times a day they must worship in a religious service. They must fast from sunrise to sunset every day during the ninth month of the lunar calendar (Ramadan). They must give charity to the poor. And at least once in their life they must make a pilgrimage to the holy city of Mecca. Muhammad's teachings were written down in the holy scriptures known as the Qur'an.	Muslims split into two factions over a dispute as to who would be Muhammad's successor. The Sunni argued the successor should be an elected member of a certain Meccan tribe, whereas the Shi'a preferred Muhammad's direct descendant. Today, most Muslims are Sunni. Wahhabism, a Sunni fundamentalist movement, originated in the eighteenth century and is the state religion of Saudi Arabia. It rejects the teachings of any but Muhammad and bans the worship of Islamic historical religious sites. Most Shi'a Muslims, concentrated in Iran, southern Iraq and Bahrain, are "Twelvers"; they follow the teachings of twelve infallible imams (preachers) descended from Muhammad, the last of whom, they believe, will one day be revealed as the ultimate saviour of humanity. Different Shi'a offshoots disagree over who qualifies as a perfect imam. Thus, Ismailis are "Seveners" and Zaidi are "Fivers." Sufism is a mystical sect within Shi'a Islam.

(*Continued*)

TABLE 16.1 *(Continued)*

	Origins	Beliefs	Divisions
Hinduism 	Hinduism originated about 2000 BCE in India in unknown circumstances. It had no single founder.	Hinduism has many gods, all of which are aspects of the one true God. There is no single holy book, but rather a collection of different texts including four Vedas that contain hymns, incantations, and rituals. Hindus are also guided by epic poems such as the Bhagavad Gita. Only the body dies in Hindu belief. The soul returns in a new form after death. The form in which it returns depends on how one lives one's life. Hindus believe that people who live in a way that is appropriate to their position in society will live better future lives. One may reach a state of spiritual perfection (*nirvana*) that allows the soul to escape the cycle of birth and rebirth, and reunite with God. But people who do not live in a way that is appropriate to their position in society supposedly live an inferior life when they are reincarnated. These ideas made upward social mobility nearly impossible because, according to Hindu belief, striving to move out of one's station in life ensures reincarnation in a lower form.	Unlike the Western religions, Hinduism assimilates rather than excludes other religious beliefs and practices. Traditionally, Western religions rejected non-believers unless they converted. God tells Moses on Mount Sinai, "You shall have no other gods before me." In contrast, in the Bhagavad Gita, Krishna says that "whatever god a man worships, it is I who answer the prayer." This attitude of acceptance helped Hinduism absorb many of the ancient religions of the peoples on the Indian subcontinent. It also explains the wide regional and class variations in Hindu beliefs and practices. Hinduism as it is practised bears the stamp of many other religions
Buddhism 	About 480-400 BCE, Siddhartha Gautama Sakya, a young prince, left his life of privilege to seek the meaning of life. He was dissatisfied with the instruction he received from leading Hindu teachers and objected to what he regarded as the stale ritualism of Hinduism. Seeking to achieve a direct relationship with God, he came to be known as Buddha, "the awakened one." He rejected Hindu ideas of caste and reincarnation, and offered a new way for everyone to achieve spiritual enlightenment, promising salvation to everyone.	Buddha promoted the "Four Noble Truths": (1) Life is suffering. Moments of joy are overshadowed by sorrow. (2) All suffering derives from the inability to see the world as it really is. (3) Suffering ceases by training ourselves to eliminate desire, aversion, and delusion. (4) The path to end suffering requires undertaking a moral life, meditating, and achieving wisdom. Buddhism does not presume the existence of one true god. Rather, it holds out the possibility of everyone becoming a god of sorts. Similarly, it does not have a central church or text, such as the Bible.	Buddhism is notable for the diversity of its beliefs and practices. Buddhism spread rapidly across Asia after India's ruler adopted it as his own religion in the third century BCE. He sent missionaries to convert people in Tibet, Cambodia (Kampuchea), Nepal, Sri Lanka (formerly Ceylon), Myanmar (formerly Burma), China, Korea, and Japan. The influence of Buddhism in the land of its birth started to die out after the fifth century CE and is negligible in India today. One of the reasons for the popularity of Buddhism in East and Southeast Asia is that Buddhism is often able to co-exist with local religious practices. Unlike Western religions, Buddhism does not insist on holding a monopoly on religious truth.

Sources: Boteach, 2012; Fenn, 2013; Gajjar, 2013; Goldberg, 2013; Heine, 2013; Kemp, 2013; Sharify-Funk and Dickson, 2013.

Religion and Class Inequality

If, after becoming routinized, religion has often supported gender inequality, it has also often supported class inequality. In medieval and early modern Europe, Christianity promoted the view that the Almighty ordains class inequality, promising rewards to the lowly in the afterlife ("the meek shall inherit the earth"). The Hindu scriptures say that the highest caste sprang from the lips of the supreme creator, the next highest caste from his shoulders, the next highest from his thighs, and the lowest, "polluted" caste from his feet. They warn that if people attempt to achieve upward mobility, they will be reincarnated as animals. And the Qur'an says that social inequality is due to the will of Allah (Surah al-An'am 6: 165).

Religion and Social Conflict

In the sociological sense of the term, a **church** is any bureaucratic religious organization that has accommodated itself to mainstream society and culture. As we have seen, church authorities often support gender and class inequality. However, religiously inspired protest against inequality often erupts from below.

A **church** is a bureaucratic religious organization that has accommodated itself to mainstream society and culture.

A famous example of such protest involves the role of black churches in spearheading the American civil rights movement during the 1950s and 1960s (Morris, 1984). Their impact was both organizational and inspirational. Organizationally, black churches supplied the ministers who formed the civil rights movement's leadership and the congregations whose members marched, boycotted, and engaged in other forms of protest. Additionally, Christian doctrine inspired the protesters. Perhaps their most powerful religious idea was that blacks, like the Jews in Egypt, were slaves who would be freed. (It was, after all, Michael—regarded by Christians as the patron saint of the Jews—who rowed the boat ashore.) Some white segregationists reacted strongly against efforts at integration, often meeting the peaceful protesters with deadly violence. But the American South was never the same again. Religion had helped promote the conflict needed to make the South a more egalitarian and racially integrated place.

Closer to home, it is worth remembering the important role played in the creation of Canada's medicare system and our social welfare network by the radical Christianity of the early twentieth-century Social Gospel movement. The Social Gospel movement took on force in the depths of the Great Depression (1929–39). It emphasized that Christians should be as concerned with improving the here and now as with life in the hereafter. The efforts of Tommy Douglas, a Baptist minister with an M.A. in sociology, the leader of the Co-operative Commonwealth Federation (precursor of the New Democratic Party), and the father of medicare in Canada, exemplify the Social Gospel's concern with social justice. In Canada too, then, religion has sometimes promoted conflict and change.

In sum, religion can maintain social order under some circumstances, as Durkheim said. When it does so, however, it often reinforces social inequality. Moreover, under other circumstances religion can promote social conflict and social change.

Weber and the Problem of Social Change: A Symbolic Interactionist Interpretation

If Durkheim highlighted the way religion contributes to social order, Max Weber stressed the way religion can contribute to social change. Weber captured the core of his argument in a memorable image: If history is like a train, pushed along its tracks by economic and political interests, then religious ideas are like railroad switches, determining exactly which tracks the train will follow (Weber, 1946: 280).

Weber's most famous illustration of his thesis is his short book *The Protestant Ethic and Spirit of Capitalism*. Like Marx, Weber was interested in explaining the rise of modern capitalism. Again like Marx, he was prepared to recognize the "fundamental importance of the economic factor" in his explanation (Weber, 1958 [1904–05]: 26). But Weber was also bent on proving the one-sidedness of any exclusively economic interpretation. He did so by offering what we would today call a symbolic interactionist interpretation of religion.

True, the term "symbolic interactionism" was not introduced into sociology until more than half a century after Weber wrote *The Protestant Ethic*. Yet Weber's focus on the worldly significance of the meanings people attach to religious ideas makes him a forerunner of the symbolic interactionist tradition.

For specifically religious reasons, wrote Weber, followers of the Protestant theologian John Calvin stressed the need to engage in intense worldly activity and to display industry, punctuality, and frugality in their everyday life. In the view of men like John Wesley and Benjamin Franklin, people could reduce their religious doubts and ensure a state of grace by working diligently and living simply. Many Protestants took up this idea. Weber called it the Protestant ethic (Weber, 1958 [1904–5]: 183). According to Weber, the Protestant ethic had wholly unexpected economic consequences. Where it took root, and where economic conditions were favourable, early capitalist enterprise grew most robustly.

Subsequent research showed that the correlation between the Protestant ethic and the strength of capitalist development is weaker than Weber thought. In some places, Catholicism has coexisted with vigorous capitalist growth and Protestantism with relative economic stagnation (Samuelsson, 1961 [1957]). Nonetheless, Weber's treatment of the religious factor underlying social change is a useful corrective to Durkheim's emphasis on religion as a source of social stability. Along with Durkheim's work, Weber's contribution stands as one of the most important insights into the influence of religion on society.

TIME FOR REVIEW

- What evidence supports the idea that hockey is a religion in Canada?
- On what grounds do conflict and feminist theorists criticize Durkheim's theory of religion?
- How does Weber's concept of the Protestant ethic enhance our understanding of the rise of modern capitalism?

THE RISE, DECLINE, AND PARTIAL REVIVAL OF RELIGION

The Rise of Religion

In 1651, British political philosopher Thomas Hobbes described life as "poore, nasty, brutish, and short" (Hobbes, 1968 [1651]: 150). His description fit the recent past. The standard of living in medieval and early modern Europe was abysmally low. On average, a person lived only about 35 years. The forces of nature and human affairs seemed entirely unpredictable. In this context, magic was popular. It offered easy answers to mysterious, painful, and capricious events.

As material conditions improved, popular belief in magic, astrology, and witchcraft gradually lost ground (Thomas, 1971). Christianity substantially replaced these beliefs. The better and more predictable times made Europeans more open to the teachings of organized religion. In addition, the Church campaigned vigorously to stamp out opposing belief systems and practices. The persecution of witches in this era was partly an effort to eliminate competition and establish a Christian monopoly over spiritual life.

The Church succeeded in its efforts. In medieval and early modern Europe, Christianity became a powerful presence in religious affairs, music, art, architecture, literature, and philosophy. Popes and saints were the rock musicians and movie stars of their day. The Church was the centre of life in both its spiritual and its worldly dimensions. Church authority was

© Bettmann/Corbis/Magma

The persecution of witches in the early modern era was partly an effort to eliminate competition and establish a Christian monopoly over spiritual life. *Burning of Witches by Inquisition in a German Marketplace.* After a drawing by H. Grobert.

supreme in marriage, education, morality, economic affairs, politics, and so forth. European countries proclaimed official state religions. They persecuted members of religious minorities.

In contrast, a few hundred years later, Weber remarked on how the world had become thoroughly "disenchanted." By the turn of the twentieth century, he said, scientific and other forms of rationalism were replacing religious authority. He and many others, including Durkheim, Marx, and Comte, subscribed to what came to be known as the **secularization thesis**, undoubtedly the most widely accepted argument in the sociology of religion until the 1990s. According to the secularization thesis, religious institutions, actions, and consciousness would fade in importance and eventually lose their significance altogether (Norris and Inglehart, 2011; Tschannen, 1991).

The **secularization thesis** says that religious institutions, actions, and consciousness are on the decline worldwide and will one day disappear altogether.

The End of Religion?

Despite the consensus about secularization that was evident in the 1980s, many sociologists modified their judgments in the 1990s. That was because the secularization hypothesis was becoming increasingly out of touch with what was happening in the world. Some of its basic tenets were demonstrably false. One leading sociologist of religion famously recanted (Berger, 1999), and another declared secularization a failed theory that deserved to be buried once and for all (Stark, 1999).

As it turns out, the proposed burial of secularization theory also proved premature. Today, sociologists are more likely to suggest secularization should be understood as a tendency rather than an iron law (Norris and Inglehart, 2011). Accordingly, the **revised secularization thesis** directs researchers to explore why wide variation exists in the process of secularization, such that the scope of religious authority and religious adherence are declining in some parts of the world, but stable or rising in other areas (Gorski and Altinordu, 2008; Turner, 2011). Let us explore some of the ways traditional secularization theory has fallen short.

The **revised secularization thesis** holds that an overall trend toward the diminishing importance of religion is unfolding in different ways throughout the world.

First, traditional secularization theory stated that all societies undergo a process called differentiation, where worldly institutions break off from the institution of religion over time (Tschannen, 1991). One such worldly institution is the education system. On the surface, one might conclude that differentiation has occurred. Whereas religious bodies once ran schools and institutions of higher learning, today, modern educational systems are run almost exclusively by non-religious authorities. Moreover, the educational system is generally concerned with worldly affairs rather than with spiritual matters.

A closer look, however, suggests that the divide between religion and the educational system is murky. In the United States, religious education is prohibited in public schools, and religious schools do not receive any public funding (Gorski and Altinordu, 2008). Parents in Germany, however, send their children to state-funded schools designated as either Catholic or Protestant, and all German students receive mandatory religious instruction. In Canada, education is a provincial responsibility and thus funding for religious education varies. Alberta, Saskatchewan, and Ontario fully fund Catholic schools. British Columbia, Alberta, Saskatchewan, Manitoba, and Québec pay for about half of the budget of religious schools that meet certain criteria (Canadian Secular Alliance, 2009). Québec requires all students to take a course in religion and ethics. Elsewhere in Canada, religious instruction is optional. Thus, religion has yet to completely sever its ties to the education system. (See Box 16.2 for another example of how some religious groups attempt to retain their influence on educational institutions.)

Similarly, there appears to be no obvious movement toward greater separation between church and state. A case can be made for the view that modern states are increasingly compelled to intervene in disputes over religion (Turner, 2011). In particular, liberal democracies must balance three constitutionally enshrined rights: religious freedom, equality, and

BOX 16.2

SOCIOLOGY AT THE MOVIES

HARRY POTTER AND THE DEATHLY HALLOWS: PART I AND PART II

Harry Potter and the Deathly Hallows: Part I and *Part II* are the seventh and eighth movies in the highly popular series about a magical world of witches and wizards. In the first movie of the series, we learned that the hero, Harry Potter (played by Daniel Radcliffe) was orphaned at the age of one when the most evil wizard of all, Lord Voldemort, murdered Harry's parents and tried to kill Harry. Harry went to live with his unwelcoming relatives, the Dursleys, who housed him in a closet under their stairs.

Shortly before his eleventh birthday, Harry's life is turned upside down. He learns that his dead parents were wizards, and so is he. He is summoned by a blizzard of letters to Hogwarts School of Witchcraft and Wizardry. The school, housed in a thousand-year-old castle and headed by the renowned Professor Dumbledore, provides select students with a seven-year program of instruction.

Harry Potter and the Deathly Hallows: Part I follows the story of Harry and his friends Hermione Granger (Emma Watson) and Ron Weasley (Rupert Grint) into maturity. The movie opens with the horrifying Lord Voldemort (Ralph Fiennes) and his Death Eaters plotting the destruction of Harry and his friends. When Harry and his friends get wind of the plot, they fly off to mysterious and remote locations so they can hide from Lord Voldemort while searching out clues to the whereabouts of missing bits of his soul. Presumably, if they can make his soul whole again, he will end his evil ways. The final showdown between Harry and Lord Voldemort takes place in the final movie of the series. Voldemort succeeds in destroying Hogwarts, and the students who survive must choose between the hero and the villain.

All entries in the Harry Potter series have been enormously successful at the box office. Children are prominent in the lineups, many of them outfitted as if for Halloween. Some of them come to the movies on school field trips after studying the Harry Potter books at school.

Although most people view the Harry Potter series as harmless, others see things differently. They

freedom of speech (Malik, 2011). Finding the right balance is a delicate task. For example, in countries like Canada where same-sex marriage is legal, do church pastors have the right to refuse to perform same-sex marriages based on their religious beliefs? When someone threatens to burn the Qur'an, should this threat be considered hate speech or protected free speech? Should polygamy be permitted as a religious freedom, or must the state forbid the practice to protect the rights of women and girls who are exploited in such relationships? Should universities permit the separation of men and women when a visiting speaker presents a lecture on Islam? How does the state appease those who insist on freedom *from* religion by demanding that all religious symbols be removed from government buildings? Each of these examples is real. Moreover, they are just a small sampling of the types of dilemmas that face democratic governments everywhere, frustrating attempts to maintain a division between religion and state.

Importantly, much evidence shows that both religious groups and the state make incursions on each other's territory when it suits their interests. In the United States, conservative Christian groups contribute to the political campaigns of candidates who share their worldview. During the twentieth century, the Catholic Church played a critically important role in undermining communism in Poland, and Catholic "liberation theology" animated the successful fight against right-wing governments in Latin America (Kepel, 1994 [1991]; Smith, 1991). Similarly, ultra-Orthodox Jews have been important players in Israeli political life, often holding the balance of power in government (Kimmerling, 2003).

Scene from *Harry Potter and the Deathly Hallows: Part I*

denounce both the films and the books on which they are based as "demonic." Many of the detractors are conservative Christians who claim that the books glorify witchcraft, make "evil look innocent," and subtly draw "children into an unhealthy interest in a darker world that is occultic and dangerous to physical, psychological and spiritual well-being" (Shaw, 2001). The controversy about the Potter series eased to some degree after some conservative Christian commentators identified Christian themes in the movies and the books ("Finding God," 2005).

Do you agree with efforts to ban the Harry Potter books and condemn the movies? In general, should religious organizations be able influence schools to ban books and movies? If so, where do you draw the line? For example, would it be acceptable for a white religious organization to recommend that a predominantly white school ban the works of Toni Morrison and Maya Angelou because they say derogatory things about whites? Would it be acceptable for a Jewish religious organization to ask a Jewish school to ban Shakespeare's *The Merchant of Venice* because it portrays Jews in an unflattering way? Would it be acceptable for a religious organization strongly influenced by feminism to convince students in an all-girls school to ban the works of Ernest Hemingway ("too sexist") or for an anti-feminist religious organization to convince students in an all-boys school to ban the writings of Margaret Atwood ("too anti-male")? In general, should religious organizations be allowed to influence schools to censor?

In other places, religious groups have successfully imposed religious rule. An Islamic revival originating in Iran has swept through the Middle East, Africa, and parts of Asia since the 1970s. In a number of these countries, secular rule of law gave way to Islamic religious law (*shari'a*). The shift to *shari'a* law gained momentum following 9/11. For example, Bahrain, which had widely adopted Western ways of dress and lifestyle, subsequently banned Western garb, particularly for women, and retreated sharply into traditional practices (Pandya, 2012).

Conversely, in some instances the state co-opts the functions of the church. Prior to the 1917 revolution, the Russian Orthodox Church was closely allied with the state. Following the revolution, the Soviet Union tried to eliminate religion altogether by taking over church property, prohibiting religious artifacts, and jailing or murdering church officials and believers. By the late 1980s, the Soviet Union had crumbled. Russia's new leader, Mikhail Gorbachev, restored religious freedom. Church activities were once again permitted. Did this mean that the church was free to operate independently? Not at all. Instead, the Russian Orthodox Church, reverting to its previous function as an arm of the state, was used for propaganda purposes to generate national pride and bolster support for political leaders. Today, 80 percent of the population now identify themselves as belonging to the Russian Orthodox Church (Evans and Northmore-Ball, 2012).

AFP/GettyImages

Members of Pussy Riot on trial

It was in this context that the punk rock band, Pussy Riot, stormed a Russian Orthodox Church in Moscow in 2012 and performed their piece, "Mother of God, Chase Putin Away." The three band members were arrested and imprisoned for "hooliganism motivated by religious hatred" but in fact they were engaged in political protest. Granted amnesty in 2013 by President Putin as a means of avoiding controversy while Russia hosted the 2014 winter Olympics, the members of Pussy Riot remained defiant, declaring that they would have preferred to stay in prison and vowing to continue their fight.

Thus far, our evaluation of the secularization thesis has focused on social institutions. However, the traditional secularization thesis also contends that religion will hold less appeal for *individuals*. Supposedly, science, with its insistence on rigorous empirical standards for proof, provides a better explanation for worldly phenomena than does religion, so religion loses its plausibility.

Religiosity refers to how important religion is to people.

How does the traditional secularization thesis fare in predicting declining rates of **religiosity**? (Religiosity refers to how important religion is to people.) There has in fact been a worldwide rise in the number of people who declare they are not affiliated with any religion. If the religiously unaffiliated were a religion, it would be the third largest in the world, accounting for one in every six people (Pew Research Centre, 2012). According to the 2011 National Household Survey, 23.9 percent of Canadians have no religious affiliation, up from 16.5 percent in 2001(Brym, 2014c: 20).

Nonetheless, closer inspection of differences around the world reveals wide variation in religious behaviour (see Figure 16.2). Weekly attendance at a religious service tends to be very high in Jordan (> 90 percent), but is very low in Russia, Japan, and Sweden (< 5 percent). We cannot say that people everywhere are turning away from religion.

In sum, secularization theory works best when it describes the decline of religion in broad strokes. At the level of institutions, religion no longer exercises the same authority over the population as it did 200 or even 50 years ago. Similarly, for many individuals, religion has less to say about education, family issues, politics, and economic affairs than it did in the past, even though it may continue to be an important source of spiritual belief and practice. The secularization thesis loses its force when it predicts that religiosity will continue to follow a downward trajectory or posits that all countries are changing in the same way. Instead, the revised secularization thesis, with its recognition of variability in the process, has come to provide a much more reasonable framework.

That is not to say that the revised secularization thesis is the only theory favoured by sociologists of religion. In the next section, we describe an alternative, the market theory of religion, and then assess how well it explains patterns of religious behaviour over time and place.

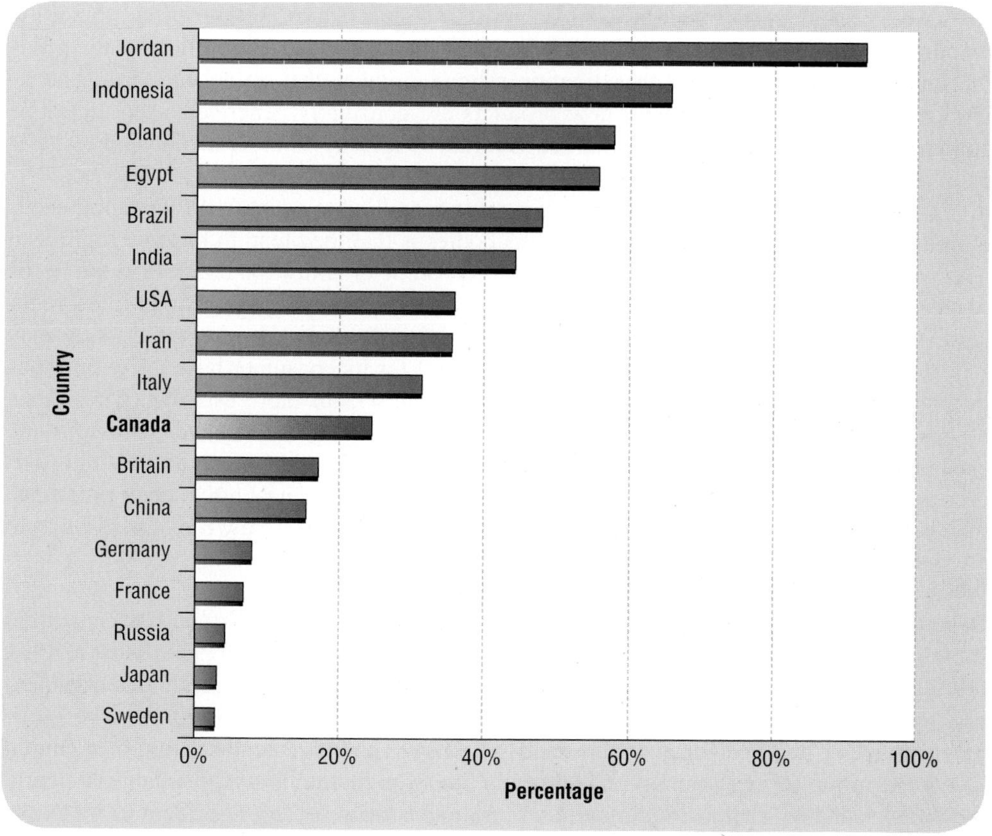

FIGURE 16.2

Weekly Attendance at Religious Services, Selected Countries

Source: Putnam and Campbell (2010). *Amazing Grace: How Religion Divides and Unites Us*. New York: Simon and Shuster. Page 9

The Market Theory

To understand why secularization has not taken its predicted course, sociologists have proposed viewing religion as a market. In this view, religious organizations are suppliers of services such as counselling, pastoral care, youth activities, men's and women's social groups, performance groups, lectures, and discussions. These services are demanded by people who desire religious activities. To meet this demand, religious organizations compete with one another, each offering their own brand or "flavour" of religious experience (Finke and Stark, 2005; Iannaccone, Finke and Stark, 1997). Success in attracting adherents depends on factors such as the organizational structure of the religious body and the quality of its sales representatives, its product, and its marketing techniques.

Importantly, not all societies encourage or permit competition among religions. Where monopolies and other forms of market regulation exist, the market theory predicts growing secularization. Conversely, an open market allowing competition among religions should give rise to greater religiosity.

Let us first see why religious monopolies squelch religious tendencies. A religious monopoly exists when one religious body has acquired special privileges from the state, preventing other religious bodies from selling their brand to consumers. When consumers can access only one brand, satisfaction is limited to those whose needs match what is offered. Everyone else will be dissatisfied. Lacking options, some consumers might resort to underground movements, but most will become indifferent to religion altogether. Apathy also grows among the clergy, who are paid by the state and thus enjoy a secure income regardless of their ability to attract people to their organization.

Sweden is one example of a religious monopoly that exhibits high levels of secularization. Three out of four citizens belong to the Church of Sweden, the country's official religion. Thus, the monopoly is not absolute. Nonetheless, the church remains heavily subsidized by the state, creating little incentive within the church to attract consumers to its product. Not surprisingly, as we observed earlier, Sweden has one of the lowest rates of church attendance in the world.

In contrast, countries such as Canada and the United States permit open competition among religions. Here, the market rewards religious bodies that successfully meet the needs of consumers and punishes with extinction religious bodies that do not attract consumer interest. In such an environment, new products are constantly generated in the quest to conquer different segments of the market. Overall, religiosity flourishes. The end result is **religious pluralism**: a diverse array of religions and religious beliefs in a given area.

Religious pluralism refers to the diverse array of religions and religious beliefs in a given area.

To retain market share, religious groups must be willing to adapt to the changing needs of consumers. The challenge for all religious bodies is that they tend to become routinized over time. That is, they start to focus on the needs of the organization rather than the needs of congregants. If religious organizations are to sustain themselves, they require rules, regulations, and a clearly defined hierarchy of roles. Inwardly focused, a religious body may fail to notice that it no longer holds the same appeal for its consumer base. New religious groups step in to fill the void, siphoning off members from more established religious bodies and making new converts. Because they are uninterested or unable to compete, some established religious groups stagnate. Others cease to exist. As they grow, all new religious groups encounter the pressures of routinization. If or when they succumb to these pressures, they risk losing their competitive edge, making way once again for new flavours to emerge.

Religious Organization

Depending on how routinized a religious organization, it occupies a different place in what sociologists call the "church-sect typology" (Stark and Bainbridge, 1979; Troeltsch, 1931 [1923]; see Figure 16.3). As noted earlier, a *church* is any bureaucratic religious organization that has fully accommodated itself to mainstream society and culture. As a result, it may endure for hundreds or even thousands of years. The bureaucratic nature of a church is evident in the formal training of its leaders, its strict hierarchy of roles, and its clearly drawn rules and regulations. Its integration into mainstream society is evident in its teachings, which are generally abstract and do not challenge worldly authority. As in the case of Russia and Sweden, many citizens may equate church membership with citizenship.

Sects usually form by breaking away from churches because of disagreement about church doctrine. Sects are less integrated into society and less bureaucratized than churches are.

At the other end of the church-sect typology are **sects**. Whereas churches are in a low state of tension with their environment, sects are in a high state of tension. Sects typically form by breaking away from churches because of disagreement about church doctrine. When a church evolves into a bureaucratic and worldly institution, sectarians launch a new movement advocating a return to the church's founding principles. Consequently, sects are less integrated into society and less bureaucratized than are churches.

Cults, or new religious movements (NRMs), are groups headed by charismatic leaders with a unique religious vision that rejects mainstream culture and society.

In contrast, **cults** form without breaking off from an established religious organization, although there are some exceptions. Although *cult* was once an accepted sociological term, labelling a religious group as a cult is now viewed as being derogatory. From now on, we will instead use the preferred term, **new religious movement** (NRM). By forming its own religious vision, an NRM sets itself in opposition to mainstream culture and society, so it too is in a high state of tension with the environment. Leaders of an NRM tend to be highly charismatic; they can attract devoted followers with ease.

Sects and NRMs experience one of three outcomes. First, sects and NRMs may disappear, having failed to generate enough buzz in the marketplace to stimulate and maintain consumer interest. This fate is the most common.

FIGURE 16.3
Church-Sect Typology

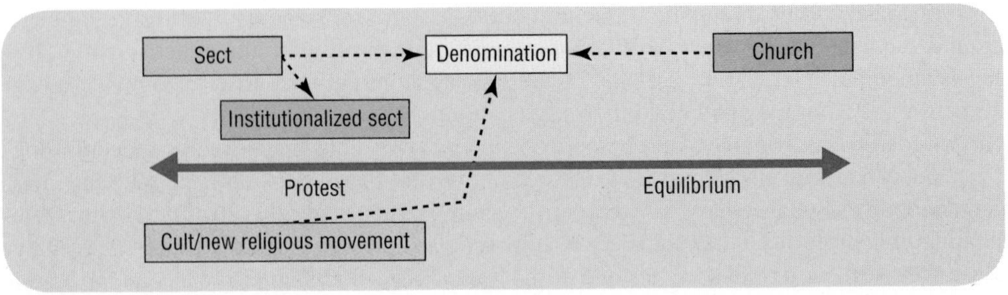

A second potential outcome is that the group persists, but in the process becomes more church-like. If the market for religion is unregulated, a sect or NRM may evolve into a **denomination**. A denomination lies midway on the continuum between church and sect. Unlike sects or NRMs, a denomination does not seek to distance itself from the world and is bureaucratically organized. Hence, it is routinized. Denominations tend to be fairly tolerant toward other denominations. Denominations can also come into being when churches lose their religious monopoly. United Church, Baptist, Lutheran, Missionary Alliance, Pentecostal Assembly and Presbyterian are some of the many Protestant denominations that exist in Canada today.

Midway on the continuum between church and sect, a **denomination** is not in tension with the world, is bureaucratically organized, and generally maintains a tolerant relationship with other denominations.

The third and final potential outcome for a sect or NRM is that it may become institutionalized. It does so by deliberately resisting assimilation into society. In some instances, sect members separate themselves geographically, as the Hutterites do in their 200 or so colonies, mostly in the Western provinces. However, even in urban settings, sect members can be separated from the larger society because of their strictly enforced rules concerning dress, diet, prayer, and intimate contact with outsiders. Hasidic Jews in Toronto and Montreal illustrate the viability of this isolation strategy.

Are you confused by the ambiguity in the descriptions of these different types of religious groups? Don't be. Sociologists are well aware that these labels can be problematic—not all religious groups fit easily into a given category. An example of a religious group that defies easy classification is the Church of Scientology. Its founder, Ron Hubbard, created the Church of Scientology in the United States in 1953. Since then, it has grown rapidly and now claims millions of members worldwide, including celebrities such as Tom Cruise, John Travolta, and Kirstie Alley. Scientologists believe that they are immortal beings who must undergo a lengthy and costly process called auditing, which helps rid themselves of negative energy (engrams) and reconnect with their true spiritual character (the thetan).

Having been in existence for more than 50 years, has Scientology made the transition from an NRM to a denomination? It is difficult to say. On one hand, it has become highly bureaucratized, suggesting that it has acquired some of the characteristics of a denomination. On the other hand, Scientology remains on the fringes of society. Governments in many countries have refused to grant Scientology status as a religion, and where it is allowed to operate, it remains in tension with the state. Because Scientology charges its members for the services they receive, many governments say the organization is really a business. Only recently have a handful of countries, including the Netherlands and the United Kingdom, recognized Scientology as a religion.

At any one time, some religious groups are on the rise while others are in decline. In the Canadian context, declining membership has been occurring in mainstream Protestant denominations such as Presbyterianism, Pentecostalism, and the United Church. In contrast, conservative, evangelical or fundamentalist Protestant denominations are gaining popularity. At the other end of the religious spectrum, the New Atheist movement has recently formed organizations that cater to the interests of the nonreligious (Guenther, Mulligan, and Papp, 2013).

The market theory of religion is not watertight. Some researchers note that a near-monopoly in religion exists in many Muslim-majority countries but religious observance is widespread, contrary to the prediction of the market theory. Other researchers note that both Canada and the United States have unregulated markets but the United States is a more religious nation than Canada is (refer back to Figure 16.2). The discrepancy must necessarily mean that other factors play a role. Are the differences due to higher levels of income insecurity in the United States than in Canada? Some think so. Because poverty rates are higher in the United States than they are in Canada, it has been proposed that more Americans than Canadians may need the comfort and tangible benefits that religious organizations provide (Norris and Inglehart, 2011). Others additionally point out that both Canada and the United States accept a high number of immigrants annually, which is changing the religious landscape but in different ways for each country. American immigrants, drawn disproportionately from Latin America, tend to be more religious than are immigrants to Canada, many of whom come from non-religious Asian countries (Marger, 2013). How these ideas may one day lead to further revisions of the market theory of religion or produce entirely new theories remains to be seen.

The Future of Religion

In the twenty-first century, gradual secularization will likely continue. At the same time, the expanded menu that is available to Canadians today will likely foster even greater religious pluralism in the future. What will be the net result of the contradictory social processes of secularization and religious pluralism as they unfold alongside one another? At least one sociologist suggests we are heading toward religious polarization (Bibby, 2011). Polarization occurs when fewer Canadians appear in the ambiguous middle, choosing instead to either embrace or reject religion. It is possible that polarization may one day test the limits of religious tolerance in this country.

However, as you might now appreciate, when it comes to predicting the future of religion, even the most careful forecasts have a way of being confounded by events. Therefore, in the next section, we turn our attention to better understanding the current divides in religion across the world, considering places where religious tolerance can sometimes be in short supply.

TIME FOR REVIEW

- What is the secularization thesis? Why did sociologists revise the secularization thesis in the 1990s?
- In what ways do churches, sects, NRMs, and denominations differ from one another?
- What are the three possible outcomes for sects and NRMs?
- According to the market theory, under what conditions is religious pluralism most likely to flourish?

RELIGION AROUND THE WORLD

Religious Tolerance

For many people, religious affiliation corresponds with the dominant religion of their country (see Figure 16.4). Almost all Hindus, for example, live in the three Hindu-majority countries (India, Mauritius, and Nepal). Similarly, the majority of Christians, Muslims, and the religiously unaffiliated are found in countries where their respective religious affiliation is dominant. Apart from these four categories (which together make up 86 percent of the world's population), those who belong to other religions are almost always in the minority. For example, most Jews live outside of Israel, the only country where Judaism is dominant. There are no countries where faiths such as Baha'i, Sikhism, Jainism, Shintoism, or Aboriginal traditions are in the majority.

Religious minorities can sometimes be at risk from those who belong to the dominant religion. Religious differences lie at the heart of many civil wars, including those in Mali, the Central African Republic, South Sudan, and Iraq. When a militant Islamist group seized control of northern Mali for a short time in 2012, it destroyed cultural and historic sites in Timbuktu and harassed and murdered religious minorities (a mixture of moderate Muslims and Christians). Coptic Christians in Egypt experienced church bombings and beatings when the Muslim Brotherhood took power for a short time following the Arab

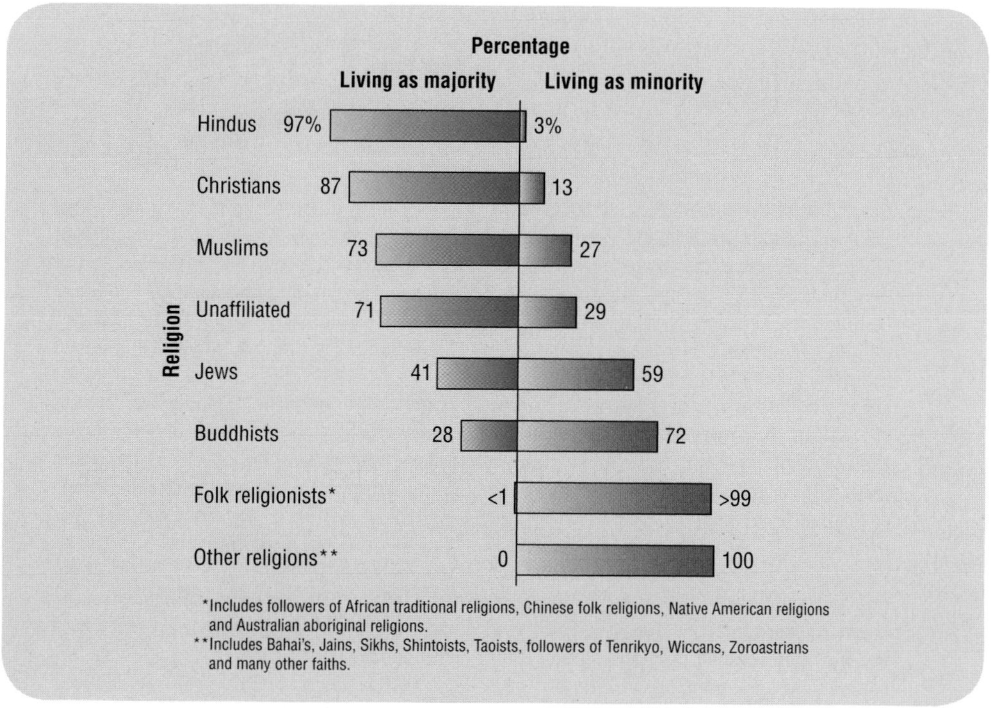

FIGURE 16.4

Percentage of Religious Groups That Live as a Majority or Minority Religion in Their Own Country, 2010.

Source: Pew Research Center. "The Global Religious landscape." © 2012. http://www.pewforum.org/2012/12/18/global-religious-landscape-exec/

Spring. Suicide bombers from the radical Muslim group Boko Haram continue to target Christian churches in Nigeria. In Myanmar, Buddhists systematically persecute minority Muslims. In Iraq, members of the Islamic State murder Shi'a, Christians, and Zaidis.

Social hostilities between religious groups appear to be on the rise, particularly in the Middle East and North Africa (Pew Research Centre, 2013a). Some observers suggest globalization is the reason. Globalization has facilitated the movement of people and cultures to other countries. Growing religious diversity may create opportunities for conflict. Yet such conflict is not evident in Canada. Although immigrants to Canada have contributed to greater religious diversity, attacks against religious minorities in this country are isolated events. Consequently, Canada's leaders have argued that the country is a model for encouraging greater religious tolerance worldwide (see Box 16.3).

Religious Affiliation in Canada

Europeans who first settled Canada were overwhelmingly Christian. They were divided between English-speaking Protestants and French-speaking Roman Catholic. Friction between the two religious groups was embedded in the larger struggle between Britain and France for political dominance. When settlements changed hands in a conflict, the religion also changed (Scott, 2012). Yet when British forces prevailed, the treaties that established the boundaries of Canada also guaranteed religious freedom for Catholics. Consequently, both religions thrived.

Jews arrived in Canada beginning in the eighteenth century. As a religious minority, they were initially afforded few rights. For example, the state restricted the registration of births, deaths, and marriages to the Anglican and Roman Catholic churches. Although it took until 1831 for Jews to be granted full religious freedom and political emancipation, Canada was the first jurisdiction in the British Empire to do so.

Muslims, Hindu, Sikhs, and Buddhists did not start arriving in Canada in discernible numbers until the twentieth century, due in part to racist ideologies that prohibited certain ethnic and racial minorities from immigrating to Canada. For this reason, prior to

BOX 16.3

IT'S YOUR CHOICE

THE OFFICE OF RELIGIOUS FREEDOM

In 2013, the Canadian government established the Office of Religious Freedom (ORF). Its purpose is to promote freedom of religion as a key Canadian foreign policy priority. In particular, the ORF will advocate on behalf of religious minorities under threat, oppose religious hatred and intolerance, and promote Canadian values of pluralism and tolerance to the rest of the world. At the official opening, Prime Minister Stephen Harper made clear that the ORF is integral to introducing democracy to the rest of the world: "Today, as many centuries ago, democracy will not find, democracy cannot find, fertile ground in any society where notions of freedom of personal conscience and faith are not permitted" (Chase, 2013).

Not everyone shares the Prime Minister's viewpoint. Some critics wonder about the credibility of the ORF given that Canada's record on religious issues at home is less than stellar. For example, in 2012, the federal government cancelled the contracts of non-Christian chaplains in prisons, leaving only Christian chaplains in place to offer interfaith counselling to inmates. Calling this decision a violation of their religious freedom, a prisoners' rights group in British Columbia subsequently launched a lawsuit against the government. Similarly, the federal government's persistent stance that women wearing veils must remove them to take the citizenship oath has been construed by Muslims as a violation of their religious rights. Finally, in Québec, a proposed law to ban public servants from wearing symbols of their faith (turbans, kipot, hijabs, kirpans, large crucifixes, and the like) has enraged religious groups. They contend the new principle of religious neutrality (which assures freedom *from* religion) violates Canadians' freedom *of* religion as enshrined in the Charter of Rights. If the Canadian government cannot or will not protect the rights of all faith groups within its own borders, how does it expect to speak with authority when it comes to the violation of religious rights elsewhere?

These domestic controversies raise doubts about how Canada will be able to avoid being drawn into conflicts on the international stage. For example, Canada is eager to establish stronger trade relations with China. Yet China is widely condemned for its human rights abuses, including its violent and ongoing suppression of the political and religious aspirations of the Tibetan people and adherents of the Falun Gong religion. Given the extreme sensitivity the Chinese government has displayed whenever a foreign power criticizes its treatment of Tibet and the Falun Gong, any intervention by the ORF necessarily risks jeopardizing relations between China and Canada.

What do you think? Should Canada have an Office of Religious Freedom? If so, how far should it go to protect religious freedom around the world? How important is it to encourage greater religious tolerance in Canada and worldwide? Can the ORF accomplish the objectives it has set for itself or will it be drawn into conflict wherever it intervenes?

the 1970s, immigrants came mainly from European countries, and most of them identified themselves as Christian. Today, most immigrants come from Asia and the Middle East, enriching Canada with their diverse cultural and religious traditions. Consequently, there have been increases in the proportion of Canadians who identify as Muslim, Hindu, and Sikh (see Table 16.2). Non-religious immigrants, mainly from Asia, also contribute to

TABLE 16.2
Religious Affiliation, Canada, 2001 and 2011 (in percent)

Sources: Statistics Canada, 2003, 2013g.

Religion	Percent, 2001	Percent, 2011
Roman Catholic	43.2	38.7
Protestant	29.2	28.6
No religious identification	16.2	23.9
Muslim	2.0	3.2
Hindu	1.0	1.5
Sikh	0.9	1.4
Buddhist	1.0	1.1
Jewish	1.1	1.0
Traditional Aboriginal	0.1	0.2
Other	5.3	0.4
Total	100.0	100.0

the growing proportion of the non-religious. The proportion of Canadians identifying as Christians fell from more than 70 percent to just over 66 percent between 2001 and 2011, while the proportion without religious identification increased from around one-sixth to nearly one-quarter.

Religiosity

It is now time to conclude our discussion by considering some social factors that determine how important religion is to people—that is, their religiosity. We can measure religiosity in various ways. In survey research, sociologists often operationalize what are known as the three Bs of religiosity: belonging, beliefs, and behaviour. Religious affiliation is a measure of belonging; that is, whether a respondent identifies with any particular religion. As noted earlier, religious affiliation among Canadians has been declining over time. Beliefs can be assessed by asking people whether they believe God exists or by asking them how familiar they are with the main tenets of their faith. We have already seen that most Canadians say that God is real. We know much less about their familiarity with church doctrine. Finally, behaviours reflect how often a person engages in religious activities, which may include the frequency of attendance at religious services, of seeking spiritual comfort from a religious authority or of praying or meditating. Today, only one in four Canadians attends religious services regularly (Bibby, 2012).

You can see that religious behaviours do not match patterns of belonging and belief. Whereas nearly 80 percent of Canadians say they believe God exists and about 75 percent identify with a specific religion, most Canadians do not attend religious services on a regular basis. We should not assume, however, that these categories are simply subsets of one another such that behaviours represent the most stringent measure of religiosity. Behaviours may exist in the absence of affiliation, and vice versa. For example, nearly one in five Americans who indicated they were not affiliated with a religion said they attend a church service at least once a year (Pew Research Center, 2012).

Religious behaviour depends on social factors. Figure 16.5 focuses on weekly church attendance by age group. The Canadians most heavily involved in religious activities are seniors. How can we explain this? First, elderly people have more time and need for religion. Because they are not usually in school, employed in the paid labour force, or busy raising a family, they have more opportunity than younger people do to

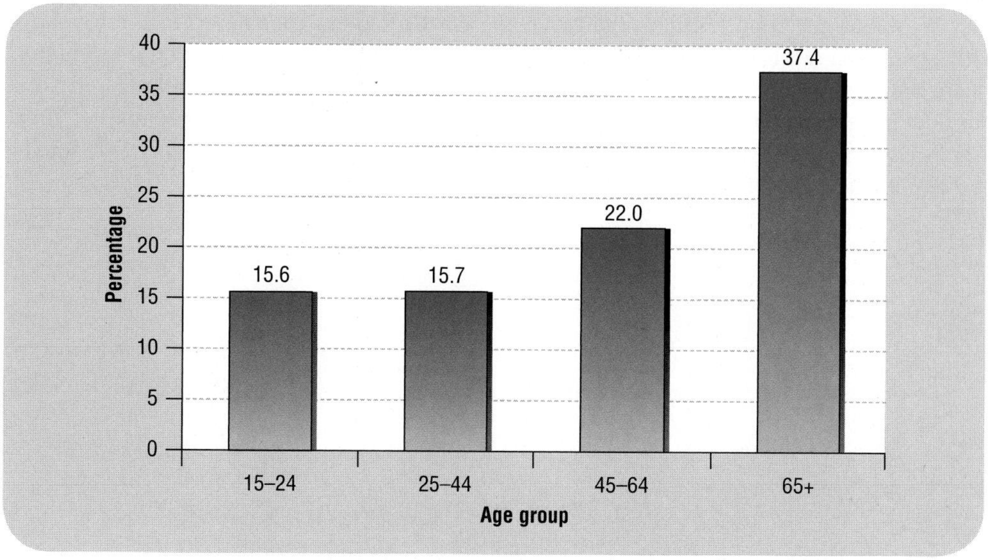

FIGURE 16.5
Canadians' Weekly Church Attendance by Age Group

Source: Adapted from Lindsay, Colin. 2008. "Canadians Attend Weekly Religious Services Less than 20 years Ago." Matter of Fact, Catalogue no. 89-630-X. Ottawa, ON: Statistics Canada.

Religiosity is partly a learned behaviour. Whether parents give a child a religious upbringing is likely to have a lasting impact on the child.

Omni Photo Communications Inc./Index Stock

attend church, synagogue, mosque, or temple. Moreover, because seniors are generally closer to illness and death than are younger people, they are more likely to require the solace of religion. To a degree, then, involvement in religious activities is a life-cycle issue.

There is also another explanation. Different age groups live through different times, and today's older people reached maturity when religion was a more authoritative force in society. A person's current religious involvement depends partly on whether he or she grew up in more religious times. Thus, although people are likely to become more religiously involved as they age, they are unlikely ever to become as involved as seniors are today.

In addition, people whose parents attended religious services frequently are more likely to do so themselves (Jones, 2000). That is because religiosity is partly a *learned* behaviour. (Freud said that people learn religion like they learn the multiplication tables.) Whether parents give a child a religious upbringing is likely to have a lasting impact on the child.

We have not supplied an exhaustive list of the factors that determine religiosity. However, even our brief overview suggests that religiosity depends in part on opportunity, need, and learning. The people who are most religiously involved and attend religious services most frequently are those who need organized religion most because of their advanced age, those who have the most time to go to services, and those who were taught to be religious as children.

TIME FOR REVIEW

- In what ways have immigration patterns contributed to religious diversity in Canada?
- Why are Canadian seniors in, say 25 years, likely to exhibit lower levels of religiosity than seniors do today?

SUMMARY

1. How does religion operate as a force for both social cohesion and social conflict?
   Durkheim argued that the main function of religion is to increase social cohesion by providing ritualized opportunities for people to experience the collective conscience. In contrast, Marx held that religion reinforces social inequality. For example, feminists note the patriarchal nature of all major world religions, which promote the idea that men should hold authority over women in all matters.
2. Why was it necessary to revise the secularization thesis?
   The secularization thesis holds that religious institutions, actions, and consciousness are on the decline worldwide. Because evidence suggests that patterns of religious authority and religious adherence are highly variable, the revised secularization thesis instead attempts to explain these variations in different contexts while maintaining that secularization continues as an overarching influence.
3. How does the market theory of religion address variation in patterns of secularization?
   The market theory of religion characterizes religious organizations as suppliers of services that are in demand by people who desire religious activities. In areas where religion has established a monopoly, too few consumers will have their religious needs met, generating mass indifference and high levels of secularization. When religious organizations are free to compete with one another, consumers can choose from a diverse and changing religious menu. Competition creates greater overall interest in religion.
4. Where is religious freedom and tolerance under threat?
   The majority of the world's Christians, Muslims, Hindus, and the nonreligious live in countries where their respective religion is dominant. Religious minorities may face limits on religious freedom and threats to personal safety. Social hostilities between religious groups are on the upswing, particularly in the Middle East and North Africa.
5. What social factors predict religiosity?
   An individual's religiosity is determined by such factors as the individual's age and socialization (whether he or she was brought up in a religious family).

CHAPTER 17

EDUCATION

IN THIS CHAPTER, YOU WILL LEARN TO

- Describe how expanding school systems increase national wealth.
- Compare the two main effects of schooling: homogenizing students into a common cultural system and sorting them into different social classes.
- Contrast the functionalist argument that education establishes a socioeconomic hierarchy based on merit with the conflict theory that education ensures the persistence of privilege.
- Distinguish the manifest functions of education, such as increasing literacy and numeracy, from the latent functions of education, such as increasing national solidarity.
- Explain how social interaction in schools reproduces inequalities by means of a "hidden curriculum" that values middle-class manners and attitudes; testing and tracking that segregate students by class background; and a self-fulfilling prophecy that lower-class students are bound to perform poorly.
- Identify the advances that women have made toward educational equality and the challenges that Aboriginal people face in making similar progress.

THE RIOT IN ST. LÉONARD

On the night of September 10, 1969, a confrontation that had long been brewing in the Montréal suburb of St. Léonard boiled over. A march organized by the French unilinguist *Ligue pour l'intégration scolaire* paraded through a predominantly Italian neighbourhood. Despite pleas for calm from leaders on both sides, many people turned out to march, while others, hostile to the marchers' cause, showed up to line the route. Scuffles broke out and a full-scale brawl ensued. Roughly a thousand people participated. Police read the riot act and made about 50 arrests.

Commentators of all political persuasions deplored the violence, but today the St. Léonard riot is recognized as a turning point in Québec history. It culminated in Bill 101, the law making French the language of public administration, imposing French language tests for admission to the professions, requiring most businesses with more than 50 employees to operate mainly in French, and requiring collective agreements to be drafted in French. Bill 101 also ensured that in Québec children of immigrants are required to receive primary and secondary schooling in French.

A year before the street violence erupted, the language of instruction in public schools emerged as a hotly contested issue. Political commentators raised concerns that French was in demographic decline and that francophones were at risk of becoming a minority in the province's biggest city, Montréal. They noted that in 1963, the St. Léonard school board had responded to an influx of new residents of Italian descent by establishing the option of bilingual education. Soon, more than 90 percent of children with neither English nor French background ("allophones") were enrolling in the bilingual track and, of those, 85 percent continued to English secondary schools. The public school system was contributing heavily to the anglicization of Montréal.

Godong/UIG/AGE Fotostock

In Québec, immigrant children are restricted to French-language schools by law.

In 1968, the St. Léonard school board eliminated bilingual programs, setting off a cycle of protests and counter-protests. Allophone parents, mainly of Italian descent and forming 30 percent of the community, withdrew their children from the public schools and organized their own "basement schools" where class were conducted in English. Meanwhile, francophone unilinguists mobilized and were able to dominate school board elections and win a referendum requiring a unilingual school system. Elites tried but failed to find a middle ground. Ultimately, in 1976, the Parti Québécois won its first election, Bill 101 was enacted, and immigrants' children were restricted to French schools by law.

It is hardly surprising that schooling in Québec has evoked sharp controversy. Schools are hugely important institutions. They teach students a common culture that forms a framework for social life. They shape work, politics, and much else. Moreover, which children have access to which schools is the starting point for sorting children into adult jobs and social classes. Not surprisingly, therefore, fierce conflicts often arise around such educational issues as who can or must go to what kinds of schools and what will be taught.

Schools are important and sometimes controversial because they endow young people with the key capacities of communication, coordination, and economic productivity. They create homogeneity out of diversity by instructing all students in a uniform curriculum. However, they also sort students into paths that terminate in different social classes. Homogeneity is achieved by enforcing common standards that serve as a cultural common denominator. Sorting favours students who develop the greatest facility in the common culture, while confining those of lesser skills to subordinate work roles and lower ranks in the class structure.

Homogenizing and sorting occur at primary, secondary, and postsecondary levels, and, within those levels, in public and private institutions. Individuals typically move in a regulated way from one educational site to the next. Curricula are adapted to what has been taught earlier, often in other places, and to prepare students for subsequent studies.

To fully understand education, we must grasp its broader implications. For example, mass schooling is a relatively recent development that is closely tied to industrialism and to maintaining a modern, productive economy. However, industrialism needs interchangeable workers who can move among ever-changing, sophisticated work facilities. Potential workers need to be culturally homogenized so they share similar outlooks and a common language, but some also need to be identified as able and willing to receive specialized training to carry out intellectually demanding tasks.

Although the number of years people devote to education has steadily risen, more education is easier to obtain when you are born in a rich country and into a prosperous family. In turn, more education ensures better treatment in labour markets, such as lower rates of unemployment and higher earnings. Thus, education not only turns students into citizens by giving them a common outlook but also reproduces the class structure and the structure of global inequality.

TIME FOR REVIEW

- What are the two main functions of schools?
- Identify specific events or processes in your own schooling that led you to develop a common outlook with your schoolmates and that segregated you and your schoolmates into different streams.

MASS EDUCATION: AN OVERVIEW

The education system has displaced organized religion as the main purveyor of formal knowledge, and it is second in importance only to the family as an agent of socialization. By the time you finished high school, you had spent nearly 13 000 hours in a classroom.

Three hundred years ago, only a small minority of people learned to read and write. A century ago, most people in the world never attended school. As late as 1950, only about 10 percent of the world's countries boasted systems of compulsory mass education (Meyer, Ramirez, and Soysal, 1992). Even today, many countries in Africa have literacy rates below 50 percent, while in India and Egypt a quarter of the population is illiterate.

In contrast, Canada has just over 15 500 elementary and secondary schools employing nearly 310 000 educators, who teach more than five million children. (Elementary schools are primary schools, high schools are secondary schools, and colleges and universities are postsecondary institutions.) In 2012, postsecondary enrolment stood at 1.9 million (Statistics Canada, 2012b). Sixty-four percent of Canadians between the ages of 25 and 64 have attained some postsecondary education (Statistics Canada, 2013b). This level of participation is higher than in any other country (Japan is in second place and the United States in third; see Human Resources and Skills Development Canada [HRSDC], 2011b). Enrolment rates are more than 95 percent for five-year-olds and remain at about that level through the mandatory schooling age of 16–18 years. Since 1990, the proportion of Canadians over the age of 14 with trade or college certification or a university degree has increased from about 30 percent to more than 50 percent (HRSDC, 2011b). Clearly, education is part of the Canadian way of life.

Universal mass education is a recent phenomenon and is limited to relatively wealthy countries (see Figure 17.1). Around 1900, Canada and the United States were the first countries to approach universal educational participation by young people. Societies that today are highly advanced in terms of economy and technology, such as Japan, Italy, and England, lagged far behind.

For most of history, families were chiefly responsible for socializing the young and training them to perform adult roles. In preindustrial Europe, the vast majority of children learned to work as adults by observing and helping their elders in the largely agricultural economy. Only a small urban minority had much use for such skills as reading and arithmetic. The literate and numerate few were typically trained in religious institutions. In fact, before the rise of Protestantism, priests held a virtual monopoly on literacy. The Catholic Church's authority depended on the *in*ability of ordinary people to read the Bible. It even went so far as to persecute people who made the Bible available in local languages. William Tyndale, whose English translation became the standard King James Bible, was burned at the stake for his efforts in 1536.

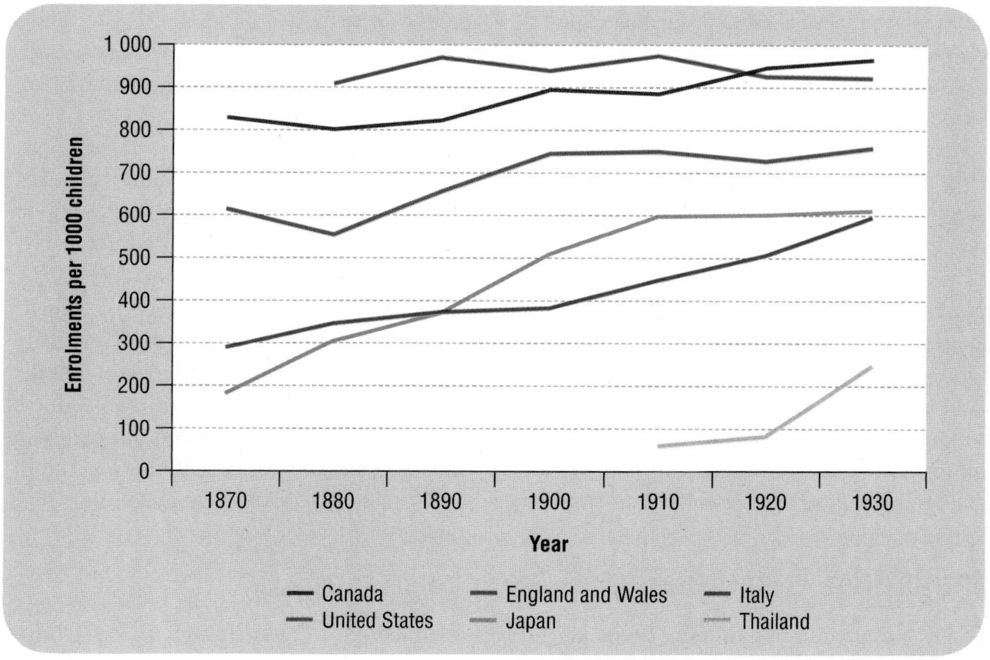

FIGURE 17.1
Elementary School Enrolments per 1000 Children Aged 5–14 for Various Countries, 1870–1930

Source: Peter H. Lindert, *Growing Public: Social Spending and Economic Growth since the Eighteenth Century* (Cambridge, UK, New York: 2004), pp. 91–93. Reprinted with the permission of Cambridge University Press.

Uniform Socialization

Creating systems of education with sufficient resources to include all children was a social change of breathtaking scope. Training in families had been decentralized, unorganized, and uneven in quality. Religious training was never widely available and tended to set people apart from the surrounding community. Replacing these forms of instruction with a centralized and rationalized system created strong pressures toward uniformity and standardization. Diversity among families, regions, and religious traditions gradually gave way to homogenized indoctrination into a common culture.

Canada was in some ways exceptional because, in the nineteenth century, the provinces recognized separate school systems for Catholics and Protestants; doing so was necessary to convince Québec to join Confederation. However, the postsecondary institutions' lack of recognition of distinct religious tracks pressured secondary schools to cover the same topics in the same fashion in their efforts to prepare their students for more advanced training. As a result, students today can travel thousands of kilometres for higher education and experience no more discontinuity than do those who attend the nearest school.

Surrendering children to state control was not universally popular, especially at first. Some students preferred skipping class to sitting in school, and special police (truant officers) were charged with tracking down absentees, who were then punished. Effective mass education was achieved only through laws that made attendance compulsory. All Canadian provinces and territories now require parents to ensure their children are educated up to a certain age. Although about 6 percent of Canadian families send their children to private schools, and about 80000 children are home-schooled (Fraser Institute, 2007), some 94 percent of families place their children in public schools (Statistics Canada, 2013k). Some children resist schooling's forced drill toward cultural ideals that are at odds with their other experiences, but they are in a minority.

Rising Levels of Education

Making education available to everyone, whether they liked it or not, was only a starting point. The amount of education that people receive has risen steadily, and this trend shows no sign of abating. In 1951, fewer than 1 in 50 Canadians had completed a university degree. Then, completing university allowed a person entry into a small elite. Today, more than a quarter of Canadians over the age of 14 have a university degree, and almost two-thirds have some postsecondary education. In half a century, a rarity has become commonplace. Between 1990 and 2011, the percentage of Canadians over the age of 14 without a high-school diploma fell from 38 percent to 13 percent. Those with a university degree rose from 11 percent to 26 percent of Canadians (Statistics Canada, 2011e).

Educational achievement is the learning of valuable skills and knowledge.

Educational attainment is the number of years of schooling successfully completed or, for higher learning, the degrees or certificates earned.

Sociologists distinguish educational attainment from educational achievement. **Educational achievement** is the knowledge or skills that an individual acquires. Achievement refers to mastery of educational content. In principle, grades reflect achievement. We say "in principle" because the validity of grades is a matter of debate (see Box 17.1). **Educational attainment** reflects participation in educational programs. It is measured by the number of years of schooling completed or, for higher levels, certificates and degrees earned. Educational attainment and achievement are correlated. Generally, more time in educational institutions leads to the acquisition of more knowledge and skills. However, the correlation is not as strong as you may think. Some students learn more in school than others do. Moreover, being selected to continue one's education depends on more than educational achievement. In practice, non-academic factors, including family background, play a large role in determining who completes an advanced education.

Individual Advantages and Disadvantages

Higher educational attainment helps people get jobs and earn more. Figure 17.2 illustrates how education level influences rates of unemployment among younger Canadians. Lower

BOX 17.1

SOCIAL POLICY: WHAT DO YOU THINK?

IS GRADE INFLATION HARMFUL?

In schools and universities, grades are the main indicator of educational achievement. Grades are intended to reflect what students know. But do they? We can assess the validity of school grades by comparing the grades teachers assign to standardized examination results. When this comparison was completed in New Brunswick and Newfoundland and Labrador, the results revealed substantial grade inflation (Laurie, 2007). In math, for example, the average standardized exam score was 60 percent, while school grades in math averaged 74 percent.

Two sociologists (Côté and Allahar, 2007) report that grade inflation is a clear trend in Canadian universities. By their estimate, fewer than half of undergraduate students in the 1970s received grades of A or B. Today, comparable figures range between 60 percent and 80 percent, depending on the institution and course. In the early 1980s, about 40 percent of students applying to Ontario's universities had A averages; now more than 60 percent do.

Some commentators attribute grade inflation to an attitude of entitlement among the current generation of students (Laurie, 2007; Schwartz, 2013). Many in this generation attended elementary schools that had "no-fail" policies and now consider high grades to be their right. Failure is not considered a possible outcome, and Cs are no longer considered average. In a recent survey of first-year university students, 70 percent rated themselves as above average, which is, of course, statistically impossible (Côté and Allahar, 2007). Many students now come to university with the orientation of consumers who expect to receive good grades in exchange for paying tuition.

Educational institutions are agents of socialization, and setting expectations is an important part of this process. But grade inflation promotes lowered expectations. If high grades are easily awarded, good students are not challenged to strive for excellence. Likewise, grade inflation gives weaker students a false sense of competence and little incentive to improve. Schools and universities that participate in grade inflation are shifting their mandate from the promotion of excellence to keeping more students in the education system longer.

What do you think? Did you work hard to get good grades? Do your university courses challenge you to achieve excellence? Does paying tuition give students a right to high grades or even passing grades? What consequences does grade inflation in the educational system have for the economy and for society? What causes grade inflation?

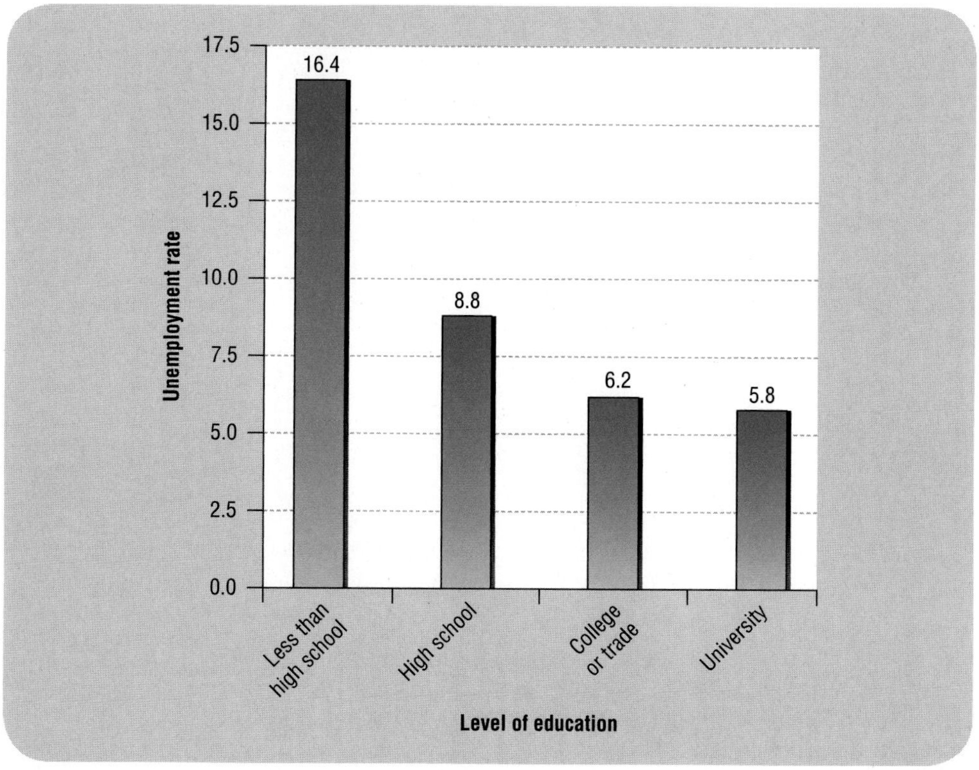

FIGURE 17.2

Unemployment Rate among 25- to 29-Year-Olds by Highest Level of Education Completed, Canada, 2012 (in percent)

Source: Statistics Canada. 2013l. "Unemployment Rates of 25–29-Year-Olds by Educational Attainment." Labour Force Survey, Table E3.2. Updated May 1, 2013. Retrieved February 17, 2014 (www.statcan.gc.ca/pub/81-582-x/2013001/tbl/tble3.2-eng.htm).

rates of unemployment are associated with more education. Young people who do not finish high school have an unemployment rate three times higher than do people with a university degree.

Education also increases earnings. As Figure 17.3 shows, the odds of earning high pay steadily improve as educational attainment increases. Among the richest 10 percent of Canadians, more than half have a university education, while only a few percent have not finished high school. The relationship of education to income pattern is imperfect. People at every level of education are found at each level of earnings. However, the pattern is clear: more education and better earnings tend to go together.

In the next section, we examine how mass education arose. We then examine theories that connect the rise of mass education to industrialization, arguing that education provides a basis for collective and individual wealth and motivates widespread loyalty to culture and society. We will see how education reproduces class inequality. We conclude by reviewing a series of recent developments and future challenges for Canada's system of mass schooling.

The Rise of Mass Schooling

What accounts for the spread of mass schooling? Sociologists usually highlight four factors: the development of the printing press that led to inexpensive book production, the Protestant Reformation, the spread of democracy, and industrialism. Let us consider each of these factors in turn.

First, the printing press: In 1436, Johannes Gutenberg introduced the printing press with movable type in Europe. The effect was revolutionary. Books were expensive when scribes were the only source of new copies. The printing press led to a dramatic fall in book prices and an explosion of supply. Many of the new printed books were in the vernacular—languages used every day by common folk—and not in the Latin that only scholars understood. Literacy spread beyond elite circles, first in cities and eventually into rural areas, as inexpensive books fostered demand for schools to teach children the useful art of reading (Eisenstein, 1983).

Second, Protestantism: The Catholic Church relied on priests to convey dogma to believers. The education of priests was a primary motivation for the foundation of European

FIGURE 17.3

Income Group by Highest Level of Educational Attainment, Canada, 2011

Source: Statistics Canada. 2011c. "Education and Occupation of High-Income Canadians." National Household Survey. Retrieved February 27, 2014 (www12.statcan.gc.ca/nhs-enm/2011/as-sa/99-014-x/99-014-x2011003_2-eng.cfm).

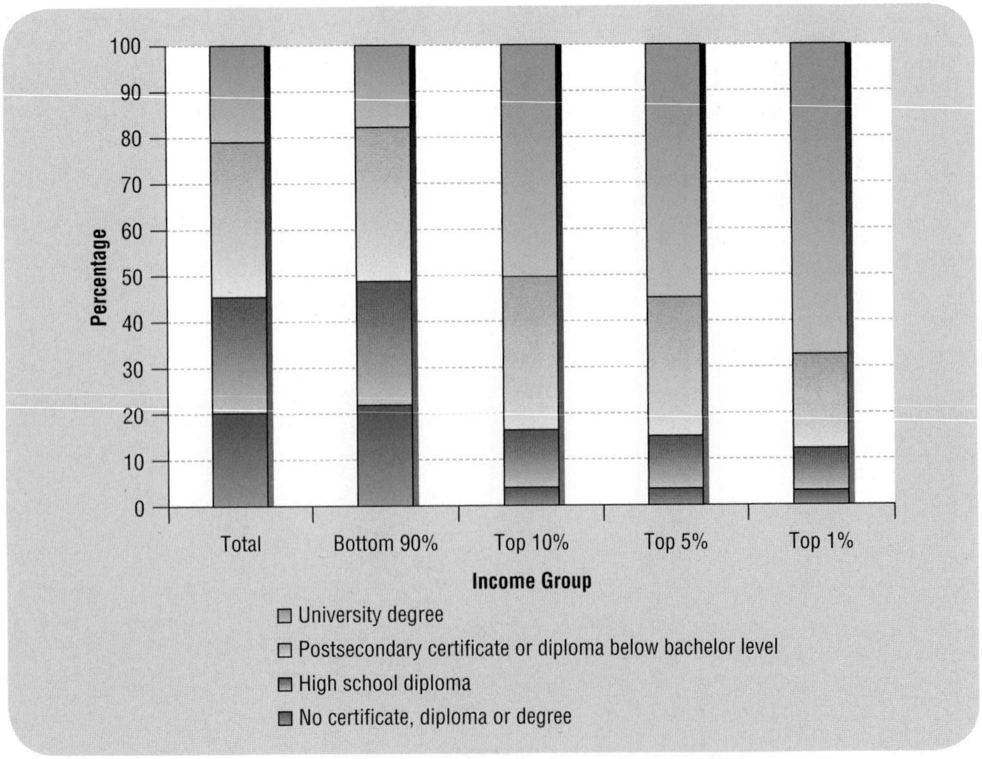

universities in the Middles Ages. However, in the early sixteenth century, Martin Luther, a German monk, began to criticize the Catholic Church. Protestantism grew out of his criticisms. The Protestants believed that the Bible alone, and not Church doctrine, should guide Christians. They expected Christians to have more direct contact with the word of God than was allowed by the Catholic Church. Accordingly, Protestants needed to be able to read the scriptures for themselves. The rise of Protestantism was thus a spur to popular literacy.

Third, democracy: The rise of political democracy led to free education for all children. Where local populations acquired the democratic means to tax themselves, tax-supported schools arose. France, which gave all men voting rights in 1848, expanded education earlier than did England, where the right to vote was not widespread until a few decades later. This side of the Atlantic followed a similar pattern (Lindert, 2004: 107). The earliest school systems were established in Upper Canada and the northern United States about 1870. By 1900, Canada and the United States were the first countries in the world in which enrolment rates for all children ages 5 to 14 exceeded 90 percent. Another first: at least in elementary education, girls were enrolled at almost the same rate as boys were.

Mass Schooling and National Wealth

The fourth and most important reason for the rise of mass schooling was industrialization. Mass education was widely recognized as an absolute necessity for creating an industrial economy.

The Industrial Revolution began in England in the 1780s. Germany and the United States soon sought to catch up to England, and by the turn of the twentieth century, they had surpassed it. Observers noted that both Germany and the United States had school systems that offered places to nearly all young people. Literacy and numeracy were widespread, although what counted as literacy in those days would not impress us today. Historians assess the literacy of that period by counting the rate at which people signed marriage registers or similar documents with a name and not merely an X or another mark. However, as the number of people achieving such minimal performance rose, so did the number of people with much higher levels of literacy. Eventually, it was evident that a highly productive economy requires an education system large enough to create a mass labour force, and rich enough to train and employ researchers able to work at the cutting edge of modern science. Democratic countries led the way, but communist countries, like the former Soviet Union, also invested heavily in education to foster economic development.

Today, investment in education is acknowledged as an important step in achieving great national wealth. However, the connection between education and wealth is by no means automatic. Some countries educate a relatively small proportion or a relatively large proportion of their population given their level of wealth (United Nations Educational, Scientific and Cultural Organization [UNESCO], 2014).

Education is not only a *source* of wealth; it is also a *product* of wealth. After all, education is expensive. Raising education levels for entire populations requires overcoming a vicious cycle: A significant fraction of a country's population must invest a great deal of time and money to become educated before a sufficient number of teachers have been trained to instruct nearly everyone. This time and money must be saved from the time and income that are needed to supply necessities like food and shelter. What is true for individuals is also true for societies: Education enhances the ability to generate earnings and wealth, but educational accumulation is greatly facilitated by an earlier accumulation of wealth (see Box 17.2).

TIME FOR REVIEW

- What is the connection between education and income?
- What factors contributed to the rise of mass schooling?
- What connections exist between education and national wealth?

BOX 17.2

SOCIAL POLICY: WHAT DO YOU THINK?

ARE VIRTUAL CLASSROOMS NEXT?

Because education is so expensive, governments, universities, and public school boards are always looking for ways to cut costs. In recent years, online courses have become increasingly popular in Canada and elsewhere. They maximize revenue by accommodating more students than can be fit into a classroom and they minimize the cost of overhead (building construction and maintenance) and labour (instructors' salaries). Are virtual classrooms—online courses without instructors—next?

You can imagine Naomi Baptiste's surprise when she arrived at her pre-calculus class at North Miami Beach Senior High School in September 2010 and found a bank of computers instead of a teacher (Herrera, 2011). Naomi is one of 7000 students in Miami-Dade public schools who were enrolled in classes without teachers in the academic year 2010–11. Only a classroom "facilitator" was available to ensure students progressed and to deal with technical issues.

While virtual classrooms save money, the quality of learning is a separate issue. Alix Braun, a sophomore at Miami Beach High taking Advanced Placement macroeconomics in a virtual classroom, said, "none of [my classmates] want to be there." According to Chris Kirchner, an English teacher at Coral Reef Senior High School in Miami, "the way our state is dealing with class size is nearly criminal" (quoted in Herrera, 2011).

Virtual classrooms (sometimes blended with intermittent, real classroom instruction) are spreading to K–8 public schools in Florida and to public schools in other states, such as Illinois and Nebraska. Can Canada be far behind? What kinds of students are most likely to be required to take classes in virtual classrooms? How will the spread of virtual classrooms likely affect social stratification?

THE FUNCTIONS OF EDUCATION

Latent Functions

Schools do not merely carry out training; they also concentrate young people for extended periods in common locations. In children's early years, the law requires attendance. In more advanced programs, economic incentives and family pressures encourage student attendance. Certain latent or unintended consequences arise from segregating people by age and forcing them to spend much of their time together.

One result is that schools encourage the development of a separate youth culture that can conflict with parents' values (Coleman, 1961). When students are asked to rank the popularity of fellow students, rankings don't centre on academic achievement. Instead, they signify athletic and social success. Many students who are low on such peer rankings find the youth culture of school alienating.

Role conflict occurs when a person's situation presents incompatible demands. One result of role conflict is alienation or disconnection from others, as Lance Roberts recalls from his own high-school experience. "I attended high school in the 1960s and, besides girls, had two major interests—grades and basketball. These interests were connected since, if your grades were poor, you were ineligible to play on the varsity basketball team. In my school, unacceptable grades were below 45 percent. For students on athletic teams, unacceptable grades were circled in red on your report card. Three red circles and you were off the team.

"During basketball season, our team practised three times a day. Report cards were distributed just before lunch, so at the noon practice, the locker room was full of inquiries and boasts about red circles. Statements like 'How many did you get?' and 'I was damn lucky, I thought Mr. Charles would give me a third one for sure' filled the room. Since our top three players were routinely in danger of ineligibility, their opinions set the standard. The norm was clear: Getting red circles was acceptable (even preferable), as long as you remained eligible to play.

"In my first year on the team, a teammate asked, 'Hey, how many red circles?' My report of 'none' was greeted with mean-spirited laughter from several players and endless chiding, bordering on harassment. As an impressionable adolescent who desperately wanted my teammates to accept me, the chastisement hurt.

"When I mentioned this situation at dinner that evening, my parents gave a united, emphatic reply: 'Anything less than your best school performance is unacceptable.' This external demand reinforced the lesson I took away from my just-completed summer job as a labourer. Hard work was important to my family and me.

"Nonetheless, I found the conflicting expectations of parents and teammates stressful. In class and out, I was awash with anxiety. I obsessed over the red-circle issue. I withdrew and felt lonely, isolated, and powerless. I dreaded going to practice for fear of hearing my new nickname, 'Egghead.' My performance both on the court and in class suffered. The coach inquired about what was troubling me, but I was too embarrassed to tell my story.

"On the next round of report cards, my grades dropped—but not nearly enough to qualify for membership in the red-circle club. Lower grades produced a predictable response from my parents, and I was still stuck with an outsider stigma by key teammates. I was irritable and felt overwhelmed and sad. Role conflict generated debilitating stress.

"The conclusion of the basketball season brought relief. However, my experience was so stressful I decided not to play basketball the following year. I matured during my season off and returned to the courts in my final year of high school, but not without lasting memories of what role conflict can do."

CP Picture Archive/Jacques Boissinot

Schools concentrate young people into a small number of places for extended periods of time. This segregation of young people has unintended consequences, such as encouraging the growth of a separate youth culture.

Encouraging the development of a separate youth culture is only one of the latent functions performed by schools. At higher levels, educational institutions also serve as a "marriage market" that brings potential mates together. Students in educational institutions often share a common social class and related background characteristics. Moreover, since most students postpone mate selection until they complete their education, potential mates often share similar educational qualifications. In these ways, educational settings encourage the choice of partners who share social origins and destinations (Rytina et al., 1988). The result is **assortative mating**—choosing a mate who is similar to oneself on various ranking criteria.

Assortative mating occurs when marriage partners are selected so that spouses are similar on various criteria of social rank.

Schools also perform other unintended functions. For example, in children's early years, schools provide the custodial service of keeping children under close surveillance for much of the day and freeing parents to work. University and college attendance postpones full-time labour force participation, which helps restrict job competition and support wage levels (Bowles and Gintis, 2011). Through their encouragement of critical, independent thinking, educational institutions can also become "schools of dissent" that challenge authoritarian regimes and promote social change (Brower, 1975; Freire, 1972).

Manifest Functions: The Logic of Industrialism

The characteristics of institutions in preindustrial societies vary widely. Functionalists argue that industrialism causes convergence among societies, dictating that social institutions develop according to a common pattern. Said differently, social institutions must perform certain common, manifest (or intended) functions to make industrialism possible. In particular, industrialism requires the widespread application of science and technology in the economy, making work more specialized and technical, and changing working conditions. The education system mirrors these trends (Brown, Reay, and Vincent, 2013).

Cultural Homogeneity and Solidarity

Durkheim saw people as continuously torn between egoistic needs and moral impulses, with schools enhancing the moral side by working to create cultural uniformity and social solidarity. By instilling a sense of authority, discipline, and morality in children, schools make society cohesive (Durkheim, 1956, 1961 [1925]).

Contemporary sociologists acknowledge Durkheim's argument and broaden it. They point to a variety of manifest functions schools perform that are aimed at creating solidarity through cultural homogeneity. For example, Canadian schools teach students civic responsibility, pride in their nation, and respect for the law. Students also learn to think of democracy as the best form of government and capitalism as the best type of economic system (Callahan, 1962). Schools also transmit shared knowledge and culture between generations, thereby fostering a common cultural identity.

Common School Standards

The uniformity of much industrial work requires an education system that teaches workers common standards. Staffing schools to meet this goal was a huge challenge. A large number of student teachers needed to be taught the same outlook and skills. Language was a problem too because, until recently, substantial variations in language and dialect existed within small areas. Creating cultural conformity required designating certain conventions of grammar, spelling, and pronunciation as correct and imposing these conventions on teacher-candidates and certification centres. A demanding and expensive system needed to be created in which a privileged few were recruited to elite institutions, socialized to the new standards, and then sent back to peripheral regions to impose the uniform standards on students. By this means, the language conventions at such university centres as Oxford and the Sorbonne were established as the cultural ideal against which student performances were judged.

National Solidarity

Before the rise of public education, an individual identified with the idiosyncratic worldview of his or her local community. As public education grew, mass socialization shifted to a common set of cultural beliefs, norms, and values directed by a central state. In this way, public education promoted membership in a national community composed of individuals who were mostly strangers but who felt connected because of a shared culture. They became part of an "imagined community" known as the nation.

The loyalties of imagined communities were centred on states because only states could afford the enormous expense of mass education. States provided classrooms with flags, rituals, patriotic songs, and historical myths, along with adults who supplied enthusiastic leadership. Legal requirements meant participation was not a matter of choice. Upper Canada led the world in not only providing universal education but requiring it. In 1871, Ontario pioneered compulsory education by fining parents whose children ages 7 to 12 did not attend school for at least four months each year. Since then, all provinces and territories have gradually tightened such requirements; most now require that students stay in school until they turn 16. Tightening requirements had the desired effect of increasing the number of years children spent in school and, subsequently, reducing unemployment rates (Oreopoulos, 2005). Such benefits soften the harsh realities of required participation imposed on those who unwillingly participate in state-sponsored public schooling.

Functionalists are correct in saying that mass education offers many people a ticket to economic, social, and cultural success. They also have a point when they argue that mass education socializes students into a common culture that enhances economic development. Nonetheless, the functionalist view of education is one-sided. While education can produce these positive individual and social outcomes, it does not do so for everyone. Institutionalized education also produces division and disadvantage, as you will now learn.

TIME FOR REVIEW

- What are the latent functions of public education?
- How do the manifest functions of mass education fit the requirements of industrialism?

SORTING INTO CLASSES AND HIERARCHIES: A CONFLICT PERSPECTIVE

Functionalists argue that modern educational institutions provide all students with equal opportunity to excel. In this view, differences in ability, motivation, and effort allow some students to perform better than others do. Those who learn poorly get inferior jobs, but that's the nature of a **meritocracy**—a social hierarchy in which rank is allocated by tests of individual merit. In a meritocracy, some children are born to lower-ranked families but if they perform well in school they can expect upward mobility. Likewise, some children are born to higher-ranked families but if they perform poorly in school they can expect downward mobility (Bell, 1973; McNamee and Miller, 2009).

A **meritocracy** is a social hierarchy in which rank corresponds to individual capacities fairly tested against a common standard.

Conflict theorists challenge the functionalist assumption that educational attainment and subsequent social ranking are regulated by performance based on individual merit (see Box 17.3). They identify other factors that contribute to educational and economic success, and we survey several of them here. We also examine several prominent features of primary and secondary schooling that tend to preserve the stratification system. We begin by first examining how higher education and advanced degrees are forms of privilege that are less accessible to those with lower-class backgrounds.

Economic Barriers to Higher Education

It might be possible to create an education system in which academic performance is the sole criterion for allocating people to the stratification system. However, few academic programs

BOX 17.3

SOCIOLOGY ON THE TUBE

MR. D

In *Mr. D*, Gerry Dee plays a teacher in a private school. Mr. D is clearly underqualified and relies on bluffing his way through the school day. Much of the show's humour is generated by contrasting the way Mr. D actually behaves with the norms defining how he is expected to act in his role of teacher. In one scene, Mr. D explains to his friend how he grades tests. "If these were regular tests, I would find the smartest student, Mia, and I would grade hers first. Then I'd use that as my answer key. But these are essay questions. If I were to read these it would take forever, so I don't. So I look at their mark going into it..." Mr. D uses each student's previous grades as the baseline for their current performance and then adjusts the grade according to how much he likes the student. This method is not exactly how a merit-based grading system is supposed to be implemented.

Topsail Entertainment Limited. Used with permission.

Mr. D

Teachers are held in high esteem because they have supposedly mastered the curriculum and know how to pass it along to students. Unfortunately, Mr. D's knowledge of history is weak. Confronted in one class with having to explain the Renaissance to his class, he says, "I'm not going to spoon-feed you. You need to do some of this yourself. Look this up tonight, for homework: What caused the Renaissance?" This response is hardly the kind of informed, supportive answer that we expect from qualified teachers.

Gerry Dee claims his sitcom character's conduct is loosely based on his 10-year experience as a teacher in Toronto, filtered through his career as a stand-up comic (Szklarski, 2012). Given the gross misconduct of his Mr. D character, we can only hope that Gerry Dee is pulling our leg when he reports he is "merely lifting the veil on little-known secrets of the classroom."

admit only qualified people and supply all who do qualify with funding to meet all expenses. In most cases, higher education in Canada and elsewhere requires students and their families to shoulder significant financial burdens. Tuition fees are rising. On average, Canadian full-time undergraduates paid $5772 in tuition fees in 2010–11, up from $1185 in 1988–89. Taking inflation into account, this difference represents a more than 200 percent increase. During the 1990s, undergraduate tuition increased at an annual average rate of nearly 10 percent, and since 2000 it has increased at an annual average rate of nearly 4 percent (Statistics Canada, 2013m). Moreover, tuition is only part of the cost of a year at school, particularly for those who leave home to pursue their studies.

Social class origin strongly affects how much formal education people attain (see Box 17.4) (Perry and Francis, 2010). Many countries, Canada among them, have greatly expanded postsecondary education in the past 50 or 60 years. Expansion has lessened class effects, but it has not eliminated them.

How exactly does family income affect postsecondary participation rates? The evidence shows a clear social gradient in which postsecondary education increases at every step of the family income ladder. While access to postsecondary education is much less restricted by family income in Canada than it is in the United States, substantial social inequality remains. About a third of students from families in the bottom quarter of the income distribution attend postsecondary institutions, while about half from families in the top quarter do (Belley, Frenette, and Lochner, 2011; Statistics Canada, 2007). In addition, while the average student loan on completion of university was $16 341 in 2008–9 ($10 085 on completion of college), students from less affluent families often need to borrow more money to complete their education, so they face a significantly weightier economic burden when they graduate (HRSDC, 2011a).

BOX 17.4

SOCIOLOGY AT THE MOVIES

THE LOTTERY

Students from disadvantaged backgrounds generally do less well in public schools than students from more privileged classes do. One policy response to this situation encourages alternative schools with different approaches, including private and charter schools. Charter schools receive public funding for a specific schooling mandate or charter that includes latitude to explore creative educational approaches. While common in the United States, Alberta is the only Canadian province that allows charter schools.

The Lottery is a documentary about the Harlem Success Academy, a high-achieving charter school in New York City. Public schools in New York serve specific geographic regions. Where a family lives determines the school their child may attend. In disadvantaged, predominantly black areas of the city, the schools are generally poor. Parents who want their children to experience better quality education can only turn to private and charter schools. For families living in poverty, private-school tuitions are a restrictive barrier, which leaves charter schools as the only alternative. The track record of success of the Harlem Success Academy ensures demand for entry will exceed supply. To ensure fairness, the school selects student by lottery.

The Lottery inspires the audience to consider educational reform by contrasting the deficiencies of the public system with the success of this model charter school. In the United States, teachers at charter schools are generally not unionized, which is a pointed difference between them and their counterparts in public schools. The opposition of teachers unions to the charter schools is one thread running through the documentary. Beyond the unionization issue, *The Lottery* highlights two important sociological themes worth considering in discussions of educational reform in Canada.

The first issue concerns the emphasis on poverty and race as explanatory factors in students' academic performance. In New York, public-school administrators and supportive politicians generally use the systemic inequalities in the lives of children as a justification for their

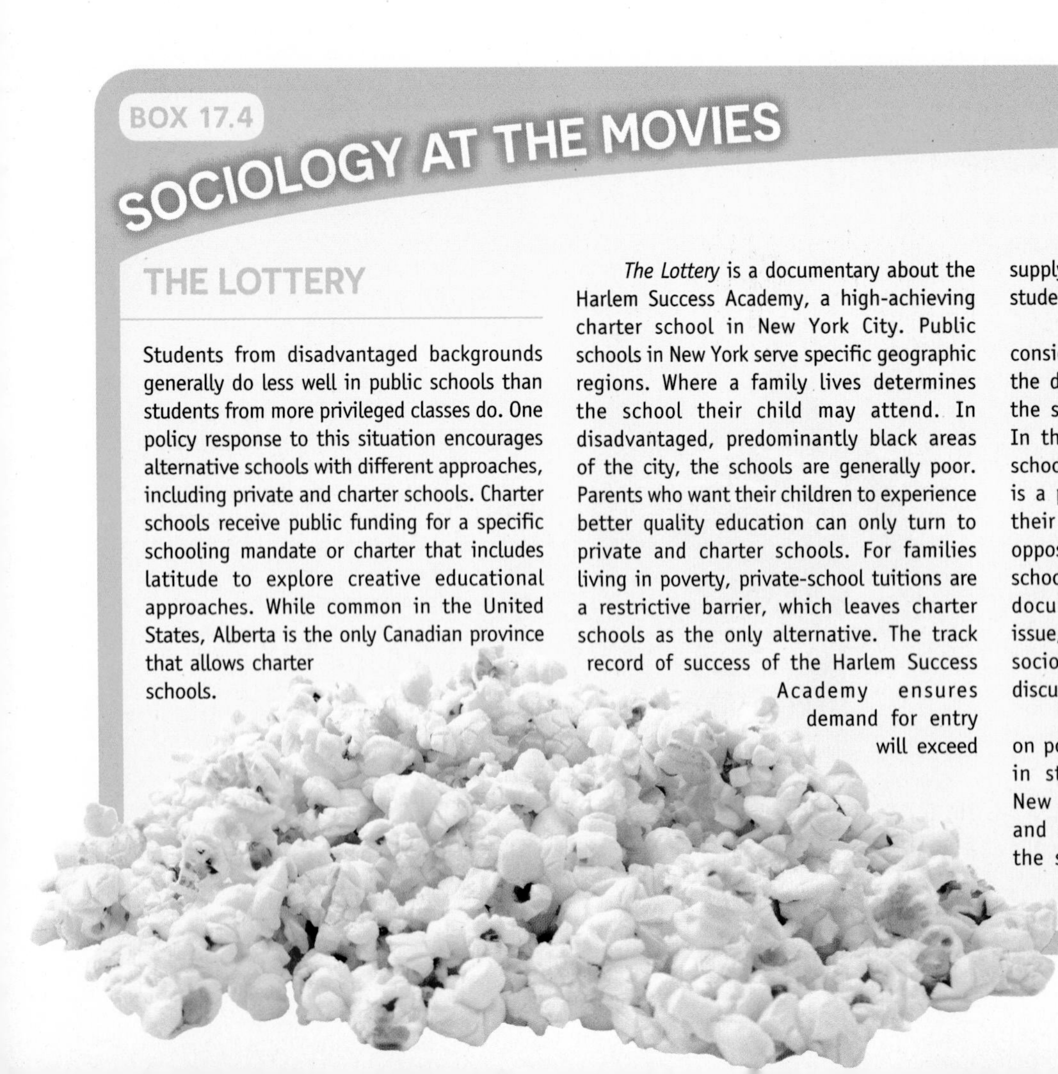

Exclusion, Credentialism, and Professionalization

Because postsecondary education is a valuable asset that children from richer families are more likely to obtain, education becomes a tool for **social exclusion**—setting up boundaries so that certain social opportunities and positions are not open to all (Wright and Rogers, 2010). Exclusion occurs when some groups have more resources than others do, allowing them to obtain educational credentials that allow them to amass still more privileges. Note that social exclusion takes place even if advanced education does not lead to useful knowledge or genuine skills; esoteric skills, such as knowledge of classical music or fine art, may still be used to distinguish insiders from outsiders.

Social exclusion is achieved by creating barriers so that certain social opportunities and positions are not open to all.

Exclusion also occurs by disregarding the knowledge that minority groups possess. Aboriginal people, for example, have vast stores of traditional, accurate knowledge about the operation and cycles of the environment (Battiste, 2012). Until recently, however, this detailed understanding of ecology was not considered knowledge since it was not generated by scientific methods (Canadian Environmental Assessment Agency, 2013). Foucault used the term **subjugated knowledge** to refer to an entire class of understandings about the nature, causes, and solutions of events that dominant groups selectively devalue or ignore (Foucault, 2003). In doing so, dominant groups maintain control by disqualifying competing perspectives from serious consideration. In curricula from grade school through graduate school, individuals and committees have the power to decide what students are assigned to study and what gets ignored. More often than not, the curriculum supports rather than challenges existing social arrangements (Margolis and Romero, 1998).

Subjugated knowledge includes descriptions and explanations of events that dominant groups selectively devalue or ignore.

Credential inflation takes place when, over time, qualifying for specific jobs requires more and more certificates and degrees. Because certificates and degrees are expensive,

Credential inflation occurs when, over time, qualifying for specific jobs requires ever more certificates or degrees.

Courtesy of Great Curve Films

Increasing educational opportunities improves educational achievement.

poor academic performance. Their overdetermined view almost takes it for granted that poor black and Hispanic children will not be able to read at their appropriate grade levels or have other academic success. The Harlem Success Academy takes the opposite view and assumes that all children are capable when given appropriate opportunities. In this charter school's view, all children, regardless of race or income, need to overcome challenges. Over-emphasizing these challenges and the lack of students' success is a failure of the education system and its administrators, not a failure of children or their parents.

Related to this first issue is a second one, expressed in the following quotation from an interview in the film: "Public schools see time as the constant and achievement as the variable. Charter schools see achievement as the constant and time as the variable." The interviewee goes on to explain that, in public schools, the school day has a specified length, whereas in charter schools teachers and students stay late and work on weekends to ensure success. This message is summed up in the mission statement of the Harlem Success Academy, "All students go to college." All lesson plans, activities, special approaches, and extracurricular studying are drawn from this mission. The charter school approaches education with a success mentality and a belief in each and every child.

The successful charter school documented in this film operates from the sociological insight that the interaction of appropriate opportunities and individual effort shapes success. If self-fulfilling prophecies restrict either opportunities or effort, outcomes are dramatically diminished. While *The Lottery* highlights the impressive educational outcomes that are possible with the correct mix of character and social structure, viewers are cautioned about overgeneralization. Achieving the optimal mixture is not easy or formulaic, as the weak performance of many charter schools shows (Tate, 2011).

credential inflation contributes to social exclusion. Credential inflation occurs in part because the technical knowledge required for jobs has increased. For example, because aircraft engines and avionics systems are more complex than they were, say, 75 years ago, working as an airplane mechanic today requires more expertise than it used to. Certification ensures that the airplane mechanic can meet the high technical demands of the job. However, in many jobs there is a poor fit between credentials and responsibilities. On-the-job training, not a diploma or a degree, often gives people the skills they need to get the job done. Nonetheless, credential inflation takes place partly because employers find it a convenient sorting mechanism. For example, an employer may assume that a university graduate has certain manners, attitudes, and tastes that will be useful in a high-profile managerial position. The effect is to exclude people from less advantaged families from such positions, while favouring individuals from families and groups with the advantages that facilitate education (Collins, 1979; McLean and Rollwagen 2010; Van de Werfhorst, 2005).

Professionalization occurs to the degree that certain levels and types of schooling are established as criteria for gaining access to an occupation.

Credential inflation is fuelled by **professionalization**, which occurs when members of an occupation insist that people earn certain credentials to enter the occupation. Professionalization ensures the maintenance of standards. It also keeps earnings high. After all, if "too many" people enter a given profession, the cost of services offered by that profession is bound to fall. Professionalization helps explain why, on average, physicians earn more than university professors who have Ph.D.s. The Canadian Medical Association is a powerful organization that regulates and effectively limits entry into the medical professions (Chapter 19, Health and Medicine). Canadian professors have never been in a position to form such a powerful organization. Because professionalism promotes high standards and high earnings, it has spread widely.

Cultural Capital and Control

French sociologist Pierre Bourdieu wrote extensively about the role of education in maintaining social inequality. His central theme grew out of an analogy with the theories of Karl Marx. Marx had emphasized the role of economic capital—ownership of the physical means of producing wealth—in sustaining inequality. Bourdieu argued that education was central to the creation and transmission of **cultural capital**—learning and skills that ensured superior positions in productive activity (Bourdieu, 1998b; Bourdieu and Passeron, 1979).

Cultural capital is the stock of learning and skills that increases the chance of securing a superior job.

Pedagogic violence is Bourdieu's term for teachers' application of punishments intended to discourage deviation from the dominant culture.

Cultural capital is expensive and difficult to acquire. Bourdieu emphasized that learning in school involves **pedagogic violence**, the application by teachers of punishments intended to discourage deviation from the dominant culture. Teachers routinely insist on one "correct" way to speak, spell, or do arithmetic. They lay down intricate rules, and individuals must learn to follow them with little pause for reflection or judgment. Such learning involves long periods of disciplinary pressure.

Pedagogic violence requires that students be treated as "docile bodies," to use Foucault's term (Foucault, 1995). That is, education institutions typically treat students as objects that need to be transformed and improved. Foucault's studies show that docile bodies are optimally shaped in environments where space is protected and controlled, where performance expectations are clearly conveyed, where power is centralized, and where surveillance is high. These are characteristics of modern school systems (Monahan and Torres, 2009).

For Bourdieu and Foucault, then, schools are institutions of social control where much of what is taught centres on how to evaluate people. Peoples' tastes in books, music, food, and clothing come to reflect their level of schooling. That is, the books and music that people discuss signal their place in the class structure. Docile bodies are shaped into instruments of conformity and the perpetuation of privilege.

Although schools pressure all students to internalize shared cultural standards, students are not equally receptive. The cultural standard designated as correct or proper in schools matches what families practise at home *to varying degrees*. If your parents are university professors, from your earliest babbling, you will be imitating the speech patterns of the dominant cultural group. Families from less advantaged countries or regions enjoy the least overlap with the ideal. If your parents come from rural Newfoundland and Labrador or Bangladesh,

TABLE 17.1
Rates of Participation in Postsecondary Education by Parental Education for Canadians Age 21, 2011

	Participation rate in . . .	
Parental Education	**College**	**University**
No Postsecondary Education	33	24
At Least Some Postsecondary Education	30	47

Source: Adapted from Statistics Canada PISA Data, "Participation in Post-Secondary Education." Retrieved March 17, 2011 (http://www.pisa.gc.ca/eng/participation.shtml).

and especially if they lack a higher education, teachers are likely to spend a lot of time correcting your English. Children from such families often struggle to meet teachers' standards.

When teachers evaluate performance, they inevitably reward students who are close to the standards of the dominant culture. Although some students from all backgrounds succeed, a student's stock of cultural capital—of disciplined familiarity with the dominant culture—will influence how difficult or easy it is to achieve success. Advantaged children will find rewards easier to achieve. Children from families with less cultural capital will be punished more and will tend to have less pleasant experiences of school.

A key part of Bourdieu's argument is readily confirmed. Table 17.1 shows how much growing up with parents who are highly educated enhances one's educational attainment. University attendance is nearly twice as common among students whose parents have some postsecondary degree than among those whose parents had none. In Canada, parents' lower education is a bigger barrier to postsecondary education than is lower family income (Finnie et al., 2011).

TIME FOR REVIEW

- Explain how economic barriers restricting access to higher education challenge the idea of meritocracy.
- How do credentialism and professionalism in education act as mechanisms of social exclusion?
- How does cultural capital restrict higher educational achievement?

REPRODUCING INEQUALITY: THE CONTRIBUTION OF SYMBOLIC INTERACTIONISM

Most sociologists find the conflict perspective on education more credible than the functionalist view. Based on the evidence, they believe that the benefits of education are unequally distributed and lead to the **reproduction of the existing stratification system** (Bowles and Gintis, 2011).

The **reproduction of the existing stratification system** refers to social processes that ensure that offspring enter a rank or class similar or identical to that of their parents.

Factors other than class also matter. Students with higher grades are more likely to advance to higher education. Parental encouragement plays a role, as does support from peers and teachers. However, research consistently finds that such social supports are part of how class advantage is transmitted; wealthier students with more highly educated parents are likely to enjoy more parental, peer, and teacher support. Furthermore, family income and parental education contribute to educational attainment over and above any influence they exert on academic performance and social support, insofar as they provide students with cultural capital that assists their advancement (Collins, 2009; Lambert et al., 2004).

Why do schools fail to overcome class differences? Symbolic interactionists emphasize three social mechanisms that operate to reproduce inequality: the hidden curriculum, testing and tracking, and self-fulfilling prophecies.

The Hidden Curriculum

The **hidden curriculum** in school teaches obedience to authority and conformity to cultural norms.

Apart from academic and vocational subjects, students learn a **hidden curriculum** in school (Snyder, 1971; Chapter 4, Socialization). Teachers and school administrators never state that understanding the hidden curriculum contributes powerfully to educational achievement, and they never teach it formally, but "getting it" is central to success.

The content of the hidden curriculum centres on obedience to authority and conformity to cultural norms. Teachers expect students to accept the curriculum, institutional routines, and grading system without question. The hidden curriculum is related to the concepts of cultural capital and docile bodies, introduced earlier. Students who comply do well; those who do not are headed for trouble. Success stories are most common among middle- and upper-class children who are well-endowed with cultural capital and whose socialization at home has cultivated the hidden curriculum's standards of dress, speech, motivation, and deferred gratification.

Students' connection to and conformity with the hidden curriculum is class-based; it is rooted in their parents' socialization styles. Think about your own early socialization. Did your parents regularly shuttle you from one scheduled appointment to the next, from dental appointments to sports practices to music lessons? Did they check that you did your homework? When you got a B on an assignment, did they encourage you to ask the teacher how you could do better? When supper was being prepared, did they consult you about salad dressing preferences, vegetable choices, and the like? If so, your experience was typically middle-class; you experienced **concerted cultivation** (Lareau, 1987, 2011). Concerted cultivation is a middle-class parenting style that emphasizes the organization of children's after-school time with activities that encourage critical thinking, autonomy, confidence, negotiation with adults, and cultural competencies. Concerted cultivation stands in clear contrast to the parenting style of working- and lower-class families, which Lareau labels **natural growth**. Parents using this style are much less involved in structuring their children's lives. And when they are involved, it is more to provide direction and orders. Given such differential socialization, it is no surprise that middle-class children are better prepared to engage with teachers, the curriculum, and school expectations. They have been preparing for it since birth.

Concerted cultivation is the middle-class parenting style that systematically organizes and directs children's time to activities that prepare them for success in school.

Natural growth is the parenting style of working- and lower-class families that leaves children largely to their own devices, except when parents demand obedience to authority.

Staying in school requires accepting the terms of the hidden curriculum and feeling positively involved. Researchers at Statistics Canada explored this phenomenon by developing measures of academic and social involvement. Social involvement was defined as not feeling like an outsider and believing that people cared what a student said. Academic involvement consisted of liking teachers, not skipping classes, and regarding class content as "not useless." Chances of continuing to higher education were twice as high for students who reported social acceptance or positive attitudes toward the formal organization, authority, and procedures of the school (Shaienks and Gluszynski, 2007).

Testing and Tracking

Most schools in Canada are composed of children from various socioeconomic, racial, and ethnic backgrounds. Apart from the hidden curriculum, testing and tracking maintain these social inequalities in schools. IQ tests sort students, who are then channelled into high-ability (enriched), middle-ability, and low-ability (special needs) classrooms based on their test scores. Often, the results are classrooms that are stratified by socioeconomic status, race, and ethnicity, much like the larger society. For example, Toronto Board of Education research showed that while 20 percent of black students were enrolled in low-level academic programming, only 10 percent of white students and 3 percent of Asian students were similarly streamed (Henry et al., 2000: 239). Research on four provinces west of Québec shows that, compared with other students, students of parents with higher education are much more likely to be on tracks leading to postsecondary education (Krahn and Taylor, 2007).

Nobody denies that students vary in their abilities and that high-ability students require special challenges to reach their full potential. Nor does anyone deny that underprivileged students tend to score low on IQ tests. The controversial question is whether IQ is mainly genetic or social in origin. If IQ is genetic in origin, then it cannot be changed, so improving the quality of schooling for the underprivileged is arguably a waste of money (Herrnstein and Murray, 1994). If IQ is social in origin, IQ tests and tracking only reinforce social differences that could otherwise be reduced by changing the social circumstances of students.

Most sociologists believe that IQ reflects social standing in great part. That is because all that IQ tests can ever measure is a person's acquired proficiency with a cultural system. How much exposure a person has had to whatever examiners count as correct will play a large role in testing. Even the most able Canadian children would perform abysmally if tested in Mongolian. IQ test results turn on a combination of two factors: (1) how effectively an individual absorbs what his or her environment offers, and (2) how closely his or her environment reflects what the test includes.

Most sociologists believe that members of underprivileged groups tend to score low on IQ tests because they do not have the training and the cultural background needed to score high (Fischer et al., 1996). To support their argument, they point to cases in which changing social circumstances result in changes in IQ scores. For instance, in the first decades of the twentieth century, most Jewish immigrants to North America tested well below average on IQ tests. Their low scores were sometimes used as an argument against Jewish immigration (Gould, 1996; Steinberg, 1989). By 1960, North American Jews tested above average in IQ (Backman, 1972). Since the genetic makeup of Jews has not changed in the past century, why the change in IQ scores? Sociologists point to upward mobility. During the twentieth century, most Jewish immigrants worked hard and moved up the stratification system. As their fortunes improved, they made sure their children had the skills and the cultural resources needed to do well in school. Average IQ scores rose as the social standing of Jews improved.

Tracking (also known as streaming or ability-grouping) was originally implemented as a way of tailoring the school experience to the diverse abilities of students. It relied on IQ tests as assessments of ability. However, IQ tests are not objective assessments of innate potential; they are value-laden social constructions. Consequently, the streaming of students in classrooms stratifies opportunities to learn. High-track students, who generally come from privileged backgrounds, are given better educational options that are denied to low-track, less privileged students (Oakes, 2005). As hundreds of research studies demonstrate, tracking in schools generates inequities that reproduce rather than reduce social inequalities (Mathis, 2013).

Consider also the "Flynn effect," named after political scientist James R. Flynn, who first pointed it out (Flynn, 1987). Flynn showed that average IQ scores increase over time on every major test, in every age range, and in every industrialized country (Neisser, 1997: 2). He observed increases of as much as 21 points in only 30 years. Typical improvements in test performance were large. For example, differences between children and their grandparents were far greater than differences observed across race and class divides in contemporary societies. This evidence suggests that IQ tests do not provide a fixed measuring rod that captures innate abilities or, for that matter, any sort of trait fixed by genetic endowment. It therefore makes sense to invest in the early education of children from underprivileged families (see Box 17.5).

Self-Fulfilling Prophecies

A third social mechanism that operates in schools to reproduce inequality is the self-fulfilling prophecy. A self-fulfilling prophecy is an expectation that helps to cause what it predicts. In a classic study, Ray Rist (1970) revealed how a self-fulfilling prophecy can influence a person's life chances. He found that after just eight days of observing students in a kindergarten classroom, and without giving a formal intelligence test, the teacher felt she could confidently assign the children to one of three tables. She assigned "fast learners" to Table 1, closest to her own desk and "slow learners" to Table 3, at the back of the class. Students she judged to be "average" were seated at Table 2, in the middle of the classroom. On what basis did she make these distinctions? Probing the issue, Rist found that the key variable distinguishing

BOX 17.5

IT'S YOUR CHOICE

IS SCHOOL ENOUGH?

Sociologists began to understand how little schools could do on their own to encourage upward mobility and end poverty in the 1960s, when American sociologist James Coleman and his colleagues conducted a monumental study of academic performance (Coleman et al., 1966). What they found was that differences in the quality of schools—measured by assessment of such factors as school facilities and curriculum—accounted at most for about a third of the variation in students' academic performance. At least two-thirds of the variation in academic performance was due to inequalities imposed on children by their homes, neighbourhoods, and peers. Fifty years later, little research contradicts Coleman's finding.

Native Child and Family Services

Head Start programs have increased the educational achievement of Aboriginal children.

Various social commentators have argued that if we are to improve the success of disadvantaged students, we must develop policies aimed at improving the social environment of young, disadvantaged children *before* they enter the formal education system (Heckman and Masterov, 2007). Compensatory education programs for preschool children were largely developed in the United States and attempt to meet the needs of children who are socially and economically disadvantaged. In Canada, such programs have also been aimed at "children with special needs" and "at-risk children"—those who, because of one or more factors in their background, are believed to face a heightened risk of poor academic performance or social adjustment. Although the traditional focus of early childhood education has been on children's social and emotional development, some of these compensatory education programs focus on children's intellectual development.

Survey research shows that household income is associated with developmental maturity and future success at school (Duncan and Murnane, 2013). In addition, as family income decreases, the likelihood increases that children will experience a host of other problems that will negatively influence their school performance. For example, poor health, hyperactivity, and delayed vocabulary development are all higher among children in low-income families than among children in middle- and high-income families. Children who score low on school readiness are also more likely to have mothers with low levels of education and to be living in neighbourhoods that their mothers characterize as unsafe or as lacking in social cohesiveness (Derosiers, Tétreault, and Boivin, 2012).

Some observers believe that early developmental programs can decrease the chances of children's developmental problems and enhance their school performance. For example, Head Start programs are based on the belief that to assist children, the entire family must be helped. They provide access to food banks, nutrition programs, literacy programs, parental support groups, and parenting courses. Promoting child readiness for school is also a key element of Head Start. Evaluations of Head Start programs in Canada report such benefits as more students completing school with better grades, students requiring fewer medical and mental health services, and students' reduced exposure to violent and alcoholic parents (Government of Canada, 2001). Head Start programs have been identified as particularly successful in increasing the educational success of Aboriginal students (Health Canada, 2010).

While the cost of providing early childhood intervention programs is substantial, investments made in the critical early years of a child's life benefit not only Canada's children but also the economy. One study reports that "every dollar spent in early intervention can save seven dollars in future expenditures in health and social spending" (Health Canada, 1999: 88).

Do you believe that early childhood intervention programs are useful in improving the educational success of children? If so, do you feel that attendance in these programs should be compulsory? Should parents be penalized if they refuse to send their children to such programs? What background factors should be used to select children and their families for inclusion in such programs?

the students was social class. Children at Table 1 were overwhelmingly middle class, while those assigned to Tables 2 and 3 were more likely to come from less advantaged homes. The assignment of these children was consequential because the children at Table 1 received more attention, were treated better, and, as the year progressed, came to see themselves as superior to the other children. In contrast, the other students tended to be ignored by the teacher and were referred to by the Table 1 children as "dumb." Unsurprisingly, they did not fare well. The following year, the grade 1 teacher took note of what the children had accomplished in kindergarten. The Table 1 children were once again assigned to places in the classroom that marked them as superior.

monkeybusinessimages/Thinkstock.com

Canada was one of the first countries in the world to link its student body to the Internet. By 1997, almost all Canadian schools had Internet access through the SchoolNet electronic network.

Rist's findings suggest that, rather than valuing all students equally and treating them as if they have equally good prospects, teachers may suspect that disadvantaged students and students who are members of some minority groups are intellectually inferior. In turn, these students may come to feel rejected by teachers, other classmates, and the curriculum. Students from minority groups may also be disadvantaged by overt racism and discrimination. In response, students presumed to be inferior and marginalized in the classroom often cluster together out of resentment and in defiance of authority. Some of them eventually reject academic achievement as a goal. Discipline problems, ranging from apathy to disruptive and illegal behaviour, can result. Consistent with this argument, the dropout rate for Aboriginal children (22.6 percent) is about three times as high as it is for non-Aboriginal children (HRSDC, 2011b). In contrast, research shows that certain strategies can explode the self-fulfilling prophecy and improve academic performance: challenging students from disadvantaged families and those from minority groups, providing them with emotional support and encouragement, including greater recognition in the curriculum to the accomplishments of the groups from which they originate, and creating an environment in which they can relax and achieve.

In sum, schools reproduce the stratification system because of the hidden curriculum, IQ testing and tracking, and the self-fulfilling prophecy that disadvantaged students and students from minority groups are bound to do poorly. These social mechanisms increase the chance that students who are socially marginal and already disadvantaged will earn low grades and will later work at jobs near the bottom of the occupational structure.

TIME FOR REVIEW

- How does the hidden curriculum operate to restrict the educational success of less advantaged students?
- How do IQ testing and tracking result in schools perpetuating social inequality rather than reducing it?
- How can self-fulfilling prophecies contribute to either success or failure in school?

PROSPECTS AND CHALLENGES FOR EDUCATION IN CANADA

Gender Differences: A Feminist Perspective

With every passing decade, Canadians spend more time in school, and with every passing decade, women's level of education increases relative to men's. Table 17.2 displays the trend. In two decades, the percentage of women with a university degree more than doubled. Women currently receive more than 60 percent of university degrees awarded annually (Hango, 2013). After decades of catching up, university-educated women now outnumber university-educated men.

TABLE 17.2
Sex Differences in Educational Achievement, Ages 25–34, 1990 and 2009, Canada

Highest Level of Educational Attainment	1990		2009	
	Women	Men	Women	Men
0 to 8 years	3.9	4.6	1.4	1.5
Some high school	15.5	17.9	5.2	8.0
High-school diploma	27.3	23.0	15.0	19.3
Some postsecondary	9.9	9.7	7.4	8.2
Postsecondary certificate/diploma	28.3	29.3	36.7	37.0
University degree	15.0	15.6	34.3	26.0

Source: Adapted from Turcotte, Martin. 2011. Women and Education: A Gender-Based Statistical Report. "Table 1 Distribution of women and men, by age group and highest level of educational attainment, Canada, 1990 and 2009." Ottawa: Statistics Canada. Catalogue no. 89-503-X. Accessed March 15, 2014.

However, as feminists note, these figures mask the ways in which greater female participation in postsecondary education still conforms to traditional gender divisions. Figure 17.4 shows gender differences in fields of study at university. Canada, like other developed nations, systematically encourages students to study STEM fields (science, technology, engineering, mathematics and computer science). Nationally, STEM courses are a strategic focus because these areas directly contribute to economic competitiveness and prosperity. In a knowledge-based economy, STEM fields lead to high-paying jobs (Knowles, 2013). The top ten highest-paying bachelor's degrees are all in STEM fields (Dehaas, 2011). However, as Figure 17.4 illustrates, women participate in STEM fields at less than half the rate that men do. Despite their remarkable high participation rate in university, women tend to concentrate their studies in less scientifically oriented, lower-paying fields.

Participation and Aboriginal Background

The Aboriginal Challenge

Barriers to education other than gender are also substantial. Aboriginal educational achievement in Canada is particularly problematic. Aboriginal peoples currently comprise 4 percent of the population and this proportion will grow in the upcoming decades. Aboriginal people

FIGURE 17.4
Number of STEM University Graduates, 2011

Source: Hango, Darcy. 2013. Gender Differences in Science, Technology, Engineering, Mathematics and Computer Science (STEM) Programs at University. Ottawa: Statistics Canada. Catalogue no. 75-006-X. Retrieved March 15, 2014 (www.statcan.gc.ca/pub/75-006-x/2013001/article/11874-eng.pdf).

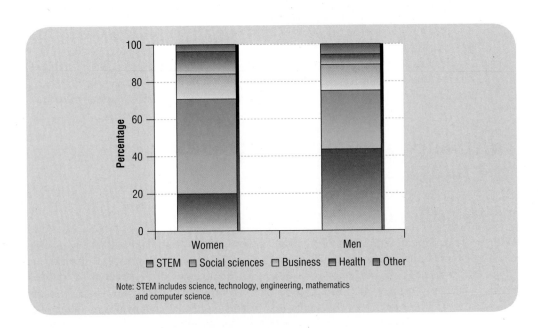

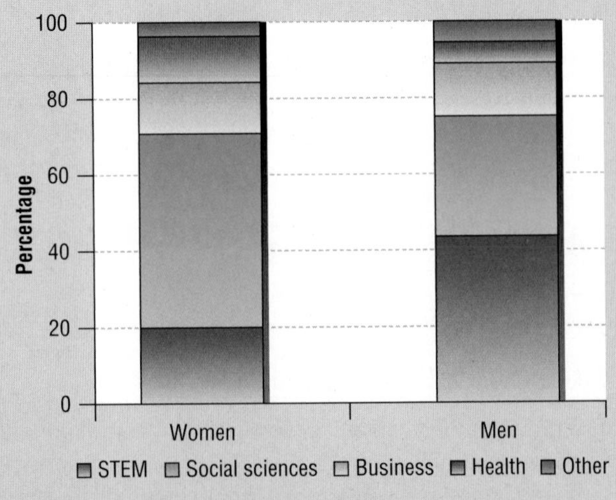

Note: STEM includes science, technology, engineering, mathematics and computer science.

are relatively young, with a median age of 26.5 years, compared with an average age of 39.5 years for other Canadians. As the general Canadian population ages, Aboriginal people will comprise a growing share of the labour force. Yet despite their strategic importance, Aboriginal education outcomes are comparatively weak.

Table 17.3 shows the trend and current situation. Almost 40 percent of Aboriginal Canadians do not complete high school. This rate is double that of non-Aboriginal Canadians, and the gap has not changed much over time. Some Aboriginal people have some postsecondary education, but their educational achievements are still substantially and consistently below those of non-Aboriginal people. And, similar to the case of women, Aboriginal people with a university education are seriously under-represented in the high-demand, high-paying STEM areas (Fong and Gulati, 2013: 4). According to the best estimates, the educational achievement gap between Aboriginal people and non-Aboriginal people will either remain at current levels or worsen in the foreseeable future (Gordon and White, 2013).

The pattern of low educational achievement among Aboriginal peoples is no coincidence. The systematic operation of social forces over time produced this result (Sengupta, 2013). To begin with, Aboriginal treaty rights were routinely ignored or their terms reduced (Mercredi and Turpel, 1993). Since before Confederation, Aboriginal peoples have not been provided an adequate standard of living that was their right and Canada's constitutional obligation. In addition, residential schools (the last of which closed in 1996) produced a legacy of personal and social dysfunction that continues over generations. The goal of these schools was to "take the Indian out of the child" and it attempted to do so with an appalling mixture of physical, mental, emotional, and sexual abuse (Truth and Reconciliation Commission of Canada, 2012b). The history of social mistreatment was compounded in the 1960s, when policies permitted more than 20 000 Aboriginal children to be adopted or fostered by middle-class white families. These children were separated from their families and cultures, and now that they are adults, they face cultural and identity confusion (Sinclair, 2007). In short, a multi-generational assault on the integrity of Aboriginal cultures has left a large proportion of these people at the margins of Canadian society, where self-respect is low and personal and social dysfunction are high (Frideres and Gadacz, 2011).

Low educational achievement is only one outcome of this social legacy, but it is one that holds promise for change. Closing the gap between Aboriginal and non-Aboriginal educational achievement would have positive effects on suicide and incarceration rates, family stability, civic participation, and health outcomes. The economic returns of closing the educational gap are enormous (Sharpe and Arsenault, 2009). For economic and

TABLE 17.3

Educational Attainment Rates by Aboriginal Identity (in percent)

	Aboriginal People			Non-Aboriginal People			Gap		
	2001	2006	2011	2001	2006	2011	2001	2006	2011
Less than high school	48.0	43.7	38.0	30.8	23.1	19.4	17.2	20.6	18.5
High school only	22.4	21.8	23.9	25.0	25.7	25.6	−2.6	−3.9	−1.7
Apprenticeship & trades	12.1	11.4	11.8	10.8	10.8	10.8	1.3	0.6	1.0
Post-secondary education less than bachelor's degree	13.0	17.3	18.9	17.6	21.9	22.8	−4.6	−4.5	−3.9
Bachelor's degree and above	4.4	5.8	7.4	15.7	18.5	21.4	−11.3	−12.7	−13.9
Total Postsecondary Education	**29.5**	**34.5**	**38.1**	**44.2**	**51.2**	**54.9**	**−14.6**	**−16.7**	**−16.8**

Source: Francis Fong, and Sonya Gulati. 2013. Employment and Education among Aboriginal Peoples. Special Report TD Economics. October 7. Retrieved March 10, 2014 (www.td.com/document/PDF/economics/special/EmploymentAndEducationAmongAboriginalPeoples.pdf).

TABLE 17.4

Completion of Post-Secondary Education, Various OECD Countries, 2010

Source: Organisation for Economic Co-operation and Development (OECD). 2012. Education at a Glance 2012: OECD Indicators, Table A1.3a, Population that has attained tertiary education (2010). Available at: Employment and Social Development Canada www4.hrsdc.gc.ca/.3ndic.1t.4r@-eng.jsp?iid=29#M_7.

Country	Percentage of Adult Population
Canada	51
Japan	45
United States	42
United Kingdom	38
OECD – 34 countries, average	31
France	29
Germany	27
Italy	15

humanistic reasons, the social inequalities of Aboriginal education deserve the attention of every Canadian.

International Competition

Although access to higher education in Canada remains uneven, the Canadian accomplishment in higher education is impressive when compared with that of other countries. Table 17.4 shows rankings of a selection of highly developed, high-income countries. With 51 percent of Canadians between the ages of 25 and 64 completing post-secondary education, we rank first in the world.

In the 1990s, some observers raised doubts about the quality of Canada's education system. Suspicions grew that students were not applying themselves and not learning enough, and that curricula and requirements had become lax. Critics were in for a surprise. The Organisation for Economic Co-operation and Development (OECD) organized a Programme for International Student Assessment (PISA) to assess the academic performance of 15-year-olds. In the first PISA survey in 2000, Canada scored among the top countries in educational achievement. The PISA research has been repeated regularly since then. The 2012 results included 61 countries and five other jurisdictions. Table 17.5 displays the country results. Canada placed seventh overall and ninth in math, fifth in reading, and eighth in science. Canada's consistently high performance across all three testing dimensions is a result that should make all Canadians proud.

TABLE 17.5

Top Ten Countries in Educational Achievement, 2012

	Total Score	Math (rank)	Reading (rank)	Science (rank)
Singapore	1666	1	1	1
South Korea	1628	2	3	5
Japan	1621	3	2	2
Finland	1588	8	4	3
Estonia	1578	7	8	4
Liechtenstein	1576	4	9	9
Canada	**1566**	**9**	**5**	**8**
Poland	1562	9	7	7
Netherlands	1556	6	12	10
Switzerland	1555	5	13	15

Source: Sedghi, Ami, George Arnett, and Mona Chalabi. 2013. "Pisa 2012 Results: Which Country Does Best at Reading, Maths and Science?" *The Guardian* Datablog, December 3. Retrieved July 17, 2014 (www.theguardian.com/news/datablog/2013/dec/03/pisa-results-country-best-reading-maths-science).

TIME FOR REVIEW

- In terms of social equality, how is women's performance in higher education encouraging? How is it discouraging?
- What is the sociological response to someone who asserts that Aboriginal people must take individual responsibility for their low educational achievement?
- What is Canada's international standing in terms of educational achievement?

SUMMARY

1. What role does mass education play in industrialized societies?
   Industrialized societies must provide complete systems of schooling that take in nearly all children and allow many of them to remain in school for many years. This approach is necessary because jobs in industrialized societies require not only basic literacy and numeracy but also specialized knowledge and skills.
2. What basic functions are performed by school systems?
   Mass education produces nearly universal literacy and numeracy. In doing so, schools homogenize future citizens by indoctrination into a common culture that is the basis of national solidarity. Schools also sort students and steer them to different class positions as adults. In addition to these manifest functions, schools perform latent functions, including the creation of a youth culture, a marriage market, a custodial and surveillance system for children, a means of maintaining wage levels by keeping college and university students temporarily out of the job market, and occasionally a "school of dissent" that opposes authorities.
3. How does the functionalist view of education differ from the conflict theory view of education?
   Functionalists argue that education is critically important for industrialization. The provision of mass public education generates equal opportunities for all citizens. Consequently, differential educational achievement and resulting employment success are the result of individual merit. By contrast, conflict theorists argue that the educational system is biased toward the perpetuation of existing social inequalities. Children from privileged social backgrounds come to school with higher human, social, and cultural capital, which supports high achievement. They are also more attuned to the hidden curriculum.
4. What advances have women made toward educational equality and what challenges do Aboriginal people face in making similar progress?
   In recent decades, women have made remarkable gains in educational achievement. Today, substantially more women than men graduate from university. Still, as feminist scholars point out, gender segregation remains. Women are much less likely to complete degrees in the STEM fields, and they are less likely to attain the high-paying jobs that usually come with such degrees. Aboriginal educational achievement is growing but not at a rate that is closing the gap with non-Aboriginal people. Aboriginal people with university education are concentrated in non-STEM fields. A social legacy of colonialism, residential schools, segregation, and discrimination shape the trend in Aboriginal educational achievement.

CHAPTER 18

MASS MEDIA AND MASS COMMUNICATION

Seamus Murphy/VII Photo Agency

IN THIS CHAPTER, YOU WILL LEARN TO

- Appreciate that the growth of the mass media is rooted in the rise of Protestantism, democracy, and capitalism, although the most popular mass media are products of the twentieth century.
- Identify the ways in which the mass media make society more cohesive.
- Recognize how the mass media foster social inequality.
- Describe how audiences filter, interpret, resist, and even reject media messages that are inconsistent with their beliefs and experiences.
- Analyze how the mass media misrepresent women and members of racial minorities.
- Recognize that the Internet and social media offer users more freedom than other mass media do.

THE SIGNIFICANCE OF THE MASS MEDIA

Illusion Becomes Reality

In *Oblivion* (2013), Jack and Victoria, played by Tom Cruise and Andrea Riseborough, live in, and work from, a pod mounted on a pole hundreds of metres above the surface of the Earth. It is 2070. The planet is nearly dead. Years earlier, an alien race started a war that humans won. It left the Earth a nuclear wasteland. Most of the human survivors live in a giant space vehicle called Tet, which circles the Earth and will soon evacuate the remains of humanity to Titan, Saturn's biggest moon.

Jack and Victoria remain on Earth to repair drones that hunt down the remaining aliens and guard the nuclear reactors that suck up water and send power to Tet. They have had their memories wiped so they won't reveal strategic information if the aliens capture them. They receive their orders from Sally (Melissa Leo) via video transmission from Tet.

Sally provides Jack and Victoria with their entire definition of reality; the whole story of the tragedy that befell Earth comes from the screen on which Sally regularly and frequently appears. Then Jack starts having memory flashbacks. Could their world be an illusion? Were the aliens the real victors? Are they using Jack and Victoria to mop up the remaining humans? These are the questions that begin to slowly surface as the movie unfolds.

Oblivion may be taken as a symbol for the fantasy worlds that the mass media create for us. Increasingly the only realities we know, the illusions created by the mass media are every bit as pervasive and influential as religion was 500 or 600 years ago. If you think this idea is an exaggeration, consider that the average Canadian spends more than three hours a day watching television, over two-and-a-half hours listening to the radio, and just under an hour reading magazines, newspapers, and books (Statistics Canada, 2008d). Add the time we spend using the Internet, going to the movies, listening to music downloads, and playing video games, and it becomes clear that about 40 percent of our time is spent interacting with the mass media—more than we spend sleeping, working, or going to school. You might want to keep a tally of your activities for a couple of days to see how you fit into this pattern of activity. Ask yourself, too, what you get out of your interactions with the mass media. Where do you get your ideas about how to dress, how to style your hair, and what music to listen to? Where do your hopes, aspirations,

Harold Innis, 1920s, photograph by H. James. Library and Archives Canada

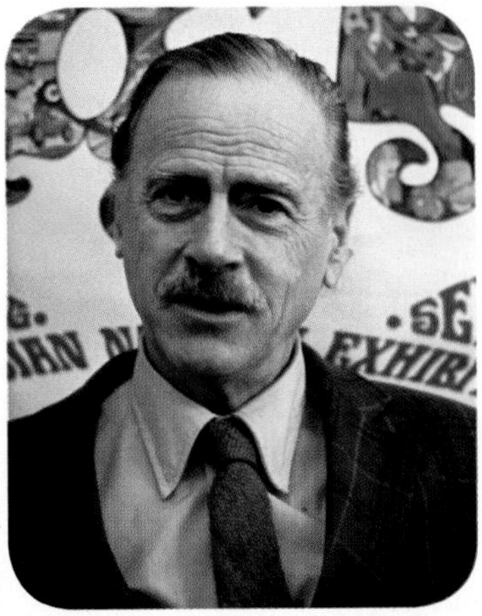

Bettman/CORBIS

Harold Innis (1894–52) and his student, Marshall McLuhan (1911–1980), were Canadian pioneers in the study of mass media and mass communication. Innis (1951) distinguished time-based media that endure but are relatively immobile (such as writing on stone tablets) from space-based media that are relatively short-lived but mobile (such as radio signals). He argued that different types of media help to create different kinds of institutions and values; time-based media foster traditionalism and established religion while space-based media encourage colonization, empire-building, and the growth of secular states and armies. McLuhan (1964) added that the introduction of new media changes the way we perceive and think. For example, printing undermined oral communication, which affected cultures based on hearing. Print media encouraged the development of cultures that are more visually oriented, abstract, individualistic, and rational. Electronic media subsequently undermined print-based culture. For instance, TV, which integrates seeing and hearing, affects its audience more deeply than print does and is more socially inclusive than print is. Moreover, TV allows communication to occur at the speed of light. It thus shrinks the world, creating what McLuhan called a "global village."

and dreams come from? If you're like most people, much of your reality is generated by the mass media. Canadian media guru Marshall McLuhan, who coined the term *global village* in the early 1960s, said the media are extensions of the human body and mind (McLuhan, 1964). More than half a century later, it is perhaps equally valid to claim that the human body and mind are extensions of the mass media (Baudrillard, 1983, 1988; Bourdieu, 1998a).

What Are the Mass Media?

The term **mass media** refers to print, radio, television, and other communication technologies. Often, *mass media* and *mass communication* are used interchangeably to refer to the transmission of information from one person or group to another. The word *mass* implies that the media reach many people. The word *media* signifies that communication does not take place directly through face-to-face interaction. Instead, technology intervenes or mediates in transmitting messages from senders to receivers. Furthermore, communication via the mass media is usually one-way, or at least one-sided. Typically, mass media have few senders (or producers) and many receivers (or audience members). Thus, most newspapers print a few readers' letters in each edition, but journalists and advertisers write virtually everything else. Ordinary people may appear on the *Dr. Phil* show or even delight in a slice of fame on *Survivor*. However, producers choose the guests and create the program content.

Usually, then, members of the audience cannot exert much influence on the mass media. They can choose only to tune in or tune out. And even tuning out is difficult because it excludes us from the styles, news, gossip, and entertainment most people depend on to grease the wheels of social interaction. Few people want to be cultural misfits. However, our apparent need to access the mass media does not mean that we are always passive consumers of the mass media. As noted below, we filter, interpret, and resist what we see and hear if it contradicts our experiences and beliefs. Even so, in the interaction between audiences and media sources, the media sources usually dominate.

To appreciate fully the impact of the mass media on life today, we need to trace their historical development. That is the first task we set ourselves in the following discussion. We then critically review theories of the mass media's effects on social life. As you will see, each of these theories contributes to our appreciation of media effects. Finally, we assess developments on the media frontier formed by the Internet, television, and other mass media. We show that, to a degree, the new media frontier blurs the distinction between producer and consumer and has the potential to make the mass media more democratic for those who can afford access.

The **mass media** are print, radio, television, and other communication technologies. The word mass implies that the media reach many people. The word media signifies that communication does not take place directly through face-to-face interaction.

The Rise of the Mass Media

It may be difficult for you to imagine a world without the mass media. Yet, as Table 18.1 shows, most of the mass media are recent inventions. The first developed systems of writing appeared only about 5500 years ago in Egypt and Mesopotamia (now southern Iraq). The print media became truly a mass phenomenon only in the nineteenth century. The inexpensive daily newspaper, costing a penny, first appeared in the United States in the 1830s. At that time, long-distance communication required physical transportation. To spread the news, you needed a horse, a railroad, or a ship. The slow speed of communication was costly. For instance, the last military engagement between Britain

TABLE 18.1
The Development of the Mass Media

Source: Berners-Lee 1999, Croteau and Hoynes, 1997: 9–10; "The Silent Boom," 1998

Year	Media Development
1450	Movable metal type used in Germany, leading to the Gutenberg Bible
1702	First daily newspaper, London's *Daily Courant*
1833	First mass-circulation newspaper, *New York Sun*
1837	Louis Daguerre invents a practical method of photography in France
1844	Samuel Morse sends the first telegraph message between Washington and Baltimore
1875	Alexander Graham Bell sends the first telephone message
1877	Thomas Edison develops the first phonograph
1895	Motion pictures are invented
1901	Italian inventor Guglielmo Marconi transmits the first transatlantic wireless message from England to St. John's, Newfoundland
1906	First radio voice transmission
1920	First regularly scheduled radio broadcast, Pittsburgh
1928	First commercial TV broadcast in United States; Canada follows in 1931
1949	Network TV begins in the United States
1952	VCR invented
1961	First cable television, San Diego
1969	First four nodes of the United States Department of Defense's ARPANET (precursor of the Internet) set up at Stanford University; University of California, Los Angeles; University of California, Santa Barbara; and the University of Utah
1975	First microcomputer marketed
1976	First satellite TV broadcast
1983	Cellphone invented
1989	World Wide Web conceived by Tim Berners-Lee at the European Laboratory for Particle Physics in Switzerland
1990	Windows 3.0 released (first mass-marketed graphical operating system)
1991	The World Wide Web becomes publicly accessible
1999	Wi-Fi (wireless Internet) becomes publicly available
2001	First iPod released Digital satellite radio introduced
2003	Camera phone invented First BlackBerry smartphone released in Waterloo, Ontario
2005	Facebook.com becomes public YouTube founded
2007	First iPhone released
2010	E Ink (Pearl display) invented, making e-readers like Kindle and Kobo widely available

and the United States in the War of 1812–14 was the Battle of New Orleans. It took place 15 days *after* a peace treaty had been signed. The good news did not reach the troops near the mouth of the Mississippi until they had suffered 2100 casualties, including 320 dead.

The newspaper was the dominant mass medium as late as 1950 (Schudson, 1991; Smith, 1980). However, change was already in the air in 1844, when Samuel Morse sent the first telegraphic signal (Pred, 1973). From that time on, long-distance communication no longer required physical transportation. The transformative power of the new medium was soon evident. For example, until 1883, hundreds of local time zones existed in North America. The correct time was determined by local solar time and was typically maintained by a clock located in either a church steeple or a respected jeweller's shop window. Virtually instant communication by telegraph made it possible to coordinate time and establish just six time zones in Canada. Railroad companies spearheaded the move to standardize time. A Canadian civil and railway engineer, Sir Sandford Fleming, was the driving force behind the worldwide adoption of standard time (Blaise, 2001).

Most of the electronic media are creatures of the twentieth century. The first commercial television broadcasts date from the 1920s. The U.S. Department of Defense established ARPANET in 1969. It was designed as a system of communication between computers that would automatically find alternative transmission routes if one or more nodes in the network broke down because of, say, nuclear attack. ARPANET begat the Internet, which in turn begat the hyperlinked system of texts, images, and sounds known as the World Wide Web in 1991. By 2013, about two-and-a-half billion people worldwide used the Web. It was a quick trip—a mere 140 years separate the Pony Express from the home videoconference.

© MachineHeadz /Istockphoto.com

Parents often find teenagers' "addiction" to electronic media bewildering—and expensive.

Communication Speed-Up

Young people's culture has always been faster than the culture of older people. Older people process information more slowly than young people do because, as we age, we have fewer and less efficient neurons. However, in recent years, technological innovation has encouraged young people's attention spans to shorten and the generational gap in processing speed to grow (Fox and Brym, 2009).

In particular, electronic media make it possible to cater to the neurological advantages that young people have over older people. When *Sesame Street* became a huge TV hit in 1969, part of its appeal was that its story segments were shorter than those on other children's programs. Decades of research by the Children's Television Workshop suggests that shows like *Sesame Street* condition children to regard brevity as the normal pace of life. The widespread adoption of the personal computer and the Internet in the 1980s and 1990s reinforced the need for speed. Quick information gathering, instant communication, and rapid-fire gaming, once considered spectacular, are now routine.

The speed with which teenagers check Facebook, channel-surf, listen to music, and engage in instant messaging often bewilders parents, who are unable to process what appear to them to be lightning-fast events. Many teenagers seem unable to listen to an entire song without becoming distracted. They often use MP3 players to skim songs, listening to each for less than a minute. A fast-paced media- and technology-rich environment affords plenty of opportunities to multitask. At clubs, DJs playing for a young crowd find it necessary to mix songs quickly to maintain a tight dance floor and excite people. In contrast, quick mixing represents information overload for an older crowd, which quickly becomes irritated unless the DJ plays songs in their entirety. Thus, although built on neurological foundations that have always separated younger from older generations, shortening attention spans have been nurtured by technological change in the electronic media.

Causes of Media Growth

The rise of the mass media can be explained by three main factors: one religious, one political, and one economic:

1. *The Protestant Reformation.* In the sixteenth century, Catholic people relied on priests to tell them what was in the Bible. In 1517, however, Martin Luther protested certain practices of the Church. Among other things, he wanted people to develop a more personal relationship with the Bible. Within 40 years, Luther's new form of Christianity, known as Protestantism, was established in half of Europe. Suddenly, millions of people were being encouraged to read. The Bible became the first mass media product in the West and by far the best-selling book.

   Technological improvements in papermaking and printing made the diffusion of the Bible and other books possible (Febvre and Martin, 1976 [1958]). The most significant landmark was Johann Gutenberg's invention of the printing press. In the 50 years after Gutenberg produced his monumental Bible in 1455, more books were produced than in the previous 1000 years. The printed book enabled the widespread diffusion and exchange of ideas. It contributed to the Renaissance (a scholarly and artistic revival that began in Italy around 1300 and spread to all of Europe by 1600) and to the rise of modern science (Johns, 1998).

   A remarkable feature of the book is its durability. Many electronic storage media became obsolete just a few years after being introduced. For instance, eight-track tapes are icons of the 1970s and 5.25-inch floppy disks are icons of the early 1980s. They are barely remembered today. In contrast, books are still being published today, 560 years after Gutenberg published his Bible. More than 23 000 books are published in Canada each year (UNESCO, 2008).
2. *Democratic movements.* A second force that promoted the growth of the mass media was political democracy. From the eighteenth century on, the citizens of France, the United States, and other countries demanded and achieved representation in government. At the same time, they wanted to become literate and gain access to previously restricted centres of learning. Democratic governments, in turn, depended on an informed citizenry and therefore encouraged popular literacy and the growth of a free press (Habermas, 1989).

   Today, the mass media, and especially TV, mould our entire outlook on politics. TV's influence first became evident in the 1960 U.S. presidential election. That was the year of the first televised presidential debate—between John F. Kennedy and Richard Nixon. One of the four reporters who asked questions during the debate later recalled: "The people who watched the debate on their television sets apparently thought Kennedy came off better than Nixon. Those who heard the debate on radio thought Nixon was superior to Kennedy" (quoted in "The Candidates Debate," 1998). Kennedy smiled. Nixon perspired. Kennedy relaxed. Nixon fidgeted. The election was close, and most analysts believe that Kennedy got the edge simply because 70 million viewers thought he looked better on TV. Television was thus beginning to redefine the very nature of politics.

   Soon, Canadian politicians were hiring "image consultants." Often, image manipulation used techniques that had been honed in the United States. Usually the media consultants' advice led to the desired results. Their recommendations included much maligned "negative advertising" techniques. While voters claim they do not approve of negative advertising, it is effective (Kinsella, 2007). For instance, the Conservative Party's use of negative advertising, such as its branding of then Liberal Party leader Michael Ignatieff as disloyal and power-hungry, is widely

CP Picture Archive/National Archives

One of the most famous photographs in Canadian history is the driving of the last spike of the Canadian Pacific Railway (CPR) on November 7, 1885, at Craigellachie, British Columbia. The man holding the hammer is Donald Smith, who financed much of the construction of the CPR. The taller man standing behind him to his right in the stovepipe hat is Sir Sandford Fleming, the mastermind behind standard time. The railroads spearheaded the introduction of standard time, which could be coordinated thanks to the introduction of the telegraph.

believed to be one reason why the Conservatives won the 2011 election and were able to form a majority government.

It is commonly claimed that television and other mass media have over-simplified politics. Some analysts say that politics has been reduced to a series of more or less well-managed images, catchy slogans, and ever-shorter uninterrupted comments or "sound bites." From this point of view, candidates are marketed for high office in much the same way that Kellogg's sells breakfast cereal, and a politician's stage presence is more important than his or her policies in determining success at the polls.

3. *Capitalist industrialization.* The third major force stimulating the growth of the mass media was capitalist industrialization. Modern industries required a literate and numerate workforce. They also needed rapid means of communication to do business efficiently. Moreover, the mass media turned out to be a major source of profit in their own right.

We thus see that the sources of the mass media are deeply embedded in the religious, political, and economic needs of our society. Moreover, the mass media are among the most influential institutions today. How, then, do sociologists explain the effects of the mass media on society? To answer this question, we now summarize the relevant sociological theories.

TIME FOR REVIEW

- The mass media shape perceptions of reality.
- Print media dominated until the mid-twentieth century. Since then, electronic media have dominated.
- The Protestant Reformation and the growth of democracy and capitalism were the major factors underlying the growth of the mass media.

BOX 18.1

SOCIAL POLICY: WHAT DO YOU THINK?

SHOULD CANADA'S BROADCASTERS BE SUBJECT TO MORE GOVERNMENT REGULATION?

In the 1930s, it was not at all obvious that more than 90 percent of the Canadian mass media would be privately owned and controlled. Here is what Prime Minister R.B. Bennett had to say on the subject in 1932:

The use of the air ... that lies over the ... land of Canada is a natural resource over which we have complete jurisdiction.... I cannot think that any government would be warranted in leaving the air to private exploitation and not reserving it for ... the use of the people. Without [complete government control of broadcasting from Canadian sources, radio] can never become the agency by which national consciousness may be fostered and national unity ... strengthened (quoted in Competition Bureau, 2002).

What was self-evident to Prime Minister Bennett more than 80 years ago is a matter of controversy today. Some Canadians, like Bennett, still argue for strict government control of the mass media. Like Bennett, they believe that the mass media should be used to strengthen Canadian culture. Others want a more or less free market in which the great bulk of programming is American in origin or, failing that, American in style.

The Canadian Radio-television and Telecommunications Commission (CRTC) was established by an act of Parliament in 1968 as an independent agency responsible for regulating Canada's broadcasting and telecommunications systems. Its self-described mandate is to promote Canadian culture and economic competitiveness ("The CRTC's Mandate," 2002). In practice, promoting Canadian culture means ensuring that Canadian content represents 35 percent of the popular music played on English-language commercial radio stations between 6 a.m. and 6 p.m., Monday through Friday. Other regulations oversee the content of "ethnic" and French-language stations. Privately owned television stations must achieve a yearly Canadian content level of 60 percent between midnight and 6 p.m. and 50 percent between 6 p.m. and midnight. Canadian content rules for the CBC are more demanding. "Canadian" means that the producer of the program is Canadian, key creative personnel are Canadian, and 75 percent of service costs and postproduction lab costs are paid to Canadians.

As a result of these regulations, about half of TV broadcasts in English Canada and 65 percent of popular music broadcasts are *American*. Moreover, many American TV and radio stations are widely available in Canada via cable, satellite, or the airwaves. (More than 90 percent of Canadian households subscribe to cable or use satellite services; Canadian Media Research, 2006). It seems reasonable to conclude that at least three-quarters of the TV and popular music to which Canadians have access is American.

Bearing the above facts in mind, does the Canadian government do enough or too much to ensure the preservation and enrichment of Canadian culture through the broadcast industry? Should the government be in the business of protecting Canadian culture? Or should it allow free-market forces to shape the structure and content of Canadian broadcasting? Would a free-market approach to broadcasting enable Canadians to get what they really want, or would it allow powerful American broadcasters to completely dominate the marketplace and virtually eliminate Canadian content?

Media Bias

Does the concentration of the mass media in fewer and fewer hands deprive the public of independent sources of information, limit the diversity of opinion, and encourage the public to accept their society as it is? Conflict theorists think so. They argue that when a few conglomerates dominate the production of news in particular, they squeeze out alternative points of view.

Quebecor Media's launch of Sun News Network in 2011 illustrates the conflict theorists' view. As noted above, Quebecor is one of the largest media conglomerates in Canada. Sun News Network is a 24-hour television news network with an unapologetically right-wing, conservative slant. Kory Teneycke, Conservative Prime Minister Harper's former press secretary, holds a key post in the organization, while Ezra Levant and other well-known conservative commentators are regular contributors. The network has been labelled "Fox News North" by its detractors since it is modelled on the popular American right-wing programming of Fox News.

Sun News Network is a blatant example of corporate-controlled media using its power to promote its ideological interests. However, according to Edward Herman and Noam Chomsky (1988), several other, more subtle mechanisms help to bias the news in a way that

BOX 18.2

SOCIOLOGY ON THE TUBE

THE NEWSROOM

The Newsroom takes place behind the scenes of the fictional Atlantis Cable News (ACN) channel. At first, ACN is a news organization like any other. It seeks to turn a profit, and if that means it has to shade the truth, appeal to the lowest common denominator, and avoid offending corporate interests and political authorities, then it is only trying to survive a tough competitive environment. Enter news anchor and former attorney, Will McAvoy (played by Jeff Daniels). Mad as hell and unwilling to take it anymore, McAvoy convinces his immediate boss that the network's flagship program, *News Night*, must speak truth to power. From now on, ACN alone will decide what is aired and how it is presented. As McAvoy announces to his television audience in an early episode, "network newscasts ... [are] in the exact same business as the producers of *Jersey Shore*. And that business was good to us, but *News Night* is quitting that business right now."

The Kobal Collection at Art Resource, NY

Will McAvoy (Jeff Daniels) in *The Newsroom*

News Night faces a powerful opponent in Leona Lansing (Jane Fonda), CEO of Atlantis World Media, the parent company of ACN. When McAvoy interviews Republican members of Congress, he humiliates them, infuriating Lansing. She reminds McAvoy's boss that members of Congress and the corporate interests they represent are ACN's bread and butter. If McAvoy continues his errant ways, advertisers will bolt, and members of Congress will refuse to appear on air. She insists that McAvoy stop his crusade or be fired.

McAvoy refuses to bend. Then, on the verge of defeat, McAvoy and his boss get hold of information proving that Lansing's son was involved in a massive business fraud. They blackmail her. If she fires McAvoy, they will go public with the incriminating information. Lansing relents, and the first season of *The Newsroom* ends with Will McAvoy continuing to lead the charge against corporate and political authority. It is, of course, a fairy-tale ending.

supports powerful corporate interests and political groups (see Box 18.2). These biasing mechanisms include advertising, sourcing, and flak:

- *Advertising*. Most of the revenue earned by television stations, radio stations, newspapers, and magazines comes from advertising by large corporations. According to Herman and Chomsky, these corporations routinely seek to influence the news so it will reflect well on them. In one American survey, 93 percent of newspaper editors said advertisers have tried to influence their news reports. Thirty-seven percent of newspaper editors admitted to being influenced by advertisers (Bagdikian, 1997). In addition, big advertisers may influence the news even without overtly trying to influence news carriers. For fear of losing business, news carriers may soften stories that big advertisers might find offensive.
- *Sourcing*. Studies of news-gathering methods show that most news agencies rely heavily on press releases, news conferences, and interviews organized by large corporations and government agencies. These sources routinely slant information to reflect favourably on their policies and preferences. Unofficial news sources are consulted less often. Moreover, unofficial sources tend to be used only to provide reactions and minority viewpoints that are secondary to the official story.
- *Flak*. Governments and big corporations routinely attack journalists who depart from official and corporate points of view. For example, Brian Ross, the leading investigative reporter for *20/20*, prepared a segment about Disney World in 1998. Ross claimed that Disney was so lax in doing background checks on employees that it had hired pedophiles. ABC killed the story before airtime. It is no coincidence that ABC is owned by Disney (McChesney, 1999). Similarly, tobacco companies have systematically tried to discredit media reports that cigarettes cause cancer. In a notorious case, the respected public affairs show *60 Minutes* refused to broadcast a damaging interview with a former Philip Morris

executive because the tobacco company threatened legal action against CBS. (This incident is the subject of the Oscar-nominated movie *The Insider*, released in 1999.)

On the whole, the conflict theorists' arguments are compelling. However, we do not find them completely convincing (Gans, 1979). After all, if 37 percent of newspaper editors have been influenced by advertisers, then 63 percent have not. News agencies may rely heavily on government and corporate sources, but their reliance does not stop them from routinely biting the hand that offers to feed them and evading flak shot their way. The daily newspaper is full of examples of mainstream journalistic opposition to government and corporate viewpoints. Even mainstream news sources, although owned by media conglomerates, do not always act like the lapdogs of the powerful (Hall, 1980).

Still, conflict theorists make a valid point when they restrict their argument to how the mass media support core societal values. In their defence of core values, the mass media *are* virtually unanimous (see Box 18.3). For example, the mass media enthusiastically support

BOX 18.3

SOCIOLOGY AT THE MOVIES

REDACTED

The Canadian Press/© Magnolia Pictures/courtesy Everett Collection

"In war, truth is the first casualty." Aeschylus

War is an ugly business, which creates a problem for elected governments that decide to wage war. If the electorate is fully informed about the facts of war, they are less likely to support it. To manage this issue, governments use the mass media to provide the public with a selective view of a war's causes, conditions, and consequences.

The United States invasion of Iraq in 2003 was initiated by questionable motives. Declarations that Iraq was non-compliant with United Nations resolutions were questionable; assertions that the regime had weapons of mass destruction were never demonstrated; Iraq's al-Qaeda connections to the 9/11 tragedy were non-existent. President Bush's administration had good reason to think that public support of "Operation Iraqi Freedom" was soft. Accordingly, they launched an expensive mass media campaign to "sell the war" through advertising.

To express his opposition to the Iraq War, director Brian De Palma produced *Redacted*, a fictional film based on real events. The main characters are a group of U.S. soldiers who control a surveillance checkpoint. The central real event is the rape of a teenage girl who ends up murdered, along with the rest of her family.

In the film, the director shows that the realities of war are often brutal and always multisided. In one scene, for instance, a car speeds through a U.S.-controlled checkpoint. From the soldiers' viewpoint, the driver received clear warnings to stop for inspection. Because they were ignored, the soldiers fire repeatedly and kill a woman in the passenger seat. It turns out, however, that the driver was a young Iraqi man hurriedly driving his pregnant sister to the hospital to have her baby. He entered the checkpoint and saw the U.S. soldiers waving him through. He couldn't understand why they began firing. Two different versions of these events were reported to the American and Iraqi publics.

This movie's main point is that the mass media inevitably present a selective version of events. Their version of "truth" aims at shaping the views of their audience toward particular goals. This use of the mass media becomes especially evident when reporting events like wars that are full of ambiguity, contradiction, and harshness. Redaction, the deliberate censoring and obscuring of actual events, is central to the power of all mass media.

Like De Palma's earlier film about the Vietnam War (*Casualties of War*, 1989), *Redacted* sensitizes viewers to how mass media presentations bias their understanding of events. The fact that De Palma is making the same point about American foreign wars two decades after his first attempt is disheartening. However, during those two decades the mass media experienced encouraging democratization. Digitization allows a wide range of audiences to record and broadcast alternative views of reality. New social media have changed the mass media. The director exploits this change by blending all manner of social media accounts into *Redacted*. The multidimensional portrait of Iraqi reality includes a collage of cellphone photos, surveillance camera footage, video segments, and documentary excerpts. Effective war propaganda relies on audiences receiving a uniform message. De Palma's film suggests that social media may provide an effective challenge to such a monopoly of interpretation and encourage independent assessments about the worthiness of war.

democracy and capitalism. We cannot think of a single instance of a major Canadian news outlet advocating a fascist government or a socialist economy in Canada. Moreover, when conservative media critics complain of liberal bias in the media, they routinely use the CBC as their example. If the CBC is the best example of left-wing bias, the range of mass media opinion is narrow indeed.

Similarly, the mass media virtually unanimously endorse consumerism as a way of life. As discussed in Chapter 3, Culture, consumerism is the tendency to define ourselves in terms of the goods and services we purchase. Endorsement of consumerism is evident in the fact that advertising fills the mass media and is its lifeblood. Advertising expenditures in Canada are now more than $23 billion a year, compared with about $28 billion a year for universities (TNS Canadian Facts and Canada Post, 2012; Statistics Canada, 2010f). We are exposed to a staggering number of ads each day; in fact, some estimates place the number in the thousands. Companies even pay filmmakers to use their brand-name products conspicuously in their movies. In some magazines, ads figure so prominently a reader must search for the articles.

It is only when the mass media deal with news stories that touch on less central values that we can witness a diversity of media opinion. *Specific* government and corporate policies are often the subject of heated debate in the mass media. Thus, despite the indisputable concentration of media ownership, the mass media are diverse and often contentious on specific issues that do not touch on core values.

Interpretive Approaches

The **two-step flow of communication** between mass media and audience members involves (1) respected people of high status and independent judgment evaluating media messages, and (2) other members of the community being influenced to varying degrees by these opinion leaders. Because of the two-step flow of communication, opinion leaders filter media messages.

Cultural studies refer to popular interdisciplinary area of research. In research on the mass media, these studies focus not just on the cultural meanings producers try to transmit but also on the way audiences filter and interpret mass media messages in the context of their own interests, experiences, and values.

The view that the mass media powerfully influence a passive public is common to both functionalists and conflict theorists. Many people believe that violence on TV causes violence in real life, pornography on the magazine stands or online leads to immoral sexual behaviour, and adolescents are more likely to start smoking cigarettes when they see popular movie stars lighting up.

There are, however, reasons for questioning the strength of media effects. For one thing, researchers have known for half a century that people do not change their attitudes and behaviours just because the media tell them to do so. That is because the link between persuasive media messages and actual behaviour is indirect. A **two-step flow of communication** takes place (Katz, 1957; Schiller, 1989; Schudson, 1995). In step one, respected people of high status evaluate media messages. They are the opinion leaders of a neighbourhood or a community, people who are usually more highly educated, well-to-do, or politically powerful than others in their circle are. Because of their high status, they exercise considerable independence of judgment. In step two, opinion leaders *may* influence the attitudes and behaviours of others. In this way, opinion leaders filter media messages. The two-step flow of communication limits the media effects. If people are influenced to vote for certain candidates, buy certain products, or smoke cigarettes, it is less because the media tell them to and more because opinion leaders suggest they should.

Yet another persuasive argument that leads us to question the effects of the mass media comes from interpretive sociologists, such as symbolic interactionists and interdisciplinary **cultural studies** experts. They use in-depth interviewing and participant observation to study how people actually interpret media messages.

British sociologist Stuart Hall (1980), one of the foremost proponents of this approach, emphasizes that people are not empty vessels into which the mass media pour a defined assortment of beliefs, values, and ideas. Rather, audience members take an active role in consuming the products of the mass media. They filter and interpret mass media messages in the context of their own interests, experiences, and values. Thus, in Hall's view, any adequate analysis of the mass media needs to take into account both the production and the consumption of media products. First, he says, we need to study the meanings intended by the producers. Then we need to study how audiences consume or evaluate media products. Intended and received meanings may diverge; audience members may interpret media messages in ways other than those intended by the producers (Hall, 1980; Seiter, 1999).

Here is a personal example of the way audiences may interpret media messages in unexpected ways: When John Lie's parents were preparing to immigrate to the United States in the late 1960s, his mother watched many American movies and television shows. One of her favourite TV programs was *My Three Sons*, a sitcom about three boys living with their father and grandfather. From the show she learned that boys wash dishes and vacuum the house in the United States. When the Lie family immigrated to Hawaii, John and his brother—but not his sister—had to wash dishes every night. When John complained, his mother reassured him that "in America, only boys wash dishes."

Even children's television viewing turns out to be complex when viewed through an interpretive lens. Research shows that young children distinguish "make-believe" media violence from real-life violence (Hodge and Tripp, 1986). That may explain why watching *South Park* has not produced a nation of *South Park* clones. Similarly, research shows differences in the way working-class and middle-class women relate to TV. Working-class women, more so than middle-class women, tend to evaluate TV programs in terms of how realistic they are. This critical attitude reduces their ability to identify strongly with many characters, personalities, and storylines. For instance, working-class women know from their own experience that families often don't work the way they are shown on TV. They view the idealized, middle-class nuclear family depicted in many television shows with a mixture of nostalgia and skepticism (Press, 1991). Age also affects how we relate to television. Senior viewers tend to be selective and focused in their television viewing. In contrast, people who grew up with cable TV and a remote control often engage in channel surfing, conversation, eating, and housework, zoning in and out of programs in anything but an absorbed fashion (Press, 1991). It is inaccurate to think that viewers passively soak up the values embedded in TV programs and then mechanically act on them.

Feminist Approaches

Finally, let us consider feminist approaches to the study of mass media effects. In the 1970s, feminist researchers focused on the representation—more accurately, the misrepresentation—of women in the mass media. They found that in TV dramas, women tended to be cast as homemakers, as secretaries, and in other subordinate roles, while men tended to be cast as professionals and authority figures. Women usually appeared in domestic settings, men in public settings. Advertising targeted women only as purchasers of household products and appliances. Furthermore, researchers discovered that the news rarely mentioned issues of importance for many women, such as wage discrimination in the paid labour force, sexual harassment and abuse, child-care problems, and so on. News reports sometimes trivialized or denounced the women's movement. Newsworthy issues (the economy, party politics, international affairs, and crime) were associated with men, and men were much more likely than women were to be used as news sources and to deliver the news (Watkins and Emerson, 2000: 152–53).

Most of this early feminist research assumed that audiences are passive. Analysts argued that the mass media portray women in stereotypical fashion; audience members recognize and accept the stereotypes as normal and even natural; and the mass media thereby reinforce existing gender inequalities. However, in the 1980s and 1990s, feminist researchers criticized this simple formula. Influenced by cultural studies, they realized that audience members selectively interpret media messages and sometimes even contest them.

A good example of this subtler and less deterministic approach is a study by Andrea Press and Elizabeth Cole (1999) of audience reaction to abortion as portrayed on TV shows. Over a four-year period, Press and Cole conducted 34 discussion groups involving 108 women. The women watched three TV programs focusing on abortion and then discussed their own attitudes and their reactions to the shows. The programs were pro-choice and dealt with women who chose abortion to avoid poverty.

Press and Cole found complex, ambivalent, and sometimes contradictory attitudes toward abortion among audience members. However, four distinct clusters of opinion emerged:

1. *Pro-life women from all social classes* form the most homogeneous group. They think abortion is never justified. On principle, they reject the mass media's justifications for abortion.
2. *Pro-choice working-class women who think of themselves as members of the working class* adopt a pro-choice stand as a survival strategy, not on principle. They do not condone abortion, but they fear that laws restricting abortion would be applied prejudicially against women of their class. Therefore, they oppose any such restrictions. At the same time, they reject the TV message that financial hardship justifies abortion.
3. *Pro-choice working-class women who aspire to middle-class status* distance themselves from the "reckless" members of their own class who sought abortions on the TV shows. They tolerate abortion for such people but they reject it for themselves and for other "responsible" women.
4. *Pro-choice middle-class women* believe that only an individual woman's feelings can determine whether abortion is right or wrong in her own case. Many pro-choice middle-class women have deep reservations about abortion, and many of them reject it as an option for themselves. However, they staunchly defend the right of all women, especially the kind of women portrayed in the TV shows they watched, to choose abortion.

One of the most striking aspects of Press and Cole's findings is that, for different reasons, three of the four categories of audience members (categories 1, 2, and 3) are highly skeptical of TV portrayals of the abortion issue. Their class position and attitudes act as filters influencing how they react to TV shows and how they view the abortion issue. Moreover, three of the four categories of audience members (categories 2, 3, and 4) reject the simple pro-choice versus pro-life dichotomy often portrayed by the mass media. Many pro-choice women express ambivalence about abortion and even reject it as an option for themselves. We must conclude that real women are typically more complicated than the stereotypes promoted in the mass media, and that women in the audience typically are aware of this discrepancy.

In recent years, some feminists have focused on the capacity of the mass media to reproduce and change the system of racial inequality in North American society. In the work of these scholars, the twin issues of female misrepresentation and active audience interpretation reappear, this time with a racial twist. On the one hand, they find that certain stereotypical images of women of colour recur in the mass media. Black women, for example, often appear in the role of the welfare mother, the highly sexualized Jezebel, or the mammy. On the other hand, feminist scholars also recognize that some mass media, especially independent filmmaking and popular music, have enabled women of colour to challenge these stereotypes. Especially noteworthy in this regard are the music and videos of Erykah Badu, Missy Elliott, Lauryn Hill, Beyoncé Knowles, and Alicia Keys. These artists write and produce their own music. They often direct their own videos. Their work is a running critical commentary on real-world issues confronting young black women. Thus, in terms of both production and content, their work breaks down the established roles and images of black women in North America (Watkins and Emerson, 2000).

Still, stereotypes persist. One study of North American prime-time TV found men predominating in law enforcement, professional, and criminal roles. Portrayals of men working in the paid labour force were twice as frequent as such portrayals of women (Signorielli,

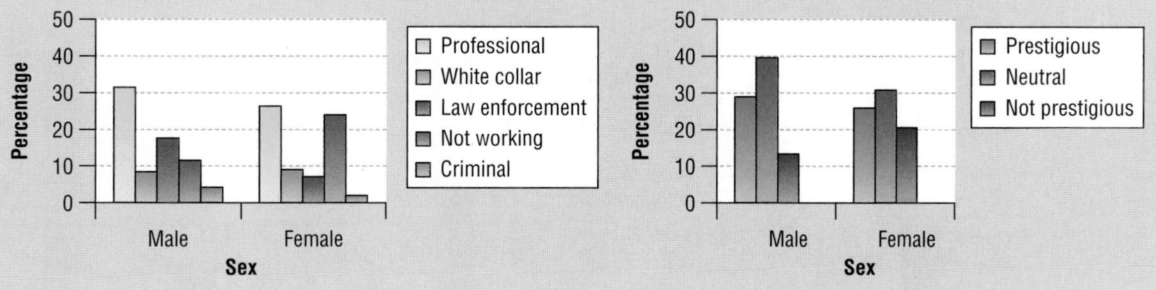

FIGURE 18.1
Gender Differences in Prime-Time TV Characters (percentages)

Note: Percentages do not add up to 100 because the "unknown" category has been omitted.

Adapted from Signorielli, 2009.

2009). Women's prime-time TV characters played "non-prestigious" roles 21 percent of the time, while only 13 percent of male characters were of this type (Figure 18.1).

The way in which the mass media treat women and members of various minority groups has for the most part improved over time. We have come a long way since the 1950s, when virtually the only blacks on TV were men who played butlers and buffoons. Research suggests that the mass media still have a long way to go before they cease reinforcing traditional stereotypes in North America (Signorielli, 2009). But research also suggests that audiences and artists are hardly passive vehicles of these stereotypes, instead struggling to diversify the way the mass media characterize them.

TIME FOR REVIEW

- Functionalism identifies the main social effects of mass media as coordination, socialization, social control, and entertainment. By performing these functions, the mass media help make social order possible.
- Conflict theory qualifies the functionalist perspective by noting that media concentration and control by a privileged minority contribute to economic inequality and maintain the core values of a stratified social order.
- Interpretive approaches remind us that audience members are people, not programmable robots. We filter, interpret, resist, and sometimes reject media messages according to our own interests and values.
- Feminist approaches highlight the misrepresentation of women and members of racial minorities in the mass media. They also emphasize the ways in which women and members of racial minorities have successfully challenged these misrepresentations and sought to diversify the characterization of race and gender by the mass media.

CENTRALIZED CONTROL AND RESISTANCE ON THE INTERNET

We have emphasized that the interaction between audiences and the traditional mass media (television, radio, and newspapers) is generally weighted in favour of the media. Audience members do not mindlessly absorb messages from these sources. However, they exercise little control over content.

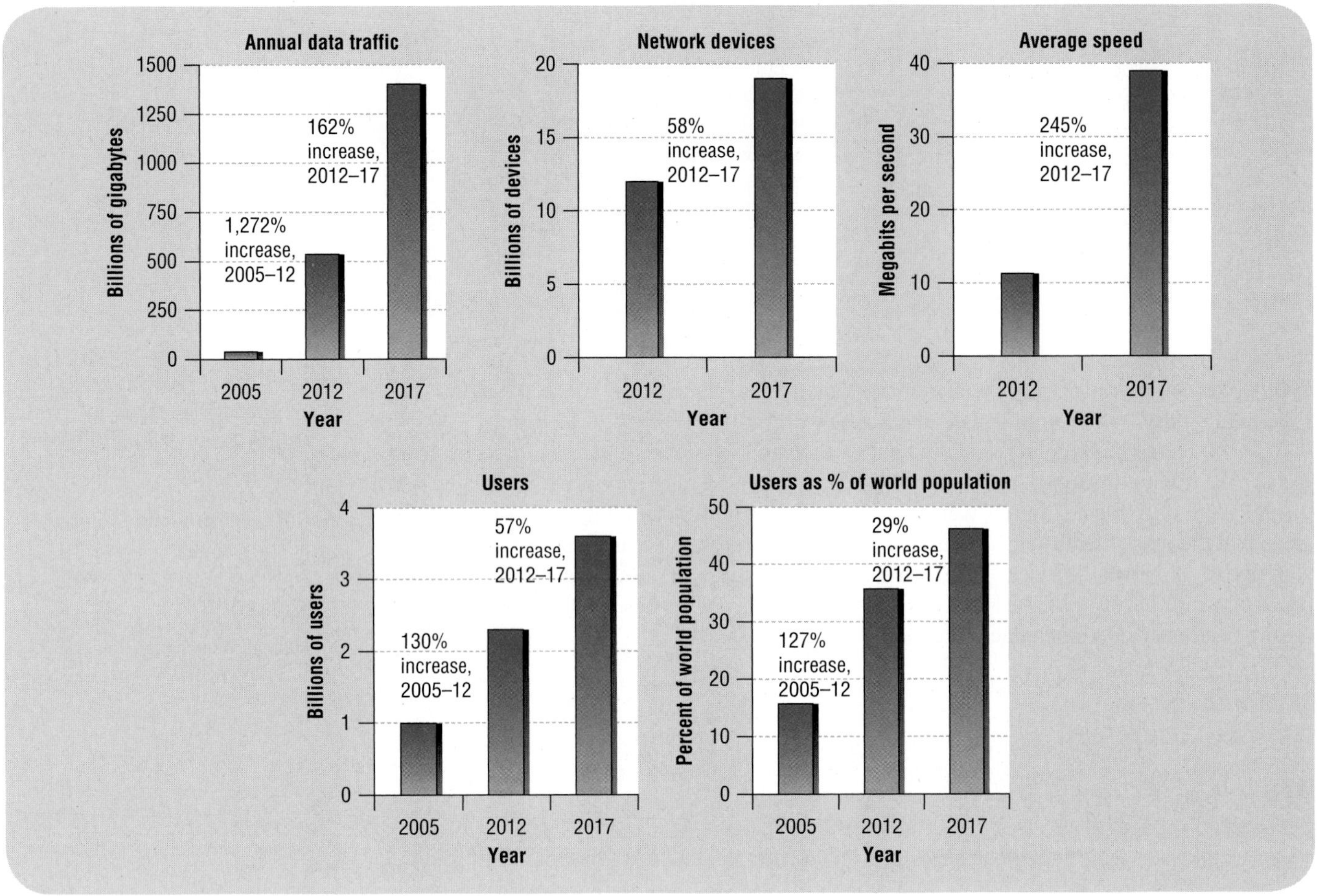

FIGURE 18.2
Internet Growth Projected to 2017

Sources: CISCO. 2013. "Visual Networking Index (VNI)." http://www.cisco.com/en/US/netsol/ns827/networking_solutions_sub_solution.html (retrieved August 18, 2013); Internet World Stats. 2013a. "Internet Growth Statistics." http://www.internetworldstats.com/emarketing.htm (retrieved August 18, 2013); United States Census Bureau. 2011. "World Population, 1950–2050." http://www.census.gov/population/international/data/idb/worldpopgraph.php (retrieved August 18, 2013).

In contrast, the Internet, especially its social media applications, offers more opportunity for audience influence than do the traditional mass media. The Internet is by far the fastest growing means of mass communication (see Figure 18.2). It provides fresh opportunities for media conglomerates to restrict access to paying customers and thereby accumulate vast wealth. However, the Internet also gives consumers new creative capabilities, partially blurring the distinction between producer and consumer. In short, the Internet makes the mass media more democratic.

To develop this idea, we first consider the forces that restrict Internet access and augment the power of media conglomerates. We then discuss countertrends.

Access

The Internet requires an expensive infrastructure of personal computers, servers, and routers; an elaborate network of fibre-optic, copper-twist, and coaxial cables; and many other components. This expensive infrastructure needs to be paid for, primarily by individual users. As a result, access is not open to everyone—far from it. In Canada, for example, households that are richer, better educated, urban, and younger are most likely to enjoy Internet access (Statistics Canada, 2010c).

Nor is Internet access evenly distributed globally. In the Scandinavian countries and the Netherlands, more than 90 percent of the population is connected. In Canada, the United States, Singapore, and South Korea, penetration rates are around 80 percent. By contrast, many underdeveloped regions have rates in the single digits. Globally, the rate of Internet connectivity is much higher in rich countries than in poor countries (Internet World Stats, 2013b).

Content

According to some analysts, American domination is another striking feature of Internet content. The world's top search engine is Google, with Facebook, YouTube, and Yahoo! rounding out the most visited sites (Alexa, 2013). Some analysts say that American domination of the web is an example of **media imperialism**, the control of a mass medium by a single national culture and the undermining of other national cultures.

© Fox Searchlight/courtesy Everett Collection

When *Who Wants to Be a Millionaire*? met Bollywood, the winner of the 2009 Academy Award for Best Picture was born. Was *Slumdog Millionaire* an example of media imperialism?

Internet Advertising

Advertising is the major source of revenue for many big Internet companies. To cite just one example, in 2012, Google earned more than US$50 billion. Nearly 90 percent of that sum came from advertising (U.S. Securities and Exchange Commission, 2013: 42).

Advertising seeks to influence (some would say "manipulate") consumers to buy products and services. Companies invest a lot in advertising because it works—and the Internet provides advertisers with ways to influence consumers more effectively than newspaper, magazine, radio, and TV ads do. For instance, targeted ads are widely used on the Internet. Google Search, YouTube (which is owned by Google), and other Internet services routinely collect information on which websites you visit, what you buy online, your locale, and your demographic characteristics. Advertisers buy this information so they can target specific market segments. It is no accident that when Indigo or Amazon suggests books for you to consider purchasing, they recommend titles that actually interest you. Nor should you be surprised to see a pop-up announcing that your favourite rock star is holding a concert in your city next month. Such ads are tailored to suit your interests and are therefore more cost-effective than, say, a roadside billboard for a refrigerator you don't need.

Top-down influence on the Internet is also enhanced by "web herding" and "sparking." Web herding is "getting viewers to click through to a goal" (that is, to make a purchase) by offering small enticements along the way—telling an interesting story, offering a small reward, encouraging consumer-to-company interaction, and so on (DC Interactive Group, 2013). Once a relationship has been formed between the consumer and the company, it is time to start sparking, defined by one advertising firm as "a soup-to-nuts process where we work with your staff (and become a virtual extension of your staff) to combine social media, interactive marketing, blogging, content creation, online events, advertising and reputation management all into one neat and powerful little package that recruits, romances and nurtures relationships with our client's prospective customers and clients" (Demi and Copper Advertising, 2013). Once the sheep have been properly herded and sparked, the probability of their making a purchase increases, serving as another reminder that the Web has hardly rendered top-down influence extinct.

Media imperialism is the domination of a mass medium by a single national culture and the undermining of other national cultures.

Media Convergence

Some researchers argue that the Internet not only restricts access, promotes American content, and manipulates audiences but also increases the power of media conglomerates. Such effects are evident, for example, in the realm of media convergence. **Media convergence** is the blending of the World Wide Web, television, telephone, and other communications media into new, hybrid media forms. The cellphone is the centrepiece of media convergence. It allows you to watch TV shows and videos, send and receive emails and text messages, browse the Web, and much else.

Media convergence is the blending of the telephone, the World Wide Web, television, and other communications media as new, hybrid media forms.

Media conglomerates like Bell and Rogers compete against each other to offer the most appealing content at the fastest speeds, but they are united on industry-wide tactics to maximize profit. For instance, both companies strongly favour user-based billing (the more you use, the more you pay). Opponents argue that technology has lowered costs so much that user-based billing is just a money grab by some of the most profitable businesses in Canada—an unfair practice that restricts the poorest Canadians' access to the Internet and cellphones.

Efforts by huge media conglomerates to shape media convergence may seem like an old story. In some respects it is. Ownership of every mass medium has become more concentrated over time. Because entry costs are so high, only media giants can play the game. However, the Internet story comes with a twist. Media conglomerates can never fully dominate the Internet because it is the first mass medium that makes it relatively easy for consumers to become producers.

The Rise of Social Media

Every minute, people upload 72 hours of digital video to YouTube (Reisinger, 2012). About 80 percent of laptops sport webcams and more than 80 percent of university and college students own laptops, so video chats through Skype or other services are commonplace ("Webcam Penetration Rates ...," 2011). In June 2014, Facebook boasted 1.28 billion monthly active users, 62 percent of whom log on daily. Canadians are the most active Facebook users in the world. Teens on Facebook have an average of 300 friends (Smith, 2014). There were 645.8 million Twitter accounts in 2014, and some celebrities have millions of followers. Canadian Justin Bieber was second on the list with 52.9 million followers as of 20 July 2014; Katy Perry topped the list at 54.5 million followers (Statistic Brain, 2014; Twitaholic.com, 2014). Add to this picture the many millions of personal websites, public-access cameras, alternate reality and multiple-user gaming sites, and discussion groups devoted to every imaginable topic, and we must temper the image of the Internet as a medium that is subject to increasing domination by large conglomerates. In many respects, the trend is the contrary. Individual users are making independent, creative contributions to Internet growth.

Our use of social media affects our identity (how we see ourselves), our social relations (the patterned connections we form with others), and our social activism (the ways in which we seek to cause social change) (Bookman, 2014). Let us briefly consider each of these issues in turn.

Identity

Social media offer people opportunities to manipulate the way they present themselves to others and to explore aspects of their selves that they may suppress in embodied social interaction. Of course, people do not shift shapes, as it were, just because they can. For most of us, the difference between self-presentation offline and online is typically modest. Nonetheless, differences exist, and they change our self-conceptions in ways that are usually minor but sometimes major. For example, we hypothesize that many people learn to become more assertive online than they are offline, and we expect that once they learn to be bolder, many carry the lesson into real life to a degree. We also hypothesize that, in far fewer cases, people "in the closet" with respect to their sexual preferences use social media as a gateway to "coming out." In these and other ways, social media often serve as "identity workshops" (Turkle, 1995).

Many users find that social media have taken over a large slice of life. They spend so much time managing online profiles and relationships, and instantly responding to emails, tweets, and Facebook messages, that their online identity performances start to feel like their real selves (Turkle, 2011: 12). Some people say that social media are causing a decline in the depth and quality of social interaction. Whether or not this is the case, it is clear that going on holiday with the family, having dinner with friends, and other traditional ways of enjoying the presence of others are now punctuated with social media interruptions and distractions that change who we are and how we think of ourselves.

Social Relations

In the 1990s, some analysts expected the Internet to isolate people, creating private worlds that would lead to the decline of family and community life. Others held the opposite opinion—that the Internet would create opportunities for people to form new communities based not on geographical proximity or blood ties but on common interests. Both scenarios contain an element of truth but both fail as assessments of the overall impact on social relations by the Internet in general, and social media in particular. A few people do retire to the basement, keep the curtains on their windows tightly drawn, avoid face-to-face interaction, and spend their days in virtual worlds. Some people do form close and even intimate friendships online in communities of common interest, dropping nearly all real-world social relations. For most people, however, social media have not replaced real life but burrowed into it and become part of it (Wellman, 2014).

Thus, research shows that people tend to use social media to *augment* telephone and face-to-face communication, not to replace them. Most of the people we email, message and text are people we already know, and when we use social media to contact people we don't know, it is often to see whether we want to proceed to a phone call or a face-to-face meeting.

For most people, then, social media increase interaction and build community—but not community in the traditional sense. Traditional communities are fixed locations. To interact in them, you need to reside in them physically. You don't get to select community members. Everybody knows your business. In contrast, social media allow for the crystallization of communities that are multiplex (you can belong to many of them), variegated (you can decide how intimately you want to interact with different members of different communities), personalized (you can decide who to allow in and who to exclude), portable (you can take them with you) and ubiquitous (you can take them anywhere you please). Social media thus breed what sociologist Barry Wellman calls "networked individualism" (Wellman, 2014).

Social Activism

Finally, social media open up new ways of engaging in social change. People advocate and spread awareness of a wide variety of environmental, human rights, and other causes using blogs, Twitter, Facebook, and activist websites containing reports, news, videos, announcements, and Web links. People also use social media to mobilize others for demonstrations, petitions, meetings, support concerts, and fundraising. The most celebrated use of social media for these purposes occurred during the heyday of the Occupy movement and the Arab Spring in 2010–11 and the Idle No More movement in Canada in 2012. Most analysts expect that the role of social media in advocating and mobilizing for social change will grow in the coming years.

In sum, the Internet is a mass medium unlike any other in the sense that it provides unique opportunities for user autonomy and creativity. To be sure, it also increases opportunities for corporations and authorities to engage in the homogenization, surveillance, and possible control of users, but at least on this mass medium, users enjoy many means of resistance (Lyon, 2007).

Even so-called American media imperialism seems to be less threatening than some analysts assume because of the decentralized nature of the Internet. Non-American influence is growing rapidly on the Web, while websites based in the United States adopt content liberally from Latin America, Asia, and elsewhere. Just as international influences are evident in today's hairstyles, clothing fashions, foods, and popular music, so we can see the Internet less as a site of American media imperialism than a site of globalization (Widyastuti, 2010). In 2013, the world's ten most popular websites included three from China: Baidu.com (a search engine), QQ.COM (an Internet portal), and Taobao.com (a consumer-to-consumer marketplace). The top 20 included a fourth website from China and one from each of India, Japan, and Russia (Alexa, 2013). Since 1996, Al Jazeera, the news and information station operating on the Web and via satellite out of Doha, Qatar, has competed with the BBC and CNN for coverage of world events. Broadcasting in Arabic and English, it has helped to liberalize and democratize the political culture of the Middle East and North Africa, and it provides insights into that region and beyond that are otherwise unavailable to Western audiences (Lynch, 2005).

Of course, nobody knows exactly how the social forces we have outlined will play themselves out. In 1999, Napster emerged, enabling millions of people to share recorded music freely on the Web using a central server. Some analysts pointed to Napster as evidence of Internet democratization. Then the media conglomerates took Napster to court, forcing it to stop the giveaway on the grounds it was effectively stealing royalties from musicians and profits from music companies. Some analysts saw the court case as evidence of growing corporate control on the Web. However, a few years later, BitTorrent emerged, allowing people to share recorded music and videos *without* a central server, making it virtually impossible to shut it down. Despite repeated legal actions to try to curb organizations like the Pirate Bay (a large torrent hub in Sweden), the dispersed locations of management, servers, developers, and users make litigation and enforcement extremely problematic. And so the tug of war between central control and democratization continues, with no end in sight. One thing is clear, however. The speed of technological innovation and the many possibilities for individual creativity on the Internet make this era an exciting time to be involved in the mass media and to study it sociologically.

TIME FOR REVIEW

- Internet access is unequally distributed. Richer categories of people enjoy more access.
- Internet content is dominated by Western, particularly American, perspectives and interests, although non-Western sources are quickly increasing their presence.
- Media convergence is creating new forms of mass media.
- As the rise of social media demonstrates, corporate domination of Internet-based mass media is continuously challenged by the creative contributions individuals and groups of content producers.

SUMMARY

1. Which historical forces stimulated the growth of the mass media?
The Protestant Reformation of the sixteenth century encouraged people to read the Bible themselves. The democratic movements that began in the late eighteenth century encouraged people to demand literacy. Beginning in the late nineteenth century, capitalist industrialization required rapid means of communication and fostered the mass media as important sources of profit.

2. What effects do the mass media have on society?
According to functionalists, the mass media coordinate society, exercise social control, and socialize and entertain people. Conflict theorists stress that the mass media reinforce social inequality by acting as sources of profit for the few people who control media conglomerates and promoting core values that help legitimize the existing social order. Interpretive sociologists, including symbolic interactionists, argue that audiences actively filter, interpret, and sometimes even resist and reject media messages according to their interests and values. Feminist approaches concur and also emphasize the degree to which the mass media perpetuate gender and racial stereotypes.

3. How does the Internet differ from other mass media?
The Internet offers users more opportunities to create content than do other mass media. Social media in particular allow people more freedom to mould their identities, forge new types of social relations, and engage in activism.

CHAPTER 19

HEALTH AND MEDICINE

© Jeffrey M. Levine MD.

IN THIS CHAPTER, YOU WILL LEARN TO

- Describe how and why population health has improved over time.
- Identify how death and disease rates vary by socioeconomic position, race, ethnicity, and gender.
- Explain the contribution of the health care system to population health.
- Analyze the key features and challenges of Canada's health care system.
- Explain how medicine exercises authority over issues involving illness.
- Evaluate evidence suggesting medical authority is weakening.

THE BLACK DEATH

In 1346, rumours reached Europe of a plague sweeping the East. Originating in Asia, the epidemic spread along trade routes to China and Russia. A year later, 12 galleys sailed from southern Russia to Italy. Diseased sailors were aboard. Their lymph nodes were swollen and eventually burst, causing a painful death. Anyone who came in contact with the sailors was soon infected. As a result, their ships were driven out of several Italian and French ports in succession. Yet the disease spread relentlessly, again moving along trade routes to Spain, Portugal, and England. Within two years, the Black Death, as it came to be known, had killed a third of Europe's population. Six hundred and fifty years later, the plague still ranks as the most devastating catastrophe in human history (Herlihy, 1998; McNeill, 1976; Zinsser, 1935).

Museo del Prado, Madrid, Spain/Giraudon, Paris/SuperStock

The Black Death

Today we know that the cause of the plague was a bacillus that spread from fleas to rats to people. It spread so efficiently because many people lived close together in unsanitary conditions. In the middle of the fourteenth century, however, nobody knew anything about germs. Therefore, Pope Clement VI sent a delegation to Europe's leading medical school in Paris to discover the cause of the plague. The learned professors studied the problem. They reported that a particularly unfortunate conjunction of Saturn, Jupiter, and Mars in the sign of Aquarius had occurred in 1345. The resulting hot, humid conditions caused the earth to emit poisonous vapours. To prevent the plague, they said, people should refrain from eating poultry, waterfowl, pork, beef, fish, and olive oil. They should not sleep during the daytime or engage in excessive exercise. Nothing should be cooked in rainwater. Bathing should be avoided at all costs.

We do not know whether the pope followed the professors' advice. We do know he made a practice of sitting between two large fires to breathe pure air. Because heat destroys the plague bacillus, this practice may have saved his life. Other people were less fortunate. Some rang church bells and fired cannons to drive the plague away. Others burned incense, wore charms, and cast spells. However, other than the pope, the only people to have much luck in avoiding the plague were the well-to-do (who could afford to flee the densely populated cities for the countryside) and the Jews (whose religion required that they wash their hands before meals, bathe once a week, and conduct burials soon after death).

Some of the main themes of the sociology of health and medicine are embedded in the story of the Black Death, or at least implied by it. First, when we consider the causes of death in the twenty-first century, we recognize that health problems have changed dramatically since the Black Death. Long ago, infectious diseases such as tuberculosis, pneumonia and scarlet fever were major killers. Today, the leading causes of death are chronic conditions such as cancer and heart disease. You might think this change occurred because advances in medical science introduced wonder drugs and other life-saving therapies to combat infectious disease. In fact, other social changes were improving population long health before these drugs were available (Markle and McCrea, 2008). Advances in agriculture and transportation in the nineteenth century resulted in higher-quality crops and more rapid distribution of food to the market. These innovations enhanced the nutritional status of the population and boosted their immune systems. Consequently, people were generally better equipped than they had been in the past to ward off illness and survive it if they did become ill. In addition, improvements in sanitation and hygiene minimized exposure to harmful germs and bacteria. Together, these changes produced a steady decline in infectious disease. When vaccines arrived nearly a century later, the threat of infectious disease had already been substantially reduced. This example illustrates why health problems have changed dramatically over time.

The history of the Black Death hints at another theme of this chapter. Recall that some groups were more likely to die of the plague than others were. This pattern is common. Health risks are almost always unevenly distributed. Women and men, upper and lower classes, and privileged and disadvantaged members of racial and ethnic groups are exposed to health risks to varying degrees. This variation suggests that health is not just a medical issue but also a sociological one. Understanding the social patterning of health risks is one of the issues we address in this chapter.

The story of the Black Death raises a third issue, too. We cannot help being struck by the superstition and ignorance surrounding the treatment of the ill in medieval times. Remedies were often herbal but also included earthworms, urine, and animal excrement. People believed it was possible to maintain good health by keeping body fluids in balance. Therefore, cures that released body fluids were common. They included hot baths, laxatives, and diuretics, which increase urination. If these treatments didn't work, bloodletting was often prescribed. No special qualifications were required to administer medical treatment. Barbers doubled as doctors.

However, the backwardness of medieval medical practice, and the advantages of modern scientific medicine, can easily be exaggerated. For example, medieval doctors stressed the importance of prevention, exercise, a balanced diet, and a congenial environment in maintaining good health. We know this advice is sound. Conversely, one of the great shortcomings of modern medicine is its emphasis on high-tech cures rather than on preventive measures. Therefore, in the final section of this chapter, we investigate how medical doctors gained substantial control over health issues and promoted their own approach to well-being. We also evaluate how medicine has been challenged in recent years.

HEALTH AND INEQUALITY

Defining and Measuring Health

How does one measure a population's health? In most countries, government-run statistical agencies routinely collect data on births, deaths, and the causes of death. Armed with these data, researchers can calculate the risk for death at different ages or for specific conditions. For example, the number of deaths of children under the age of one relative to the number of live births over a one-year period produces the **infant mortality rate**. Similarly, the administrative databases of health care systems can be analyzed for the diagnostic codes that doctors record for their patients. From these data, sociologists calculate **morbidity rates**—that is, the number of people who suffer from particular illnesses per 100 000 members of the population. Finally, surveys can shed insight into how people view their own health status.

The **Infant mortality rate** is the number of deaths before the age of one for every 1000 live births in a population in one year.

Morbidity rates indicate the number of people who suffer from particular illnesses per 100 000 members of a population.

For example, do they see their health as being excellent, very good, good, fair, or poor? Note that statistical agencies, health care records, and surveys each focus on a different outcome—death, illness, and subjective well-being, respectively. Because health is an abstract concept, it is often operationalized in different ways. We draw on different measures of health throughout this chapter.

Life expectancy is the average age at death of the members of a population.

Sociologists analyze measures of population health to understand how and why patterns change over time and place. For example, **life expectancy**, the average age at death of the members of a population, is calculated from mortality statistics. A population with a longer life expectancy is said to be healthier than is a population with a shorter life expectancy. By charting changes in life expectancy in Canada over the past two centuries, we find the health of the Canadian population has greatly improved. Although record-keeping was rudimentary in Canada's early years as a nation, researchers estimate that life expectancy in 1831 was approximately 40 years for men and 42 years for women (Lavoie and Oderkirk, 2000: 3). By 2013, life expectancy had doubled, rising to 79 years for men and 84 years for women (Martel, 2013).

Epidemiological transition refers to the shift from a society characterized by infectious and parasitic disease and low life expectancy to a society where chronic and degenerative diseases dominate and life expectancy is high.

Remember too that chronic and degenerative conditions are now the leading causes of death, whereas just a century ago, deaths were mostly attributable to infectious disease (see Table 19.1). Thus, Canada has made the **epidemiological transition**. Said differently, Canada is no longer a society characterized by infectious and parasitic disease and low life

TABLE 19.1
Leading Causes of Death, Canada, 1901 and 2009

1901	Percentage of Deaths
1. Tuberculosis	12.0
2. Bronchitis and pneumonia	10.0
3. Affections of the intestines	9.1
4. Senile debility	7.4
5. Congenital debility	7.0
6. Diseases of the heart	5.6
7. Apoplexy and paralysis	4.4
8. Diphtheria and croup	3.9
9. Accidents	3.4
10. Cancer	2.8
Other	34.4
Total	100.0
2009	
1. Cancer	29.9
2. Major heart disease	19.7
3. Stroke	5.5
4. Chronic lower respiratory diseases	4.6
5. Accidents	4.4
6. Diabetes	3.0
7. Alzheimer's disease	2.6
8. Influenza and pneumonia	2.4
9. Intentional self harm (suicide)	1.5
10. Kidney disease	1.4
Other	23.6
Total	100.0

Note: Totals may not add up to 100 percent due to rounding.

Sources: Dawson, 1906; Statistics Canada, 2014c.

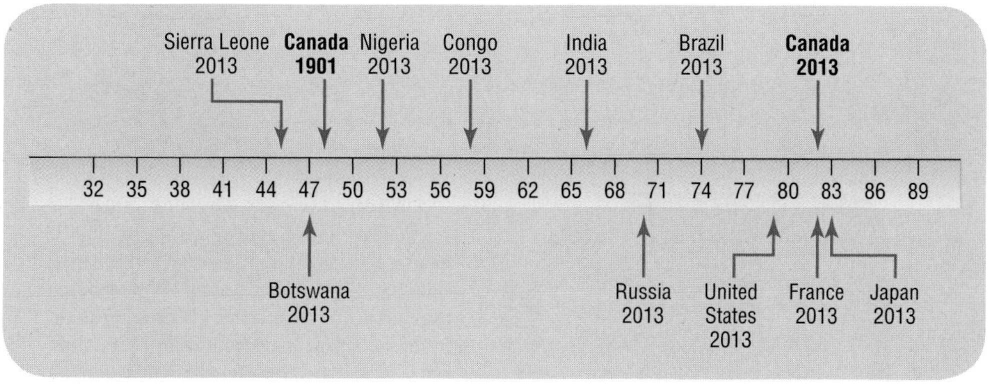

FIGURE 19.1

Life Expectancy, Selected Countries and Years

Sources: Population Reference Bureau, 2013; Statistics Canada, 2001.

expectancy; it has become a society in which chronic and degenerative diseases dominate and life expectancy is high. All developed countries and a growing number of developing countries have undergone the epidemiological transition.

We can also compare life expectancy between Canada and other countries. Life expectancy in Canada is one of the highest in the world, exceeded only by a handful of European countries and Japan, where life expectancy is unmatched (80 for men and 86 for women). Yet in desperately poor countries that have been ravaged by war and exploited by dictators or foreign powers, life expectancy is as low as 45 (in Sierra Leone) (Population Reference Bureau, 2013). Emerging economies, such as India and Brazil, occupy an intermediate position, with life expectancy at 66 and 74, respectively. Even though Russia is often regarded as an emerging economy, life expectancy there has dropped over the past few decades, indicating to sociologists that much of the population is under stress (Cockerham, 2012a). Figure 19.1 shows life expectancy in selected countries.

Assuming ideal conditions, how long can a person live? To date, the record is held by Jeanne Louise Calment, a French woman who died in 1997 at the age of 122. Calment was an extraordinary individual. She took up fencing at age 85, rode a bicycle until she was 100, gave up smoking at 120, and released a rap CD at age 121 (Matalon, 1997). The record holder for men is Jiroemon Kimura who died in June 2013 of natural causes at the age of 116 in Japan. The gap in the age of death between Calment and Kimura reflects another fact about life expectancy: on average, women live longer than men do.

CP Picture Archive/Associated Press AP

Currently, the record for longevity is held by Jeanne Louise Calment, a French woman who died in 1997 at the age of 122.

The Social Causes of Illness and Death

It might seem that disease and death are biologically caused—that people get sick because they have a genetic predisposition to a certain illness or because they come into contact with a deadly virus or carcinogen. Common sense also tells us that choosing a healthy lifestyle—eating the right type and amount of food, exercising regularly, avoiding tobacco and excessive alcohol consumption, and so on—can help us avoid disease. These two factors, a person's biological characteristics and health behaviours, are *individual-level* factors. However, sociologists typically broaden their focus by also examining *social* factors that have a profound, but often unacknowledged, influence on health. Taking into account the full range of individual and social factors that shape our health provides a better understanding of the causes of disease and death than considering individual factors alone.

When people examine factors at the level of the individual, they often find it easier to blame people who are ill for their condition. For example, when people develop diabetes, one might be inclined to say it is their own fault because they chose an unhealthy diet. Similarly, one might attribute lung cancer to a lifetime of smoking cigarettes. These sentiments convey the message that diseases stem from people's unwise choices.

A different picture emerges when we consider individual behaviours in light of the social and environmental context. If unhealthy behaviours are freely chosen, they should

BOX 19.1

SOCIOLOGY AT THE MOVIES

SILVER LININGS PLAYBOOK

Released from a mental health institution where he has spent the past eight months, Pat Solatano (played by Bradley Cooper) has one thing on his mind. He wants to find his wife, Nikki, and get back together with her. It doesn't matter that Nikki has a restraining order against him. It doesn't even matter that the reason he was institutionalized was because he beat up a colleague that he caught in the shower with his wife. Trapped in a delusion generated by his bipolar disorder, Pat is convinced that his wife still loves him and wants him back.

His re-entry into normal life is rocky. Pat lives with his parents, whom he manages to upset with his bizarre behaviour, in one scene throwing an Ernest Hemingway novel out of his bedroom window in the middle of the night and waking up his parents to complain about the book's ending. Believing that he needs to get fit so Nikki will once again find him attractive, Pat takes up jogging, wearing a garbage bag over his sweatsuit so he will perspire more and lose weight faster. Moreover, Pat is convinced he doesn't need his medication. It doesn't make him feel good and, besides, he has adopted a new philosophy. Summed up in the word "excelsior," Pat believes that if he chooses to see the good in everything—the silver linings—life will turn out right for him.

His friends, looking for a way to help Pat move on with his life, invite him over for dinner to meet Tiffany Maxwell (played by Jennifer Lawrence, whose performance won her the 2012 Academy Award for best actress). Tiffany is a recent widow struggling to get over sex addiction and depression. Pat and Tiffany take to one another right away. They reject social convention, asking each other inappropriate questions and happily exchanging information on the unpleasant side effects of their medication in front of their hosts.

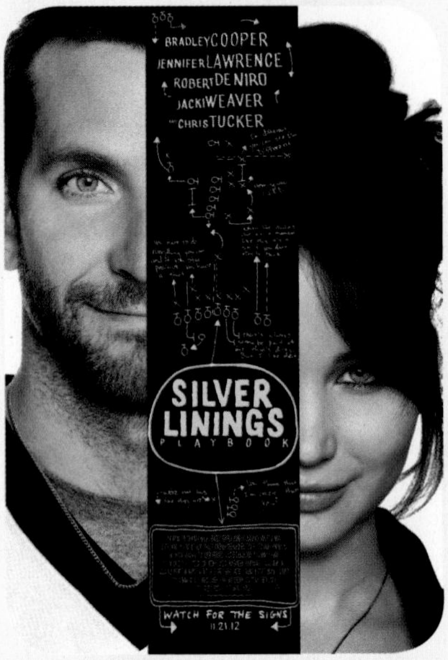

The Kobal Collection at Art Resource, NY

Pat and Tiffany in *Silver Linings Playbook*

It turns out that Tiffany knows Nikki, so Pat and Tiffany strike an odd bargain. Tiffany promises to deliver Pat's love letters to Nikki in violation of the restraining order. In exchange, Pat agrees to be Tiffany's dance partner in an upcoming competition. Over the next several weeks, the couple work hard practising for the competition. They grow close, even though Tiffany gives Pat a letter from Nikki that appears to show that his wife is open to reconciliation. In the end, a crisis causes Pat to look at Tiffany with new eyes. In doing so, he realizes that it is Tiffany whom he loves. His delusions drop away as he reaches for his silver lining.

Silver Linings Playbook takes a stridently individualistic approach to mental illness. It portrays Pat's resolve to find the silver lining as the singular force that helps him overcome his delusions and shed the shackles of mental illness. At the same time, the film ignores social factors that are the background causes of mental illness. Note that it takes nothing more than a random and unexpected moment of catching his wife with another man to propel Pat into madness. The implication is that we are all equally at risk for mental illness. Sociologists would beg to differ—some social groups are at greater risk than are other social groups. For example, how might socioeconomic position function as a predisposing factor in this film? The audience is never invited to ponder that question.

Similarly, *Silver Linings Playbook* ends on a triumphant note, implying that Pat's future is bright because he found his silver lining. But are his problems over? Pat and Tiffany lack jobs. Each lives with their parents. One of their small circle of friends includes a recovering meth addict (played by Chris Tucker) who routinely escapes from a mental institution. In the community, Pat and Tiffany have a reputation for being mentally unstable and socially abrasive. These obstacles are formidable for anyone, let alone someone who has been labelled mentally ill. As discussed earlier, labels are powerful—they have the potential to change how we see a person. Because people with mental illness are often perceived as dangerous and unpredictable, they are often socially rejected. Thus, despite the optimism we feel when Pat finds love, we know there is no guarantee that members of the community will abandon their negative perceptions and welcome him back.

be randomly distributed in the population. But they are not. Instead, behaviours such as cigarette smoking and the consumption of fatty, calorie-dense foods vary by gender, race and ethnicity, and social class. The social patterning of health behaviours tells us that even when people think they are exercising free choice, part of what drives their choices comes from their social context (see Box 19.1). Let's look more closely at the link between diet and diabetes to explore the effects of the social environment.

Canada is in the midst of a diabetes epidemic. The diabetes rate has doubled over the past decade. Two million people had diabetes in 2012, and the number is expected to rise to three million by the end of the decade (Statistics Canada, 2013a). The health care costs of treating the illness are high. Moreover, people with diabetes are vulnerable to heart disease, kidney failure, and limb amputation, so their mortality rate is more than twice that of people who do not have the disease (Public Health Agency of Canada, 2011). The biggest risk factor for diabetes is excess weight. As such, public health announcements focus on encouraging Canadians to eat healthy food. But this important message assumes that everybody has the same opportunity to consume healthy food.

Is access to healthy food the same for everyone? Certainly not. In both Canada and the United States, processed foods that are dense in calories and fat are cheaper than are fresh fruits and vegetables. Because of the greater cost of healthy food, people on a limited budget may face enormous difficulty eating the recommended diet (Drewnowski, 2009). Moreover, poorer neighbourhoods generally have a higher proportion of fast-food outlets and convenience stores and house fewer grocery stores than wealthier neighbourhoods do. Neighbourhoods with limited access to grocery stores and farmers' markets are often called "food deserts." Although food deserts are more common in the United States than in Canada, researchers have identified food deserts in Canada, especially in poor neighbourhoods (Gould, Apparicio, and Cloutier, 2012; Smoyer-Tomic, Spence, and Amrhein, 2006). Consequently, telling people to improve their eating habits without making healthy foods less expensive and more accessible is unlikely to result in change, particularly for those who are poor and therefore least able to alter their behaviour. In this case, focusing only on individual behaviours prevents us from seeing how economic circumstances constrain food choices.

Once we take social context into account, we can evaluate how health is influenced by forces that lie beyond the ability of individuals to control. Let us now review some of these social forces.

Socioeconomic Inequalities and Health

More than 30 years ago, a government study in the United Kingdom, the Black Report, made an important discovery that changed how we think about the relationship between poverty and health. It had been obvious that people living in poverty were on average sicker and more vulnerable to death than the rest of the population was. Even in the nineteenth century, social reformers devoted their lives to drawing attention to the miserable and unhealthy conditions of people living in poverty. However, by carefully documenting the unequal distribution of mortality and morbidity by social class in the United Kingdom, the Black Report described a **socioeconomic gradient in health**. Simply put, *every* increase in class position was accompanied by an improvement in health status.

The **socioeconomic gradient in health** refers to the existence of a positive correlation between socio-economic position and health.

As news of this finding spread, researchers began to look for similar patterns in their own populations. The socioeconomic gradient in health has since been detected in numerous countries using various measures of socioeconomic position, including income and education. Figure 19.2 shows Canadian data for women and men (Tjepkema, Wilkins, and Long, 2013). Risk of death in Canada is highest for those in the poorest fifth of the income distribution and decreases as income level rises. If all Canadians enjoyed the same risk for mortality as the wealthiest fifth of the population, 40 000 fewer Canadians would die every year.

Income affects health because it enables people to buy the things they need to sustain good health, including nutritious meals, well-built homes that are free from environmental hazards and are located in areas where crime is low, cultural and recreational activities that enhance physical and mental well-being, and so on. Health, however, is affected by more than economic deprivation. Independent of income, education and stress also matter.

While people with higher education tend to earn more than do people with less education, education has its own health benefits. Higher levels of education typically provide access to jobs that are more enjoyable. People with more education tend to have better job security than do people with little education. Education also provides people with opportunities to become more knowledgeable about how to stay healthy.

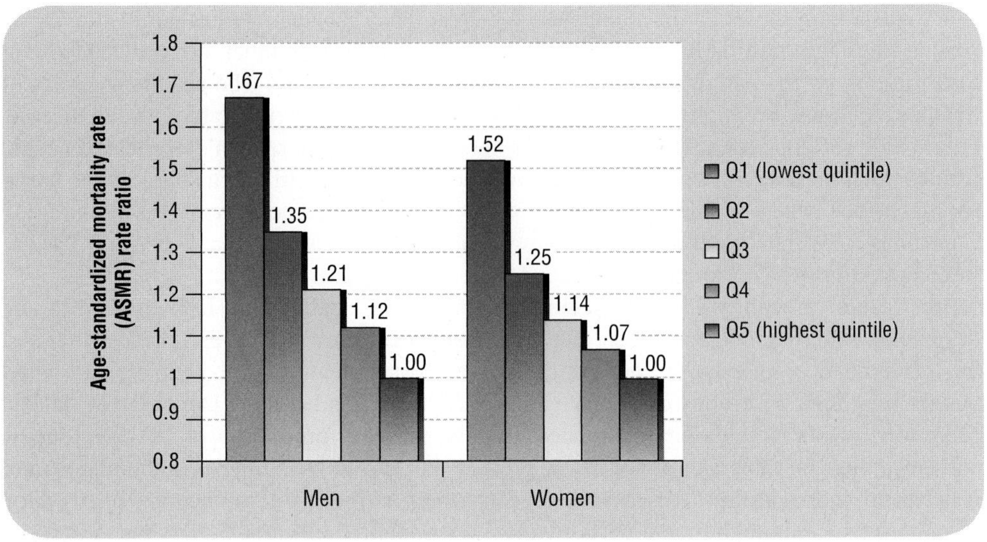

FIGURE 19.2
Relative Risk for Mortality by Sex and Income Quintile, Canadians Aged 25 and Older, 1991–2006.

Source: Adapted from Tjepkema, Michael, Russell Wilkins, and Andrea Long. 2013. "Cause-specific Mortality by Income Adequacy in Canada: A 16-Year Follow-up Study." *Health Reports 24*(7): 14–22.

Moreover, the graded nature of the association between socioeconomic position and health means that economic deprivation cannot be the sole cause of ill health. That is, middle-class people generally have enough resources to stay healthy, yet their health is still not as good as the health of upper-class people. Instead, socioeconomic differences in health are partly caused by the fact that that the higher you are in the socioeconomic hierarchy, the less stress you experience—and stress levels are associated with high rates of cardiovascular disease, cancer, and other ailments (Marmot, 2012). Simply stated, the richer you are, the less you are exposed to stressful situations and the better equipped you are to avoid them.

The socioeconomic gradient in health has endured despite the changing nature of disease, increased life expectancy that occurred during the epidemiological transition, and changes in the risk factors for disease. For this reason, some sociologists have proposed that socioeconomic position is a *fundamental* cause of disease, serving as a "cause of other causes" (Link and Phelan, 1995). In other words, economic circumstances influence how people are individually and collectively able to avoid risks for disease and death. Those in privileged positions have access to resources that enhance health under any circumstance (Phelan, Link, and Tehranifar, 2010, p. S28). Thus, when cholera was the main threat to health, more advantaged individuals and groups could avoid areas where disease was most prevalent and keep those who were infected from entering their communities. Now that heart disease is a major killer, those who are more advantaged can adopt a heart-healthy lifestyle and make use of advanced technologies to minimize their risk. As these examples illustrate, the socioeconomic gradient persists even as the causes of disease and their risk factors change over time. We must conclude that the ways in which our societies are organized are a more powerful determinant of health than are individual behaviours or choices.

Racial Inequalities in Health

Just as socioeconomic position affects health, so too do race and ethnicity. Throughout the world, disadvantaged racial and ethnic groups experience a higher risk of disease and death than do advantaged racial and ethnic groups. For example, the life expectancy of Aboriginal Canadians is from five to twelve years shorter than that of non-Aboriginal Canadians, depending on region, data source, and whether one is Métis, Inuit, or First Nations (Tjepkema et al., 2010; Statistics Canada, 2012k; Wilkins et al., 2008). Similarly, diabetes is more prevalent among First Nations peoples than in the Canadian population as a whole (Auditor General of Canada, 2013). As Figure 19.3 illustrates, the highest rates occur among First Nations peoples who live on-reserve. They experience a rate of diabetes that is more than three times above the Canadian average.

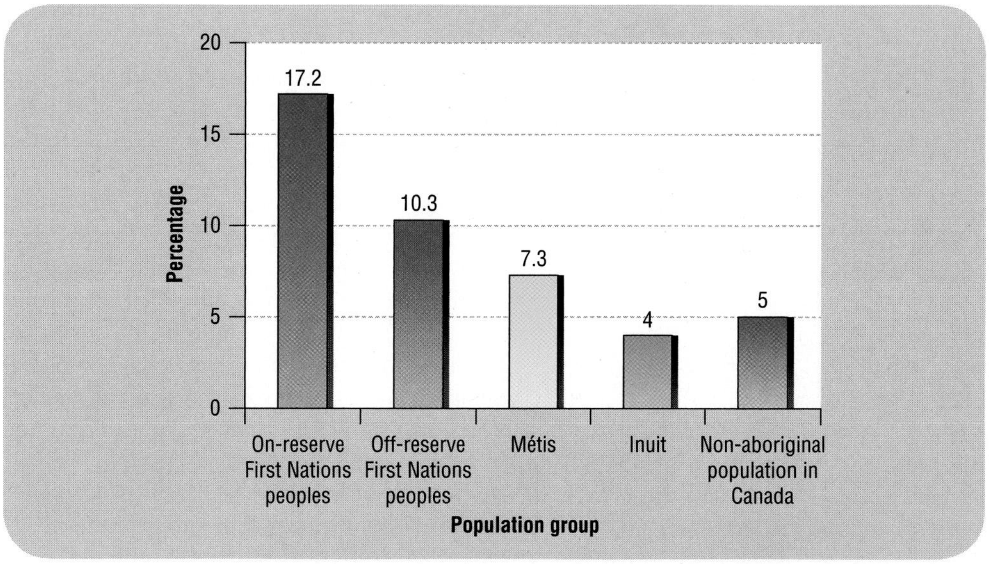

FIGURE 19.3
The Prevalence of Self-Reported Diabetes among Aboriginal People and the Non-Aboriginal Population in Canada, Aged 12 Years and Older

Source: Public Health Agency of Canada, 2013. Reproduced with permission from the Minister of Health, 2014.

How can we explain the health deficit among Canada's Aboriginal people? First and most obviously, the health deficit can be traced to economic deprivation. Compared with other Canadians, Canada's Aboriginal people are more likely to live in poverty. Thus, 17 percent of all Canadian children live in poverty compared with 40 percent of Aboriginal children (Macdonald and Wilson, 2013). Poverty early in life is particularly troubling because children whose bodies are still developing are more sensitive to their environment than adults are. Adversities associated with poverty can alter the biology of young children in ways that predispose them to illness later in life (Hertzman and Boyce, 2010). Moreover, children who are poor may display less school readiness and less early academic success than more advantaged children do. Class differences in early school outcomes may persist or widen over the course of childhood, eventually contributing to lower educational attainment in adulthood and lower lifetime earnings, which in turn increase risk for illness and shortened lives (Duncan et al., 2012).

However, economic disadvantage accounts for only some of the variation in health by race and ethnicity. Many researchers believe that the remaining difference stems from the way racially or ethnically marginalized groups react to the cumulative effects of discrimination (Williams and Sternthal, 2010). At the individual level, discrimination can result in health-harming behaviours such as using drugs or alcohol as a coping mechanism or avoiding seeking help for health problems. At the institutional level, segregation on reserves and in urban neighbourhoods concentrates poverty, disorder, and despair, thus deepening problems.

European settlers in the New World seized lands that were suitable for farming, forcing Aboriginal people to move onto distant reserves. Relocation made it difficult for Aboriginal people to adapt their traditional hunting and fishing practices to strange environments. Eventually, many of them abandoned their traditions and started relying on purchased food. The loss of traditional hunting methods, which assured physical fitness and contributed to a shared cultural identity, accompanied by the shift to a market-based diet and increasingly sedentary lifestyle, are central to understanding the high prevalence of diabetes in the Aboriginal population (Haman et al., 2010; Willows, Hanley, and Delormier, 2012).

In addition, starting in the 1870s, the Canadian government snatched thousands of Aboriginal children from their families and forced them into residential schools. The purpose of residential schools was to assimilate Aboriginal children into European culture. To ensure that they would no longer be influenced by their "inferior" culture, many Aboriginal children never saw their parents again.

Under institutional care, Aboriginal children were socialized to despise their cultural heritage. Children who used their own language and followed their own customs

The message on the blackboard of this Anglican-run school in Lac la Ronge, Saskatchewan, in 1945 is "Thou Shalt Not Tell Lies."

were harshly punished. They were forced to adopt European ways. In some schools, children were also subjected to physical and sexual abuse. An unknown number of children died—few schools kept records of who and why.

Less obviously, children in residential schools lacked role models from whom they could learn parenting skills. When Aboriginal children reached adulthood, they left the institution and began to have children. Most had no idea how to raise them. These psychological wounds launched a cycle of abuse and neglect that is only now being recognized (Truth and Reconciliation Commission, 2012a).

In sum, deficits in the health of Canada's Aboriginal people must be placed in the historical context of colonization. Health outcomes are as much the consequence of social forces as individual choices.

Gender Inequalities in Health: A Feminist Approach

As noted earlier, men and women differ in their risk for disease and death. Some of these differences are biological. Others are due to social factors. In societies characterized by gender inequality, women enjoy fewer rights than men do. Women's rights are especially weak in the Middle East, Africa, and South Asia (Brym, 2014b: 106–27).

The higher value placed on males than on females often begins before birth, when sex-selective abortion allows families to terminate unwanted female fetuses (Dyson, 2012). This practice is widespread in India and China. As boys grow up, they often receive preferential treatment from their families in terms of more food and better access to health care and education. Children of both sexes are socialized to believe that males are superior to females (Bharadwaj and Lakdawala, 2013; Singh, 2012). Because of social pressure to ensure that daughters are pure and thus marriageable, parents control where their daughters go and what they do to a far greater extent than they do for sons (Ram, Strohschein, and Gaur, 2014).

Indeed, in many parts of the world, daughters are seen as a burden to their family. Arranged, unexpected, and unwanted marriages are common in such places (United Nations Population Fund, 2012). Thus, despite laws against it, child marriage remains common. Child marriage is a major health risk for girls because it generally occurs before they are ready for adulthood, both physically and psychologically (Erulkar, 2013). Isolated in the household of her husband, a young bride is vulnerable in many ways. She is economically dependent. She has limited power to refuse sex and demand that her husband wear a condom during intercourse. She is at risk for partner violence, sexually transmitted disease, and sexual abuse. She may be treated as little more than domestic help until she starts producing sons. She often lacks the skill and knowledge to care properly for herself during pregnancy (Erulkar, 2013; Godha, Hotchkiss, and Gage, 2013). Where gender inequality is entrenched in political and legal systems, girls and women are powerless to protect themselves from harm. As a result, they typically experience disease and mental disorder at far higher rates than boys and men do.

In countries where women have the same rights as men do, gender differences in health are less marked. For example, in Canada, an equal proportion of men and women (about 60 percent) report being in excellent or very good health (Statistics Canada, 2011f). Nonetheless, we should not assume that wherever women are afforded the same rights as men are, both genders experience similar risks for disease and death.

To fully understand and explain gender differences, researchers must consider the interplay of biological and social factors in specific health outcomes. These complexities can be seen, for example, when we examine gender differences in heart disease. From a biological standpoint, hormones lower women's risk for heart disease until women reach menopause (Read and Gorman, 2010). When women develop heart disease, on average 10 years later than men, they are more likely than men are to have additional health problems. Therefore, heart disease kills more women than men in later life. Men and women also experience different symptoms during a heart attack, with men reporting chest and arm pain, and women reporting fatigue, nausea, and shortness of breath (Low, Thurston, and Matthews, 2010). Because women's symptoms differ from men's, women are more likely to be misdiagnosed and thus less likely than men are to receive appropriate and timely treatment. The widespread assumption that heart disease is largely a male condition has meant that women are underrepresented in clinical trials. Consequently, men tend to benefit more from treatment than women do (Worrall-Carter et al., 2011). Thus, whereas biological factors play a protective role in women's risk for heart disease until menopause, social assumptions about the disease translate into medical practices that confer greater risk on women.

Thus far, we have illustrated how health varies by socioeconomic position, race and ethnicity, and gender. While each of these areas of research continues to grow, we should recognize that these statuses do not occur in isolation from one another. According to **intersectionality theory**, the effects of socioeconomic position, race and ethnicity, and gender on health are multiplicative, not additive. Being poor may cause people to experience X health deficits, and being an Aboriginal Canadian may cause people to experience Y health deficits, but the effect of being poor and Aboriginal is XY, not X + Y (Veenstra, 2013). This argument implies that sociologists need to understand how various dimensions of inequality combine to affect health. Do First Nations women living in poverty experience triple jeopardy in their risk for heart disease or diabetes? Does privilege in one status provide protection against disease, despite a disadvantage in other statuses? Currently, answers to these questions are elusive. Addressing them is an important area for future research.

Intersectionality theory holds that the effects of socioeconomic position, race and ethnicity, and gender on health are multiplicative, not additive. For instance, being poor may cause people to experience X health deficits and being an Aboriginal may cause people to experience Y health deficits, but the effect of being poor and Aboriginal on health is XY, not X + Y.

Health Care as a Determinant of Health

A nation's health depends on a comprehensive infrastructure that provides citizens with access to clean drinking water, basic sewage and sanitation services, agricultural technologies, and efficient transportation systems. Where these systems are absent, we find high rates of disease and low life expectancy. For example, the Democratic Republic of Congo is rich in copper, diamonds, and gold; enjoys lush farmlands that produce coffee, sugar cane, and maize in abundance; and offers unrealized opportunities for generating massive amounts of hydroelectric power. Yet it is the site of the deadliest conflict since World War II. Decades of civil strife have left the country in ruins. Millions have been killed. Nearly 75 percent of Congolese people lack access to safe drinking water, and about 80 percent do not have a flush toilet (World Bank, 2012). Travelling by vehicle on dirt roads is extremely dangerous, and most of the country's railway system has been shut down. It should come as no surprise that, despite its rich resources, life expectancy in the Congo is 58 years, among the lowest in the world.

The **health care system** merits special attention. It comprises a nation's clinics, hospitals, and other facilities for treating illness. A country's health care system plays a unique role insofar as it is designed to help people when they are sick, whereas other institutions play a bigger role in preventing people from becoming ill in the first place. A health care system is important for population health because rapidly restoring ill citizens to a state of health enables them to live longer lives free from disability and disease.

The **health care system** is composed of a nation's clinics, hospitals, and other facilities for treating illness.

To what extent does the health care system matter for improving population health? One way of tackling this question is to evaluate which features of a health care system are associated with better health. For example, researchers have investigated whether a country with more doctors per capita has better health outcomes than do countries with fewer doctors. They have also examined whether a relationship exists between population health and health care spending.

Their findings may surprise you. Researchers have shown that, in high-income countries, the number of physicians per capita is unrelated to population health (Watson and McGrail, 2009). Canada has more doctors per capita than does Japan, yet life expectancy is higher in Japan than in Canada. Similarly, Portugal and Germany have more doctors per capita than does Canada but life expectancy is higher in Canada than in those countries.

These findings are intriguing because Canadian doctors have long argued that Canada has a doctor shortage. As recently as 2011, a report by the conservative think tank, the Fraser Institute, criticized the federal government for imposing restrictions on the number of medical students and suggested that Canadians are poorly served because too few doctors are available to meet Canadians' growing demand for health care (Esmail, 2011). Yet a report published by the Royal College of Physician and Surgeons of Canada found instead that the unemployment rate among newly graduated medical specialists in the fall of 2013 was more than two times greater than was the average unemployment rate (Fréchette et al., 2013). From this report, one might logically conclude that Canada has an oversupply of medical specialists. Debate over the optimal number of doctors is clearly a complex issue. Nonetheless, in light of research showing little relation between doctor supply and population health in high-income countries, we might want to look elsewhere for ways to improve health in Canada.

Researchers have also found that the amount high-income countries spend on their health care system has little relation to population health. The United States has the most expensive health care system in the world, with costs accounting for nearly 18 percent of its gross domestic product (GDP) (Canadian Institute for Health Information [CIHI], 2013). Annual expenditures on health care amount to $8508 per person. (Box 19.2 illustrates one reason why health care expenditures are much higher in the United States than elsewhere.) Yet life expectancy in the United States is the lowest among high-income countries. Conversely, Japan enjoys the world's highest life expectancy but allocates less than 10 percent of GDP to health care—just $3213 per person. Canada occupies an intermediate position: health care costs are the fifth highest in the world, representing about 11 percent

BOX 19.2

SOCIAL POLICY: WHAT DO YOU THINK?

Vote

THE HIGH COST OF PRESCRIPTION DRUGS

Americans pay more for prescription drugs than people in any other country do—in 2012, double the price Canadians paid (Patented Medicine Prices Review Board, 2013). The price of prescription drugs in the United States has increased rapidly over the past few decades, generally more quickly than the rate of inflation and the price of other items in that nation's health care budget (Health Care Cost Institute, 2013).

Unlike the United States, other high-income countries keep prescription drug prices down through government regulation. In Japan, the Department of Health, Labour, and Welfare negotiates the price of pharmaceuticals directly with manufacturers. Additionally, the Japanese government can lower the price if a drug proves more popular than the drug manufacturer predicts (Ikegami and Anderson, 2012). In France, a new policy of substituting cheaper generic drugs for expensive patented drugs saved more than €1.3 billion in a single year (World Health Organization, 2010).

How well does Canada fare in its efforts to lower the cost of prescription drugs? Because each province negotiates directly with pharmaceutical industries, the provinces have historically achieved significant costs savings (Silversides, 2009). Federal regulation also keeps prices low. Since 1987, Canadian drug companies have not been able to increase prices of brand-name drugs above the inflation rate. New brand-name drugs cannot exceed the highest Canadian price of comparable drugs used to treat the same disease. Most provincial drug plans encourage the substitution of generic drugs for patented medications.

Despite these savings, one study suggests that Canada could do more to lower costs. If Ontarians paid the best international prices for its top 100 generic drugs, they would save $245 million annually (Law, 2013). Why do you think the cost of prescription drugs is relatively high in Canada? What more should be done to reduce these costs? Do you think it is reasonable to compare Canadian prices with the prices that people in other rich countries pay for their prescription drugs? Why or why not?

Country	% of GDP Spent on Health Care	Infant Mortality Rate (per 1000 live births)
United States	17.7	5.9
Netherlands	11.9	3.7
France	11.6	3.3
Germany	11.3	3.3
Canada	11.2	4.9
Japan	9.6	2.4
Norway	9.3	2.2

TABLE 19.2
Health Care Costs and Infant Mortality Rate, Selected Countries

Source: Canadian Institutes for Health Information, 2013. National Health Expenditure Trends, 1975–2013. Ottawa, On: Author; Population Reference Bureau, 2013. 2013 World Population Data Sheet. Washington, DC: Author

of GDP, or $4522 per person. Of the four countries that spend more (the United States, Netherlands, France, and Germany), only France has a longer life expectancy than Canada does. Table 19.2 illustrates the lack of a relationship between health care costs and infant mortality rates for rich countries. As with life expectancy, little evidence suggests that rich countries that spend more on health care achieve lower infant mortality rates.

TIME FOR REVIEW

- What three measures do sociologists use to operationalize the health of a population?
- Why is it important to look beyond individual choices to understand the risk for disease and death?
- In what ways does the broader social context explain variations in health by socioeconomic position, race and ethnicity, and gender?
- What evidence supports the view that the health care system plays an important but overstated role in improving the health of the population?

HEALTH CARE AND MEDICINE

The Canadian Health Care System: A Conflict Approach

Earlier we noted that the health care system affects the population's health by making it possible for sick or injured citizens to regain their health. But this observation is not the extent of sociological interest in health care. Sociologists also investigate health care as a socially organized response to the problem of illness. Among other issues, they find the powerful position that medical doctors occupy to be a subject of enduring significance. On the next few pages, we describe how medical doctors rose to prominence and show how doctors have used their power to shape health care in Canada.

More than two centuries ago, the practice of medicine was disorganized and unregulated. Herbalists, faith healers, midwives, homeopaths, druggists, and medical doctors vied to meet the health needs of the public, selling their services to anyone willing to pay for them. As scientific thinking began to permeate Western societies, medical doctors were among the first to grasp its importance in treating illness. The adoption of the scientific method led to remarkable breakthroughs that identified the bacteria and viruses responsible for various diseases, facilitating the development of effective treatments to combat them. These and subsequent triumphs convinced most people of the superiority of medical science over other approaches to health. Medical science worked, or at least it seemed to work more effectively and more often than other therapies did.

It would be wrong, however, to think that scientific medicine came to dominate the treatment of illness only because it produced beneficial results. A second, sociological reason for the rise to dominance of scientific medicine is that doctors were able to professionalize. As noted in Chapter 13, Work and the Economy, a profession is an occupation that requires extensive formal education. Professionals regulate their own training and practice. They restrict competition within the profession, mainly by limiting the recruitment of practitioners. They minimize competition with other professions, partly by laying exclusive claim to a field of expertise. They exercise considerable authority over their clients. They profess to be motivated mainly by the desire to serve their community even though they earn a lot of money in the process. Professionalization, then, is the process by which people gain control and authority over their occupation and their clients. It results in professionals enjoying high occupational prestige and income, and considerable social and political power (Freidson, 1986; Timmermans and Oh, 2010).

The professional organization of Canadian doctors, the Canadian Medical Association (CMA), was founded in 1867 in Québec City. It quickly set about broadcasting the successes of medical science and criticizing alternative approaches to health as quackery. The CMA was able to have laws passed to restrict medical licences to graduates of approved schools and to ensure that only graduates of those schools could train the next generation of doctors. By restricting entry into the profession, and by specifying what "paramedical" practitioners could and could not do, the medical establishment ensured its own status, prestige, and high income. In short, when medicine became a profession, it also became a monopoly.

Medical doctors controlled the practice of medicine well before Canada's modern health care system came into being. As a result, medical doctors played an important role in the formation of Canada's health care system. Fiercely opposed to the idea of government-sponsored health insurance, medical doctors were able to delay its implementation. Physicians viewed government-sponsored health insurance as a threat to their autonomy, including their ability to set prices. Private insurance companies also viewed government-sponsored insurance as an intrusion on the existing market-based system. Their collective lobbying ensured that one promising discussion on health care, when federal and provincial governments met to rebuild the country in the aftermath of World War II, ended in failure.

Frustrated by the lack of progress, Tommy Douglas, then premier of Saskatchewan, resolved to introduce health care without federal assistance. His move earned him the title, "the father of medicare." Douglas began his career as a Baptist minister and was strongly influenced by the Christian social gospel, which called for progressive social reform. In 1933, he earned an M.A. in sociology from McMaster University. He led the Co-operative Commonwealth Federation (CCF) to victory in Saskatchewan in 1944, making it the first democratic socialist party to win a North American election. (Subsequently, Douglas helped turn the CCF into the New Democratic Party.) He served as premier of Saskatchewan from 1944 to 1961, introducing many social reforms, including universal medical care. Many medical doctors opposed Douglas, and some even launched a province-wide physicians' strike, but Saskatchewan's government prevailed. Health care in Saskatchewan became a model for the whole country and helped shape the five principles of the 1984 Canada Health Act that regulates health care (see Table 19.3).

In countries with **socialized medicine**, the government (1) directly controls the financing and organization of health services, (2) directly pays providers, (3) guarantees equal access to health care, and (4) allows some private care for individuals willing to pay for their medical expenses.

Under the umbrella of the Canada Health Act, Canada's health care system can be loosely described as **socialized medicine**. Despite differences in how socialized medicine works in such countries as the United Kingdom, Sweden, and Italy, common to these systems is that the government (1) directly controls the financing and organization of health services, (2) directly pays providers, (3) guarantees equal access to health care, and (4) allows some private care for individuals willing to pay for their medical expenses (Cockerham, 2012b). Canada does not have a true system of socialized medicine, however,

TABLE 19.3
Five Principles of the 1984 Canada Health Act

Principle	Description
Universal	Public health care insurance must be available to all Canadians.
Accessible	All insured persons must have reasonable access to health care services.
Publicly administered	Each province must set up a not-for-profit public authority to administer health care, e.g., the Ontario Health Insurance Plan.
Comprehensive	The plan must insure all medically necessary services provided in hospital and by medical doctors.
Portable	Residents are entitled to coverage when they travel or move to another province.

in that the government does not directly employ Canadian physicians. Most of Canada's physicians are independent practitioners who are paid on a fee-for-service basis and submit claims to the provincial or territorial health insurance plan for payment.

The costs of health care are distributed between the provinces and the federal government. Over time, the funding agreement has evolved from a 50–50 split to block-funding, whereby the federal government transfers a fixed amount to each province. In other words, when health care costs rise more rapidly than annual increases in federal transfer payments, the provinces end up shouldering a bigger burden. The gradual downloading of health care costs to the provinces, with the federal contribution falling to around 25 percent of the total cost of health care, has fuelled resentment toward the federal government in recent decades.

Ongoing debate persists regarding whether Canada can afford its health care system and who should pay for it, raising questions about its future. Following nearly a decade of cutbacks to health care, the Liberal Party under Paul Martin won the 2004 election on a pledge to shore up the system. During Martin's brief time in office, the Liberals invested billions of dollars in health care and guaranteed an annual 6 percent increase in federal transfers for the next 10 years. With the agreement set to expire in 2014, Stephen Harper, leader of the Conservative government, unilaterally established the new 10-year funding arrangement. The agreement signalled the federal government's reduced commitment to national health care. First, the annual increase in federal transfers was reduced from 6 percent to 3 percent, despite health care costs having been on the rise by about 5 percent annually (Canadian Institute of Actuaries, 2013). Second, the Harper government eliminated federal funding for improving the performance of the system and lowering costs. The eliminated programs included the Wait Times Reduction Fund and initiatives to promote information-sharing among provinces. Finally, the government ended the equalization payments that had previously transferred money from richer to poorer provinces. This policy had helped ensure high standards of care in every province. As the changes laid out in the new agreement begin to be felt across the country, the provinces will need to find their own solutions, which may in turn erode their commitment to the Canada Health Act and increase the use of privatized medical services.

Canada's health care system is also under threat from other sources. In 2005, the Supreme Court ruled in favour of a man who had sued the province of Québec after he had been told that he was forbidden from privately purchasing a hip replacement to avoid a year-long wait in the public system. The Supreme Court ruled that delays in access amounted to denial of access. Many commentators believe that the ruling opened the door to a two-tier system in which private insurance and service provision operate alongside the public system. Implicit in such a system is preferred treatment for the well-to-do who are better able to afford private care. Some individuals and organizations, notably the Canadian Medical Association, welcomed the decision, but supporters of equal access feared its consequences. The Supreme Court decision applies only to Québec but lawsuits underway in other provinces also seek to overturn the Canada Health Act. It remains to be seen how these lawsuits will play out.

TIME FOR REVIEW

- How did medical doctors come to dominate other health practitioners in the nineteenth century?
- Why is Canada's health care system not a true example of socialized medicine?
- What threats are jeopardizing the future of Canada's health care system?

The Power of Medicine

The **sick role** is the social mechanism that allows doctors to confer a diagnosis on an individual so that a person who is sick or injured can legitimately step away from daily responsibilities and take the requisite time to recover.

Although Canada's doctors failed to prevent government-sponsored health care, doctors do not lack influence. In fact, medical doctors wield immense power, as Talcott Parsons, a prominent functionalist, noted when he first described the sick role in 1951. According to Parsons, the **sick role** is the social mechanism that society has created to deal with the problem of illness (Parsons, 1951: 428 ff.). When people become ill, their condition may require them to step away from their normal responsibilities for a time. Before they may legitimately do so, they must present themselves to a doctor, who holds ultimate authority in deciding whether a person is ill. (Students who have fallen ill on the day of a test are familiar with this process.) Once labelled ill, patients are obliged to follow the advice of their physician and strive to get well. For their part, doctors are required to be technically competent and objective—that is, not to be emotionally involved with, or prejudiced against, the patient or biased in any other way. As such, physicians serve to maintain social order. They ensure that people who are sick are permitted to shed their daily obligations and not regain them until they can recover. Similarly, doctors deny these privileges to people who fraudulently claim to be ill in an effort to avoid their social responsibilities.

In addition to their power to determine who can legitimately claim the sick role, doctors maintain the exclusive right to decide which conditions will be recognized as illness. In an earlier era, when medicine held less sway, behaviours that were deviant might have been labelled as "evil." Deviants tended to be chastised, punished, and otherwise socially controlled by religious leaders. Today, however, a person prone to alcohol-fuelled drinking sprees is more likely to be declared an alcoholic and treated in a detoxification centre. A person predisposed to violent rages might be diagnosed with intermittent explosive disorder and prescribed medication.

Medicalization is the process by which a condition or behaviour becomes defined as a medical problem requiring a medical solution.

These examples illustrate that the problems people encounter in their everyday lives are increasingly framed as medical issues. Sociologists use the term **medicalization** to refer to the process by which "human problems or experiences become defined as medical problems, usually in terms of illnesses, diseases, or syndromes" (Conrad and Barker, 2010: S75). Once a problem has been defined as a medical condition, doctors become the only experts who are able exercise authority over it. Thus, the process of medicalization serves to increase the power of medical doctors while reducing the power of other authorities, including judges, the police, religious leaders, and legislators.

Over time, medicalization has transformed mundane aspects of life into medical problems. Wrinkles and sagging body parts are no longer seen as part of the normal process of aging but as evidence of decline to be reversed through cosmetic surgery (Adams, 2013). Ironically, risks to health sometimes accompany cosmetic procedures. Botox injections and laser treatments to remove wrinkles may entail minor risks, but surgical interventions can have serious complications. For example, implants to reshape sagging breasts may result in painful hardening of the tissue around the implant, numbness, rupture, infection, and cell death (necrosis).

Medicalization has also transformed childbirth into an event managed by sophisticated medical technologies in the hospital, with the consequence that unmedicated vaginal delivery in the home has become rare and undesirable (Shaw, 2013). Importantly, these medical practices persist despite evidence that hospital births are more costly but no more beneficial to mothers or their babies than traditional home births are. Moreover, some women have come to resent the disempowerment that childbirth represents because physicians oversee and control every step of the process.

Medicalization is ongoing. For example, in 2013, the American Medical Association officially recognized obesity as a disease, setting aside its previous designation as either a symptom or a risk factor for illness. The decision has both positive and negative implications. A benefit of labelling obesity a disease is that researchers and governments may be encouraged to invest more money into learning about obesity. The resulting research could well translate into better treatments. The investment in obesity research could make it easier for people who seek treatment for obesity to have their expenses covered through health insurance, rather than out of their own pocket. Moreover, people diagnosed with obesity may no longer be viewed as lazy or undisciplined. It may also be more difficult to hold obese people personally responsible for a condition to which they might be biologically or genetically predisposed.

Included in the disadvantages of recognizing obesity as a disease is that surgical interventions and medication for weight loss will increasingly be seen as reasonable solutions. Consequently, obese people will face greater pressure to undergo medical procedures even when these interventions are known to be ineffective, produce harmful side effects, or be potentially fatal. An example of such an intervention is gastric bypass surgery. Although celebrities such as Sharon Osbourne, Randy Jackson, Lisa Lampanelli, and New Jersey governor Chris Christie have successfully undergone gastric bypass surgery to lose weight, not everyone who has the surgery is able to keep the weight off. Risks associated with gastric bypass surgery include bone loss, kidney stones, ulcers, and bowel obstruction. About four in a hundred people die as a result of gastric bypass surgery (Karmali et al., 2012), including some who commit suicide when weight loss does not improve the quality of their lives.

A second problem with defining obesity as a disease is that it tries to fix people rather than the underlying social causes of their ailment. The problem of food deserts, for example, may fade in importance if doctors can convince the public that medical procedures are the best way to solve the problem of obesity.

Just as the medical profession has the power to medicalize certain conditions, it has the ability to demedicalize other conditions. This dual capacity becomes evident when we consider the field of psychiatry.

Medical Power and Mental Illness: A Symbolic Interactionist Approach

In 1974, a condition that had been considered a psychiatric disorder for more than a century ceased to be labelled as such by the American Psychiatric Association (APA). Did the condition disappear because it had become rare to the point of extinction? No. Did the discovery of a new wonder drug eradicate the condition virtually overnight? Again, no. In fact, in 1974, the condition was perhaps more widespread and certainly more public than ever before. Paradoxically, just as the extent of the condition was becoming more widely appreciated, the APA's "bible," the *Diagnostic and Statistical Manual of Mental Disorders* (DSM), ceased to define it as a psychiatric disorder.

The "condition" we are referring to is homosexuality. In preparing the third edition of the DSM for publication, a squabble broke out among psychiatrists over whether homosexuality is in fact a psychiatric disorder. Gay and lesbian activists, who sought to destigmatize homosexuality, were partly responsible for a shift in the views of many psychiatrists on this subject. In the end, the APA decided that homosexuality is not a psychiatric disorder.

The controversy over homosexuality is only one example out of many illustrating an important fact: Decisions about which disorders to include in the DSM are sometimes based less on science than on changing values and power struggles. Another example concerns post-traumatic stress disorder (PTSD). When veterans of the Vietnam War began returning to the United States in the early 1970s, they faced great difficulty re-entering American society. The war was unpopular, so veterans were not widely greeted as heroes. The U.S. economy went into a tailspin in 1973, making jobs difficult to find. Finally, the veterans had suffered high levels of stress during the war itself. Many of them believed their troubles were psychiatric in nature, and soon a nationwide campaign was underway, urging the APA to recognize PTSD in its manual. Many psychiatrists were reluctant to do so. Nonetheless, DSM-III listed the disorder. To be sure, the campaign succeeded partly on the strength of evidence that extreme trauma has psychological (and at times physiological) effects. However, in addition, as one activist later explained, the PTSD campaign succeeded because "[we] were better organized, more politically active, and enjoyed more lucky breaks than [our] opposition" did (Chaim Shatan, quoted in Scott, 1990: 308).

Over time, the DSM has broadened what is considered to be mental illness. In 1968, DSM-II recognized 182 mental disorders. By 1994, DSM-IV listed 357 mental disorders and 25 "culture-bound syndromes." Not only did the number of mental disorders grow but successive changes have made it easier to meet the criteria for a mental disorder. For example, when PTSD was first listed in DSM-III, a person needed to exhibit symptoms for at least six months before being diagnosed with the condition. In DSM-IV, the duration was reduced to one month. In DSM-III, the traumatic event that precipitated PTSD needed to be an incident that was beyond the range of normal human experience, such as being in a horrific traffic accident or surviving a natural disaster. DSM-IV stipulated that the event only needed to be experienced as stressful, making it possible for many more situations to be considered as legitimate PTSD triggers.

The trend toward increasing the number of categories of mental illnesses and relaxing the criteria for diagnosis has resulted in substantially higher rates of mental illness. Whereas fewer than 5 percent of the population would have met the criteria for anxiety disorder in 1980, anxiety disorders today affect nearly 20 percent of the population (Horwitz and Wakefield 2012). A similar rise has been observed in cases of clinical depression. Attention Deficit Hyperactivity Disorder (ADHD), which was unknown nearly a half century ago, is now the most common mental disorder of childhood, diagnosed in about 5 percent of children.

Increased usage of psychiatric medication has accompanied rising rates of mental disorder. Antidepressants such as Prozac, Paxil, and Zoloft became bestselling drugs in the 1990s, recording a spectacular 1300 percent increase in global sales over the decade (Rose, 2003). They have since been replaced in popularity by drugs such as Abilify and Seroquel, two antipsychotic medications used to treat people who do not respond well to antidepressants. Similarly, the use of medication for Canadian children diagnosed with ADHD nearly doubled between 1994 and 2007 (Brault and LaCourse, 2012).

Perhaps in response to growing skepticism about the rapid growth of mental illness in the past few decades, the American Psychiatric Association did not noticeably expand the number of mental disorders in the latest edition of DSM (DSM-5), released in 2013. While some new categories were added, including disruptive mood dysregulation disorder (DMDD), which pathologizes temper tantrums in children, other disorders have disappeared, including Asperger's syndrome and the 25 culture-bound syndromes first listed in DSM-IV.

Lisa Strohschein

DSM-5 was published in 2013.

Changing what counts as mental illness can profoundly alter both how society regards those who have been diagnosed and how diagnosed individuals see themselves. You will recall from our earlier discussion of deviance that symbolic interactionism is preoccupied with the labelling process (Chapter 7, Deviance and Crime). In essence, how we behave toward others is determined by the meanings we give to their actions. When a person is diagnosed as mentally ill, we respond differently to that person. For example, a young man diagnosed with schizophrenia may be treated as if he is unpredictable, strange, dangerous, and unable to care for himself properly. Consequently, we may shun or avoid him. If, on the other hand, unusual behaviours are not labelled as mental illness, we may regard the behaviour as quirkiness or perhaps something else altogether.

Consider Miley Cyrus's sexually charged performance at the 2013 MTV Music Video Awards. It drew worldwide attention, with millions taking to social media either to condemn or praise her twerking. Her actions were largely interpreted as an attempt to shed her squeaky-clean image as Hannah Montana and reinvent herself as an adult pop star. Nobody suggested Miley was mentally ill. Yet, nearly a century ago, such behaviour would have been grounds for admission to a mental institution and perhaps sexual sterilization (Boschma, 2008). How can responses to the same behaviour vary so widely? The reason is that the meanings attributed to behaviour continually change over time as society itself changes and sees things differently. Consequently, medical doctors may exercise considerable authority in making claims about the human condition, but their power is not absolute.

Symbolic interactionism also suggests that acquiring a label has implications for one's identity. Because the way we see ourselves comes, in part, from imagining how others look at us, people who are labelled with a mental illness may come to see themselves as damaged or worthless. Not all mental conditions, however, result in a negative self-identity. As Box 19.3 illustrates, being labelled with a mental illness may sometimes generate a new, positive identity.

The Social Limits of Modern Medicine

The epidemiological transition lulled most people into thinking that the threat of infectious diseases had been vanquished. Yet the public has periodically had to face new infectious diseases that have threatened to wipe out populations, such as HIV/AIDS (human immunodeficiency virus/acquired immunodeficiency syndrome), SARS (severe acute respiratory syndrome), H1N1 influenza, and Ebola. What many people do not realize is that even larger challenges face us in the future.

In 2009, a Swede who had been hospitalized in New Delhi, India, was the first person to acquire a bacterial infection resistant to all known antibiotic treatments. The superbug, known as NDM-1, has since spread to other countries. It is believed that all Canadian cases occurred as a result of citizens receiving hospital care in another country, but investigation of a recent outbreak in a Toronto hospital revealed two initial cases, one of which did not involve international travel (Lowe et al., 2013).

NDM-1 is deeply worrying because it is difficult to detect using standard laboratory techniques, requiring instead time-consuming methods for positive identification. In an outbreak, rapid identification is critical to stopping the spread of disease, so delays can be catastrophic. Moreover, a growing number of NDM-1 cases appear to have been acquired in the community rather than in hospital, where people have historically come into contact with superbugs. In India, Pakistan, and Bangladesh, NDM-1 has been found in food and drinking water. Because international travel is increasingly common, such superbugs pose a worldwide environmental threat. Finally, NDM-1 is unique in its ability to transmit its drug resistance to other bacteria. This means that other microbes that have been successfully treated with a standard regimen of antibiotics are now as drug-resistant as NDM-1 is. No wonder the U.S. Centers for Disease Control and Prevention issued a first-of-its-kind report in 2013 on antibiotic-resistant organisms, noting that the post-antibiotic era is rapidly approaching, if not already here. If antibiotics are indeed on their way out, we will no longer have any viable way to treat many infections, setting medical care back by more than a century.

How have we allowed this crisis to creep up on us? One thing we did wrong was to invest disproportionately in expensive, high-tech diagnostic equipment and treatment to the neglect of preventative measures. Typically, 55 cents of every dollar we spend on cancer research goes to investigating the biology and causes of the disease. Another 43 cents goes to research on detection, diagnosis, prognosis, treatment, and related efforts. Just 2 percent is allocated for research on prevention (Brym, 2014b: 92). Our second error was to overprescribe antibiotics, thus encouraging drug-resistant mutations. Labour-intensive, time-consuming hygiene was used to halt the spread of infectious disease in hospitals as

BOX 19.3

SOCIOLOGY ON THE TUBE

BIG BANG THEORY

Sheldon Cooper, the quirky character played by Jim Parsons, is a theoretical physicist on the wildly popular TV show, *Big Bang Theory*. The show follows the lives of Sheldon and his roommate, Leonard Hofstadter, an experimental physicist, together with their socially awkward but scientifically inclined friends, Howard and Raj. While Leonard is smitten with Penny, an aspiring actress who works as a waitress and lives in the apartment across the hall, Sheldon is more interested in advancing his own career and lording his intellectual superiority over others. He is, however, oblivious to his social deficits. Sheldon often interprets language literally, so most jokes confuse him. His emotionally flat demeanour amuses and frustrates his friends. He is so afraid of germs that he makes Leonard sign a landlord–tenant agreement ensuring that their apartment remains antiseptic. He follows strict routines that only he understands, such as knocking on a friend's door precisely three times and then uttering the person's name. On the many occasions others question his sanity, Sheldon's invariable response is that he couldn't be insane because his mother had him tested.

These unusual behaviours have led many people to speculate that Sheldon may have Asperger's syndrome, a mental illness that affects a small but growing proportion of the population. Although the show's creators dispute that Sheldon has Asperger's, Jim Parsons himself acknowledges that his inspiration for the role comes from reading and learning about the disorder.

Sheldon Cooper *in Big Bang Theory*

Sonja Flemming/CBS via Getty Images

Ironically, the question as to whether Sheldon has Asperger's may soon be moot. As predicted, DSM-5 dropped the diagnosis of Asperger's. Instead, Asperger's was combined with other diagnoses into a single illness called autism spectrum disorder (ASD). While the disappearance of Asperger's from DSM-5 will be felt most acutely by those who proudly identify themselves as "Aspies," the change raises a number of interesting issues for sociologists. What happens to a person's identity when someone previously diagnosed with Asperger's can no longer use the label? Will people who received help in the past be barred from future treatment because they no longer meet the criteria for the more narrowly defined ASD? Will people who embrace the quirkiness that their illness entails be dismayed if they are now forced to acquire the more negatively viewed label "autistic"?

These questions illustrate that diagnosis has both a medical purpose and a range of social consequences. Diagnosis can reassure the diagnosed that their condition is real. Knowing that they are not alone can give them comfort. They may gain hope that treatment exists. If the condition is chronic, diagnosis may permanently alter people's perception of who they are. More broadly, a diagnosis helps others respond appropriately when they encounter those who are ill. That is, a diagnosis may help people recognize that unusual behaviours are symptoms of the disorder. Finally, a diagnosis also makes it easier to justify the use of health care resources and other health-related services.

late as the 1940s, but by the 1950s it was cheaper—in the short run—to prescribe antibiotics to treat infections. Animal populations have also been subject to the overuse of antibiotics. Crammed in close quarters and thus susceptible to disease, livestock routinely receive low doses of antibiotics to reduce infection and enhance growth. We then eat the livestock, so microorganisms in our body become resistant to antibiotics (Sibbald, 2012). Finally, with bigger profits to be made by treating chronic conditions that turn patients into lifelong drug consumers, pharmaceutical companies have little incentive to find cures for short-lived infections. Consequently, research and development in antibiotic treatment has lagged.

These explanations suggest that social circumstances can constrain the success of modern medicine. High-tech solutions to medical problems sometimes collide with social realities, failing to produce desired outcomes.

At the same time, people are growing skeptical of the claims of modern medicine. Many people choose to challenge traditional medicine and to explore alternatives that rely less on technology and drugs. In concluding this chapter, we explore some of these challenges and alternatives.

Challenges to Traditional Medical Science

Patient Activism

By the mid-twentieth century, the dominance of medical science in Canada was virtually complete. Any departure from the dictates of scientific medicine was considered deviant. Parsons accurately described the sick role. Patients respected the authority of doctors and passively submitted to medical advice and treatment.

How things have changed in the last five or six decades! Today, it is commonplace for patients to learn about medical treatments on their own and for doctors to involve patients in deciding on the appropriate treatment options. Change in the relationship between patient and doctor is the result of people acquiring the knowledge, vocabulary, self-confidence, and political organization to challenge medical authority. Compared with people in the 1950s, we are more educated today. We have access to more medical information. Through the Internet, those who are newly diagnosed can reach out to others who have the same ailment. Advocacy groups such as the Schizophrenia Society of Canada and the Canadian Cancer Society offer support and a voice for those affected by schizophrenia and cancer. Because people who are ill have more places to turn to for advice than they did in the past, they are not completely dependent on their doctors. Therefore, doctors today exert less control than they once did when they interact with patients.

Alternative Therapies

The growing popularity of treatments outside of mainstream medicine also threatens medical dominance. "Complementary and alternative medicine," as it is often called, appears to fulfill an unmet need in health care. Providers of complementary and alternative medicine are more likely than doctors are to approach patient care holistically, which is to say they value the experience and knowledge of their clients and see themselves as working collaboratively with clients to achieve wellness in body and mind.

Between 12 percent and 17 percent of Canadians report having used complementary and alternative medicine in the past year (Harris et al., 2012). This approach to health care is not as popular as it is in some other countries, such as the United States. Nonetheless, Canadian doctors seem to be as threatened by it as American doctors are. In both countries, most doctors insist that complementary and alternative medicine not be permitted unless properly conducted experiments can demonstrate their beneficial effects. They argue that practitioners of complementary and alternative medicine are unqualified and inferior to physicians, and they generally seek to exclude them from medical decision making, even when patients request their involvement. The message Canadians seem to be getting is that complementary and alternative medicine may be acceptable when used in conjunction with conventional medicine but should never be used on its own (Clarke et al., 2010).

Notwithstanding these cautions, a substantial number of people are apparently influenced to turn to alternative healing practices when their celebrity idols do (Ernst and Pittler, 2006). For example, Catherine Zeta-Jones, Pamela Anderson, Whoopi Goldberg, and former British prime minister Tony Blair have all used homeopathic medicine. Similarly, ayurvedic medicine has been used by Madonna, Demi Moore, and supermodel Christy Turlington. The attraction of these therapies, despite the lack of scientific evidence to support them, further demonstrates that the public relies on many sources for help in treating illness, and no longer attends solely to the advice of medical doctors.

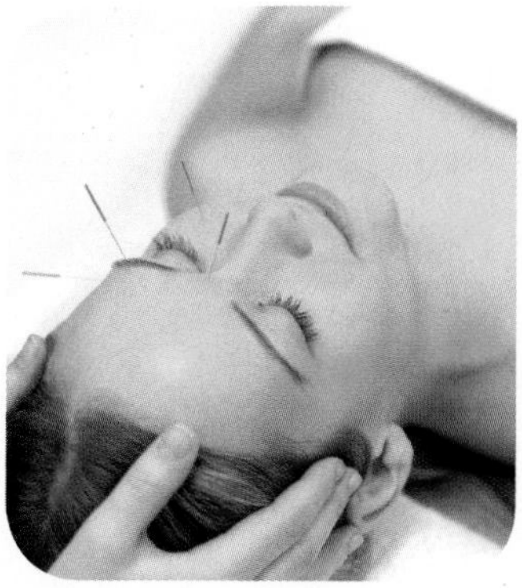

Acupuncture is one of the most widely accepted forms of alternative medicine.

TIME FOR REVIEW

- What are the advantages and disadvantages of medicalization?
- How does the crisis of the post-antibiotic era indicate that scientific medicine both solves and creates problems?
- Why do medical doctors have less authority today than they did in the past?

SUMMARY

1. What accounts for the rise in life expectancy beginning in the eighteenth century?
Several factors are responsible for the epidemiological transition (the shift from infectious disease and low life expectancy to chronic disease and high life expectancy). Although medical discovery was a contributing factor, improvements in agriculture, transportation, sanitation, and hygiene all played an earlier and more influential role.

2. Are all causes of illness and death biological?
Ultimately, yes. However, when we look beyond the immediate cause of death and instead take into account its social context, we see that social factors are often background causes of immediate causes. Specifically, health risks are lower among upper classes, rich countries, and members of privileged racial and ethnic groups than among lower classes, poor countries, and members of disadvantaged racial and ethnic groups. In some respects related to health, men are in a more advantageous position than women are.

3. How much does a health care system contribute to the health of the population?
The health care system plays a unique role in population health but its importance can be exaggerated. The health care system treats people after they have been diagnosed as ill but is not designed to prevent people from becoming sick in the first place. To the extent that the supply of doctors and the costs of health care have little influence on population health in rich countries, identifying other social factors that do matter remains an important task.

4. Why is the future of health care in Canada in jeopardy?
Health care as we know it faces two potential threats. First, conflict between the federal and provincial governments over who will pay for health care may result in provinces withdrawing from the Canada Health Act. Second, lawsuits attempting to expand a two-tier system to provide quick treatment for people who can afford it may lead the Supreme Court of Canada to declare the Canada Health Act unconstitutional.

5. How does medicine exert social control over issues relating to health and illness?
Medical doctors retain exclusive control over who is allowed to take on the sick role and what conditions qualify as disease. Their decision to label a growing number of conditions as illness is an inherent feature of medicalization, with profound consequences, both for how others respond to labelled individuals and for the self-perception of those who have been so labelled.

6. What are the limits of medical authority in contemporary society?
High-tech solutions to medical problems sometimes collide with social realities, failing to produce desired outcomes. For instance, largely economic incentives have led to the neglect of basic hygiene in hospitals, the overuse of antibiotics in human and animal populations, and the failure of pharmaceutical companies to develop new treatments for infectious diseases. These circumstances have facilitated the spread of drug-resistant germs, which may one day render ineffective existing medical treatments for infection. Compared to the past, an educated and informed public is increasingly likely to challenge medical authority by demanding greater say in their own care and greater choice in health practitioners, including healers outside mainstream medicine.

PART 5

SOCIAL CHANGE

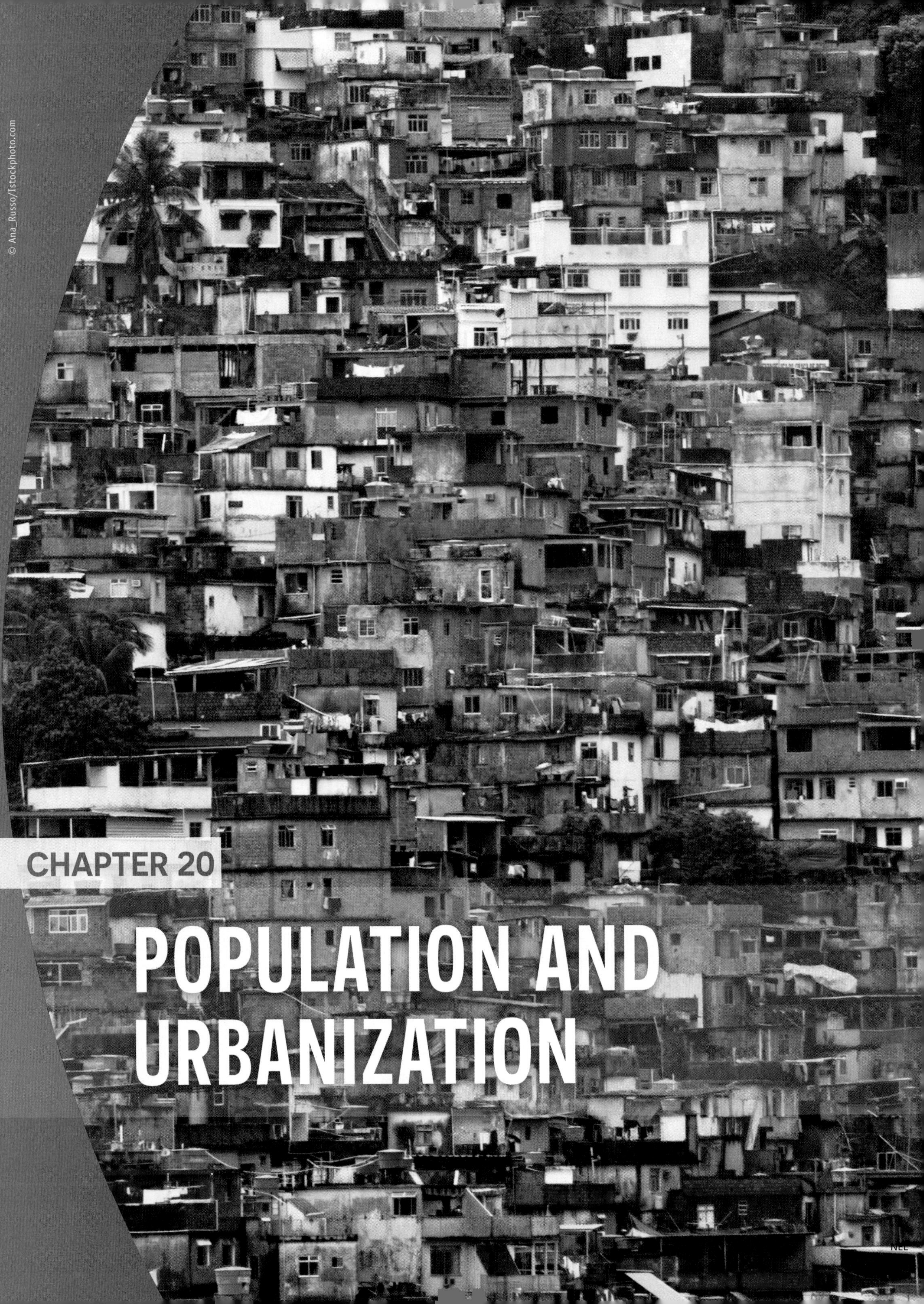

© Ana_Russo/Istockphoto.com

CHAPTER 20

POPULATION AND URBANIZATION

IN THIS CHAPTER, YOU WILL LEARN TO

- Assess the prediction that we are facing an imminent population explosion.
- Describe how social inequality and industrialization influence human population growth.
- Evaluate the impact of industrialization and other factors on urbanization.
- Contrast the strengths and weaknesses of the Chicago school's analysis of cities.
- Recognize that the spatial and cultural form of cities depends largely on the level of development of the societies in which cities are found.

POPULATION

The City of God

Rio de Janeiro, Brazil, site of the 2016 Summer Olympics, is one of the world's most beautiful cities. Along the warm, blue waters of its bays lie flawless beaches, guarded by four- and five-star hotels and pricey shops. Rising abruptly behind them is a mountain range, partly populated, partly covered by luxuriant tropical forest. The climate seems perpetually balanced between spring and summer. The inner city of Rio is a place of great wealth and beauty, devoted to commerce and the pursuit of leisure.

Rio is also a large city. With a metropolitan population of approximately 12 million people in 2013, it is the twenty-sixth biggest metropolitan area in the world. Not all of its inhabitants are well off, however. Brazil is characterized by more inequality of wealth than most other countries in the world. Slums started climbing up the hillsides of Rio about a century ago. Fed by a high birth rate and people migrating from the surrounding countryside in search of a better life, slums, such as the one shown in the photo, are now home to about 20 percent of the city's residents (Unger and Riley, 2007).

Don Klein/SuperStock

A slum in Rio

Some of Rio's slums began as government housing projects designed to segregate the poor. One such slum, as famous in its own way as the beaches of Copacabana and Ipanema, is *Cidade de Deus* (the "City of God"). Founded in the 1960s, it had become one of the most lawless and dangerous areas of Rio by the 1980s. It is a place where some families of four live on $50 a month in houses made of cardboard and discarded scraps of tin, a place where roofs leak and rats run freely. For many inhabitants, crime is survival. Drug traffickers wage a daily battle for control of territory, and children as young as six perch in key locations with walkie-talkies to feed information to their bosses on the comings and goings of passersby.

Cidade de Deus is also the name of a brilliant movie released in 2002. Based in part on the true-life story of Paulo Lins, who grew up in a slum and became a novelist, *Cidade de Deus* chronicles the gang wars of the 1970s and 1980s. It leaves us with the nearly hopeless message that, in a war without end, each generation of drug traffickers starts younger and is more ruthless than its predecessor.

Paulo Lins escaped Brazil's grinding poverty. So did Luiz Inácio Lula da Silva, Brazil's president from 2003 to 2010. Both are inspiring models of what is possible. They are also reminders that the closely related problems of population growth and urbanization are more serious now than ever. Brazil's 41 million people in 1940 multiplied to about 200 million in 2013. The country is now as urbanized as Canada, with more than 80 percent of its population living in urban areas.

This chapter tackles the closely connected problems of population growth and urbanization. We first show that population growth is a process governed less by natural laws than by social forces. We argue that these social forces are not related exclusively to industrialization, as social scientists commonly believed just a few decades ago. Instead, social inequality also plays a major role in shaping population growth.

We next turn to the problem of urbanization. Today, population growth is typically accompanied by the increasing concentration of the world's people in urban centres. As recently as 50 years ago, sociologists typically believed that cities were alienating and anomic (or normless). We argue that this view is an oversimplification. We also outline the social roots of the city's physical and cultural evolution from preindustrial to postindustrial times.

The Purcell Group/Corbis

A "population explosion"? Hong Kong is one of the most densely populated places on Earth.

The Population "Explosion"

Twelve thousand years ago, the world population was only about 6 million. Ten thousand years later, the world population had risen to 250 million, and it increased to some 760 million by 1750. After that, world population skyrocketed. The number of humans reached 1 billion in 1804 and 6 billion in 1999. In 2011, the world population reached 7 billion (see Figure 20.1). Where one person stood 12 000 years ago, there are now 1050 people; statistical projections suggest that, by 2100, that number will have increased to about 1700 people. Of those 1700, fewer than 250 will be standing in the rich countries of the world. More than 1450 of them will be in the developing countries of South America, Asia, and Africa.

Many analysts project that, after passing the 9.4 billion mark around 2150, world population will level off. But given the numbers cited previously, is it any wonder that some population analysts say we're now in the midst of a population "explosion"? Explosions are horrifying events. They cause widespread and severe damage. They are fast and unstoppable. And that is exactly the imagery some population analysts, or **demographers**, want to convey (e.g., Ehrlich and Ornstein, 2010; Figure 20.2). Many books, articles, and television programs deal with the population explosion. Images of an overflowing multitude in,

Demographers are social-scientific analysts of human population.

FIGURE 20.1
World Population, 1950–2050 (in billions, projected)

Source: Population Reference Bureau, 2013.

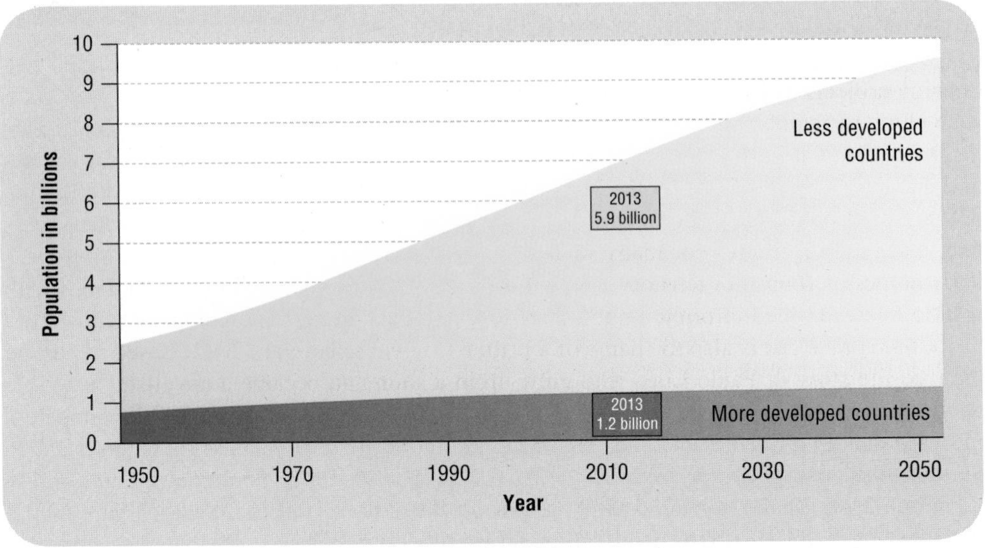

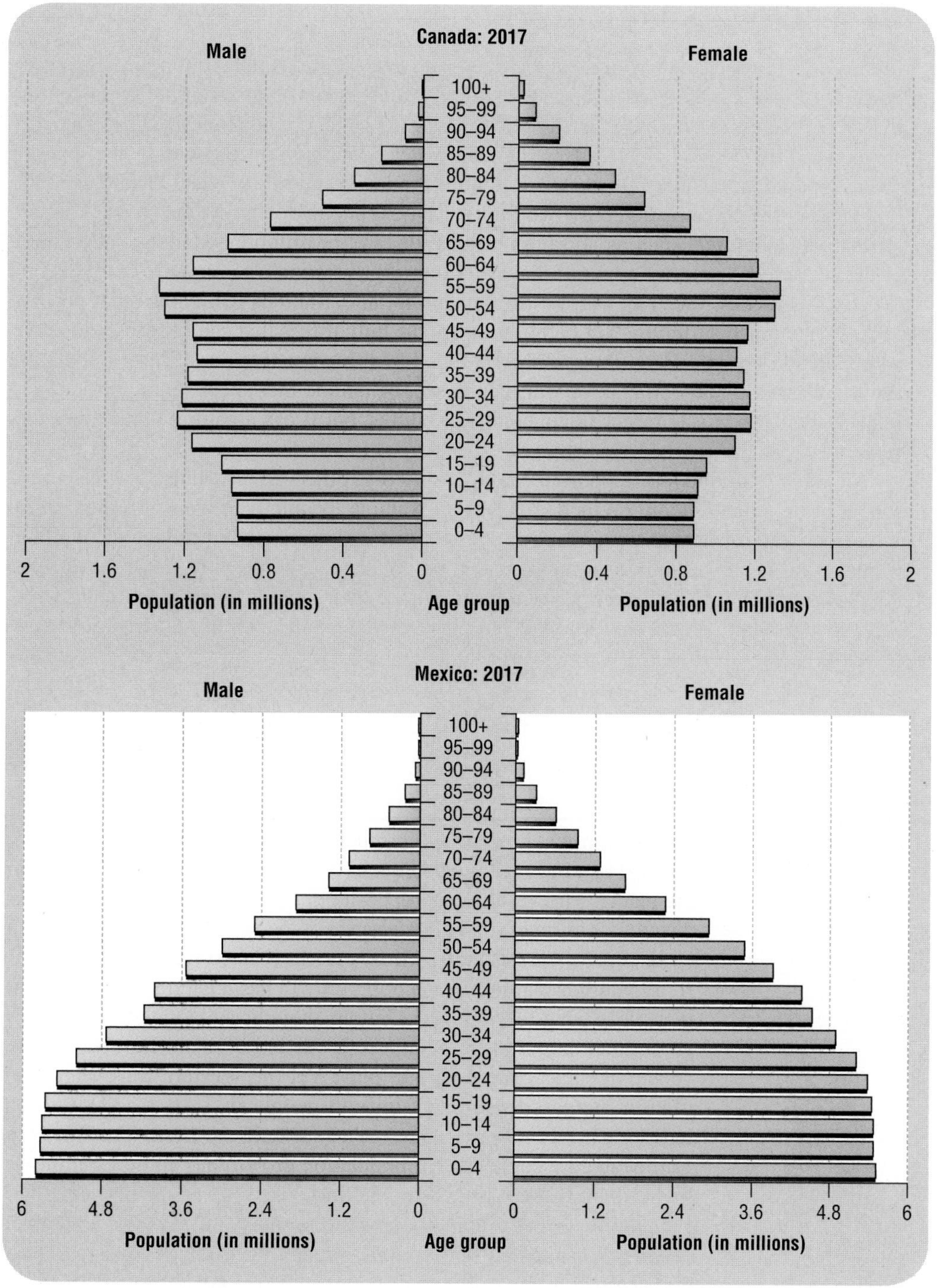

FIGURE 20.2

How Demographers Analyze Population Composition and Change

The main purpose of demography is to understand why the size, geographical distribution, and social composition of human populations change over time. The basic equation of population change is $P2 = P1 + B - D + I - E$, where $P2$ is population size at a given time, $P1$ is population size at an earlier time, B is the number of births in the interval, D is the number of deaths in the interval, I is the number of immigrants arriving in the interval, and E is the number of emigrants leaving in the interval. A basic tool for analyzing the composition of a population is the "age–sex pyramid," which shows the number of males and females in each age cohort of the population at a given time. Age–sex pyramids for Canada and Mexico are shown here for 2017. Why do you think they look so different? Compare your answer with that of the theory of the demographic transition, discussed later in this section.

Source: U.S. Census Bureau, 2014.

say, Bangladesh, Nigeria, or Brazil remain fixed in our minds. Some people are frightened enough to refer to overpopulation as catastrophic. They link it to recurrent famine, brutal ethnic warfare, and other massive and seemingly intractable problems.

If this imagery makes you feel that the world's rich countries must do something about overpopulation, you're not alone. In fact, concern about the population "bomb" is as old as the social sciences. In 1798, Thomas Robert Malthus, a British clergyman of the Anglican faith, proposed a highly influential theory of human population (Malthus, 1966 [1798]). As you will soon see, contemporary sociologists have criticized, qualified, and in part rejected his theory. But because much of the sociological study of population is, in effect, a debate with Malthus's ghost, we must confront the man's ideas squarely.

The Malthusian Trap

Malthus's theory rests on two undeniable facts and one questionable assumption. The facts: People must eat, and they are driven by a strong sexual urge. The assumption: Although the food supply increases slowly and arithmetically (1, 2, 3, 4, etc.), population size grows quickly and geometrically (1, 2, 4, 8, etc.). Based on these ideas, Malthus concluded that "the superior power of population cannot be checked without producing misery or vice" (Malthus, 1966 [1798]): 217–18). Specifically, only two forces can hold population growth in check. First are "preventive" measures, such as abortion, infanticide, and prostitution. Malthus called these "vices" because he morally opposed them and thought everyone else ought to also. Second are "positive checks," such as war, pestilence, and famine. Malthus recognized that positive checks create much suffering. Yet he felt they are the only forces that can be allowed to control population growth. Here, then, is the so-called **Malthusian trap**: a cycle of population growth followed by an outbreak of war, pestilence, or famine that keeps population growth in check. Population size might fluctuate, said Malthus, but it has a natural upper limit that Western Europe has reached.

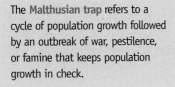

The **Malthusian trap** refers to a cycle of population growth followed by an outbreak of war, pestilence, or famine that keeps population growth in check.

Although many people supported Malthus's theory, others reviled him as a misguided prophet of doom and gloom (Winch, 1987). For example, people who wanted to help those living in poverty disagreed with Malthus. He felt such aid was counterproductive. Welfare, he said, would enable the poor to buy more food. With more food, they would have more children. And having more children would only make them poorer than they already were. Better to leave them alone, said Malthus, and thereby reduce the sum of human suffering in the world.

A Critique of Malthus

Although Malthus's ideas are in some respects compelling, events have cast doubt on several of them. Specifically:

- Since Malthus proposed his theory, technological advances have allowed rapid growth in how much food is produced for each person on the planet. This result is the opposite of the slow growth Malthus predicted. For instance, in the first decade of the twenty-first century, world production of cereals increased 19 percent (United Nations, 2010a).
- If, as Malthus claimed, population growth has a natural upper limit, it is unclear what that limit is. Malthus thought the population couldn't grow much larger in late–eighteenth-century Western Europe without "positive checks" coming into play. Yet the Western European population increased from 187 million people in 1801 to 321 million in 1900. It has now stabilized at about half a billion. The Western European case suggests that population growth has an upper limit far higher than that envisaged by Malthus.
- Population growth does not always produce misery. For example, despite Western Europe's rapid population increase over the past 200 years, it is one of the most prosperous regions in the world.
- Helping those living in poverty does not generally result in their having more children. For example, in Western Europe, social welfare policies (employment insurance, state-funded medical care, paid maternity leave, pensions, etc.) are the most generous on the planet. Yet the size of the population is quite stable. In fact, as you will learn, some forms of social welfare produce rapid and large *decreases* in population growth, especially in poor, developing countries.
- Although the human sexual urge is as strong as Malthus thought, people have developed contraceptive devices and techniques to control the consequences of their sexual activity (World Health Organization, 2007). Thus, sexual activity does not necessarily lead to childbirth.

Scala/Art Resource, NY

Albrecht Dürer's *The Four Horsemen of the Apocalypse* (woodcut, 1498). According to Malthus, only war, pestilence, and famine could keep population growth in check.

BOX 20.1

SOCIOLOGY AT THE MOVIES

WORLD WAR Z

Soon after Gerry Lane, his wife, Karin, and their two daughters get stuck in traffic in downtown Philadelphia, all hell breaks loose. Terrified people run for their lives, a garbage truck plows through a row of cars, something explodes. Then you see them: the undead, the post-humans, the mobile deceased, the differently animated—in short, brain-eating zombies. They are everywhere. And after they bite, their victims become zombified, too.

Lane, played by Brad Pitt in *World War Z*, is a former UN troubleshooter, and his planet-saving skills are in high demand as the world tries to figure out the cause and cure of the zombie problem. To that end, Lane scours the world to find the first victim, and as he does so, we are horrified to realize two things. First, the zombies are winning, chomping their way through entire cities and countries. Second, they represent what was described in *Ghostbusters* three decades earlier as "a disaster of biblical proportions ... The dead rising from the grave! ... Mass hysteria!" In short, the zombies are a metaphor for one of our biggest fears: a population explosion that entirely depletes the world's life-sustaining resources.

The Kobal Collection at Art Resource, NY

Zombies: a metaphor for overpopulation

If this interpretation seems far-fetched, you might want to consider what Marc Forster, the director of *World War Z*, had to say about the meaning of his movie in a 2013 interview:

Population is growing and in 2050, there will be around ten billion people on the planet. So overpopulation becomes more and more of a concern with less and less resources, and if you're looking all around in regards to politics and economics, it seems like we are all going after the last resources. There is almost a mindlessness to it and I thought that would be a great metaphor (Flores, 2013).

Forster, a neo-Malthusian, is not alone in his fear that our species could be extinguishing itself because of mindless overpopulation. Nor is *World War Z* alone in expressing this fear. From wildly popular TV shows like *The Walking Dead* to blockbuster video games like *Resident Evil*, the mass media feed us a seemingly endless supply of zombies. We are only too eager to consume them, perhaps as an act of psychic self-defence, a way of making light of our deep anxieties about the future. In this context, the sociological view that the limits to growth are as much social as they are natural and therefore avoidable rather than inevitable may be, at the very least, therapeutic. At best, it may be the basis for valuable public policy, perhaps even superior to relying on a hero like Gerry Lane to save the planet.

The developments listed here all point to one conclusion. Malthus's pessimism was overstated. Human ingenuity seems to have enabled us to wriggle free of the Malthusian trap, at least for the time being.

We are not, however, home free. Today, many people have voiced renewed fears that industrialization and population growth are putting severe strains on the planet's resources. As established by the online chapter that accompanies this book, Chapter 22, Technology and the Global Environment, we must take these fears seriously. It is encouraging to learn that the limits to growth are as much social as they are natural, and therefore avoidable rather than inevitable. However, we will see that our ability to avoid the Malthusian trap in the twenty-first century requires all the ingenuity and self-sacrifice we can muster (see Box 20.1). For the time being, however, let us consider the second main theory of population growth, the theory of the demographic transition.

Demographic Transition Theory

Demographic transition theory explains how changes in fertility and mortality affected population growth from preindustrial to postindustrial times.

According to **demographic transition theory**, the main factors underlying population dynamics are industrialization and the growth of modern cultural values (Chesnais, 1992 [1986]; Coale, 1974; Notestein, 1945). This theory is based on the observation that the European population developed in four distinct stages (see Figure 20.3).

FIGURE 20.3
Democratic Transition Theory

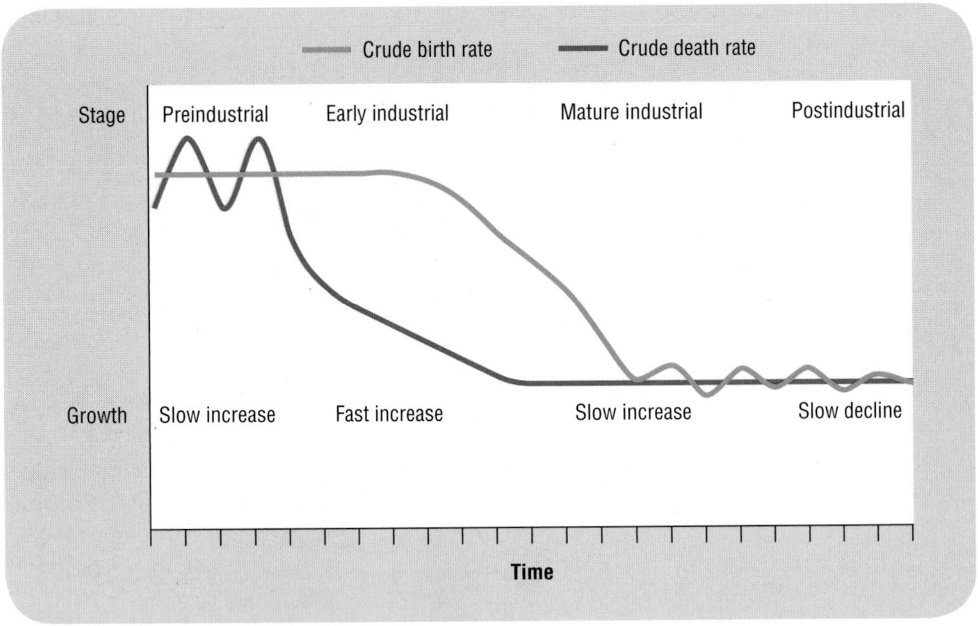

The Preindustrial Period

The **crude death rate** is the annual number of deaths per 1000 people in a population.

The **crude birth rate** is the annual number of live births per 1000 people in a population.

In the first, preindustrial stage of growth, a large proportion of the population died every year from inadequate nutrition, poor hygiene, and uncontrollable disease. In other words, the **crude death rate** was high. The crude death rate is the annual number of deaths (or "mortality") per 1000 people in a population. During this period, the **crude birth rate** was also high. The crude birth rate is the annual number of live births per 1000 people in a population. In the preindustrial era, most people wanted to have as many children as possible. That was partly because relatively few children survived till adulthood. In addition, children were considered a valuable source of agricultural labour and a form of old age security in a society consisting largely of peasants and lacking anything resembling a modern welfare state.

The Early Industrial Period

The second stage of European population growth was the early industrial, or transition, period. At this stage, the crude death rate dropped. People's life expectancy, or average lifespan, increased because economic growth led to improved nutrition and hygiene. However, the crude birth rate remained high. With people living longer and women having nearly as many babies as in the preindustrial era, the population grew rapidly. Malthus lived during this period of rapid population growth, which, in part, may account for his alarm.

The Mature Industrial Period

Cultural lag refers to the gap that occurs between rapid technological change and slower changes in norms and values.

The third stage of European population growth was the mature industrial period. At this stage, the crude death rate continued to fall. The crude birth rate fell even more dramatically. It declined because economic growth eventually changed people's traditional beliefs about the value of having many children. Having many children made sense in an agricultural society, where children were a valuable economic resource. In contrast, children were more of an economic burden in an industrial society since breadwinners were employed outside the home and children contributed little, if anything, to the economic welfare of the family. Note, however, that the crude birth rate took longer to decline than the crude death rate did. This phenomenon is called **cultural lag** and refers to conditions in which people's values change more slowly than their technologies do. For example, installing a sewer system or a water purification plant can lower the crude death rate faster than people can change their minds about something as fundamental as how many children to have. Eventually, however, the technologies and outlooks that accompanied modernity led people to postpone getting married and to choose to use contraceptives and other birth-control methods. As a result, population stabilized during the mature industrial period. This effect demonstrates the validity of the demographer's favourite saying: "Economic development is the best contraceptive."

The Postindustrial Period

In the last two decades, the total fertility rate has continued to fall. (Recall our definition of the total fertility rate in Chapter 15, Families: the average number of children that would be born to a woman if she lived to the end of her childbearing years and experienced the same age-specific fertility rates observed in a given year.) In fact, in some countries, the total fertility rate fell below the **replacement level**. The replacement level is the number of children each woman must have on average for population size to remain stable. Ignoring any inflow of settlers from other countries (**immigration,** or in-migration) and any outflow to other countries (**emigration**, or out-migration), the replacement level is 2.1. In other words, on average, each woman must give birth to slightly more than the two children needed to replace herself and her mate. Slightly more than two children are required because some children die before they reach reproductive age.

The **replacement level** is the number of children that each woman must have on average for population size to remain stable, ignoring migration. The replacement level is 2.1.

Immigration, or in-migration, is the inflow of people into one country from one or more other countries and their settlement in the destination country.

Emigration, or out-migration, is the outflow of people from one country and their settlement in one or more other countries.

By the 1990s, some Europeans were worrying about declining fertility and its possible effects on population size. As you can see in Table 20.1, Europe as a whole has a fertility rate below the replacement level. In fact, about a third of the world's countries, including Canada, China, and South Korea, now have a fertility level below the replacement level, and the number of such countries is growing. Because of the proliferation of low-fertility societies, some scholars suggest that we have now entered a fourth, postindustrial stage of population development. In this fourth stage of the demographic transition, the number of deaths per year exceeds the number of births (Powell and Leedham, 2009).

As outlined earlier, the demographic transition theory provides a rough picture of how industrialization affects population growth. However, research has revealed several inconsistencies in the theory. Most of the inconsistencies are due to the theory placing too much emphasis on industrialization as the main force underlying population growth (Coale

TABLE 20.1
Total Fertility Rate by Region and Selected Countries, 2013

Source: Population Reference Bureau, 2013.

Niger	7.6
Chad	7.0
Somalia	6.8
Africa	4.8
India	2.4
Asia	2.2
South America	2.1
United States	1.9
Sweden	1.9
Canada	1.6
Europe	1.6
China	1.5
Poland	1.3
South Korea	1.3
Bosnia-Herzegovina	1.2

and Watkins, 1986). For example, demographers have found that reductions in fertility sometimes occur when standards of living stagnate or decline, not just when they improve through industrialization. Thus, in Russia and some developing countries today, declining living standards have led to deterioration in general health and a subsequent decline in fertility. Because of such findings, many scholars have concluded that an adequate theory of population growth must pay more attention to social factors other than industrialization and, in particular, to the role of social inequality.

Population and Social Inequality

Karl Marx

One of Malthus's staunchest intellectual opponents was Karl Marx. Marx argued that the problem of overpopulation is specific to capitalism (Meek, 1971). In his view, overpopulation is not a problem of too many people. Rather, it is a problem of too much poverty. Do away with the exploitation of workers by their employers, said Marx, and poverty will disappear. If a society is rich enough to eliminate poverty, then by definition its population is not too large. In Marx's view, by eliminating poverty, we also solve the problem of overpopulation.

Marx's analysis makes it seem that capitalism can never generate enough prosperity to solve the overpopulation problem. He was evidently wrong. Today, overpopulation is not a serious problem in Canada, the United States, Japan, or Germany.[1] It *is* a problem in most of Africa, where capitalism is weakly developed and the level of social inequality is much higher than in postindustrial societies. Still, a core idea in Marx's analysis of the overpopulation problem rings true. As some contemporary demographers argue, social inequality is an important cause of overpopulation. We now illustrate this argument by first considering how gender inequality influences population growth. Then we discuss the effects of class inequality on population growth.

Gender Inequality and Overpopulation

The effect of gender inequality on population growth is well illustrated by the case of Kerala, a state in India with more than 33 million people. The most recent census shows Kerala's total fertility rate at 1.7, about two-thirds of India's national rate and below the replacement level of 2.1. How did Kerala achieve this remarkable feat? Is it a highly industrialized oasis in the midst of a semi-industrialized country, as we might expect, given the arguments of demographic transition theory? No. Although Kerala is no longer one of the poorest states in India, it is not highly industrialized. Then has the government of Kerala strictly enforced a state childbirth policy similar to China's? Again, no. Since 1979, the Chinese government has strongly penalized families with more than one child (although it announced a relaxation of the policy at the end of 2013). It even allows abortion 8.5 months into a pregnancy. Consequently, China had a total fertility rate of 1.5 in 2013. In contrast, the government of Kerala provides ready access to contraceptive services but the decision to have children remains a strictly private affair (Vithayathil, 2013).

The women of Kerala have achieved a low total fertility rate partly because, historically, their family system was matrilineal (Nair, 2010). Unlike other Indian states, the rights of inheritance in Kerala were traditionally passed to female offspring, giving Keralan women a greater voice in domestic affairs and in public life than was the case elsewhere in the country (Jeffrey, 2004). In such an environment, females are considered to be assets to their families. Girls are expected to be educated, and it is acceptable for women to engage in paid employment. Therefore, among all women in India, Keralan women enjoy the highest literacy rate, the highest labour force participation rate, and the highest rate of political participation. Given their desire for education, work, and political involvement, Keralan women marry at a much later age than do women in the rest of India and, once married, use contraception to prevent unwanted births more often than other married Indian women (George, 2010). Later

BOX 20.2

SOCIAL POLICY: WHAT DO YOU THINK?

HOW CAN WE FIND 100 MILLION MISSING WOMEN?

Agricultural societies need many children to help with farming, but industrial societies require fewer children. Because many developing countries are industrializing, the rate of world population growth is falling. Another important reason for the declining growth rate is the improving economic status and education of women. Once women become literate and enter the nonagricultural paid labour force, they quickly recognize the advantages of having few children. The birth rate plummets. In many developing countries, that is just what is happening.

However, in other respects, the position of women is less satisfactory. We can see this by examining the **sex ratio**, the ratio of men to 100 women. In most developed countries, women outnumber men. However, in some less developed countries, the picture is reversed. For instance, in India and China, there are 106 men for every 100 women. What accounts for differences in the sex ratio across countries?

The sex ratio favours men where women have less access to health services, medicine, and adequate nutrition (Borooah and Dubey, 2009; Dyson, 2012). These factors are associated with high female mortality. Another factor is significant in China, India, South Korea, and some other Asian countries. Widely available ultrasound scans make it possible for families to know the sex of the fetus, and many parents so strongly prefer sons over daughters they abort female fetuses (Brym, 2014b). Globally, about 100 million women are "missing" in the sense that they would be alive today if different circumstances had allowed the world sex ratio to fall to the level of the developed countries.

The question of how to eliminate sex-selective abortions is complex. You might think that improving economic conditions would be a viable solution. However, economic factors may contribute to the problem. In some affluent parts of Asia, such as South Korea, sex-selective abortions are common. India's highest sex ratio can be found in the wealthy northern states of Punjab and Haryana (Guilmoto, 2012). The high sex ratio is partly explained by the high cost of ultrasound scans, which only the middle-class and the rich can afford. In addition, to the extent that improved economic status encourages women to have fewer children, the pressure to have a male child may be magnified. In the past, a woman would bear children until she gave birth to a boy. Today, few women think this way.

Laws outlawing the use of ultrasound technology for determining the sex of the fetus have proved useless. India banned the practice in 1994, but it continues unabated. China also outlawed sex-determining ultrasounds and sex-selective abortions—but to no avail.

This situation leaves wide open the question of how reformers might rectify the situation. In the meantime, a strong preference for sons over daughters adds millions to the number of missing women every year. What other solutions might make a difference? How can such deeply ingrained cultural norms be changed?

age at marriage and use of contraceptive methods drive down the number of children that a woman has in her lifetime. In general, where

> women tend to have more power, [the society has] low rather than high mortality and fertility. Education and employment, for example, often accord women wider power and influence, which enhance their status. But attending school and working often compete with childbearing and child rearing. Women may choose to have fewer children in order to hold a job or increase their education. (Riley, 1997)

The **sex ratio** is the ratio of men to 100 women in a given society at a given time.

Unfortunately, in many of the world's less developed regions, women fare less well than they do in Kerala (see Box 20.2).

Class Inequality and Overpopulation

Unravelling the Keralan mystery is an instructive exercise. It establishes that population growth depends not just on a society's level of industrialization but also on its level of gender inequality. *Class* inequality influences population growth, too. We turn to the South Korean case to illustrate this point.

In 1960, South Korea had a total fertility rate of 6.0. Knowledge of this high fertility rate prompted one American official to remark that "if these Koreans don't stop overbreeding, we may have the choice of supporting them forever, watching them starve to death, or washing our hands of the problem" (quoted in Lie, 1998: 21). Yet by 1989, South Korea's total fertility rate had dropped to a mere 1.6. By 2013 it fell to 1.3. Why? The first chapter in this story involves land reform, not industrialization. The government took land from big landowners and gave it to small farmers. Consequently, small farmers' standard of living improved, which eliminated a major reason for high fertility. Once economic uncertainty decreased, so did the need both for child labour and for adult offspring to support their elderly. Soon, the total fertility rate began to fall. Subsequent declines in the South Korean total fertility rate were due to industrialization, urbanization, and the higher educational attainment of the population. But a decline in class inequality in the countryside first set the process in motion.

The reverse is also true. Increasing social inequality can lead to overpopulation, war, and famine. For example, in the 1960s, the governments of El Salvador and Honduras encouraged the expansion of commercial agriculture and the acquisition of large farms by wealthy landowners. The landowners drove peasants off the land. The peasants migrated to the cities, where they hoped to find employment and a better life. Instead, they often found squalor, unemployment, and disease. Suddenly, two countries with a combined population of fewer than five million people had a big "overpopulation" problem. Competition for land increased and contributed to rising tensions. This conflict eventually led to the outbreak of war between El Salvador and Honduras in 1969 (Durham, 1979).

Similarly, economic inequality helps to create famines. As Nobel Prize–winning economist Amartya Sen notes, "Famine is the characteristic of some people not *having* enough food to eat. It is not the characteristic of there not *being* enough food to eat" (Sen, 1981: 1; our emphasis). Sen's distinction is crucial, as his analysis of several famines shows. Sen found that, in some cases, although food supplies did decline, enough food was available to keep the stricken population fed. However, suppliers and speculators took advantage of the short supply. They hoarded grain, which increased prices beyond the means of most people. In other cases, the food supply did not decline at all. Food was simply withheld for political reasons—that is, to subdue a population, or because the authorities decided that certain people were not entitled to receive it. For example, in 1932–33, Stalin instigated a famine in Ukraine that killed millions. His purpose: to bring the Ukrainian people to their knees and force them to give up their privately owned farms and join state-owned, collective farms. The source of famine, Sen concludes, is not underproduction or overpopulation but inequality of access to food (Drèze and Sen, 1989).

TIME FOR REVIEW

- According to Malthus, what factors prevent population explosions?
- In what ways was Malthus's predictions about the causes of overpopulation correct? In what ways were they incorrect?
- According to demographic transition theory, what factors are responsible for the trend toward low birth and death rates?
- How do class and gender inequalities influence population growth?

URBANIZATION

We have seen that overpopulation remains a troubling problem in much of the world because of lack of industrialization and too much gender and class inequality. We may now add that overpopulation is in substantial measure an *urban* problem. Driven by lack of economic opportunity in the countryside, political unrest, and other factors, many millions of people flock to big cities in the world's poor countries every year. Thus, most of the fastest-growing cities in the world today are in semi-industrialized countries. As Table 20.2 shows, in 1900, 9 of the 10 biggest cities in the world were in industrialized Europe and the United States. By 2025, in contrast, 7 of the world's 10 biggest cities will be in Asia, 1 will be in Mexico, and 1 in Brazil.

TABLE 20.2
World's 10 Largest Metropolitan Areas, 1900 and 2025, Projected (in Millions)

1900		2025	
London, England	6.5	Tokyo, Japan	38.7
New York, United States	4.2	Delhi, India	32.9
Paris, France	3.3	Shanghai, China	28.4
Berlin, Germany	2.4	Mumbai, India	26.6
Chicago, United States	1.7	Mexico City, Mexico	24.6
Vienna, Austria	1.6	New York-Newark, U.S.	23.6
Tokyo, Japan	1.5	São Paulo, Brazil	23.2
Saint Petersburg, Russia	1.4	Dhaka, Bangladesh	22.9
Philadelphia, United States	1.4	Beijing, China	22.6
Manchester, England	1.3	Karachi, Pakistan	20.2

Sources: Department of Geography, Slippery Rock University, 1997, 2003. United Nations, 2012. *World Urbanization Prospects, The 2011 Revision*. New York: Author. (page 23)

Urbanization is taking place in the world's rich countries too. According to the 2011 census, more than 1 in 3 Canadians resides in the three largest cities: Toronto, Montreal, and Vancouver (Statistics Canada, 2012e). In North America as a whole, the urban population is expected to increase to 84 percent of the total population by 2030. In Africa and Asia, however, the urban population is expected to increase much faster to 62 percent of the total population by 2050 (United Nations, 2011).

Marcus Mok/Getty Images

Shanghai during one of its frequent smog alerts.

From the Preindustrial to the Industrial City

To a degree, urbanization results from industrialization. Many great cities of the world grew up along with the modern factory, which drew hundreds of millions of people out of the countryside and transformed them into urban, industrial workers. Industrialization is not, however, the whole story behind the growth of cities. As we have just seen, the connection between industrialization and urbanization is weak in the world's less developed countries today. Moreover, cities first emerged in Syria, Mesopotamia, and Egypt 5000 or 6000 years ago, long before the growth of the modern factory. These early cities served as centres of religious worship and political administration. Similarly, it was not industry but international trade in spices, gold, cloth, and other precious goods that stimulated the growth of cities in preindustrial Europe and the Middle East. Thus, the correlation between urbanization and industrialization is far from perfect (Bairoch, 1988 [1985]; Jacobs, 1969; Mumford, 1961; Sjöberg, 1960).

Preindustrial cities differed from those that developed in the industrial era in several ways. Preindustrial cities were typically smaller, less densely populated, built within protective walls, and organized around a central square and places of worship. The industrial cities that began to emerge at the end of the eighteenth century were more dynamic and complex social systems. Accompanying their growth were a host of social problems, including poverty, pollution, and crime. The complexity, dynamism, and social problems of the industrial city were all evident in Chicago at the turn of the twentieth century. Not surprisingly, therefore, it was at the University of Chicago that modern urban sociology was born.

The **Chicago school** founded urban sociology in the United States in the first decades of the twentieth century.

The Chicago School and the Industrial City

From the 1910s to the 1930s, the members of the **Chicago school** of sociology distinguished themselves by their vividly detailed descriptions and analyses of urban life, backed up by careful in-depth interviews, surveys, and maps showing the distribution of various features of the social landscape, all expressed in plain yet evocative language (Lindner, 1996 [1990]). Three of its leading members, Robert Park, Ernest Burgess, and Roderick McKenzie, proposed a theory of **human ecology** to illuminate the process of urbanization (Park, Burgess, and McKenzie, 1967 [1925]). Borrowing from biology and ecology,

Human ecology is a theoretical approach to urban sociology that borrows ideas from biology and ecology to highlight the links between the physical and social dimensions of cities and identify the dynamics and patterns of urban growth.

Jonathan S. Blair/National Geographic/Getty Images

Carcassonne, France, a medieval walled city

Differentiation in the theory of human ecology refers to the process by which urban populations and their activities become more complex and heterogeneous over time.

In the theory of human ecology, **competition** refers to the struggle by different groups for optimal locations in which to reside and set up their businesses.

Ecological succession in the theory of human ecology refers to the process by which a distinct urban group moves from one area to another and a second group comes in to replace the group that has moved out.

Urbanism is a way of life that, according to Louis Wirth, involves increased tolerance but also emotional withdrawal and specialized, impersonal, and self-interested interaction.

the theory highlights the links between the physical and social dimensions of cities and identifies the dynamics and patterns of urban growth.

The theory of human ecology, as applied to urban settings, holds that cities grow in ever-expanding concentric circles. It is sometimes called the "concentric zone model" of the city. Three social processes animate this growth (Hawley, 1950). **Differentiation** refers to the process by which urban populations and their activities become more complex and heterogeneous over time. For instance, a small town may have a diner, a pizza parlour, and a Chinese restaurant. But if that small town grows into a city, it will likely boast a variety of ethnic restaurants reflecting its more heterogeneous population. Moreover, in a city, members of different ethnic and racial groups and socioeconomic classes may vie with one another for dominance in particular areas. Businesses may also try to push residents out of certain areas to establish commercial zones. When this happens, people are engaging in **competition**, an ongoing struggle by different groups to inhabit optimal locations. Finally, **ecological succession** takes place when a distinct group of people moves from one area to another, and a second group moves into the old area to replace the first group. For example, a recurrent pattern of ecological succession involves members of the middle class moving to the suburbs, with working-class and poor immigrants moving into the inner city. In Chicago in the 1920s, differentiation, competition, and ecological succession resulted in the zonal pattern illustrated by Figure 20.4.

For members of the Chicago school, the city was more than just a collection of socially segregated buildings, places, and people. It also involved a way of life they called **urbanism**. They defined urbanism as "a state of mind, a body of customs[,] … traditions, … attitudes and sentiments" specifically linked to city dwelling (Park, Burgess, and McKenzie, 1967 [1925]: 1). Louis Wirth (1938) developed this theme. According to Wirth, rural life involves frequent face-to-face interaction among a few people. Most of these people are familiar with one another, share common values and a collective identity, and strongly respect traditional ways of doing things. Urban life, in contrast, involves the absence of community and of close personal relationships. Extensive exposure to many socially different people leads city dwellers to become more tolerant than rural folk are. However, urban dwellers also withdraw emotionally and reduce the intensity of their social interaction with others. In Wirth's view, interaction in cities is therefore superficial, impersonal, and focused on specific goals. People become more individualistic. Weak social control leads to a high incidence of deviance and crime.

After Chicago: A Critique

The Chicago school dominated North American urban sociology for decades and still inspires much interesting research (Sampson, 2012; Wilson and Taub, 2006). However, three major criticisms of this approach to understanding city growth have gained credibility over the years.

One criticism focuses on Wirth's characterization of the "urban way of life." Research shows that social isolation, emotional withdrawal, stress, and other problems may be just as common in rural as in urban areas (Crothers, 1979; Webb and Collette, 1977, 1979). After all, in a small community a person may not be able to find anyone with whom to share a particular interest or passion. Moreover, farm work can be every bit as stressful as work on an assembly line.

Research conducted in Toronto and other North American cities also shows that urban life is less impersonal, anomic, and devoid of community than the Chicago sociologists made it appear. True, newcomers (of whom there were admittedly many in Chicago in the

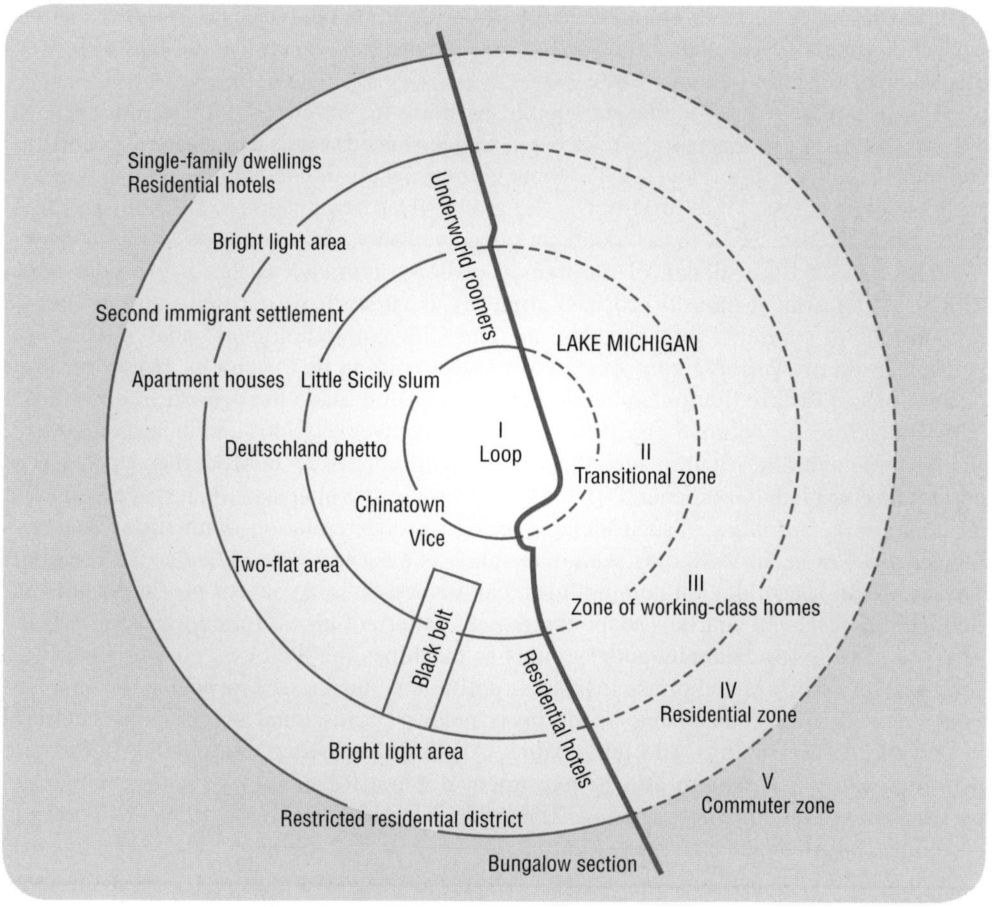

FIGURE 20.4

The Concentric Zone Model of Chicago, about 1920

Source: From "The Growth of the City: An Introduction to a Research Project," Ernest W. Burgess, pp. 47–62, in *The City* by Robert E. Park et al. Copyright © 1967 University of Chicago Press. Used with permission.

1920s) may find city life bewildering if not frightening. Neighbourliness and friendliness to strangers are less common in cities than in small communities (Fischer, 1981). However, even in the largest cities, most residents create social networks and subcultures that serve functions similar to those performed by the small community. Forming the bases of these urban networks and subcultures are friendship, kinship, ethnic and racial ties, and work and leisure relationships (Fischer, 1984 [1976]; Jacobs, 1961; Wellman, 1979). Consider in this context that the United Nations identifies Toronto as among the most multicultural cities in the world. Cities, it turns out, are clusters of many different communities, prompting one sociologist to refer to city dwellers as "urban villagers" (Gans, 1962).

A second problem with the Chicago school's approach concerns the applicability of the concentric zone model to other times and places. Canada, for example, has managed to avoid the American "ghetto" syndrome. Canada lacks the deep and enduring poverty that characterizes so many central-city neighbourhoods in the United States (Janigan, 2002: 26). True, the total urban population is growing more slowly than is the urban population living in poverty, and Canada's urban population includes many immigrants and Aboriginal people. Research also shows that in the last few decades, socioeconomic and ethnic residential segregation has increased in Canada's large cities, leading one urban sociologist to conclude that "[t]he socioeconomic status of urbanites increases directly with the distance of their residence from the city centre" (Gillis, 1995: 13.17; see also Kazemipur and Halli, 2000). Still, the core areas of most Canadian cities remain economically vibrant and socially viable, and many such areas boast desirable and expensive housing. We conclude that the concentric zone theory has limited applicability to Canada.

Evidence from preindustrial cities supports the view that the concentric zone model was most applicable to American industrial cities in the first quarter of the twentieth century. In preindustrial cities, slums were more likely to be found on the outskirts. Wealthy districts were more likely to be found in the city core. Commercial and residential buildings were often not segregated (Sjöberg, 1960).

Finally, we note that after the automobile became a major means of transportation, some cities expanded not in concentric circles but in wedge-shaped sectors along natural boundaries and transportation routes (Hoyt, 1939). Other cities grew up around not one but many nuclei, each attracting similar kinds of activities and groups (Harris and Ullman, 1945; Figure 20.5). All of this evidence serves to cast doubt on the universality of the concentric zone theory.

The third main criticism of the human ecology approach is that it presents urban growth as an almost natural process, slighting its historical, political, and economic foundations in capitalist industrialization. The Chicago sociologists' analysis of competition in the transitional zone came closest to avoiding this problem. However, their discussions of differentiation and ecological succession made the growth of cities seem more like a force of nature than a process rooted in power relations and the urge to profit.

The **new urban sociology** emerged in the 1970s and stressed that city growth is a process rooted in power relations and the urge to profit.

The so-called **new urban sociology**, heavily influenced by conflict theory, sought to correct this problem (Gottdiener, 2010). For new urban sociologists, urban space is not just an arena for the unfolding of such social processes as differentiation, competition, and ecological succession. Instead, they see urban space as a set of *commodified* social relations. That is, urban space, like all commodities, can be bought and sold for profit. As a result, political interests and conflicts shape the growth pattern of cities. John Logan and Harvey Molotch (1987), for example, portray cities as machines fuelled by a "growth coalition." This growth coalition comprises investors, politicians, businesses, property owners, real estate developers, urban planners, the mass media, professional sports teams, cultural institutions, labour unions, and universities. All these partners try to obtain government subsidies and tax breaks to attract investment dollars. Reversing the pattern identified by the Chicago sociologists, this investment has been used since the 1950s to redevelop decaying downtown areas in many North American cities. In Canada, this approach is evident in the development of Harbourfront Centre, a four-hectare (10-acre) property along Toronto's Lake Ontario that mixes recreational, cultural, residential, and commercial elements. It is also notable in the re-invigoration of Gastown and the former Expo '86 lands in Vancouver, Quebec City's thriving Lower Town, the inviting green spaces and markets at The Forks in downtown Winnipeg, and Hamilton's waterfront park reclaimed from former industrial lands.

According to Logan and Molotch (1987), members of the growth coalition present redevelopment as a public good that benefits everyone. This ideology tends to silence critics, prevent discussion of alternative ideas and plans, and veil the question of who benefits and who does not. In reality, the benefits of redevelopment are often unevenly distributed. Most redevelopments are "pockets of revitalization surrounded by areas of extreme poverty" (Hannigan, 1998a: 53). That is, local residents often enjoy few if any direct benefits from

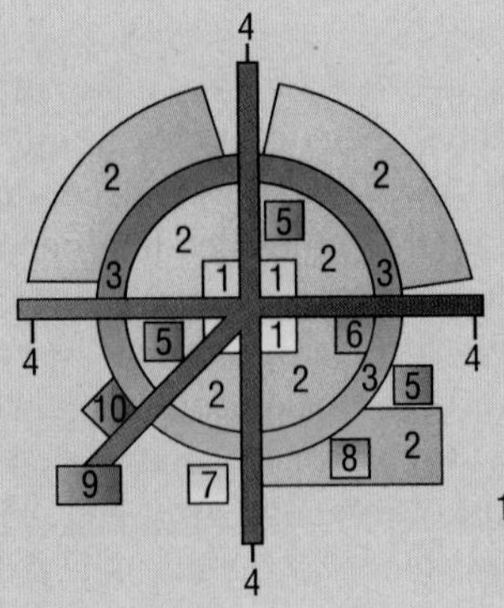

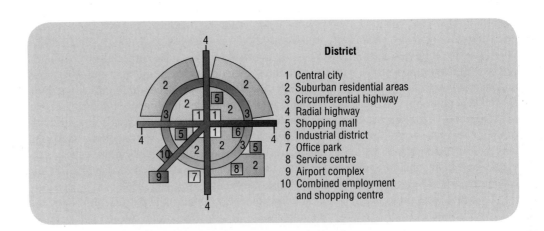

FIGURE 20.5
The Peripheral Model of Cities: An Alternative to the Concentric Zone Model

Source: Harris (1997).

Bob Brooks/Nova Scotia Archives and Records Management

Africville relocation meeting, Seaview Baptist Church, circa 1962. Halifax's Africville relocation project illustrates how poor urban residents typically have little say over redevelopment plans (Clairmont and Magill, 1999). Africville was settled around 1850 by blacks fleeing slavery in the United States, but it suffered drastic decline after World War I. In 1963, against the wishes of its residents, the Halifax municipal government began to phase Africville out of existence. The city promised generous financial compensation and alternative housing, but some residents still refused to move. They were threatened with the expropriation of their property and eventually the community was bulldozed.

redevelopment. Indirectly, they may suffer when budgets for public schooling, public transportation, and other amenities are cut to help pay for development subsidies and tax breaks. The growth coalition is not, however, all-powerful. Community activism often targets local governments and corporations that seek unrestricted growth. Sometimes activists meet with success (Castells, 1983). Yet for the past 50 years, the growth coalition has managed to reshape the face of North American cities, more or less in its own image.

The Corporate City

Through the efforts of the growth coalition, the North American industrial city, typified by Chicago in the 1920s, gave way after World War II to the **corporate city**. Sociologist John Hannigan defines the corporate city as "a vehicle for capital accumulation—that is, … a money-making machine" (Hannigan, 1998b: 345).

The **corporate city** refers to the growing post–World War II perception and organization of the North American city as a vehicle for capital accumulation.

In the suburbs, urbanized areas outside the political boundaries of cities, developers built millions of single-family detached homes for the corporate middle class. These homes boasted large backyards and a car or two in every garage. A new way of life developed, which sociologists dubbed **suburbanism**. Every bit as distinctive as urbanism, suburbanism organized life mainly around the needs of children. It also involved higher levels of conformity and sociability than did life in the central city (Fava, 1956). Suburbanism became fully entrenched as developers built shopping malls to serve the needs of suburbanites. Malls reduced the need to travel to the central city for consumer goods.

Suburbanism is a way of life outside city centres that is organized mainly around the needs of children and involves higher levels of conformity and sociability than life in the central city.

The suburbs were at first restricted to the well-to-do. However, following World War II, brisk economic growth and government assistance to veterans put the suburban lifestyle within the reach of middle-class Canadians. Also stimulating mushroom-like suburban growth were extensive road-building programs, the falling price of automobiles, and the baby boom that began in 1946.

Because of the expansion of the suburbs, urban sociologists today often focus their attention not on cities but on **census metropolitan areas (CMAs)**, a term coined by Statistics Canada (see Table 20.3). Each CMA includes a large urban area (known as the urban core) along with adjacent urban and rural areas (urban and rural "fringes") that are highly integrated into the urban core. The Statistics Canada definition of a CMA also specifies that it has an urban core population of at least 100 000 at the time of the most recent census. As of the 2011 Census, Canada had 33 CMAs (Statistics Canada, 2012c).

Census metropolitan areas (CMA) include a large urban area (known as the urban core) along with adjacent urban and rural areas (urban and rural "fringes") that are highly integrated into the urban core.

TABLE 20.3
The 10 Largest Census Metropolitan Areas in Canada, 1901 and 2011

Sources: Adapted from Kearney and Ray, 1999: 147; Statistics Canada, 2014d. Population and Dwelling Counts, for Census Metropolitan Areas, 2011 and 2006 Census Areas. Retrieved January 2014 (www12.statcan.gc.ca/census-recensement/2011/dp-pd/hlt-fst/pd-pl/Table-Tableau.cfm?T=205&S=3&RPP=50).

1901		2011	
CMA	Population	CMA	Population
Montreal	266 826	Toronto	5 583 064
Toronto	207 971	Montreal	3 824 221
Quebec City	68 834	Vancouver	2 313 328
Ottawa	59 902	Ottawa-Gatineau	1 236 324
Hamilton	52 550	Calgary	1 214 839
Winnipeg	42 336	Edmonton	1 159 869
Halifax	40 787	Quebec City	765 706
Saint John	40 711	Winnipeg	730 018
London	37 983	Hamilton	721 053
Vancouver	26 196	Kitchener-Waterloo	477 160

CMAs also include two recent developments that indicate the continuing decentralization of urban Canada: the growth of rural residential areas within commuting distance of a city and the emergence of **edge cities** where clusters of malls, offices, and entertainment complexes arise, often beside major highways (Garrau, 1991). Edge cities are the "sprawling outer suburbs" of major metropolitan areas (Janigan, 2002: 25). The growth of edge cities in Canada, though less pronounced than in the United States, has been stimulated by many factors. Among the most important are the mounting costs of operating businesses in city cores and the growth of new telecommunication technologies that are changing the location of work. Home offices, mobile employees, and decentralized business locations are all made possible by these technologies.

Edge cities are clusters of malls, offices, and entertainment complexes that arise at the convergence point of major highways.

In the early 1960s, Toronto urban critic Jane Jacobs (1961) warned of the dangers of sprawling suburbs and decaying downtowns in her classic work, *The Death and Life of Great American Cities*. Her forecast proved to be less valid for Canada than for the United States. The municipal governments of Vancouver, Quebec City, Calgary, and other Canadian cities decided to reinvigorate their downtowns. In addition, deteriorating conditions in many of Canada's central cities were reduced by **gentrification**—the process of middle-class and high-income people moving into rundown areas of the inner city and restoring them (Ley, 1996).

Gentrification is the process of middle-class and high-income people moving into rundown areas of the inner city and restoring them.

Some analysts suggest that many of the problems confronting cities are best resolved by amalgamation—the creation of "megacities," such as Toronto, now the fourth-largest city in North America. They argue that when it comes to building adequate roads and public transit systems, improving the environment, providing efficient and cost-effective services, and negotiating with provincial or territorial and federal governments—bigger is better.

Although Winnipeg, Halifax, Saint John, Hamilton, and Fort McMurray are among the Canadian cities that have opted for amalgamation, some analysts maintain that "smaller is smarter." Critics argue that amalgamation often *increases* costs (Istar, 2001). They also contend that, when compared with large government units, small units are more democratic, more accountable, and more responsive to their citizens; more sensitive to local, community, and neighbourhood issues; and capable of responding to local opinion on the types and levels of services desired. Large governments, they claim, are difficult to control, show greater resistance to innovation and government reform, and are more likely to be influenced by special interests and lobbyists (Cox, 1997).

Rural Communities

Springhill, Nova Scotia, is a town not far from the New Brunswick border, the hometown of singer Anne Murray. It became a thriving coal-mining centre in the 1870s and by 1941 its population had reached more than 7000. However, its large mines started to shut down in the 1950s, and in 1958 a devastating explosion killed 88 miners, hastening the mine's decline. By 2011, only about 3800 residents remained. On March 4, 2014, it was announced that Springhill could no longer afford to remain a town and that it would legally dissolve on 1 April 2015 ("Farewell to Springhill," 2014). Many small towns in Nova Scotia face a similar fate.

Nance Ackerman

A man walks by a shuttered business on Main St. in Springhill, Nova Scotia, in 2014.

Is smaller always better? It depends on whom you ask. Not all residents of rural communities would agree that smaller is better. And there are plenty of rural Canadians that one *could* ask because, despite the waning popularity of rural living, nearly one in five Canadians still resides in a rural community (see Figure 20.6).

Just as urban sociologists study cities, rural sociologists are interested in the dynamics of small communities. The concerns of the two types of sociologists are hardly the same. Urbanization creates unique challenges for cities, to be sure, but rural communities face an entirely different set of issues. For example, young people are drawn to large urban centres for education and employment, and rarely move back to the towns and villages where they grew up. As a result, rural communities tend to have older populations on average than do cities. Because specialized health care services tend to be concentrated in cities, older rural residents, who generally require more services because of their age, are forced to travel longer distances to obtain care. Access to health care is clearly a pressing issue in rural settings.

In addition, rural sociologists are concerned about the ways in which depopulation threatens the viability of rural towns and villages. When large cities wield the gravitational pull of political power, decision-makers can easily overlook the needs of towns and villages, leading to policies that are balanced in favour of city-dwellers. These problems intensify when towns and villages themselves lack the structure and resources to protect their own interests. Such experiences leave residents feeling isolated and powerless. The real state of small-town Canada contrasts starkly with the idyllic rural life many people imagine. The evidence also lends little weight to the argument that smaller is always better.

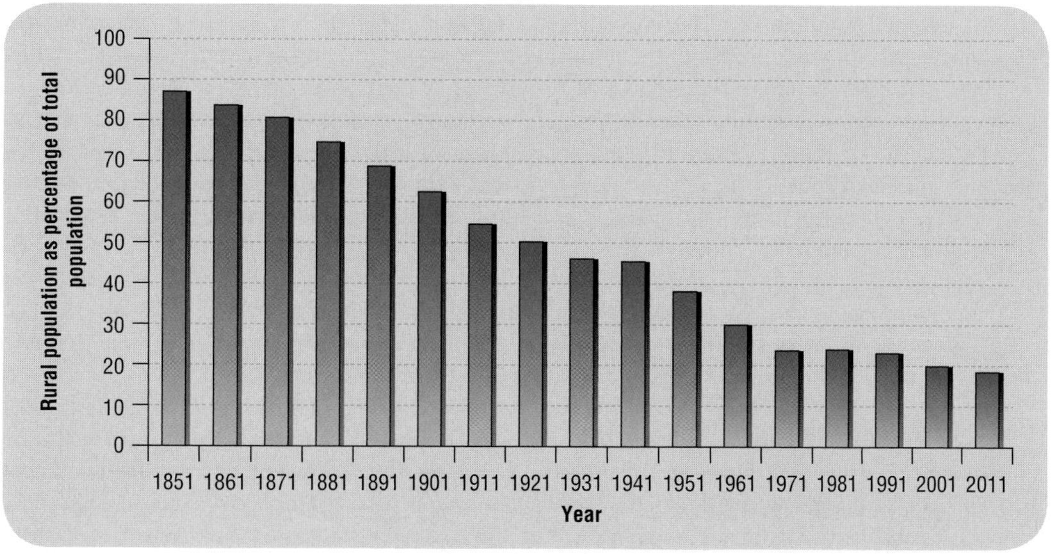

FIGURE 20.6
Rural Population, Canada, 1851– 2011

Source: Statistics Canada. 2012c. Canada's Rural Population Since 1851. Catalogue no. 98-310-X2011003. Ottawa: Minister of Industry: 2.

The Postmodern City

The **postmodern city** is a new urban form that is more privatized, more socially and culturally fragmented, and more globalized than the corporate city is.

Many of the conditions that plagued the industrial city—poverty, inadequate housing, structural employment—are evident in Canadian cities today. However, since about 1970, a new urban phenomenon has emerged alongside the legacy of old urban forms—the **postmodern city** (Hannigan, 1995a). The postmodern city has three main features.

1. The postmodern city is more *privatized* than is the corporate city is because access to formerly public spaces is increasingly limited to those who can afford to pay. Privatization is evident in closed-off "gated communities" that boast controlled-access front gates and foot patrols on the lookout for intruders. Privatization is also apparent in the construction of gleaming office towers and shopping areas that sometimes replace public urban green spaces. It is evident in pay-for-use public toilets and "patrons-only" washrooms. In the United States, the tendency is even more notable. For example, the private areas of downtown Los Angeles are increasingly intended for exclusive use by middle-class visitors and professionals who work in the information sector, including financial services, the computer industry, telecommunications, entertainment, and so on.
2. The postmodern city is also more *fragmented* than the corporate city is. That is, it lacks a single way of life, such as urbanism or suburbanism. Instead, a variety of lifestyles and subcultures proliferate in the postmodern city. They are based on race, ethnicity, immigrant status, class, and sexual orientation.
3. The postmodern city is more *globalized* than is the corporate city. New York, London, and Tokyo epitomize the global city (Sassen, 1991; 2005). They are centres of economic and financial decision making. They are also sites of innovation, where new products and fashions originate. They have become the command posts of the globalized economy and its culture.

The processes of privatization, fragmentation, and globalization are evident in the way the postmodern city has come to reflect the priorities of the global entertainment industry. Especially in the 1990s, the city and its outlying districts came to resemble so many Disneyfied "Magic Kingdoms" based on capital and technologies from the United States, Japan, Britain, Canada, and elsewhere. There, we find the latest entertainment technologies and spectacular thrills to suit nearly every taste. The postmodern city gets its distinctive flavour from its theme parks, restaurants and nightclubs, waterfront developments, refurbished casinos, giant malls, megaplex cinemas, IMAX theatres, virtual-reality arcades, ride simulators, sports complexes, book and CD megastores, aquariums, and hands-on science "museums." In the postmodern city, nearly everything becomes entertainment or, more accurately, combines entertainment with standard consumer activities. This trend has led to hybrid activities, such as "shoppertainment," "eatertainment," and "edutainment."

John Hannigan has shown how the new venues of high-tech urban entertainment manage to provide excitement—but all within a thoroughly clean, controlled, predictable, and safe environment (Hannigan, 2005). The new Magic Kingdoms are kept spotless, in excellent repair, and fully temperature- and humidity-controlled. They also provide a sense of security by touting familiar brand names and rigorously excluding anything and anybody that might disrupt the fun. For example, entertainment developments often enforce dress codes, teenager curfews, and rules that ban striking workers and groups espousing social or political causes from their premises. The most effective barriers to potentially disruptive elements, however, are affordability and access. User surveys show that the new forms of urban entertainment tend to attract middle-class and upper-middle-class patrons, especially whites. That is because the new forms of urban entertainment are pricey, and some are inaccessible by public transit and too expensive for most people to reach by taxi.

Referring to the major role played by the Disney Corporation in developing the new urban entertainment complexes, an architect once said that North American downtowns would be "saved by a mouse" (quoted in Hannigan, 1998a: 193). But do the new forms of entertainment that dot the urban landscape increase the economic well-being of the communities in which they are established? Not much, beyond creating some low-level, dead-end jobs, such as security guard, wait staff, and janitor. Do they provide ways of meeting new people, seeing old friends and neighbours, and in general improving urban sociability? Not really. You visit a theme park with family or friends, but you generally stick close to your group and rarely have chance encounters with other patrons or bump into acquaintances. Does the high-tech world of globalized urban entertainment enable cities and neighbourhoods to retain and enhance their distinct traditions, architectural styles, and ambience? It would be difficult to destroy the distinctive character of such cities as New York, Montreal, or Vancouver, but many large North American cities are becoming homogenized as they provide the same entertainment services—and the same global brands—as Tokyo, Paris, and Sydney. If the mouse is saving our cities, perhaps, in the process, he is also gnawing away at something valuable (see Box 20.3).

BOX 20.3

SOCIOLOGY ON THE TUBE

GIRLS

Launched on HBO in 2012, *Girls* is a comedy that follows the adventures of four single women in their twenties living in New York City. The award-winning show is inevitably compared with *Sex and the City*, another HBO hit show in the late 1990s and early 2000s that centred on the lives of four single women in their thirties living in New York City. The choice of New York City in both cases is no accident: "the Big Apple" epitomizes the postmodern city. As such, it presents the perfect backdrop for the consumer-driven lifestyle and self-centered existential angst of the characters in both shows.

In *Girls*, the show's creator, Lena Dunham, plays one of its central characters. Hannah Horvath is an aspiring writer who has just been informed by her parents that they are withdrawing their financial support. Now, she must make it on her own. Hannah comes up with a desperate scheme to be compensated for her unpaid internship, but ends up without any job at all. For a while, the only job she can get to support herself is in a friend's coffee shop. Unlike *Sex and the City*, then, the characters in *Girls* are not just younger, but far less certain of themselves and of their future. For Hannah and her friends, the struggle to launch meaningful careers often ends in setback and failure. Their sex lives are unsatisfying, demeaning, and sometimes uncomfortable to watch. In contrast, the women on *Sex and the City* also bemoan the sorry state of their sex lives, but they do so as self-assured and financially independent career women. Their sexual exploits are presented humorously and with irony, so that taboo subjects such as anal sex, masturbation, and abortion are open for discussion. What a difference a decade makes!

Aby Baker/Getty Images

Postmodern anguish in *Girls*

Despite the awards and accolades bestowed on the show, *Girls* has no shortage of detractors. One criticism has to do with its lack of diversity. The four young women are all white and from privileged backgrounds. Critics charge that this is a jarring oversight given that New York City is one of the most racially diverse cities in the world. Others criticize the show for its anti-feminist slant. For example, one television critic wonders what there is "to celebrate for feminism when a show depicts four entirely self-interested young women and a lead character having the most depressing, disempowered sexual relationships imaginable?" (Scott, 2012). Take, for example, Hannah's boyfriend, Adam. Beyond his sexual hang-ups, which include child rape fantasies, he is an immature, abusive, and self-absorbed jerk. Deep down, Hannah knows she deserves better but she can't make herself leave him.

It may be, however, that *Girls* could be read as an indictment of the lifestyle that is celebrated in the postmodern city. To the extent that a postmodern city serves only the fleeting needs of economically privileged, white consumers, it comes as no surprise to learn that the lives of such individuals lack emotional fulfillment and engagement with the wider world. In short, a decade later, the promise of the postmodern city via *Sex and the City* has lost most of its lustre. If men are simply brands to experiment with and then discard in favour of new varieties, as the women in *Sex and the City* see it, then the emptiness of such pursuits is made fully manifest in the lives of the characters in *Girls*. The characters of *Sex and the City* revel in their sexual misadventures; the same experiences serve to defeat and diminish the characters in *Girls*. Do these contrasting perspectives provide a compelling argument for the need to transform and re-imagine cities in the twenty-first century?

TIME FOR REVIEW

- What distinguishes industrialization from urbanization?
- According to the Chicago school, what three forces shape urban environments into concentric zones?
- In what ways do the corporate city and the postmodern city accurately reflect urban centres today?

SUMMARY

1. In what ways was Malthus's prediction of an impending population explosion inaccurate?
Malthus argued that although food supplies increase slowly, populations grow quickly. Because of these presumed natural laws, only war, pestilence, and famine can keep human population growth in check. Several developments cast doubt on Malthus's theory. Food production has increased rapidly. The limits to population size are higher than Malthus expected. Some populations are large yet prosperous. Some countries provide generous social welfare and still maintain low population growth rates. The use of contraception is widespread, allowing women to better manage the number of births.

2. What is demographic transition theory?
Demographic transition theory holds that the main factors underlying population dynamics are industrialization and the growth of modern cultural values. In the preindustrial era, crude birth rates and crude death rates were high, and population growth was therefore slow. In the first stage of industrialization, crude death rates fell, so population growth was rapid. As industrialization progressed and people's values about having children changed, the crude birth rate fell, resulting in slow growth again. Finally, in the postindustrial era, the crude death rate has risen above the crude birth rate in many countries. As a result, their populations shrink unless in-migration augments their numbers.

3. What factors aside from the level of industrialization influence growth in human populations?
Population growth is influenced by both the level of inequality between women and men and the level of inequality between classes. Low levels of gender and class inequality typically result in low crude birth rates and less competition for resources.

4. Aside from the level of industrialization, what factors affect urbanization?
Much urbanization is associated with the growth of factories. However, religious, political, and commercial needs gave rise to cities in the preindustrial era. Moreover, the fastest-growing cities in the world today are in semi-industrialized countries.

5. What did members of the Chicago school contribute to our understanding of the growth of cities?
The members of the Chicago school famously described and explained the spatial and social dimensions of the industrial city. They developed a theory of human ecology that explained urban growth as the outcome of differentiation, competition, and ecological succession. They described the spatial arrangement of the industrial city as a series of expanding concentric circles. The main business, entertainment, and shopping area stood in the centre, with the class position of residents increasing as they moved from

inner to outer rings. By identifying the weaknesses of the Chicago school's analysis of cities, sociologists came to better understand cities as social phenomena. In particular, they showed that the city is not as anomic as the Chicago sociologists made it appear. Moreover, the concentric zone pattern applies best to the American industrial city in the first quarter of the twentieth century. Finally, the new urban sociology criticized the Chicago school for making city growth seem like an almost natural process, playing down the power conflicts and profit motives that prompt the development of cities.

6. In what ways do the spatial and cultural forms of cities today reflect the societies in which they are found?
The corporate city that emerged after World War II was a vehicle for capital accumulation that stimulated the growth of the suburbs and the decline of inner cities. The postmodern city that took shape in the last decades of the twentieth century is characterized by the increased globalization of culture, fragmentation of lifestyles, and privatization of space.

NOTE

1. However, because people in the world's rich countries consume so much energy and other resources, they have a substantial negative impact on the global environment. See the online chapter that accompanies this book, Chapter 22, Technology and the Global Environment.

CHAPTER 21

COLLECTIVE ACTION AND SOCIAL MOVEMENTS

IN THIS CHAPTER, YOU WILL LEARN TO

- Recognize that when people act together to correct perceived injustice, their actions may appear spontaneous, but they are usually calculated and reflect underlying social organization.
- Identify the structural conditions associated with aggrieved groups acting in unison to correct perceived injustice.
- Analyze how successful social movement leaders make their activities, ideas, and goals congruent with the interests, beliefs, and values of potential recruits to their movement.
- Trace the history of social movements as a struggle for the acquisition of constantly broadening citizenship rights—and opposition to those struggles.

HOW TO SPARK A RIOT

Robert Brym almost sparked a small riot once. "It happened in grade 11," says Robert, "shortly after I learned that water combined with sulphur dioxide produces sulphurous acid. The news shocked me. To understand why, you have to know that I lived in Saint John, New Brunswick, about 100 metres downwind of one of the largest pulp-and-paper mills in Canada. Waves of sulphur dioxide billowed from the mill's smokestacks day and night. The town's pervasive rotten-egg smell was a long-standing complaint in the area. But, for me, disgust turned to upset when I realized the fumes were toxic. Suddenly it was clear why many people I knew—especially people living near the mill—woke up in the morning with a kind of 'smoker's cough.' Through the simple act of breathing we were causing the gas to mix with the moisture in our bodies and form an acid that our lungs tried to expunge, with only partial success.

Akabei/Thinkstock.com

Students of social movements want to know why people sometimes rebel against established social practices.

"Twenty years later, I read the results of a medical research report showing that area residents suffered from rates of lung disease, including emphysema and lung cancer, significantly above the North American average. But even in 1968 it was evident my hometown had a serious problem. I therefore hatched a plan. Our high school was about to hold its annual model parliament. The event was notoriously boring, partly because, year in year out, virtually everyone voted for the same party, the Conservatives. But here was an issue, I thought, that could turn things around. A local man, K.C. Irving, owned the pulp and paper mill. *Forbes* magazine ranked him as one of the richest men in the world. I figured that when I told my fellow students what I had discovered, they would quickly demand the closure of the mill until Irving guaranteed a clean operation.

"Was *I* naive. As head of the tiny Liberal Party, I had to address the entire student body during assembly on election day to outline the party platform and rally votes. When I got to the part of my speech that explained why Irving was our enemy, the murmuring in the audience, which had been growing like the sound of a hungry animal about to pounce on its prey, erupted into loud boos. A couple of students rushed the stage. The principal suddenly appeared from the wings and commanded the student body to settle down. He then took me by the arm and informed me that, for my own safety, my speech was finished. So, I discovered on election day, was our high school's Liberal Party. And so, it emerged, was my high-school political career.

"This incident troubled me for many years, partly because of the embarrassment it caused, partly because of the puzzles it presented. Why did I almost spark a small riot? Why didn't my fellow students rebel in the way I thought they would? Why did they continue to support an arrangement that was enriching one man at the cost of a community's health? Couldn't they see the injustice? Other people did. Nineteen sixty-eight was not just the year of my political failure in high school; it was also the year that student riots in France nearly toppled that country's government. In Mexico, the suppression of student strikes by the government left dozens of students dead. In the United States, students at Berkeley, Michigan, and other universities demonstrated and staged sit-ins with unprecedented vigour. They supported free speech on their campuses, an end to American involvement in the war in Vietnam, increased civil rights for African Americans, and an expanded role for women in public affairs. It was, after all, the 1960s."

The Study of Collective Action and Social Movements

Robert didn't know it at the time, but by asking why students in Paris, Mexico City, and Berkeley rebelled while his fellow high-school students did not, he was raising the main question that animates the study of collective action and social movements. Under what social conditions do people act in unison to change, or resist change to, society? That is the main issue we address in this chapter.

We have divided the chapter into three sections:

Collective action occurs when people act in unison to bring about or resist social, political, and economic change.

1. We first discuss the social conditions leading to the formation of lynch mobs, riots, and other types of non-routine **collective action**. When people engage in collective action, they act in unison to bring about or resist social, political, and economic change (Schweingruber and McPhail, 1999: 453). Some collective actions are "routine" and others are "non-routine" (Useem, 1998: 219). Routine collective actions tend to be nonviolent and usually follow established patterns of behaviour in bureaucratic social structures. For instance, when Mothers Against Drunk Driving (MADD) lobbies for tougher laws against driving under the influence of alcohol, when members of a community organize a campaign against abortion or for freedom of reproductive choice, and when workers form a union, they are typically engaging in routine collective action. Sometimes, however, "usual conventions cease to guide social action and people transcend, bypass, or subvert established institutional patterns and structures" (Turner and Killian, 1987: 3). On such occasions, people engage in non-routine collective action, which tends to be short-lived and sometimes violent. They may, for example, form mobs and engage in riots. Until the early 1970s, it was widely believed that people who engage in non-routine collective action lose their individuality and capacity for reason. Mobs and riots were often seen as wild and uncoordinated affairs, more like stampedes of frightened cattle than structured social processes. As you will see, however, sociologists later showed that this portrayal is an exaggeration. It deflects attention from the social organization and inner logic of extraordinary sociological events.

Social movements are collective attempts to change all or part of the political or social order by means of rioting, petitioning, striking, demonstrating, and establishing pressure groups, unions, and political parties.

2. We next outline the conditions underlying the formation of **social movements**. To varying degrees, social movements are enduring and bureaucratically organized collective attempts to change (or resist change to) part or all of the social order by petitioning, striking, demonstrating, and establishing lobbies, unions, and political parties. We will see that an adequate explanation of institutionalized protest also requires the introduction of a set of distinctively sociological issues. These issues concern the distribution of power in society and the framing of political issues in ways that appeal to many people.
3. Finally, we make some observations about the changing character of social movements. We argue that much of the history of social movements is the history of attempts by underprivileged groups to broaden their members' citizenship rights and increase the scope of protest from the local to the national to the global level.

We begin by considering the riot, a well-studied form of non-routine collective action.

NON-ROUTINE COLLECTIVE ACTION

The Vancouver Riot of 1907

Just after 9 p.m. on September 7, 1907, following a rousing chorus of "Rule Britannia," A.E. Fowler rose to address a crowd of several thousand people outside Vancouver City Hall. Fowler was secretary of the Seattle branch of the Asiatic Exclusion League, an organization of white trade unionists who were trying to convince the American and Canadian governments to keep Chinese, Japanese, Hindus, and Sikhs out of North America. Fowler was a fanatic. He was discharged from the U.S. Army for "unfitness by character and temperament" (quoted in Wynne, 1996). According to rumour, he had spent time in the Washington State Asylum at Steilacoom. He certainly knew how to whip up a crowd's emotions. Just two days earlier, he had participated in an anti-Asian riot in Bellingham, Washington, 80 kilometres southeast of Vancouver. He described how 500 white men had invaded the lodgings of more than 1100 Sikh and Hindu mill workers under cover of night, dragged them half-naked from their beds, and beat them. Six of the victims were in hospital. Four hundred were in jail, guarded by police. Seven hundred and fifty had been driven across the U.S.–Canada border.

The Vancouver crowd liked what it heard. They cheered Fowler's impassioned description of the Bellingham violence as they waved little flags inscribed "A white Canada for us." According to one source, Fowler "whipped the crowd into a frenzy" by calling for a "straight-from-the-shoulder blow" against Asian immigration ("Chinese Community," 2001). Suddenly, someone threw a stone. It shattered a window in a nearby Chinese-owned shop. The crowd, its prejudices having been reinforced and inflamed by Fowler, took this act as its cue. Members of the crowd surged uncontrollably into Vancouver's Chinatown, hurling insults, throwing rocks through windows, and beating and occasionally stabbing any Chinese people who were unable to flee or hide. With Chinatown reduced to a mass of broken glass, the crowd then moved on to the Japanese quarter, a few blocks away. The rioting continued for about three hours.

Rare Books and Special Collections, University of British Columbia Library, Photo XXXVI-17

Aftermath of the Vancouver riot, 1907

The next morning's papers in Toronto, Manchester, and London agreed on the main reason for the riot. The Toronto *Globe* said the riot was caused by "a gang of men from Bellingham." The *Manchester Guardian* said it had "proof of the correctness of the theory ... that the anti-Japanese rioting in Vancouver was due to American agitators" (quoted in Wynne, 1996). In short, according to the papers, the riot resulted less from local social conditions than from the incitement of foreign hoodlums, the half-crazed Fowler foremost among them. Surely, the newspapers suggested, good white Canadian citizens could not be responsible for such an outrage.

Breakdown Theory: A Functionalist Approach to Collective Action

Until about 1970, most sociologists believed at least one of three conditions needed to be met for non-routine collective action to emerge, as exemplified by the 1907 Vancouver riot. First, a group of people—leaders, those who are led, or both—must be socially marginal or poorly integrated in society. Second, their norms must be strained or disrupted. Third, they must lose their capacity to act rationally as a result of being caught up in the supposedly inherent madness of crowds. Following Charles Tilly and his associates, we group these three factors together as the **breakdown theory** of collective action because all three factors assume collective action results from the disruption or breakdown of traditional norms, expectations, and patterns of behaviour (Tilly, Tilly, and Tilly, 1975: 4–6). At a more abstract level,

Breakdown theory suggests that social movements emerge when traditional norms and patterns of social organization are disrupted.

breakdown theory may be seen as a variant of functionalism, for it regards collective action as a form of social imbalance that results from various institutions functioning improperly (Chapter 1, A Sociological Compass). Specifically, most pre-1970 sociologists would have said that the Vancouver riot was caused by one or more of the following factors:

1. *The discontent of socially marginal people.* This factor was emphasized by the Ontario and British newspapers when they singled out "foreign agitators" as the main cause of the disturbance. According to the papers, the Vancouver rioters were galvanized by people from outside the community who had little in common with the solid citizens of Vancouver and who were skilled in whipping crowds into a frenzy and getting them to act in extraordinary and violent ways. Breakdown theorists often single out such socially marginal, outside agitators as a principal cause of riots and other forms of collective action.

   Sometimes, however, breakdown theorists focus on the social marginality of those who are led. Often, they say, a large number of the ordinary people who participate in riots, mobs, lynchings, and the like are poorly integrated in society. For example, they may be recent migrants to the area, that is, people who are unsettled and unfamiliar with the peaceable norms and conventions of the community. Pre-1970 sociologists could have made a case for the presence of many such people in Vancouver. The completion of the Canadian Pacific Railway more than two decades earlier and the ongoing construction of other railways had stimulated rapid economic growth and urbanization in British Columbia. Construction, mining, and lumbering were all boom industries. It is at least possible (although it has not been demonstrated empirically) that a large proportion of the rioters in 1907 were poorly integrated newcomers.

Strain is the breakdown in traditional norms that supposedly precedes collective action.

2. *The violation of norms* (sometimes called **strain**) is the second factor that pre-1970 sociologists would have stressed in trying to account for the 1907 Vancouver riot (Smelser, 1963: 47–48, 75). Arguably, two norms were violated in Vancouver in 1907, one cultural, the other economic. With rapid economic growth stimulating demand for labour, the number of Asian immigrants in British Columbia grew quickly in the early part of the twentieth century. By 1907, one-quarter of male workers in the province were of Asian origin. Their languages, styles of dress, religions, foods—in short, their entire way of life—offended many residents, who were of British origin. They regarded the Asian immigrants as "a threat to their cultural integrity" (Citizenship and Immigration Canada, 2000). From their point of view, Asian Canadian cultural practices were violations of fundamental Anglo-Canadian norms.

   A second source of strain may have been the result of rapid economic growth causing British Columbians' material expectations to grow out of line with reality. According to proponents of breakdown theory, it is not grinding poverty, or **absolute deprivation**, that generates riots and other forms of collective action so much as **relative deprivation** (see Figure 21.1). Relative deprivation refers to the growth of an intolerable gap between the social rewards people expect to receive and those they actually receive. Social rewards are widely valued goods, such as money, education, security, prestige, and so on. Accordingly, people are most likely to engage in collective action when rising expectations (brought on by, say, rapid economic growth and migration) exceed social rewards (sometimes brought on by economic recession or war; Davies, 1969; Gurr, 1970). Neither recession nor war affected Vancouver in 1907. But in that era of heady economic expansion, economic expectations may have risen beyond what society was able to provide. Hence, the mounting frustration of Vancouver's workers that left them open to the influence of men like Fowler.

Absolute deprivation is a condition of extreme poverty.

Relative deprivation is an intolerable gap between the social rewards people feel they deserve and the social rewards they expect to receive.

3. *The inherent irrationality of crowd behaviour* is the third factor likely to be stressed in any pre-1970 explanation of the Vancouver riot. Gustave Le Bon, an early French interpreter of crowd behaviour, wrote that an isolated person might be a cultivated individual. In a crowd, however, the individual is transformed into a "barbarian," a "creature acting by instinct" possessing the "spontaneity, violence," and "ferocity" of "primitive beings" (Le Bon, 1969 [1895]: 28). Le Bon argued that this transformation occurs because people lose their individuality and willpower when they join a crowd. Simultaneously, they gain a sense of invincible group power that derives from the

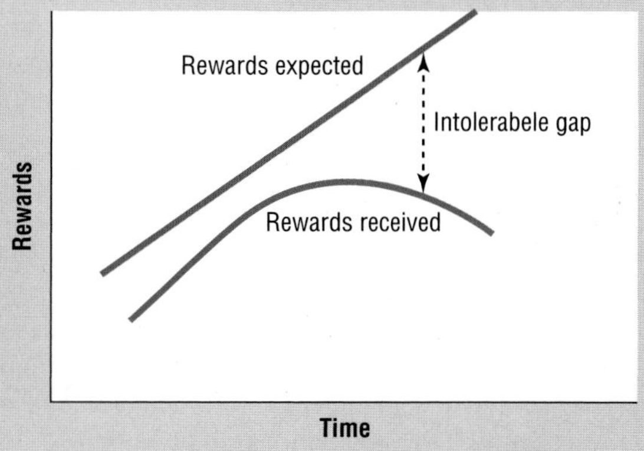

FIGURE 21.1
Relative Deprivation Theory

People feel relatively deprived when they experience an intolerable gap between the social rewards they think they deserve and the social rewards they expect to receive.

From BRYM/LIE. *Sociology*, 1E. © 2009 Nelson Education Ltd. Reproduced by permission. www.cengage.com/permissions

crowd's sheer size. Their feeling of invincibility allows them to yield to instincts they would normally hold in check. Moreover, if people remain in a crowd long enough, they enter something like a hypnotic state. As a result, people are left open to the suggestions of manipulative leaders, which ensures that extreme passions spread through the crowd like a contagious disease. (Sociologists call Le Bon's argument the **contagion** theory of crowd behaviour.) For all these reasons, Le Bon held, people in crowds are often able to perform extraordinary and sometimes outrageous acts. "Extraordinary" and "outrageous" certainly describe the actions of the citizens of Vancouver in 1907.

Contagion is the process by which extreme passions supposedly spread rapidly through a crowd like a contagious disease.

Assessing Breakdown Theory

Can social marginality, contagion, and strain fully explain what happened in Vancouver in 1907? Can breakdown theory adequately account for collective action in general? The short answer is no. Increasingly since 1970, sociologists have uncovered flaws in all three elements of breakdown theory and proposed alternative frameworks for understanding collective action. To help you appreciate the need for these alternative frameworks, let us reconsider the three elements of breakdown theory in the context of the Vancouver riot.

Social Marginality

Although it is true that Fowler and some of his associates were "outside agitators," the plain fact is that "if there had not been many local people who were deeply concerned about Oriental immigration, no amount of propaganda from the outside would have aroused the crowds" (Wynne, 1996). Moreover, the parade of 7000 to 9000 people who marched to city hall to hear Fowler's incendiary speech was organized locally by pillars of the community: Vancouver trade unionists, ex-servicemen, and clergymen. Their role fits a general pattern. In most cases of collective action, leaders and early joiners tend to be well-integrated members of their communities, not socially marginal outsiders (Brym, 2010a [1980]; Lipset, 1971 [1951]).

Contagion

No evidence suggests that the violence of September 7, 1907, was premeditated. But neither were the day's events spontaneous and unorganized acts of "contagion." A Vancouver branch of the Asiatic Exclusion League had been formed more than a month earlier and held three meetings before September 7. Two hundred people attended its third meeting on August 23. They carefully mapped out the route for the parade, ending at city hall. They decided to hire a brass band. They arranged for the manufacture of flags emblazoned with racist slogans. They arranged to mobilize various local organizations to participate in the parade. They decided who would be invited to speak at city hall and what demands would be made of the government. Sophisticated planning went into organizing the day's events.

As the Vancouver example shows, and as much research on riots, crowds, and demonstrations has confirmed, non-routine collective action may be wild and violent, but it is usually socially structured. In the first place, non-routine collective action is socially structured by the predispositions that unite crowd members and predate their collective action. Thus, if the Vancouver rioters had not shared racist attitudes, they never would have organized and assembled for the parade and engaged in the riot in the first place (Berk, 1974; Couch, 1968; McPhail, 1991). Second, non-routine collective action is socially structured by ideas and norms that emerge in the crowd itself, such as the idea to throw rocks through the windows of Chinese- and Japanese-owned shops in Vancouver (Turner and Killian, 1987). Third, non-routine collective action is structured by the degree to which different types of participants adhere to emergent and preexisting norms. Leaders, rank-and-file participants, and bystanders adhere to such norms to varying degrees (Zurcher and Snow, 1981). Fourth, preexisting social relationships among participants structure non-routine collective action. For instance, relatives, friends, and acquaintances are more likely than strangers are to cluster together and interact in riots, crowds, demonstrations, and lynchings (McPhail, 1991; McPhail and Wohlstein, 1983; Weller and Quarantelli, 1973). Thus, non-routine collective action is socially organized in many ways, none of which is highlighted by focusing on contagion.

Strain

Contrary to the argument of many breakdown theorists, a large body of post-1970 research shows that, in general, levels of deprivation, whether absolute or relative, are not commonly associated with the frequency or intensity of outbursts of collective action, either in Canada or elsewhere (McPhail, 1994; Torrance, 1986: 115–45). In other words, although feelings of deprivation are undoubtedly common among people who engage in collective action, they are also common among people who do not engage in collective action. Deprivation may therefore be viewed as a necessary, but not a sufficient, condition for collective action. For example, although Asian immigration upset many Anglo-Canadians in Vancouver, the roots of the 1907 riot ran deeper than the violation of their cultural norms. They were embedded in the way the local labour market was organized. Typically, where low-wage workers of one race and high-wage workers of another race compete for the same jobs, racist attitudes develop or are reinforced because high-wage workers resent the presence of low-wage competitors (Chapter 10, Race and Ethnicity). Conflict almost inevitably results. This situation happened when black Americans first migrated from the South to northern and western American cities in the early twentieth century. In Chicago, New York, and Los Angeles, the split labour market fuelled deep resentment, animosity, and even anti-black riots on the part of working-class whites (Bonacich, 1972). Similarly, the 1907 Vancouver riot was ultimately the result of the way social life and, in particular, the labour market were organized in the city.

We conclude that non-routine collective action is a two-sided phenomenon. Breakdown theory alerts us to one side. Collective action is partly a reaction to the violation of norms that threaten to *disorganize* traditional social life. But breakdown theory diverts attention from the other side of the phenomenon. Collective action is also a response to the *organization* of social life. And so we arrive at the starting point of post-1970 theories of collective action and social movements. For the past four decades, most students of the subject have recognized that collective action is often not a short-term reaction to disorganization and deprivation. Instead, it is a long-term attempt to correct perceived injustice that requires a sound social-organizational basis.

TIME FOR REVIEW

- Breakdown theory attributes non-routine collective action to the discontent of socially marginal people, the violation of core norms ("strain"), and the inherent rationality of crowds.
- Research shows that none of the factors listed earlier correlates with non-routine collective action.

SOCIAL MOVEMENTS

According to breakdown theory, people typically engage in non-routine collective action soon after social breakdown occurs. In this view, rapid urbanization, industrialization, mass migration, unemployment, and war often lead to a buildup of deprivations or the violation of important norms. Under these conditions, people soon take to the streets.

In reality, however, people often find it difficult to turn their discontent into an enduring social movement. Social movements emerge from collective action only when those who are discontent succeed in building up a more or less stable membership and organizational base. Once this foundation has been established, they typically move from an exclusive focus on short-lived actions, such as demonstrations and riots, to more enduring and routine activities. Such activities may include establishing a publicity centre, founding a newspaper or other regularly published means of communication, and running for public office. These and similar endeavours require hiring personnel to work full-time on various movement activities. The creation of a movement bureaucracy takes time, energy, and money. On these grounds alone, we should not expect social breakdown to result immediately in the formation of a social movement.

Solidarity Theory: A Conflict Approach

Research conducted since 1970 shows that, in fact, social breakdown often does not have the expected short-term effect. That is because several social-structural factors modify the effects of social breakdown on collective action. For example, Charles Tilly and his associates studied collective action in France, Italy, and Germany in the nineteenth and twentieth centuries (Lodhi and Tilly, 1973; Snyder and Tilly, 1972; Tilly, 1979a; Tilly, Tilly, and Tilly, 1975). They systematically read newspapers, government reports, and other sources so they could analyze a representative sample of strikes, demonstrations, and acts of collective violence. (They defined acts of collective violence as events in which groups of people seized or damaged other people or property.) They measured social breakdown by collecting data on rates of urban growth, suicide, major crime, prices, wages, and the value of industrial production. Breakdown theory would be supported if they found that levels of social breakdown rose and fell with rates of collective action. But they did not.

As the top panel of Table 21.1 shows for France, nearly all the correlations between collective violence and indicators of breakdown are close to zero. In other words, acts of

	Correlation with Frequency of Collective Violence
Breakdown variables	
Number of suicides	0.00
Number of major crimes	−0.16
Deprivation variables	
Manufactured goods prices	0.05
Food prices	0.08
Value of industrial production	0.10
Real wages	0.03
Organizational variable	
Number of union members	0.40
Political process variable	
National elections	0.17
State repression variable	
Days in jail	−0.22

TABLE 21.1

Correlates of Collective Violence, France, 1830–1960

Notes: Correlations can range from −1.0 (indicating a perfect, inversely proportional relationship) to 1.0 (indicating a perfect, directly proportional relationship). A correlation of zero indicates no relationship. The correlation between the major crime and the rate of collective violence is negative, but it should be positive according to breakdown theory. The years covered by each correlation vary.

Source: Adapted from Tilly, Tilly, and Tilly, 1975: 81–82.

collective violence did not increase in the wake of mounting social breakdown, nor did they decrease in periods marked by less breakdown.

Significantly, however, Tilly and his associates found stronger correlations between collective violence and some other variables. You will find them in the bottom panel of Table 21.1. These correlations hint at the three fundamental lessons of the **solidarity theory** of social movements, a variant of conflict theory (Chapter 1, A Sociological Compass) and the most influential approach to the subject since the 1970s:

Solidarity theory suggests that social movements are social organizations that emerge when potential members can mobilize resources, take advantage of new political opportunities, and avoid high levels of social control by authorities.

1. Inspecting Table 21.1, we first observe that collective violence in France increased when the number of union members rose. It decreased when the number of union members fell. Why? Because union organization gave workers more power, which increased their capacity to pursue their aims—if necessary, by demonstrating, striking, and engaging in collective violence. We can generalize from the French case as follows: Most collective action is part of a power struggle. The struggle usually intensifies as groups whose members feel disadvantaged become more powerful relative to other groups. How do disadvantaged groups become more powerful? By gaining new members, becoming better organized, and increasing their access to scarce resources, such as money, jobs, and means of communication (Bierstedt, 1974). French unionization is thus only one example of **resource mobilization**, a process by which groups engage in more collective action as their power increases because of their growing size and increasing organizational, material, and other resources (Gamson, 1975; Jenkins, 1983; McCarthy and Zald, 1977; Oberschall, 1973; Tilly, 1978; Zald and McCarthy, 1979).
2. Table 21.1 also shows that more collective violence occurred in France when national elections were held. Again, why? Because elections gave people new political opportunities to protest. By providing a focus for discontent and a chance to put new representatives with new policies in positions of authority, election campaigns often serve as invitations to engage in collective action. Chances for protest also emerge when influential allies offer support, when ruling political alignments become unstable, and when elite groups are divided and come into conflict with one another (Tarrow, 1994: 86–9; Useem, 1998). Said differently, collective action takes place and social movements crystallize not just when disadvantaged groups become more powerful but also when privileged groups and the institutions they control are divided and therefore become weaker. As economist John Kenneth Galbraith once said about the weakness of the Russian ruling class at the time of the 1917 revolution, if someone kicks in a rotten door, some credit has to be given to the door. In short, this second important insight of solidarity theory links the timing of collective action and social movement formation to the emergence of new **political opportunities** (McAdam, 1982; Piven and Cloward, 1977; Tarrow, 1994).
3. The third main lesson of solidarity theory is that government reactions to protest influence subsequent protest (see Box 21.1). Specifically, governments can try to lower the frequency and intensity of protest by taking various **social control** measures (Oberschall, 1973: 242–83). These measures include making concessions to protesters, co-opting the most troublesome leaders (for example, by appointing them advisers), and violently repressing collective action. The last point explains the modest correlation in Table 21.1 between frequency of collective violence and governments throwing more people into jail for longer periods. In France, more violent protest often resulted in more state repression. However, the correlation is modest because social control measures do not always have the desired effect. For instance, if grievances are very deeply felt, and yielding to protesters' demands greatly increases their hopes, resources, and political opportunities, government concessions may encourage protesters to press their claims further. And although the firm and decisive use of force usually stops protest, using force moderately or inconsistently often backfires. That is because unrest typically intensifies when protesters are led to believe that the government is weak or indecisive (Piven and Cloward, 1977: 27–36; Tilly, Tilly, and Tilly, 1975: 244).

Resource mobilization refers to the process by which social movements crystallize because of the increasing organizational, material, and other resources of movement members.

Political opportunities for collective action and social movement growth occur most frequently during election campaigns, when influential allies offer insurgents support, when ruling political alignments become unstable, and when elite groups become divided and conflict with one another.

Social control refers to methods of ensuring conformity, for example, the means by which authorities seek to contain collective action through co-optation, concessions, and coercion.

Discussions of strain, deprivation, and contagion dominated analyses of collective action and social movements before 1970. Afterward, analyses of resource mobilization, political

BOX 21.1

SOCIAL POLICY: WHAT DO YOU THINK?

STATE SURVEILLANCE OF DEMONSTRATIONS

CP Picture Archive/Maclean's Photo/Phill Snel

OCAP versus then Ontario premier Mike Harris, Toronto, June 15, 2000

On June 15, 2000, members of the Ontario Coalition Against Poverty (OCAP) organized a demonstration of about 1000 people in front of the provincial legislature at Queen's Park to protest the policies of Mike Harris's Progressive Conservative government toward people who are homeless and those living in poverty. It didn't take long before a violent confrontation developed between protesters and the police. Gary Morton, one of the demonstrators, described the events as follows:

An angry crowd of protesters ... marches across the city to the legislature at Queen's Park. They make noise, bang drums and chant. When they arrive, huge numbers of riot police meet them. . . . [T]he protesters send a delegation to the barricades at the front. Their demand—that they be allowed to address the legislature on homeless issues. The response is that no such thing will be allowed and no representative of the Harris Government will be speaking to them. The delegation informs the crowd of this and they surge forward to [the] barricades. . . . The people at the front grab the barricades and walk backward with them, opening a hole for the crowd to get through. Then all hell breaks loose. Gas smoke rolls and police charge out swinging batons. Some protesters struggle with them and others throw a few things like small water bottles. Horseback cops follow up, riding in from the north to force the crowd back and then swinging back in from the south. Between the horse sweeps the riot cops charge out and then get pushed back in. The police slowly gain ground. People are being picked off and beaten and cops begin to charge viciously into the larger body of peaceful protesters. At this point many people, myself included, begin to throw anything they can at the police. Bottles of water, mud and stones from the garden, picket signs. Brutality increases; anarchists tear apart a sidewalk and throw the chunks of stone at police. Horse charges swing in through the grassy area of the park and as the fight continues for some time we get forced out on the road, which we block. . . . The police are now saying that they are going to review their videos frame by frame. (Morton, 2000)

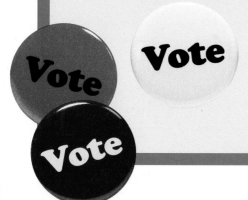

The videos to which Morton refers came from seven cameras police set up to record the demonstration. In addition, police had a still photographer and several on-duty plainclothes officers with disposable cameras. Two cameras belonging to Queen's Park security officers were also rolling during the melee. Finally, after the demonstration, the police seized film and videotape of the demonstration from television networks and newspapers.

What effect might police surveillance of demonstrations have on collective action? In the first place, if journalists fear their film and videos might be seized, they may be less likely to report what they see. For example, a journalist might be disinclined to film a demonstrator being beaten by the police knowing that the film could be edited and used to identify and prosecute the demonstrator (Canadian Journalists for Free Expression, 2000). Moreover, according to sociologist Gary Marx, surveillance systems can be "used against those with the 'wrong' political beliefs; against racial, ethnic, or religious minorities; and against those with lifestyles that offend the majority" (quoted in Boal, 1998). One journalist comments: "Social psychologists say that taping political events can affect a participant's self-image, since being surveilled is unconsciously associated with criminality. Ordinary citizens shy away from politics when they see activists subjected to scrutiny. As this footage is splayed across the nightly news, everyone gets the meta-message: hang with dissenters and you'll end up in a police video" (Boal, 1998). In short, police surveillance of demonstrations may limit dissent and the free expression of political opinion.

In 2013, it was revealed that the United States Department of Homeland Security had developed a system of tower-mounted cameras and face recognition software that could correctly identify 80 percent to 90 percent of people at a distance of 100 meters. Experts expect that a near-perfect system will be ready by 2018 (Savage, 2013). In the interest of maintaining law and order, should the police be entirely free to record demonstrations by using such equipment? Should they be allowed to seize film and videos from journalists? Or do such actions infringe the fundamental democratic rights of both the media and the citizenry?

opportunities, and social control dominated the field. Let us now make the new ideas more concrete. We do so by analyzing the ups and downs of one of the most important social movements in twentieth-century Canada, the union movement, and its major weapon, the strike.

Strikes and the Union Movement in Canada

You can appreciate the significance of solidarity theory by considering patterns of strike activity in Canada. When blue-collar and white-collar workers go out on strike, they withhold their labour to extract concessions from employers or governments in the form of higher wages and improved social welfare benefits. How do resource mobilization, political opportunity, and social control influence the willingness of workers to challenge the authority of employers and governments in this way?

Resource Mobilization

Consider first the effect of resource mobilization on the frequency of strikes. Research shows that in Canada between the mid-1940s and the mid-1970s, strike activity was high when (1) unemployment was low, (2) union membership was high, and (3) governments were generous in their provision of social welfare benefits. Low unemployment indicates a strong economy. Workers are inclined to strike when business activity is robust because they know employers and governments can afford to make concessions. (During economic booms, employers make bigger profits and governments collect more taxes.) A high level of unionization is also conducive to more strike activity because unions provide workers with leadership, strike funds, and coordination. Thus, as resource mobilization principles suggest, strong social ties among workers (as indicated by a high level of unionization) and access to jobs and money (as indicated by a booming economy) increase challenges to authority (as indicated by strikes).[1]

Figure 21.2 shows the pattern of strike activity in Canada between the end of World War II and 2011. The observed trend adds substance to the resource mobilization approach. Until 1974, the trend in strike activity was upward. In fact, in the 1970s, Canada was the most strike-prone country in the world. This decade was a period of growing prosperity, low unemployment, expanding state benefits, and increasing unionization. Armed with greater access to organizational and material resources, workers challenged authority increasingly more often in the three decades after World War II.

In 1973, however, economic crisis struck. Because of war and revolution in the Middle East, oil prices tripled, and then tripled again at the end of the decade. Inflation increased and unemployment rose. Soon, the government was strapped for funds and

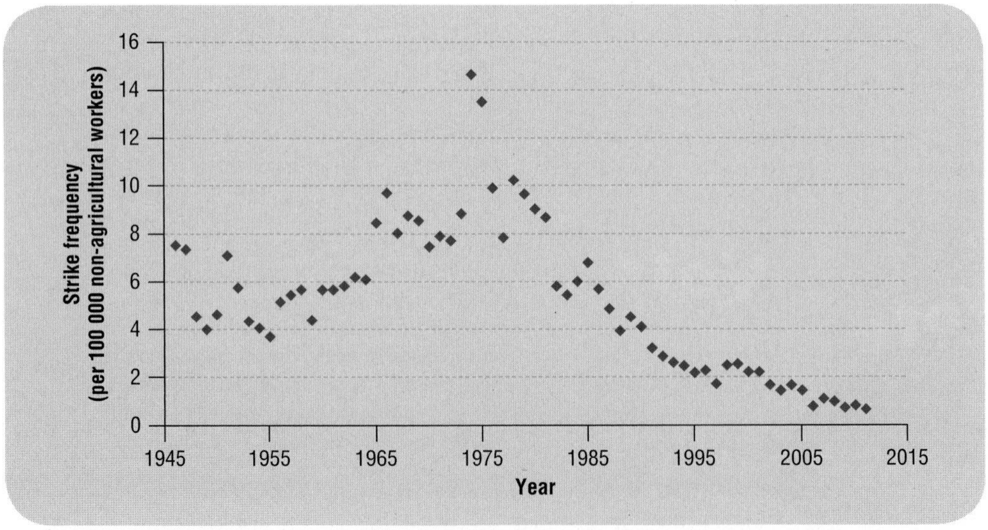

FIGURE 21.2
Weighted Frequency of Strikes, Canada, 1946–2011

Source: Brym, Robert, Louise Birdsell Bauer, and Mitch McIvor. 2013. "Is Industrial Unrest Reviving in Canada? Strike Duration in the Early 21st Century." *Canadian Review of Sociology* (50) 227–38.

needed to borrow heavily to maintain health, education and welfare programs. Eventually, the debt burden was so heavy the government felt obliged to make deep program cuts. At the same time, federal, provincial, and territorial governments introduced laws and regulations limiting the right of some workers to strike and limiting the wage gains that workers could demand. Unionization reached a peak in 1978, stabilized, and then began to decline. Today, just under 30 percent of non-agricultural workers are unionized in Canada. In the public sector, seven out of ten public sector workers remain union members. However, in the private sector, the figure has dropped to just one out of six ("Unions on Decline...," 2012).

Strike action was made even more difficult when Canada signed the free trade deal with the United States and Mexico in 1994. In the face of protracted strikes, many employers could now threaten to relocate to the United States or Mexico. In addition, governments passed laws making it more difficult for many public employees to strike and forcing striking workers back to work. Thus, in the post-1973 climate, the organizational and material resources of workers fell. Consequently, strike activity plummeted. In 1974, nearly 16 strikes took place for every 100 000 Canadian non-agricultural workers. By 2011, that number had fallen to 0.66.

Political Opportunities

Comparing Canada with the United States allows us to highlight the effect of *political opportunities* on the health of the union movement. These two cases illustrate that opportunities for union growth are greater when privileged groups and the institutions they control are divided and therefore become weaker. Opportunities for union growth are fewer when privileged groups are socially cohesive and are backed by strong institutions.

The United States and Canada have similar industrial and occupational structures. As the world's two largest trading partners, and linked by a free trade agreement, they are subject to most of the same economic forces. Yet trends in **union density** (the percentage of the non-agricultural labour force that is unionized) started to diverge in the mid-1960s. By 2013, just 11 percent of non-agricultural employees in the United States were members of a union while the figure in Canada was close to 30 percent (U.S. Bureau of Labor Statistics, 2013b). Why the divergence?

Union density is the number of union members in a given location as a percentage of non-agricultural workers. It measures the organizational power of unions.

John F. Kennedy won the closely contested American presidential election of 1960 partly because of the union movement's support. Because of his victory, government employees were awarded the right to unionize in 1961. Their rights were sharply restricted, however. They were not allowed to strike, bargain collectively over wages and benefits, or make union membership compulsory. Therefore, public-sector unions did not become a very effective or popular means for furthering employee interests.

The situation differed in Canada in the early 1960s. A new pro-labour political party, the New Democratic Party (NDP), was established in Canada in 1961 with the support of the union movement. The NDP gained enough popularity among voters to be able to exert considerable influence over government policy. In fact, in the mid-1960s, the ruling Liberal Party would have lost office without NDP support. The NDP used its political leverage to convince the government to extend full union rights to public-sector workers, including the rights to strike and to bargain collectively. Government employees soon joined unions in droves—and to a considerably greater extent than in the United States. Moreover, partly as a result of NDP influence, restrictions on private-sector unionization were eased. Thus, in Canada, union density increased after the mid-1960s because political forces made unions attractive vehicles for furthering workers' interests.

Why, then, has the union movement been more successful in Canada than in the United States since the 1960s? In the United States, a unified political establishment was able to prevent the union movement from gaining rights that would have made it attractive to more workers. Meanwhile, in Canada, a more divided political establishment could not prevent the creation of a legal environment that was favourable to union growth. In both cases, we see how political opportunities affect the growth or decline of social movements.

Social Control

Finally, we turn to the most disruptive and violent strike in Canadian history—the Winnipeg General Strike of 1919—because it illustrates well three features of the use of *social control* on social movements:

1. *If authorities show indecision or weakness, movement partisans often become bolder.* In April 1918, three unions of Winnipeg city employees walked off the job, demanding higher wages. A month later, the strikers and their employers had nearly hammered out a settlement. Just before signing off on the deal, however, the Winnipeg city council added a clause demanding that city workers pledge never to go on strike again. In angry reaction, nearly all city employees walked off the job. The same day, the city council capitulated. The striking workers got almost everything they demanded. After many bitter defeats, this victory convinced Winnipeg's workers they could get what they wanted by participating in a general strike, that is, a strike in which all employees walk off the job. The city council's capitulation emboldened the workers (Bercuson, 1974: 7).
2. The second thing the Winnipeg strike teaches us about the use of social control on social movements is that *violence, especially the most extreme forms of violence, is most often initiated by authorities, not movement partisans.* On May 15, 1919, negotiations broke down over demands from workers in the building and metal trades for union recognition and higher wages. They called a general strike. The next morning, the city was paralyzed. Nearly all workers walked off the job. The strike leaders made every effort to keep the streets peaceful. The police, who supported the strike, even agreed to continue working to help maintain law and order. The city council, however, was opposed to having pro-strike police officers on duty. So they fired the entire police force, replacing them with a large group of untrained "special police" who were hostile to the strike. The special police celebrated their first day of service

National Archives of Canada/PA163001

The Winnipeg General Strike of 1919 was the most disruptive and violent strike in Canadian history.

by riding their horses and swinging their batons into a crowd listening to a speech downtown. That was the first act of violence during the Winnipeg General Strike, but it was by no means the last. In addition to the special police, a mobile military force of 800 men armed with rifles and machine guns was recruited and trained to deal with the strikers. On the afternoon of Saturday, June 21, that is just what they did. Striking workers had been gathering downtown to hold a parade in defiance of a ban issued by the mayor. They spotted a streetcar driven by a scab (replacement worker), cut the electricity powering it, smashed its windows, slashed its seats, and set the interior on fire. Fifty-four Royal North-West Mounted Police on horses and 36 more in trucks were dispatched to break up the crowd. They charged twice. The crowd responded by throwing rocks and bottles. The Mounties then opened fire on the crowd and continued firing for several minutes. One worker was killed and many more were wounded. There is no evidence that workers fired any shots (Bercuson, 1974: 27). As is usually the case when we compare the violence exercised by authorities with the violence exercised by movement partisans, the authorities came out on top (Tilly, Tilly, and Tilly, 1975).

3. Finally, the Winnipeg strike teaches us that *violent repression can still discontent, at least for a time*. That was certainly the case in Winnipeg. Four days after "Bloody Saturday," as June 21 came to be known, the Strike Committee called off the walkout, the strikers having failed to achieve any of their objectives. It took another quarter-century of strikes, many of them bitterly fought, before a larger and more powerful Canadian working class achieved the main demand of the Winnipeg General Strike and won the legal right to form unions.

TIME FOR REVIEW

- Solidarity theory focuses on how social movement formation is influenced by shifts in the balance of power between disadvantaged and privileged groups, the opening and closing of political opportunities, and the exercise of social control by authorities.

FRAMING DISCONTENT: A SYMBOLIC INTERACTIONIST APPROACH

As we have seen, solidarity theory helps to explain the emergence of many social movements. Still, the rise of a social movement sometimes takes solidarity theorists by surprise. So does the failure of an aggrieved group to press its claims by means of collective action. It seems, therefore, that something lies between (1) the capacity of disadvantaged people to mobilize resources for collective action and (2) the recruitment of a substantial number of movement members. That "something" is **frame alignment** (Benford, 1997; Carroll and Ratner, 1996a, 1996b; Goffman, 1974; Snow et al., 1986; Valocchi, 1996). Frame alignment is the process by which social movement leaders make their activities, ideas, and goals congruent with the interests, beliefs, and values of potential new recruits to their movement—or fail to do so. Thanks to the efforts of scholars operating mainly in the symbolic interactionist tradition (Chapter 1, A Sociological Compass), frame alignment has recently become the subject of sustained sociological investigation.

Frame alignment is the process by which individual interests, beliefs, and values become congruent and complementary with the activities, goals, and ideology of a social movement.

Examples of Frame Alignment

Frame alignment can be encouraged in several ways. For example:

1. Social movement leaders can reach out to other organizations that, they believe, include people who may be sympathetic to their movement's cause. Thus, leaders of an anti-nuclear movement may use the mass media, telephone campaigns, and direct mail to appeal to feminist, anti-racist, and environmental organizations. In doing so, they assume these organizations are likely to have members who would agree at least in general terms with the anti-nuclear platform.
2. Movement activists can stress popular values that have so far not featured prominently in the thinking of potential recruits. They can also elevate the importance of positive beliefs about the movement and what it stands for. For instance, in trying to win new recruits, movement members might emphasize the seriousness of the social movement's purpose. They might analyze the causes of the problem the movement is trying to solve in a clear and convincing way. Or they might stress the likelihood of the movement's success. By doing so, they can increase the movement's appeal to potential recruits and perhaps win them over to the cause.
3. Social movements can stretch their objectives and activities to win recruits who were not initially sympathetic to the movement's original aims. This approach may involve a watering down of the movement's ideals. Alternatively, movement leaders may decide to take action calculated to appeal to non-sympathizers on grounds that have little or nothing to do with the movement's purpose. For example, when rock, punk, or reggae bands play at nuclear disarmament rallies or gay liberation festivals, it is not necessarily because the music is relevant to the movement's goals. Nor do bands play just because movement members want to be entertained. The purpose is also to attract non-members. Once attracted by the music, non-members may make friends and acquaintances in the movement and then be encouraged to attend a more serious-minded meeting.

As we see, then, social movements can use many strategies to make their ideas more appealing to a larger number of people. However, movements must also face the reality that their opponents routinely seek to do just the opposite. That is, although movements seek

CP Photo/Adrian Wyld

The Live 8 concert to fight global poverty in Barrie, Ontario, July 2005, featured Bruce Cockburn, Kevin Hearn of the Barenaked Ladies, Neil Young, Gordon Lightfoot, and many other Canadian music stars.

to align their goals, ideas, and activities with the way potential recruits frame issues, their adversaries seek to *disalign* the way issues are framed by movements and potential recruits.

The B.C. Forest Alliance provides a good illustration of this process (Doyle, Elliott, and Tindall, 1997). Launched in British Columbia in 1991, the B.C. Forest Alliance was created and bankrolled by a group of senior forest industry executives and guided by the world's largest public relations firm. Its goal was to counter the province's environmental movement. It did so in two main ways. First, in its TV and print ads, the alliance claimed it represented the "middle ground" in the debate between forest companies and environmentalists. In practice, the alliance rarely criticized forest companies while it routinely characterized environmentalists as dope-smoking hippies with untenable ideas, such as shutting down the entire forest industry. Actually, very few environmentalists hold such extreme opinions, and research shows that the middle class in British Columbia broadly supports environmental groups. The second way the alliance sought to counter the environmental movement was by arguing that more environmentalism means fewer jobs. This claim was a huge oversimplification. Job losses in the forest industry were also caused by the introduction of new technologies in some areas, aging equipment in others, First Nations land claims, and resource depletion through overharvesting and inadequate reforestation.

Muddying the waters in this way is typical of social movement opponents. Frame alignment should therefore be viewed as a conflict-ridden process in which social movement partisans and their opponents use the resources at their disposal to compete for potential recruits and sympathizers.

An Application of Frame Alignment Theory: Back to 1968

Frame alignment theory stresses the strategies employed by movement members to recruit non-members who are like-minded, apathetic, or even initially opposed to the movement's goals. Resource mobilization theory focuses on the broad social-structural conditions that facilitate the emergence of social movements. One theory usefully supplements the other.

The two theories certainly help clarify the 1968 high-school incident described at the beginning of this chapter. In light of our discussion, it seems evident that two main factors prevented Robert Brym from influencing his classmates when he spoke to them about the dangers of industrial pollution from the local pulp and paper mill.

First, he lived in a poor and relatively unindustrialized region of Canada where people had few resources they could mobilize on their own behalf. Per capita income and the level of unionization were among the lowest of any state, province, or territory in North America. The unemployment rate was among the highest. In contrast, K.C. Irving, who owned the pulp and paper mill, was so powerful that most people in the region could not even conceive of the need to rebel against the conditions of life he had created for them. He owned most of the industrial establishments in the province. He also owned every daily newspaper, most of the weeklies, all of the TV stations, and most of the radio stations. Little wonder people rarely heard a critical word about his operations. Many people believed that Irving could single-handedly make or break local governments. Should we therefore be surprised that mere high-school students refused to take him on? In their reluctance, Robert's fellow students were only mimicking their parents, who, on the whole, were as powerless as Irving was mighty (Brym, 1979).

Second, many of Robert's classmates did not share his sense of injustice. Most of them regarded Irving as the great provider. They were grateful that his pulp and paper mill, and his myriad other industrial establishments, provided many people with jobs. They regarded that fact as more important for their lives and the lives of their families than the pollution problem Robert raised. Frame alignment theory suggests Robert needed to figure out how to build bridges between their understanding and his. He did not. Therefore, he received an unsympathetic hearing.

We can briefly summarize what we have learned about the causes of collective action and social movement formation with the aid of Figure 21.3.

FIGURE 21.3
Determinants of Collective Action and Social Movement Formation

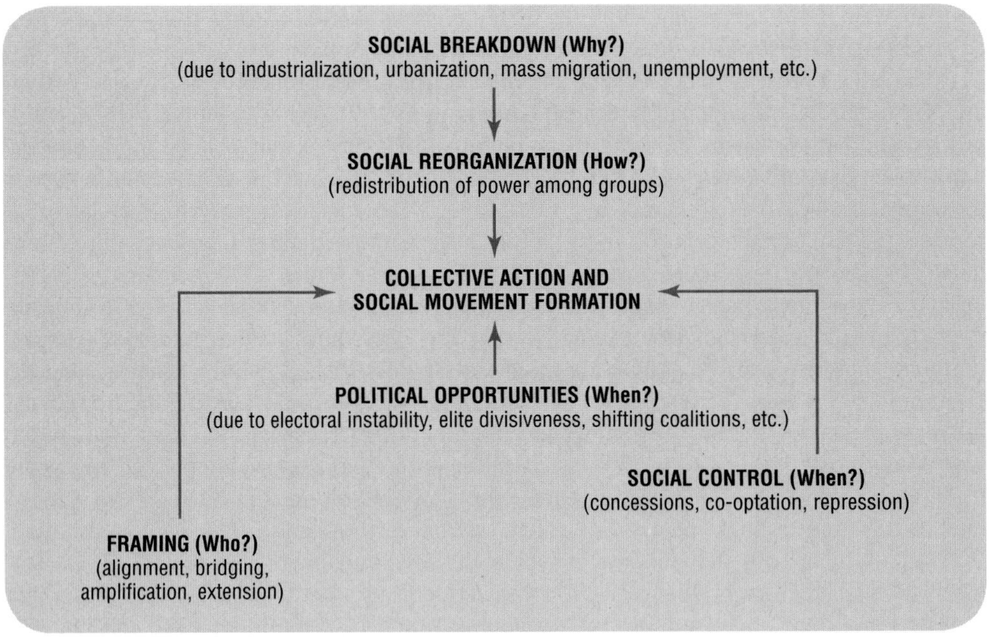

TIME FOR REVIEW

- Frame alignment theory analyzes the process by which individual interests, beliefs, and values become congruent and complementary with the activities, goals, and ideology of a social movement or fail to do so, thereby facilitating or preventing the formation of social movements.

THE HISTORY AND FUTURE OF SOCIAL MOVEMENTS

The Past 300 Years

Repertories of contention are historically specific forms of protest that include what people know how to do when they protest, what others expect them to do when they protest, and the actual form of protest they engage in.

In 1700, social movements were typically small, localized, and violent. In Europe, poor residents of a city might riot against public officials in reaction to a rise in bread prices or taxes. Peasants on an estate might burn their landowner's barns (or their landowner) in response to his demand for a larger share of the crop. However, as the state grew, **repertories of contention** changed. Repertoires of contention involve what people know how to do when they protest, what others expect them to do when they protest, and the actual form of protest they engage in (Tarrow, 2011: 29–30, 39, 55–6; Tilly, 1995). Repertoires of contention are historically specific forms of protest that include everything from food riots and banditry 300 years ago, to demonstrations and strikes in the modern era, to online petitions and "hacktivism" in the digital age (Earl and Kimport 2011: 16).

The state started taxing nearly all its citizens at higher and higher rates as government services expanded. It imposed a uniform language and a common curriculum in a compulsory education system. It drafted most young men for army service. It instilled in its citizens all the ideological trappings of modern nationalism, from anthems to flags to historical myths. As the state came to encompass most aspects of life, social movements changed in three

Bibliotheque Nationale de France

In medieval Europe, social movements were small, localized, and violent. For example, in 1358, a French historian reported "very strange and terrible happenings in several parts of the kingdom.... They began when some of the men from the country towns came together in the Beauvais region. They had no leaders and at first they numbered scarcely a hundred. One of them got up and said that the nobility of France ... were disgracing and betraying the realm, and that it would be a good thing if they were all destroyed. At this they all shouted: 'He's right! He's right! Shame on any man who saves the gentry from being wiped out!' They banded together and went off, without further deliberation and unarmed except for pikes and knives, to the house of a knight who lived near by. They broke in and killed the knight, with his lady and children, big and small, and set fire to the house" (Froissart, 1968 [c. 1365]: 151).

ways. First, they became national in scope. That is, they typically directed themselves against central governments rather than local targets. Second, their membership grew. Growth was helped in part because potential recruits were now literate and could communicate by using the printed word. In addition, big new social settings—factories, offices, densely populated urban neighbourhoods—could serve as recruitment bases. Third, social movements became less violent. That is, their size and organization often allowed them to bureaucratize, stabilize, and become sufficiently powerful to get their way without frequently resorting to extreme measures. Repertoires of contention now included strikes, demonstrations, petitioning, and sit-ins (Tilly, 1978, 1979a, 1979b; Tilly, Tilly, and Tilly, 1975).

Social movements often used their power to expand the rights of citizens. We may identify four stages in this process, focusing on Britain and the United States. In eighteenth-century Britain, rich property owners fought against the king for the right to **civil citizenship**. Civil citizenship is the right to free speech, freedom of religion, and justice before the law. In the nineteenth century, the male middle class and the more prosperous strata of the working class fought against rich property owners for the right to **political citizenship**. Political citizenship is the right to vote and run for office. In early twentieth-century Britain, women and poorer workers succeeded in achieving these same rights despite the opposition of many, in particular, well-to-do men. During the remainder of the century, blue-collar and white-collar workers fought against the well-to-do for the right to **social citizenship**. Social citizenship is the right to have a certain level of economic security and full participation in social life with the help of the modern welfare state (Marshall, 1965).

The timing of the struggle for citizenship rights differed in the United States. Universal suffrage for white males was won earlier in the nineteenth century than in Europe. This timing accounts in part for the greater radicalism of the European working class who engaged in a long and bitter struggle for the right to vote, while the American working class was already incorporated into the political system (Lipset, 1977). Another important distinguishing feature of the United States concerns black Americans. The 15th Amendment to the Constitution gave them the right to vote in 1870. However, most of them were unable to exercise that right, at least in the South, from the late nineteenth

Civil citizenship recognizes the right to free speech, freedom of religion, and justice before the law.

Political citizenship recognizes the right to run for office and vote.

Social citizenship recognizes the right to a certain level of economic security and full participation in the social life of the country.

century until the 1960s. That was because of various restrictions on voter registration, including poll taxes and literacy tests. The civil rights movement of the 1960s was in part a struggle over this issue. It helped to create a community that is more politically radical than its white counterpart is.

New Social Movements

New social movements became prominent in the 1970s. They attract a disproportionately large number of highly educated people in the social, educational, and cultural fields, and universalize the struggle for citizenship.

So-called **new social movements** emerged in the 1970s (Melucci, 1980, 1995). What is new about new social movements is the breadth of their goals, the kinds of people they attract, their potential for globalization, and the repertories of action they employ. Let us consider each of these issues in turn.

Goals

Some new social movements promote the rights not of specific groups but of humanity as a whole to peace, security, and a clean environment. Such movements include the peace movement, the environmental movement, and the human rights movement. Other new social movements, such as the women's movement and the gay rights movement, promote the rights of particular groups that have been excluded from full social participation. Accordingly, gay rights groups have fought for laws that eliminate all forms of discrimination based on sexual orientation. They have also fought for the repeal of laws that discriminate on the basis of sexual orientation, such as anti-sodomy laws and laws that negatively affect parental custody of children (Adam, Duyvendak, and Krouwel, 1999). Since the 1960s, the women's movement has succeeded in getting admission practices altered in professional schools, winning more freedom of reproductive choice for women, and opening up opportunities for women in the political, religious, military, educational, medical, and business systems (Adamson, Briskin, and McPhail, 1988). The Idle No More movement emerged in 2011 to promote land claims and environmental protection, among other issues of particular concern to First Nations people in Canada. The emergence of such movements marked the beginning of a fourth stage in the history of social movements, involving the promotion of **universal citizenship**, or the extension of citizenship rights to all adult members of society and to society as a whole (Roche, 1995; Turner, 1986: 85–105).

Universal citizenship recognizes the right of marginal groups to full citizenship and the rights of humanity as a whole.

Membership

New social movements are also novel in that they attract a disproportionately large number of highly educated, relatively well-to-do people from the social, educational, and cultural fields. Such people include teachers, professors, journalists, social workers, artists, actors, writers, and student apprentices to these occupations. For several reasons, people in these occupations are more likely to participate in new social movements than are people in other occupations. Their higher education exposes them to radical ideas and makes those ideas appealing. They tend to hold jobs outside the business community, which often opposes their values. And they often become personally involved in the issues facing their clients and audiences, sometimes even becoming their advocates (Brint, 1984; Rootes, 1995). Not coincidentally, the explosion of Native activism that Canada has recently witnessed with the emergence of the Idle No More movement is largely the doing of university-educated Aboriginal people. There were just a few hundred Aboriginal students in Canada's colleges and universities in the 1970s, but they now number around 30 000, two-thirds of whom are women. They have high expectations about their careers, they are eager to achieve equality with the rest of the country, and they have given a resounding, articulate voice to the aspirations of their community (Friesen, 2013).

Globalization Potential

Finally, new social movements are new in that they have more potential for globalization than did previous social movements.

Until the 1960s, social movements were typically *national* in scope. That is why, for example, the intensity and frequency of urban race riots in the United States in the 1960s

PATRICK BAZ/AFP/Getty Images

A protester in Tahrir Square, Cairo, Egypt, 2011, helping to overthrow the authoritarian regime of President Hosni Mubarak. In late 2010, Mohamed Bouazizi, a 27-year-old Tunisian street vendor, set himself on fire to protest harassment and humiliation by local officials. His action catalyzed an uprising that overthrew the Tunisian government and then spread to Egypt, Yemen, Bahrain, Libya, Syria, and elsewhere in the Middle East and North Africa. By the end of 2011, the "Arab Spring" had stimulated the growth of the "Occupy" movement in North America and Western Europe. Although global communication networks helped these movements spread, we must be careful not to exaggerate their causal importance, as Box 21.2 explains.

did not depend on such local conditions as the degree of black–white inequality in a given city (Spilerman, 1970, 1976). Instead, black Americans came to believe that racial problems were nationwide and capable of solution only by the federal government. Congressional and presidential action (and inaction) on civil rights issues, national TV coverage of race issues, and growing black consciousness and solidarity helped shape this belief (Myers, 1997; Olzak and Shanahan, 1996; Olzak, Shanahan, and McEneaney, 1996).

Many new social movements that gained force in the 1970s increased the scope of protest beyond the national level. For example, members of the peace movement viewed federal laws banning nuclear weapons as necessary. Environmentalists felt the same way about federal laws protecting the environment. However, environmentalists also recognized that the condition of the Brazilian rain forest affects climactic conditions worldwide. Similarly, peace activists understood that the spread of weapons of mass destruction could destroy all of humanity. Therefore, members of the peace and environmental movements pressed for *international* agreements binding all countries to protect the environment and stop the spread of nuclear weapons. Social movements went global (Smith, 1998).

Inexpensive international travel and communication facilitate the globalization of social movements. New technologies make it easier for people in various national movements to work with like-minded activists in other countries. In the age of CNN, inexpensive jet travel, websites, instant messaging, email, Facebook, and Twitter, it is easier than ever to see the connection between apparently local problems and their global sources and to act both locally and globally (see Box 21.2).

New Repertories of Contention

New repertories of contention have accompanied the changing goals, membership, and globalization of social movements in the digital era. Digital forms of protest include online petitioning, online fundraising, and hacking government or business websites to disrupt service or get hold of confidential information. Digital repertories of contention differ from traditional repertories (such as food riots) and modern repertories (such as demonstrations) in four ways (Earl and Kimport, 2011: 181; Brym et al., 2014). First, in traditional and modern forms of contention, protesters needed to be in one another's presence. In contrast,

BOX 21.2

SOCIOLOGY AT THE MOVIES

V FOR VENDETTA

On November 5, 1605, Guy Fawkes tried to blow up the British Parliament because he wanted to restore a Catholic monarch to the English throne. It is now November 5, 2020, and children in London are burning effigies of Guy Fawkes, as they have on this day for the past four centuries. However, in 2020, Britain is ruled by a brutal dictator. And on this particular day, a man (played by Hugo Weaving) appears wearing a Guy Fawkes mask. He rescues a young female reporter (played by Natalie Portman) from a gang rape, and then proceeds to blow up the Old Bailey, the Central Criminal Court of England and Wales. He goes by the name of V, and over the next year he almost single-handedly seeks to overthrow the dictatorship. Among other feats, he hacks into the national TV system to thwart the state propaganda machine, proclaiming that "people should not be afraid of their governments. Governments should be afraid of their people."

The idea that a single person can overthrow a regime is of course the stuff of fiction, but *V for Vendetta* resonated with a real social movement that spread across the world in 2011. After Vancouver's anti-consumerist magazine, *Adbusters*, urged people to occupy Wall Street in protest against growing economic inequalities and the ravages of Great Recession of 2008–09, scores of thousands of people in nearly a hundred cities in 82 countries took over parks and other public areas, set up tent communities, and demanded justice. When they demonstrated, many of them put on the Guy Fawkes mask that V wore.

© Ted Soqui/Ted Soqui Photography/Corbis

Protester wearing Guy Fawkes mask.

The remarkable spread of the Occupy Movement was facilitated by television stations with global reach, such as CNN, the BBC, and al Jazeera. Facebook, Twitter, Skype, and other Internet applications were widely used to coordinate protest activities. These media demonstrated something of the potential of new social movements to mobilize large numbers of people quickly and effectively in the era of instant, globalized communication.

Still, one must be careful not to exaggerate the role of the Internet in fostering the emergence and spread of global social movements. For example, some analysts have referred to the democracy movement that swept the Middle East and North Africa in 2010–11 as a "Twitter Revolution" or a "Facebook Revolution" because these Internet applications were used as organizing tools during the uprising in Tunisia, Egypt, and elsewhere in the region. However, survey research among Egyptian activists paints a more subtle picture. While using new electronic communications media was associated with being a demonstrator, other factors were more important in distinguishing demonstrators from mere sympathetic onlookers. Protestors tended to be people with strong grievances over unemployment, poverty, and corruption. They were more available for protest activities than others were because they tended to be unmarried men living in cities. And they tended to have strong, preexisting ties to various civic associations. The use of new electronic communications media was less important than were strong grievances, high availability, and dense social connections in distinguishing demonstrators from sympathetic onlookers (Brym et al., 2014).

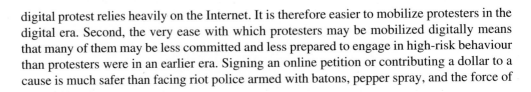

digital protest relies heavily on the Internet. It is therefore easier to mobilize protesters in the digital era. Second, the very ease with which protesters may be mobilized digitally means that many of them may be less committed and less prepared to engage in high-risk behaviour than protesters were in an earlier era. Signing an online petition or contributing a dollar to a cause is much safer than facing riot police armed with batons, pepper spray, and the force of the law. Third, while demonstrations and other forms of protest in the modern era were typically sustained and connected to social movements, digital contention may be sporadic and unconnected to larger social movements. Fourth, while protest tended to be political in an earlier era, some digital campaigns are intended to redress specific grievances rather than effect political change.

The globalization of social movements can be further illustrated by coming full circle and returning to the anecdote that began this chapter. In 1991, Robert Brym visited his hometown. He hadn't been back in years. As he entered the city, he vaguely sensed that something was different. "I wasn't able to identify the change until I reached the pulp and paper mill," says Robert. "Suddenly, it was obvious. The rotten-egg smell was virtually gone. I discovered that in the 1970s a local woman whose son developed a serious case of asthma took legal action against the mill and eventually won. The mill owner was forced by law to install a 'scrubber' in the main smokestack to remove most of the sulphur dioxide emissions. Soon, the federal government was putting pressure on the mill owner to purify the polluted water that poured out of the plant and into the local river system." Apparently, local citizens and the environmental movement had caused a deep change in the climate of opinion. This change influenced the government to force the mill owner to spend millions of dollars to clean up his operation. It took decades, but what was political heresy in 1968 became established practice by 1991. That is because environmental concerns had been amplified by the voice of a movement that had grown to global proportions. In general, as this case illustrates, globalization helps to ensure that many new social movements transcend local and national boundaries and promote universalistic goals.

Michael Wheatley/Alamy

Greenpeace is a highly successful environmental movement that originated in Vancouver in the mid-1970s. It now has offices in 40 countries.

TIME FOR REVIEW

- Over the past 300 years, the scope of social movements has grown from local to national to international dimensions.
- As the scope of social movements grew, so did demands for civil, political, social, and universal citizenship.

SUMMARY

1. **How accurate is the view that riots and other forms of collective action are irrational and unstructured actions that take place when people are angry and deprived?**
   Deprivation and strain from rapid social change are generally *not* associated with increased collective action and social movement formation. Mobs, riots, and other forms of collective action may be wild and violent, but social organization and rationality underlie most collective action.
2. **Which aspects of social organization facilitate rebellion against the status quo?**
   People are more inclined to rebel against the status quo when social ties bind them to many other people who feel similarly wronged and when they have the time, money, organization, and other resources needed to protest. In addition, collective action and social movement formation are more likely to occur when political opportunities allow them to occur. Political opportunities emerge through elections, increased support by influential allies, the instability of ruling political alignments, and divisions among elite groups. Finally, authorities' attempts to control unrest mainly influence the timing of

collective action. Authorities may offer concessions to insurgents, co-opt leaders, and employ coercion.

3. What is framing?
For social movements to grow, members must make the activities, goals, and ideology of the movement congruent with the interests, beliefs, and values of potential new recruits. The process of doing so is known as framing.

4. How have social movements changed in the past three centuries?
In 1700, social movements were typically small, localized, and violent. By the mid-twentieth century, social movements were typically large, national, and less violent. In the late twentieth century, new social movements developed broader goals, recruited more highly educated people, and developed global potential for growth. Because of these changes, the struggle for the acquisition of citizenship rights came to include (1) the right to free speech, religion, and justice before the law (civil citizenship), (2) the right to vote and run for office (political citizenship), (3) the right to a certain level of economic security and full participation in the life of society (social citizenship), and (4) the right of marginal groups to full citizenship and the right of humanity as a whole to peace and security (universal citizenship).

NOTE

1. Some of these generalizations do not apply to countries with a long tradition of labour government. For example, since World War II, Sweden has experienced high levels of unionization and low strike rates. That is because Swedish workers and their representatives are involved in government policymaking. Decisions about wages and benefits tend to be made not on the picket line, but during negotiations among unions, employer associations, and governments.

REFERENCES

Abbott, Elizabeth. 2011. *A History of Marriage*. New York: Seven Stories Press.

Abrahams, Naeemah, Karen Devries, Charlotte Watts, Christina Pallitto, Max Petzold, Simukai Shamu, and Claudia García-Moreno. 2014. "Worldwide Prevalence of Non-Partner Sexual Violence: A Systematic Review." *The Lancet* 6736(13): 6243–46.

Adam, Barry, Jan Willem Duyvendak, and Andre Krouwel. 1999. *The Global Emergence of Gay and Lesbian Politics*. Philadelphia: Temple University Press.

Adams, Henry E., Lester W. Wright, Jr., and Bethany A. Lohr. 1996. "Is Homophobia Associated with Homosexual Arousal?" *Journal of Abnormal Psychology* 105: 440–45.

Adams, Josh. 2013. "Medicalization and the Market Economy: Constructing Cosmetic Surgery as Consumable Health Care." *Sociological Spectrum* 33(4): 374–89.

Adams, Michael. 1997. *Sex in the Snow: Canadian Social Values at the End of the Millennium*. Toronto: Penguin.

———. 2004. "Canadians Are Nothing Like Americans." *Walrus*. April/May.

———. 2007. *Unlikely Utopia: The Surprising Triumph of Canadian Pluralism*. Toronto: Viking.

"Adams Mine." 2000. Retrieved October 8, 2000 (http://server1.nt.net/customers/13/tpc/www/togarbag.htm#Anchor-First-14210).

Adams, Roy J., Gordon Betcherman, and Beth Bilson. 1995. *Good Job, Bad Jobs, No Jobs: Tough Choices for Canadian Labor Law*. Toronto: C.D. Howe Institute.

Adamson, Nancy, Linda Briskin, and Margaret McPhail. 1988. *Feminist Organizing for Change: The Contemporary Women's Movement in Canada*. Toronto: Oxford University Press.

Adler, Patricia A., and Peter Adler. 1998. *Peer Power: Preadolescent Culture and Identity*. New Brunswick, NJ: Rutgers University Press.

Agboola, Akinlolu, and Rafiu Salawu. 2011. "Managing Deviant Behavior and Resistance to Change." *International Journal of Business & Management* 6(1): 235–42.

"Agricultural Subsidies." 2012. *The Economist* 22 September. Retrieved August 11, 2013 (www.economist.com/node/21563323).

Ainsworth, Sarah E., and K. Maner, 2012. "Sex Begets Violence: Mating Motives, Social Dominance, and Physical Aggression in Men." *Journal of Personality and Social Psychology* 103(5): 819–29.

Albas, Daniel, and Cheryl Albas. 1989. "Modern Magic: The Case of Examinations." *The Sociological Quarterly* 30: 603–13.

Albelda, Randy, and Chris Tilly. 1997. *Glass Ceilings and Bottomless Pits: Women's Work, Women's Poverty*. Boston, MA: South End Press.

Albrow, Martin. 1997. *The Global Age: State and Society Beyond Modernity*. Stanford, CA: Stanford University Press.

Aldrich, Howard E. 1979. *Organizations and Environments*. Englewood Cliffs, NJ: Prentice-Hall.

Alexa. 2013. "Top Sites." Retrieved 2 April 2013 (www.alexa.com/topsites).

Alford, Robert R., and Roger Friedland. 1985. *Powers of Theory: Capitalism, the State, and Democracy*. Cambridge, UK: Cambridge University Press.

Allen, Robert C. 1999. *Education and Technological Revolutions: The Role of the Social Sciences and the Humanities in the Knowledge Based Economy*. Ottawa: Social Sciences and Humanities Research Council of Canada. Retrieved May 8, 2001 (www.sshrc.ca/english/resnews/researchresults/allen99.pdf).

Allen, Vanessa, Claire Ellicott, and Louise Eccles. 2011. "'I Couldn't Give My Baby Away . . . They Only Wanted a Toy': Surrogate Mother Fought Legal Battle after Learning That Would-Be Parents Were Violent." *MailOnline*. Retrieved July 13, 2011 (www.dailymail.co.uk/news/article-1356176/Surrogate-mother-wins-case-baby-giving-birth.html).

Amato, Paul R. 2000. "The Consequences of Divorce for Adults and Children." *Journal of Marriage and the Family* 62: 1269–87.

———. 2003. "Reconciling Divergent Perspectives: Judith Wallerstein, Quantitative Family Research, and Children of Divorce." *Family Relations* 52(4): 332–39.

———. 2010. "Research on Divorce: Continuing Trends and New Developments." *Journal of Marriage and Family* 72: 650–66.

Amato, Paul R., and Joan G. Gilbreth. 1999. "Nonresident Fathers and Children's Well-being: A Meta-analysis." *Journal of Marriage and the Family* 61(3): 557–73.

Amato, Paul R., Jennifer B. Kane, and Spencer James. 2011. "Reconsidering the 'Good Divorce.'" *Family Relations* 60: 511–24.

American Psychological Association. 1998. "Answers to Your Questions About Sexual Orientation and Homosexuality." Retrieved June 14, 2000 (www.apa.org/pubinfo/orient.html).

American Society of Plastic Surgeons. 2013. "2013 Cosmetic Plastic Surgery Statistics." Retrieved May 2, 2014. (www.plasticsurgery.org/Documents/news-resources/statistics/2013-statistics/cosmetic-procedures-national-trends-2013.pdf).

Anderson, Benedict R. O'G. 1991. *Imagined Communities: Reflections on the Origin and Spread of Nationalism*. London, UK: Verso.

Anderson, Cameron D., and Laura B. Stephenson, Laura B., eds. 2011. *Voting Behaviour in Canada*. Vancouver: University of British Columbia Press.

Anderson, Siwan, and Debraj Ray. 2012. "The Age Distribution of Missing Women in India." *Economic and Political Weekly* December 1, pp. 87–95.

Andersson, Gunnar, Turid Noack, Ane Seierstad, and Harald Weedon-Fekjaer. 2006. "The Demographics of Same-Sex Marriage in Norway and Sweden." *Demography* 43(1): 79–98.

Andriessen, Karl, and Karolina Krysinska. 2009. "Can Sports Events Affect Suicidal Behavior? A Review of the Literature and Implications for Prevention." *Crisis* 30(3): 144–52.

Angus Reid Global. 2013. "Three-in-Five Canadians Would Bring Back Death Penalty." March 20. Retrieved December 6, 2013 (www.angusreidglobal.com/polls/48709/three-in-five-canadians-would-bring-back-death-penalty/).

Anschutz, Doeschka J., and Rutger C. M. E. Engels. 2010. "The Effects of Playing with Thin Dolls on Body Image and Food Intake in Young Girls." *Sex Roles* 63: 621–30.

Ariès, Phillipe. 1962 [1960]. *Centuries of Childhood: A Social History of Family Life*, Robert Baldick, trans. New York: Knopf.

———. 1982. *The Hour of Our Death*. New York: Knopf.

Armstrong, Elizabeth A., Laura Hamilton, and Brian Sweeney. 2006. "Sexual Assault on Campus: A Multilevel, Integrative Approach to Party Rape." *Social Problems* 53(4): 483–99.

Arsenault, Jean-Francois, and Andrew Sharpe. 2009. "The Economic Crisis through the Lens of Economic Well-Being." *Canadian Index of Well-Being*. Retrieved February 15, 2014 (https://uwaterloo.ca/canadian-index-wellbeing/resources/infographics/time-use).

Asch, Solomon. 1955. "Opinion and Social Pressure." *Scientific American* July: 31–35.

Asia Pacific Foundation of Canada. 2002. "Generous at Heart, Prudent at Pocket. Foreign Aid and Trade: What Do Canadians Think?" Retrieved May 13, 2006 (www.asiapacific.ca/analysis/pubs/listing.cfm?ID_Publication=222).

Atkinson, Michael. 2003. *Tattooed: The Sociogenesis of a Body Art*. Toronto, ON: Toronto University Press.

Aubrey, Jennifer Stevens. 2010. "Looking Good versus Feeling Good: An Investigation of Media Frames of Health Advice and their Effects on Women's Body-related Self-Perceptions." *Sex Roles* 63(1/2): 50–63.

Auditor General of Canada. 2013. *Promoting Diabetes Prevention and Control*. Ottawa, ON: Author.

Ayalon, Hanna, and Idit Livneh. 2013. "Educational Standardization and Gender Differences in Mathematics Achievement: A Comparative Study." *Social Science Research* 42: 432–55.

Aylward, Carol A. 1999. *Canadian Critical Race Theory: Racism and the Law*. Halifax: Fernwood.

Azumio Inc. 2014 "Stress Check Pro by Azumio." Retrieved March 29, 2014. (https://itunes.apple.com/us/app/stress-check-pro-by-azumio/id439500612).

Babad, Michael. 2014. "Canadians Richer than Ever, and Cutting Back on Mortgage Debt." *Globe and Mail* June 20. Retrieved June 25, 2014 (www.theglobeandmail.com/report-on-business/top-business-stories/canadians-richer-than-ever-and-cutting-back-on-mortgage-debt/article19256176/).

Babbie, Earl. 2000. *The Practice of Social Research*, rev. 9th ed. Belmont, CA: Wadsworth.

———. 2004. "Laud Humphreys and Research Ethics." *International Journal of Sociology and Social Policy* 24(3/4/5): 12–19.

Babbie, Earl, and Benaquisto, Lucia. 2010. *Fundamentals of Social Research*, 2nd Canadian ed. Toronto: Nelson Education.

Backman, M. E. 1972. "Patterns of Mental Abilities: Ethnio, Socioeconomic, and Sex Differences." *American Educational Research Journal* 9: 1–12.

Baer, Doug. 1999. "Educational Credentials and the Changing Occupational Structure." Pp. 92–106 in J. Curtis, E. Grabb, and N. Guppy, eds. *Social Inequality in Canada: Patterns, Problems, Policies*, 3rd ed. Scarborough, ON: Prentice Hall Allyn and Bacon Canada.

Bagdikian, Ben H. 1997. *The Media Monopoly*, 5th ed. Boston: Beacon.

Bairoch, Paul. 1988 [1985]. *Cities and Economic Development: From the Dawn of History to the Present*, Christopher Braider, trans. Chicago: University of Chicago Press.

Baker, Michael, and Marie Drolet. 2010. "A New View of the Male/Female Pay Gap." *Canadian Public Policy* 36(4): 429–64.

Baran, Paul A. 1957. *The Political Economy of Growth*. New York: Monthly Review Press.

Barber, Benjamin. 1996. *Jihad vs. McWorld: How Globalism and Tribalism Are Reshaping the World.* New York: Ballantine Books.

Barker, Eileen. 1984. *The Making of a Moonie: Choice or Brainwashing?* New York: Blackwell Publishers.

Barlow, Maude, and Elizabeth May. 2000. *Frederick Street: Life and Death on Canada's Love Canal*. Toronto: HarperCollins.

Barnard, Chester, I. 1938. *The Functions of the Executive*. Cambridge, MA: Harvard University Press.

Barnes, Colin, and Geof Mercer. 2003. *Disability*. Cambridge, UK: Polity Press.

Barnet, Richard J., and John Cavanagh. 1994. *Global Dreams: Imperial Corporations and the New World Order*. New York: Simon & Schuster.

Barnett, Laura, Julia Nicol, and Julian Walker. 2012. *An Examination of the Duty to Accommodate in the Canadian Human Rights Context*. Publications No. 2012-01-E. Ottawa, ON: Library of Parliament.

Bar-On, D. 1999. *The Indescribable and the Undiscussable: Reconstructing Human Discourse after Trauma*. Ithaca, NY: Cornell University Press.

Barth, Fredrik, ed. 1969. *Ethnic Groups and Boundaries: The Social Organization of Cultural Difference*. Boston: Little, Brown.

Bashevkin, Sylvia. 1993. *Toeing the Line: Women and Party Politics in English Canada*, 2nd ed. Toronto: Oxford University Press.

Batson, C. Daniel. 2011. *Altruism in Humans*. New York: Oxford University Press.

Battams, Nathan. 2013. *Disability and Employment in Canada*. Ottawa: Vanier Institute of the Family.

Battiste, Marie. 2012. "Enabling the Autumn Seed: Toward a Decolonized Approach to Aboriginal Knowledge, Language, and Education." Pp. 253–87, in Sara Burke and Patrice Milewski, eds. *Schooling in Transition: Readings in Canadian History of Education*. Toronto: University of Toronto Press.

Battle, Ken. 2011. *Restoring Minimum Wages in Canada*. Ottawa: The Caledon Institute of Social Policy. Retrieved April 14, 2014 (www.caledoninst.org/publications/pdf/931eng.pdf).

Baudrillard, Jean. 1983. *Simulations*. New York: Semiotext(e).

———. 1988. *America*. Chris Turner, trans. London: Verso.

Bauer, Nancy. 2010. "Lady Power." *New York Times* June 20. www.nytimes.com (retrieved January 4, 2011)

Bauman, Zygmunt. 1991. *Modernity and the Holocaust*. Ithaca, NY: Cornell University Press.

Bauman, Zygmunt, and David Lyon. 2013. *Liquid Surveillance*. Malden, MA: Polity Press.

Beck, Ulrich. 1992 [1986]. *Risk Society: Towards a New Modernity*, Mark Ritter, trans. London, UK: Sage.

Beck, Ulrich, and Elisabeth Beck-Gernsheim. 1995. *The Normal Chaos of Love*. Cambridge, UK: Polity Press.

Becker, Dominik. 2013. "The Impact of Teachers' Expectations on Students' Educational Opportunities in the Life Course: An Empirical Test of a Subjective Expected Utility Explanation." *Rationality and Society* 25(4): 422–69.

Becker, Gary. 1976. *The Economic Approach to Human Behavior*. Chicago: University of Chicago Press.

Becker, Howard S. 1963. *Outsiders: Studies in the Sociology of Deviance*. New York: Free Press.

Beer, Frances A. 1974. *How Much War in History: Definitions, Estimates, Extrapolations and Trends*. Beverly Hills, CA: Sage.

Bélanger, Claude. 2000. "Readings in Quebec History: Opting Out." Retrieved February 18, 2001 (http://members.nbci.com/history_1/his951/readings/opting.htm).

Bell, Daniel. 1973. *The Coming of Post-Industrial Society: A Venture in Social Forecasting*. New York: Basic Books.

Belley, Philippe, Marc Frenette, and Lance Lochner. 2011. "Post-Secondary Attendance by Parental Income in the U.S. and Canada: What Role for Financial Aid Policy?" National Bureau of Economic Research Working Paper No. 17218. Retrieved July 18, 2014 (www.nber.org/papers/w17218.pdf).

Bellow, Saul. 1964. *Herzog*. New York: Fawcett World Library.

Beltrame, Julian. 2014. "Temporary Foreign Worker Program Abusers to Be Slapped With Big Fines." *Huff Post Business Canada* March 28. Retrieved April 12, 2014 (www.huffingtonpost.ca/2014/03/28/temporary-foreign-worker-fines_n_5049295.html).

Benford, Robert D. 1997. "An Insider's Critique of the Social Movement Framing Perspective." *Sociological Inquiry* 67: 409–39.

Benoit, Cecilia, Mikael Jansson, Martha Jansenberger, and Rachel Phillips. 2013. "Disability Stigmatization as a Barrier to Employment Equity for Legally-blind Canadians." *Disability & Society* 28(7): 970–83.

Benzaquen, Adriana S. 2006. *Encounters with Wild Children: Temptations and Disappointment in the Study of Human Nature*. Montreal: McGill-Queen's University Press.

Bercuson, David. 1974. "The Winnipeg General Strike." Pp. 1–32 in Irving Abella, ed. *On Strike: Six Key Labour Struggles in Canada, 1919–1949*. Toronto: James Lewis & Samuel.

Berger, Peter. 1999. *The Desecularization of the World: Resurgent Religion and World Politics*. Washington, DC: Ethics and Public Policy Center.

Berger, Peter L., and Thomas Luckmann. 1966. *The Social Construction of Reality: A Treatise in the Sociology of Knowledge*. Garden City, NY: Doubleday.

Berger, Suzanne, and Ronald Dore, eds. 1996. *National Diversity and Capitalism*. Ithaca, NY: Cornell University Press.

Berk, Richard A. 1974. *Collective Behavior*. Dubuque, IO: Brown.

Berkowitz, S. D. 1982. *An Introduction to Structural Analysis: The Network Approach to Social Research*. Toronto: Butterworths.

Berners-Lee, Tim. 1999. "Tim Berners-Lee." Retrieved May 2, 2000 (www.w3.org/People/Berners-Lee/Overview.html).

Berry, John W. 2013. "Research on Multiculturalism in Canada." *International Journal of Intercultural Relations* 37: 663–75.

Berry, John W. and D. L. Sam. 2013. "Accommodating Cultural Diversity and Achieving Equity." *European Psychologist* 18(3): 151–57.

Betcherman, G., and G. Lowe. 1997. *The Future of Work in Canada: A Synthesis Report*. Ottawa: Canadian Policy Research Networks.

Bharadwaj, Prashant, and Leah K. Lakdawala. 2013. "Discrimination Begins in the Womb: Evidence of Sex-Selective Prenatal Investments." *Journal of Human Resources* 48(1): 71–113.

Bhatt, Chetan. 2012. "Human Rights and the Transformations of War." *Sociology* 46(5): 813–28.

Bianchi, Suzanne, M., Liana C. Sayer, Melissa A. Milkie, and John P. Robinson. 2012. "Housework: Who Did, Does or Will Do It, and How Much Does It Matter?" *Social Forces* 91(1): 55–63.

Bianchi, Suzanne M., and Daphne Spain. 1996. "Women, Work, and Family in America." *Population Bulletin* 51, 3: 2–48.

Bibby, Reginald W. 2001. *Canada's Teens: Today, Yesterday, and Tomorrow*. Toronto: Stoddart.

———. 2009. *The Emerging Millennials*. Toronto: Project Canada Books.

———. 2011. *Beyond the Gods and Back*. Toronto: Project Canada Books.

———. 2012. "Continuing the Conversation on Canada: Changing Patterns of Religious Service Attendance." *Journal for the Scientific Study of Religion* 50(4): 831–39.

———. 2013. "The Future as an Allusion: What Social Forecasts Tell Us about Explicit and Implicit Religion." Paper Presented at the 36th Denton Conference in Implicit Religion, Ilkley, England. May 10–12, 2013. Retrieved November 4, 2013 (www.reginaldbibby.com/images/Reginald_Bibby_Implicit_Religion_Denton_May_2013.pdf).

Bierstedt, Robert. 1963. *The Social Order*. New York: McGraw-Hill.

———. 1974. "An Analysis of Social Power." Pp. 220–41 in *Power and Progress: Essays in Sociological Theory*. New York: McGraw-Hill.

Bjorhus, J. 2000. "Gap Between Execs, Rank and File Grows Wider." *San Jose Mercury News* June 18. Retrieved June 20, 2000 (http://www.mercurycenter.com/premium/business/docs/disparity18.htm).

Blaise, Clark. 2001. *Time Lord: The Remarkable Canadian Who Missed His Train and Changed the World*. Toronto: Knopf Canada.

Blankenhorn, David. 2007. *The Future of Marriage*. New York: Encounter Books.

Blau, Peter M. 1963. *The Dynamics of Bureaucracy: A Study of Interpersonal Relationships in Two Government Agencies*, rev. ed. Chicago: University of Chicago Press.

Blauner, R. 1972. *Racial Oppression in America*. New York: Harper & Row.

Bliss, Michael. 2006. "Has Canada Failed?" *Literary Review of Canada* 14(2): 3–6.

Block, Fred. 1979. "The Ruling Class Does Not Rule." Pp. 128–40 in R. Quinney, ed. *Capitalist Society*. Homewood, IL: Dorsey Press.

Block, Sheila. 2013. "Who Is Working for Minimum Wage in Ontario?" Toronto: Wellesley Institute. http://www.wellesleyinstitute.com/wp-content/uploads/2013/10/Who-Makes-Minimum-Wage.pdf (retrieved 13 September 2014).

Bloemraad, Irene. 2006. *Becoming a Citizen: Incorporating Immigrants and Refugees in the United States and Canada*. Berkeley, CA: University of California Press.

"Bloomberg Game Changers: Mark Zuckerberg." 2010. [Video]. Retrieved October 9, 2010 (http://www.bloomberg.com/video/63583008/).

Blossfeld, H., and Y. Shavit, eds. 1993. *Persistent Inequality: Changing Educational Attainment in Thirteen Countries.* Boulder, CO: Westview Press.

Blumberg, Paul. 1989. *The Predatory Society: Deception in the American Marketplace.* New York: Oxford University Press.

Blumer, Herbert. 1969. *Symbolic Interactionism: Perspective and Method.* Englewood Cliffs, NJ: Prentice-Hall.

Boal, Mark. 1998. "Spycam City." *The Village Voice* (September 30–October 6). Retrieved March 26, 2001 (www.villagevoice.com/issues/9840/boal.shtml).

Bonacich, Edna. 1972. "A Theory of Ethnic Antagonism: The Split Labor Market." *American Sociological Review* 37: 547–59.

Bookman, Sonia. 2014. "Social Media: Implications for Social Life." Pp. 64–74 in Robert Brym, ed. *Society in Question*, 7th ed. Toronto: Nelson Education.

Boorstein, Michelle. 2010. "Children of Moon Church's Mass-Wedding Age Face a Crossroads." *Washington Post* January 3. Retrieved March 31, 2014. (www.washingtonpost.com/wp-dyn/content/article/2010/01/02/AR2010010200621.html?hpid=moreheadlines&sid=ST2010010201386)

Boroditsky, Lera. 2010. "Lost in Translation." *The Wall Street Journal* July 23. Retrieved June 7, 2011 (http://online.wsj.com/article/SB10001424052748703467304575383131592767868.html).

Borooah, Vani K., and Amaresh Dubey. 2009 "Measuring Regional Backwardness: Poverty, Gender, and Children in the Districts of India." *Margin—The Journal of Applied Economic Research* 1, 4: 403–40.

Boschma, Geertje. 2008. "A Family Point of View: Negotiating Asylum Care in Alberta, 1905–30." *Canadian Bulletin of Medical History* 25(2): 367–89.

Boteach, Shmuley. 2012. *The Modern Guide to Judaism.* New York: Overlook Duckworth.

Bouchard, Thomas J., Jr., David T. Lykken, Matthew McGue, Nancy L. Segal, and Auke Tellegen. 1990. "Sources of Human Psychological Differences: The Minnesota Study of Twins Reared Apart." *Science* 250, 4978: 223–26.

Boucher, Christian. 2013. "Canada–US Values Distinct, Inevitable Carbon Copy, or Narcissism of Small Differences?" Ottawa: Policy Horizons Canada. Retrieved November 3, 2013 (www.horizons.gc.ca/eng/content/feature-article-canada-us-values-distinct-inevitably-carbon-copy-or-narcissism-small).

Boulding, Elise. 1976. *The Underside of History.* Boulder, CO: Westview.

Bourdieu, Pierre. 1977 [1972]. *Outline of a Theory of Practice*, Richard Nice, trans. Cambridge, UK: Cambridge University Press.

———. 1986. "The Forms of Capital." Pp. 241–58 in John Richardson, ed. *Handbook of Theory and Research for the Sociology of Education.* New York: Greenwood.

———. 1998a. *On Television.* New York: New Press.

———. 1998b. *Practical Reason: On the Theory of Action.* Stanford, CA: Stanford University Press.

Bourdieu, Pierre, and Jean Claude Passeron. 1979. *The Inheritors: French Students and Their Relation to Culture.* Chicago: University of Chicago Press.

———. 1990. *Reproduction in Education, Society and Culture*, 2nd ed. R. Nice, trans. London: Sage.

Bowen, Glenn A. 2006. "Grounded Theory and Sensitizing Concepts." *International Journal of Qualitative Methods* 5(3): 1–9.

Bowles Samuel, and Herbert Gintis. 2011. *Schooling in Capitalist America: Educational Reform and the Contradictions of Economic Life.* Chicago: Haymarket Books.

Boyce, Jillian. 2013. "Adult Criminal Court Statistics in Canada, 2011/2012." *Juristat* (85-002-X). Retrieved December 5, 2013 (www.statcan.gc.Sca/pub/85-002-x/2013001/article/11804-eng.htm).

Boyd, Monica. 1997. "Feminizing Paid Work." *Current Sociology* 45, 2 (April): 49–73.

———. 1999. "Canadian, eh? Ethnic Origin Shifts in the Canadian Census." *Canadian Ethnic Studies* 31, 3: 1–19.

———. 2001. "Gender Inequality." Pp. 178–207 in Robert J. Brym, ed. *New Society: Sociology for the 21st Century*, 3rd ed. Toronto: Harcourt Canada.

———. 2002. "Educational Attainments of Immigrant Offspring: Success or Segmented Assimilation?" *International Migration Review* 36, 4: 1037–60.

Boyd, Monica, John Goyder, Frank E. Jones, Hugh A. McRoberts, Peter C. Pineo, and John Porter. 1985. *Ascription and Achievement: Studies on Mobility and Status Attainment in Canada.* Ottawa: Carleton University Press.

Boyd, Monica, and Doug Norris. 2001. "Who Are the 'Canadians'? Changing Census Responses, 1986–1996." *Canadian Ethnic Studies* 33, 1: 1–25.

Bozoyan, Christiane, and Tobias Wolbring. 2012. "Fat, Muscles, and Wages." *Economics and Human Biology* 9: 356–63.

Braithwaite, John. 1981. "The Myth of Social Class and Criminality Revisited." *American Sociological Review* 46: 36–57.

———. 1989. *Crime, Shame and Reintegration.* New York: Cambridge University Press.

Brault, Marie-Christine, and Eric LaCourse. 2010. "Prevalence of Prescribed Attention-Deficit Hyperactivity Disorder Medications and Diagnosis among Canadian Preschoolers and School-Age Children: 1994-2007." *Canadian Journal of Psychiatry* 57(2): 93–101.

Brave, Ralph. 2003. "James Watson Wants to Build a Better Human." *AlterNet* May 29. Retrieved January 19, 2005 (www.alternet.org/story/16026).

Braverman, H. 1974. *Labour and Monopoly Capital: The Degradation of Work in the Twentieth Century.* New York: Monthly Review Press.

Brechin, Steven R., and Willett Kempton. 1994. "Global Environmentalism: A Challenge to the Postmaterialism Thesis." *Social Science Quarterly* 75: 245–69.

Brennan, Shannon. 2012. "Youth Court Statistics in Canada, 2010/2011." *Juristat* (85-002-X). Retrieved December 5, 2013 (www.statcan.gc.ca/pub/85-002-x/2012001/article/11645-eng.htm).

Brennan, Teresa. 2003. *Globalization and Its Terrors: Daily Life in the West.* London: Routledge.

Brimelow, Peter. "The Silent Boom." *Forbes*, July 7, 1998.

Brint, Stephen. 1984. "New Class and Cumulative Trend Explanations of the Liberal Political Attitudes of Professionals." *American Journal of Sociology* 90: 30–71.

Broad, William J. 2014. "Billionaires with Big Ideas Are Privatizing American Science." *New York Times* 15 March. Retrieved 16 March 2014 (www.nytimes.com).

Brodie, Janine. 1991. "Women and the Electoral Process in Canada." Pp. 3–59 in Kathy Megyery, ed. *Women in Canadian Politics: Toward Equity in Representation*. Toronto: Dundurn Press.

Bronowski, J. 1965. *Science and Human Values*, revised ed. New York: Harper & Row.

Brooker, Ann-Sylvia, and Ilene Hyman. 2010. *Time Use: A Report of the Canadian Index of Well-Being*. Retrieved November 7, 2013. (https://uwaterloo.ca/canadian-index-wellbeing/sites/ca.canadian-index-wellbeing/files/uploads/files/Time_Use-Full_Report.sflb_.pdf).

Brooks, Clem, and Jeff Manza. 1997. "Social Cleavages and Political Alignments: U.S. Presidential Elections, 1960 to 1992." *American Sociological Review* 62: 937–46.

Brower, David. 1975. *Training the Nihilists: Education and Radicalism in Tsarist Russia*. Ithaca, NY: Cornell University Press.

Brown, Jennifer. 2012. "Feds Get Tough on White-Collar Crimes." *The Canadian Lawyer*. 26 November. Retrieved December 10, 2013 (www.canadianlawyermag.com/4425/Feds-get-tough-on-white-collar-crimes.html).

Brown, Phillip, Diane Reay, and Carol Vincent. 2013. "Education and Social Mobility." *British Journal of Sociology of Education* 34(5): 637–43.

Brown, Susan. 2010. "Marriage and Child Well-Being: Research and Policy Perspectives." *Journal of Marriage and Family* 72: 1059–77.

Brown, Susan L., and Manning Wendy D. 2009. "Family Boundary Ambiguity and the Measurement of Family Structure: The Significance of Cohabitation." *Demography* 46: 85–101.

Browning, Christopher R. 1992. *Ordinary Men: Reserve Police Battalion 101 and the Final Solution in Poland*. New York: HarperCollins.

Bumpass, Larry L., and Hsien-Hen Lu. 2000. "Trends in Cohabitation and Implications for Children's Family Contexts in the United States." *Population Studies: A Journal of Demography* 54: 29–41.

Brym, Robert J. 1979. "Political Conservatism in Atlantic Canada." Pp. 59–79 in Robert J. Brym and R. James Sacouman, eds. *Underdevelopment and Social Movements in Atlantic Canada*. Toronto: New Hogtown Press.

———. 1989. "Canada." Pp. 177–206 in Tom Bottomore and Robert J. Brym, eds. *The Capitalist Class: An International Study*. New York: New York University Press.

———. 1990. "Sociology, *Perestroika*, and Soviet Society." *Canadian Journal of Sociology* 15: 207–15.

———. 1992. "Some Advantages of Canadian Disunity: How Quebec Sovereignty Might Aid Economic Development in English-speaking Canada." *Canadian Review of Sociology and Anthropology* 29: 210–26.

———. 1995. "Voters Quietly Reveal Greater Communist Leanings." *Transition: Events and Issues in the Former Soviet Union and East-Central and Southeastern Europe* 1, 16: 32–35.

———. 1996. "The Turning Point in the Presidential Campaign." Pp. 44–49 in *The 1996 Presidential Election and Public Opinion*. Moscow: VTsIOM. [In Russian.]

———. 2001. "Jewish Immigrants from the Former Soviet Union in Canada, 1996." *East European Jewish Affairs* 31: 36–43.

———. 2010a [1980]. *Intellectuals and Politics*, facsimile ed. London, UK: Routledge.

———. 2010b. "Survey of SOC01 Students." University of Toronto.

———. 2014a. "Gender Risk." Pp. 106–27 in *Sociology as a Life or Death Issue*, 3rd ed. Toronto: Nelson Education.

———. 2014b. *Sociology as a Life or Death Issue*. Toronto: Nelson Education.8,

———. 2014c. *2011 Census Update: A Critical Interpretation*. Toronto: Nelson Education.

Brym, Robert, Louise Birdsell Bauer, and Mitch McIvor. 2013. "Is Industrial Unrest Reviving in Canada? Strike Duration in the Early 21st Century." *Canadian Review of Sociology* (50): 227–38.

Brym, Robert, Melissa Godbout, Andreas Hoffbauer, Gabe Menard, and Tony Huiquan Zhang. 2014. "Social Media in the 2011 Egyptian Uprising." *British Journal of Sociology* 65(2): 266–92.

Brym, Robert, and Howard Ramos. 2013. "Actually, Now's the Perfect Time to 'Commit Sociology.'" *iPolitics* 26 April. Retrieved 25 July 2014 (http://projects.chass.utoronto.ca/brym/commit.htm).

Brym, Robert J., et al. 2011. "The Social Bases of Cancer." Pp. 80–102 in *Sociology as a Life or Death Issue*, 2nd. Canadian ed. Toronto: Nelson.

Brym, Robert J., with Bonnie J. Fox. 1989. *From Culture to Power: The Sociology of English Canada*. Toronto: Oxford University Press.

Brym, Robert J., Michael Gillespie, and Rhonda L. Lenton. 1989. "Class Power, Class Mobilization, and Class Voting: The Canadian Case." *Canadian Journal of Sociology* 14: 25–44.

Brym, Robert J., and Rhonda Lenton. 2001. "Love Online: A Report on Digital Dating in Canada." Toronto: MSN.CA. Retrieved December 20, 2001 (http://www.nelson.com/nelson/harcourt/sociology/newsociety3e/loveonline.pdf).

Brym, Robert J., and John Lie. 2009. *Sociology: The Points of the Compass*. Toronto: Nelson Education Ltd.

Brym, Robert J., with the assistance of Rozalina Ryvkina. 1994. *The Jews of Moscow, Kiev and Minsk: Identity, Antisemitism, Emigration*. New York: New York University Press.

Brym, Robert J., William Shaffir, and Morton Weinfeld, eds. 1993. *The Jews in Canada*. Toronto: Oxford University Press.

Bryman, A. and Teevan, J. 2005. *Social Research Methods*. Toronto: Oxford University Press.

Brynjolfsson, Erik, and Andrew McAfee. 2014. *The Second Machine Age*. New York: W.W. Norton and Company.

Brzezinski, Zbigniew. 1993. *Out of Control: Global Turmoil on the Eve of the Twenty-First Century*. New York: Scribner.

Bullard, Robert D. 1994. *Dumping in Dixie: Race, Class and Environmental Quality*, 2nd ed. Boulder, CO: Westview Press.

Burgess, Ernest. W. 1967 [1925]. "The Growth of the City: An Introduction to a Research Project." Pp. 47–62 in Robert E. Park, Ernest W. Burgess, and Roderick D. McKenzie. *The City*. Chicago: University of Chicago Press.

Burleigh, Michael. 2000. *The Third Reich: A New History*. New York: Hill & Wang.

Burns, Tom, and G. M. Stalker. 1961. *The Management of Innovation*. London, UK: Tavistock.

Bush, Irene R., and Anthony Sainz. 2001. "Competencies at the Intersection of Difference, Tolerance, and Prevention of Hate Crimes." Pp. 205–24 in Mary E. Swigonski and Robin S. Mama, eds. *From Hate Crimes to Human Rights: A Tribute to Matthew Shepard*. New York: Haworth Press.

Buss, David M. 2000. *Dangerous Passion: Why Jealousy Is as Necessary as Love and Sex*. New York: Free Press.

———. 2013. "Sexual Jealousy." *Psychological Topics* 22(2): 155–82.

Butovsky, Jonah. 2001. *The Decline of the New Democrats: The Politics of Postmaterialism or Neoliberalism*? Ph.D. dissertation, Department of Sociology, University of Toronto.

Buxton, L. H. D. 1963. "Races of Mankind." Pp. 864–66 in *Encyclopedia Britannica*, vol. 18. Chicago: Encyclopedia Britannica, Inc.

"By the Numbers: How Much Does Daycare Really Cost in Canada?" *The Globe and Mail*, October 22, 2013.

Calasanti, Toni. 2007. "Bodacious Berry, Potency Wood and the Aging Monster: Gender and Age Relations in Anti-Aging Ads." *Social Forces* 86(1): 335–55.

Callahan, Raymond E. 1962. *Education and the Cult of Efficiency: A Study of the Social Forces That Have Shaped the Administration of the Public Schools*. Chicago: University of Chicago Press.

Cameron, Michelle. 2005. "Two-Spirited Aboriginal People." *Canadian Woman Studies* 24, 2/3: 123–27.

"Campaign for Labor Rights." 2004. Retrieved February 8, 2011 (www.clrlabor.org/alerts/1997/nikey001.html).

Campbell, D., and J. Stanley. 1963. *Experimental and Quasi-experimental Designs for Research*. Chicago: Rand McNally.

Campbell, Jane, and Mike Oliver. 1996. *Disability Politics: Understanding Our Past, Changing Our Future*. London: Routledge.

Canadian Business Journal. 2013. "White Collar Crime." 9 October. Retrieved December 10, 2013 (www.cbj.ca/features/oct_09_features/white_collar_crime.html).

Canadian Child Care Federation. 2013. *Child Care: A Canadian Snapshot—The numbers on Early Childhood Care and Education in Canada*. Ottawa, ON: Author.

Canadian Coalition for Nuclear Responsibility. 2000. Retrieved October 8, 2000 (www.ccnr.org/#topics).

Canadian Environmental Assessment Agency. 2013. *Considering Aboriginal Traditional Knowledge in Environmental Assessments Conducted under the Canadian Environmental Assessment Act—Interim Principles*. Retrieved February 28, 2014 (www.ceaa-acee.gc.ca/default.asp?lang=En&n=4A795E76-1).

Canadian Institute for Health Information. 2013. *National Health Expenditure Trends, 1975–2013*. Ottawa: Author.

———. 2014. "Annual Abortion Rates." Retrieved July 14, 2014 (http://abortionincanada.ca/stats/annual-abortion-rates/).

Canadian Institute of Actuaries. 2013. *Sustainability of the Canadian Health Care System and Impact of the 2014 Revision to the Canada Health Transfer*. Ottawa: Author.

Canadian Journalists for Free Expression. 2000. "CJFE Disappointed at Ontario Superior Court Ruling Against Media Freedom." Retrieved March 22, 2001 (www.cjfe.org/releases/2000/seizures.html).

Canadian Media Research. 2006. "How Many Canadians Subscribe to Cable TV or Satellite TV?" Canadian Radio-television and Telecommunications Commission. Retrieved October 20, 2011 (www.crtc.gc.ca/eng/publications/reports/radio/cmri.htm).

Canadian Press. 2012. "Once Vibrant Aboriginal Languages Struggle for Survival." October 24, 2013. Retrieved November 4, 2013. (www.cbc.ca/news/canada/once-vibrant-aboriginal-languages-struggle-for-survival-1.11736590).

Canadian Resource Centre for Victims of Crime. 2013. "Understanding How the Media Reports Crime." Retrieved December 12, 2013 (http://crcvc.ca/publications/media-guide/understanding/#fn3).

Canadian Secular Alliance. 2009. "Public Financing of Religious Schools." Retrieved February 3, 2014 (http://secularalliance.ca/about/policies/public-financing-of-religious-schools/).

Cancer Care Nova Scotia. n.d. "Cancer Statistics in Nova Scotia: An Overview, 1995–1999." Retrieved January 12, 2008 (http://cancercare.ns.ca/media/documents/CancerinNS_Overview.pdf).

Cancio, A. S., T. D. Evans, and D. J. Maume. 1996. "Reconsidering the Declining Significance of Race: Racial Differences in Early Career Wages." *American Sociological Review* 61: 541–56.

"The Candidates Debate." 1998. MSNBC News. Retrieved May 2, 2000 (http://msnbc.com/onair/msnbc/TimeAndAgain/archive/ken-nix/Default.asp?cp1=1).

Carbon Tracker Initiative. 2012. "Unburnable Carbon—Are the World's Financial Markets Carrying a Carbon Bubble?" Retrieved 31 March 2013 (www.carbontracker.org/wp-content/uploads/downloads/2012/08/Unburnable-Carbon-Full1.pdf).

Cardinal, H. 1977. *The Rebirth of Canada's Indians*. Edmonton: Hurtig Publishers.

Cardoso, Fernando Henrique, and Enzo Faletto. 1979. *Dependency and Development in Latin America*, Marjory Mattingly Urquidi, trans. Berkeley: University of California Press.

Caron, Roger. 1979. *Go-Boy! The True Story of a Life Behind Bars*. London, UK: Arrow Books.

Carpenter, Dave. 2003. "McDonald's High-Tech with Kitchen, Kiosks." Kiosk.com. Retrieved October 23, 2003 (www.kiosk.com/articles_detail.php?ident=1856).

Carrier, Roch. 1979. *The Hockey Sweater and Other Stories*, Sheila Fischman, trans. Toronto: Anansi.

Carroll, William, and Robert S. Ratner. 1996a. "Master Frames and Counter-Hegemony: Political Sensibilities in Contemporary Social Movements." *Canadian Review of Sociology and Anthropology* 33: 407–35.

———. 1996b. "Master Framing and Cross-Movement Networking in Contemporary Social Movements." *The Sociological Quarterly* 37, 4: 601–25.

Case, Anne, and Christina Paxson. 2008. "Stature and Status: Height, Ability, and Labor Market Outcomes." *Journal of Political Economy* 116: 499–532.

Cassidy, B., R. Lord, and N. Mandell. 1998. "Silenced and Forgotten Women: Race, Poverty and Disability." Pp. 26–54 in Nancy Mandell, ed. *Race, Class and Sexuality*, 2nd ed. Scarborough: Prentice-Hall Allyn and Bacon.

Castells, Manuel. 1983. *The City and the Grassroots: A Cross-Cultural Theory of Urban Social Movements*. Berkeley, CA: University of California Press.

Cavalli-Sforza, L. L., P. Menozzi, and A. Piazza. 1994. *The History and Geography of Human Genes*. Princeton, NJ: Princeton University Press.

CBC News. 2007. "Casualties in the IRAQ War." Retrieved January 13, 2008 (www.cbc.ca/news/background/iraq/casualties.html).

———. 2010. "Cheese Recall Affects Sandwich Businesses." December 6. Retrieved December 7, 20110 (www.cbc.ca/consumer/story/2010/12/06/con-saputo-cheese-sandwich.html).

———. 2013. "Bangladesh Garment Workers' Lives Still at Risk, the Fifth Estate Finds." Retrieved April 14, 2014 (www.cbc.ca/news/world/bangladesh-garment-workers-lives-still-at-risk-the-fifth-estate-finds-1.1959518).

Central Intelligence Agency. 2001. *The World Factbook 2001*. Retrieved June 25, 2002 (www.cia.gov/cia/publications/factbook).

Chagnon, Napoleon. 1992. *Yanomamö: The Last Days of Eden*. New York: Harcourt, Brace Yovanovich.

Chang, Ha-Joon. 2002. *Kicking away the Ladder: Development Strategy in Historical Perspective*. London: Anthem Press.

Chard, Jennifer. 2000. "Women in a Visible Minority." Pp. 219–44 in *Women in Canada, 2000: A Gender-Based Statistical Report*. Ottawa: Statistics Canada.

Chase, Steven. "Religious-Freedom Envoy to Ensure That 'Canada Will Not Be Silent,' PM Says." *Globe and Mail* February 19, 2013. Retrieved December 23, 2013 (www.theglobeandmail.com/news/politics/religious-freedom-envoy-to-ensure-that-canada-will-not-be-silent-pm-says/article8806344/).

Chauncey, George. 2005. *Why Marriage? The History Shaping Today's Debate over Gay Equality*. New York: Basic Books.

Cheadle, Bruce. 2012. "Unions Disappearing from Private Sector as Canadian Labour Movement Struggles." *National Post* September 2. Retrieved April 14, 2014 (http://news.nationalpost.com/2012/09/02/unions-disappearing-from-private-sector-as-labour-movement-struggles/).

Cherlin, Andrew J. 2009. *The Marriage-Go-Round: The State of Marriage and the Family in America Today*. New York: Alfred A. Knopf.

———. 2010. "Demographic Trends in the United States: A Review of Research in the 2000s." *Journal of Marriage and Family* 72: 403–19.

Cherlin, Andrew J., P. Lindsay Chase-Lansdale, and Christine McRae. 1998. "Effects of Parental Divorce on Mental Health Throughout the Life Course." *American Sociological Review* 63: 239–49.

Chesnais, Jean-Claude. 1992 [1986]. *The Demographic Transition: Stages, Patterns, and Economic Implications*, Elizabeth Kreager and Philip Kreager, trans. Oxford, UK: Clarendon Press.

"Chinese Community." 2001. Retrieved March 15, 2001 (www.direct.ca/news/cchi/chin02.shtml).

Chomsky, Noam. 1991. *Deterring Democracy*. London: Verso.

Cicourel, Aaron. 1968. *The Social Organization of Juvenile Justice*. New York: Wiley.

Cisco. 2013. "Visual Networking Index (VNI)." Retrieved 18 August 2013 (www.cisco.com/en/US/netsol/ns827/networking_solutions_sub_solution.html).

Citizenship and Immigration Canada. 2000. "The Vancouver Riot of 1907." Retrieved March 16, 2001.

Citrin, Jack, Richard Johnson, and Matthew Wright. 2012. "Do Patriotism and Multiculturalism Collide? Competing Perspectives from Canada and the United States." *Canadian Journal of Political Science* 45(3): 531–52.

Clairmont, Donald H., and Dennis W. Magill. 1999. *Africville: The Life and Death of a Canadian Black Community*, 3rd ed. Toronto: Canadian Scholars' Press.

Clancey, William J. 2001. "Field Science Ethnography: Methods for Systematic Observation of an Arctic Expedition." *Field Methods* 13: 223–43.

Clark, Samuel Delbert. 1968. *The Developing Canadian Community*, 2nd ed. Toronto: University of Toronto Press.

Clark, Terry Nichols, and Seymour Martin Lipset. 1991. "Are Social Classes Dying?" *International Sociology* 6: 397–410.

Clark, Terry Nichols, Seymour Martin Lipset, and Michael Rempel. 1993. "The Declining Political Significance of Class." *International Sociology* 8: 293–316.

Clark, Warren, and Susan Crompton. 2006. "Til Death Do Us Part? The Risk of First and Second Marriage Dissolution." *Canadian Social Trends* summer: 23–33.

Clarke, Juanne, Amy Romagnoli, Cristal Sargent, and Gudrun van Amerom. 2010. "The Portrayal of Complementary and Alternative Medicine in Mass Print Magazines Since 1980." *Journal of Alternative and Complementary Medicine* 16(1): 25–30.

Clarke, Lynda, and Ceridwen Roberts. 2004. "The Meaning of Grandparenthood and its Contribution to the Quality of Life of Older People." Pp. 188–208 in Alan Walker and Catherine H. Hennessy, eds. *Growing Older: Quality of Life in Old Age*. Maidenhead: Open University Press.

Clarke-Stewart, K. Alison, Christian P. Gruber, and Linda May Fitzgerald. 1994. *Children at Home and in Day Care*. Hillsdale, NJ: Lawrence Erlbaum.

Clement, Wallace. 1975. *The Canadian Corporate Elite: An Analysis of Economic Power*. Toronto: McClelland & Stewart.

Clement, Wallace, and John Myles. 1994. *Relations of Ruling: Class and Gender in Postindustrial Societies*. Montreal and Kingston: McGill-Queen's University Press.

Clement, William Henry Pope. 1897. *The History of the Dominion of Canada*. Toronto: William Briggs.

Cleveland, Gordon, and Michael Krashinsky. 1998. *The Benefits and Costs of Good Child Care: The Economic Rationale for Public Investment in Young Children*. Toronto: University of Toronto.

Clifton, Rodney, and Lance Roberts. 1993. *Authority in Schools*. Toronto: Prentice-Hall.

Clinard, Marshall B., and Peter C. Yeager. 1980. *Corporate Crime*. New York: Free Press.

Cloward, Richard A., and Lloyd E. Ohlin. 1960. *Delinquency and Opportunity: A Theory of Delinquent Gangs*. New York: Free Press.

Coale, Ansley J. 1974. "The History of Human Population." *Scientific American* 23, 3: 41–51.

Coale, Ansley J., and Susan C. Watkins, eds. 1986. *The Decline of Fertility in Europe*. Princeton, NJ: Princeton University Press.

Cockerham, William C. 2012a. "The Intersection of Life Expectancy and Gender in a Transitional State: The Case of Russia." *Sociology of Health and Illness* 34(6): 943–57.

———. 2012b. *Medical Sociology*, 12th ed. Upper Saddle River, NJ: Pearson.

Coghlan, Banjamin, Richard J. Brennan, Pascal Ngoy, David Dofara, Brad Otto, Mark Clements, and Tony Stewart. 2006. "Mortality in the Democratic Republic of Congo: A Nationwide Survey." *The Lancet* 367: 44–51.

Cohen, Albert. 1955. *Delinquent Boys: The Subculture of a Gang*. New York: Free Press.

Cohen, I. Glenn. 2013. "Transplant Tourism: The Ethics and Regulation of International Markets for Organs." *Journal of Law, Medicine and Ethics* 41(1): 269–85.

Colapinto, John. 1997. "The True Story of John/Joan." *Rolling Stone* December 11: 54–73, 92–97.

———. 2001. *As Nature Made Him: The Boy Who Was Raised as a Girl*. Toronto: HarperCollins.

Cole, S., D. Denny, A. E. Eyler, and S. L. Samons. 2000. "Issues of Transgender." Pp. 149–95 in L. T. Szuchman and F. Mascarella, eds. *Psychological Perspectives on Human Sexuality*. New York: Wiley.

Coleman, James, Ernest Campbell, Carol Hobson, James McPartland, Alexander Mood, Frederic Weinfeld, and Robert York. 1966. *Equality of Educational Opportunity*. Washington, DC: United States Department of Health, Education, and Welfare, Office of Education.

Coleman, James S. 1961. *The Adolescent Society*. New York: Free Press.

———. 1988. "Social Capital in the Creation of Human Capital." *American Journal of Sociology* 94: 95–120.

———. 1990. *Foundations of Social Theory*. Cambridge, MA: Harvard University Press.

Collins, James. 2009. "Social Reproduction in Classrooms and Schools." *Annual Review of Anthropology* 38: 33–48.

Collins, Randall. 1979. *The Credential Society: An Historical Sociology of Education*. New York: Academic Press.

———. 1982. *Sociological Insight: An Introduction to Non-obvious Sociology*. New York: Oxford University Press.

———. 2013. "Goffman and Garfinkel in the Intellectual Life of the 20th Century." *The Sociological Eye* October 20. Retrieved November 26, 2013. (http://sociological-eye.blogspot.ca/).

Collins, Rebecca L. 2011. "Content Analysis of Gender Roles in Media: Where Are We Now and Where Should We Go?" *Sex Roles* 64: 290–98.

Competition Bureau. 2002. "Comments of the Commissioner of Competition to the Standing Committee on Canadian Heritage on the Study of the State of the Canadian Broadcasting System." Ottawa: Government of Canada. Retrieved May 19, 2002 (http://strategis.ic.gc.ca/pics/ct/writtensubmission.pdf).

Conference Board of Canada. 2013. "Income Inequality." Retrieved April 8, 2014. (www.conferenceboard.ca/hcp/details/society/income-inequality.aspx).

Conley, Dalton. 1999. *Being Black, Living in the Red: Race, Wealth, and Social Policy in America*. Berkeley: University of California Press.

Connell, Tula. 2011. "The Triangle Fire: Still Burning Before Our Nation." AFL-CIO Now. March 24. Retrieved April 14, 201. (www.aflcio.org/Blog/Organizing-Bargaining/The-Triangle-Fire-Still-Burning-Before-Our-Nation).

Connidis, Ingrid A. 2010. *Family Ties and Aging*, 2nd ed. Los Angeles, CA: Pine Forge Press.

Conrad, Peter, and Kristin K. Barker. 2010. "The Social Construction of Illness: Key Insights and Policy Implications." *Journal of Health and Social Behavior* 51: S67–S79.

Cook, Karen S., and J. Whitmeyer. 1992. "Two Approaches to Social Structure: Exchange Theory and Network Analysis." *Annual Review of Sociology* 18: 109–27.

Cook, Steve, Duncan Watson, and Louise Parker. 2014. "New Evidence on the Importance of Gender and Asymmetry in the Crime–Unemployment Relationship." *Applied Economics* 46(2): 119–26.

Cooley, Charles Horton. 1902. *Human Nature and the Social Order*. New York: Scribner's.

Coontz, Stephanie. 2004. "The World Historical Transformation of Marriage." *Journal of Marriage and Family* 66: 974–79.

Coontz, Stephanie, and Peta Henderson. 1986. *Women's Work, Men's Property: The Origins of Gender and Class*. London: Verso.

Copen, Casey E., Kimberly Daniels, Jonathan Vespa, and William D. Mosher. 2012. "First Marriages in the United States: Data from the 2006–2010 National Survey of Family Growth." *National Health Statistics Reports* 49. Washington, DC: U.S. Department of Health and Human Services, Centers for Disease Control, National Center for Health Statistics.

Côté, James, and Anton L. Allahar. 2007. *Ivory Tower Blues: A University System in Crisis*. Toronto: University of Toronto Press.

Couch, Carl J. 1968. "Collective Behavior: An Examination of Some Stereotypes." *Social Problems* 15: 310–22.

Coupland, Douglas. 1991. *Generation X: Tales for an Accelerated Culture*. New York: St. Martin's Press.

Cox, Wendell. 1997. "Local and Regional Governance in the Greater Toronto Area: A Review of Alternatives." Retrieved March 27, 2001 (www.publicpurpose.com/tor-demo.htm).

Creighton, Sarah M., Lina Michala, Imran Mushtaq, and Michal Yaron. 2014. "Childhood Surgery for Ambiguous Genitalia: Glimpses of Practice Changes or More of the Same?" *Psychology & Sexuality* 5: 34–43.

Crompton, Susan. 2011. "What's Stressing the Stressed? Main Sources of Stress among Workers." *Canadian Social Trends* no. 92. Statistics Canada Catalogue no. 11-008-X.

Crompton, Susan, and Michael Vickers. 2000. "One Hundred Years of Labour Force." *Canadian Social Trends* Summer: 2–5.

Crosnoe, Robert, and Monica Kirkpatrick Johnson. 2011. "Research on Adolescence in the Twenty-First Century." *Annual Review of Sociology* 37: 439–60.

Croteau, David, and William Hoynes. 1997. *Media/Society: Industries, Images, and Audiences*. Thousand Oaks, CA: Pine Forge Press.

Crothers, Charles. 1979. "On the Myth of Rural Tranquility: Comment on Webb and Collette." *American Journal of Sociology* 84: 429–37.

Crozier, Michel. 1964 [1963]. *The Bureaucratic Phenomenon*. Chicago: University of Chicago Press.

"The CRTC's Mandate." 2002. Retrieved May 15, 2003 (www.crtc.gc.ca/eng/BACKGRND/Brochures/B29903.htm).

Cui, Ming, Jared A. Durtschi, M. Brent Donnellan, Frederick O. Lorenz, and Rand D. Conger. 2011. Intergenerational Transmission of Relationship Aggression: A Prospective Longitudinal Study. *Journal of Family Psychology* 24(6): 688–97.

Cullum, Brannon. 2011. "Music of the Revolution: How Songs of Protest Have Rallied Demonstrators." *Citizen Media, Sustaining Protest Movements*. Retrieved April 9, 2014 (http://movements.org/movements/blog/entry/music-of-the-revolution-how-songs-of-protest-have-rallied-demonstrators/index.html).

Curran, John. 2000. "Thinner Miss Americas: Study: Some Contestants Undernourished." ABCNEWS.com. Retrieved February 15, 2001 (wysiwyg://7/http://abcnews.go.com/sections/living/DailyNews/missamerica000322.htmk).

Currier, Danielle M. 2013. "Strategic Ambiguity: Protecting Emphasized Femininity and Hegemonic Masculinity in the Hookup Culture." *Gender & Society* 27(5): 704–27.

CyberPress. 2001. "The Recidivist Roger Caron Stopped Once Again" (translated from the French), October 14. Retrieved October 10, 2002 (http://216.239.37.120/transl).

Dahl, Robert A. 1961. *Who Governs*? New Haven, CT: Yale University Press.

Dailymash, 2014. "Undercover Boss Participant Finally Gets Punched in the Face." Retrieved March 26, 2014. (www.thedailymash.co.uk/news/arts-entertainment/undercover-boss-participant-finally-gets-punched-in-the-face-2012071834713)

Dan, Jill. 2008. *Emotional Intelligence*. London: Hodder Education.

Darwin, Charles. 1859. *On the Origin of Species by Means of Natural Selection*. London: John Murray.

———. 1871. *The Descent of Man*. London: John Murray.

Dauvergne, Mia. 2012. "Adult Correctional Statistics in Canada, 2010/2011." *Juristat*. (85-002-X). Retrieved April 4, 2014. (www.statcan.gc.ca/pub/85-002-x/2012001/article/11715-eng.htm#a3).

Davies, James B. 1999. "Distribution of Wealth and Economic Inequality." Pp. 138–50 in J. Curtis, E. Grabb, and N. Guppy, eds. *Social Inequality in Canada: Patterns, Problems, Policies*, 3rd ed. Scarborough, ON: Prentice Hall Allyn and Bacon Canada.

Davies, James C. 1969. "Toward a Theory of Revolution." Pp. 85–108 in Barry McLaughlin, ed. *Studies in Social Movements: A Social Psychological Perspective*. New York: Free Press.

Davis, Cindy. 2013. "Mindhole Blowers: 20 Strange, Inane and Stupid Things Celebrities Said." Retrieved March 26, 2014. (www.pajiba.com/seriously_random_lists/mindhole-blowers-20-strange-inane-and-stupid-things-celebrities-said.php#.UzLiXahdW3o).

Davis, Fred. 1992. *Fashion, Culture, and Identity*. Chicago: University of Chicago Press.

Davis, Kingsley, and Wilbert. E. Moore. 1944. "Some Principles of Stratification." *American Sociological Review* 10: 242–49.

Davis, Mike. 1990. City of Quartz: Excavating the Future in Los Angeles. New York: Verso.

Dawson, S. E. 1906. "Principal Causes of Death." Table IV. *Fourth Census of Canada, 1901*, Volume IV. Ottawa: Library and Archives Canada.

DC Interactive Group. 2013. "Web Herding: Everything Online Links to You." Retrieved 21 August 2013 (www.dcinteractivegroup.com/what-we-offer/web-herding-everything-online-leads-to-you/).

Death Penalty Information Center. 2012. "Deterrence: States without the Death Penalty Have Had Consistently Lower Murder Rates." Retrieved December 6 2013 (www.deathpenaltyinfo.org/deterr ence-states-without-death-penalty-have-had-consistently-lower-murder-rates).

Dehass, Josh. 2011. "Students Are Fleeing STEM Degrees: And Why They May Want to Reconsider." *Maclean's on Campus* November 7. Retrieved March 16, 2014 (www.macleans.ca/work/jobs/students-are-fleeing-stem-degrees/).

de Jong Gierverld, Jenny, and Eva-Maria Merz. 2013. "Parents' Partnership Decision Making after Divorce or Widowhood: The Role of (Step)children." *Journal of Marriage and Family* 75: 1098–1113.

DeKeseredy, Walter S., and Katherine Kelly. 1993. "The Incidence and Prevalence of Woman Abuse in Canadian University and College Dating Relationships." *Canadian Journal of Sociology* 18: 137–59.

"Delhi Gang-Rape Victim as Guilty as Her Rapists, Asaram Bapu Says." 2013. *Times of India* January 7. Retrieved April 19, 2013 (http://articles.timesofindia.indiatimes.com/2013-01-07/india/36192073_1_asaram-bapu-sharma-and-akshay-thakur-chargesheet).

Demi and Cooper Advertising. 2013. "Sparking." Retrieved 21 August 2013 (http://sparking.demicooper.com/).

Deming, Michelle E., Eleanor Krassen Covan, Suzanne C. Swan, and Deborah L. Billings. 2013. "Exploring Rape Myths, Gendered Norms, Group Processing, and the Social Context of Rape Among College Women: A Qualitative Analysis." *Violence Against Women* 19(4): 465–85.

Demleitner, Nora V. 2010. "Replacing Incarceration: The Need for Dramatic Change." *Federal Sentencing Reporter* 22(1): 1–5.

Denton, Margaret, Jennifer Plenderleith, and James Chowhan. 2013. "Health and Disability as Determinants for Involuntary Retirement of People with Disabilities." *Canadian Journal of Aging* 32(2): 159–72.

Department of Geography, Slippery Rock University. 1997. "World's Largest Cities, 1900." Retrieved May 2, 2000 (www.sru.edu/depts/artsci/ges/discover/d-6-8.htm).

———. 2003. "World's Largest Urban Agglomerations, 2015." Retrieved August 2, 2006 (http://www.sru.edu/gge/faculty/hughes/100/100-6/d-6-9b.htm).

Department of Justice, Canada. 2013. Sentencing of Young Persons. Retrieved April 4, 2014. (www.justice.gc.ca/eng/cj-jp/yj-jj/ycja-lsjpa/sheets-feuillets/pdf/syp-dpaa.pdf).

Derber, Charles. 1979. *The Pursuit of Attention: Power and Individualism in Everyday Life*. New York: Oxford University Press.

Derosiers, Hélène, Karine Tétreault, and Michel Boivin. 2012. "Demographic, Socioeconomic, and Neighbourhood Characteristics of Vulnerable Children at School Entry." *Profiles and Pathways* December 2012. Retrieved July 21, 2014 (www.stat.gouv.qc.ca/statistiques/sante/bulletins/portrait-201205_an.pdf).

Derrida, Jacques. 2004. *Positions*, Alan Bass, trans. London: Continuum.

Deutscher, Guy. 2010. "Does Your Language Shape How You Think?" *The New York Times* August 26. Retrieved June 7, 2011 (www.nytimes.com).

Diamond, Larry. 1996. "Is the Third Wave Over?" *Journal of Democracy* 7, 3: 20–37. Retrieved May 1, 2000 (http://muse.jhu.edu/demo/jod/7.3diamond.html).

Diamond, Milton, and H. Keith Sigmundson. 1999. "Sex Reassignment at Birth." Pp. 55–75 in Stephen J. Ceci and

Wendy W. Williams, eds. *The Nature–Nurture Debate: The Essential Readings*. Maldan, MA: Blackwell.

Dickinson, John A., and Brian Young. 2008. *A Short History of Quebec*. Montreal and Kingston: McGill-Queen's University Press.

DiMaggio, Paul, and Walter Powell. 1983. "The Iron Cage Revisited: Institutional Isomorphism and Collective Rationality in Organizational Fields." *American Sociological Review* 48: 147–60.

Dittmar, Helga, Emma Halliwell, and Suzaane Ive. 2006. "Does Barbie Make Girls Want to Be Thin? The Effect of Experimental Exposure to Images of Dolls on the Body Image of 5- to 8-Year-Old Girls." *Developmental Psychology* 42(2): 283–82.

Dolnick, Edward. 1993. "Deafness as Culture." *The Atlantic Monthly* 272(3): 37–48.

Donahue, John J., III, and Steven D. Levitt. 2001. "The Impact of Legalized Abortion on Crime." *Quarterly Journal of Economics* 116: 379–420.

Dore, Ronald. 1983. "Goodwill and the Spirit of Market Capitalism." *British Journal of Sociology* 34: 459–82.

Doremus, P. N., W. W. Keller, L. W. Pauly, and S. Reich. 1998. *The Myth of the Global Corporation*. Princeton, NJ: Princeton University Press.

Dougherty, Kevin. 2013. "It's Official: PQ Will Present Charter of Quebec Values on Thursday." *Montreal Gazette* November 6. Retrieved November 15, 2013 (www.montrealgazette.com/news/official+will+present+Charter+Quebec+Values+Thursday/9131967/story.html).

Douglas, Jack D. 1967. *The Social Meanings of Suicide*. Princeton, NJ: Princeton University Press.

Downs, Edward, and Stacy L. Smith. 2010. "Keeping Abreast of Hypersexuality: A Video Game Character Content Analysis." *Sex Roles* 62: 721–33.

Doyle, Aaron, Brian Elliott, and David Tindall. 1997. "Framing the Forests: Corporations, the B.C. Forest Alliance, and the Media." Pp. 240–68 in William Carroll, ed. *Organizing Dissent: Contemporary Social Movements in Theory and Practice,* 2nd ed. Toronto: Garamond Press.

Dranoff, Linda Silver. 2001. *Everyone's Guide to the Law*. Toronto: HarperCollins.

Drewnowski, Adam. 2009. "Obesity, Diets and Social Inequalities." *Nutrition Reviews* 67(S1): S36–S39.

Drèze, Jean, and Amartya Sen. 1989. *Hunger and Public Action*. Oxford, UK: Clarendon Press.

Dugan, Daniel O. 2004. "Appreciating the Legacy of Kübler -Ross: One Clinical Ethicist's Perspective." *American Journal of Bioethics* 4(4): W24–W28.

Duncan, Greg G., Katherine Magnuson, Ariel Kalil, and Kathleen Zio-Guest. 2012. "The Importance of Early Childhood Poverty." *Social Indicators Research* 108: 87–98.

Duncan, Greg, and Richard Murnane. 2013. *Whither Opportunity? Rising Inequality, Schools, and Children's Life Chances*. New York: Russell Sage Foundation.

Duncan, Simon, and Miranda Phillips. 2011. "People Who Live Apart Together (LATs): New Family Form or Just a Stage?" *International Review of Sociology* 21: 3, 513–32.

Dunk, T. 1991. *It's a Working Man's Town: Male Working Class Culture in Northwestern Ontario*. Montreal: McGill-Queen's University Press.

Durham, William H. 1979. *Scarcity and Survival in Central America: Ecological Origins of the Soccer War*. Stanford, CA: Stanford University Press.

Durkheim, Émile. 1938. *The Rules of Sociological Method*, S. Solovay and J. Mueller, trans.; G.E.G. Catlin, ed. Chicago: University of Chicago Press.

———. 1951 [1897]. *Suicide: A Study in Sociology*, G. Simpson, ed., J. Spaulding and G. Simpson, trans. New York: Free Press.

———. 1956. *Education and Sociology,* Sherwood D. Fox, trans. New York: Free Press.

———. 1961 [1925]. *Moral Education: A Study in the Theory and Application of the Sociology of Education*, Everett K. Wilson and Herman Schnurer, trans. New York: Free Press.

———. 1964 [1895]. *The Division of Labor in Society*, George Simpson, trans. London: Free Press of Glencoe.

———. 1973 [1899–1900]. "Two Laws of Penal Evolution." *Economy and Society* 2: 285–308.

———. 1976 [1915]. *The Elementary Forms of the Religious Life*, Joseph Ward Swain, trans. New York: Free Press.

Dworkin, Shari L., and Faye Linda Wachs. 2009. *Body Panic: Gender, Health and the Selling of Fitness*. New York: New York University.

Dyer, Gwynne. 2012. "English Triumphs over Other Languages." May 23. 2012. Retrieved November 4, 2013. (http://dawn.com/news/720835/the-triumph-of-english).

Dyson, Freeman. 1999. *The Sun, the Genome, and the Internet*. New York: Oxford University Press.

Dyson, Tim. 2012. "Causes and Consequences of Skewed Sex Ratios." *Annual Review of Sociology* 38: 443–61.

Eagles, Munroe. 1993. "Money and Votes in Canada: Campaign Spending and Parliamentary Election Outcomes, 1984 and 1988." *Canadian Public Policy* 19: 432–49.

Eagly, Alice H., and Wendy Wood. 1999. "The Origins of Sex Differences in Human Behavior: Evolved Dispositions versus Social Roles." *American Psychologist* 54: 408–23.

———. 2013. "The Nature–Nurture Debates: 25 Years of Challenges in Understanding the Psychology of Gender." *Perspectives on Psychological Science* 8(3): 340–57.

Earl, Jennifer and Katrina Kimport. 2011. *Digitially Enabled Social Change: Activism in the Internet Age*. Cambridge MA: MIT Press.

Easton, Thomas. 2011. *Taking Sides: Clashing Views in Science, Technology, and Society*. Guilford, CT: McGraw-Hill/Dushkin.

"Eating a Burger King 'Super Seven Incher' Is Just Like Giving a Blow Job." 2009. Retrieved 21 July 2014 (http://gawker.com/5301856/eating-a-burger-king-super-seven-incher-is-just-like-giving-a-blow-job).

Economist. 2007. "In Praise of Multiculturalism." June 14. Retrieved February 3, 2014 (www.economist.com/node/9337695?zid=315&ah=ee087c5cc3198fc82970cd65083f5281).

Edel, Abraham. 1965. "Social Science and Value: A Study in Interrelations." Pp. 218–38 in Irving Louis Horowitz, ed. *The New Sociology: Essays in Social Science and Social Theory in Honor of C. Wright Mills*. New York: Oxford University Press.

Ehrlich, Paul R., Gretchen C. Daily, Scott C. Daily, Norman Myers, and James Salzman. 1997. "No Middle Way on the Environment." *Atlantic Monthly* 280, 6: 98–104. Retrieved October 8, 2000 (www.theatlantic.com/issues/97dec/enviro.htm).

Ehrlich, Paul, and Robert Ornstein. 2010. *Humanity on a Tightrope: Thoughts on Empathy, Family, and Big Changes for a Viable Future*. Lanham, MD: Rowman & Littlefield.

Eichler, Margrit. 1987. *Nonsexist Research Methods*. Boston: Allen & Unwin.

———. 1988a. *Families in Canada Today*, 2nd ed. Toronto: Gage.

———. 1988b. *Nonsexist Research Methods: A Practical Guide*. Boston: Unwin Hyman.

Einstein, Albert. 1954. *Ideas and Opinions*, Carl Seelig, ed., Sonja Bargmann, trans. New York: Crown.

Eisenstadt, S. N. 1956. *From Generation to Generation*. New York: Free Press.

Eisenstein, Elizabeth L. 1983. *The Printing Revolution in Early Modern Europe*. Cambridge/New York: Cambridge University Press.

Eisler, Riane. 1987. *The Chalice and the Blade: Our History, Our Future*. New York: HarperCollins.

Ekman, Paul. 1999. "Basic Emotions." Pp 45–60 in Tim Dalgleish and Mick Power, eds. *Handbook of Cognition and Emotion*. New York: John Wiley & Sons.

Elections Canada. 2011. "Official Voting Results: Forty-First General Election 2011." Retrieved September 6, 2011 (www.elections.ca/scripts/ovr2011/default.html).

———. 2013. "Voter Turnout at Federal Elections and Referendums." Retrieved 14 August 2013 (www.elections.ca/content.aspx?section=ele&dir=turn&document=index&lang=e).

Elias, Norbert. 1994 [1939]. *The Civilizing Process*, Edmund Jephcott, trans. Cambridge, MA: Blackwell.

Ellis, Lee, Brian Robb, and Donald Burke. 2005. "Sexual Orientation in United States and Canadian College Students." *Archives of Sexual Behavior* 34: 569–81.

Ellison, Nicole B., Charles Steinfeld, and Cliff Lampe. 2007. "The Benefits of Facebook 'Friends:' Social Capital and College Students' Use of Online Social Network Sites." *Journal of Computer-Mediated Communication* 12(4): 1143–68. Retrieved August 8, 2013 (http://jcmc.indiana.edu/vol12/issue4/ellison.html).

Ellul, Jacques. 1964 [1954]. *The Technological Society*, John Wilkinson, trans. New York: Vintage.

Employment and Social Development Canada. 2014. "Family Life–Marriage." Retrieved July 14, 2014 (www4.hrsdc.gc.ca/.3ndic.1t.4r@-eng.jsp?iid=78&bw=1).

Encrenaz, Gaelle, Benjamin Contrand, Karen Leffondre, Raphaelle Queinec, Albertine Aouba, Eric Jougla, Alain Miras, and Emmanuel Legarde. 2012. "Impact of the 1998 Football World Cup on Suicide Rates in France: Results from the National Death Registry." *Suicide and Life-Threatening Behavior* 42(2): 129–35.

Engels, Frederick. 1970 [1884]. *The Origins of the Family, Private Property and the State*, Eleanor Burke Leacock, ed., Alec West, trans. New York: International Publishers.

England, Paula. 1992. *Comparable Worth: Theories and Evidence*. Hawthorne, NY: Aldine de Gruyter.

———. 2010. "The Gender Revolution: Uneven and Stalled." *Gender and Society* 24(2), 149–66.

Entine, J. 2000. *Taboo: Why Black Athletes Dominate Sports and Why We Are Afraid to Talk about It*. New York: Public Affairs.

Environics Institute. 2011. *Focus Canada 2011*. Ottawa, ON: Author.

Equal Voice. 2005. "The Facts, Ma'am." Retrieved June 12, 2006 (www.equalvoice.ca/research.html).

Ernst, Edzard, and Max H. Pittler. 2006. "Celebrity-Based Medicine." *Medical Journal of Australia* 185(11/12): 680–81.

Erulkar, Annabel. 2013. "Adolescence Lost: The Realities of Child Marriage." *Journal of Adolescent Health* 52: 513–14.

Esmail, Nadeem. 2011. "Canada's Physician Supply." *Fraser Forum* (March/April): 12–18.

Esping-Andersen, Gøsta. 1990. *The Three Worlds of Welfare Capitalism*. Princeton, NJ: Princeton University Press.

Espinoza, Penelope, Ana B. Arêas da Luz Fontes, and Clarissa J. Arms-Chavez. 2014. "Attributional Gender Bias: Teachers' Ability and Effort Explanations for Students' Math Performance." *Social Psychology of Education* 17: 105–26.

Estrich, Susan. 1987. *Real Rape*. Cambridge, MA: Harvard University Press.

Etheridge, D. M., L. P. Steele, R. L. Langenfelds, R. J. Francey, J.-M. Barnola, and V. I. Morgan. 1998. "Historical CO_2 Record from the Law Dome DE08, DE08-2, and DSS ice cores." Retrieved 31 March 2013 (http://cdiac.ornl.gov/ftp/trends/co2/lawdome.combined.dat).

"Ethnic Groups in the World." 2001. *Scientific American*. Retrieved December 4, 2001 (www.sciam.com/1998/0998issue/0998numbers.html).

Evans, Geoffrey, and Ksenia Northmore-Ball. 2012. "The Limits of Secularization? The Resurgence of Orthodoxy in Post-Soviet Russia." *Journal for the Scientific Study of Religion* 51(4): 795–808.

Evans, Peter B., Dietrich Rueschemeyer, and Theda Skocpol. 1985. *Bringing the State Back In*. Cambridge, UK: Cambridge University Press.

Everingham, Christine, Deborah Stevenson, and Penny Warner-Smith. 2007. "'Things Are Getting Better All the Time?' Challenging the Narrative of Women's Progress from a Generational Perspective." *Sociology* 41(3): 419–37.

Evertsson, Marie. 2014. "Gender Ideology and the Sharing of Housework and Child Care in Sweden." *Journal of Family Issues* 35: 929–49.

"Eye-Stinging Beijing Air Risks Lifelong Harm to Babies." 2013. *Bloomberg News* 6 February. Retrieved 6 February 2013 (www.bloomberg.com/news/print/2013-02-06/eye-string-beijing-air-risks-lifelong-harm-to-babies.html).

Fagot, Berly I., Caire S. Rodgers, and Mary D. Leinbach. 2000. "Theories of Gender Socialization." Pp. 65–89 in Thomas Eckes, ed. *The Developmental Social Psychology of Gender*. Mahwah, NJ: Lawrence Erlbaum Associates.

Fallon, Elizabeth A., Brandonn S. Harris, and Paige Johnson. 2014. "Prevalence of Body Dissatisfaction among a United States Adult Sample." *Eating Behaviors* 15: 151–58.

"Farewell to Springhill: N.S. Coal-Mining Town to Be Dissolved, Amalgamated." *Globe and Mail* 15 March 2014. Retrieved

15 March 2014 (www.theglobeandmail.com/news/national/farewell-to-springhill-ns-coal-mining-town-to-be-dissolved-amalgamated/article17507611/).

Farrell, Colin. n.d. "The Canadian Prison Strap." Retrieved May 12, 2006 (www.corpun.com/canada2.html).

Fattah, Ezzat A. 1991. *Understanding Criminal Victimization: An Introduction to Theoretical Victimology*. Scarborough, ON: Prentice Hall.

Faulkner, Anne H., and Kevin Cranston. 1998. "Correlates of Same-Sex Sexual Behavior in a Random Sample of Massachusetts High School Students." *Journal of Public Health* 88, February: 262–66.

Fausto-Sterling, Anne, Cynthia Garcia Coll, and Meaghann Lamarre. 2012. "Sexing the Baby: Part 2—Applying Dynamic Systems Theory to the Emergences of Sex-Related Differences in Infants and Toddlers." *Social Science and Medicine* 75: 1693–1702.

Fava, Sylvia Fleis. 1956. "Suburbanism as a Way of Life." *American Sociological Review* 21: 34–37.

Febvre, Lucien, and Henri-Jean Martin. 1976 [1958]. *The Coming of the Book: The Impact of Printing 1450–1800*, David Gerard, trans. London: NLB.

Federal Accountability Initiative for Reform. 2013. "White-Collar Crime in Canada." Retrieved December 10, 2013 (http://fairwhistleblower.ca/issues/white_collar_crime_overview.html).

Feeley, Malcolm M., and Jonathan Simon. 1992. "The New Penology: Notes on the Emerging Strategy of Corrections and its Implications." *Criminology* 30: 449–74.

Fenn, Mavis L. 2013. "Buddhism." Pp. 156–203 in Doris R. Jakobsh, ed. *World Religions, Canadian Perspectives: Eastern Traditions*. Toronto: Nelson Education.

Fernandez, Sofia, and Mary Pritchard. 2012. "Relationships between Self-esteem, Media Influence, and Drive for Thinness." *Eating Behaviors* 13: 321–25.

Fernandez-Dols, Jose-Miguel, Flor Sanchez, Pilar Carrera, and Maria-Angeles Ruiz-Belda. 1997. "Are Spontaneous Expressions and Emotions Linked? An Experimental Test of Coherence." *Journal of Nonverbal Behavior* 21: 163–77.

Ferraro, Vincent. 2010. *Women in Canada: A Gender-based Statistical Report, Paid Work*. Ottawa, ON: Minister of Industry.

Ferree, Myra Marx. 2010. "Filling the Glass: Gender Perspectives on Families." *Journal of Marriage and Family* 72: 420–39.

Figart, Deborah M., and June Lapidus. 1996. "The Impact of Comparable Worth on Earnings Inequality." *Work and Occupations* 23: 297–318.

Fikkan, Janna L., and Esther D. Rothblum. 2012. "We Agree: Fat Is a Feminist Issue." *Sex Roles* 66: 632–35.

Finch, Frank D., and Steven R. H. Beacham. 2010. "Marriage in the New Millennium: A Decade in Review." *Journal of Marriage and Family* 72: 630–49.

"Finding God in Harry Potter." 2005. *The Christian Post* 16 July. Retrieved December 14, 2005 (www.christianpost.com/article/education/895/section/finding.god.in.harry.potter/1.htm).

Finke, Roger, and Rodney Starke. 1992. *The Churching of America, 1776–1990: Winners and Losers in Our Religious Economy*. New Brunswick, NJ: Rutgers University Press.

Finnie, Ross, Stephen Childs, and Andrew Wismer. 2011. *Under-Represented Groups in Postsecondary Education in Ontario: Evidence from the Youth in Transition Survey*. Toronto: Higher Education Quality Council of Ontario.

Fischer, Claude S. 1981. "The Public and Private Worlds of City Life." *American Sociological Review* 46: 306–16.

———. 1984 [1976]. *The Urban Experience*, 2nd ed. New York: Harcourt Brace Jovanovich.

Fischer, Claude S., Michael Hout, Martín Sánchez Jankowski, Samuel R. Lucas, Ann Swidler, and Kim Voss. 1996. *Inequality by Design: Cracking the Bell Curve Myth*. Princeton, NJ: Princeton University Press.

Fischer, Nancy L. 2013. "Seeing "Straight": Contemporary Critical Heterosexuality Studies and Sociology: An Introduction." *The Sociological Quarterly* 54: 501–10.

Fisher, John. 1999. *A Report on Lesbian, Gay and Bisexual Youth*. Ottawa: EGALE.

Fisher, Max. 2013. "This Map Shows Where the World's 30 Million Slaves Live. There Are 60,000 in the U.S." *The Washington Post* 17 October Retrieved 8 March 2014 (www.washingtonpost.com/blogs/worldviews/wp/2013/10/17/this-map-shows-where-the-worlds-30-million-slaves-live-there-are-60000-in-the-u-s/).

Fleras, Augie. 2009. *The Politics of Multiculturalism: Multicultural Governance in Comparative Perspective*. New York: Palgrave.

Flores, Lucien. 2013. "Interview: 'World War Z' Director Marc Forster." *The Daily Free Press* 21 June. Retrieved March 12, 2014 (http://dailyfreepress.com/2013/06/21/interview-marc-forster-chases-zombies-in-world-war-z/).

Flowers, Paul, and Katie Buston. 2001. "'I Was Terrified of Being Different': Exploring Gay Men's Accounts of Growing-Up in a Heterosexist Society." *Journal of Adolescence, Special Issue: Gay, Lesbian, and Bisexual Youth* 24, 1 (February): 51–65.

Flynn, James R. 1987. "Massive IQ Gains in 14 Nations: What IQ Tests Really Measure." *Psychological Bulletin* 101: 171–91.

Fomby, Paula, and Andrew J. Cherlin. 2007. "Family Instability and Child Well-being." *American Sociological Review* 72: 181–204.

Fomby, Paula, and Christie Sennott. 2013. "Family Structure Instability and Mobility: The Consequences for Adolescents' Problem Behavior." *Social Science Research* 42: 181–206.

Fong, Francis, and Sonya Gulati. 2013. *Employment and Education among Aboriginal Peoples*. Special Report TD Economics. October 7. Retrieved March 10, 2014 (www.td.com/document/PDF/economics/special/EmploymentAndEducationAmongAboriginalPeoples.pdf).

Forbes, Gordon B., Jachee Jung, Juan Diego Vaamonde, Alice Omar, Laura Paris, and Nilton Soreas Formiga. 2012. "Body Dissatisfaction and Disordered Eating in Three Cultures: Argentina, Brazil and the U.S." *Sex Roles* 66: 677–94.

"Foreign Direct Investment in 2007." 2008. *EconomyWatch*. Retrieved November 16, 2010 (http://www.economywatch.com/foreign-direct-investment/2007.html).

Fortin, Nicole, David Green, Thomas Lemieux, Kevin Milligan, and Craig Riddell. 2012. "Canadian Inequality: Recent Development and Policy Options." *Canadian Public Policy* 38(2): 121–45.

Forum Research. 2013. "More than Two Thirds Support Decriminalization/Legalization of Marijuana." Press release, August 24, 2013. Retrieved April 1, 2014 (www.forumresearch.com/forms/News%20Archives/News%20Releases/50140_Federal_Trudeau_-_Marijuana_%2824082013%29_Forum_Research.pdf).

Foucault, Michel. 1973. *The Birth of the Clinic: An Archaeology of Medical Perception*, A. M. Sheridan, trans. London, UK: Routledge.

———. 1977. *Discipline and Punish: The Birth of the Prison*, Alan Sheridan, trans. New York: Pantheon.

———. 1981. *The History of Sexuality: Volume 1, an Introduction.* Harmondsworth, UK: Penguin.

———. 1988. *Madness and Civilization: A History of Insanity in the Age of Reason*, Richard Howard, trans. New York: Random House.

———. 1995. *Discipline and Punish: The Birth of the Prison.* New York: Vintage.

———. 2003. *Society Must Be Defended: Lectures at the College de France, 1975–76.* New York: St. Martin's Press.

Fournier, Patrick, Fred Cutler, Stuart Soroka, and Dietlind Stolle. 2011. "The 2011 Canadian Election Study." Retrieved 14 August 2013 ([dataset] http://ces-eec.org/pagesE/surveys.html).

Fox, Nick J. 2012. *The Body*. Cambridge, UK: Polity Press.

Fox, Yale, and Robert J. Brym. 2009. "Musical Attention Deficit Disorder." Darwin vs. The Machine. Retrieved May 30, 2010 (www.darwinversusthemachine.com/2009/10/musical-attention-deficit-disorder).

Francis, D. 1992. *The Imaginary Indian: The Image of the Indian in Canadian Culture*. Vancouver, BC: Arsenal Pulp Press.

Franco, Zeno, and Philip Zimbardo. 2006–07. "The Banality of Heroism." *Greater Good* 3, 2: 33–4. Retrieved January 3, 2008 (http://greatergood.berkeley.edu/greatergood/archive/2006fallwinter/francozimbardo.html).

Frank Porter Graham Child Development Center. 1999. "Early Learning, Later Success: The Abecedarian Study." Retrieved August 10, 2000 (www.fpg.unc.edu/~abc/abcedarianWeb/index.htm).

Frank, Thomas. 2009. "Dissent Commodified." *The Huffington Post* August 19. Retrieved November 2, 2013. (www.huffingtonpost.com/thomas-frank/dissent-commodified_b_263496.html).

Frankel, Glenn. 1996. "U.S. Aided Cigarette Firms in Conquests Across Asia." *Washington Post* November 17: A01. Retrieved February 8, 2003 (www.washingtonpost.com/wp-srv/national/longterm/tobacco/stories/asia.htm).

Franklin, Cortney A., and Glen A. Kercher. 2012. "The Intergenerational Transmission of Intimate Partner Violence: Differentiating Correlates in a Random Community Sample." *Journal of Family Violence* 27: 187–99.

Franklin, Karen. 1998. "Psychosocial Motivations of Hate Crime Perpetrators." Paper presented at the annual meetings of the American Psychological Association (San Francisco: 16 August).

Fraser Institute. 2007 *Home Schooling: From the Extreme to the Mainstream.* Studies in Educational Policy. Retrieved March 10, 2011 (www.fraserinstitute.org/research-news/display.aspx?id=13089).

Fréchette, Danielle, Daniel Hollenberg, Arun Shrichand, Carole Jacob, and Indraneel Datta. 2013. *What's Really Behind Canada's Unemployed Specialists? Too many, Too Few Doctors? Findings from the Royal College's Employment Study.* Ottawa, ON: The Royal College of Physicians and Surgeons of Canada.

Fredericks, Jennifer A., and Jacquelynne S. Eccles. 2005. "Family Socialization, Gender, and Sport Motivation and Involvement." *Journal of Sport and Exercise Psychology* 27(1): 3–31.

Freedman, Samuel G. 2011. "Waging a One-Man War on American Muslims." *New York Times* 16 December. Retrieved January 13, 2013 (www.nytimes.com/2011/12/17/us/on-religion-a-one-man-war-on-american-muslims.html?_r=1&).

Freedom House. 2013. "*Freedom in the World* Country Rankings." Retrieved August 11, 2013 (www.freedomhouse.org/sites/default/files/Country%20Status%20%26%20Ratings%20Overview%2C%201973-2013.pdf).

Freidson, Eliot. 1986. *Professional Powers: A Study of the Institutionalization of Formal Knowledge*. Chicago: University of Chicago Press.

Freire, Paolo. 1972. *The Pedagogy of the Oppressed*. New York: Herder and Herder.

Frere-Jones, Sasha. 2012. "Cold Facts." *The New Yorker* August 3. Retrieved April 11, 2014 (www.newyorker.com/online/blogs/sashafrerejones/2012/08/searching-for-sugar-man-malik-bendjellou.html).

Freud, Sigmund. 1962 [1930]. *Civilization and Its Discontents*, James Strachey, trans. New York: Norton.

———. 1973 [1915–17]. *Introductory Lectures on Psychoanalysis*, James Strachey, trans., James Strachey and Angela Richards, eds. Harmondsworth, UK: Penguin.

———. 1977 [1905]. *On Sexuality*, James Strachey, trans., Angela Richards, comp., and ed. Harmondsworth, UK: Penguin.

Freudenburg, William R. 1997. "Contamination, Corrosion and the Social Order: An Overview." *Current Sociology* 45, 3: 19–39.

Frideres, James, and Rene Gadacz. 2011. *Aboriginal Peoples of Canada*, 9th ed. Toronto: Pearson Education.

Fried, Martha Nemes, and Morton H. Fried. 1980. *Transitions: Four Rituals in Eight Cultures*. New York: Norton.

Friesen, Joe. 2013. "The Future Belongs to the Young." *Globe and Mail* 19 January: A4.

Fröbel, Folker, Jürgen Heinrichs, and Otto Kreyre. 1980. *The New International Division of Labour: Structural Unemployment in Industrialised Countries and Industrialisation in Developing Countries*. Pete Burgess, trans. Cambridge: Cambridge University Press.

Froissart, Jean. 1968 [c. 1365]. *Chronicles*, selected and translated by Geoffrey Brereton. Harmondsworth, UK: Penguin.

"Fuel." 2013. Giantbomb.com. Retrieved 1 April 2013 (www.giantbomb.com/fuel/61-23461/).

Furstenberg, Frank F., Jr. 2010. "On a New Schedule: Transitions to Adulthood and Family Change." *The Future of Children* 20(1): 67–87.

Fussell, Elizabeth. 2006. "Leaving New Orleans: Social Stratification, Networks, and Hurricane Evacuation." Retrieve April 3, 2014 (http://understandingkatrina.ssrc.org/Fussell).

Gadalla, Tahany M. 2008. "Impact of Marital Dissolution on Men's and Women's Incomes: A Longitudinal Study." *Journal of Divorce and Marriage* 50(1): 55–65.

Gaetz, Stephen, Jesse Donaldson, Tim Richter, and Tanya Gulliver. 2013. *The State of Homelessness in Canada 2013*. Toronto: Canadian Homelessness Research Network Press.

Gajjar, Irina N. 2013. *On Hinduism*. Edinburg, VA: Axioms Press.

Galarneau, Diane, and Marian Radulescu. 2009. "Employment among the Disabled." *Perspectives*: 5–15. Catalogue No. 75-001-X. Ottawa: Statistics Canada.

Gambetta, Diego, ed. 1988. *Trust: Making and Breaking Cooperative Relations*. Oxford, UK: Blackwell.

Gammon, Katherine. 2009. "Infoporn: Today's Playmates Are More Like Anime Figures Than Real Humans." *Wired* 17(2). Retrieved 14 January 2013 (www.wired.com/special multimedia/2009/st_infoporn_1702 (retrieved 14 January 2013).

Gamson, William A. 1975. *The Strategy of Social Protest*. Homewood, IL: Dorsey Press.

Gamson, William A., Bruce Fireman, and Steven Rytina. 1982. *Encounters with Unjust Authority*. Homewood, IL: Dorsey Press.

Gans, Herbert. 1962. *The Urban Villagers: Group and Class in the Life of Italian*-Americans. New York: Free Press.

———. 1972. "The Positive Functions of Poverty." *American Journal of Sociology* 78(2): 275–29.

———. 1979. *Deciding What's News: A Study of CBS Evening News, NBC Nightly News, Newsweek and Time*. New York: Pantheon.

———. 1991. "Symbolic Ethnicity: The Future of Ethnic Groups and Cultures in America." Pp. 430–43 in Norman R. Yetman, ed. *Majority and Minority: The Dynamics of Race and Ethnicity in American Life*, 5th ed. Boston, MA: Allyn and Bacon.

Ganns, George E., ed. 1991. *Ignatius of Loyola: The Spiritual Exercises and Selected Works*. New York: Paulist Press.

Garfinkel, Harold. 1967. *Studies in Ethnomethodology*. Englewood Cliffs, NJ: Prentice-Hall.

Garland, David. 1990. *Punishment and Modern Society: A Study in Social Theory*. Chicago: University of Chicago Press.

Garrau, Joel. 1991. *Edge City: Life on the New Frontier*. New York: Doubleday.

Gauvain, Mary, Beverly I. Fagot, Craig Leve, and Kate Kavanagh. 2002. "Instruction by Mothers and Fathers During Problem Solving with Their Young Children." *Journal of Family Psychology* 6, 1 (March): 81–90.

Gauvreau, Michael. 2008. *The Catholic Origins of Quebec's Quiet Revolution, 1931–1970*. Montreal and Kingston: McGill-Queen's University Press.

Gawley, Tim, Thomas Perks, and James Curtis. 2009. "Height, Gender, and Authority Status at Work: Analyses for a National Sample of Canadian Workers." *Sex Roles* 60: 208–22.

Gelbspan, Ross. 1999. "Trading Away Our Chances to End Global Warming." *Boston Globe* May 16: E2.

Gelfand, Michele J., J. L. Raver, L. Nishii, L. M. Leslie, J. Lun, B. C. Lim, L. Duan, A. Almaliach, S. Ang, J. Arnadottir, Z. Aycan, K. Boehnke, P. Boski, R. Cabecinhas, D. Chan, J. Chhokar, A. D'Amato, M. Ferrer, I. C. Fischlmayr, R. Fischer, M. Fülöp, J. Georgas, E. S. Kashima, Y. Kashima, K. Kim, A. Lempereur, P. Marquez, R. Othman, B. Overlaet, P. Panagiotopoulou, K. Peltzer, L. R. Perez-Florizno, L. Ponomarenko, A. Realo, V. Schei, M. Schmitt, P. B. Smith, N. Soomro, E. Szabo, N. Taveesin, M. Toyama, E. Van de Vliert, N. Vohra, C. Ward, and S. Yamaguchi, S. 2011. "Differences between Tight and Loose Cultures: A 33-Nation Study." *Science* 332: 1100–04.

Gellner, E. 1988. *Plough, Sword and Book: The Structure of Human History*. Chicago: University of Chicago Press.

Gelman, Susan A. 2003. *The Essential Child: Origins of Essentialism in Everyday Thought*. New York: Oxford University Press.

George, Moolamattom V. 2010. "The Fertility Decline in India's Kerala State: A Unique Example of Below Replacement Fertility in a High Fertility Country." *Canadian Studies in Population* 37 (3/4): 563–600.

Gerber, Theodore P., and Michael Hout. 1998. "More Shock than Therapy: Market Transition, Employment, and Income in Russia, 1991–1995." *American Journal of Sociology* 104: 1–50.

Germani, Gino, and Kalman Silvert. 1961. "Politics, Social Structure and Military Intervention in Latin America." *European Journal of Sociology* 11: 62–81.

Gerrits, Trudie, Ria Reis, Didi D.M. Braat, Jan A.M. Kremer, and Anita P. Hardon. 2013. "Bioethics in Practice: Addressing Ethically Sensitive Requests in a Dutch Fertility Clinic." *Social Science and Medicine* 98: 330–339.

Gerschenkron, Alexander. 1962. *Economic Backwardness in Historical Perspective: A Book of Essays*. Cambridge, MA: Harvard University Press.

Ghosh, Bobby. 2011. "Rage, Rap and Revolution: Inside the Arab Youth Quake." *Time.com* February 17. Retrieved February 17, 2011 (http://www.time.com/time/world/article/0,8599,2049808,00.html).

Giddens, Anthony. 1990. *Sociology: A Brief But Critical Introduction*, 3rd ed. New York: Harcourt Brace Jovanovich.

Gidengil, Elisabeth. 1992. "Canada Votes: A Quarter Century of Canadian National Election Studies." *Canadian Journal of Political Science* 25: 219–48.

Gignac, Clément. 2014. "Quebec's Child Care Program: How Social Innovation Can Create Wealth." *Globe and Mail* 16 April. Retrieved April 16, 2014 (www.theglobeandmail.com/).

Gill, Ritu and Angela R. Febbraro. 2013. "Experiences and Perceptions of Sexual Harassment in the Canadian Forces Combat Arms." *Violence Against Women* 19(2): 269–87.

Gilliom, John, and Torrin Monahan. 2012. *SuperVision: An Introduction to the Surveillance Society*. Chicago: University of Chicago Press.

Gillis, A. R. 1995. "Urbanization." Pp. 13.1–13.35 in Robert J. Brym, ed. *New Society Brief Edition: Sociology for the 21st Century*. Toronto: Harcourt Brace.

Gillis, John R. 1981. *Youth and History: Tradition and Change in European Age Relations, 1770–Present*, expanded student ed. New York: Academic Press.

Gilman, S. L. 1991. *The Jew's Body*. New York: Routledge.

Gilmore, Jason, and Sabastien LaRochelle-Cote. 2011. "Inside the Labour Market Downturn." *Perspectives on Labour and Income*. Ottawa: Statistics Canada.

Gilpin, Robert. 2001. *Global Political Economy: Understanding the International Economic Order*. Princeton, NJ: Princeton University Press.

Giordano, Peggy C. 2014. "Gender, Crime, and Desistance: Toward a Theory of Cognitive Transformation." Pp. 41–62 in John A. Humphrey and Peter Cordella, eds. *Effective Interventions in the Lives of Criminal Offenders*. New York: Springer.

Gitlin, Todd. 1983. *Inside Prime Time*. New York: Pantheon.

Goddard Institute for Space Studies, National Aeronautics and Space Administration. 2013. "GLOBAL Land-Ocean Temperature Index in 0.01 Degrees Celsius Base Period: 1951–1980." Retrieved 31 March 2013 (http://data.giss.nasa.gov/gistemp/tabledata_v3/GLB.Ts+dSST.txt).

Godha, Deepali, David R. Hotchkiss, and Anastasia J. Gage. 2013. "Association between Child Marriage and Reproductive Health Outcomes and Service Utilization: A Multi-Country Study From South Asia." *Journal of Adolescent Health* 52: 552–58.

Goffman, Erving. 1959. *The Presentation of Self in Everyday Life*. Garden City, NY: Anchor.

———. 1961. *Asylums: Essays on the Social Situation of Mental Patients and Other Inmates*. Garden City, NY: Anchor Books.

———. 1963. *Stigma: Notes on the Management of Spoiled Identity*. Englewood Cliffs, NJ: Prentice-Hall.

———. 1971. *Relations in Public: Microstudies of the Public Order*. New York: Basic Books.

———. 1974. *Frame Analysis*. Cambridge, MA: Harvard University Press.

Gold, Raymond. 1958. "Roles in Sociological Field Observations." *Social Forces* 36: 217–23.

Goldberg, Abbie E., Julianna Z. Smith, and Maureen Perry-Jenkins. 2012. "The Division of Labor in Lesbian, Gay, and Heterosexual New Adoptive Parents." *Journal of Marriage and Family* 74(4): 812–28.

Goldberg, Sharon. 2013. "Judaism." Pp. 30–87 in Doris R. Jakobs, ed. *World Religions, Canadian Perspectives: Eastern Traditions*. Toronto, ON: Nelson Education.

Goldie, Terry. 2001. *In a Queer Country: Gay & Lesbian Studies in the Canadian Context*. Vancouver: Arsenal Pulp Press.

"Gold Medal Men's Hockey Game Gets Record Canadian TV Audience." *The Province* 1 March. Retrieved March 28, 2010 (www.theprovince.com/entertainment/Gold+medal+hockey+game+gets+record+Canadian+audience/2628644/story.html).

Goll, David. 2002. "True Priority of Office Ethics Clouded by Scandals." *East Bay Business Times* August 19. Retrieved January 13, 2003 (http://eastbay.bizjournals.com/eastbay/stories/2002/08/19/smallb3.html).

Gollom, Mark. 2014. "Temporary Foreign Workers Have Better Work Ethic, Some Employers Believe." *CBC News*. Retrieved April 12, 2014 (www.cbc.ca/news/temporary-foreign-workers-have-better-work-ethic-some-employers-believe-1.2600864).

Goodin, Samantha M., Alyssa Van Denburg, Sarah K. Murnen, and Linda Smolak. 2011. "'Putting on' Sexiness: A Content Analysis of the Presence of Sexualizing Characteristics in Girls' Clothing." *Sex Roles* 65: 1–12.

Gordinier, Jeff. 2008. *X Saves the World: How Generation X Got the Shaft But Can Still Keep Everything from Sucking*. New York: Viking.

Gordon, Catherine, and Jerry P. White. 2013. *Supply Side of Aboriginal Post-secondary Education in Canada*. Paper presented at the conference on Indigenous Issues in Post-Secondary Education: Transitions to the Workplace, Toronto. Accessed March 15, 2014 (http://ir.lib.uwo.ca/cgi/viewcontent.cgi?article=1178&context=iipj).

Gordon, D. M., R. Edwards, and M. Reich. 1982. *Segmented Work, Divided Workers: The Historical Transformation of Labor in the United States*. New York: Cambridge University Press.

Gordon, Sarah. 1984. *Hitler, Germans, and the Jewish Question*. Princeton, NJ: Princeton University Press.

Gorman, Christine. 1997. "A Boy without a Penis." *Time* March 24: 83.

Gorski, Philip S., and Ates Altinordu. 2008. "After Secularization?" *Annual Review of Sociology* 34: 55–85.

Gottdiener, Mark. 2010. *The New Urban Sociology*. Boulder, CO: Westview Press.

Gottfredson, Michael, and Travis Hirschi. 1990. *A General Theory of Crime*. Stanford, CA: Stanford University Press.

Gould, Adrian C., Philippe Apparicio, and Marie-Soleil Cloutier. 2012. "Classifying Neighbourhoods by Level of Access to Stores Selling Fresh Fruit and Vegetables and Groceries: Identifying Problematic Areas in the City of Gatineau, Quebec." *Canadian Journal of Public Health* 103(6): 433–37.

Gould, Stephen Jay. 1988. "Kropotkin Was No Crackpot." *Natural History* 97, 7: 12–18.

———. 1996. *The Mismeasure of Man*, rev. ed. New York: Norton.

Government of Canada. 1971. "Multiculturalism Policy." Statement to the House of Commons, November.

———. 2001. "Early Intervention Programs." Retrieved February 14, 2003 (www.crime-prevention.org/english/publications/youth/mobilize/early_e.html).

Graff, Kaitlin, Sarah K. Murnen, and Linda Smolak. 2012. "Too Sexualized to be Taken Seriously? Perceptions of a Girl in Childlike versus Sexualizing Clothing." *Sex Roles* 66: 764–75.

Gramigna, Remo. 2012. "Between Cultural Studies and Semiotics of Culture: The Case of Culture Jamming." *Acta Semiotica Estica* 9: 66–89.

Gramsci, Antonio. 1957. *The Modern Prince and Other Writings*, Louis Marks, trans. New York: International Publishers.

———. 1971. *Selections from the Prison Notebooks*, Q. Hoare and G. Smith, eds. London, UK: Lawrence & Wishart.

Granovetter, Mark. 1973. "The Strength of Weak Ties." *American Sociological Review* 78: 1360–80.

———. 1995. *Getting a Job: A Study of Contacts and Careers*. Chicago: University of Chicago Press.

Grant, Tavia. 2014. "Working for Nothing: Canada Joins the Global Minimum Wage Debate." *The Globe and Mail* January 30. Retrieved February 15, 2014 (www.theglobeandmail.com/report-on-business/economy/working-for-nothing-canada-joins-global-minimum-wage-debate/article16508375/?page=all).

Gray, Richard. 2012. "Internet May Save Endangered Languages." *The Telegraph* February 18. Retrieved November 4, 2013. (www.telegraph.co.uk/technology/internet/9090885/Internet-may-save-endangered-languages.html).

Green, Adam Isaiah. 2007. "Queer Theory and Sociology: Locating the Subject and the Self in Sexuality Studies." *Sociological Theory* 25: 26–45.

Greenhill, Pauline. 2001. "Can You See the Difference: Queerying the Nation, Ethnicity, Festival, and Culture in Winnipeg." Pp. 103–21 in Terry Goldie, ed. *In a Queer Country: Gay & Lesbian Studies in the Canadian Context*. Vancouver: Arsenal Pulp Press.

Greenstein, Theodore N. 1996. "Husbands' Participation in Domestic Labor: Interactive Effects of Wives' and Husbands' Gender Ideologies." *Journal of Marriage and the Family* 58: 585–95.

Gregg, Allan. 2006. "Identity Crisis: Multiculturalism: A Twentieth-Century Dream Becomes a Twenty-First Century Conundrum." *The Walrus* 3/2 (March). Retrieved November 4, 2013. (http://walrusmagazine.com/articles/2006.03-society-canada-multiculturism/).

Gregory, Derek. 2011. "From a View to a Kill: Drones and Late Modern War." *Theory, Culture and Society* 28: 188–215.

Grekul, Jana, Harvey Krahn, and Dave Odynak. 2004. "Sterilizing the 'Feeble-minded': Eugenics in Alberta, Canada, 1929–1972." *Journal of Historical Sociology* 17: 358–84.

Grimmett, Richard F. 2006. "Conventional Arms Transfers to Developing Nations, 1998–2005." Congressional Research Service. Retrieved January 12, 2008 (www.fas.org/sgp/crs/weapons/RL33696.pdf).

Groce, Nora Ellen. 1985. *Everyone Here Spoke Sign Language: Hereditary Deafness on Martha's Vineyard*. Cambridge, MA: Harvard University Press.

Gu, Wulong, and Ambrose Wong. 2010. *Estimates of Human Capital in Canada: The Lifetime Income Approach*. Economic Analysis Research Paper Series. Catalogue no. 11F0027M — No. 062. Ottawa: Statistics Canada.

Guenther, Katja, Kerry Mulligan, and Cameron Papp. 2013. "From the Outside In: Crossing Boundaries to Build Collective Identity in the New Atheist Movement." *Social Problems* 60(4): 457–75.

Guillén, Mauro F. 2001. "Is Globalization Civilizing, Destructive or Feeble? A Critique of Five Key Debates in the Social-Science Literature." *Annual Review of Sociology* 27: 235–60. Retrieved February 6, 2003 (http://knowledge.wharton.upenn.edu/PDFs/938.pdf).

Guilmoto, Christophe Z. 2012. *Sex Imbalances at Birth: Current Trends, Consequences and Policy Implications*. Bangkok, Thailand: UNFPA.

Gunderson, Elizabeth A., Gerardo Ramirez, Susan C. Levine, and Sian L. Beilock. 2012. "The Role of Parents and Teachers in the Development of Gender-Related Math Attitudes." *Sex Roles* 66: 153–66.

Guppy, Neil, and Scott Davies. 1998. *Education in Canada: Recent Trends and Future Challenges*. Ottawa: Ministry of Industry.

Guppy, Neil, and R. Alan Hedley. 1993. *Opportunities in Sociology*. Montreal: Canadian Sociology and Anthropology Association.

Gurr, Ted Robert. 1970. *Why Men Rebel*. Princeton, NJ: Princeton University Press.

Guven, Cahit, Claudia Senik, and Holger Stichnoth. 2012. "You Can't Be Happier than Your Wife: Happiness Gaps and Divorce." *Journal of Economic Behavior and Organization* 82: 110–30.

Haas, Jack and William Shaffir. 1987. Becoming Doctors: The Adoption of a Cloak of Competence. Greenwich, CT: JAI Press.

Habermas, Jürgen. 1989. *The Structural Transformation of the Public Sphere*, Thomas Burger, trans. Cambridge, MA: MIT Press.

Hagan, John. 1989. *Structuralist Criminology*. New Brunswick, NJ: Rutgers University Press.

———. 1994. *Crime and Disrepute*. Thousand Oaks, CA: Pine Forge Press.

Hagan, John, John Simpson, and A. R. Gillis. 1987. "Class in the Household: A Power-Control Theory of Gender and Delinquency." *American Journal of Sociology* 92: 788–816.

Haines, Herbert H. 1996. *Against Capital Punishment: The Anti–Death Penalty Movement in America, 1972–1994*. New York: Oxford University Press.

Hall, Edward. 1959. *The Silent Language*. New York: Doubleday.

———. 1966. *The Hidden Dimension*. New York: Doubleday.

Hall, Stuart. 1980. "Encoding/Decoding." Pp. 128–38 in Stuart Hall, Dorothy Hobson, Andrew Lowe, and Paul Willis, eds. *Culture, Media, Language: Working Papers in Cultural Studies, 1972–79*. London: Hutchinson.

Haman, F., B. Fontaine-Bisson, M. Batal, P. Imbeault, J. M. Blais, and M. A. Robidoux. 2010. "Obesity and Type 2 Diabetes in Northern Canada's Remote First Nations Communities: The Dietary Dilemma." *International Journal of Obesity* 34: S24–S31.

Hamilton, Roberta. 1996. *Gendering the Vertical Mosaic: Feminist Perspectives on Canadian Society*. Toronto: Copp-Clark.

Hancock, Graham. 1989. *Lords of Poverty: The Power, Prestige, and Corruption of the International Aid Business*. New York: Atlantic Monthly Press.

Hancock, Philip, Bill Hughes, Elizabeth Jagger, Kevin Paterson, Rachel Russell, Emmanuelle Tulle-Watson, and Melissa Tyler. 2000. *The Body, Culture, and Society: An Introduction*. Buckingham, UK: Open University Press.

Haney, Craig, W. Curtis Banks, and Philip G. Zimbardo. 1973. "Interpersonal Dynamics in a Simulated Prison." *International Journal of Criminology and Penology* 1: 69–97.

Hango, Darcy. 2013. *Gender Differences in Science, Technology, Engineering, Mathematics and Computer Science (STEM) Programs at University*. Ottawa: Statistics Canada. Catalogue no. 75-006-X. Retrieved March 15, 2014 (www.statcan.gc.ca/pub/75-006-x/2013001/article/11874-eng.pdf).

Hannigan, John. 1995a. "The Postmodern City: A New Urbanization?" *Current Sociology* 43, 1: 151–217.

———. 1995b. *Environmental Sociology: A Social Constructionist Perspective*. London: Routledge.

———. 1998a. *Fantasy City: Pleasure and Profit in the Postmodern Metropolis*. New York: Routledge.

———. 1998b. "Urbanization." Pp. 337–59 in Robert J. Brym, ed. *New Society: Sociology for the 21st Century*, 2nd ed. Toronto: Harcourt Brace Canada.

———. 2005. *Fantasy City: Pleasure and Profit in the Postmodern City*. London: Routledge.

Hannon, Roseann, David S. Hall, Todd Kuntz, Van Laar, and Jennifer Williams. 1995. "Dating Characteristics Leading to Unwanted vs. Wanted Sexual Behavior." *Sex Roles* 33: 767–83.

Haraway, Donna. 1991. *Cyborgs, Simians and Women*. London: Free Association Books.

Hari, Johann. 2009. "You are being lied to about pirates." *Huffington Post* 4 January. http://www.huffingtonpost.com/johann-hari/you-are-being-lied-to-abo_b_155147.html (6 November 2013).

Harris, Chauncy D. 1997. "The Nature of Cities and Urban Geography in the Last Half Century." *Urban Geography* 18: 15–35.

Harris, Chauncy D., and Edward L. Ullman. 1945. "The Nature of Cities." *Annals of the American Academy of Political and Social Science* 242: 7–17.

Harris, Gardiner. 2013. "India's New Focus on Rape Shows Only the Surface of Women's Perils." *New York Times* January 12. Retrieved April 19, 2013 (www.nytimes.com/2013/01/13/world/asia/in-rapes-aftermath-india-debates-violence-against-women.html).

Harris, Marvin. 1974. *Cows, Pigs, Wars and Witches: The Riddles of Culture*. New York: Random House.

Harris, Philip E., Katy L. Cooper, Clare Relton, and Kate J. Thomas. 2012. "Prevalence of Complementary and Alternative Medicine (CAM) Use by the General Population: A Systematic Review and Update." *International Journal of Clinical Practice* 66(10): 924–39.

Harrison, Bennett. 1994. *Lean and Mean: The Changing Landscape of Corporate Power in the Age of Flexibility*. New York: Basic Books.

Hartnagel, Timothy F. 2000. "Correlates of Criminal Behaviour." Pp. 94–136 in Rick Linden, ed. *Criminology: A Canadian Perspective*, 4th ed. Toronto: Harcourt Canada.

Harvey, Edward B., and Richard Kalwa. 1983. "Occupational Status Attainments of University Graduates: Individual Attributes and Labour Market Effects Compared." *Canadian Review of Sociology and Anthropology* 20: 435–53.

Harvey, Elizabeth. 1999. "Short-Term and Long-Term Effects of Early Parental Employment on Children of the National Longitudinal Survey of Youth." *Developmental Psychology* 35: 445–49.

Hatton, Timothy J., and Bernice E. Bray. 2010. "Long Run Trends in the Heights of European Men, 19th–20th Centuries." *Economics and Human Biology* 8: 405–13.

Haub, Carl. 2011. "How Many People Have Ever Lived on Earth?" *Population Reference Bureau*. Retrieved 14 August 2013 (www.prb.org/Publications/Articles/2011/HowManyPeopleHaveEverLivedonEarth.aspx).

Hawley, Amos. 1950. *Human Ecology: A Theory of Community Structure*. New York: Ronald Press.

Häyry, Matti, and Tuija Lehto. 1998. "Genetic Engineering and the Risk of Harm." Paper presented at the 20th World Congress of Philosophy. Boston. Retrieved January 17, 2005 (www.bu.edu/wcp/Papers/Bioe/BioeHay2.htm).

Haythornthwaite, Caroline, and Barry Wellman. 2002. "The Internet in Everyday Life: An Introduction." Pp. 3–41 in B. Wellman and C. Haythornthwaite, eds. *The Internet in Everyday Life*. Oxford: Blackwell.

Health Canada. n.d. "Canadian Cancer Statistics, 2003." Retrieved January 12, 2008 (www.cancer.ca/vgn/images/portal/cit_776/61/38/56158640niw_stats_en.pdf).

———. 1999. "Statistical Report on the Health of Canadians." Retrieved December 25, 1999 (www.hc-sc.gc.ca/hppb/phdd/report/state/englover.html).

———. 2010. "Aboriginal Head Start On Reserve—Backgrounder." Retrieved March 12, 2014 (www.hc-sc.gc.ca/fniah-spnia/famil/develop/ahsor-bckgr-info-eng.php).

Health Care Cost Institute. 2013. *2012 Health Care Cost and Utilization Report.* Washington, DC: Author. Retrieved July 21, 2014 (www.healthcostinstitute.org/ files/HCCI_HCCUR2012.pdf).

Health Service Bureau. 2009. *National Health and Nutrition Survey in Japan*. Ministry of Health and Labour Welfare. Tokyo, Japan: Author.

Heart and Stroke Foundation. 2011. "Time Crunch Is Stealing Healthy Years from Canadians." Retrieved February 19, 2014 (www.heartandstroke.com/site/c.ikIQLcMWJtE/b.7883473/k.3B77/2011_Report__Time_crunch_is_stealing_healthy_years_from_Canadians.htm).

Hechter, M. 1974. *Internal Colonialism: The Celtic Fringe in British National Development, 1536–1966*. Berkeley, CA: University of California Press.

Heckman, James J. 2011. "The American Family in Black and White: A Post-Racial Strategy for Improving Skills to Promote Equality." *Daedalus* 140 (2): 70–89.

Heckman, James, and Dimitriy Masterov. 2007. *The Productivity Argument for Investing in Young Children*. Cambridge, MA: National Bureau of Economic Research. Retrieved March 11, 2014 (www.nber.org/papers/w13016).

Heine, Ronald E. 2013. *Classical Christian Doctrine: Introducing the Essentials of the Christian Faith*. Grand Rapids, MI: Baker Academic.

Held, David. 1987. *Models of Democracy*. Stanford, CA: Stanford University Press.

Henry, Frances, Carol Tator, Winston Mattis, and Tim Rees. 2000. *The Colour of Democracy: Racism in Canadian Society*, 2nd ed. Toronto: Harcourt Brace Canada.

Henry, Frances, et al. 2001. "The Victimization of Racial Minorities in Canada." Pp. 145–60 in Robert J. Brym, ed. *Society in Question: Sociological Readings for the 21st Century*. Toronto: Harcourt Canada.

Herdt, Gilbert. 2001. "Social Change, Sexual Diversity, and Tolerance for Bisexuality in the United States." Pp. 267–83 in Anthony R. D'Augelli and Charlotte J. Patterson, eds. *Lesbian, Gay, and Bisexual Identities and Youth: Psychological Perspectives*. New York: Oxford University Press.

Herlihy, David. 1998. *The Black Death and the Transformation of the West*. Cambridge, MA: Harvard University Press.

Herman, Edward S., and Noam Chomsky. 1988. *Manufacturing Consent: The Political Economy of the Mass Media*. New York: Pantheon.

Herrera, Laura. 2011. "In Florida, Virtual Classrooms with No Teachers." *The New York Times* January 17. Retrieved May 24, 2011 (www.nytimes.com).

Herrnstein, Richard J., and Charles Murray. 1994. *The Bell Curve: Intelligence and Class Structure in American Life*. New York: Free Press.

Hersch, Patricia. 1998. *A Tribe Apart: A Journey into the Heart of American Adolescence*. New York: Ballantine Books.

Hertzman, Clyde, and Thomas Boyce. 2010. "How Experience Gets under the Skin to Create Gradients in Developmental Health." *Annual Review of Public Health* 31: 329–46.

Hess, Alexander. 2013. "On Holiday: Countries with the Most Vacation Days." *Wall Street Journal* June 8. Accessed April 15, 2014. (www.usatoday.com/story/money/business/2013/06/08/countries-most-vacation-days/2400193/).

Hesse-Biber, Sharlene. 1996. *Am I Thin Enough Yet? The Cult of Thinness and the Commercialization of Identity*. New York: Oxford University Press.

Heuveline Patrick, and Jeffrey M. Timberlake. 2004. "The Role of Cohabitation in Family Formation: The United States in Comparative Perspective." *Journal of Marriage and Family* 66: 1214–30.

Hewitt, Belinda, and David de Vaus, D. 2009. Change in the Association between Premarital Cohabitation and Separation, Australia 1945–2000. *Journal of Marriage and Family* 71: 353–61.

Hewitt, J. Joseph, Jonathan Wilkenfeld, and Ted Robert Gurr with Birger Heldt. 2012. *Peace and Conflict 2012*. College Park MD: Center for International Development and Conflict Management, University of Maryland.

Hier, Sean P. 2011. "Tightening the Focus: Moral Panic, Moral Regulation and Liberal Government." *British Journal of Sociology* 62(3): 523–41.

Higgs, Paul, and Chris Gilleard. 2010. "Generational Conflict, Consumption and the Ageing Welfare State in the United Kingdom." *Aging and Society* 30(8): 1439–51.

Hirschi, Travis. 1969. *Causes of Delinquency*. Berkeley, CA: University of California Press.

Hirschman, Albert O. 1970. *Exit, Voice, and Loyalty: Responses to Decline in Firms, Organizations, and States*. Cambridge, MA: Harvard University Press.

Hirst, Paul, and Grahame Thompson. 1999. *Globalization in Question: The International Economy and the Possibilities of Governance*, 2nd ed. London: Polity.

Hobbes, Thomas. 1968 [1651]). *Leviathan*. Middlesex, UK: Penguin.

Hobsbawm, Eric. 1979. "Emotion Work, Feeling Rules, and Social Structure." *American Journal of Sociology* 85: 551–75.

———. 1983. *The Managed Heart: Commercialization of Human Feeling*. Berkeley: University of California Press.

———. 1994. *Age of Extremes: The Short Twentieth Century, 1914–1991*. London: Abacus.

———. 2012. *The Outsourced Self*. New York: Metropolitan Books.

Hochschild, Arlie Russell, with Anne Machung. 1989. *The Second Shift: Working Parents and the Revolution at Home*. New York: Viking.

Hodge, Robert, and David Tripp. 1986. *Children and Television: A Semiotic Approach*. Cambridge, UK: Polity.

Hodson, R., and T. Sullivan. 1995. *The Social Organization of Work*, 2nd ed. Belmont CA: Wadsworth.

Holmqvist, Caroline. 2013. "Undoing War: War Ontologies and the Materiality of Drone Warfare." *Millennium Journal of International Studies* 41(3): 535–52.

hooks, bell. 1984. *Feminist Theory: From Margin to Center*. Boston: South End Press.

Hopkins, Terence K., and Immanuel Wallerstein. 1986. "Commodity Chains in the World Economy Prior to 1800." *Review* 10: 157–70.

Horkheimer, Max, and Theodor W. Adorno. 1986 [1944]. *Dialectic of Enlightenment*, John Cumming, trans. London: Verso.

Horwitz, Allan V., and Jerome C. Wakefield. 2012. *All We Have to Fear: Psychiatry's Transformation of Natural Anxieties into Mental Disorders*. Oxford, UK: Oxford University Press.

Hossain, Emram. 2013. "Rana Plaza Collapse Victims Still Waiting for Compensation." *Huffington Post Canada* 6 August. Retrieved August 11, 2013 (www.huffingtonpost.com/2013/08/06/rana-plaza-collapse-victims-compensation_n_3713408.html)

Howe, Neil and William Strauss. 2009. *Millennials Rising: The Next Great Generation*. New York: Vintage Books.

Hoyt, Homer. 1939. *The Structure and Growth of Residential Neighborhoods in American Cities*. Washington, DC: Federal Housing Authority.

Hughes, Fergus P. 1995. *Children, Play and Development*, 2nd ed. Boston: Allyn and Bacon.

Hughes, H. Stuart. 1967. *Consciousness and Society: The Reorientation of European Social Thought, 1890–1930*. London: Macgibbon and Kee.

Hughes, I. A., C. Houk, S. F. Ahmed, P. A. Lee, and LWPES1/ESPE2 Consensus Group. 2006. "Consensus Statement on Management of Intersex Disorders." *Archives of Diseases in Childhood* 91(7): 554–63.

Hui, Ann. 2013. "Canadian Teens Lead Developed World in Cannabis Use: UNICEF Report." *Globe and Mail* April 15. Retrieved April 3, 2014 (www.theglobeandmail.com/news/national/canadian-teens-lead-developed-world-in-cannabis-use-unicef-report/article11221668/).

Human Resources Development Canada. 2000. "Job Futures 2000." Retrieved June 2001 (http://jobfutures.ca/doc/jf/emerging/emerging.shtml#sample).

Human Resources and Skills Development Canada. 2011a. "Average Student Loan Balance at Completion of Studies." Retrieved May 23, 2011 (www.hrsdc.gc.ca/eng/learning/canada_student_loan/Publications/annual_report/2008-2009/tables/loan_balances.shtml).

———. 2011b. "Learning—Educational Attainment." *Indicators of Well-Being in Canada*. Retrieved April 29, 2011 (www4.hrsdc.gc.ca/.3ndic.1t.4r@-eng.jsp?iid=29).

Hume, Stephen. 2013. "Minor Hockey's Archaic Attitudes about Violence Demand Change." *Vancouver Sun* November 11. Retrieved December 3, 2013. (www.vancouversun.com/news/Stephen+Hume+Minor+hockey+archaic+attitudes+about+violence+demand+change/8900451/story.html).

Humphrey, Laud. 1970. *Tearoom Trade: Impersonal Sex in Public Places*. New Brunswick, NJ: Transaction Publishers.

Huntington, Samuel. 1991. *The Third Wave: Democratization in the Late Twentieth Century*. Norman, OK: University of Oklahoma Press.

Hyde, Janet S., and Janet E. Mertz. 2009. "Gender, Culture, and Mathematics Performance." *Proceedings of the National Academy of Sciences in the United States of America* 106(22): 8801–07.

Ignatiev, N. 1995. *How the Irish Became White*. New York: Routledge.

Ikegami, Naoki, and Gerard F. Anderson 2012. "In Japan, All-Payer Rate Setting under Tight Government Control Has to Be an Effective Approach to Containing Costs." *Health Affairs* 31(5): 1049–56.

IMD International. 2010. "The World Competitiveness Yearbook 2010." Retrieved March 1, 2011 (www.imd.org/research/publications/wcy/upload/PressRelease.pdf).

Inglehart, Ronald. 1997. *Modernization and Postmodernization: Cultural, Economic, and Political Change in 43 Societies*. Princeton, NJ: Princeton University Press.

Ingram, Gordon Brent. 2001. "Redesigning Wreck: Beach Meets Forest as Location of Male Homoerotic Culture in Placemaking in Pacific Canada." Pp. 188–208 in Terry Goldie, ed. *In a Queer Country: Gay & Lesbian Studies in the Canadian Context*. Vancouver: Arsenal Pulp Press.

Inkeles, Alex, and David H. Smith. 1976. *Becoming Modern: Individual Change in Six Developing Countries*. Cambridge, MA: Harvard University Press.

Innis, Harold. 1951. *The Bias of Communication*. Toronto: University of Toronto Press.

Intergovernmental Panel on Climate Change. 2007. "Climate Change 2007." Retrieved May 2, 2007 (www.ipcc.ch).

International Gay, Lesbian, Bisexual, Trans and Intersex Association. "Punishment for Male–Male Sexual Relations. Retrieved November 21, 2010 (http://ilga.org).

"International Tourism Challenged by Deteriorating Global Economy." 2009. *UNWTO World Tourist Barometer* 7, 1. Retrieved November 16, 2010 (www.unwto.org/facts/eng/pdf/barometer/UNWTO_Barom09_1_en_excerpt.pdf).

International Union for Conservation of Nature. 2013. "Table 1: Number of Threatened Species by Major Groups of Organisms (1996–2013)." Retrieved 26 August 2013 (www.iucnredlist.org/documents/summarystatistics/2013_1_RL_Stats_Table1.pdf).

Internet Systems Consortium. 2010. "Internet host count history: Number of Internet hosts." Retrieved November 16, 2010 (http://www.isc.org/solutions/survey/history).

———. 2013a. "Internet Growth Statistics." Retrieved 18 August 2013 (www.internetworldstats.com/emarketing.htm)

———. 2013b. "Internet World Stats 2013: Usage and Population Statistics." Retrieved May 2, 2014. (www.internetworldstats.com/stats.htm).

———. 2013c. "ISC Domain Survey." Retrieved August 10, 2013 (www.isc.org/services/survey/).

"Iraq Body Count." 2008. Retrieved January 12, 2008 (www.iraqbodycount.org).

"Iraq Coalition Casualty Count." 2008. Retrieved January 12, 2008 (http://icasualties.org/oif).

Isajiw, W. W. 1978. "Olga in Wonderland: Ethnicity in a Technological Society." Pp. 29–39 in L. Driedger, ed. *The Canadian Ethnic Mosaic: A Quest for Identity*. Toronto: McClelland & Stewart.

istar. 2001. "Why Small Is Smarter." Retrieved June 12, 2004 (http://home.istar.ca/~gskarzn/go/SMALL.HTM).

Itaborahy Lucas Paoli, and Jingshu Zhu. 2013. *State-Sponsored Homophobia: A World Survey of Laws: Criminalisation, Protection and Recognition of Same-Sex Love*. Washington, DC: International Lesbian Gay Bisexual Trans and Intersex Association.

Iyengar, Shanto. 1991. *Is Anyone Responsible? How Television Frames Political Issues*. Chicago: University of Chicago Press.

Jacobs, Jane. 1961. *The Death and Life of Great American Cities*. New York: Random House.

———. 1969. *The Economy of Cities*. New York: Random House.

James, Harold. 2001. *The End of Globalization: Lessons from the Great Depression*. Cambridge, MA: Harvard University Press.

James, William. 1890. *Principles of Psychology*. New York: H. Holt.

———. 1976 [1902]. *The Varieties of Religious Experience: A Study in Human Nature*. New York: Collier Books.

Janigan, Mary. 2002. "Saving Our Cities." *Maclean's* 3 June: 22–27.

Janis, Irving. 1972. *Victims of Groupthink*. Boston: Houghton Mifflin.

Jannini, Emmanuelle A., Ray Blanchard, Andrea Camperio-Cianai, and John Bancroft. 2010. "Male Homosexuality: Nature or Culture?" *Controversies in Sexual Medicine* 7: 3245–53.

Jeffords, Shawn. 2013. "Karla Homolka Has Tried to Dodge Public Eye." *Toronto Sun* September 26. Retrieved December 8, 2013 (www.torontosun.com/2013/09/26/karla-homolka-has-tried-to-dodge-public-eye).

Jeffrey, Robin. 2004. "Legacies of Matriliny: The Place of Women and the 'Kerala Model.'" *Pacific Affairs* 78: 647–64.

Jenkins, J. Craig. 1983. "Resource Mobilization Theory and the Study of Social Movements." *Annual Review of Sociology* 9: 527–53.

Johns, Adrian. 1998. *The Nature of the Book: Print and Knowledge in the Making*. Chicago: University of Chicago Press.

Johnson, Chalmers. 2000. *Blowback: The Costs and Consequences of American Empire*. New York: Metropolitan Books.

Johnson, Holly. 2006. "Measuring Violence against Women: Statistical Trends, 2006." Ottawa: Statistics Canada. Retrieved May 2, 2008 (www.statcan.ca/english/research/85-570-XIE/85-570-XIE2006001.pdf).

Johnson, Michael P. 1995. "Patriarchal Terrorism and Common Couple Violence: Two Forms of Violence Against Women." *Journal of Marriage and the Family* 57: 283–94.

Johnson, Michael P., and Kathleeen J. Ferraro. 2000. "Research on Domestic Violence in the 1990s: Making Distinctions." *Journal of Marriage and the Family* 62: 948–63.

Joiner, Thomas E., Jr., Daniel Hollar, and Kimberly Van Orden. 2006. "On Buckeyes, Gators, Super Bowl Sunday, and the Miracle on Ice: 'Pulling together' is associated with lower suicide rates." *Journal of Social & Clinical Psychology* 25(2): 179–95.

Jones, Frank. 2000. "Are Children Going to Religious Services?" Pp. 202–05 in *Canadian Social Trends* 3. Toronto: Thompson Educational Publishing.

Jones, Laura. 1997. "Global Warming Is All the Rage These Days ... Which Enrages Many Doubting Scientists." The Fraser Institute. Retrieved May 5, 2002 (http://oldfraser.lexi.net/media/media_releases/1997/19971201a.html).

Jones, Melanie K. 2008. "Disability and the Labour Market: A Review of the Empirical Evidence." *Journal of Economic Studies* 35(5): 405–24.

Joshee, Reva, and Ivor Sinfield. 2012. "The Canadian Education Multicultural Policy Web: Lessons to Learn, Pitfalls to Avoid." *Multicultural Education Review* 2(1): 55–75.

Joudrey, Allan D., and Jean E. Wallace. 2009. "Leisure as a Coping Resource: A Test of the Job Demand-Control-Support Model." *Human Relations* 62: 195–217.

Jubilee Debt Campaign. 2010. "Getting into Debt." Retrieved February 12, 2011 (http://www.jubileedebtcampaign.org.uk/Getting%20into%20Debt+6281.twl).

Juby, Heather, Nicole Marcil-Gratton, and Celine LeBourdais. 2005. *When Parents Separate: Further Findings from the National Longitudinal Survey of Children and Youth*. Ottawa: Justice Canada.

Judge, Timothy A., and Daniel M. Cable. 2011. "When It Comes to Pay, Do the Thin Win? The Effect of Weight on Pay for Men and Women." *Journal of Applied Psychology* 96(1): 95–112.

Kalbach, Madeline. A., and Warren. E. Kalbach. 1998. "Becoming Canadian: Problems of an Emerging Identity." *Canadian Ethnic Studies* 31, 2: 1–17.

Kalleberg, Arne L. 2013. *Good Jobs, Bad Jobs*. New York: Russell Sage Foundation.

Kalmijn, Matthijs, Anneke Loeve, and Dorien Manting. 2007. "Income Dynamics in Couples and the Dissolution of Marriage and Cohabitation." *Demography* 44(1): 159–79.

Kanter, Rosabeth Moss. 1977. *Men and Women of the Corporation*. New York: Basic Books.

———. 1989. *When Giants Learn to Dance: Mastering the Challenges of Strategy, Management, and Careers in the 1990s*. New York: Simon and Schuster.

Kark, Malin, and Nina Karnehed. 2012. "Weight Status at Age 18 Influences Marriage Prospects: A Population-based Study of Swedish Men." *BMC Public Health* 12(833): 1–7.

Karlsen, Monica, and Bente Træen. 2013. "Identifying 'Friends with Benefits' Scripts among Young Adults in the Norwegian Cultural Context." *Sexuality and Culture* 17: 83–99.

Karlsson, Sofie, and Klas Borell. 2002. "Intimacy and Autonomy, Gender and Ageing: Living Apart Together." *Ageing International* 27(4): 11–26.

Karmali, Shahzeer, Carlene Johnson Stoklossa, Arya Sharma, Janet Stadnyk, Sandra Christiansen, Danielle Cottreau, and Daniel W. Birch. 2012. "Bariatric Surgery: A Primer." *Canadian Family Physician* 56: 873–79.

Katz, Elihu. 1957. "The Two-Step Flow of Communication: An Up-to-Date Report on an Hypothesis." *Public Opinion Quarterly* 21: 61–78.

Kaul, Rhythma. 2012. "Rape Victim Still Critical, Writes to Mother 'I Want to Live.' " *Hindustan Times* December 20. Retrieved April 19, 2013 (www.hindustantimes.com/India-news/NewDelhi/Delhi-gang-rape-victim-writes-on-a-piece-of-paper-Mother-I-want-to-live/Article1-976798.aspx).

Kauri, Vidya. 2012. "Canada Migrant Workers Prone to Abuse, Exploitation Due to Lax Government Oversight: Advocates." *The Huffington Post Canada* January 21. Retrieved April 14, 2014 (www.huffingtonpost.ca/2012/01/21/canada-migrant-workers-abuse_n_1210725.html).

Kay, Fiona, and John Hagan. 1998. "Raising the Bar: The Gender Stratification of Law Firm Capitalization." *American Sociological Review* 63: 728–43.

Kazemipur, Abdolmohammad, and Shiva S. Halli. 2000. *The New Poverty: Ethnic Groups and Ghetto Neighbourhoods*. Toronto: Thompson Educational Publishing, Inc.

———. 2001. "The Changing Colour of Poverty in Canada." *Canadian Review of Sociology and Anthropology* 38, 2: 217–38.

Kearney, Mark, and Randy Ray. 1999. *The Great Canadian Book of Lists*. Toronto: Dundurn Group.

Kelly, Mary B. 2012. "Divorce Cases in Court, 2010/2011." *Juristat*, Catalogue No. 85-002-X, Vol. 5-23. Ottawa, ON: Minister of Industry.

Kemp, Hugh P. 2013. *The One-Stop Guide to World Religions*. Oxford, UK: Lion Books.

Kennedy, Paul. 1993. *Preparing for the Twenty-First Century*. New York: HarperCollins.

Kepel, Gilles. 1994 [1991]. *The Revenge of God: The Resurgence of Islam, Christianity and Judaism in the Modern World,* Alan Braley, trans. University Park, PA: Pennsylvania State University Press.

Kerig, Patricia K., Philip A. Cowan, and Carolyn Pape Cowan. 1993. "Marital Quality and Gender Differences in Parent–Child Interaction." *Developmental Psychology* 29: 931–39.

Kerr, Don, Melissa Moyser, and Roderic Beaujot. 2006. "Marriage and Cohabitation: Demographic and Sociodemographic Differences in Quebec and Canada." *Canadian Studies in Population* 33: 83–117.

Kimmerling, Baruch. 2003. *Politicide: Ariel Sharon's War against the Palestinians*. London: Verso.

King, Melanie. 2008. *The Dying Game: A Curious History of Death*. Oxford, UK: OneWorld.

Kingsbury, Nancy, and John Scanzoni. 1993. "Structural-Functionalism." Pp. 195–217 in Pauline G. Boss, William J. Doherty, Ralph LaRossa, Walter R. Schumm, and Suzanne K. Steinmetz, eds. *Sourcebook of Family Theories and Methods: A Contextual Approach*. New York: Plenum.

Kinkartz, L., K. Wells, and A. Hillyard, 2013. *Safe Spaces Campus Climate Survey Report: Gauging the Environment for Sexual and Gender Minorities at the University of Alberta*. Edmonton, AB: Institute for Sexual Minority Studies and Services.

Kinsella, Warren. 2007. *The War Room: Political Strategies for Business, NGOs, and Anyone Who Wants to Win*. Toronto: Dundurn.

Kinsey, Alfred C., Wardell B. Pomeroy, and Clyde E. Martin. 1948. *Sexual Behavior in the Human Male*. Philadelphia: W. B. Saunders.

Kinsey, Alfred C., Wardell B. Pomeroy, Clyde E. Martin, and Paul H. Gebhard. 1953. *Sexual Behavior in the Human Female*. Philadelphia: W. B. Saunders.

Kleege, Georgina. 1999. *Sight Unseen*. New Haven, CT: Yale University Press.

Klein, Jeff Z. 2013. "Rinks in Canada's Arctic Turn to Cooling Systems." *New York Times* 4 January. Retrieved 4 January 2013 (www.nytimes.com).

Klein, Naomi. 2000. *No Logo: Taking Aim at the Brand Bullies*. New York: HarperCollins.

Klingemann, Hans-Dieter. 1999. "Mapping Political Support in the 1990s: A Global Analysis." In Pippa Norris, ed. *Critical Citizens: Global Support for Democratic Governance*. Oxford, UK: Oxford University Press. Retrieved October 20, 2001 (http://ksgwww.harvard.edu/people/pnorris/Chapter_2.htm).

Knowles, Angie. 2013. "Growing STEM: Careers Abound in Science, Technology, Engineering and Mathematics." *Industry Trends* October 17. Retrieved March 10, 2014 (https://www.eco.ca/community/blog/growing-stem-careers-abound-in-science-technology-engineering-and-mathematics/81945).

"Kobe Bryant Resumes Endorsement Career." 2005. *USA Today* July 10. Retrieved February 8, 2011 (http://www.usatoday.com/life/people/2005-07-10-kobe-bryant_x.htm).

Koepke, Leslie, Jan Hare, and Patricia B. Moran. 1992. "Relationship Quality in a Sample of Lesbian Couples with Children and Child-Free Lesbian Couples." *Family Relations* 41: 224–29.

Kohlberg, Lawrence. 1981. *The Psychology of Moral Development: The Nature and Validity of Moral Stages*. New York: Harper and Row.

Kohn, Alfie. 1988. "Make Love, Not War." *Psychology Today* 22, 6: 35–38.

Kolko, Gabriel. 2002. *Another Century of War?* New York: New Press.

Konrath, Sara. 2010. "Changes in Dispositional Empathy in American College Students Over Time: A Meta-Analysis." *Personality and Social Psychology Review* 15 (May): 180–98.

Korpi, Walter. 1983. *The Democratic Class Struggle*. London: Routledge and Kegan Paul.

Krahn, Harvey, and Graham S. Lowe, eds. 1998. *Work, Industry, and Canadian Society,* 3rd ed. Scarborough, ON: Nelson.

Krahn, Harvey, and Alison Taylor. 2007. "Streaming in 10th Grade in Four Canadian Provinces in 2000." *Education Matters* 4(2). Retrieved March 10, 2014 (www.statcan.gc.ca/pub/81-004-x/2007002/9994-eng.htm).

Kraus, Michael W., and Dacher Keltner. 2009. "Signs of Socioeconomic Status." *Psychological Science* 20: 99–106.

Kreager, Derek A., Richard B. Felson, Cody Warner, and Marin R. Wenger. 2013. "Women's Education, Marital Violence, and Divorce: A Social Exchange Perspective." *Journal of Marriage and Family* 75: 565–81.

Krieger, Tim, and Jens Ruhose. 2013. "Honey, I Shrunk the Kids' Benefits—Revisiting Intergenerational Conflict in OECD Countries." *Public Choice* 157: 115–43.

Kropotkin, Petr. 1908. *Mutual Aid: A Factor of Evolution*, revised ed. London: W. Heinemann.

Kübler-Ross, Elisabeth. 1969. *On Death and Dying*. New York: Macmillan.

Kuhn, Thomas. 1970 [1962]. *The Structure of Scientific Revolutions*, 2nd ed. Chicago: University of Chicago Press.

Kulik, Carol T., Pepper, Molly B., Shapiro, Debra L., and Cregan, Christina. 2012. "The Electronic Water Cooler: Insiders and Outsiders Talk about Organizational Justice on the Internet." *Communication Research* 39 (5): 565–91.

Kurdek, Lawrence A. 1998. "Relationship Outcomes and Their Predictors: Longitudinal Evidence from Heterosexual Married, Gay Cohabiting and Lesbian Cohabiting Couples." *Journal of Marriage and the Family* 60, 3: 553–68.

Kuther, Tara L., and Erin McDonald. 2004. "Early Adolescents' Experiences with and Views of Barbie." *Adolescence* 39, 39–52.

Kymlicka, Will. 2010. *The Current State of Multiculturalism in Canada and Research Themes on Canadian Multiculturalism.* Ottawa: Citizenship and Immigration Canada.

LaFeber, Walter. 1993. *Inevitable Revolutions: The United States in Central America*, 2nd ed. New York: Norton.

———. 1999. *Michael Jordan and the New Global Capitalism.* New York: Norton.

LaFree, Gary, and Laura Dugan. 2012. "Trends in Global Terrorism, 1970–2008." Pp. 39–52 in J. Joseph Hewitt, Jonathan Wilkenfeld, and Ted Robert Gurr with Birger Heldt. eds. *Peace and Conflict 2012*. College Park, MD: Center for International Development and Conflict Management, University of Maryland.

Lamanna, Mary Ann, and Agnes Riedmann. 2009. *Marriages and Families: Making Choices in a Diverse Society*, 10th ed. Belmont, CA: Thomson Wadsworth.

Lambert, M., Klarka Zeman, Mary Allen, and Patrick Bussière. 2004. "Who Pursues Postsecondary Education, Who Leaves and Why: Results from the Youth in Transition Survey." Ottawa, Statistics Canada. Retrieved May 27, 2006 (www.statcan.ca/cgi-bin/downpub/listpub.cgi?catno=81-595-MIE2004026).

Lane, Harlan. 1976. *The Wild Boy of Aveyron*. Cambridge, MA: Harvard University Press.

Lang, Sabine. 1998. *Men as Women, Women as Men: Changing Gender in Native American Cultures*. Austin, TX: University of Texas Press.

Lapchick, Richard. 2011. *2011 Racial and Gender Report Card*. Orlando, FL: University of Central Florida. Retrieved January 28, 2014 (http://dl.dropboxusercontent.com/u/11322904/RGRC/2011_RGRC_FINAL.pdf).

Lapidus, Gail Warshofsky. 1978. *Women in Soviet Society: Equality, Development, and Social Change*. Berkeley, CA: University of California Press.

Laplante, Benoit. 2013. "Normative Groups: The Rise of the Formation of the First Union through Cohabitation in Québec, a Comparative Approach." *Population Research and Policy Review*, DOI 10.1007/s11113-013-9279-4.

Lareau, Annette. 1987. "Social Class Differences in Family–School Relationships: The Importance of Cultural Capital." *Sociology of Education* 60: 73–85.

———. 2011. *Unequal Childhoods: Class, Race and Family Life*. Berkeley, CA: University of California Press.

LaRochelle-Côté, Sébastien, John Myles, and Garnett Picot. 2012. "Income Replacement Rates among Canadian Seniors: The Effect of Widowhood and Divorce." *Canadian Public Policy* 38(2): 471–95.

Lasswell, Harold. 1936. *Politics: Who Gets What, When and How*. New York: McGraw-Hill.

Lau, Charles Q. 2012. "The Stability of Same-Sex Cohabitation, Different-Sex Cohabitation, and Marriage." *Journal of Marriage and Family* 74: 973–88.

Laumann, Edward O., John H. Gagnon, Robert T. Michael, and Stuart Michaels. 1994. *The Social Organization of Sexuality: Sexual Practices in the United States*. Chicago: University of Chicago Press.

Laureys, Steven, Adrian N. Owen, and Nicholas D. Schiff. 2004. "Brain Function in Coma, Vegetative State, and Related Disorders." *The Lancet Neurology* 3: 537–46.

Laurie, Robert. 2007. "Are We Setting Up Students to Fail?" *Atlantic Institute for Market Studies* June 5. Retrieved May 24, 2011 (www.macleans.ca/article.jsp?content=20070605_153207_13228).

Lautard, Hugh, and Neil Guppy. 2014. "Multiculturalism or Vertical Mosaic? Occupational Stratification among Canadian Ethnic Groups." Pp. 137–51 in Robert Brym, ed. *Society in Question,* 7th ed. Toronto: Nelson Education.

Lavoie, Yolande, and Jillian Oderkirk. 2000. "Social Consequences of Demographic Change." Pp. 2–5 in *Canadian Social Trends,* Volume 3. Toronto: Thompson Educational Publishing.

Law, Danielle M., Jennifer D. Shapka, Shelley Hymel, Brent F. Olson, and Terry Waterhouse. 2012. The Changing Face of Bullying: An Empirical Comparison between Traditional and Internet Bullying and Victimization. *Computers in Human Behavior* 28: 226–32.

Law, Michael R. 2013. "Money Left on the Table: Generic Drug Prices in Canada." *Healthcare Policy* 8(3): 17–25.

Laxer, Gordon. 1989. *Open for Business: The Roots of Foreign Ownership in Canada*. Toronto: Oxford University Press.

Leacock, Eleanor Burke. 1981. *Myths of Male Dominance: Collected Articles on Women Cross-Culturally*. New York: Monthly Review Press.

Le Bon, Gustave. 1969 [1895]. *The Crowd: A Study of the Popular Mind*. New York: Ballantine Books.

LeBourdais, Celine, and Evelyne Lapierre-Adamcyk. 2004. "Changes in Conjugal Life in Canada: Is Cohabitation Progressively Replacing Marriage?" *Journal of Marriage and Family* 66: 929–42.

Lee, Richard B. 1979. *The !Kung San: Men, Women and Work in a Foraging Society*. Cambridge, UK: Cambridge University Press.

Lefkowitz, Bernard. 1997a. *Our Guys: The Glen Ridge Rape and the Secret Life of the Perfect Suburb*. Berkeley, CA: University of California Press.

———. 1997b. "Boys Town: Did Glen Ridge Raise Its Sons to Be Rapists?" *Salon* August 13. Retrieved March 20, 2003 (www.salon.com/aug97/mothers/guys970813.html).

Leidner, Robin. 1993. *Fast Food, Fast Talk: Service Work and the Routinization of Everyday Life*. Berkeley, CA: University of California Press.

Le Mare, Lucy, and Karyn Audet. 2006. "A Longitudinal Study of the Physical Growth and Health of Post-institutionalized Romanian Adoptees." *Pediatric and Child Health* 11(2): 85–91.

Lenski, G., P. Nolan, and J. Lenski. 1995. *Human Societies: An Introduction to Macrosociology*, 7th ed. New York: McGraw-Hill.

Lerner, Gerda. 1986. *The Creation of Patriarchy*. New York: Oxford University Press.

Lever. J. 1994. "The 1994 Advocate Survey of Sexuality and Relationships." *Advocate* 23: 16–24.

Levine, R. A., and D. T. Campbell. 1972. *Ethnocentrism: Theories of Conflict, Ethnic Attitudes, and Group Behavior*. New York: Wiley.

Lewin, Simon, and Scott Reeves. 2011. "Enacting 'Team' and 'Teamwork': Using Goffman's Theory of Impression Management to Illuminate Interprofessional Practice on Hospital Wards." *Social Science & Medicine* 72(10): 1595–1602.

Lewontin, R. C. 1991. *Biology as Ideology: The Doctrine of DNA*. New York: HarperCollins.

Ley, David. 1996. *The New Middle Class and the Remaking of the Central City*. Oxford, UK: Oxford University Press.

Li, Peter. 1995. "Racial Supremacism under Social Democracy." *Canadian Ethnic Studies* 27, 1: 1–17.

———. 1998. *The Chinese in Canada*, 2nd ed. Toronto: Oxford University Press.

———. 2000. "Earning Disparities between Immigrants and Native-Born Canadians." *Canadian Review of Sociology and Anthropology* 37, 3: 289–311.

Lian, J. Z., and D. R. Matthews. 1998. "Does the Vertical Mosaic Still Exist? Ethnicity and Income in Canada, 1991." *Canadian Review of Sociology and Anthropology* 35: 461–81.

Lie, John. 1992. "The Concept of Mode of Exchange." *American Sociological Review* 57: 508–23.

———. 1998. *Han Unbound: The Political Economy of South Korea*. Stanford, CA: Stanford University Press.

———. 2001. *Multiethnic Japan*. Cambridge, MA: Harvard University Press.

Liebow, Elliott. 1967. *Tally's Corner*. Boston: Little, Brown.

Liefbroer, Aart C., and Edith Dourleijn. 2006. "Unmarried Cohabitation and Union Stability: Testing the Role of Diffusion using Data from 16 European Countries." *Demography* 43(2): 203–21.

Light, I. 1991. "Immigrant and Ethnic Enterprise in North America." Pp. 307–18 in N. R. Yetman, ed. *Majority and Minority: The Dynamics of Race and Ethnicity in American Life*, 5th ed. Boston: Allyn and Bacon.

Lincoln, Abraham. 1860. "Cooper Union Address." Retrieved 13 August 2013 (www.abrahamlincolnonline.org/lincoln/speeches/cooper.htm).

Lindert, Peter H. 2004. *Growing Public: Social Spending and Economic Growth Since the Eighteenth Century*. New York: Cambridge.

Lindner, Rolf. 1996 [1990]. *The Reportage of Urban Culture: Robert Park and the Chicago School,* Adrian Morris, trans. Cambridge, UK: Cambridge University Press.

Lindqvist, Erik. 2012. "Height and Leadership." *Review of Economics and Statistics* 94(4): 1191–96.

Lindsay, Colin. 2008a. *Are Women Spending More Time on Unpaid Domestic Work than Men in Canada? Matter of Fact*. Catalogue no. 89-630-X. Ottawa, ON: Statistics Canada.

———. 2008b. "Canadians Attend Weekly Religious Services Less Than 20 Years Ago." *Matter of Fact,* Catalogue no. 89-630-X. Ottawa, ON: Statistics Canada.

Link, Bruce G., and Jo Phelan. 1995. "Social Conditions as Fundamental Causes of Disease." *Journal of Health and Social Behavior* 35: 80–94.

Lips, Hilary M. 1999. *A New Psychology of Women: Gender, Culture and Ethnicity*. Mountain View, CA: Mayfield Publishing.

Lipset, Seymour Martin. 1963. "Value Differences, Absolute or Relative: The English-Speaking Democracies." Pp. 248–73 in *The First New Nation: The United States in Historical Perspective*. New York: Basic Books.

———. 1971 [1951]. *Agrarian Socialism: The Cooperative Commonwealth Federation in Saskatchewan*, revised ed. Berkeley, CA: University of California Press.

———. 1977. "Why No Socialism in the United States?" Pp. 31–363 in Seweryn Bialer and Sophia Sluzar, eds. *Sources of Contemporary Radicalism*. Boulder, CO: Westview Press.

———. 1981. *Political Man: The Social Bases of Politics*, 2nd ed. Baltimore: Johns Hopkins University Press.

Lipset, Seymour Martin, and Stein Rokkan. 1967. "Cleavage Structures, Party Systems, and Voter Alignments: An Introduction." Pp. 1–64 in Seymour Martin Lipset and Stein Rokkan, eds. *Party Systems and Voter Alignments: Cross-National Perspectives*. New York: Free Press.

Lipset, Seymour Martin, Martin A. Trow, and James S. Coleman. 1956. *Union Democracy: The Internal Politics of the International Typographical Union*. Glencoe, IL: Free Press.

Lisak, David. 1992. "Sexual Aggression, Masculinity, and Fathers." *Signs* 16: 238–62.

Livernash, Robert, and Eric Rodenburg. 1998. "Population Change, Resources, and the Environment." *Population Bulletin* 53, 1. Retrieved October 8, 2000 (www.prb.org/pubs/population_bulletin/bu53-1.htm).

Livingstone, Andrew. 2013. "Son Defends Scientist behind Aboriginal Nutrition Experiments." *Toronto Star* July 24. Retrieved March 28, 2014 (www.thestar.com/news/canada/2013/07/24/son_defends_scientist_behind_aboriginal_nutrition_experiments.html).

Lodhi, Abdul Qaiyum, and Charles Tilly. 1973. "Urbanization, Crime, and Collective Violence in 19th Century France." *American Journal of Sociology* 79: 296–318.

Lofland, L. H. 1985. "The Social Shaping of Emotion: Grief in Historical Perspective." *Symbolic Interaction* 8: 171–90.

Logan, John R., and Harvey L. Molotch. 1987. *Urban Fortunes: The Political Economy of Place*. Berkeley, CA: University of California Press.

Longmore, Paul K. 2003. *Why I Burned My Book and Other Essays on Disability*. Philadelphia: Temple University Press.

Lonmo, Charlene. 2001. "Adult Correctional Services in Canada, 1999–2000." *Juristat* 21, 5 (July). Catalogue no. 85-002-XPE.

Low, Carissa A., Rebecca C. Thurston, and Karen A. Matthews. 2010. "Psychosocial Factors in the Development of Heart Disease in Women: Current Research and Future Directions." *Psychosomatic Medicine* 72: 842–54.

Lowe, Christopher F., Julianne V. Kus, Natasha Salt, Sandra Callery, Lisa Louie, Mohammed A. Khan, Mary Vearncombe, and Andrew E. Simor. 2013. "Nosocomial Transmission of New Delhi Metallo-β-Lactamase-1-Producing Klebsiella pneumonia in Toronto, Canada." *Infection Control and Hospital Epidemiology* 31(1): 49–55.

Lowe, Graham S. 1987. *Women in the Administrative Revolution: The Feminization of Clerical Work*. Toronto: University of Toronto Press.

———. 2000. *The Quality of Work: A People-Centred Agenda*. Don Mills, ON: Oxford University Press.

Lowman, John, Robert T. Menzies, and Ted S. Palys. 1987. *Transcarceration: Essays in the Sociology of Social Control*. Aldershot, ON: Gower.

Lynch, Marc. 2005. "Watching Al-Jazeera." *The Wilson Quarterly* 29(3): 36–45.

Lyngstad, Torkild Hovde, and Marika Jalovaara. 2010. "A Review of the Antecedents of Union Dissolution." *Demographic Research* 23(10): 257–92.

Lyon, David. 2007. *Surveillance Studies: An Overview*. Oxford UK: Polity Press.

Macdonald, David. 2014. *Outrageous Fortune: Documenting Canada's Wealth Gap*. Ottawa: Canadian Centre for Policy Alternatives. Retrieved April 5, 2014 (www.policyalternatives.ca/outrageous-fortune).

Macdonald, David, and Daniel Wilson 2013. *Poverty or Prosperity: Indigenous Children in Canada*. Ottawa, ON: Canadian Centre for Policy Alternatives.

MacKinnon, Catharine A. 1979. *Sexual Harassment of Working Women*. New Haven, CT: Yale University Press.

Maclean's. 2002. "Acceptable but Not Equal." 3 June: 12.

MacLennan, Hugh. 1945. *Two Solitudes*. Toronto: Collins.

Magro, Albert M. 1997. "Why Barbie Is Perceived as Beautiful." *Perceptual & Motor Skills* 85, 1 (August): 363–74.

Malik, Maleiha. 2011. "Religious Freedom, Free Speech and Equality: Conflict or Cohesion?" *Res Publica* 17: 21–40.

Malthus, Thomas Robert. 1966 [1798]. *An Essay on the Principle of Population*, J. R. Bodnar, ed. London: Macmillan.

Mankiw, N. G. 1998. *Principles of Macroeconomics.* Fort Worth, TX: Dryden Press.

Mannheim, Karl. 1952. "The Problem of Generations." Pp. 276–320 in *Essays on the Sociology of Knowledge*, Paul Kecskemeti, ed. New York: Oxford University Press.

Manning, Wendy D., and Jessica A. Cohen. 2012. "Premarital Cohabitation and Marital Dissolution: An Examination of Recent Marriages." *Journal of Marriage and Family* 74: 377–87.

Manza, Jeff, Michael Hout, and Clem Brooks. 1995. "Class Voting in Capitalist Democracies since World War II: Dealignment, Realignment, or Trendless Fluctuation?" *Annual Review of Sociology* 21: 137–62.

Marchak, M. P. 1991. *The Integrated Circus: The New Right and the Restructuring of Global Markets*. Montreal: McGill-Queen's University Press.

Marger, Martin. 2013. "Religiosity in Canada and the United States: Diverging Paths." *American Review of Canadian Studies* 43(1): 70–85.

Margolis, Eric, and Mary Romero. 1998. "The Department Is Very Male, Very White, Very Old, and Very Conservative: The Functioning of Hidden Curriculum in Graduate Sociology Departments." *Harvard Educational Review* 68(1): 1–32.

Markle, Gerald E., and Frances B. McCrea. 2008. *What If Medicine Disappeared*? Albany, NY: State University of New York Press.

Markowitz, Fran. 1993. *A Community in Spite of Itself: Soviet Jewish Émigrés in New York*. Washington, DC: Smithsonian Institute Press.

Marmot, Michael. 2012. "Why Should the Rich Care about the Health of the Poor?" *Canadian Medical Association Journal* 184(11): 1231–32.

Marshall, Katherine. 2001. "Part-Time by Choice." *Perspectives on Labour and Income* 13, 1: 20–27. Retrieved June 3, 2009 (http://dsp-psd.pwgsc.gc.ca/dsp-psd/Pilot/Statcan/75-001-XIE/75-001-XIE.html).

———. 2011. "Paid and Unpaid Work over Three Generations." *Perspectives on Labour and Income*. Catalogue no. 11-008-X. Ottawa, ON: Statistics Canada.

Marshall, Monty G., and Ted Robert Gurr. 2003. "Peace and Conflict 2003." College Park: Department of Government and Politics, University of Maryland. Retrieved June 3, 2003 (www.cidcm.umd.edu/inscr/PC03print.pdf).

Marshall, Samuel L. A. 1947. *Men against Fire: The Problem of Battle Command in Future War*. New York: Morrow.

Marshall, Thomas Humphrey. 1965. "Citizenship and Social Class." Pp. 71–134 in Thomas Humphrey Marshall, ed. *Class, Citizenship, and Social Development: Essays by T.H. Marshall*. Garden City, NY: Anchor.

Martel, Laurent. 2013. *Mortality: An Overview, 2010 and 2011*. Catalogue no. 91-209-X. Ottawa, ON: Minister of Industry.

Marx, Karl. 1904 [1859]. *A Contribution to the Critique of Political Economy,* N. Stone, trans. Chicago: Charles H. Kerr.

———. 1970 [1843]. *Critique of Hegel's "Philosophy of Right,"* Annette Jolin and Joseph O'Malley, trans. Cambridge, MA: Harvard University Press.

Marx, Karl, and Friedrich Engels. 1972 [1848]. "Manifesto of the Communist Party." Pp. 331–62 in R. Tucker, ed. *The Marx-Engels Reader*. New York: Norton.

Matalon, Jean-Marc. 1997. "Jeanne Calment, World's Oldest Person, Dead at 122." *The Shawnee News-Star* August 5. Retrieved May 2, 2000 (www.news-star.com/stories/080597/life1.html).

Mathis, William. 2013. "Moving beyond Tracking." *Research-Based Policy Options*. School of Education, University of Colorado Boulder. Retrieved March 11, 2014 (http://nepc.colorado.edu/files/pb-options-10-tracking.pdf).

Matsueda, Ross L. 1988. "The Current State of Differential Association Theory." *Crime and Delinquency* 34: 277–306.

———. 1992. "Reflected Appraisals, Parental Labeling, and Delinquency: Specifying a Symbolic Interactionist Theory." *American Journal of Sociology* 97: 1577–611.

McAdam, Doug. 1982. *Political Process and the Development of Black Insurgency, 1930–1970*. Chicago: University of Chicago Press.

McCarthy, John D., and Mayer N. Zald. 1977. "Resource Mobilization and Social Movements: A Partial Theory." *American Journal of Sociology* 82: 1212–41.

McChesney, Robert W. 1999. "Oligopoly: The Big Media Game Has Fewer and Fewer Players." *The Progressive* November: 20–24. Retrieved August 7, 2000 (www.progressive.org/mcc1199.htm).

McClelland, W. R. 1931. "Precautions for Workers in the Treating of Radium Ores." *Investigations in Ore Dressing and Metallurgy*. Ottawa: Bureau of Mines. Retrieved October 8, 2000 (www.ccnr.org/radium_warning.html).

McConaghy, Nathaniel. 1999. "Unresolved Issues in Scientific Sexology." *Archives of Sexual Behavior* 28, 4: 285–318.

McDonald's Corporation. 2005. "Poutine-large." Retrieved December 1, 2005 (http://www.mcdonalds.ca/en/food/ingredient.aspx?menuid=262).

———. 2012. *Annual Report*. Retrieved November 4, 2013 (www.aboutmcdonalds.com/content/dam/AboutMcDonalds/Investors/Investor%202013/2012%20Annual%20Report%20Final.pdf).

McGinn, Anne Platt. 1998. "Promoting Sustainable Fisheries." Pp. 59–78 in Lester R. Brown, Christopher Flavin, Hilary French et al. *State of the World 1998*. New York: Norton.

McHale, Susan M., Ann C. Crouter, and Shawn D. Whiteman. 2003. "The Family Contexts of Gender Development in Childhood and Adolescence." *Social Development* 12(1): 125–48.

McKinley, Nita Mary 2011. "Feminist Consciousness and Objectified Body Consciousness." *Psychology of Women Quarterly* 35(4): 684–88.

McLanahan, Sara, Laura Tach, and Daniel Schneider. 2013. "The Causal Effects of Father Absence." *Annual Review of Sociology* 39: 399–427.

McLaren, A. 1990. *Our Own Master Race: Eugenics in Canada*, 1885–1945. Toronto: McClelland & Stewart.

McLean, Scott, and Heather Rollwagen. 2010. "Educational Expansion or Credential Inflation? The Evolution of Part-Time Study by Adults at McGill University, Canada." *International Journal of Lifelong Education* 29(6): 739–55.

McLuhan, Marshall. 1964. *Understanding Media: The Extensions of Man*. New York: Mentor Books.

McMahon, Maeve W. 1992. *The Persistent Prison? Rethinking Decarceration and Penal Reform*. Toronto: University of Toronto Press.

McManus, Ruth. 2013. *Death in a Global Age*. New York: Palgrave Macmillan.

McNamee, Stephen, and Robert Miller. 2009. *The Meritocracy Myth*, 2nd ed. Lanham, MD: Rowman and Littlefield.

McNeill, William H. 1976. *Plagues and Peoples*. Garden City, NY: Anchor Press.

McPhail, Clark. 1991. *The Myth of the Madding Crowd*. New York: Aldine de Gruyter.

———. 1994. "The Dark Side of Purpose: Individual and Collective Violence in Riots." *The Sociological Quarterly* 35: 1–32.

McPhail, Clark, and Ronald T. Wohlstein. 1983. "Individual and Collective Behaviors within Gatherings, Demonstrations, and Riots." *Annual Review of Sociology* 9: 579–600.

McRoberts, Kenneth. 1988. *Quebec: Social Change and Political Crisis*, 3rd ed. Toronto: McClelland & Stewart.

McVey, Wayne W., Jr., and Warren E. Kalbach. 1995. *Canadian Population*. Scarborough, ON: Nelson.

Mead, G. H. 1934. *Mind, Self and Society*. Chicago: University of Chicago Press.

Meahan, Lynn. 2010. "Statement on 2011 Census." Office of the Honourable Tony Clement, Minister of Industry. Retrieved November 27, 2012. (www.ic.gc.ca/eic/site/064.nsf/eng/05709.html).

Mealey, Linda. 2010. "The Sociobiology of Sociopathy: An Integrated Evolutionary Model." *Behavioral and Brain Sciences* 18 (3): 523–41.

Meek, Ronald L., ed. 1971. *Marx and Engels on the Population Bomb: Selections from the Writings of Marx and Engels Dealing with the Theories of Thomas Robert Malthus*. Dorothea L. Meek and Ronald L. Meek, trans. Berkeley, CA: Ramparts Press.

Melby, Melissa K., Margaret Lock, and Patricia Kaufert. 2005. "Culture and Symptom Reporting at Menopause." *Human Reproduction Update* 41(5): 495–512.

Melucci, Alberto. 1980. "The New Social Movements: A Theoretical Approach." *Social Science Information* 19: 199–226.

———. 1995. "The New Social Movements Revisited: Reflections on a Sociological Misunderstanding." Pp. 107–19 in Louis Maheu, ed. *Social Classes and Social Movements: The Future of Collective Action*. London, UK: Sage.

Mendes, Vânia, Joana Araújo, Carla Lopes, and Elisabete Ramos. 2014. "Determinants of Weight Loss Dieting Among Adolescents: A Longitudinal Analysis." *Journal of Adolescent Health* 54: 360–63.

Menzies, C. R. 1999. "First Nations, Inequality and the Legacy of Colonialism." Pp. 236–44 in J. Curtis, E. Grabb, and N. Guppy, eds. *Social Inequality in Canada*, 3rd ed. Scarborough, ON: Prentice Hall Allyn and Bacon Canada Inc.

Mercredi, Ovid, and Mary Turpel. 1993. I*n the Rapids: Navigating the Future of First Nations*. New York: Viking.

Merton, Robert K. 1938. "Social Structure and Anomie." *American Sociological Review* 3: 672–82.

———. 1968 [1949]. *Social Theory and Social Structure*. New York: Free Press.

Messerschmidt, J. W. 1993. M*asculinities and Crime: Critique and Reconceptualization of Theory*. Lanham, MD: Roman and Littlefield.

Messner, Michael. 1995. "Boyhood, Organized Sports, and the Construction of Masculinities." Pp. 102–14 in Michael S. Kimmel and Michael A. Messner. *Men's Lives*, 3rd ed. Boston: Allyn and Bacon.

———. 2000. "Barbie Girls versus Sea Monsters: Children Constructing Gender." *Gender & Society*, Special Issue 14, 6 (December): 765–84.

Meyer, John W., Francisco O. Ramirez, and Yasemin Nuhoglu Soysal. 1992. "World Expansion of Mass Education, 1870–1980." *Sociology of Education* 65: 128–49.

Meyer, John W., and W. Richard Scott. 1983. *Organizational Environments: Ritual and Rationality*. Beverly Hills, CA: Sage.

Michelle, Carolyn. 2012. "Co-constructions of Gender and Ethnicity in New Zealand Television Advertising." *Sex Roles* 66: 21–37.

Michels, Robert. 1949 [1911]. *Political Parties: A Sociological Study of the Oligarchical Tendencies of Modern Democracy*, E. Paul and C. Paul, trans. New York: Free Press.

Milanovic, Branko. 2010. "The Consequences of Inequality and Wealth Distribution." Retrieved February 16, 2010 (http://ineteconomics.org/people/participants/branko-milanovic)

Miles, R. 1989. *Racism*. London: Routledge.

Milgram, Stanley. 1974. *Obedience to Authority: An Experimental View*. New York: Harper.

Miliband, Ralph. 1973 [1969]. *The State in Capitalist Society*. London: Fontana.

Milligan, Kevin. 2008. "Evolution of Elderly Poverty in Canada." *Canadian Public Policy* 34 (S1): 79–94.

Milloy, John S. 1999. *A National Crime: The Canadian Government and the Residential School System, 1879 to 1986*. Winnipeg: University of Manitoba Press.

Mills, C. Wright. 1956. *The Power Elite*. New York: Oxford University Press.

———. 1959. *The Sociological Imagination*. New York: Oxford University Press.

Minois, George. 1989 [1987]. *History of Old Age: From Antiquity to the Renaissance,* Sarah Hanbury Tenison, trans. Chicago: University of Chicago Press.

Mishna, Faye, Mona Khoury-Kassabri, Tahany Gadalla, and Joanne Daciuk. 2012. "Risk Factors for Involvement in Cyber Bullying: Victims, Bullies and Bully–Victims." *Children and Youth Services Review* 34: 63–70.

Mitchell, Nia S., Victoria A. Catenacci, Holly R. Wyatt, and James O. Hill. 2011. "Obesity: Overview of an Epidemic." *Psychiatric Clinics of North America* 34: 717–32.

Mittelman, James H. 2000. *The Globalization Syndrome: Transformation and Resistance*. Princeton, NJ: Princeton University Press.

Mizruchi, M. S. 1982. *The American Corporate Network, 1904–1974.* Beverly Hills, CA: Sage.

———. 1992. *The Structure of Corporate Political Action: Interfirm Relations and Their Consequences*. Cambridge, MA: Harvard University Press.

Monahan, Torin, and Rodolfo Torres. 2009. *Schools under Surveillance: Cultures of Control in Public Education*. New Brunswick, NJ: Rutgers University Press.

Money, John, and Anke Ehrhardt. 1972. *Man and Woman, Boy and Girl*. Boston: Little Brown.

Montgomery, M. 1965. "The Six Nations and the Macdonald Franchise." *Ontario History* 57: 13.

Mooney, Elaine, Heather Farley, and Chris J. Strugnell. 2010. "Body Dissatisfaction and Dieting among Adolescent Females in the Republic of Ireland." *Nutrition and Food Science* 40(2): 176–85.

Moore, Barrington, Jr. 1967. *Social Origins of Dictatorship and Democracy: Lord and Peasant in the Making of the Modern World*. Boston: Beacon.

Moore, Oliver. 2010. "Smuggled alcohol recalls tragedy of Davis Inlet." *The Globe and Mail* 2 October: A6.

Morris, Aldon D. 1984. *The Origins of the Civil Rights Movement: Black Communities Organizing for Change*. New York: Free Press.

Morris, Norval, and David J. Rothman, eds. 1995. *The Oxford History of the Prison: The Practice of Punishment in Western Society*. New York: Oxford University Press.

Morrison, Donna R., and Mary Jo Coiro. 1999. "Parent Conflict and Marital Disruption: Do Children Benefit When High-Conflict Marriages Are Dissolved?" *Journal of Marriage and the Family* 61: 626–37.

Morrison, Nancy. 1987. "Separation and Divorce." Pp. 125–43 in M. J. Dymond, ed. *The Canadian Woman's Legal Guide*. Toronto: Doubleday.

Morton, Gary. 2000. "Showdown at Queen's Park." Retrieved March 22, 2001 (www.tao.ca/earth/toronto/archive/1999/toronto01278.html).

Mosby, Ian. 2013. "Administering Colonial Science: Nutrition Research and Human Biomedical Experimentation in Aboriginal Communities and Residential Schools, 1942–1952." *Histoire sociale/Social History* 46(91): 145–72.

Mumford, Lewis. 1961. The City in History: Its Origins, Its Transformations, and Its Prospects. New York: Harcourt, Brace, and World.

Munch, Christopher. 2012. "Youth Correctional Statistics in Canada, 2010/2011." *Juristat*. (85-002-X). Retrieved April 4, 2014 (www.statcan.gc.ca/pub/85-002-x/2012001/article/11716-eng.pdf3).

Mundell, Helen. 1993. "How the Color Mafia Chooses Your Clothes." *American Demographics* November. Retrieved May 2, 2000 (www.demographics.com/publications/ad/93_ad/9311_ad/ad281.htm).

Murdock, George Peter. 1949. *Social Structure*. New York: Macmillan.

Murnen, Sarah K., Annette Perot, and Don Byrne. 1989. "Coping with Unwanted Sexual Activity: Normative Responses, Situational Determinants and Individual Differences." *Journal of Sex Research* 26: 85–106.

Murphy, Brian, Xuelin Zhang, and Claude Dionne. 2012. "Low Income in Canada: A Multi-Line and Multi- Index Perspective." Income Research Paper Series. Catalogue No. 75F0002M— No. 001. Ottawa: Statistics Canada. Retrieved December 25, 2012 (www.statcan.gc.ca/pub/75f0002m/75f0002m2012001- eng.pdf).

Murrell, Amy R., Karen A. Christoff, and Kris R. Henning. 2007. "Characteristics of Domestic Violence Offenders: Associations with Childhood Exposure to Violence." *Journal of Family Violence* 22: 523–32.

Myers, Daniel J. 1997. "Racial Rioting in the 1960s: An Event History Analysis of Local Conditions." *American Sociological Review* 62: 94–112.

Myles, John. 1989. *Old Age in the Welfare State: The Political Economy of Public Pensions*, 2nd ed. Lawrence, KA: University Press of Kansas.

Nair, P. Sadasivan 2010. "Understanding Below-replacement Fertility in Kerala, India." *Journal of Health and Population Nutrition* 28(4): 405–12.

Nakhaie, M. R. 1997. "Vertical Mosaic among the Elites: The New Imagery Revisited." *Canadian Review of Sociology and Anthropology* 34, 1: 1–24.

National Basketball Association. 2000. "New York Knicks History." Retrieved May 29, 2000 (http://nba.com/knicks/00400499.html#2).

National Council of Welfare. 1998. *Banking and Poor People: Talk Is Cheap*. Ottawa: The Council.

National Oceanic and Atmospheric Administration, U.S. Department of Commerce. 2013. "CO_2 Expressed as a Mole Fraction in Dry Air, Micromol/Mol, Abbreviated as ppm." Retrieved 31 March 2013 (ftp://ftp.cmdl.noaa.gov/ccg/co2/trends/co2_annmean_mlo.txt).

National Opinion Research Center. 2004. *General Social Survey, 1972–2002*. Chicago: University of Chicago. Machine readable file.

National Union of Public and General Employees. 2013. "Migrant Workers Account for Most New Jobs: CLC." Retrieved April 12, 2014 (http://nupge.ca/content/5815/migrant-workers-account-most-new-jobs-clc).

Nawfal, Wissam. 2011. *Interlocking Directors: Impact on Canadian Merger and Acquisition Outcomes*. Masters thesis, Concordia University. Retrieved February 18, 2014 (http://spectrum.library.concordia.ca/7348/)

Neal, Mark Anthony. 1999. *What the Music Said: Black Popular Music and Black Public Culture*. New York: Routledge.

Neisser, Ulric. 1997. "Rising Scores on Intelligence Tests." *American Scientist* 85, 5: 440–47.

Nelson, Adie, and Barrie W. Robinson. 2002. *Gender in Canada*, 2nd ed. Toronto: Prentice Hall.

Nelson, Charles, A., Nathan A. Fox, and Charles H. Zeanah. 2014. *Romania's Abandoned Children: Deprivation, Brain Development and the Struggle for Recovery*. Boston: Harvard University Press.

Nelson, Dean, and Barney Henderson. 2009. "Slumdog Child Stars Miss Out on the Movie Millions." *Telegraph.co.uk* 26 January. Retrieved January 2, 2010 (www.telegraph.co.uk/news/worldnews/asia/4347472/Poor-parents-of-Slumdog-millionaire-stars-say-children-were-exploited.html).

Neuberg, Steven L., Douglas T. Kenrick, and Mark Schaller. 2010. "Evolutionary Social Psychology." Pp. 761–96 in Susan T. Fiske, Daniel T. Gilbert, and Gardner Lindzey, eds., *Handbook of Social Psychology*, 5th ed., Vol. 2. New York: John Wiley & Sons.

Nevitte, Neil. 1996. *The Decline of Deference*. Peterborough, ON: Broadview Press.

Newman, K. 1999. *No Shame in My Game: The Working Poor in the Inner City*. New York: Knopf and the Russell Sage Foundation.

Neyer, Gerda, and Laura Bernardi. 2011. "Feminist Perspectives on Motherhood and Reproduction." *Historical Social Research* 36(2): 162–76.

Nikiforuk, Andrew. 1998. "Echoes of the Atomic Age: Cancer Kills Fourteen Aboriginal Uranium Workers." *Calgary Herald* March 14: A1, A4. Retrieved October 8, 2000 (www.ccnr.org/deline_deaths.html).

Nisbett, Richard E. 2011. "The Achievement Gap: Past, Present & Future." *Daedalus* 140(2): 90–100.

Nisbett, Richard E., Kaiping Peng, Incheol Choi, and Ara Norenzayan. 2001. "Culture and Systems of Thought: Holistic versus Analytic Cognition." *Psychological Review* 108: 291–310.

Nisen, Max. 2011. "How Nike Solved Its Sweatshop Problem." *Business Insider* May 9. Retrieved February 18, 2014 (www.businessinsider.com/how-nike-solved-its-sweatshop-problem-2013-5).

Nock, Steven L. 2009. "The Growing Importance of Marriage in America." Pp. 302–24 in H. Elizabeth Peters and Claire M. Kamp Dush, eds. *Marriage and Family: Perspectives and Complexities*. New York: Columbia University Press.

Nolan, Patrick, and Gerhard Lenski. 2005. *Human Societies*. Boulder CO: Paradigm.

Nolen, Stephanie. 1999. "Gender: The Third Way." *The Globe and Mail* September 25: D1, D4.

Nomaguchi, Kei M., and Melissa A. Milkie. 2003. "Costs and Rewards of Children: The Effects of Becoming a Parent on Adults' Lives." *Journal of Marriage and Family* 65: 356–74.

Norris, Pippa, and Ronald Inglehart. 2011. *Sacred and Secular: Religion and Politics Worldwide*, 2nd ed. Cambridge, UK: Cambridge University Press.

Northup, Solomon. 1855. *Twelve Years a Slave: Narrative of Solomon Northup, A Citizen of New York, Kidnapped in Washington City in 1841 and Rescued in 1853, from a Cotton Plantation near the Red River, in Louisiana*. New York: Miller, Orton and Mulligan.

Norton, Kevin I., Timothy S. Olds, Scott Olive, and Stephen Dank. 1996. "Ken and Barbie at Life Size." *Sex Roles* 34, 3–4 (February): 287–94.

Notestein, F.W. 1945. "Population—The Long View." Pp. 36–57 in T.W. Schultz, ed. *Food for the World*. Chicago: University of Chicago Press.

Nowak, Martin A., Robert M. May, and Karl Sigmund. 1995. "The Arithmetics of Mutual Help." *Scientific American* 272, 6: 76–81.

O'Connor, Joe. 2013. "Ex-NHL Players' Lawsuit Blames Don Cherry for Being Don Cherry." *National Post* November 26. Retrieved November 28, 2013 (http://fullcomment.nationalpost.com/2013/11/26/joe-oconnor-ex-nhl-players-lawsuit-blames-don-cherry-for-being-don-cherry/).

O'Connor, Julia S., and Robert J. Brym. 1988. "Public Welfare Expenditure in OECD Countries: Towards a Reconciliation of Inconsistent Findings." *British Journal of Sociology* 39: 47–68.

O'Connor, Julia S., and Gregg M. Olsen, eds. 1998. *Power Resources Theory and the Welfare State: A Critical Approach*. Toronto: University of Toronto Press.

O'Malley, Martin, and Amina Ali. 2001. "Sticks, Stones and Bullies." CBC.ca. Retrieved June 23, 2002 (http://cbc.ca/national/news/bully).

O'Neil, Dennis. 2004. "Patterns of Subsistence: Classification of Cultures Based on the Sources and Techniques of Acquiring Food and other Necessities." Retrieved January 12, 2005 (http://anthro.palomar.edu/subsistence).

Oakes, Jeannie. 2005. *Keeping Track: How Schools Structure Social Inequality*. New Haven, CT: Yale University Press.

Oberschall, Anthony. 1973. *Social Conflict and Social Movements*. Englewood Cliffs, NJ: Prentice-Hall.

OECD. 2008. "Aid Targets Slipping Out of Reach?" Retrieved February 12, 2011 (www.oecd.org/dataoecd/47/25/41724314.pdf).

———. 2011. *Doing Better for Families*. Paris, France: OECD Publishing.

———. 2012. *Education at a Glance 2012: OECD Indicators*, Table A1.3a, Population that has attained tertiary education (2010). Available at: Employment and Social Development Canada (www4.hrsdc.gc.ca/.3ndic.1t.4r@-eng.jsp?iid=29#M_7).

———. 2013a. "FDI in Figures." Retrieved August 10, 2013 (www.oecd.org/daf/inv/FDI%20in%20figures.pdf).

———. 2013b. "Overweight and Obesity." In *OECD Factbook 2013: Economic, Environmental and Social Statistics*, OECD Publishing. Retrieved July 7, 2014 (http://dx.doi.org/10.1787/factbook-2013-100-en).

———. 2013c. "Pensions at a Glance: Canada." Paris: Author.

———. 2014a. "Average Usual Weekly Hours Worked on the Main Job." *OECD StatExtracts*. Retrieved February 15, 2014 (http://stats.oecd.org/Index.aspx?DataSetCode=ANHRS).

———. 2014b. "Union Density." *OECD StatExtracts*. Retrieved February 15, 2014 (http://stats.oecd.org/Index.aspx?QueryId=20167).

Office of Correctional Investigator. 2013. *Annual Report of the Office of the Correctional Investigator 2012–2013*. Retrieveed July 2, 2014 (www.oci-bec.gc.ca/cnt/rpt/annrpt/annrpt20122013-eng.aspx).

Ogmundson, R., and J. McLaughlin. 1992. "Trends in the Ethnic Origins of Canadian Elites: The Decline of the BRITS?" *The Canadian Review of Sociology and Anthropology* 29: 227–42.

Oliveira, Michael. 2013. "How Do You Compare? New Report Reveals Stats about Social Media Usage in Canada." *Maclean's* 29 April. Retrieved 21 August 2013 (www2.macleans.ca/2013/04/29/how-do-you-compare-new-report-reveals-stats-about-social-media-usage-in-canada/).

Oliver, Melvin L., and Thomas M. Shapiro. 1995. *Black Wealth/White Wealth: A New Perspective on Racial Inequality*. New York: Routledge.

Olsen, Dennis. 1980. *The State Elite*. Toronto: McClelland & Stewart.

Olsen, Gregg M. 2002. *The Politics of the Welfare State: Canada, Sweden, and the United States*. Don Mills, ON: Oxford University Press Canada.

Olsen, Gregg, and Robert J. Brym. 1996. "Between American Exceptionalism and Swedish Social Democracy: Public and Private Pensions in Canada." Pp. 261–79 in Michael Shalev, ed. *The Privatization of Social Policy? Occupational Welfare and the Welfare State in America, Scandinavia and Japan*. London: Macmillan.

Olzak, Susan, and Suzanne Shanahan. 1996. "Deprivation and Race Riots: An Extension of Spilerman's Analysis." *Social Forces* 74: 931–62.

Olzak, Susan, Suzanne Shanahan, and Elizabeth H. McEneaney. 1996. "Poverty, Segregation, and Race Riots: 1960 to 1993." *American Sociological Review* 61: 590–614.

Omi, M., and H. Winant. 1986. *Racial Formation in the United States*. New York: Routledge.

Oreopoulos, Philip. 2005. "Canadian Compulsory School Laws and Their Impact on Educational Attainment and Future Earnings." Ottawa: Statistics Canada. Retrieved May 27, 2006 (www.statcan.ca/english/research/11F0019MIE/11F0019MIE2005251.pdf).

Organisation Mondiale pour l'Education Préscolaire [OMEP]. 2014. Retrieved March 11, 2014 (www.worldomep.org/en/).

Orsorio, Marisa. 2014. "Ethnic Groups Clamor for Reparations." *UCLA Today*. Retrieved February 5, 2014 (http://www.today.ucla.edu/portal/ut/PRN-010522reparations.aspx).

Ouimet, M. 2002. "Explaining the American and Canadian Crime 'Drop' in the 1990s." *Canadian Journal of Criminology* 44, 1: 33–50.

Ouldzeidoune Nacerdine, Joseph Keating, Jane Bertrand, and Janet Rice. 2013. "A Description of Female Genital Mutilation and Force-Feeding Practices in Mauritania: Implications for the Protection of Child Rights and Health." *PLoS ONE* 8(4): e60594. doi:10.1371/journal.pone.0060594

Owen, Jesse, Frank D. Funcham, and Megan Manthos. 2013. "Friendship after a Friends with Benefits Relationship: Deception, Psychological Functioning, and Social Connectedness." *Archives of Sexual Behavior* 42: 1443–49.

Owen, Michelle K. 2001. "'Family' as a Site of Contestation: Queering the Normal or Normalizing the Queer?" Pp. 86–102 in Terry Goldie, ed. *In a Queer Country: Gay and Lesbian Studies in the Canadian Context*. Vancouver: Arsenal Pulp Press.

Paasonen, Susanna, Kaarina Nikunen, and Laura Saarenmaa. 2007. *Pornification: Sex and Sexuality in Media Culture*. Oxford: Berg.

Pabilonia, Sabrina Wulff, and Cindy Zoghi. 2005a. "Returning to the Returns to Computer Use." BLS Working Paper 377. Washington DC: U.S. Department of Labor, Bureau of Labor Statistics.

———. 2005b. "Who Gains from Computer Use?" *Perspectives on Labor and Income* 6, 7: 5–11.

Pacey, Arnold. 1983. *The Culture of Technology*. Cambridge, MA: MIT Press.

Paek, Hye-Jin, Michelle R. Nelson, and Alexandra M. Vilela. 2010. "Examination of Gender-role Portrayals in Television Advertising across Seven Countries." *Sex Roles* 64: 192–207.

Pammett, Jon H. 1997. "Getting Ahead Around the World." Pp. 67–86 in Alan Frizzell and Jon H. Pammett, eds. *Social Inequality in Canada*. Ottawa: Carleton University Press.

Pandya, Sophia. 2012. *Muslim Women and Islamic Resurgence: Religion, Education and Identity Politics in Bahrain*. New York: Palgrave Macmillan.

Pape, Robert A. 2003 "The Strategic Logic of Suicide Terrorism." *American Political Science Review* 97: 343–61.

Paperny, Anna Mehler. 2011. "Antibullying Movement Is in the Pink." *The Globe and Mail*, March 14. Retrieved April 24, 2011 (www.globeandmail.com).

Park, Robert Ezra, Ernest W. Burgess, and Roderick D. McKenzie. 1967 [1925]. *The City*. Chicago: University of Chicago Press.

Parke, Ross D. 2001. "Paternal Involvement in Infancy: The Role of Maternal and Paternal Attitudes." *Journal of Family Psychology* 15, 4 (December): 555–58.

———. 2002. "Parenting in the New Millennium: Prospects, Promises and Pitfalls." Pp. 65–93 in James P. McHale and Wendy S. Grolnick, eds. *Retrospect and Prospect in the Psychological Study of Families*. Mahwah, NJ: Lawrence Erlbaum Associates, Inc.

Parshall, Gerald. 1998. "Brotherhood of the Bomb." *US News and World Report* 125, 7 (17–24 August): 64–68.

Parsons, Talcott. 1942. "Age and Sex in the Social Structure of the United States." *American Sociological Review* 7: 604–16.

———. 1951. *The Social System.* New York: Free Press.

———. 1955. "The American Family: Its Relation to Personality and to the Social Structure." Pp. 3–33 in Talcott Parsons and Robert F. Bales, eds. *Family, Socialization and Interaction Process*. New York: Free Press.

———. 1963. "On the Concept of Political Power." *Proceedings of the American Philosophical Society* 107, 3: 232–62.

Patented Medicine Prices Review Board. 2013. *Annual Report, 2012*. Ottawa: Author.

Patsiurko, Natalka, John L. Campbell, and John A. Hall. 2012. "Measuring Cultural Diversity: Ethnic, Linguistic and Religious Fractionalization in the OECD." *Ethnic and Racial Studies* 35(2): 195–217.

Pazol, Karen, Andreea A. Creanga, Kim D. Burley, Brenda Hayes, and Denise J. Jamieson. 2013. "Abortion Surveillance—United States, 2010." *Morbidity and Mortality Weekly Report Surveillance Summaries*. 62(8): 1–44.

Pence, Leah, and Monique Jacobs. 2001. "Tracking the Elusive Traditional Family." *UVic KnowlEDGE* 2, 9. Retrieved June 12, 2006 (http://communications.uvic.ca/edge/v2n09_17sep01.pdf).

Pendakur, K., and R. Pendakur. 1998. "The Colour of Money: Earnings Differentials among Ethnic Groups in Canada." *Canadian Journal of Economics* 31: 518–48.

Pendakur, R. 2000. *Immigrants and the Labour Force: Policy, Regulation and Impact*. Montreal: McGill-Queen's University Press.

Perelli-Harris, Brienna, Michaela Kreyenfeld, Wendy Sigle-Rushton, Renske Keizer, Trude Laapegard, Aiva Jasilioneone, Caroline Berghammer, and Paola di Guilio. 2012. "Changes in Union Status during the Transition to Parenthood in Eleven European Countries, 1970s to Early 2000s." *Population Studies: A Journal of Demography* 66: 167–82.

perezhilton. 2013. "Celebrities Who Believe in Ghosts!" Retrieved March 26, 2014 (http://perezhilton.com/galleries/celebrities-who-believe-in-ghosts-ahhh/?id=398628#.UzLmoqhdW3p)

Perks, Thomas A. 2005. *Height as a Factor in Social Inequality: Analyses Based on Five Canadian National Surveys*. Ph.D. dissertation, Department of Sociology, University of Waterloo.

Perreault, Samuel. 2009. "The Incarceration of Aboriginal people in Adult Correctional Services." Statistics Canada. Retrieved November 10, 2010 (www.statcan.gc.ca/pub/85-002-x/2009003/article/10903-eng.htm).

———. 2013. "Police-Reported Crime Statistics in Canada, 2012." *Juristat* summer (85-002-X). Retrieved November 25, 3013 (www.statcan.gc.ca/pub/85-002-x/2013001/article/11854-eng.htm).

Perreault, Samuel and Shannon Brennan. 2010. "Criminal Victimization in Canada, 2009." *Juristat* summer (85-002-X). Retrieved November 25, 2013 (www.statcan.gc.ca/pub/85-002-x/2010002/article/11340-eng.htm).

Perrow, Charles B. 1984. *Normal Accidents*. New York: Basic Books.

Perry, Emma, and Becky Francis. 2010. *The Social Class Gap for Educational Achievement: A Review of the Literature*. London, UK: RSA Action and Research Centre. Retrieved February 26, 2014 (www.thersa.org/action-research-centre/learning,-cognition-and-creativity/education/social-justice/the-social-class-gap-for-educational-achievement-a-review-of-the-literature).

Peters, John F. 1994. "Gender Socialization of Adolescents in the Home: Research and Discussion." *Adolescence* 29: 913–34.

Pettersson, Jan. 2003. "Democracy, Regime Stability, and Growth." *Scandinavian Working Papers in Economics*. Retrieved February 13, 2003 (http://swopec.hhs.se/sunrpe/abs/sunrpe2002_0016.htm).

Pew Research Center. 2012. *The Global Religious Landscape: A Report on the Size and Distribution of the World's Major Religious Groups as of 2010*. Washington, DC: Author.

———. 2013a. *Arab Spring Adds to Global Restrictions on Religion*. Washington, DC: Author.

———. 2013b. *The Global Divide on Homosexuality: Greater Acceptance in More Secular and Affluent Countries*. Washington, DC: Author.

———. 2014. *Millennials in Adulthood: Detached from Institutions, Networked with Friends*. Washington, DC: Author.

Pew Research Center for the People and the Press. 2002. "Among Wealthy Nations U.S. Stands Alone in its Embrace of Religion." Retrieved May 3, 2003 (http://people-press.org/reports/display.php3? ReportID_167).

Phelan, Jo C., Bruce G. Link, and Parisa Tehranifar. 2010. "Social Conditions as Fundamental Causes of Disease: Theory, Evidence and Policy Implications." *Journal of Health and Social Behavior* 51: S28–S40.

Phelps, Edmund S. 2010. "Short-termism Is Undermining America." *New Perspectives Quarterly* 27(4): 17–19.

Piaget, Jean, and Bärbel Inhelder. 1969. *The Psychology of the Child*, Helen Weaver, trans. New York: Basic Books.

Picard, Andre. 2013. "Canadian Medical Association Comes Down Hard on NHL Owners over Hockey Violence." *The Globe and Mail* August 21. Retrieved December 1, 2013 (www.theglobeandmail.com/news/national/canadian-medical-association-comes-down-hard-on-nhl-owners-over-hockey-violence/article13897652/).

Pineo, P. C., and J. Porter. 1985. "Ethnic Origin and Occupational Attainment." In M. Boyd, J. Goyder, F. E. Jones, H. A. McRoberts, P. C. Pineo, and J. Porter, eds. *Ascription and Achievement: Studies in Mobility and Status Attainment*. Ottawa: Carleton University Press.

Pinker, Steven. 2002. *The Blank Slate: The Modern Denial of Human Nature*. New York: Viking.

Piven, Frances Fox, and Richard A. Cloward. 1977. *Poor People's Movements: Why They Succeed, How They Fail*. New York: Vintage.

———. 1993 [1971]. *Regulating the Poor: The Functions of Public Welfare*, updated ed. New York: Vintage.

Plummer, Kenneth. 1995. *Telling Sexual Stories: Power, Change and Social Worlds*. London, UK: Routledge.

Podolny, Joel M., and Karen L. Page. 1998. "Network Forms of Organization." *Annual Review of Sociology* 24: 57–76.

Pollard, Michael S., and Wu, Zheng. 1998. "Divergence in Marriage Patterns in Quebec and Elsewhere in Canada." *Population and Development Review* 24: 329–56.

Pollution Watch. 2008. "An examination of pollution and poverty in the City of Toronto." Retrieved December 7, 2010 (www.toronto.ca/demographics/pdf/pollutionwatch_toronto_fact_sheet.pdf).

Polsby, Nelson W. 1959. "Three Problems in the Analysis of Community Power." *American Sociological Review* 24: 796–803.

Pool, Robert. 1997. *Beyond Engineering: How Society Shapes Technology*. New York: Oxford University Press.

Popenoe, David. 1998. "The Decline of Marriage and Fatherhood." Pp. 312–19 in John J. Macionis and Nicole V. Benokraitis, eds. *Seeing Ourselves: Classic, Contemporary and Cross-Cultural Readings in Sociology*, 4th ed. Upper Saddle River, NJ: Prentice Hall.

Population Reference Bureau. 2013. *2013 World Population Data Sheet*. Washington, DC: Author.

Porter, John. 1965. *The Vertical Mosaic: An Analysis of Social Class and Power in Canada*. Toronto: University of Toronto Press.

———. 1979. *The Measure of Canadian Society: Education, Equality, and Opportunity*. Toronto: Gage.

Portes, A., and R. D. Manning. 1991. "The Immigrant Enclave: Theory and Empirical Examples." Pp. 319–32 in N. R. Yetman, ed. *Majority and Minority: The Dynamics of Race and Ethnicity in American Life*, 5th ed. Boston: Allyn and Bacon.

Postel, Sandra. 1994. "Carrying Capacity: Earth's Bottom Line." Pp. 3–21 in Linda Starke, ed. *State of the World 1994*. New York: Norton.

Poulantzas, Nicos. 1975 [1968]. *Political Power and Social Classes*, T. O'Hagan, trans. London: New Left Books.

Powell, J., and C. Leedham. 2009. "Comparative Aging in Post-Industrial Society." Pp. 141–60 in J. Powell and J. Hendricks, eds. *The Welfare State in Postindustrial Society: A Global Analysis*. New York: Springer.

Powers, Ann. 2009. "Frank Talk with Lady Gaga." *Los Angeles Times* December 13. Retrieved January 4, 2010 (http://articles.latimes.com/2009/dec/13/entertainment/la-ca-lady-gaga13-2009dec13).

Pred, Allan R. 1973. *Urban Growth and the Circulation of Information*. Cambridge, MA: Harvard University Press.

Press, Andrea. 1991. *Women Watching Television: Gender, Class and Generation in the American Television Experience*. Philadelphia: University of Pennsylvania Press.

Press, Andrea L., and Elizabeth R. Cole. 1999. *Speaking of Abortion: Television and Authority in the Lives of Women*. Chicago: University of Chicago Press.

Proctor, Robert N. 1988. *Racial Hygiene: Medicine under the Nazis*. Cambridge, MA: Harvard University Press.

Province of Nova Scotia. 2008. "Counties of Nova Scotia." Retrieved January 12, 2008 (www.gov.ns.ca/snsmr/muns/info/mapping/counties.asp).

Provine, Robert R. 2000. *Laughter: A Scientific Investigation*. New York: Penguin.

Public Health Agency of Canada. 2011. *Diabetes in Canada: Facts and Figures from a Public Health Perspective*. Ottawa: Public Health Agency of Canada.

Puhl, Rebecca M., and Chelsea A. Heuer. 2009. "The Stigma of *Obesity*: A Review and Update." Obesity 17: 941–64.

Putnam, Robert D., and David E. Campbell. 2010. *Amazing Grace: How Religion Divides and Unites Us*. New York: Simon & Shuster.

Raag, Tarja, and Christine L. Rackliff. 1998. "Preschoolers' Awareness of Social Expectations of Gender: Relationships to Toy Choices." *Sex Roles* 38: 685–700.

Ram, Usha, Lisa Strohschein, and Kirti Gaur. 2014. "Gender Socialization: Differences between Male and Female Youth in India and Associations with Mental Health." *International Journal of Population Research*. (http://dx.doi.org/10.1155/2014/357145).

Ramos, Howard. "Do Canadians Know How Increasing Numbers of Temporary Foreign Workers Is Changing Immigration?" *In Focus* January 1. Retrieved April 12, 2014 (https://www.policyalternatives.ca/sites/default/files/uploads/publications/Nova%20Scotia%20Office/2012/02/tempforeignworkersinfocus.pdf).

Ravanera, Zenaida, and Roderic Beaujot. 2009. "Life Course and Structural Factors in Childlessness: The Waiting Game and Constrained Choices in the Second Demographic Transition," *PSC Discussion Papers Series* 23(6), Article 1. Available at: (http://ir.lib.uwo.ca/pscpapers/vol23/iss6/1).

———. 2014. "Childlessness of Men in Canada: Result of a Waiting Game in a Changing Family Context." *Canadian Studies in Population* 41(1/2): 38–60.

Ray, Rebecca, Milla Sanes, and John Schmitt. 2013. *No-Vacation Nation Revisited*. Washington, DC: Center for Economic and Policy Research. Retrieved July 9, 2014 (www.cepr.net/documents/publications/no-vacation-update-2013-05.pdf).

Read, Jen'nan Ghazal, and Bridget K. Gorman. 2010. "Gender and Health Inequality." *Annual Review of Sociology* 36: 371–86.

Reardon, Sean. 2011. "The Widening Academic Achievement Gap Between the Rich and the Poor: New Evidence and Possible Explanations." Pp. 91–116 in Greg Duncan and Richard Murnane, eds. *Whither Opportunity? Rising Inequality, Schools, and Children's Life Chances*. New York: Russell Sage Foundation.

Reisinger, Don. 2012. "YouTube Users Uploading 72 Hours of Video Each Minute." CNet.com. Retrieved 4 April 2013 (http://news.cnet.com/8301-1023_3-57438332-93/youtube-users-uploading-72-hours-of-video-each-minute/).

Reiter, Ester. 1991. *Making Fast Food: From the Frying Pan into the Fryer*. Montreal: McGill-Queen's University Press.

Reitz, Jeffrey G. 2010. "Getting Past 'Yes' or 'No.'" *Literary Review of Canada* July/August: 3–4.

———. 2011. "Tapping Immigrants' Skills." Pp. 178–93 in Robert J. Brym, ed., *Society in Question*, 6th ed. Toronto: Nelson.

Reitz, Jeffrey G., and Raymond Breton. 1994. *The Illusion of Difference: Realities of Ethnicity in Canada and the United States*. Toronto: C.D. Howe Institute.

Reitz, Jeffrey G., Raymond Breton, Karen Dion, and Kenneth Dion. 2009. *Multiculturalism and Social Cohesion: Potentials and Challenges of Diversity*. Dordrecht, Netherlands: Springer.

Reputation Institute. 2013. "Canada Has the Best Reputation in the World According to Reputation Institute's 2013 Country Retrack Study." Retrieved November 3, 2013 (www.reputationinstitute.com/frames/events/2013_Country_RepTrak_Press_Release_Final.pdf).

Retail Council of Canada. 2014. "Minimum Wage by Province." Retrieved July 2, 2014 (www.retailcouncil.org/quickfacts/minimum-wage).

Reuters. 2013. "Alberta Oil Sands Production Likely to Double by 2022—Regulator." 8 May. Retrieved 26 August 2013 (www.reuters.com/article/2013/05/08/canada-alberta-reserves-idUSL2N0DP2HI20130508).

Richardson, John. 1832. *Wacousta; Or the Prophecy: A Tale of the Canadas*. London, UK: Cadell.

Richardson, R. Jack. 1996. "Canada and Free Trade: Why Did It Happen?" Pp. 200–09 in Robert J. Brym, ed. *Society in Question*. Toronto: Harcourt Brace Canada.

Richler, Mordecai. 1959. *The Apprenticeship of Duddy Kravitz*. Don Mills, ON: A. Deutsch.

Ridgeway, Cecilia L. 1983. *The Dynamics of Small Groups*. New York: St. Martin's Press.

Rifkin, Jeremy. 1998. *The Biotech Century: Harnessing the Gene and Remaking the World*. New York: Jeremy P. Tarcher/Putnam.

Riley, Matilda White, Anne Foner, and Joan Waring. 1988. "Sociology of Age." Pp. 243–90 in Neil Smelser, ed. *Handbook of Sociology*. Newbury Park, CA: Sage.

Riley, Nancy. 1997. "Gender, Power, and Population Change." *Population Bulletin* 52, 1. Retrieved August 25, 2000 (www.prb.org/pubs/population_bulletin/bu52-1.htm).

Rist, Ray. 1970. "Student Social Class and Teacher Expectations: The Self-Fulfilling Prophecy in Ghetto Education." *Harvard Educational Review* 40, 3 (August): 411–51.

Ritzer, George. 1996. "The McDonalidzation Thesis: Is Expansion Inevitable?" *International Sociology* 11: 291–307.

Robbins, Liz. 2005. "Nash Displays Polished Look: On the Court, of Course." *The New York Times* January 19. Retrieved January 19, 2005 (www.nytimes.com).

Roberts, C. G. D. 1915. *A History of Canada for High Schools and Academics*. Toronto: Macmillan.

Roberts, Julian, and Thomas Gabor. 1990. "Race and Crime: A Critique." *Canadian Journal of Criminology* 92, 2 (April): 291–313.

Roberts, Lance W., Rodney A. Clifton, Barry Ferguson, Karen Kampen, and Simon Langlois. 2005. *Recent Social Trends in Canada, 1960–2000*. Montreal and Kingston: McGill-Queen's University Press.

Roberts, Lance W., Barry Ferguson, Mathias Boes, and Susanne von Below, eds. 2013. *Multicultural Variations: Social Incorporation in Europe and North America*. Montreal and Kingston: McGill-Queens University Press.

Robertson, Ian. 1987. *Sociology*, 3rd ed. New York: Worth Publishing.

Robertson, Roland. 1992. *Globalization: Social Theory and Global Culture*. Newbury Park, CA: Sage.

Roche, Maurice. 1995. "Rethinking Citizenship and Social Movements: Themes in Contemporary Sociology and Neoconservative Ideology." Pp. 186–219 in Louis Maheu, ed. *Social Classes and Social Movements: The Future of Collective Action*. London, UK: Sage.

Rochon, Paula A., Andrea Gruneir, Wei Wu, Sudeep S. Gill, Susan E. Bronskill, Dallas P. Seitz, Chaim M. Bell, Hadas D. Fischer, Anne L. Stephenson, Xuesong Wang, Andrea S. Gershon, and Geoffrey M. Anderson. 2014. "Demographic Characteristics and Health Care Use of Centenarians: A Population-based Cohort Study." *Journal of the American Geriatrics Society* 62(1): 86–93.

Roediger, D. R. 1991. *The Wages of Whiteness: Race and the Making of the American Working Class*. London: Verso.

Roethlisberger, Fritz J., and William J. Dickson. 1939. *Management and the Worker*. Cambridge, MA: Harvard University Press.

Rogan, Mary. 2001. "An Epidemic of Gas Sniffing Decimates Arctic Indian Tribe." *The New York Times on the Web*. Retrieved March 4 (www.uwec.edu/Academic/Curric/majstos/p390/Articles/030301gas-sniffing-Indians.htm).

Rogers, Jackie Krasas, and Kevin D. Henson. 1997. "'Hey, Why Don't You Wear a Shorter Skirt?' Structural Vulnerability and the Organization of Sexual Harassment in Temporary Clerical Employment." *Gender and Society* 11: 215–37.

Romaniuc, A. 1984. "Fertility in Canada: From Baby-boom to Baby-bust." *Current Demographic Analysis*. Ottawa: Statistics Canada.

Ron, James. 2007. Personal communication. Norman Paterson School of International Affairs, Carleton University, Ottawa. December 20.

Rootes, Chris. 1995. "A New Class? The Higher Educated and the New Politics." Pp. 220–35 in Louis Maheu, ed. *Social Classes and Social Movements: The Future of Collective Action*. London, UK: Sage.

Roscigno, Vincent. 2012. "Power, Sociologically Speaking." Retrieved October 23, 2013 (http://thesocietypages.org/specials/power/).

Rose, Nikolas. 2003. "Neurochemical Selves." *Society* 1(267): 46–59.

———. 2007. "Molecular Biopolitics, Somatic Ethics and the Spirit of Biocapital." *Social Theory and Health* 5: 3–29.

Rosenbloom, Stephanie. 2007. "On Facebook, Scholars Link up with Data." *The New York Times* 17 December. Retrieved October 9, 2010 (www.nytimes.com).

Rosenbluth, Susan C. 1997. "Is Sexual Orientation a Matter of Choice?" *Psychology of Women Quarterly* 21: 595–610.

Rosenhan, David L. 1973. "On Being Sane in Insane Places." *Science* 179: 250–58.

Rosenthal, Robert, and Lenore Jacobson. 1968. *Pygmalion in the Classroom: Teacher Expectation and Pupils' Intellectual Development*. New York: Holt, Rinehart, and Winston.

Rosin, Hanna, and Richard Morin. 1999. "In One Area, Americans Still Draw a Line on Acceptability." *Washington Post*, National Weekly Edition, 16, 11 (11 January): 8.

Rostow, W. W. 1960. *The Stages of Economic Growth: A Non-Communist Manifesto*. New York: Cambridge University Press.

Rothman, David J. 1998. "The International Organ Traffic." *New York Review of Books* 45, 5: 14–17.

Royal Canadian Mounted Police. 2012. "Community Policing and Crime Prevention." Retrieved December 3, 2013 (www.rcmp-grc.gc.ca/mb/yir-bilan-11-12/community-polic-communautaire-eng.htm).

Rubie-Davis, Christine, John Hattie, and Richard Hamilton. 2006. "Expecting the Best for Students: Teacher Expectations and Academic Outcomes." *British Journal of Educational Psychology* 76: 429–44.

Rueschemeyer, Dietrich, Evelyne Huber Stephens, and John Stephens. 1992. *Capitalist Development and Democracy*. Chicago: University of Chicago Press.

Ruggles, Steven. 1997. *Prolonged Connections: The Rise of the Extended Family in 19th-Century England and America*. Madison, WI: University of Wisconsin Press.

Rupp, Leila J., and Verta Taylor. 2010. "Straight Girls Kissing." *Contexts* 9, 4: 28–32.

Rural Advancement Foundation International. 1999. "The Gene Giants." Retrieved May 2, 2000 (www.rafi.org/web/allpub-one.shtml?dfl=allpub.db&tfl=allpub-one-frag.ptml&operation=display&ro1=recNo&rf1=34&rt1=34&usebrs=true).

Rushton, J. Philippe. 1995. *Race, Evolution and Behaviour: A Life History Perspective*. New Brunswick, NJ: Transaction Publishers.

Rushton, J. Philippe, and C. Davison Ankney. 2009 "Whole Brain Size and General Mental Ability: A Review." *International Journal of Neuroscience* 119(5): 692–732.

Russett, Cynthia Eagle. 1966. *The Concept of Equilibrium in American Social Thought*. New Haven, CT: Yale University Press.

Ryan, Louise, Eleonore Kofman, and Pauline Aaron. 2011 "Insiders and Outsiders: Working with Peer Researchers in Researching Muslim Communities." *International Journal of Social Research Methodology* 14(1): 49–60.

Ryan, Phil. 2010. *Multicultiphobia*. Toronto: University of Toronto Press.

Ryerson, Stanley. 1973. *Unequal Union: Roots of Crisis in the Canadas, 1815–1873*, 2nd ed. Toronto: Progress.

Rytina, Steven, Peter M. Blau, Terry Blum, and Joseph Schwartz. 1988. "Inequality and Intermarriage: A Paradox of Motive and Constraint." *Social Forces* 66: 645–75.

Sahlins, Marshall D. 1972. *Stone Age Economics*. Chicago: Aldine.

Sampson, Robert J. 2012. *Great American City: Chicago and the Enduring Neighborhood Effect*. Chicago: Chicago University Press.

Sampson, Robert, and John H. Laub. 1993. *Crime in the Making: Pathways and Turning Points through Life*. Cambridge, MA: Harvard University Press.

Samson, Colin, James Wilson, and Jonathan Mazower. 1999. *Canada's Tibet: The Killing of the Innu*. London UK: Survival. Retrieved May 1, 2001 (www.survival.org.uk/pdf/Innu%20report.pdf).

Samuelsson, Kurt. 1961 [1957]. *Religion and Economic Action*, E. French, trans. Stockholm: Scandinavian University Books.

Sanchez, F. J. P., and Roda, M. D. S. 2003. "Relationships between Self-Concept and Academic Achievement in Primary Students." *Electronic Journal of Research in Educational Psychology and Psychpedagogy* 1, 1: 95–120.

Sanctuary for Families. 2013. *Female Genital Mutilation in the United States: Protecting Girls and Women in the US from FGM and Vacation Cutting*. Retrieved November 3, 2013 (www.sanctuaryforfamilies.org/storage/sanctuary/documents/report_onfgm_w_cover.pdf).

Sandel, Michael. 2007. *The Case against Perfection: Ethics in the Age of Genetic Engineering*. New York: Harvard University Press.

Saner, Emine. 2012. "I Was a Moonie Cult Leader." *The Guardian* September 3. Retrieved March 31, 2014 (www.theguardian.com/world/2012/sep/03/moonie-cult-leader).

Sapers, Howard. 2012. "Behind the Bars: Howard Sapers, Correctional Investigator—Sun News Network Interview." Retrieved July 2, 2014 (www.youtube.com/watch?v=g2OCmATMbAM).

Sarlo, C. 2001. *Measuring Poverty in Canada*. Vancouver: Fraser Institute.

Sartre, J. 1965 [1948]. *Anti-Semite and Jew*, G. J. Becker, trans. New York: Schocken.

Sassen, Saskia. 1991. *The Global City: New York, London, Tokyo*. Princeton, NJ: Princeton University Press.

———. 2005. "The Global City: Introducing a Concept." *Brown Journal of World Affairs* 11(2): 27–43.

Sassler, Sharon. 2010. "Partnering across the Life Course: Sex, Relationships, and Mate Selection." *Journal of Marriage and Family* 72: 557–75.

Savage, Charlie. 2013. "Researchers Making Gains on Computerized Facial Recognition." *Pittsburgh Post-Gazette* 21 August. Retrieved 27 August 2013 (www.post-gazette.com/stories/news/us/researchers-making-gains-on-computerized-facial-recognition-700126/).

Sayer, Liana C., Paula England, Paul D. Allison, and Nicole Kangas. 2011. "She Left, He Left: How Employment and Satisfaction Affect Women's and Men's Decisions to Leave Marriages." *American Journal of Sociology* 116(6): 1982–2018.

Scarr, Sandra, and Richard A. Weinberg. 1978. "The Influence of 'Family Background' on Intellectual Attainment." *American Sociological Review* 43: 674–92.

Schiff, Michel, and Richard Lewontin. 1986. *Education and Class: The Irrelevance of IQ Genetic Studies*. Oxford, UK: Clarendon Press.

Schiller, Herbert I. 1989. *Culture Inc.: The Corporate Takeover of Public Expression*. New York: Oxford University Press.

Schirle, Tammy. 2013. "Senior Poverty in Canada: A Decomposition Analysis." *Canadian Public Policy* 39(4): 517–40.

Schor, Juliet B. 1992. *The Overworked American: The Unexpected Decline of Leisure*. New York: Basic Books.

Schudson, Michael. 1991. "National News Culture and the Rise of the Informational Citizen." Pp. 265–82 in Alan Wolfe, ed. *America at Century's End*. Berkeley, CA: University of California Press.

———. 1995. *The Power of News*. Cambridge, MA: Harvard University Press.

Schuettler, Darren. 2002. "Earth Summit Bogs Down in Bitter Trade Debate." *Yahoo! Canada News* 28 August. Retrieved February 12, 2002 (http://ca.news.yahoo.com/020828/5/olia.html).

Schwartz, Zane. 2013. "High School Grade Inflation Balloon Ready to Pop." *The Globe and Mail* March 29, 2013. Retrieved February 19, 2014 (www.theglobeandmail.com/news/national/education/high-school-grade-inflation-balloon-ready-to-pop/article10452197/).

Schweingruber, David, and Clark McPhail. 1999. "A Method for Systematically Observing and Recording Collective Action." *Sociological Methods and Research* 27: 451–98.

Scott, Catherine. 2012. "'Girls' Is Not Diverse, Not Feminist and Not Empowering." *The Independent* 14 April. Retrieved April 14 2014 (www.independent.co.uk/voices/comment/girls-is-not-diverse-not-feminist-and-not-empowering-8224704.html).

Scott, Jamie S. 2012. *The Religions of Canadians*. Toronto: University of Toronto Press.

Scott, Janny. 1998. "Manners and Civil Society." *Journal* 2(3). Retrieved April 12, 2003 (www.civnet.org/journal/issue7/ftjscott.htm).

Scott, Wilbur J. 1990. "PTSD in DSM-III: A Case in the Politics of Diagnosis and Disease." *Social Problems* 37: 294–310.

Seale, Clive. 1998. *Constructing Death: The Sociology of Dying and Bereavement*. Cambridge, UK: Cambridge University Press.

Sedgh, Gilda, Susheela Singh, Iqbal H. Shah, Elisabeth Ahman, Stanley K. Henshaw, and Akinrinola Bankola. 2012. "Induced Abortion: Incidence and Trends Worldwide from 1995–2008." *The Lancet* 379: 625–32.

Sedghi, Ami, George Arnett, and Mona Chalabi. 2013. "Pisa 2012 Results: Which Country Does Best at Reading, Maths and Science?" *The Guardian Datablog* December 3. Retrieved July 17, 2014 (www.theguardian.com/news/datablog/2013/dec/03/pisa-results-country-best-reading-maths-science).

Seiter, Ellen. 1999. *Television and New Media Audiences*. Oxford, UK: Clarendon Press.

Seltzer, Judith A., and Suzanne M. Bianchi. 2013. Demographic Change and Parent-Child Relationships in Adulthood." *Annual Review of Sociology* 39: 275–290.

Sen, Amartya. 1981. *Poverty and Famines: An Essay on Entitlement and Deprivation*. Oxford, UK: Clarendon Press.

Sengupta, Ushnish. 2013. "The War on Canada's Aboriginal Youth." McMaster Centre for Scholarship in the Public Interest. Retrieved March 16, 2014 (http://mcspi.ca/summer-institute/2013-the-war-on-youth/student-projects/ushnish-sengupta/).

Senn, Charlene Y., Serge Desmarais, Norine Veryberg, and Eileen Wood. 2000. "Predicting Coercive Sexual Behavior across the Lifespan in a Random Sample of Canadian Men." *Journal of Social and Personal Relationships* 17, 1 (February): 95–113.

Sepinwall, Alan. 2012. *The Revolution Was Televised: The Cops, Crooks, Slingers and Slayers Who Changed TV Drama Forever*. N.p.: Alan Sepinwall.

Shaienks, Danielle, and Tomasz Gluszynski. 2007. "Participation in Postsecondary Education: Graduates, Continuers and Drop Outs, Results from YITS Cycle 4. Programme for International Student Assessment, Government of Canada." Retrieved March 17, 2011 (www.pisa.gc.ca/eng/participation.shtml).

Shakur, Sanyika (a.k.a. Monster Kody Scott). 1993. *Monster: The Autobiography of an L.A. Gang Member*. New York: Penguin.

Shalev, Michael. 1983. "Class Politics and the Western Welfare State." Pp. 27–50 in S. E. Spiro and E. Yuchtman-Yaar, eds. *Evaluating the Welfare State: Social and Political Perspectives*. New York: Academic Press.

Shallcross, Sandra L., and Jeffry A. Simpson. 2012. "Trust and Responsiveness in Strain-Test Situations." *Journal of Personality and Social Psychology* 102(5): 1031–44.

Shanahan, Michael J., and Ross Macmillan. 2008. *Biography and the Sociological Imagination: Contexts and Contingencies*. New York: W.W. Norton and Company.

Sharify-Funk, Meena, and William Rory Dickson. 2013. "Islam." Pp. 150–201 in Doris R. Jakobsh, ed. *World Religions, Canadian Perspectives: Eastern Traditions*. Toronto: Nelson Education.

Sharpe, Andrew, and Jean-Francois Arsenault. 2009. *Investing in Aboriginal Education in Canada: An Economic Perspective*. Ottawa, Canada: Canadian Policy Research Networks.

Shaw, Jessica C.A. 2013. "The Medicalization of Birth and Midwifery as Resistance." *Health Care for Women International* 34(6): 522–36.

Shaw, Karen. 2001. "Harry Potter Books: My Concerns." Retrieved June 15, 2003 (www.reachouttrust.org/regulars/articles/occult/hpotter2.htm).

Shaw, Martin. 2000. *Theory of the Global State: Globality as Unfinished Revolution*. Cambridge: Cambridge University Press.

Sherif, M., L. J. Harvey, B. J. White, W. R. Hood, and C. W. Sherif. 1988 [1961]. *The Robber's Cave Experiment: Intergroup Conflict and Cooperation*. Middletown, CT: Wesleyan University Press.

Sherrill, Robert. 1997. "A Year in Corporate Crime." *The Nation* 7 April: 11–20.

Shields, M. 1999. "Long Working Hours and Health." *Health Reports* 11, 2: 33–48.

Shilling, Chris. 2013. *The Body and Social Theory*, 3rd ed. London: Sage.

Shkilnyk, Anastasia. 1985. *A Poison Stronger Than Love: The Destruction of an Ojibway Community*. New Haven, CT: Yale University Press.

"Short Guys Finish Last." 1995–96. *The Economist* December 23–January 5: 19–22.

Sibbald, Barbara. 2012. "Farm-grown Superbugs: While the World Acts, Canada Dawdles." *Canadian Medical Association Journal* 184(14): 1553.

Signorielli, Nancy. 2009. "Race and Sex in Prime Time: A Look at Occupations and Occupational Prestige." *Mass Communication and Society* 12: 332–52.

Silberman, Steve. 2000. "Talking to Strangers." *Wired* 8, 5: 225–33, 288–96. Retrieved May 23, 2002 (http://www.wired.com/wired/archive/8.05/translation.html).

"The Silent Boom." 1998. *Fortune* 7 July: 170–71.

Silventoinen, Karri. 2003. "Determinants of Variation in Adult Body Height." *Journal of Biosocial Science* 35: 263–85.

Silversides, Ann. 2009. "Provincial Experiments Aim to Lower Public Drug Plan Costs." *Canadian Medical Association Journal* 181: 80–82.

Simmel, Georg. 1950. *The Sociology of Georg Simmel*, Kurt H. Wolff, trans. and ed. New York: Free Press.

Simon, Jonathan. 1993. *Poor Discipline: Parole and the Social Control of the Underclass, 1890–1990*. Chicago: University of Chicago Press.

Simons-Morton, B., and R. Chen. 2009. "Peer and Parent Influences on School Engagement among Early Adolescents." *Youth & Society*, 41: 3–25.

Sinclair, Raven. 2007. "Identity Lost and Found: Lessons from the Sixties Scoop." *First Peoples Child and Family Review* 3(1): 65–82.

Singh, Ashish. 2012. "Gender Based Within-Household Inequality in Childhood Immunization in India: Changes over Time and across Regions." *PLoS ONE* 7(4) e35045. doi:10.1371/journal.pone.0035045.

Sinha, Maire. 2013. *Family Violence in Canada: A Statistical Profile, 2011*. Catalog. No. 85-002-X. Ottawa, ON: Minister of Industry.

———. 2014. *Parenting and Child Support after Separation or Divorce*. Catalogue No. 89-652-X. Ottawa, ON: Minister of Industry.

Sissing, T. W. 1996. "The Black Community in the History of Québec and Canada." Retrieved June 14, 2003 (www.qesnrecit.qc.ca/mpages/title.htm).

Sjöberg, Gideon. 1960. *The Preindustrial City: Past and Present.* New York: Free Press.

Skerrett, Delaney Michael. 2010. "Can the Sapir–Whorf Hypothesis Save the Planet? Lessons from Cross-Cultural Psychology for Critical Language Policy." *Current Issues in Language Planning* 11(4): 331–40.

Skinner, B. F. 1953. *Science and Human Behavior.* New York: Macmillan.

Skocpol, Theda. 1979. *States and Revolutions: A Comparative Analysis of France, Russia, and China.* Cambridge, UK: Cambridge University Press.

Smeeding, Timothy M. 2004. "Public Policy and Economic Inequality: The United States in Comparative Perspective." Working Paper No. 367. Syracuse NY: Maxwell School of Citizenship and Public Affairs, Syracuse University. Retrieved January 30, 2005 (www.lisproject.org/publictions/LISwps/367.pdf).

Smelser, Neil. 1963. *Theory of Collective Behavior.* New York: Free Press.

Smiler, Andrew P. 2011. "Sexual Strategies Theory: Built for the Short Term or the Long Term?" *Sex Roles* 64: 603–12.

———. 2013. *Challenging Casanova: Beyond the Stereotype of the Promiscuous Young Male.* San Francisco, CA: Jossey-Bass.

Smith, Anthony. 1980. *Goodbye Gutenberg: The Newspaper Revolution of the 1980s.* New York: Oxford University Press.

Smith, Christian. 1991. *The Emergence of Liberation Theology: Radical Religion and Social Movement Theory.* Chicago: University of Chicago Press.

Smith, Christine A. 2012. "The Confounding of Fat, Control, and Physical Attractiveness for Women." *Sex Roles* 66: 628–31.

Smith, Craig. 2014. "By the Numbers: 125 Amazing Facebook User Statistics." *Digital Marketing Ramblings* 13 July. Retrieved July 20, 2014 (http://expandedramblings.com/index.php/by-the-numbers-17-amazing-facebook-stats/#.U8vhlN3igvI).

Smith, Elliot. 2012. "American Dream Fades for Generation Y Professionals." Bloomberg.com, December 21. Retrieved December 28, 2013 (www.bloomberg. com/news/2012-12-21/american- dream-fades-for-generation-y - professionals.html).

Smith, Jackie. 1998. "Global Civil Society? Transnational Social Movement Organizations and Social Capital." *American Behavioral Scientist* 42: 93–107.

Smith, Paula, and Myrinda Schweitzer. 2013. "The Therapeutic Prison." *Journal of Contemporary Criminal Justice* 28(1): 7–22.

Smith, Stacy L., Katherine M. Pieper, Amy Granados, and Mare Choueiti. 2010. "Assessing Gender-related Portrayals in Top-Crossing G-rated Films." *Sex Roles* 62: 774–86.

Smoyer-Tomic, Karen E., John C. Spence, and Carl Amrhein. 2006. "Food Deserts in the Prairies? Supermarket Accessibility and Neighborhood Need in Edmonton, Canada." *The Professional Geographer* 58(3): 307–26.

Smyth, Julie. 2003. "Sweden Ranked as Best Place to Have a Baby: Canada Places Fifth on Maternity Leave, 15th for Benefits." *National Post* 17 January. Retrieved June 27, 2004 (www.childcarecanada.org/ccin/2003/ccin1_17_03.html).

Snider, Laureen. 1999. "White-Collar Crime." P. 2504 in James H. Marsh, editor in chief. *The Canadian Encyclopedia, Year 2000 Edition.* Toronto: McClelland & Stewart Inc.

Snow, David A., E. Burke Rochford Jr., Steven K. Worden, and Robert D. Benford. 1986. "Frame Alignment Processes, Micromobilization, and Movement Participation." *American Sociological Review* 51: 464–81.

Snyder, Benson R. 1971. *The Hidden Curriculum.* New York: Alfred A. Knopf.

Snyder, David, and Charles Tilly. 1972. "Hardship and Collective Violence in France, 1830–1960." *American Sociological Review* 37: 520–32.

Sobal, Jeffery, and Karla L. Hanson. 2011. "Marital Status, Marital History, Body Weight, and Obesity." *Marriage and Family Review* 47: 474–504.

Sobolewski, Juliana M., and Valarie King. 2005. "The Importance of the Coparental Relationship for Nonresident Fathers' Ties to Children." *Journal of Marriage and Family* 67: 1196–212.

Sobotka, Tomáš, and Laurent Toulemon. 2008. "Changing Family and Partnership Behaviour: Common Trends and Persistent Diversity across Europe." *Demographic Research* 19(6): 85–138.

Sofsky, Wolfgang. 1997 [1993]. *The Order of Terror: The Concentration Camp*, William Templer, trans. Princeton, NJ: Princeton University Press.

Sone, Emmanuel N. 2010. Piracy in the Horn of Africa: The Role of Somalia's Fishermen. MSc thesis, Naval Postgraduate School, Monterey, California. http://www.hsdl.org/?view&did=10985 (retrieved 6 November 2013).

Sorenson, Elaine. 1994. *Comparable Worth: Is It a Worthy Policy?* Princeton, NJ: Princeton University Press.

Sparrow, Robert. 2010. "Implants and Ethnocide: Learning from the Cochlear Implant Controversy." *Disability and Society* 25(4): 455–66.

Speer, Susan, and Elizabeth Stokoe, eds. 2011. *Conversation and Gender.* Cambridge, UK: University Press.

Spencer, Herbert. 1975 [1897–1906]. *The Principles of Sociology*, 3rd ed. Westport, CT: Greenwood Press.

Spilerman, Seymour. 1970. "The Causes of Racial Disturbances: A Comparison of Alternative Explanations." *American Sociological Review* 35: 627–49.

———. 1976. "Structural Characteristics of Cities and the Severity of Racial Disorders." *American Sociological Review* 41: 771–93.

Spines, Christine. 2010. "Lady Gaga Wants You." *Cosmopolitan*, UK edition. May: 50–54.

Spitzer, Steven. 1980. "Toward a Marxian Theory of Deviance." Pp. 175–91 in Delos H. Kelly, ed. *Criminal Behavior: Readings in Criminology.* New York: St. Martin's Press.

Stalker, Glenn, and Michael Ornstein. 2013. "Quebec, Daycare, and the Household Strategies of Couples with Young Children." *Canadian Public Policy* 39(2): 241–62.

Standing, Guy. 2011. *The Precariat: The New Dangerous Class.* London: Bloomsbury Academic.

Stankiewicz, Julie, and Francine Rosselli. 2008. "Women as Sex Objects and Victims in Print Advertisements." *Sex Roles* 58: 579–89.

Stark, Rodney. 1999. "Secularization: RIP." *Sociology of Religion* 60: 249–73.

Stark, Rodney, and William Sims Bainbridge. 1979. "Of Churches, Sects, and Cults: Preliminary Concepts for a Theory of

Religious Movements." *Journal for the Scientific Study of Religion* 18: 117–31.

Statistic Brain. 2013. "Twitter Statistics." Retrieved 20 August 2013 (www.statisticbrain.com/twitter-statistics/).

Statistics Canada. 2000a. "Household Environmental Practices." Retrieved October 7, 2000 (www.statcan.ca/english/Pgdb/Land/Environment/envir01a.htm).

———. 2000b. "Income in Canada, 1998." Ottawa: Ministry of Industry.

———. 2000c. "Population." Retrieved October 7, 2000 (www.statcan.ca/english/Pgdb/People/Population/demo02.htm).

———. 2000d. "Population by Aboriginal Group, 1996 Census." Retrieved October 7, 2000 (www.statcan.ca/english/Pgdb/People/Population/demo39a.htm).

———. 2001. "Death: Shifting Trends." *Health Reports* 12(3): 41–46.

———. 2003. "Religions in Canada." *2001 Census Analysis Series*. Retrieved November 28, 2005 (www12.statcan.ca/english/census01/Products/Analytic/companion/rel/canada.cfm).

———. 2005a. "Labour Force Survey Estimates by National Occupational Classification for Statistics and Sex, Annual." Table 282-0010. On the World Wide Web at http://cansim2.statcan.ca/cgi-win/CNSMCGI . EXE? LANG=E&SDDSLOC=//www.statcan .ca/english/ sdds/*.htm&ROOTDIR=CII/&RESULTTEMPLATE=CII/CII PICK&ARRAY PICK=1&ARRAYID=2820010 (retrieved 25 July 2005).

———. 2005b. "2001 Microdata Files." Retrieved November 30, 2005 (http://dc1.chass.utoronto.ca.myaccess.library .utoronto.ca/census/mainmicro.html).

———. 2007. "Highest Certificate, Diploma or Degree (14), Age Groups (10A) and Sex (3) for the Population 15 Years and Over of Canada, Provinces, Territories, Census Metropolitan Areas and Census Agglomerations, 2006 Census—20% Sample Data." Retrieved March 5, 2011 (www12.statcan.ca/english/census06/data/topics/RetrieveProductTable.cfm ?Temporal=2006&PID=93609&GID=837928&METH =1&APATH=3&PTYPE=88971&THEME=75&AID= &FREE=0&FOCUS=&VID=0&GC=99&GK=NA&RL =0&d1=1).

———. 2008a. "Distribution of Total Income, by Economic Family Type, 2005 Constant Dollars, Annual." CANSIM, Table 202-0401. Retrieved January 12, 2008 (http://cansim2.statcan.ca/cgi-win/cnsmcgi.exe?Lang=E&RootDir=CII/&ResultTemplate=CII/CII &Array Pick=1&ArrayId=2020401).

———. 2008b. "Earnings of Individuals, by Selected Characteristics and National Occupational Classification (NOC-S)" (CANSIM Table 202-0106). Retrieved November 20, 1010 (http://dc1.chass.utoronto.ca.myaccess.library .utoronto.ca/cgi-bin/cansimdim/c2 getArrayDim.pl).

———. 2008c. "Labour Force Survey Estimates (LFS), by National Occupational Classification for Statistics (NOC-S) and Sex" (CANSIM Table 282-0010). Retrieved November 20, 2010 (http://dc1.chass.utoronto.ca.myaccess.library .utoronto.ca/cgi-bin/cansimdim/c2 getArrayDim.pl).

———. 2008d. "Screen Time among Canadian Adults: A Profile." *Health Reports* 19, 2: June. Retrieved February 22, 2010 (www.statcan.gc.ca/pub/82-003-x/2008002/article/10600-eng.pdf).

———. 2010a. "Aboriginal Statistics at a Glance." Retrieved January 4, 2013 (www.statcan.gc.ca/pub/89-645-x/89-645-x2010001-eng.htm (retrieved 4 January 2013).

———. 2010b. "Age Groups (13) and Sex (3) for the Population of Canada, Provinces and Territories, 1921 to 2006 Censuses - 100% Data." Retrieved November 10, 2010 (http://www12.statcan.gc.ca/census-recensement/2006/dp-pd/tbt/Rp-eng.cfm?LANG=E&APATH=3&DETAIL =0&DIM=0&FL=A&FREE=0&GC=0&GID=0&GK =0&GRP=1&PID=88977&PRID=0&PTYPE=88971,97 154&S=0&SHOWALL=0&SUB=0&Temporal=2006 &THEME=66&VID=0&VNAMEE=&VNAMEF=).

———. 2010c. "Canadian Internet Use Survey." Retrieved September 20, 2011 (www.statcan.gc.ca/daily -quotidien/110525/dq110525b-eng.htm).

———. 2010d. "Persistence of Low Income, by Selected Characteristics, Every 3 Years." CANSIM Table 202087.

———. 2010e. "Projections of the Diversity of the Canadian Population." Retrieved March 13, 2010 (www.statcan.gc.ca/pub/91-551-x/91-551-x2010001-eng.pdf).

———. 2010f. "University Expenditures, by Type of Expenditure, Canada an Provinces, 1999/2000 and 2004/2005 to 2008/2009" (Table B.2.13). Retrieved September 20, 2011 (www.satcan.gc.ca/pub/81-582-x/2010004/tbl/tblb2.13 -eng.htm).

———. 2011a. *Census of Population*. Statistics Canada Catalogue no. 98-312-XCB2011046.

———. 2011b. "Divorce Database and Marriage Database." Health Statistics Division, Canadian Vital Statistics.

———. 2011c. "Education and Occupation of High-Income Canadians." *National Household Survey*. Retrieved February 27, 2014 (www12.statcan.gc.ca/nhs-enm/2011/as-sa/99-014-x/99-014-x2011003 2-eng.cfm).

———. 2011d. *General Social Survey—2010: Overview of the Time Use of Canadians*. Retrieved June 23, 2014. (www.statcan.gc.ca/pub/89-647-x/89-647-x2011001-eng.pdf).

———. 2011e. National Household Survey. Retrieved July 21, 2014. (www12.statcan.gc.ca/nhs-enm/2011/as-sa/99-012-x/2011001/tbl/tbl01-eng.cfm).

———. 2011f. *Women in Canada: A Gender-based Statistical*, 6th ed. Catalogue no. 89-503-X. Ottawa, On: Minister of Industry.

———. 2012a. "Average Hours Worked Per Week, Canada, 1976–2012. Labour Force Survey Estimates (LFS), by Total and Average Usual and Actual Hours Worked." Table 282-0028. Retrieved February 18, 2014 (www4.hrsdc.gc.ca/.3ndic.1t.4r@-eng.jsp?iid=19).

———. 2012b. *Back to School By the Numbers, 2012*. Retrieved February 19, 2014 (www42.statcan.ca/smr08/2012/smr08 167 2012-eng.htm).

———. 2012c. *Canada's Rural Population Since 1851*. Catalogue no. 98-310-X2011003. Ottawa: Minister of Industry.

———. 2012d. *The Canadian Population in 2011: Age and Sex*. Ottawa: Minister of Industry.

———. 2012e. *The Canadian Population in 2011: Population Counts and Growth, Population and Dwelling Counts, 2011 Census*. Catalogue no. 98-310-X2011001. Ottawa: Minister of Industry.

———. 2012f. *Centenarians in Canada: Age and Sex, 2011 Census*. Catalogue no. 98-311-X2011003. Ottawa: Minister of Industry.

———. 2012g. "Conjugal Status, Opposite/Same-sex Status and Presence of Children for the Couple Census Families in Private Households of Canada, Provinces, Territories and Census Metropolitan Areas, 2011 Census." Retrieved July 14, 2014 (www12.statcan.gc.ca/census-recensement/2011/dp-pd/tbt-tt/Rp-eng.cfm?LANG=E&APATH=3&DETAIL=0&DIM=0&FL=A&FREE=0&GC=0&GID=0&GK=0&GRP=1&PID=102659&PRID=0&PTYPE=101955&S=0&SHOWALL=0&SUB=0&Temporal=2011&THEME=89&VID=0&VNAMEE=&VNAMEF=).

———. 2012h. "Earnings of individuals, by selected characteristics and National Occupational Classification (NOC-S), 2010 constant dollars, annually." CANSIM Table 2020106. Retrieved December 25, 2012 http://dc2.chass.utoronto.ca.myaccess.library.utoronto.ca/cgi-bin/cansimdim/c2_getArrayDim.pl.

———. 2012i. *Fifty Years of Families in Canada, 1961–2011: Families, Households and Marital Status, 2011 Census of Population*. Catalogue no. 98-312-X2011003. Ottawa, ON: Minister of Industry.

———. 2012j. "Generations in Canada: Age and Sex, 2011 Census." Catalogue no. 98-311-X2011003. Ottawa: Minister of Industry.

———. 2012k. Living Arrangements of Seniors: Families, Households and Marital Status: Structural Type of Dwelling and Collectives, 2011 Census of Population. Catalogue no. 98-312-X2011003. Ottawa: Author.

———. 2012l. "Low Income Lines, 2010–2011." Retrieved December 25, 2012 (www.statcan.gc.ca/pub/75f0002m/75f0002m2012002-eng.htm).

———. 2012m. *Portrait of Families and Living Arrangements in Canada. Families, Households, and Marital Status, 2011 Census of Population*. Catalogue no. 98-312-X2011001 Ottawa, ON: Minister of Industry.

———. 2012n. "Suicide and Suicide Rate, by Sex and Age Group." Retrieved 5 August 2013 (www.statcan.gc.ca/tables-tableaux/sum-som/l01/cst01/hlth66a-eng.htm).

———. 2013. "Table 2: Low income cut-offs (1992 base) before tax." http://www.statcan.gc.ca/pub/75f0002m/2013002/tbl/tbl02-eng.htm (retrieved 13 September 2014).

———. 2013a. "Diabetes by Age Group and Sex." Retrieved July 21, 2014 (www.statcan.gc.ca/tables-tableauxsum-som/l01/cst01/health53b-eng.htm).

———. 2013b. *Disability in Canada: Initial findings from the Canadian Survey on Disability*. Catalogue no. 89-654-X — No. 002. Ottawa, ON: Author.

———. 2013c. "Education in Canada: Attainment, Field of Study and Location of Study." Catalogue no. 99-012-X2011001. Ottawa: Minister of Industry.

———. 2013d. "Ethnic Origin (264), Single and Multiple Ethnic Origin Responses (3), Generation Status (4), Age Groups (10) and Sex (3) for the Population in Private Households of Canada, Provinces, Territories, Census Metropolitan Areas and Census Agglomerations, 2011 National Household Survey." Retrieved February 10, 2014 (www12.statcan.gc.ca/nhs-enm/2011/dp-pd/dt-td/Rp-eng.cfm?LANG=E&APATH=3&DETAIL=0&DIM=0&FL=A&FREE=0&GC=0&GID=0&GK=0&GRP=1&PID=105396&PRID=0&PTYPE=105277&S=0&SHOWALL=0&SUB=0&Temporal=2013&THEME=95&VID=0&VNAMEE=&VNAMEF=).

———. 2013e. "Family Violence in Canada: A Statistical Profile, 2011." Ottawa: Minister of Industry.

———. 2013f. "Fertility: Overview, 2009 to 2011." Catalogue no. 91-209-X. Ottawa, ON: Minister of Industry.

———. 2013g. *Immigration and Ethnocultural Diversity in Canada: National Household Survey, 2011*. Catalogue no. 99-010-X2011001. Ottawa, ON: Minister of Industry.

———. 2013h. "Labour Force Characteristics by Age and Sex—Seasonally Adjusted." Retrieved August 5, 2013 (http://www.statcan.gc.ca/daily-quotidien/130705/t130705a001-eng.htm).

———. 2013i. National Household Survey (NHS) Profile. 2011 National Household Survey. Retrieved November 4, 2013 (www12.statcan.gc.ca/nhs-enm/2011/dp-pd/prof/index.cfm?Lang=E).

———. 2013j. "Study: Long-term Trends in Unionization, 1981 to 2012." *The Daily* November 26.

———. 2013k. "Summary Elementary and Secondary School Indicators for Canada." *The Daily* December 4, 2013. Retrieved February 15, 2014 (www.statcan.gc.ca/access_acces/alternative_alternatif.action?teng=The%20Daily,%20Wednesday,%20December%204,%202013:%20Summary%20elementary%20and%20secondary%20school%20indicators%20for%20Canada,%20the%20provinces%20and%20territories,%202011/2012&tfra=Le%20Quotidien,%20le%20mercredi%204%20décembre%202013%20:%20Indicateurs%20sommaires%20des%20écoles%20primaires%20et%20secondaires%20pour%20le%20Canada,%20les%20provinces%20et%20les%20territoires,%202011-2012&l=eng&loc=dq131204c-eng.pdf).

———. 2013l. "Unemployment Rates of 25- 29-Year-Olds by Educational Attainment." *Labour Force Survey*, Table E3.2. Updated May 1, 2013. Retrieved February 17, 2014 (www.statcan.gc.ca/pub/81-582-x/2013001/tbl/tble3.2-eng.htm).

———. 2013m "University Tuition Fees, 2013–14." *The Daily* September 12, 2013. Retrieved February 26, 2014 (www.statcan.gc.ca/access_acces/alternative_alternatif.action?teng=The%20Daily,%20Thursday,%20September%2012,%202013:%20University%20tuition%20fees,%202013/2014&tfra=Le%20Quotidien,%20le%20jeudi%2012%20septembre%202013%20:%20Frais%20de%20scolarité%20universitaires,%202013-2014&l=eng&loc=dq130912b-eng.pdf).

———. 2014. "Ethnic Origin (264), Single and Multiple Ethnic Origin Responses (3), Generation Status (4), Age Groups (10) and Sex (3) for the Population in Private Households of Canada, Provinces, Territories, Census Metropolitan Areas and Census Agglomerations, 2011 National Household Survey." http://www12.statcan.gc.ca/nhs-enm/2011/dp-pd/dt-td/Rp-eng.cfm?LANG=E&APATH=3&DETAIL=0&DIM=0&FL=A&FREE=0&GC=0&GID=0&GK=0&GRP=1&PID=105396&PRID=0&PTYPE=105277&S=0&SHOWALL=0&SUB=0&Temporal=2013&THEME=95&VID=0&VNAMEE&VNAMEF (retrieved 12 August 2014).

———. 2014a. "Distribution of Earnings, by Sex, 2011 Constant Dollars, Annual, 1976–2011." CANSIM (database), Table 202-0101.

———. 2014b. "Labour Force Survey Estimates, by North American Industry Classification System, Sex and Age Group, Annual." CANSIM (database) Table 282-0008. Retrieved February 12, 2013 (www.statcan.gc.ca/tables-tableaux/sum-som/l01/cst01/labor12-eng.htm).

———. 2014c. "Leading Causes of Death, Total Population, by Age Group and Sex, Canada." Table 102-0561. Retrieved May 9, 2014 (www5.statcan.gc.ca/cansim/a26?lang=eng&retrLang=eng&id=1020561&pattern=&csid).

———. 2014d. "Population and Dwelling Counts, for Census Metropolitan Areas, 2001 and 2006 Census Areas." Retrieved July 21, 2014 (www.statcan.gc.ca/census-recensement/2011/dp-pd/hlt-fst/pd-pl/Table-Tableau.cfm?T=205&S=3&RPP=50).

Stearns, Carol Zisowitz, and Peter N. Stearns. 1985. "Emotionology: Clarifying the History of Emotions and Emotional Standards." *American Historical Review* 90: 813–36.

———. 1986. *Anger: The Struggle for Emotional Control in America's History*. Chicago: University of Chicago Press.

Steckel, Richard H. 2013. "Biological Measures of Economic History." *Annual Reviews of Economics* 5: 401–23.

Steel, Freda M. 1987. "Alimony and Maintenance Orders." Pp. 155–67 in Sheilah L. Martin and Kathleen E. Mahoney, eds. *Equality and Judicial Neutrality*. Toronto: Carswell.

Steinberg, Stephen. 1989. *The Ethnic Myth: Race, Ethnicity, and Class in America*, updated ed. Boston: Beacon Press.

Sternberg, Robert J. 1986. "A Triangular Theory of Love." *Psychological Review* 93: 119–35.

———. 1998. *In Search of the Human Mind,* 2nd ed. Fort Worth, TX: Harcourt Brace.

Stewart, Donna, Harriet MacMillan, and Nadine Wathen. 2013. "Intimate Partner Violence." *Canadian Journal of Psychiatry* 58(6): 1–15.

Sticca, Fabio, and Sonja Perren. 2013. "Is Cyberbullying Worse than Traditional Bullying? Examining the Differential Roles of Medium, Publicity, and Anonymity for the Perceived Severity of Bullying." *Journal of Youth and Adolescence* 42(5): 739–50.

Stiglitz, Joseph E. 2002. *Globalization and Its Discontents*. New York: Norton.

Stopford, John M., and Susan Strange. 1991. *Rival States, Rival Firms: Competition for World Market Shares*. Cambridge: Cambridge University Press.

Stouffer, Samuel A., Edward A. Suchman, Leland C. De Vinney, Shirley A. Star, and Robin M. Williams, Jr. 1949. *The American Soldier*, 4 vols. Princeton, NJ: Princeton University Press.

Strauss, Anselm L. 1993. *Continual Permutations of Action*. New York: Aldine de Gruyter.

Stretesky, Paul, and Michael J. Hogan. 1998. Environmental Justice: An Analysis of Superfund Sites in Florida." *Social Problems* 45: 268–87.

Strohschein, Lisa. 2005. "Parental Divorce and Child Mental Health Trajectories." *Journal of Marriage and Family* 67: 1286–1300.

———. 2012. "Parental Divorce and Child Mental Health: Understanding Predisruption Effects." *Journal of Divorce and Remarriage* 53(6): 489–502.

Strohschein, Lisa, Noralou Roos, and Marni Brownell. 2009. "Family Structure Histories and High School Completion: Evidence from a Population Based Registry." *Canadian Journal of Sociology* 34(1): 83–103.

Stuhldreher, Katie. 2008. "To turn the tide on piracy in Somalia, bring justice to its fisheries." *Christian Science Monitor* 20 November. http://www.csmonitor.com/Commentary/Opinion/2008/1120/p09s01-coop.html (retrieved 6 November 2013).

Subra, Baptiste, Muller, Dominique, Bègue, Laurent, Bushman, Brad J., and Delmas, Florian. 2010. "Effects of Alcohol and Weapon Cues on Aggressive Thoughts and Behaviors." *Personality and Social Psychology Bulletin* 36(8): 1052–57.

Subrahmanyam, Kaveri, and Patricia M. Greenfield. 1998. "Computer Games for Girls: What Makes Them Play?" Pp. 46–71 in Justine Cassell and Henry Jenkins, eds. *From Barbie to Mortal Kombat: Gender and Computer Games*. Cambridge, MA: MIT Press.

Sumner, William Graham. 1940 [1907]. *Folkways*. Boston: Ginn.

Sutherland, Edwin H. 1939. *Principles of Criminology*. Philadelphia: Lippincott.

———. 1949. *White Collar Crime*. New York: Dryden.

Swami, Viren, et al. 2010. "The Attractive Female Body Weight and Female Body Dissatisfaction in 26 Countries across 10 World Regions: Results of the International Body Project I." *Personality and Social Psychology Bulletin* 36, 3: 309–25.

Swanson, Scott R., Yinghau Huang, and Baoheng Wang. 2014. "Hospitality-Based Critical Incidents: A Cross-Cultural Comparison." *International Journal of Contemporary Hospitality Management* 26(1): 50–68.

Sweezy, Kate, and Jill Tiefenthaler. 1996. "Do State-Level Variables Affect Divorce Rates?" *Review of Social Economy* 54: 47–65.

Swiss Re. 2005 "Sigma Natural Catastrophes and Man-Made Disasters in 2004." Retrieved March 2, 2005 (http://www.swissre.com).

———. 2007. "Natural Catastrophes and Man-Made Disasters in 2006." Retrieved July 24, 2014 (http://media.swissre.com/documents/sigma2_2007_en.pdf).

———. 2009. "Natural Catastrophes and Man-Made Disasters in 2008." *Sigma* 2. Retrieved December 2, 2010 (http://media.swissre.com/documents/sigma2_2009_en.pdf).

———. 2010. "Natural Catastrophes and Man-Made Disasters in 2009." *Sigma* 1. Retrieved December 2, 2010 (http://media.swissre.com/documents/sigma2_2009_en.pdf).

———. 2013. "Sigma: Natural Catastrophes and Man-Made Disasters in 2012." Retrieved 31 March 2013 (http://media.swissre.com/documents/sigma2_2013_en.pdf).

Sykes, Gresham, and David Matza. 1957. "Techniques of Neutralization: A Theory of Delinquency." *American Sociological Review* 22: 664–70.

Sylwester, Kevin. 2002. "Democracy and Changes in Income Inequality." *International Journal of Business and Economics* 1: 167–78.

Szasz, Andrew, and Michael Meuser. 1997. "Environmental Inequalities: Literature Review and Proposals for New Directions in Research and Theory." *Current Sociology* 45, 3: 99–120.

Szklarski, Cassandra. 2012. "Gerry Dee Turns Teaching Antics into Sitcom." *Halifax Herald* January 8, 2012. Retrieved April 13, 2014 (http://thechronicleherald.ca/artslife/49955-gerry-dee-turns-teaching-antics-sitcom).

Tajfel, Henri. 1981. *Human Groups and Social Categories: Studies in Social Psychology*. Cambridge, UK: Cambridge University Press.

Takala, Jukka, Päivi Hämäläinen, Kaija Leena Saarela, Yoke Yun Loke, Kathiresan Manickam, Wee Jin Tan, Peggy Heng, Caleb Tjong, Guan Kheng Lim, Samuel Lim, Siok Lin Gan. 2013. "Global Estimates of the Burden of Injury and Illness at Work in 2012." *Journal of Occupational and Environmental Hygiene* 11(5): 326–337.

Tam, Pui-Wing. 2012. "Average Silicon Valley Tech Salary Passes $100,000." *Wall Street Journal* January 24. Retrieved February 12, 2014 (http://online.wsj.com/news/articles/SB10001424052970204624204577179193752435590 0).

Tannen, Deborah. 1990. *You Just Don't Understand Me: Women and Men in Conversation*. New York: William Morrow.

———. 1994. *Talking from 9 to 5: How Women's and Men's Conversational Styles Affect Who Gets Heard, Who Gets Credit, and What Gets Done at Work*. New York: William Morrow.

Tarrow, Sidney. 1994. *Power in Movement: Social Movements, Collective Action and Politics*. Cambridge, UK: Cambridge University Press.

———. 2011. *Power in Movement: Social Movements and Contentious Politics*, 3rd ed. Cambridge UK: Cambridge University Press.

Tasker, Fiona L., and Susan Golombok. 1997. *Growing Up in a Lesbian Family: Effects on Child Development*. New York: Guilford Press.

Tate, Geoffrey, and Liu Yang. 2012. "The Bright Side of Corporate Diversification: Evidence from Internal Labor Markets." Retrieved February 16, 2014 (http://papers.ssrn.com/sol3/papers.cfm?abstract_id=1787776).

Tate, William. 2011. "Review of *The Lottery*." Boulder, CO: National Education Policy Centre. Retrieved April 13, 2014 (http://nepc.colorado.edu/files/TTR-Lottery-Tate_0.pdf).

Tavris, C. 1992. *The Mismeasure of Woman*. New York: Simon & Schuster.

Tec, Nechama. 1986. *When Light Pierced the Darkness: Christian Rescue of Jews in Nazi-Occupied Poland*. New York: Oxford University Press.

Television Bureau of Canada. 2014. "TV Basics, 2013–14." Toronto: Author.

"TFW2005." Retrieved 1 April 2013 (www.tfw2005.com/boards/transformers-fan-art/487030-tf-prime-eradicon-commander-torvek-crew.html).

Thoits, Peggy A. 1989. "The Sociology of Emotions." *Annual Review of Sociology* 15: 317–42.

Thomas, Carol. 1999. *Female Forms: Experiencing and Understanding Disability*. Buckingham, UK: Open University Press.

Thomas, Keith. 1971. *Religion and the Decline of Magic*. London: Weidenfeld and Nicholson.

Thomas, Mikhail. 2002. "Adult Criminal Court Statistics, 2000–01." *Juristat* 22, 2. Statistics Canada Catalogue no. 85-002-XPE.

Thomas, William Isaac. 1966 [1931]. "The Relation of Research to the Social Process." Pp. 289–305 in Morris Janowitz, ed. *W.I. Thomas on Social Organization and Social Personality*. Chicago: University of Chicago Press.

Thompson, E. P. 1967. "Time, Work Discipline, and Industrial Capitalism." *Past and Present* 38: 59–67.

Thompson, Kenneth, ed. 1975. *Auguste Comte: The Foundation of Sociology*, New York: Wiley.

Thorne, Barrie. 1993. *Gender Play: Girls and Boys in School*. New Brunswick, NJ: Rutgers University Press.

Thornton, Arland, William G. Axinn, and Yu Xie. 2007. *Marriage and Cohabitation*. Chicago: University of Chicago Press.

Tilly, Charles. 1978. *From Mobilization to Revolution*. Reading, MA: Addison-Wesley.

———. 1979a. "Collective Violence in European Perspective." Pp. 83–118 in H. Graham and T. Gurr, eds. *Violence in America: Historical and Comparative Perspective*, 2nd ed. Beverly Hills: Sage.

———. 1979b. "Repertoires of Contention in America and Britain, 1750–1830." Pp. 126–55 in Mayer N. Zald and John D. McCarthy, eds. *The Dynamics of Social Movements: Resource Mobilization, Social Control, and Tactics*. Cambridge, MA: Winthrop Publishers.

———. 1995. "Cycles of Collective Action between Moments of Madness and the Repertoire of Contention." Pp. 89–116 in Mark Traugot, ed. *Repertoires and Cycles of Collective Action*. Durham NC: Duke University Press.

———. 2002. "Violence, Terror, and Politics as Usual." Unpublished paper, Department of Sociology, Columbia University.

Tilly, Charles, Louise Tilly, and Richard Tilly. 1975. T*he Rebellious Century, 1830–1930*. Cambridge, MA: Harvard University Press.

Timmermans, Stefan, and Hyejoung Oh. 2010. "The Continued Social Transformation of the Medical Profession." *Journal of Health and Social Behavior* 51: S94–S106.

Titlestad, Michael. 2013. "Searching for the Sugar-coated Man." *Safundi: The Journal of South African and American Studies* 14(4): 466–70.

Tjepkema, Michael. 2006. *Measured Obesity: Adult Obesity in Canada—Measured Height and Weight*. Ottawa, ON: Statistics Canada.

———. 2008. "Health Care Use among Gay, Lesbian and Bisexual Canadians." *Health Reports* 19(1): 53–64.

Tjepkema, Michael, Russell Wilkins, and Andrea Long. 2013. "Cause-specific Mortality by Income Adequacy in Canada: A 16-year Follow-up Study." *Health Reports* 24(7): 14–22.

Tjepkema, Michael, Russell Wilkins, S. Senecal, E. Guimond, and C. Penney 2010. "Mortality of Urban Aboriginal Adults in Canada, 1991–2001." *Chronic Diseases in Canada* 31(1): 4–21.

Tkacik, Maureen. 2002. "The Return of Grunge." *The Wall Street Journal* December 11: B1, B10.

TNS Canadian Facts and Canada Post. 2012. "The Implications of Marketing Trends." Retrieved August 21, 2013 (www.canadapost.ca/cpo/mr/assets/pdf/business/marketingtrendsimplications_en.pdf).

Toffler, Alvin. 1990. *Powershift: Knowledge, Wealth, and Violence at the Edge of the 21st Century*. New York: Bantam.

Tolich, Martin. 1993. "Alienating and Liberating Emotions at Work: Supermarket Clerks' Performance of Customer Service." *Journal of Contemporary Ethnography* 22: 361–81.

Tomlinson, Kathy. 2013. "RBC Replaces Canadian Staff with Foreign Workers." *CBC News*. Retrieved April 12, 2014 (www.cbc.ca/news/canada/british-columbia/rbc-replaces-canadian-staff-with-foreign-workers-1.1315008).

Tönnies, Ferdinand. 1988 [1887]. *Community and Society (Gemeinschaft and Gesselschaft)*. New Brunswick, NJ: Transaction.

"Top Canadian CEOs Earn Annual Worker's Salary by Jan. 2." 2014. *CBC News*. Retrieved January 7, 2014 (www.cbc.ca/news/canada/top-canadian-ceos-earn-annual-worker-s-salary-by-lunchtime-on-jan-2-1.2481494).

"Top 1000: Exclusive Rankings of Canada's Most Profitable Companies." 2013. *Globe and Mail* 28 June. Retrieved August 21, 2013 (www.theglobeandmail.com/report-on-business/rob-magazine/top-1000/top-1000/article12829649/).

Torrance, Judy M. 1986. *Public Violence in Canada*. Toronto: University of Toronto Press.

Totten, Mark. 2001. "Legal, Ethical, and Clinical Implications of Doing Fieldwork with Youth Gang Members Who Engage in Serious Violence." *Journal of Gang Research* 8: 35–49.

Tovee, M. J., S. M. Mason, J. L. Emery, S. E. McClusky, and E. M. Cohen-Tovee. 1997. "Supermodels: Stick Insects or Hourglasses?" *Lancet* 350: 1474–75.

Trading Economics. 2010. "Canada GDP Growth Rate." Retrieved November 10, 2010 (www.tradingeconomics.com/Economics/GDP-Growth.aspx?Symbol=CAD).

Travers, Jeffrey, and Stanley Milgram. 1969. "An Experimental Study of the Small World Problem." *Sociometry* 32: 425–43.

Troeltsch, Ernst. 1931 [1923]. *The Social Teaching of the Christian Churches*, Olive Wyon, trans. 2 vols. London, UK: Allen and Unwin.

Trovato, Frank. 1998. "The Stanley Cup of Hockey and Suicide in Quebec, 1951–1992." *Social Forces* 77, 1 (September): 105–27.

Trudeau Foundation. 2006. "Backgrounder: Environics Research Group Poll for the Trudeau Foundation." Retrieved January 13, 2013 (www.trudeaufoundation.ca/sites/default/files/resultats_en1.pdf).

———. 2011 *The Making of Citizens: A National Survey of Canadians*. Retrieved April 12, 2014 (www.trudeaufoundation.ca/sites/default/files/u5/trudeau_foundation_immigration_survey_-_backgrounder_-_final_e.pdf).

Truth and Reconciliation Commission of Canada. 2012a. *They Came for the Children: Canada, Aboriginal Peoples, and Residential Schools*. Winnipeg, MB: Author.

———. 2012b. *Truth and Reconciliation Commission of Canada: Interim Report*. Retrieved March 14, 2014 (www.trc.ca/websites/trcinstitution/index.php?p=9).

Truzzi, Marcello. 1974. *Verstehen: Subjective Understanding in the Social Sciences*. Reading, MA: Addison-Wesley.

Tschannen, Olivier. 1991. "The Secularization Paradigm: A Systematization." *Journal for the Scientific Study of Religion* 30: 395–415.

Tsutsui, William M. 1998. *Manufacturing Ideology: Scientific Management in Twentieth-Century Japan*. Princeton, NJ: Princeton University Press.

Tumin, M. 1953. "Some Principles of Stratification: A Critical Analysis." *American Sociological Review* 18: 387–94.

Turcotte, Martin. 2011. *Women and Education: A Gender-Based Statistical Report*. Catalogue no. 89-503-X. Ottawa: Statistics Canada.

———. 2013. *Living Apart Together*. Cat. 75-006-X. Ottawa: Minister of Industry.

Turkle, Sherry. 1995. *Life on the Screen: Identity in the Age of the Internet*. New York: Simon & Schuster.

———. 2011. *Alone Together: Why We Expect More from Technology and Less from Each Other*. New York: Basic Books.

Turner, Bryan S. 1986. *Citizenship and Capitalism: The Debate over Reformism*. London, UK: Allen and Unwin.

———. 1996. *The Body and Society: Explorations in Social Theory*, 2nd ed. London: Sage.

———. 2011. *Religion and Modern Society: Citizenship, Secularisation and the State*. Cambridge: Cambridge University Press.

Turner, Ralph H., and Lewis M. Killian. 1987. *Collective Behavior*, 3rd ed. Englewood Cliffs, NJ: Prentice-Hall.

Twenge, Jean M. 2006. *Generation Me: Why Today's Young Americans Are More Confident, Assertive, Entitled—and More Miserable Than Ever Before*. New York: Random House.

Twenge, Jean M., and W. Keith Campbell. 2009. *The Narcissism Epidemic: Living in the Age of Entitlement*. New York: Simon & Schuster.

Twitaholic.com. 2013. "The Twitaholic.com Top 100 Twitterholics Based on Followers." Retrieved April 2, 2013 (http://twitaholic.com/).

"U.K. Panel Calls Climate Data Valid." 2010. *The New York Times* 30 March. Retrieved April 1, 2010 (www.nytimes.com).

Ungar, Sheldon. 1992. "The Rise and (Relative) Decline of Global Warming as a Social Problem." Sociological Quarterly 33: 483–501.

———. 1995. "Social Scares and Global Warming: Beyond the Rio Convention." Society and Natural Resources 8: 443–56.

———. 1998. "Bringing the Issue Back In: Comparing the Marketability of the Ozone Hole and Global Warming." *Social Problems* 45: 510–27.

———. 1999. "Is Strange Weather in the Air? A Study of U.S. National Network News Coverage of Extreme Weather Events." *Climatic Change* 41: 133–50.

Unger, Alon, and Lee W. Riley. 2007. "Slum Health: From Understanding to Action." *PLOS Medicine* 4, 10: e295. Retrieved October 20, 2010 (www.plosmedicine.org/article/info:doi/10.1371/journal.pmed.0040295).

UNICEF. 2008. *The Child Care Transition: Innocenti Report Card 8*. Florence: UNICEF Innocenti Research Centre.

______. 2013. "Female Genital Mutilation/Cutting: A Statistical Overview and Exploration of the Dynamics of Change." http://www.unicef.org/esaro/FGCM_Lo_res.pdf (retrieved 12 August 2014); World Health Organization. (2014). "Female Genital Mutilation." On the World Wide Web at http://www.who.int/mediacentre/factsheets/fs241/en/ (retrieved 12 August 2014).

Union of International Associations. 2001. "International Organizations by Year and Type, 1909–1999 (Table 2)." *Yearbook of International Organizations*. Retrieved February 14, 2006 (http://www.uia.org/statistics/organizations/ytb299.php).

———. 2010. "Yearbook of International Organizations." Retrieved November 16, 2010 (http://www.uia.be/yearbook).

———. 2013. "The Yearbook of International Organizations." Retrieved August 10, 2013 (www.uia.org/yearbook?qt-yb_intl_orgs=2#qt-yb_intl_orgs).

"Unions on Decline in Private Sector." 2012. *CBC News* 3 September 2012. Retrieved 24 August 2013 (www.cbc.ca/news/canada/story/2012/09/02/unions-labour-canada-decline.html).

United Church of Canada. 2013. "Statistics." Retrieved December 19, 2013 (www.united-church.ca/organization/statistics).

United Nations. 1998. "Universal Declaration of Human Rights." Retrieved January 25, 2003 (www.un.org/Overview/rights.html).

———. 2002. "Human Development Report 2002." New York: Oxford University Press. Retrieved April 16, 2003 (http://hdr.undp.org/reports/global/2002/en).

———. 2004. "UNAIDS 2004 Report on the Global AIDS Epidemic 2004 (PDF version)." Retrieved June 26, 2005 (www.unaids.org/bangkok2004/report_pdf.html).

———. 2007. "AIDS Epidemic Update 07." Geneva. Retrieved January 16, 2008 (http://data.unaids.org/pub/EPISlides/2007/2007_epiupdate_en.pdf).

———. 2010a. "FAO Cereal Supply and Demand." Retrieved June 10, 2011 (www.fao.org/worldfoodsituation/wfs-home/csdb/en).

———. 2010b. "Human Development Statistical Tables." *Human Development Report 2010*. Retrieved November 16, 2010 (http://hdr.undp.org/en/media/HDR_2010_EN_Tables.pdf).

———. 2011. "World Population to Reach 10 Billion by 2100 if Fertility in All Countries Converges to Replacement Level." May 3. Retrieved September 6, 2011 (http://esa.un.org/unpd/wpp/other-information/Press_Release_WPP2010.pdf).

———. 2012. World Urbanization Prospects, The 2011 Revision. New York: Author.

———. 2013. "2013 Human Development Report: Data Repository." Retrieved August 10, 2013 (http://hdr.undp.org/opendata/).

United Nations Children's Fund (UNICEF). 2013. *Female Genital Mutilation/Cutting: A Statistical Overview and Exploration of the Dynamics of Change*. New York: UNICDF. Retrieved November 3, 2013 (www.unicef.org/media/files/FGCM_Lo_res.pdf).

United Nations Conference on Trade and Development. 2007. *World Investment Report 2007*. Geneva. Retrieved December 19, 2007 (http://www.unctad.org/en/docs/wir2007p1_en.pdf).

United Nations Development Programme. 2013. *Human Development Report 2013. The Rise of the South: Human Progress in a Diverse World*. New York: UNDP.

United Nations Educational, Scientific and Cultural Organization (UNESCO). 2008. "International Literacy Statistics: A Review of Concepts, Methodology and Current Data." Retrieved March 27, 2010 (www.uis.unesco.org/template/pdf/Literacy/LiteracyReport2008.pdf).

———. 2014. "Poverty Reduction: The Millennium Development Goals." Retrieved February 27, 2014 (www.unesco.org/new/en/education/themes/leading-the-international-agenda/education-for-sustainable-development/poverty-reduction).

United Nations Population Fund. 2012. *Marrying Too Young: End Child Marriage*. New York: UNPF.

United Nations World Tourism Organization. 2007. "International Tourist Arrivals." Retrieved December 19, 2007 (http://unwto.org/facts/eng/pdf/historical/ITA_1950_2005.pdf).

University of Ottawa. 2014. "Facts and Figures: Marijuana in Canada." Retrieved April 3, 2014 (www.med.uottawa.ca/sim/data/Marijuana_e.htm).

Uppal, Sharanjit. 2011. "Unionization 2011." Ottawa: Statistics Canada. Retrieved February 16, 2014 (www.statcan.gc.ca/pub/75-001-x/2011004/article/11579-eng.htm).

U.S. Bureau of Labor Statistics. 2013a. "CPI Inflation Calculator." Retrieved 31 March 2013 (www.bls.gov/data/inflation_calculator.htm).

———. 2013b. "Union Members Summary." Retrieved 24 August 2013 (www.bls.gov/news.release/union2.nr0.htm).

U.S. Census Bureau. 2011. "World Population, 1950–2050." Retrieved 18 August 2013 (www.census.gov/population/international/data/idb/worldpopgraph.php).

———. 2014. "International Data Base: Population Pyramid Graph—Custom Region—Canada." Retrieved April 11, 2014 (www.census.gov/population/international/data/idb/region.php?N=%20Results%20&T=12&A=separate&RT=0&Y=2017&R=-1&C=CA).

U.S. Department of Commerce. 1998. "Statistical Abstract of the United States: 1998." Retrieved October 8, 2000 (www.census.gov/prod/3/98pubs/98statab/sasec1.pdf).

U.S. Environmental Protection Agency, Office of Air Quality Planning and Standards. 2000. "National Air Pollutant Emission Trends, 1900–1998." Retrieved August 3, 2000 (www.epa.gov/ttn/chief/trends98/emtrnd.html).

U.S. Information Agency. 1998–99. *The People Have Spoken: Global Views of Democracy*, 2 vols. Washington, DC: Office of Research and Media Reaction.

U.S. Securities and Exchange Commission. 2013. "Form 10-K: Google Inc." Retrieved 21 August 2013 (www.sec.gov/Archives/edgar/data/1288776/000119312513028362/d452134d10k.htm).

Useem, Bert. 1998. "Breakdown Theories of Collective Action." *Annual Review of Sociology* 24: 215–38.

Valocchi, Steve. 1996. "The Emergence of the Integrationist Ideology in the Civil Rights Movement." *Social Problems* 43: 116–30.

Van de Werfhorst, Herman G. 2005 "Social Background, Credential Inflation and Educational Strategies." *Acta Sociologica* 48(4): 321–40.

Veenstra, Gerry. 2013. "Race, Gender, Class, Sexuality (RGCS) and Hypertension." *Social Science and Medicine* 89: 16–24.

Veugelers, John. 1997. "Social Cleavage and the Revival of Far Right Parties: The Case of France's National Front." *Acta Sociologica* 40: 31–49.

Vezina, Mireille. 2012. 2011 *General Social Survey: Overview of Families in Canada—Being a Parent in a Stepfamily: A Profile*. Catalogue no. 89-650-X—No. 002. Ottawa, ON: Minister of Industry.

Vithayathil, Trina. 2013. "Pathways to Low Fertility in India." *Asian Population Studies* 9: 3, 301–21.

Von Below, Susanne, Justin Powell, and Lance W. Roberts. 2013. "Educational Systems and Rising Inequality: Eastern Germany after Unification." *Sociology of Education* 86(4): 362–75.

Wade, Lisa. 2010. "How to Spot Fake Smiles." Retrieved November 20, 2013 (http://thesocietypages.org/socimages/2010/11/14/how-to-spot-fake-smiles-spoiler-alert/).

———. 2013. "Gender and the Body Language of Power." Retrieved November 18, 2013 (http://thesocietypages.org/socimages/2013/09/10/gendered-and-the-body-language-of-power/).

Wade, Robert, and Martin Wolf. 2002. "Are Global Poverty and Inequality Getting Worse?" *Prospect* March: 16–21.

Wald, Matthew L., and John Schwartz. 2003. "Alerts Were Lacking, NASA Shuttle Manager Says." *The New York Times* July 23. Retrieved July 23, 2003 (www.nytimes.com).

Waldfogel, Jane. 1997. "The Effect of Children on Women's Wages." *American Sociological Review* 62: 209–17.

Walker, Alan. 2012. "The New Ageism." *The Political Quarterly* 83(4): 812–19.

Wallace, James, and Jim Erickson. 1992. *Hard Drive: Bill Gates and the Making of the Microsoft Empire*. New York: Wiley.

Wallerstein, Immanuel. 1974–89. *The Modern World-System*, 3 vols. New York: Academic Press.

Wallerstein, Judith S., Julia Lewis, and Sandra Blakeslee. 2000. *The Unexpected Legacy of Divorce: A 25 Year Landmark Study*. New York: Hyperion.

Wanner, Richard. 1999. "Expansion and Ascription: Trends in Educational Opportunity in Canada, 1920–1994." *Canadian Review of Sociology and Anthropology* 36 (August): 409–42.

Warner, Remi. 2006. *Theoretical Framework for the Racism, Violence and Health Project: A Working Paper.* Retrieved February 2, 2014 (http://rvh.socialwork.dal.ca/resources.html).

Wasserman, Stanley, and Katherine Faust. 1994. *Social Network Analysis: Methods and Applications*. Cambridge: Cambridge University Press.

Watkins, S. Craig, and Rana A. Emerson. 2000. "Feminist Media Criticism and Feminist Media Practices." *Annals of the American Academy of Political and Social Science* 571: 151–66.

Watson, Diane E., and Kimberlyn M. McGrail. 2009. "More Doctors or Better Care." *Healthcare Policy* 5: 26–31.

Watson, Elwood. 2013. *Generation X: Professor Speak*. Plymouth, UK: Scarecrow Press.

Watson, James D. 1968. *The Double Helix: A Personal Account of the Discovery of the Structure of DNA*. New York: Atheneum.

———. 2000. *A Passion for DNA: Genes, Genomes, and Society*. Cold Spring Harbor, NY: Cold Spring Harbor Laboratory Press.

Watson, James L., ed. 1997. *Golden Arches East: McDonald's in East Asia*. Stanford, CA: Stanford University Press.

Webb, Stephen D., and John Collette. 1977. "Rural–Urban Differences in the Use of Stress-Alleviating Drugs." *American Journal of Sociology* 83: 700–707.

———. 1979. "Reply to Comment on Rural–Urban Differences in the Use of Stress-Alleviating Drugs." *American Journal of Sociology* 84: 1446–52.

"Webcam Penetration Rates & Adoption." 2011. Weareorganizedchaos.com. Retreived 4 April 2013 (http://weareorganizedchaos.com/webcam-penetration-rates-adoption/).

Weber, Brenda R., and Karen W. Tice. 2009. "Are You Finally Comfortable in Your Own Skin?" Genders 49. Retrieved May 2, 2014 (www.genders.org/g49/g49_webertice.html).

Weber, Max. 1946. *From Max Weber: Essays in Sociology*, rev. ed., H. Gerth and C. W. Mills, eds., and trans. New York: Oxford University Press.

———. 1947. *The Theory of Social and Economic Organization*, T. Parsons, ed., A. M. Henderson and T. Parsons, trans. New York: Free Press.

———. 1958 [1904–5]. *The Protestant Ethic and the Spirit of Capitalism*. New York: Scribner.

———. 1978. *Economy and Society*, Guenther Roth and Claus Wittich, eds. Berkeley, CA: University of California Press.

Weeks, Carly. 2009. "The Dark Side of 'Free-Range' Chickens." *The Globe and Mail* January 15. Retrieved December 7, 2010 (www.theglobeandmail.com/life/article966564.ece).

Wegenstein, Bernadette, and Nora Ruck. 2011. "Physiognomy, Reality Television and the Cosmetic Gaze." *Body and Society* 17(4): 27–55.

Weis, Joseph G. 1987. "Class and Crime." Pp. 71–90 in Michael Gottfredson and Travis Hirschi, eds. *Positive Criminology*. Beverly Hills, CA: Sage.

Weller, Jack M., and E. L. Quarantelli. 1973. "Neglected Characteristics of Collective Behavior." *American Journal of Sociology* 79: 665–85.

Wellesley Institute. 2010. *Precarious Housing in Canada*. Retrieved December 17, 2013 (www.wellesleyinstitute.com/wp-content/uploads/2010/08/Precarious_Housing_In_Canada.pdf).

Wellman, Barry. 1979. "The Community Question: The Intimate Networks of East Yorkers." *American Journal of Sociology* 84: 201–31.

———. 2014. "Connecting Communities On and Offline." Pp. 54–63 in Robert Brym, ed. *Society in Question*, 7th ed. Toronto: Nelson Education.

Wellman, Barry, and Stephen Berkowitz, eds. 1997. *Social Structures: A Network Approach*, updated ed. Greenwich, CT: JAI Press.

Wellman, Barry, Peter J. Carrington, and Alan Hall. 1997. "Networks as Personal Communities." Pp.130–184 in Barry Wellman and S. D. Berkowitz, eds. *Social Structures: A Network Approach*, updated ed. Greenwich, CT: JAI Press.

Wells, H. G. 1927. "The Country of the Blind." Pp. 123–46 in *Selected Short Stories*. Harmondsworth, UK: Penguin. Retrieved April 24, 2003 (http://www.fantasticfiction.co.uk/etexts/y3800.htm).

Welsh, Sandy. 1999. "Gender and Sexual Harassment." *Annual Review of Sociology* 25: 169–90.

Wendell, Susan. 1996. *The Rejected Body*. New York: Routledge.

West, Candace, and Don Zimmerman. 1987. "Doing Gender." *Gender and Society* 1: 125–51.

———. 2009. "Accounting for Doing Gender." *Gender & Society* 23(1): 112–22.

Wheeler, Stanton. 1961. "Socialization in Correctional Communities." *American Sociological Review* 26: 697–712.

Whitaker, Reg. 1987. *Double Standard*. Toronto: Lester and Orpen Dennys.

Whitefield, S., and G. Evans. 1994. "The Russian Election of 1993: Public Opinion and the Transition Experience." *Post-Soviet Affairs* 10: 38–60.

Whittington, L. 1999. *The Banks: The Ongoing Battle for Control of Canada's Richest Business*. Toronto: Stoddart.

Whorf, Benjamin Lee. 1956. *Language, Thought, and Reality*, John B. Carroll, ed. Cambridge, MA: MIT Press.

Whyte, William F. 1943. *Street Corner Society*. Chicago: University of Chicago Press.

Widyastuti, Adeline. 2010. *The Globalization of New Media Exposure: The Dependency on the Internet*. Saarbrücken, Germany: Lambert.

Wilensky, Harold L. 1967. *Organizational Intelligence: Knowledge and Policy in Government and Industry*. New York: Basic Books.

———. 1997. "Social Science and the Public Agenda: Reflections on the Relation of Knowledge to Policy in the United States and Abroad." *Journal of Health Politics, Policy and Law* 22: 1241–65.

Wilkins, Russell, Sharanjit Uppal, Philippe Finès, Sacha Senècal, Éric Guimond, and Rene Dion. 2008. "Life Expectancy in the Inuit-inhabited Areas of Canada, 1989 to 2003." *Health Reports* 19(1), 7–19.

Wilkinson, Richard, and Kate Pickett. 2010. *The Spirit Level: Why Equality Is Better For Everyone*. New York: Penguin.

Williams, Cara. 2006. "Disability in the Workplace." Perspectives Catalogue No. 75-001-XIE. Ottawa: Statistics Canada.

Williams, David R., and Michelle Sternthal. 2010. "Understanding Racial-Ethnic Disparities in Health: Sociological Contributions." *Journal of Health and Social Behavior* 51: S1–S15.

Williams, Eric. 1944. *Capitalism and Slavery*. Chapel Hill, NC: University of North Carolina Press.

Williams, Lela Rankin, and Heidi L. Adams. 2013. "Friends with Benefits or 'Friends' with Deficits? The Meaning and Contexts of Uncommitted Sexual Relationships among Mexican American and European American Adolescents." *Children and Youth Services Review* 35: 1110–17.

Willis, Paul. 1984 [1977]. *Learning to Labour: How Working-Class Kids Get Working-Class Jobs*. New York: Columbia University Press.

Willows, Noreen D., Anthony J. G. Hanley, and Treena Delormier. 2012. "A Socioecological Framework to Understand Weight-related Issues in Aboriginal Children in Canada." *Applied Physiology, Nutrition and Metabolism* 37: 1–13.

Wilson, Brian. 2002. "The Canadian Rave Scene and Five Theories on Youth Resistance." *Canadian Journal of Sociology* 27: 373–412.

Wilson, James Q., and Joan Petersilia. 2011. *Crime and Public Policy*. New York: Oxford University Press.

Wilson, William Julius. 1987. *The Truly Disadvantaged: The Inner City, the Underclass, and Public Policy*. Chicago: University of Chicago Press.

Wilson, William Julius, and Richard P. Taub. 2006. *Racial, Ethnics and Class Tensions in Four Chicago Neighbourhoods and Their Meaning for America*. New York: Random House.

Winch, Donald. 1987. *Malthus*. Oxford, UK: Oxford University Press.

Winograd, Morley, and Michael D. Hais. 2011. *Millennial Momentum: How a New Generation Is Remaking America*. New Brunswick, NJ: Rutgers University Press.

Wirth, Louis. 1938. "Urbanism as a Way of Life." *American Journal of Sociology* 44: 1–24.

Wister, Andrew V. 2005. *Baby Boomer Health Dynamics: How Are We Aging?* Toronto: University of Toronto Press.

Wolf, D. L. 1992. *Factory Daughters: Gender, Household Dynamics, and Rural Industrialization in Java*. Berkeley, CA: University of California Press.

Wolfinger, Nicholas H. 2011. "More Evidence for Trends in the Intergenerational Transmission of Divorce: A Completed Cohort Approach Using Data from the General Social Survey." *Demography* 48: 581–92.

"The Women of Battlestar Galactica." n.d. SpacePlay. Retrieved 1 April 2013 (http://titch1992.wordpress.com/the-women-of-battlestar-galactica/).

Wong, L., and M. Ng. 1998. "Chinese Immigrant Entrepreneurs in Vancouver: A Case Study of Ethnic Business Development." *Canadian Ethnic Studies* 30: 64–85.

Wood, William. 2012. "Victim Offender Reconciliation Programs." Pp. 442–468 in S.M. Barton-Bellessa, ed. *Encyclopedia of Community Corrections*. Thousand Oaks, CA: Sage.

Woodrow Federal Reserve Bank of Minneapolis. 2000. "What's a Dollar Worth?" Retrieved October 8, 2000 (http://woodrow.mpls.frb.fed.us/economy/calc/cpihome.html).

Woods, Lakeesha N., and Robert E. Emery. 2002. "The Cohabitation Effect on Divorce." *Journal of Divorce and Remarriage* 37: 101–22.

World Bank. 2012. *Water Supply and Sanitation in the Democratic Republic of Congo: Turning Finance into Services for 2015 and Beyond*. Washington, DC: World Bank.

World Economic Forum. 2007. "Core Health Indicators." Retrieved January 16, 2008 (www.who.int/whosis/database/core/core_select.cfm).

———. 2010. Health Systems Financing: The Path Universal Coverage. Geneva, Switzerland: Author.

———. 2011. *Global Health and Aging*. Switzerland: Author.

______. 2013. *The Global Gender Gap Report, 2013*. Switzerland: Author.

———. 2013a. "Female Genital Mutilation." Retrieved November 3, 2013 (www.who.int/mediacentre/factsheets/fs241/en/).

———. 2013b. "Suicide Prevention (SUPRE)." Retrieved August 5, 2013 (www.who.int/mental_health/prevention/suicide/suicideprevent/en/index.html).

World Tourism Organization. 2013. "International Tourism to Continue Robust Growth in 2013." Retrieved 3 July 2014 (http://media.unwto.org/en/press-release/2013-01-28/international-tourism-continue-robust-growth-2013).

World Values Survey. 2005. Machine readable data set. Ann Arbor, MI: Inter-University Consortium for Political and Social Research.

Worrall-Carter, Linda, Chantal Ski, Elizabeth Scruth, Michelle Campbell, and Karen Page. 2011. "Systematic Review of Cardiovascular Disease in Women: Assessing the Risk." *Nursing and Health Sciences* 13: 529–35.

Wortley, Scot, and Julian Tanner. 2011. "The Racial Profiling Debate: Data, Denials, and Confusion." Pp. 295–302 in Robert J. Brym, ed. *Society in Question*. Toronto: Nelson.

Wright, Charles Robert. 1975. *Mass Communication: A Sociological Perspective*. New York: Random House.

Wright, Erik Olin, and Joel Rogers. 2010. *American Society: How It Really Works*. New York: W.W. Norton and Company.

Wright, Robert. 2010. "Zuckerberg: Non-Evil Non-Genius." *The New York Times* 5 October. Retrieved October 9, 2010 (www.nytimes.com).

Wu, Zheng, and Michael S. Pollard. 2000. "Economic Circumstances and the Stability of Nonmarital Cohabitation." *Journal of Family Issues* 21(3): 303–28.

Wynne, Robert E. 1996. "American Labor Leaders and the Vancouver Anti-Oriental Riot." *Pacific Northwest Quarterly* 86: 172–79. Retrieved March 15, 2001 (www.vcn.bc.ca/acww/html/body_riot.html).

Yancey, W. L, E. P. Ericksen, and G. H. Leon. 1979. "Emergent Ethnicity: A Review and Reformulation." *American Sociological Review* 41: 391–403.

Yap, Andy, Abbie Wazlawek, Brian Lucas, Amy Cuddy, and Dana Carney. 2013. "The Ergonomics of Dishonesty: The Effect of Incidental Posture on Stealing, Cheating, and Traffic Violations." *Psychological Science* 24(11): 2281–89.

Yates, Gayle Graham, ed. 1985. *Harriet Martineau on Women*. New Brunswick, NJ: Rutgers University Press.

Zakaria, Fareed. 1997. "The Rise of Illiberal Democracy." *Foreign Affairs* 76, 6: 22–43.

Zald, Meyer N., and John D. McCarthy. 1979. *The Dynamics of Social Movements*. Cambridge, MA: Winthrop.

Zaslavsky, Victor, and Robert J. Brym. 1978. "The Functions of Elections in the USSR." *Soviet Studies* 30: 62–71.

Zayer, Linda Tuncay, Katherine Sredl, Marie-Agnès Parmentier, and Catherine Coleman. 2012. "Consumption and Gender Identity in Popular Media: Discourses of Domesticity, Authenticity, and Sexuality." *Consumption Markets and Culture* 15(4): 333–57.

Zhao, Zuo, and Shengbing Zhang. 2013. "Research on Influence of Weak ties to Information Spreading in Online Social Networks." Communication and Information Technologies, International Symposium. Accessed February 17, 2014 (http://ieeexplore.ieee.org/xpl/login.jsp?tp=&arnumber=6645851&url=http%3A%2F%2Fieeexplore.ieee.org%2Fxpls%2Fabs_all.jsp%3Farnumber%3D6645851).

Zimbardo, Philip. 1972. "Pathology of Imprisonment." *Society* 9, 6: 4–8.

———. 2008. *The Lucifer Effect: Understanding How Good People Turn Evil*. New York: Random House.

Zimring, Franklin E., and Gordon Hawkins. 1995. *Incapacitation: Penal Confinement and the Restraint of Crime*. New York: Oxford University Press.

Zinsser, Hans. 1935. *Rats, Lice and History*. Boston: Little, Brown.

Zuboff, S. 1988. *In the Age of the Smart Machine: The Future of Work and Power*. New York: Basic Books.

Zurbriggen, Eileen L. et al. 2010. *Report of the APA Task Force on the Sexualization of Girls*. Washington, DC: American Psychological Association. Retrieved January 16, 2013 (www.apa.org/pi/women/programs/girls/report-full.pdf).

Zurcher, Louis A., and David A. Snow. 1981. "Collective Behavior and Social Movements." Pp. 447–82 in Morris Rosenberg and Ralph Turner, eds. *Social Psychology: Sociological Perspectives*. New York: Basic Books.

INDEX

Note: Bolded entries and page references indicate key terms and the page on which they are defined; page references followed by *t* indicate tables; page references followed by *i* indicate pictures and captions; and page references followed by *f* indicate figures.

K

L

M

N

S